# PROFESSIONAL LIABILITY:
## LAW AND INSURANCE

LLOYD'S COMMERCIAL LAW LIBRARY

*Interests in Goods*
by Norman Palmer and
Ewan McKendrick
(1993)

*The Law of Insurance Contracts*
second edition
by Malcolm A. Clarke
(1994)

*EC Banking Law*
second edition
by Marc Dassesse, Stuart Isaacs QC
and Graham Penn
(1994)

*The Law and Practice
Relating to
Appeals from Arbitration Awards*
by D. Rhidian Thomas
(1994)

*Force Majeure and Frustration
of Contract*
second edition
Edited by Ewan McKendrick
(1995)

*The Practice and Procedure
of the Commercial Court*
fourth edition
by The Hon. Sir Anthony Colman
and Victor Lyon
(1995)

*Arbitration Law*
by Robert Merkin
(looseleaf)

*Professional Liability:
Law and Insurance*
by Ray Hodgin
(1996)

# PROFESSIONAL LIABILITY:
## LAW AND INSURANCE

EDITED BY

### RAY HODGIN, LL.M.

*Senior Lecturer in Law*
*University of Birmingham*
*Consultant, Pinsent Curtis, Solicitors*

LONDON   NEW YORK   HONG KONG
1996

LLP Limited
Legal & Business Publishing Division
27 Swinton Street
London WC1X 9NW

USA AND CANADA
LLP Inc.
Suite 308, 611 Broadway
New York, NY 10012, USA

SOUTH EAST ASIA
LLP Asia Limited
Room 1101, Hollywood Centre
233 Hollywood Road
Hong Kong

©

R. W. Hodgin and contributors
1996

*British Library Cataloguing in Publication Data*
A catalogue record for this book is
available from the British Library

ISBN 1–85978–034–2

Text set in 10/12pt Times by
Mendip Communications Ltd.
Frome, Somerset
Printed in Great Britain by
Hartnolls Ltd.
Bodmin, Cornwall

# PREFACE

"A professional person should wear a halo but need not wear a hair shirt", *per* Lord Justice Slade in *La Banque Financière de la Cité SA* v. *Westgate Insurance Co Ltd* [1988] 2 Lloyd's Rep. 513, C.A. Perhaps his Lordship should have added that, on the other hand, a flak jacket would not go amiss! Formerly it was "awe not law" that prevailed in professional negligence cases, but those days are fast disappearing as we become a more litigious nation.

Even the 1980s television advertisement, "get the strength of the insurance companies around you" is now restricted (if it was ever true at all) to domestic insurance. It is clear from very recent evidence that some professionals can no longer obtain sufficient cover or only on terms that require massive deductibles.

"Negligence", that most illusive of legal concepts, has itself undergone very considerable changes in the last few years. If "proximity" is currently the favourite ingredient required for proving that a duty of care is owed, one should bear in mind Lord Oliver's words in *Murphy* v. *Brentwood District Council* [1991] 1 A.C. 398 that proximity "is an expression which persistently defies definition".

The superior courts have been hyperactive and not necessarily in a predictable way. *Anns* v. *London Borough of Merton* [1978] A.C. 728 has been reversed by *Murphy* (above) presenting a unique example, certainly in tort law, of the House of Lords reversing its own previous decision within such a short period. The *Murphy* decision has notched up another "first" in that it has proved to be immediately unacceptable to the courts of Australia, Canada and New Zealand as exemplified in the Privy Council on appeal from New Zealand in *Invercargill City Council* v. *Hamlin* [1996] 1 All E.R. 756.

*Hedley Byrne & Co Ltd* v. *Heller & Partners Ltd* [1964] A.C. 465, the "other arm" to *Anns*, however, lives on. First in a reformulated and perhaps somewhat truncated form in *Caparo Industries plc* v. *Dickman* [1990] 2 A.C. 605, and second only to find a, potentially, massively expanded role to play in *White* v. *Jones* [1995] 1 All E.R. 691. Thus for the professional the difference between words and acts becomes a major concern; a matter of liability or no liability.

While that battle goes on the House of Lords in *Henderson* v. *Merrett Syndicates* [1994] 3 All E.R. 506 has decided that a professional can owe a concurrent liability to a client in both contract and in negligence. This brings with it problems of the contrasting results in contract and tort as to limitation periods, contributory negligence and remoteness of damage rules.

Again in *Spring* v. *Guardian Assurance plc* [1994] 3 All E.R. 129 the House decided that there can be liability to a former employee for a negligently drafted reference thus allowing the plaintiff to avoid all the problems that beset any litigant who has to embark along the, often, disastrously costly defamation trail.

In all of these cases of expanding liability the House has left open the door of avoiding liability by means of adequately framed "exclusion/exemption" wording. Future decisions will show just how that will be done, while still meeting the requirements of the Unfair Contract Terms Act 1977 and the Unfair Terms in Consumer Contract Regulations 1994, where applicable.

Of considerable concern to both sides of any professional negligence action has been the publication, in January 1996, of the initial feasibility study of the common law team of the Law Commission as to whether changes should be made to the law relating to joint and several liability. To the dismay of the professions the overall conclusions were that no changes should be made. However it has been published with a view to obtaining a cross-section of opinions to assist government in their decision-making. Despite their conclusions the team did offer a number of different views to the abolition of joint and several liability. One tentative suggestion was that auditors might be permitted to limit their liability or that a statutory cap on liability might be worth considering.

The chapters in this book cover a wide range of "professionals". The definition of "professional" is no easy matter and some would argue that some of those included do not fit within their definition of the word. The driving force has been to look at who has been the subject-matter of litigation in recent years.

In addition the mutual recognition of professional qualifications and the possible growth in the movement of professionals within the EU indicated that an explanation of how this can be done was merited. The underpinning of professional indemnity insurance is referred to briefly in the final chapter although several chapters refer to the specific requirements of their particular profession. Finally, several chapters discuss, briefly, the ever-growing amount of professional regulation, codes of conduct and disciplinary procedures applicable to their individual professions.

Most of the professions in this book have been the subject-matter of monographs by the contributing authors. It is hoped, however, that this publication will bring those discussions together within one book to act as a first port of call for the busy reader.

*June 1996*                                                          RAY HODGIN

# EDITOR

RAY HODGIN is a Senior Lecturer at the University of Birmingham and consultant to Pinsent Curtis, Solicitors. His books include *Insurance Intermediaries: Law and Regulation* (looseleaf) and *Protection of the Insured* (both published by LLP Limited). He is also the editor of *Leading Decisions Affecting Insurance* (4 volumes) and consultant editor of *Houseman and Davies, Law of Life Assurance* (11th edition, Butterworths).

# CONTRIBUTORS

DAVID ALLEN is Head of the Department of Law at Leicester University. He is also in practice at the Bar. He is the General Editor of the *Personal Injuries and Quantum Reports* and is Managing Editor of the journal *Professional Negligence*. He has written a number of books and articles in the area of contract and tort.

LESLEY JANE ANDERSON graduated in 1984 from the University of Manchester and stayed on as a lecturer in law. She was called to the Bar in 1989 and then employed as training manager to Norton Rose M5 Group of solicitors' practices with overall responsibility for training and education within the Group. In June 1991 she joined 40 King Street in Manchester and has been in practice there since that date in all fields of professional negligence, commercial litigation, individual and corporate insolvency and landlord and tenant. She is the author of a number of academic and professional articles and notes in various journals.

MICHAEL DAVIES is currently Senior Tutor in law at Leicester University and consultant in medical negligence litigation to Coffee, Randall & Warnock, Solicitors. He has published in the field of medical law and is the author of *Textbook on Medical Law* (1996, Blackstone Press). His other research interests are in civil justice and criminal law, having formerly worked for the Crown Prosecution Service.

JON HOLYOAK is a barrister and lecturer in law at Leicester University. He has written extensively on tort and intellectual property law and has been involved with the editing of the journal *Professional Negligence* since its inception in 1985.

JULIAN LONBAY is a Senior Lecturer and the Director of the Institute of European Law at the University of Birmingham. He is the editor and co-author of *Training Lawyers in the European Community* and *International Professional Practice* and is the reporter on "Free movement of persons, recognition of qualifications, and working conditions" for the *International and Comparative Law Quarterly* and has published many articles in these and related fields.

ANDREW MCGEE is Professor of Business Law at Leeds University, having previously held the same post at Lancaster University. His research interests cover limitation of actions, insurance and financial services, company law and European law. He is the author of *Limitation Periods, 2nd edition* (1994, Sweet & Maxwell), *Insurance Contract Law* (1988), *The Law and Practice of Life Assurance Contracts* (1995) and *The Business of Company Law* (1995). He is the General Editor of the *Encyclopaedia of Insurance Law* (Sweet & Maxwell), a member of the Editorial Board of *Professional Negligence* and a Public Interest Member of the Council of the PIA Ombudsman Bureau.

FRANK MEISEL is a Senior Lecturer at Birmingham University. With Professor Brian Harvey, he is author of *Auctions: Law and Practice, 2nd edition* (1995, Oxford University Press) and has published articles in the fields of commercial law and civil justice. His current research is for a work on international sale of goods. He is Assistant Editor of the *Civil Justice Quarterly*.

MARK MILDRED qualified as a solicitor in 1975. He was in partnership from then until 1995 specialising in civil litigation, with a particular interest in professional negligence, product liability and group actions. In 1995 he became the Sweet & Maxwell Professor of Advanced Litigation at Nottingham Law School. He combines this with consultancy to leading solicitors' firms in the litigation field. He is the General Editor of *Product Liability: Law and Insurance* (looseleaf, LLP Limited) and a contributor to *Miller: Product Liability and Safety Encyclopaedia* (looseleaf, Butterworths) and *Medical Negligence* (1995, Butterworths) and to several legal journals.

JOHN MURDOCH, LLB, ACIArb, is a Senior Lecturer in law at the University of Reading, where he specialises in the law relating to the property and construction professions. His recent publications include books on estate agency and auctions, surveys and valuations, property misdescriptions and building contracts. In addition, he has for many years contributed to the weekly "Legal Notes" column of the *Estates Gazette*.

ROY PARR, MA (OXON), FCII, is a registered insurance broker and is currently a consultant to Anthony K. Falcon Ltd. He is a longstanding member of the Insurance Institute of London Debating Committee, a frequent lecturer and chairman of seminars relating to insurance and liability issues and a regular contributor to numerous professional journals and publications.

IAN YULE is a Solicitor and Partner in Neil F Jones & Co, Solicitors of Birmingham. He specialises in construction and engineering litigation and arbitration and related professional indemnity work. He has lectured and written for various journals on these topics and contributed to the firm's book *Professional Negligence and Insurance Law, 2nd edition* (1994, LLP Limited). He is a Fellow of the Chartered Institute of Arbitrators.

# CONTENTS

## CHAPTER 5   AUDITORS AND ACCOUNTANTS
*Andrew McGee*

# TABLE OF CASES

xlix

# TABLE OF LEGISLATION

CHAPTER 1

# THE MUTUAL RECOGNITION OF PROFESSIONAL QUALIFICATIONS IN THE EC

## 1 INTRODUCTION

This chapter seeks to outline the main principles of the European Community (hereafter EC) rules on mutual recognition of professional qualifications operating with regard to the professions covered in this book. It will outline the general rules on free provision of services and establishment within the EC and then concentrate on the rules on the mutual recognition of qualifications and includes particular observations on some of the professions covered in this book. This chapter does not deal with the wider international issues represented by the adoption of GATS—the general agreement on trade and services.[1] Article VII of the GATS contains details on how members should recognise training education or experience where any licence or certifications or diplomas are required. However, the article is broad brush and further negotiation is necessary before concrete rules emerge in this world arena. Similarly, no further mention is made of the EEA Treaty which essentially extends the EU rules to Norway, Liechtenstein and Iceland.[2]

For the professions under discussion, this chapter primarily looks to the position in the UK. It is beyond the scope of the chapter to look at how all the individual professions in all the Member States have or have not accepted and implemented rights of mobility according to Community law. The body of Community law in this area continues to grow and the case-law advances joltingly in line with the chances of litigation. This chapter focuses on the principle of mutual recognition of professional qualifications, and does not cover all the EC rules dealing with mobility for particular professions as such. It is hoped, nevertheless, that it will provide useful guidance and insight for those seeking an understanding of how the EC rules operate and affect professions. It may also help to throw some light on the meaning of the term "profession".

After discussing the rules on mutual recognition of qualifications in general terms, the chapter has short sections on how the rules apply to the main professions covered in this book.

---

1. For a useful general survey of this area, see M Footer, "The International Regulation of Trade and Services following completion of the Uruguay Round" (1995) 29 *The International Lawyer* 453.
2. European Economic Area Treaty, 1994 OJ L 1/3.

1

## 2 FREE MOVEMENT OF PROFESSIONALS

The Treaty of Rome establishing the European Community[3] covers all economic activities in their cross-border dimensions. Sporting activities, for example, have their economic dimension as the recent *Bosman* case illustrates.[4] As the European Court has stated[5]:

"... the provisions of the Treaty relating to freedom of movement of persons are intended to facilitate the pursuit by Community citizens of occupational activities of all kinds throughout the Community, and to preclude measures which might place Community citizens at a disadvantage when they wish to pursue an economic activity in the territory of another Member State."

The rights of mobility conferred by EC law include immigration rights for workers, the self-employed and businesses.[6] Access to a national market cannot be refused on grounds of nationality or residence.[7] The benefits of such mobility are normally conferred only on nationals of a Member State and their families.[8] Rights conferred by Community law mean that providers of professional services who are Community citizens,[9] in principle, can take advantage of the immigration rights granted by the Treaty to provide services on a temporary basis or establish businesses or agencies or to work as an employee in another Member State of the EU.[10] Moreover, any rules impeding their ability to do so, regardless of their origin, can be subject to scrutiny to assess their legitimacy in the eyes of Community law.[11]

In "purely internal" cases Community law simply does not operate at all. In *Openbaar Ministerie* v. *Geert van Buynder*[12] Mr van Buynder, a Belgian national, carried out operations on animals in Belgium contrary to a Belgian law which "allegedly" reserved such activities to registered vets who had appropriate qualifications. The operations consisted of grinding down horses' teeth and involved no use

---

3. Hereinafter referred to as the EC Treaty, as amended by the Treaty on European Union (1993) OJ C-172/1.

4. C-415/95 *Union Royale Belge des Sociétés de Football Association ASBL* v. *Jean-Marc Bosman* and *Royal Club Liégois SA* v. *Jean-Marc Bosman, SA d'Économie Mixte Sportive de l'Union Sportive du Littoral de Dunkerque, Union Royal Belges des Sociétés de Football Association ASBL, Union des Associations Européennes de Football (UEFA)* and *Jean-Marc Bosman* v. *Union des Associations Européennes de Football (UEFA)* (15 December 1995).

5. *Bosman* (above) at para. 94.

6. Their spouses and families can also obtain rights, not dealt with here. For example, see case 131/85 *Gül* v. *Regierungs-präsident Düsseldorf* [1986] E.C.R. 1573.

7. This was established in the early cases 2/74 *Reyners* v. *Belgian State* [1974] E.C.R. 631 (as regards Article 52 and nationality requirements) and 33/74 *Van Binsbergen* v. *Bestuur van de Bedrijfsvereneging voor de Metaalnijverheid* [1974] E.C.R. 1299 (as regards Article 59 and residence requirements).

8. Generally speaking, non-EU nationals cannot utilise EC-based mobility rights. This cannot be considered a watertight rule. For example, the lawyers' services Directive, 77/249/EEC ((1977) OJ L 78/17) (as amended) applies to all relevant lawyers who are established in a Member State regardless of nationality.

9. This means nationals of a Member State: see Article 8(1) of the EC Treaty, more generally, D O'Keeffe, "Union Citizenship" in O'Keeffe and Twomey (Eds) *Legal Issues of the Maastricht Treaty* (Chancery Law, 1994) p. 87; Closa, "Citizenship of the Union and Nationality of Member States" in O'Keeffe and Twomey (Eds) *Legal Issues of the Maastricht Treaty* (Chancery Law, 1994) p. 109.

10. See generally, Marenco, "The notion of Restriction on the Freedom of Establishment and Provision of Services in the case-law of the Court" (1991) 11 Y.E.L. 111; Lonbay, "Picking over the bones: Rights of establishment reviewed" (1991) 16 E.L.Rev. 507.

11. *Bosman* (above) at paras 69–87.

12. Case C-152/94 *Openbaar Ministerie* v. *Geert van Buynder* (16 November 1995).

of medicine or anaesthetic. The national court was aware that such activities could be carried out in neighbouring States (the Netherlands, France and Germany) without any qualifications and wondered whether Article 52 of the EC Treaty could protect Mr van Buynder from a criminal charge that he had acted contrary to the relevant Belgian law. The European Court made it clear that Community law was inapplicable in such circumstances as there was no cross-border element involved. Community law allows reverse discrimination whereby nationals of a Member State can be discriminated against by their own State if there is no element in their case with a cross-border dimension.[13] In *Aubertin*[14] French hairdressers were unable to avail themselves of Directive 82/489/EEC laying down measures to facilitate the effective exercise of the right of establishment and freedom to provide services in hairdressing.[15] They had operated hairdressing salons in France without the necessary (under French law) diplomas. They argued as a defence to their criminal prosecution that as hairdressers with the requisite experience outside France (within the EU) were exempt from this requirement, according to the (correct) French implementation of the Directive they too should benefit even though they had no such (non-French) experience. The European Court following its case-law ruled that they were unable to rely on Community law in such circumstances as there was no cross-border element in their case. Thus France was harsher to its own nationals than foreigners, and this was permitted by Community law.

This chapter does not deal with the basic immigration rights which are already clearly established,[16] but rather with the secondary barriers to cross-border activity thrown up by national differences in ways of organising professions and professional activities. These differences create difficulties for Community law. How can one reconcile the principle of national regulation of professional activities with the right of professionals to move either temporarily or permanently to practice their profession or activity in another Member State? The next section briefly illustrates the general scope of EC law granting rights to those providing cross-border services under these Articles.[17]

Professionals exercising their rights of mobility can do this either on a permanent basis by virtue of Article 52 of the EC Treaty *et seq.* or on a temporary basis in which case the provisions of Articles 59 of the EC Treaty *et seq.* apply.[18] As workers (employees) they would rely principally on Articles 48 of the EC Treaty *et seq.*[19]

13. See case C-132/93 *Steen* v. *Deutsche Bundespost* [1992] E.C.R. I-341.

14. Joined cases C-29/94–C-35/94 *Ministère Public* v. *Jean-Louis Aubertin and others* (16 February 1995).

15. 1982 OJ L 218/24.

16. For excellent general overviews, see J Handoll, *Free Movement of Persons in the EU* (Wiley, 1995) and HG Schermers *et al.* (Eds), *Free Movement of Persons in Europe* (TMC Asser Institute—Martinus Nijhoff, 1993).

17. For a fuller treatment, see works cited at fns 10 and 16 above. Also Wyatt & Dashwood, *European Community Law* (3rd edn, Sweet & Maxwell, 1993) chapters 9 and 10; P Craig and G de Búrca, *EC Law* (OUP, 1995) chapters 15 and 16; Weatherill and Beaumont, *EC Law* (2nd edn, Penguin, 1995) chapter 19; N Green, T Hartley and J Usher, *The Legal Foundations of the Single European Market* (OUP, 1991), part II.

18. See C-55/94 *Reinhard Gebhard* v. *Consiglio dell'Ordine degli Avvocati e Procuratori de Milano* (30 November 1995), where the E.C.J. set out some guidelines distinguishing "establishment" from "services", at para. 27. It is clear that Article 52 is the dominant article with Article 59 playing a residual role.

19. Articles 48, 52 and 59 though are interlinked and, as the case of *Ramrath* (below) illustrates, the rights of a worker may turn on the interpretation of Article 52 of the EC Treaty.

Articles 48, 52 and 59 of the EC Treaty all have direct effect.[20] The rights of mobility granted by Articles 48, 52 and 59 are not dependent, for the most part, on measures adopted under Article 57,[21] which in paragraph 1 allows legislative attempts "to make it easier for persons to take up and pursue activities as self-employed persons" by issuing "directives for the mutual recognition of diplomas, certificates and other evidence of formal qualifications". Paragraph 2 allows for the issuing of "directives for the co-ordination of the provisions laid down by law, regulation or administrative action in Member States concerning the taking up and pursuit of activities as self-employed persons".

Article 57 is the key article of the Treaty as regards the mutual recognition of qualifications. It must be borne in mind that for most of the professions covered by this book the conditions under which the professional activities are undertaken are set out and regulated by national law, regulation or administrative action. It is rare for EC law to intervene in the operation of the national rules except to ensure that EC rights of mobility, in particular, are respected. The principle of subsidiarity, incorporated in Article 3b of the EC Treaty, will help to ensure national autonomy in the regulation of professional activities. The sectoral directives emanating from Article 57 do, however, co-ordinate professional training and Community law does require full respect for the principle of non-discrimination on grounds of nationality.

Professionals are often employed persons, though in some countries, for some professions, this is prohibited. Few of those active in the professions covered in this book are likely to upset so spectacularly their existing professional order as Jean-Marc Bosman, a Belgian professional footballer, who successfully invoked Article 48 to challenge the "transfer fees" system used by national football associations and UEFA as well as the nationality rule which hitherto had limited the number of nationals of other Member States who could play in match competitions. However, all professionals are entitled to challenge national rules which impede their genuine access to a national market for their professional services. Community law does not grant a de-regulatory judicial *carte blanche* to professionals who dislike regulatory aspects of their new professional environment, though it can be helpful in mitigating the effects of national regulation.[22]

In *Ramrath*[23] the importance of the free movement of persons rules were emphasised in the context of an auditor whose authorisation to practice in Luxembourg was withdrawn by the Minister of Justice on the grounds that he had no "establishment" in Luxembourg, and because, as the employee of a German firm of auditors, under the law of Luxembourg, he lacked the necessary professional

20. This was established in the early cases, 2/74 *Reyners* v. *Belgian State* [1974] E.C.R. 631 (as regards Article 52) and 33/74 *Van Binsbergen* v. *Bestuur van de Bedrijfsvereneging voor de Metaalnijverheid* [1974] E.C.R. 1299 (as regards Article 59), and case 167/73 *Commission* v. *France* [1974] E.C.R. 359 (as regards Article 48).

21. Case 2/74 *Reyners* v. *Belgian State* [1974] E.C.R. 631; case 71/76 *Thieffry* v. *Conseil de l'Ordre des Avocats à la Cour de Paris* [1977] E.C.R. 765, para. 17; case C-104/91 *Borrell*, fn. 170 below.

22. *Plenderleith* v. *Royal College of Veterinary Surgeons* (1995) *The Times*, 19 December, where a veterinary surgeon was saved from a four-month suspension for "disgraceful conduct in a professional respect" imposed for his unlawful conduct in respect of employing unregistered veterinary surgeons who, however, did hold appropriate national (Irish and Dutch) qualifications according to Directive 78/1026/EEC (1978 OJ L 362/1) as implemented by the Veterinary Surgeons Act 1966, s. 5A, as amended, and were thus entitled to register, and had in fact applied to register.

23. C-106/91 *Ramrath* v. *Ministre de la Justice* [1992] E.C.R. I-3351.

independence to practice in Luxembourg. The European Court firmly emphasised that establishment in another Member State could not be a grounds for such an act,[24] and secondly, whilst recognising a Member State's right to impose conditions on practice as an auditor, those proportionate "requirements" had to be justified by "compelling reasons in the general interest which justify restrictions on freedom of movement" such rationales not being already safeguarded by the rules in place in the State of provenance.[25] Thus Member State rules are legitimately subject to assessment as to their "objective necessity".[26] The right of Ramrath to practise as an employed auditor in Luxembourg was secured in part by a wide interpretation of Article 52. It is clear that a Member State cannot apply rules which prohibit cross-border practice as such. In case 107/83 *Ordre des Avocats au Barreau de Paris* v. *Klopp* the French rule requiring the maintenance of only one office (*unicité de cabinet*: single practice rule) was applied to a German lawyer who was qualified as a French lawyer to prevent him from practising in Paris, as he already had an office in Germany. The European Court, applying Article 52, rejected the application of this rule here as it had the effect of preventing mobility.[27] In *Gullung*,[28] a *Rechtsanwalt* (German lawyer) sought to work in France where he had earlier been disbarred. The European Court did not explicitly answer the point raised concerning establishment under home State title, but did make it clear that Gullung could not automatically become a member of the French Bar by virtue of his German qualification. Whether he could establish in France as a *Rechtsanwalt* was not decided. France was entitled to maintain its professional standards and Gullung could not use the lawyers' services Directive[29] to avoid the effects of disbarment in France.

In *Commission* v. *Luxembourg* the European Court of Justice ruled that the single practice rule in medicine[30] was not justified by considerations of patient care. Thus a general prohibition on practitioners established or employed in another Member State from working within the host State was unduly restrictive and not justified under Articles 48 and 52. This application of the principles in Article 48 and 52 emphasises that restrictions on the medical profession's rights of mobility have to be assessed and justified in the light of Community law. The Court had no difficulty coming to this conclusion relying on the case of *Klopp* primarily and also on *Commission* v. *France*.[31]

A further illustration of the scope of Article 52 is given by the case of *Kraus*.[32] Mr Kraus, a German, who wished to use his (Scottish) "LLM" title in Germany, challenged the German rules that obliged him to pay a fee and get authorisation prior to using the academic designation. The referring German court recognised the utility

24. *Ibid.*, p. 3382, paras 20–22, where the important case of *Klopp* is cited.
25. *Ibid.*, pp. 3384–3385, para. 31.
26. *Ibid.*, p. 3385, para. 32.
27. Case 107/83 *Ordre des Avocats au Barreau de Paris* v. *Klopp* [1984] E.C.R. 2971.
28. Case 292/86 *Claude Gullung* v. *Conseil de l'Ordre des Avocats du Barreau de Colmar and Conseil de l'Ordre des Avocats du Barreau de Saverne* [1988] E.C.R. 111. See J Lonbay, "Free movement of professionals" (1988) 13 E.L.Rev. 275–279.
29. Directive 77/249/EEC, fn. 8 above.
30. This Luxembourg rule applied to medical practitioners, dentists and veterinary surgeons: case C-351/90 *Commission* v. *Luxembourg* [1992] E.C.R. I-3945.
31. Case 96/85 *Commission* v. *France* [1986] E.C.R. 1475 where similar restrictions in France had struck down.
32. Case C-19/92 *Kraus* v. *Land Baden-Württemburg* [1993] E.C.R. I-1663.

of the qualification for professional purposes, yet the European Court declined to find that the German administrative requirements of individual approval and a 130DM fee were contrary to Article 48(2) of the EC Treaty. It held that the German measures were necessary to protect a legitimate state interest in preventing abusive use of academic titles. The European Court had laid down strict requirements for such an administrative procedure, including amenability of the process to judicial review.[33] Advocate General Van Gerven in his liberal opinion had found the German measures to be disproportionate on several grounds.[34] The European Court, interestingly, did not leave it to the national court to assess the necessity of the restrictive rule but made this assessment itself. The case strongly indicates that Article 52 reaches beyond discriminatory measures and can apply to "indistinctly applicable" national measures.[35] This has recently been confirmed by the case of *Gebhard*.[36]

Reinhard Gebhard was a German national who joined the Stuttgart Bar as a *Rechtsanwalt* in 1977. In 1978 Gebhard joined the Milan legal partnership of Bergmann & Scamoni becoming a partner from 1 January 1980 until the middle of 1989 at which point he opened his own Chambers in Milan. Gebhard mainly advised and represented the interests of German-speaking citizens and also represented Italian nationals in courts in Germany and Austria. He considered that 30 per cent of his turnover involved helping Italian businessmen seeking to do business in Germany, Austria and Switzerland. He also helped Italian practitioners dealing with issues of German law on behalf of their clients (5 per cent of his turnover) and 65 per cent of his turnover related to nationals of German-speaking countries who wished to pursue their interests in Italy using a German-speaking lawyer. Mr Gebhard did not himself practise Italian law though he supervised work of Italian lawyers in this field. In addition to his work in Italy Mr Gebhard belonged to a *Burgogemeinschaft* (office-sharing arrangement) in Germany.

The case in Milan arose against Mr Gebhard after complaints from an Italian lawyer that Gebhard had used the title *Avvocato* on his headed paper in 1989. Further complaints to the Milan Bar Association arose because he appeared in court using that title. He also opened a chambers with the name *Studio Legale Gebhard*. Further complaints prompted the Bar Association in Milan to initiate disciplinary proceedings on the grounds that he had used the title *Avvocato*, thus failing to comply with the law number 31/82 (which implemented the EC Directive 77/249 in Italy). The Milan Bar imposed a disciplinary sanction of suspension for six months. Mr Gebhard appealed against the decision to the *Consiglio Nazionale Forense*. Mr Gebhard applied to become an *avvocato*[37] but his application was rejected in February 1993. The *Consiglio Nazionale Forense* stayed their proceedings and referred questions to the European Court under Article 177 of the EC Treaty for an interpretation of Directive 77/249 and Articles 52 and 59 of the Treaty. The following questions were asked:

33. See paras 37–41.
34. See para. 13 of the Opinion, 13 January 1993.
35. Earlier cases had suggested that Article 52 would not reach non-discriminatory national measures that applied equally to all: case 221/85 *Commission* v. *Belgium* [1987] E.C.R. 719.
36. Case C-55/94 *Reinhard Gebhard* v. *Consiglio dell'Ordine degli Avvocati e Procuratori di Milano* (30 November 1995): see *The Times*, 13 December 1995 and *The Financial Times*, 12 December 1995.
37. Under Directive 89/48/EEC dealt with below: see fn. 73 and accompanying text.

1. Is Article 2 of law number 81 of 9 February 1982 on "Freedom for lawyers who are nationals of the Member States of the European Communities to provide services", enacted in implementation of the Community directive of 22 March 1977, which prohibits "The establishment on the territory of the Italian republic either of an office or of a principal or branch office", compatible with the rules laid down by that Directive, given that in the Directive there is no reference to the fact that the possibility of opening an office could be interpreted as reflecting a practitioner's intention to carry on his activities not on a temporary or occasional basis, but on a regular basis?
2. What are the criteria to be applied in assessing whether activities are of a temporary nature, with respect to the continuous and repetitive nature of the services provided by lawyers practising under the system referred to in the above-mentioned Directive of 22 March 1977?

The European Court followed the Advocate General's Opinion that the provision of services does not necessarily exclude the presence of permanent infrastructure in the Member State where the service is actually provided, as long as it could be shown to be necessary,[38] and also adopted his criteria for distinguishing services from establishment, namely that the provider of services is there on a temporary basis. The temporary nature of services is to be determined by duration of the activities and their regularity, periodicity or continuity.[39] *Gebhard*'s case was clearly a question of establishment.

The European Court affirmed that establishment, as such, was not dependent on belonging to a professional body of the host State.[40] It allowed, however, the argument that it depended on the activities that the professional was going to undertake in the host State. Bearing in mind that the second paragraph of Article 52 indicated that freedom of establishment was "to be exercised under the conditions laid down for its own nationals by the law of the country where establishment is to be effected" the Court ruled that if the activities to be pursued were unregulated, calling for no qualifications for example, then the migrant should have free and unfettered access to establish in that State. Whereas if the activity to be pursued were regulated then "*in principle*" the migrant must comply with such rules. However, such national rules which are "liable to hinder or make less attractive the exercise to fundamental freedoms guaranteed by the Treaty" had to conform to four conditions imposed by the Treaty. They must:

— be applied in a non-discriminatory manner;
— be justified by imperative requirements in the general interest;
— be suitable for securing the attainment of the objective which they pursue; and
— not go beyond what is necessary in order to obtain it.[41]

In laying out these conditions the European Court was stricter than Advocate General Léger who indicated briefly that Community law did not reach into the

---

38. Léger, para. 41, European Court, para. 27.
39. European Court, para. 27.
40. *Ibid.*, paras 29–31.
41. *Ibid.*, para. 37 and final ruling.

7

scope of national rules regulating activities on a national basis.[42] The Court did not apply these rules to the situation before it as this was a matter for the national court. Thus it is not decided definitively whether *l'établissement sauvage* (establishing in another Member State under one's home State title) is permitted. Clearly, in Member States which permit it there is no difficulty for the migrant lawyer. In those States which regulate the activities of lawyers and allow local monopolies of particular types of legal activity it is now clear that these rules can be scrutinised at the Community level using the four conditions set out by the Court.

In the *Säger* case[43] the European Court ruled that Article 59 of the EC Treaty prevented Germany from prohibiting a foreign company from providing the services of patent renewal. Säger complained that Dennemeyer, an English company specialising in the renewal of patents, was engaging in unfair competition and infringing the German *Rechtsberatungsgesetz*. Dennemeyer charged lower rates for its services than those generally applied by German lawyers. Mr Säger argued that under the German law only specified persons could perform these tasks, and companies could never perform these tasks. The Court ruled that a ban on Dennemeyer would be disproportionate, given the limited nature of the services it provided, and thus the German monopoly law could not be maintained. The case confirms that Article 59 reaches beyond the "discrimination" analysis, and actually reaches directly Member State regulation of professional activities. The Court will allow a "necessity challenge" to any regulations, by those utilising Article 59 of the EC Treaty.[44] The main rationale for the lightness of the regulatory burden on those providing cross-border services is that their provision of a service is on a temporary basis. Thus it would be inequitable for the full weight of local regulation to be imposed on them. Such a burden would dampen the cross-border provision of services with a consequent loss of competition and decline in consumer choice. In the tourist guide cases,[45] the European Court affirmed the right of the Member States, in principle, to require those providing a service to obtain certain qualifications if there were imperative reasons in the public interest that justified the requirement, and as long as the requirements imposed were proportionate, and in the case of cross-border service providers the requirements were not already met by equivalent qualifications. In the particular cases, a general licensing requirement for guides accompanying the coach loads of tourists was held to be disproportionate.

Nationals of a Member State cannot, however, seek to evade local regulation by utilising their right to free movement.[46] Thus reasonable local regulation is permissible as was seen in the *Kraus* case above.

So in relation to the provision of services, the free movement of workers and the right of establishment, the European Court is allowing Community law a role in assessing the proportionality of Member State regulation that without being discriminatory (whether directly or indirectly) nevertheless hinders cross-border

42. Advocate General Léger, para. 92.
43. Case C-76/90 *M Säger* v. *Dennemeyer & Co. Ltd* [1991] E.C.R. I-4211.
44. Commission Communication (1993) OJ C-334/03.
45. C-154/89 *Commission* v. *France* [1991] E.C.R. 659; C-180/89 *Commission* v. *Italy* [1991] E.C.R. 709; C-198/89 *Commission* v. *Hellenic Republic* [1991] E.C.R. 691.
46. Case 115/78 *Knoors* [1979] E.C.R. 399 and case C-61/89 *Bouchoucha* [1990] E.C.R. I-3551, noted by Lonbay, *op. cit.*, E.L.Rev., fn. 54 below. Cf. case C-384/93 *Alpine Investments BV* v. *Minister van Financiën* [1995] E.C.R. I-1167.

economic activity. Thus professionals are entitled to practice their arts in other Member States. However, as we have seen, the general national rules on liberal professions are essentially a matter for national competence. It now falls for us to assess how the national rules on professional qualifications are affected by these principles.

The demarcation of professional frontiers between professions are set differently in most Member States. For example, legal services are provided by a host of particular professions in Spain and the UK. However, the UK jurisdictions have no exact equivalent of the notary, nor the *procurador*, and in Spain the role which a solicitor plays in the UK jurisdictions is split between several professions.[47] This uneven allocation of activity between professions causes some difficulty for the cross-border movement of professionals or professional services. The EC Treaty recognised these potential difficulties from the start and provided in Article 57 for the co-ordination and mutual recognition of professional qualifications. This provides (as amended by Article G(13) of the Treaty on European Union):

"1. In order to make it easier for persons to take up and pursue activities as self-employed persons, the Council shall, acting in accordance with the procedure referred to in Article 189b, issue directives for the mutual recognition of diplomas, certificates and other evidence of formal qualifications.
2. For the same purpose, the Council shall, before the end of the transitional period, issue directives for the co-ordination of the provisions laid down by law, regulation or administrative action in Member States concerning the taking up and pursuit of activities as self-employed persons. The Council, acting unanimously on a proposal from the Commission and after consulting the European Parliament, shall decide on directives the implementation of which involves in at least one Member State amendment of the existing principles laid down by law governing the professions with respect to training and conditions of access for natural persons. In other cases the Council shall act in accordance with the procedure referred to in Article 189b.
3. In the case of the medical and allied and pharmaceutical professions, the progressive abolition of restrictions shall be dependent upon co-ordination of the conditions for their exercise in the various Member States."

This, however, is not the same as providing for the co-ordinating of the professional structures themselves. Before searching for a Community definition of professional activity it might be helpful to set out some of the ways in which professions can be regulated under national regimes. The great diversity of practice and the difficulties for the Community in confronting these in their cross-border dimensions can then be better appreciated.

The national regulation of a profession generally takes one of several forms. The activity in question, for example the giving of legal advice, can be reserved to members of a particular group or professional body, entrance to which is normally controlled by educational and other criteria. For example, in France the *avocats* have such a monopoly with narrow exceptions. In Germany the monopoly is also maintained but with larger categories of exception, including one for EEA lawyers which permits them to give legal advice on their own national law as well as

---

47. See generally on the legal professions, Lonbay *et al.*, *Training Lawyers in the European Community* (The Law Society, 1990); Lonbay and Spedding, *International Professional Practice* (Wiley, 1992); CCBE, *Cross-border Practice Compendium* (LBE, 1991); H Adamson, *Free Movement of Lawyers* (The Law Society/Butterworths, 1992).

international and EC law, but not on German law. In England and Wales anyone can give legal advice, but the title of "solicitor" is reserved to those meeting the specialist entry requirements set out by the Law Society of England and Wales. If the activity is not reserved to a specialist profession, membership of such a professional body may in fact nevertheless confer significant market advantages, and yet entry could be restricted to such a professional group, again using educational and other criteria. Further illustrations will be seen later[48] in the context of applicable Community law.

### 3 COMMUNITY LAW ON MUTUAL RECOGNITION OF QUALIFICATIONS[49]

In the *Patrick*[50] case an English architect sought to have his qualifications recognised in France which refused to register him. In this case, which preceded the architects' Directive by many years,[51] France was obliged to recognise the UK qualification as a French ministerial decree of 1964 had recognised his type of certificate. Thus the French refusal to recognise Patrick's authorisation as an architect in 1973 could not be maintained. The rights flowing from Article 52 did not need to wait for a Directive under Article 57 to be enforceable. The Court applied its *Reyners* jurisprudence and maintained the rule of equal treatment. The Court here re-emphasised that Directives under Article 57 merely made the freedom of establishment easier but were not a prerequisite to the application of the rule in Article 52.[52] Thus as France had recognised the UK qualification it was not entitled to refuse authorisation to practice. The French were not entitled to rely on the requirement, under French law, that a diplomatic convention should exist between France and the UK before the recognition was automatic. As the French rules had recognised the equivalent of the diploma, Patrick was entitled immediately to rely on that equivalence by virtue of Article 52 as interpreted in the *Reyners* case and the case of *Thieffry*.[53]

The general law on Article 52 was considerably advanced by the case of *Vlassopoulou*.[54] Here, a Greek lawyer was refused admission to the German Bar as she did not hold the necessary diplomas under German law. As the facts in the case

48. See, for example, fn. 154 (engineers), fn. 172 (chartered surveyors) and accompanying text.

49. See generally, J Pertek (Ed), *General Recognition of Diplomas and Free Movement of Professionals* (European Institute of Public Administration, 1992); J Laslett, "The mutual recognition of diplomas, certificates and other evidences of formal qualifications in the European Community" (1990) L.I.E.I. 1; J Lonbay, "Diplomas Directive: Recognising Legal Qualifications in the EEC" (1991) *Lawyers in Europe*, Issue 7, pp. 10–13, Issue 8, pp. 5–10; J Pertek, *L'Europe des Diplomes et des professions* (Bruylant, 1994); H Schneider, *Die Anerkennung von Diplomen in der Europäischen Gemeinschaft* (Metro, 1995); D Lasok, *The Professions and Services in the European Economic Community* (Kluwer, 1986).

50. Case 11/77 *Patrick* v. *Ministere des Affaires Culturelles* [1977] E.C.R. 1199.

51. See fn. 137 below and accompanying text for a detailed look at the architects' Directive.

52. Paragraph 17 of the judgment. In particular, the Court stated: "... the fact that those Directives have not yet been issued does not entitle a Member State to deny the practical benefit of that freedom to a person subject to Community law in the freedom of establishment provided for by Article 52 can be ensured in the Member State by virtue in particular of the provisions of the laws and regulations already in force".

53. Case 71/76 *Thieffry* v. *Conseil de l'Ordre des Avocats* [1977] E.C.R. 765.

54. Case C-340/89 *Vlassopoulou* v. *Ministerium für Justiz, Bundes-und Europaangelegenheiten Baden-Württemberg* [1991] E.C.R. I-2357. Noted by J Lonbay, "Picking over the bones; the rights of establishment reviewed" (1991) 16 *European Law Review* 507–520 and Stein, (1992) 29 C.M.L.Rev. 625; see also J Lonbay, "Current Developments in EC law—Free movement of persons, recognition of qualifications and working conditions" (1994) 43 I.C.L.Q. 217.

arose before Directive 89/48/EEC[55] was in force the case was considered under Article 52. The European Court considered that national authorities had to have regard to knowledge and qualification acquired by the migrant in order to assess whether or not there was an equivalence of content. In the *Borell* case[56] the European Court applied the *Vlassopoulou* jurisprudence in the case of an English estate agent who, using Article 52EC, had sought recognition by the appropriate Spanish authorities to practice as such in Spain. There was no appropriate recognition machinery in place in Spain, and the European Court consequently ruled that the Spanish authorities were not entitled to impose penal sanctions for his exercise of the profession in Spain. Thus an EC citizen is entitled to expect that when he applies to practice a profession elsewhere in the Community the relevant authorities must have established proper recognition machinery (in accordance with the *Vlassopoulou* doctrine) prior to imposing any penalties. In *Haim* the applicant did not hold one of the necessary qualifications under Directive 78/686,[57] but the Court ruled that the competent authority in Germany was required to take into account his professional experience in assessing whether or not he would have to complete a further training period as required under German law.[58] Thus the *Vlassopoulou* principle can be applied in relation to Community secondary law.

Thus in principle *Vlassopoulou* and *Borrell*[59] together with *Haim*[60] indicate that the competent authorities of Member States must scrutinise carefully individual migrants to assess whether or not their own experience and knowledge are sufficient to comply with the local "qualifications" regime. The *Aranitis* case, discussed below,[60a] seems to extend the doctrine of mutual recognition to cover situations where qualifications are not required as a matter of regulation.

In the earlier *Heylens*[61] case important procedural safeguards had been established, which the European Court in *Vlassopoulou* re-endorsed. There a football trainer from Belgium worked in Lille, France. His application to have his qualifications recognised was refused without any reasons being given and with no right of appeal. The European Court firmly established that reasons had to be given as such a refusal could seriously impinge a migrant's right to mobility and that due rights of appeal should also be allowed. Thus incoming migrants can expect their knowledge and experience to be taken into account when the local competent authority assesses whether or not they fulfil the local qualification criteria.[62]

55. See fn. 73 below and accompanying text.

56. C-104/91 *Colegio Oficial de Agentes de la Propriedad Inmobiliaria* v. *Borrell, Newman, et al.* [1992] E.C.R. I-3003. The Spanish applicants' cases were dismissed as their situation did not fall within the domain of Community law.

57. The dentists sectoral Directive. Haim was qualified in Turkey. This qualification had been recognised in Belgium.

58. Case C-319/92 *Haim* v. *Kassenzahnärztliche Vereinigung Nordrhein* [1994] E.C.R. I-425.

59. Briefly noted by Lonbay (1992) 42 I.C.L.Q. 212 at 215).

60. See J Lonbay, "Current Developments in EC law—Free movement of persons, recognition of qualifications and working conditions" (1995) 44 I.C.L.Q. 705 at 710 *et seq.*

60a. See pp. 18 *et seq.*

61. Case 222/86 *Union Nationale des Entraineurs et Cadres Techniques Professionnels du Football (UNECTEF)* v. *Heylens* [1987] E.C.R. 4097. See R Wallace, "Remedies for foul play" (1988) 13 E.L.Rev. 267. See also J Lonbay, "Current Developments in EC law—Free movement of persons, recognition of qualifications and working conditions" (1989) 38 I.C.L.Q. 211 at 213.

62. Case C-419/92 *Scholtz* v. *Universitaria Cagliari* [1994] E.C.R. I-505 makes it clear that the experience of workers must also be taken into account where relevant.

The particular rules for individual professions are in some cases dealt with by specialised secondary Community law, to which we can now turn. There are three main types of Community secondary law in this field, the transitional Directives, the sectoral Directives and the general Directives. Each will be briefly explained below before turning to a more detailed assessment of their provisions, as relevant to the professions covered elsewhere in this book.

## 3.1 The transitional Directives

A series of early "transitional" Directives cover some regulated activities, such as insurance activities (agents and brokers[63]; all risk insurers[64]) and sundry trade and craft activities.[65] These transitional Directives were largely confined to removing discriminatory barriers, and did not attempt to co-ordinate qualifications nor provide for mutual recognition.[66] The insurance agents and brokers Directive,[67] for example, lists the professions covered in Article 2(2), Article 2(1) having defined the activities covered. Articles 4, 5 and 6 set out the levels of experience, knowledge or ability that must be accepted if a Member State subjects the activity to "possession of general commercial or professional knowledge of ability". Insurance practitioners who are chartered under the Chartered Insurance Institute are covered by Directive 89/48/EEC.[68] Another type of Directive in the field of qualifications is known as the sectoral Directive. We now turn to examine the role of the sectoral Directives issued under Article 57 of the EC Treaty.

## 3.2 The sectoral Directives

The medical and allied and pharmaceutical professions were considered relatively similar in the range of their activities and as Article 57(3) of the EC Treaty indicates that the "abolition of restrictions shall be dependent upon co-ordination of the conditions for their exercise in the various Member States" they received early attention and most of the medical and pharmaceutical professions have their own specialised sectoral Directives.[69] Typically these Directives come in pairs. First,

63. Directive 77/92/EEC (1977) OJ L 26/14.
64. Directive 88/357/EEC amending Directive 73/239/EEC (1988) OJ L 172/1.
65. E.g., Directive 64/224/EEC, OJ Sp. Ed. 1963–1964, p. 126.
66. The Commission proposes to consolidate and update these Directives to include these features. See "Proposal for a European Parliament and Council Directive establishing a mechanism for the recognition of qualifications in respect of professional activities covered by the Directives on liberalisation and transitional measures and supplementing the general systems for the recognition of qualifications", COM(96) final (8 February 1996). The proposal does not include any suggested alteration of Directive 77/92/EEC as it already includes provision for "certificates of aptitude". See generally Vaughan (Ed.) *Law of the European Communities* (Butterworths) paras 16.34 *et seq.*
67. The general rules are set out in chapter 8. The Insurance Brokers Registration Council applies rules established under s. 8 of the Insurance Brokers (Registration) Act 1977. Those wishing to register can do so according to s. 3 of the Act. Those applying from other Member States can rely on Directive 77/92/EEC (1977) OJ L 26/14 and have their overseas experience recognised (attested by a Certificate of Experience (see Article 9 of the Directive)). There is a Commission recommendation on insurance intermediaries (92/48/EEC (1992) OJ L 19/32) which sets out various professional requirements and competence levels.
68. The title "insurance broker" is protected by the Insurance Brokers (Registration) Act 1977, s. 22. However, insurance brokers are not covered by the general Directives as entry is by experience, and Directive 92/51/EEC excludes them in Article 2(2), annex a.
69. Doctors (general practice and specialists), nurses (general care), dentists, midwives, veterinary surgeons and pharmacists all have sectoral Directives.

training is co-ordinated so that there is a common minimum level of training, then the qualifications meeting these requirements are listed and those holding them are entitled to have them recognised in other Member States. The Directives also deal with matters relating to establishment and the provision of services and thus additionally have rules on recognising things such as "good character" and so on which are frequently required prior to being granted practice rights. In this sphere these Directives are referred to as "sectoral" Directives. Some other professions also have sectoral Directives, for example, architects,[70] and, at the time of writing there is also a controversial proposed Directive on the establishment of rights for lawyers.[71] Lawyers also currently have a services Directive.[72]

## 3.3 The general Directives[73]

For professions which are not covered by such "sectoral" or transitional Directives the scheme of the general Directives will normally operate, as long as the profession is in fact regulated.[74] Many Member States have yet to implement these Directives fully and the Commission has taken several successful Article 169 actions against several countries.[75] A reference has been made by the Administrative Court of First Instance in Athens regarding Directive 89/48/EEC, asking whether it entails rights in favour of individuals to whom it relates and whether these rights are directly effective and whether there are any infringements of Article 12 and questions of compensation for the damage the applicants claim to have suffered. There has as yet

70. As we shall see, this Directive is more properly considered a "mixed" Directive. See text accompanying fn. 137 below.

71. Proposal for a European Parliament and Council Directive to facilitate practice of the profession of lawyer on a permanent basis in a Member State other than that in which the qualification was obtained, COM(94)572; (1995) OJ C-128/6. See House of Lords Select Committee of the European Communities, Report on *The Right of Establishment for lawyers* (Session 1994–1995, HL paper 82; 14th Report). See Xavier de Roux, *Vers l'Europe des avocats,* Assemblée Nationale Rapport d'information No 2262 (1995) for a French parliamentary view of the proposal. J Lonbay, "Lawyers bounding over the borders: the Draft Directive on lawyers establishment" (1996) 21 E.L.Rev. 50.

72. Council Directive 77/249/EEC to facilitate the effective exercise by lawyers of freedom to provide services: (1977) OJ L 78/17.

73. The general Directives are: Council Directive 89/48/EEC on a general system for the recognition of higher-education diplomas awarded on completion of professional education and training of at least three years' duration (1989) OJ L 19/16 and Council Directive 92/51/EEC on a second general system for the recognition of professional education and training to supplement Directive 89/48/EEC (1992) OJ L 209/25 as amended (most recently by Commission Directive 95/43/EC of 20 July 1995) OJ L 184/21. See generally Commission, "Report to the European Parliament and the Council on the state of application of the general system for the recognition of higher education diplomas", COM(96) 46 final (15 February 1996), which indicates that the system has been used by 12,000 people since its inception.

74. This issue is dealt with at fns 82–93 below and accompanying text.

75. See case C-216/94 *Commission* v. *Belgium* (13 July 1995); case C-365/93 *Commission* v. *Hellenic Republic* (23 March 1995). Generally, see the Pack Report (A4-261/950) of the European Parliament, debated in November 1995. Note there is an Article 169 Reasoned Opinion currently pending against Germany with regard to its failure to implement the Directive for Teachers in four Laender, against France under Directive 92/51 for its failure as regards ski instructors, against Greece for failure to implement the doctors Directive correctly, and its failure to implement properly the transitional Directive 68/366/EEC as regards hotel managers (failure to recognise experience and requiring local qualifications/courses) and against the UK for failing to implement fully Directive 89/594/EEC which modifies sectoral Directives on nurses, doctors, dental practitioners, veterinary surgeons and midwives. See *Agence Europe* No 6636 (29 December 1995). See also COM(96) 46, *op. cit.*

been no Opinion by the Advocate General on this case which is awaited with interest.[76]

The general system Directives were adopted as it was clear that the sectoral method[77] would take many years to complete, if it could ever be completed. The architects' Directive,[78] for example, took over 17 years to agree. With this rate of progress there was no hope for a scheme to be in place allowing professionals to migrate within the "1992" target. Moreover, the sectoral scheme of co-ordination had its detractions, notably a lack of flexibility. Alterations to training or qualifications have to be routed through Brussels machinery, and there were fears and doubts about the quality of incoming professionals with non-national qualifications.[79]

At the Fontainebleau Summit in June 1984 the European Council asked the Council of Ministers to consider the introduction of "a general system for ensuring the equivalence of university diplomas in order to bring about the effective freedom of establishment within the Community". The *ad hoc* Adonninno Committee report, supported by the European Council Summit in March 1985 (Brussels), suggested mutual recognition of higher educational qualifications, the content of which would not be affected in any way. Any major "structural differences" between training programmes could be compensated by two to three years of professional experience.

The Commission recognised this new approach in its famous White Paper, and duly proposed a Directive (COM(85) 355 final) along these lines. This was modified after the European Parliament and Economic and Social Committee had commented and the amended proposal was published in May 1986. The German Presidency managed to get a "common position" on the Directive on mutual recognition adopted in June 1988, and the Directive itself was decided in December 1988. Directive 89/48/EEC "on a general system for the recognition of higher education diplomas awarded on completion of professional education and training of at least three years' duration" was adopted in the spirit of "1992", though the Member States and the affected professions are likely to have had any worries soothed by the low take-up rate by non-nationals of the professions liberalised beforehand. By 1987, for example, only 187 midwives had exercised their rights of mobility available since 1983. It should be recognised that the path taken by the Community, though sanctioned by Summit meetings, was also sign-posted by the case-law of the European Court in Luxembourg, in particular the line of cases leading to the *Heylens* decision.[80]

These general Directives cover "regulated professions" when certain training criteria are met. Directive 89/48/EEC dealing with higher-level qualifications is the most relevant for the professions covered by this book and thus I concentrate on it. The core of the Directive is found in Article 3 which states:

"Where, in a host Member State, the taking up or pursuit of a regulated profession is subject to possession of a diploma, the Competent Authority may not, on the grounds of inadequate

---

76. Cases C-225/95, C-226/95 and C-227/95 *Kapasakalis, Skiathitis and Kouyangas* v. *Greece* (1995) OJ C-229/13.

77. Sectoral Directives are still possible, and the Commission has proposed a Directive for lawyers: see 1995 OJ C-128/6. This follows the agreement of the CCBE at Lisbon in 1992 on the text of a draft Directive.

78. See fn. 137 below.

79. These are still present, see fns 132 and 133 below.

80. See fn. 61 above.

qualifications, refuse to authorise a national of a Member State to take up or pursue that profession on the same conditions as apply to its own nationals:

(a) if the applicant holds the diploma required in another Member State for the taking up or pursuit of the profession in question in its territory, such diploma having been awarded in a Member State; or

(b) if the applicant has pursued the profession in question full-time for two years during the previous ten years in another Member State which does not regulate that profession, within the meaning of Article 1(c) and the first subparagraph of Article 1(d), and possesses evidence of one or more formal qualifications:

— which have been awarded by a Competent Authority in a Member State, designated in accordance with the laws, regulations or administrative provisions of such State,

— which show that the holder has successfully completed a post-secondary course of at least three years' duration, or of an equivalent duration part-time, at a university or establishment of higher education or another establishment of similar level of a Member State and, where appropriate, that he has successfully completed the professional training required in addition to the post-secondary course and

— which have prepared the holder for the pursuit of his profession.

The following shall be treated in the same way as the evidence of formal qualifications referred to in the first subparagraph: any formal qualifications or any set of such formal qualifications awarded by a Competent Authority in a Member State if it is awarded on the successful completion of training received in the Community and is recognised by that Member State as being of an equivalent level, provided that the other Member States and the Commission have been notified of this recognition."

Thus under Article 3 of the Directive, migrants have the right to have their qualifications submitted for recognition, but do not receive automatic recognition of their right to practice their profession in the host State. Article 4 provides the "so-called" compensation mechanisms.

"(1) Notwithstanding Article 3, the host Member State may also require the applicant:

(a) to provide evidence of professional experience, where the duration of the education and training adduced in support of his application, as laid down in Article 3(a) and (b), is at least one year less than that required in the host Member State. In this event, the period of professional experience required:

— may not exceed twice the shortfall in duration of education and training where the shortfall relates to post-secondary studies and/or to a period of probationary practice carried out under the control of a supervising professional person and ending with an examination,

— may not exceed the shortfall where the shortfall relates to professional practice acquired with the assistance of a qualified member of the profession.

In the case of diplomas within the meaning of the last subparagraph of Article 1(a), the duration of education and training recognised as being of an equivalent level shall be determined as for the education and training defined in the first subparagraph of Article 1(a).

When applying these provisions, account must be taken of the professional experience referred to in Article 3(b).

At all events, the professional experience required may not exceed four years;

(b) to complete an adaptation period not exceeding three years or take an aptitude test:

— where the matters covered by the education and training he has received as laid down in Article 3(a) and (b), differ substantially from those covered by the diploma required in the host Member State, or

— where, in the case referred to in Article 3(a), the profession regulated in the host Member State comprises one or more regulated professional activities which are not in the profession regulated in the Member State from which the applicant originates or comes and that difference corresponds to specific education and training required in the host Member State and covers matters which differ substantially from those covered by the diploma adduced by the applicant, or

— where, in the case referred to in Article 3(b), the profession regulated in the host Member State comprises one or more regulated professional activities which are not in the profession pursued by the applicant in the Member State from which he originates or comes, and that difference corresponds to specific education and training required in the host Member State and covers matters which differ substantially from those covered by the evidence of formal qualifications adduced by the applicant.

Should the host Member State make use of this possibility, it must give the applicant the right to choose between an adaptation period and an aptitude test. By way of derogation from this principle, for professions whose practice requires precise knowledge of national law and in respect of which the provision of advice and/or assistance concerning national law is an essential and constant aspect of the professional activity, the host Member State may stipulate either an adaptation period or an aptitude test. Where the host Member State intends to introduce derogations for other professions as regards an applicant's right to choose, the procedure laid down in Article 10 shall apply.

(2) However, the host Member State may not apply the provisions of paragraph 1(a) and (b) cumulatively."

The Directive allows migrants entry to the local "profession on the same conditions as apply to its own nationals".[81] They must have equivalent qualifications, and if they do not then Article 4 can be applied "in compensation". In this way the Directive can "bend" and be applied to many professions that have different training requirements or scope of activities. The Directive only applies to regulated professions. How are these defined?

## 3.4 What is a regulated profession?

The general Directives do not seek, at the Community level, to ascertain equivalence of training as such (as do the sectoral Directives), but rather consider that activities which are similar will require similar training, and that mutual recognition can piggy-back this fact.[82] The Directive accords with the spirit of subsidiarity in that it does not seek to alter in any way the local professional regulation, except to force the local profession to accept suitably qualified and experienced migrants. Clearly the burden under the general Directive's scheme is on the competent national authorities who have the duty to assess first whether the migrant's profession is "the same" and, secondly, whether the training the migrant has received is sufficient and if not which compensation mechanism at which level to deploy.[83] For the purposes of the Directive there must be definition of what comprises a "profession". However, as we shall see, this is a complex question.

---

81. This is emphasised by Article 7(1) of the Directive which provides:
"The Competent Authorities of host Member States shall recognise the right of nationals of Member States who fulfil the conditions for the taking up and pursuit of a regulated profession in their territory to use the professional title of the host Member State corresponding to that profession."

82. J Beuve-Méry, "La reconnaissance des diplômes: le système générale adopté le 21.12.1989 par le conseil des communautés européennes" (1990) 336 *Revue du marché commun* 293; see Council Resolution of 1974 OJ C-98/1.

83. Subject to Article 4 of Directive 89/48/EEC.

The issue of what amounts to a profession or professional activity is rather avoided in Community legislation. As we shall see with the architects' Directive[84] the use of the designation itself is alone mentioned with no definition of the activities which architects undertake attempted. This is because architects and what they do varies considerably from country to country,[85] and there are overlaps with other professions. One might think that the general Directives on mutual recognition of professional qualifications would provide a definition. They do in part, but the definitions appear at first sight to be tautologous. As they deal potentially with many professions the definition used can be expected to be somewhat wide. In Directive 89/48/EEC Article 2 dictates:

"This Directive shall apply to any national of a Member State wishing to pursue a *regulated profession*[86] in a host Member State in a self-employed capacity or as an employed person.

This Directive shall not apply to professions which are the subject of a separate Directive establishing arrangements for the mutual recognition of diplomas by Member States."

What amounts to a "regulated profession" within the Directive is defined in Article 1 of the Directive as follows:

"(c) a regulated profession: the regulated professional activity or range of activities which constitute this profession in a Member State; ..."

This is not much help, but Article 1(d) then defines "regulated professional activity" as follows:

"(d) regulated professional activity: a professional activity, in so far as the taking up or pursuit of such activity or one of its modes of pursuit in a Member State is subject, directly or indirectly by virtue of laws, regulations or administrative provisions, to the possession of a diploma. The following in particular shall constitute a mode of pursuit of a regulated professional activity:
— pursuit of an activity under a professional title, in so far as the use of such a title is reserved to the holders of a diploma governed by laws, regulations or administrative provisions,
— pursuit of a professional activity relating to health, in so far as remuneration and/or reimbursement for such an activity is subject by virtue of national social security arrangements to the possession of a diploma.

Where the first subparagraph does not apply, a professional activity shall be deemed to be a regulated professional activity if it is pursued by the members of an association or organisation the purpose of which is, in particular, to promote and maintain a high standard in the professional field concerned and which, to achieve that purpose, is recognised in a special form by a Member State and:
— awards a diploma to its members,
— ensures that its members respect the rules of professional conduct which it prescribes, and
— confers on them the right to use a title or designatory letters, or to benefit from a status corresponding to that diploma.

A non-exhaustive list of associations or organisations which, when this Directive is adopted, satisfy the conditions of the second subparagraph is contained in the annex. Whenever a Member State grants the recognition referred to in the second subparagraph to an association or organisation, it shall inform the Commission thereof, which shall publish this information in the Official Journal of the European Communities."

84. See fn. 137 below and accompanying text.
85. Even this minimalist approach causes problems in cross-border activities: see fn. 186 below and accompanying text.
86. My emphasis. Note that the Directive covers both the employed and the self-employed.

The definition of "diploma" thus becomes important in determining what amounts to a regulated professional activity under the Directive.

Regulated professional activity is defined in terms of activities which are directly or indirectly regulated by the requirement of possession of a diploma. The examples given in the Article are those activities which are only pursued under a "reserved"[87] professional title. The term "diploma" is itself defined in Article 1(a) as:

"(a)  diploma: any diploma, certificate or other evidence of formal qualifications or any set of such diplomas, certificates or other evidence:
— which has been awarded by a Competent Authority in a Member State, designated in accordance with its own laws, regulations or administrative provisions;
— which shows that the holder has successfully completed a post-secondary course of at least three years' duration, or of an equivalent duration part-time, at a university or establishment of higher education or another establishment of similar level and, where appropriate, that he has successfully completed the professional training required in addition to the post-secondary course; and
— which shows that the holder has the professional qualifications required for the taking up or pursuit of a regulated profession in that Member State, provided that the education and training attested by the diploma, certificate or other evidence of formal qualifications were received mainly in the Community, or the holder thereof has three years' professional experience certified by the Member State which recognised a third-country diploma, certificate or other evidence of formal qualifications.[88]
The following shall be treated in the same way as a diploma, within the meaning of the first subparagraph: any diploma, certificate or other evidence of formal qualifications or any set of such diplomas, certificates or other evidence awarded by a Competent Authority in a Member State if it is awarded on the successful completion of education and training received in the Community and recognised by a Competent Authority in that Member State as being of an equivalent level and if it confers the same rights in respect of the taking up and pursuit of a regulated profession in that Member State; ..."

It will be seen that the Directive is not very clear and the *Aranitis*[89] case was the first opportunity for the European Court to analyse its provisions. The issue of what amounts to professional regulation was raised in litigation in Germany, where professional titles have great importance and considerable regulation attached to them. Georgios Aranitis held a Greek diploma "Ptichiouchos Geologikos" which is awarded after four years of university studies in geology. He had worked as a geologist in Greece for over a decade. He then moved to Berlin where he wished to carry on as a geologist. The local employment office in Berlin classified him as an "unskilled assistant". He challenged this classification relying on the general Directive on mutual recognition of professional qualifications, Directive 89/48/

---

87. Reserved either "by laws, regulations or administrative provisions" (first indent) or by the action of "an association or organisation" which is recognised in a special form by a Member State and:
— awards a diploma to its members,
— ensures that its members respect the rules of professional conduct which it prescribes, and
— confers on them the right to use a title or designatory letters, or to benefit from a status corresponding to that diploma.
88. Directive 89/48/EEC deals with those holding third-country diplomas by the definition of diplomas whereby diplomas obtained in third countries by EU nationals who can show at least three years' experience certified by the Member State recognising their diploma will have their diploma recognised. See also Council recommendation 89/49 OJ L 19/24. See fn. 187 below and accompanying text.
89. Case C-164/94 *Georgios Aranitis* v. *Land Berlin* Advocate General Léger Opinion delivered on 26 October 1995, judgment, 1 February 1996.

EEC.[90] The *Arbeitsamt* allowed him a literal translation of his Greek title, but refused to allow him to use the equivalent German qualification *Diplom-Geologe*. The profession of geologist was not considered to be regulated in Germany and the German authorities thus considered that Aranitis was unable to rely on Directive 89/48/EEC.

Advocate General Léger in his Opinion first considered the question as to whether or not geologists were regulated in Germany (under the terms of the Directive). It was clear that there was no required "diploma" but rather that in order to succeed *de facto* geologists practising in Germany all had the *Diplom-Geologe*. Was this fact sufficient to make the practice of geology in Germany a "regulated activity"? The Advocate General went for a narrow definition of the meaning of "regulated profession", confining it to professions "where the State has directly or indirectly laid down rules governing the taking up and pursuit of the profession and where penalties are imposed for failure to comply with those rules". This interpretation was adopted by the European Court and meant that Aranitis could not rely on the general Directive itself to force the German authorities to recognise his qualification as equivalent to the German qualification. Léger stated that the Directive should not be used to "turn truth upside down by allowing persons who do not possess a certain diploma to make use of a diploma which they do not have".[91] The European Court was much more positive and indicated[91a] that Aranatis should be able to rely on the *Vlassopoulou* jurisprudence which it extended to cover qualifications for unregulated occupations which could help holders gain employment.

Thus it is submitted that should an element of knowledge or ability not be attested to in Aranitis's Greek qualification then the German authorities could refuse such recognition unless his practical or other academic experience compensated for the deficit. It seems that the general case-law may have extended to require competent authorities to assess the equivalence of the diploma? And if missing elements are found then experience, knowledge and ability subsequently acquired should be taken into account. Confusion could be averted by a tag indicating the qualification of origin. There are numerous professions where it is not certain whether the profession is regulated throughout the EC. For example, in the Netherlands the academic title of engineer is protected and is used for professional purposes though not legally required.[92] Is it a regulated profession? As *Aranitis* extends *Vlassopoulou* to cover such situations the question of regulation becomes less important. It is arguable then that *Aranitis* extends *Vlassopoulou* to cover the mutual recognition of academic qualifications where these are important assets for job-seekers or self-employed persons.

The general Directives in particular have spawned a surge by "wannabe" professions towards wishing to be regulated on the grounds that this will increase the ease with which one might be accepted as a professional in other European states. This is because the general Directive requires them to have two years professional

90. 1989 OJ L 19/16.
91. Paragraph 45.
91a. Paras 30–32 of the judgment.
92. See Parkins, N, "Directive 89/48/EEC: Progress Towards implementation" in Pertek (Ed.) *General Recognition of Diplomas and Free Movement of Professionals, op. cit.*, p. 37 at pp. 49 *et seq.*

experience before recognition in another member State. The Commission is proposing to remove this requirement by revising Directive 89/48/EEC.[92a] An illustration of this is shown in the *Operational Research Newsletter* where the case for "regulation" has recently been discussed.[93]

Many of the paramedical professions are covered by the general system, for example physiotherapists. Peter Burley in his paper[94] indicates the variety of types of regulation for the medical professions. Where an activity is reserved to a particular profession he describes this as a "functional closure", for example for the profession of midwife, the criminal law makes it an offence for anyone except a midwife to practice midwifery as defined by Parliament. Other professions are protected by a title. So, for example, the nurse regulated by the UKCC has a protected title. Other medical professions have a partially protected title. Thus "state registered" chiropodists have specific sectors reserved to them, but anybody can describe themselves as a simple "chiropodist". Other professions such as the drama therapist have their training regulated and have some specific employment sectors reserved for those with particular qualifications by the Department of Health. Others are indirectly regulated. Thus, for example, for orthotists each and every separate contract for orthotic services has a specific level of required qualifications. All these Burley considers as regulated professions in terms of Community law. On the threshold of "regulation" are the professions where the market-enforced employment rules operate—for example for the ambulance paramedics only those with the relevant qualifications are likely to be employed, but there is no rule maintaining this position. Or again, psychotherapists where there is a voluntary self-regulation by the professional body. It is in these cases that the *Aranitis* ruling will be important.

Where Community secondary law does not apply, for example in activities outwith the scope of the sectoral or transitional Directives and for which no qualifications are required, then the principles set out in the EC Treaty, as interpreted by the European Court of Justice and set out above, will operate. These principles will also guide the interpretation of the EC secondary legislation.

We can now turn to view the Community rules affecting some of the particular professions covered in this book which will enable a fuller explanation of these types of secondary law in context. Lawyers and accounts are dealt with by the first general Directive and so follow on immediately. Then the reader will find sections on doctors and architects who are dealt with by sectoral Directives. Thereafter, engineers and estate agents are covered. As both are extremely varied in how they are dealt with at national level and EC-wide, and as they both overlap in function, at least to some degree with architects they are presented partially as a case study of the issues raised by such overlapping of professional functions.

---

92a. See COM(96) 46, *op. cit.*, p. 36.

93. See issues of the *Operational Research Newsletter* from November 1994. Articles by Lynn Thomas (president), Robert Simons, Maurice Shutler, TMF Smith and Jonathan Rosenhead.

94. Sent to the author: see P Burley, "The General Directives on Mutual Recognition of Higher Education Diplomas," in P Neale, *Creating European Professional* (Leeds, 1994), p. 29.

## 4 LAWYERS[95]

As regards lawyers, one can say that there are lots of professional bodies and legal professions in Europe.[96] The objective differences between the legal systems is such as to make it difficult for an immediate cross-border application of mutual recognition of qualifications. It is only in exceptional circumstances, for example, that a German lawyer will be well versed in English law or Scots law and vice versa. This fact was in part recognised by the early adoption of a Directive allowing cross-border mobility for lawyers as regards services. It is beyond the scope of this chapter to describe in detail this Directive which allows the provision of legal services on a temporary cross-border basis.[97] The fact that one is on a temporary cross-border activity does not preclude one from establishing an office if this is necessary.[98] However, lawyers wishing to establish on a more permanent basis have come across the same difficulties as other professions where their activities, for example the giving of legal advice, is reserved to a particular profession or professions as in France and Germany and some other Member States. They may wish to practice their own law for the benefit of expatriates and yet are prevented from establishing as such. Difficulties and uncertainties about the scope of Article 52 which have not been fully resolved by the *Gebhard* case have led to the adoption by the Commission of a proposal for a lawyers establishment rights Directive.[99] It is not appropriate to rehearse the entire history of this saga but suffice it to say that this proposal is currently in the doldrums following disagreement about the nature of the rights that should be established within it. The larger faction promotes the idea of a right of establishment on a home State title basis but a strong rearguard action by Luxembourg and France maintain that establishment must be on host State terms i.e., under the regulation and control of the local profession. A compromise solution proposed within the CCBE is currently being discussed, and may be used by the Commission in a revised proposal expected shortly.[100]

Lawyers can, of course, utilise the provisions of Directive 89/48/EEC. This has not been implemented throughout the EC yet[101] and in some cases the implementation is of questionable legality, for example, in the Netherlands. It is not proposed to detail all the types of aptitude tests which have been established in the different Member

95. See generally D Edward, "Freedom of Movement for the Regulated Professions" in White & Smythe (Eds), *Current Issues in European and International Law*; R Goebel, "Lawyers in the European Community: Progress towards Community-wide rights of practice" in (1991–1992) 15 *Fordham International Law Journal* 556; N Skarlatos, "European Lawyer's right to transnational legal practice" (1991) L.I.E.I. 49; J Pertek, "Professions juridiques et judiciares" (1994) *Juris-Classeur*; Lonbay and Spedding, *International Professional Practice* (Chancery Law, 1992).

96. Lonbay, Brown, Tridimas, Platt, *Training Lawyers in the European Community* (The Law Society, 1990).

97. The issue has been before the European Court in several important cases and both German and French implementation has been found to be faulty. See case 427/85 *Commission* v. *Germany* [1988] E.C.R. 1123, commented on by J Lonbay, in "Cross-frontier provision of services by lawyers" (1988) 13 E.L.Rev. 347–350; and case 294/89 *Commission* v. *France* [1991] E.C.R. I-3591.

98. The *Gebhard* case, *op. cit.*

99. See fn. 71 above.

100. See J Lonbay, "Lawyers bounding over Borders" (1996) 21 E.L.Rev. 50.

101. For example, in Spain and Belgium there is no implementation yet as regards lawyers. Where the Directive has been implemented the numbers utilising it have been small. For example, in Germany around 50 have attempted entry, in Greece there have been two applicants and in England solicitors have admitted over 350 applicants (though 270 were Irish solicitors).

States,[102] but as the training lawyers receive in the different European countries is mostly very different, one can imagine that cross-qualification is not a particularly easy route.[103]

## 5 ACCOUNTANTS AND AUDITORS

Accountants are in a similar position to lawyers relative to Community law on mutual recognition of qualifications. An illustration used by the DTI shows that someone wishing to work as an accountant throughout the Community would have to spend 50 years training to get all the necessary different national qualifications. For lawyers 50 years' study would not even provide one with the basic academic stage of qualification in all the Member States; a similar further period of professional training would be required to be fully qualified throughout the Community!

Auditors hold a slightly different position in that Directive 84/253/EEC[104] sets out specific knowledge requirements which auditors must have together with levels of practical training to be undertaken. The chapter on auditors and accountants deals very thoroughly with the UK implementation of these rules.[105] Thus an auditor is in a slightly different position from the accountant and lawyer in that some level of qualification is required by the EC law on companies.

Generally, the provision of general accounting services such as tax advice or management consultancy is not regulated in the UK. Anybody may provide such services and need not belong to any UK accountancy organisation. One does find, however, that auditing[106] (as mentioned above), insolvency practice[107] and investment business[108] is regulated. Migrants coming into the UK wishing to maintain an auditing practice will have to pass a test to include the law on auditing of accounts in the UK. There will also be a series of regulations to be complied with (for example, rules relating to maintenance of competence by registered auditors).

102. For details of the first few systems adopted, see J Lonbay, "Diplomas Directive: Recognising Legal Qualifications in the EEC" (1991) *Lawyers in Europe*, Issue 7, pp. 10–13, Issue 8, pp. 5–10; for a sketch of the French system, see I Jacobs, "Requalification for EC lawyers in France" (1993) *International Legal Practitioner* 117. The Institute of European Law of the University of Birmingham will shortly have a worldwide web site giving all the relevant details.

103. See J Lonbay, "Differences in the legal education in the Member States of the European Community" in Bruno de Witte and Caroline Forder (Eds), *The common law of Europe and the future of legal education* (Kluwer, 1992) pp. 75–94; also Lonbay *et al.*, *Training Lawyers in the European Community* (The Law Society, 1990).

104. Directive 84/253/EEC (1984) OJ L 126. This Directive is based on Article 54(3)(g) and is primarily a company law Directive not dealing mainly with rights of establishment or rights to provide services.

105. See chapter 5.

106. The auditing recognised supervisory bodies include the Institute of Chartered Accountants in England and Wales ("ICAEW"); the Institute of Chartered Accountants of Scotland ("ICAS"); the Institute of Chartered Accountants in Ireland ("ICAI"); the Chartered Association of Certified Accountants ("ACCA"); and the Association of Authorised Public Accountants ("AAPA").

107. Insolvency practice is regulated by the Insolvency Act 1986 and the Insolvency (Northern Ireland) Order (1989, SI 1989/2405), which require persons to hold an insolvency licence if they wish to undertake insolvency work in relation to UK companies.

108. Investment services are regulated by the Financial Services Act 1986. There are numerous authorising bodies for work in this field including the Securities and Investments Board ("SIB"), five self-regulating organisations and nine recognised professional bodies including the ICAEW, the ICAS, the ICAI and ACCA.

The use of the title "chartered accountant" is reserved for members of the ICAEW, ICAS or ICAI. There is no restriction on the use of the term "accountant" or "public accountant" nor indeed on using a home title qualification.[109] Thus one can see that chartered accountants are in a similar position to lawyers in that the bulk of their activity is unregulated, but their professional title (at least for some groups)[110] is protected and thus the terms of the general Directive 89/48/EEC will apply.[111]

## 6 THE MEDICAL PROFESSIONS

The assumption that the medical professions were similar, and thus amenable to the sectoral approach, did not always hold true. As Zilioli relates with regards to Italian dentistry which had to be completely "created" following the adoption of the EC dentists' Directives.[112] This is illustrated by the recent case against Italy under Article 169 of the EC Treaty.[113] In this case Italy was condemned for delaying in its implementation of the dentistry Directives. The Dentists' Recognition Directive[114] laid down the principle that Member States will recognise each others' dentistry diplomas. This was made possible by the co-ordination Directive which laid down the conditions of training by which Member States limit the right to take up with the dental profession. The criteria control of training relate to both quality and the total duration of training. Article 3 then sets out an exhaustive list of national diplomas which will be automatically recognised.

In 1985 Italy created the profession of dental practitioner. It is to be noted that Article 5 of the Dentists' Co-ordination Directive actually specifies the definition of dentists' work. The medical Directives do not do this for doctors. The situation was that prior to 1978 the dental profession in Italy was unregulated and ordinary doctors could practise dentistry. Thus the dentist Directive essentially meant that Italy had to create a new training system and new profession of dentistry and Article 19 allowed Italy a slight delay to allow for this. This delay meant that Italy had about a four-and-a-half year period extra grace allowing it six years to set up a new system. However, the Commission's patience had run out by 1988 when the Italians sought to further delay implementation of the Directive. In essence Italy was maintaining the *status quo*, thus creating a category of dental practitioner who would only be able to practise in Italy as they had failed to comply with the requirements of the dentists'

---

109. Of the six UK professional accountancy bodies, the members of the three mentioned are granted the status of "chartered" accountant. The Chartered Association of Certified Accountants ("ACCA") and the Chartered Institute of Management Accountants ("CIMA") have applied to the Privy Council for the right to use the title. See Kelly, *Financial Times*, 10 September 1995.

110. Certified accountants ("ACCA") are also covered by the general directive.

111. The aptitude test established by the Institute of Chartered Accountants in England and Wales, of Scotland, and in Ireland are set out in a useful publication, *Practice Rights in the UK and Ireland for EC Nationals*, prepared by the Chartered Accountants Joint International Committee. This body is also producing information on practice rights and other Member States for UK and Irish Chartered Accountants.

112. C Zilioli, "The recognition of diplomas and its impact on educational policies" in B De Witte (Ed.), *European Community Law of Education* (Nomos, 1989).

113. Case C-40/93 *Commission* v. *Italy* (1 June 1995).

114. Directive 78/686/EEC (1978) OJ L 233/1.

Directive. Advocate General Léger was scathing and indicated that "the Italian Republic is wrecking the principle of mutual trust established by the system and the principle of automatic recognition of diplomas which was introduced on the implementation of the 1978 Directives". The case confirms that the Directives exclusively set out the training requirements of dentists and Member States "may not create a category of dental practitioners which does not correspond to any category provided for by the Directives in question."[115]

This case is important as it made clear that in the case of sectoral Directives there could be, where the scope of the activities definitely defined, an exclusion of Member State recognition of alternative professions in that sector.

Although doctors, dentists, vets, nurses and midwives are covered by the EC sectoral Directives there are specialities which have yet to be covered by these measures.[116] As Nicholas points out, for example, accident and emergency medicine are not included as a speciality.[117] Additionally other (para-)medical professions notably those dealt with in the UK by The Council For Professions Supplementary to Medicine fall under Directives 89/48/EEC and 92/51/EEC.[118] In the field of professions related to medicine—for example chiropody, dieticians, occupational therapy, orthoptics, physiotherapy and radiography—there have been a considerable number of migrants. The bulk of these are comprised of physiotherapists and occupational therapists. Since 1991 the numbers have been high,[119] largely as a result of the UK's open door policy and a shortage of relevantly qualified personnel. Also the UK is considered a staging post for continental migrants on their way to the USA. A dental surgery assistant or hygienist, for example, would fall under the second general Directive, a dietician under the first general Directive; whereas a surgeon would come under the sectoral Directive. Thus one cannot generalise about the medically related professions. Each activity and profession must be assessed on its merits to determine what Community law applies. Many of the professions are covered by the general Directives, for example the chartered psychologists,[120] and the rules of Directive 89/48/EEC will apply. It is now appropriate to look at the doctors' Directives though it is not proposed to go through all the requirements established by the doctors' Directives here, but rather to give an overall explanation of how they work.[121]

The movement of doctors in Europe has an interesting history and has provided

---

115. Paragraph 24.

116. For a general survey, see W Boesken, H-H Kühne and W Heusel, *Postgraduate studies for medical specialists and freedom of establishment for doctors in the internal market* (Bundesanzeige, 1994).

117. S Nicholas, "Mobility of Doctors—the Theory and the Practice" in P Neale, *Creating European Professionals* (Leeds, 1994) at pp. 16 and 17.

118. Professions covered by the Council include chiropodists, dieticians, medical laboratories' scientific officers, occupational therapists, orthoptists, physiotherapists and radiographers. The professions of Art, Music and Drama therapists have observer status: P Burley, "The General Directives on Mutual Recognition of Higher Education Diplomas", in P Neale, *Creating European Professionals, op. cit.*, p. 29.

119. Over 3,000 have been admitted: Letter (8 August 1995) from Peter Burley, Acting Registrar of the Council for the Professions Supplementary to Medicine. See generally, P Burley, "European Community Directive 89/48/EEC and the Council for Professions Supplementary to Medicine", *op. cit.*

120. The practice of psychology itself is not protected, though the title "chartered psychologist" is. Anybody can style themselves as a psychologist. They are thus in a similar position to accountants as regards EC law.

121. For fuller treatment, see Vaughan, *op. cit.*, N Foster, *Common Market Reporter*, para. 1772 (CCH).

some interesting cases. For our purposes the history will concentrate on the implementation of the sectoral Directives which were adopted in 1975 and provided for co-ordination and mutual recognition of medical training.[122] The sundry medical Directives have now been consolidated into Directive 93/16/EEC.[123] The Directives follow the classic mode of the sectoral Directives; thus the training is first co-ordinated and a second companion Directive provides for mutual recognition of qualifications which comply with the terms of the co-ordination Directive, and additionally lists the earlier qualifications covered.

Directive 93/16[124] includes long lists of diplomas, certificates and other evidence of qualifications in medicine, country by country. The lists are found in Article 3 for basic qualifications and Articles 5 and 7[125] for specialisations. Articles 23–29 require the Member States to ensure that persons wishing to take up and pursue such medical professions hold such diplomas.[126] The qualifications and training period are designed to ensure adequate knowledge and understanding of the necessary disciplines and sciences as well as to provide suitable clinical experience. The Directive sets out basic requirements below which Member States may not fall. Thus medical training must comprise at least a six-year course of 5,500 hours of theoretical and practical instruction given under the supervision of the university. Those whose diplomas do not satisfy the requirements of Articles 3, 5 and 7 can supplement their training and attach a certificate of equivalence according to Article 9. The Directive includes provisions for cases where Member States suspect that the requirements of the diplomas Directive are not being complied with. It also deals with supervision on the use of academic and professional titles[127] and linguistic requirements.[128] The Directive has provisions on both establishment and the provision of services by doctors.[129] Decision 75/364 set up an advisory committee on medical training[130] and there is a review committee of senior officials on public health established by Council Decision 75/365.[131] These Decisions allow for Community-wide review of the Directives on medical training. This procedure has been insufficient to satisfy some professional bodies.[132] Similar fears are expressed by vets who threatened to breach

---

122. The Nuffield Foundation's *Education and Training of Personnel, Auxiliary to Dentistry* outlines at p. 32 the history of regulation and registration in medicine and dentistry in the UK.

123. Directive 93/16/EEC (1993) OJ L165/1; itself now the subject of a proposal to amend it: (COM/94/626/fin. 1994/12/16/8p.) Proposal for European Parliament and Council Directive amending Directive 93/16/EEC which facilitates the free movement of doctors and provides for the mutual recognition of their diplomas, certificates and other evidence of formal qualifications, and conferring implementing powers on the Commission for the updating of certain articles thereof.

124. Directive 93/16 also incorporates Council Directive 81/1057 (1981) OJ L 35/25.

125. Article 7 includes, for example, geriatrics and renal diseases in the UK.

126. This is a mandatory obligation: see Case 306/84 *Commission* v. *Belgium* [1987] E.C.R. 675.

127. Articles 10 and 19 respectively.

128. Article 20. Some "medical" professions (not covered by Directive 93/16) are particularly concerned that their language requirements are complied with, for example, the Royal College of Speech and Language Therapists. This is because of the nature of speech and language therapy and the need for highly developed English language skills. Since 1991 the Royal College has approved approximately 25 applicants under Directive 89/48/EEC. This College acts as gatekeeper for those wishing to practise as speech therapists within the NHS.

129. Articles 11–19. These Articles deal with such matters as proof of good character, health, disciplinary matters, procedural issues and registration.

130. OJ L 167/17.

131. As amended by Council Decision 77/455 OJ 1977 L 176/13.

132. See S Nicholas, *op. cit.*, at p. 21, who indicates fears of inadequate training of doctors.

EC law by refusing to allow vets from some Member States to work in the UK. Barry Johnson, the President of the Royal College of Veterinary Surgeons, expressed concern over training in Italy, Greece and Spain in particular.[133]

In the UK it is the General Medical Council that deals with recognition of qualifications for doctors. For incoming EU-doctors[134] there are three requirements which must be met:

(1) one must be a national of an EC Member State;
(2) one must possess a primary qualification in that State; and
(3) one must be in good standing with the regulatory authorities in his/her home State.

An acknowledged failure of the UK to implement properly the Directives was illustrated in a case brought by Anthony Goldstein, a London rheumatologist, in a High Court writ against the Health Secretary.[135] The UK criteria for awarding specialist medical accreditation were admitted in the High Court to be in breach of EC law, namely the doctors' diplomas Directive. The result has been a report by the Government's Chief Medical Officer on reforming hospital doctors' training for the future.[136] Annex C of this report explains the structure and duration of training required by the EC Directives. These are too lengthy for inclusion in this work but, for example, the Annex includes a list (at least three pages long) of specialist doctors covered by the Directives.

## 7 ARCHITECTS

In some Member States, architects form part of a creative artistic occupation rather than hands-on construction team members. The content and training in Germany is considerably higher than elsewhere and there is less formal distinction between architects and engineers than in the UK.[137] In France the architectural profession has a strong technical foundation and is associated strongly with the fine arts. Since 1968 there has been a greater emphasis on technical matters in educational training of architects.[138] In the UK, as the chapter on architects and engineers[139] indicates,

133. (1994) *The Financial Times*, 24 March. It was also reported that they were dismayed at a proposal to cease EU-level inspections of veterinary schools throughout the EU. This was the only quality check which they had to rely on.

134. It is clear from the case of *R* v. *General Medical Council ex parte Virik* (1995) *The Times*, 31 October that the differentiation between EU and other overseas doctors in terms of recognition and registration is upheld or can be maintained. Thus a Malaysian and Indian qualified doctor who had experience within the UK was unable to argue that he should be treated similarly to an EU doctor.

135. *R* v. *Secretary of State for Health ex parte Goldstein* (1993), *The Times*, 5 April; see C Newdick, "The UK report", in Boesken *et al.* (Eds), *op. cit.*, p. 59. Case C-277/93 *Commission* v. *Spain* [1994] I-5515 gives an illustration of a Spanish failure to comply with the Directives, by not complying with the obligation to provide remuneration for training periods of certain specialists.

136. Report of the Working Group on Specialist Medical Training, *Hospital Doctors: Training for the Future* (1993).

137. See Button and Fleming, "The Professions in the Single European Market; A Case Study of Architects in the UK" (1992) 30 J.C.M.S. 403.

138. The varied roles of architects in three Member States (Germany, France, and the UK) are briefly set out in K Button, and M Fleming, "The Changing Regulatory Regime Confronting the Professions in Europe" (1992) *The Anti-Trust Bulletin* 429 at 436–441.

139. See chapter 3.

architects are those with aesthetic as well as practical knowledge and skills.[140] The structure of the UK profession is set out in chapter 3. Under the Architects Registration Act 1938 the designation "architect" is protected by criminal sanctions. The UK has implemented the architects' Directive[141] by the Architects' Qualifications (EEC Recognition) Order 1987.[142] As the architects' Directive contains a list of all recognised architectural qualifications in the European Union the UK statutory instrument, which amends the UK statute itself, simply allows the ARCUK to register architects with the appropriate qualifications under the statute.

The architects' Directive is a mixed Directive, falling somewhere between the sectoral and general Directives. The Directive provides for mutual recognition of architectural degrees providing they cover certain areas. It is noteworthy that the architects' Directive does not actually define the activities pursued under the title of architect but refers instead to Member State practice as it existed up to that point. For the future, minimum qualifications are required but there is no attempt here to co-ordinate the education and training of architects. The EC Directive applies to "activities in the field of architecture". Such activities are those usually "pursued under the professional title of architect".[143]

By Article 2 of the Directive each Member State has to recognise:

> "the diplomas, certificates and other evidence of formal qualifications acquired as a result of education and training fulfilling the requirements of Articles 3 and 4".

Article 3 then defines the education and training leading to such diplomas. The requirement is that such studies "shall be balanced between the theoretical and practical aspects of architectural training" and then eleven sets of abilities, skills and knowledge are set out. For example, architects' training must lead to "an understanding of the structural design, constructional and engineering problems associated with building design".[144] Moreover, such training must be at university level. Article 4 sets out a minimum length of education and training, which is either four years' full-time studies or comparable period of part-time studies, though at least three years must be full-time.[145]

The Directive calls for a list of diplomas, certificates and other evidence of formal qualifications to be drawn up by each Member State for the purposes of the Directive and this eases the implementation of the Directive itself. An Advisory Committee on Education and Training in the field of architecture is established at the Community level and any doubts about whether the diplomas are appropriate can be drawn to that Committee's attention.[146] The list is published in the Official Journal of the

---

140. Readers will find a brief and helpful description of architectural training in some of the Member States of the EC in A Hughes, *Developing European Professions* (University of Bristol, 1994). Information on UK professions is available in J Shapland and J Allaker *Organising UK Professions: Information about the Professions* (Institute for the Study of the Legal Profession, Sheffield 1995).

141. Council Directive of 10 June 1985 on the mutual recognition of diplomas, certificates and other evidence of formal qualifications in architecture, including measures to facilitate the effective exercise of the right of establishment and freedom to provide services: Directive 85/384/EEC (1985) OJ L 223/15.

142. SI 1987/1824.

143. Article 1.

144. Article 3(8).

145. Article 4(1)(a). Special provision is made for the German *Fachhochschulen*.

146. Decision of 85/385/EEC (1985) OJ L 233/15 sets up the Advisory Committee (1985) OJ L 223/26 (as amended by Directive 85/614/EEC (1985) OJ L 376/1 which amends the original Directive to account for the accession of Spain and Portugal).

European Communities. The Advisory Committee can be called into action if a Member State or the Commission feel that the diploma certificate or other evidence of formal qualifications previously published has subsequently failed to meet the requirements of Articles 3 and 4 of the Directive. The Commission is entitled to withdraw the diploma from the lists either with the agreement of the Member State concerned or by following a ruling of the European Court.

Article 11 sets out the lists of diplomas and qualifications in architecture that were current at the time of the passing of the Directive, and these must be recognised whether or not they comply with the prior conditions set out in Articles 3 and 4. Article 11(a) was interpreted by the European Court in *Bauer* v. *Conseil National de l'Ordre des Architectes*.[147] Mr Bauer, a German residing in Belgium, applied to register with the Association of Architects for the province of Brussels in Belgium. He held a diploma issued by the Department of Architecture for the *Fachhochschulen* of Stuttgart, having completed four years of studies, including two practical semesters in accordance with the law of Baden Württenberg. The European Court of Justice applied its ruling in *Nationale Raad van der Order van Architecten* v. *Egle*[148] where the Court had indicated that Article 4(1)(a) of the Directive had to be interpreted in such a way "that education and training lasting four years which includes practical semesters organised and supervised by the *Fachhochschulen* must be regarded as four years of full time studies".

In *Dreessen*[149] a more complex situation arose. A Belgian who had been awarded a German construction engineers' diploma in 1966 and had been employed in an architects' firm in Belgium until 1991, sought to have his qualifications recognised in Belgium. His diplomas were not listed in Article 11 of Directive 85/384.[150] The European Court, spurred on by Advocate General Darmon, who in several instances reminded the Court of Justice not to "act as a legislature", took the view that Belgium was not bound to recognise Dreessen's qualification.

*Dreessen*'s case has been criticised for its narrow interpretation of the Directive, but the European Court was only answering the question asked which was itself narrow. An application of the principles of *Vlassopoulou*, *Haim*, *Borrell* and *Aranitis* would indicate that Mr Dreessen should be entitled to require the Belgian competent authority to take account of his professional experience in Belgium itself, subject to the reverse discrimination difficulties.

The *Dreessen* case[151] highlights one of the weaknesses and rigidities of the sectoral Directives' approach. Any alterations to training requirements, including existing training requirements as opposed to merely prospective alterations, must, in order for the machinery to recognise the new requirement, go through Brussels to have the appropriate alterations made and published in the Official Journal. In the case of architects, this is not as serious as in the earlier sectoral Directives, for there was no co-ordination of training requirements in any detail at all. This is not the situation in the medical and paramedical fields, as we have seen.

147. Case C-166/91 *Bauer* v. *Conseil National de l'Ordre des Architectes* [1992] E.C.R. I-2797.
148. Case C-310/90 *Nationale Raad van der Order van Architecten* v. *Egle* [1992] E.C.R. I-177.
149. Case C-447/93 *Nicholas Dreessen* v. *Conseil National de l'Ordre des Architectes* [1994] E.C.R. I-4087.
150. Directive 85/384/EEC (1985) OJ L 223/15.
151. Case C-447/93 *Nicholas Dreessen* v. *Conseil National de l'Ordre des Architectes* [1994] E.C.R. I-4087 noted by Lonbay (1995) I.C.L.Q., *op. cit.* at 711.

Article 16 of the architects' Directive allows the migrant national architect to use his or her lawful academic title from the State of origin or its abbreviation in the language of that State. Host Member States are entitled to require that the name and location of the establishment or examining board which awarded the qualification be also attached. To avoid confusion where titles are similar but the training or education is not, the host State is entitled to designate the form to be specified for such use of title. Article 20 of the Directive requires that the procedure for authorising a person to take up the activities or architecture must "be completed as soon as possible" and in any event not later than three months after presentation of all the necessary documents. In Articles 17 and 18, the Directive calls for co-operation procedures with regard to proof of good character or reputation and for cross border co-operation in cases of serious doubts as to the veracity of certificates of good character of reputation or disciplinary matters. Article 23 provides that where the title architect is protected, migrants complying with the provisions of the Directive have the right to use the local professional title once they have fulfilled any conditions as to practical training experience laid down by that State. Such practical experience if undertaken elsewhere can be recognised under Article 23(2).[152] Article 27 allows host States to require competent authorities of another State to confirm the authenticity of diplomas "where legitimate doubt exists".

The procedures set up by the Directive as implemented in the UK provide a relatively straightforward way for the UK to recognise architects from other Member States.

The European Court of Justice has dealt with architects in several cases. The first was the case of *Patrick*.[153] The linkage between architects with other building and construction professions (for example, certain engineers and chartered surveyors) has caused complications in the application of Community law rules on the mutual recognition of qualifications which are dealt with below.

## 8 ENGINEERS

Engineers form a very complex set of professions. The description of the main engineers covered in this book is set out in the chapter on architects and engineers. In the UK alone there are over 39 individual engineering institutions under the umbrella of the Engineering Council. The professional engineering institutions themselves control the education and training of engineers. Anybody can be described as an engineer in the UK. The protected title is "chartered engineer". There are at least seventeen chartered professional engineering institutions in the UK. The activity of engineer is not regulated in the UK and there are no legal barriers for foreign engineers working in the UK. In Germany an engineer has a protected academic title. The Engineering Council operates a British National Committee for International Affairs. This body itself belongs to the World Federation of Engineering Organisations and the Commonwealth Engineers Council and the Federation of

152. Article 26(3) allows Member States, where appropriate to ensure that persons, in the interests of their clients and themselves, acquire the necessary linguistic knowledge to follow their profession in the host State.

153. Case 11/77 *Patrick* v. *Ministere des Affaires Culturelles* [1977] E.C.R. 1199 (dealt with above: see fn. 50 and accompanying text).

European National Engineering Organisations ("FEANI"). FEANI has been recognised by the Commission as the voice of the engineering profession in Europe. The FEANI register sets a minimum of a seven years' period after completion of secondary education as being necessary for competence as an engineer entitled to the "Eur Ing" designation which is used as a prefix.[154] 19,000 engineers have been registered in this fashion.[155]

The *Guide To Engineering Institutions* published by the Engineering Council lists the numerous British Institutes. The details are impossible to relate in this short chapter, but they range from the Institution of Mechanical Engineers through Lighting Engineers, Gas Engineers and Plant Engineers, for example. Each of these groups have particular and specialised qualification requirements and levels of membership. The Chartered Institution of Building Service Engineers, for example, has a useful publication, the *General Membership Guide*, which indicates the different levels of membership available to individuals and the requirements for reaching these levels. One can see why the engineer's sectoral Directive was abandoned.

The diversity found in the UK is reflected elsewhere. Effectively, the professional branches of activity vary from country to country within Europe. The engineers themselves cannot agree on a basic definition of what an engineer is, although it is recognised that they practise their calling in the field of *applied science*.[156] Engineers in the fields of agronomy, cartography, meteorology and biochemistry as well as biotechnology are not universally accepted as engineers. The professional structures then of engineers are different in terms of the subject-matters undertaken but also in terms of whether they are regulated or not and the level of education required to become an engineer varies considerably. Work did start in 1969 on a sectoral Directive for engineers, but this work was given up and they are now covered, if at all, by the general Directives.

The surveying professions have recently agreed a Eur Geo qualification which should be available to professionally qualified surveyors practising within the Community.[157] It is clear that some engineering occupations will be considered unregulated, others would fall within the first general Directive and some would fall within the second general Directive. The second general Directive 92/51,[158] which was due to be implemented in Member States by 18 June 1994,[159] supplements the first general Directive by covering shorter courses. The Directive applies, as does the first, to those who wish to pursue a regulated profession, whether self-employed or employed. The structure of the Directive is similar to that of 89/48/EEC; however, there are three levels of qualifications covered. It is not proposed to go into detail into this Directive as the liberal professions covered by this book are unlikely to fall under it.

154. The FEANI register is divided into group 1 and group 2; group 1 engineers being those of chartered status and having at least seven years of training. The group 2 register is for technical level engineers.

155. This information was kindly sent to me by the Engineering Council.

156. M Guerin, Secretary General, FEANI, "Does engineering as a profession exist in Europe?", *Civil and Structural Weekly* (1991) p. 9.

157. A Pearce, "Eur Geo; Passport to Europe" (1991) *ASI Journal*, p. 15.

158. Council Directive 92/51/EEC 1992 OJ L 209/25.

159. Directive 92/51/EEC of 18 June, 1992; OJ L 209/25.

## 9 ESTATE AGENTS

Where a core activity is not protected, and the professional title is equally not protected, it may still be that paticular acts typically performed in providing a service are regulated. Thus in England an estate agent's main activity in the residential housing market is open to all, as is the title "estate agent", yet if the estate agent receives certain client funds he is bound by the Estate Agents Act 1979, section 14, and has certain obligations with regard to annual audit reports.[160] Thus aspects of the work of an estate agent are regulated, though the core activity and title are not.[161] In this situation the incoming migrant is free to establish himself and to use the local title. The incoming migrant estate agent must also comply with the general regulatory norms. In other words, where there is no regulatory element in the host State with regard to either the professional title or professional activity, then the migrant professional will meet no regulatory barrier and so will be able to establish, work or provide a service freely utilising Articles 48, 52 or 59 as appropriate.

Nevertheless, even in these circumstances it may be that an academic or professional title would be helpful. We have seen in the *Kraus* case that academic designations can be "imported" though their use can be the subject of host State regulatory controls. If the migrant wished to use a local title (the migrant might want to use the local form, which, even if not required, might confer marketing advantage), can he rely on Community law to translate his title to the local style? The *Aranitis* case suggests that he can request parity under the extended *Vlassopoulou* doctrine.

Where a profession is "unregulated", for example estate agents in England,[162] then the incoming migrant professional will meet no barrier of a professional nature and thus will be able to rely on the general right of free movement. Such unregulated professions or trades may be covered by the EC transitional Directives. These Directives are currently being regrouped and consolidated.[163]

The estate agent leaving the UK to set up elsewhere will be able to do so, but the regulatory structure he will encounter will depend upon which country he migrates to. The extent to which local requirements can be imposed against him will depend on his own personal qualifications and experience (even if these are not required by the home State for the exercise of similar activities there). If there is a total monopoly reserved to a particular national profession, then he has the right to become a member of that local profession, but must fulfil the entry requirements. He may be helped in doing so by provisions of EC law.[164] Directive 67/43/EEC covers the right to take up and pursue the activities of self-employed persons in the matter of

160. The Estate Agents (Accounts) Regulations 1981, SI 1981/1520.

161. Naturally, there are also other aspects of the work of an estate agent which entail obligations owed to third parties, for example, under the Town and Country Planning (Control of Advertisements) Regulations 1989 and the Property Misdescriptions Act 1991.

162. Section 22 of the Estate Agents Act 1979 makes provision for regulations to be enacted prescribing professional or academic qualifications and experience requirements, for those wishing to become estate agents, but no regulations have yet been made. See more fully, chapter 7, "Estate Agents", fn. 2.

163. See COM(96) 22, fn. 66 above.

164. But not by Council Directive 64/224/EC concerning the attainment of freedom of establishment and freedom to provide services in respect of activities of intermediaries in commerce, industry and small craft industries (1963) OJ L 364/224 (English Sp. Ed. 1963–1964, p. 118) as "matters concerning immovable property" are specifically excluded from its scope by Article 4(1).

immovable property (excluding land surveyors).[165] The Directive obliges Member States to remove restrictions on taking up such activities by EU nationals,[166] and essentially implements the principle of equal treatment with nationals. It does not seek to co-ordinate or harmonise such activities. EU citizens have the right to join the national professional or trade associations.[167]

Thus, for example, if English (unqualified) estate agents wished to move and establish, in Spain, on a permanent basis, they would have to join the relevant Spanish professional group, probably the Spanish *Colegio de Oficial Agentes de la Propriedad Inmobiliaria* ("API").[168] This is because the activity of estate agent in Spain is reserved[169] to members of the *Colegio Oficial de Agentes de la Propriedad Inmobiliaria*.[170] Membership of API would entail taking and passing the relevant Spanish examinations. The applicant's previous qualifications, knowledge and ability would have to be taken into account in the setting of any examination. He could challenge the appropriateness of the local monopoly under the *Gebhard* conditions as EC law partially recognises a right of establishment under home State title.[171]

Estate agents from the UK may, however, be qualified. They frequently join the Royal Institution of Chartered Surveyors ("RICS")[172] for example. Auctioneers[173] are also often members of RICS and so what follows applies *mutatis mutandis* to them as well.[174] RICS is quite active internationally[175] and has an office in Brussels.[176]

---

165. Council Directive 67/43/EEC concerning freedom of establishment and freedom to provide services in respect of self-employed persons (OJ Engl. Sp. Ed. 1967, p. 3).

166. The restrictions removed are mainly set out in Article 5 of the Directive.

167. Article 6(1) of the Directive.

168. The National Association of Estate Agents considers that membership of the *Asociacion de Gestores Intermediarios en Promociones de Edificaciones* ("GIPE") might also be an appropriate alternative body. For a lay view, see the National Association of Estate Agents, *An Information Manual for Estate Agents interested in Overseas Property Sales* (NAEA, 1994). Council Directive 67/43/EEC concerning freedom of establishment and freedom to provide services in respect of self-employed persons (OJ Engl. Sp. Ed. 1967, p. 3) prohibits discrimination on grounds of nationality, but does not attempt to regulate professional qualifications.

169. Article 1 of Spanish Decree No 3248/69 indicates the reserved activities of members of the *Colegio Oficial de Agentes de la Propriedad Inmobiliaria* as mediation and brokerage in buying and selling property, letting property, granting of loans secured by mortgages and the provision of valuations in relation to immovable property. See Opinion of Advocate General Jacobs in Case C-104/91 *Colegio Oficial de Agentes de la Propriedad Inmobiliaria* v. *José Luis Aguirre Borrell and Others* [1992] E.C.R. I-3003 at 3015.

170. This is enforced by penal sanctions under Spanish law (i.e. Article 572 of the Spanish Penal Code). See generally the facts stated in case C-104/91 *Colegio Oficial de Agentes de la Propriedad Inmobiliaria* v. *José Luis Aguirre Borrell and Others* [1992] E.C.R. I-3003.

171. See fn. 36 above and accompanying text.

172. Membership of RICS is formed into seven major divisions, described in their *Chartered Surveyors Regional Directory* (1994) pp. xvi–xxviii. Briefly, they comprise building surveying; general practice; land and hydrographic surveying; minerals surveying; planning and development; quantity surveying; and rural practice. See also RICS, *Information for Members*.

173. Although the activity is unregulated in the UK, in other Member States the activity is reserved. Thus apparently Article 169 action is currently being taken against France, where the *commissaires priseurs* are apparently blocking UK access to the French market: House of Lords, Hansard (13 July 1995) cols 1829–1830. (I am grateful to Frank Meisel and Nick Wikely for pointing this out to me.)

174. They also belong to the Incorporated Society of Valuers and Auctioneers ("ISVA"), which is also a founding member of CEPI in Brussels. See fn. 176 below.

175. It has over 91,000 members world-wide, including 2,000 who work outside the UK but within the EU.

176. It is a founder member of the European Society of Chartered Surveyors ("ESC") or *Conseil Européen des Professions Immobiliers* ("CEPI").

It sets out educational and training requirements for members[177] and lays down a common Standard Code of Conduct. Its members can use the professional designation "chartered". The organisation thus fulfils the criteria set out in the general Directive on mutual recognition of qualifications and is mentioned as one of the 38 bodies to which Article 1(d) refers.[178] This means that estate agents (and others) who are members of the RICS can utilise the Directive's recognition machinery.[179] Only one incoming migrant has so far utilised the Directive's machinery.[180]

However, except in Ireland,[181] where a similar situation prevails, there is no direct equivalent of the chartered surveyors' title in the rest of Europe.[182] The range of activities undertaken is dissimilar, and there are no similar self-regulating bodies. In particular, their role as valuers as well as estate agents is not mirrored in other European countries.[183]

The RICS itself is setting out to rectify this. It has adopted a policy of inviting leading property specialists to become members (with no examination) and thus seeks to promote the profession of chartered surveyor. By 1995, 62 such persons had been admitted to membership.[184] The RICS also admits EU non-migrants to membership on relatively liberal terms and is accrediting courses in other Member States. So far three courses in Germany have been approved, and members having taken these courses have been admitted as chartered surveyors (having undertaken all their training and supervised practice in Germany in German).

The differences in professional structures across Europe has led to difficulties. For example, in France RICS members were refused the *carte professionnelle* authorising them to practise as estate agents, on the grounds that their qualification was not equivalent to the French baccalaureate and that the RICS could not deprive members of their university degree. This situation has now been resolved.[185] Another problem arises from a recent Spanish decree which reserves the right of valuation for the Bank of Spain to architects (*aparejador*). Chartered surveyors are not recognised as "architects" in Spain as the Competent Authority indicates that they are not "the same profession" and thus they are unable to cross-qualify. Currently then, chartered surveyors are excluded from this market in Spain. Further difficulties are caused by the fact that under the sectoral architects' Directive[186] some of the activities which

---

177. Now holding a degree and at least two years' practical training.
178. The last paragraph of Article 1(d) states:
"A non-exhaustive list of associations or organisations which, when this Directive is adopted, satisfy the conditions of the second subparagraph is contained in the annex. Whenever a Member State grants the recognition referred to in the second subparagraph to an association or organisation, it shall inform the Commission thereof, which shall publish this information in the Official Journal of the European Communities."
179. The provisions of the European Communities (Recognition of professional Qualifications) Regulations 1991, SI 1991/824, therefore apply and the RICS has made appropriate information and application forms available and is the "Competent Authority" under the terms of the Directive.
180. I am indebted to Lesley Reid (ESCS Secretary) for this information which is incorporated in a reply to an EC Commission discussion document (COM(94)596 fin, para. 3.10).
181. Here, the Society of Chartered Surveyors plays a similar role to that of RICS in the UK.
182. Reid, *op. cit.*
183. *Ibid.*, para. 2.4.
184. *Ibid.*, para. 3.5.
185. *Ibid.*, para. 2.5.
186. See text accompanying fn. 137 above.

chartered building surveyors undertake could be classified as "activities of an architect" and thus appear to be reserved to architects in some countries. This is by no means a unique difficulty for this profession. Many professional activities overlap and underlap in this way, and the prime cause of the problem is the reservation of an "activity" itself to members of a particular profession (or even several professions).

Before concluding, it is helpful to have a brief section outlining how the EU rules on mutual recognition cope with non-EU qualifications held by EU nationals.

## 10 THIRD COUNTRY DIPLOMAS

The Community law rules are not always consistent between professions in this matter. A dentistry case helps to illuminate how the Community rules deal with third country qualifications. In the case of *Tawil-Albertini*[187] a French national with Lebanese dental qualifications which had been recognised by the Belgian authorities (as well as those of the UK and Ireland) could not get his qualifications recognised by France. EC Dentistry qualifications had been co-ordinated in Directive 76/686[188] and the Member States were entitled to rely on those qualifications listed there.[189] This was not the case with qualifications awarded outside the EC and France was able to not recognise Tawil-Albertini's qualifications despite his recognition elsewhere in the Community. Tawil-Albertini was unable to rely on Directive 89/48 as that Directive, in Article 2, specifically excludes professions covered by the sectoral Directives. However, this does not prevent him from relying on the *Vlassopoulou*, *Haim* and *Aranitis* doctrines whereby professional experience and knowledge must be assessed where it is taking place within the Community, including within the host State. The referring court asked no questions as to this matter and thus received no answer on this particular point.

One interesting anomaly with regard to the medical Directives as opposed to the general Directives is that there is no provision for those with non-EU qualification which is subsequently recognised in a Member State.[190] Under the general Directive, such persons with three years' experience in a Member State which has recognised their qualifications are entitled to have their qualifications recognised by other Member States.[191]

---

187. Case C-154/93 *Tawil-Albertini* v. *Ministre des Affaires Sociales* [1994] E.C.R. I-451.
188. Directive 78/686/EEC 1978 OJ L233/1.
189. As we saw in *Commission* v. *Italy* the standard is maintained.
190. Article 23 does allow Member States to accept non-Member State qualifications, but this does not confer rights of mobility with the EU to such persons.
191. See Article 1(a) of Directive 89/48/EEC. See also Council recommendation 21 December 1988 concerning nationals of Member States who hold a diploma conferred in a third State (89/49/EEC) OJ L019/24:

> "Council recommendation 21 December 1988 concerning nationals of Member States who hold a diploma conferred in a third state (89/49/EEC) the Council of the European Communities, approving Council Directive 89/48/EEC of 21 December 1988 on a general system for the recognition of higher-education diplomas awarded on completion of professional education and training of at least three years' duration; noting that this directive refers only to diplomas, certificates and other evidence of formal qualifications awarded in Member States to nationals of Member States; anxious however, to take account of the special position of nationals of Member States who hold diplomas, certificates or other evidence of formal qualifications awarded in third states and who are thus in a position

## 11 CONCLUSION

As one can appreciate from reading this chapter, there is no easy way to sum up the EC rules on mutual recognition of qualifications. One could say that there are three main sets of EC rules available to those seeking to enforce a right of mobility, and which is to be used will depend on whether the relevant profession is regulated or unregulated in both the host and home State. The professional will also need to check whether:

(1) there are particular sectoral Directives which might be applicable; or
(2) the transitional Directives are applicable; or
(3) the general system Directives are applicable.

Overlaying this is the European Court's general case-law.

There is no doubting that Community rules have had a strong impact on the professions. As we saw in Italy the profession of dentistry had to be created. Those effected by sectoral Directives have a long Euro-shadow cast on their future evolution. In the UK and Ireland the historical commonality of professions was rediscovered, leaving solicitors, for example, to recognise each other and drop the previous "protectionist" barriers. The first non-UK professional entrants under the diplomas Directive were several hundred Irish solicitors who had their qualifications automatically recognised. In other places a seemingly more protectionist attitude was provoked. Thus both France and Luxembourg introduced monopolies on the giving of legal advice. It is, however, now clear that such rules are amenable to Community assessment under the four *Gebhard* conditions. One can expect some challenges to Member State regulations.[191a]

The Community law rules have also thrown a narrow beam of light on the nature of professions. The Community's rules focus on the regulatory aspects of professions as it is these that tend to form barriers to cross-border mobility. In applying a Community-wide assessment of the validity and proportionality of national rules, even where they are non-discriminatory on their face, the EC will force professions to confront their protectionist tendencies and to question their traditional way of doing things. As it has in the sphere of indirect taxation,[192] the Community may have more influence over the regulatory environment in which professions operate by having no rules directly on the subject matter. National professional regulation

---

comparable to one of those described in Article 3 of the directive hereby recommends: that the governments of the Member States should allow the persons referred to above to take up and pursue regulated professions within the community by recognising these diplomas, certificates and other evidence of formal qualifications in their territories."
A similar recommendation is attached to the architects' Directive:
"Council recommendation of 10 June 1985 concerning holders of a diploma in architecture awarded in a third country (85/386/EEC) the Council of the European Communities, in adopting Council Directive 85/384/EEC of 10 June 1985 on the mutual recognition of diplomas, certificates and other evidence of formal qualifications in architecture, including measures to facilitate the effective exercise of the right of establishment and freedom to provide services."
191a. The Commission has launched an Article 169 action against France with regard to its lawyers monopoly. See Lonbay (1996) 21 E.L.Rev. 50.
192. See J Lonbay, "A Review of recent tax cases ..." (1989) 14 E.L.Rev. 48–56.

protected by the principles of subsidiarity and host State control is confronted nevertheless by Community-level scrutiny on the one hand (where the courts are assessing the appropriateness and necessity of national rules),[193] and centripetal political forces on the other provided by the interaction of national regulatory authorities.

One clear outcome of the rules has been a growth in the mutual understanding of how each others systems operate.[194] There has been a wave of European level associations established[195] and currently in formation. This has led in some cases to the development of European-wide qualifications, most evidently in the engineering sectors. These forces willl slowly bear down on unnecesary national idiosyncrasies, and yet Member States and their professionals will be able to maintain "necessary" national rules and regulations. It will only be by voluntary action that uniformity might emerge.[196]

It can be seen, for example in the case of lawyers, how difficult it is to develop a Community dimension to national rules. The conflicting visions of the scope of Article 52 will need to be resolved for progress to be made. The *Gebhard* case provides some useful guidelines that will need to be fleshed out in the proposed Directive. It seems to indicate that establishment as a German lawyer in Italy might be possible and that any Italian restrictions on such a right would need to be justified. Thus both France and Luxembourg, for example, would need to show that their broad legal advice monoplies were necessary, and that a system, such as applied in Germany, where the monopoly really bites to prevent advice being given on German law would not suffice. Given the Anglo-Saxon tradition and the even more liberal regime on lawyers found in Sweden, can even the German regime be justified? The particular case of lawyers is likely to be settled by the proposed establishment Directive when it finally emerges from the legislative process.

In other professions where there are considerable overlaps and "underlaps" in the types of activity undertaken, as well as types of qualifications required for undertaking such activities (ranging from none to higher level qualifications), the Community regimes described in this chapter will be hard-pressed to establish commonality, but this is not their goal. High-level professions will seek to safeguard their turf and will resent and try to block members from "lower-level" professions (especially emanating from other Member States) taking their "business". The fact that in some countries the same activities can be carried out by unqualified (or even just less-qualified) persons is not a convincing argument for de-professionalisation in the first State. Community law does not force a downward pressure on national

193. Is it really necessary to be under 35 years of age in order to be admitted as a Greek *dikigoros* (lawyer) or eat so many dinners in order to become a barrister in England?

194. This informational awareness is accelerated by the system of co-ordinators adopted by the two general Directives and specialised committees under the sectoral Directives. See D Hoefnagel, "The work of the co-ordinators' Group" in Pertek (Ed.), *General Recognition of Diplomas and Free Movement of Professionals, op. cit.*

195. For example, the European Federation of Professional Psychological Associations is currently working on a common code of ethics.

196. It must be pointed out, in fairness, that some overtures were initially misinterpreted or rebutted. See, for example, the reception given by continental physicists to UK approaches; see D Jefferies, "An EC Directive as catalyst for the development of physicists in Europe" in P Neale, *op. cit.*, p. 51, where he relates how initial contacts "lead to a heated exchange and hostile reaction", though collaboration is now more fruitful and includes discussions on a pan-European qualification for physicists.

qualification requirements. A high-level profession can maintain those requirements, but as the *Säger* case shows the reserved activities may not be all protected from foreign encroachment. This should sharpen the professions' competitiveness.[197] The effects of future *Gebhard* challenges will add to the deregulatory pressure.

It should be noted that even in the professions covered by sectoral Directives and thus benefiting from nearly automatic rights to practise anywhere in the Community, there has not been a massive cross-border flow of professionals. Linguistic, cultural and family ties still seem to be dominating factors. In highly organised professions, where the clientele have international operations, there has been considerable professional integration regardless of Community rules on qualifications. The big accountancy firms and, to a lesser extent, the emergence of large legal firms in Europe are evidence of this.

The Community, in tackling the question of mutual recognition of qualifications, as it must, to establish the "internal market", has only just started. The main legislative framework is now in place. Further clarification is needed as to the scope of the exceptions permitted by Community law (see, for example, Article 55) and there remain difficult issues which need to be resolved clearly; for example, the role of the competitive entry systems in some States which seem to favour national candidates.[198]

However, the main challenge is in successfully ensuring the correct implementation of Community law in this sphere and in promoting information about the opportunities which it opens up for EU citizens. There are considerable administrative burdens imposed on national Competent Authorities in administering the general system as we have seen. As they tackle these, the process of integration is furthered, for part of the burden is to understand how other non-national regimes operate. A blanket protectionist stance is likely to provoke a legal challenge. The judicial authorities of the Member States will also increasingly play a role. The right of appeal against admission decisions by Competent Authorities is secured by general Community law and they will also be called upon to assess the *Gebhard* conditions in particular cases. This bodes a busy future for those active in this field.

JULIAN LONBAY

---

197. It is clear that national professional regulations can themselves fall foul of the EC competition rules: see COAPI decision 95/188/EC, (1995) OJ L 122/37.

198. These issues were not tackled here for reasons of space.

CHAPTER 2

# NEGLIGENCE AND THE PROFESSIONS

## 1 CONTRACTUAL LIABILITY FOR PROVISION OF SERVICES

The basis of professional liability in contract has of course always depended on the terms of the contract with the client. Those terms, as with any other contract, are subject to the general principles of contract law, which it is not proposed to analyse here, except where the context specifically demands it. Contracts of professionals tend only exceptionally to contain mention of the level of duty towards the client; as we shall see, the implied term is the norm in that regard.

The nature of the activities of professionals is such that the law has not deemed it appropriate to impose liability on the basis of failure to succeed in performing the task in question, or providing the service in question. A doctor cannot be expected to guarantee the success of an operation; a solicitor cannot be expected to promise a successful outcome to litigation. As we shall see, express warranties can be given by professionals, but that is the consequence of personal choice rather than imposition by the courts or, Parliament. As early as the decision in *Lanphier* v. *Phipos*[1] it was said by Tindal CJ that "Every person who enters into a learned profession undertakes to bring to the exercise of it a reasonable degree of care and skill", and such is the nature of the term that the law will imply into the contracts of professional men. The principle is also to be found in section 13 of the Supply of Goods and Services Act 1982, which provides: "In a contract for the supply of a service where the supplier is acting in the course of a business, there is an implied term that the supplier will carry out the service with reasonable care and skill."

As was noted above, the law, in effect, provides a minimum standard, and a professional may be prepared to go beyond his basic duty and guarantee a result, effectively therefore extending his liability from fault-based to strict. Thus, in *Thake* v. *Maurice*[2] it was held by the trial judge, though reversed by the Court of Appeal, that the defendant surgeon had guaranteed the successs of a vasectomy. Such an undertaking would be exceptional, and might also carry the risk that the professional's indemnity insurance would not extend to liability for breach of warranty, leaving him without cover as a consequence.

A further, again exceptional, possibility, is that a strict duty may be implied from the terms of the retainer. Thus, in *Greaves & Co (Contractors) Ltd* v. *Baynham*

---

1. (1838) 8 C. & P. 475.
2. [1986] Q.B. 644. See also *Edwards* v. *Mallan* [1908] 1 K.B. 1002 at 1005.

*Meikle and Partners*[3] contractors engaged the services of the defendant consulting engineers to design a warehouse to be built by the contractors. The defendants were informed that the floors would have to be strong enough to cope with the weight of stacker trucks, but in the event the floors proved unequal to the task and cracked. The Court of Appeal held that there was, in the circumstances of the case, an implied term that the design was to be fit for the purpose for which it was required.

Subsequently, in *IBA* v. *EMI and BICC*[4] the House of Lords had to consider the nature of design duties of contractor and consultant, and consider their relationship to each other. EMI had been appointed by IBA to design and supply a television mast. EMI sub-contracted the design and construction to BICC, nominated sub-contractors. The mast failed due to design faults. It was held that EMI had warranted the quality of the design to IBA, and held that BICC had given EMI the same warranty. Although it was held that the design was negligent, Lord Scarman argued strongly that one who contracts to design an article for a purpose made known to him undertakes that the design is reasonably fit for its purpose.

An authority relied upon by Lord Scarman was *Samuels* v. *Davis*,[5] where it was said that a dentist who agrees to make a denture for his patient is under an obligation to produce a denture which will be fit for its purpose, not simply a duty to exercise reasonable care and skill. In other words, there may be cases where the professional is required to achieve a particular result, and will be liable for his failure to do so, irrespective of his exercise of reasonable care. It may be that in such cases the analogy with a sale of goods, where strict duties are implied as a matter of law,[6] is closer than that of the provision of services only, imparting, as we have seen, a duty of reasonable care only, a point made by Du Parcq LJ in *Samuels*,[7] drawing a distinction between a dentist extracting a tooth (duty of care only) and a dentist supplying a denture (strict undertaking of fitness for purpose). Most cases of professional advice will involve the provision of professional services only, and thus cases where stricter duties are imposed are very much the exception rather than the rule.

The *IBA* case illustrates the aspect of a not infrequent situation; the ability of the professional in certain circumstances to delegate work. The professional's duties, frequently reinforced by professional ethical codes, are personal, involving duties of confidence[8] and avoidance of conflicts of interest.[9] The fact that the duties are personal does not preclude delegation, but the professional remains personally responsible for the performance.

This responsibility will extend to liability for defective performance by the person to whom the work was delegated, even where the professional exercised reasonable care in engaging that person,[10] though such liability is limited to the scope of the retainer: thus liability will not extend to negligent work carried out by others where that work falls outside the remit of the professional.[11]

3. [1975] 2 All E.R. 99.
4. (1980) 14 B.L.R. 1.
5. [1943] 1 K.B. 526.
6. Sale of Goods Act 1979, ss. 13 and 14.
7. [1943] 1 K.B. 526 at 529.
8. See, e.g., *Tournier* v. *National Provincial and Union Bank of England* [1924] 1 K.B. 461.
9. See, e.g., *Spector* v. *Ageda* [1973] Ch. 30.
10. See, e.g., *Bevan Investments Ltd* v. *Blackhall and Struthers (No 2)* [1973] 2 N.Z.L.R. 45.
11. See, e.g., *Morris* v. *Winsbury-White* [1937] 4 All E.R. 494.

The prudent professional who considers that expert advice or work beyond his own expertise will be needed in relation to a particular task will limit the scope of his retainer by recommending to the client that he engage the services of a specialist to do that aspect of the work. Thus a surveyor might consider that specialist skills were needed in respect of a very old building, or in relation to particular aspects of potential defects in a building. In this way the professional will be able to avoid liability for the defective work of the specialist, but must exercise reasonable care in recommending the person: in one case, not surprisingly, recommendation by a solicitor of a surveyor who was a known alcoholic led to liability of the solicitor for the surveyor's defective work.[12] Also, the professional cannot assume the accuracy of the specialist's advice or work, but he should examine it and, if he disagrees, point this out to the client.

It is of great importance to ensure that the duties to be undertaken are clearly set out in the retainer, especially where more than one professional may be involved in advising the client. Thus, there are real risks of overlap where a solicitor and a surveyor are advising in connection with a property transaction, or an accountant and a solicitor in connection with tax and business concerns of the client. Clear definition of the respective obligations of those involved is especially necessary in such cases, so as to avoid on the one hand both professionals performing the same task, or some aspects of the same task, or on the other hand some vital piece of work or advice falling between them, each assuming that the other will do it. Difficulties may also arise from excessive vagueness in the terms of the retainer even where only one profession is involved: the professional and the client may easily in such cases have entirely different ideas as to the nature and/or extent of the services to be provided.

An aspect of the scope of the retainer is the issue of whether or not the professional is authorised to act as an agent on the client's behalf. If he acts without actual or implied authority from the client, he will be in breach of his retainer, and liable to indemnify the client against losses resulting from his actions. If he acts without either actual or apparent authority, the client will not be bound, and the professional, as agent, will be liable to the person to whom he represented that he had authority. Even where he does have actual or apparent authority, he may be personally liable for breach of contracts he makes on the client's behalf, as well as the client, as principal, being liable. This will especially be the case where he has failed to disclose that he was acting as agent; such a failure can result in serious personal liability, as can be seen from *Yeung Kai Yung* v. *Hong Kong and Shanghai Banking Corporation*[13] where stockbrokers were held liable when they failed to make clear in a letter accompanying share transfer documents (which had been forged by a client, and which were sent to a bank, asking the bank to transfer the shares to the client) that the request was made only by the client and not by the brokers personally. The true owner of the documents claimed compensation from the bank in respect of their lost shares, and the brokers were held liable to indemnify the bank, on the basis that a promise of indemnity was deemed to have been made by them in making the request together with the client, and that promise was accepted by the bank in acting on the request.

12. *Mercer* v. *King* (1859) 1 F. & F. 490.
13. [1981] A.C. 787.

A further important aspect of the professional's duties to his client arises from the confidential nature of the relationship between them. Information of a confidential nature disclosed by the client to the professional must not be disclosed to others, and the client's interests may be protected by injunctive relief and damages for breach of an implied contractual term. It was made clear in *Tournier* v. *National Provincial and Union Bank of England* [14] that the duty of confidence extends to information concerning the client which the professional acquires in the course of professional work, and is not limited to information obtained from the client. Further, the duty extends after the retainer has been terminated. It is not, however, an absolute duty; confidential information may be disclosed where the law [15] or public interest require it, or where the interests of the professional himself require disclosure, or where the client consents to disclosure.

Breach of duty may also occur where the professional acts in a situation where either there is a conflict between his own interests and those of the client, or there is a conflict between the interests of two separate clients. Thus, in *Spector* v. *Ageda* [16] a solicitor was held to be in breach of her duty to her client where she lent the client money to pay off a loan from an unlicensed moneylender who was a close relative of the solicitor, without advising the client that such a loan was illegal and might not have to be repaid.

In cases where the conflict lies in the interests of two (or more) clients, the breach of duty arises where there is an actual conflict, but not where that conflict is merely a possibility, for that risk exists as between any two clients. Where problems arise, it may become necessary to advise both clients to obtain independent representation, though in an appropriate case, e.g., non-contentious business by a solicitor, it may be sufficient to determine the retainer for at least one party, though even in that situation there is a real risk of inevitable liability to one client or the other.

## 2 EXCLUSION AND LIMITATION OF LIABILITY

### 2.1 Introduction

It is usually the case that professionals do not seek to exclude or limit their liability, since this is seen as being essentially incompatible with the status of a professional. There are also statutory provisions precluding solicitors [17] and auditors [18] excluding their liability in particular situations. Otherwise, it is clear from the Unfair Contract Terms Act, section 2(1) that attempts to exclude or restrict liability for death or personal injury resulting from negligence (which includes breach of any contractual obligation to exercise reasonable care and skill) by reference to any contract term or to a notice given to persons generally or to a particular person, cannot succeed. This

---

14. [1924] 1 K.B. 461.

15. Though this is subject to the ability of the professional man to refuse to disclose privileged information.

16. [1973] Ch. 30; see also *Thornton Hall and Partners* v. *Wembley Electrical Appliances Ltd* [1947] 2 All E.R. 630. See chapter 10 for other examples.

17. Solicitors Act 1974, s. 60(5).

18. Companies Act 1985, s. 310.

has clear implications for professionals whose negligence might result in death or personal injury.

Attempts to exclude or restrict liability for negligence resulting in damage other than personal injury or death are subject to section 2(2) of the Act. Such attempts will be unsuccessful unless the term or notice in question satisfies the requirement of reasonableness, which is defined in section 11 of the Act, with guidelines set out in Schedule 2 to the Act. A distinction is drawn in section 11 between contract terms and notices which are not of contractual effect. The former are required by section 11(1) to have been a fair and reasonable term to be included having regard to the circumstances which were, or ought reasonably to have been, known to or in the contemplation of the parties when the contract was made, and the matters specified in the Schedule, such as the relative bargaining strength of the parties, are in particular to be taken into account. Under section 11(3), the requirement of reasonableness in relation to a non-contractual notice is that it should be fair and reasonable to allow reliance on it, having regard to all the circumstances obtaining when the liability arose or (but for the notice) would have arisen. This would appear to be potentially somewhat broader than the test under section 11(1), in taking account of a wider range of circumstances.

Insofar as a professional man is not precluded by statute or rules of professional conduct from excluding or limiting his liability, it seems unlikely in any event that a blanket exclusion would be regarded as satisfying the requirement of reasonableness *vis-à-vis* a client. Specific provision for restricting liability to a specified sum of money is to be found in section 11(4), which directs the court, in deciding whether such a provision satisfies the requirement of reasonableness, to have regard (a) to the resources which the person seeking to restrict liability could expect to be available to him for the purpose of meeting the liability, should it arise, and (b) how far it was open to him to cover himself by insurance. It may be therefore that restricting liability to a particular figure based on what a professional considers to be a reasonable level of insurance cover would enable him to avoid liability beyond that figure, but this of course begs the very difficult question of what a reasonable level of insurance (or premium) would be.

If a professional seeks to exclude or limit his liability to a third party, not only will he find the rules and mores of his professional association taking a more relaxed view of such an effort, but also the various statutory provisions governing the professions may be silent on the point. Thus, section 60(5) of the Solicitors Act 1974 precludes exclusion of liability for negligence or breach of duty in a contentious business agreement, which would appear not to preclude such exclusion if it relates to a potential liability to a third party, since such a person would not be privy to the agreement. By the same token, privity will of course deprive a purported exclusion of contractual liability of any force where the claim is brought by a third party.

The possibility remains, however, of excluding or limiting tortious liability to third parties, insofar as such liability is capable of arising. Such exclusion or limitation may be attempted to be done either by an express notice seeking to exclude or limit an existing duty or by means of a definition of the limits of the professional's undertaking. The context in which these issues have arisen in professional negligence cases is that of valuations of property by surveyors for mortgagees, with the actual content of the valuation report or its purport being allegedly relied upon by the mortgagor in agreeing to buy the property in question. It was held in *Yianni* v. *Edwin Evans & Sons*[19] that a duty of care was owed by the valuer to the mortgagor in a case where the building society mortgagee's handbook stated, *inter alia*, that the valuer's report was exclusively for the use of the society's directors and officers in determining whether a loan should be made and, if so, for what amount.

Subsequently, in *Smith* v. *Eric S Bush*[20] the House of Lords had to consider disclaimers of liability contained in mortgage application forms and in a mortgage valuation report. The disclaimers asserted that the valuation was for the benefit of the lender and that no responsibility was implied or accepted for the value or condition of the property by reason of the inspection report. It was argued, *inter alia*, that such a provision did not fall within the control of the Unfair Contract Terms Act, and hence was not required to satisfy the requirement of reasonableness. It was held that section 13 of the Act, dealing with varieties of exemption clause, was apt to cover this type of provision. Section 13(1) provides:

"To the extent that this Part of this Act prevents the exclusion or restriction of any liability it also prevents—
    (a) making the liability or its enforcement subject to restrictive or onerous conditions;
    (b) excluding or restricting any right or remedy in respect of the liability, or subjecting a person to any prejudice in consequence of his pursuing any such right or remedy;
    (c) excluding or restricting rules of evidence or procedure;
and (to that extent) sections 2 and 5 to 7 also prevent excluding or restricting liability by reference to terms and notices which exclude or restrict the relevant obligation or duty..."

The disclaimers were held to be notices to which the Act applied, and it was also held that they did not satisfy the requirement of reasonableness. It was said that in deciding whether the surveyor had discharged the onus of establishing that the disclaimer was fair and reasonable, and indeed in any case where this issue arose, it would always be necessary to consider: (a) whether the parties were of equal bargaining power; (b) whether, in the case of advice, it would have been reasonably practicable to obtain the advice from an alternative source, taking into account considerations of costs and time; (c) how difficult was the task for which liability was being excluded; (d) what were the practical consequences of the decision on the question of reasonableness. Lord Griffiths pointed out that it would not, in his view, be unreasonable for professionals in all circumstances to seek to exclude or limit their liability for negligence; for example where enormous sums of money were at stake it might be reasonable to exclude liability entirely, or limit it to the extent of the adviser's insurance cover. Indeed, in the earlier case of *Stevenson* v. *Nationwide Building Society*[21] a disclaimer was held to be reasonable, though it was of particular relevance in that case that the plaintiff was an estate agent, who therefore had professional expertise with regard to the matters about which he was complaining, and also that he was buying a relatively expensive property, including commercial elements. In *Smith* v. *Bush* it was remarked that the property in question was a dwelling-house of modest value in which it was widely recognised by surveyors that the purchasers were in fact relying on their care and skill, and the position might be otherwise in respect of valuations of industrial property, large blocks of flats or very

19. [1982] Q.B. 438.
20. [1990] 1 A.C. 831.
21. (1984) 272 E.G. 663.

expensive houses, where the general expectation of the behaviour of the purchaser might be quite different; prudence in such cases might seem to demand the commissioning of a structural survey by the would-be purchaser, and exclusion or limitation of liability by the surveyor valuing on behalf of the provider of the finance might be reasonable. This should not mean that every definition of responsibility by a professional is subject to the controls of the Unfair Contract Terms Act. Thus, a solicitor who gives advice on tax matters and specifies that such is the range of his expertise should not be treated as potentially unreasonably excluding liability for negligence concerning other aspects of the law not related to his advice, especially if he emphasises the areas in relation to which advice is not being provided.

The nature of the duty of care may also operate so as to exclude particular persons from the range of those who can claim against a professional for negligent advice. Thus in *Shankie-Williams* v. *Heavey*[22] a dry rot specialist inspected a ground floor flat and gave it a clean bill of health. The report was commissioned by the vendor of the flat, who wished to use it to show to prospective purchasers. It was held that, though a duty of care was owed to purchasers, since the specialist knew the purpose for which the report had been commissioned, no duty was owed to the purchaser of the first floor flat, since the instructions and report related to the ground floor flat only. Again, the nature of the duty of care in cases of negligent misstatement[23] as evidenced by *Caparo* v. *Dickman*[24] makes it clear that the ambit of the duty of care is circumscribed in such cases such that reliance by third parties on advice or information from a professional man may not be reasonable.

## 3 CONCURRENT LIABILITY IN TORT AND CONTRACT

Tortious claims can arise from contractual situations. As an example an accountant who is paid by his client for investment advice and who gives carelessly framed advice may, in principle, be faced with a claim by the client either for breach of the contractual term (express or implied) to take reasonable care in giving of the advice or an action based on a tortious duty of care to a similar effect. The purpose of this section of the chapter is to consider whether, and why, the prospective plaintiff may choose between the two potential remedies. It will accordingly cover:

(a) the distinctions between tortious and contractual actions;
(b) the ability to select a cause of action;
(c) the influence of the contractual setting on tortious liability.

### 3.1 Tort and contract: the differences

Some plaintiffs are constrained by rules of law and never have the opportunity to choose between tort and contract. Mrs Donoghue was barred from suing on a

22. [1986] 2 E.G.L.R. 139.
23. See p. 60 below.
24. [1990] 2 A.C. 605.

contract with the vendor of the famous contaminated ginger beer by reason of the established rules of privity of contract. However, in many cases there may exist a potential choice of cause of action and plaintiffs may be persuaded or at times forced into one cause of action rather than another by reason of the differences which exist between them.

Arguably the biggest cause of the recent growth in tort actions, especially in cases against construction professionals, has been the vital difference between the rules on limitation of actions. By virtue of the Limitation Act 1980 in both tort[25] and in contract[26] an action will be time-barred in each case six years after the date on which the relevant cause of action accrues. This apparent similarity conceals a vital distinction, however, since the date of accrual is vitally different in the two forms of action. Most tort actions, and all negligence actions, have the necessity for damage to have occurred as an essential element of the cause of action and therefore no cause of action accrues until damage occurs.[27] On the other hand, contract is about the creation of expectations and, accordingly, the cause of action here is complete as soon as there is a breach of contract. Thus a house built in 1996 with inherent defects resulting from the construction work cannot be the subject of a contract action beyond 2002, since the six-year period from the date of the breach must end during that year. It may well be, however, that no damage will occur until the defect in the building is triggered off by exceptionally hot or wet weather conditions in 2000; in such a case, the tort period will only begin to run at that date and thus continue to 2006.[28]

It should also be noted that a further distinction occurs in relation to claims in respect for personal injuries framed in negligence, nuisance or breach of duty. In such cases the tortious limitation period is reduced to three years from the date of the cause of action's accrual or, more generously to the plaintiff, from the date of the victim's knowledge of his cause of action.[29] On the other hand, cases where the law of tort extends its protection to the economic interests of the plaintiff[30] have the effect of concealing the distinction between actions in tort and in contract since the damage here is to the expectation of value which clearly is created as soon as the plaintiff is committed, for instance, to the purchase of a property carelessly over-valued by a surveyor[31] and time will thus run at a much earlier date than may be the case if the purchaser had to wait for actual physical damage to occur.

Vital differences also exist between contract and tort actions in relation to the award of damages. In tort, cases from the *Wagon Mound (No 1)* onwards[32] have established a broad test of foreseeability of the general type of harm[33] as being sufficient to ground a valid cause of action. On the other hand, the law of contract requires that, in order to be claimable, damage must be likely to result,[34] and this distinction may be justified by reference to the fact that an unsuspecting tortfeasor

25. Limitation Act 1980, s. 2.
26. *Ibid.*, s. 5.
27. *Pirelli General Cable Works Ltd* v. *Oscar Faber & Co.* [1983] 2 A.C. 1.
28. Subject also to the provisions of the Latent Damage Act 1986. See p. 91 below.
29. Limitation Act 1980, s. 11.
30. See p. 57 below.
31. *Dept of the Environment* v. *Essex, Goodman & Suggitt* (1985) 276 E.G. 308.
32. [1961] A.C. 388. See p. 81 below.
33. See e.g., *Draper* v. *Hodder* [1972] 2 Q.B. 556 at 573.
34. *Heron II* [1969] 1 A.C. 350.

should be entitled to protection against relatively unusual losses of which he has, by definition, no warning while a party to a contract can negotiate in advance about relatively unlikely consequences of a potential breach.[35]

The range of protection of purely economic interests of plaintiffs in tort and in contract is reflected in the rules about the measure of damage. Future economic losses are readily capable of compensation in contract actions. For example, future revenues due for three years under a contract which was purportedly repudiated by the respondent on the very day that the contract was made could be fully claimed accordingly to the House of Lords in *White and Carter (Councils) Ltd* v. *McGregor*,[36] while the law of tort takes a highly restrictive view of such claims, as will be seen from subsequent discussion of the duty of care in economic loss cases.[37]

Other distinctions also exist. Mention may be made of a procedural rule not devoid of significance. Court rules[38] ordain that a writ may be issued outside the jurisdiction of the English courts in respect of most contractual disputes, so long as the contract was either made within the jurisdiction or is otherwise governed by English Law or where the breach occurs within the jurisdiction; claims in tort may only be pursued by means of the service of a writ outside the local jurisdiction if the damage complained of occurred within the jurisdiction. Although the relevant rules have altered in certain respects, the case of *Matthews* v. *Kuwait Bechtel Corporation*[39] remains a classic example of what would for most be categorised as a tort case—an industrial accident on a site in Kuwait—which had to be reformulated as a contract case—breach of an implied term to take reasonable care of workers on the site—so as to enable service out of the jurisdiction to occur.

A final distinction worthy of note is one that arises as an issue of defences to liability rather than of liability itself, but can be of considerable practical significance. The question is whether a defendant's own contributory negligence can be a (partial)[40] defence not only to an action framed in tort but also to one framed in breach of contract. The answer appears now to be clear, namely that contributory negligence will be a defence in certain contractual cases only. The defence will operate where the defendants' contractual liability is, effectively, identical to their tortious liability, in other words where their contractual failing is a lack of reasonable care, rather than any stricter duty. This was established by the Court of Appeal in *Forsikringsaktieselskapet Vesta* v. *Butcher*[41] where the plaintiffs' deficient lack of care of their fish farm was held relevant to the calculation of their claim of damages against their insurers. Equally, the defence of contributory negligence does not apply where the defendants are strictly liable under their contracts.[42]

## 3.2 Tort and contract: the choice

Given that there are ample reasons for plaintiffs to select between tortious and contractual claims, it is at the least surprising that for decades the simple question of

35. *Ibid.* at 385 *per* Lord Reid.
36. [1962] A.C. 413.
37. See p. 57 below.
38. R.S.C., Ord. 11, r. 1, paras (d)–(f).
39. [1959] 2 Q.B. 57.
40. *Pitts* v. *Hunt* [1990] 3 All E.R. 344.
41. [1989] A.C. 852; appeal on other grounds to the House of Lords.
42. *Barclays Bank plc* v. *Fairclough Building Ltd* [1995] Q.B. 214.

whether such a choice exists has been one shrouded in mystery. That said, a reasonably clear solution does appear to have come into sight recently and only the briefest of historical introductions is now necessary. A clear rejection of concurrent liability in cases of professional negligence stemming from such cases as *Groom* v. *Crocker*[43] was still being upheld as late as the mid-1960s[44] by which time the tide of events was very clearly moving against the validity of such a view. This was entirely due to the epoch-making decision of the House of Lords in *Hedley Byrne & Co Ltd* v. *Heller & Partners Ltd*[45] where the then new liability for economic losses caused by negligent misrepresentation was stated to arise irrespective of whether a contract existed or not.[46] The impact of this decision dominates the scene still. Confirmation of the role of the *Hedley Byrne* principle in cases where, unlike in *Hedley Byrne* itself, the parties had gone on to form a contractual relationship was duly provided by such cases as *Esso Petroleum Co Ltd* v. *Mardon*[47] and *Midland Bank Trust Co Ltd* v. *Hett, Stubbs & Kemp*,[48] and the free availability of choice of cause of action appeared to be clearly established.

However, this clear picture did not last. In 1985 Lord Scarman attacked the idea of concurrent liability with considerable force, if not considerable authority, in the Privy Council case of *Tai Hing Cotton Mill Ltd* v. *Liu Chong Hing Bank Ltd.*[49] Here, a woefully incompetently managed company allowed procedures of financial management to arise which enabled the accounts clerk to defraud the company of HK $5.5m and the company alleged the bank was itself negligent in honouring the cheques, the bank counterclaiming on the grounds of the company's own lack of care. This turned out to be the focal point of the litigation, with a finding with reference to the law of banking contracts that the company owed no duty of care to its bankers then being coupled with a finding that the law of tort should therefore also refuse to owe a duty.

Lord Scarman[50] was emphatic on the point, in words which still are of some effect today. There was, he stated, "nothing to the advantage of the law's development in searching for a liability in tort where the parties in a contractual relationship". This was for reasons both of principle and of pragmatism; concurrent liability should not be allowed, particularly in the context of a commercial relationship, "on principle because it is a relationship in which the parties have, subject to a few exceptions, the right to determine their obligations to each other, and for the avoidance of confusion because different consequences do follow according to whether liability arises from contract or tort e.g., in the limitation of action". Bizarrely evading the possible freely agreed use of clauses excluding tortious liability and simultaneously providing an example of precisely why the choice of cause of action might be useful, Lord Scarman's words nevertheless dominated consideration of the issue for much of the following decade. The outright rejection of concurrent liability was generally felt to be overstated,[51] but equally there was some validity in the view taken at least on the

---

43. [1939] 1 K.B. 194.
44. E.g., in *Bagot* v. *Stevens Scanlan & Co Ltd* [1966] 1 Q.B. 197.
45. [1964] A.C. 465.
46. *Ibid.* at 494 *per* Lord Morris of Borth-y-Gest.
47. [1976] Q.B. 801.
48. [1979] Ch. 384.
49. [1986] A.C. 80.
50. *Ibid.* at 107.
51. See, e.g., Holyoak (1990) P.N. 113.

facts of *Tai Hing* since the parties had decided, or at least were taken by the law of banking contracts to have decided, that the customer of a bank did not owe it a duty to take care and the imposition of such a duty by the law of tort would contradict their clear contractual stance.

Subsequent litigation took a range of varying approaches to the difficult conundrum created by *Tai Hing*,[52] and some of this will be noted in due course. Happily, however, a definitive answer has now been given by the House of Lords in the important case of *Henderson* v. *Merrett Syndicates Ltd.*[53] This is one of the many cases arising from the losses incurred by underwriting members at Lloyd's who, seemingly unaware that insurance and risk are not unconnected, turned to the agents who managed the affairs of their syndicate and sought redress from them in respect of their negligence. There were a variety of different legal structures linking the members and their agents but in most instances a lack of privity indicated that a tortious action was the appropriate way forward.

The House of Lords found that a tortious duty of care was present on these facts. In the principal speech Lord Goff of Chievely found that the law of tort, in the particular form of the *Hedley Byrne* doctrine, was of overriding significance, tort being a general rule which may be added to or subtracted from by the contractual agreement of the parties. He notes[54] that the general rule is that the fact that the duty in tort is imposed by the general law while that in contract is then added on by the will of the parties means that there should be no objection to the plaintiff exercising his choice of preferred cause of action and that a plaintiff "may choose that remedy which appears to him to be the most advantageous".

However, this does not mean that the decision in *Tai Hing* is entirely overwhelmed. Lord Goff notes[55] at the outset that it was a case where the alleged duty in tort was clearly more extensive than that which the parties had agreed in their contractual relationship and that in such a case the courts should be careful not to contradict the parties' expressed intention. Thus the rule in favour of concurrent liability would not apply where "the tortious duty is so inconsistent with the applicable contract that, in accordance with ordinary principles, the parties must be taken to have agreed that the tortious remedy is to be limited or excluded".[56] Thus an implied exclusion clause ruling out the applicability of tort law would seem to arise where it had the effect of fulfilling the intentions of the parties to the contract. In the words of Lord Browne-Wilkinson,[57] "the agreement of the parties evidenced by the contract can modify and shape the tortious duties which, in the absence of contract, would be applicable".

This sensible approach has the effect of subjecting the general principle that concurrent liability should apply to the intention of the parties as expressed by their contractual agreement; this makes sense especially in the commercial context noted by Lord Scarman in *Tai Hing* and it seems that the courts will continue to afford due priority to contractual provisions in cases such as *Bank of Nova Scotia* v. *Hellenic*

---

52. *Ibid.*
53. [1995] A.C. 145.
54. *Ibid.* at 194.
55. *Ibid.* at 186.
56. *Ibid.* at 194.
57. *Ibid.* at 206.

*Mutual War Risks Association (Bermuda) Ltd.*[58] Here, *Tai Hing* was used to deny the existence of a duty in tort by insurers, aware that the ship *Good Luck* was sailing into the Persian Gulf where insurance cover was invalid, to tell the bank whose financial support was secured on the ill-named vessel of the lack of cover when a missile struck the ship. Likewise, the decision in *National Bank of Greece SA* v. *Pinios Shipping Co (No 1)*[59] that a bank who had agreed with a shipowner that the vessel in question should be managed by agents owed no duty to the shipowner to ensure that the agents in question took proper insurance cover for the vessel; such a tortious claim would, if allowed, give protection beyond that which was stipulated by the agreed contractual provision. Such cases still represent good law even after *Henderson*.

### 3.3 Tort in a contractual context

In the previous section we have been examining the way in which contracts between the parties affect their tortious rights. Now, however, we must turn to consider cases where contracts *other* than between the parties to an action may also be of relevance in determining the nature and extent of relevant tortious duties. A starting-point is the decision in *Ernst & Whinney* v. *Willard Engineering (Dagenham) Ltd.*[60] Here, the plaintiffs took on the lease of an office building with defective air conditioning which had been installed by sub-contractors. Clearly there was no contractual nexus as between the parties, but it was held that no action could be brought in tort given the background of network[61] of contracts which provided a complete pattern of protection for the parties without the need to encompass tortious duties. Certainly complex contractual relationships in construction or other such complex claims are planned to fully reflect the wishes of the various parties concerned but, that said, it seems somewhat strange to hold the existence of other contracts between other parties relevant to the issue of a tortious duty between non-contracting parties. The "Privity of Contract Fallacy" i.e., that the doctrine of privity can affect non-contractual liability, seems alive and well in this field.

However, this limitation on tortious liability seems to be clearly possible. In *Southern Water Authority* v. *Carey*[62] the plaintiff's predecessor in title had promised sub-contractors some measure of immunity from suit and it was held that this became a factor which would negative or reduce the scope of the duty of care in tort, even though the plaintiff was obviously not privy to the earlier deal. The earlier deal in effect acted as a policy factor reducing what might otherwise have been a clear duty of care in tort at that time. Likewise, a sub-contractor could avoid the burden of a tortious duty by reference to the main contractors' contractual freedom from liability according to the Court of Appeal in *Norwich City Council* v. *Harvey*,[63] irrespective of the lack of privity on the part of the sub-contractor.[64]

---

58. [1990] 1 Q.B. 818.
59. [1990] 1 A.C. 637; appeal on other grounds to the House of Lords.
60. (1987) 40 B.L.R. 67.
61. Or "fasciculus", *per* Judge Davies Q.C., *ibid.* at 80.
62. [1985] 2 All E.R. 1077.
63. [1989] 1 W.L.R. 928.
64. See also *Pacific Associates Inc* v. *Baxter* [1990] 1 Q.B. 993 especially at 1020–1023.

There thus clearly exists the possibility of the overall background of other contracts affecting the existence and extent of a tortious duty between the plaintiff and the defendant. The existence of these contracts acts not as a fact of contractual liability for non-parties to them, but as evidence of factual circumstances which may as a matter of policy alter or limit the normal ambit of the duty of care imposed by the law of tort. But such cases fail to pass the test of why the parties, in such cases clearly involved in prior dealings, did not themselves expressly create a contractual relationship and exclude tortious liability from it. This would clearly represent best practice.

It is clear that there are many factors which may influence the choice the plaintiff now often has as between actions in tort and contract. It is also clear that in most cases the plaintiff will be able to exercise that choice given the picture that has emerged of the basic general duties in tort being then supplemented by contractual obligations. However, it is also clear that the creation of contractual obligations, or a background of them may mean that the clear intention of the parties not to owe a duty may overcome the general rule of tort. Tort may be the baseline obligation, but we know now that it can be trumped, explicitly or implicitly, by the provisions of the contract.

## 4 TORT: THE DUTY OF CARE

The jurisprudence on the issue of a duty of care in the law of tort in the six or so decades since Mrs Donoghue endured her fateful encounter with the alleged snail has led the issue to reach the House of Lords alone on dozens of occasions. However, in describing the current position on duties owed by professionals it is hoped to establish that a reasonably clear position has now evolved and it is one which may bring stability for a while. That said, the one complication clearly still present in the law is that there is no one single overall test for duty of care, the search for such a test being memorably compared by Lord Oliver to the pursuit of a will-o'-the-wisp in *Caparo Industries plc* v. *Dickman*.[65] So it is necessary to bear in mind that different formulae for finding a duty of care apply in different cases.

### 4.1 Duty: the general test in physical damage cases

Most negligence actions centre on the physical damage caused to the person or property of the plaintiff. Professional defendants are more likely than most to stray into the disputed territory of economic loss, but it is important to start with physical damage partly as it is the trunk from which the outer branches of duty have grown but also because clearly many professionals can prove to be responsible for physical damage e.g., an architect who designs a building which collapses onto its occupants, or a surveyor who fails to spot defects in a ship which subsequently sinks. This latter example is based on the facts of the recent House of Lords' decision in *Marc Rich & Co AG* v. *Bishop Rock Marine Co Ltd*[66] which provides a most useful reminder that it is the law as between physical damage and economic loss that is the main division within the duty issue, rather than arising as between negligent acts and statements. In

---

65. [1990] 2 A.C. 605.
66. [1995] 3 All E.R. 307. See also p. 53 below.

51

the case a classification society surveyor approved the departure of a ship from port after a repair. The ship sank during its voyage and the House of Lords made it clear that it was a case to be decided on the standard negligence principles employed in physical damage cases even though it was a statement rather than an act which caused the loss. This seems implicit in Lord Steyn's speech[67] and explicit in the dissent of Lord Lloyd.[68]

So what are the relevant standard negligence principles that shape liability here? *Donoghue* v. *Stevenson*[69] is, once more, the starting-point since the criteria laid down at the start of the modern tort of negligence remain at centre stage. It is vital to an understanding of the impact of this decision to realise that, in formulating a generally applicable principle of duty of care, Lord Atkin's famous "neighbour" speech was aimed at creating a test that would restrict claims. Rules of law were being created, said Lord Atkin,[70] to "limit the range of complainants and the extent of their remedy". Thus it was, and still is, that a duty of care is only owed to "persons who are so closely and directly affected by my act that I ought to have them in contemplation".[71] That this approach should be the norm became rapidly accepted and confirmed by the House of Lords in *Home Office* v. *Dorset Yacht Co*,[72] but the law in its current form has only finally come into being as a result of reactions to the controversial case of *Anns* v. *London Borough of Merton*.[73]

In this landmark premises liability case a clear and simple twofold test for duty was formulated by Lord Wilberforce.[74] The first question to ask was whether the defendant ought to have realised that harm to the plaintiff was in reasonable contemplation: if so a *prima facie* duty of care arose. Then the second question was whether there were any policy factors which should limit that duty. There was nothing wrong with these questions but the answer to the first question created a presumption in favour of duty which ran against the spirit of Lord Atkin's approach and created a spate of claims, many of which were directed at the professions. Also, to add to the problems, the courts appeared to forget to ask Lord Wilberforce's second question for the best part of the following decade.[75] However, in the second part of the 1980s, efforts were made to curb these excesses and these give us the law on duty of care today. The arguments have focused on both proximity and policy issues.

## 4.2 Proximity

It has clearly been the case right from *Donoghue* to the present day that no duty is owed by a defendant unless there has been harm to the plaintiff in question, but after *Anns* this seemed to be the sole criterion of liability. Clearly this could give rise to a

67. *Ibid.* at 327. His assertion is that policy issues alone are common to both types of claim.
68. *Ibid.* at 321. See also *Mobil Oil Hong Kong Ltd* v. *Hong Kong United Dockyards Ltd* [1991] 1 Lloyds Rep 309 especially at 328.
69. [1932] A.C. 562.
70. *Ibid.* at 579.
71. *Ibid.* at 580.
72. [1970] A.C. 1004 especially at 1026.
73. [1978] A.C. 728.
74. *Ibid.* at 751.
75. With the honourable exception of Ewbank J, in *Ashton* v. *Turner* [1981] Q.B. 137.

potentially very large number of claims. One false move by an auditor of a large company could deprive thousands of shareholders of their profits and tens of thousands of employees of their livelihoods. This fear seems to have been in the collective mind of the Privy Council when hearing an appeal from Hong Kong in the Barlow Clowes lookalike case of *Yuen Kun-Yeu* v. *Attorney General of Hong Kong*[76] when the factor of "close and direct proximity", highlighted as being necessary by Lord Atkin in *Donoghue* but since rather forgotten, should be restored to the centre of the stage. This enabled the Hong Kong Government to avoid liability to an investor in a fraudulent company who claimed that Government officials had failed to exercise statutory powers which would have prevented the fraud. Harm to the plaintiff was foreseeable as a result of these alleged failures but the plaintiff could hardly be said to be either closely or directly proximate to the Government. He was no closer to the Government than any other of the myriad of investors on the Hong Kong Stock Exchange and it was the fraudsters, not the Government, who directly deprived him of his money.[77]

It has already been seen that *Caparo Industries plc* v. *Dickman*[78] purported to deny the existence of a universal test for duty of care, but it seems clear that the principles outlined above extend to all physical damage cases. This seems clear most recently from *Marc Rich & Co AG* v. *Bishop Rock Marine Co Ltd*[79] where Lord Steyn[80] notes that both the principles of foreseeability and proximity have to be employed, as well as the consideration of policy factors.

To whom then may professional defendants owe a duty of care? The key element will clearly be the presence of a relationship of close and direct proximity. This will be easy to establish in many cases where there is direct dealing between the parties. Clearly, a NHS doctor is in such a relationship with his patients and their immediate families while a solicitor's dealings with a client will inevitably also satisfy the test, though the presence of a parallel contractual relationship may, as has been seen,[81] create its own particular difficulties. Classic examples from the case-law of professionals being held to be under a duty not to cause physical harm include any of the innumerable medical negligence decisions,[82] the failure of a solicitor to hold on to a passport thus enabling the client's estranged husband to abduct their children out of the jurisdiction,[83] and the careless advice of an architect which led to a wall collapsing and causing personal injury and property damage.[84]

It is harder, however, to draw a precise line around these concepts. Foreseeability of the particular plaintiff being harmed is inevitably going to be a fact-led question,[85] as will the closeness of the relationship for the purposes of proximity. How close must the patient's relatives be before the doctor in our example owes them a duty of care? Only time, and litigation, will tell.

---

76. [1988] A.C. 175.
77. There were also similar reasons that sounded in policy to refuse the claim. See p. 54 below.
78. [1990] 2 A.C. 605.
79. [1995] 3 All E.R. 307.
80. *Ibid.* at 326.
81. See p. 49 above.
82. See, e.g., *Thake* v. *Maurice* [1986] Q.B. 644.
83. *Al-Kandari* v. *JR Brown & Co* [1988] Q.B. 665.
84. *Clay* v. *AJ Crump & Sons Ltd* [1964] 1 Q.B. 533.
85. Cf. *Bourhill* v. *Young* [1943] A.C. 92 and *Haley* v. *London Electricity Board* [1965] A.C. 778.

What is clearer, however, is that the need to show directness will give rise to problems for plaintiffs in all cases where a professional harms them indirectly, for example by allowing them to be harmed by someone else. This goes far to explain the decision in *Yuen-Kun-Yeu*, though this is perhaps better categorised as an economic loss decision, and also the decision that the police owed no duty to the victim of a murderer whom they had failed to apprehend in *Hill* v. *Chief Constable of West Yorkshire*[86] (though here special police-related policy reasons were also in play). Even this, however, is not an invariable rule, for instance if the intervention of the third party is highly likely.[87] In any event, rules of law are not the sole relevant criterion.

### 4.3 Policy

This has been at the heart of the duty question ever since it became a question. In *Donoghue* v. *Stevenson*,[88] it is the speech of Lord Macmillan which is clearest on the point. In warning, presciently, that "the categories of negligence are never closed"[89] he was not saying that the role of negligence was eternally unpredictable but rather was making the comment in the context of the fact that the law of duty of care existed not in the abstract but in the real world of human relations; this means that the law will always try and reflect the then prevalent view of society. Again the words of Lord Macmillan are still of significance—"The criterion of judgement must adjust and adapt itself to the circumstances of life".[90]

If policy was, for a while, rather downgraded as part of the discussion of duty of care, its central role was reasserted in the construction law case of *Governors of the Peabody Donation Fund* v. *Sir Lindsay Parkinson & Co.*[91] Here, building development took place on clay soils and the original plan was that the drainage system for the development should be flexible in character. It seems likely that cost factors subsequently caused the substitution of a rigid drainage system, this being with the approval of the project's architects. This did not work and action by the developer against builder and architect led to the local authority being joined to the case, the argument against them being that they had failed to utilise their powers to insist on the provision of the flexible drainage system. The House of Lords rejected the notion of liability on the part of the local authority and insisted that any responsibility was that of the contractors, engineers and architects, and not that of the local authority. This was on the basis of policy: "in determining whether or not a duty of care was incumbent upon a defendant it is material to take into consideration whether it is just and reasonable that it should be so".[92] Clearly on such facts the primary, indeed the sole, responsibility lay on the highly qualified building professionals involved with the project rather than the lesser qualified and doubtless overworked officials of the local authority.

But the case has a broader significance simply by reason of its restoration of policy

---

86. [1989] A.C. 453.
87. *Smith* v. *Littlewoods Organisation Ltd* [1987] A.C. 241.
88. [1932] A.C. 562.
89. *Ibid.* at 618.
90. *Ibid.*
91. [1985] A.C. 210.
92. *Ibid.* at 241, *per* Lord Keith.

issues at the centre of the law of negligence agenda. Since *Peabody* the courts have regularly taken on board issues of policy and, although the issue has the age-old reputation of being an unruly horse, in fact some clear lines of approach have emerged from the case-law of the last decade.

It is suggested that the following policy factors may militate against a finding that there should be, on the basis of foreseeability and proximity, a duty of care. These are:

    (a) illegal conduct;
    (b) the presence of legislation;
    (c) the risk of defensive conduct;
    (d) the presence of alternative routes to justice;
    (e) the low likelihood of breaches of any duties; ·
    (f) "floodgates"; and
    (g) the proper allocation of responsibility.

The illegal conduct of the plaintiff is a matter that may arise in any case, not just those of professional liability. Case-law indicates that those who are the victims of wrongs when they are jointly engaged with the defendant in what may be broadly, if not euphemistically, described as joint misbehaviour will lose their right to sue in tort on policy grounds.[93] Of greater significance is the notion that a duty may be circumscribed by the intervention (or non-intervention) of Parliament in the form of legislation. Thus, in *Curran* v. *Northern Ireland Co-Ownership Association Ltd*[94] the failure of the housing authorities to note defects while inspecting work done on the plaintiff's property did not give rise to a duty of care since the purpose of the inspection was to prevent financial fraud rather than to guarantee housing quality.[95]

The courts increasingly seem to cite the risk of defendants responding to the imposition of a duty of care by resort to unduly defensive practices as a reason for restricting duty of care. The most notorious instance is the group of police cases starting from the decision of the House of Lords that the police owed no duty to the victim of a murder and her family in relation to their failure to apprehend the murderer in *Hill* v. *Chief Constable of West Yorkshire*[96] and culminating in the remarkable decision of the Court of Appeal in *Osman* v. *Ferguson.*[97] Whereas earlier police cases could be justified on the grounds that proximity was hard to establish,[98] this excuse was less easy to run in *Osman* where a schoolteacher obsessed with one of his pupils had told the police that he might well take violent action against the family of the plaintiffs. Nonetheless no duty was held to arise on the basis purely of policy viz the diversion of police resources from the investigation of crime to litigation if such a tortious liability were to be established.

It is clear that such an argument would be equally available in principle to many other professional groups. The courts have accepted that the risk of overly defensive conduct should negate the existence of what would otherwise be a clear duty of care

93. E.g., *Ashton* v. *Turner* [1981] Q.B. 137; *Pitts* v. *Hunt* [1991] 1 Q.B. 24.
94. [1987] A.C. 718.
95. See also *Investors in Industry Ltd* v. *South Bedfordshire District Council* [1986] Q.B. 1034 especially at 1062.
96. [1989] A.C. 453.
97. [1993] 4 All E.R. 344.
98. E.g., *Alexandrou* v. *Oxford* [1993] 4 All E.R. 328.

in a fascinating range of cases thus exempting from the embrace of duty government ministers,[99] coastguards[100] and supervisory authorities.[101] However, the clearest evidence of the courts citing the time and effort expended on litigation as a reason to negate rather than encourage the existence of a duty of care comes from the cases concerning the immunity from suit of barristers and others directly involved in the judicial process.[102]

The time and effort taken to, in effect, rehear cases where there has been an allegation of incompetence by a barrister acting in it is expressly cited in *Rondel* v. *Worsley* as a justification of the immunity of counsel.[103] But equally these cases also testify to the importance of the next policy ground, viz the availability of other forms of redress. If incompetent counsel cause their client to lose at, say, a High Court trial, the simplest method of redress is not an agonising rehearing of the conduct of the trial in an action against counsel framed in negligence but lies in the shape of an appeal to the Court of Appeal. Likewise, courts have found against claims in negligence against the social security authorities because of the existence of a tribunal structure[104] and against claims against the police force by members who could avail themselves of disciplinary procedures[105] and against the Charity Commissioners where internal appeals remained available.[106]

The big question underlying all this is whether these (at least internally) coherent arguments will be allowed in cases where as yet they do not appear to have been put. A doctor can surely argue at least as well as counsel that time is better spent on treatment rather than litigation especially when, as is so often the case, that litigation involves the detailed re-enactment of the events of an operation or of a trial. Yet at present this argument has not been applied in medical negligence, or indeed most professional negligence, cases. If the immunity of lawyers is, as cynics maintain, self-serving, it should be removed. But if it has a valid underpinning, it is difficult to confine it to only a small and select group of professionals.

The notion that no duty is owed because of the low likelihood of breach is more controversial. The argument can be found in at least two leading cases. In *Rowling* v. *Takaro Properties*[107] a government minister in New Zealand was held by the Privy Council not to owe a duty of care to a company to whom he had refused financial support, allegedly unlawfully. Lord Keith expressly noted[108] the futility of imposing a duty in circumstances where it was unlikely that a breach could be established. The same distinguished judge also noted in the *Hill* case[109] that the "general sense of public duty" felt by the police did not need the support of a tortious duty of care and

99. *Rowling* v. *Takaro Properties Ltd* [1988] A.C. 473.
100. *Skinner* v. *Secretary of State for Transport* (1995) *The Times*, 3 January.
101. *Philcox* v. *Civil Aviation Authority* (1985) *The Times*, 8 June.
102. On barristers, see *Rondel* v. *Worsley* [1969] 1 A.C. 191; on others engaged in court and related work, see *Saif Ali* v. *Sydney Mitchell & Co* [1980] A.C. 198; on judges, see *Sirros* v. *Moore* [1975] Q.B. 118 and on witnesses (including those making pre-trial statements in contemplation of litigation), see *Evans* v. *London Hospital Medical College* [1981] 1 W.L.R. 184.
103. [1969] 1 A.C. 191 at 230 *per* Lord Reid and at 249 *per* Lord Morris of Borth-y-Gest.
104. *Jones* v. *Department of Employment* [1989] Q.B. 1 at 22.
105. *Calveley* v. *Chief Constable of Merseyside* [1989] A.C. 1228.
106. *Mills* v. *Winchester Diocesan Board of Finance* [1989] Ch. 428 at 452.
107. [1988] A.C. 473.
108. *Ibid.* at 502.
109. [1989] A.C. 53 at 63.

that they would in any event use their best endeavours to suppress and investigate crime. It is submitted strongly that these views, though expressed at a senior level, are incorrect. Duty and breach are separate issues; to cite breach issues as part of the formulation of duty is a *non sequitur*. If there is no breach, the law in relation to breach is the appropriate method of dealing with the matter.

The "floodgates" argument falls to be considered next. This is when the fear of liability for too much to too many is cited as a ground for denial of a duty of care. It appeared at one stage that the courts might accept that the denial of a remedy to one on the grounds of the potential use of the remedy by many multiplies rather than negates any injustice,[110] but clearly the threat of widespread litigation lies at the root of the restrictive decisions in *Hill* and in *Yuen Kun-Yeu* and was regarded as a justification to wait for appropriate legislation rather than for the courts to impose a duty in *Caparo Industries plc* v. *Dickman.*[111]

The final policy factor to be borne in mind is a broader one. It is suggested that running through many of these cases is a theme of individual responsibility. That this accorded with prevalent political thinking is doubtless no coincidence since, as we have already seen,[112] policy factors will vary in accordance with the views of the real world. What is happening, it is suggested, is that the courts are pausing to identify who is really responsible and ascribing duties accordingly. The plaintiffs in *Curran* v. *Northern Ireland Co-Ownership Associated Ltd*[113] could have and should have employed their own surveyor to assess the state of their property and could not rely on the inspection by the housing authorities to secure a guarantee that the house was sound. In *Hill* the bottom line must be that it was the murderer, not the police, who was directly responsible for the murder. In *Van Oppen* v. *Clerk to the Bradford Charity Trustees*[114] it was for a schoolboy and his family to arrange insurance against injuries incurred while playing school rugby, and the school was not liable for not arranging or advising on insurance.

There will always be the opportunity for any policy factors to intervene and alter the legal picture of duty of care; however, the foregoing discussion hopefully offers a guide to factors which frequently do strike a chord and elicit a response from the judiciary in cases where the duty issue is significant.

## 4.4 Duty: economic loss cases

The law of tort possesses its own set of values, values which hopefully accord with those of contemporary society. These values point to the restrictive nature of duty of care becoming yet more restrictive in cases where the interests for which protection is being sought are regarded as less worthy than other interests—we know from *Donoghue* that not every loss can be compensated. So it is that the law of negligence has been historically reluctant to compensate losses that are economic rather than physical in character. This may be justified with reference to a value judgment that,

---

110. *Junior Books* v. *Veitchi & Co Ltd* [1983] 1 A.C. 520 at 539 *per* Lord Roskill.
111. [1990] 2 A.C. 605 at 623 *per* Lord Bridge.
112. See p. 54 above.
113. [1987] A.C. 718.
114. [1990] 1 W.L.R. 235.

say, broken legs are more worthy of compensation than bruised wallets but also, more pragmatically, by reference to the fact that the law of contract also exists and, *inter alia*, can assist in the protection of economic interests.

Clearly, this area is of significance to many professional groups. An auditor who fails to assess accurately the value of the stocks of the company may cause harm to the value of the company and to the value of the holdings of the shareholders. A solicitor who fails to execute properly the wishes of a testator may well harm the economic interests of a disappointed beneficiary. Such economic losses or, perhaps better, failures to make a gain, have been a bone of contention in the law of tort, and only now is a clear(-ish) picture of liability beginning to emerge. In its earlier formulation, the law of negligence set itself against allowing any recovery for this type of loss,[115] but in its recent expansionary phase it did (and does) allow such claims in restricted circumstances. This is the case, once again, whether acts or statements are the basis of the action.[116]

However, before considering what liabilities arise in relation to economic losses it is important to consider fully what counts as an economic loss. This is of particular importance given that the courts have, in their efforts to curtail the tort of negligence in recent years, redefined losses which may in the past have been thought of by lawyers as examples of physical damage (and still would be by laymen) into the category of economic losses for which, as will be seen, only more restrictive liability exists.

The key change in this area came from the House of Lords decision in the case of *Murphy* v. *Brentwood District Council*.[117] This was a classic post-*Anns* case where a local authority was alleged to have been careless in its inspection of the foundations of a property with the result that cracks developed after the premises had been occupied. Cracks, it may well be thought, are items of physical damage—you can put your fingers in them and feel them. This analysis, however, was too simplistic for the House of Lords.[118] The house in question, like any other similarly defective premise or product, was regarded as suffering from economic loss, on the basis that the defects were defects in quality which had existed within the building ever since its initial construction. As such, then, the house had never been worth the price paid for it by Murphy and thus, in economic terms, had never had the value which had been ascribed to it at the time of purchase. The question then logically arises as to what circumstances will give rise to a tortious right of action in respect of such economic losses.

## 4.5 Liability for economic loss

The first clear evidence that the tort of negligence was prepared to get involved with the world of economic loss came in the headline case of *Hedley Byrne & Co Ltd* v. *Heller and Partners Ltd*.[119] This was a case where a bank gave a careless positive reference about the creditworthiness of one of its corporate customers to another bank at the instigation of their customer who then extended credit to the company

---

115. *Cattle* v. *Stockton Waterworks Ltd* (1875) L.R. 10 Q.B. 453 is the *locus classicus*.
116. See *Murphy* v. *Brentwood District Council* [1991] 1 A.C. 398 at 481 *per* Lord Bridge.
117. [1991] 1 A.C. 398.
118. See *ibid.*, particularly Lord Bridge at 475.
119. [1964] A.C. 465.

with resultant economic loss. The House of Lords found that, for the first time, a duty of care would be capable of arising (on the facts a disclaimer of responsibility prevented the duty from arising) in respect of a negligent misstatement made by the defendant which caused economic loss. At this stage in the development of the law it was found that words should be treated differently from deeds since words can be all too easily transmitted (and of course potentially altered) as they are passed from person to person, unlike a chattel. This was found to justify a more restrictive liability for damage caused by words rather than by things. Liability would be created in particular where the parties were in a special relationship, whether contractual or otherwise, that relationship being one where the plaintiff was relying on the defendant's skill and judgment to the knowledge of the defendant. This, of course, is of particular relevance to a professional defendant and the examples given at the outset of coverage of economic losses[120] are classic instances of post-*Hedley Byrne* liability and are, in themselves, leading cases in the evolution of this type of tort action. It is therefore important to trace the evolution of this significant cause of action.

Although there is no doubt that a valid cause of action exists in respect of economic loss caused by careless misstatements, the precise form of the action has altered subtly. Initially, the Privy Council found that the duty would only arise when the maker of the statement was a professional giver of advice,[121] but such a restrictive view did not survive the dramatic expansion of negligence liability later in the 1970s and it was the view of the minority rather than of the majority of the speeches which found favour in subsequent litigation. It was found that there was no reason why any appropriate case where reliance was found should not be one where a *Hedley Byrne* duty could arise.[122]

More recently, the House of Lords have had several opportunities to review this area of the law. The first came in the case of *Smith* v. *Eric S Bush; Harris* v. *Wyre Forest District Council*.[123] Two joined appeals were heard in cases where surveyors had allegedly misvalued properties but where, as is the norm, the initial report was made to the valuer's employer (a building society and local authority respectively) who in turn passed on details of the valuation to the customer. Thus there was no personal link between the parties from which the key concept of reliance could flow. This, however, was no bar to a finding that a duty of care existed on the part of the valuer; the valuer knew that it was common, almost invariable, practice to pass on the details of the survey report to the purchaser and that the purchaser would rely on those views, apparently in 90 per cent of all cases.[124] The valuer's actual knowledge that their opinions would be passed on to the plaintiffs is vital to a proper understanding of the case.

But what the law can give it can also take away. A more restrictive (though not incompatible) approach was taken by the House of Lords in the subsequent case of *Caparo Industries plc* v. *Dickman*[125] where a company's auditor was held not to owe a

---

120. See p. 58 above.
121. *Mutual Life and Citizens' Assurance Co Ltd* v. *Evatt* [1971] A.C. 793.
122. See, e.g., *Howard Marine and Dredging Co Ltd* v. *A Ogden & Sons (Excavations) Ltd* [1978] Q.B. 54.
123. [1990] 1 A.C. 831.
124. *Ibid.* at 864 *per* Lord Griffiths and at 871 *per* Lord Jauncey.
125. [1990] 2 A.C. 605.

duty of care to the purchasers of shares who claimed to have relied on the audited accounts during a, from their point of view sadly, successful takeover bid. As in *Smith* there was clearly no direct personal relationship between the parties, but unlike in *Smith* there was no reason for the auditors of a public company to be aware that the accounts of the company were being perused by a corporate predator. Lord Bridge responded to the ever-present fear of unlimited liability by restricting the duty of care to cases where[126]:

"the defendant knew that his statement would be communicated to the plaintiff, either as an individual or as a member of an identifiable class, specifically in connection with a particular transaction or transactions of a particular kind ... and that the plaintiff would be very likely to rely on it for the purpose of deciding whether or not to enter upon that transaction or upon a transaction of that kind."

On such a formulation it is clearly still possible to uphold the judgment in the *Smith* case but on the facts of *Caparo* itself a general statement made in public accounts to, at least potentially, the whole world cannot satisfy the rigour required by Lord Bridge. Indeed, even the statement in *Hedley Byrne* itself may have been too vague and general in character to satisfy the post-*Caparo* requirements.

Three further cases have also reached the House of Lords recently and help to further define the parameters of *Hedley Byrne* liability. In *Spring* v. *Guardian Assurance plc*[127] a negligently drafted reference for an official of an insurance company meant that the industry's regulatory body was unable to approve his appointment. This was held to be a case where there was a duty of care owed by the employer to the employee not to make careless statements but the basis of the finding varied. Lord Goff directly applied *Hedley Byrne* principles to the facts, finding that this was a case where a special relationship had arisen, this forming the basis of an assumption of responsibility on the part of the defendants—this now being once again regarded as the true intellectual basis of the *Hedley Byrne* line of authority[128]— which would render them liable for breaches of duty taking place within the ambit of the relationship. Lord Woolf thought that the imposition of a duty was a logical development of the *Hedley Byrne* principle, while the other two judges in the majority (Lord Keith dissented from the majority view) found for Spring on broader (even vaguer) grounds. The case demonstrates that there is life in the *Hedley Byrne* principle even after its restriction in *Caparo*, and reinforces that the voluntary assumption of responsibility by the defendant lies at the heart of that liability.

This latter point was reinforced and developed by Lord Goff, in particular in the next case where the House of Lords addressed this area of the law. *Henderson* v. *Merrett Syndicates Ltd*[129] arose from the problems in the insurance market at Lloyd's of London. Again a duty was found to exist on the part of various agents of Lloyd's Names to those Names. He found[130] that the assumption of responsibility in offering professional services was crucial to an understanding of why there should be liability for any losses, including here the perfectly foreseeable economic losses, arising out of breaches of the duties created by that assumption of responsibility, and that acts and

---

126. *Ibid.* at 621.
127. [1995] 2 A.C. 296.
128. Cf. *Smith* v. *Eric S Bush* [1990] 1 A.C. 831 at 864–865 *per* Lord Griffiths.
129. [1995] 2 A.C. 145.
130. [1995] 2 A.C. 145 at 181.

omissions might equally give rise to liability under the *Hedley Byrne* principle.[131] This time Lord Goff enjoyed the full support of his fellow Law Lords.

The assumption of responsibilities by the defendants lay at the heart of the third of this modern trilogy of cases, the appeal in *White* v. *Jones*.[132] This was a re-run of the issue decided in the High Court in the plaintiff's favour in *Ross* v. *Caunters*,[133] namely whether a solicitor could be sued for a failure to draft a will properly on the instructions of the testator by the disappointed beneficiary. Again, a positive answer was given by the House of Lords, confirming *Ross* albeit only by a bare majority. The essence of the decision lies[134] in what was accepted to be an expansion of *Hedley Byrne* principles, albeit an incremental one, whereby the ambit of the assumption of responsibility is extended beyond the obvious assumption of a relationship to the testator to cover in addition the foreseeable, though personally unknown, beneficiaries.

These major recent cases all provide clear evidence that the imposition of a duty of care under *Hedley Byrne* principles can continue to evolve into new forms. But it must be noted that the duty said to be owed to the unknown beneficiaries in *White* v. *Jones* contradicts the spirit, if not the letter, of the approach taken in *Caparo*. But the consistent line taken in the three most recent cases suggests that a departure from the earlier harder line has unequivocally taken place.

Not all economic losses are caused by negligently made statements. Negligent acts may also create such losses, for example where a solicitor's writing of a conveyance is negligent and causes a delay in the transfer of a property which in turn delays the starting date of the plaintiff's use of the property as a (presumably profitable) hotel. In such a case it is submitted that what was once a separate strand of authority has now been subsumed into the mainstream principles of liability for negligently caused economic loss, as under the *Hedley Byrne* decision and the subsequent line of cases that builds upon it.

The pivotal case on tortious acts that cause economic loss is of course the decision in *Junior Books* v. *Veitchi & Co Ltd*[135] where a duty was found to exist on the part of a sub-contractor to provide a floor for the plaintiff's book warehouse that was capable of maximising the profitability of the warehouse rather than, in fact, harming its profitability. Such a duty to avoid economic loss arose, in the view of a majority of the House of Lords, because of the particularly close relationship between the parties; the plaintiffs had nominated the defendants as their sub-contractors and had relied on their evident expertise. This,[136] and the close similarity with a contractual relationship, were reasons to impose this hitherto unprecedented duty of care.

The decision in *Junior Books* was not greeted with unalloyed pleasure. Indeed it is difficult to find a case that directly follows the judgment.[137] However, the case has not been totally abandoned but rather has been explained as part of the *Hedley Byrne*

---

131. Following *Midland Bank Trust Co Ltd* v. *Hett, Stubbs and Kemp* [1979] Ch. 384 at 416.
132. [1995] 2 A.C. 207.
133. [1980] Ch. 297.
134. [1995] 2 A.C. 207 at 268.
135. [1983] 1 A.C. 520.
136. See particularly Lord Roskill at 546.
137. See the negative comments of Dillon LJ in *Simaan General Contracting Co* v. *Pilkington Glass Ltd* [1988] Q.B. 758 at 784: "I found it difficult to see that future citation from the *Junior Books* case can ever serve any useful purpose".

approach. This view stems, once again, from the decision in the House of Lords in *Murphy* v. *Brentwood District Council*[138] where Lord Bridge expressed cogently that[139]:

"even in the absence of contract, there is a special relationship between the builder and building owner which is sufficiently akin to contract to introduce the element of reliance so that the scope of the duty of care owed by the builder to the owner is wide enough to embrace purely economic loss. The decision in *Junior Books* v. *Veitchi Co Ltd* can, I believe, only be understood on this basis".

It is difficult, if not impossible, to distinguish this approach from that in the *Hedley Byrne* line of cases, in the words of Lord Keith in the *Murphy* case[140]: "I would regard *Junior Books* v. *Veitchi Co Ltd* as being an application of that principle", this being a direct reference to the principle established in the *Hedley Byrne* decision. Thus the decision in the controversial *Junior Books* case survives, albeit in a restrictive form.

### 4.6 Duty: nervous shock cases

A third category of cases where separate rules apply in relation to duty of care is where the damage complained of is psychiatric rather than physical damage. Happily this is not an area where too many professionals are likely to become liable, but it is easy to imagine a case, for example, where a professional employer causes stress amongst his workforce and becomes liable as a result of this.[141]

It now seems clear that the law will accept in an appropriate case that psychiatric damage is as foreseeable as physical injury on the part of a victim who is personally a participant in the tortious events.[142] However, where shock is caused by a reaction to the news of an unfortunate event, rather than by the incident itself, liability is restricted to cases where there is a high level of proximity based upon the close personal relationship between plaintiff and actual victim, and the closeness in time of hearing news of the events in question.[143]

Thus care must be taken to avoid taking steps which will cause psychiatric damage to those directly in contemplation of a potential defendant; on the other hand liability for indirectly caused psychiatric harm seems to be compensatable on a highly restrictive basis.

### 4.7 Duty: other cases

Other instances do exist where the rules in relation to duty of care vary from the norm. *Caparo plc* v. *Dickman*[144] indicates some others and points[145] to liability caused by the act of a third party as being based on stricter notions of foreseeability,[146] while

138. [1991] 1 A.C. 398.
139. *Ibid.* at 481.
140. *Ibid.* at 466.
141. See, e.g., *Walker* v. *Northumberland County Council* [1995] 1 All E.R. 737.
142. See *Alcock* v. *Chief Constable of South Yorkshire* [1992] 1 A.C. 310 especially at 407 *per* Lord Oliver.
143. *Ibid.* especially at 411.
144. [1990] 2 A.C. 605.
145. *Ibid.* at 635 *per* Lord Oliver.
146. See *Smith* v. *Littlewoods Organisation Ltd* [1987] 2 A.C. 241.

rules also differ between policy and operational activities of public bodies[147] as well, as we have seen, in relation to misrepresentations which cause economic loss.

Duty of care may now be likened to an archipelago of islands such as the West Indies where each island is a separate nation with, often, similar but not identical rules. Likewise different but not dissimilar rules apply within the tort of negligence on the different "islands" of, for instance, physical harm, economic loss or nervous shock. There is no one universal principle, but general principles must, and do, survive.

## 5 BREACH OF DUTY

The issue of duty of care may have dominated the headlines of *The Times* law reports in recent years, and it is an issue which prefaces all negligence litigation. That said, in many cases the issue can be disposed of cursorily—of course doctors owe a duty of care to their patients; of course solicitors owe such a duty to their clients. However, in every instance of negligence litigation the issue of breach of duty arises, and arises at the very heart of the litigation, because it embodies the key question as to whether the defendant was actually careless or negligent in his conduct or not. It is also appropriate to note at the outset that the question will ultimately be a factual one, albeit one assessed in accordance with the underlying broad principles of the law and this means that related issues arise concerning the proof of those facts and thus of any breach of duty that may have occurred.

### 5.1 Breach: general principles

The law of negligence does not, unlike contract, set ideals or guarantee results. Rather, its basic approach is to ensure that reasonable care, no more, is taken. In order to decide this issue the courts have resorted to the mythical character of the reasonable man[148] and liability in negligence arises when a defendant fails to avoid an accident which the reasonable man would have avoided,[149] or which, rather, the court thinks the reasonable man should have avoided. The test is on the face of it an objective one[150] but one which in the last resort has to be carried out by an individual judge or judges.

The reasonable man has been described often enough; he is ordinary, average, normal; he is "free both from over-apprehension and from over-confidence".[151] However, these basic tests are of only limited validity in a professional context, since the fabled "man on the Clapham omnibus" is not a highly trained doctor, a qualified solicitor or an expert in building design. Thus the basic test has evolved in cases of professional liability into the assessment of negligence by reference to the notional reasonable skilled man in a particular profession and it is by reference to his standard of care that that of the defendant is analysed. The classic formulation of this is the

---

147. *Anns* v. *Merton London Borough Council* [1978] A.C. 728.
148. See, e.g., *Hall* v. *Brooklands Racing Club* [1933] 1 K.B. 205 especially at 224.
149. See, e.g., *Glasgow Corporation* v. *Muir* [1943] A.C. 448.
150. *Ibid.* at 457 *per* Lord Macmillan.
151. *Ibid.*

famous *Bolam* test. *Bolam* v. *Friern Hospital Management Committee*[152] was a case where a doctor treated a mental patient by giving him electro-convulsive treatment without any restraint or sedation, this latter aspect being the subject of debate within the medical profession at the time. The patient was injured, and sued. In due course McNair J addressed the jury hearing the case on the issue of standard of care. "The test is the standard of the ordinary skilled man exercising and professing to have that special skill. A man need not possess the highest expert skill; it is well established that it is sufficient if he exercises the ordinary skill of an ordinary competent man exercising that particular art."[153] He went on later to say to the jury "the real question . . . is whether the defendants, in acting in the way they did, were acting in accordance with a practice of competent respected professional opinion".

The wide ramifications of this need to be explored in due course, but it is important to establish the centrality of the *Bolam* test in all professional negligence cases. Its continuing relevance in all cases of medical negligence has been reaffirmed in *Gold* v. *Haringey Area Health Authority*[154] while its relevance to non-medical cases was identified by Lord Denning MR in *Greaves* v. *Baynham Meikle*[155]: "in the ordinary employment of a professional man, whether it is a medical man, a lawyer, or an accountant, an architect or an engineer, his duty is to use reasonable care and skill".[156] The *Bolam* test has been upheld by the House of Lords[157] and represents the appropriate test in all professional liability cases.[158]

Such a general formula for liability is bound to raise its own complications. These will now be considered. First comes the problem of where professional views vary and differing views prevail. *Bolam* was indeed such a case. The answer to the problem lies in the form of the view that the defendant needed to find the support of any "reasonably competent medical men".[159] This statement suggests that it is the quality, not the quantity, of support that is relevant to the finding of negligence. Many doctors may have moved on, as in *Bolam*, to more modern forms of treatment, but the doctor in question was perfectly entitled to be found to have behaved in a non-negligent manner while enjoying the support of other competent professionals.

The full significance of this approach did not become fully clear, perhaps until the decision of the House of Lords in *Maynard* v. *West Midlands Regional Health Authority*.[160] A trial judge had found for the plaintiff on the basis of his preference for the views of her expert witnesses rather than those of the equally distinguished defence witnesses. In overturning that judgment, it was noted that "a court may prefer one body of opinion to the other: but that is no basis for a conclusion of negligence".[161] In other words, the fact that the defendants could point to the support for them by any body of opinion which satisfied the test of competence was enough to make the court give judgment against the plaintiffs. "Competence" is all and the

---

152. [1957] 1 W.L.R. 852.
153. *Ibid.* at 856.
154. [1988] Q.B. 481.
155. [1975] 1 W.L.R. 1095.
156. *Ibid.* at 1101.
157. See, e.g., *Whitehouse* v. *Jordan* [1981] 1 W.L.R. 246.
158. See also the view of Lord Ackner extra-judicially. See [1992] 8 P.N. 54 at 55.
159. [1957] 1 W.L.R. 852.
160. [1984] 1 W.L.R. 634.
161. *Ibid.* at 638 *per* Lord Scarman.

amount and even the accuracy of rival contrary opinion is not relevant. This is the remorseless logic of the *Bolam* approach.

Also stemming directly from the *Bolam* approach is the relevance, or rather irrelevance, of hindsight in the assessment of negligence liability. In cases such as *Roe* v. *Minister of Health*[162] the fact that medical practice had subsequently changed after the accident but before the trial was deemed rightly to be irrelevant. The assessment of the situation by the reasonable man can only be made with reference to the facts then known, and not with regard to future developments. In this context it might be noted that the frequent habit of citing subsequent changes to practice as evidence of prior negligence seems inappropriate unless the previous situation was so dangerous, to the mind of the reasonable man, crying out for reform.

Yet another consequence of the *Bolam* formula is that many errors by professionals will not result in any compensation for the victims of them. This is because the professional man will in reality make mistakes from time to time and will thus be only held liable for those errors of judgment which the notional reasonable man would have avoided. The tragic mistake made by the doctor in *Whitehouse* v. *Jordan*[163] was in a very difficult situation, such that the reasonable doctor in that situation might very well have made the same mistake. Yes, there was an error but, no, there was no negligence.

A particular aspect of the *Whitehouse* case is that the situation was a difficult one. On the one hand action had to be taken speedily to bring to an end the prolonged period of labour being experienced by a patient in some difficulty, but equally there were risks whether a Caesarean operation or a forceps delivery was carried out. Clearly, the likelihood of error in such a concatenation of circumstances is greatly increased, and finding negligence accordingly less likely. But care must be taken. Some professionals, most obviously in the medical and related professions, must be expected to cope with emergency situations in their daily work—it must be assumed that *Whitehouse* was an unusually severe case and the relevance of an emergency situation can only ever provide a reduction in the standard of care, not a total removal of it.[164]

Clearly, such general issues as this which can arise in litigation will also be relevant to professional liability cases. Whether driving to work or treating a patient, the reasonable doctor will act to avoid major risks but will be entitled to ignore minor ones.[165] But equally, liability will arise where obvious risks are ignored, especially where they may be easily remedied and/or where the risk is of a particularly serious injury. All these factors were present in *Black* v. *Kent County Council*[166] where a school authority was held liable for eye injury caused by the use of sharp scissors in a classroom where much less sharp scissors were adequate and available.

So far consideration has been given to a range of factors which point to the legal picture of the professional defendant as being a relatively happy one. The defendant, it seems, does not have to achieve a result but merely has to exercise ordinary skill and judgment. Mistakes can be made, hindsight is never relevant and the support of

---

162. [1954] 2 Q.B. 66.
163. [1981] 1 W.L.R. 246. See particularly Lord Edmund-Davies at 257 and Lord Fraser at 263.
164. E.g., *Watt* v. *Hertfordshire County Council* [1954] 1 W.L.R. 835. See Denning J at 838.
165. As, classically, in *Bolton* v. *Stone* [1951] A.C. 850.
166. (1984) 82 L.G.R. 39.

even a small minority of professionals will obviate liability. Yet if this was the case professional negligence cases would be few and far between and insurance premiums low. Anecdotal experience suggests that this is far from being so. Why is there present this apparent discrepancy between legal reality and worldly reality?

Several factors may be mentioned. Litigation does not equate to liability and in an ever more litigious age it is inevitable that more claims may be made against professionals who may, in past, more deferential, days have been held in awe not sued in law. All these claims have to be defended and that process is long and time- and energy-consuming even if the foregoing legal analysis suggests that they will be ultimately successful. Only empirical work on a huge scale can ever provide a true picture of the eventual outcome of all professional liability litigation.

However it may be that, in deciding cases, the courts are in practice imposing ever higher standards of care on professionals, perhaps moved by the plight of the plaintiff or simply using the disguise of the reasonable man to hide that they are imposing their own standards of prejudices. Again, proof is almost impossible to find other than from within the lurking suspicions of professionals, usually that their particular profession is harshly treated. It may well be that the courts are less willing to impose their views on more specialist professions such as medicine, though equally other factors in the whole litigation equation may have the same effect.[167]

However, there are two areas of some significance where the law itself takes a harsher view and, indeed, obliges the defendant to attain a standard of care that is in practice going to be beyond that individual's capabilities. The first area where this may arise is in relation to the liability of the novice or trainee. At the beginning of almost every professional's working life there is likely to arise some instance where inexperience, over-eagerness or over-promotion leads to the position where the young professional realises that he has bitten off more than he can chew. This fact of life has caused the argument to be put that a novice or trainee professional should be able to offer a lower standard of care than that provided by his more experienced counterparts. The argument may reflect reality, but does not represent the law.

This can be expressed unhesitatingly after the decision of the Court of Appeal in the case of *Wilsher* v. *Essex Area Health Authority*.[168] Here, a prematurely born baby was in need of highly specialist care in a specialist unit of the defendant's hospital. The doctor in charge was a fully qualified specialist but was holding his first post in his specialism. It was alleged that the doctor made a mistake which injured the baby which, perhaps, a more experienced doctor would have avoided. However, the relative inexperience of the doctor was not a factor that would justify any variation in the standard of care to be expected from the reasonable (i.e., reasonably experienced) doctor of that speciality. Mustill LJ[169] summed up the view of the majority of the court by rejecting the view that standards of care should vary as between different individual doctors (in respect of whom the patient will very often not have a choice); he said that "this notion of a duty tailored to the actor rather than to the act which he elects to perform, has no place in the law of tort". In other words, by holding himself out as a doctor, the employee of the defendant was holding himself out as offering the standard of care to be expected from a reasonable doctor, in the same way as by

167. See Lord Ackner, extra-judicially [1992] 8 P.N. 54.
168. [1987] Q.B. 730 (appealed on other grounds: [1988] A.C. 1074. See p. 69 below.
169. *Ibid.*

sitting in the driver's seat of a car, one holds oneself out as being able to offer the skills of the reasonable driver,[170] even if in fact one is only a learner.

*Wilsher* is not without its critics; there is without doubt a cogency within the dissenting judgment of Browne-Wilkinson V-C and the High Court of Australia takes the contrary approach too, as in *Cook* v. *Cook*.[171] The obligation of the novice or trainee to reach a standard of care which he may never be able to attain seems harsh but can be justified on the grounds of efficiency in litigation, since a standard of care is applicable to a whole profession rather than each practitioner of it, and also may be justified on policy grounds too since it obliges an employer to devote appropriate resources to the supervision and training of newer employees.[172]

This notion of an obligation to act appropriately being applied in an objective way then raises the question of whether a particularly excellent and/or experienced doctor (for instance) may be expected to offer a higher standard of care than the reasonable doctor. On the face of it such a proposition does not sit easily with the *dicta* in *Wilsher* but it could equally be argued that behind *Wilsher* lies a policy decision to entitle all patients to a certain minimum standard of care and to apply *Wilsher* so as to allow the lowering of the standard offered by the best is far from compatible with this policy. There is scant authority on this point; prior to *Wilsher* it was suggested *obiter* by a trial judge that *if* there was any variation in the standard of care in such a case it would be in favour of the eminent surgeon offering a higher standard of care.[173] On the other hand such an argument was rejected in *George Wimpey & Co* v. *Poole*[174] but this was an odd case where the plaintiffs were trying to be found negligent for insurance reasons and it may be readily confined to its own facts. In any event, there is a clash between the letter of and the policy behind the *Wilsher* decision when applied to highly experienced professionals and the case may arise when the issue of potentially higher standards of care from such defendants will be raised in due course.

A second area where the test of standard of care may be varied is rare in its application but significant in its approach. It has so far always been assumed that compliance with ordinary professional standards by a defendant will release him from any further tortious obligation. However, it is clear that in what must be emphasised to be exceptional cases, the courts will find a defendant to be liable even though there has been compliance with those standards where those standards are found to be unacceptable. This will happen where the courts take the view that to follow the established standard is to follow a path so obviously deficient that it would be folly to follow it.[175] This is easy to apply in cases where ordinary common sense shows the obvious folly of accepted ways[176] but the courts will occasionally be prepared to use the "obvious folly" approach in cases where it is professional standards of care that are at issue in litigation. Thus the Privy Council found that compliance with standard methods of conveyancing of commercial property in Hong Kong could none the less be regarded as negligent since the system was evidently over-reliant on

---

170. As in *Nettleship* v. *Weston* [1971] 2 Q.B. 691.
171. (1987) 61 A.L.J. 25.
172. See p. 70 below.
173. *Ashcroft* v. *Mersey Regional Health Authority* [1983] 2 All E.R. 245 at 247 *per* Kilner Brown J.
174. [1984] 2 Lloyd's Rep. 499.
175. *Morton* v. *William Dixon*, 1909 S.C. 807 at 809 *per* Lord Dunedin. See *Holyoak* [1990] L.S. 201.
176. See, e.g., *Cavanagh* v. *Ulster Weaving Co Ltd* [1960] A.C. 145.

trust.[177] Standard practice amongst captains of a particular type of car ferry was seen as evidence not of reasonable care but of "general and culpable complacency" in a hearing arising from the Zeebrugge ferry disaster.[178] Even the medical profession is not free from the possibility of judicial criticism of its established practices,[179] though it is fair to note that few would disagree with the judgment in the Canadian case of *Anderson* v. *Chesney*[180] that it was obviously wrong to use common practice to defend a case where a patient suffocated where a sponge had been left in his throat after an operation. There it is clearly appropriate to question common practice, but it should not be ignored that so to do in many other cases of professional liability in effect amounts to the substitution of the opinion of the relevant profession by that of the court and that comes to be close to judicial legislation. Thankfully, as has been emphasised, such cases are exceptional and, to date, unexceptionable.

## 5.2 Breach: issues in professional liability

The general principles of breach of duty that have been discussed already always are relevant to, and often derive from, professional negligence litigation. However, some issues seem to arise exclusively in such litigation and, while accepting that the dividing line is a hard one to draw precisely, it is now appropriate to turn to specific issues in professional liability.

The first and perhaps most important issue is to attempt to discern what the appropriate profession is when ascertaining the appropriate professional standard of care. Clearly a different standard of care may be expected from a specialist heart surgeon than from a general practitioner, and the law reflects this. The leading case is *Maynard* v. *West Midlands Regional Health Authority*,[181] where the issue arose as to whether there had been negligence by two consultants expert in the treatment of chest diseases. Lord Scarman made clear[182] that the appropriate standard of care was not that of the reasonable doctor *per se* but rather was that of the reasonable doctor exercising "the ordinary skills of his speciality".[183] This seems only sensible or, indeed, self-evident, but this clear approach can still lead to problems.

Within any profession there may be many sub-specialisms; the question therefore arises as to whether each single small unit within a profession is entitled to assert that it has its own separate set of professional practices. The case of *De Freitas* v. *O'Brien*[184] provides authority here where a group of fewer than a dozen doctors of a particular speciality were held to be capable of forming a distinct responsible body of opinion even though they were such a small group. The decision appears to be compatible with the *Bolam* test but, while in no way commenting on the group of specialists involved, there must be a risk of professional collusion when such a small group of specialists, who inevitably are highly likely to know one another, are regarded as forming an independent body of responsible professional opinion.

177. *Edward Wong Finance Ltd* v. *Johnson, Stokes & Masters* [1984] A.C. 296.
178. *Re The Herald of Free Enterprise* (1987) *The Independent*, 18 December.
179. See *Sidaway* v. *Board of Governors of the Bethlem Royal Hospital* [1984] Q.B. 493 at 513–514.
180. [1949] 4 D.L.R. 71, affirmed [1950] 4 D.L.R. 223.
181. [1984] 1 W.L.R. 634.
182. *Ibid.* at 638.
183. *Ibid.*
184. (1995) *The Times*, 17 February.

Likewise within different professions different members possess varying expertise. A small town solicitor will typically be a generalist, a "jack of all trades" and is a figure who is a very different figure from an expert partner in a large City law firm who will typically be an expert not just in, say, company law or professional negligence, but on some arcane matter located deep within such a speciality. Here, too, the courts have recognised the problem, and have resolved it sensibly. A clear formulation is provided by the Court of Appeal in its decision in *Luxmoore-May* v. *Messenger May Baverstock*.[185] The defendants, a firm of auctioneers based in the Surrey town of Godalming, made an initial valuation of £30–£50 for a pair of paintings which subsequently turned out to have been painted by the famous painter George Stubbs and were ultimately auctioned by a later owner at Sotheby's for no less than £88,000. It was held that, in spite of this seemingly wide discrepancy, the defendants were not liable; they should be judged by the standard of the reasonable exemplar of what they actually were, namely a firm of ordinary provincial auctioneers who were not in the same league as, and were not holding themselves out as offering the same standards of care as, a major international auctioneers such as Sotheby's or Christie's. The case is best explained as establishing in effect that a firm such as Messenger May Baverstock are in a different profession from the more expert and, doubtless, more resourced, firms of auctioneers of international repute.

It is important to distinguish the precise areas in which the professional defendant is able to rely on his unique qualifications to defend his actions. To use medical negligence as an example, it is clear that only a fellow surgeon (or to be precise his notional reasonable counterpart) can assess the appropriate standard of care but, equally, there are other aspects of the surgeon's job where a different test of liability is appropriate, for example in the organisation of the workload of the surgeon, or the establishment of appropriate support mechanisms, rather than just in the process of surgery itself.

All this is well-illustrated by, once again, *Wilsher* v. *Essex Area Health Authority*.[186] It will be recalled that a premature baby was allegedly injured by the negligence of a young doctor. The Court of Appeal took the view that, irrespective of whether the doctor in question was negligent or not, a matter on which the court was divided, there should also be a liability potentially to be ascribed to the doctor's employer, the local health authority, not just on the basis of vicarious liability, but as a matter of primary liability. It was under a duty, in the view of both Browne-Wilkinson V-C and Glidewell LJ, who were not *ad idem* on the issue of the doctor's own liability, to take reasonable care to organise its hospital in such a way as to ensure that appropriately qualified staff were in place to ensure an appropriate standard of health care for all patients. It could clearly be argued that to leave a newly qualified doctor in charge of a highly specialist premature baby unit was a breach of the basic primary duty of care of the health authority.

Such a decision has, it is suggested, broad implications. The organisation of a business or similar trading activity is a matter in which the surgeon, to use our example again, can in no way be able to argue that his own professional skills place him in any different position from any other person engaged in any trade or business.

185. [1990] 1 W.L.R. 1009.
186. [1987] Q.B. 730. See also p. 66 above.

It is accordingly easier to hold professional defendants liable for the manner in which they organise their professional activity rather than for the precise exercise of their professional skills.

Professional defendants have further problems. They may in many cases be as the cliché has it, at the cutting edge of their particular specialism. The law has to adapt its standard tests of professional liability to cases where, by virtue of being ahead of the pack of co-professionals, a defendant is unable to find a responsible body of opinion which follows, or even understands, the approach being followed by the defendant. In such a case the "reasonable skilled professional" test needs to be applied in a different way. The answer must be that, in such a case, the innovator must take whatever reasonable steps other reasonable innovators would take and the obvious precaution that is appropriate to take is to, at the least, carry out trials and experiments with a new product or technique so as to ensure that if not safe, it is at least reasonably safe in the light of the reasoning that has led to the innovation.[187]

In other cases, however, it is easier to establish whether the professional defendant is liable or not. In this (over-)regulated age there are many both statutory and non-statutory sets of rules and regulations that are vital in establishing the appropriate professional standards. A simple example is provided by *Budden* v. *BP Oil Ltd*[188] where an action alleging that the defendants were liable in negligence for putting excessive amounts of lead in their petrol failed on the simple ground that the amounts of lead complied with the then legislation. Not only was it not reasonable to ask BP to reach a higher standard than that ordained by Parliament, it was indeed, in the view of the Court of Appeal, unconstitutional for a court to require any different or higher standard. Clearly voluntary standards created as a result of self-regulation will also go a long way to defining the appropriate standard of professional care,[189] though of course there is always the outside risk that those standards will be seen to represent a folly which it would be obvious to avoid.[190]

There is a further area where a professional defendant may be in a distinct position as opposed to that of an "ordinary" defendant. In consulting a professional, a client puts himself under the control of that professional, whether it is in an instance of medical treatmnt by a doctor or one of financial advice from an accountant. This then raises the question of whether the relevant professional becomes under what may be described as a higher duty to act positively to control his client's affairs or, at the least, to give positive advice and/or warnings to attempt to affect their position. The standard rule remains in the law of negligence against such positive duties,[191] but it seems clear that within the specific context of a professional–client relationship that such positive duties may exist[192] though, at least in cases of negligent advice, there may be only a restricted duty to subsequently update that advice.[193]

There is no doubt that, by virtue of both their special skills and special responsibilities, defendants in actions who come from a professional background owe higher duties of care and therefore are at greater risk of negligence liability.

---

187. *Landan* v. *Werner* (1961) 105 S.J. 1008.
188. (1980) 124 S.J. 376.
189. E.g., *Lord Cheyham & Co Ltd* v. *Littlejohn & Co* (1985) 2 P.N. 154.
190. See p. 65 above.
191. *Yuen Kun-Yeu* v. *Attorney-General of Hong Kong* [1988] A.C. 175 at 192 *per* Lord Keith.
192. As classically in *Rivtow Marine Ltd* v. *Washington Ironworks Ltd* (1973) 40 D.L.R. (3d) 530.
193. *Eckersley* v. *Binnie, Nuttall and North West Water Authority* (1988) 18 Con. L.R. 1.

## 5.3 Proof of fault

It is the case in professional negligence disputes as in any other case that the plaintiff is under an obligation to prove the elements of the claim that he makes, including the vital factor for breach of duty. But it is equally evident that this may be difficult for an unskilled plaintiff attempting to unravel the arcane mysteries of what may well be a highly specialist vocation carried out by the defendant. It is therefore of particular importance to the plaintiff in such a case to see what, if any, help the law will provide to him and it is to the doctrine of *res ipsa loquitur* that such a plaintiff may well turn. It is necessary to consider both the applicability and the impact of the doctrine.

*Res ipsa loquitur*—loosely translated as "let the thing speak for itself"—is a doctrine that can be used where the facts are redolent of negligence (and this is essential) and where the negligence is that of the defendant. Thus if a routine operation ends in a tragedy it may well not be obvious whether, for example, it is the surgeon or the anaesthetist who will be responsible and *res ipsa* will be hard to employ. But if all the relevant staff are employed by the same health authority then it may well be possible to employ the doctrine against that body.[194] Clearly, therefore, the doctrine will be of limited use in multi-party actions such as a typical building dispute involving builders, architects, surveyors, engineers and representatives of local authorities.

Even if the plaintiff can overcome these obstacles, he will then find that the doctrine of *res ipsa loquitur* will only be of relatively marginal assistance. For some time there had been debate as to whether the doctrine actually reversed the burden of proof and placed it on the defendant who would have to disprove that he had been negligent or whether it created some lesser obligation on the defendant. The decision of the Privy Council in *Ng Chun Pui* v. *Lee Chuen Tat*[195] makes it clear that the effect of the doctrine is merely, when it applies, to create a presumption of negligence that can be overturned but which does not have to be proven by him. In this way, then, the burden of proof as such never removes itself from the plaintiff and the *res ipsa* doctrine becomes of relatively limited utility.

## 5.4 Proof of causation

An abstract breach of duty is not sufficient to ground liability. There must also, for a negligence claim to be successfully brought, be damage, the type of which must be of a foreseeable character[196] and the type of which may cause the definition of the relevant duty of care to vary.[197] However, there is also a need to link the breach and the damage together to ensure that causation exists between the two elements.[198] It has been recently emphasised by the House of Lords in the appeal in *Wilsher* v. *Essex Area Health Authority*[199] that the element of causation can only be satisfied by the

---

194. See, e.g., *Saunders* v. *Leeds Western Health Authority* [1985] L.S. G92 1491.
195. [1988] R.T.R. 298.
196. See p. 80 below.
197. See p. 81 below.
198. See, classically, *Barnett* v. *Chelsea & Kensington Hospital Management Committee* [1969] 1 Q.B. 428.
199. [1988] A.C. 1074.

proof, on the balance of probabilities, by the plaintiff that the act of the defendant complained of made a "material contribution"[200] to the harm suffered by the plaintiff.

That said, the issue is normally seen as an inherently factual one. Whether, for instance, a pregnancy occurs because of the failure of a sterilisation operation or for other reasons[201] is a matter which must be for the judge to decide and, as a finding of fact, is unlikely to be disturbed by any appellate tribunal. Equally, though, it is possible for issues of law to arise. In *Hotson* v. *East Berkshire Area Health Authority*[202] the House of Lords reiterated the need to prove causation in an appropriate way but failed to answer, by a process of evasion whether in tort law it is possible to claim in tort for negligence which deprives a plaintiff not of a cure but merely of the chance of a cure.[203] It would seem logical to allow such a claim only when it is more likely than not that the cure would have been effective.

It is clear that breach of duty and related issues represent a hurdle for plaintiffs (and equally a comfort for defendants) far more effectively than ever the mid-1990s picture of duty of care. This remains the heartland of litigation.

# 6 MISREPRESENTATION

## 6.1 Introduction

There are a number of types of liability that exist where a person is induced to rely to his detriment upon the untrue statement of another. Such liability may be tortious, contractual, equitable or comprise a breach of statutory duty. All these types of liability may be relevant to a professional: especially, perhaps, liability for negligent misstatement at common law, but none of the other bases of liability examined below can be ignored in considering the position of the professional man as a whole.

## 6.2 Misrepresentation

A misrepresentation may be defined as an untrue statement of fact which induces the representee to contract with the representor. Such a statement must be material and unambiguous.

### 6.2.1 Statement of fact

Mere descriptive words which are too imprecise to be reasonably relied on will not amount to a misrepresentation. In *Scott* v. *Hanson*[204] an auctioneer who described land in particulars of sale as a lot consisting of 14 acres of uncommonly rich water meadow was held not to have made a misrepresentation. The more specific the description, the greater the likelihood that it will be held to be a misrepresentation.

A statement of opinion will not generally be held to be a misrepresentation, unless it can be shown either that the maker of the statement did not hold that opinion or

---

200. *Ibid.* at 1090 *per* Lord Bridge.
201. Based on the facts of *Thake* v. *Maurice* [1986] Q.B. 644.
202. [1987] A.C. 750.
203. Claimable in contract; *Chaplin* v. *Hicks* [1911] 2 Q.B. 786.
204. (1829) 1 Russ. & M. 128.

that a reasonable person equipped with his knowledge could not honestly have held that opinion. Thus, in *Bisset* v. *Williamson*[205] a vendor of land which had never been used for sheep-farming was held not to be liable for misrepresentation when he gave an estimate of the number of sheep the land would carry. All he had provided was an honest opinion, not a representation of the actual capacity of the land.

A promise to do something in the future is, on the face of it, not a statement of fact, and as such can only give rise to contractual liability. However, if there is, at the time of making the promise, no intention of keeping it, there is a misrepresentation of the state of mind of the representor, and, as was held in *Edgington* v. *Fitzmaurice*[206] this is a misstatement of fact and as such actionable as a misrepresentation. In *Edgington* the directors of a company stated in a prospectus that they intended to use money which they were inviting the public to lend them to improve the buildings and extend the business. In fact they intended to use the money to discharge outstanding liabilities. This was held to amount to a misrepresentation.

A misrepresentation of law, as opposed to a misrepresentation of fact, is not actionable. Beyond this apparently unproblematical statement lies the difficulty of statements of mixed law and fact. As the case-law shows, it is necessary to identify the essence of the statement: does the untruth refer to the proportion of law or to the facts to which the (accurately stated) proposition of law refers?[207]

### 6.2.2 Inducement

The causal link between the misrepresentation and the subsequent contract must be established. Non-reliance on,[208] or testing the accuracy of,[209] the statement made will preclude relief for misrepresentation, though failure to take advantage of an opportunity to check the truth of a statement will not, as in *Redgrave* v. *Hurd*,[210] where the failure by the purchaser of a solicitor's practice to check the accounts, which could have revealed the misrepresentations of the vendor concerning the annual income derived from the practice, did not prevent a successful argument of misrepresentation. However, the statement need not be the sole factor inducing the representee to contract. In *Edgington* v. *Fitzmaurice*[211] the representee was induced to make the loan partly because of the directors' representation as to the use to which the money would be put, and partly as a result of his mistaken belief that he would have a charge on the company's property. He was still entitled to succeed.

### 6.2.3 Materiality/unambiguity

The requirement that a misrepresentation, to be actionable, must be material, involves no more than the commonsense factor that the statement must be one that would have affected the judgement of a reasonable man in deciding whether to

---

205. [1927] A.C. 177; cf. *Smith* v. *Land and Home Property Corporation* (1885) 28 Ch.D. 7.
206. (1885) 29 Ch.D. 459.
207. Cf. *Solle* v. *Butcher* [1950] 1 K.B. 671 and *Territorial & Auxiliary Forces Association* v. *Nichols* [1949] 1 K.B. 35.
208. See, e.g., *Smith* v. *Chadwick* (1884) 9 App.Cas. 187.
209. *S Pearson & Son Ltd* v. *Dublin Corporation* [1907] A.C. 351 at 353–354.
210. (1881) 20 Ch.D. 1.
211. See fn. 206 above.

contract with the representor, and, if so, on what terms. The test is therefore an objective one. Similarly, in requiring that the statement be unambiguous, the law does no more than require that it be reasonable to enter into the subsequent contract.

### 6.3 Remedies for misrepresentation

Assuming that it has been shown that a misrepresentation fulfilling the above criteria has been made, the next issue is that of the available remedies for the representee. A misrepresentation renders voidable the contract it induces,[212] and the remedy is rescission of the contract. The availability of damages in such cases is discussed below.

#### 6.3.1 Rescission

Positive action must be taken by the representee to indicate that he will not be bound by the terms of the contract; passive inactivity will leave the contract alive, and, as we shall see, may ultimately preclude any relief at all. The practicalities of notification of the decision to rescind may be denied to the representee in cases of fraudulent misrepresentation, but in such cases a notional indication of rescission may suffice, as in *Car and Universal Finance Co Ltd* v. *Caldwell*,[213] where the representee informed the police and the Automobile Association following the dishonouring of a cheque presented to him by the representor in exchange for his car. The Court of Appeal held that where rescission cannot be notified due to the deliberate disappearance of the representor, an overt expression of intention to rescind, as in the instant case, might suffice.

Where rescission is effective, it may be accompanied by an element of financial compensation in the form of an indemnity, if such is necessary to achieve the purpose of rescission or *restitutio in integrum*. Thus, in *Whittington* v. *Seale-Hayne*[214] it was held that a representee who had entered into a leasehold agreement on the strength of a representation that the premises were sanitary was entitled, in addition to rescission, to obtain compensation for rates paid and the cost of repairing the drains, both being obligations imposed by the lease.

Since rescission is an equitable remedy, it is not automatically available, and the right to rescind may be lost. Since the object of rescission is *restitutio in integrum*, an inability to restore the status quo may deny the representee the ability to rescind. Earlier cases indicated the need for a precise restitution; thus in *Clarke* v. *Dickson*[215] a representee who had been induced to take shares in a partnership was denied relief, since, by the time he sought to rescind, the partnership had become a limited liability company. The nature of the corporate body and of his shares in it had changed; an exact restitution could therefore not be effected. Subsequently a more flexible approach was developed, thus in *Armstrong* v. *Jackson*[216] the fact that shares,

212. See, e.g., *Clough* v. *London and North Western Railway Co* (1871) L.R. 7 Ex. 26.
213. [1965] 1 Q.B. 525.
214. (1900) 82 L.T. 49.
215. (1858) E.B. & E. 148.
216. [1917] 2 K.B. 822.

originally purchased when worth nearly £3, were worth only five shillings by the time proceedings were instituted, did not preclude relief, provided that the representee returned the shares and the dividends he had received.

Again, affirmation of the contract by the representee may preclude rescission, as being inconsistent with an intention to rescind. If, for example, a person purchases shares in reliance on a misrepresentation, learns the true facts and yet continues to receive dividends, it is unlikely that rescission would still be available. Delay may be seen as evidence of affirmation, and indeed the court may in any event decide that an excessive lapse of time in its own right prevents rescission from remaining available. In *Leaf* v. *International Galleries*[217] the plaintiff bought a painting, represented as being by Constable, in 1944. In 1949 he attempted to resell it, was told that it was not a Constable, and unsuccessfully sought to rescind the contract, the court holding that he had not acted within a reasonable time.

A consequence of misrepresentation rendering a contract voidable rather than void is that, prior to the contract being avoided by the representee, the opportunity exists for third parties to acquire rights in the subject-matter of the contract, so as to render rescission impossible. Thus, in the *Car and Universal Finance Co Ltd* v. *Caldwell*[218] situation, if a third party bought the car from the rogue before the purported act of rescission by the representee, the attempt to rescind would be ineffective, and the third party would obtain a good title to the car.

The enactment of the Misrepresentation Act in 1967 followed a report by the Law Reform Committee which identified a number of areas of the law of misrepresentation in need of reform. One weakness of the pre-1967 law was the inflexibility that made provision for no remedy other than rescission for misrepresentation, even where the effects of rescission might be disproportionate to the nature of the misrepresentation perpetuated, and also inconvenient to the parties to the contract. This state of affairs was remedied by section 2(2) of the Misrepresentation Act 1967, which enables the court to grant damages in lieu of rescission "if of opinion that it would be equitable to do so, having regard to the nature of the misrepresentation and the loss that would be caused by it if the contract were upheld, as well as to the loss that rescission would cause to the other party". It is clear therefore that this is another situation where the right to rescind may be lost, although there is at least in this situation the consolation for the representee that the alternative remedy of damages is available.[219] It has been held that damages in lieu of rescission can only be awarded if rescission is otherwise available at the time when the court is being asked to exercise its discretion.[220]

Two further aspects of rescission taken account of in the Misrepresentation Act 1967 are the right of the representee to rescind (provided rescission is otherwise available) even if the misrepresentation has become a term of the contract, and the right to rescind, again if rescission is available still, where the contract has been performed.

217. [1950] 2 K.B. 86.
218. See p. 74 above.
219. For the measure of damages under s. 2(2), see p. 77 below.
220. *Alton House Garages (Bromley) Ltd* v. *Monk* (unreported) 31 July 1981 (Lexis transcript).

### 6.3.2 *Damages*

#### 6.3.2.1 FRAUDULENT MISREPRESENTATION

Clearly consequential losses may result from a misrepresentation, such that rescission, even with an indemnity, does not adequately compensate the representee for the misrepresentation. It has long been the case that damages may be sought in the tort of deceit for a fraudulent misrepresentation, where it must be shown, as was held by the House of Lords in *Derry* v. *Peek*,[221] that there was an absence of honest belief by the representor in the truth of the statement made. As a common law remedy, damages have the further advantage that the right to claim cannot be precluded by the kind of factors that may bar the right to rescission, subject to the rules on limitation of actions.[222] Clearly, the measure of damages in cases of deceit is tortious, but it was further held in *Doyle* v. *Olby (Ironmongers) Ltd*[223] that the defendant was liable to compensate the plaintiff for all the losses flowing directly from his deceit unless they were rendered too remote by the plaintiff's own conduct. Such losses may well go beyond those recoverable in a negligence claim where the rules of remoteness are less generous to the plaintiff, in an appropriate case perhaps justifying the effort involved in proving fraud, but, as we shall see, even that advantage is of less significance today.

It is possible to seek rescission of the ensuing contract, as well as damages in deceit, provided that the effect is not such as to allow the plaintiff to duplicate his claim. The objective of *restituto in integrum* remains the fundamental aim.

#### 6.3.2.2. NEGLIGENT MISREPRESENTATION

A further consequence of the deliberations of the Law Reform Committee was the enactment, in section 2(1) of the Misrepresentation Act 1967, of a statutory remedy in damages for misrepresentation. Section 2(1) provides:

"where a person has entered into a contract after a misrepresentation has been made to him by another party thereto and as a result thereof he has suffered loss, then, if the person making the misrepresentation would be liable to damages in respect thereof had the misrepresentation been made fraudulently, that person shall be so liable notwithstanding that the misrepresentation was not made fraudulently, unless he proves that he had reasonable ground to believe and did believe up to the time the contract was made that the facts represented were true".

The effect of this provision is that, once the representee has shown that the statement made by the representor was an actionable misrepresentation, the burden shifts to the representor to show that he had reasonable grounds to believe that the statement was true. As with fraudulent misrepresentation, it is clear that in an appropriate case rescission and damages may be sought.[224]

It is also clearly established that the measure of damages under section 2(1) is tortious.[225] However, perhaps somewhat surprisingly in *Royscot Trust* v. *Rogerson*,[226]

---

221. (1889) 15 App. Cas. 337.
222. See p. 87 below.
223. [1969] 2 Q.B. 158. See also *Archer* v. *Brown* [1985] Q.B. 401; *East* v. *Maurer* (1991) 2 All E.R. 733.
224. See, e.g., *F & H Entertainments Ltd* v. *Leisure Enterprises Ltd* (1976) 120 S.J. 331.
225. See, e.g., *Sharneyford Supplies Ltd* v. *Edge* [1985] 1 All E.R. 976.
226. [1991] 3 All E.R. 294.

the Court of Appeal was of the view that the use of the words "so liable" in the subsection meant that Parliament had intended damages recoverable under section 2(1) to be recoverable to the same extent as if the misrepresentation had been made fraudulently. Consequently, all losses resulting directly from the misrepresentation will be recoverable under section 2(1), thus effectively equating a careless representor with a fraudulent one, and almost entirely removing the need for an action for fraudulent misrepresentation ever to be brought.

As regards damages under section 2(2) (damages in lieu of rescission), some guidance was provided by the Court of Appeal in *William Sindall plc* v. *Cambridgeshire County Council*[227] where it was said that the proper measure of damages was the cost of remedying the defect or the reduced market value attributable to the defect.

## 6.4 Liability for non-disclosure

The general rule is that silence does not amount to a misrepresentation, though there may be misrepresentation by conduct[228] and in certain circumstances there may be liability for a partial non-disclosure, as in *With* v. *O'Flanagan*[229] where the initial representation by the would-be vendor of a medical practice as to the annual takings was overtaken by events during the course of the negotiations, such that it was significantly untrue by the time the contract was made some months later. The vendor's failure to inform the purchaser of the change of circumstances was held to entitle the purchaser to rescission.

Fiduciary relationships may give rise to a duty of disclosure. For example, the relationship between a solicitor and his client is one involving the necessary degree of confidence such as to fall into this category, and disclosure will be required of the solicitor. The *locus classicus* is *Nocton* v. *Lord Ashburton*[230] where the defendant solicitor advised and induced the plaintiff to advance £65,000 on a mortgage made by other clients of the defendant, a transaction in which the defendant was entitled to be compensated for the defendant's breach of fiduciary duty. It is clear from this and other cases[231] that the solicitor's duty will exist in situations where he has an interest in a particular transaction, where only full disclosure will preclude the risk of a claim for damages for breach of fiduciary duty.

## 6.5 Contract

The distinction between representations and terms is notoriously difficult to define and identify. In the case of an oral contract it may be especially difficult to locate the point at which negotiation ends and agreement begins. Lord Denning explained succinctly in *Esso Petroleum Co Ltd* v. *Mardon* the historical reason why the distinction has had much importance[232]:

"Ever since *Heilbut, Symons & Co* v. *Buckleton* ([1913] AC 30) we have had to contend with the law as laid down by the House of Lords that an innocent misrepresentation gives us no right

227. [1994] 3 All E.R. 932.
228. See, e.g., *Walters* v. *Morgan* (1861) 3 D.F. & J. 718 at 723–724.
229. [1936] Ch. 575.
230. [1914] A.C. 932.
231. E.g., *Spector* v. *Ageda* [1973] Ch. 30; *Day* v. *Mead* [1987] 2 N.Z.L.R. 443.
232. [1976] Q.B. 801 at 817.

to damages. In order to escape from that rule, the pleader used to allege—I often did it myself—that the misrepresentation was fraudulent, or alternatively a collateral warranty. At the trial we nearly always succeeded on collateral warranty."

Of course, since 1967 there has been a statutory remedy in damages for negligent misrepresentation, and in addition since 1964 the alternative claim at common law for damages for negligent misrepresentation has existed,[233] for some purposes eliminating the need to attempt to characterise the defendant's untrue statement as a warranty. However, there remains some practical significance in cases where the measure of damages in contract enables recovery beyond what would be recoverable in tort. Thus a plaintiff representee who has suffered expectation losses will seek still to argue that the statement was a term, or alternatively a separate collateral contract[234]; though since *Royscot* the significance of the distinction between a contractual claim and a claim under section 2(1) of the Misrepresentation Act 1967 is further eroded.

In cases where there remains significance in the characterisation of the plaintiff's statement the courts have emphasised the importance of the intention of the parties in particular whether the maker of the statement had the intention (assessed objectively) of warranting the truth of his statement or not. This may be evidenced by the relative knowledge of the parties,[235] on the basis that special knowledge on the part of the representor in contrast to a lack thereof on the part of the representee may be relevant in assessing intention. Again, a statement is more likely to be regarded as being made with contractual intention if it is of such importance that without it the representee would not have entered into the contract.[236] As another relevant factor, the making of a statement followed by advice to the other party to verify its accuracy is likely to be regarded as a representation rather than a term,[237] and indeed may not even amount to a misrepresentation if it leads the representee to contract on the basis of his own judgement rather than the statement. It is clear, however, that these are factors only, none of which provides a decisive test for gleaning the intention of the parties, which can only be deduced from the totality of the evidence.

In certain circumstances it may be necessary to argue that the statement operates, not as a collateral warranty, but as a separate collateral contract in its own right. In *Heilbut, Symons & Co* v. *Buckleton*[238] the House of Lords emphasised the exceptional nature of this device, and the need to show an intention to make a collateral contract. Historically, use has been made of the collateral contract to circumvent the requirements of the Statute of Frauds, which, *inter alia*, required agreements to transfer interests in land and contracts for the sale of goods worth more than £10 to be in writing under signature. An oral statement concerning the subject-matter of such a contract could clearly not operate as a warranty collateral to the contract, so it became necessary, in order to give the statement contractual effect, to argue that it operated as a separate oral contract, collateral to the written

233. *Hedley Byrne & Co Ltd* v. *Heller & Partners Ltd* [1964] A.C. 465.
234. See below.
235. See, e.g., *Oscar Chess Ltd* v. *Williams* [1957] 1 W.L.R. 370; *Dick Bentley Productions Ltd* v. *Harold Smith (Motors) Ltd* [1965] 1 W.L.R. 623.
236. See, e.g., *Couchman* v. *Hill* [1947] K.B. 554; *Bannerman* v. *White and Others* (1861) 10 C.B. (N.S.) 844.
237. See, e.g., *Ecay* v. *Godfrey* (1974) 80 Ll.L.Rep. 286.
238. [1913] A.C. 30.

agreement. Such a collateral contract may even be given effect when it contradicts a written agreement, as in *City and Westminster Properties (1934) Ltd* v. *Mudd*,[239] where an oral undertaking not to enforce a particular clause in a lease was held to be binding as a collateral contract.

## 6.6 Tort

It has been clear since 1964 that in appropriate circumstances tortious liability may attach to a negligent misstatement which results in detrimental reliance by the recipient of the statement. This category of liability for untrue statements, which is examined in detail elsewhere in this chapter,[240] has greater practical implications for the professional, as the case-law shows, than the other types of such liability. Professionals, especially in an increasingly competitive climate, may, no less than others, be tempted to induce clients to contract with them on the basis of over-zealous promotion of their skills and expertise, hence the need to bear in mind the framework of liability examined above.

## 6.7 Exclusion/limitation of liability

Elsewhere in this chapter we examine the general rules governing the ability of the professional to exclude or limit his liability.[241] What was said there is, of course, equally true in this context, and the extent to which a professional remains free, to exclude or limit his liability for misrepresentation has to be seen in the light of the various legal and professional restrictions described above.

Section 3 of the Misrepresentation Act provides as follows:

". . . if a contract contains a term which would exclude or restrict—
    (a) any liability to which a party to a contract may be subject by reason of any misrepresentation made by him before the contract was made; or
    (b) any remedy available to another party to the contract by reason of such a misrepresentation,
that term shall be of no effect except in so far as it satisfies the requirement of reasonableness as stated in section 2(1) of the Unfair Contract Terms Act 1977; and it is for those claiming that the term satisfies that requirement to show that it does."

Section 2(1) requires the term to have been a fair and reasonable one to be included having regard to the circumstances which were, or ought reasonably to have been, known to or in the contemplation of the parties when the contract was made.

In *Overbrooke Estates Ltd* v. *Glencombe Estates Ltd*[242] it was held that conditions of sale at an auction which provided that the vendors did not make representations and the auctioneers (the vendors' agent) had no authority to make representations did not fall within the statutory control, being a public limitation for the otherwise ostensible authority of the agent rather than a clause excluding or restricting liability.

In *Walker* v. *Boyle*[243] a vendor and purchaser of land entered into an agreement which was subject to the National Conditions of Sale (19th edn), condition 17(1) of

---

239. [1959] Ch. 129.
240. See pp. 58–61 above.
241. See p. 42 above.
242. [1974] 1 W.L.R. 1335.
243. [1982] 1 All E.R. 634.

which provided that "No error misstatement or omission in any preliminary answer concerning the property ... shall annul the sale". The answer to a pre-contract inquiry concerning awareness of any boundary dispute comprised an innocent misrepresentation. It was held that condition 17 had not been shown to satisfy the requirement of reasonableness, and hence the vendor was not entitled to an order for specific performance. The purchaser was entitled to the return of the deposit paid. Such a decision seems consistent with the consumerist ethos of the Unfair Contract Terms Act 1977, and underlies the difficulties likely to be faced by a professional in seeking to exclude liability for misrepresentation albeit that, as can be seen from the discussion in *Smith* v. *Bush*,[244] the position may be different when the bargaining position is more equal, thus potentially granting the professional greater scope for protection where the client is a businessman or a commercial entity.

## 7 DAMAGES[245]

### 7.1 Introduction

The fundamental object of the award of damages, in contract and tort, is to put the plaintiff in the position he would have been in had the breach of duty not occurred. The range of services undertaken by professionals is such that the type of interest represented by the amount of damages for breach of duty ranges broadly, from personal injury or fatal accident damages in the case of medical negligence to difference in the value of a property between actual and represented value in the case of surveyors' negligence; from mental distress and upset caused to a solicitor's client by negligent handling of non-molestation proceedings to compensation for financial loss resulting from an accountant's negligence. The measure of damages in cases of professional liability is not founded upon any special principle, but the particular implications of the basic principles for individual professions are considered in detail in the chapters that follow. Certain general principles applicable to all cases are considered below however.

### 7.2 Foreseeability of damage

In all cases of professional liability, whether in tort or in contract, the plaintiff is obliged to satisfy the requirement that the loss which he suffers is not too remote from the breach of duty; remoteness, will defeat a claim. In contractual claims guidance is provided primarily by the *Heron II* decision.[246] Here, delay in the execution of a contract for the carriage of goods by sea meant that a consignment of sugar was late in its delivery and missed a favourable market opportunity. The consequent loss of value was held to be claimable and, although different speeches in the House of Lords utilised different words,[247] a consensus does appear to emerge that damage can only be claimed if it is clearly anticipatable as being, to use the

---

244. See p. 44 above.
245. See *McGregor on Damages*; Burrows, *Remedies for Torts and Breach of Contract* (2nd edn, 1994).
246. [1969] 1 A.C. 350.
247. E.g., Lord Reid, *ibid.* at 388, Lord Morris of Borth-y-Gest at 406, Lord Hodson at 410, Lords Pearce and Upjohn at 414–415 and 425.

particular phraseology of Lord Reid,[248] "not unlikely to occur". While not representing, perhaps, the most precise language ever used, a clear message none the less emerges that a clear likelihood of the harm that arises being anticipatable, and further, being anticipatable at the time at which the contract is made,[249] is essential to ground a claim based on the contract.

The test in tort, however, differs in several ways.[250] First, the test of remoteness is more generous; it appears that all that is needed is that the general type of harm which in fact occurs is foreseeable[251] and that this more generous approach than in contract may be justified by the contrast between the contracting parties' ability to negotiate over the result of possible, if unlikely, future events on their contract as opposed to the inherent problem of the victim of a tort being under the disability of not knowing what torts may affect him and thus not being able to engage in any similar type of pre-planning. Equally in negligence cases the time of the assessment of the likely risk must be at the time of the tort, rather than at any earlier time and it is, as ever, through the eyes of the reasonable man rather than, as in contract, through the eyes of the actual parties that that assessment is made.[252] It should also be noted that the replacement of a remoteness test based on directness by one based on foreseeability in the *Wagon Mound (No 1)*[253] applies only to negligence liability and, in a different form, to nuisance cases,[254] but does not apply to other torts where the original approach based on the need to establish that the damage complained of was a direct result[255] remains as the basis of other tort claims such as those in deceit or its non-fraudulent counterpart under section 2(1) of the Misrepresentation Act 1967.[256]

The law of negligence, however, has appeared to make full use of the opportunities that its more flexible formulation of a remoteness test offers. It is clear that the precise method of the infliction of harm is immaterial, so long as the general type of harm can be foreseen,[257] while the fact that the extent of the harm suffered is in fact much greater than what may be reasonably foreseen is also no bar to a claim.[258] Even if the harm that occurs is due to the particular individual propensities of the plaintiff, the classic "eggshell skull" example, here too liability will arise for what in reality is unforeseeable harm so long as it remains within the overall type of harm which is foreseeable.[259] Loss caused by what might be characterised as an "eggshell wallet" i.e., the poverty of the plaintiff, may also be claimed,[260] so long as it does not amount to the dreaded state of impecuniosity that defeated the claim of the plaintiff in *Liesbosch Dredger* v. *S/S "Edison" (Owners)*.[261] Whether an intervening act will

---

248. *Ibid.* at 388.
249. *Ibid.*
250. Cf. the generally discredited views of Lord Denning MR in *H Parsons (Livestock) Ltd* v. *Uttley Ingham & Co Ltd* [1978] Q.B. 791.
251. See, e.g., *Hughes* v. *Lord Advocate* [1963] A.C. 837, especially at 857 *per* Lord Pearce.
252. *Wagon Mound (No 1)* [1961] A.C. 388 at 423 *per* Viscount Simonds.
253. [1961] A.C. 388.
254. *Wagon Mound (No 2)* [1967] 1 A.C. 617 especially at 639 *per* Lord Reid.
255. *Re Polemis* [1921] 3 K.B. 560.
256. See *Royscot Trust Ltd* v. *Rogerson* [1991] 2 Q.B. 297.
257. E.g., *Hughes* v. *Lord Advocate* [1963] A.C. 837.
258. E.g., *Bradford* v. *Robinson Rentals* [1967] 1 W.L.R. 337.
259. *Smith* v. *Leech Brain & Co Ltd* [1962] 2 Q.B. 405; more dubiously *Brice* v. *Brown* [1984] 1 All E.R. 997.
260. *Dodd Properties Ltd* v. *Canterbury City Council* [1980] 1 W.L.R. 433.
261. [1933] A.C. 449. The decision has, however, been much criticised and distinguished. See p. 83 below.

break the chain of causation depends, once again, on the foreseeability (or otherwise) of that intervention[262]; for instance relevant experts can be expected to exercise that expertise in an appropriately professional manner.[263]

All of these facts combine to give a clear danger signal to professional defendants in particular. In contrast to their position under contract, where they can in broad measure define and, often, exclude their legal responsibilities in advance, the position in tort law is that the courts will be reluctant to allow a defendant to plead that the consequence of his action is too remote; rather, by embarking on a negligent course of conduct, he is taking the risk of whatever consequences may transpire.

## 7.3 Mitigation

An economically efficient aspect of the law of damages is the requirement that the innocent party acts reasonably to mitigate the damage. The basic principle is contained in the statement of Viscount Haldane LC in *British Westinghouse Electric* v. *Underground Electric Railways Co of London Ltd*[264] who described the principle as one "which imposes on a plaintiff the duty of taking all reasonable steps to mitigate the loss consequent on the breach, and debars him from claiming any part of the damage which is due to his neglect to take such steps".

Much will depend on the facts of the case in determining what is reasonable. In the context of medical negligence, the decision in *McAuley* v. *London Transport Executive*,[265] though not a case of medical negligence, is of relevance. The plaintiff had been injured in a work accident due to his employers' negligence. He was advised to have an operation which would give him a 90 per cent chance of being able to continue to work as a labourer. He refused to have the operation, and the Court of Appeal held that the refusal was unreasonable, and his claim was limited to loss of earnings up to the time when he could have had the operation. The fact that the doctor who made the recommendation was acting on behalf of the defendants did not make the refusal reasonable, though, as Jenkins LJ pointed out, if there had been conflicting medical opinions the court would by no means necessarily have taken the same view.

As an aspect of reasonableness, it is established that the plaintiff need not embark on complicated litigation in order to minimise the damage. In *Pilkington* v. *Wood*[266] the plaintiff attempted to resell a property which he had bought the previous year, only to discover that the title was defective. The defendant solicitor admitted negligence, but argued that the plaintiff, who was awarded damages to reflect the difference between the market price of the property at date of purchase with and without the defect in title, should have sued the vendor on the convenant for title implied in the Law of Property Act 1925. The court held that he was not under a duty

---

262. *Banque Bruxelles Lambert SA* v. *Eagle Star Insurance Co Ltd* [1995] 2 W.L.R. 607.
263. E.g., *Knightley* v. *Johns* [1982] 1 W.L.R. 349.
264. [1912] A.C. 673 at 689.
265. [1957] 2 Lloyd's Rep. 500. Cf. *Selvanayagam* v. *University of West Indies* [1983] 1 All E.R. 824; *Savage* v. *T Wallis Ltd* [1966] 1 Lloyd's Rep. 357.
266. [1953] Ch. 770.

to embark on complicated and difficult litigation to protect his solicitor from the consequences of his own carelessness, although the solicitor offered to indemnify the plaintiff against the cost of the action.

In *Buckley* v. *Lane Herdman & Co*,[267] the defendant solicitors in breach of duty exchanged contracts for the sale of the plaintiffs' house before exchanging contracts for the purchase of the house they wished to buy. The plaintiffs incurred expenditure in unsuccessfully defending specific performance proceedings brought against them, and they were able to recover the cost of that in their claim against the solicitors, which included damages for distress, anguish and inconvenience.

In *The Liesbosch*[268] it was held that loss resulting from the plaintiff's weak financial position was irrecoverable, as being too remote. Subsequent cases have frequently sought to distinguish this criticised judgment,[269] one approach being to treat the issue in terms of the duty to mitigate.[270] In *Perry* v. *Sidney Phillips & Son*[271] the plaintiff bought a house, relying upon a survey carried out by the defendants. Subsequently he discovered the existence of serious defects which had not been identified in the report. The plaintiff did not carry out the necessary repairs, claiming that he could not afford to do so and that the defendants' denial of liability deterred him from doing so. He also claimed to be entitled to damages for the distress and discomfort of living in a house which was in a defective condition. It was held that he was entitled to damages for vexation if it was a reasonably foreseeable consequence of the defects which the defendants negligently failed to disclose in their report that he would suffer distress and discomfort until the repairs were carried out, and if it was reasonable for him not to carry out the repairs immediately. His impecuniosity was held not to be the only reason for his not carrying out the repairs, and in the face of the defendants' denial of liability it was reasonable for him not to carry out the repairs immediately. He was thus entitled to damages for inconvenience, distress and discomfort. In addition, *The Liesbosch* was distinguished on the grounds that in that case the plaintiff's loss resulting from his impecuniosity was too remote, whereas in the instant case it was reasonably foreseeable. Though other cases have similarly interpreted *The Liesbosch* restrictively,[272] it was applied in a case of insurance brokers' negligence in *Ramwade Ltd* v. *WJ Emson & Co Ltd*.[273] The plaintiffs' lorry was written off in a road accident. They incurred hiring charges, and sought to recover these as well as damages for the value of the lorry, against the defendants who had negligently failed to provide them with comprehensive insurance coverage, with the result that the lorry was not covered. The trial judge's award was reversed by the Court of Appeal as regards the hiring charges, on the basis that, as a loss resulting from the plaintiffs' impecuniosity, it was unreasonable under *The Liesbosch*, the authority of which cannot, therefore, be ignored, though its application remains somewhat unpredictable.

---

267. [1977] C.L.Y. 3143.
268. *Owners of Dredger Liesbosch* v. *Owners of Steamship Edison, The Liesbosch* [1933] A.C. 449.
269. See, e.g., *Dodd Properties (Kent) Ltd* v. *Canterbury City Council* [1980] 1 All E.R. 928.
270. See, e.g., *Robbins of Putney Ltd* v. *Meek* [1971] R.T.R. 345.
271. [1982] 3 All E.R. 705.
272. E.g., *Archer* v. *Brown* [1984] 2 All E.R. 267.
273. [1987] R.T.R. 72.

## 7.4 Contributory negligence

Contributory negligence has been a partial defence since the enactment of the Law Reform (Contributory Negligence) Act 1945, which provides in section 1(1):

"Where any person suffers damage as a result partly of his own fault and partly of the fault of any other person or persons, a claim in respect of that damage shall not be defeated by reason of the fault of the person suffering the damage, but the damages recoverable in respect thereof shall be reduced to such extent as the court thinks just and equitable having regard to the claimant's share in the responsibility for the damage."

Clearly, such a formula is designed to allow the trial judge to exercise his discretion in accordance with the facts of the particular case. Where the plaintiff is a professional or a businessman it is perhaps more likely that contributory negligence may be held to exist, given the higher expectations the court may have of such a person (*a fortiori* if the plaintiff is an entity such as a professional firm or a business). Thus in *De Meza* v. *Apple*[274] the plaintiffs were a firm of solicitors who instructed a firm of auditors to complete consequential loss insurance certificates. It was held that losses suffered by the plaintiffs as a result of under-insurance were a consequence of negligence by the defendants, but the plaintiffs had also been negligent, having failed to notice a mistake made by the defendants and the degree of contributory negligence was assessed as being 30 per cent.

## 7.5 Applicability of the Act

"Fault" in section 1(1) of the Act is defined under section 4 as meaning "negligence, breach of statutory duty or other act or omission which gives rise to a liability in tort, or would, apart from this Act, give rise to the defence of contributory negligence". Reference to the common law is necessary in order to determine which torts give rise to the defence of contributory negligence. Thus it has been made clear that contributory negligence is not applicable to deceit,[275] though it seems to be applicable to intentional trespass to the person,[276] and is applicable to claims for negligent misrepresentation under section 2(1) of the Misrepresentation Act 1967.[277]

Of especial relevance to the professional is the question of whether contributory negligence is available where the claim is one for breach of contract. Following a good deal of earlier, often conflicting authority[278] the Court of Appeal in *Forsikrings-aktieselskapet Vesta* v. *Butcher*[279] affirmed the thorough analysis by Hobhouse J at trial,[280] upholding his finding of contributory negligence against the plaintiff insurance company in its action against the defendant reinsurers. The Court of

---

274. [1974] 1 Lloyd's Rep. 508; [1975] 1 Lloyd's Rep. 498, C.A.
275. *Alliance & Leicester Building Society* v. *Edgestop Ltd* [1993] 1 W.L.R. 1462.
276. See *Murphy* v. *Culhane* [1977] Q.B. 94.
277. *Gran Gelato Ltd* v. *Richcliff (Group) Ltd* [1992] 1 All E.R. 865.
278. See, e.g., *Sole* v. *Hallt Ltd* [1973] Q.B. 574; *Marintrans AB* v. *Comet Shipping Co Ltd* [1985] 3 All E.R. 442 (contributory negligence inapplicable); *Quinn* v. *Burch Bros (Builders) Ltd* [1966] 2 Q.B. 370; *De Meza* v. *Apple* (see fn. 274 above) (contributory negligence applicable).
279. [1988] 2 All E.R. 43.
280. [1986] 2 All E.R. 488.

Appeal upheld Hobhouse J's classification of cases of contributory negligence into three categories: category 1 cases where the defendant is in breach of a strict contractual duty; category 2 comprising cases where the defendant is in breach of a contractual duty of care; and category 3 where the defendant is in breach of a contractual duty of care and also is liable in the tort of negligence, independent of the existence of any contract. It was held that contributory negligence only applies to category 3 cases.[281]

This is potentially helpful to the client of the professional, since most cases of professional negligence will involve parallel contractual and tortious duties of care, though the comments elsewhere in this chapter[282] should be borne in mind on the issue of concurrent liability.

## 7.6 Apportionment

A further issue of concern to the professional is that, if he is found to be at fault, he will bear no more than his fair share of culpability in comparison with any other defendants. Frequently, cases involving professional liability involve advice from more than one profession; e.g., solicitor and accountant in tax cases, surveyor and architect in building cases, solicitor and counsel in litigation; and a determination of the proper allocation of responsibility between them is frequently a complicated and difficult task.

An appropriate starting-point is the Law Reform (Married Women and Tort-feasors) Act 1935, section 6 of which provides that a tortfeasor who is liable in respect of damage may recover a contribution from any other tortfeasor who is liable in respect of the same damage. An immediate comment that may be made on this provision is that it applies only to tortfeasors, not contract-breakers, and had an especially restrictive effect therefore in the era when the court had set its face against concurrent liability. The basis of apportionment is set out in section 6(2), on principles very similar to those for contributory negligence, in that the amount of contribution is to be such amount as the court finds to be just and equitable, having regard to the extent of the contributor's responsibility for the damage. As an example of apportionment in a building case, it was held in *Clay* v. *AT Crump & Sons Ltd*[283] that an architect, demolition contractor and builder were liable respectively 42 per cent, 38 per cent and 20 per cent towards a workman who suffered injury when a wall, which should have been removed from the site, collapsed on him.

The Civil Liability (Contribution) Act 1978 was passed in order to remove the deficiencies of the earlier legislation. It provides that any person liable in respect of any damage may recover contribution from any other person liable in respect of the same damage, thus bringing persons whose sole liability is contractual within its scope. The Act also provides that a person may recover contribution even if he or she has ceased to be liable for the damage in question since the time when the damage occurred, provided that they were liable immediately before the payment in respect of which contribution was sought was ordered or agreed to be made. Further, a

---

281. See, Burrows, *op. cit.*, note 1 for a thorough analysis of the general implications of this decision.
282. See p. 45 above.
283. [1964] 1 Q.B. 533.

person who has settled or agreed to settle a claim by means of a payment can obtain contribution, whether or not they are or ever were liable in respect of the damage, provided that they would have been liable assuming that the factual basis of the claim against them could be established. The principles of apportionment are essentially the same as those under the earlier legislation.

### 7.7 Loss of a chance

Two recent decisions of the Court of Appeal are of interest in the context of professional negligence generally, and solicitors' negligence in particular. Historically, this issue had arisen especially in the context of breach of contract; thus in *Chaplin* v. *Hicks*[284] a breach of contract by the defendant prevented the plaintiff from participating in a beauty contest, in which she had the chance to win a cash prize. She was awarded £25 damages, on the basis that although it was not certain that she would have won, she had been deprived of the chance of so doing.

The applicability of this principle to cases of medical negligence was considered by the House of Lords in *Hotson* v. *East Berkshire Health Authority*.[285] The plaintiff suffered a fracture on the left femoral epiphysis in a fall and, due to a delay in treatment by the defendant, subsequently developed avascular necrosis of the epiphysis. The judge (with whom the Court of Appeal agreed) held that there was a 75 per cent chance that so many blood vessels had been ruptured by the fall that avascular necrosis was bound to result, and awarded 25 per cent of the full damages for the injury for loss of a 25 per cent chance of recovery. The House of Lords, however, held that since, on a balance of probabilities the epiphysis was doomed prior to the defendant coming under a duty to the plaintiff, he had failed to prove causation. The issue of whether damages could be awarded for loss of a chance in that context was avoided therefore, though the House of Lords expressed doubts concerning such a claim, without ruling it out. More recently, however, in *Spring* v. *Guardian Assurance plc*,[286] in holding that an employer might be liable in damages to an ex-employee for whom he negligently gave a bad reference, it was said by Lord Lowry that once duty and breach had been established, the plaintiff only had to show that by reason of the negligence he had lost a reasonable chance of employment (which would have to be evaluated) and had thereby suffered loss: there was no need to prove that, but for the negligent reference the putative employer would have employed him.

More recently, the Court of Appeal in *Allied Maples Group Ltd* v. *Simmons & Simmons*[287] considered the issue, again in the contractual context. The defendants advised the plaintiffs in connection with a takeover. In order to obtain certain properties from a third party it was necessary to obtain the shares in a subsidiary company of the third party, with a view to transferring out the unwanted properties and liabilities and keeping the desired properties. However, some of the properties

---

284. [1911] 2 K.B. 786. See also cases such as *Kitchen* v. *Royal Air Force Association* [1958] 3 All E.R. 241 where it was held, in a case of solicitors' negligent failure to issue proceedings within the limitation period, that the plaintiff had to prove on a balance of probabilities that she would have succeeded in the claim. She was awarded two-thirds of the full liability value of the claim.
285. [1987] A.C. 750.
286. [1994] 3 All E.R. 129.
287. (1995) 145 N.L.J. 1646.

owned by the subsidiary had first tenant liabilities which, subsequent to the acquisition, resulted in claims against the plaintiffs, who sought compensation for the losses they sustained resulting from those claims, in an action against the defendants. At trial (on a preliminary issue as to liability) Turner J held that the defendants were liable since, if they had given the advice on first tenant liability which they ought to have given, the plaintiffs would have taken steps to obtain a warranty from the parent company or to protect themselves in some other way.

On appeal it was held that, where a plaintiff's loss resulting from the defendant's negligence depends on the hypothetical action of a third party, either in addition to action by the plaintiff or independent of it, the plaintiff's success depends on his showing that he had a substantial chance, rather than a speculative one, the evaluation of the substantial chance being a question of quantification of damages. It was not necessary to prove on the balance of probabilities that the third party would have acted so as to confer the benefit on or avoid the risk to the plaintiff. If the plaintiff established that he had a real chance, the evaluation of that chance was part of the assessment of the damages, on a range from something that just qualified as real or substantial to near certainty.

This decision was followed in *Stovold* v. *Barlows*.[288] The defendant solicitors acted for the plaintiff, in connection with the sale of his house. He wished to complete as soon as possible (as did the purchaser) since he had already bought a new house and had a substantial bridging loan. Unfortunately, the defendants sent the documents by DX to a firm of tailors, who shared the same name as the purchaser's solicitors, and were in the same town, but were not on the DX system. There was a five-day delay, and the purchaser withdrew from the transaction. The plaintiff's house was subsequently sold at a lower price, and he sued the defendants for damages. The Court of Appeal held that the proper approach, in a case where the plaintiff's loss depended on the action of an independent third party in circumstances which, *ex hypothesi*, did not arise, the proper approach was to evaluate the chance for the plaintiff that if the documents had arrived the sale would have gone ahead. The court assessed the chance that the purchaser would have bought the other property as 50 per cent and reduced the award of the trial judge (price difference plus interest on the bridging loan) accordingly. It will be interesting to see in due course if the House of Lords' should the opportunity arise, assert what might be called the causation approach rather than the quantum approach on this issue.

## 8 LIMITATION PERIODS[289]

### 8.1 Introduction

The basic rules concerning limitation periods in contract and tort can be briefly stated, but, as will be seen, they hide a number of complexities that can be especially problematical in the context of professional liability. Section 2 of the Limitation Act 1980 provides that claims founded on tort or simple contract are barred after the expiration of six years from the date on which the cause of action accrues. Section 28

---

288. (1995) 145 N.L.J. 1649.
289. See, *inter alia*, McGee, *Limitation Periods* (Sweet & Maxwell, 2nd edn, 1994).

of the Act provides that where a person is under a disability (by reason of infancy or being a person of unsound mind) a claim may be brought within six years from the date when the person ceases to be under a disability or dies, whichever occurs first. Section 32 of the Act makes provision for postponement of the running of the limitation period in cases of fraud, concealment or mistake, time not beginning to run until the fraud or concealment has been discovered by the plaintiff or ought with reasonable diligence to have been discovered.[290] The main difficulties that have arisen stem from the need to establish the date on which the cause of action accrued, which has been an especial problem in the law of negligence.

## 8.2 Contract

On the whole the courts have faced relatively few problems in establishing when time began to run in cases of breach of contract, since the cause of action accrues upon breach, irrespective of whether damage was suffered at that time. Where the breach consists of a positive act which goes contrary to the obligations of a professional under his or her contract, the issue of limitation is likely to be especially unproblematical. Cases of omissions have given rise to greater difficulty, especially where the court has found there to be a continuing obligation, such as in the case of an architect who may have a continuing duty to supervise and/or keep under review the particular project.[291] A rather restrictive view was taken by the Court of Appeal in *Bell* v. *Peter Browne & Co*[292] where solicitors failed to protect the interest of a man who in 1978 transferred the former matrimonial home to his wife on the basis that he would receive one-sixth of the proceeds whenever it was sold. It was held that the breach of contract occurred in 1978 rather than in 1986 when the former wife sold the house and spent the proceeds, and hence the proceedings that were commenced in 1987 were time-barred.

## 8.3 Tort

In cases of negligence it has long been established that the cause of action accrues when damage occurs. This generally gives rise to no difficulty in cases where the damage is immediately apparent, but it has proved extremely problematical in cases of latent damage, both in the context of personal injuries and other forms of damage.

### 8.3.1 Personal injuries

The separate regime established for limitation purposes in the case of personal injuries must be borne in mind in certain cases of professional liability. In general, cases of medical negligence will be cases which are, in the words of section 11(1) of the Limitation Act 1980, "in respect of personal injuries", though, in some cases the issue may essentially be one of financial loss, as in *Salih* v. *Enfield Health Authority*[293]

---

290. See p. 94 below.
291. See, e.g., *Birchfield Properties Ltd* v. *Newton* [1971] 1 W.L.R. 862 at 873F; *University of Glasgow* v. *William Whitfield* (1988) 42 B.L.R. 66; chapter 3 below.
292. [1990] 2 Q.B. 495. See also *Lee* v. *Thompson* [1989] 2 E.G.L.R. 131. Cf. *Midland Bank Trust Co Ltd* v. *Hett, Stubbs & Kemp* [1979] Ch. 384.
293. [1991] 3 All E.R. 400.

where the parents of a child born suffering from congenital rubella syndrome were awarded damages against the health authority which had negligently failed to diagnose and warn the mother that the child might be infected with rubella, with the result that she was unable to have the pregnancy terminated. Damages were awarded for the additional cost of bringing up a handicapped child (his birth had caused the parents to decide not to have further children). General damages for the mother were also awarded. Clearly a case against a solicitor who has negligently failed to institute proceedings within the limitation period in a personal injuries case would not be a personal injuries case for limitation purposes, for the case against the solicitor is an economic loss case, but *quantum* in such a case will clearly reflect what the award (if any) to the accident victim would have been.[294]

A major catalyst in the reform of personal injury limitation periods was the decision of the House of Lords in *Cartledge* v. *Jopling (E) & Sons*[295] where the plaintiff suffered from pneumoconiosis as a result of inhaling asbestos dust over a number of years. Proceedings were issued more than six years after the damage had occurred to his lungs, albeit that he was not aware of that damage. Concern was understandably expressed that the right to obtain compensation could be lost in such circumstances, and the law was subsequently amended to produce a regime which is much fairer on plaintiffs, though still not without its difficulties.

The position now[296] is that the limitation period for cases where damages are claimed for negligence, nuisance or breach of duty in respect of personal injuries is a three-year period, beginning on the date when the cause of action accrued, or on "the date of knowledge", whichever is the later. The "date of knowledge" is the date on which the plaintiff or his personal representative first knew:

"(a) that the injury in question was significant; and
 (b) that the injury was attributable in whole or in part to the act or omission which is alleged to constitute negligence, nuisance or breach of duty; and
 (c) the identity of the defendant; and
 (d) if it is alleged that the act or omission was that of a person other than the defendant, the identity of that person and the additional facts supporting the bringing of an action against the defendant;
and knowledge that any acts or omissions did or did not, as a matter of law, involve negligence, nuisance or breach of duty is irrelevant."

In a number of medical negligence cases, the "date of knowledge" has been an important issue. Thus, in *Dobbie* v. *Medway Health Authority*[297] it was held that a woman who had a mastectomy which later (it was alleged) proved to have been unnecessary, had the relevant knowledge from the time when her breast was removed, and the fact that she did not know at that time that the defendant's act or omission was (arguably) negligent or blameworthy did not prevent time from running.

Another fruitful source of litigation has been section 33 of the Limitation Act, which, in cases of personal injury or death[298] gives the court a discretion to disapply

---

294. See chapter 9.
295. [1963] A.C. 758.
296. Limitation Act 1980, s. 11.
297. [1994] 1 W.L.R. 1235. See also *Broadley* v. *Guy Clapham & Co* [1994] 4 All E.R. 439; *Whitfield* v. *North Durham Health Authority* [1995] P.I.Q.R. 361.
298. The three-year limitation in fatal accident cases runs from the date of death or the date of knowledge of the person for whose benefit the claim is brought, whichever date is the later: s. 12.

the time-limits if it considers it would be equitable to allow the action to proceed, having regard to the degree to which the provisions of section 11 or section 12 prejudice the plaintiff or any person whom he represents, and any decision of the court under the section would prejudice the defendant or any person whom he represents. Various specific circumstances are set out in section 33(3) to which the court is directed to have regard in acting under the section, though it is required in any event to have regard to all the circumstances of the case. Thus for example a claim for medical negligence may be revived despite proceedings being issued out of time[299]; conversely a potential solicitors' negligence action may be avoided by exercise of the court's discretion. The fact that the plaintiff might be able to claim against his solicitor if the discretion is not exercised is not a circumstance specifically adverted to in section 33(3), but it is a general circumstance to which the court must have regard.

### 8.3.2 Other cases

In the 1970s a number of non-personal injury latent damage cases came before the courts and exposed the same problem in such cases that legislation had been required to solve in the light of *Cartledge* v. *Jopling*. This issue again was that of proceedings being issued some years after the occurrence of damage of which the plaintiff was unaware; typically where a building had been constructed on inadequate foundations, but the occupier of the building only became aware of this problem a number of years later when large cracks developed in the walls of the property. The Court of Appeal, in *Sparham-Souter* v. *Town and Country Developments (Essex) Ltd*[300] in effect transposed the statutory solution to the personal injuries problem into the context of a defective building, holding that the limitation period in an action against an allegedly negligent local authority began to run from the time when the owner discovered, or with reasonable diligence ought to have discovered, the defective state of the property. Subsequently, in *Anns* v. *Merton London Borough Council*,[301] the House of Lords expressed the view that the cause of action, again in a case where the defendant was a local authority, arose when the state of the building was such that there was present or imminent danger to the health or safety of persons occupying it.

Clearly the approach in *Sparham-Souter* and *Anns* involved a view of the occurrence of damage which was not immediately reconcilable with *Cartledge*. The authority of *Cartledge* was reasserted by the House of Lords in *Pirelli General Cable Works Ltd* v. *Oscar Faber & Partners*.[302] The defendants, a firm of consulting engineers, designed a chimney for the plaintiffs' factory. Cracks were discovered in the chimney in November 1977, and the plaintiffs issued proceedings claiming damages for negligent design. The judge held that damage to the chimney had occurred no later than April 1970, and hence, as was subsequently held by the House of Lords, the action was time-barred. It was held to be irrelevant that the damage could not have been discovered with reasonable diligence by the plaintiffs in 1970; it was the date of physical damage to the chimney that caused time to begin to run.

---

299. See, e.g., *Hills* v. *Potter* [1984] 1 W.L.R. 641; cf., however, *Dobbie* v. *Medway Health Authority* (above).
300. [1976] Q.B. 858.
301. [1978] A.C. 728.
302. [1983] 2 A.C. 1.

The Law Reform Committee had already been examining the law on limitation where latent defects were involved, and in the light of *Pirelli* it produced its 24th Report[303] which in turn led to the enactment of the Latent Damage Act 1986.

The Latent Damage Act is concerned with latent damage not involving personal injuries, and was designed to balance the right of plaintiffs to have a fair and sufficient opportunity of pursuing their remedy against the right of defendants to be protected against stale claims, with uncertainty in the law being avoided wherever possible. The Act provides for a new section 14A to be inserted into the Limitation Act 1980. Section 14A provides that in any action for damages for negligence (other than personal injuries), an action shall not be brought after whichever is the later of six years from the date on which the cause of action accrued or three years from the "starting date" which is "the earliest date on which the plaintiff or any person in whom the cause of action was vested before him first had both the knowledge required for bringing an action for damages in respect of the relevant damage and a right to bring such an action".[304] The "knowledge required" means knowledge both[305]:

"(a) of the material facts about the damage in respect of which damages are claimed; and
 (b) of the other facts relevant to the current action ..."

The "material facts" referred to in (a) are defined as[306]:

"Such facts about the damage as would lead a reasonable person who had suffered such damage to consider it sufficiently serious to justify his instituting proceedings for damages against a defendant who did not dispute liability and was able to satisfy a judgment".

The "other facts" referred to in (b) above are[307]:

"(a) that the damage was attributable in whole or in part to the act or omission which is alleged to constitute negligence; and
 (b) the identity of the defendant; and
 (c) if it is alleged that the act or omission was that of a person other than the defendant, the identity of that person and the additional facts supporting the bringing of an action against the defendant".

All this is subject, however, to an overall long stop of 15 years from the date on which there occurred any act or omission which is alleged to constitute negligence and to which it is claimed the damage concerning which damages are claimed is attributable, in whole or in part.[308]

The Act also makes provision, in section 2,[309] for extension of the limitation period in cases to which section 14A applies, where the right of action has accrued to a person suffering from a disability. Also in section 3, provision is made for successive owners of a property subject to latent damage. It is provided that where a person acquires an interest in a property after the date on which a cause of action has accrued to the previous owner, but before the material facts about the damage had become known, a fresh cause of action shall accrue to that subsequent purchaser on the date

303. Latent Damage: Cmnd 9390.
304. Section 14A(5).
305. Section 14A(6).
306. Section 14A(7).
307. Section 14A(8).
308. Section 14B.
309. Inserting s. 28A into the 1980 Act.

on which they acquire their interest in the property, but for limitation purposes the cause of action is deemed to have accrued on the date when a cause of action accrued to the predecessor in title.

The Act came into force on 18 September 1986, and does not affect any actions commenced before that date; nor does it revive actions which had become time-barred by that date. A matter that the Act does not make clear is the meaning of the word "negligence", the particular difficulty being whether it is limited to tortious negligence or extends to cases where breach of a statutory duty or of a contractual duty entails a breach of a duty of reasonable care. The better view appears to be that "negligence" in the Act means tortious negligence[310] which carries implications for the cases where concurrent liability is an issue.[311]

There is a sense in which some of the importance of the Latent Damage Act has been overtaken by subsequent events, particularly the decision of the House of Lords in *Murphy* v. *Brentwood District Council*.[312] In severely limiting as it did the range of claims for pure economic loss resulting from negligent acts, and holding that defects in buildings should be characterised as economic loss, the House of Lords effectively restricted the ambit of the Latent Damage Act 1986. *Pirelli* was explained by Lord Keith in *Murphy* as being a case falling within the principles of *Hedley Byrne* v. *Heller & Partners Ltd*,[313] and it is clear that such cases of economic loss resulting from a negligent misstatement remain actionable after *Murphy*. It was held, however, by May J in *Nitrigin Eireann Teoranta* v. *Inca Alloys Ltd*[314] that the fact that the defendants in *Pirelli* were a firm of professional consulting engineers on whom it was reasonable to rely was significant, in contrast to the case in *Nitrigin* where the defendants were specialist manufacturers of proprietary alloy tubing, who knew or ought to have known the purpose for which the specialist pipe they provided was needed. That, however, was held to amount neither to "a professional relationship in the sense in which the law treats professional negligence nor a *Hedley Byrne* relationship".[315] Clearly, a significant number of professional negligence cases will arise as a consequence of negligent misstatement, and to such cases the changes effected by the Latent Damage Act 1986 will be of great significance.

The essence of a negligent misstatement is detrimental reliance, and consequently it has been held in surveyors' negligence cases that the damage is done, and the cause of action accrues, when the would-be purchaser (or lessee) who relies on the defective survey report acts in reliance on the report and irrevocably commits theirself to the transaction in question.[316] Again, in cases of solicitors' negligence such as *Forster* v. *Outred*[317] it has been held that where the plaintiff acts to his detriment in reliance on negligent advice, damage is suffered and the cause of action accrues.

An example of how a pre-Latent Damage Act case might be dealt with today is the

---

310. See *Iron Trade Mutual Insurance Co Ltd* v. *J K Buckenham Ltd* [1990] 1 All E.R. 808.
311. See p. 45 above.
312. [1991] 1 A.C. 398.
313. [1964] A.C. 465.
314. [1992] 1 All E.R. 854.
315. *Ibid.* at 860.
316. See *Secretary of State for the Environment* v. *Essex, Goodman & Suggitt* [1986] 1 W.L.R. 1432; *Horbury* v. *Craig Hall & Rutley* [1991] E.G.C.S. 81.
317. [1982] 1 W.L.R. 86; *Costa* v. *Georghion* [1984] P.N. 201; cf. *UBAF Ltd* v. *European American Banking Corporation* [1984] 1 Q.B. 713. In the context of insurance brokers, see *Iron Trade Mutual Insurance Co Ltd* v. *J K Buckenham Ltd* (see fn. 22 above) to similar effect.

case of *DW Moore & Co Ltd* v. *Ferrier*.[318] In 1971 the plaintiffs, who were insurance brokers, instructed the defendants, a firm of solicitors, to draft an agreement between them and F who was to become an employee director and shareholder of the plaintiffs' company. The agreement contained a restrictive covenant restraining him from setting up as an insurance broker if he ceased to be a member of the company. A further agreement containing similar terms was entered into in 1975. In 1980 F decided to set up business on his own in an area within the geographical restrictions of the restrictive covenants. He resigned as a director and employee of the company, but remained a shareholder. It transpired, however, that the restrictive covenants did not take effect on F's ceasing to be a director or employee, but only on his ceasing to be a shareholder. Consequently, the plaintiffs were unable to enforce the restrictive covenants against F, and in 1985 they brought proceedings in negligence against the defendants. It was held that actual damage capable of quantification had been sustained by the plaintiffs at the time when the agreements were executed, in 1971 and 1975, and hence the action was time-barred. If such a defective restrictive covenant contained in an agreement created in (say) 1987, the Latent Damage Act would apply, and there would need to be a determination of when the starting date, as defined in section 14A(5) of the Limitation Act occurred. That would presumably be the point at which the director/employee resigned, set up in rivalry and the defective nature of the covenant was discovered. Such discovery could occur as late as 1999 for the plaintiff to have three years in which to bring a claim before the overall long stop under section 14B cut off the claim.[319]

As was noted above, Lord Keith in *Murphy* described the nature of the engineers' liability in *Pirelli* as being in negligent misstatement, and hence actionable as a recoverable economic loss even in the light of *Murphy*. Prior to that decision, there had been a run of cases picking up a remark of Lord Frazer's in *Pirelli* that[320]:

"... except perhaps where the advice of an architect or a consulting engineer leads to the erection of a building which is so defective as to be doomed from the start, the cause of action accrues only when physical damage occurs to the building."

Some ingenuity was expended by defendants seeking to argue that the defects in their design were so serious as to cause the building to have been doomed from the start, with time beginning to run from that point.[321] In *Ketteman* v. *Hansel Properties Ltd*[322] Lawton LJ pointed out that although the trial judge in *Pirelli* found that, as a consequence of unsuitable materials, cracks were bound to occur in the chimney, nevertheless it was not regarded as being doomed from the start, and the House of Lords[323] held that the mere fact that the houses in that case had been constructed in such a way that damage was bound to occur did not mean that they had been doomed from the start. This reassertion of damage rather than defect as the basis of the cause of action is surely to be welcomed. However, if the basis of the engineer or architect's

---

318. [1988] 1 All E.R. 400.
319. Though on the facts of *Moore*, even if the events had occurred since the coming into force of the Latent Damage Act 1986, s. 14A would not appear to avail the plaintiff, given the delay of more than three years between the realisation that the covenant was defective and the issue of proceedings.
320. [1983] 2 A.C. 1 at 18.
321. See, e.g., *Dove* v. *Banhams Patent Locks Ltd* [1983] 2 All E.R. 833; *London Congregational Union Inc* v. *Harriss* [1985] 1 All E.R. 335.
322. [1985] 1 All E.R. 353.
323. [1987] A.C. 189.

liability is the reliance by the plaintiff on careless advice, the cause of action will arguably accrue in a case such as *Pirelli* on the date of reliance rather than the date of physical damage to the building.

### 8.4 Fraud, concealment or mistake

A further important aspect of the Limitation Act is the provision in section 32(1) for extension of the date from which time begins to run in cases of fraud, concealment or mistake. The subsection provides that:

"... where in the case of any action for which a period of limitation is prescribed by this Act, either—

(a) the action is based upon the fraud of the defendant; or

(b) any fact relevant to the plaintiff's right of action has been deliberately concealed from him by the defendant; or

(c) the action is for relief from the consequences of a mistake;

the period of limitation shall not begin to run until the plaintiff has discovered the fraud, concealment or mistake (as the case may be) or could with reasonable diligence have discovered it."

Section 32(2) provides:

"For the purposes of subsection (1) above, deliberate commission of a breach of duty in circumstances in which it is unlikely to be discovered for some time amounts to deliberate concealment of the facts involved in that breach of duty."

As an example of the operation of this provision (in fact its predecessor, section 26 of the Limitation Act 1939), in *Kitchen* v. *Royal Air Forces Association*[324] the second defendants, a firm of solicitors, negligently failed to issue proceedings under the Fatal Accidents Act within the limitation period. Subsequently an *ex gratia* payment was made to the solicitors in 1946, a few months after the action became time-barred, by the potential defendants to the Fatal Accidents claim, it being agreed between them and the solicitors that the plaintiff (the widow) should not be informed who the donor was. The solicitor/client relationship still existed at that time between the plaintiff and the solicitors. The plaintiff brought an action against the solicitors in 1955 for professional negligence in connection with the fatal accident litigation. The Court of Appeal held that the word "fraud" in section 26 was not confined to deceit or dishonesty, and the conduct by the solicitors in concealing that payment was made by the potential defendants in 1946 for the plaintiff's benefit amounted to concealment by fraud, for the purposes of the section, of the plaintiff's right of action against the solicitors at that time, hence her claim against them was not time-barred.

In *Sheldon* v. *RHM Outhwaite (Underwriting Agencies) Ltd*[325] it was argued that an alleged deliberate concealment from the plaintiffs after their cause of action had arisen of facts relevant to their right of action against the defendant underwriting agency, caused the running of the limitation period to be postponed under section 32(1)(b). It was held that on a true construction of the subsection it did not suspend or postpone the running of the limitation period in cases where the defendant had deliberately concealed facts relevant to the plaintiff's claim after his action had arisen

---

324. [1958] 2 All E.R. 241. See also *King* v. *Victor Parsons & Co* [1973] 1 All E.R. 206, for a more obvious case.

325. [1994] 4 All E.R. 481, C.A.; [1995] 2 All E.R. 558, H.L.

until the discovery of the concealment. As Staughton LJ (who dissented), pointed out,[326] either solution to the problem raised by the appeal could give rise to absurdity. The House of Lords held (by a majority of three to two) that it was clear that in actions based on fraud under section 32(1)(a) and actions for relief from the consequences of a mistake under section 32(1)(c), time did not begin to run until the fraud or mistake was discoverable, and it was therefore to be assumed that the same was true of section 32(1)(b) (concealment). The difficulties remain, and it may be that a legislative solution will be the most desirable outcome.

JON HOLYOAK
DAVID ALLEN

326. [1994] 4 All E.R. 481 at 495.

CHAPTER 3

# ARCHITECTS AND ENGINEERS

## 1 THE TWO PROFESSIONS AND HOW THEY ARE REGULATED

### 1.1 Architects

#### 1.1.1 Definition

The word "architect" has been defined by the High Court as follows[1]:

"One who possesses, with due regard to aesthetic as well as practical considerations, adequate skill and knowledge to enable him (i) to originate, (ii) to design and plan, (iii) to arrange for and supervise the erection of such buildings or other works calling for skill in design and planning as he might, in the course of his business, reasonably be asked to carry out or in respect of which he offers his services as a specialist ..."

A leading textbook defines an architect as "a person who professes skill in the art of designing buildings to meet his client's needs, in the organisation of the contractual arrangements for their construction, and in the supervision of work and contractual administration until final completion".[2]

Thus an architect is concerned with the design of buildings and the consequential contractual and supervisory aspects of construction.

#### 1.1.2 Regulation by statute

There are currently three statutes dealing directly with architects. However, at the time of going to press, the Housing Grants, Construction and Regeneration Bill is passing through Parliament, and is expected to become law during 1996. What follows is an exposition of the current law, followed by a brief note of the changes proposed by the Bill. The statutes are as follows.

##### 1.1.2.1 THE ARCHITECTS (REGISTRATION) ACT 1931

This Act established the Architects Registration Council of the United Kingdom ("ARCUK"). ARCUK has a duty to maintain a register ("the Register of Architects") containing the names and addresses of all those entitled to inclusion under that Act (i.e., anyone who has satisfied ARCUK's Admissions Committee that

---

1. *R* v. *Architects Registration Tribunal, ex parte Jagger* [1945] 2 All E.R. 131.
2. I Duncan-Wallace QC, *Hudson's Building and Engineering Contracts* (11th edn), Volume 1, para. 2–006.

he has passed relevant examinations or holds appropriate qualifications, including EC qualifications,[3] or is a member of one or more specified bodies).

Section 7 of the Act creates a Disciplinary Committee and empowers ARCUK to direct it to hold inquiries into allegations that a person on the Register is guilty of disgraceful conduct or a criminal offence. The Council has the power, after considering the Disciplinary Committee's findings and recommendations, to remove the offender from the Register. A full description of ARCUK's inquiry procedure is set out below.[4]

### 1.1.2.2 THE ARCHITECTS REGISTRATION ACT 1938

Under this Act it is a criminal offence to practise or carry on business under any name, title or style containing the word "architect" unless that person is on the Register. Exceptions are provided for anyone describing themselves as a "naval architect", "landscape architect" or "golf course architect". Visiting architects from the EC are also allowed to describe themselves as architects subject to certain provisions.[5]

### 1.1.2.3 THE ARCHITECTS REGISTRATION (AMENDMENT) ACT 1969

This short Act establishes ARCUK's Education Fund, which is administered by the Board of Architectural Education (itself established by the 1931 Act), through its Awards Panel, which considers applications for research and maintenance grants.

### 1.1.2.4 ARCUK

ARCUK has two committees concerned with discipline:

(a) The Professional Purposes Committee which is established under ARCUK's own regulations made under the 1931 Act. The committee deals with aspects of professional conduct falling short of "disgraceful conduct" and may make recommendations to the Council. It also advises architects regarding professional conduct matters, especially with regard to ARCUK's document "Conduct and Discipline", which from June 1981 replaced ARCUK's former Code of Professional Conduct. "Conduct and Discipline" describes the "Standard of Conduct for Architects" as follows:

   (i) before making an engagement the architect will have *defined* the terms of his engagement beyond reasonable doubt;

   (ii) the architect will have *declared* to the other parties to the engagement any business interests which might be, or appear to be, prejudicial to the proper performance of the engagement;

   (iii) the architect will, if he finds that his interests conflict so as to put his integrity in question, *inform* without delay anyone who may be concerned and withdraw from the engagement if necessary.

   The document also contains eight points constituting ARCUK's "Advice to Architects" issued in March 1989. To a large degree these elaborate the

---

3. Sections 6 and 6A. The fourth and fifth Schedules to the Act contain a comprehensive list of the relevant qualifications, country by country.
4. See section 1.1.2.5 below.
5. Section 1A, inserted by the Architects' Qualifications (EEC Recognition) Order 1987, SI 1987/1824, art. 8.

principles above regarding architects' integrity and the need to put agreements in writing.

(b) The Discipline Committee, which has greater powers. Its authority derives from the 1931 Act direct (s. 7). It has eight members and investigates disgraceful conduct and allegations of criminal offences. It is appropriate at this stage to examine ARCUK's disciplinary procedure in a little more detail.[6]

### 1.1.2.5 ARCUK'S DISCIPLINARY PROCEDURE

Any complaints regarding a registered architect are reported first to the Professional Purposes Committee (PPC) at its quarterly meeting. This Committee investigates the matter. The PPC may adopt one of four conclusions.

First, it may decide that the matter lies outside the scope of the Standard of Conduct (the three principles set out above) or outside its jurisdiction altogether, in which case the matter proceeds no further. Secondly, it may decide that the facts indicate conduct not in compliance with the Standard, but not amounting to "disgraceful conduct", in which case the PPC may warn against any repetition, and may pass the relevant papers to RIBA. Thirdly, in the case of a criminal conviction relevant to the person's activity as an architect, the PPC may submit a report to the full Council which, subject to the architect's rights to representations may then remove the architect from the Register for any period of time.

Fourthly, the PPC may decide that the facts disclose what appears to be "disgraceful conduct". In this case:

(a) the PPC ceases its investigation and directs the Registrar to instruct ARCUK's Solicitor Complainant to prepare an affidavit and apply to the Council to require the person to answer the allegations;

(b) the Council considers the application and the affidavit and decides whether an inquiry is necessary, i.e., where there is a *prima facie* case to answer. If it decides that there is, it directs the Disciplinary Committee to hold an inquiry;

(c) the Discipline Committee reports to the Council by way of findings of fact and recommendations. It may make three possible findings/ recommendations:

  (i) *not guilty*—the Council must accept this finding;

  (ii) *guilty*, with a recommendation that the name not be removed—the council must accept the finding and decide whether to adopt the recommendation. If it wishes to remove the name from the Register, it must act as under (iii) below;

  (iii) *guilty*, with a recommendation to remove the name—again, the Council must accept the finding and decide only on the question of whether it intends to remove the name. If it does, the person concerned is advised of his right to make representations, and the Council will decide at its next following meeting whether to confirm its intention to remove.

---

6. See Appendix 3 of "Conduct and Discipline".

The Council has not only power to remove a name but also to disqualify a person for registration. This is more serious than removal, as it prevents the architect from applying *de novo* for registration, at least while the disqualification lasts. (ARCUK's notes in "Conduct and Discipline" state that a decision to disqualify may be added to a removal in the interests of the public or the profession to prevent the person from practising under the title for a significant period. The notes envisage that, if a disqualification is imposed, it will generally be for a period of between one and ten years.)

### 1.1.2.6 THE HOUSING GRANTS, CONSTRUCTION AND REGENERATION BILL 1996—PROPOSED CHANGES

The following changes are envisaged by the Bill:

— ARCUK will be known as the Architect's Registration Board.
— The Board will appoint a "Registrar of Architects", who will maintain the Register of Architects. Entry on the Register will be open to those who have appropriate qualifications, experience or competence. The Board may, in addition, require a person to pass a prescribed examination in architecture.
— The Board will issue a new code of professional conduct and practice (which will presumably replace "Conduct and Discipline").
— The Discipline Committee under the 1931 Act will be abolished. Matters of professional conduct will be dealt with by a Professional Conduct Committee of the Board. The somewhat antiquated term "disgraceful conduct" will be replaced. The Committee will now investigate "unacceptable professional conduct" (defined as conduct falling short of the standard required by a registered architect) or professional incompetence. Relevant criminal offences may still result in disciplinary procedures. The Professional Conduct Committee will have similar powers to the current ones to reprimand, find, suspend or remove from the Register (an order for removal will now be known as an "erasure order"). It is to be hoped that the rather cumbersome procedure described in section 1.1.2.5 above will thus be streamlined.
— Certain other amendments are made to the 1931 and 1938 Acts.

### 1.1.3 Regulation by the Royal Institute of British Architects

The Royal Institute of British Architects ("RIBA") is the main professional body for architects. Its objects as described in its Charter are "The advancement of Architecture and the promotion of the acquirement of the knowledge of the Arts and sciences connected therewith". It is an important constituent body on the Joint Contracts Tribunal which is responsible for drafting many of the standard construction forms of contract. Consultant achitects, i.e., those in private practice, may also (or additionally) belong to the Association of Consultant Architects which has itself produced standard contract forms.[7] Architects are not prohibited from practising as limited companies.

7. The ACA Form of Building Agreement 1982 and its associated sub-contract.

100

RIBA provides a Code of Professional Conduct. This consists of three principles and a number of related rules. The Code uses the word "client" throughout to denote the person for whom the architect is providing services.

The three principles, with their associated rules, are as follows:

(a) Principle 1: "A member shall faithfully carry out the duties which he undertakes. He shall also have a proper regard for the interests both of those who commission and those who may be expected to use or enjoy the product of his work".

There are four rules relating to this principle. The first requires a member to have defined "beyond reasonable doubt" (and recorded) the terms of the engagement including the scope of the service allocation of responsibilities and limitation of liability, calculation of remuneration and the provision for termination. These are onerous obligations, and go a little further than ARCUK's own Standard of Conduct, which, to some degree, they otherwise parallel.

The other rules state that an architect:
— must ensure that his office and any branch office is under the control of an architect;
— must not sub-commission or sub-let work without the prior agreement of his client or without defining the changes in the responsibilities of those concerned;
— must act fairly and impartially beteween parties where he is appointed under a building contract or in any similar circumstances.[8]

(b) Principle 2: "A member shall avoid actions and situations inconsistent with his professional obligations or likely to raise doubts about his integrity".

There are 10 rules relating to conflicts of interest (for example rules preventing an architect acting as a purportedly "independent" architect under a building contract when he or his firm is the contractor; prohibiting the taking of discounts, commissions or gifts as an inducement to show favour to anyone etc.).

(c) Principle 3: "A member shall rely only on ability and achievement as the basis for his advancement".

There are seven rules under this principle. Amongst these are that a member shall not attempt to oust another architect from his engagement; and if he is approached to take on work in which he can ascertain by reasonable inquiry, or knows, that another architect has an engagement with the same client, he must notify that other architect of the fact.

RIBA's Professional Conduct Committee deals with complaints against members. In the first instance the complainant should write to The Professional Conduct Secretary, The Royal Institute of British Architects, 66 Portland Place, London, W1N 4AD. RIBA will require conformation that the complainant has no objection to his letter being sent to the architect in question, and will also require details of any second opinions or independent advice obtained by the complainant. The Com-

---

8. See section 5 below.

mittee then proceeds to deal with the matter at one or more of its six-weekly meetings.

### 1.1.4 Summary of a complainant's options

Assuming that an architect is a member of RIBA, a complainant has four possible courses of action, which he may take separately or in combination:

    (1) To complain to ARCUK[8a] (73 Hallam Street, London, W1N 6EE). This may be done if the behaviour is alleged to be disgraceful conduct or a criminal offence (which can result in removal from the Register, thus preventing the architect from practising); or a breach of ARCUK's "Conduct and Discipline", or indeed is any behaviour falling short of disgraceful conduct (which may result in warnings).

    (2) To refer the matter to RIBA's Professional Conduct Committee (see above).

    (3) To apply for a conciliator to be appointed under the RIBA conciliation scheme. Conciliation is a form of alternative dispute resolution ("ADR"). ADR is a term loosely used to describe various methods of resolving disputes outside the traditional litigation or arbitration routes. The doctrine originated from the USA and has been growing in influence in the UK in the early 1990s.[9] Like all forms of ADR, conciliation is:

      (a) *consensual*—it cannot go forward without both parties' agreement; and

      (b) *non-binding*—any opinions or recommendations of the conciliator are not legally enforceable.

The RIBA scheme has the following characteristics:

—     it may be used for fee disputes where the sum in dispute does not exceed £15,000, or for other disputes where the total sums in dispute do not exceed £50,000;

—     it is not available where litigation or arbitration has already been commenced;

—     it is not available for disputes between two architects.

    Fees are payable to the RIBA conciliator. RIBA have published notes for guidance of conciliators and parties under the scheme, dated July/August 1993, to which further reference should be made. Full details of the scheme are available from RIBA at the address stated above.

    (4) To commence proceedings either by way of arbitration or litigation. If any of the standard forms of appointment of architects have been used (SFA/92, for example) the dispute will prima facie be referable to aribration, subject to incorporation of the arbitration clause.[10]

---

8a. To be replaced by a new body, the Architects' Registration Board, under the Housing Grants, Construction and Regeneration Bill 1996. See section 1.1.2.6 above.

9. See Philip Naughton QC, "Alternative Forms of Dispute Resolution—Their Strengths and Weaknesses" (1990) 6 Const. L.J. for an outline of the various forms of ADR. In High Court actions, *Practice Direction* (*Civil Litigation: Case Management*) of 24 January 1995 requires the parties' solicitors to state, as part of the pre-trial checklist, whether they have considered alternative dispute resolution with their clients.

10. See section 8.1 below.

## 1.2 Engineers

### 1.2.1 Definition

"Engineer" is a looser term than "architect". There is no statutory system of regulation as there is with architects. Nor is there any restriction on the use of the word "engineer", although the description by a person of himself as a "chartered engineer" implies membership of one of the professional bodies and, if incorrect, might therefore give rise to civil liability at common law or under the Misrepresentation Act 1967.

Civil engineers are primarily concerned with the design and construction of roads, bridges, canals, railways, embankments, drains and waterways etc. Civil engineering work is notable for the fact that some of it usually takes place underground, and it is not always clear at the outset what obstacles may be encountered, or how much excavation will be required. This has important contractual consequences in terms of how the contractor is paid, i.e., usually on a "remeasurement" basis for quantities actually excavated, rather than on a "lump sum" basis as is the case for traditional building contracts.

The main professional body is the Institution of Civil Engineers which publishes the main form of civil engineering contract between employers and contractors (ICE Conditions, 6th edn). There are various other types of engineers with their own professional bodies (mechanical and electrical, structural, chemical). The Association of Consulting Engineers, which produces the standard conditions of engagement for the profession, is primarily for engineers in private practice.

The various professional bodies are now considered with particular reference to their systems of regulation.

### 1.2.2 The Institution of Civil Engineers

The Institution of Civil Engineers ("ICE") was granted a Royal Charter originally in 1828. In 1975 a number of supplemental Charters were revoked and consolidated into a further Royal Charter of 11 June 1975. The object of ICE is "to foster and promote the art and science of Civil Engineering" (Article 3 of the 1977 Charter). On 1 April 1984 the Institution of Municipal Engineers was merged with ICE, and an Association of Municipal Engineers was then formed as a sub-division of ICE.

ICE's functions and system of regulation are to be found in four documents which are conveniently published together in one booklet by ICE, namely:

(1) *The Royal Charter of 11 June 1995*   This is the source of ICE's powers, in particular that of its council, to make byelaws and regulations. It is necessarily framed in general terms.

(2) *Byelaws*   The 119 byelaws contain a comprehensive system of rules for the running of ICE. Byelaw 35 defines "improper conduct" (see below).

(3) *Disciplinary regulations*   These are procedural rules for the investigation of complaints, made by ICE's Council, under byelaw 85.

(4) *Rules for Professional Conduct*   There are thirteen rules, many of which are similar in content to those of RIBA. The following may be noted:
*Rule 1*: a member must have full regard to the public interest particularly in the matters of health and safety.

*Rule 2*: a member shall discharge his professional responsibilities with integrity.

*Rule 6*: a member must not in self-laudatory language, or in any manner derogatory to the dignity of the profession, advertise, or write articles for publication.

*Rule 11*: a member shall not attempt to supplant another engineer, or attempt to intervene in connection with any other engineering work which he knows has been entrusted to another engineer.

It may be seen that there is a three-tier framework of authority. The Disciplinary Regulations and Rules for Professional Conduct are made under powers given in the byelaws, which themselves are made pursuant to the powers granted in the Royal Charter.

### 1.2.2.1 DISCIPLINARY PROCEDURE

ICE has two bodies, set up under its byelaws, that deal with complaints:

(a) an Investigating Panel consisting of Fellows of ICE;
(b) a Disciplinary Board consisting of past or present members of the Council.

ICE will consider any complaint of "improper conduct". This is defined in byelaw 35 as:

"(a) any breach of the provisions of the Charter, or of the byelaws, or of any regulations or rules made under the Charter or byelaws; or
(b) any other conduct which will indicate unfitness to be a member or shall otherwise be unbefitting to a member as such."

Complaints of improper conduct must be made to ICE at Great George Street, Westminster, London, SW1P 3AA. ICE require full details of the breach, and confirmation that a copy of the complaint may be forwarded to the member concerned.

In the first instance the Investigating Panel has to consider whether there is a prima facie case of improper conduct. If it considers that there is not, it may dismiss the case without informing the member concerned and without hearing the person making the allegation (reg. 9). In all other cases, it must send written notice to the member of the allegations and invite his observations. It may then dismiss the case if satisfied that the allegation is unfounded, does not disclose a prima facie case or is of a trivial nature. Otherwise it must refer the case on to the Disciplinary Board.

The Board then deals with the allegation in a quasi-judicial manner. Five members of the Board sit. They may appoint a practising barrister or solicitor to sit with them. Proper notice to the member must be given and the member has the opportunity to call witnesses, cross-examine, and be represented by solicitors or counsel or a fellow member of the ICE.

If the Board finds the member guilty it has power to make "such order as it may consider appropriate" including expulsion or suspension. It also has various costs powers (byelaw 36).

The Board must cause the finding and the particulars of its order to be displayed in the Institution and published (if an allegation is dismissed, the accused member is entitled to demand similar publication of the dismissal).

### 1.2.3 The Institution of Mechanical Engineers

The Institution of Mechanical Engineers ("IMechE") of 1 Birdcage Walk, London, SW1H 9JJ published the third edition of its Professional Code of Conduct in August 1989. This states that the Institution has three main functions: to promote the development of mechanical engineering, to govern the qualifications of its members, and to control their professional conduct. Byelaw 32 and its associated Rules of Conduct deals with the conduct of members. The dignity and reputation of the Institution, and the obligation to act with fairness and integrity to all persons with whom the work is connected, are both stressed.

IMechE has its own disciplinary system for investigating improper conduct. Rule 6 states that a court judgment against a member accused of professional negligence may be taken as prima facie evidence of improper conduct, but "this is not necessarily so and will always depend upon all the circumstances of the case". While it is of course proper that the Institution's disciplinary procedures are independent of any findings by a court, it will presumably be a rare case where professional negligence does not also amount to improper conduct.

### 1.2.4 The Institution of Electrical Engineers

This Institution was founded in 1871 and incorporated by Royal Charter in 1921. The Institution publishes Rules of Conduct. Members must take all reasonable care to ensure that their work and products constitute no avoidable danger of death or injury or ill-health to any person. There is a positive obligation to take all reasonable steps to maintain and develop professional competence by attention to new developments in science and engineering. Rule 7 states that where a member has offered professional advice that is not accepted, he must take all reasonable steps to ensure that the person overruling or neglecting his advice is aware of any danger which the member believes may result from such overruling or neglect. This may be a matter that a potential plaintiff could pray in aid in litigation, although it probably adds little, if anything, to an engineer's common law duties.

Byelaw 41 deals with disciplinary action. The Institution has also published disciplinary regulations made under that byelaw. These are aimed at improper conduct, which is defined as the making of any false representation in applying for election or transfer to any class of membership; any breach of the byelaws, regulations, rules or directions; or any conduct injurious to the Institution.

The regulations lay down the procedure for investigation of any complaints. These are very similar to those of ICE. Like ICE, the Council has an Investigating Panel, and a Disciplinary Board, and a "two-stage" procedure is adopted similar to that of ICE.

### 1.2.5 The Association of Consulting Engineers

This Association of Alliance House, 12 Caxton Street, London, SW1H 0QL also has a Code of Professional Conduct for members running to seven paragraphs with sub-divisions. It publishes the standard form of professional conduct for engineers, the ACE Conditions of Engagement 1995 (see section 2.2 below).

## 2 THE STANDARD FORMS OF CONTRACT

This section focuses on three standard forms of contract for the appointment of professionals. The first two are the forms produced by the Royal Institute of British Architects and the Association of Consulting Engineers. The third is the Professional Services Contract ("PSC") published in 1994 by the Institution of Civil Engineers. This form has been drafted for use with the New Engineering Contract ("NEC"), also published by the Institution of Civil Engineers, though it can be used separately. The NEC (revised and republished in 1995 as The Engineering and Construction Contract) was endorsed by the 1994 Latham Report, "Constructing the Team". As this contract becomes more popular, it is likely that the PSC itself will be widely used, and that this will therefore be a form of contract that those involved in the field of professional negligence for architects and engineers will need to become familiar with.

The Appendix to this chapter contains a brief summary, in tabular form, of some of the more important clauses in these forms.

### 2.1 SFA/92

The Standard Form of Agreement for the Appointment of an Architect (SFA/92) was published in July 1992 by RIBA. It is the successor to RIBA's "The Architect's Appointment", also known as "the Blue Book" (1982). The form was updated in April 1995 to provide a clause allowing architects to claim an extra fee for work carried out pursuant to the Construction (Design and Management) Regulations 1994. SFA/92 consists of:

   (a) a memorandum of agreement;
   (b) conditions of appointment;
      These are in four parts, namely:
      (i) conditions applicable to all appointments;
      (ii) conditions specific to the design of building projects (work stages A–H of RIBA's document "Plan of Work");
      (iii) conditions specific to contract administration and administration (work stages J–L of the "Plan of Work");
      (iv) conditions specific to the appointment of consultants and specialists where the architect is the lead consultant;
   (c) four schedules, namely: information to be supplied by the client; services that will be performed by the architect; payment; and matters relating to the appointment of other consultants where the architect is the "lead" consultant. The schedules need to be completed with the specific details of the appointment.

The overriding "care and skill" obligation is contained in clause 1.2.1 which states:

"The Architect shall in providing the Services exercise reasonable skill and care in conformity with the normal standards of the Architect's profession."

Although the foreword to the Guidance Notes prepared by RIBA states that it is "balanced fairly between the parties and in the interests of both", there are a number of exclusions and restrictions of the architect's liability, some of which were not present in the Architect's Appointment, that might be said to tilt the balance somewhat in favour of the architect. In particular:

— no action may be taken against the architect after the expiry of a stated number of years from practical completion (Article 5)—the architect may thus impose a shorter limitation period than would exist at law;

— liability for loss or damage is limited to a stated figure (Article 6.2);

— liability in any event is limited to a "fair contribution", in cases where others are partly to blame, and irrespective of whether those others are sued (Article 6.1);

— the architect does not warrant that his services can be completed within the timetable agreed with the client (cl. 1.3.7);

— the architect is not responsible for work on site, although he has a duty to inspect (cll. 3.2.2 and 3.2.3);

— the architect is not responsible for design or work carried out by another specialist (cl. 4.2.5) or a consultant (cl. 4.1.7);

— all rights of set-off are excluded (cl. 1.5.15)—specifically, the clause provides that the client may not withhold or reduce any sum payable to the architect by reason of claims or alleged claims against the architect. There appear to be two methods by which the client might circumvent this. First, he might argue that no sum is "payable" under the clause at all, because of defective performance; secondly, it is possible that the Unfair Contract Terms Act 1977 might apply[11];

— extra payment is due for "delay for any [other] reason beyond the architect's control" (cl. 1.5.7).

## 2.2 The Association of Consulting Engineers' Conditions of Engagement 1995

These conditions come in six forms:

*Agreement A(1)*—for use where the consulting engineer is engaged as a lead consultant;

*Agreement B(1)*—where the consulting engineer is engaged directly by the client, but not as lead consultant;

*Agreement C(1)*—where the consulting engineer is providing design services for a "design and construct" contractor;

*Agreement D*—where the engineer is engaged to provide reporting and advisory services;

*Agreement E*—where the consulting engineer is engaged as a project manager;

---

11. Section 3 of the Act applies where one party contracts on the other's written terms of business. There seems no reason why this should not include a form that has been drafted by the governing body of the professional in questions. Section 3(2)(b) prevents a party from seeking to exclude his liability where he renders a performance substantially different from that to be reasonably expected of him, or renders no performance at all—except insofar as the exclusion is reasonable. If an architect claims to be entitled without any set-off to payment for (say) completing work stages A–L, in the face of evidence before the court that such performance was defective, it might be argued that cl. 1.5.15 of SFA/92 is caught by the section.

*Agreement F*—where the consulting engineer acts as planning supervisor in accordance with the Construction (Design and Management) Regulations 1994.

Agreements A, B and C only are published in two variants, the first for civil and structural engineering, the second for electrical and mechanical services engineering. There are further agreements for minor works (Agreement G), where the engineer acts as client's representative for design and construct work (Agreement H) and for sub-consultancy (Agreement I).

References in this chapter and Appendix are to Agreement A(1).

The agreements themselves comprise:

  (i) a memorandum of agreement;
 (ii) conditions of engagement;
(iii) Appendix 1—the services of the consulting engineer;
(iv) Appendix 2—the remuneration of the consulting engineer.

(The two appendices obviously have to be completed.)

These conditions supersede the previous conditions of engagement of 1991, and follow many of the clauses that limit liability in SFA/92. In particular, liability is limited to a certain number of years from practical completion; there is an overall financial limit to liability; and the "fair contribution" approach is also adopted. The engineer is only obliged to use "reasonable endeavours" to adhere to any agreed programme—and even then "subject always to conditions beyond [his] reasonable control" (cl. 2.10).

The British Property Federation has issued a three-page "health warning" advising members to use this form of appointment with "utmost care", apparently being unhappy with changes that were not made after the consultation process.[12]

Clause 2.4 defines the skill and care obligation as follows:

"The Consulting Engineer shall exercise reasonable skill, care and diligence in the performance of the Services."

## 2.3 The Professional Services Contract

The first edition of this was published in September 1994 to complement the New Engineering Contract. It is published by the Institution of Civil Engineers. It uses the same style of language as the New Engineering Contract/the Engineering and Construction Contract, in that obligations are put in the present tense, and coupled with a general obligation on all parties to act as stated in the contract. The professional is, unusually, redefined as virtually another contractor, offering his services to the client. It should be noted that the language itself is untested in the courts.

The brief is the single most important document and it is essential that it is properly drafted if the contract is to work. It is prepared jointly by the client and the professional. It sets out the scope of the consultant's duties, and defines the client's objectives. The principle of "fair contribution" between parties jointly liable is contained in this agreement, as in SFA/92 and the ACE Conditions, although the

12. "Building", 2 June 1995.

PSC seeks to reduce the professional's contribution where there is contributory fault on the client's part (cl. 82.1).

A timetable is introduced for the professional to follow. Either party may be in breach: the client, if he does not provide information in time; the professional, if he does not keep to his timetable. There are "compensation events" which can adjust the professional's fee up or down, and give more time. Both parties are under obligations to give "early warnings" where they have reason to believe that a compensation event will occur. In general, the professional is obliged to "correct a defect" (which does not necessarily imply fault—a "defect" is defined as anything that does not comply with the brief), and argue about fault afterwards. The contract allows various procurement options ranging from "cost reimbursable" to lump sum and target contract. There is no option of a simple percentage of the cost of the work.

The reasonable skill and care obligation mirrors the common law one, although the Guidance Notes to the form suggest that clients might wish to impose a "fitness for purpose" obligation. Although this suggestion is a logical consequence of the treatment of the professional as just another contractor, such an obligation is not generally implied at common law (see section 4.3.1 below) and a professional would be well advised not to take it on unless he is prepared to warrant the outcome of his work, independent of fault.

# 3 LIABILITY GENERALLY

## 3.1 The usual standard of care

It is well established that the law requires of the professional man that he live up to the standard of the ordinary skilled man exercising and professing to have his special skills. McNair J directed the jury in the medical negligence case of *Bolam* v. *Friern Hospital Management Committee*[13] thus:

"[He] need not possess the highest expert skill ... It is enough if he exercises the ordinary skill of an ordinary competent man exercising that particular art."

The test has been applied and approved "time without number"[14] and is acknowledged to be applicable in cases of architects' and engineers' negligence as much as in cases involving negligence of other professionals. The professional man is not liable for errors of judgment, unless the error is such that no reasonably well-informed and competent member of the profession could have made it.[15]

The following are typical statements of the nature of architects' and engineers' obligations:

"It follows that a professional man should command the corpus of knowledge which forms part of the professional equipment of the ordinary member of his profession. He should not lag

---

13. [1957] 1 W.L.R. 582.
14. Bingham LJ in *Eckersley* v. *Binnie* (1988) 18 Con. L.R. 1 at 80.
15. *Saif Ali* v. *Sydney Mitchell & Co.* [1978] 3 All E.R. 1033 at 1043 (Lord Diplock).

behind other ordinarily assiduous and intelligent members of his profession in knowledge of new advances, discoveries and developments in his field. He should have such awareness as an ordinarily competent practitioner would have of the deficiencies in his knowledge and the limitations on his skill. He should be alert to the hazards and risks inherent in any professional task he undertakes to the extent that other ordinary competent members of the profession would be alert. He must bring to any professional task he undertakes no less expertise, skill and care than other ordinarily competent members of his profession would bring, but need bring no more. The standard is that of the reasonable average. The law does not require of a professional man that he be a paragon, combining the qualities of polymath and prophet."[16]

"An architect undertaking any work in the way of his profession accepts the ordinary liabilities of any man who follows a skilled calling. He is bound to exercise due care, skill and diligence. He is not required to have an extraordinary degree of skill or the highest professional attainments. But he must bring to the task he undertakes the competence and skill that is usual among architects practising their profession. And he must use due care."[17]

## 3.2 Circumstances where the standard of care may be lower than normal

It is of course open to parties to agree that, perhaps in return for a reduction in fees, an architect or engineer will carry out his work to a lower standard than would normally be required. However, such an arrangement would be unusual. What is perhaps more common is the issue of whether the parties can by virtue of their actions be said to have *impliedly* agreed a lower standard.

In respect of surveyors, it has been said that the undertaking of a straightforward valuation does not connote a lower standard of care than is applicable for a full survey.[18] However, in *Cotton* v. *Wallis*[19] the Court of Appeal (Denning LJ dissenting) held that the trial judge had not erred in principle in holding that there must be "some tolerance" in assessing the standard of care where a house had been "built down to a price". There it was held that the architect had not been negligent in issuing a final certificate (thus effectively passing as satisfactory certain items of defective work). The principle was followed in *Brown & Brown* v. *Gilbert-Scott & Another*,[20] where the plaintiffs required the defendant architect to design a conservatory on a relatively low budget.

Although these decisions suggest that, in certain factual circumstances, the architect in a low-budget project may avoid a finding of negligence in cases where an architect in a higher value project might be liable, it would be wrong, it is submitted, to regard the value of the project as an item of major significance—otherwise there would be a two-tier standard of care.[21]

Mere agreement by a client to a matter being dealt with at a relatively junior level (within a firm of architects or engineers) is unlikely, without more, to place the firm under a lower standard of care. In such cases, the contract is between the client and

---

16. *Eckersley* v. *Binnie* (1988) 18 Con. L.R. 1 (a case of engineers' negligence).
17. *Voli* v. *Inglewood Shire Council and Lockwood* (1963) 56 Queensland Law Reports 256 (an Australian case where an architect was found liable in tort for negligent design of a stage which collapsed in a meeting at a public hall).
18. *Roberts* v. *Hampson* [1989] 2 All E.R. 504.
19. [1955] 1 W.L.R. 1168.
20. (1992) 35 Con. L.R. 120.
21. *Hudson's Building and Engineering Contracts* (11th edn), noting that the *Cotton* v. *Wallis* decision is "otherwise difficult", argues that the architect was held not liable because he honestly adopted one of two possible interpretations of the contract (para. 2–198 at p. 353).

the firm itself (in whose name invoices will be rendered, for example). It will then be the firm that is under an obligation to carry out work with reasonable care and skill, and that will involve selecting the appropriate members of staff to do the work in question.[22]

### 3.3 Circumstances where the standard of care may be higher than normal

If the standard of care may be lower than normal in certain cases, it would logically follow that it may also, on occasions, be higher. In *Duchess of Argyll* v. *Beuselinck*,[23] a solicitor's negligence action, Megarry J considered the hypothetical position of a client employing a solicitor of high standard and great experience and said:

"If the client engages an expert, and doubtless expects to pay commensurate fees, is he not entitled to expect something more than the standard of the reasonably competent?"

However, Megarry J's obiter suggestion, which he noted might "one day ... require further consideration", has not been taken up subsequently. In particular, in *George Wimpey & Co* v. *DV Poole*[24] Webster J was not inclined to put such a gloss on the "*Bolam*" test. However, he did accept that it is not open to a professional man who *in fact* possesses a particularly high level of knowledge to argue that he should be judged only by reference to that lesser degree of knowledge possessed by the ordinary practitioner.[25]

### 3.4 The liability of the individual within a firm

Professional negligence actions are generally brought against the firm or company responsible for the work, although the performance of the individual architect or engineer actually carrying out the work is of course a vital issue. To what extent, however, is the employee of the firm personally at risk?[26] There are two possibilities, neither of which appears likely in practice to lead to widespread liability of individual employees.

The first is the possibility of a direct action against the employee instead of, or in addition to, an action against the firm. In *Punjab National Bank* v. *De Boinville*[27] such an action was successful. A bank sued Lloyd's underwriters as insurers under policies placed by two individual brokers who had been employed by two Lloyd's broking companies. It was held that the individual brokers owed duties of care in tort to the bank. However, the facts were unusual and will not be easily applied by analogy to

---

22. In *Wilsher* v. *Essex AMA* [1988] A.C. 1074, the Court of Appeal held that the standard of skill and care of medical staff related not to the individuals, but to the level of position within the authority at which the work was carried out. Thus a junior doctor carrying out a consultant's task was to be judged by the standard of the reasonably competent consultant. Where a similar hierarchy exists within an architect's or engineer's firm, the same principles would probably apply.

23. [1972] 2 Lloyd's Rep. 172.

24. (1984) 27 B.L.R. 58.

25. *Ibid.* at 78.

26. The situation where an architect or engineer does not disclose that he is acting as agent for a company or firm (e.g., *Sika Contracts Ltd* v. *BL Gill & Closeglen Properties Ltd* (1978) 9 B.L.R. 11) is a different sort of situation. If the individual in question is a partner in a firm, and is sued as such, he will be entitled to an indemnity from the other partners at the time when the cause of action arose either under the partnership agreement or under the Partnership Act 1890—provided of course that he had the firm's authority to act as its agent.

27. [1992] 1 Lloyd's Rep. 7.

the ordinary case of architects' or engineers' negligence. The bank clearly dealt primarily with the individual brokers, rather than with the firms with whom they happened to be employed at the time, making their proximity to the bank particularly close and justifying the imposition of a duty of care. Staughton LJ said (citing Cross LJ in *Ministry of Housing & Local Government* v. *Sharp* [1970] 1 All ER at 1038):

"It is not every employee of a firm or company providing professional services that owes a personal duty of care to the client; it depends what he is employed to do."

Therefore, it seems likely that only where the client deals almost incidentally with the firm as opposed to the individual, and where the identity of the firm or company is almost irrelevant to the client, is there likely to be any possibility of bringing a direct action against the employee.

The second is the possibility of the employer himself claiming an indemnity against his negligent employee in respect of damages payable. In *Lister* v. *Romford Ice & Cold Storage Co*[28] the House of Lords held that the employers of a lorry driver, for whose negligence they had been held liable, were entitled to be indemnified by the driver on the basis of the driver's breach of an implied term in his contract of employment to use reasonable care and skill while performing his duties. The Civil Liability (Contribution) Act 1978 would allow a similar claim.[29] In practice, however, such claims appear to be rare. Actions against individual uninsured employees would not usually be considered viable; and insurers of employers are perhaps unlikely to wish to be seen as pursuing this kind of action. Indeed, the Association of British Insurers' "gentlemen's agreement" stresses this approach.[30]

## 4 LIABILITY FOR DESIGN

### 4.1 The Construction (Design and Management) Regulations 1994

On 31 March 1995 the Construction (Design and Management) Regulations 1994,[31] commonly referred to as the "CDM" or "Condam" Regulations, came into force.[32] The Regulations give effect to EC Directive 92/57/EEC on the implementation of minimum health and safety requirements on construction sites. These obligations are imposed on clients, contractors, project supervisors and designers. The obligations relating to project supervisors (called "planning supervisors") are contained in regulation 14.

A "designer" is defined in regulations 2(1) as any person who carries on a trade, business or other undertaking, in connection with which he prepares a design relating to a "structure", or arranges for an employee or other person under his control to do so. "Structure" is defined widely under regulation 2(1). It includes roads, railways, tunnels, pipes and cables; temporary items such as scaffold, formwork and falsework; and even certain items of fixed plant (specifically, plant used for work that entails a risk of a person falling more than two metres).

---

28. [1957] A.C. 555.
29. See para. 4.31 below.
30. See *Morris* v. *Ford Motor Co* [1973] 1 Q.B. 792.
31. S.I. 1994/3140, made under the Health and Safety at Work etc. Act 1974.
32. There are transitional provisions for projects begun before that date.

The Regulations *as a whole* apply only to "construction work" (reg. 3). They do not apply to small projects.[33] However, regulation 13, which sets out the obligations of a designer, applies to *all* projects of construction work[34] and architects and engineers will therefore need to consider health and safety aspects of their design.

The obligations imposed on a designer under regulation 13 are broadly threefold:

    (a) to ensure that the design has positive regard for the health and safety of persons carrying out the construction work;

    (b) to ensure that the design contains information regarding any aspect of the project, including materials, that might affect such health and safety;

    (c) to co-operate with the client's "planning supervisor" and any other designer involved.

The sanctions are criminal, and are enforceable by the Health and Safety Executive. Although the Regulations specifically do not confer a right of action in civil proceedings[35] architects and engineers need to consider the possibility of professional negligence actions from the following persons where the design fails to take into account health and safety matters:

    (a) from any person injured on site because of the design that fails to comply with the Regulations (a designer would probably owe a duty of care in tort to such a person);

    (b) from the client (a client, facing a personal injury claim from a construction site worker, might issue third party proceedings claiming a contribution or indemnity from his designer, on the basis that the designer expressly or impliedly promised that his design would comply with the Regulations);

    (c) from the planning supervisor, principal contractor, or others (e.g. sub-contractors, other designers).

Any of the above persons, faced with a similar personal injury claim based on negligence, and in particular the negligent failure to comply with statutory obligations under the Regulations, might issue proceedings under the Civil Liability (Contribution) Act 1978 against the designer on the basis that he was negligent in respect of the same damage as that for which the above person is being sued, and should therefore contribute to it.[36]

---

33. The Regulations do not apply if:
    (a) the largest number of persons carrying out the work at any one time is less than five; and
    (b) the construction phase will not last longer than 30 days or involve more than 500 person-days of construction work; and
    (c) the work does not involve dismantling or demolition of a structure. Since "structure" includes scaffolding—see above—it seems that many small projects will nevertheless be caught by the legislation.
34. Regulation 3(2).
35. Regulation 21.
36. Section 1(1) of the 1978 Act provides that:
    "... Any person liable in respect of any damage suffered by another person may recover contribution from any other person liable in respect of the same damage (whether jointly with him or otherwise)."
Proceedings under the Act can be issued when the putative contributing party is already a party to the proceedings (in which case the contribution notice is served, in the High Court, under R.S.C. Ord. 16, r. 8); and also where he is not (in which case the proceedings are begun by a writ). See section 8.2.2 below.

## 4.2 Delegation or transfer of design duties

### 4.2.1 Generally

Although this section deals with delegation of design duties, it is of course possible, though less usual, for a professional to delegate supervisory or other duties.

A consequence of the increasingly complex nature of modern construction techniques is that often some of the design needs to be carried out by one or more specialists. An employer may retain a number of design consultants to deal with different aspects of the project. Thus while an architect may be responsible for the overall design and (usually) co-ordination of the design team, aspects such as mechanical and electrical works or structural design may be dealt with by specialists. The design responsibility of the various persons on the employer's "team" should be clearly addressed in the contract conditions by which each professional is engaged, failing which there may be gaps leaving the employer potentially without redress against anyone.

Another possibility is for the designer to delegate or sub-contract his duties to someone else. Questions then arise as to whether a designer can delegate and, if he does, whether, and to what extent, he remains liable for the work of the delegate.

It is important to establish what is meant by delegation. There are broadly three ways in which a contractual obligation may be transferred to another party:

(a) *By assignment of a benefit of the contract*
Where A promises B that he will perform certain duties in return for a fee, it may be possible for A to assign his right to the fee, or for B to assign his right to performance, to a third party. Whether such a unilateral right exists depends on a number of factors.[37] In general the benefit of a contract is only assignable in "cases where it can make no difference to the person on whom the obligation lies to which of two persons he is to discharge it".[38]

(b) *By novation of the contract*
A novation, which may be expressed or implied, is an arrangement whereby a contract between A and B is transformed, by way of a three-party agreement, into a contract between A and C. Effectively C steps into B's shoes, with the consent of all parties, and assumes the rights and obligations that B originally had. Novation is discussed further below in the context of construction projects.

(c) *By sub-contracting*
Where B sub-contracts to C an obligation that he owes to A, he continues to remain liable to A for damages for breach of the obligation (in contrast therefore to assignment and novation). However, he may of course have his own remedies against C for breach.

We are principally concerned here with delegation as in type (c).

### 4.2.2 The power to delegate; and obligations of the designer after delegation

#### 4.2.2.1 UNDER THE STANDARD FORMS OF CONTRACT

(i) Under SFA/92 the architect may sub-contract work if the client consents in writing, but the client cannot unreasonably withhold such consent (cl. 1.4.2).

---

37. See *Chitty on Contracts* (27th edn), Volume 1, para. 19–024.
38. *Tolhurst* v. *Associated Portland Cement Manufacturers Ltd* [1902] K.B. 660 at 668.

The architect is not responsible for the work of other "specialists" (cl. 4.2.5), who are defined as designer-suppliers of goods or components. Nor is he responsible for work of consultants (cl. 4.1.7). By virtue of condition 1.3.7 it seems that liability for services sub-contracted is *also* excluded (that clause states that the architect does not warrant the work or products of "others").

(ii) The ACE Conditions allow the engineer to recommend that the client sub-lets any services (the client must not unreasonably withhold consent). The engineer remains responsible for the performance of any sub-contractor (cl. 2.7). The engineer may recommend that the *detailed design* be carried out by a specialist, and again the client cannot unreasonably withhold his consent to this (cl. 2.8). In this case however, the engineer is *not* responsible for the designer's perform-ance. Similarly clause 2.6 excludes liability for design by other consultants.

(iii) The PSC treats assignment and sub-contracting together as "sub-consulting" under clause 24.1. The professional cannot sub-contract without the consent of the employer who can however object on any one of three grounds (broadly, to the effect that the proposed delegate will not be able to perform as well as the professional). However, unlike SFA/92 or the ACE conditions (in part), the *professional* is entirely responsible for the sub-consultant's performance as if he, the professional, had performed himself. This is in line with the PSC's treatment of the professional as just another contractor.

To summarise: all three forms allow sub-contracting with consent, which cannot be unreasonably refused. SFA/92 excludes the architect's liability for the sub-contract-or; the ACE Conditions exclude it only for "detailed design"; the PSA does not exclude such liability at all.

It should be noted that although SFA/92 and the ACE Conditions generally exclude liability for the work of other specialists, the architect or engineer may be negligent if he fails to recommend to the client that the client enter into a direct warranty with that specialist.

## 4.2.2.2 AT COMMON LAW

Whether performance of an obligation can lawfully be sub-contracted depends upon the proper inference to be drawn from the contract itself, the subject-matter of it and other material surrounding circumstances.[39] Some contractual obligations are personal and must be performed by the party who has contracted to perform them and nobody else.[40] In *Southway Group Ltd* v. *Wolff & Wolff*[41] Bingham LJ said:

"In some classes of contract, as where B commissions A to write a book or paint a picture or teach him to play the violin, it would usually be clear that personal performance by A was required. In other cases, as where A undertakes to repair B's shoes, or mend B's watch or drive B to the airport, it may be open to A to perform the contract vicariously by employing the services of C."

Save in the rare cases where a contractual obligation consists of merely fulfilling a functional role that might be carried out by almost anyone, the obligations of a

39. *Davies* v. *Collins* [1945] 1 All E.R. 247 at 250, C.A.
40. Staughton LJ in *Linden Gardens Trust Ltd* v. *Lenesta Sludge Disposals Ltd* (1992) 57 B.L.R. 57 at 81. The case subsequently went to the House of Lords, but Staughton LJ's point was unaffected.
41. (1991) 57 B.L.R. 33 at 52.

designer have more in common with Bingham LJ's first category of contracts than with his second. Thus it will rarely be that a designer can unilaterally delegate all, or most, of his obligations.[42]

However, where an architect or engineer seeks to argue for the right to delegate a particular *part* of his obligations—perhaps of a small, but specialised area—the position is less clear cut. The two cases most usually cited are *Moresk Cleaners Ltd* v. *Thomas Henwood Hicks*[43] and *Merton London Borough Council* v. *Lowe*.[44]

### The Moresk case

*Facts*
The plaintiff employed the defendant architect to design an extension for a laundry. Unknown to the plaintiff, the architect invited the main contractor, with whom he was acquainted, to design the structure. The design was defective, in that the purlins were too weak to support the roof; and the portal frames, which should have been tied together, had spread, causing them to come apart from the cladding.

The judge held that there was no implied term in the contract giving the architect the power to delegate the design duty at all, and certainly not to the contractor whose interests were "entirely opposed" to those of the plaintiff. He also rejected a further argument that the architect had implied authority to act as the plaintiff's agent in employing the contractor to carry out his design.[45]

### The Merton LBC case

*Facts*
The defendant architects were retained to design a swimming pool and to supervise its erection. Their design incorporated the use of Pyrok, a material used in the suspended ceilings. This was a proprietary product produced by Pyrok Ltd who became nominated sub-contractors. The ceilings later developed cracks because the mix used in the Pyrok coat was stronger than that used in the underlying coat; and also because of poor workmanship.

The architects were held not liable for the design error, even though it had undoubtedly been their obligation to design the pool (in fact they were held liable on other grounds, namely failure to supervise). Waller LJ entirely agreed with the judge in *Moresk* but saw it as clearly distinguishable[46]:

"There the architect had virtually handed over to another the whole task of design. The architect could not escape responsibility for the work which he was supposed to do by handing it over to another.

42. This does not mean that an architect's firm cannot have someone other than the person who took the instructions from the client actually carry out at least some of the work. Mundane work on a project may be carried out by a junior member of staff, but this does not amount to sub-contracting.
43. (1966) 4 B.L.R. 50.
44. (1981) 18 B.L.R. 130, C.A.
45. The Official Referee went on to say that if the architect had felt out of his depth in dealing with the form of reinforced concrete construction that was, in technical terms, relatively new at the time of this case, he might pay for a structural engineer himself to carry out that work. In view of the personal nature of an architect's retainer in such cases, it is questionable whether this is correct.
46. 18 B.L.R. at 148.

This case was different. Pyrok were nominated sub-contractors employed for a specialised task of making a ceiling with their own proprietary material. It was the defendants' duty to use reasonable care as architects. In view of successful work done elsewhere [it was reasonable to employ Pyrok]."

*Summary of the common law position*  Read together, the two cases, coupled with the cases referred to previously, appear to suggest that the position is as follows:

(i) An architect or engineer cannot delegate any major area of the design where that area is one that the employer reasonably expects him to perform personally.

However,

(ii) In certain circumstances, the architect's or engineer's contract may be construed as to allow him to discharge his design obligations (relating to a particular, specialised area) by reasonably choosing a particular skilled specialist to carry out that work.
It is submitted that a court will be less likely to adopt this analysis where it would leave the employer without a remedy against a specialist designer.[47]

It is always important to distinguish the two questions:

(a) Has the designer the contractual power to have someone other than himself personally carry out the work? (In *Moresk*, the answer was no.)
(b) If he has, is he still liable to the employer for the delegate's breach (sub-contracting); or was his contractual obligation such that merely exercising a reasonable choice of delegate discharges him of his obligations (as in *Merton*)?

*Novation*  There may be cases where the court will hold that a novation has taken place, e.g., where, part-way through a design, the architect explains to his employer that a particular aspect of the design is proving difficult, that he requires a specialist, and where the employer then enters into a direct arrangement with a third party specialist.

Finally, it is not uncommon for employers on "design and build" projects to have an arrangement whereby the employer instructs his own design consultants to carry out certain work, after which, by novation, the design and build contractor takes on the future obligations, and indeed even the accrued design liabilities of the consultants, as part of the "package". The architect or engineer who is the consultant in such an arrangement should consider the contractual position with care, in particular whether he is relieved of his obligations to the employer.[48]

47. In *Merton* the remedy was presumably available. The designer, Pyrok Ltd, was a sub-contractor nominated under the main contract, a JCT 1963 standard form, and would therefore normally enter into a direct warranty with the employer, although the report does not make specific mention of this and the point does not appear to have been a material consideration for the court. See generally on the reconciliation of these two cases, *Hudson's Building and Engineering Contracts* (11th edn), Volume 1, para. 2–119 at p. 304.
48. See P McNicholas, "Novation of Consultants to Design Build Contractors" (1993) 9 Const. L.J. 263.

## 4.3 Design obligations and fitness for purpose

### 4.3.1 The general rule

At common law a supplier of goods impliedly promises:

— that his goods are of satisfactory quality[49];
— that his goods are reasonably fit for any intended purpose expressly or impliedly made known to him by the buyer.[50]

Similar warranties are implied at common law in the case of a building contractor regarding the goods that he supplies.[51] This is so, even though a building contract is one for the provision of work and materials, not materials alone, so that the sale of goods legislation itself does not directly apply.[52] However, it is reasonably well established that the designer, indeed the professional in general, who performs services (rather than supplies goods), has the duty only to use reasonable care and skill and does not have to comply with the higher fitness for purpose obligation (as it is sometimes alternatively put, he is not under an obligation to achieve a particular result).[53]

The distinction is important for practical purposes. It means that where, for example, an employer has commissioned a design of an office building, which is then found to suffer from condensation; or a bridge which is unusable without reinforcement to take the load of heavy traffic intended for it; the employer cannot simply point to the failure as establishing a breach of the designer's contract—he must still show a failure to use reasonable care and skill and will usually need to call expert evidence to do so.[54]

### 4.3.2 Where might a fitness for purpose obligation apply?

There appear to be three possible areas:

(1) Where the designer not only designs but also supplies the item: In *Samuels* v. *Davis*[55] the Court of Appeal held that where a dentist (i.e., a professional) undertakes to make a denture for a patient, he impliedly promises that the denture will be fit for its intended purpose, even though the dentist removing a tooth is only bound to perform with care and skill and does not warrant a particular result. The distinction was endorsed in *Independent Broadcasting Authority* v. *EMI Electronics Ltd and BICC Construction Ltd*.[56] That case followed the collapse on Emley Moor in Yorkshire of a 1,250-foot high television aerial mast constructed by EMI as main contractor for IBA, and designed by EMI's nominated sub-contractors, BICC. The House of Lords held that BICC had been negligent in their design, and since a duty of

---

49. Sale of Goods Act 1979, s. 14(2), as amended by the Sale and Supply of Goods Act 1994, s. 1.
50. Sale of Goods Act 1979, s. 14(3), as amended by the Sale and Supply of Goods Act 1994, Sch. 2, para. 5. The promises as to satisfactory quality and fitness for purpose are now implied terms, not necessarily conditions, by virtue of amendments made to the Sale of Goods Act 1979 by the 1994 Act.
51. *Young & Marten Ltd* v. *McManus Childs Ltd* (1968) 9 B.L.R. 77.
52. *Dawber-Williamson* v. *Humberside County Council* (1979) 14 B.L.R. 70 at 77.
53. See section 3 above.
54. See section 9 below.
55. [1943] K.B. 526.
56. (1980) 14 B.L.R. 1.

care was admitted, there was no need to consider the contractual aspects. However, Lord Scarman, obiter, approved the words of du Parcq LJ in *Samuels* and added[57]:

"I see no reason why one who in the course of his business contracts to design, supply and erect a television aerial mast is not under an obligation to ensure that it is reasonably fit for the purpose for which he knows it is intended to be used ... However I do not accept that the design and obligation of the supplier of an article is to be equated with the obligation of a professional man in the practice of his profession."

(2) In certain "design and build" or joint venture projects: In *Consultants Group International* v. *John Worman Ltd*[58] the position was as follows:

*Facts*
Worman were engaged as building contractors to renovate an abattoir for Turner. Worman engaged architects, CGI, to provide design services. The assumed facts were that the work, as designed, failed to comply with the relevant UK EC standards that would have otherwise enabled the employer to receive the benefit of certain EC grants. Judge Davies QC construed the building contract as putting Worman under an obligation to ensure that the works achieved the necessary standard. Further, the architects, CGI, were under a similar obligation to Worman. This was because they were the "prime movers" in the project from start to finish; they were not retained by the contractor to provide architectural services in the usual way—rather, the relationship was "a joint venture" with the architects as project manager; and the contract relied on the architects' skill and professional expertise. These circumstances therefore justified the imposition of the higher obligation.

It may be noted that the standard form of "design and build" contract JCT 81 "With Contractor's Design" defines the contractor's design obligations by reference to the usual professional criterion (he has "the like liability ... as would an architect or ... other appropriate professional designer ..." who designs without supplying— cl. 2.5). However, since the employer in this contract may require specific performance criteria to be achieved in the "Employer's Requirements", it is possible that the contractor may sometimes be under the higher fitness for purpose obligation.

(3) Where the evidence indicates that, unusually, the professional has agreed to achieve a result, as in *Greaves (Contractors) Ltd* v. *Baynham Meikle & Partners*[59]:

*Facts*
Baynham Meikle were structural engineers employed by a design and build contractor to design a structure of a warehouse. The trial judge found that the warehouse floors were not designed with sufficient strength to withstand the vibrations produced by fork-lift trucks carrying oil drums, as intended. In the Court of appeal, Lord Denning began by noting that the surgeon does not promise to cure his patient, or the solicitor to win his client's case. However, there were two reasons for imposing an obligation on the engineer to ensure that the design allowed for the load in question:
 (i) in cross-examination, the engineer had admitted that "it was his job" to produce a building that would be fit to be used to store oil drums, and for use by stacker-trucks;
(ii) in its pleading, the engineer had originally admitted the existence of a fitness for purpose criterion, but had been given leave on the second day of the trial to amend so as to withdraw the concession. The fact that the term had been initially accepted was held to be evidence of the fact that it was indeed a term of the contract.

It is submitted that the case is not authority for imposing a fitness for purpose

57. 14 B.L.R. at 47.
58. (1985) 9 Con. L.R. 46.
59. (1975) 4 B.L.R. 56, C.A.

obligation on designers in general. The two factors above were clearly all-important and will not be present in most cases. Geoffrey Lane LJ in the Court of Appeal saw the case as deciding "no great issue of principle".

### 4.3.3 The orthodox view illustrated

*George Hawkins* v. *Chrysler (UK) Ltd*[60] exemplifies the general rule:

Facts
A foundry worker sued his employer, Chrysler, when he slipped and fell on a shower room floor. Chrysler joined as a third party the engineer who had designed the floor. The trial judge found that the engineer's decision to use a type of flooring called "Altro Standard" was wrong, but not negligent, since the engineer had, inter alia, considered various alternatives, taken specialist advice from a flooring firm and tested the floor himself. However, the trial judge held that the engineer had also *warranted* the floor's safety, and it was on this issue that the Court of Appeal had to rule.

In overturning the trial judge's decision, the court rejected two of Chrysler's arguments, both of which bear examination. The first was that it was anomalous that a contractor who designs and constructs the building should be under a higher obligation *in respect of his design obligations* than the architect who merely designs it. Nourse LJ acknowledged the anomaly but held that it was established in law. The distinction has been defended on the grounds that a designer who also supplies material (e.g., the design and build contractor) is under unavoidable competitive pressures to "design down" to a price, and thus save costs by aiming for only minimum standards of quality and durability; whereas a professional (whose percentage fee indeed would usually *increase* in line with the cost of the work) is under no such pressures; so that the employer is entitled to the added protection in the former case.[61]

The second was that the engineer had been asked in cross-examination:

"It was your job to produce a floor that was safe in [those] circumstances?"

And had answered:

"As safe as I possibly could, yes."

Dillon LJ dismissed the significance of this:

"It seems to me that that is the sort of answer which might be given by any professional man.
  'Q: It was your job to provide medicines which would cure the patient's illness?
  A: Insofar as I possibly could, yes.
  Q: It was your job to provide a tax avoidance scheme which would save your client an enormous amount of tax?
  A: Insofar as I possibly could, yes.'
The answer indicates the objective which the professional man would have in advising—what he would be hoping to achieve—but I cannot think that it is, just by itself, enough to extend his obligation, from an obligation to use reasonable care and skill in his profession, to a guarantee that his advice would be successful if any advice could be successful."

However, it may be noted that the answer given in cross-examination by the defendant in *Greaves*, which proved fatal to his case, was not very different from that

---

60. (1986) 38 B.L.R. 36, C.A.
61. *Hudson's Building and Engineering Contracts* (11th edn), Volume 1, para. 2–105 at p. 296.

given by the engineer in *Hawkins*,[62] as was indeed acknowledged by the Court of Appeal in *Hawkins*[63]—thus suggesting further that *Greaves* should perhaps be limited to its own facts.

## 4.4 Design obligations: miscellaneous aspects

### 4.4.1 The scope of the architect's/engineer's responsibilities

Where an employer retains a team of consultants on a project, the architect is often recognised as being the "lead" consultant, since, traditionally, it is he who is responsible for the overall design, co-ordination and supervision of construction of the work.[64] It is particularly important therefore that an architect establishes the limits of his design (and other) responsibilities, since he may otherwise be held to have taken on wide-ranging duties, because of the nature of his position and the reliance and the trust that the employer often places in him. *Richard Roberts Holdings Ltd* v. *Douglas Smith Stimson Partnership*[65] is a striking illustration of this:

*Facts*
The plaintiff retained the defendant to design an effluent tank for use in a dye works. Both parties knew that the tank would need to be lined. The architects' design assumed that this would be with stainless steel. Discussions then followed between the plaintiff and the defendant's representatives regarding the choice of lining. The parties jointly investigated a number of possible firms to supply the lining including ECC, also defendants in the action. At the plaintiff's suggestion, the architects asked ECC to quote. Their quotation was accepted after the architects had confirmed to the plaintiff that they felt that the plaintiff's outstanding queries had been answered. The plaintiff then entered into a direct contract with ECC. Subsequently large areas of the lining became detached causing erosion of the concrete walls.

The architects pointed to the following facts:
    (i) they had charged no fee for their work in relation to the choice of linings;
   (ii) the plaintiff was aware that they had no knowledge of linings;
  (iii) the plaintiff had taken independent advice from a trade association about linings[66];
  (iv) the input regarding the linings had primarily been directed to helping the plaintiff to perform its part in the project.

Nonetheless, his Honour Judge Newey QC held that the architects' duty extended to the lining, on the basis that they were employed as architects for the creation of the *whole* dye works, and that the lining was an integral part of the tank. The architects

---

62. In *Greaves* the cross-examination was as follows:
   "**Q**: And it was your job, was it not, to produce a building which was going to be fit to be used as a store for oil drums and for stacker-truck use?
   **A**: Yes.
   **Q**: That was what you were being engaged to do and that is what you were being paid your fee for?
   **A**: Correct."
63. (1986) 38 B.L.R. 36 at 48 *per* Fox LJ.
64. Although the trend in recent years towards design and build contracting has operated to diminish the architect's traditional position of pre-eminence.
65. (1988) 46 B.L.R. 50.
66. In itself a prudent, though not necessarily sufficient, step to take. In *George Hawkins* (above), one of the factors contributing to the Court of Appeal's decision that an engineer designing a shower floor was not negligent was that he had taken advice from specialist flooring firms. On the other hand, in *Nye Saunders & Partners* v. *Bristow* (1987) 37 B.L.R. 92, C.A., the architect was held not to have discharged his obligation to provide cost advice, despite consulting a quantity surveyor.

were in breach of their duty: first, in failing to investigate alternative linings when they initially designed the tank; secondly, when they failed to seek independent advice from specialists or trade associations regarding the linings; and because they failed to heed certain "alarm bells" such as a "suspiciously cheap" quotation from the supplier, ECC. As between ECC and the architect, the judge held them both equally to blame.

### 4.4.2 Liability for areas outside architecture and engineering

*Holland Hannen & Cubitts (North) Ltd* v. *Welsh Health Technical Services Organisation*[67] illustrates a more restrictive interpretation of a designer's remit. The case was a complex multi-party action. The ratio of the Court of Appeal decision is not easy to establish, because of the different reasons given by the three Lords Justices, one of whom dissented in part:

*Facts*
WHTSO engaged Cubitts to construct two new hospitals at Rhyl and Gurnos in Wales. CED were nominated sub-contractors for the design of the floor. They in turn instructed Alan Marshall & Partners (AMP), structural engineers, to assist in the design. The floors suffered from some deflection, although they were usable. The employer's architects, Percy Thomas Partnership (PTP) amended the specification midway through the design stage. The floors then failed to comply with the amended specification. PTP then condemned the floors. Cubitts, whose work was thus delayed for some 20 weeks, sued WHTSO for its delay-related losses, and other parties were then brought into the action. On the 85th day of the trial, a compromise was reached whereby CED, PTP and WHTSO's own structural engineering consultants, Wallace Evans & Partners (WEP), agreed to pay Cubitts £396,681 for the delay attributable to the floor matters.

The trial judge held that:

(a) CED should pay two-thirds of Cubitts' losses, and PTP and WEP one-third between them;
(b) AMP should contribute 75 per cent of what CED had to pay.

However, the Court of Appeal held that:

(a) CED should pay only one-third of Cubitts' losses, and PTP and WEP the other two-thirds. The Court of Appeal as a whole held that the judge had failed sufficiently to take into account—except in his apportionment between PTP and WEP inter se—PTP's failure to grapple with the floor problem earlier;
(b) AMP were not negligent at all (Robert Goff LJ dissenting).

CED were held one-third liable because (per Lawton LJ) they produced floors which "visually looked wrong" and (per Robert Goff LJ, not dissenting on this point) the floors were unserviceable and CED should have properly considered their profile.

Whether AMP as structural engineers were liable to CED then depended on whether they had a duty to consider the visual and aesthetic aspects of the floor so as to warn their clients, CED, of the likely appearance after tiles were laid. Dillon LJ said:

67. (1985) 35 B.L.R. 1, C.A.

"Matters of visual appearance or aesthetic effect are matters for the architect and are not within the province of the structural engineer. It is for the structural engineer to work out what the deflections of a floor will be; it is for the architect to decide whether a floor with those deflections will be visually or aesthetically satisfactory when the finishes chosen by the architect have been applied."

Lawton LJ assessed AMP's duties partly by reference to the obligations that they had taken on when working previously with CED in patenting a different type of floor. He held that then, and in this case, AMP's responsibility as advisers ended with the putting down of the screed finish, and that what happened afterwards was a matter for the employer and his architect:

"AMP, when advising as consultant structural engineers on the floors designed by CED were under no duty to consider what they would look like when the vinyl tiles were laid."

Robert Goff LJ in a powerful and reasoned dissent, however, disagreed:

"I accept the proposition that finishes are a matter for the architect, and that in this sense the visual appearance of the structure is a matter for the architect and not for the structural engineer. But it does not follow that structural engineers are not concerned at all with visual appearance. A structural engineer is obviously concerned with the strength and stability of the structure; but is also considered with the configuration of the structure which the relevant design may produce, with regard not only to its function but also to its appearance."

Nevertheless, the case is clearly Court of Appeal authority for the following propositions:

(a) that in circumstances a structural engineer need not be concerned with visual appearance or aesthetics; and,

(b) more generally, that a professional is not liable for matters outside his own sphere of expertise, particularly where the client has retained another professional to deal with that area.

### 4.4.3 Duty to reconsider or revise design

It seems fairly clear both as a matter of principle and on authority[68] that a designer has a duty to reconsider or revise his design which continues at least until his design obligations are complete. An example of failure to reappraise is *Hubert Leach & Another* v. *Norman Crossley & Partners*.[69] There, a structural engineer produced a design for a car deck on a warehouse roof. He was held to be negligent in failing to reappraise his loading figures after becoming aware of facts that should have alerted him to the point that his client intended to use a heavier material on the roof than that for which the design had originally been made.

It also seems clear that, where the architect has supervisory or other duties, this obligation continues into the construction phase. The following words of Sachs LJ in *Brickfield Properties Ltd* v. *Newton*[70] have often been adopted:

"The architect is under a continuing duty[71] to check that his design will work in practice and to

---

68. *London Borough of Merton* v. *Lowe* 18 B.L.R. 130 at 132.
69. (1984) 8 Con. L.R. 7, C.A.
70. [1971] 1 W.L.R. 862 at 873.
71. *A fortiori, per* Sachs LJ, where the design is "experimental" or requires amplification as the construction progresses.

correct any errors which may emerge. It savours of the ridiculous for the architect to be able to say, as it was here suggested, that he could say: 'True my design was faulty, but of course I saw to it that the contractors followed it faithfully'."[72]

### 4.4.3.1 THE LENGTH OF THE CONTINUING DUTY

For how long does this duty last? In *Chelmsford District Council* v. *Evers*[73] his Honour Judge Smout QC regarded it as lasting "until the works are completed". In *Equitable Debenture Assets Corporation Ltd* v. *William Moss & Others*[74] and *Victoria University of Manchester* v. *Hugh Wilson*,[75] his Honour Judge Newey QC said that it lasted until practical completion, though in the latter case was prepared, without deciding the point, to consider that it might last longer. The reasoning behind the imposition of a continuing obligation in the construction phase, as exemplified in the words of Sachs LJ above, is that the architect is able, during this phase, to assess the workability and practicability of his design.[76] The reasoning applies with less force during the defects liability, or maintenance, period where the only work that is, or should be, being carried out is the making good of defects appearing after practical completion.

Although there is no clear authority on the point, it seems unlikely that the duties of the designer who is also a supervisor continue after his contractual obligations have otherwise ceased entirely, e.g., upon the issue of any final certificate required by the contract.[77] In *Eckersley* v. *Binnie*,[78] a fatal explosion in 1984 at Abbeystead Pumping Station in Lancashire was found to have been caused by the engineer's negligence in failing to foresee, at design stage, the possibility of a dangerous accumulation of methane gas in a tunnel and valve house. The trial judge had caused some consternation amongst insurers[79] in suggesting that the engineers were "to some slight degree negligent" in not keeping abreast with, and passing on to the current owners, developing knowledge about methane in the 4½ years between the completion of the project and the date of the explosion. Bingham LJ[80] said:

"It has never, to my knowledge, been held that a professional man who advises on a tax scheme, or on draft trading conditions, is thereafter bound to advise his client if, within a period of years, the statutory provisions or the relevant authorities change."

72. Applied by Judge Stabb QC at first instance in *London Borough of Merton* v. *Lowe* (1981) 18 B.L.R. 130 at 132; by Judge Newey QC in *Chelmsford DC* v. *Evers* (1985) 25 B.L.R. 99 at 106; and by Judge Newey QC again in *EDAC* v. *Moss* (1984) 2 Con. L.R. 1 at 24. In the latter case, his Honour Judge Newey QC said that the architect had "both the right and the duty to check their design as work proceeded and to correct it if necessary". (The B.L.R. report suggests that the judge in the *Chelmsford* case was Judge Smout QC, contrary to Judge Newey's own reference to the case as his own in *EDAC* v. *Moss*. The case is also reported (with the correct judge noted) at (1984) Const. L.J. 1).
73. (1985) 25 B.L.R. 99 at 106.
74. (1984) 2 Con. L.R. 1 at 24.
75. (1984) 2 Con. L.R. 43 at 73.
76. In *Brickfield* the court regarded the design and its workability as very much intermingled. See also *EDAC* v. *Moss* (1984) 2 Con. L.R. 1 dealt with at section 4.4.6 below.
77. In practice, the process of issuing the final certificate, and indeed dealing with other contractual formalities required after the end of the defects liability period, is frequently not carried out, for one reason or another, leaving open the possible argument to the employer that the obligation to review design continues *pro tem*.
78. (1988) 18 Con. L.R. 1.
79. *Per* Bingham LJ at 146.
80. Bingham LJ was in a minority in holding the engineers not negligent. However, this does not affect his words on the issue of continuing design obligation.

However, Bingham LJ felt that there were "persuasive examples" involving dangers to life and health where "some response by a professional man might well be called for".

It is submitted that even in cases involving danger to life and health, it will be difficult to imply any form of continuing obligation to warn or advise, in the absence of particular wording in the contract suggesting such an obligation. Although it might seem reasonable to hold a professional liable in cases where he becomes aware of such matters after termination of his retainer, such a step would be dangerously close to imposing liability for omissions rather than acts, something which English law has so far resisted.[81]

### 4.4.4. Duties in relation to recommending others

An architect may be liable for recommending a builder who subsequently carries on defective work. Such was the case in *Pratt* v. *Swanmore Builders*.[82] Architects and engineers should bear in mind that they may owe such duties to persons other than those with whom they have a contractual relationship (e.g., if they recommend a specialist sub-contractor or supplier to another contractor) under the doctrine of negligent mis-statement in *Hedley Byrne*. It may also be part of an architect's duty to his client to check the financial status of the contractor, for example, by obtaining a bank or trade credit reference or carrying out a company search.[82a]

In *EDAC* v. *Moss*[83] an architect was held liable for failing to make sufficient inquiries at tender stage of a nominated sub-contractor responsible for the installation of curtain walling. Further inquiries in respect of their "somewhat superficial tender" would have revealed that they had been in business for a short time only and that their claim to have had experience of a project similar to the one in question was misleading. In *Richard Robert Holdings* v. *Douglas Smith Stimson Partnership* (above), the architect was negligent for his input in the selection of suppliers of a lining for an effluent tank, in particular regarding their quotation which was "not only suspiciously cheap but obviously not properly considered".

### 4.4.5 Duties to warn regarding design (or similar) work carried out by others[84]

The standard forms, predictably, do not impose any duty to warn of others' shortcomings, and in view of the express disclaimers[85] relating to the work of others, it might be thought that none would be implied. However, the decision of the Court of Appeal in *Investors in Industry* v. *South Bedfordshire District Council*[86] suggests otherwise. The court considered a predecessor of SFA/92 which stated:

---

81. The act/omission distinction is re-emphasised in, for example, *Yuen Kun-Yeu* v. *Attorney General of Hong Kong* [1988] A.C. 175 at 192. However, there have been recent suggestions by the House of Lords that the distinction may not operate with the same force in the field of *Hedley Byrne* liability—see section 6.1 below.

82. (1987) 38 B.L.R. 25, C.A.

82a. *Partridge* v. *Morris* (1995) Construction Industry Law Letter 1095.

83. (1989) 2 Con. L.R. 1 at 26.

84. Duties in relation to construction work carried out by others are dealt with in section 5.5 below.

85. SFA/92 cll. 1.3.7, 4.1.7 and 4.2.5. ACE Conditions cll. 2.6 and 2.8. Under the PSC, the professional is responsible for his "sub-consultant" under cl. 24.1.

86. (1985) 32 B.L.R. 1 at 37.

"The architect will advise on the need for independent consultants and will be responsible for the direction and integration of their work but not for their detailed design, inspection and performance of the work entrusted to them."

Slade LJ, holding that the conditions clearly contemplated that an architect might recommend a specialist to his client, where the work in question was outside his own area of expertise, continued:

"If following such a recommendation a consultant with these qualifications is appointed, the architect will normally carry no legal responsibility for the work to be done by the expert which is beyond the capability of an architect of ordinary competence; in relation to the work allotted to the expert, the architect's legal responsibility will normally be confined to directing and co-ordinating the expert's work in the whole. However, this is subject to one important qualification. If any danger or problem arises in connection with the work allotted to the expert, of which an architect of ordinary competence reasonably ought to be aware and reasonably could be expected to warn the client ... the duty of the architect [is] to warn the client. In such a contingency he is not entitled to rely blindly on the expert ..."

Slade LJ was considering the situation where a "lead" designer arranges for a specialist professional to carry out part of the overall design. The obligations will be less onerous, it is submitted, where what is being considered is the liability of a professional who simply happens to be working alongside another. In such a case, the Court of Appeal majority decision in *Holland Hannen & Cubitts* v. *WHTSO* referred to earlier[87] (to the effect that a designer does not generally have responsibility outside his area of expertise), is likely to be of greater relevance, as is the decision in *Kensington and Chelsea and Westminster AHA* v. *Wettern Composites*[88] (albeit in relation to the construction period—see section 5.5 below).

It may be noted that in the above type of situation, the designer who is found to be in breach for failing to warn of another professional's error will usually be entitled to a contribution (towards his liability to the employer), often amounting to a full indemnity, from that other professional under the Civil Liability (Contribution) Act 1978.

### 4.4.6 Obligations to consider the practicability of the design

An architect or engineer must consider the practicality of his design in the context of the actual work that will be carried out on site. In *EDAC* v. *Moss*[89] his Honour Judge Newey QC held that the designer in that case was under an obligation to ensure that the work could be performed by those likely to be employed to do it, and had to take into account foreseeable conditions such as windiness, the fact that scaffolding would be needed, the fact that exceptional skill was required on site etc., and that if these were not considered properly, then the design would lack "buildability". He continued:

"Similarly, I think that if a design requires work to be carried out on site in such a way that those whose duty it is to supervise it and/or check that it has been done will encounter great difficulty in doing so, then the design will again be defective. It may perhaps be described as lacking 'supervisability'."

On the facts of the case:

87. See section 4.4.2 above.
88. (1984) 31 B.L.R. 57.
89. (1989) 2 Con. L.R. 1.

(a) as to buildability, the design of curtain walling on a "front sealed" principle dependent upon total exclusion of water (rather than on a rain screed principle which allows water to pass through an outer skim before draining away) was not flawed *per se*, but in the circumstances was inappropriate because the "ordinary fitters" who would be fitting it in a high and exposed location, would inevitably experience difficulty in applying the required sealant. The architect was therefore negligent;

(b) as to supervisability however, the application of sealant was supervisable, provided that the supervisor had "determination and persistence". There was therefore no negligence regarding this aspect.

The extent of the architect's and engineer's liability vis-à-vis the *contractor* is discussed in section 6.2 below.

### 4.4.7 Innovative design

In the case of the novel or untried design, the law appears to accept that there is a need to balance two principles. The first is that without experimentation, technical progress is not possible. Erle J directed the jury in *Turner* v. *Garland & Christopher*[90] in these terms:

"If you employ [an architect] about a novel thing about which he has had little experience, if it has not had the test of experience, failure may be consistent with skills. The history of all great improvements shows failure of those who embark in them."

The second is that particular care should be taken with innovative design. This is illustrated by the case of *IBA* v. *EMI & BICC*[91] which followed the collapse of a cylindrical television mast nearly one-quarter of a mile high but only nine feet wide in diameter at its base at Emley Moor in Yorkshire. The cause was found to be vortex shedding[92] and asymmetric ice loading on the stays. As to the latter, the designers had assumed that ice forming on the stays would crack and fall away as the stays were shaken by the wind. Lord Dilhorne held that, particularly when one considered the prospect of vortex shedding, it was negligent to make such an assumption "with regard to a design which was at and beyond the frontiers of professional knowledge". It was no answer to say that the conjunction of these two phenomena had not been previously considered. Lord Edmund-Davies added, "The law requires even pioneers to be prudent" and noted that in some circumstances, the pioneer should be prepared to consider the abandonment of the project.

It seems that the innovative designer, more than any other designer, must ensure that his client is particularly well aware of the position. In *Victoria University of Manchester* v. *Hugh Wilson*[93] the architect adopted what in the 1960s was an innovative cladding design for a university building involving the use of brick and ceramic tiles. Judge Newey QC noted that although it was not wrong in itself to use

90. 1853. Apparently unreported, but noted in *Hudson's Building and Engineering Contracts* (11th edn) at para. 2–099. Erle J's words were cited by Lord Edmund-Davies in *Independent Broadcasting Authority* v. *EMI Electronics Ltd & BICC Construction Ltd* (1980) 14 B.L.R. 1. See section 4.3.2 above.

91. (1980) 14 B.L.R. 1.

92. A phenomenon affecting cylindrical masts and chimneys and described by Lord Dilhorne at p. 12. In brief, as air flows around the cylinder, vortices are formed on both sides. These detach, alternately inducing forces on the cylinder which can cause dangerous oscillation.

93. (1984) 2 Con. L.R. 43.

untried materials or techniques (otherwise progress could never be made) the architect who was venturing into the "untried or little tried" should firstly warn his clients specifically of what he was doing and secondly obtain their express approval.

### 4.4.8 Judging by the standards of the time

In *Eckersley* v. *Binnie*,[94] Bingham LJ stated:

"In deciding whether a professional man has fallen short of the standards observed by ordinarily skilled and competent members of his profession, it is the standards prevailing at the time of his acts or omissions which provide the relevant yard stick. He is not, as the judge in this case correctly observed, to be judged by the wisdom of hindsight. This of course means that knowledge of an event which happened later should not be applied when judging acts and omissions which took place before that event ..."

Similar *dicta* appear elsewhere.[95] An application of this principle may be seen in *Imperial College of Science and Technology* v. *Norman & Dawbarn (a firm)*.[96] Architects designing in the mid-1950s did not warn their client that ceramic tiles to be used as cladding were unlikely to last more than 60 years, but were held by Judge Smout QC not to have been negligent, since the "state of the art" as indicated by articles in the RIBA journal of 1955, was that such tiling provided "excellent cladding" and that there was no reason to consider that it was of relatively short lifespan.

The principle has also been held to apply to other professionals such as surveyors.[97] It will be of particular importance as a possible defence for any designer, including innovative designers, working in a fast changing field.

### 4.4.9 Advising a client on a form of contract to be used for construction

Architects and engineers will often advise the client on the appropriate form of contract for the construction period. In a project of any size, the architect or engineer is likely to recommend one of the standard JCT forms for construction projects, or ICE forms for civil engineering projects. It has been suggested in *Hudson's Building and Engineering Contract* (11th edn) (para. 2–167 *et seq.*) that a legal adviser cannot properly recommend his client to use *any* of the current JCT or ICE forms without amendment, although it is noted in that commentary that the architect or engineer might plausibly defend himself at least to some degree on the ground that his own professional bodies have approved or sanctioned the use of these forms. The commentary contains lists of the main matters which an architect or engineer should draw to his client's attention. There appears, however, to be little or no authority on the issues.[98] Clearly, cases of alleged failure to advise of consequential loss will depend very much on their facts.

94. (1988) 18 Con. L.R. 1. See section 4.4.3 above.
95. E.g., *George Wimpey & Co* v. *DV Poole* (1984) 27 B.L.R. 58 at 78 *per* Webster J.
96. (1986) 2 Const. L.J. 280.
97. E.g., in *Last* v. *Post* (1952) 159 E.G. 240, where a surveyor was not negligent in failing to consider the possibility of disintegration of roof tiles through efflorescence, described at that time as a "rare phenomenon".
98. In *Corfield* v. *Grant* (1992) 59 B.L.R. 102, one of 28 pleaded allegations of negligence against the architect was that he had recommended a JCT Minor Works Form for a contract where the contract sum was slightly in excess of the figure suggested by the JCT in its Guidance Notes (p. 126). Rejecting the allegation, Judge Bowsher QC noted, *inter alia*, that recommendations of the JCT have to be taken "with a pinch of salt" because of the conflicting interests of those represented on it.

## 4.4.10 Provision of estimates and the need to qualify advice

### 4.4.10.1 COST ESTIMATES

Clients will generally require their architect or engineer to give them some indication of the prospective cost of a project before proceeding. An overrun on the original contract sum will not in itself be evidence of any negligence on the part of the designer, unless the designer can be held to have *warranted* that the work could be carried out for the sum, which will hardly ever be the case. In particular, it should be remembered that in most construction and engineering contracts, even those of the "lump sum" or "fixed price" variety (as opposed to remeasurement contracts, where the contractor's payment is based on the quantity of work actually carried out) the contract sum will fall to be adjusted during the contract for such matters as variations and events that caused delay to the contractor's regular progress.[99] The architect or engineer who does make his client aware of this, particularly if the client is inexperienced, may well be held to be negligent.

Although cases of alleged negligence in giving costs advice tend to depend on their facts, the following points will usually be taken into account:

(a) the amount by which the final cost exceeds the estimated cost;
(b) the context in which the estimate was given, including any qualifications made;
(c) the extent to which the architect or engineer should have indicated (and the extent to which he did indicate) that the estimate might be exceeded in practice.

An architect's failure to warn his client of a possible effect of inflation on building prices is illustrated by *Nye Saunders & Partners* v. *Bristow*[100]:

*Facts*
A firm of architects was retained by the defendant to prepare a planning application and provide services in connection with the renovation of the defendant's mansion and installation of a swimming pool. The defendant made it clear that he had approximately £250,000 to spend. In February 1974 the architects provided a written estimate of £238,000 which they had in fact obtained from an independent quantity surveyor. By September 1974 the projected costs had risen to some £440,000, and Mr Bristow aborted the project and terminated the architects' retainer. The architects then sued for their fees.

Although Mr Bristow was an experienced businessman, who might be thought to have taken into account the possible effects of inflation, the architects were held to be negligent in failing to warn him. Two factors appear to have influenced the court. First, the trial judge had been impressed by expert evidence that it was not proper practice for architects to omit a warning about inflation when giving estimates. Secondly, Mr Bristow had consistently sought, and obtained, the architects' confirmation over several months that the estimate still stood, and its accuracy was therefore clearly of great importance to him. (Although the Court of Appeal accepted it as "sensible and prudent" of the architects to consult a quantity surveyor

---

99. E.g., cl. 26 of JCT 80.
100. (1987) 37 B.L.R. 92, C.A.

about costs, it was held that such consultation did not discharge their obligations to Mr Bristow.)

### 4.4.10.2 OTHER ESTIMATES

*Gable House Estates Ltd* v. *The Halpern Partnership & Bovis Construction Ltd*[101] illustrates the architect's obligation to qualify estimates in appropriate terms:

*Facts*
The plaintiffs were owners of a building in Leadenhall Street in the City of London. Their investment options regarding the building were, broadly, to sell it, with or without refurbishment, or to redevelop and let it. They engaged the defendant architects to design the proposed redevelopment.

The client's quantity surveyor prepared three cost plans and various schedules of areas which were provided to the client, sometimes direct by the quantity surveyor, but with the architect's knowledge, as lead consultant. The architect was aware that an important factor in the client's decision to redevelop was the space that could be let. One of the schedules of areas indicated that the lettable space was some 34,000 square feet. In fact, only some 32,000 square feet could be let.

The schedules bore the phrase "all areas approximate". A later schedule referred to "usable office space" instead of "lettable areas", although the difference was not explained to the client. The client sued for damages of £32.5 million, over five times the project value, based on its getting a lower letting space than it had been led to believe would be achievable.

The judge found as follows:

(a) the use of the phrase "all areas approximate" was not a sufficient warning to the client;

(b) the architect should have warned the client of the number of uncertainties that could affect the lettable area;

(c) the architect should have explained to the client that "lettable area" and "usable office space" did not mean the same thing, and should have given the client an estimate of the effect that a change in the specification had on the "lettable area";

(d) the fact that some of the schedules of area were prepared by the quantity surveyor, who sent them direct to the client, did not operate to avoid the architects' liability. The architects were co-ordinators of the professional team and knew of the importance of these schedules to the client;

(e) the client relied on the information about lettable area and would not have redeveloped had it known of the true area.

(Aspects relating to damages are dealt with in section 7.2.2.2 below. In the judgment referred to, the court did not make final findings on damages, although it endorsed the general principle of the plaintiff's claim.)

The case thus provides a salutary reminder to architects and engineers of the enormous claims that may arise through a failure properly to qualify estimates and advice, particularly where the architect or engineer is in the position of lead consultant.

101. (1995) Construction Industry Law Letter, p. 1072.

### 4.4.10.3 A PROBLEM FOR THE COUNTERCLAIMING CLIENT

In *Nye Saunders* the client successfully defended the architects' claim for their fees. He did not apparently raise any counterclaim for damages. If he had, he might have faced the defence that the negligence caused no loss (unless the client could show that he would never have proceeded with the project had the estimate been correct in the first place as in *Gable House Estates Ltd* above). This defence will apply *a fortiori* where the client actually *does* learn of the architect's error while the option of not proceeding is still open to him, e.g., where the architect advises incorrectly of the likely cost before tenders are invited and where the tenders received greatly exceed the estimate. Here, although the client may still have claims for some wasted expenditure and, of course, a partial or even complete defence to the architect's claim for fees, the architect will be able to argue that the cause of the increased cost was the client's decision to proceed, and not the architect's negligent estimate (see, further, section 7.2.2.2 below).

## 5 LIABILITY DURING THE CONSTRUCTION PERIOD

Architects and engineers are frequently appointed as supervising officers or contract administrators on building or engineering projects, usually under a standard form of contract. The architect or engineer is generally the agent of the employer, but it is implicit in his contract with his client that he will act fairly against the contractor "holding the balance between his client and the contractor".[102] The ACE Conditions, clause 2.12 explicitly states that the engineer will exercise any discretion fairly as between client and contractor/sub-contractor. However, his direct liability to the contractor (as opposed to his liability to indemnify his client against a contractor's claim) is limited due to the decision in *Pacific Associates* v. *Baxter*[103] (see section 6.2.2 below).

In addition, architects and engineers who are appointed as "planning supervisors" under the Construction (Design and Management) Regulations 1994[104] should bear in mind their statutory duties under those Regulations. These include the checking of the design and co-ordination of designers to ensure the adequacy of the design with respect to health and safety matters; being in a position to advise the client and contractor on such matters; and preparing a health and safety file which is to be handed to the client at the end of the construction phase. The Regulations impose criminal sanctions. The possible consequences in terms of professional negligence are discussed above in section 4.1.

### 5.1 The obligation to inspect and supervise

#### 5.1.1. Generally

This section discusses liability as between the employer and architect. The architect's potential liability to third parties, including the contractor, is discussed in section 6 below.

---

102. Lord Reid in *Sutcliffe* v. *Thackrah* [1974] A.C. 727.
103. (1988) 44 B.L.R. 33, C.A.; [1990] Q.B. 993.
104. See section 4.1 above.

Inspection and supervision are usually covered by express terms. However, an obligation may be implied as in *Rowlands* v. *Callow*[105] where an employer, who had designed a driveway and certified the value of work done, was held to have impliedly taken on an obligation to supervise the work. However, this was a domestic case, involving a very informal contract, with an engineer who tendered no invoices, charging on a "semi-social" basis.

The obligation to supervise usually lasts until practical completion.[106] The owner of premises may be able to avoid liability to third parties (e.g., for personal injury) if he can show that he was entitled to rely on the supervising officer to supervise construction.[107]

An employer cannot automatically sue his architect or engineer for failure to notice a contractor's defective work. The fact that there is defective work does not necessarily imply a breach of the supervising officer's obligations. The following passage from Lord Upjohn's speech in *East Ham Corporation* v. *Bernard Sunley & Sons Ltd*[108] has consistently been cited as authoritative of the supervisory obligations in building contracts:

"As is well known the architect is not permanently on the site but appears at intervals, it may be of a week or a fortnight, and he has, of course, to inspect the progress of the work. When he arrives on the site there may be very many important matters with which he has to deal: the work may be getting behind-hand through labour trouble; some of the suppliers of materials or the sub-contractors may be lagging; there may be physical trouble on the site itself, such as finding an unexpected amount of underground water. All these are matters which may call for important decisions by the architect. He may in such circumstances think that he knows the builder sufficiently well and can rely upon him to carry out a good job; that it is more important that he should deal with urgent matters on the site than that he should make a minute inspection on the site to see that the builder is complying with the specifications laid down ... It by no means follows that, in failing to discover a defect which a reasonable examination would have disclosed, in fact the architect was necessarily thereby in breach of his duty to the building owner so as to be liable in an action for negligence. It may well be that the omission of the architect to find a defect was due to no more than an error of judgment, or was a deliberately calculated risk which, in all the circumstances of the case, was reasonable and proper."

Therefore:

    (a) mere failure to discover a defect does not necessarily involve negligence;
    (b) it is important to consider the architect's position in relation to the overall management of the project;
    (c) it may be reasonable to allocate time to urgent matters rather than to inspect minute details;
    (d) the competence and trustworthiness of the builder is a factor to be taken into consideration in deciding on the appropriate level of supervision.

A number of cases have considered point (d) in particular, which is now discussed further.

105. [1992] 1 N.Z.L.R. 1780.
106. *EDAC* v. *Moss* (1984) 2 Con. L.R. 1 at 25.
107. As in *Eckersley* v. *Binnie* (1988) 18 Con. L.R. 1, where the Court of Appeal unanimously allowed the appeal by the owners of the site, the North West Water Authority, against the judge's finding that they were 30 per cent to blame for an explosion at a pumping station. See section 4.4.3 above.
108. [1966] A.C. 406 at 443.

### 5.1.2 The contractor's competence

In *Brown* v. *Gilbert-Scott & Payne*[109] where an architect was negligent in failing to supervise, one of the important factors was that he should have borne in mind the general youth and inexperience of the builder. In *Sutcliffe* v. *Chippendale & Edmondson*[110] Judge Stabb QC said:

"I think that the degree of supervision required of an architect must be governed to some extent by his confidence in the contractor. If and when something occurs which indicates to him a lack of competence in a contractor, then, in the interest of his employer, the standard of his supervision should be higher."

Similarly, in *Oldschool* v. *Gleeson*[111] the judge pointed out that the duty of care owed by an architect or consulting engineer to a third party is limited by the assumption that the contractor who executes the work acts at all times as a competent contractor. Finally, in *Corfield* v. *Grant*[112] Judge Bowsher QC held that the builder did not need a great deal of supervision because of his reliability in workmanship, and honesty in his practices (subject to an inclination to charge up to the limit of what the market could bear).

### 5.1.3 Frequency of visits

Under SFA/92, the architect must make such visits as, at the date of his appointment, he reasonably expects to be necessary (cl. 3.1). If he believes later that more are necessary, he makes recommendations to the client, pointing out any consequential increase in fees. It appears therefore that he has no obligation to increase visits until the client takes up his recommendations.

Under the ACE Conditions, the frequency of the engineer's site meetings and site visits are specified in the memorandum. Under the Professional Services Contract, the frequency of visits will be specified in the brief, if anywhere.

At common law, the obligations as to frequency and extent of the architect's visits to site may be altered by surrounding circumstances or arrangements between the parties. In *EDAC* v. *Moss*[113] it was held that the architect was obliged to inspect on a "marginally more frequent" basis than would normally be the case, because of the employer's insistence, and also his reimbursing the architect a sum for travelling expenses for that very purpose. An architect's duty has been held not to be reduced merely because of the distance from his office to site.[114] In *Merton London Borough Council* v. *Lowe*[115] it was held not sufficient for the architect to ask the manager of a swimming pool, who was not an expert, to oversee the contractor's day-to-day work, rather than for the architect to visit himself.

---

109. (1992) 35 Con. L.R. 120.
110. (1971) 18 B.L.R. 149 at 162. The case was subsequently appealed up to the House of Lords, but the observations set out here were unaffected by the appeal.
111. (1976) 4 B.L.R. 131.
112. (1992) 59 B.L.R. 102.
113. (1984) 2 Con. L.R. 1.
114. *Brown & Brown* v. *Gilbert-Scott & Another* (1992) 35 Con. L.R. 120 at 123.
115. (1981) 18 B.L.R. 135 at 141. See section 4.2.2.2 above.

### 5.1.4 Particularly bad work, including deliberate concealment

Where a contractor deliberately or recklessly carries out sub-standard work, two opposing arguments are possible. The first is that the seriousness of what the supervising officer has allowed to go undetected suggests a strong prima facie case that he is in breach of his supervisory duties. The second is that, faced with a contractor bent on a deliberate course of action, perhaps involving speedy concealment of defective work, even a supervising officer exercising reasonable care and skill may fail to appreciate what is going on. The following two cases exemplify these two approaches.

In *Kensington and Chelsea and Westminster Area Health Authority* v. *Wettern Composites*[116] the first defendants were sub-contractors for the supply and erection of pre-cast concrete mullions for a hospital conversion. Expert evidence indicated that the defects in fixing were "startling". The vertical supports of some 85 per cent of the mullions examined, and the horizontal supports in 25 per cent, were unsatisfactory. Judge Smout QC, in holding the architects negligent, attached significance to the following three factors:

(a) the architects had been alerted relatively early on to the poor workmanship and lack of frankness of the sub-contractor;

(b) the fixing of the mullions was work that, by its nature, could be speedily covered up in the course of erection. That made close supervision all the more essential;

(c) the burden of supervision was greater where, as here, poor workmanship could result in physical danger.

Although regarding the point as without clear authority, the judge also held that the fact of the employer appointing a clerk of works did not reduce the architect's obligations, even though the clerk of works was providing "constant supervision".

In that case, on the facts, the architect should clearly have been alerted to what was going on. In *Gray* v. *TP Bennett*,[117] by contrast, the architect was not negligent in failing to discover deliberate concealment:

*Facts*
A 10-storey reinforced concrete building was designed so that concrete projections or nibs provided support for the brick cladding. Some 17 years after construction, and after bulges had appeared in the brick work, the concrete panels were opened up. It was discovered that about 90 per cent of the nibs had been "hacked back or butchered" to which the experts applied epithets such as "appalling", "destructive" and "mindless vandalism".

The judge concluded that the only possible explanation was that the operatives fitting the brick work onto the nibs had been engaged in a deliberate policy to conceal from the architect what the judge described as "destruction on a massive scale". That being so, the architect was not negligent in failing to discover what was going on on his routine visits, especially when he had other matters to consider on those visits.

Interestingly, the judge also held that even if the architect had been in breach of his duty, the deliberate act of the fixers was the true *cause* of the damage that necessitated the remedial works.

116. (1984) 31 B.L.R. 57.
117. (1987) 43 B.L.R. 63.

### 5.1.5  Getting to grips with the situation

Architects who have shown a lack of firmness and resolve have frequently been criticised in the law reports. In *EDAC* v. *Moss*,[118] the architect was described as "fundamentally honest and honourable" but "a poor organiser ... [lacking] the firmness of purpose and assertiveness required for effective supervision of a large project". Despite evidence of workmanship problems, and although employed to exercise responsibility he "simply hoped for the best".

In *Holland Hannen & Cubitts*[119] the Court of Appeal increased the architect's proportion of the overall liability, because of his failure to grapple with the floor problem at an early stage. And in *Corfield* v. *Grant*[120] his Honour Judge Bowsher QC described the project, a hotel conversion, as an "inadequately controlled muddle", and said that the plaintiff architect was in continuous breach of contract. The need for co-ordination was particularly important on this project where work could never be progressed in an orderly way stage by stage, and where the employer was particularly anxious to move speedily. In addition, the project demanded that the architect have an experienced assistant. This particular assistant was inexperienced, and problems were compounded by the architect's failure to give clear instructions or to have a detailed plan of action for him.

### 5.1.6  The inexpensive project

Can the architect argue for a reduced duty to supervise when the project is being "built down" to a price, i.e., cheaply? *Cotton* v. *Wallis*[121] suggests that he can. The Court of Appeal majority refused to disturb the judge's finding that, in the circumstances, the architect's act of issuing the final certificate, despite the presence of defects, was not negligent. However, it may be questioned whether it is right in principle to reduce the architect's obligation to inspect merely because of the employer's cost-consciousness.[122]

## 5.2  The architect's obligation to issue instructions, or to give the contractor information

This section is concerned primarily with contractual liability of the supervising officer to his client, generally where the client is seeking an indemnity in respect of a contractor's claim made against him. *Direct* claims by the contractor are dealt with in section 6 below.

### 5.2.1  Instructions leading to loss and expense

Under the standard forms of building contracts, the contractor may make claims for loss and expense caused by, *inter alia*, by failure to provide information required by the contractor or by the issue of variations by the supervising officer.[123] In addition,

---

118. (1984) 2 Con. L.R. 1.
119. (1985) 35 B.L.R. 1, C.A. For the facts, see section 4.4.2 above.
120. (1992) 59 B.L.R. 102.
121. [1955] 1 W.L.R. 1168, C.A.
122. See the discussion at section 3.2 above.
123. JCT 80, cll. 26.2.1 and 26.2.7.

the contractor may sue for damages for breaches of contract terms relating to supply of information. Architects must consider the following in particular:

(i) clause 5.4 of the JCT 80 contract stipulates that the employer must provide such further drawings or details as are reasonably necessary to explain or exemplify the contract drawings or to enable the contractor to carry out the work; (the ICE Conditions (6th edn), clause 7 is similar except that the obligation is to provide such drawings specifications and information as the engineer considers necessary);

(ii) terms will often be implied into building contracts, whether or not executed under standard forms, to the effect that the employer will not hinder or prevent the contractor from carrying out the work (which in turn obliges the architect to provide a contractor with full correct and co-ordinated information); and will do all things reasonably necessary to enable the contractor to carry out the work.[124]

Under the ICE Conditions, the employer can claim additional payment for delayed drawings or instructions, variation instructions and other matters.[125]

Inexperienced employers, faced with unexpected increases in costs, often assume that since the contractor's claim cannot be their (the employer's) fault, either it is invalid or it is due to the supervising officer's own defaults, and therefore should ultimately be borne by him. Such an approach is flawed.

First, many of the matters for which loss and expense or additional payment can be claimed (even such matters as the architect's failure to give timeous instructions to the contractor) do not necessarily imply fault on the supervising officer's part. Secondly, even if such fault is present, it does not follow that the failure amounts to negligence. For example, in a project where a large amount of information necessarily has to be communicated to the contractor during the construction phase, an architect would necessarily fall below the *Bolam* standard of care merely by failing to provide every item of information to the contractor at the time when he needs it.

This is nevertheless an area where supervising officers are vulnerable to attack from their clients.

### 5.2.2 Instructions as to how the work is to be carried out (including safety obligations)

These obligations are dealt with in section 6.2.1 below.

### 5.2.3 Failure to issue instructions

An architect may be liable to his employer for failure to issue an instruction which is needed to overcome a problem on site. In one of the sub-trials ordered in the Rhyl Hospital case, *Holland Hannen & Cubitts v. WHTSO*,[126] the position was as follows:

---

124. *London Borough of Merton* v. *Stanley Hugh Leach Ltd* (1985) 32 B.L.R. 51.

125. For example, ICE (6th edn), cll. 7(4)(a) and 5(2).

126. The judgment referred to here is that reported at (1981) 18 B.L.R. 80, dealing with the windows sub-trial. The litigation generated a further judgment, reported at (1985) 35 B.L.R. 1 on issues relating to the floors dealt with at section 4.4.2 above.

*Facts*

It was discovered during the works that the windows, designed and installed by Crittall, who were nominated sub-contractors to Cubitts, the main contractor, were letting in water. Crittall, who appeared to have been aware from an early stage that they would have to bear the greater part of the responsibility either as designers or installers[127] put forward remedial suggestions to Cubitts, and to PTP, the employer's architect. Although PTP prepared a draft variation instruction, to cover the remedial works, no instruction was ever finalised or issued, partly because of a dispute between Cubitts and PTP as to who was in the right. The works were accordingly delayed.

The judge held that PTP, by their failure to issue a variation instruction, had made it impossible for Cubitts and Crittall to carry on the work. PTP were held to be liable to the employer for breach of contract in failing to issue the instruction when it was apparent that one was needed to overcome defective work because the building contract required them to issue an instruction whenever it was "necessary" for completion of the works (alternatively, there was an implied term that they would do all things necessary to enable the contractor to complete the work). The judge criticised the architect's "passive attitude".[128]

### 5.2.4 *Issuing instructions other than in writing*

If the contract provides for the architect's instructions to be in writing, difficulties may arise where the architect gives them orally. Some forms of contract allow the contractor to confirm such verbal instructions in writing, and go on to provide that if the architect does not dissent within a certain period of time, they are deemed to be effective.[129] However, if the contract does not give the contractor this option, or he does not take it up, he may have alternative methods of recovering for work done which may involve issues of evidence and legal argument.[130] The architect should therefore be aware that negligent failure to issue instructions in the manner required by the contract may cause problems for which the employer may eventually seek redress against him.

### 5.3 Obligations to issue certificates

### 5.3.1 *Generally*

Under the standard building and civil engineering forms of contract, the certificates issued by the supervising officer include the following:

---

127. Judge Newey held as a matter of law that Crittall were indeed the designers of the window assemblies.

128. The employer, as PTP's principal, was therefore liable to Cubitts for its delay-related losses, but, in the event, the employer in turn was able to recover these from Crittall under its direct warranty. *Hudson's Building and Engineering Contracts* (11th edn) at paras 2–201 and 4–095 finds it difficult to support the decision and suggests that the analysis of the employer's obligations to the contractor under the main contract was cursory, because the existence of the direct warranty meant that ultimate liability rested with Crittall in any event.

129. JCT 80, cl. 4.3.2; ICE Conditions (6th edn) cl. 2(6).

130. For example on the basis of a separate implied contract, cf. *Wallis* v. *Robinson* 1862 3 F. & F. 307; *Liebe* v. *Molloy* (1906) 4 C.L.R. 347 (High Court of Australia).

— interim valuation certificates;

— extension of time certificates;

— a certificate of practical completion (a "Certificate of Substantial Completion" under the ICE Conditions);

— certificate of making good defects at the conclusion of the defects liability/ maintenance period;

— the final certificate.

In *Sutcliffe* v. *Thackrah*[131] the House of Lords rejected the argument, which had previously had some authoritative support,[132] that the architects acting as certifiers enjoyed an immunity from actions in negligence akin to those of an arbitrator or judge. Therefore a supervising officer may in principle face negligence or breach of contract actions for negligently certifying in the same way as he may face such action in respect of any of his other functions. Three types of certificate are now examined.

### 5.3.2. Interim valuation certificates

The value of work certified in an interim certificate may be corrected on the next, and to that extent the process of measuring and valuing work[133] done at monthly or other stages is necessarily approximate. How much latitude therefore does an architect have in making approximations as to the correct value to be certified?

In *Sutcliffe* v. *Chippendale & Edmondson*[134] Judge Stabb QC accepted that although a prolonged or detailed inspection or measurement at interim stage was impractical "more than a glance round" was to be expected. In particular, the architect's obligation to value "work properly executed" did not allow him to include defective work on the assumption that the contractor would rectify it at a later stage—the contract might be terminated for the contractor's insolvency or otherwise, leaving the employer in the position of having to repay the contractor.[135] In particular, the architect was obliged to keep the quantity surveyor continually informed of defective work that he observed.[136]

Similarly, in *Townsend* v. *Stone Toms & Partners*[137] the architect argued that he was entitled to include defective work in the valuation certificates because the retention covered the outstanding defects. The argument was rejected. The Court of

---

131. [1974] A.C. 727.
132. *Chambers* v. *Goldthorpe* [1911] 1 K.B. 624, C.A.
133. The measurement and valuing is usually carried out by a quantity surveyor. Indeed, under the standard forms, the quantity surveyor has the power to do so. However, the responsibility for issue of a certificate remains that of the architect.
134. (1971) 18 B.L.R. 149 at 165.
135. The issue of *how* to value defective work is one to which there is no clear answer. Simply making an allowance based on the contractor's rates may be insufficient if the contract is terminated and the employer is forced to arrange for remedial work to be carried out by others. In these circumstances, the architect valuing on this basis would appear to be open to the criticism made by Judge Stabb QC. However, the contract does not, at least expressly, allow the architect to take into account the potential remedial costs. *Hudson's Building and Engineering Contracts* (11th edn) at para. 5–062, acknowledging the problem, suggests that the architect/engineer should nevertheless take such costs into account.
136. *Ibid.* at p. 66.
137. (1984) 27 B.L.R. 26, C.A.

Appeal pointed out the financial consequences to the employer if the contractor had become insolvent before making good the defects.

### 5.3.3 Extension of time certificates

An architect who negligently fails to issue an extension of time certificate is in breach of contract to his client and may therefore be liable for the losses, including loss and expense, claimed by the contractor against the employer.[138]

Contractors frequently arbitrate against employers to overturn architects' extension of time certificates, so as to obtain return of liquidated damages deducted, and thus, indirectly, to establish the factual basis for a claim for loss and expense (although the contractor's rights as to extensions of time and to loss and expense are independent, so that one does not entail the other). The employer will then often consider whether the architect was negligent in certifying incorrectly. One might suppose that an employer who wished to sue his architect would first have to have established, by way of proceedings involving the contractor, what the contractor's right to extensions of time and loss and expense actually were, and therefore what loss the employer had suffered. However, *Wessex Regional Health Authority* v. *HLM Design Ltd*[139] suggests otherwise. In that case the court held that an employer could pursue the architect or contractor separately and in whichever order he pleased.

### 5.3.4 The final certificate

This certificate operates to confer finality on certain issues as between employer and contractor. JCT 80 provides that, unless arbitration proceedings have been instituted within 28 days of its issue, it is conclusive evidence of the following:

(a) in favour of the employer, that the contract sum has been adjusted in accordance with the terms of the contract;

(b) in favour of the contractor, that where and to the extent that the quality of materials or the standard or workmanship is to be to the satisfaction of the architect, that such work is to his satisfaction.

Prior to *Colbart* v. *Kumar*[140] it had been assumed that the evidential bar applied only to standards of workmanship and materials that the contract made *expressly* to be subject to the architect's satisfaction. However, in that case, in relation to the Intermediate Form of Contract (IFC 84), the Official Referee held that the bar applied to *all* matters that were "inherently" a matter for the architect's discretion, effectively including all types of defective workmanship and materials. The decision was endorsed in respect of the JCT form by the Court of Appeal in *Crown Estates Commissioners* v. *Mowlem*.[141]

---

138. In *Holland Hannen & Cubitts* v. *WHTSO* (1981) 18 B.L.R. 80, discussed earlier, the architect was found to be in breach of his obligations to his client in failing to issue an extension of time certificate (at 128). In the event, the employer recovered losses otherwise payable to the contractor by virtue of his direct warranty with the nominated sub-contractor.

139. (1995) 71 B.L.R. 32. The case is dealt with more fully in section 8.1 below.

140. (1992) 59 B.L.R. 89.

141. (1994) 70 B.L.R. 1, C.A. The decision itself, and the refusal of leave to appeal to the House of Lords, is criticised by IN Duncan-Wallace QC in (1995) 11 Const. L.J. in "Not What the RIBA/JCT Meant: Loose Cannon in the Court of Appeal". However, on a literal, as opposed to a purposive, interpretation of the clause in question, it is difficult to fault the reasoning of the Court of Appeal.

The Joint Contracts Tribunal have now issued Amendment 15 (July 1995) to JCT 80, and similar amendments to the other JCT standard forms, "correcting" the effect of these cases and therefore restoring what was presumably the intention of those drafting the standard form. However, for cases affected by the original wording, and in view of the potentially drastic consequences that employers may face, architects and engineers need to exercise particular care to ensure that final certificates are not issued where there is any likelihood of defective work.

There is no reason to suppose that the *Crown Estates* reasoning does not apply to latent defects as well as patent ones, thus leaving the employer not only with an effective 28-day limitation period instead of 6 or 12 years, but also removing his rights under the Latent Damage Act 1986 to "start the clock" in respect of latent defects, as soon as the defect was reasonably discoverable. It may be assumed that employers finding themselves in this unfortunate position will be particularly assiduous in scrutinising the supervising officer's issue of the final certificate to see whether any action can be taken against him.

### 5.4 Obligations to advise on the law

While an architect or engineer is not expected to have the expertise of a lawyer, he cannot be immune to actions based on his faulty interpretation of the law. Two cases support this view. The first is *BL Holdings* v. *Robert J Wood & Partners*[142]:

*Facts*
A planning officer incorrectly advised the architect that the local planning authority did not, as a matter of course (and was not in law required to), take into account car parking spaces when considering whether to grant office development permits (which in turn were required for planning permission). The architect, while expressing some surprise at this information, did not pass it on to his client. The building was subsequently designed without sufficient car park spaces. No permit was issued and the employer later lost rental income while the matter was being put right.

Ralph Gibson J said:

"A professional man such as an architect who agrees to act in some field of activity commonly carried out by architects, in which a knowledge and understanding of certain principles of law is required ... must have a sufficient knowledge of those principles of law in order reasonably to protect his client from damage and loss ..."

He went on to say that in many cases the duty would be discharged by advising his client that he knows little or nothing of the legal principles in question. The trial judge found the architects liable, while accepting that many architects, and even some lawyers, would have no reason to doubt the advice from the planning authority. The Court of Appeal overruled the judge's finding on negligence on the facts, but upheld his statement of the principles to be applied.

*West Faulkner* v. *Newham LBC*[143] concerned clause 25 of JCT 80, which gives the architect the power to determine a contractor's employment if, amongst other things, he fails to proceed "regularly and diligently":

142. (1979) 10 B.L.R. 48.
143. (1994) 71 B.L.R. 1, C.A.

*Facts*

The council engaged Moss Construction as contractor for the renovation of 50 dwellings on a housing estate. The contract period of 9 weeks was, as it turned out, exceeded by 28 weeks, causing a number of problems to the tenants who had been temporarily evacuated. Despite vigorous and repeated requests from the council, the architect maintained that he was unable in law to issue a determination notice. The main reason, as the Court of Appeal found, was that he thought that such a notice could be served only if Moss were failing to proceed both regularly *and* diligently (whereas by common consent, Moss were at least proceeding regularly, albeit slowly).

The Court of Appeal rejected this "conjunctive" interpretation of the clause, so that the question then was: was the architect negligent or could he argue that his interpretation of the words, though now shown to be wrong, was nevertheless a plausible one to have taken at the time?

Independent advice contained in a letter to the council from a firm of specialist solicitors appeared to indicate that the issue of whether the contractor's employment could be determined was "borderline". However, the court held that the letter was not in fact directed to the construction of the clause, but rather to what the council could do in the circumstances, given the apparent inflexibility of the architect (in particular, said the court, the advice did not deal with the rival constructions of the clause itself). Neither did it assist the architect that another professional man (the quantity surveyor) had construed the clause in the same way as the architect had. It was held that the construction of the clause was one that no reasonably competent architect could have arrived at.

The decision may be regarded as placing a heavy onus on supervising officers in construing contracts properly. A contract is a legal document, and the powers and duties of architects are inevitably therefore framed in legal terms. Moreover, the predecessor of the JCT 80 form has been criticised on more than one occasion for its lack of clarity.[144] However, it is submitted that in a case where the construction of the contract is genuinely difficult, the architect will often discharge the onus by recommending independent legal advice. He must then be sure that, in contrast to the position in *West Faulkner*, he relies on that legal advice only to the extent that the advice is directed specifically to the issue that he has to answer.

## 5.5 Obligations to warn in respect of other professionals

The obligation to alert the client to the failings of other professionals has already been dealt with in section 4.4.5 above in relation to design and the standard forms of appointment. Some of those points apply, *mutatis mutandis*, to the construction phase. One decision that particularly relates to the construction phase, however, is *Kensington and Chelsea and Westminster Area Health Authority* v. *Wettern Composites and Others*.[145] There were extensive defects in the manufacture and manner of fixing of pre-cast concrete mullions and in relation to the nature of the joints between the individual mullions. The architects were negligent in failing to be

144. The J.C.T. 63 form was described as comprising a "farrago of obscurities" by Edmund-Davies LJ in *English Industrial Estates Corporation* v. *George Wimpey & Co Ltd* [1973] 1 Lloyd's Rep. 118 at 126; and "amorphous and tortuous" by Sachs LJ in *Bickerton* v. *North West Metropolitan Regional Hospital Board* [1969] 1 All E.R. 977 at 989.
145. (1984) 31 B.L.R. 57.

sufficiently alert to the contractor's lack of competence. The issue was whether the engineers, whose duty would admittedly not ordinarily extend to supervision, had any duty to follow up the defective fixing once they had some knowledge of it. The judge held that:

(a) they had a duty to notify the architect as to those defects in the fixings of which they had *actual* knowledge (on the facts, this was discharged by a letter that they had written to the architect);

(b) they had no duty to supervise others to put the defects right. That was the job of the architect and the clerk of works.

It is submitted that the position may be different depending on circumstances, if the professional against whom the duty to warn is alleged is not merely (as in *Kensington and Chelsea and Westminster AHA*) one of the professionals on site but a lead consultant, explicitly or otherwise appointed as such.

## 5.6 Obligations post-contract

With the issue of the final certificate, the architect is probably *functus officio*, since the standard forms of contract do not envisage his doing anything after this. It seems unlikely that any obligations to the client can continue following this, since that would suggest that there is some form of continuing obligation to advise the client, owed presumably in tort, outside the contractual period. It was suggested in section 4.4.3 above that such a duty does not exist, except conceivably in cases where there is the possibility of death or personal injury.

If no final certificate is ever issued, as often seems to be the case in construction contracts[146] it is likely to be a question of fact as to when the architect's obligations under the contract have in fact been completed. It is submitted that the mere lack of issue of a final certificate will not of itself operate to extend the architect's general obligations to the client indefinitely, even though the architect's failure to issue such a certificate may, depending on the circumstances, be a breach of his obligation to the client to administer the contract properly.

## 6 LIABILITY TO THIRD PARTIES (INCLUDING LIABILITY IN TORT)

### 6.1 Liability to third parties in general

#### 6.1.1 Introduction

It is not possible to understand the current position with regard to an architect's or engineer's potential liability in tort to a third party without a brief synopsis of the development of the law of tort generally since 1964.[147]

Until that time, the main non-statutory avenue for actions in negligence was that in *Donoghue* v. *Stevenson*, where the manufacturer of a ginger beer bottle was held to be liable to an ultimate consumer for personal injuries suffered when she drank the

---

146. The architect/engineer will be even more wary of issuing final certificates since *Colbart* v. *Kumar* (1992) 59 B.L.R. 89 and *Crown Estate Commissioners* v. *John Mowlem & Co. Ltd* (1994) 70 B.L.R. 1, C.A., in cases involving the JCT forms which do not include Amendment 15 (July 1995) or similar. See section 5.3.4 above.

147. The matter is dealt with in further detail in chapter 2.

ginger beer. It was a constituent part of the doctrine that a plaintiff could not recover for "pure" economic loss, i.e., economic loss suffered in the absence of physical injury or damage. Further, damage to "the article itself" (in this case, the ginger beer) did not qualify as physical damage (so that the plaintiff was unable to recover the price of the drink).

In 1964 the House of Lords opened up a second major avenue of liability in *Hedley Byrne* v. *Heller & Partners*.[148] There it was held that pure economic loss was recoverable for negligent *statements* as opposed to negligent acts, in certain circumstances—these being where there was:

(a) sufficient proximity and some form of special relationship between the parties;

(b) a sufficient degree of reliance by the representee on the statement;

(c) circumstances making it just and reasonable to impose a duty of care.

In the 1970s the ambit of *Donoghue* v. *Stevenson* liability was widened considerably by *Dutton* v. *Bognor Regis Urban District Council*[149] and *Anns* v. *London Borough Council of Merton*.[150] In both of these cases, local authorities were held liable to plaintiffs for negligent inspection by the building inspector of foundations (*Dutton*) and negligent passing of the contractor's plans which breached byelaw requirements as to foundations (*Anns*). Both cases appeared to weaken the requirement for physical damage to be present if financial loss was to be recoverable. Both cases were, however, formally overruled by the House of Lords in *Murphy* v. *Brentwood District Council*,[151] in which the House of Lords restated the previous orthodoxy in holding that any duty of care in tort owed to occupiers of property is limited to ensuring that they or their property (other than the property the subject of the alleged negligence) do not suffer physical injury or damage. The House of Lords reiterated that there was in principle no liability in tort for pure economic loss.

### 6.1.2 The position as at 1990

The position in relation to third party liability of architects and engineers at this stage therefore appeared to be:

(a) that they could be liable under *Hedley Byrne*, subject to the plaintiff showing that the *Hedley Byrne* principles applied to the case in question. The criteria were usefully summarised by the Court of Appeal in *James McNaughton Paper Group* v. *Hicks Anderson & Co*[152] as follows:

  (i) the purpose for which the statement is made,

  (ii) the relationship between the parties,

  (iii) the size of the class of which the plaintiff is a member,

  (iv) the state of knowledge of the defendant,

  (v) whether the plaintiff was entitled to rely on the statement;

(b) that they could be liable under the Defective Premises Act 1972 in respect of *dwelling-houses*;

148. [1964] A.C. 465.
149. [1972] 1 Q.B. 373.
150. [1977] 2 W.L.R. 1024.
151. [1991] 1 A.C. 398.
152. [1991] 2 Q.B. 113.

(c) that they could be liable for negligent *acts*, as opposed to statements, but only if the acts have caused physical damage or injury to the plaintiff or to his property other than that which was the subject-matter of the act in question.[153]

### 6.1.3 The current position

As might be expected, plaintiffs faced with the virtual closing off of liability following *Dutton* and *Anns*, certainly as regards economic loss, could be expected to examine the *Hedley Byrne* misstatement avenue, to see whether it could be made to yield wider liability. It appears that it may indeed do so, following two House of Lords' decisions.

*Henderson v. Merrett Syndicates.*[154]  In this case the House of Lords held that members' agents and managing agents owed a duty of care in tort under *Hedley Byrne* to Lloyd's Names on whose behalf they wrote insurance business. Of particular significance for architects and engineers are the following *dicta* of Lord Goff:

(i) that the *Hedley Byrne* principle extends beyond mere advice to include performance on "other services";

(ii) that the correct test to apply is to ask whether there has been a "voluntary assumption of responsibility" by the defendant. It had not previously been entirely clear, following *Hedley Byrne*, whether this concept was an essential ingredient of *Hedley Byrne* liability of dicta doubting it in *Smith* v. *Eric S Bush*;[155] and *Caparo Industries plc* v. *Dickman.*[156] However, Lord Goff felt that there was no reason why recourse should not be had to the concept, and pointed out that it had been adopted by all of their Lordships, in one form or another, in *Hedley Byrne* itself;

(iii) that the "voluntary assumption of responsibility" test could give rise to liability for the professional man in respect of negligent *omissions* as well as statements.

In summary, matters other than statements, and indeed mere omissions, may now give rise to a *Hedley Byrne* liability for the professional man.

*White v. Jones.*[157]  In this case, a testator instructed his solicitor to alter a previous will so as to provide for certain named beneficiaries. The solicitor negligently failed to do so and the testator subsequently died without the will having been altered. The disappointed beneficiaries brought an action against the solicitor. The House of Lords by a 3:2 majority, endorsing the Court of Appeal's decision, found in their favour, despite the fact that:

153. Actions brought in tort against surveyors for allegedly negligent surveys have tended to be based on *Hedley Byrne* liability for misstatements, as in *Smith* v. *Eric S Bush (a firm)* and *Harris* v. *Wyre Forest District Council* [1990] 1 A.C. 831, H.L.
154. (1994) 69 B.L.R. 26, sub nom. *Arbuthnott & Others* v. *Fagan & Feltrim Underwriting Agencies Ltd* [1994] 3 All E.R. 506.
155. [1990] 1 A.C. 831 at 864–865 *per* Lord Griffiths.
156. [1990] 2 A.C. 605 at 628 *per* Lord Roskill.
157. [1995] 1 All E.R. 691.

   (i) there was apparently no relationship whatsoever (and certainly no "special relationship") between the disappointed beneficiaries and the solicitor;

  (ii) there was no reliance by the beneficiaries who only discovered the position after the testator's death;

 (iii) the solicitor's negligence consisted of an omission, not a statement, or even an act.

Lord Nolan said that "... a professional man or an artisan who undertakes to exercise his skill in a manner which, to his knowledge, may cause loss to others, if carefully performed, may therefore implicitly assume a legal responsibility towards them (i.e., in the absence of reliance)".

Lord Browne-Wilkinson said that the categories of special relationship, not all of which required reliance (citing *Nocton* v. *Lord Ashburton*[158]) could be extended incrementally. He was willing to allow the category of solicitor/intended beneficiaries to qualify as a "special relationship".

Lord Goff accepted that there was no "assumption of responsibility" by a solicitor towards the intended beneficiary "on ordinary principles", but held that the law could nevertheless "fashion a remedy to fill a lacuna in the law and so prevent [an] injustice".

### 6.1.4 Implications of Henderson v. Merrett and White v. Jones

The potential liability of architects, engineers and other professionals has now been considerably widened. The retrenchment in the law of tort following *Murphy* appears to have been reversed by an enormous widening of *Hedley Byrne* liability. The widening applies to two areas:

*The persons to whom a duty may be owed*   In appropriate circumstances, it seems that an architect or engineer, involved in the design or supervision of a construction project, may, in the absence of any contractual warranty, be liable to such people as funders, subsequent purchasers of property, tenants and sub-tenants. This follows from the relaxation in the relative tightness of the special relationship that was thought to be an important part of *Hedley Byrne* liability.

*The actions that may attract liability*   It seems that omissions, and matters other than statements, may now be covered by *Hedley Byrne* liability, although it is not easy to state definitively what the limits of this potential new liability are. In both cases (especially *Henderson*) the House of Lords, in asserting the "voluntary assumption of responsibility" test downgraded the importance of the act/statement distinction. However, it is not clear that this can be reconciled with *Caparo Industries Plc* v. *Dickman*.[159] In that case, the House of Lords held that auditors of a public company's accounts owed no duty of care to the plaintiff either as a member of the public at large or as a shareholder, and appeared to proceed on the basis that *Hedley Byrne* liability was in principle to be founded on negligent statements or advice. The law must therefore be regarded as being in something of a transitional state in this area.

158. [1914] A.C. 932.
159. [1990] 2 A.C. 605, H.L.

If the *Henderson* reasoning is followed, it seems that an architect or engineer producing drawings or a design for a client may be liable to a third party for negligent preparation of those drawings or design. In other words, the lack of a "representation" or "statement" to the third party will not be a defence.

Authority for this proposition exists at Official Referee level in the case of *Conway* v. *Crowe Kelsey & Partners*.[160] Judge Newman QC said that if there was an "assumption of responsibility" the act/statement distinction was "unsustainable" and irrelevant. He held, on a preliminary issue, that consulting engineers could be liable in tort under *Hedley Byrne* to their clients (the contractual limitation period having expired) because of negligent design and supervision consisting of *actions*.[161] There is thus likely no longer to be any distinction between an architect or engineer:

(a) providing a drawing or design (act); and
(b) advising in relation to a drawing or design, or approving the drawing of another person (statement).

### 6.1.5 Statutory liability regarding dwelling-houses—the Defective Premises Act 1972

The Act applies to dwelling-houses. Section 1 states:

"A person taking on work for or in connection with the provision of a dwelling (whether the dwelling is provided by the erection or by the conversion or enlargement of a building) owes a duty—
(a) if the dwelling is provided to the order of any person, to that person; and
(b) without prejudice to paragraph (a) above, to every person who acquired an interest (whether legal or equitable) in the dwelling;
to see that the work which he takes on is done in a workmanlike, or as the case may be, professional manner, with proper materials and so that as regards that work the dwelling will be fit for habitation when completed."

The Act thus imposes civil liability on architects and engineers (and also contractors) in respect of design, supervision and other work carried out on dwellings. The duty is owed to anyone acquiring an interest in the house and therefore includes future owners and tenants. The limitation period which, in tort, ends six years from when the cause of action accrues, runs from completion of the dwelling (s. 1(5)). It had been thought that the Act did not apply to the vast majority of new houses covered by the National House Builders' Registration Council (NHBC) scheme, by virtue of the section 2 exemption in the case of an "approved scheme", but it now appears that this is not so.[162]

---

160. (1994) 39 Con. L.R. 1.

161. In *Lancashire & Cheshire Association of Baptist Churches Inc* v. *Seddon* (1994) 65 B.L.R. 21, his Honour Judge Kershaw QC had held that where an architect submitted drawings to his employer, so that the employer could consider the design, it would be artificial to say that the architect was making a statement (for the purposes of *Hedley Byrne* liability) as opposed to carrying out an act. While as a matter of plain English that may be correct, it would mean that an architect who submits a drawing accompanied by some form of assurance that the drawing represents a workable design, or who approves as satisfactory the installation drawing of a sub-contractor, is in a less favourable position than the architect who merely submits a drawing unaccompanied by any form of statement. This "debilitating distinction" is criticised by the editors of the Building Law Reports at 69 B.L.R. 31 in their commentary on *Henderson*, and it must now be doubted as to whether, in the light of *Henderson*, the *Lancashire* case is good law.

162. See Duncan Wallace QC, "*Anns* beyond repair" (1991) L.Q.R. 243.

### 6.1.5.1 TWO LIMITATIONS ON THE DEFECTIVE PREMISES ACT 1972

The scope of the section has been somewhat limited by virtue of the Court of Appeal decision in *Alexander* v. *Mercouris*[163] and by an Official Referee's decision in *Miles Charles Thompson & Others* v. *Clive Alexander & Partners*.[164] In short, a plaintiff will be unable to establish liability against an architect or engineer unless he can show not only that the work was not done in a professional manner, but also that the failure has caused the house to be unfit for habitation. The issue revolves around whether clause 1(1)(b) imposes one obligation on the professional (to carry out work in a professional manner with proper materials *so that* it is fit for habitation) or two or three distinct obligations.

In *Alexander* v. *Mercouris* the question was not directly in issue, but the Court of Appeal felt that the words should be read conjunctively as imposing one obligation. In *Thompson* v. *Alexander* his Honour Judge Esyr Lewis QC felt obliged to follow the Court of Appeal, since their views were "intimately bound up" with their decision on the issues, and therefore very much in point. However, he would in any event have agreed with the architects' and engineers' arguments, since it seemed to him that the "plain intention" of the Act was to ensure fitness for habitation, rather than to impose liability for "trivial" defects in design and construction. In such cases, the judge felt, the plaintiff would usually have been compensated by negotiating a reduction in the purchase price anyway.

If the above two decisions are correct, the liability of architects and engineers under the Act is much restricted. Although the Act does not define "fitness for habitation" it may be assumed, particularly by reference to other Acts of Parliament that do define that phrase,[165] that only in severe cases will a dwelling fall below such a standard.

In a further decision, *Jacobs* v. *Morton & Partners*,[166] the Official Referees' Court has restricted the application of the Act yet further. In this case, it was held that the Act applies only to works involving the creation of a dwelling, and not to repair or rectification works to existing dwellings. The reasons given were:

(i) in ordinary usage the word "provision" generally refers to the initial supply of an item;

(ii) the parentheses within section 1(1) appear to be directed to the creation of new dwellings;

(iii) if Parliament had intended to include works of rectification, it would have said so expressly.

The judge also noted that the mischief to which the Act had been directed was defects in new buildings, as confirmed by the Law Commission report (No. 40 of 1979) on which the Act had been based.

---

163. [1979] 1 W.L.R. 1270, C.A.
164. (1992) 59 B.L.R. 81.
165. Under the Landlord and Tenant Act 1985, s. 10, it is provided that, for the purpose of determining under the Act whether a house is "unfit for human habitation" regard should be had to its condition in respect of: repair, stability, freedom from damp, internal arrangement, natural lighting, ventilation, water supply, drainage and sanitary conveniences and facilities for preparation and cooking of food and for the disposal of waste water. The Housing Act 1985, s. 604 (inserted by the Local Government and Housing Act 1989, s. 165) defines the phrase in a little more detail, but by reference to broadly similar criteria.
166. (1994) 72 B.L.R. 92.

## 6.2 Liability to contractors and sub-contractors

### 6.2.1 Duties regarding health and safety

In *Clayton* v. *Woodman & Son (Builders)*[167] the plaintiff, an experienced bricklayer, employed by the contractor, suggested to the architect on site that there would be difficulties in cutting a chase in an existing gable wall, and that a completely new wall should be built instead. The architect rejected this criticism. A chase was cut in the gable wall without it being sufficiently shored up, and it collapsed, injuring the plaintiff. The plaintiff sued (*inter alia*) the contractor as his own employer, and the architect. The Court of Appeal dismissed the action against the architect. Pearson LJ said:

"It is quite plain, in my view, both as a general proposition and under the particular contract in this case, that the builder, as the employer of the workman, has the responsibility at common law to provide a safe system of work ... The architect on the other hand is engaged as the agent of the owner of the building for whom the building is being erected, and his function is to make sure that in the end, when the work has been completed, the owner will have a building properly constructed in accordance with the contract and plans and specification and drawings ... The architect does not undertake (as I understand the position) to advise the builder as to what safety precautions should be taken or, in particular, as to how he should carry out his building operations. It is the function and the right of the builder to carry out his own building operations as he thinks fit and, of course, in doing so, to comply with the obligations to the workmen."

On issues of health and safety, the impact of the Construction (Design and Management) Regulations 1994 must now be borne in mind. The contractor (if he is appointed "principal contractor") and the architect (if he is appointed as "planning supervisor") will both have obligations to consider health and safety aspects of the project.[168] Although the Regulations impose criminal, not civil, sanctions, the allocation of responsibilities that they entail will undoubtedly be of significance in civil actions.[169] However, the words of Pearson LJ, in particular, are of wider application. The Court of Appeal's view clearly was that the architect's first duty is to his employer, being a duty to ensure that the building is constructed in accordance with the specification etc.; whereas *how* the building is to be built (including related issues of safety) is a matter for the builder.[170] Similarly, in *Oldschool* v. *Gleeson (Contractors) Ltd*[171] Judge Stabb QC said:

"It seems abundantly plain that the duty of care of an architect or of a consulting engineer in no way extends into the area of how the work is carried out. Not only has he no duty to instruct the builder how to do the work, or what safety precautions to take, but he has no right to do so ..."[172]

---

167. [1962] 2 Q.B. 533, 4 B.L.R. 65, C.A.
168. Amendment 14 (March 1995) to the JCT 80 Standard Form provides that, where the CDM Regulations apply, the contractor automatically takes the role of principal contractor for the purposes of the Regulations and the architect takes the role of planning supervisor.
169. See section 4.1 above.
170. An important gloss on the above is that, *qua designer*, the supervising officer must consider "buildability"—*EDAC* v. *Moss* (1984) 2 Con. L.R. 1.
171. (1976) 4 B.L.R. 105.
172. In *Victoria University of Manchester* v. *Hugh Wilson* (1984) 2 Con. L.R. 43 at 92, Judge Newey QC suggested that these words were too wide in view of the House of Lords' decision in *Sutcliffe* v. *Thackrah*. However, *Sutcliffe*, discussed above. which dealt with architects' supposed immunity in relation to the issue of certificates, preceded *Oldschool*, and does not appear to contradict anything in either *Clayton* or *Oldschool*.

*Clay* v. *AJ Crump & Sons Ltd*[173] provides an illustration of a successful action by personal representatives of a workman employed by the contractor against an architect. In this case the architect's original design provided for the demolition of a wall. When the owner asked whether it could be left standing in order to keep out intruders, the architect was willing to sanction a variation to this effect, without visiting site to satisfy himself as to its safety. The wall later collapsed, killing two workmen. The architect's failure to carry out even a cursory examination of the wall appears to have been the decisive factor, however, and the case therefore does not contravene the principle that it is for the contractor, not the architect, to decide how to build.

### 6.2.2 Duties arising from the supervisor's contractual functions, including certification

#### 6.2.2.1 PACIFIC ASSOCIATES V. BAXTER[174]

Until 1988 there was authority that a claim could be maintained in negligence by a contractor against an architect for negligent certification. The authority was an *obiter dictum* of Lord Salmon in *Arenson* v. *Arenson*.[175] The case was an action by the employer against his architect for negligent *over*-certification. Lord Salmon, suggesting that an architect owed a duty to his client under *Hedley Byrne* said:

"In *Sutcliffe* v. *Thackrah*[176] the architect negligently certified more money due than was in fact due, and he was successfully sued for the damage which this had caused his client. He might, however, have negligently certified that less money was payable than was in fact due and thereby starve the contractor of money ... This might have caused the contractor serious damage for which the architect could have been successfully sued."

The view was subsequently followed in two first instance decisions.[177] However, in 1988 the Court of Appeal gave judgment in *Pacific Associates* v. *Baxter*,[178] following which the contractor's rights against the architect or engineer appear to be limited:

*Facts*
Pacific were contractors under a FIDIC engineering contract for the dredging of a lagoon in the Persian Gulf. Halcrow were the engineers under the contract. Pacific claimed extensions of time and additional expense. The application was rejected by Halcrow. Pacific commenced arbitration proceedings against the employer, which resulted in a settlement of some £10 million. They then pursued Halcrow for the balance of the claim of some £45 million. The Court of Appeal struck the claim out as disclosing no cause of action.

The case was decided on a preliminary issue largely on principles of *Hedley Byrne*. However, it is not easy to extract clear principles for two reasons. First, the three Lords Justices gave different reasons for their decision.[179] Secondly, the issues were

---

173. (1963) 4 B.L.R. 80.
174. (1988) 44 B.L.R. 33, C.A.; [1990] Q.B. 993.
175. [1977] A.C. 405.
176. [1974] A.C. 727.
177. *Shui On Construction Ltd* v. *Shui Kay Co Ltd* (1985) 1 Const. L.J., a decision of the Hong Kong Crown Court; and *Michael Salliss & Co Ltd* v. *Calil* (1988) 4 Const. L.J. a decision of Judge Fox-Andrews QC in which the importance of cash flow to the contractor, also referred to by Lord Salmon in *Arenson*, was underlined.
178. (1988) 44 B.L.R. 33, C.A.; [1990] Q.B. 993.
179. Purchas LJ held that there was no reason to infer that the contractor was ever relying upon breach by the engineer of his obligations to the employer to recover his (the contractor's) economic loss, but on the facts did not find it necessary to distinguish between assumption of responsibility, proximity, lack of foreseeability of loss and whether it was just and reasonable to impose a duty of care (at 68). Ralph Gibson

affected by a clause in the engineer's contract excluding the engineer's liability vis-à-vis the employer for any defaults or omissions. The clause clearly features as significant in the judgments (Lord Devlin in *Hedley Byrne* itself had said, "A man cannot be said voluntarily to be undertaking a responsibility if, at the very moment when he is said to be accepting it, he declares that in fact he is not") but two of the Lords Justices[180] would have come to the same decision even in the absence of the disclaimer clause.

What was clearly crucial to all three Lords Justices was that the contractual mechanism between the three parties gave a contractor a remedy for under-certification, namely arbitration against the employer. It is submitted that it is not the presence of the arbitration clause *per se* which was of importance, but rather the fact that there was no contractual bar on the contractor opening up, reviewing and revising unfavourable architect's certificates. In the High Court of Hong Kong, Bokhary J distilled the principle of *Pacific* as follows:

"Where, first, there is adequate machinery under the contract between the employer and the contractor to enforce the contractor's rights thereunder and, secondly there is no good reason at tender stage to suppose that such rights and machinery would not together provide a contractor with an adequate remedy, then, in general, a certifying architect or engineer does not owe to the contractor a duty in tort coterminous with the obligation in contract owed to the contractor by the employer."[181]

Thus a contractor might succeed against an engineer if his contract provides for payment only on certificates, but (unusually) gives him no means, in arbitration or otherwise, to challenge such certificates—a point that may apply where there are "home-made" forms of contract, or ill-considered amendments to the standard forms.

Following the logic of *Pacific*, an engineer will not be held to have assumed a responsibility under *Hedley Byrne*, (and will not therefore be liable to the contractor), where he is carrying out his functions in *purported* performance of his duties under his terms of engagement with his client, the employer. However, where he makes some form of representation *outside* those terms, and upon which the contractor relies to his detriment, there is no reason why (subject to the usual *Hedley Byrne* criteria) he should not be liable. Giving the contractor (incorrect) information, issuing (incorrect) instructions, valuations or certificates will not be covered (provided that the contractor has the power to challenge those decisions). However, a leading commentator has suggested that, for example, the negligent assurance given by an architect to an unpaid sub-contractor that ample money will be owing to the main contractor to meet the sub-contractor's account, in reliance upon which the sub-contractor continues to carry out work, would be one such example.[182]

---

LJ did distinguish between lack of foreseeability of loss, proximity and the criterion that it must be just and reasonable to impose a duty (at 76) and held against Pacific on each point; Russell LJ regarded the test of whether it was just and reasonable to impose a duty of care as being at the heart of the appeal (at 82) and also found against Pacific on proximity (at 83) and lack of foreseeability of loss (at 85).

180. Purchas LJ at 66; Ralph Gibson LJ at 79.

181. *Leon Engineering & Construction Co Ltd* v. *Ka Duk Investment Co Ltd* (1989) 47 B.L.R. 139.

182. I Duncan Wallace QC, "Charter for the construction professional?" (1990) 6 Const. L.J. 207.

## 6.2.2.2 PRE-TENDER CONTRACTUAL INFORMATION

Where pre-tender information provided initially to a tendering contractor by an employer becomes incorporated into the contract itself, the contractor will generally have a remedy against the employer and, on the principles of *Pacific*, will be unable to sue the engineer. Where the information is not so incorporated, the position is different. As above, an important question will be whether the engineer can be said to have assumed a voluntary responsibility to the contractor. In turn, the degree to which the contractor could reasonably be expected to make his own investigations will be relevant. In *Dillingham Ltd* v. *Down*,[183] the New South Wales Supreme Court held that the person providing to the contractor site information (in this case, as it happened, the employer) was not negligent because:

— the specification required the contractor to satisfy himself about site conditions;
— the contractor made no inquiries of the employer;
— the contractor took no independent advice from a geologist or engineer;
— the contractor was clearly anxious to obtain the contract;
— the contractor submitted the low tender, in relation to which the cost of taking independent advice would have been high.

Similarly, the Canadian Supreme Court in *South Nation River Conservation Authority* v. *Auto Concrete Curb Ltd*[184] held that an engineer owed no duty to advise a prospective contractor of the need to obtain a work permit for the particular form of dredging that he proposed to carry out (which was unconventional, but not barred by the contract). The court regarded it as well established that the method by which a contractor decides to carry out work (i.e., where there is a discretion) is within his sphere of responsibility.

(By contrast, in *Edgworth Construction Ltd* v. *F Lea & Associates*[185] the same court held that an engineer liable to a contractor under *Hedley Byrne* for damage caused by inaccuracies in the specification and drawings prepared by him. It may be, however, that this case should not be too heavily relied upon in English courts. *Pacific Associates* is not referred to in the surprisingly short leading judgment; the case was tried on preliminary issues and it is rather unclear as to what the inaccuracies in the information provided by the engineer actually were; and the case is heavily criticised by the learned editor of *Hudson's Building and Engineering Contracts* (11th edn), Volume 1 p. 168, para. 1–296A.)

## 6.2.2.3 FRAUD AND PROCURING A BREACH OF CONTRACT

An architect who deliberately misapplies the contract will be liable in tort to the contractor, or to anyone else (e.g., sub-contractors and suppliers, future occupiers, funders etc.) foreseeably likely to suffer consequential loss because of interference with the contractor's contractual rights.[186] In *John Mowlem & Co Plc* v. *Eagle Star Insurance Co Ltd*[187] the Official Referee refused to strike out a claim by Mowlem that

183. (1972) 13 B.L.R. 97.
184. (1995) 11 Const. L.J. 155.
185. (1993) 3 S.C.R. 206.
186. *Lubenham Fidelities & Investments Co Ltd* v. *South Pembrokeshire District Council* (1986) 33 B.L.R. 46, C.A.
187. (1992) 62 B.L.R. 126.

the project architect had conspired with an insurance company (through its representatives on the board of the employer) to have them removed from their position as management contractors on a housing development at Carlton Gate in West London. The contractor was also allowed to proceed to trial on an allegation of wrongful interference by the architect with its economic interests under its contract with the employer.

Although actions of this nature may sometimes be the only avenue by which a contractor can achieve redress (in *Mowlem* the employer was insolvent), the difficulties involved in bringing such a claim are formidable. The contractor will have to show not merely negligence but deliberate intent. Further, if it cannot be shown that the proper administration of the contract by the architect would, on the balance of probabilities, have led to a payment before the employer's insolvency, the claim would still fail as a matter of causation. In the substantive trial in the *Mowlem* case, Mowlem, the contractor, withdrew its allegations and abandoned its action some six months after the trial began.[188]

## 7 DAMAGES

### 7.1 Generally

The guiding principle on which damages for breach of contract are awarded is clear. In a much cited passage in *Robinson* v. *Harman*[189] Parke B said:

"The rule of the common law is that where a party sustains a loss by reason of a breach of contract, he is, so far as money can do it, to be placed in the same situation with respect to damages, as if the contract had been performed."

In tort, the principle is necessarily different. Damages are to place the injured party, so far as possible, in the position that he would have been in had the negligent act not taken place (the principle of *restitutio in integrum*).[190] In practice the distinction has not featured significantly in the case-law on architects' and engineers' negligence,[191] and it is proposed here to discuss damages on the basis of the contractual principle above. It is not proposed to deal further with the rules applicable to damages generally, but two points should be borne in mind.

First, a plaintiff must establish a causal link between the breach of contract and the loss complained of. In one case[192] it was held that a firm of structural engineers was negligent in failing to obtain calculations from the designers of proprietary cladding, but that even if they had done so, it was unlikely that their clients would have decided

---

188. (1995) *The Times*, 2 August.
189. (1848) 1 Exch. 850 at 855. A similar statement by the High Court of Australia in *Bellgrove* v. *Eldridge* (1954) Aust. L.R. 929 is also often cited.
190. See, for example, Lord Blackburn's words in *Livingstone* v. *Rawyards Coal Co* (1880) 5 App. Cas. 25 at 39, that the court should award "that sum of money which will put the party who has been injured, or who has suffered, in the same position as he would have been in if he had not sustained the wrong for which he is now getting his compensation or reparation".
191. For an exception, see *Gable House Estates Ltd* v. *The Halpern Partnership & Bovis Construction Ltd* (1995) Construction Industry Law Letter 1072, where the court, in considering a claim against an architect for some £32.5 million in damages, found it necessary to consider the architect's potential liability in tort, as well as in contract, because of the different bases on which such damages are awarded (at 1074).
192. *Hill Samuel Bank Ltd* v. *Frederick Brand Partnership & Others* (1994) 45 Con. L.R. 141.

not to proceed with installation of the cladding—i.e., the loss was not caused by the negligence.

Secondly, some losses may be held to be too remote. In order to be recoverable, the loss must:

(a) arise naturally in the usual course of things; or
(b) be said to be within the actual or presumed contemplation of the parties at the time when the contract was made as being the probable[193] result of the breach.

The above two points are often referred to as the first and second limbs of the rule in *Hadley* v. *Baxendale*,[194] after the leading case of that name.

## 7.2 Damages for negligent design

### 7.2.1 Where the building is defective

#### 7.2.1.1 DIMINUTION IN VALUE OR COST OF REPAIR?

In cases of defective buildings, a distinction has often been drawn between two methods of calculating the plaintiff's loss so as to put into effect the principle in *Robinson* v. *Harman*. The first is the cost of reinstatement or repair (also sometimes referred to as "cost of cure"). The second is the diminution in value of the building, i.e., the difference between its actual value and the value that it would have had if there had been no negligence or breach of contract. There has been relatively little discussion in the English reported cases as to why, in principle, there should be any difference.[195] However, two situations where the two methods may yield different results are:

(a) where the plaintiff stipulates for a personal, non-commercial or aesthetic requirement to be fulfilled which is not necessarily translated into an increase in the value of the property in objective terms. Lord Mustill in *Ruxley Electronics & Construction Ltd* v. *Forsyth*,[196] referring to the "consumer surplus",[197] gave the examples of a stipulation for lurid bathroom tiles or a grotesque folly "so discordant with general taste that in purely economic terms the builder may be said to do the employer a favour by failing to install them";
(b) where there is a time-lag between the date of the defendant's breach and the date when the repairs are actually carried out. On the cost of repair basis, damages will either be assessed when the plaintiff paid for them (adding interest if necessary under the court's statutory powers)[198] or at the date of

---

193. Attempts were made to clarify the degree of probability required in *Czarnikow Ltd* v. *Koufos* [1969] 1 A.C. 350, where it was held that, in order to be recoverable, the loss must be held to be "not unlikely" or a "serious possibility" or "real danger".

194. 9 Exch. 341 (1854).

195. Cf. *Hudson's Building and Engineering Contracts* (11th edn) at para. 2–213. Though see below for the current position since *Ruxley* v. *Forsyth*.

196. [1995] 3 All E.R. 268 at 277, H.L.

197. A phrase taken from Harris Ogus and Philips, "Contract Remedies and the Consumer Surplus" (1979) 95 L.Q.R. 581.

198. Supreme Court Act 1981, s. 35A. County Courts Act 1984, s. 69. These rates are currently 8 per cent per annum. In addition an arbitrator has power to award interest, derived from the Arbitration Act 1950, s. 19A.

the trial (if the repairs have not yet been carried out).[199] On the diminution in value basis, the assessment is generally made at the time of the breach.[200] Therefore, changes in the statutory interest rates, and increases in building costs, may result in the two approaches giving different figures.

In actions by employers against contractors for defective buildings, the appropriate measure of damages has been held to be cost of reinstatement.[201] Conversely, in actions against surveyors for negligent pre-purchase surveys, the Court of Appeal has now stated that the correct measure is diminution in value, whether or not the plaintiff would have proceeded to purchase had he been given a proper survey.[202] What is the position in cases of negligent design?

### 7.2.1.2 NEGLIGENT DESIGN: COST OF REINSTATEMENT AS THE STARTING-POINT

In cases of negligent design leading to defective buildings, it seems, particularly in the light of *Ruxley* v. *Forsyth* (dealt with below) that neither cost of reinstatement nor diminution in value is *inflexibly* to be treated as the correct measure. However, insofar as either measure is of more significance than the other, cost of reinstatement appears to be the usual starting-point. This is shown by *Bevan Investments* v. *Blackhall & Struthers*,[203] a decision of the New Zealand Court of Appeal the reasoning of which has often been cited in English cases:

*Facts*
Mr Bevan, a businessman, instructed an architect (Blackhall) to design a recreation centre comprising an ice rink, squash courts and sauna facilities. The architect engaged a structural engineer, Struthers, to assist in the design. During construction, the design was found to be at fault. Mr Bevan's new advisers proposed a modified design to which the work could be completed. Mr Bevan claimed, *inter alia*, the cost of completion according to the modified design.

The New Zealand Court of Appeal, while noting that the cost of reinstatement was not to be regarded as the inevitable approach in all cases of defective buildings,[204] nevertheless held that it was the *prima facie* rule in actions against architects and engineers. Here the defendants' argument that it would have been more reasonable to abort the project and sell the land was rejected. The court also held that the relevant cost was that at trial, since the plaintiff was reasonable in the circumstances to wait until then.

Nevertheless, some factual situations clearly call for the diminution in value approach as being both easier to apply and obviously correct. For example, in *EH Cardy & Sons Ltd* v. *Taylor & Paul Roberts Associates*[205] the plaintiff in fact chose not to carry out repairs but instead to sell the property in question at a reduced price. There was no criticism of him by the court for doing so. In another case[206] the court

---

199. *Bevan Investments* v. *Blackhall & Struthers* (1977) 11 B.L.R. 78; *Dodd Properties (Kent) Ltd* v. *Canterbury City Council* [1980] 1 W.L.R. 433. See section 7.4 below.
200. *Watts* v. *Morrow* [1991] 4 All E.R. 937.
201. *East Ham Corporation* v. *Sunley (Bernard) & Son Ltd* [1966] A.C. 406.
202. *Watts* v. *Morrow* (above).
203. (1977) 11 B.L.R. 78.
204. *Ibid.* at 102.
205. (1994) 39 Con. L.R. 79.
206. *IMI Cornelius (UK) Ltd* v. *Bloor* (1991) 35 Con. L.R. 1.

refused to allow damages to be assessed on the cost of reinstatement basis where a plaintiff had parted with possession and therefore not only no longer had the right to repair but could derive no benefit to itself in having repairs carried out.

In cases where the diminution in value approach is applicable, the date at which the diminution should, in law, be assessed, is not clear. In *Watts* v. *Morrow*,[207] a surveyor's negligence case, Ralph Gibson LJ reserved his views as to whether it should be the date of the breach or the (later) date when damage was sustained. In *T&S Contractors Ltd* v. *Architectural Design Associates*[208] Judge Rich QC held that it was not the date of trial, but the date when "the plaintiff can fairly be said to be in a position where money can fairly compensate him for the effect of the breach", which, in that case, was the delayed date by which the plaintiff was finally able to sell the houses that were the subject of the architect's negligence.

### 7.2.1.3 ANOTHER BASIS FOR ASSESSMENT?: RUXLEY ELECTRONICS & CONSTRUCTION LTD V. FORSYTH

The whole dichotomy between cost of reinstatement and diminution in value may need to be reconsidered in the light of the above House of Lords' decision[209]:

*Facts*
The appellant contracted to build a swimming pool at the respondent's home. The respondent stipulated a requirement of a depth of 7' 6" for diving purposes, but the pool as built was only 6' 9" at its deepest point. It was found as a fact however that this did not in any way hinder diving, nor did it affect the value of the property. The pool could not be repaired and either had to be left as it was or completely replaced at a cost of £21,560, more than the contract sum.

The trial judge held that it would be unreasonable in these circumstances to replace the pool entirely and awarded Mr Forsyth £2,500 for loss of amenity represented by the lost depth. The Court of Appeal overturned this decision by a 2:1 majority and awarded the sum of £21,560. The House of Lords, in unanimously restoring the trial judge's decision, said that the choice was not between cost of repair and diminution in value. Applying the principle of *Robinson* v. *Harman*, and on the basis that it would be unreasonable to expend £21,560 to make good the fault, the plaintiff's loss was properly represented, the court held, by the trial judge's figure of £2,500 for lost amenity. It was also confirmed that a plaintiff need not, as Mr Forsyth had in fact done, undertake to spend any damages recovered on the reinstatement works; but that a plaintiff's intention regarding damages might affect the issue of reasonableness (i.e., if it could be shown as a fact that the plaintiff had no intention of rebuilding, a claim based on cost of repair would be unlikely to succeed).

Although *Ruxley Electronics* was a case on contractors' negligence, not designers' negligence, the House of Lords' flexible approach to the issue of the appropriate measure of damages is likely to be of significance in design cases. Depending on circumstances, there may be other ways in which a plaintiff can properly be compensated for negligent design or supervision.[210] However, it is submitted that

207. [1991] 4 All E.R. 937 at 953.
208. (1993) Construction Industry Law Letter, p. 842.
209. [1995] 3 All E.R. 268, H.L.
210. In *East Ham Corporation* v. *Bernard Sunley & Sons Ltd* [1966] A.C. 406, Lord Upjohn cited with approval a passage from *Hudson* (8th edn, 1959), at p. 319 that there is a further possible head of damage for defective building work over and above cost of repair and diminution in value, viz. the difference between the cost to the builder of the actual work done, and the cost of the work specified. This suggestion is elaborated on in paras 8–137 to 8–140 of the present edition of *Hudson*, where it is argued that such

there is nothing in the judgment that contradicts the *Bevan* view that cost of reinstatement is at least the *prima facie* rule to apply.

### 7.2.1.4 BETTERMENT

It is often the case that the completion or correction of a defective design results in the owner having a more valuable building than he originally contracted for, thus acquiring a degree of "betterment". Must he give credit for such a "windfall" benefit, or can he argue that the benefit is simply the consequence of the architect's or engineer's breach? The answer depends upon the degree to which the betterment was an inevitable consequence of the negligence.

In *Richard Roberts Holdings* v. *Douglas Smith Stimson*[211] the judge, rejecting the defendant's argument that damages should be reduced to take into account betterment, said:

"I think that the law can be shortly summarised. If the only practicable method of overcoming the consequences of a defendant's breach of contract is to build to a higher standard than the contract had required, the plaintiff may recover the cost of building to that higher standard. If, however, a plaintiff, needing to carry out works because of a defendant's breach of contract, chooses to build to a higher standard than is strictly necessary, the courts will, unless the new works are so different as to break the chain of causation, award him the cost of the works less a credit to the defendant in respect of betterment."

The court does not consider *de novo* what the plaintiff should have done, and a claim will not be defeated merely because, with hindsight, the plaintiff might have done something else. The test is whether the plaintiff acted reasonably at the time.[212] However, if the plaintiff *chooses* to build to a higher standard than that originally contracted for, he must generally give credit for the betterment.[213] If his proposed remedial works are radically different from the works contracted for, it may be held that the chain of causation has been broken altogether.[214]

---

damages based on this measure may sometimes be apt, particularly against contractors who have sought to save costs by delivering work and materials of an inferior quality. Further, it is argued, such a measure does not infringe on the rule that damages are to compensate the plaintiff for his loss, rather than to punish the wrongdoer.

It may readily be seen that these considerations apply where a supervising officer fails to identify defective work. They may also apply where a designer deliberately misleads a client as to the type of material that will be used, pocketing the difference in cost himself where, for example, the inferior material is not objectively any less serviceable or functional.

211. (1988) 46 B.L.R. 50 at 69.

212. *Board of Governors of the Hospital for Sick Children* v. *McLaughlan & Harvey plc* (1987) 19 Con. L.R. 25.

213. Cf. *British Westinghouse Electric & Manufacturing Co Ltd* v. *Underground Electric Railways Co of London Ltd* [1912] A.C. 673, where the plaintiff, who had been supplied with engines under a contract, replaced them with better ones.

214. *Harbutts Plasticine Ltd* v. *Wayne Tank & Pump Co Ltd* [1970] 1 Q.B. 447, C.A. The case was overruled in the House of Lords but on a different point. See also Judge Newey's words in the *Board of Governors of the Hospital for Sick Children* case (above): "A plaintiff's own action in failing to mitigate his loss by, for example, carrying out more remedial work than he needs, may in itself break the chain of causation".

In the *Bevan* case discussed above, the cost of a properly designed recreation centre would have exceeded the cost of the building design by the defendant by some $8,000. The court found as a fact that Mr Bevan would almost certainly have still gone ahead with the project, if the original price put to him had been $8,000 more than it in fact was. Therefore, damages were to be assessed on the basis of the cost of completing the works, less a credit for the benefit of the $8,000 in value that the plaintiff would effectively receive after the reinstatement works were carried out.

### 7.2.2 *Where the designer misleads the client as to cost or some other matter*

#### 7.2.2.1 THE PROBLEM IN CASES WHERE THE PLAINTIFF WOULD HAVE PROCEEDED IN ANY EVENT

Where the plaintiff's complaint is that the designer was negligent in providing a misleadingly low cost estimate, his immediate difficulty with regard to damages is as follows. Unless he can show that he would not have proceeded with the project at all had he known the true likely cost at the outset, or unless he in fact reasonably aborted the project once the true costs were known he will have suffered no loss—the building would always have cost the higher figure, and the plaintiff will have received the full value of it. In such cases, the plaintiff's claim will typically be limited to such matters as reasonably foreseeable consequential costs, associated with the re-financing arrangements including, possibly, administration costs and increased interest charges. The same applies where the misleading information was about something other than cost.[215]

#### 7.2.2.2 WHERE THE PLAINTIFF WOULD NOT HAVE PROCEEDED IF ADVISED PROPERLY

The situation is different where the plaintiff can show that he would not have started a particular project or would have taken a materially different course of action had the correct advice or information been given. Whether the plaintiff would have acted differently is a matter of fact for the court to decide. In *Gable House Estates Ltd* v. *The Halpern Partnership & Bovis Construction Ltd*[216] an architect provided to a client a schedule stating that the usable office space for a building was some 34,000 square feet. In fact it was some 2,000 square feet less. The judge found on the facts that if the client had been given the correct figure, it would not have proceeded with redevelopment but would have renovated then sold the building. Particularly important in this context was the fact that the lower figure would have been a "sudden, substantial descent" from figures previously given to the client, and also that there were other risks and uncertainties associated with redevelopment.

Assuming that a plaintiff can show that he would not have proceeded, he will in principle be able to recover, as his main head of damage, his wasted expenditure. Where he cuts his losses by selling a development site which was the subject of the design (and provided that he acts reasonably in doing so), he may also, in principle,

---

215. Cf. *Hill Samuel Bank Ltd* v. *The Frederick Brand Partnership and Others* (1994) 45 Con. L.R. 141, where the court found that an engineer's negligent failure to obtain calculations about cladding did not cause any loss, as the client would have proceeded with this form of cladding even if the calculations had been provided.
216. (1955) Construction Industry Law Letter, p. 1072.

recover damages for any fall in the value of the site between his purchase and his sale, on the authority of *Banque Bruxelles Lambert SA* v. *Eagle Star Insurance Co Ltd & Others*.[217] The principles as to causation in that case will plainly apply to similar property losses where there is negligent advice about cost or other matters, coupled with proof that the plaintiff would not otherwise have proceeded (a situation referred to by the Court of Appeal as a "no transaction" case).

### 7.3 Damages for negligent administration/supervision of the contract

A feature of claims against architects and engineers for breach of their obligations to administer or supervise the construction of a building is that the plaintiff will often join contractors, and indeed any sub-contractors with whom he has direct warranties, to the action. Thus in actions for defective work the contractor may be sued in respect of the work itself, and the architect may be sued for failing to identify the defective work. The multi-party aspect of these cases is dealt with only briefly here, and in detail in section 8 below. The typical areas are:

(a) failing to identify defects: here, the damages will generally be the cost of putting the defects right. Damages are assessed on the cost of repair basis,[218] and the architect/engineer will be able to claim a contribution or full indemnity from the contractor;

(b) failure to give information or instructions, leading to a loss and expense claim by the contractor: here, the damages will generally be the legitimate value of the loss and expense claim. Following *Wessex Regional Health Authority* v. *HLM Design Ltd*[219] an architect or engineer may have to face a claim by an employer for damages relating to a contractor's claim which has not itself been fully fought to a conclusion—see the discussion in section 8.1 below;

(c) instructions for extras, thus increasing the employer's costs; and over-certification: if an architect is negligent in instructing variation orders in the sense that to do so is outside his express or implied authority, or in the sense that the variation orders were not necessary, the plaintiff's claim may face the same difficulties outlined above, in that the plaintiff will have received the benefit (assuming there is one) of the extra work.

If the architect or engineer has negligently overvalued work and fails to correct the valuation on the next or later certificates, the employer will have suffered a real and recoverable loss. Since valuation is generally the function

---

217. [1995] 2 All E.R. 769. In that case, in which a number of similar appeals were consolidated and heard together, the various lenders had granted loans secured on properties that had been negligently under-valued by various surveyors. When the lenders came to realise their security, their losses were greater than would otherwise have been the case because of the intervening slump in the property market in the late 1980s/early 1990s. The surveyors argued that the plaintiff's damages should not extend to cover this phenomenon which was not reasonably foreseeable. However, the Court of Appeal held that the issue was one of causation, rather than reasonable foreseeability as such. The losses were caused by the negligent valuations, therefore, subject to the usual rules about the damage not being too remote (which, here, it was held not to be, as it was plainly foreseeable that a lender would suffer an increased loss if the market moved downwards) and subject to there being no other intervening cause, the surveyors were liable for the whole of the lender's loss.

218. *East Ham Corporation* v. *Sunley (Bernard) & Son Ltd* [1966] A.C. 406.

219. (1995) 71 B.L.R. 32.

of the quantity surveyor under the standard forms of contract, the supervising officer may well be able to claim a contribution from him.

## 7.4 Mitigation

In the tort case of *Liesbosch Dredger (Owners)* v. *SS Edison*[220] the House of Lords held that losses arising from a plaintiff's impecuniosity were not recoverable. The case is thus capable of being prayed in aid by negligent architects and engineers against owners who fail to carry out necessary repair work promptly, and as such is capable of causing some difficulties for owners who will often be unable or unwilling to carry out such repairs until funds are available or liability is established.

Recent cases, however, have tended to take a more sympathetic view as follows:

(i) In *Bevan* v. *Blackhall & Struthers*[221] (for the facts, see section 7.2.1.2 above) the court accepted that the owner had acted reasonably, and in a commercially sensible manner, in awaiting the outcome of the litigation on liability before embarking on costly reinstatement work. Relevant factors were that the contractor was willing to complete only on a "cost plus" basis, which would have been expensive; the plaintiff's bank was unwilling to advance monies without a firm price; the architect was uninsured so that any judgment against him might be unenforceable; and the personal assets of the plaintiff and his father-in-law would probably have had to be ploughed into the reinstatement work.

The court expressed some doubt as to whether the *Liesbosch* case still represented good law, citing similar doubts expressed in Halsbury's Laws of England (4th edn); and in any event said that it was a case of "true impecuniosity unaccompanied by other factors". The court also approved a passage from *Hudson's Building and Civil Engineering Contracts* (10th edn),[222] that the true rule should be that the delay should only be a relevant factor in reducing the damages recoverable if it has had the effect of increasing the *real* cost of repair, i.e., by increasing the *physical* amount or quality of the work to be done.

(ii) In *Dodd Properties (Kent) Ltd* v. *Canterbury City Council*,[223] a tort case, the Court of Appeal distinguished *Liesbosch* in holding that the decision to postpone reinstatement was not to be regarded as a product of impecuniosity, but to be seen as a decision based on commercial good sense.

(iii) In *Perry* v. *Sidney Philips*[224] Kerr LJ, referring in particular to *Dodd Properties*, felt that the authority of certain statements emanating from the *Liesbosch* case was "consistently being attenuated" by more recent decisions and added:

"If it is reasonably foreseeable that the plaintiff may be unable to mitigate or remedy the consequence of the other party's breach as soon as he would have done if he had been provided with the necessary means

220. [1933] A.C. 449.
221. (1977) 11 B.L.R. 78.
222. Reproduced in *Hudson's Building and Engineering Contracts* (11th edn), para. 8–148.
223. [1980] 1 W.L.R. 433.
224. (1982) 22 B.L.R. 120, C.A.

to do so from the other party, then it seems to me that the principle of the *Liesbosch* no longer applies in its full rigour."

(iv) In *Mattocks* v. *Mann*[225] it was held that only in exceptional circumstances could the impecuniosity of a plaintiff be isolated as a separate cause so as to bring the *Liesbosch* principle into consideration.

In summary it appears that, provided that a plaintiff can show that his decision to postpone work is based on reasonable commercial grounds, and is not *wholly* due to impecuniosity, he will safely be able to postpone such work. Damages will then be assessed at the date of trial.

## 7.5 Reduction of damages for contributory negligence

### 7.5.1 The employer and his clerk of works

In the area of negligent administration of a contract, a supervising officer might wish to argue that the employer, through his clerk of works, is contributorily negligent in, for example, also failing to identify defective work. To what extent can such a defence succeed?

In *Kensington and Westminster and Chelsea Area Health Authority* v. *Wettern Composites*[226] (his Honour Judge Smout QC) the architect successfully reduced the employer's damages by 20 per cent, by arguing that the employer was, through his clerk of works, contributorily negligent in failing to identify poor workmanship by the contractor. However, in *EH Cardy & Sons Ltd* v. *Paul Roberts & Associates*,[227] the root cause of the problems was the failure of the architect to survey the property before making drawings. The argument by the third party for contributory negligence was that, as a reasonably prudent person, the plaintiff ought to have checked that a survey had been made or make its own survey. It was common ground that the plaintiff company had the ability to make a survey. Judge Bowsher QC robustly rejected this argument: "There is little point in hiring a professional to do work if it is to be said that the client has a duty to check the professional's work"—or more pithily "You do not hire a dog and bark yourself".

Further, allowing claims for contributory negligence in these circumstances penalises the employer who employs a clerk of works more than the employer who does not. Also, it may be said that the employer employs a clerk of works for his own benefit, not to act as a second line of protection from the architect.[228] In view of these points and the brakes on contributory negligence as a defence discussed below, it may be that the *Kensington* case would be decided differently today.

### 7.5.2 The Law Reform (Contributory Negligence) Act 1945

The concept of contributory negligence was recognised in the above Act, section 1(1) of which states:

225. [1993] R.T.R. 13.
226. (1984) 31 B.L.R. 57. For the facts, see section 5.1.4 above.
227. (1994) 38 Con. L.R. 79 at 96.
228. See also the strong words of the Canadian Supreme Court in *Bilodeau* v. *Bergeron* 1974 (2) S.C.R. 345 at 351 cited in section 8.2.4 below, in the context of a supplier's allegation of contributory negligence against his main contractor's supervisor.

"Where any person suffers damage as the result partly of his own fault and partly of the fault of any other person or persons, a claim in respect of that damage shall not be defeated by reason of the fault of the person suffering the damage, but the damages recoverable in respect thereof shall be reduced to such extent as the court thinks just and equitable having regard to the claimant's share in the responsibility for the damage …"

In *Forsikringsaktieselskapet Vesta* v. *Butcher*[229] the Court of Appeal considered the applicability of the concept to contractual cases and held that there were three categories of contractual obligations co-existent with obligations in tort:

(i) where a party's liability arises from breach of a contractual provision which does not depend on negligence (this could, for example, apply to an obligation to design to a set standard);

(ii) where the liability arises from an express contractual obligation to take care, but which does not in fact correspond to any duty which would exist in tort (for example, an obligation to design using reasonable care and skill but again to a set standard);

(iii) where the liability for breach of contract is the same as, and co-extensive with, a liability in tort independently of the existence of a contract.

Only in the third of these cases can contributory negligence be raised as a defence.[230] In fact, most architects' and engineers' appointments will be within category (iii) by virtue of an express or implied term.

The general ambit of the contributory negligence defence has been further eroded by *Barclays Bank plc* v. *Fairclough Building Ltd.*[231] Nourse LJ said:

"It ought to be a cause of general concern that the law should have got into such a state that a contractor who was in breach of two of the main obligations expressly undertaken by him in a standard form building contract was able to persuade the judge in the court below that the building owner's damages should be reduced by 40 per cent because of his own negligence in not preventing the contractor from committing the breaches. It ought to have been perfectly obvious that the [1945 Act] was never intended to obtrude the defence of contributory negligence into an area of the law where it has no business to be."

Specifically, the Court of Appeal held that where the plaintiff complained of breach of a strict contractual obligation, contributory negligence was not available as a defence. This will not restrict the architect's or engineer's position where (as is usual) he is sued for breach of the obligation of care and skill, rather than for breach of a strict obligation. Nevertheless, the above cases exemplify something of a trend away from this particular defence.

## 7.6 Heads of damage

This subsection examines some of the heads of damage over and above the "substantial" relief (rectification costs etc., as to which see earlier) frequently claimed by employers against architects and engineers.

---

229. [1988] 2 All E.R. 43, C.A., a reinsurance case which subsequently went to the House of Lords on other points.
230. For an argument that contributory negligence should in principle be capable of being raised in the other two categories as well, see a note by A Burnett on the case of *Schering Agrochemicals Ltd* v. *Resibel Nusa* at (1993) 109 L.Q.R. 175. See also Law Commission Working Paper No. 114 (1990), "Contributory Negligence as a Defence in Contract".
231. [1995] 1 All E.R. 289, C.A.

### 7.6.1 Lost profits

Architects and engineers, whether as designers or supervisors, may be liable in damages under this head subject to the usual rules as to foreseeability. In *Victoria Laundry (Windsor) Ltd* v. *Newman Industries Ltd*[232] the defendant could not reasonably be expected to know at the time when the contract was made that the plaintiffs for whom it was to deliver a boiler intended to use it in connection not with ordinary dyeing contracts but for special dyeing contracts with the Ministry of Supply. The defendant was therefore only liable for the notional amount of lost profits corresponding to those which he could reasonably be said to have had within his contemplation at the time when the contract was made.

In *Bevan* v. *Blackhall & Struthers*[233] (for the facts, see section 7.2.1.2 above) the Court of Appeal noted the difficulties in assessing whether or not the plaintiff's recreation centre would have made a profit, and if so what, particularly bearing in mind the fact that no similar centre existed at the time from which comparable figures might be taken. However, given the plaintiff's enthusiasm, business ability in other fields and sporting prowess, which was felt in particular to be an important factor in attracting custom, the court believed that the business would have been profitable and assessed lost profits at $10,000.

### 7.6.2 Damages for inconvenience, distress and loss of amenity

The courts have always taken a restrictive view of the extent to which such damages are recoverable in contract cases. In *Addis* v. *Gramophone Co Ltd*[234] the House of Lords rejected a claim for distress following an action for unfair dismissal, and emphasised that damages for breach of contract were limited to financial losses. This head of damage must be considered in relation to three areas as follows.

#### 7.6.2.1 IN CONTRACTS WHOSE OBJECT IS THE PROVISION OF PLEASURE

If the contract is one in respect of which it can properly be said that the object of the contract is the provision of pleasure, peace of mind or freedom from distress, the plaintiff may recover such damages.[235] Typical are the cases of lost or spoilt holidays.[236] However, contracts between client and solicitor are not generally covered.[237]

In *Knott* v. *Bolton*[238] the Knotts instructed an architect, Mr Bolton, to build their "dream home". An important feature of this home was to be a wide and impressive staircase. This was not achieved. The Court of Appeal declined to hold that this was a contract whose object was pleasure. Per Russell LJ:

"The very object of the contract ... was to design [the] house. As an ancillary of that of course it was in the contemplation of Mr Bolton and of the Knotts that pleasure would be provided, but the provision of pleasure to the occupiers of the house was not the very object of the contract."

232. [1949] 1 All E.R. 997.
233. (1977) 11 B.L.R. 78.
234. [1909] A.C. 488.
235. *Bliss* v. *South East Thames Regional Health Authority* (1987) I.C.R. 700.
236. *Jarvis* v. *Swan Tours Ltd* [1973] Q.B. 233; *Jackson* v. *Horizon Holidays Ltd* [1975] 3 All E.R. 92.
237. *Hayes* v. *Dodd* [1990] 2 All E.R. 815.
238. (1995) 45 Con. L.R. 127, C.A.

The issue must be one of degree, it is submitted. A contract to build a games room, or something of purely aesthetic and non-functional value is *prima facie* a contract for the provision of pleasure.

In *Hutchinson* v. *Harris*[239] the Court of Appeal, while accepting that there could be damages for distress in architects' negligence cases, declined to award them for a plaintiff who had lost the use of premises, on the basis that she was intending to convert and renovate her house for commercial purposes only, in order to provide an income for herself and her family.

### 7.6.2.2 IN CASES WHERE OTHER MEANS OF ASSESSING DAMAGES ARE INAPPROPRIATE

In *Ruxley Electronics & Construction Ltd* v. *Forsyth*[240] the court, faced with the unpalatable alternatives of awarding the plaintiff either nothing (for an admitted breach of contract) or £21,560 (representing the reinstatement costs of a defective swimming pool, in a situation where the court felt that complete replacement was unjustified) held that there was a third measure of damages that could be properly be said to represent the plaintiff's cost, viz. £2,500 for the loss of amenity in not having the depth of pool stipulated. Clearly, if the facts had been slightly different an award of nil damages (e.g., if the discrepancy in depth had been one inch instead of nine inches) or £21,560 damages (e.g., if the discrepancy had been three feet, not nine inches) would have been appropriate. Thus the distress and inconvenience head was used by the court to "plug the gap".

It is submitted that *Ruxley* is thus now authority for the proposition that where a contract is inadequately performed in such a way as to leave a plaintiff with a legitimate right to compensation, but where the compensation is not, for whatever reason, calculable by reference to the cost of repair or diminution in value, the plaintiff's loss may best be represented by damages for loss of amenity. This rule will be particularly apposite in contracts that have a non-commercial element and *a fortiori* where a plaintiff requires something that has only subjective or idiosyncratic value.[241]

### 7.6.2.3 IN OTHER CASES

In *Watts* v. *Morrow*[242] a case of surveyors' negligence, a survey caused a husband and wife to pay too much for a weekend cottage. Bingham LJ summarised the position relating to damages for distress and inconvenience as follows:

"Where the very object of a contract is to provide pleasure, relaxation, peace of mind or freedom from molestation, damages will be awarded if the fruit of the contract is not provided or if the contrary result is procured instead. If the law did not cater for this exceptional category of case it would be defective. A contract to survey the condition of a house for a prospective purchaser does not, however, fall within this exceptional category.

In cases not falling within this exceptional category, damages are in my view recoverable for physical inconvenience and discomfort caused by the breach and mental suffering directly

239. (1978) 10 B.L.R. 19, C.A.
240. See section 7.2.1.3 above.
241. E.g., a person who requires a lurid set of bathroom tiles (Lord Mustill) or wants one course of blue bricks for his house (Lord Jauncey) or contracts for the building of a grotesque folly (Lords Mustill and Jauncey).
242. [1991] 4 All E.R. 937, C.A.

related to that inconvenience and discomfort. If those effects are foreseeably suffered during a period when defects are repaired I am prepared to accept that they sound in damages even though the cost of the repairs is not recoverable as such. But I also agree that award should be restrained."

In that case, the judge's award of £4,000 to each plaintiff was reduced by the Court of Appeal to £750 each.

*Summary*[243]  The position, it is submitted, in relation to damages for loss of amenity, distress and inconvenience in the case of architects' and engineers' negligence is as follows:

(1) Where the object of the contract is to provide pleasure, such damages are recoverable. A contract to design a house, even one with a prominent artistic feature, is not such a contract (*Knott*).

(2) Where the object of the contract is otherwise, damages are recoverable for physical inconvenience and discomfort caused by the breach, and consequential mental suffering directly related to that inconvenience and discomfort. The courts will restrain the quantum of such damages (*Watts*).

(3) However, damages for loss of amenity may also be awarded where that is the best method of compensating a plaintiff who has suffered a loss, and in respect of which damages based on any other measure are inappropriate (*Ruxley*).

### 7.6.3 Costs of alternative accommodation while repairs are being carried out

Such cases have been allowed in actions by tenants for landlords' breach of repairing covenants.[244] Although Ralph Gibson LJ in *Watts* v. *Morrow* reserved his position on whether such a claim, had it been made, would have succeeded, there seems no reason in principle why these claims should not be made where an owner reasonably moves out of accommodation while repair work is being carried out.

### 7.6.4 Managerial time and costs

A corporate plaintiff will often claim that it has suffered losses in terms of management time and costs in sorting out problems caused by an architect's or engineer's negligence. While there is no precedent for recovering these costs insofar as they are incurred in connection with *litigation* (except possibly where an employee acts as an in-house expert) there is authority that, provided a quantifiable loss can be shown to the company, such losses may be recovered.

In *Tate & Lyle Food & Distribution Ltd* v. *GLC*[245] Forbes J said:

"I have no doubt that the expenditure of managerial time in remedying an actionable wrong done to a trading concern can properly form a subject matter of a head of special damage."

243. For a thorough review of quantum, in these types of cases, see K Franklin, "Damages for Heartache: The Award of General Damages for Inconvenience and Distress in Building Cases" (1988) Const. L.J. 4 and "More Heartache: A Review of the Award of General Damages in Building Cases" (1992) Const. L.J. 8.
244. E.g., *Lubren* v. *Lambeth LBC* (1987) 20 H.L.R. 165.
245. [1982] 1 W.L.R. 149.

The principle has been applied to non-trading concerns.[246] The suggestion has also been taken further by his Honour Judge Lloyd QC in *Babcock Energy Ltd* v. *Lodge Sturtevant Ltd*.[247] The judge noted that although it could be said to be a normal part of a manager's employment to sort out problems, in this case "an untoward degree of time" had been expended. He therefore allowed a claim under this head. It is important to note that the plaintiff was able to provide detailed and extensive records of time claimed.

### 7.6.5 Lost opportunity to obtain cheaper quotations

In *Corfield* v. *Grant*[248] the Official Referee described a hotel conversion as an "inadequately controlled muddle" and held an architect to be in continuous breach of contract in failing to co-ordinate matters. The hotelier successfully argued that because of the architect's delay in progressing matters, he had lost the opportunity to obtain competitive quotations, since he had to work speedily and obtain whatever quotation he could in the time available. Judge Bowsher QC awarded £500 to represent the lost opportunity of obtaining cheaper quotations, on the principle of *Chaplin* v. *Hicks*.[249]

### 7.6.6 Experts' fees incurred by the plaintiff

In *Hutchinson* v. *Harris*[250] the plaintiff claimed against the defendant architect as one head of damage fees paid to her independent surveyor for the preparation of two reports dealing with allegedly defective work. The Court of Appeal held that although these reports had been prepared partly for the purpose of rectifying the defective work, it was clear that their main purpose was to indicate over-pricing by the builder with a view to proving that matter in the litigation, and thus to support the plaintiff's case against the architect. The fees were therefore recoverable in the same way as the plaintiff's other litigation costs, i.e., on a taxation of costs following a favourable costs order.

To the extent therefore that experts' fees can be said to be incurred primarily for matters other than the litigation, the plaintiff may be able to claim them as damages in the litigation itself. The advantages are small: damages would generally be payable before taxation of costs by the court is complete; and the plaintiff can claim interest on the fees from the time when they are incurred. However, the disadvantage is that the expert's files relating to the fees claimed become discoverable documents in the litigation.[251]

### 7.6.7 The architect's or engineer's cross-claim for fees

Plaintiffs suing architects and engineers often tend to assume that if they prove negligence, they have no liability for payment of any of the professional's fees. This is

---

246. *The Salvage Association* v. *Cap Financial Services Ltd* (unreported) 2 October 1992 (Judge Thayne Forbes QC, Official Referees' Business).
247. (1994) Construction Industry Law Letter, p. 982.
248. (1992) 59 B.L.R. 102, Q.B.D.
249. [1911] 2 Q.B. 586.
250. (1978) 10 B.L.R. 19, C.A.
251. See *Goldman* v. *Hesper* [1988] 3 All E.R. 97 for the extent to which discovery and inspection of such documents might be resisted.

not so. First, the architect's or engineer's work may be separable into various discrete elements,[252] e.g., under the RIBA stages of work or the ACE Conditions, or simply as a matter of construction of the contract. The professional is then entitled to sever the good from the bad, and the plaintiff will have to give credit in his claim for the parts that have been properly performed. Secondly, as regards fees relating to work which is found to be negligent, unless it can be said that the negligence is so fundamental that the architect or engineer has effectively failed to perform at all (i.e., a total failure of consideration) the architect or engineer may be entitled to keep or claim at least a portion of the fees in diminution of his claim.

It is submitted that the following principles apply:

(a) Where the contract is severable, the part performed properly must be paid for (see above).
(b) Where:
  (i) there is a total failure of consideration; or
  (ii) the architect's or engineer's negligence results in the plaintiff entering into a project that, had he known the true position, he would not have entered into,

he will not be entitled to keep any of his fees.

In *Moneypenny* v. *Hartland*[253] Best CJ said, "If a surveyor delivers an estimate greatly below the sum at which a work can be done and thereby induces a private person to undertake what he would not otherwise do, then I think he is not entitled to recover: ..."

Similarly, in *Nye Saunders & Partners* v. *Bristow*,[254] where the architect underestimated the potential costs of the project, the Court of Appeal held that he was not entitled to his fees.

(c) In other cases, it is submitted, the plaintiff will generally have to give some credit for the architect's or engineer's fees, though this may be offset by increased costs payable to an architect or engineer to have the work done properly, if those fees are reasonable—the overriding principle being that the plaintiff must not recover more than his actual loss.[255]

In *Hutchinson* v. *Harris*[256] the Court of Appeal held that the plaintiff had to give credit for the architect's fees in her successful damages claim, so as to avoid double recovery. Despite the court's reservation,[257] there seems no reason in principle why

252. E.g., under SFA/92 which incorporates the various work stages of the RIBA document "Plan of Work"; or under the ACE Conditions.

253. (1820–26) 2 C. & P. 378.

254. (1987) 37 B.L.R. 92, C.A. For the facts, see section 4.4.10 above.

255. For example, if the negligent architect or engineer charges £500 and the plaintiff has to pay a further £500 for an architect to do the work properly (leaving aside costs connected with litigation) the plaintiff can in principle claim £500 damages for the second architect's fee, and the negligent architect can cross-claim £500 for his own fees, the net result being that the claim and cross-claim cancel each other out while the plaintiff will have paid £500 overall (which is what he would have paid had the contract been performed properly in the first place). If the second architect charges £750, the plaintiff will still be able to put that figure into the account, subject to reasonableness of that fee.

256. See section 7.6.6 above.

257. Waller LJ was influenced by the fact that abatement was not pleaded or argued in the court below. He also held that it could lead to double recovery for the plaintiff. Stevenson LJ had "the greatest difficulty" in applying the principle to a claim for professional services though, as pointed out in the commentary by the editors of the Building Law Reports (p. 22) it is not clear why, or why the principle should not be applicable in such cases.

an architect's or engineer's fees cannot be abated under the rule in *Mondel* v. *Steel*,[258] i.e., as stated by Parke B:

"It is competent for the defendant ... not to set off, by a proceeding in the nature of a cross-action, the amount of damages which he has sustained by breach of the contract, but simply to defend himself by showing how much less the subject matter of the action was worth, by reason of the breach of contract."

# 8 ASPECTS OF MULTI-PARTY ACTIONS

A feature of construction litigation is that it often involves more than two parties. Architects and engineers may find themselves in actions involving owners, contractors, sub-contractors, suppliers and other professionals. Some consequences of these sorts of action are now considered.

## 8.1 Jurisdictional problems

The standard forms of building and engineering contracts, and those for the appointment of architects and engineers (e.g., SFA/92, the ACE Conditions and the Professional Services Appointment) contain arbitration clauses.[259] If one party seeks to litigate instead, the other, provided he has taken no step in the action, may apply for a stay to arbitration under the Arbitration Act 1950, s. 4, where the court may (i.e., in its discretion) order a stay if there is an agreement to arbitrate, which in turn requires the arbitration agreement to be in writing (s. 32).[260] In at least the following two situations, the architect or engineer may be forced to have the dispute heard in court where there is an arbitration clause:

(a) where the arbitration clause is not unequivocally incorporated into the contract of engagement: a string of construction cases,[261] explicitly or otherwise recognising the approach taken in the shipping case of *Thomas* v. *Portsea*,[262] have made clear that the courts will not force a party to arbitrate in the absence of specific agreement. Merely agreeing by letter (for example) that the contract will be based on a certain standard form or set of

---

258. (1841) 8 M. & W. 858.

259. SFA/92, cl. 1.8.1; ACE Conditions, cl. 9.6 (subject, however, to prior adjudication in certain cases—see the Appendix to this chapter); PSA, cl. 92.1, again subject to adjudication.

260. For non-domestic arbitrations the relevant statutory provision is s. 1 of the Arbitration Act 1975. Here, however, the court must (not "may") order a stay to arbitration, so long as it is shown that the contract contains an arbitration clause.

261. *Aughton* v. *MF Kent Services Ltd* (1991) 57 B.L.R. 1, C.A. (the judgment of Megaw LJ only); *Lexair Ltd (In administrative receivership)* v. *Edgar Taylor Ltd* (1933) 65 B.L.R. 87; *Smith & Gordon Ltd* v. *John Lewis Building Ltd* (1994) Construction Industry Law Letter, p. 934, C.A.; *Giffen (Electrical Contractors) Ltd* v. *Drake & Scull Engineering Ltd* (and *Femwork* v. *Drake & Scull*) (1933) 37 Con. L.R. 84; *Ben Barrett & Son (Brickwork) Ltd* v. *Henry Boot Management Ltd* (1995) Construction Industry Law Letter, p. 1026; *Co-Operative Wholesale Society Ltd* v. *Saunders & Taylor Ltd* (1994) 39 Con L.R. 77. For a discussion of these and other cases, see the writer's article "Incorporating Arbitration Clauses into Construction Contracts: Two Problems" in (1994) 61 J.C.I. Arb. 1, p. 53. For a different, and perhaps more commercial, approach to these cases, albeit in relation to Article 7(2) of the Model Law, see the decision by the Supreme Court of Hong Kong (Kaplan J) in *Astel-Peiniger Joint Venture* v. *Argos Engineering & Heavy Industry Co. Ltd* (unreported, 1994).

262. [1912] A.C. 1.

conditions may well not be enough. Architects and engineers should therefore be wary of trying to incorporate standard conditions by reference (as opposed to incorporation by actually signing the standard form);

(b) where the employer sues a number of defendants: here, the courts have often recognised, in refusing section 4 applications, that a party's "right" to arbitrate may be outweighed by the interests of justice in avoiding separate proceedings with potentially inconsistent findings by different tribunals.[263]

Conversely, an architect or engineer who *wants* a dispute resolved in the High Court may himself be able to prevent the other party from proceeding by way of arbitration. It has been held that a man whose professional capabilities are impugned is entitled to have the allegations determined in the High Court.[264] An architect or engineer in this position can simply sue for his fees, resist a section 4 application, and apply by injunction if necessary to restrain the other party's efforts to proceed with the arbitration.[265]

If an employer is faced with a claim for extra payment and/or loss and expense from a contractor, he may turn to his architect and allege negligent administration of the building contract. In such cases, the architect's power to challenge the loss and expense claim may be limited, as appears from *Wessex Regional Health Authority* v. *HLM Design Ltd.*[266]

His Honour Judge Fox-Andrews introduced the issues by commenting[267]:

"These proceedings present in stark form problems which may arise in construction/ engineering contracts where there are three parties namely the employer, the contractor and the professional man, whether he be architect, engineer or otherwise."

*Facts*
The main contractor, ARC, to whom an extension of time covering 74 of the 84 weeks' overrun had been granted by HLM, the architects, commenced an arbitration against the employer, Wessex, seeking an award that the extension of time should have been granted for the whole period of 84 weeks. HLM were of course not parties to that arbitration. Wessex, after incurring some £1 million in costs, settled the arbitration on relatively unfavourable terms and without proceeding to a final award, mainly because of evidential difficulties. Wessex then commenced High Court proceedings against HLM claiming damages comprising sums paid to the contractor, and their extensive arbitration costs. HLM objected to this course of action arguing that, if allowed, it meant that an employer could sue his architect for negligent over-certification without (or before) bringing an action against the contractor for recovery of the overpaid monies. A further difficulty was that the architect might then be unable to bring the contractor into the action in contribution proceedings under section 1 of the Civil Liability (Contribution) Act 1978 (because that section refers to liability established in an *action* whereas the contractor's liability, if any, would be established in an *arbitration*, assuming an arbitration clause).

The judge "reluctantly" held that an employer has independent causes of action against his contractor and architect. He said that there would be much to be said for contractual arrangements requiring the employer to pursue his remedy against the

---

263. *Taunton-Collins* v. *Cromie* [1964] 1 W.L.R. 633; *Berkshire Senior Citizens Housing Association Ltd* v. *McCarthy E Fitt Ltd* (1979) 15 B.L.R. 27.
264. *Turner* v. *Fenton* [1982] 1 W.L.R. 52.
265. *Doleman* v. *Ossett Corporation* [1912] 3 K.B. 257 illustrates the court's powers to restrain arbitrations by injunction.
266. (1995) 71 B.L.R. 32.
267. *Ibid.* at 39C.

contractor who had been overpaid, and only gave him limited rights against the architect, but that in the absence of such arrangements there were untrammelled independent causes of action. He rejected HLM's argument that the action must fail because the settlement in the arbitration broke the chain of causation and/or was too remote and/or that it was not reasonably foreseeable that the employer would settle the arbitration in such a manner. The case illustrates the jurisdictional problems caused by:

(a) the fact that the standard building and architects' forms do not have arbitration clauses that contemplate multi-party proceedings[268];

(b) the decision in *Northern Regional Health Authority* v. *Derek Crouch Construction Ltd*[269] where the Court of Appeal held that in the case of a standard building contract with an arbitration clause, only an arbitrator, and not the court, could open up, review and revise the architect's certificates as between the employer and contractor.[270] This would have made it likely that any attempt by the architect to involve the contractor in three-party proceedings in the High Court would have met with a successful defence based on the *Crouch* decision (the point was not actually decided in the *Wessex* case, but the judge acknowledged the force of the submissions of ARC's counsel—p. 60I).

In cases where an employer settles with one party, wishing to pass on the losses arising from a settlement with another party, the issue of the reasonableness of the settlement may arise. The courts have made clear that in this position, the settling party is not obliged to prove again every item of the claim in order to justify the settlement. Some credit is usually due to the settling party for the saving of costs that would otherwise have been incurred had the case continued—see for example *Biggin & Co* v. *Permanite*[271]; *Oxford University Press* v. *John Stedman Group*.[272] In *Wessex*, the architect unsuccessfully tried to argue that the employer was precluded in principle from "passing on" the settlement, although the reasonableness or otherwise of the settlement was not itself directly determined.

## 8.2 Apportionment

### 8.2.1 Generally

In considering apportionment, one should keep separate:

268. The standard construction sub-contract forms such as NSC/A (formerly NSC/4) and DOM/1 do provide for the same arbitrator to hear employer-contractor and contractor-sub-contractor disputes, although these are still separate arbitrations.

269. (1984) 26 B.L.R. 1, C.A.

270. The decision was in theory *obiter* but, although much criticised, has been accepted in subsequent cases as representing the law. A full criticism is contained in I Duncan-Wallace QC, "The Architect, The Arbitrator and The Courts" (1986) 2 Const. L.J. 13.

271. [1951] 2 K.B. 314.

272. (1990) 34 Con. L.R. 1. There are conflicting first instance Official Referees' decisions as to whether the settling party can call evidence as to the advice of its lawyers to it at the time when the settlement was made, as proof of the reasonableness of the settlement itself. The *Society of Lloyd's* v. *Kitsons Environmental Services Ltd* (1994) 67 B.L.R. 102 suggests that such evidence is admissible and relevant, whereas *DSL Group Ltd* v. *Unisys International Services Ltd* (1994) 67 B.L.R. 117 suggests that such evidence is irrelevant. The *DSL* case was later in time, so that the judge was able to consider the views expounded in *Lloyd's*. It is submitted that the *DSL* decision represents the better view, partly because it accords more easily with the reasoning in *Biggin* v. *Permanite*, and partly on principle.

(a) the degree to which the court decides that a plaintiff should succeed against each defendant;

(b) the degree to which the defendants *inter se* are liable to contribute to the plaintiff's loss.

Under (a), for example, it is perfectly possible for a court to hold each of the three defendants fully, and jointly and severally, liable for the plaintiff's losses, thus leaving the plaintiff free to enforce its judgment against whichever defendant it chooses (though it could not of course enforce more than once over to obtain greater damages than the overall judgment sum). Under (b) however, the apportionment between the defendants must necessarily total 100 per cent (if no apportionment is made, the co-defendants have equal rights against each other).[273]

### 8.2.2 *The Civil Liability (Contribution) Act 1978*

Section 1(1) of this Act states:

"Subject to the following provisions of this section, any person liable in respect of any damage suffered by another person may recover contribution from any other person liable in respect of the same damage (whether jointly with him or otherwise)."

The court thus has power to apportion responsibility between parties to a dispute in respect of the "same damage" and, of its own volition, irrespective of whether any contribution notices (under R.S.C. Ord. 16, r. 8 or otherwise) have been served between such parties.

The following two cases have, respectively, slightly widened and slightly narrowed the ambit of this section:

(a) in *Friends Provident Life Office* v. *Hillier Parker May & Rowden Estates & General Plc*,[274] the Court of Appeal held that a claim for restitution may be for "the same damage" within section 1;

(b) however, in *Birse Construction Ltd* v. *Haiste Ltd*[275] the Court of Appeal confirmed that liability in respect of "the same damage" under the 1978 Act necessarily implied that both of the "contributing" parties must be liable to the same *person*. Thus where an employer sued its contractor under a design and build contract, and the contractor joined its sub-contractor, the sub-contractor was not entitled to draw into the proceedings an engineer who was (so it was alleged) liable to the employer.

### 8.2.3 *The standard forms*

The "fair contribution" provisions of SFA/92 and the ACE Agreement and the Professional Services Contract all provide that the professional's liability is limited to

---

273. For an example of the distinctions, see *EDAC* v. *Moss* (1984) 2 Con. L.R. 1 at 40.
274. (Unreported) 3 April 1995.
275. (1995) Construction Industry Law Letter, p. 1034.

the sum that should reasonably be paid having regard for the responsibility that other consultants may have—see section 2 above and the Appendix to this chapter.

### 8.2.4 Case-law

It is difficult to extract principles from the cases in which apportionments have been made, since these cases tend to depend on their own facts. However, some examples may be discussed.

The point has sometimes been made that an architect or engineer supervising a job should not be held to have as large a liability as the contractor whose defective work he has failed properly to investigate. In *Eames* v. *North Hertfordshire Borough Council*[276] Judge Fay QC endorsed the view that "the blameworthiness of a policeman who fails to detect the crime is less than that of the criminal himself" and said that in typical cases involving negligent passing of defective foundations by local authorities, he had held the local authority generally to be 25 per cent to blame, and the builder 75 per cent. Although this statement of what was no more than an Official Referee's rule of thumb may have some useful value as a guide in considering supervisor/contractor apportionment, the supervisory obligations of local authorities in tort are now almost extinguished following *Murphy* v. *Brentwood District Council*.[277] Even more peremptory treatment was given by the Canadian Supreme Court to a supplier of defective concrete seeking a contribution from the main contractor's supervisor[278]:

"How could it be fairly heard to say ... Because you failed to supervise me properly, and you were bound to do so by your undertaking to the contractor, you must share with me the burden of making compensation and, to that extent, relieve me of it."

Similarly in *Oldschool* v. *Gleeson*[279] the judge refused to allow a contractor to pass the blame for incompetent work onto the consulting engineer on the grounds that he had failed to intervene to prevent it.

In *Clay* v. *Crump*[280] the architects (42 per cent) and the demolition sub-contractor (38 per cent) bore the brunt of the blame when a wall collapsed killing two workmen. The architect had failed even cursorily to examine the wall before instructing its demolition. The contractor was held responsible for the other 20 per cent.

Finally, *Holland Hannen & Cubitts* v. *WHTSO*[281] is an example of the Court of Appeal's reallocation of blame from the nominated flooring sub-contractor towards the employer's design team.

## 8.3 Costs and settlement

### 8.3.1 General

In a two-party action, the normal way for a defendant to protect himself on costs is to make a payment into court. This is more difficult in a multi-party action. If such a

---

276. (1980) 18 B.L.R. 50.
277. (1990) 50 B.L.R. 1, [1991] 1 A.C. 378, H.L.
278. *Bilodeau* v. *Bergeron* (1974) 2 S.C.R. 345 at 351 *per* Fauteux CJ.
279. (1976) 4 B.L.R. 103 at 131.
280. (1963) 4 B.L.R. 80. See section 6.2.1 above.
281. (1985) 35 B.L.R. 1, C.A. See section 4.4.2 above.

payment is made and accepted, the litigation may still continue unless the other defendant(s) can be persuaded to settle. If the plaintiff discontinues against the non-paying defendant, that defendant will be entitled to his costs. But if the plaintiff proceeds against the non-paying defendant:

(a) the plaintiff is forced to continue litigation that he might rather terminate; and the non-paying defendant can effectively take the benefit of the payment in by seeking to set it off against any damages that the plaintiff may later recover[282] (which may even leave the plaintiff in a position where he recovers nothing and is therefore himself at risk as to costs);

(b) the non-paying defendant may still be forced back into the proceedings, if the paying-in defendant serves or continues with any contribution notice under the Civil Liability (Contribution) Act 1978.

The current position is therefore unsatisfactory.[283] Particular difficulties for the plaintiff and defendant are illustrated by the following two cases.

### 8.3.2 Payments into court—difficulties for the plaintiff

In *Fell* v. *Gould Grimwade Shirbon Partnership & Malden District Council*[284] the plaintiff, faced with a problem of this nature, sought an order from the court that he be allowed to take out the monies in court, with costs against the paying-in defendant, and that the paying-in defendant should pay the other defendant's costs. Such an application could not have been made *within* the 21-day period prescribed by the High Court Rules for accepting a payment in (since, within that period, a plaintiff must either accept the payment or not). The court therefore held that the plaintiff could not obtain, by an application made outside that period, what he would not have been able to obtain by an application made within it. Nevertheless, the judge appeared to have some sympathy with the plaintiff's predicament, and mentioned the possibility of the plaintiff serving a *Calderbank* offer,[285] without however expressing an opinion as to how, or whether, this might be effective.

It follows from the above problems that it might be open to a plaintiff at trial, who has failed to beat a payment in, to argue that he was right not to accept in any event; which in turn places a defendant in difficulty when making such a payment in. At present, the parties' problems are compounded by R.S.C. Orders 22 and 62, r. 9(1) which, while allowing *Calderbank* offers, effectively provide that a payment in is the proper method by which a defendant should protect itself on costs.[286]

---

282. *Townsend* v. *Stone Toms & Partners* (1984) 27 B.L.R. 26 at 38.

283. See the commentary by the learned editors of the Building Law Reports on *South East Thames Regional Health Authority* v. *WJ Lovell (London) Ltd & Others* (1985) 32 B.L.R. 127.

284. (1993) Construction Industry Law Letter, p. 861.

285. An offer made "without prejudice save as to costs" so that the offeror has the right to draw the court's attention to the offer after issues of liability and *quantum* have been determined. If the offeree has obtained less by proceeding to trial than he would have done by accepting the offer, he may suffer a costs penalty. The name is taken from the case of *Calderbank* v. *Calderbank* [1975] 3 All E.R. 333, C.A. in which it was first used.

286. "Access to Justice", the interim report of Lord Woolf published in 1995 proposes replacing payments into court with written offers. Plaintiffs would also be able to make such offers.

### 8.3.3 Payments into court—difficulties for the paying defendant

A further example of the difficulties caused by the payment-in rules, this time for a defendant, is apparent from *Corby District Council* v. *Holst*[287]:

*Facts*
The first defendant had initiated a claim for delay-based losses against the plaintiff by way of an arbitration. That arbitration was settled on terms that the plaintiff's cross-claim for defects was dealt with in the High Court, and that the first defendant should provide a banker's bond for that cross-claim. The first defendant then joined others as third parties. The first defendant wished to protect its position as to costs, but did not wish to pay into court, having already provided an expensive bond as part of the arbitration settlement. It therefore made a *Calderbank* offer to the plaintiff and asked the court to ratify the *principle* of the *Calderbank* offer, by making an interim declaration.

The Court of Appeal held that it was inappropriate to make such a declaration as to the validity or invalidity of the *Calderbank* offer at all, since the issue of the effectiveness of the *Calderbank* offer should be left entirely to the trial judge. The first defendant was therefore faced with the difficulties of expending a further sum on a payment in (and presumably encountering the same problems as any co-defendant making a solo payment into court) or trusting that its method of trying to protect itself would be endorsed at trial, with potentially large costs consequences at trial if that were not so.

### 8.3.4 The reluctant defendant

If all but one defendant wishes to settle, there is the option, admittedly not wholly attractive, of the other parties entering into an agreement under which either the plaintiff or one of the other defendants pursues the plaintiff's case against the defendant, and on behalf of the settling parties, and jointly at their cost. In *South East Thames Regional Health Authority* v. *WJ Lovell (London) Ltd*[288] an attempt by the reluctant defendant to have such an agreement declared void for maintenance or champerty was unsuccessful. In that case, one of the *defendants* took over the plaintiff's case against the reluctant defendant. In *Victoria University Manchester* v. *Hugh Wilson and Lewis Womersley & Another*[289] an agreement was entered into on the fifth day of the trial by which the first defendants agreed to pay to the plaintiffs £1.3 million on condition that the *plaintiffs* continued the action against the second defendants, at the expense of the first defendants, and on the basis that any sum recovered in excess of £1.3 million would be paid to the second defendants. In the *South East Thames* case, Judge Newey QC, noting that both cases "illustrate the difficulties which beset defendants when one wishes to settle and another does not" did not agree with counsel's suggestion that agreement would have been champertous, had it been attacked on that ground. What was significant was that the first defendant had a "genuine commercial interest" in it.

---

287. (1984) 28 B.L.R. 35.
288. (1985) 32 B.L.R. 127.
289. (1984) 2 Con. L.R. 43.

However, the real problem with these arrangements is that the reluctant defendant is determined to open up the issue of contribution as between himself and the other defendants, by contribution proceedings or otherwise, he cannot be prevented from doing so.

## 9 EXPERT EVIDENCE

### 9.1 Expert evidence must be from the appropriate field

Only in rare cases will a plaintiff alleging negligence against an architect or engineer not need to call expert evidence from a fellow architect or engineer to support its case that the defendant has fallen below the required standard of skill and care. In *Worboys* v. *Acme Developments*[290] the Court of Appeal said that it would be "grossly unfair" to condemn a professional man without such evidence, except in straightforward cases. The court gave the example of an architect who failed to provide a front door to premises, but presumably less obvious matters such as blatantly failing to comply with clear instructions in an important respect would also be covered.

Similarly, in *Investors in Industry Ltd* v. *South Bedfordshire District Council*[291] the Court of Appeal said that little reliance could be placed on answers given by three engineering experts in the court below as to the nature and extent of an architect's duties, since the evidence related to a profession other than their own. (The House of Lords had previously suggested in a medical negligence case[292] that in certain circumstances a judge could properly come to a conclusion that disclosure of a risk was "so obviously necessary" that a court could find, even in the absence of expert evidence, that no reasonably prudent medical practitioner could have failed to disclose it. However the Court of Appeal in *Nye Saunders & Partners* v. *Bristow*,[293] observing that these words dealt with a doctrine—the doctrine of informed consent—pertaining specifically to the medical profession, doubted its applicability in the case of an architect who had failed to inform his client of the risk of inflation on building costs.)

### 9.2 The expert to have practical experience

An expert giving an opinion on an architect's or engineer's negligence must have practical day-to-day experience of the business of an architect or engineer whose standard of care and skill he is commenting on. Without it, his opinion of whether an architect or engineer has fallen below that standard is of little value. In one case the High Court described a professor of soil mechanics and consultant in geo-technical engineering as follows[294]:

"Throughout his life he has conducted original research: he has lectured on soils virtually throughout the world; he has published over 60 original papers; and he has advised on geo-technical aspects of the design or construction or remedial measures of over 300 civil

---

290. (1969) 4 B.L.R. 133, C.A.
291. (1986) 32 B.L.R. 1 at 39, C.A.; [1986] Q.B. 1034.
292. *Sidaway* v. *The Board of Governors of the Bethlem Hospital* [1985] A.C. 871.
293. (1987) 37 B.L.R. 92 at 107, C.A.
294. (1984) 27 B.L.R. 58 at 72.

engineering projects ... He is without doubt an outstandingly brilliant exponent of the complexities of soil mechanics and his work in that field has received international acclaim and recognition. He applies, however, both to himself and to others, the highest possible standards; and it can fairly be said that he is generous with his criticisms. Few people connected with the case escaped it. For these reasons, and because his experience has given him little contact with the ordinary day-to-day problems of designing structures in soil, I am able to place little if any reliance upon his evidence as to the standards to be expected of an ordinarily competent designer. On the other hand his analysis of the causes of the movement of the wall impressed me enormously, and I place very considerable reliance upon it."

Similarly, in an architect's negligence case, the Official Referee, hearing evidence on the financial viability of a small hotel project, preferred evidence from an architect with experience in that field to that of an expert accountant.[295]

## 9.3 The architect or engineer as his own expert

There is no rule of law that prevents an architect or engineer giving expert evidence on his own behalf. The lack of independence of such a witness goes only to the weight of such evidence, not to its admissibility, as confirmed by the Court of Appeal in *David Michael Lusty* v. *Finsbury Securities*.[296] There, an architect was allowed to give evidence as to the value of his drawing work. The court noted that:

"If every time a professional man sued for his fees he had to have some independent evidence for what he himself considered to be his proper fees, it would clearly be intolerable."

However, on the substantive issue of whether an architect or engineer has fallen below the required standard of skill and care, the evidence of the individual against whom the allegation is made will clearly be of little value.

## 9.4 The role of the expert

Discussion of the role of the expert and the contents of his report is outside the scope of this chapter, but reference should be made to the following cases in which these matters have been discussed: *Whitehouse* v. *Jordan*[297]; *University of Warwick* v. *Sir Robert McAlpine*[298]; *National Justice Compania Naviera SA* v. *Prudential Insurance Co Ltd (The Ikarian Reefer)*[299]; *Alliance & Leicester Building Society & Others* v. *Edgestop Ltd & Others*[300]; *Cala Homes (South) Ltd & Others* v. *Alfred McAlpine Homes (East) Ltd*[301]; see also "The preparation of experts' reports" by A Bartlett QC.[302]

IAN YULE

295. *EH Cardy & Sons Ltd* v. *Paul Roberts Associates* (1994) 38 Con. L.R. 79 at 96.
296. (1991) 58 B.L.R. 66 at 83.
297. [1981] 1 W.L.R. 246 at 256.
298. (1988) 42 B.L.R. 1 at 22.
299. [1993] 2 Lloyd's Rep. 68.
300. [1993] 1 W.L.R. 1462.
301. (1995) Construction Industry Law Letter 1083.
302. (1994) 60 J.C.I. Arb. 2, p. 94. The text in the first line of the second column, and the second paragraph of the editorial introduction, both contain errors, which are referred to and corrected by Mr Bartlett QC in his letter to "Arbitration" at (1994) 60 J.C.I. Arb. 3.

APPENDIX: A COMPARISON OF THREE PROFESSIONAL CONTRACTS

| Subject | SFA/92 (1992) | ACE Conditions (1995) | The Professional Services Contract (1994) |
|---|---|---|---|
| 1 General | Consists of Memorandum of Agreement, Conditions and Schedules. Memorandum requires various matters to be inserted, including limitations on liability. Four schedules set out information from client, architect's services, fees and expenses and appointment of consultants, specialists and site staff (where appropriate). <br><br> The conditions are in four parts, namely: <br> (1) those common to all commissions; <br> (2) those relating to design stages A–H of the "Plan of Work" published by the RIBA; <br> (3) those relating to supervision stages J–L; <br> (4) those specific to appointments of consultants and specialists where architect is lead consultant. <br><br> It is published in two editions, the RIBA edition, and the RIAS edition for Scotland. There are separate versions for design and build projects, one for use where the architect is engaged by the employer, and another for use where he is engaged by the contractor. | Comprises Memorandum of Agreement, Conditions of Engagement, and two appendices dealing with services and remuneration. It comes in six forms (A–F), with three further agreements (G–I) for minor works, design and construct works, and sub-consultancy. There are variants on forms A–C for civil and structural engineering and for mechanical and electrical engineering. | This consists of: <br> (1) nine core clauses; <br> (2) four "main option" clauses, depending on the way in which the remuneration of the professional is calculated; <br> (3) eight secondary option clauses which may or may not be inserted; <br> (4) a "Contract Data" section, the first part of which must be completed by the employer, the second by the consultant. |

| Subject | SFA/92 (1992) | ACE Conditions (1995) | The Professional Services Contract (1994) |
|---|---|---|---|
| 2 Reasonable care and skill obligation | Reasonable care and skill in conformity with the normal standards of the architect's profession (cl. 1.2.1). | Reasonable skill, care and diligence in the performance of the services (cl. 2.4). | Provision of the services using reasonable skill and care (cl. 21.2). |
| 3 Limitations on liability | Liability is limited to a period (which should be inserted) calculated from completion of the services or from practical completion (if the contract involves supervision of the work)—Memorandum, para. 5. There is no phrase "whichever is the earlier" although that is presumably intended. | Liability is limited to a period (which should be inserted) calculated from the date of practical completion (cl. 8.3 and Memorandum). | Liability is limited to the amount of insurance cover that the professional has agreed to put in place. It is also limited by reference to particulars to be inserted in the Contract Data (cl. 82.1). |
| | Liability for loss or damage is limited to the sum that the architect ought reasonably to pay having regard to the responsibility of other consultants, specialists, the contractor (the "fair contributor" clause), or a specific sum of money to be inserted in the memorandum, whichever is the lower (Memorandum 6.1 and 6.2). | Liability in connection with pollution or contamination may be excluded (cl. 8.1A). Whether or not it is, liability is in any event limited to the amount stated in the Memorandum, or the amount that the engineer ought reasonably to pay having regard to the responsibility of other consultants (the "fair contribution" clause) (cl. 8). | Follows S.F.A./92 and the Latham Report in the "fair contribution" concept, but goes further in seeking to reduce the professional's liability where there is contributory fault on the client's part (cl. 82.1). |
| | Architect does not warrant that services can be completed within the timetable (1.3.7). | The engineer will use "reasonable endeavours" to adhere to any agreed programme; and then only "subject always to conditions beyond his reasonable control" (cl. 2.10). | The consultant is obliged to carry out work in accordance with the "accepted programme", but extensions, with payment, for "compensation events" are possible. |

177

| Subject | SFA/92 (1992) | ACE Conditions (1995) | The Professional Services Contract (1994) |
|---|---|---|---|
| | The architect is not responsible for proper installation of contractors' materials, or for contractors' operational methods, or for the carrying out and completion of the works, or for health and safety provisions on site (3.2.2 and 3.2.3). | The engineer is responsible for sub-contractors (cl. 2.7) but not for anyone else doing detailed design (2.8). | |
| | The architect is not responsible for design or work carried out by specialists (4.2.5). | | |
| | The architect is not responsible for work of consultants or for the general inspection of their work (4.1.7). | The engineer is not responsible for detailed design or defects attributable to other consultants (2.6). | The consultant's legal liability is limited to the amount of insurance required under the contract (cl. 82.1). |
| | All rights of set off excluded (1.5.15). | Rights of set off are not excluded as such, although clause 6.7 says that the client must pay the uncontested part of any invoice. | No rules about set off. |
| 4 Fees | There are various possibilities. The architect is entitled to extra fees for work caused by variations, examination of notices applications and claims under the building contract, or delay or "any other reason beyond the architect's control"—cl. 1.5.7.

The April 1995 update includes a clause that allows the architect to be paid a separate fee for work done in compliance with the CDM Regulations. | There are various possibilities. Extra payments (time-based) are due for miscellaneous matters including "other reasons beyond the control of the consulting engineer" (cl. 6.4). | Fees may be based on various procurement options ranging from "cost reimbursable" to lump sum, but there is no option related to a straightforward percentage of the cost of the work. |

| Subject | SFA/92 (1992) | ACE Conditions (1995) | The Professional Services Contract (1994) |
|---|---|---|---|
| 5 Sub-contracting | The architect needs the client's written consent, but that cannot be unreasonably withheld (1.4.2). Clause 1.3.7 may mean that the architect does not warrant the work of any sub-contractor to whom he has delegated. In any event, he is not responsible for the work of "consultants" (4.1.7) or "specialists" (those who design and supply for the client) (4.2.5). | The engineer may recommend that the client sub-lets services. The client cannot unreasonably withhold consent, and the engineer is then responsible for the sub-consultant (2.7). Alternatively, the engineer may recommend that detailed design is carried out by a specialist. Again, the client must not unreasonably withhold consent, but this time the engineer is *not* responsible for performance (cl. 2.8). | Sub-contracting is called "sub-consulting". The employer's consent is necessary, but only apparently on certain grounds. The consultant is then entirely responsible for the sub-consultant (cl. 24.1). |
| 6 Assignment | Only with the written consent of the other party (1.4.1). | Only with the written consent of the other party which cannot unreasonably be withheld (2.5 and 3.4). | Prohibited altogether (cl. 24.1). There is however nothing to stop the parties consensually varying the agreement, of course. |
| 7 Visits to site | The architect must make such visits as he reasonably expected to make at the date of his appointment. If it becomes apparent that more visits are needed, he must inform the client but is entitled to further fees (3.1). | Frequency of site meetings and visits is defined in the Memorandum. | Not specifically dealt with, but might well be included in the brief. |
| 8 Disputes | Arbitration (cl. 1.8). | For any matters relating to the contesting of any invoice or to the termination of the engineer's appointment are referred to arbitration (in practice, disputes relating to the contesting of an invoice will often cover many of the disputes between the parties, since the engineer will either be asserting his right to pay, or the client his right not to pay!). For all other disputes, there is compulsory mediation, and if that fails after six weeks, compulsory adjudication. The adjudicator's decision can be challenged by either party further in arbitration (cl. 9). | Compulsory reference to adjudicator in the first instance. There is a short eight-week timetable for his decision. If that is not accepted, both parties have a right to arbitrate (cll. 90–92). |

179

CHAPTER 4

# AUCTIONEERS

## 1 INTRODUCTION

The auctioneering profession is a vitally important one. Auctions fulfil a major function in the commercial world and the importance of the auction as a mode of selling in the UK should not be underestimated. Auctions represent the principal mode of selling a wide variety of goods and land ranging from high profile sales of paintings and antiques to more mundane trades such as wholesale livestock and produce markets, second-hand motor vehicles and a range of commodities. In some cases the auction is selected because it is the only viable method available, whereas in others it may be the preferred mode of sale because it enables a market price to be fixed on the spot. Moreover, the auction has frequently been the prescribed method for selling goods or land in certain situations, e.g., sales ordered by the court—as under writs of *fieri facias*—and this bears testimony to the confidence reposed in the auction as a device for achieving the best possible, or at least an unassailable price by the immediate and direct action of competition.

The economic significance of auctions is such that considerable demands are made on the skill and expertise of auctioneers. Auctioneers occupy a pivotal position: principally they are employed by the owner of property to effect a sale but, not infrequently, they may also act as agent of the purchaser for limited purposes and may enter into a direct contractual relationship with a purchaser. In the course of transacting the business the auctioneer may additionally act in other legal capacities such as a bailee with a duty to care for the property in his possession either on behalf of the seller pending sale or the buyer thereafter.

Given this situation, it will be apparent that the potential professional liability of an auctioneer is wide and significant and liabilities may be incurred not only to his client, the seller, but also to the purchaser and other third parties. This liability may sound in contract, under the law of agency or in tort and, as we shall see, the auctioneer is also potentially liable under a number of criminal statutes, primarily those designed to achieve consumer protection, such as the Trade Descriptions Act 1968.

### 1.1 Regulation and restrictions on trading

Unlike many other professionals, auctioneers are not required to obtain any particular qualifications for practice, nor is an auctioneer required to join any professional association although most auctioneers do, in fact, belong to one of the main professional bodies: the RICS or the ISVA and these bodies have issued codes of practice to which their members are subject.

There is no legislation specifically designed to control auctioneering practices similar to that which affects estate agents,[1] but an auctioneer who engages in estate agency work will find himself subject to those controls and, for example, the criminal sanctions under the Property Misdescriptions Act 1991.

In dealing with the auctioneer's professional responsibilities, it will be convenient to deal separately with his civil law liabilities to the seller and those to the purchaser and to other parties and also to deal independently with his potential criminal liability under various regulatory statutes.

## 2 DUTIES TO THE VENDOR

The auctioneer is an agent and his duties and liabilities will be determined by the extent of his authority both actual and apparent.[2] His authority will depend ultimately upon the precise terms of the contract with his principal within the framework of the general rules of common law, in particular, the law of agency. Some specific duties will be provided for expressly in his contract but, in addition, the law lays down a number of general obligations concomitant with the agency relationship. These may conveniently be classified as:

(a) duties relating to performance;
(b) fiduciary duties;
(c) the duty to account for goods or proceeds;
(d) the duty to care for goods.

### 2.1 Duties relating to performance

#### 2.1.1 To act in accordance with his instructions

An auctioneer, like any agent, may only perform those acts which are authorised. If he fails to obey his instructions he will be liable to his principal for any loss arising. This liability will be an additional consequence to that of failing to bring about a contract between his principal and a third party with the resultant loss of commission.

If the auctioneer is in doubt as to his instructions he should seek clarification.[3]

---

1. See chapter 7.

2. For the authority of an auctioneer, see Harvey and Meisel, *Auctions Law and Practice* (2nd edn, 1995) Oxford University Press, Oxford.

3. In the unusual case of *Re Bishop, ex parte Langley, ex parte Smith* (1879) 13 Ch.D. 110, 49 L.T. Bcy. 1, it was stated that on receipt of a telegram from solicitors advising that an injunction restraining sale had been issued by the Bankruptcy Court, an auctioneer was under a duty to communicate with his principal although it was not incumbent upon him to communicate with the court. In this case the auctioneer communicated with his client, the sheriff levying execution on the goods of a judgment debtor who had subsequently filed a liquidation petition. Having received instructions to proceed with the sale, and bona fide believing the telegram to be a ruse by the debtor, he was held not liable in contempt of court when he went ahead with the sale. If the auctioneer only receives notice of an injunction after the sale, although before receipt of the proceeds, the court will not set aside the sale: see *Freehold Permanent Building Society* v. *Choate* (1871) 3 Chy. Chrs. 440.

## 2.1.2 To act with skill and care

An auctioneer, as a professional, is under a general duty under the common law to exercise proper skill and care in and about the sale of his principal's property. As Lord Ellenborough long ago put it in an oft-cited dictum[4]:

"In the present case the plaintiff appears to have been guilty of gross negligence and the defendant has suffered an injury instead of deriving any benefit from employing him. . . . I pay an auctioneer, as I do any other professional man for the exercise of skill on my behalf and I have a right to the exercise of such skill as is normally possessed by men of that profession."

That case decided that an auctioneer lost his right to commission in circumstances where he had had to return the purchaser's deposit due to the failure of the vendor of a lease to show his lessor's title. It was found that it was usual practice in such cases for the auctioneer to insert a proviso in the conditions of sale that the vendor was not to be called upon to show the title of the lessor and the auctioneer's negligence consisted of the failure to include such a provision. Whilst this case concerned only the auctioneer's liability to forgo his commission, he will also be liable in damages for loss occasioned to his principal by reason of his negligence. It is impossible to provide an exhaustive list of the circumstances in which such a liability may arise, but a number of instances are given below.[5]

## 2.1.3 What is the standard of care required?

Lord Ellenborough referred to the exercise of "such skill as is normally possessed by men of that profession". However, it is recognised that some auctioneers are specialists whereas others may be more in the way of general practitioners. Recent decisions have established that the law takes account of such matters.

In *Alchemy (International) Ltd* v. *Tattersalls Ltd*[6] the defendant auctioneers were sued by the vendor of a colt for failing to obtain an appropriate price. The main issue in the case was whether, the apparent highest bidder having disappeared, the auctioneers acted properly in delaying putting up the horse again whilst they sought (unsuccessfully) to trace and hold the successful bidder to his bargain. At the re-auction some days later, the colt achieved some 200,000 guineas less than originally.

Experts were called by both sides and gave divergent views as to what was the proper or sensible thing for the auctioneer to have done in such a dilemma. The court applied a statement of the law adopted in a medical malpractice case, *Maynard* v. *West Midlands Regional Health Authority*,[7] in which the court endorsed an earlier dictum that[8]:

"In the realm of diagnosis and treatment there is ample scope for genuine difference of opinion

---

4. *Denew* v. *Daverell* (1813) 3 Camp. 451 at 452–453. This has more recently been made the subject of statutory provision: Supply of Goods and Services Act 1982, s. 13.
5. Several examples are given by Mar J in *Fordham* v. *Christie Manson & Woods* (1977) 244 E.G. 213 at 219–220. It has been decided at first instance in *Balsamo* v. *Medici* [1984] 2 All E.R. 304, [1984] 1 W.L.R. 951, that a sub-agent can be liable in negligence to an owner of goods for damage thereto (but not for misapplication of the proceeds of sale). Thus an auctioneer instructed to sell by the agent of the owner will owe a duty of care to that owner although there is no contractual relationship between them.
6. [1985] E.G. 675.
7. [1985] 1 All E.R. 635.
8. The dictum is that of Lord President Clyde in *Hunter* v. *Hamley*, 1955 S.L.T. 213 at 217.

and one man clearly is not negligent merely because his conclusion differs from that of other professional men ...

The true test for establishing negligence in diagnosis or treatment on the part of a doctor is whether he has been proved to be guilty of such failure as no doctor of ordinary skill would be guilty if acting with ordinary care."

Thus it is not enough to show that there is a body of competent professional opinion which would have acted differently if there also exists a body of professional opinion, equally competent, which regards the actions which are called into question as reasonable in the circumstances. This approach was confirmed in the important case of *Luxmoore-May* v. *Messenger May Baverstock*.[9] In this case, which will be discussed in some detail below, the Court of Appeal, reversing the decision of the judge at first instance, held provincial auctioneers not liable for missing a "sleeper", that is a work of some quality or provenance which is not, at the time, recognised. In dealing with the standard of care Slade LJ said:

"The defendants submitted ... that they should be regarded as akin to general practitioners and that (1) the required standard of skill and care allows for differing views, and even a wrong view, without the practitioner holding that view (necessarily) being held in breach of his duty, (2) the standard is to be judged by reference only to what may be expected of the general practitioner, not the specialist, here provincial auctioneers, rather than one of the leading auction houses, and (3) compliance with the required standard is to be judged by reference to the actual circumstances confronting the practitioners at the material time, rather than with the benefit of hindsight. The judge 'unhesitatingly' accepted these propositions, and so would I."

It appears, therefore, that "general practitioners" will be regarded as negligent only if it could be said that no auctioneer of ordinary skill and care would have acted or failed to act as had occurred in the case in question.

### 2.1.4 Duty to secure a binding agreement

There is a number of old cases which establish that an auctioneer is liable in negligence if he fails to ensure that a binding contract has been entered into by the purchaser. Frequently the default of the auctioneer has consisted of a failure to ensure that a contract evidenced in writing sufficient to satisfy the requirements of the Statute of Frauds 1677, and subsequent enactments based thereon, has been procured. These requirements no longer obtain with regard to either sales of land or goods.

There are, however, other ways in which an auctioneer may fail to bring about a contract binding the purchaser; he may for example simply fail to accept a bid. In the New Zealand case of *Logie* v. *Gillies & Hislop*[10] the reserve placed on an estate at Dunedin was £2,000. A bid of that amount was made, but, inexplicably, the auctioneer did not accept it and the property was bought in at £2,100. After several subsequent abortive auctions at decreasing reserves, the estate was eventually sold for £1,250. It was held that the auctioneer was liable to his principal-vendor for damages, the proper measure of which was the difference between the wrongfully unaccepted bid and the true market value of the property at that time, the subsequent sale price achieved being only one means of ascertaining that value. In this case the

9.  [1990] 1 All E.R. 1067.
10.  (1885) 4 N.Z.L.R. 65

court found the market price to have been £1,775 so that the loss was £225 plus £12 regarding the expenses of the abortive sale. It is clear then that a negligent failure to accept a bid will render an auctioneer liable in damages for any loss arising. Many auctioneers' conditions of sale reserve the right to refuse any bid, but it is questionable whether such a provision would protect an auctioneer in this type of situation where he does not exercise a discretion to refuse a bid but carelessly fails to accept it to the detriment of the vendor.[11]

In these days when international auctions have become more commonplace, it appears that an auctioneer is at risk of a negligence action if his, or his audience's, linguistic skills are lacking so that a mistake is made as to the price which a lot has reached, entitling a purchaser to set aside the contract. This occurred in *Friedrich* v. *A Monnickendam Ltd*[12] where the chairman of Christie's himself conducted a major jewellery auction in Geneva. According to the law of Geneva the auction had to be conducted in French. Many of the potential purchasers invited to the sale were from England and the USA. The auctioneer's French was not good and a genuine mistake occurred whereby the defendant purchaser thought that a lot had reached 190,000 Swiss francs, whereas it had in fact reached 290,000 Swiss francs, an extravagantly high price. Under Swiss law the purchaser, an English diamond-cutter, was held entitled to avoid the contract on the grounds of mistake. The case involved an action by a vendor against the purchaser, but the question of negligence by the auctioneer was considered. Lord Denning said[13]:

"There was concurrent negligence on the part of the auctioneer. He should have known that the bid of 290,000 Swiss francs was not such a sum as Mr Monnickendam the expert diamond-cutter would knowingly bid. The auctioneer should therefore have assured himself by the clearest words in English that Mr Monnickendam appreciated that the figure was 290,000 Swiss francs."

Stamp LJ was of the view that the lack of care consisted not so much in the imperfection of the auctioneer's French as in a failure to give the bids in English as well, given that the auction particulars were printed in both English and French and that English-speaking people were specifically solicited to attend.

### 2.1.5 Duty to describe the property accurately

Property put up for auction, whether land or goods, is likely to have some description applied. This may be fairly short or there may be a detailed description of any given lot. In addition to whatever may be said in the catalogue, the auctioneer may comment on the property, its condition and so forth, from the rostrum.

It is probably true to say that no aspect of auctioneering is so fraught with potential hazard as the application of description to lots to be sold.[14] Misdescriptions may give rise to criminal sanctions under the Trade Descriptions Act 1968, in the case of goods, or under the Property Misdescriptions Act 1991, in the case of land. Additionally, misdescribing the property may subject the auctioneer to civil liability at the suit of

---

11. For a discussion of the position relating to disputed bids, see Harvey and Meisel, *op. cit.*, chapter 6.
12. (1973) 228 E.G. 1311.
13. *Ibid.* at 1315.
14. A misrepresentation can take the form of a misleading photograph: see *Atlantic Estates* v. *Ezekiel* [1991] 2 E.G.L.R. 202, where a photograph depicted a thriving wine bar, but the liquor licence had been revoked; see also *St Marylebone Property Co Ltd* v. *Payne* [1994] E.G. 156.

his client, the seller, and the purchaser. It is in relation to such potential civil liability, particularly in relation to the purchaser of goods, that auctioneer's conditions frequently contain exclusion clauses. The viability of these is discussed in detail in chapter 2.

In this part of this chapter we shall deal with the potential liability of the auctioneer vis-à-vis his client, the seller.

There are two aspects to this: first an auctioneer may, by misdescribing the property, render the seller liable to compensate a purchaser misled thereby and the auctioneer will be under a civil liability to the seller to indemnify him in respect of that loss. Secondly, and quite separately, an auctioneer may directly cause loss to his client as a result of a failure to describe the property to its optimum value.

EXPOSING THE VENDOR TO LIABILITY TO THE PURCHASER

This may arise in two ways:

*Sale of Goods Act 1979, section 13, as amended.*   Section 13(1) provides:

"Where there is a contract for the sale of goods by description, there is an implied term that the goods will correspond with the description ..."

Section 13(3) provides that:

"... a sale of goods is not prevented from being a sale by description by reason only that, being exposed for sale or hire, they are selected by the buyer ..."

Auction sales are clearly within the definition of sales by description within this statutory provision. Thus, if the purchaser can show that the goods are not as described, either in the auction particulars or orally from the rostrum, he may be entitled to reject them and claim his purchase money back. Alternatively, he may claim damages being the difference between the goods he has actually bought and their value as described.

To the extent that the auctioneer is responsible for applying the description to the lot in question, he will be liable to indemnify his principal-seller for any loss to which the latter will have been exposed as against the purchaser.

A fairly early illustration of the principle involved, though the case concerned land, is *Parker* v. *Fairebrother*[15] where an auctioneer engaged to sell certain properties described them as three-storey buildings. In fact they were only comprised of two-storeys. The vendor was liable to compensate the purchaser as a result of this misdescription and the auctioneer was held bound to indemnify him.

*Liability under the Misrepresentation Act 1967.*   An additional hazard for auctioneers is the possibility that the purchaser may be able to claim rescission of the contract and, or alternatively, damages for misrepresentation which emanates either from catalogue descriptions, or, once again, from oral statements made from the rostrum. This is an alternative route for the buyer of goods at auctions and is also available in land auctions.[16]

---

15. (1853) 21 L.T.O.S. 128, I.C.R. 323.
16. Such a right existed prior to the 1967 Act—see *Flight* v. *Booth* (1834) 1 Bing. N.C. 370 and *King Brothers (Finance) Ltd* v. *North Western British Road Services Ltd* [1986] 2 E.G.L.R. 253.

Whilst it is clear that the auctioneer, as agent, incurs no direct liability to the purchaser under the Act, he can expose the seller to action under the Act and, to the extent that the seller is made liable for an actionable misrepresentation, the auctioneer will be liable to indemnify him.

An action under the Misrepresentation Act 1967 will lie not only for fraudulent and negligent misrepresentations but also for those which are innocently made, that is, where the auctioneer has a reasonable belief in the truth of the statement he makes.

A detailed discussion of the remedies for misrepresentation under the Act is provided in chapter 2, but a purchaser induced to enter into a contract by a material misrepresentation is normally entitled to rescind the contract or to damages in lieu of rescission. The purchaser who is a victim of an innocent misrepresentation may be denied rescission and be awarded damages instead. The right to rescind may be lost also where there is a lapse of time.[17]

Where damages are awarded it may be possible for the purchaser to recover not only reliance losses, i.e., the difference between the price paid and the value of the asset acquired, but also incidental losses which he incurs in respect of the item bought. This is illustrated by the case of *Norton* v. *O'Callaghan*[18] where there was a claim against the vendor directly by the purchaser in misrepresentation under the Misrepresentation Act 1967. The facts were as follows:

Lot 200 in the September yearling sales at Newmarket in September 1981 was a chestnut colt named Fondu. Contained in the description of the colt was its pedigree and this included the information that his sire was Nonalco and his dam was Habanna whose sire in turn was Habitat. It was established that the Habitat line was an important factor because at that time he was beginning to establish himself with a reputation as a sire of good brood mares. The trainer acting on behalf of the plaintiffs in this action recommended the horse and was eventually the successful bidder for him at 26,000 guineas. (The trainer in fact "kept a leg", i.e., 25 per cent interest in the horse for himself.)

Fondu had no success whatever in his various races including a complete flop in a trainer's invitation race. In June or July 1983 it was discovered that a mistake had been made, apparently at the stud where Fondu was born, and that Fondu was not a son of Habanna at all. In fact his dam was an American horse called Moon Min, a horse whose pedigree suggested that he might well be able to perform on the dirt tracks of America but not on the turf of England.

The owners kept the horse in training until October 1983 and thereafter partly at home and with other stables in the hope that he might provide a useful point-to-point horse for the owner's son. Thus training and upkeep fees continued to be incurred until August 1984.

Subsequently, a writ was issued claiming damages for breach of contract and/or misrepresentation, and judgment in default was obtained; that is to say the sellers did not defend. The reason for this was that they had brought in the stud owners as third parties and had obtained judgment in default from them. The case was, therefore, not

---

17. See, for example, *Leaf* v. *International Galleries* [1950] 2 K.B. 86, where a buyer of a painting wrongly described as a Constable was held disentitled to rescind the contract when he discovered the error five years after the sale.
18. [1990] 3 All E.R. 191.

concerned with liability but with damages assessment. It should be noted that the buyers did not claim a right to reject the horse and, given the delays that had occurred post-discovery of the "defect" after 1983, such a claim would probably have been unsuccessful. Nor, it should be noted, did the buyers claim for "loss of bargain", i.e., they did not claim for any loss in respect of potential resale at a profit, stud value etc. They claimed merely for their "reliance losses", namely the difference between the price they paid and the value of the horse actually acquired. They also claimed the cost of training fees and upkeep. These two elements need to be dealt with separately.

### 2.1.5.1 RELIANCE LOSS

The buyer claimed the difference between 26,000 guineas and £1,500 which was the value of Fondu by the end of May/June 1983 when the defect was discovered, such value having been "achieved" by the then known track record of Fondu.

The judge thought that this raised a difficult point because if Fondu had been correctly described as a Moon Min foal he would have had a substantial value to perhaps another purchaser and perhaps a value at least as high as the price paid, i.e., 26,000 guineas. It was also the received legal wisdom at that time[19] that the normal rule for the measure of damages in such situations is the difference between the price paid and the value at acquisition of the item. Thus subsequent falls, e.g., in market price are not taken into account. However, the judge held that in this case, despite that normal rule, the buyers were entitled to the difference between the price paid and the value at discovery of the breach, i.e., £1,500.

With respect, this seems right: the misdescription masked a latent defect, viz: the inability of the horse to perform on turf. The fall in value after acquisition was due to that latent defect, extant at the time of sale.

### 2.1.5.2 TRAINING EXPENSES

The defendants argued here that the training expenses, which ran to several thousand pounds, were not recoverable because the buyers would have incurred such fees whatever horse they had bought: if the horse had been as described and they had bought him they would have incurred such expenses. The judge held this to be irrelevant. The fact that they might have spent such or similar sums on another animal did not preclude their recovery of the expenses which flowed from their purchasing of this animal which they would not have purchased had he been correctly described.

It should be noted that in this case the disappointed buyers sued the vendor direct, but the principles would apply equally to an action against the auctioneers.

In the non-auction case of *East and Another* v. *Mara and Another*[20] the Court of Appeal held that where a purchaser was fraudulently induced to enter into a contract to buy a business, the measure of damages was to be assessed on the basis of compensating the plaintiff for all the loss he had suffered and not, as in breach of

19. But see now the important Court of Appeal decision in *Banque Bruxelles Lambert SA* v. *Eagle Star Insurance Co Ltd* [1995] 2 All E.R. 769, where it was held that a negligent valuer was liable for losses attributable to falls in property values subsequent to his breach of duty. This case is discussed in chapter 11.

20. [1991] 2 All E.R. 733.

contract, on the basis of putting him in as good a position as if a statement had been true. Therefore, in addition to reliance losses, a purchaser would be able to recover loss of profits that he might have expected to make had he instead invested his money in an alternative business bought for a similar sum. This hypothetical profit element is somewhat crudely assessed.

It can, therefore, be seen that, perhaps not surprisingly, the law has traditionally been prepared to allow recovery for a greater range of losses in the case of fraud than would be the case where misrepresentations are made merely carelessly or, indeed, innocently. But where a plaintiff recovers under the Misrepresentation Act 1967, the courts have now construed the Act in such a way that whatever type of misrepresentation is involved the fraud basis of recovery is appropriate.

This discussion has proceeded on the basis that the auctioneer would be liable to his client if he, the auctioneer, has exposed him to liability for misdescription vis-à-vis the buyer. Of course, if the auctioneer has made statements which are expressly authorised by the seller, the auctioneer will not be under any duty to indemnify him. In *Museprime Properties Ltd* v. *Adhill Properties Ltd*[21] the auctioneer gave an assurance to the ultimately successful bidder about the status of rent reviews on business properties being sold. The auctioneer had directly sought confirmation of the accuracy of these statements from the vendor. When these turned out to be inaccurate and the purchaser sued, the auctioneer was held not liable to indemnify his vendor-client.

### 2.1.6 Failure to describe the property to its best advantage

Conditions of sale frequently make express the right of the auctioneer to apply his own description to the properties offered for sale. In the absence of such, an auctioneer will be liable in damages to his principal if he departs from his descriptions to the detriment of the vendor in circumstances where the vendor expressly or impliedly instructs him to sell under his descriptions. In *Brown* v. *Draper & Co*[22] the vendor handed the auctioneer a box of items together with a list describing them. The auctioneers sold them under different descriptions and the vendor sued in negligence. He recovered damages, being the difference between the prices which the goods would probably have achieved had they been sold under the vendor's descriptions, and the prices they actually fetched.

It is important, therefore, that auctioneers expressly reserve the right to sell under their own descriptions. However, if they do, it is equally important that they take care to describe the property accurately to its best advantage. Failure to do so, so that the sale fails to attract the appropriate class of bidders, or the optimum price, may render the auctioneers liable in negligence. An instructive case is *Cuckmere Brick Co Ltd* v. *Mutual Finance Ltd*,[23] which involved a dispute between mortgagors and mortgagees of certain development land. The plaintiff mortgagors obtained finance to develop a site with 100 flats and obtained planning permission therefor. Subsequently, due to financial difficulties, they resolved instead to build 33 houses, a less lucrative, but less

21. [1990] E.G.C.S. 29.
22. (1975) 119 Sol.J. 300, 233 E.G. 929.
23. [1971] Ch. 949, [1971] 2 All E.R. 633. For observations as to valuation evidence, see *Johnson* v. *Ribbins* (1975) 235 E.G. 757 *per* Walton J at 761.

expensive scheme. They obtained planning permission for this revision. Subsequently, they defaulted on the mortgage. The defendant bankers entered into possession and, in exercise of their power of sale under the mortgage, put the site up for auction. The auctioneers described the property as having planning permission for 33 houses, but omitted to mention the permission for the more valuable flat development scheme. The main reason for this omission was that they took a pessimistic view as to the economic value of such a development and decided that it was not an attractive proposition. The sale of the site, as described, realised £44,000. The judge at first instance awarded damages against the mortgagees on the basis that, properly described to include the planning consent for 100 flats, the land would have realised £65,000. Although this was not in issue in this decision, it seems clear that auctioneers would be liable to indemnify their principals in such a case. The Court of Appeal upheld the decision. Two of the judges considered that the conscious omission of the auctioneers amounted to negligence but one, Cross LJ, considered it to be merely an error of judgment. However, whilst the pessimistic evaluation of the property was not itself negligent, Cross LJ held them negligent in being so confident of its correctness as not to see to it that the earlier planning permission for flats was mentioned in the particulars in the hope at least of attracting some developers prepared to bid more for the property for that purpose.

### 2.1.7  Underselling the vendor's goods

However, the real nightmare for many auctioneers will probably be that of missing a "sleeper", and we now turn to the *Luxmoore-May* case which requires detailed consideration. When the High Court judgment was handed down in 1989 it set alarm bells ringing in auctioneers' offices around the country because it seemed to suggest that a misattribution, even in so notoriously difficult a field as fine art, could easily be negligent.

Mrs Luxmoore-May instructed her late husband's firm to sell two paintings, which had hung unadmired in a dark corner of the plaintiff's hallway, and an employee came round to look at them. She thought they might be worth about £30 but agreed to value them and gave Mrs Luxmoore-May a receipt for them on which was written "for research" (this, it was held, gave rise to an express contractual duty to carry out research into the pictures which may or may not be a significant factor—see later).

The employee, Mrs Z, showed them to the firms' fine art consultant. He did not think much of them and valued them at between some £30–£50 the pair. Mrs Z, next time she happened to be going to Christie's, took them along as an afterthought and asked them at the front counter what they thought of them. Five to ten minutes later, an employee of Christie's returned them without favourable comment.

Subsequently, the paintings were put up for sale as lot 394 out of a total of 417 lots. The catalogue described them blandly as: "English school. Hounds by Rocky Seashore. Panel pair. Oil on paper. 5.75 inches × 9 inches". A reserve of £40 was placed upon them. To the surprise of all they fetched £840, but five months later the paintings were sold at Sotheby's for £88,000 as a pair of Foxhounds by Stubbs. Mrs Luxmoore-May was held, at first instance, entitled to recover the difference between the price obtained on her sale and the subsequent sale at Sotheby's.

Whilst the judge was at pains to point out that not every auctioneer who missed a "sleeper" would necessarily be negligent, in this particular case the auctioneers were because, in his view, any competent valuer would have appreciated in these pictures a substantially greater potential than crossed their mind.

Thus the liability was squarely based on a failure to spot the potential and do the necessary further investigative work. It should also be noted that, whilst it was clear in this case that there was a direct and specific contractual duty to research the pictures, it is thought that the judge was prepared to find that the duty existed independently as a commitment to the contract as agent for sale.

The Court of Appeal, no doubt to the relief of the auctions world, reversed the decision. A number of important issues arose:

### 2.1.7.1 WHAT WAS THE DUTY OF CARE?

The duty was found to be one to express a considered opinion as to the sale value of the Foxhound pictures and for that purpose to take further appropriate advice.

### 2.1.7.2 WHAT IS THE STANDARD OF CARE REQUIRED?

Very importantly, the Court of Appeal confirmed the finding at first instance that a valid distinction should be made between those who may fairly be described, by analogy with the medical profession, as "general practitioners" and specialists or consultants. This provincial firm of auctioneers fell squarely within the general practitioner group and the Court of Appeal held that, as in the case of the medical man, in the realm of diagnosis and treatment, "there is ample scope for genuine difference of opinion and one man clearly is not negligent merely because his conclusion differs from that of other professional men". Thus the true test is not to see whether or not the auctioneer got his "diagnosis" wrong, but whether he has been guilty of such failure as no auctioneer of ordinary skill would be guilty of acting with ordinary care.

It is clear, therefore, that the degree of skill and care which one is entitled to demand of a provincial auction house in such matters is rather less than one would be entitled to demand from, say, Christie's or Sotheby's. As regards the duty in this case, Slade LJ pointed out[24]:

"Attribution ... is not an exact science, the judgment in the very nature of things may be fallible and may turn out to be wrong. Accordingly provided that the valuer has done his job honestly and with due diligence I think that the court should be cautious before convicting him of professional negligence merely because he has failed to be the first to spot a sleeper."

### 2.1.7.3 DISCHARGE OF THE DUTY OF CARE

The Court of Appeal found that the auctioneers would have been acting in discharge of their duty if they had simply passed on the views of their consultant, so the court did not have to consider whether or not they had discharged their duty by getting the advice they did from Christie's. However, the judges opined that that would have sufficed.

24. [1990] 1 All E.R. 1067 at 1076.

### 2.1.7.4 QUANTUM OF DAMAGES

Since no liability was found, the issue of damages did not arise for consideration, but the Court of Appeal was by no means satisfied that the correct measure would have been the difference between the £840 and the £88,000 obtained at the Sotheby's sale. There were a number of factors which contributed to the achievement of this price and such might not necessarily recur. It is important to note that the pictures were considerably "tarted up" by Sotheby's before the sale and looked very different from the neglected articles sold by the defendant auctioneers.

The case is one of immense interest and, whilst it leaves auction houses happier than they will have been at the end of the High Court hearing, there is no doubt that auctioneers remain potentially liable for misattributions which depress the price obtained at auction and also for advice on values and reserves which is given carelessly.

Auctioneers may regard themselves, with some justification, as being "between a rock and a hard place": if they fail to describe a lot to its full potential, they may incur liability to the seller; if they over-describe it, they may be liable directly to the purchaser.[25]

### 2.1.8 Duty to obtain the deposit and price

In the absence of an express contractual duty, an auctioneer will not be liable for failing to obtain a deposit from the purchaser, but it has been established that it may be negligent for an auctioneer to allow a purchaser to take away lots without paying for them.[26]

Auction conditions of sale today frequently give auctioneers a discretion whether to allow the purchaser credit. In *Cyril Andrade Ltd* v. *Sotheby & Co*[27] the auctioneers knocked down a fine suit of armour, belonging originally to Count Von Trapp, to a Mr Bartel who had previously acted, and they believed presently to be acting, for the American newspaper tycoon William Randolph Hearst. The sale price was £5,000 and, acting on this belief, the auctioneers allowed Mr Bartel to depart without taking a deposit from him. The conditions of sale provided that a deposit was payable "if required". The sale was repudiated by Mr Hearst who said that Mr Bartel was not his agent and the auctioneers returned the armour to their clients. The plaintiff-vendors claimed £2,500 being the 50 per cent deposit they alleged ought to have been taken.

Sotheby's gave evidence that they did not normally demand deposits unless they did not know or trust the purchaser. On these facts it was held that there was no breach of duty by the auctioneers.

The issue as to whether an auctioneer is liable to the seller if he causes loss by delaying in re-offering a lot where the purchaser disappears was considered in *Alchemy (International) Ltd* v. *Tattersalls Ltd*.[28] The auctioneer defendants designated the first day of the September 1983 bloodstock sales at Newmarket for yearlings of exceptional pedigree vetted by the auctioneers. The sales were to be called the "High-flyer Premier Yearling Sales" and the object was obviously to

---

25. See *De Balkany* v. *Christie Manson & Woods Ltd* (unreported, 1995) discussed below.
26. See 2 *Halsbury's Laws of England* (4th edn, reissue) para. 915.
27. (1931) 47 T.L.R. 244.
28. [1985] 2 E.G.L.R. 17.

attract the big money to that opening day. In this, the auctioneers were successful because they did attract, amongst others, several of the sons of the ruler of Dubai and on that day lot 117, a foal of "Hello gorgeous", achieved a European record price of 15 million guineas.

The immediately preceding lot, 116, was a "Riverman" colt and it was with this lot that the case is concerned. This colt had a reserve of 150,000 guineas and was brought into the ring towards the end of the day at 8pm. Bidding proceeded briskly and the colt was knocked down to a Mr Flood for 430,000 guineas. However, Flood denied that he had made a bid of that figure, claiming that he withdrew at 410,000 guineas; one Omar Assi was the underbidder though whether at 420,000 or only at 400,000 guineas, as he claimed, was in dispute. The bidding was video-recorded and there seems little doubt that the colt was properly knocked down to Mr Flood at the price of 430,000 guineas. However, he refused to give his name and address to the auctioneers, denied that he was the successful bidder and absented himself from the scene. He was subsequently arrested at Heathrow.

Little or no blame was attached by the sellers to Tattersalls over this, but they complained that Tattersalls were negligent in not there and then, or at the latest at the end of that first day, re-auctioning the colt or at least announcing that they would be doing so. The colt was not in fact put up again until three days later, after unsuccessful attempts either to get Flood to honour his bid or to track down the underbidder and secure a private treaty sale with him at the underbid price. The colt was knocked down for 200,000 guineas some days later. It is clear that by that date some of the big money had been expended. There was no dispute about the scope of the duty owed by the auctioneers, *viz* to exercise reasonable care to obtain the best price for their vendor-client. Condition 4 of the conditions of sale of Tattersalls in terms gave the auctioneers the option, in the circumstances which arose, of putting the lot up again or selling privately either immediately or later.

Experts were called on both sides and, not surprisingly, gave divergent views as to what was the proper or sensible thing for the auctioneer to have done in such a dilemma. But the interest in the case lies in the formulation of the proper approach and role of the court in such cases involving a conflict of expert evidence. As indicated earlier, the court applied by analogy tests which had been applied in cases involving alleged medical malpractice. Under these tests it was recognised that a specialist (which clearly Tattersalls here were) would not be liable merely because they had acted in a way which was contrary to that in which similar specialists might have done, provided there was a respectable body of opinion which would have accepted their actions as proper. The judge concluded that the relevant expert evidence taken as a whole demonstrated that the auctioneers' actions and decisions were fully in line with a respectable body of professional opinion. Therefore Tattersalls were not negligent.

## 2.2 Fiduciary duties

An agent is in a fiduciary position vis-à-vis his principal and, as a consequence, owes him certain duties.[29] These may variously be described as duties of loyalty or duties of

---

29. For a detailed analysis of the fiduciary relationship, see *Bowstead on Agency* (15th edn, 1985) Sweet & Maxwell, arts. 45–55.

good faith. Essentially this means that an agent must not so place himself that his personal interests may conflict with his duty to his principal. The main instances include:

    (a)  taking commission from both parties,
    (b)  purchasing the principal's property,
    (c)  obtaining a secret profit.

### 2.2.1 Taking commission from both parties

The practice of auctioneers charging buyers a commission or premium on sales in addition to that payable by the vendor is commonplace today. As such it is often much objected to by buyers, but it may also act to the detriment of the vendor-principal. As Sargeant LJ explained in a case involving an hotel broker who sought to charge both his principal and the buyer commissions[30]:

"He is seeking to impose an onerous condition on the purchaser which might very well prevent the purchaser ever taking advantage of the order to view; and to impose such a condition would be in flagrant violation of his duty to the vendor which is to bring along any purchaser who can be found on the terms of the vendor paying ... the agreed commission ... [The] condition ... might have the effect of stalling off a purchaser and preventing the plaintiff from securing for the vendor such a purchaser as would be acceptable to the vendor."

As regards auctions, it is clear that the imposition of a buyer's premium could have the effect of, at least, depressing the price which a buyer would be prepared to pay and this is obviously contrary to the vendor's interests.

It is not a situation, however, where the auctioneer's interests and duty conflict since it will be likewise in his and his vendor's interests to obtain the highest possible price and, therefore, taking commission from the buyer will not involve a breach of fiduciary duty provided that the auctioneer fully discloses to his vendor-principal the existence of a contractual provision entitling him so to do.

Another situation where there may appear to be a potential conflict of interest is where an auctioneer, for gain or otherwise, agrees to bid on behalf of a prospective purchaser; for then he is acting as agent for two parties whose interests are antithetical. That such activity is quite lawful is nowadays not a matter for much doubt. In *Fullwood* v. *Hurley*, which concerned the taking of remuneration from both sides, Lord Hamworth MR stated categorically:

"If and so long as the agent is the agent of one party he cannot engage to become the agent of another principal without leave of the first principal with whom he has originally established his agency."

The crucial words are "without leave". It is thought that provided the auctioneer notifies the vendor and obtains his consent, actual or tacit, the practice will not involve a breach of fiduciary duty.

Sotheby's (condition 34) provide that they will execute bids for buyers (whilst discouraging the practice somewhat by warning them that their interests are best

---

30. *Fullwood* v. *Hurley* [1928] 1 K.B. 498 at 505, 96 L.J.K.B. 976.

served by personal attendance). Christie's similarly notify their willingness to accept "commissions" (condition A 12).[31]

### 2.2.2 Purchasing the principal's property

The purchase by an auctioneer of his principal's property is another activity giving rise to a potential conflict of interest and duty, and, once again, he is enjoined from so doing unless he has made the fullest disclosure of all relevant facts to his principal. As it was put by a textbook writer in the nineteenth century[32]:

"If then, the seller were permitted as the agent of another, to become the purchaser, his duty to his principal and his own interest would stand in direct opposition to each other; and thus a temptation, perhaps in many cases too strong for resistance by men of flexible morals or hackneyed in the common devices of worldly business, would be held out, which would betray them into gross misconduct ..."

If an auctioneer docs, without the requisite disclosure and consent, buy his client's property,[33] two consequences may flow. First, he will not be able to keep the property purchased but will hold it as a trustee on trust[34] for his principal at whose suit the sale will be set aside. In *Oliver* v. *Court*,[35] where an auctioneer who had also valued an estate carelessly omitting to take account of valuable timber thereon, bought it himself after an abortive auction, the principal was held entitled to set the sale aside even after a lapse of 13 years. However, whilst delay may not, of itself, preclude the setting aside of the sale, it was stressed in *Wentworth* v. *Lloyd*[36] that where the principal delays and, as a result, evidence may have been lost, the defendant agent is "entitled to every fair and reasonable presumption that may be drawn in favour of the direct testimony [he] adduces".[37] This case also shows that the burden of proving that he made full disclosure and that the vendor acquiesced in his purchase lies on the agent.

The second consequence of such a breach of his fiduciary duty is that the auctioneer will be disentitled to his commission and this will be so whether the principal has elected to set the sale aside or has affirmed it. As Pollock CB put it in *Salomons* v. *Pender*[38]:

"The argument has failed to convince me that a person can, in the same transaction buy in the character of a principal, and at the same time charge the seller as his agent. I cannot agree that, because the seller has chosen to abide by the sale he is therefore to be held to have acknowledged the claims of the plaintiff both as agent and purchaser."

This seems a correct result. If the auctioneer has not shown that he made full disclosure to the vendor and that the latter acquiesced in the sale to him, he has

---

31. The practice was commented on with approval (albeit *obiter*) in *Fordham* v. *Christie Manson & Woods Ltd* (1977) 244 E.G. 213 at 215 *per* May J.

32. *Story on Agency*, p. 262, para. 210, cited in *Salomons* v. *Pender* (1856) 3 H. & C. 639 at 643.

33. By himself or in consortium with others; see *Wentworth* v. *Lloyd* (1863) 32 Beav. 467; *Dunne* v. *English* (1874) L.R. 18 Eq. 524; 31 L.T. 75.

34. See *Lees* v. *Nuttall* (1829) 1 Russ. and M. 53; affd. (1834) 2 My. & K. 819.

35. (1820) Dan. 301, 8 Price 127.

36. (1863) 32 Beav. 467.

37. (1863) 32 Beav. 467 *per* Sir John Romilly MR at 474.

38. (1856) 3 H. & C. 639 at 641.

simply acted outside his authority and thus, on general principles,[39] has not earned his commission; he was employed to sell to third parties and has sold instead to himself.

Given these consequences, it is obviously vital that an auctioneer ensures that he does satisfy the disclosure requirements and obtains the express consent to his purchase from his client. However, he will be free to buy when his agency has terminated. In the New Zealand case of *Young* v. *Hill Ford & Newton*[40] auctioneers were instructed by a mortgagor to sell his land. The auction having proved abortive, the auctioneers bought the land concerned from unpaid mortgagees who had subsequently instructed them to sell. The mortgagor claimed that the auctioneers had remained his agents.

The Court of Appeal held that the onus of proof that the auctioneers had divested themselves of their fiduciary character lay on them and that once an agency existed, subsequent purchases by an agent would be closely scrutinised. However, in the circumstances of this case, the agency had terminated and the auctioneers' purchase of the property was, vis-à-vis the mortgagor, unobjectionable. Here the auctioneers had subsequently become agents for the mortgagees from whom they had bought. As to this Williams J said[41]:

"It appears that they were employed by the mortgagees to sell the property by auction; the auction proved abortive as no bid was received, and the agency of Ford and Newton so far as regards the mortgagees had therefore determined. An auctioneer is agent *pro hac vice*, and whether he succeeds in effecting the sale or not his agency is determined after the auction."

Such a categorical statement has to be treated with some caution. Much will depend upon the circumstances of the auctioneer's appointment, his conduct of the auction and so on. In *Oliver* v. *Court*,[42] for example, it was held that the agency of the auctioneer continued after he had descended from the rostrum and that he had in any event already determined to purchase the property himself when he commenced conduct of the auction. On that basis, his agency was extant when he purchased the estate and the sale to him was set aside.

### 2.2.3  Obtaining a secret profit

It is an inexorable rule, derived from the law of trusts, that an agent must not use his position to acquire for himself any secret profit from a third party. This is so even if the principal has suffered no actual loss. There are numerous circumstances in which a "secret profit" can arise. At one extreme the notion will include a bribe, and at the other, the relatively innocent receipt of commission from a third party for the introduction of the principal's business. The leading case as regards auctioneers is *Hippisley* v. *Knee Bros.*[43] There the defendant auctioneers had been instructed to sell goods on terms that they were to be paid a lump sum by way of commission together with disbursements, including the costs of printing and advertising. The auctioneer contracted with printers for posters, catalogues and newspaper advertisements for which they were invoiced at the normal rate. However, the auctioneers were allowed,

---

39. See Harvey and Meisel, *op. cit.*, chapter 4.
40. (1883) 2 N.Z.L.R. 62.
41. *Ibid.* at 88.
42. (1820) Dan. 301, 8 Price 127.
43. [1905] 1 K.B. 1.

in fact, a 10 per cent discount. When accounting to their client, however, the auctioneers charged these expenses at the normal invoice price. On discovering these facts the plaintiff sued to recover the discounts and also the commission paid. As regards the discounts it was held that these were repayable to the client. The auctioneers' claim to a trade custom entitling them to such discounts did not succeed. Lord Alvestone CJ adverted to "an extraordinary laxity in the view taken of the earning of secret profits by agents" within commercial circles.[44] Whilst the auctioneers' honest belief in their right to retain these discounts as additional profit for themselves did not affect their duty to account for them to their principal, their *bona fides* in this regard was relevant in the context of the claim for return of the commission. The Chief Justice said[45]:

"If the court is satisfied that there has been no fraud or dishonesty upon the agent's part, I think that the receipt by him of a discount will not disentitle him to his commission unless the discount is in some way connected with the contract which the agent is employed to make or the duty which he is called upon to perform. In my opinion the neglect by the defendants to account for the discounts in the present case is not sufficiently connected with the real subject-matter of their employment. If the discount had been received from the purchasers the case would have been covered by *Andrews* v. *R Ramsey*[46] but here it was received in respect of a purely incidental matter. It had nothing to do with the duty of selling. It cannot be suggested that the plaintiff got one penny a lower price than he would otherwise have got. Therefore I come to the conclusion that, so far as the £20 commission is concerned, the plaintiff is not entitled to succeed."

Whilst the *bona fides* of these auctioneers was accepted by the court, auctioneers must ensure today that they disclose and account for such commissions to their clients.

## 2.3 Duty to account

The duty to account is one of the duties owed by an agent to his principal which arises out of the fiduciary relationship which exists between them, but it warrants separate treatment. It is the duty of every agent to keep the property and money of his principal separate from his own and to preserve and keep accounts of all his dealings in the course of his agency. He must also be prepared to produce all relevant books and documents relating to his principal's affairs.[47] If an agent fails to keep proper accounts or fails to pay or transfer to his principal money or property received for him, the agent is liable to an action for an account,[48] normally brought in the Chancery Division of the High Court.

The significance of the fact that the duty to account arises out of the fiduciary relationship between the agent and his principal lies in the remedies available against a defaulting agent, namely that the principal can trace the property belonging to him in the hands of his agent in priority to that agent's ordinary creditors. Thus in *Re Cotton, ex parte Cook*,[49] the deceased, Cotton, was instructed in cattle sales in

---

44. *Ibid.* at 7.
45. *Ibid.* at 8.
46. [1903] 2 K.B. 635.
47. See generally *Bowstead on Agency* (15th edn, 1985) Sweet & Maxwell, art. 52.
48. See the Supreme Court Act 1981, s. 61(1) and Sch. 1. The relevant rules are to be found in R.S.C. Ord. 43.
49. (1913) 108 L.T. 310.

Bromsgrove and four other towns. It appears that he generally sold in his own name and made himself personally liable for all money received. Occasionally he gave credit to purchasers and allowed set-offs to those who were also vendors. Cook instructed him to sell certain cattle and this was duly effected but the proceeds were not immediately collected. Thereafter, the auctioneer committed suicide but his son obtained outstanding payments due and paid the money into a separate bank account. The auctioneer's estate being insolvent, the question arose whether a sum of £40 17s 6d in respect of the proceeds of sale of Cook's cattle was recoverable by Cook or whether it was properly kept by the trustee in bankruptcy as part of the general assets of the estate into which Cook could prove his debt together with the other creditors. The Divisional Court held that the auctioneer had established a course of dealing in which he became a principal, buying and selling on his own account and that Cook merely looked to him as a debtor. The Court of Appeal, however, found such a course of dealing negatived by the express conditions of business of the auctioneer and held that the question was whether Cook was entitled to say, "These cattle of mine were entrusted to you for a particular purpose, as commission agent to sell for me. That is a fiduciary position and the fiduciary relation applies to the money received from the sale of cattle entrusted to you for sale".[50] This question was, on the facts, answered in the affirmative; the proceeds belonged to the principal and he could trace into the insolvent auctioneer's estate ahead of the general creditors by virtue of the fiduciary relationship existing between them. If, however, the facts had been as the Divisional Court had found them, that the auctioneer in fact sold as principal on his own account having bought them from his client, no fiduciary relationship would have existed nor attached to the proceeds and the seller would merely have been an unpaid creditor. This kind of arrangement is not uncommon in cattle auctions where sales are effected outside the ring and booked with the auctioneers.[51]

The right to trace property exists both at law and in equity. The latter remedy is more efficacious when money is involved because at common law the right to trace is lost when the true owner's property is no longer identifiable. Equity, however, is prepared to unscramble bank accounts containing monies belonging to several persons. It is beyond the scope of this chapter to examine the remedy in any detail, but the right to trace would be lost if the property were taken by another without notice of the rights of the true owner, having given value for it. So in *Marten* v. *Rocke Eyton & Co*,[52] unpaid vendors were held unable to trace into the bank account of the defaulting auctioneer when the bankers had taken the balance therein in satisfaction of an overdraft, without notice that the balance comprised monies due to the vendors.

It is clear, therefore, that an auctioneer is at risk if he fails properly to account and he will in the absence of express authority to the contrary only escape liability if he does so direct to the principal himself. There is no implied authority to pay proceeds

---

50. *Ibid.* at 311 *per* Cozens-Hardy MR.
51. See, e.g., *Murphy* v. *Howlett* (1960) 176 E.G. 311, and Harvey and Meisel, *op. cit.*, chapter 10.
52. (1885) 53 L.T. 946, 34 W.R. 253.

or a deposit to his client's solicitors.[53] The auctioneer must remain willing and able to account to his principal. In *Lowe* v. *Gallimore*[54] it was held that a principal could enforce this duty after having revoked an earlier instruction to pay proceeds of sale into a bank account pending resolution of a dispute surrounding them. Further, in *Crosskey* v. *Mills*[55] the defendant auctioneer was instructed to sell goods by one W Crosskey, the brother of a deceased who had given the plaintiff a bill of sale. The deceased's widow instructed the auctioneer to hold the proceeds to satisfy all the creditors of the deceased. It is unclear whether the plaintiff concurred in such an arrangement, but in any event he subsequently instructed the auctioneer to account to him. It was held that the auctioneer was bound to do so: "the plaintiff was the person who originally employed the defendant to sell. Therefore *prima facie*, the defendant was bound to account to the plaintiff".[56]

The problem in these cases can be regarded as stemming from conflicting instructions from the principal. However, the major area of difficulty for an auctioneer exists where a third party lays claim to the goods or their proceeds. As we shall see later, if the third party's claim is justified, the auctioneer is exposed to an action in tort for conversion of the true owner's property. The auctioneer may, therefore, be caught on the horns of a dilemma, but in certain circumstances may be able to escape liability for failing to account to his principal where he invokes the right and title of a third party: the *jus tertii* defence.

### 2.3.1 The jus tertii defence

In *Crosskey* v. *Mills*[57] it was expressly held that there no third party had shown any title to the money, but that if such had been shown the auctioneer might have had a defence to an action by the principal. The precise circumstances where this defence will be available now fall to be briefly considered. The common law position has been affected by the Torts (Interference with Goods) Act 1977. The Act does not represent a masterpiece of clear draftsmanship and it may well be that its provisions do not apply at all to cases where a principal sues an agent for failure to account to him for the proceeds of sale. We shall, therefore, first outline the position at common law, and then consider the impact of the statute.

### 2.3.1.1 COMMON LAW

In *Hardman* v. *Willcock*[58] an auctioneer was instructed by the plaintiff to sell certain goods he possessed. Before the sale the auctioneer was given notice by assignees of an insolvent that the goods belonged to them and that the plaintiff had obtained them

---

53. See *Brown* v. *Farebrother* (1880) 58 L.J.Ch. 3 at 4 *per* Kekewich J, although in that case auctioneers instructed to sell by the plaintiff acting under a court order and under a duty to pay proceeds into court were held discharged when they paid the proceeds over to solicitors for the vendor for that purpose. It seems that in this case the auctioneers did have actual authority so to do.
54. (1851) 18 L.T.O.S. 63, 241.
55. (1834) 1 Cr. M. & R. 298, 3 L.J.Ex. 297.
56. (1834) 1 Cr. M. & R. 298 at 301–302 *per* Parke B.
57. See fn. 55 above.
58. (1831) 9 Bing. 382n.

from the insolvent under a fraudulent arrangement devised to defeat their claim. Having subsequently sold the goods, the auctioneer refused to account to the plaintiff for the proceeds. The plaintiff duly brought an action for money had and received to his use and the auctioneer pleaded the defence of *jus tertii*, that is, the right of the assignees as third parties entitled to the property. The court accepted the general proposition that an agent is under a duty to account to his principal, but held the defence good on the ground that the principal had taken the goods as part of a fraudulent scheme to defeat the rights of the true owners. A defence based on a notion of fraud by the client is somewhat narrow and the principle was explained and extended a few years later in *Biddle* v. *Bond*[59] where an auctioneer refused to account to his principal, a landlord selling a tenant's goods under distraint for rent. Here again, the auctioneer received notice just before the sale from the tenant claiming that the distress was void. The court held that the defence of *jus tertii* was available against the principal. Blackburn J explained the rationale thus[60]:

"We do not question the general rule that one who has received property from another as his bailee or agent or servant must restore or account for that property to him from whom he received it ... But the bailee has no better title than the bailor and consequently if a person entitled as against the bailor to the property claims it, the bailee has no defence against him."

Whereas, normally, an agent is estopped from denying the title of his principal, the estoppel ceases when the possession on which it is founded is determined by the agent being "evicted" by someone with a better title. There must be something in the nature of an eviction or dispossession (although this need not be physical); mere notice of another's claim does not suffice. The agent can set up the *jus tertii* only if he defends by virtue of the title and on the authority of the true owner.[61] And the defence is not restricted to cases where the principal has been guilty of fraud on the true owner.

An auctioneer then, in order to have a valid defence to an action brought by his principal for failure in his duty to account, must prove two things: first, he must prove the title of the adverse claimant by whose authority he is defending the claim and, secondly, he must show that he has not by his conduct estopped himself from setting up that adverse claim. Where an auctioneer knows of an adverse claim but disregards it and sells for his principal, he cannot then deny his principal's title by invoking that of the third party whose claim he has disregarded. This was the difficulty into which the auctioneer placed himself in *Re Sadler, ex parte Davies*.[62] Here, the auctioneer with due notice of two claims effectively took sides. He was held to be estopped from denying the title of one of two persons who had concurrently instructed him to sell. This case is distinguishable from *Biddle* v. *Bond*,[63] where the notice of the conflicting claim came only a short time before the sale was due to be commenced so that it could not properly be said that the auctioneer made an election. The obvious course for an auctioneer who has notice of rival claims to property is to interplead.[64]

---

59. (1865) 122 E.R. 1179, 6 B. & S. 225.

60. (1865) 122 E.R. 1179 at 1181.

61. See *Rogers Sons & Co* v. *Lambert & Co* [1891] 1 Q.B. 318, 60 L.J.Q.B. 187, C.A.

62. (1881) 19 Ch.D. 86, 45 L.T. 632, C.A.

63. See fn. 59 above.

64. On interpleader, see Harvey and Meisel, *op. cit.*, chapter 4. Essentially, it is a court procedure which enables a person being made subject to adverse claims to property to bring the property or fund into court and let the disputants contest it. The procedure is set out in R.S.C. Ord. 17, r. 3 and C.C.R. Ord. 33, r. 6.

## 2.3.1.2 STATUTORY MODIFICATIONS

The Torts (Interference with Goods) Act 1977, s. 8(1) provides:

"The defendant in an action for wrongful interference shall be entitled to show, in accordance with rules of court, that a third party has a better right than the plaintiff as respects all or any part of the interest claimed by the plaintiff, or in right of which he sues, and any rule of law (sometimes called *jus tertii*) to the contrary is abolished."

There is an immediate difficulty over the parenthesis in section 8(1). It is not the defence based on the invocation of the *jus tertii* that is abolished, but the *limitations* on that defence outlined above. Thus, if the 1977 Act applies in the situations under consideration, the basic rule laid down by the common law—that generally a bailee cannot deny the title of his bailor—is abrogated. *Rogers Sons & Co* v. *Lambert*[65] is therefore no longer good law and an auctioneer defendant will always be able to invoke the defence of *jus tertii*.

But does the Torts (Interference with Goods) Act 1977 apply where the auctioneer fails to account for proceeds of sale to his principal? Section 8 refers to the rights of the defendant "in an action for wrongful interference". Section 1 defines such as:

(a) conversion of goods (also called trover);
(b) trespass to goods;
(c) negligence so far as it results in damage to goods or to an interest in goods;
(d) subject to section 2, any other tort so far as it results in damage to goods or an interest in goods.

The problems with this definition are twofold. First, it is doubtful whether a fund representing proceeds of sale of goods would be regarded as "goods" within the definition.[66] Secondly, and more difficult to surmount, is the fact that a vendor seeking such proceeds could invariably bring an action for breach of contract. A right to the proceeds of sale is usually expressly provided and, if it is not, such will be implied into his contract with the auctioneer. Thus the action would not be one for conversion, trespass, negligence or any other tort.

One is driven to the conclusion that the 1977 Act simply does not apply to a retention by the auctioneer of the proceeds of sale. This is rather unfortunate; the consequence is that an auctioneer who before sale learns of a rival claim to goods may freely invoke the *jus tertii* and enjoin the rival in any action against him for their return. Whereas if he sells the goods and seeks to set up the *jus tertii* as a defence to an action in respect of the proceeds, framed in contract, he can only invoke the *jus tertii* subject to the strict common law rules outlined above.

It is thought that despite the very general wording of section 8(1) of the Torts (Interference with Goods) Act 1977, even where the Act does apply, a specific estoppel such as that which was found in *Re Sadler*[67] could still operate to prevent the auctioneer setting up the defence. The 1977 Act seeks to ameliorate the position of a defendant who finds himself subject to two or more rival claims. If he has chosen to

---

65. See fn. 61 above.
66. Money is specifically excluded: Torts (Interference with Goods) Act 1977, s. 14(1).
67. See fn. 62 above.

throw in his lot with one of the rivals, he should account to him and face the legal wrath of the other.

Where the provisions of the Act are available to the defendant he is permitted to name any interested rival, and apply for his being joined. The Rules of Court referred to in section 8(2) are to be found in R.S.C. Ord. 15, r. 10A(2) for the High Court, and C.C.R. 1981, Ord. 15, r. 4(1) for the county court.

An auctioneer will also have a defence to an action for money had and received where his receipt of the proceeds of sale or deposit is only conditional so that the purchaser's claim to its return is valid. In *Hardingham* v. *Allen*,[68] for example, a horse was sold at auction under the contractual condition that if it was warranted quiet in harness it could be returned within a prescribed period if it did not correspond with that description. The horse was then to be tried and examined by an impartial person whose decision would be final. A purchaser returned a horse under this condition and the auctioneer duly paid back the purchase money. The vendor-plaintiff's claim for the purchase price as money had and received failed. Coltman J held[69]:

"With regard to the money received by the defendant as the price of the horse [it] was received conditionally only and never in fact became money had and received to the use of the plaintiff."

The decision in *Murray* v. *Mann*[70] where the purchaser justifiably rescinded the contract for fraud is to similar effect. However, the question whether an auctioneer is entitled, in the absence of express authority, vis-à-vis his principal to accept rescission of a contract is not entirely free from doubt. If he unjustifiably does so he will be liable to account for the money he ought to have received and retained.[71]

### 2.3.2 Interest

We have already seen that, by virtue of his fiduciary relationship with his principal, an auctioneer may not make any profit out of his agency. It is perhaps obvious, therefore, that where an auctioneer holds money which belongs to his principal, any interest which it earns must be accounted for to him.[72] The question arises whether an agent holding money for his principal is under a duty to invest it so that it yields interest and is liable for such interest as could have been earned if he fails to do so. At common law the agent was only liable if he dealt with his principal's money wrongfully or made any use of it.

The common law has been rendered somewhat obsolete by the Law Reform (Miscellaneous Provisions) Act 1934, which gives the court a wide general discretion to award interest on any debt or damages between the date when the cause of action arose and the judgment.

---

68. (1848) 5 C.B. 793.
69. *Ibid.* at 797–798.
70. (1848) 2 Exch. 538, 17 L.J.Ex. 256.
71. See *Nelson* v. *Aldridge* (1818) 2 Stark 435 and contrast *Stevens* v. *Legh* (1853) 2 C.L.R. 251, 22 L.T.O.S. 84.
72. The general principles are discussed in *Bowstead on Agency* (15th edn, 1985) Sweet & Maxwell, art. 54.

## 2.4 Duty to care for the goods

The main legal relationship between a vendor and an auctioneer is that of agency, but in addition there exists in connection with goods a relationship of bailment. Bailment is a legal institution of some antiquity and complexity and it is possible within the scope of this chapter to discuss its impact in the field of auctions only in rather brief and general terms.[73]

The central feature of bailment involves the delivery of goods by the bailor into the custody of another, the bailee. Bailment is usually but not invariably for reward. Although an auctioneer will generally be a bailee for reward there are situations where the bailment may be gratuitous—as where he is in possession of a prospective vendor's goods for valuation purposes if he does not charge for such or, vis-à-vis the purchaser, after a sale but before collection by him.[74] Originally it was thought that bailment presupposed redelivery by the bailee, but this is no longer so. A bailment can clearly exist where it is envisaged, as is the case with auctions, that the bailee will deliver the goods to a third party—the purchaser after the sale. But if the sale is abortive, the auctioneer will again be holding the goods as a bailee for the vendor with the concomitant rights and duties created by the relationship. A failure to return such goods without lawful excuse such as in exercise of his lien, or pleading the *jus tertii*, will render the auctioneer liable in conversion.

In the case of auctions the bailment will usually be contractual and its terms will depend upon the precise terms of that contract. Subject to such provisions, the duty of the auctioneer at common law will be to take reasonable care of the goods in his custody. In the old case of *Maltby* v. *Christie*[75] an auctioneer was instructed to sell a quantity of plate glass. A dispute arose as to whether the auctioneer was entitled to deduct commission at the rate of 7½ per cent. No commission had been agreed between the parties but the defendant claimed there to be a trade custom that such an amount was usual in view of the extraordinary risks attending the sale of such goods. Lord Kenyon, in denying the auctioneer's claim, said that he was of the opinion that the auctioneer as bailee was only bound to take such care of the goods as he would exercise in respect of his own, and that for a loss arising from misfortune or unavoidable accident he was not liable.

Such a general statement as to the duty and standard of care must be treated with some caution. Some bailments involve benefit to both bailor and bailee, some create benefits only to the bailor, and some create benefits only to the bailee. According to *Halsbury's Laws of England*[76]:

"an ordinary degree of care and skill is usually required where both benefit from the transaction; slighter diligence, perhaps, where the benefit is wholly that of the bailor ... and greater diligence where the benefit accrues only to the bailee".

---

73. The major modern work of reference is N E Palmer, *Bailment* (2nd edn, 1991) Sweet and Maxwell. See also 2 *Halsbury's Laws of England* (4th edn, reissue).

74. The classic classification of the various sorts of bailment is to be found in *Coggs* v. *Bernard* (1703) 2 Ld. Raym. 909; 1 Com. 133 *per* Holt CJ, *viz*: (a) custody of goods without reward, (b) loan of goods, (c) hire of goods, (d) pawn or pledge of goods, (e) carriage of goods or other performance of service for reward, and (f) the same, without reward.

75. (1795) 1 Esp. 340.

76. 2 *Halsbury's Laws of England* (4th edn, reissue) para. 1803.

However, in *Houghland* v. *R R Low (Luxury Coaches) Ltd*,[77] the Court of Appeal preferred simply to say that the standard of care depended upon the circumstances of the particular case, it being artificial frequently to try to fit a particular case into the various rigid categories.[78] Moreover, it has been held that where the bailment is contractual, as with auctions it usually is, if the bailee deals with the property entrusted to him in an unauthorised manner, he takes upon himself the risks of so doing. Thus if, for example, an auctioneer were to warehouse his principal's goods with a third person, in breach of contract, whereupon the goods became destroyed by fire, the auctioneer would be liable.[79] This raises the question whether in the absence of express provision, a bailee may sub-contract out his duties. The answer turns on whether the contract involved is one the essence of which is the personal skill and care of the bailee employed.[80]

### 2.4.1 Liability for negligence

The most obvious situations in which the auctioneer will be liable to his vendor-principal will be where he fails to take reasonable care of the latter's goods either prior to the sale or whilst they remain in the auctioneer's custody and control after the sale pending delivery to the buyer or redelivery to the seller (where there is an abortive sale).

An instructive cases is *Spriggs* v. *Sotheby Parke Bernet and Co.*[81] In that case the plaintiff decided to sell a diamond valued at some £22,000 and deposited it with Sotheby's for inclusion in their next important diamond sale. It was envisaged that the auctioneers would make the stone available for viewing before the sale, and viewing arrangements, and security procedures therefor, were established. The contract between Spriggs and Sotheby's provided, *inter alia*, by clause 2:

"I accept that whilst you take all reasonable care in handling the property on behalf of clients, you are not responsible for loss or damage of any kind whether caused by negligence or otherwise, the property being accepted at owner's risk."

Mr Sprigg's diamond, lot 290, was stolen by a viewer while the porter's attention had been diverted by another customer.

At first instance the judge held that Sotheby's had not been negligent: they had employed a retired Detective Chief Inspector as head of security; security guards were posted in the room; if gems were to be sold reasonable facilities had to be provided for their viewing; even if it could be said that the porter should not have allowed his attention to have been distracted by another viewer, it was impossible to impose a duty to maintain such vigilance as to prevent a theft which might occur in seconds.

On appeal, however, it was held that the duty of Sotheby's as bailees for reward was to take reasonable care of the goods entrusted to them and that such a bailee had

---

77. [1962] 1 Q.B. 694, [1962] 2 All E.R. 159.
78. For a detailed consideration of this question, see *Palmer* (fn. 73 above).
79. See, e.g., *Lilley* v. *Doubleday* (1881) 7 Q.B.D. 510, 51 L.J.Q.B. 310; *McMahon* v. *Field* (1881) 7 Q.B.D. 591, 50 L.J.Q.B. 552.
80. See *Edwards* v. *Newland & Co* [1950] 2 K.B. 534, C.A. *per* Denning LJ at 542.
81. [1986] 1 Lloyd's Rep. 487.

to show, and the onus was on him, that the loss or damage occurred without his neglect or any neglect of his servant to whom the duty was delegated. The court held that the duty involved two aspects: the provision of a safe system of security and, secondly, the diligent operation of it. In this case it was held that there was not in operation a safe system. It was defective insofar as it allowed extremely small but valuable items to be handled by persons who were strangers to Sotheby's in circumstances where the porter would have to turn his back on them; moreover, the security guards could not be certain of having an uninterrupted view of proceedings.

Exemption clauses are dealt with specifically in chapter 2, but it may be convenient here to look briefly at the impact of the exempting provision referred to earlier. The clause appeared on the reverse of the form which the customer signed. However, immediately above the place where he signed was printed a notice referring to the conditions of sale. The exclusion clause provided for insurance by Sotheby's at an extra cost at seller's option, although in fact this was excluded in this case as Mr Spriggs had insured the diamond himself.

There was much arcane argument as to the construction of the clause, particularly as to the effect of the opening words, "I accept that whilst you take all reasonable care...", but the court was satisfied that the words "whether caused by negligence or otherwise" were clear and adequate to exclude any liability for any act of negligence by Sotheby's or any person for whom they would be responsible. Therefore, and ultimately quite simply, the auctioneers escaped liability because they had incorporated a suitably worded exclusion clause in their contract with their customer. It is important to note, however, that this contract was entered into in 1977, just before the coming into force of the Unfair Contract Terms Act. Thus the exclusion clause in this particular case did not have to satisfy the statutory test of "reasonableness" as would now be the case.

The final problem in relation to the duty of care concerns the question whether a bailee is responsible for the loss of the bailor's goods due to their theft or other depredations by an employee. There are two possible bases for such a liability: first, the bailee may be liable personally insofar as his selection of the employee may have been negligent.[82] Auctioneers frequently deal with very valuable merchandise and it is incumbent upon them to select and supervise their staff with care. In the absence of negligent selection, will he be liable, secondly, for the actions of his employee—i.e. vicariously? Broadly speaking, an employer will be vicariously liable for the torts of his servant acting within the course of employment. Thus a bailee will be liable for the theft or conversion of his bailor's goods committed by an employee who is employed in some part to perform tasks involving care of the goods. He may not, however, be liable if the goods are stolen by an employee engaged in work unconnected with the lost goods.

As we have said, these duties are subject to express contractual variations. Auctioneers' contracts frequently make some provision for their potential liability[83] and their efficacy now depends upon the ordinary rules of common law and the provisions of the Unfair Contract Terms Act 1977 discussed more particularly in chapter 2 of this book.

---

82. See *Jobson* v. *Palmer* [1893] 1 Ch. 71, 62 L.J.Ch. 180.
83. See Christie's Conditions of Acceptance 7 and Sotheby's Conditions of Business 20.

## 3 DUTIES AND LIABILITIES OWED TO THE PURCHASER

An auctioneer may be liable to the purchaser of lots in a variety of ways. To a limited extent he has been regarded as the purchaser's agent. More significantly, he will in certain circumstances be personally liable in contract. Finally, the general law imposes certain duties on auctioneers in and about the conduct of their business.

### 3.1 The auctioneer as agent of the purchaser

It seems to have been well settled by the early nineteenth century[84] that the auctioneer was the agent of the purchaser for the purpose of signing the memorandum then required to make enforceable certain contracts of sale. Both contracts for the sale etc. of land and those for the sale of goods, where the value exceeded £10, were required to be evidenced in writing, but today only contracts for the sale of land concluded prior to 27 September 1989 are significant in this context. After that date, a contract for the disposition of an interest in land by auction sale is concluded, as with goods, on the fall of the hammer.[85]

The agency of the auctioneer vis-à-vis the purchaser has been described as follows[86]:

"Where there is a sale by public auction and the property is knocked down by the auctioneer to the highest bidder, the auctioneer is not only the agent of the vendor, but he is also the agent of the purchaser, the highest bidder, and ... he is the purchaser's agent clearly to this extent, that he is entitled to sign in the name and on behalf of the purchaser, a memorandum sufficient to satisfy the provisions of the Statute of Frauds ... "

Most of the cases where this agency has been invoked have involved claims by vendors or auctioneers against defendant purchasers seeking to resile from their bargains. The question arose, however, to what extent if at all, this agency involved obligations on the part of the auctioneer to the purchaser. In other words, did this agency involve duties to sign the memorandum on the part of the purchaser so that he could insist that he became a party to the contract, and, if so, did it follow that he could further insist that the auctioneer sign on behalf of the vendor so that the contract became enforceable? It is clear from the cases cited earlier that the authority to sign on behalf of the purchaser is irrevocable after the property is knocked down to him[87] and it would be surprising, not to say commercially unfortunate, if an irretrievably bound purchaser could not be certain that the vendor, too, would be bound or that if he was not, a remedy would lie against him or through his agent, the auctioneer.

It must be accepted that there is no conclusive authority on these questions. Although the abolition of formalities in auction sales of land is comparatively recent,

---

84. See *Emmerson* v. *Heelis* (1809) 2 Taunt. 38; *White* v. *Proctor* (1811) 4 Taunt. 209; *Farebrother* v. *Simmons* (1822) 5 B. & Ald. 333; *Eden* v. *Blake* (1845) 13 M. & W. 614, 14 L.J.Ex. 194.

85. Law of Property (Miscellaneous Provisions) Act 1989, s. 2(5).

86. *Sims* v. *Landray* [1894] 2 Ch. 318 *per* Romer J at 310. Compare *Chaney* v. *Maclow* [1929] 1 Ch. 461, 98 L.J.Ch. 345, C.A.; *Bell* v. *Balls* [1897] 1 Ch. 663, 66 L.J.Ch. 397; *Van Praagh* v. *Everidge* [1902] 2 Ch. 266, 71 L.J.Ch. 598 (revsd [1903] 1 Ch. 434, 72 L.T. Ch. 260, C.A., on the ground that there was no sufficient memorandum).

87. *Chancey* v. *Maclow* [1929] 1 Ch. 461 above; see also (1929) 45 L.Q.R. 289.

it is not proposed here to consider the pre-Act authorities in detail.[88] In *Richards* v. *Phillips*,[89] Pennycuick J, responding to the contention that the auctioneer was bound to sign on behalf of the vendor rendering the contract enforceable at the suit of the highest bidder, said[90]:

"The ... contention raises a question of law which has been the subject of one or two inconclusive *dicta*, but ... not of any actual decision ... An auctioneer is primarily the agent of the vendor ... there is no doubt that he becomes also the implied agent of a purchaser to sign the memorandum on behalf of the purchaser. But it is not at all clear to me how this implied agency on behalf of the purchaser can make it part of his duty to the purchaser to sign the memorandum on behalf of the vendor."

In this case the question did not, in the result, arise for decision because it was held that there had been a genuine dispute about rival bids justifying the withdrawal of the lot and its re-offer for sale. On this aspect of the case, the decision was upheld on appeal.

The duty, it is suggested, can be regarded as arising in this way: the purchaser, as highest bidder impliedly or expressly authorises the auctioneer to effect an enforceable contract by adding his signature to the requisite memorandum. As part of this agency relationship, and impliedly imported into it to give it business efficacy, is a corresponding duty to ensure that the contract is mutually enforceable; that the purchaser effectively *is* the purchaser by obtaining or supplying the vendor's signature. The auctioneer has power to sign on behalf of and to bind both parties. This authority is, as regards each party, irrevocable after the property is knocked down. It is difficult to see why a purchaser should be left without a remedy if the vendor is not bound (as we have seen, a vendor can recover from the auctioneer if he fails to secure an agreement binding the purchaser).[91] Were it otherwise, the agency between auctioneer and purchaser would largely be, as it has been called, a spurious agency enuring exclusively to the benefit of the vendor.

### 3.2 Personal contractual liability to the purchaser

An auctioneer may be personally liable to the purchaser in contract[92] in three distinct ways, and we shall consider each in turn.

### 3.2.1 Breach of warranty of authority

If an agent, including an auctioneer, sells property without or in excess of his authority, he will be liable to the purchaser in damages for breach of the implied warranty that he does, in fact, possess the authority exercised. The simplest situation is where the agent has no authority to sell at all. In *Anderson* v. *John Croall & Sons Ltd*[93] auctioneers sold a mare after a selling race, the trainer's lad having failed to remove her from the paddock after the weighing up so that the auctioneers were

---

88. An analysis is to be found in Harvey and Meisel, *op. cit.*, chapter 9.
89. [1969] 1 Ch. 39.
90. *Ibid.* at 52.
91. See the discussion in the section of this chapter entitled "Duties to the vendor".
92. Liability for breach of warranty of authority may alternatively lie in tort where it is negligent or fraudulent: *Bowstead on Agency, op. cit.*, art. 120 *et seq.*
93. 1903 6 F. (Ct. of Sess.) 153, 41 Sc.L.R. 95.

misled into believing that she was being offered for sale. The owners refused to deliver her and the purchaser claimed against the auctioneer for 35 guineas, being the difference in price between that at which she had been knocked down to him and the price which she had fetched six months later. The Court of Session in Scotland allowed such a claim and awarded damages for breach of the warranty that they were authorised to sell, 10 guineas being deducted in respect of costs of upkeep.

More problematic is the position where the auctioneer has some authority to sell but exceeds it. The obvious case where this may arise is where the auctioneer is instructed to sell subject to a reserve and sells below it. The seller is not bound on the contract of sale because the bids and any acceptance remain conditional, but the question arises whether the auctioneer is liable to the purchaser for breach of warranty of authority. If the fact that a reserve is or may be fixed is notified to purchasers, as it usually is through the auction particulars, the auctioneer will not normally be liable for breach of warranty because the purchaser has notice of the restriction on that authority, or notice of the possibility that it may be restricted and he is put on inquiry as to whether it has been. That was decided in *McManus* v. *Fortescue*.[94] However, in *Fay* v. *Miller Wilkins & Co*[95] auctioneers were held liable to the purchaser because they went further than merely knocking the property down: they proceeded to sign the then requisite memorandum on his behalf. This was held to amount to a waiver of the condition that the property was sold subject to the reserve. Until the abolition of section 40 of the Law of Property Act 1925 in 1989 the position was, therefore (after the abolition of similar evidentiary requirements in relation to certain goods in 1954), that an auctioneer could only be liable for breach of warranty of authority for selling below the reserve in the case of land. The distinction thus drawn in the treatment of sales was difficult to justify. The difficulty for the purchaser is that even if he knows that there is or may be a reserve placed on the property, he will not know whether it has in fact been reached. Should he not be entitled to assume that it has if the auctioneer knocks the property down to him, or, at any rate, should he not have redress against the auctioneer in such circumstances? The liability would not attach for falsely representing that he had authority to sell without reserve but for representing that the reserve had been reached. In *Fay* v. *Miller Wilkins & Co* the auction conditions empowered the vendor to fix a reserve. Clauson LJ, after reiterating that in such circumstance the purchaser took the risk that in selling at the knock-down price the auctioneer might be exceeding this authority, went on to say that the purchaser relies[96]:

"... in practice on the care and honesty of the auctioneer as a professional man, and in law on his ... right to sue the auctioneer on the warranty of authority implied in the fact of his selling on the principal's behalf at the figure named in the note."

Whilst this dictum is not entirely free from ambiguity, it lends some judicial support to the proposition that an auctioneer, in concluding the formalities required for the sale of the property which is or may be subject to a reserve, represents that the property has reached or exceeded the reserve price and that if it has not, whilst he cannot enforce the sale against the vendor, the purchaser can sue the auctioneer on

---

94. [1907] 2 K.B. 1, 76 L.J.K.B. 393.
95. [1941] Ch. 360.
96. *Ibid.* at 367.

that representation. However, since now, both in respect of land and chattels, the contract is both valid and enforceable on the fall of the hammer without more, it is suggested that no action will now lie for breach of warranty of authority where property is knocked down below the reserve price.[97]

### 3.2.2 Liability on the contract of sale

Whilst the general rule is that an agent is not liable on the contract which he makes on behalf of his principal, there is a number of exceptions. Liability may attach because of particular strict rules relating to certain kinds of contract. Thus an agent will be liable where he makes a contract by deed and himself executes it. He is liable even though he is described as acting for and on behalf of his principal.[98] Additionally, an agent will be liable if his principal is undisclosed. This is axiomatic in that, in such circumstances, the fact of his agency is not revealed to the purchaser at all. Here the purchaser may also sue the principal once he discovers his existence. It might have been arguable that an auctioneer could never sell for an undisclosed principal in that, *qua* auctioneer, he inevitably sells only the property of another. Indeed there have been judicial suggestions to this effect.[99] Unfortunately, however, this is not the case. It has been settled, at least since the case of *Flint* v. *Woodin*[100] in 1852, that there is no objection to an auctioneer selling his own property to the purchaser. In such a case, clearly, the auctioneer sells as principal.

More uncertain, however, is the question whether an auctioneer may be liable personally in contract if the fact of his agency is disclosed but the identity of his principal is not. It is very important here to distinguish between the case where the principal is undisclosed, where the agent will always be liable, and the case where the existence of the principal is disclosed but his identity is not.[101] In such circumstances it is not possible to be dogmatic as to whether the agent incurs personal liability on the contract. In some cases the identity of the vendor may be important to the purchaser so that a purchaser who contracts with an agent who declines to name his principal may be taken to do so only on the basis that the agent undertakes some concurrent liability. In other circumstances the identity of the seller may be of no interest. In *Teheran-Europe Co Ltd* v. *S T Belton (Tractors) Ltd* Diplock LJ said[102]:

97. The position would, it is argued, be different in land sales if the conditions stipulate that the purchaser enter into a written contract and the auctioneer is empowered to sign such on behalf of the purchaser and purports to do so notwithstanding the failure to reach the reserve. Where the auctioneer thus takes these further steps he can be regarded as representing that he has authority to waive the condition inherent in a subject to reserve sale.
98. See *Bowstead on Agency*, art. 109, and see also art. 110 reliability on bills of exchange etc.
99. See, e.g., *per* Blackburn J in *Mainprice* v. *Westley* (1865) 6 B. & S. 420 at 429, reporting the opinions of Cockburn CJ and Shee J: "In the employment of an auctioneer the character of an agent is necessarily implied and the party bidding at auction knowingly deals with him as such ..."; see also in similar vein at first instance, *Anderson* v. *John Croall & Sons Ltd* 1904 6 F. (Ct. of Sess.) 153, 41 Sc.L.R. 95.
100. (1852) 9 Hare. 618, 22 L.J.Ch. 92.
101. Regrettably, the judges have not always made such distinctions with care: "the case [is] one of disclosed agency and undisclosed principal" (*Benton* v. *Campbell Parker & Co* [1925] 2 K.B. 410 *per* Salter J at 414); see also *per* Blackburn J in *Mainprice* v. *Westley* (above) at 429 where, speaking of the sale in *Warlow* v. *Harrison* (1859) 1 E. & E. 309, 27 L.J.Q.B. 14 (involving the sale of a horse sold as "the property of a gentleman"), his Lordship said, "the principal was not disclosed ... he was a concealed principal".
102. [1968] 2 Q.B. 545 at 555.

"A person may enter into a contract through an agent whom he has actually authorised to enter into the contract on his behalf or whom he has led the other party to believe he has so authorised but we are concerned here only with actual authority. Where an agent has such actual authority and enters into a contract with another party intending to do so on behalf of his principal it matters not whether he discloses to the other party the identity of the principals or even that he is contracting on behalf of a principal at all, if the other party is willing or leads the agent to believe that he is willing to treat as a party to the contract anyone on whose behalf the agent may have been authorised to contract. In the case of an ordinary commercial contract such willingness of the other party may be assumed by the agent unless either the other party manifests his unwillingness or there are other circumstances which should leave the agent to realise that the other party was not so willing."

However, there are several cases involving auctions which suggest that where the name of the principal-vendor is not given, the auctioneer invariably incurs contractual liability to the purchaser. As long ago as 1792,[103] Lord Kenyon held an auctioneer liable where a bond was not assigned to the purchaser within the contractual period. Although it is not clear from the brief report of this case, it appears[104] that the fact of agency was disclosed but the name of the principal was not. The purchaser was said to be entitled to look to the auctioneer "personally for the completion of the contract". In *Franklyn* v. *Lamond*[105] it was held that the auctioneer was liable for the non-transfer of certain company shares sold at auction. Here the judge, Wilde CJ, said that the auctioneer had contracted personally. The auctioneers were described as such in the catalogue and they argued unsuccessfully that this sufficed as an indication of agency absolving them from personal liability. The case is not particularly strong on the question of personal liability where the fact of agency is disclosed, because the Chief Justice observed that "their character as agents was no [sic] otherwise intimated to the purchaser" and that "this is the simple case of parties who have sold as principals, turning round and saying that they are merely agents". However, more modern cases have reiterated the principle that[106]:

"Where an agent purports to make a contract for a principal, disclosing the fact that he is acting as an agent, but not naming his principal the rule is that, unless a contrary intention appears, he makes himself personally liable on the authorised contract."

The nature and scope of this personal liability will now be considered. In *Wood* v. *Baxter*[107] the purchaser of wheat and straw sold by a tenant sued the auctioneers when the landlord refused to allow him to remove the straw, invoking a custom that such was to remain on the land. It was held that the claim failed because the auctioneer had done all he could to effect delivery and was not responsible for the vendor's lack of title (if such there was) to sell. Williams J said[108]:

"What is the character and extent of the contract entered into by the auctioneer when he sells without disclosing the name of his principal? The answer to this is, that it depends upon the conditions of sale, upon what is said by the auctioneer at the time, upon the surrounding circumstances, and upon the nature of the subject-matter of the sale. In the first place, it would

103. *Hanson* v. *Roberdeau* (1792) Peake 120.
104. *Per* Salter J in *Benton* v. *Campbell Parker & Co* [1925] 2 K.B. 410 at 417.
105. (1847) 4 C.B. 637, 16 L.J.C.P. 221.
106. *Benton* v. *Campbell Parker & Co* [1925] 2 K.B. 410 *per* Salter J at 414.
107. (1883) 49 L.T. 45.
108. *Ibid.* at 46; see also *Payne* v. *Elsden* (1900) 17 T.L.R. 161.

certainly be going too far to say that an auctioneer, selling without disclosing the name of his principal makes himself a contracting party in the same way and to the same extent that another agent acting for an undisclosed principal does. The auctioneer sells, not as an owner having a right to sell by virtue of his own right of property, but as an auctioneer empowered and entrusted by his employer to sell. If he is selling livestock or implements in the market place or furniture in a room, the extent of his contract would ordinarily be to deliver the goods to the buyer; if he was selling shares in a joint stock company, it would be to procure a transfer to the purchaser; if he was selling timber stacked in a yard or loaded on board ship or growing crops on a farm, it would be in each case to give such constructive delivery as according to the nature of the subject-matter was practicable and usual. Upon making such delivery, his obligation would ordinarily be fulfilled."

Thus it appears that the liability of an auctioneer in these circumstances is essentially only for non-delivery. Despite that Williams J says that "his contract is very nearly that of an ordinary vendor",[109] it is clear from the decision in that case, and also from *Benton* v. *Campbell, Parker & Co,*[110] that no liability attaches to the auctioneer for any want of title (logically, because as an expressed agent he does not claim to have any). The earlier cases of *Hanson* v. *Roberdeau*[111] and *Franklyn* v. *Lamond*[112] are consistent with a limited liability to deliver, since failure to deliver was in each case the complaint, but the question arises whether such a limitation is consonant with principle. If the rationale of fixing the auctioneer with personal liability is that given by Salter J in *Benton's* case,[113] namely that "a purchaser is willing to contract with an unknown man ... but only if the agent will make himself personally liable if called upon to perform the contract",[114] there seems little justification or commercial logic in limiting the duty of performance to delivery only. Should not the purchaser have recourse against the auctioneer if the goods are defective or unfit for their purpose too?

It is suggested, however, that the reason for rendering the auctioneer liable is not because of any assumption that the identity of the vendor is crucial, but simply because the duty to deliver is the reverse of the coin that an auctioneer may sue for the price.[115] The auctioneer's right to sue for the price is based upon his implied contract arising out of the delivery up of possession of the goods sold, and this contract is quite separate from the contract of sale. Although Williams J suggested in *Wood* v. *Baxter*[116] that the auctioneer could be sued upon the contract of sale, the better view is that expressed in *Benton* v. *Campbell, Parker & Co* that[117]:

"These rights and liabilities do not arise from the contract of sale which binds only the buyer and the principal. They arise from the contract which the auctioneer makes upon his own account with the buyer ... The duty to deliver and the right to receive the price are usually expressed in the conditions of sale. But whatever its terms may be, the contract is entirely independent of the contract of sale."

Finally, it could be argued that the best reason for making the auctioneer

109. See fn. 108 above.
110. [1925] 2 K.B. 410.
111. See fn. 103 above.
112. See fn. 105 above.
113. [1925] 2 K.B. 410.
114. *Ibid.* at 414.
115. See, e.g., *per* Field J in *Woolf* v. *Horne* (1877) 2 Q.B.D. 355 at 360, and *per* Rowlatt J in *Page* v. *Sully* (1918) 63 Sol.J. 55.
116. See fn. 107 above.
117. [1925] 2 K.B. 410 at 415–416.

personally liable where he declines to name the vendor[118] is that if the auctioneer fails to identify him, the purchaser will be unable to bring actions against the vendor. However, it is suggested that this practical obstacle can be overcome by an action for discovery.

### 3.2.3 Independent contractual liability

It may be that, as a matter of specific contractual agreement, the auctioneer will owe duties to the buyer. So, in the recent decision in *De Balkany* v. *Christie Manson & Woods*[119] where the auctioneers expressly promised, through their conditions, on their own account to "repurchase" a deliberate forgery, the court held that this created an independent contractual liability to the buyer. This was significant in that the ability of the buyer in that case to pursue relevant remedies under the contract of sale against the seller may have been less extensive.

The foregoing discussion has proceeded on the assumption that the auctioneer has sold goods. Hitherto, an auctioneer would not sign a contract of sale concerning land in such a way as to render himself liable personally. Now, under the Law of Property (Miscellaneous Provisions) Act 1989 the contract itself—and not merely the evidentiary memorandum—may be signed by an agent. If the auction particulars stipulate both that the purchaser enter into a written agreement and that the auctioneer may sign such on behalf of the vendor he may, in appropriate circumstances—e.g., where the vendor is unnamed—attract personal liability.

### 3.3 Other liability

Under the general law an auctioneer may incur liability to the purchaser in a variety of circumstances. Generally speaking, the liability will arise from a failure to take proper care either of the purchaser's goods, or his person, or for misstatements in and about the sale of the property.

### 3.3.1 Duty with regard to the goods purchased

When specific goods are sold to a purchaser ownership of them will, unless a contrary intention appears, pass to the purchaser when the contract is made,[120] i.e., on the fall of the hammer. Thereafter they are the purchaser's goods. If the auctioneer retains possession of them, he will become the bailee of the purchaser. As such he will be under a duty to take reasonable care of them, apart from any express exclusion of liability provision which will be subject to the test of reasonableness under the Unfair Contract Terms Act 1977.[121] In practice, however, it is rare to find that title to property passes to the purchaser on the sale. Both Sotheby's and Christie's

---

118. A principal remains unnamed where the property is described as "the property of a gentleman" as in *Warlow* v. *Harrison* (1859) 1 E. & E. 309, 29 L.J.Q.B. 14, and also, it seems, where the sale is expressed to be "By order of Mr J Spurling and Others" (even if it later transpired that the named person was the seller of the particular lot) as in *Page* v. *Sully*, above.

119. *The Independent*, 19 January 1995.

120. Sale of Goods Act 1979, s. 18, r. 1.

121. See generally chapter 2 and see the discussion above relating to the liability of the auctioneer as bailee of the seller; the principles apply, *mutatis mutandis*, as between auctioneer and purchaser.

conditions provide that ownership shall not pass until payment and that credit may be given. Sotheby's give the buyer five days in which to remove the goods purchased where they have been paid for or where credit has been given, and provide further that after collection or the five-day period the buyer will be responsible for any loss. This leaves open the potential liability of the auctioneers during the collection period. Christie's conditions are of similar effect. Those earlier in use provided that the risk passed to the buyer from the fall of the hammer.

The effect of such a clause requires consideration. Where the ownership passes to the buyer and the auctioneer retains possession during a period when the purchaser may collect, the auctioneer, as stated, becomes the bailee of the purchaser and, as such, owes him a duty to take reasonable care of his goods. Where the property does not pass to the purchaser pending payment, the analysis is different. Neither ownership nor possession passes to the buyer and, therefore, he cannot be a bailor although he has an interest in the preservation of the goods. The law is clear that such a person cannot, in the absence of a contract with the person in whose custody they were—e.g., carrier or warehouseman—sue in negligence for any failure to take care of them. This is because in order to maintain such an action a party has to be their owner; if he is not, then none of *his* property is damaged or lost and his loss is purely economic and not recoverable.[122] However, in the case of auctions, there is a separate contract with the buyer on the terms of the conditions of sale. Whether such a contract would include an implied term, in the absence of the exclusions commonly found, to care for the goods of a purchaser who has not become their owner, is, however, doubtful.

### 3.3.2  Liability for physical injury

An auctioneer may be liable in negligence if those attending the auction are damaged by goods, e.g., by a frisky horse, or by the state of the auctioneer's premises. This duty of care is owed not only to one who becomes a purchaser but to all those who are lawfully present at the auction, and the ambit of this liability will be considered briefly in the following section of this chapter, "Duties and liabilities to third parties" (section 4.2.1 *et seq.*).

Additionally, an auctioneer may incur civil liability to those injured by the goods that he sells. There is a general potential, though secondary, liability in limited circumstances for defective goods under the Consumer Protection Act 1987. The legislation is largely aimed at manufacturers and importers, but an auctioneer who is required to name his supplier and fails to do so will be liable for the defect and losses caused thereby to the person injured.[123] Criminal liability under this Act is discussed below.

### 3.3.3  Liability for misrepresentations

In dealing with the duty owed to the vendor to describe the property accurately the point is made that whereas the vendor may be liable for misrepresentations, including those made quite innocently, under the Misrepresentation Act 1967, no

---

122. See *Leigh and Sillivan Ltd* v. *Aliakmon Shipping Co Ltd* [1986] 2 W.L.R. 902.
123. Section 2(3). An auctioneer would be well advised to obtain an indemnity from his vendor.

direct liability thereunder attaches to the auctioneer acting within his authority. However, an auctioneer may still render himself civilly liable to the purchaser for misstatements made in the auction particulars or orally from the rostrum, under the common law. What follows is necessarily a truncated account. Readers are referred to the standard works on contract and tort for detailed consideration. There are several separate possible bases of liability, and these are given below.

### 3.3.4 In deceit

A person who causes loss to another by means of fraud will be liable to an action in tort for deceit. Fraud is a serious charge to be levelled at anyone, but especially at a professional person and, in order for it to be made out, fairly stringent tests have to be satisfied. The House of Lords has held that it cannot be proved unless it can be said of a person that, "he knowingly made a false statement or one which he did not believe to be true, or was careless whether what he stated be true or false".[124] A prerequisite to a successful action against an auctioneer under this tort is, therefore, that it be shown that he did not honestly believe what he said was true. If he did have that honest belief, however foolish, credulous or negligent he might have been, he will not be liable to the purchaser for deceit.

### 3.3.5 Negligent misstatement

For 70 years after the decision in *Derry* v. *Peek* it was thought that no liability could attach for misstatements if they were made merely negligently. In 1963, however, the House of Lords delivered a judgment of exceptional importance for professional men in *Hedley Byrne & Co Ltd* v. *Heller & Partners Ltd*.[125] That case concerned a banker's reference on which another party relied, but the decision is of very wide scope. The House of Lords said that a person could owe a duty of care to another in giving information or advice and that such a duty would exist where there was some "special relationship" between the parties. The precise circumstances when such a special relationship will be held to exist have not been exhaustively stated, but in general it can be said to arise whenever someone possessed of special skill undertakes to apply it for the assistance of another person who relies upon it.[126] There appears to be no reported instance of an auctioneer being held liable under the *Hedley Byrne* v. *Heller* doctrine, probably because purchasers will normally prefer to take recourse against the vendor in cases of negligent misstatement made by the auctioneer as his

124. *Derry* v. *Peek* (1889) 14 App.Cas. 337, 58 L.J.Ch. 864, H.L.
125. [1964] A.C. 465, [1963] 2 All E.R. 575, H.L. Detailed consideration is given in chapter 2 to liability under this case-law.
126. The more restrictive test suggested by the majority of the Privy Council in *Mutual Life and Citizens' Assurance Co Ltd* v. *Evatt* [1971] A.C. 793, [1971] 1 All E.R. 150, P.C., that the adviser should be in business as the supplier of information or advice or expressly have claimed to possess special skill, has not been regarded as conclusively limiting the English authority. However, even on the basis of such a narrow interpretation, an auctioneer would normally be, *prima facie*, regarded as owing a duty of care. More recently the House of Lords has restricted the circumstances in which the duty would be owed by a professional man. In *Caparo* v. *Dickman* [1990] 2 A.C. 605 auditors of a public company were held not liable to investors for carelessly given financial information: the information was given not for investment purposes but merely to fulfil statutory requirements as to provision of accounts. Thus the purpose for which the statement is made is critical: only if it is given for the purpose upon which it was relied, will liability lie.

agent. The reason for this is that the vendor's liability under s. 2(1) of the Misrepresentation Act 1967 is somewhat easier to establish, because under the Act it is for the vendor positively to disprove negligence, whereas at common law the onus would be on the purchaser to prove it. However, there can be little doubt that an auctioneer is in a special relationship vis-à-vis a purchaser.[127]

A difficulty arises as to exclusion of liability. The impact of the Unfair Contract Terms Act 1977 has been alluded to and it is clear that a vendor seeking to rely on the exclusion of liability clauses commonly found in auctioneers' conditions would have to show that such reliance was reasonable. As regards the auctioneer seeking to avoid liability for negligent misstatements, the position is the same. In *Hedley Byrne* v. *Heller* the bank was, in the result, held not liable because it had expressly disclaimed liability by heading its advice "without responsibility". Normally a person cannot avoid liability for negligence simply by broadcasting that he does not incur it, but the basis of the duty in this area is that the defendant has expressly or impliedly undertaken that he will give his advice or information with care. Obviously, if he says in advance that he undertakes no such thing, no duty will arise. This kind of disclaimer differs from exclusion clauses as traditionally construed in that it does not seek to avoid the loss arising from a breach of duty but, rather, prevents the duty arising in the first place[128]:

"a man cannot be said voluntarily to be undertaking a responsibility if at the very moment that he is said to be accepting it he declares that he is not".

The Unfair Contract Terms Act 1977, s. 2(2), subjects to a test of reasonableness a term or notice excluding or restricting "liability for negligence" and it was once thought that this did not cover a term which negates the existence of the duty. However, the House of Lords has now clarified the position and held that the Act applies equally to disclaimers of this sort. They, too, must, therefore, satisfy the test of reasonableness.[129]

### 3.3.6  On a collateral warranty

As stated, whilst tort imposes liability on auctioneers for deceit or negligence, there is no liability for purely innocent misstatements. However, such liability may be imposed contractually on the basis that the auctioneer has made a collateral warranty. Essentially, the collateral contract is construed on this basis: the auctioneer effectively says to the successful purchaser, "if you will make the contract of sale with the vendor I promise that (for example) the horse is sound etc.". Thus the promise by the auctioneer is said to be part of a contract collateral to the main contract of sale and which contains a representation which induces the formation of that main

---

127. An estate agent has been held to be potentially liable to the buyer for negligently misdescribing the acreage of property in *McCullagh* v. *Lane Fox & Partners* (1995) *The Times*, 22 December, C.A., although, in the result, the claim failed because the agent had successfully disclaimed responsibility. Whilst in *Gran Gelato Ltd* v. *Richcliff (Group) Ltd* [1992] 1 All E.R. 873, the court suggested that there was no need for separate personal liability to attach to an agent acting within his authority, this seems to be limited to the case of solicitors' agents employed in conveyancing transactions.

128. *Per* Lord Devlin in *Hedley Byrne* v. *Heller* [1964] A.C. 465 at 533.

129. See *Smith* v. *Eric S Bush* [1989] 2 All E.R. 514.

contract, though it may not become incorporated in it. In such a way an auctioneer can be made liable for a representation, including one made innocently, which induces the formation of the main contract. Since the representation amounts, independently, to a term of a separate, collateral contract, the auctioneer will be liable for breach of it unless he can point to an exclusion clause which is apt to protect him. Once again, therefore, he will have to show that such a clause is reasonable.

### 3.4 Duties relating to the deposit

Invariably, in the case of sales of land by auction, and sometimes in chattel auctions, the conditions of sale require the purchaser to pay a deposit to the auctioneer. In such cases the auctioneer incurs certain liabilities with regard to the sums so paid. The requiring of a deposit has a twofold purpose: first, to provide a part-payment of the purchase price—provided that the sale goes ahead to completion—but secondly and primarily, it is to "guarantee that the purchaser means business" or to provide "a security for the performance of the contract".[130]

When such a deposit is paid to an auctioneer, the duties and liabilities which ensue depend largely upon whether he receives it as agent for one of the parties (usually the vendor) or as a stakeholder. The contract will usually explicitly provide for this[131] but, if it fails to denote the capacity, the law presumes that an auctioneer receiving a deposit does so as stakeholder,[132] whereas an estate agent and a solicitor do so as agent for the vendor. The significance of the distinction was explained by Bowen LJ in *Ellis* v. *Goulton* as follows[133]:

"When a deposit is paid by a purchaser under a contract for the sale of land, the person who makes the payment may enter into an agreement with the vendor that the money shall be held by the recipient as agent for both vendor and the purchaser. If this is done, the person who receives it becomes a stakeholder, liable in certain events to return the money to the person who paid it. In the absence of such agreement the money is paid to a person who has not the character of stakeholder; and it follows that, when the money reaches his hands it is the same thing so far as the person who pays it is concerned as if it had reached the hands of the principal. If so it is impossible to treat money paid under these circumstances and remaining in the hands of the agent as there under any condition or subject to any trust in relation to the payer."

Thus, as a stakeholder, the duty of the auctioneer is to hold the deposit money as agent for both parties and not to part with it until the event upon which it becomes payable to one party or the other takes place. If he pays the money over to the vendor before completion or while a dispute is continuing relating to the contract of sale, he will be liable for it as money had and received to the purchaser's use; whereas if he receives it as agent, it is the vendor who will be accountable to the purchaser in the event that the sale falls through, since payment to the agent is virtually payment to the principal.

130. *Soper* v. *Arnold* (1889) 14 App.Cas. 429, H.L., *per* Lord MacNaghten at 435, and Lord Herschell at 433.
131. See, e.g., National Conditions of Sale, which provide for the deposit to be paid to the auctioneer as stakeholder; see also Standard Conditions of Sale (2nd edn), which incorporate the Law Society's Conditions of Sale 1992 and are to similar effect.
132. Conceded in *Furtado* v. *Lumley* (1890) 54 J.P. 47, 6 T.L.R. 168, but if the receipt for the deposit is signed by the auctioneer as agent for the vendor, he will hold it as such: *Barnford* v. *Shuttleworth* (1840) 11 Ad. & El. 926; *Ellis* v. *Goulton* [1893] 1 Q.B. 350.
133. [1893] 1 Q.B. 350 at 352–353.

An auctioneer holding as stakeholder should, therefore, not pay over any deposit to his vendor until he has satisfied himself that the sale has been satisfactorily completed. Most of the old cases cited concerned protracted disputes about title. If, however, his vendor is importunate for payment to him of what is, after all, part-payment of the price, the auctioneer may pay it over but he should ensure that he obtains an indemnity from him.

The basic duty of the auctioneer as described above is well settled. Two important questions remain, however, as to which a certain degree of doubt may be entertained. The first relates to liability to pay interest on the deposit and the second concerns responsibility where the deposit is lost.

### 3.4.1 Interest on the deposit

There are two questions: first, whether the auctioneer is liable to invest the deposit money so that it yields interest and, in default, is liable for sums which could have been earned to the party ultimately entitled; and secondly, even where the answer to that question is "No", whether if the auctioneer does in fact invest the deposit, he is entitled to keep the interest yielded.

#### 3.4.1.1 LIABILITY FOR NON-INVESTMENT

The answer to the first question is relatively clear: no interest is payable on deposit monies whilst properly in the auctioneer's hands as stakeholder.[134] in *Gaby* v. *Driver*[135] the purchaser's contention that interest would automatically run from the contractual completion date when the vendor failed to meet it was rejected, but it was suggested that a claim for interest could be maintained after a valid demand and refusal. The purchaser's remedy, where the vendor is in breach of contract, is to sue the vendor and claim loss of income on the deposit monies as special damages.[136]

#### 3.4.1.2 LIABILITY FOR INTEREST EARNED

Less certain is the position where the auctioneer does, in fact, invest the deposit monies. Here there is some division of opinion amongst the judges. The earliest case in which the question seems to have received detailed consideration is *Harington* v. *Hoggart* in 1830.[137] Here the auctioneer was requested by the vendor's solicitors to invest the deposit in certain government securities and the vendor offered an indemnity in case such investment caused loss. The auctioneers, who held the deposit as stakeholders, said they would do as asked but only if the purchaser concurred. He did not, and the fund was not invested. In the result the sale was only completed some eight years after the deposit had been paid, due to protracted title disputes. The

---

134. See, e.g., *Lee* v. *Munn* (1817) 8 Taunt. 45 where a purchaser claimed back his deposit with interest from the auctioneer when the vendor was unable to make title but the court held that no interest could be recovered by him since negotiations for the sale had been continuing throughout. It was suggested, *obiter*, in this case that the auctioneer could be liable for interest if the contract was rescinded and the auctioneer wrongly retained the deposit after demand had been duly made.

135. (1828) 2 Y. & J. 549.

136. See *Curling* v. *Shuttleworth* (1829) 6 Bing. 121, 3 Moo. & P. 368.

137. (1830) 1 B. & Ad. 577.

purchaser claimed interest on the deposit. Lord Tenterden, the Chief Justice, was clear that the auctioneers as stakeholders dealt correctly with the request of the vendors to invest the money. However, he went on to consider what the position would have been had the sum yielded interest, and concluded that if a stakeholder chose to invest the funds he would be liable for any loss accruing, and "if he is to answer for the loss it seems to me he has a right to any intermediate advantage which may arise".[138] Moreover, whilst it was in the stakeholder's possession, the deposit fund belonged to neither vendor nor purchaser so that any interest yielded belonged to the stakeholder. This last point is not thought to be compelling: there is no reason why a stakeholder should not hold the interest as an accretion to the principal sum for whomsoever of the parties ultimately becomes entitled to it. Moreover, the notion that the right to any profit is the corollary of his potential loss is also objectionable. There are many situations where an agent may be liable to disgorge profits made even though he would be also liable to make good losses. The real question is whether the stakeholder should be distinguished from one who holds a fund as an agent. Such a distinction has been carefully maintained with regard to basic duties relating to the deposit. On the other hand it might be argued that the stakeholder is, as has frequently been stressed, the agent of both vendor and purchaser and that, as such, he should never be able to keep profits yielded by a fund which belongs to one of them. However, a rationale for such a distinction was suggested in the modern case of *Potters (a firm)* v. *Loppert*[139] *viz*[140]:

"The interest represents not merely a reward for the agent's trouble but also as a recompense for the sterilisation of the property vis-à-vis the estate agent during the period between payment of the deposit and the conclusion of the contract or its breakdown with the consequences that the agent has no prospect of earning a commission on its sale to any other party so long as the property remains sterilised."

As will be obvious, all this was said in connection with an estate agent's position, but it is arguable that similar reasoning can be applied to that of an auctioneer engaged to sell property; a vendor's solicitor, for example, instructed to receive a deposit as agent, is in an entirely different position. But the simplest rationale is that given by Harman J in *Smith* v. *Hamilton*, namely that, "the stakeholder is not bound to pay interest. He retains the benefit of it; that is his reward for holding the stake".[141]

### 3.4.2 Loss of the deposit

The argument in favour of permitting the auctioneer, when stakeholder, to retain profits made out of the deposit monies is based, at the end of the day, on the maintenance of a distinction between the capacity of the stakeholder and that of one who is merely an agent. A final question arises as to upon whom the liability should fall in the event that the auctioneer, through infraction or otherwise, causes the deposit to be lost, usually by reason of his insolvency. If he is the agent of one party,

138. *Ibid.* at 586–587.
139. [1973] Ch. 399, [1973] E.R. 658. This case concerned a pre-contract deposit paid to an estate agent, but much of the discussion concerned the liability of an auctioneer-stakeholder of a contract deposit.
140. [1973] 1 All E.R. 658 at 669 *per* Pennycuick V-C.
141. [1951] Ch. 174 at 184.

one would expect that the risk of loss would fall on that party and, indeed, that is the position. Conversely, if the auctioneer is a stakeholder and as such is liable "to hold it *in medio* pending the outcome of a future event"[142] one might have expected the risk of loss to fall equally on either party, vendor or purchaser, who subsequently became entitled to it; he is equally the agent of both. However, it appears[143] to be the law that the vendor will bear the risk of loss so that he will be liable to recompense a purchaser who becomes entitled to its return and must give credit for it as part-payment once it has been paid to the auctioneer. Were the auctioneer the vendor's agent, this conclusion would be unremarkable. If, however, the courts are assimilating the position of stakeholder and agent, it is contrary to principle. There is, however, one explanation for this line of cases which can, it is suggested, be supported. In *Fenton* v. *Browne* Sir William Grant MR rationalised the result in this way[144]:

"Upon a sale by auction the vendor determines who is to receive the deposit. The auctioneer is not a stakeholder of the purchaser: at least not of his choice ... Under these circumstances it would be too hard to throw [the] loss upon this purchaser."

Where the parties are put at risk as to the honesty or financial stability of the auctioneer-stakeholder it is justifiable to render the vendor liable for any loss, since it is the vendor who selects the stakeholder—the purchaser has no choice but to entrust the auctioneer with the stake. The antiquity of the cases in this area may be a happy sign that today these risks are minimal.

## 4 DUTIES AND LIABILITIES TO THIRD PARTIES

### 4.1 Conversion and acts amounting to conversion

An auctioneer may owe a number of general duties—for example under the law relating to negligence (which we consider briefly below)—and he may also incur liabilities to a third party who is not either a seller or buyer concerned with the sale. The prime example of the latter is the liability which attaches when an auctioneer wrongly converts the property of another. This will arise if the auctioneer sells the property on behalf of a principal who is not entitled to sell, or where he wrongfully delivers property to one who is not entitled to receive it with notice of that fact, or where he retains property to which a third party is entitled. A conversion may be defined as an unlawful act of interference with goods inconsistent with the right of a third party whereby the latter is deprived of their use and possession. It is a tort for which the remedy is primarily damages; but where goods are detained by a person being sued, the court has the power to order their delivery up to the successful claimant. Where such a remedy is available, the court may give the defendant the option of retaining them and paying damages instead.[145] Damages will be assessed by

---

142. *Per* Denning MR in *Burt* v. *Claude Cousins & Co Ltd* [1971] 2 Q.B. 426.
143. See 2 *Halsbury's Laws of England* (4th edn, reissue) para. 949, but the authorities are not entirely convincing and are of some age.
144. (1807) 14 Ves. 144 at 150. Approved in *Burt* v. *Claude Cousins & Co Ltd* [1971] 2 Q.B. 426 at 450 *per* Sachs LJ.
145. Torts (Interference with Goods) Act 1977, s. 3.

reference to the value of the goods, which in the case of a sale by auction will not necessarily be the hammer price.[146] In addition, damages may be awarded for any consequential loss arising out of the conversion.

### 4.1.1 Sale without the authority of the true owner

The principal may simply have stolen them, or he may have a right of possession but not yet have become their owner, such as where he is in possession under a hire-purchase agreement. Where a car is sold in this way, the "buyer" in fact is given possession and the intention is that the property will become his. However, the legal analysis is that unless and until the hirer exercises an option to purchase, on paying the final instalment, he remains simply a hirer. As such he is entitled only to possession. The finance company which finances the deal is the true owner of the vehicle. If the hirer during the currency of the agreement sells the car, the finance company will be able to maintain an action in conversion against him and if he sells through an auctioneer, the latter too will be liable if the purchaser gets title or if the auctioneer delivers the car to the purchaser with the intention of transferring title.[147]

It must be emphasised here that the liability of the auctioneer does not depend upon any deliberate or negligent wrongdoing: he is liable in conversion to the true owner even if he is totally innocent and acts in complete good faith.[148] In 1971 the Law Reform Committee considered whether the "innocent handler" (as opposed to the innocent acquirer, i.e., the purchaser) should be protected but concluded, on balance, that he should not. It was felt that auctioneers and others in a similar position carry on a business to which this risk is incidental and for which insurance is available.

There may remain, however, an argument open to the auctioneer that in certain circumstances he did not in fact effect the sale at all but merely acted in a lesser capacity to bring the seller and buyer together. In *Cochrane* v. *Rymill*,[149] one Peggs borrowed money from Cochrane and the loan was secured on a number of cabs and carriage horses, the borrower effecting a bill of sale in favour of Cochrane. Subsequently, Peggs instructed the defendant auctioneer to sell the charged goods. The auctioneer gave the seller an advance on the proceeds of sale, sold the goods and, after deduction of the advance, paid the proceeds to Peggs. The holder of the bill of sale sued the auctioneer in conversion. Notwithstanding that Cochrane had been at fault in failing to register the bill of sale, the auctioneers were held liable. Bramwell LJ held that here there had been a clear dealing with the property and an exercise of dominion over it coupled with its delivery to another. However, he distinguished

---

146. *Davis* v. *Artingstall* (1880) 49 L.J.Ch. 609, 42 L.T. 507: "the plaintiff is entitled to the real value of the goods sold, and not merely to what they fetched at auction, which cannot be assumed to be the real value of the goods" (*per* Fry J, (1880) 49 L.J.Ch. 609 at 610).

147. Although conversion is essentially a wrong against possession, the finance company by law has a right to possession if, prior to the wrongful sale, it exercises the right to terminate the hiring, for, e.g., non-payment of an instalment, normally contained in the contract. It also seems that the owner can establish a sufficient right to possession as a result of the hirer's delivery up of the vehicle to the auctioneer for sale since this is anathematic to the bailment. See *Union Transport Finance Ltd* v. *British Car Auctions Ltd* [1978] 2 All E.R. 385; *North Central (or General) Wagon & Finance Co Ltd* v. *Graham* [1950] 2 K.B. 7, [1950] 1 All E.R. 780.

148. *Union Transport Finance Ltd* v. *British Car Auctions Ltd* (fn. 147 above).

149. (1879) 40 L.T. 744, 43 J.P. 572.

such a dealing by auctioneers from one where the auctioneer would not be liable in conversion thus[150]:

"Supposing a man were to come into an auctioneer's yard holding a horse ... and say 'I want to sell my horse; if you will find a purchaser I will pay commission' and the auctioneer says: 'Here is a man who wants to sell a horse; will anyone buy him?' If he then and there finds him a purchaser and the seller himself hands over the horse there could be no act on the part of the auctioneer which could render him liable for conversion."

This dictum has given rise to considerable difficulty. The fact that in this case the auctioneer, having made the vendor an advance, had a lien on the goods sold, clearly, of itself, took the case out of the "mere conduit" example given, but it would not be correct to conclude that where the auctioneer does not have such an interest in the sale, he will automatically be within its scope. In a subsequent case against the same auctioneer a couple of years later,[151] the court held the defendant not liable in conversion. There the horses were sold by private contract before the auction and the auctioneer took his commission and gave a delivery order to the purchaser. The Court of Appeal found the auctioneer not to have converted the goods as against the rights of the holder of a bill of sale relating to the horses. The auctioneer was held to be a mere conduit. *Cochrane* v. *Rymill* was distinguished on the ground that here there was no question of the auctioneer selling for his own benefit but the salient distinction must be simply that the auctioneer did not effect the sale at all.[152] The case of *Turner* v. *Hockey*[153] does, at first sight, suggest that whenever the auctioneer sells without having a personal interest in the sale, he does so merely as a conduit pipe, but that decision has been doubted and explained on the basis that there all the auctioneer did was to communicate an offer, the sale being concluded privately by the vendor with the purchaser. Whether, in such circumstances, the auctioneer generally escapes liability must again be doubted however.

This situation arose in somewhat special circumstances in *R H Willis & Son (a firm)* v. *British Car Auctions Ltd.*[154] Here a hire-purchase buyer, in breach of his agreement, placed the car in the hands of the defendant auctioneers for sale subject to a reserve. The property did not reach its reserve and the auctioneers, in pursuance of their usual practice, invited the purchaser and vendor to join them at their "provisional bid office", where the vendor agreed to accept the bid. It was argued that here the auctioneers had done something less than effect the sale; no sale at auction had been concluded because since the goods had not reached their reserve the bids and acceptance remained conditional. Nor, it was argued, had they sold the property themselves by private treaty; they had merely introduced a prospective purchaser to the vendor. However, the Court of Appeal rejected that argument. The judges looked to the business purpose behind the fairly elaborate provisional bid procedure, namely that it was to bring about a sale, and to the fact that in such cases, as also in those where a sale was effected through the fall of the hammer, the buyer is required to pay an indemnity fee[155] and he concludes a contract on the terms of the conditions

---

150. (1879) 40 L.T. 744 at 746.
151. *National Mercantile Bank* v. *Rymill* (1881) 44 L.T. 767.
152. See the observations of Collins J in *Consolidated Co* v. *Curtis & Son* [1892] 1 Q.B. 495 at 501–502.
153. (1887) 56 L.J.Q.B. 301.
154. [1978] 2 All E.R. 392, [1978] 1 W.L.R. 432.
155. The insurance point pressed heavily on Lord Denning in particular, as did the fact that the auctioneers took their commission (albeit at reduced rate).

of sale. In all these circumstances the court held the auctioneer liable for conversion of the car since they had effectively sold it. The court doubted the correctness of both *National Mercantile Bank* v. *Rymill* and *Turner* v. *Hockey*.

It can be concluded, therefore, that where the auctioneer effects the sale (whether at auction or by private treaty) of property which his principal is not entitled to sell, he will be guilty of conversion.

It is a general principle of commercial law that where the seller is not the true owner, the purchaser from him will not get title: *nemo dat quod non habet*. However, the desirability of protecting commercial transactions is also of crucial concern. Thus the law permits certain exceptions to this general principle. If the auctioneer knocks down goods to a bidder he will be liable in conversion if he couples that act with a dealing with intent to pass the title, whether or not the purchaser does, in fact, get title to them. If the purchaser *does* get a good title so that the true owner is divested of his ownership of the goods, then, *a fortiori*, the auctioneer will incur liability in conversion. But in such a case the purchaser will not also be liable—he gets title and cannot be sued by the former owner. Where he does not get title both he and the auctioner will be potentially liable. Thus, it may be in the interests of the auctioneer to show that the purchaser does not become the owner of the goods, because if the true owner elects to sue the purchaser rather than the auctioneer, the latter may escape.

A purchaser liable in conversion to the true owner may seek to sue the auctioneer in turn. However, the appropriate cause of action here would be for breach of warranty of authority. But an auctioneer will only be liable for such a breach if he has expressly warranted the vendor's title: *Benton* v. *Campbell Parker & Co.*[156] (Failing a remedy against the auctioneer, a purchaser who finds himself answerable to the true owner in conversion will be left with a right of action against the seller himself on the contract of sale. In every contract for the sale of goods there is an implied condition that the seller has title or the right to sell them by virtue of section 12 of the Sale of Goods Act 1979 and that term cannot be excluded in any contract whether the sale is a consumer or non-consumer sale.)

Thus it is important to be aware of those circumstances where the purchaser will get a good title, leaving the auctioneer alone[157] liable to the former owner of the goods. Both the common law and statute have provided exceptions to the basic principle that the rights of the true owner should remain inviolable, and these will now briefly be noted.[158]

### 4.1.2 Estoppel

Section 21(1) of the Sale of Goods Act 1979 provides that a purchaser shall obtain on sale no better title than the seller had, "unless the owner of the goods is by his conduct

---

156. [1925] 2 K.B. 410, 94 L.J.K.B. 881. If the purchaser has no contractual claim against the auctioneer, he has a right to contribution (Civil Liability (Contribution) Act 1978, s. 1), but the amount of such is entirely at the discretion of the court.

157. His client, the non-owner seller, will also be liable and the auctioneer will be entitled to join him as co-defendant or claim an indemnity but, in many of these cases, recovery against the seller will, in practice, prove difficult.

158. For a detailed account, readers are directed to *Benjamin's Sale of Goods* (4th edn, 1992) Sweet & Maxwell.

precluded from denying the seller's authority to sell". The quoted words indicate that a general exception arises by way of estoppel when the true owner's conduct has led the purchaser to believe that the seller is entitled to sell. Many of the other specific statutory exceptions appear to be based on this notion, too. It is a question of fact whether an owner of goods has sufficiently invested the seller with the indicia of property as opposed merely to possession.[159]

### 4.1.3 Sale in market overt

Another general, and, until its repeal in 1994, very long-established common law exception, formerly enshrined in the Sale of Goods Act 1979,[160] is where property has been sold in market overt. Market overt is an open, public and legally constituted market. Such a market could be set up by statute or under a charter. It was also established by custom that every shop within the City of London was market overt. There is nothing in the character of auction sales that made them, *ipso facto*, sales in market overt and relatively few were. Market overt is more usually a pertinent factor when the vendor, against whom it is alleged that he is not the owner, claims he became such because he bought the goods previously in market overt. The potency of this exception may remain, therefore, for some time after its abolition.

### 4.1.4 Sale under a voidable title

Where the seller has a voidable title, e.g., where he has obtained the property in the goods by fraud, the owner may take steps to avoid the title of the seller, but until he does so the seller may pass a good title to a bona fide purchaser. However, if the seller has obtained title by inducing a material mistake, the sale to him is absolutely void and he will have no title to pass to such a purchaser.

### 4.1.5 Sale by a mercantile agent

Section 2(1) of the Factors Act 1889 provides:

"Where a mercantile agent is with the consent of the owner, in possession of goods, or of the documents of title to goods, any sale, pledge or other disposition of the goods made by him when acting in the ordinary course of business of a mercantile agent, shall, subject to the provisions of this Act be as valid as if he were expressly authorised by the owner of the goods to make the same; provided that the person taking under the disposition acts in good faith and has not at the time of the disposition notice that the person making the disposition has not authority to make the same."

An auctioneer is such a mercantile agent but in this context the provision is of no avail to a purchaser of stolen goods, for the auctioneer is not in possession of them or their documents of title "with the consent of the owner". However, where an auctioneer is in possession of goods with the consent of the true owner he may pass a

---

159. Estoppel was successfully pleaded in *Eastern Distributors Ltd* v. *Goldring* [1957] 2 Q.B. 600, [1957] 2 All E.R. 525, a case involving a complicated hire-purchase swindle.
160. Section 22 repealed by the Sale of Goods (Amendment) Act 1994, s. 1 as from 3 January 1995.

valid title to a purchaser of them under this section even if the possession was given to him for a purpose other than sale.[161]

This section may be relevant where an auctioneer receives goods for sale from a mercantile agent, and we consider this briefly below.

### 4.1.6 Sale by seller remaining in possession

Where a seller sells goods to a purchaser but retains possession of them or their documents of title, a second sale to another purchaser will effectively pass title to the latter if he acts in good faith and without notice of the prior sale. This exception was provided by section 8 of the Factors Act 1889 and substantially reproduced by section 24 of the Sale of Goods Act 1979. It is immaterial in what capacity the seller has been left in possession. So, for example, it suffices if the original buyer leaves the goods with the seller merely as bailee to care for them.

### 4.1.7 Sale by buyer in possession

Somewhat more complicated is the position where a buyer is given possession of the goods although the title in the property is not passed to him until some later date. This is covered now by section 25(1) of the Sale of Goods Act 1979 which provides that a sale by such a buyer shall "have the same effect as if the person making the delivery or transfer were a mercantile agent in possession of the goods or documents of title with the consent of the owner". A sale by a mercantile agent in such circumstances will, as we have seen, pass a good title to the purchaser under section 2(1) of the Factors Act 1889 provided the purchaser acts in good faith and without notice of any restriction on the agent's authority to sell.

A sale under a hire-purchase agreement does not fall within section 25(1) of the Sale of Goods Act 1979, and special provisions are made for sales by hirers under certain such contracts. Also excluded is a "conditional sale" where the price is payable by instalments with title to the property remaining in the seller until payment of the last instalment.

Where, however, the original sale to the buyer is merely conditional upon, e.g., the price being paid but the buyer is given possession of the goods, a subsequent sale by that buyer is within the exception. Section 25 of the Sale of Goods Act 1979 does not provide that the effect of the sale is as if the buyer had the authority of the owner, as it does under section 24, but rather that the effect is the same "as if" the original buyer was selling as a mercantile agent. This rather odd provision has been construed to mean that the subsequent purchaser only gets a good title and is thus immune from an action for conversion if the original buyer in possession sold to him in the manner in which a mercantile agent would have sold such goods in the ordinary course of his business. Thus, if an original buyer sells a car without releasing the log-book, the subsequent purchaser from him will not get a good title because a mercantile agent would, selling in the ordinary course of business, have delivered up the log-book.[162]

---

161. As Denning LJ explained in *Pearson* v. *Rose & Young Ltd* [1951] 1 K.B. 275 at 288: "the owner must consent to the agent having them for a purpose which is in some way or other connected with his business as a mercantile agent. It may be for display or to get offers, or merely to put in his showroom; but there must be a consent to something of that kind before the owner can be deprived of his goods".

162. See *Newtons of Wembley Ltd* v. *Williams* [1965] 1 Q.B. 560, [1964] 3 All E.R. 532.

## 4.1.8 Sales of motor vehicles subject to hire-purchase agreements

Sales of motor vehicles under hire-purchase agreements were dealt with separately by statute when they became especially prevalent in the 1950s and 1960s. It is relatively easy for hirers to pass themselves off as owners and sell the cars to unsuspecting purchasers. Section 27 of the Hire-Purchase Act 1964, as re-enacted by the Consumer Credit Act 1974, provides that where the purchaser of the car from the hire-purchase "buyer" is a "private purchaser" as defined, acting in good faith and without notice of the hire-purchase (or conditional sale) agreement, that purchaser will get a good title to the vehicle.

It must be reiterated that the effect of all these exceptions is to protect the purchaser who thereby gets a good title. They do nothing to prevent the auctioneer from being liable in conversion for selling the particular goods. Indeed, they place it beyond doubt that he is liable since the sale and delivery not only has the intention of passing the property to the purchaser but is actually effective to do so.

The only way in which an auctioneer could protect himself from suit would be if he could show that the delivery *to* him of the goods in question amounted to a disposition under those exceptions as a result of which he, the auctioneer, got title—a subsequent sale or retention would then be of the auctioneer's own property and not that of another. Although such an argument was successfully advanced on the basis of the Factors Act 1889 in *Shenstone* v. *Hilton*,[163] it is difficult to see how such a mere transfer of possession could be regarded as a disposition so as to protect the auctioneer from a conversion action in these circumstances. The "disposition" (if indeed such it would be) in any event, on the terms of the section, only has "the same effect as if the person making the delivery or transfer were a mercantile agent". The effect of a delivery by a mercantile agent would be to give the auctioneers at most a right to possession but it would not, it is submitted, give them any title, so that any subsequent sale by them would still interfere with the title of another.

## 4.1.9 Refusal to deliver up to the owner

It is well settled that conversion can be committed by a wrongful refusal to deliver up possession of goods to the person entitled to them upon his demand. An auctioneer may obviously be in some difficulty if goods are being claimed by both his principal and a third party. In appropriate cases the auctioneer should interplead, as discussed earlier. However, short of such action, an auctioneer is entitled to make reasonable inquiries to ascertain the true ownership of the goods.[164]

## 4.1.10 Other acts short of a sale

For the sake of completeness, it should be mentioned that conversion can be committed by the transfer of possession without sale. A redelivery to the vendor after notice of a third party's title would probably amount to such. Additionally, although it is difficult to conceive of many situations in which such depredations might occur in the context of auctions, a deliberate destruction of goods is also conversion, but if loss

---

163. [1894] 2 Q.B. 452. Contrast, however, *Waddington & Sons* v. *Neale & Sons* (1907) 96 L.T. 786, 2 B.T.L.R. 464.
164. See *Lee* v. *Bayes & Robinson* (1856) 18 C.B. 599 and also *Turner* v. *Ford* (1846) 15 N.W. 212.

is caused simply negligently, it is not, However, in such a case the ordinary law of negligence would provide a remedy against the careless auctioneer.

All the foregoing discussion assumes that the sale by auction has been on the instructions of one who has not the right to sell them. If he has, no question of conversion can arise. So, even if the goods had previously been stolen, if the principal has obtained them in circumstances rendering him the true owner, for instance where he bought them in market overt, the auctioneer will be able to sell them with impunity. Usually, of course, the question whether the vendor had, or had acquired, the right to sell will be determined by the English law principles discussed above but occasionally foreign law is involved.

In *Winkworth* v. *Christie Manson & Woods Ltd*[165] Winkworth had owned certain works of art in England and these were stolen. They found their way to Italy where they were bought by an Italian. Subsequently, this buyer sent them to Christie's for auction and some were sold. Winkworth, having obtained an undertaking from Christie's that they would not part with the remaining articles or the proceeds of sale, sued the Italian vendor in conversion. A preliminary question of law arose before the High Court in England, namely whether English or Italian law should be applied to the issue whether the Italian defendant had title to the goods and the proceeds of sale. The court decided that, using English principles of private international law, on these facts the appropriate law to be applied was Italian.

Thus the rights of a true owner of English goods, situated in England, can be defeated by a transaction in another country in accordance with the law of that country, even though the original owner had never consented to their going there.

## 4.2 Other duties to third parties

### 4.2.1 Negligence

As mentioned above, an auctioneer may be liable under the tort of negligence for carelessly damaging a person's goods or for injuring him. There is little to be gained from an attempt at listing the variety of instances in which such a liability might be incurred, but there is one area worthy of special—albeit brief—mention, namely the liability attaching to the occupier of premises.

Although all persons are under a general duty to take reasonable care not to injure those who would with reasonable foreseeability be harmed if care were not taken, statute has provided especially for the liability of those who occupy or control premises.

The Occupier's Liability Act 1957, as amended, provides that the "occupier" owes to all his visitors (which include those permitted to enter under a licence) a common duty of care. This duty of care is defined by section 2(2) of the Act as:

"a duty to take such care as in all the circumstances of the case is reasonable to see that the visitor is reasonably safe in using the premises for the purpose for which he is invited or permitted to be there."

The duty relates both to the state of the premises themselves and also to activities

---

165. [1980] Ch. 496, [1980] 1 All E.R. 1121.

carried on there. So an auctioneer might, not too fancifully, be liable if improperly penned cattle injured persons attending the auction or if a bidder were injured falling as a result of a defective step in the auction rooms.

Whilst the 1957 Act applies not only to those who actually occupy premises but also to those in control of them, it is thought that an auctioneer would not, normally, be regarded as having sufficient control of, e.g., the principal-vendor's house or place of business in which he is conducting the auction. In *Walker* v. *Crabb*,[166] however, where a mare which was being auctioned on the vendor's premises injured the plaintiff, the vendor himself was held not liable in negligence on the ground that the control of the entire sale and responsibility for the chattels lay on the auctioneer.

It is open to an occupier to satisfy the duty imposed on him by strategically placed warning notices where such a warning given is in fact sufficient to render the visitor safe. However, exclusion of liability is a different matter. The Occupier's Liability Act 1957 permitted an occupier to modify the common duty of care "so far as he is free to". This has now been greatly affected by the Unfair Contract Terms Act 1977 which makes any purported exclusion of liability for negligence causing death or personal injury wholly ineffective, and, as has been said, renders any other type of exclusion subject to a test of reasonableness. On the other hand a warning notice is still useful since, even if it does not render the duty of care satisfied, it may make it easier to point to some contributory negligence by the visitor with the result that any compensatory damages will be apportioned under the Law Reform (Contributory Negligence) Act 1945.

### 4.2.2 Nuisance

A nuisance is a use of land so that the use and enjoyment of neighbouring land by another is diminished. Clearly, the business of auctioneering may constitute a nuisance to others and may be actionable. In the nineteenth century the owner of a coffee-house near Covent Garden succeeded in an action against a defendant auctioneer when the latter's vans obstructed the door and the stench from the horses rendered the coffee-shop "incommodious and uncomfortable".[167] This lone reported case may be somewhat outmoded on its facts, but doubtless in appropriate circumstances an action would lie today.

## 5 CRIMINAL LIABILITY

As indicated in the introduction to this chapter, an auctioneer can expose himself not only to civil liability but also, in certain circumstances, to criminal liability. It is not proposed here to consider such matters as conducting mock auctions[168] or simple cases of theft of a seller's property but, rather, with criminal liability which attaches as a result of the circumstances in which certain goods are sold, i.e., the descriptions under which they are sold, their condition or the status of seller or purchaser.

---

166. [1916] W.N. 433, 33 T.L.R. 119.
167. *Benjamin* v. *Storr* (1874) L.R. 9 C.P. 400, 43 L.J.C.P. 162.
168. See Harvey and Meisel, *op. cit.*, pp. 206–209.

## 5.1 False trade descriptions

A major piece of consumer protection legislation is the Trade Descriptions Act 1968. Section 1(1) provides:

"Any person who in the course of a trade or business—
(a) applies a false trade description to any goods; or
(b) supplies or offers to supply any goods to which a false trade description is applied,
shall, subject to the provisions of this Act be guilty of an offence."

It will be observed that there are two possible charges, one of applying a false trade description and, the second, of supplying or offering to supply goods to which a false trade description has been applied. There have been some well-publicised prosecutions of auctioneers under this legislation and auctioneers need to be careful to avoid committing these offences. Although the offences are of strict liability—there is no requirement of intention or any other specific state of mind—there are some fairly technical defences.[169]

### 5.1.1 Disclaimers

In the well-publicised case of *May* v. *Vincent*,[170] the auctioneers had described a painting as "by JMW Turner RA, a water colour . . . " The name of the artist appeared on the frame. This turned out to be false and when prosecuted under section 1 of the Act the defendant auctioneers, first, argued that the Act did not apply to auctioneers and, secondly, relied on the presence of a comprehensive disclaimer in the sale catalogue.

The first argument was dismissed without ado. The second argument, based on the presence of the disclaimer, was also, ultimately, rejected.

The Act does not specifically mention disclaimers, but case-law development has established that a disclaimer can be effective so long as, first, the false trade description has not been applied by the disclaimer himself and, secondly, that the disclaimer is "as bold, precise and compelling" as the description itself.[171]

Thus, provided that the false description has been applied by another, an auctioneer can disclaim his liability by an appropriate clause in the sale catalogue or possibly by oral announcement from the rostrum.

A more subtle approach by auctioneers might involve assertions in the conditions of sale to the effect that:

"Care is taken to ensure that any statement as to authorisation, attribution, origin, state, age, provenance and condition is reliable and accurate but all such statements are statements of opinion only and are not to be taken as statements or representations of fact."

This may work as a valid disclaimer, provided it is sufficiently prominent (small print will not suffice) but such a disclaimer can be double-edged: if it can be shown not to be true, that is to say, if it can be shown that care is not taken etc., then it may itself amount to a false trade description as to services under section 14 of the Act.

169. The Trade Descriptions Act 1968 is more extensively analysed in, e.g., Harvey and Parry, *The Law of Consumer Protection and Fair Trading* (4th edn, 1992) Butterworths. See also Butterworth's *Trading and Consumer Law*.
170. [1991] E.G. 144.
171. See, e.g., *Norman* v. *Bennett* [1974] 3 All E.R. 351.

It has been pointed out that the Act is one of strict liability, but the rigor of this has been mitigated by a specific defence contained in section 24 of the Act, namely one of "due diligence".

### 5.1.2 Due diligence

The defendant must establish, first, that the offence was due to a mistake or to reliance on information supplied to him or to the act or default of another person or some other cause beyond his control *and*, secondly, that he took all reasonable precautions and exercised all due diligence to avoid the commission of the offence by himself or any person under his control, such as an employee.

The due diligence requirement is a substantial hurdle to overcome. There is a considerable body of case-law on what amounts to due diligence derived both from this Act and from other legislation of a consumer protection character containing similar defences.

In broad terms the following can be advanced:

1. "All reasonable precautions" means setting up a control system but not necessarily a fool-proof system. Due diligence means ensuring that the system works.
2. The system must be tailored to the needs of the particular company or firm concerned.
3. The system must be under the "directing mind and will" of the firm, although day-to-day functioning can be delegated to appropriately senior employees or agents.
4. The extent of control varies in proportion to the risk involved and the resources of the firm.
5. The system should be reduced to writing with adequate instructions and training being given to staff.
6. The system needs to be both proactive and reactive, i.e., it must be capable of acting preventatively and also curatively.
7. The system should be reviewed by senior management at appropriate intervals and its operation should be monitored, adjusted or amended as necessary.

Where an auctioneer may not be in a position to check information for himself, there may be a duty on him to find out from his suppliers what system or systems they may have operated to ensure that no offence under the Act is likely to take place.

Section 24 of the Trade Descriptions Act, in fact, provides a specific defence with regard to misdescription. The section states:

"In any proceedings for an offence under this Act of supplying or offering to supply goods to which a false trade description is applied it shall be a defence for the person charged to prove that he did not know and could not with reasonable diligence have ascertained that the goods did not conform to the description or that the description had been applied to the goods."

This further element in the defence will only apply to an offence of "supplying or offering to supply goods to which a false trade description is applied", i.e., a section

1(1)(b) offence. It will not be available when an auctioneer is charged with *applying* a false trade description to any goods. It will be noted that under section 1(3) he does not have to show that he exercised "all due diligence" as under section 1(2) but merely that he could not "with reasonable diligence" have ascertained that the goods did not conform to the description.

## 5.2 Property misdescriptions

One of the criticisms which the consumer lobby has often directed at the Trade Descriptions Act 1968 is that it does not apply to land. The selling of houses by auction or private treaty is not covered. Considerable agitation, directed primarily at estate agents' activities, brought about legislative reform in the form of the Property Misdescriptions Act 1991.

### 5.2.1 Scope of the Act

The Act makes it an offence to make a false or misleading statement in the course of "estate agency business" as defined, about any "prescribed matter". The maximum penalty per offence is £5,000 on a summary conviction or an unlimited fine on indictment. Once again, whilst the offence is one of strict liability, there is a defence of due diligence available. The Act is enforced by local authorities and they are given express powers of entry, inspection and seizure.

### 5.2.2 Estate agency business

The Act creates an offence "where a false or misleading statement about a prescribed matter is made in the course of estate agency business ... ".[172] A statement is made in the course of estate agency business only if the making of the statement is a thing done "as mentioned in subsection (1) of section 1 of the Estate Agents Act 1979 and that Act applies to it".[173] Whilst the position is not entirely free from doubt, it is thought that auctioneers selling land are performing "estate agency work" by effecting the introduction of two parties who wish respectively to acquire and to dispose of an interest in land.[174]

The Act is dealt with in detail in chapter 7 and what follows is, therefore, only an outline of the main provisions. Many of these are, in any event, mirrors of those in other consumer protection enactments such as the Trade Descriptions Act, dealt with earlier.

The Act came into force, effectively, as from 4 April 1993 when the Property Misdescriptions (Specified Matters) Order 1992[175] was effected. That statutory instrument specified the various "prescribed matters" for the purposes of section 1 of the Act.

172. Property Misdescriptions Act 1991, s. 1(1).
173. Section 1(5).
174. See Murdoch, *The Estate Agents and Property Misdescriptions Acts* (3rd edn, 1993) The Estates Gazette Ltd, London, p. 27.
175. S.I. 1992/2834.

## 5.2.3 *Specified matters*

Specified matters include:

    (i) the location or address of property;
    (ii) aspect, view, outlook or environment;
    (iii) availability and nature of services, facilities and amenities;
    (iv) accommodation, measurement or sizes;
    (v) fixtures or fittings;
    (vi) physical or structural characteristics or condition;
    (vii) surveys etc. and the results thereof;
    (viii) history, including the age, ownership or use of land or any building or fixture and the date of any alterations thereto;
    (ix) tenure or estate;
    (x) existence or nature of any planning permission or proposals for development, construction or change of use;
    (xi) existence and extent of any public or private right of way.

As one commentator somewhat wryly put it[176]:

"Interpretative semantics and linguistic law may soon become an essential qualification for anyone dealing in property not to mention advanced hair-splitting telepathy and clairvoyance".

Auctioneers with a penchant for a poetic term of phrase will find that the Act takes away their poetic licence!

## 5.2.4 *Due diligence defence*

Once again, this strict liability offence is mitigated by the provision of a due diligence defence in section 2 of the Act. Section 2 provides as follows:

"(1) In proceedings against a person for an offence under section 1 above it shall be a defence for him to show that he took all reasonable steps and exercised all due diligence to avoid committing the offence.

(2) A person shall not be entitled to rely on the defence provided by sub-section (1) by reason of his reliance on the information given by another unless he shows that it was reasonable in all the circumstances for him to have relied on the information, having regard in particular—
    (a) to the steps which he took, and those which might reasonably have been taken, for the purpose of verifying the information, and
    (b) to whether he had any reasons to disbelieve the information."

We have already seen the kinds of factors which are relevant in deciding whether a defendant has shown the exercise of due diligence, in discussing the position under the Trade Descriptions Act 1968. It is obvious that with factual matters, such as measurements and dimensions or the existence of surveys or planning permission, checks can be instituted. What is more difficult for the auctioneer is to avoid misdescriptions when it comes to matters which might be regarded as appertaining to judgment or aesthetics. There is evidence that those engaged in estate agency work are modifying their practices and tending toward the giving of purely factual information, eschewing opinions, value judgments and the more fanciful phrases.

---

176. See *Estates Gazette*, Issue 9121, June 1991, p. 62.

There is evidence, too, that estate agents are putting in place systems to ensure the updating of factual information and the like in order to avoid inadvertent contraventions of this new legislation. Auctioneers will have to be particularly careful when answering questions from the rostrum about particular properties.

### 5.3 Unsafe goods[177]

Another aspect of consumer protection is concerned with the safety of goods bought rather than with the bargain made by the consumer. There is a number of statutes which create offences relating to the sale of substances or goods which may be harmful. These include the Food Safety Act 1990, which is concerned with the sale of food rendered unfit for human consumption; the Agriculture Act 1970—sale of material for use as feeding stuff which is discovered to be unwholesome or dangerous to animals or human beings; the Medicines Act 1968, which proscribes the retailing of certain drugs; and the Consumer Protection Act 1987 and a large number of Regulations made under it as supplemented by the General Product Safety Regulations issued by the European Community. The following discussion will limit itself to the selling of unsafe goods.

The discussion is best followed by realising that there are three possible routes by which a person can attract criminal liability in this area.

### 5.3.1 The general safety requirement under the Consumer Protection Act 1987

Section 10 makes it a criminal offence for a person to supply, offer or agree to supply or expose or possess any consumer goods which fail to comply with a general safety requirement. However, under section 10(4)(c) it is a defence for a person to show that the terms on which he supplied the goods indicated that they were not supplied or to be supplied as new. Normally, of course, an auctioneer will not be selling new goods but it may be that the liquidator of a company might decide to sell unsold stock by auction and in those circumstances, of course, the goods will be new and will be subject to this provision.

### 5.3.2 Safety regulations

The safety regulations do not themselves provide for their contravention to be an offence,[178] but section 12(1) of the Act provides that:

"where safety regulations prohibit a person from supplying or offering or agreeing to supply any goods or from exposing or possessing any goods for supply, that person shall be guilty of an offence if he contravenes the prohibition."

Section 39(1) provides a due diligence defence. There is no exception under the safety regulations for goods which are not supplied as new.

There has been a plethora of regulations under the 1987 Act. These include regulations relating to low voltage electrical equipment, gas cooking appliances, ceramic ware, several regulations relating to the manufacture of toys, stands

---

177. We deal here with general goods. There is a specific offence of strict liability for supplying unroadworthy motor vehicles contrary to the Road Traffic Act 1988, s. 75.
178. See s. 11(4).

for carry cots and a range of regulations relating to such items as bunk-beds, pedal cycles, oil lamps and pencils and graphic instruments.

An auctioneer, particularly a provincial auctioneer of a non-specialist nature, may well find himself engaged in selling such items, perhaps in the course of a house clearance sale, and he can very easily fall foul of these regulations. They cover all goods whether new or second-hand and the only exemption appears to be under section 46 of the 1987 Act which excludes sales to professional repairers or sales of articles as scrap.

An auctioneer engaged in such sales should ensure that he checks the Regulations carefully to see whether the particular item is covered and, where appropriate, subjects certain goods to tests. If he is about to sell a second-hand vacuum cleaner this should be tested by an electrician to ensure that it does not fail to comply with the relevant Regulations.[179] Testing is inexpensive and should enable the auctioneer to mount a successful defence of due diligence.

### 5.3.3  General Product Safety Regulations 1994

New and additional safety regulations are issued pursuant to the 1994 Regulations which implement the General Product Safety Directive[180] emanating from the European Community. These Regulations have two principal effects:

(1) They require producers to place only safe products on the market: "the general safety requirement".
(2) They require distributors to abstain from supplying products which do not comply therewith.

Auctioneers are most likely to be concerned with the second of these two principles and it should be noted that under the 1994 Regulations second-hand goods are covered. However, regulation 3(a) provides that the Regulations do not apply to products which are "sold as antiques". The antiques exception is useful to auctioneers. Presumably, if a catalogue legitimately describes, expressly or by implication, a particular lot as an antique no question under these Regulations will arise. It is debatable how far a general condition in the catalogue that all goods are supplied as antiques unless the contrary is stipulated would be held to be effective.

The duty of an auctioneer distributing such goods is to act with due care in order to assist in ensuring compliance with the general safety requirement. There is the usual due diligence defence.[181]

---

179. Alarm was caused in auctioneering circles a few years ago by the report of a prosecution of a firm by the Suffolk County Council Trading Standards Department for breach of the Low Voltage Electrical Equipment (Safety) Regulations 1989. The auctioneers were found guilty of selling a Hoover "Junior" vacuum cleaner which had live parts which were accessible contrary to those regulations and they were fined £500, plus costs, having pleaded guilty.

180. 92/59/EEC.

181. There is also specific criminal liability attaching to the selling of unroadworthy vehicles. Sales by auctions of motor vehicles have rapidly increased in popularity in recent years. The potential to commit an offence, under s. 75 of the Road Traffic Act 1988 (selling unroadworthy vehicles) is considerable. The section makes it an offence for a person to supply vehicles in an unroadworthy condition or altered so as to

## 5.4 Prohibitions on sales

There are some goods which cannot be sold at all or can only be sold in certain circumstances to certain persons. Amongst these the most important for auctioneers are wild animals and firearms.

### 5.4.1 Wild animals and endangered species

The sale or the offering or exposing for sale or possessing for sale of certain live or dead wild birds or part of such or their eggs is made a criminal offence by the Wildlife and Countryside Act 1981. The relevant birds are listed in Schedule 3 to the Act. Similarly, by section 9 it is an offence to sell or to offer or expose for sale or to possess those wild animals, whether live or dead, listed in Schedule 5 to the Act.

As regards birds there are a number of interlinking provisions within the Act which are relevant. First, section 1(2) provides:

"Subject to the provisions of this Part, if any person has in his possession or control—
    (a) any live or dead wild bird or any part of or anything derived from, such a bird; or
    (b) an egg of a wild bird or any part of such an egg, he shall be guilty of an offence."

There is then a defence under subsection (3) whereby a person shall not be guilty if he can show that the bird or egg had not been killed or taken, or if it had been killed or taken, such was otherwise than in contravention of the relevant provisions. There are also specific exceptions to section 1 contained in sections 2 and 4.

In addition to the offence in section 1(2) there is an offence provided by section 6 in relation to the sale of live or dead wild birds. Section 6(1) provides as follows:

"Subject to the provisions of this Part, if any person—
    (a) sells, offers or exposes for sale, or has in his possession or transports for the purpose of sale, any live wild bird ... or an egg of a wild bird or any part of such an egg; or
    (b) publishes or causes to be published any advertisement likely to be understood as conveying that he buys or sells, or intends to buy or sell any of these things,
he shall be guilty of an offence."

Whereas it is relatively unlikely that an auctioneer will sell live wild birds, he may find himself selling or possessing for sale stuffed birds. The sale of such appears to be caught by section 6(2) which provides:

"Subject to the provisions of this Part, if any person who is not for the time being registered in accordance with regulations made by the Secretary of State—
    (a) sells, offers or exposes for sale or has in his possession or transports for the purpose of sale, any dead wild bird other than a bird included in Part 2 or 3 of Schedule 3, or any part of, or anything derived from, such a wild bird; or
    (b) publishes or causes to be published any advertisement likely to be understood as conveying that he buys or sells, or intends to buy or sell, any of these things,
he shall be guilty of an offence."

Thus, as regards the sale of dead birds it appears only to be an offence if the person is not registered in accordance with regulations made by the Secretary of State. These

---

be unroadworthy. "Supply" is defined so as to cover selling, offering to sell or supplying and exposing for sale. The offence is one of strict liability, once again, but it will be a defence for the auctioneer to show that he had reasonable cause to believe that the vehicle would not be used on a road in Great Britain, or would not be used until it had been put into a condition in which it might lawfully be so used.

regulations are provided by the Wildlife and Countryside (Registration to Sell etc. Certain Dead Wild Birds) (Amendment) Regulations 1991.[182]

There has been one reported prosecution of auctioneers under this legislation. In *Robinson* v. *Everett and Another*[183] a taxidermist and auctioneers were both prosecuted with offences under section 1(2)(a) in that they had in their possession or under their control at the auctioneers' premises in Chelsea, a dead Golden Eagle which is a species of wild bird included in Schedule 1 to the Wildlife and Countryside Act 1981. The bird had been found by a tourist in Scotland and subsequently stuffed and mounted in a glass case by the first defendant and then placed with the second defendant for sale by auction. Prosecution was brought before the stipendiary magistrate in London and the defendants were acquitted, but the prosecutor appealed. On appeal, a number of ingenious defences were run but, oddly, it seems to have been conceded that section 6(2) did not provide a defence to the charge under section 1(2)(a). However, the appeal court had specifically been asked the question whether section 6(2) of the Act was of any relevance whatsoever. The judges responded:

"Without finding it necessary to enlarge upon the matter we say it has not."

On this basis the case was remitted for re-trial by another Bench. Subsequently both defendants were convicted and fined. The report of the case is not full and there are a number of uncertainties which remain about the case. However, it seems that both the taxidermist and the auctioneers were registered under the regulations provided for in section 6(2) and whilst the offence under section 1(2)(a) of being in possession or control is clearly separate from the offence of selling or having in one's possession for sale under section 6 it would be unfortunate, to say the least, if the registration of auctioneers under section 6 did not protect them from a charge of an offence contrary to section 1(2)(a).

## 5.4.1.1 IMPORTATION OR EXPORTATION

The Endangered Species (Import and Export) Act 1976, as amended by the Wildlife and Countryside Act 1981, restricts the import and export of certain animals and plants and renders it an offence to sell or offer or expose them for sale to the public unless imported or exported as the case may be in accordance with the terms of the licence.

## 5.4.2 *Firearms and other offensive weapons*

There is an established auction tradition in firearms sales and it is no surprise to find that this area of activity is subject to considerable legal control. The possession and sale of firearms is now largely controlled by the Firearms Act 1968, as amended by the Firearms (Amendment) Act 1988. Criminal offences may be committed by auctioneers who fall foul of the legislation in respect of three activities:

182. 1991/479.
183. (1988) *The Times*, 20 May.

(1) possession;
(2) sale or transfer;
(3) failure to take reasonable care of firearms and ammunition.

### 5.4.2.1 POSSESSION

Section 1 of the 1968 Act makes it an offence to possess certain firearms without a firearms certificate. However, an auctioneer does not need a certificate in order to possess a firearm in the ordinary course of his business by virtue of the Firearms Act 1968, s. 9(1). There should, therefore, be little problem for auctioneers as regards possession.

### 5.4.2.2 SALE OR TRANSFER

Section 3 of the 1968 Act provides two separate offences:

"(1) A person commits an offence if by way of trade or business he—
    (a) manufactures, sells, transfers ... any firearm or ammunition to which section 1 of this Act applies or a shotgun; or
    (b) exposes for sale or transfer or has in his possession for sale, transfer, ... any such firearm or ammunition or a shotgun, without being registered under this Act as a firearms dealer.

(2) It is an offence for a person to sell or transfer to any other person in the United Kingdom, other than a registered firearms dealer, any firearm or ammunition to which section 1 of this Act applies or a shotgun, unless that other produces a firearms certificate authorising him to purchase or acquire it or as the case may be his shotgun certificate or shows that he is by virtue of this Act entitled to purchase or acquire it without holding a certificate."

It is relatively easy for an auctioneer to avoid penalties under subsection (1) by being registered as a firearms dealer. Those who regularly sell such items will, no doubt, be so registered. However, auctioneers may sometimes find themselves being asked to sell a firearm (which includes, incidentally, a replica) on an *ad hoc* basis. If this does occur, he should obtain a permit for that purpose from the Chief Officer of Police for his area.

The real difficulty lies with subsection (2), in that it is an offence to sell to anyone other than a dealer unless that other person holds a certificate authorising him to purchase the weapon. The difficulty is that the sale is, technically, effected on the fall of the hammer and at that point the auctioneer may well not know whether the successful bidder holds the relevant certificate. It is, therefore, strongly recommended that anyone selling a firearm should include an express contractual provision in the conditions of sale to the effect that no ownership shall pass to the buyer unless and until he produces the requisite certificate.

It will be noted that section 3(2) also makes it an offence to *transfer* a firearm, ammunition or a shotgun to anyone who fails to show he is entitled to purchase or acquire it. "Transfer" is defined in section 57(4) of the Act as including "let on hire, give lend and part with possession". Thus it would seem that an offence would be committed by an auctioneer who merely returned the firearm to his vendor-client if the latter has not got the requisite permit.

Unsold firearms may, therefore, pose a problem for auctioneers. Auctioneers should either retain such unsold firearms until they can find a registered dealer willing to acquire them or, if the vendor-client agrees, ensure that they are de-activated so that they are no longer capable of being discharged. Section 8 of the Firearms (Amendment) Act 1988 deals with the procedures for that, such as the obtaining of a certificate from either the London or Birmingham gunmakers or proof house respectively.

### 5.4.2.3 LACK OF CARE IN CUSTODY OF THE FIREARM

There is an offence provided by the Firearms (Amendment) Act 1988, section 14(1) of failing to take reasonable precautions for the safe custody of a firearm or ammunition or failing to report its loss or theft forthwith to the police.

### 5.4.3 Antique firearms

The offences provided by sections 1 and 3 of the 1968 Act relating to possession and transfer do not apply to "antique firearms ... sold, transferred, purchased, acquired or possessed as a curiosity or ornament".

Thus it would not be an offence to sell an antique firearm for that purpose to a person who failed to produce the requisite certificate.

However, whereas in the case of offensive weapons other than firearms the law simply regards those over 100 years old as being antique, the position with regard to firearms is not quite so clearcut. All those over 100 years old will be antique, but it is possible that those of lesser age may be also. In *Richards* v. *Curwen*[184] the defendant was acquitted of charges of possessing firearms without a certificate. He had bought a German and a Belgian revolver dating from 1891 and 1893 respectively. The case was brought in 1975. He had clearly bought them for ornament and the issue was squarely one of whether they were antique. The magistrates decided that they were antique and the Divisional Court, on appeal, held that the magistrates had approached the matter quite properly.

On the other hand in *Bennett* v. *Brown* in 1980 the court held that a post-1905 Mauser rifle in working order and a Mauser pistol, circa 1910, modified but capable of firing a .22 cartridge, were not antiques. The defendant was a collector who had bought them for ornament, but the Court of Appeal refused to find that weapons of that vintage which might well have been used as weapons in the Great War were antiques. Watkins J held[185]:

"I am prepared to say that no reasonable Bench of justices could conclude, regardless of whether or not a firearm could be used in a war at any time, that a firearm which has been manufactured during this century is an antique. To that limited extent I offer with humility some assistance to justices who will continue to be faced with difficulty when called upon to decide the seemingly insoluble problem created by Parliament."

Thus it seems that any weapon manufactured this century will not (for the next few years at any rate) qualify as an antique.

### 5.4.3.1 HONEST BELIEF

The uncertainty which surrounds the meaning of "antique" for these purposes is problematic for auctioneers. These problems are exacerbated by the fact that if a

184. [1977] 3 All E.R. 426, [1977] 1 W.L.R. 747.
185. (1980) 71 Cr.App.R. 109 at 112.

firearm is not, in law, an antique, an auctioneer will have no defence by showing that he honestly believed it to be one.[186]

### 5.4.3.2 CURIOSITY OR ORNAMENT

If a firearm is sold or transferred to a buyer who does not produce a firearms certificate, he will only escape criminal sanction if the auctioneer shows, both, that the firearm is antique and that the purchaser acquired it "as a curiosity or ornament".

In *R* v. *Howells* the judge said to the jury[187]:

"Now, I am not going to attempt to go to a dictionary and define for you what keeping something as a curiosity means and what keeping something as an ornament means. I am going to assume that you know perfectly well what it means."

This obviously involves a subjective element and auctioneers might be well advised to stipulate expressly with antique firearms that they are sold for those purposes only.

### 5.4.3.3 OTHER OFFENSIVE WEAPONS

The 1988 Act deals in detail with a whole host of other offensive weapons which it is an offence to sell, hire, lend, import etc. unless they are antique (over 100 years old at the time of the alleged offence). The list includes sword-sticks and knives and a number of exotic oriental weapons, together with more prosaic items such as knuckledusters.

FRANK MEISEL*

---

186. See *R* v. *Howells* [1977] Q.B. 614.
187. [1977] Q.B. 614 at 619.
* The structure and much of the content of this chapter draws upon the treatment of similar subject-matter in Harvey and Meisel, *Auctions Law and Practice* (2nd edn, 1995) Oxford University Press, chapters 5 and 8. Whilst that work is co-authored, responsibility for any errors which may occur in this chapter remains solely mine.

# CHAPTER 5

# AUDITORS AND ACCOUNTANTS

This chapter deals with the legal responsibilities and liabilities of both auditors and accountants, and it is important to begin by distinguishing between the two groups. Auditors are those who are engaged to carry out the audit of a company's accounts required by the Companies Acts 1985 and 1989. The nature of their work and the right to engage in it are quite closely regulated by statute. Accountants may be described as those who give accounting, financial (and often other) advice to businesses (incorporated and unincorporated) and individuals. If the boundaries of the definition of an accountant seem less precise than those of the definition of an auditor, that is because there is a statutory definition of accountancy and because admission to the profession of accountant is a matter which is regulated by the profession itself. In practice all auditors will also be accountants (though not all accountants are authorised to act as auditors). Another important feature of accounting and auditing practice in the United Kingdom is that the accounts of a company are usually audited by the same firm which provides the company with accounting advice, despite the apparent conflict of interest involved in this arrangement.

It will be seen that the greatest part of this chapter is devoted to the position of auditors rather than to the position of accountants. There are two reasons for this. First, the section on regulatory issues necessarily deals exclusively with auditors, for reasons already given. Secondly, the great majority of the cases involving firms of accountants will be seen on careful examination to relate to audit work rather than to more general accountancy work, whilst the few cases which do relate to accountancy work mostly involve no principle particular to accounting, turning instead on more general principles of contractual or tortious liability which are dealt with in chapter 1 of this book and which will therefore not be repeated here.

## 1 REGULATION OF AUDITING

The regulation of auditing may conveniently be divided into two branches. The first consists of the legal rules which govern the right to act as auditor, whilst the second consists of the technical rules governing the audit process. These rules are made by the auditing profession itself, mainly through the Auditing Practices Board. The rules themselves are not considered in any detail in this chapter, though their legal status is discussed below.

## 1.1 The legal rules

The right to act as auditor is now governed by Part II of the Companies Act 1989, enacted to implement the Eighth Directive on Company Law.[1] Section 25 of that Act provides that a person is eligible for appointment as company auditor if, but only if, he is a member of a registered supervisory body and is eligible for appointment under the rules of that body.

### 1.1.1 The requirement of independence

Section 27 declares certain classes of persons ineligible for appointment as auditor. These are officers and employees of the company, partners or employees of such persons and partnerships of which such persons are members. The prohibition extends to anyone who is on these grounds ineligible for appointment as auditor of an associated undertaking of the company, "associated company" being defined[2] as a parent or subsidiary of the company or any subsidiary on any parent of the company.

A person who is ineligible for appointment as auditor is forbidden to act in that capacity.[3] Contravention of this rule is an offence punishable by a fine.[4] Further, a person who has been properly appointed as auditor but who becomes ineligible during his term of office must forthwith vacate the office, giving the company notice in writing that he has vacated office for this reason.[5] Failure to comply is again an offence punishable by fine.[6] Section 28(5) provides a defence for a person who shows that he did not know and had no reason to believe that he was or had become ineligible for appointment.

Where an audit has been performed by a person who was ineligible for appointment during any part of the period in which the audit was conducted, the Secretary of State may require the company within 21 days to retain an eligible person either to perform a fresh audit or to review the first audit and state with reasons whether a second audit is needed.[7] If a second audit is recommended, the company must comply with the recommendation.[8] Failure by the company to comply with a direction to retain an eligible person or with a recommendation of a second audit is an offence punishable by fine.[9] An ineligible auditor who has acted in that capacity knowing himself to be ineligible is liable to the company for any costs incurred by it in complying with section 29.[10]

### 1.1.2 Appointment of partnership

The appointment may be of a person or a firm.[11] Where a firm is appointed, it is assumed that the appointment is of the firm as such and not of the persons who are

1. Directive EEC 84/253.
2. Companies Act 1989, s. 27(4).
3. *Ibid.*, s. 28(1).
4. *Ibid.*, s. 28(3).
5. *Ibid.*, s. 28(2).
6. *Ibid.*, s. 28(3).
7. *Ibid.*, s. 29(1).
8. *Ibid.*, s. 29(2).
9. *Ibid.*, s. 29(5).
10. *Ibid.*, s. 29(7).
11. *Ibid.*, s. 25(2).

partners for the time being.[12] Consequently, if the partnership ceases, the appointment is treated as extending to any partnership which succeeds to the practice of that partnership and any person who succeeds to the practice, having previously carried it on in partnership, provided in both cases that this successor is eligible for appointment as auditor.[13] However, a partnership is to be regarded as succeeding to the practice of another partnership only if its members are substantially the same as those of the former partnership, whilst an individual is treated as succeeding to the practice of a former partnership only if he succeeds to the whole or substantially the whole of that practice.[14] These rules are intended to deal with the situation where the composition of the partnership changes or the partnership is dissolved entirely. The effect of the rules is that there will inevitably be cases where no person or firm is treated as succeeding to the practice of the former auditors. In this case the company will need to consider who are to be its auditors for the time being. Section 26(5) allows the appointment to be treated, with the consent of the company, as extending to any person or partnership succeeding to all or part of the *business* of the former partnership (as distinct from succeeding to the *practice* of the former partnership in the sense defined above). It is not clear that this section adds anything to the law, since this option would presumably have been open to the company in any case, and since the company is not required to treat the appointment as extended in this way—if the firm which acted as auditors no longer exists and there is no person or firm entitled to succeed as auditor under section 26(4), it must be open to the company to appoint any qualified person or firm to that position.

### 1.1.3 *Supervisory bodies*

Section 30 of the Companies Act 1989 defines a supervisory body as a body established in the United Kingdom which maintains and enforces rules as to eligibility to act as company auditor and as to the conduct of company audit work which are binding on persons seeking appointment as company auditors whether through their membership of that body or otherwise. Schedule 11 to the Act then sets out the conditions under which supervisory bodies may become recognised for the purposes of entitling their members to act as auditors. Such bodies may apply to the Secretary of State for recognition.[15] He may grant or refuse the application,[16] but must not grant it unless satisfied that the rules and practices of the body are satisfactory[17] and may refuse it anyway if the granting of it appears to be unnecessary because of the existence of one or more other bodies fulfilling the same function.[18] In other words, he is entitled to take into account the fact that there are already enough supervisory bodies to perform the task of supervision adequately. Recognition which has been granted may be revoked by the Secretary of State if he considers that the recognised body has failed to discharge its obligations, that it is no

---

12. *Ibid.*, s. 26(2).
13. *Ibid.*, s. 26(3).
14. *Ibid.*, s. 26(4).
15. *Ibid.*, Sch. 11, para. 1(1).
16. *Ibid.*, Sch. 11, para. 2(1).
17. *Ibid.*, Sch. 11, para. 2(2); see p. 243 below.
18. *Ibid.*, Sch. 11, para. 2(3).

longer eligible for recognition under the Act[19] or that its continued recognition is undesirable because of the existence of other bodies which have been or are to be recognised.[20]

Part II of Schedule 11 goes on to set out the prerequisites to recognition of a supervisory body. These are couched in terms of the rules which the body is required to have. First, the body must have rules to the effect that a person is not eligible for appointment as auditor unless, in the case of an individual, he holds an appropriate qualification or, in the case of a firm, the individuals within it engaged in audit work hold appropriate qualifications and the firm is controlled by qualified persons,[21] i.e., persons holding appropriate qualifications[22] or firms which are eligible for appointment as company auditor. The rules may permit a firm which ceases to meet these requirements to remain eligible for appointment as auditor for a maximum period of three months after ceasing to meet the requirements.[23] This will allow for the situation where a firm inadvertently ceases to qualify but promptly takes steps to correct the situation.

A firm is treated as controlled by qualified persons if, but only if, a majority[24] of its members are qualified persons and, where its affairs are controlled by a management body, a majority of the members of that body (or at least one if there are only two members) are qualified persons.

### 1.1.4 Auditors to be fit and proper persons

The body must have adequate rules and practices designed to ensure that the persons whom it recognises as eligible for appointment as company auditor are fit and proper persons to be so appointed.[25] Matters which may be taken into account in determining whether a person is fit and proper include, but are not limited to, matters relating to any person who will be employed by or associated with the eligible person in connection with company audit work; in the case of a body corporate they include anything relating to any director or controller of it, or to any other body corporate in the same group or any director or controller of such other body; in the case of a partnership they include anything relating to any of the partners, any director or controller of any of the partners, any body corporate in the same group as any of the partners and any director or controller of any such other body.[26]

### 1.1.5 Professional integrity and independence

The rules and practices of the body must be adequate to ensure that company audit work is conducted properly and with integrity and that persons are not appointed company auditor in circumstances in which they have any interest likely to conflict

---

19. See pp. 243–244 below.
20. Companies Act 1989, Sch. 11, para. 3(1).
21. *Ibid.*, Sch. 11, para. 4(1).
22. As defined in s. 31 of the Companies Act 1989; see further p. 245 below.
23. Companies Act 1989, Sch. 11, para. 4(3).
24. Majority is determined according to voting rights rather than according to simple numbers, in any case where the two are different: Companies Act 1989, Sch. 11, para. 5(4) and (5).
25. Companies Act 1989, Sch. 11, para. 6(1).
26. *Ibid.*, Sch. 11, para. 6(2).

with the proper conduct of the audit.[27] The body's rules and practices must also be designed to ensure that no firm is eligible under its rules for appointment as company auditor unless the rules of that firm prevent non-members of the firm and persons without an appropriate qualification from exercising any influence over the conduct of the audit in circumstances in which that influence would be likely to affect the integrity and independence of the audit.[28]

### 1.1.6 Technical standards

The body must have rules and practices as to the technical standards to be applied in company audit work and as to the manner in which those standards are to be applied in practice.[29] The Schedule says nothing about the nature and content of those technical standards.

### 1.1.7 Procedures for maintaining competence

The body must have rules and practices designed to ensure that persons eligible under its rules for appointment as company auditor continue to maintain an appropriate level of competence in the conduct of company audits.[30]

### 1.1.8 Monitoring and enforcement

The body must have adequate arrangements and resources for the effective monitoring and enforcement of compliance with its rules,[31] though that function may be performed on behalf of the body by some other person or body, the responsibility for effective performance of the task remaining with the recognised supervisory body.[32]

### 1.1.9 Membership, eligibility and discipline

The body must have fair and reasonable rules relating to the admission and expulsion of members, the grant and withdrawal of eligibility for appointment as company auditor and the discipline it exercises over its members. These rules must make adequate provision for appeals.[33] In this way it is sought to strike an appropriate balance between the freedom of auditors to carry on their profession and the protection of the general public by taking measures against the dishonest and the incompetent.

### 1.1.10 Investigation of complaints

The body must have effective arrangements for the investigation of complaints against persons who are eligible under its rules for appointment as company auditor

---

27. *Ibid.*, Sch. 11, para. 7(1).
28. *Ibid.*, Sch. 11, para. 7(2).
29. *Ibid.*, Sch. 11, para. 8.
30. *Ibid.*, Sch. 11, para. 9.
31. *Ibid.*, Sch. 11, para. 10(1).
32. *Ibid.*, Sch. 11, para. 10(2).
33. *Ibid.*, Sch. 11, para. 11.

or against the body in relation to matters arising out of its functions as a supervisory body.[34] It appears that the complaints against individuals need not be directly related to audit work, and this conclusion is a desirable one, since evidence of, for example, dishonesty, even in a matter unconnected with audit, may reflect on the person's fitness to be appointed as auditor. The investigation of complaints may be wholly or partly delegated to a body independent of the recognised supervisory body.[35] This would seem to include an arbitration scheme or an appropriate Ombudsman scheme.

### 1.1.11  Meeting of claims arising out of audit work

The body must have adequate rules or arrangements designed to ensure that persons eligible under its rules for appointment as company auditor take such steps as can reasonably be expected of them to secure that they are able to meet claims against them arising out of company audit work.[36] This may be done by professional indemnity insurance or by other appropriate means.[37] All the recognised bodies have rules which make the holding of suitable professional indemnity insurance compulsory for those carrying on audit work.

### 1.1.12  Register of auditors and other information to be made available

The body must have rules requiring persons eligible under its rules to comply with obligations imposed on them under sections 35 and 36 of the Companies Act 1989, which deal with information to be made public by auditors.[38]

### 1.1.13  Taking account of costs of compliance

The body must have satisfactory arrangements for taking account, in framing its rules, of the cost to those subject to the rules of complying with the rules and with any other controls to which they are subject.[39]

### 1.1.14  Promotion and maintenance of standards

The body must be able and willing to promote and maintain high standards of integrity in the conduct of company audit work and to co-operate, by the sharing of information and otherwise, with the Secretary of State and any other authority, body or person having responsibility in the United Kingdom for the qualification, supervision or regulation of auditors.[40]

---

34. *Ibid.*, Sch. 11, para. 12(1).
35. *Ibid.*, Sch. 11, para. 12(2).
36. *Ibid.*, Sch. 11, para. 13(1).
37. *Ibid.*, Sch. 11, para. 13(2).
38. *Ibid.*, Sch. 11, para. 14; see p. 259 below.
39. *Ibid.*, Sch. 11, para. 15.
40. *Ibid.*, Sch. 11, para. 16.

## 1.2 Appropriate qualification

Section 31 of the Companies Act 1989 defines what is meant by "appropriate qualification", a phrase which has occurred a number of times above. There are three types of appropriate qualification recognised for these purposes. The first is derived from having been qualified for appointment as company auditor by virtue of membership of a body recognised under section 389(1)(a) of the Companies Act 1985 immediately before 1 January 1990 and immediately before the coming into force of section 25 of the 1989 Act, which came into force on 1 March 1990. This is what might be called an "old qualification" and the effect is that those who were authorised to act as auditors under the old law remain so authorised under the new law without having to re-qualify. This entitlement is subject to the person concerned having notified the Secretary of State of his wish to retain his old qualification; such notice must have been given not later than 1 March 1991, being 12 months from the day when section 25 of the Companies Act 1989 came into force,[41] though the Secretary of State does have discretion to allow a late application if satisfied that there was good reason why the applicant did not give notice in time and that the applicant genuinely intends to practice as an auditor in the United Kingdom.[42] There are transitional arrangements under which a person who began studying or training to qualify as an accountant before 1 January 1990 and who obtained the qualification on or after that date but before 1 January 1996 may be treated as having an old qualification if the Secretary of State approves his qualification.[43] Such approval shall not be given unless the Secretary of State is satisfied that the body awarding the qualification has or had at the relevant time adequate arrangements to ensure that its qualification was awarded only to persons trained to a standard at least equivalent to that required in the case of a recognised professional qualification.[44]

The second type of appropriate qualification is a recognised professional qualification obtained in the United Kingdom.[45] The recognition of professional qualifications is governed by Schedule 12 to the Companies Act 1989.

A qualifying body may apply to the Secretary of State for an order declaring a qualification offered by it to be a recognised professional qualification.[46] A qualifying body is any body established in the United Kingdom which offers a professional qualification in accountancy.[47] The Secretary of State may grant the application, but only if satisfied that the requirements for recognition, discussed below, are met.[48] Recognition may subsequently be revoked if it appears to the Secretary of State that those requirements are no longer met or that the body has failed to comply with any obligation to which it is subject under these provisions,[49] though the body concerned has the right to make representations to the Secretary of State to try to persuade him not to make such an order.[50]

41. *Ibid.*, s. 31(2).
42. *Ibid.*, s. 31(3).
43. *Ibid.*, s. 31(4).
44. *Ibid.*, s. 31(5).
45. *Ibid.*, s. 31(1)(b).
46. *Ibid.*, Sch. 12, para. 1(1).
47. *Ibid.*, s. 32(1).
48. *Ibid.*, Sch. 12, para. 2(2).
49. *Ibid.*, Sch. 12, para. 3(1).
50. *Ibid.*, Sch. 12, para. 3(4).

### 1.2.1 Requirements for recognition

The requirements for recognition are contained in Part II of Schedule 12 to the Companies Act 1989, discussed in the following paragraphs.

### 1.2.2 Entry requirements

The qualification must only be open to those who have attained university entrance level or who have a sufficient period of professional experience.[51] A candidate who has not in fact been admitted to higher education in the United Kingdom may demonstrate the necessary standard by reference to academic or professional qualifications obtained in the United Kingdom or elsewhere and recognised by the Secretary of State as appropriate for the purpose[52] or by passing written and/or oral tests so recognised.[53]

### 1.2.3 Course of theoretical instruction

The qualification must be restricted to those who have completed a course of theoretical instruction in the subjects prescribed for the examination considered in the next paragraph or who have a sufficient period of professional experience.[54]

### 1.2.4 Examination

The examination mentioned in the previous paragraph must be at least partly in writing and must test to a level at least equivalent to the standard of a first degree in the United Kingdom theoretical knowledge of such subjects as may be prescribed by regulations made by the Secretary of State, together with the ability to apply that knowledge in practice.[55] An appropriate university examination may be substituted for a test of theoretical knowledge administered by the professional body[56] and a period of practical training attested by diploma or examination may be substituted for an examination testing practical application of knowledge.[57]

51. *Ibid.*, Sch. 12, para. 4(1).
52. *Ibid.*, Sch. 12, para. 4(2).
53. *Ibid.*, Sch. 12, para. 4(2).
54. *Ibid.*, Sch. 12, para. 5.
55. *Ibid.*, Sch. 12, para. 7(1); the subjects of the examination are prescribed by the Company Auditors (Examinations) Regulations 1990 (S.I. 1990/1146) and are 1. Auditing; 2. Analysis and critical assessment of annual accounts; 3. General accounting; 4. Cost and management accounting; 5. Consolidated accounts; 6. Internal control; 7. Standards relating to the preparation of annual and consolidated accounts and to methods of valuing balance sheet items and of computing profits and losses; 8. Legal and professional standards and professional guidance relating to the statutory auditing of accounting documents and to those carrying out such audits; 9. Those aspects of the following which are relevant to auditing:
    (a) company law;
    (b) the law of insolvency and similar procedures;
    (c) tax law;
    (d) civil and commercial law;
    (e) social security law and law of employment;
    (f) information and computer systems;
    (g) business, general and financial economics;
    (h) mathematics and statistics; and
    (i) basic principles of financial management of undertakings.
56. *Ibid.*, Sch. 12, para. 7(2).
57. *Ibid.*, Sch. 12, para. 7(3).

## 1.2.5 Practical training

The qualification must be restricted to those who have completed at least three years' practical training, part of which was spent being trained in company audit work and a substantial part of which was spent being trained in company audit work or other audit work of a description approved by the Secretary of State as being similar to company audit work.[58] The training must be given by persons approved by the body offering the qualification as suitable for the purpose, i.e., people whom the body accepts, in the light of its supervision of them and any undertakings given by them, as persons who will provide adequate training.[59] At least two-thirds of the training must be given by a fully qualified auditor, i.e., a person eligible to be appointed as company auditor in one or more member states of the European Union.[60]

## 1.2.6 Sufficient period of professional experience

The period of professional experience which was mentioned above as being sufficient to substitute for the entry requirement of university admission level is a period of not less than seven years' experience in law, finance and accountancy.[61] Periods of theoretical instruction in these fields may be deducted from the seven years (up to a maximum of four years' deductions), provided that they have lasted at least one year and are attested by an examination recognised by the Secretary of State for the purpose.[62] In the case of a person whose professional experience is recognised as an adequate substitute, the period of professional experience together with the practical training must not be shorter than the total of the theoretical instruction and the practical training required of people who qualify by that route.[63]

## 1.2.7 The body offering the qualification

The body offering the qualification must have rules and arrangements adequate to ensure compliance with the above requirements and arrangements adequate to monitor that compliance on a continuing basis.[64] These arrangements must include arrangements for monitoring the standard of the examinations and the adequacy of the practical training.[65]

The third type of appropriate qualification is an approved overseas qualification. This is dealt with in section 33 of the 1989 Act. This allows the Secretary of State to recognise as holding approved overseas qualifications persons who are qualified under the law of some other country to audit accounts or who hold a specified professional qualification in accountancy recognised under the law of some other country.[66] Such recognition is not to be granted unless the Secretary of State is

---

58. *Ibid.*, Sch. 12, para. 8(1).
59. *Ibid.*, Sch. 12, para. 8(2).
60. *Ibid.*, Sch. 12, para. 8(3).
61. *Ibid.*, Sch. 12, para. 6(1).
62. *Ibid.*, Sch. 12, para. 6(2).
63. *Ibid.*, Sch. 12, para. 6(3).
64. *Ibid.*, Sch. 12, para. 9(1).
65. *Ibid.*, Sch. 12, para. 9(2).
66. *Ibid.*, s. 33(1).

satisfied that the qualification in question offers an assurance of professional competence equivalent to that afforded by a recognised domestic professional qualification.[67] In deciding whether to recognise an overseas qualification the Secretary of State may have regard to the extent to which the other country concerned recognises qualifications obtained in the United Kingdom.[68] In granting recognition the Secretary of State may impose additional educational requirements for the purpose of ensuring that persons qualifying by this route have an adequate knowledge of the law and practice in the United Kingdom relating to the audit of accounts.[69]

The bodies who currently have recognition orders in force are:

The Institute of Chartered Accountants in England and Wales;
The Chartered Association of Certified Accountants;
The Institute of Chartered Accountants of Scotland;
The Institute of Chartered Accountants in Ireland;
The Institute of Authorised Practitioners of Accountancy.

### 1.3 1967 Act qualifications

Audit qualifications granted under section 13(1) of the Companies Act 1967 continue to be valid, but a person who holds no other qualification to act as auditor may act as auditor only to an unquoted company,[70] i.e., a company whose shares and whose parent company's shares have never been offered on a stock exchange.[71]

## 2 THE PROFESSIONAL RULES

### 2.1 The requirement for an audit

Audit requirements appeared at an early stage in the history of company law.[72] The Joint Stock Companies Act 1844 required companies to produce audited accounts. The rule disappeared in 1856, but was gradually restored for specialised companies such as banks and insurers. The Companies Act 1900 restored it for all companies, and it has remained ever since. It may be worth noticing that in 1900 there was no such thing as a private company (these first appeared in the Companies Act 1907), so the question of whether the requirement was appropriate for private companies could not have been asked at that time.

#### 2.1.1 Financial Services Act 1986

Sections 107–111 of the Financial Services Act 1986 allow the Secretary of State to make rules requiring persons authorised to conduct investment business within the

---

67. *Ibid.*, s. 33(2).
68. *Ibid.*, s. 33(3).
69. *Ibid.*, s. 33(4).
70. *Ibid.*, s. 34(1).
71. *Ibid.*, s. 34(2).
72. Gwilliam (1992) 8 P.N. 147.

meaning of that Act[73] or members of recognised self-regulating organisations under that Act[74] to appoint auditors even if they are not limited companies and would therefore not otherwise be required to do so. Section 108 of the Act allows the Secretary of State to require a second audit of the accounts of a person authorised to carry on investment business if it appears to him that there is good reason to do so. Section 109 creates an exception to the general rules about client confidentiality in relation to auditors by providing that no duty to which the auditor of an authorised person is subject shall be treated as contravened by reason of his communicating to the Secretary of State any information of which the auditor has become aware in his capacity as auditor of that person and which is relevant to any of the functions of the Secretary of State under the Act. This provision effectively allows auditors to report to the Secretary of State when the audit reveals anything which might cast doubts on the fitness of the authorised person to retain his authorisation.

## 2.2 The duty to appoint auditors

In principle every company is required to appoint auditors.[75] The relaxation of the auditing requirements in the case of very small companies introduced by the Companies Act 1985 (Audit Exemption) Regulations 1994[76] create an important exception to this principle by allowing companies with a turnover not exceeding £90,000 per annum to provide only an accountant's report and by allowing a much simplified audit report in the case of companies with a turnover not exceeding £350,000 per annum.

Another exception occurs in the case of a dormant company which, under section 250 of the Companies Act 1985, is exempt from the requirement to have its accounts audited. There is obviously no reason why such a company should be required to have auditors, and section 388A of the Companies Act 1985 exempts it from that requirement. Save in the case of a private company taking advantage of the elective regime, as to which see below, auditors must be appointed at each general meeting at which accounts are laid (normally this will be the annual general meeting) to hold office from the end of that meeting until the end of the next meeting at which accounts are laid.[77] The first auditors may be appointed by the directors at any time before the first general meeting at which accounts are laid, and hold office until the termination of that meeting.[78]

A private company which has dispensed under section 252 of the Companies Act 1985 with the need to lay annual accounts before the general meeting is still required to have auditors, since dispensng with the requirement to lay accounts is not the same as dispensing with the need to have accounts, but the procedure laid down in section 385 is obviously inappropriate, since there will be no meeting at which accounts are laid. Section 385A applies to such companies. Auditors shall be appointed by the

73. Financial Services Act 1986, s. 107.
74. *Ibid.*, s. 107A.
75. Companies Act 1985, s. 384(1).
76. S.I. 1994/1935.
77. Companies Act 1985, s. 385(2).
78. *Ibid.*, s. 385(3).

company in general meeting within 28 days of the day on which the accounts for the previous financial year are sent to the members, or, if a member has given notice under section 253(2) requiring the laying of the accounts before a general meeting, before the conclusion of that meeting.[79] Auditors so appointed then hold office until the end of the time for appointing auditors for the following financial year.[80] The first auditors of such a company may be appointed by the directors at any time up to 28 days after the company's first annual accounts are sent to the members or before the beginning of the meeting at which those accounts are laid in cases where there has been notice under section 253(2) requiring the laying of the accounts before the general meeting. The general meeting may exercise these powers if the directors neglect to do so.[81] If the election to dispense with the laying of accounts is made when the company has been in existence for some time, there will normally be auditors in office at the time of the election. Such auditors hold office until the end of the time for appointing auditors for the following financial year under section 385A(2)[82] (and are eligible for reappointment). Where an election to dispense with laying accounts is in force and is then revoked the auditors holding office at the time of the revocation continue to hold office until the conclusion of the next general meeting of the company at which accounts are laid.[83]

### 2.2.1 Casual vacancies

Any casual vacancy in the office of auditor may be filled by the directors or by the company in general meeting.[84] Until such a vacancy is filled any surviving or continuing auditor or auditors may continue to act.[85] Special notice to the company is required for a resolution at a general meeting filling a casual vacancy or reappointing an auditor who was appointed by the directors to fill a casual vacancy.[86] A copy of the notice must be sent by the company to the person proposed to be appointed and, if the casual vacancy was caused by the resignation of an auditor, to the auditor who resigned.[87]

### 2.2.2 Secretary of State's powers

If a company fails to appoint auditors within the time laid down for doing so according to the circumstances of the company, the Secretary of State may appoint auditors for the company.[88] The company is required to give notice to the Secretary of State that this power has become exercisable within one week of the date on which it does so. Failure to comply is an offence.[89]

79. *Ibid.*, s. 385A(2).
80. *Ibid.*, s. 385A(3).
81. *Ibid.*, s. 385A(4).
82. *Ibid.*, s. 385A(5).
83. *Ibid.*
84. *Ibid.*, s. 388(1).
85. *Ibid.*, s. 388(2).
86. *Ibid.*, s. 388(3).
87. *Ibid.*, s. 388(4).
88. *Ibid.*, s. 387(1).
89. *Ibid.*, s. 387(2).

## 2.3 Rights of auditors

The auditors are entitled at all times to access to the company's books, accounts and vouchers and are entitled to require from the company's officers such information and explanations as they think necessary for the performance of their duties as auditors.[90] These powers are not restricted to the period during which the audit is conducted, though no doubt in practice they are likely to be exercised primarily, if not exclusively, during that period. The duty extends to the officers and auditors of a subsidiary company, who must also supply all necessary information and explanations to the auditors of the parent company.[91] It is an offence for an officer of a company to make any misleading, false or deceptive statement to the auditors when conveying or purporting to convey any information to which the auditors are entitled.[92]

The auditors also have the same right to receive all notices of and other communications relating to any general meeting as do members of the company. They are also entitled to attend general meetings of the company, where they have the right to be heard on any part of the business which concerns them as auditors.[93] Where it is proposed to agree anything by means of a written resolution, a procedure generally permitted in the case of a private company by section 381A of the Companies Act 1985, the auditors are entitled to receive the same communications relating to the proposed resolution as must be supplied to members of the company, to give notice to the company that in their opinion the resolution concerns them as auditors and should be considered by a general meeting of the company, to attend any such meeting and to be heard at any such meeting on that part of the business which concerns them as auditors.[94]

## 2.4 The requirement to keep accounts

The statutory requirements are set out in Part VII of the Companies Act 1985, as amended by the Companies Act 1989. These rules deal both with the keeping of accounts by the company and with the auditing of accounts by independent auditors. Part VII of the Act divides the detailed provisions into a number of smaller headings, and for convenience these headings are largely followed in this chapter.

### 2.4.1 Accounting records

Every company is required to keep proper accounts[95] which are sufficient to show with reasonable accuracy the financial position of the company at any given time and to enable the directors to prepare the statutory accounts required under other provisions of Part VII of the Act. A private company must keep accounts for three years from the date on which they are made.[96] The accounting records are normally

90. *Ibid.*, s. 389A(1).
91. *Ibid.*, s. 389A(3).
92. *Ibid.*, s. 389A(2).
93. *Ibid.*, s. 390(1).
94. *Ibid.*, s. 390(2).
95. *Ibid.*, s. 221(1).
96. *Ibid.*, s. 222(5).

kept at the company's registered office, though they may alternatively be kept in such other place as the directors think fit.[97]

### 2.4.2 Financial years and accounting reference periods

Companies are allowed to choose the date on which their financial year ends.[98] This date is known as the accounting reference date.[99] If the company does not make a choice as to its accounting reference date, then that date falls on 31 March for companies incorporated before 1 April 1990 and on the last day of the month in which the anniversary of the company's incorporation falls for companies incorporated after 1 April 1990. A particular difficulty arises when a company is first formed if it wants to choose an accounting reference date which would give it an initial accounting reference period of more or less than one year. Section 224(4) requires that the initial accounting reference period must be at least six months and no more than 18 months long. Subsequent accounting reference periods are always exactly 12 months long, unless the company exercises its option under section 225 of the 1985 Act to alter an established accounting reference date. In such a case the company must give notice of the change to the Registrar of Companies, and must state whether it wishes to extend its current accounting reference period to the second occasion on which the new accounting reference date falls after the change or to shorten it so that it expires on the first occasion when that date falls after the change.[100] A change involving an extension of the accounting reference period cannot be made more than once in any five-year period.[101] The accounting reference period is important because it is to this date that the accounts must be made up.

### 2.4.3 Annual accounts

It is the duty of the directors of the company to prepare annual accounts. These accounts consist principally of two documents, namely the profit and loss account and the balance sheet. The former shows the profit or loss of the company for the accounting reference period, whereas the latter shows the financial position of the company as at the end of the accounting reference period. Schedule 4 to the Act contains detailed requirements as to the form in which these documents must be presented. However, the most important single provision about the accounts is to be found in section 226(2), which requires that the profit and loss account shall give a true and fair view of the profit or loss of the company for the financial year and that the balance sheet shall give a true and fair view of the state of affairs of the company as at the balance sheet date.

### 2.4.4 Groups

Sections 227–230 of the 1985 Act deal with the operation of the accounting rules in relation to groups of companies. Section 227 requires the directors of the parent

97. *Ibid.*, s. 222(5).
98. *Ibid.*, s. 224(2).
99. *Ibid.*, s. 224(3).
100. *Ibid.*, s. 225(3).
101. *Ibid.*, s. 225(4).

company to prepare group accounts as well as the individual accounts for the parent company. Group accounts consist of a consolidated profit and loss account and a consolidated balance sheet for the group as a whole. The true and fair view requirement applies to the group accounts in the same way as it applies to the individual accounts of the parent company, though obviously it is the position of the group which must be fairly described. The normal rule is that all subsidiaries of the parent company must be included in the consolidation, though section 229 allows certain limited exceptions to this principle. The most important exception in relation to groups of small companies is that contained in section 229(4), which states that subsidiaries must be excluded from the consolidation where their activities are so different from those of the parent company that to include them in the consolidation would be incompatible with the requirement to give a true and fair view. This is merely a specific application of the general principle that the requirement to give a true and fair view overrides all other rules and requirements of the Companies Acts relating to the form and content of accounts. However, it is to be noted that it is not open to the directors of a company to invoke this exception merely because the activities of the subsidiary companies involve different goods or services than those of the parent company.

Section 232 (and Schedule 6, to which that section gives effect) imposes requirements of disclosure in relation to the emoluments and other benefits of directors and certain other persons. The purpose of these provisions is to bring to the attention of the members of the company the level of emoluments and compensation for loss of office (if any) paid to the directors.

### 2.4.5 Approval and signing of accounts

Section 233 of the Companies Act 1985 is a very important provision. It imposes a requirement that the accounts be signed by one director on behalf of the board as a whole. The significance of this is that in signing the accounts the directors take responsibility for their accuracy. Under section 235(5) it is an offence for directors knowingly to approve accounts which do not comply with the requirements of the Companies Acts as to form or content or as to the giving of a true and fair view.[102]

### 2.4.6 Directors' report

Under section 234 of the Companies Act 1985 the directors of a company are required to prepare for each financial year of the company a report containing a fair review of the development of the business of the company and its subsidiary undertakings during the financial year and of their position at the end of it and stating the amount if any which the directors propose should be declared as dividend and the amount if any which they propose to carry to reserves. The amount recommended by the directors as dividend is the maximum amount which may be paid, since it is not open to the general meeting to decide upon a dividend larger than that recommended by the directors (though the general meeting may decide upon a lower amount than recommended). The report must also give the names of all persons who have been

---

102. Prosecutions under this section are, however, very rare. The only known instance is that of the prosecution of the directors of the Argyll Group in 1979.

directors during the year in question and must give certain other factual information about the company. Section 234A requires the directors' report to be signed on their behalf by a director or by the company secretary. As with the accounts, it is an offence knowingly to be party to the signing of an inaccurate directors' report.

### 2.4.7 Small and medium-sized companies and groups

In addition to the rules introduced in 1994 exempting very small companies from all or part of the audit requirement,[103] the detailed accounting requirements of the Companies Acts are somewhat relaxed in relation to smaller companies and groups. The provisions relating to this are contained in sections 246–249 of the 1985 Act. The concepts of "small" and "medium-sized" are defined by reference to three tests, namely turnover, balance sheet total and number of employees. In order to qualify for the exemption a company or group of companies must satisfy any two of the three tests in the year for which it wishes to claim the exemption and in the previous accounting year (unless it is claiming the exemption in respect of its first accounting year). The table below shows the limits under each of the three headings for the exemption.[104]

|  | Turnover | Balance Sheet | Employees |
| --- | --- | --- | --- |
| Small company | £2m | £975k | 50 |
| Medium-sized company | £8m | £3.9m | 250 |
| Small group | £2m | £1m | 50 |
| Medium-sized group | £8m | £3.9m | 250 |

These exemptions are not available to public companies[105] even if they qualify according to the above table, nor to any group of companies which includes a public company.[106] In determining whether the group includes a public company, the question is whether such a company is included within the group accounts for which the exemption is being claimed. Schedule 8 to the Act sets out the details of the exemptions granted to small and medium-sized companies. There is no need to disclose whether accounting standards have been complied with in the preparation of the accounts; a much-abbreviated version of the balance sheet may be delivered to the Registrar, and the profit and loss account and directors' report need not be delivered to the Registrar at all. However, this does not relieve the directors from the obligation to prepare these documents, to submit them to the auditors and to lay them before the company in general meeting. In the case of medium-sized companies, the exemption with respect to accounting standards is again applicable and an abbreviated balance sheet may be delivered to the Registrar, but the profit and loss account and the directors' report must be delivered. The value of these exemptions is somewhat questionable. Small and medium-sized companies and groups are given limited protection from the disclosure requirements imposed on larger companies, but there is unlikely to be any significant saving in time or cost, since full versions of the accounts are still required for internal purposes, and will of

103. S.I. 1994/1935, discussed above.
104. Companies Act 1985, ss. 246 and 249.
105. *Ibid.*, s. 246(3).
106. *Ibid.*, s. 248(2).

course be demanded by loan creditors under the terms of any debenture. Indeed, it is arguable that taking advantage of the exemptions may involve greater cost, since it will then be necessary to produce an additional abbreviated version of the balance sheet which would not otherwise have been required.

### 2.4.8 Publication of accounts and reports

The accounts and the directors' report must be sent to every member of the company and every debenture holder at least 21 days before the general meeting at which copies of the accounts are to be presented. The requirement to send the accounts to a debenture holder seems unnecessary, since he could get them after filing anyway, and is not entitled to vote at the meeting. It may be observed, however, that in practice it is usual for the debenture to confer an express right to receive at least the statutory accounts and often the management accounts as well. Section 241 is the section which requires that the accounts and report, together with the auditors' report, shall be laid before the company in general meeting. These documents must also be sent to the Registrar of Companies within 10 months of the end of the accounting period to which they relate (seven months in the case of a public company).[107] These requirements form an essential element in the disclosure rules in company law, which aim to ensure that significant information about limited companies is in the public domain,[108] though it may be noted that the vigour with which they have been enforced has varied from time to time.

## 3 THE AUDITOR'S DUTIES

In relation to each stage of the audit the crucial questions concern the nature and standard of the duty imposed on the auditor. Before considering these questions in detail it is necessary to be clear about the role of the audit and what it is intended to produce.

### 3.1 Preparation

There is virtually no authority on the duties of the auditors when preparing to conduct an audit, perhaps because those cases where difficulty later arises are nearly always concerned with the outcome of the auditing process rather than with the preparation for it. It is nevertheless suggested that appropriate preparation is part of the auditors' duties and that good preparation can significantly reduce the risk of problems occurring at a later stage. In particular it is essential for the auditors to acquire a good working knowledge of the nature and operation of the company's business, so as to be able to understand the way in which the accounting system relates to that business. In this way the auditors are well placed to choose suitable

---

107. *Ibid.*, s. 244.
108. See also chapter 1.

sample transactions to examine and to know where difficulties and discrepancies are most likely to arise.

## 3.2 Execution

*3.2.1 Re London & General Bank (No 2)*[109] was the first case to give authoritative consideration to the duties of an auditor. In a passage relied on in later cases[110] Lindley LJ, drawing on the decision of Stirling J in *Leeds Estate Building and Investment Co* v. *Shepherd*,[111] laid down a number of important propositions:

(1) The auditor must ascertain and state the true financial position at the time of the audit by examining the books and taking reasonable care to see that they show the true position. In *Re City Equitable Fire Insurance Co Ltd*,[112] Romer J added to this the qualificiation that "He is not an insurer; he does not guarantee that the books do correctly show the true position of the company's affairs; he does not even guarantee that his balance sheet is accurate according to the books of the company".[113] As far as it goes this statement may be regarded as being still good law, but it is necessary to add that the auditor must have taken all reasonable steps to satisfy himself as to the accuracy of the books and must be able to demonstrate that he has adopted appropriate systems for the task before him. In particular, he will need to obtain a proper understanding of the company's accounting system.

(2) The auditor has nothing to do with the prudent/imprudent or profitable/unprofitable management of the company, nor with proper/improper declaration of dividends. In particular an auditor has nothing to do with the prudence or imprudence of making a loan without security.[114]

(3) The auditor must be honest; he must not certify without believing and must not believe without reasonable grounds. It may be observed that auditors do not at the present day "certify" the accuracy of a company's accounts. They merely express an opinion on them. Subject to the rephrasing, this proposition must still be good law today.

(4) The duty is only to take reasonable care. This may be regarded as uncontentious, since it is clear that this is not an area of strict liability.

(5) The usual practice is to sample a number of transactions, and this is legally acceptable. It should be added that at the present day it would hardly be acceptable to select merely a random sample. The availability of computerised record-keeping should allow auditors to select a proper cross-sample and to check them without great difficulty.

(6) The auditor is justified in acting on expert opinion where special knowledge is required.[115]

The crucial point here concerns the auditor's duty to detect fraud, and, in line with

---

109. [1895] 2 Ch. 673, C.A.
110. Notably *Re City Equitable Fire Insurance Co Ltd* [1925] Ch. 407, C.A. (Romer J).
111. (1887) 36 Ch.D. 787.
112. [1925] Ch. 407.
113. *Ibid.*
114. *Re City Equitable Fire Insurance Co Ltd.*
115. *Ibid.* at 482.

the low standard approved elsewhere in the case for directors, the court here sets the auditor's duty at a low level This point was further developed in the next case to be considered.

### 3.2.2 Watchdog, not bloodhound

In *Fomento (Sterling Area)* v. *Selsdon Fountain Pen Co Ltd*[116] Viscount Simmonds, relying on *Re Kingston Cotton Mill*,[117] laid down the much-quoted dictum that an auditor is a watchdog, not a bloodhound. Although Viscount Simmonds dissented from the eventual decision in the case,[118] and although his remarks on the functions of auditors cannot properly be regarded as forming even part of the *ratio decidendi* of the decision he would have made (indeed the case as a whole has nothing to do with the statutory functions of auditors, since the powers and duties with which it was concerned arose under a license agreement), the principle which he stated has achieved general acceptance. Its importance lies in the approach which it requires auditors to take in the conduct of the audit. It must be remembered that the auditors are not preparing the accounts, nor, as was stated in the earlier cases, do they guarantee the accuracy of those accounts. If in the course of their examination they become aware of discrepancies or inaccuracies they must draw attention to these. Initially, no doubt, they will seek to persuade the directors to modify the accounts so that they are accurate, but if this fails they will have to point them out to the shareholders. They are not, however, required actively to seek out such problems. A case which illustrates the duties of the auditors to see problems which are put before them is *Re Thomas Gerrard & Son Ltd*,[119] where auditors were for years fooled by false accounts, having accepted the managing director's word without making proper checks. This had continued even after the auditors noticed that some invoice dates had been altered. Profits were greatly overstated, illegal dividends had been declared and too much tax had been paid. Eventually the company collapsed. The liquidator recovered damages for misfeasance from the managing director (who was imprisoned for his fraudulent conduct) but also sought to sue the auditors. It was held that the audit had not been conducted with proper care and skill. The changes in invoice dates should have put the auditors on inquiry. Although the duty is only to conduct the audit with reasonable care and skill, standards have risen since the days of *Re Kingston Cotton Mill*. As the auditors' breach of duty was the direct cause of the loss arising from the unlawful distributions, this was recoverable from the auditors, less credit for the recovery of overpaid tax and the amount recovered from the managing director.[120]

### 3.2.3 Report to the members

In *Re London & General Bank (No 2)*[121] the auditor knew that the value of some loans was questionable, but contented himself with saying in his report that the

116. [1958] 1 All E.R. 11, H.L.
117. [1896] 2 Ch. 279.
118. See p. 275.
119. [1967] 2 All E.R. 525 (Pennycuick J).
120. For the questions of causation arising on this part of the decision, see pp. 273–274.
121. [1895] 2 Ch. 673, C.A. For other aspects of this case, see above.

value depended on realisation. He did make a confidential report to the directors setting out the true position. The Court of Appeal held that this was a breach of duty. The auditor reports to the members and must put the proper information before them. Another case which illustrates the same principle is *Norton* v. *Birmingham Small Arms Co Ltd.*[122] In that case the company's articles authorised creation of a secret reserve fund, which was not to appear in the balance sheet. No details were to be given to shareholders. Auditors were to get details but were not to pass them on. Buckley J held that these provisions were void because they were capable of preventing the auditors from reporting on the true state of affairs. The judge went on to suggest that a report disclosing the existence of the fund and its omission from the balance sheet might still give a true and fair view. This observation is only an *obiter dictum* and it is submitted that it is wrong. It cannot be right to say that failure to disclose the value of the company's funds is consistent with a true and fair view—the matter may be tested by supposing a set of accounts which disclosed that the company had cash at the bank but failed to say how much it was. It is inconceivable that such a set of accounts would be considered to give a true and fair view, and there is no material distinction between that case and the secret fund in *Norton* v. *Birmingham Small Arms Co Ltd.*

### 3.2.4 Choice of accounting treatment

In *Lloyd Cheyham & Co Ltd* v. *Littlejohn & Co*[123] the plaintiff company agreed a financial support package for a company after seeing its audited accounts. Soon afterwards the company collapsed. The plaintiff company sued the auditors for negligence. The gist of the dispute was that the company hired out trailers and the auditors had accepted the idea of not charging replacement costs for the tyres in the accounts until the tyres actually had to be replaced. Plaintiffs claimed that this made the company's position look much better than it was. Defendants said that plaintiffs were not always responsible for tyre replacement, since this depended on the length of the lease of the trailer. It was held that the auditors owed P a duty of care in auditing the accounts because they knew that P would see these accounts and would rely on them.[124] The question then was whether the auditors had in fact been negligent. It was held that they had not. Their method of accounting for cost of replacement tyres was not the only one, but it was legitimate and was therefore sufficient to provide a true and fair view. This aspect of the case illustrates a very important point, namely that the law requires the giving of *a* true and fair view, not *the* true and fair view. In many cases there is more than one way in which the information can be presented; the formulation of a set of accounts is a matter of art, not a purely arithmetical exercise. The purpose of accounts is to present information about the company in such a way as to give a true and fair view, but the facts of the case illustrate the difficulty of deciding what would be true and fair in relation to a particular case. In one sense it could be said that the potential cost of replacement was constantly accruing and therefore ought to be charged on a proportionate basis for all tyres. This argument might have succeeded if the company had always been

---

122. [1906] 2 Ch. 378 (Buckley J).
123. [1987] B.C.L.C. 303 (Woolf J).
124. For this aspect of the case, see p. 269.

responsible for tyre replacement, but the uncertainties about where the cost of replacement would fall weakened the argument significantly. Another possibility would have been to make some assumption about the proportion of tyres which the company would have been responsible for replacing and to base the accounts on a proportion of that cost, but such accounts would necessarily have involved an estimate which might well prove to be wrong in due course. On the other hand not charging any part of the cost until it fell due could be seen as inevitably understating the liabilities and therefore overstating the profits. Nevertheless, given the complexities of the situation the court was prepared to accept that this was a legitimate approach. It was also relevant in this case that the treatment adopted was in line with the relevant SSAP.[125] Although these do not have the force of law, they are of persuasive value and the court will tend to favour an accounting treatment which is in line with them. Naturally, the choice of accounting policy in this respect needed to be disclosed in the accounts, and the question of disclosure of policies also plays an important role in the giving of a true and fair view. If the accounts make clear what approach has been adopted, then an intelligent reader of them can draw conclusions about what they really show.

## 3.3 Reporting

The auditors are required to make a report to the members on all annual accounts which are laid before the company in general meeting while they are in office.[126] This report must state whether in the auditors' view the annual accounts have been properly prepared in accordance with the Companies Act 1985 and in particular whether they give a true and fair view of the position of the company (or group in the case of group accounts) at the balance sheet date and of the profit or loss for the relevant accounting period.[127] The auditors must also consider whether the information given in the directors' report is consistent with the accounts. If they think that it is not, they must say so in their report,[128] though there is no requirement to make any statement on the subject if they accept that the information in the report is consistent with the accounts. In *Re London & General Bank (No 2)*[129] the auditor knew that the value of some loans was questionable, but contented himself with saying in his report that the value depended on realisation. He did make a confidential report to the directors setting out the true position. It was held that this was a breach of duty. The auditor reports to the members and must put the proper information before them. It is thought that this case needs to be treated with some care. It is in every case a question of fact whether the accounts have been properly prepared and whether they show a true and fair view, and there may well be more than one way to comply with these requirements. Under the present legislation it appears that the auditor would have to decide first whether the accounts did comply. If they did, he would be able simply to state that fact without more. If they did not, he

---

125. For the role of SSAPs and FRSs see p. 260.
126. Companies Act 1985, s. 235(1).
127. *Ibid.*, s. 235(2).
128. *Ibid.*, s. 235(3).
129. [1895] 2 Ch. 673.

would presumably wish to discuss the situation with the directors and invite them to amend the accounts. If they refused to do so, the auditor would have to qualify the accounts by drawing attention to the respects in which they did not show a true and fair view.

The auditors' report must state the names of the auditors and must be signed by them.[130] The copy of the report sent to the Registrar must also comply with this requirement,[131] whilst copies laid before the general meeting or otherwise published or issued must state the names of the auditors but need not be signed by them.[132] Failure to comply with the requirements in relation to the copy sent to the Registrar or copies otherwise issued is an offence on the part of the company and every officer of it who is party to the default.[133]

In *Re Allen, Craig & Co*[134] auditors sent their report to the company secretary, but no general meeting was ever called. It was held that the auditors had committed no breach of duty, having correctly submitted their report. It was no concern of theirs what then became of it. Although the point is not expressly dealt with in the present legislation, it appears that this decision remains good law. Section 241 of the 1985 Act requires the laying of accounts before the general meeting, whilst section 242 requires that a copy be sent to the Registrar, but both sections impose the relevant duty on the directors, not on the auditors, and subject the directors, but not the auditors, to a fine in case of non-compliance. Section 242A imposes an additional civil penalty on the company, but again says nothing about the auditors.

### 3.4 The role of the statutory audit

The question of the role of the statutory audit is more difficult than might at first appear. It is also a question of some practical significance when considering the consequences which ought to follow from failure by the auditors to carry out their duties properly. A fundamental question is, whom is the audit intended to protect? It is possible to identify two extreme approaches to this question.[135] According to one approach the audit report is a public good, i.e., it provides benefits to the public at large. For this reason it is imposed on companies, which are also required to bear the cost of it, in the expectation that there will be significant public benefits. The logic of this analysis would be that the audit is there for the benefit of the public at large and that there should be liability to the public at large for failure to conduct it properly. At the other extreme is the view that the audit is there essentially for the benefit of the company itself, i.e., that it is a private good. The logic of this analysis would be that the scope and nature of the audit would be a matter to be agreed contractually between the company and the auditors (presumably on this analysis a company could choose to dispense with an audit entirely) and there would be no liability to third parties for the way in which the audit was conducted. As appears from the following

130. Companies Act 1985, s. 236(1).
131. *Ibid.*, s. 236(3).
132. *Ibid.*, s. 236(2).
133. *Ibid.*, s. 236(4).
134. [1934] Ch. 483 (Bennett J).
135. Gwilliam (1992) 8 P.N. 147.

analysis of the statutory scheme and supporting case law, the present United Kingdom system is something of a hybrid between these two approaches.

Section 235(1) describes the auditors' report as being a report to the members of the company, rather than to the company itself or to the directors, and this wording appears to represent the original idea behind the statutory audit requirement, namely that the accounts are the major means by which the directors keep the shareholders informed of the progress of the company, and the role of the auditors is to provide an independent check on the legitimacy of those accounts. Unfortunately, there are at the present day a number of significant difficulties with this theory. The first is that the auditors are not liable to the members at large for any errors in the accounts. This important principle was established by the decision of the House of Lords in *Caparo* v. *Dickman*,[136] where an action was brought against the auditors by shareholders in the company who had relied on the audited accounts in buying enough shares in the company to acquire control of it, but who alleged that after taking control they had discovered that the accounts were inaccurate and misleading. The House of Lords held that the auditors owed no duty of care to prospective shareholders who bought shares on the faith of the accounts since the purpose of the accounts is to allow shareholders to exercise informed control over the company and not to provide information to possible speculative investors. At the same time there is no duty to individual shareholders, since the duty is owed to the shareholders as a whole rather than to individuals. It is not clear from this decision whether it would be possible for the shareholders to bring an action if they all agreed to participate in it. Although this would seem a logical possibility, it should be remembered that English law does not normally recognise the concept of a class action such as this. It is of course open to the company to bring a contractual action against the auditors, but in such an action the damages recoverable would be limited to the loss suffered by the company as a result of the faults in the accounts. In most cases this damage will be negligible or non-existent, and the action will not enable the recovery of any losses suffered by individual shareholders who have relied on the accounts.

Even if these difficulties can be overcome in an individual case, there are further problems in bringing an action against the auditors because of defects in the accounts. Section 235 requires the auditors to express an opinion as to whether the accounts have been properly prepared. It is not correct to say that the auditors certify the accuracy of the accounts—their function is a much more limited one than that. The accounts are essentially the directors' accounts, and it is the directors who must take responsibility for the accuracy of the accounts. On the other side of the case it may be argued that section 237 of the 1985 Act requires the auditors to take such steps as are necessary to enable them to form an opinion as to whether the accounts have been properly prepared and whether they show the necessary true and fair view. In some cases this will no doubt expose the auditors to liability, but their liability is not established merely by showing that there are defects in the accounts, since these defects may exist despite the taking of all reasonable steps by them—it has been said judicially that the task of the auditor is to be a watchdog, not a bloodhound,[137] and this means that the auditor is not required actively to look for irregularities, though

---

136. [1990] 1 All E.R. 568, H.L.
137. *Re Kingston Cotton Mill (No 2)* [1896] 2 Ch. 279 at 288 *per* Lopes LJ.

he must of course draw attention to them if he sees any. It might justly be added that another duty of a watchdog is not to let his attention wander while on duty, thereby missing evidence of wrongdoing when it passes before him.

### 3.5 The true and fair view

Section 226 also provides that compliance with the provisions of Schedule 4 to the Act and with the other provisions of the Act is not sufficient if it does not result in compliance with the true and fair view requirement. The company is required to give whatever additional information is necessary or to depart from the requirements of the Act in whatever other way is necessary in order to produce a true and fair view. The expression "true and fair view" is not defined anywhere in the legislation, and its meaning is a matter of some considerable dispute.[138] It is sometimes argued that compliance with the standards is of itself sufficient to give a true and fair view. Unfortunately, this simple view of the matter cannot be sustained, for Schedule 4 to the 1985 Act provides (in para. 36A) that the accounts shall include particulars of any departure from accounting standards, together with an explanation of the reasons for them. Although this provision emphasises the weight given to accounting standards, it also makes clear that in some cases it will not be appropriate to follow them (for how else could there ever be a case where a company consciously chose not to follow them and was able to justify this decision?). It follows that the concept of true and fair view must involve something more than mere compliance with accounting standards. The question what more it involves is linked with the complex question of the purpose of the accounts, which is also explored later in this chapter.

#### 3.5.1 The role of accounting standards in relation to company accounts

Section 256 of the Act empowers the Secretary of State to make regulations about bodies preparing and issuing accounting standards, and this power has been exercised by designating the Financial Reporting Council and its subsidiary organ the Accounting Standards Board as the appropriate bodies for these purposes. The Accounting Standards Board has undertaken a fundamental review of all accounting standards with the intention of making company accounts more relevant to the real state of the company and more readily comprehensible to shareholders. The first Financial Reporting Standards have now been issued. Although these standards continue to have no statutory force, it is clear that they will be taken seriously by auditors, and it is to be hoped that the Accounting Standards Board will continue in a determined effort to remove some of the artificialities which presently afflict the form and content of company accounts.

#### 3.5.2 Qualifications to the accounts and the true and fair view

Where the auditors find it necessary to qualify the accounts of a company, this does not mean that the accounts do not present a true and fair view, for the effect of a

138. (1991) 54 M.L.R. 874; (1989) 10 *Company Lawyer* 13; [1990] L.M.C.L.Q. 255.

qualification ought to be that it clarifies the details of the accounts to the point where they, taken in conjunction with the qualification, do present a true and fair view.


### 3.5.3 Conclusion

The unfortunate fact is that the statutory audited accounts give the reader relatively little of the information which he might wish to know about the state of the company and about trends within it. These accounts operate within a number of highly artificial constraints (especially in relation to the balance sheet) and they have to be considered within the terms of those constraints. Thus, the balance sheet does not state the value of the company at any given date. Rather, it states the assets and liabilities as calculated and expressed in accordance with accounting conventions. The profit and loss account is rather less artificial, though the calculation of profit is again done in accordance with specific accounting conventions, especially in relation to such items as depreciation and the treatment of work in progress. The profit and loss account can only give an overall result for the last accounting year: it cannot identify trends within that year. The reality is that the accounts are a poor basis for evaluating the company. Any shareholder who is seriously interested in financial questions, as well as any potential investor in the company, whether in the form of equity or of debt, should not rely on them, but should insist instead on seeing the company's management accounts, which the directors will prepare regularly (if only to satisfy the requirements of the bank) including particularly the cash-flow analysis and projections.

The points made above lead inevitably to the questioning of the value of the statutory accounting requirements. Fundamentally there are two linked questions. The first is, for whom are the accounts intended, whilst the second is, what are the accounts supposed to do? The legislation does not provide a clear answer to either question. The usual assumption in relation to the first question has been that expressed in *Caparo* v. *Dickman*,[139] namely that the accounts are intended for the benefit of the shareholders. However, this assumption becomes problematic when the directors and the shareholders are largely the same people, since the accounts are then a report by the directors to themselves in a different capacity, and the value of requiring such a report is not obvious. A further problem occurs even where the directors and the shareholders are not the same people, for it now appears that the shareholders as such are not entitled to rely on the audited accounts, or at least that they do so at their own risk, since neither the directors nor the auditors are liable to individual shareholders for errors in the accounts which cause them loss. Apparently the only remedy which shareholders have is their power to dismiss the directors if they do not like what the accounts reveal, or if they subsequently discover that the accounts have been negligently or dishonestly prepared. Even this is, of course, meaningless where the directors and the shareholders are the same people. So far as the second question is concerned, it seems impossible to deny that the present rules on form and content of accounts do little to promote the production of helpful and informative accounts, and may even impede that process, though the work of the

---

139. [1990] 1 All E.R. 568, H.L., discussed above.

Financial Reporting Council may lead to some progress in this respect. It is hard to resist the conclusion that in relation to private companies the statutory audit requirement serves little or no purpose (though it does impose costs on the company) and that the advantages of abolishing it considerably outweigh the disadvantages. From the point of view of the auditors it might plausibly be argued that the audit is a source of income without being a significant source of legal liability. Such an argument does nothing to enhance the status of the audit process. Unfortunately, the audit requirements are now enshrined in European Community Directives,[140] and it would not be possible for the United Kingdom unilaterally to abolish them, even if Parliament were to become convinced of the merits of doing so. For the smallest companies, the Companies Act 1985 (Audit Exemption) Regulations 1994[141] have eased the position somewhat, as discussed above.[142]

### 3.6 To whom is the auditors' duty owed?

This is a question of fundamental importance, for it determines the range of possible plaintiffs in an action based on the negligence of the auditors, as well as defining the losses which might be recoverable in such an action. The present position is to be deduced from the judgment of the House of Lords in *Caparo* v. *Dickman*.[143] The plaintiffs were shareholders in Fidelity plc, who alleged that they had retained their existing shares and launched a takeover bid for the company on the basis of the annual accounts for the year ending 31 March 1984, which had been audited by the defendants. The case reached the House of Lords on the preliminary question whether the defendants owed any duty to the plaintiffs. The House of Lords unanimously held that no duty was owed. The imposition of a duty of care in tort requires foreseeability of damage, proximity of relationship and the reasonableness of imposing such a duty.[144] Much of the importance of this decision has to do with general principles of the law of tort which lie beyond the scope of the present work.[145] However, some discussion of the specific company law and auditing implications is also appropriate.

The two principal speeches, those of Lord Bridge and Lord Oliver, both contain extensive citation from the dissenting judgment of Denning LJ in *Candler* v. *Crane Christmas & Co*,[146] a judgment later approved by the House of Lords in *Hedley Byrne* v. *Heller*.[147] The passages relied on are those where Denning LJ, advocating the view that an accountant might be liable for the economic loss suffered by a third party who relies on his accounts, seeks to limit that liability to those persons who were known to be going to act in reliance on the accounts. Such a restriction would of course be

140. The Fourth Directive (Directive 78/660 OJ 1978 L222/11) and the Seventh Directive (Directive 83/349 OJ 1983 L193/1).
141. S.I. 1994/1935; see also p. 249.
142. At p. 249.
143. [1990] 1 All E.R. 568.
144. *Per* Lord Bridge.
145. For commentary, see Evans (1989) 5 P.N. 16 and (1990) 6 P.N. 76; James (1990) 6 P.N. 69. Subsequent cases considering the general tort law implications of the case include *Morgan Crucible Co plc* v. *Hill Samuel Bank* [1990] 3 All E.R. 330; [1991] 1 All E.R. 148; *Lonrho plc* v. *Tebbit* [1991] 4 All E.R. 973.
146. [1951] 1 All E.R. 426, C.A.
147. [1964] A.C. 465.

highly significant in *Caparo*-type situations, since for the most part the auditors will not have specific knowledge that anyone is going to rely on the accounts.

There is also in these speeches some interesting consideration of three cases from other jurisdictions. In *Scott Group Ltd* v. *McFarlane*[148] a public company's accounts contained significant errors. Its financial circumstances made it vulnerable to a takeover bid, which duly materialised. The purchasers later discovered the errors and sought to sue the auditors. Their action failed, though the majority of the New Zealand Court of Appeal held that a duty of care was owed because it was foreseeably likely that someone would make a bid. Lord Bridge approved[149] the minority opinion of Richmond P to the effect that no duty of care could arise merely from the abstract possibility of a takeover bid where it was not shown that the auditor ought to have had in mind some particular bidder. Lord Oliver made the point[150] that the views of the majority were based on the test for liability laid down by Lord Wilberforce in *Anns* v. *Merton LBC*,[151] a test which has since been substantially modified by other decisions of the House of Lords.

In the well-known case of *Ultramares Corporation* v. *Touche*[152] the auditors were aware that the audited accounts would be shown to others as the basis of the company's financial dealings, but did not know that the company was specifically planning to seek financial help from the plaintiff. The plaintiff's claim against the auditors failed.

The final foreign case considered was the decision of the Outer House of the Court of Session in *Twomax Ltd* v. *Dickson McFarlane & Robinson*.[153] In that case three investors (one company and two individuals) had bought shares in a company which shortly thereafter went into liquidation. They sued the auditors, claiming that they had relied on the audited accounts and that these were materially inaccurate. The Lord Ordinary (Sewart) followed the majority view of the New Zealand Court of Appeal in *Scott Group Ltd* v. *McFarlane*, and thus by implication the views of Lord Wilberforce in *Anns* v. *Merton LBC*. Lord Oliver was thus able to dismiss this case also as founded on an obsolete notion of duties of care.

These cases taken together show an interesting common pattern of auditors being unaware of any specific likely reliance on the accounts, though obviously they will be aware that the accounts are likely to be relied on in some way at some point. This in turn raises the fundamental question, considered by both Lord Bridge and Lord Oliver, of the purpose of the statutory accounts, a question which has also been considered elsewhere in this chapter. Both their Lordships took a restrictive view of the purpose of the accounts, holding that this was restricted to the making of management decision by the shareholders in general meeting and did not extend to investment decisions by existing shareholders or others. This view is almost certainly unrealistic in a public company, where shareholders do not exercise any effective management powers and where the principal effect of the publication of the accounts is seen in movements of the share prices (largely based on the profit or loss figure)

---

148. [1978] 1 N.Z.L.R. 553.
149. [1990] 1 All E.R. 568 at 579.
150. *Ibid.* at 596.
151. [1977] 2 All E.R. 477 at 525.
152. (1931) 255 N.Y. 170.
153. 1982 S.C. 113.

which in turn will probably trigger buying and selling of the shares. In truth, the decision in this case must be seen as part of the more general trend to limit the scope of recovery in tort rather than being based on any very strong logic.

### 3.7 Case-law since Caparo

A number of subsequent cases have considered and developed the scope of the rule laid down in *Caparo* v. *Dickman*.

In *McNaughton* v. *Hicks Anderson*[154] the plaintiffs entered into negotiations to take over a rival company which was in financial difficulty. The target company's chairman asked its accountants to prepare draft accounts as quickly as possible. At a meeting between the plaintiffs and the target company these accounts were shown to the plaintiffs and a representative of the defendants told them that the company was breaking even or making a modest loss. The plaintiffs' case was that after completing the takeover they found that the target company was in a much worse position than this. The Court of Appeal held that the defendants had owed no duty of care to the plaintiffs in preparing the accounts or in making the oral statement at the meeting. The accounts were draft accounts and were prepared for the benefit of the target company; the defendants could not reasonably have foreseen that the plaintiffs would rely on them. The oral statement was intended only as a very general statement, and the defendants could not reasonably have foreseen that the plaintiffs would rely on it without further inquiry. The plaintiffs' case accordingly failed. Although the decision may be regarded as depending primarily on its own facts, those facts are sufficiently commonplace to make the case of some general interest. It will commonly happen that the accounts are prepared at the request of the target company rather than at the request of the bidder, just as the accounts will often be only draft accounts because of the need to produce them at short notice. It appears that in takeover situations a bidder wishing to rely on accounts must be prepared to commission the preparation of those accounts (and presumably to pay for them) and may have to wait long enough for the preparation of proper accounts. In *Morgan Crucible* v. *Hill Samuel*[155] the plaintiffs launched a contested takeover bid for another listed company. In the course of the takeover battle the target company and its advisers produced various defence documents, which included (on the facts assumed for the purposes of the preliminary hearing) untrue representations by the auditors as to the company's audited accounts and profit forecast. The auditors (and the other defendants, the target's directors and merchant bank) relied on *Caparo* as the basis for having the action struck out, but the Court of Appeal rejected this application. The representations made by the defendants were made after an identified bidder (the plaintiff company) had emerged and in the context of a takeover battle, which clearly made it much easier to argue that reliance by the plaintiffs on the statements was both foreseeable and reasonable. As against this it was argued for the auditors[156] that Morgan Crucible had not asked the defendants for this information, that the information was addressed to the directors and shareholders of the company, not to Morgan Crucible, that the interests of the shareholders of the company were in

154. [1991] 1 All E.R. 134, C.A.
155. [1991] 1 All E.R. 148, C.A.
156. *Ibid.* at 163g.

conflict with those of Morgan Crucible, that there was no financial or other connection between the auditors and Morgan Crucible and that the auditors at all times had access to separate advisers of their own. The Court of Appeal accepted that these were relevant arguments (though the relevance of the last point is not easy to see) and that at the trial of the substantive action they might well lead the judge, operating on the basis of known facts rather than assumed facts, to conclude that no duty of care was owed by the auditors. The limits of this case should therefore be understood. It decides only that it is possible for auditors to owe duties of care to identified bidders, if they make statements, knowing that those bidders are likely to rely on them as part of the takeover process.

*Berg* v. *Mervyn Hampton Adams*[157] was an action against auditors of an insolvent company for failure to qualify the 1982 accounts in relation to the recoverability of certain bills. The action was brought by the company and by a discount house which had discounted the bills. The company collapsed in 1985. At all material times all shares in the company were under the ultimate beneficial ownership of the sole executive director of the company. On the basis of *Caparo* v. *Dickman* it was held that the auditors owed no duty to the discounters of the bills. It is difficult to see how this conclusion could have been avoided. The company succeeded in its action against the auditors (an action founded on contract) but it was held that the company was entitled only to nominal damages. The executive director had not been misled by the accounts and had not relied on them. Moreover, there was no evidence that the error in relation to the 1982 accounts had contributed to the collapse of the company. The logic of this is difficult to challenge, but its practical effect appears to be that there will be virtually no case where mistakes in the accounts will entitle the company to substantial damages.

In *Anthony* v. *Wright*[158] the plaintiffs had placed money with a company for investment, and this money had been held on trust for them and had initially been segregated from other money of the company. At some stage the trust money had been fraudulently mixed with the funds of the company by the directors. The plaintiffs' action against the auditors was based upon the failure of the auditors to discover his fraud at an early stage. The auditors successfully applied to have the action struck out under R.S.C., Ord. 18, r. 19 as disclosing no cause of action and being an abuse of process. Lightman J observed that there was no apparent assumption by the auditors of any duty towards the plaintiffs and that the plaintiffs had expressly disavowed any reliance on the audit reports. In these circumstances the decision in *Caparo* v. *Dickman*[159] effectively precluded any possibility of holding that any duty of care existed.

In *White* v. *Jones*,[160] the House of Lords held that a solicitor who negligently prepares a will can be liable to an intended beneficiary who loses a bequest as a result of that negligence. This decision, in line with the controversial decision of Megarry V-C in *Ross* v. *Caunters*[161] (though the reasoning in that case was expressly

---

157. [1993] B.C.L.C. 1045, Hobhouse J.
158. (1994) *The Independent*, September 27 (Lightman J).
159. See fn. 143 above.
160. [1995] 1 All E.R. 691, H.L.
161. [1980] Ch. 297.

disapproved by Lord Goff[162]), might be thought to be at odds with the principles laid down in *Caparo* v. *Dickman*, since it accepts the idea of a tortious duty owed to third parties, even those third parties who cannot be considered to have relied on the solicitor. In *Anthony* v. *Wright* Lightman J dealt with an argument along these lines by describing *White* v. *Jones* as "in a category of its own". This pragmatic approach to determining the limits of liability may be regarded as typical of the English judicial method, though it may also be observed that the approach proposed by Lord Goff in *White* v. *Jones*, namely the extension of the *Hedley Byrne* special relationship to cases of this kind, would allow a legitimate distinction between *White* v. *Jones* and *Anthony* v. *Wright*, since it may be said that in the former case the contract (between solicitor and client) is entered into with the intention of benefiting the eventual plaintiff, whereas in the latter case the contract (between company and auditors) is not entered into for the benefit of the shareholders who would be the ultimate plaintiffs.

### 3.7.1  Foreseeability of damage

It is essential to show that the defendant could reasonably have foreseen that his negligence would lead to the plaintiff suffering damage of the type which in fact occurred, though such foreseeability of itself will not found liability.

### 3.7.2  Proximity of relationship

In addressing this question the court should look at the class of cases in which such duties have previously been held to exist, and should develop the law incrementally by analogy,[163] rather than trying to deduce some general principle which can then be applied to all cases. A relevant factor in deciding whether the duty to take care should be extended to a new situation is whether the type of loss which has been suffered is one which the defendant was under a duty to prevent; the court should ask whether this is the kind of case where it is pragmatically possible to conclude that a duty to take care exists.

### 3.7.3  Reasonableness of imposing a duty

This may be regarded as the least important of the three criteria, but it is clear from *Caparo* v. *Dickman* that it is now more important than it appeared to be at the time of *Anns* v. *Merton*[164] when Lord Wilberforce[165] characterised the question of whether there were policy grounds which ought to limit, exclude or restrict the scope of the duty as the second stage of the inquiry into the existence of a duty, with the implication that the burden was on the defendant to establish such grounds once the issue of foreseeability had been resolved in favour of the plaintiff. It is under this

---

162. *White* v. *Jones* [1995] 1 All E.R. at 710.
163. *Ibid*. at 712.
164. [1977] 2 All E.R. 492.
165. *Ibid*. at 525.

head that the court should consider the question whether the damage which occurred was damage of the type which it was the defendant's duty to prevent. This question is of course only another way of saying that the court must consider whether it is reasonable for liability for this loss to be imposed on the defendant. Indeed, the question itself may be regarded as circular, for it is impossible to decide whether it was the duty of the defendant to prevent this harm without also asking whether the defendant owed the plaintiff a duty in the first place. In the particular context of auditors' duties, however, it may be possible to make some sense of this question by asking whom the statutory audit is intended to protect and in relation to what. As indicated above,[166] this approach was regarded in *Caparo* v. *Dickman* as producing the answer that the accounts are designed to provide shareholders with information on which they can evaluate the performance of management and make appropriate strategic decisions, but not to be used as the basis for decisions about selling, retaining or buying shares in the company.

The conclusion to be drawn from *Caparo* v. *Dickman* must be that auditors conducting a statutory audit owe their duties to the company, but not to individual shareholders. Although Lord Bridge in *Caparo* v. *Dickman*[167] left open the possibility that the duty might be owed to shareholders as a class, it is not possible to take seriously any suggestion that this might allow a class action to be brought by all shareholders acting together. English law does not generally recognise actions of this kind, and there is anyway no possible basis for the action, since no individual shareholder could claim that any duty is owed to him. The only possible sensible interpretation of Lord Bridge's remarks is that the duty is owed to the company, and that the company is in a sense the shareholders collectively (though of course the doctrine of corporate personality means that the company is something separate from its body of corporators).

If the duty is not owed to individual current shareholders, it must follow that it is not owed to potential shareholders or to any other party (apart from the company). Thus it has been held that no duty is owed to a discount house which accepts bills drawn on the company, allegedly on the faith of the audited accounts.[168]

On the other hand there are cases which accept that duties can be owed to actual or potential investors, at least where auditors in auditing accounts know that those accounts will be relied upon for the purposes of making investment decisions. This was the situation in *Lloyd Cheyham & Co Ltd* v. *Littlejohn & Co*,[169] but that case could be dismissed on the ground that it pre-dates *Caparo* v. *Dickman* and should be treated as overruled by it. That argument is not available, however, in dealing with *Galoo* v. *Bright Grahame Murray*,[170] where on materially similar facts the court appears to have assumed without argument that a duty of care was owed. It is of course true that *Caparo* v. *Dickman* was not directly concerned with such cases and might be open to distinction on that ground, and it is interesting to observe that recent cases do seem to hold out once again the possibility of a duty of care on these facts.

---

166. See p. 265.
167. [1990] 1 All E.R. 568 at 580.
168. *Berg Sons & Co* v. *Mervyn Hampton Adams* [1993] B.C.L.C. 1045 (Hobhouse J).
169. [1987] B.C.L.C. 303 (Woolf J). For other aspects of this case, see p. 258.
170. [1995] 1 All E.R. 16, C.A.

### 3.8 Action by company

Where the accounts are negligently audited, it is clear that the auditors are in breach of duty to the company. Indeed, in such cases it will normally be possible for the company to sue in contract, since there will be a contract under which the auditors are engaged, and it will be at least an implied term of that contract that the audit be conducted with reasonable care and skill.[171] It may well be that the same duty will be owed in tort, though this point is unlikely to be of practical importance except in those cases where limitation of actions is in issue.[172]

The biggest difficulty likely to be faced by the company in bringing an action against the auditors is that of identifying any loss which it has suffered. The negligence will presumably contribute to the presentation to the annual general meeting and eventual filing at Companies House of inaccurate accounts, but this is unlikely to cause the company any immediate loss, whether the error overstates the profits or understates them. Management do not generally place great reliance on the audited accounts for internal purposes, since most companies will be required by their financiers to produce regular management accounts, which are more detailed and more up to date, and thus more reliable. Even where the audited accounts wrongly fail to reveal that the company is insolvent, it is unlikely that the failure to discover this promptly will cause further loss to the company (though it may of course cause loss to creditors, and even to directors if they are subsequently held liable for wrongful trading). This state of affairs may at first seem very odd, but it must be appreciated that it is the consequence of holding that the auditors owe their duties only to the company. The difficulties in this area are well illustrated by *Galoo* v. *Bright Grahame Murray*[173] where the plaintiffs included companies which had been taken over, allegedly in reliance on defective accounts. The new parent company had made substantial loans to them, but these loans had become irrecoverable when the companies went into liquidation. It was alleged by the plaintiffs that the acceptance of these loans caused the subsidiaries losses, and that the loans would never have been made if the accounts had been properly prepared, since they would then have shown that the subsidiaries were unprofitable and worthless. The Court of Appeal upheld the decision of the deputy judge to strike out these elements of the statement of claim on the ground that the mere acceptance of the loan could not amount to a loss—the company receiving the loan incurred a liability to repay the loan but received an asset of equal value, i.e., the loan itself. Of course, the use then made of the borrowed money might cause the company to incur losses, but that use was determined by the decisions of the company's directors, not by the defendants in the case.[174]

Another interesting and as yet unresolved question arises from the role at the present day of the rules of the Stock Exchange in relation to listed companies. These rules are for the most part delegated legislation under the Financial Services Act 1986, whereas at the time of *Caparo* v. *Dickman* they were merely the internal rules

---

171. Such a term would be implied by the Supply of Goods and Services Act 1982, s. 13: "In a contract for the supply of a service where the supplier is acting in the course of a business, there is an implied term that the supplier will carry out the service with reasonable care and skill."

172. As to this see below.

173. [1995] 1 All E.R. 16, C.A.

174. *Per* Glidewell LJ at 24c–d.

of an entirely self-regulating organisation.[175] The present rules require listed companies to produce audited accounts for the purpose of informing the investing public. Clearly, this falls short of overruling the decision in *Caparo* v. *Dickman*, even in the context of limited companies (it could have no application to unlisted companies) but it remains to be seen whether the new rules could be used as the basis for an argument that the auditors of listed companies owe their duties to shareholders individually. The major difficulty is that the listing rules impose burdens on companies not on auditors, and a failing in the accounts would thus seem to be a breach of duty by the auditors but not by anyone else.

## 3.9 Action by the directors

A question which has not yet been resolved by case-law concerns the extent to which directors who have been held liable as a result of errors in the accounts can pass any of that liability on to auditors. Such liability may be of various kinds. First, a director who signs accounts which fail to give the necessary true and fair view thereby commits a criminal offence[176] and may incur a fine. Secondly, the company may wish to sue a director for loss caused to it by the errors in the accounts. Finally, directors who have continued to trade on the basis of inaccurate accounts may possibly be held liable to contribute to the company's assets on the grounds of wrongful trading under the Insolvency Act 1986, s. 214. The various possibilities require to be considered separately.

### 3.9.1 Criminal penalties

The criminal penalties imposed on directors reflect and emphasise the fact that the accounts are the directors' accounts, not the auditors' accounts. The auditors merely express an opinion on those accounts—despite the contrary observations of Lord Bridge in *Caparo* v. *Dickman*,[177] echoing an error perpetrated by Denning LJ in *Candler* v. *Crane Christmas & Co*,[178] the auditors do not "certify" the accounts.[179] This contention is supported by the words of s. 235 of the Companies Act 1985, which requires the auditors to "state whether, *in their opinion*, the accounts have been properly prepared ... " (Emphasis added.)

### 3.9.2 Wrongful trading

Where the company is in financial difficulties, the question will at some point arise, whether there remains any reasonable prospect of avoiding insolvent liquidation. If the directors know or ought reasonably to know that there is no such prospect, then it becomes their duty to take "every step" with a view to minimising loss to creditors.[180] Failure to do so will render the directors liable on the insolvent liquidation of the company to make such contribution to the company's assets as the court, at the suit of

---

175. Evans (1990) 6 P.N. 76.
176. Companies Act 1985, s. 233(5).
177. [1990] 1 All E.R. 568, H.L.
178. [1951] 1 All E.R. 426, C.A.
179. On the question of "certificates" issued by the auditors, see fn. 258 below.
180. Insolvency Act 1986, s. 214.

271

the liquidator, may think just. In practice the requirement to take every step to minimise creditors' losses will often mean that the company must be put into liquidation as soon as the directors conclude that insolvent liquidation is inevitable (even if it would be possible to struggle on for somewhat longer). Inaccuracies in the accounts, involving overstatements of the profits and/or current shareholders' funds, may well be influential in causing the directors to misinterpret the company's prospects and thus to continue with the business after the time when it should have been put into liquidation. It is not clear that in such a case the directors will be liable for wrongful trading anyway, since it might be open to them to argue that they had no reason to know the true position. In this event, there would be no liability to pass on to the auditors. However, the difficulty with this argument is in principle the same as that previously discussed, namely that the accounts are the directors' accounts and they ought to be aware of the company's financial position, notwithstanding that the auditors do not spot errors in the accounts. If this view is followed strictly, then any loss to the company arising from the failure to take prompt action is not to be laid at the door of the auditors, whose errors cannot be considered to have caused that loss.

## 4 BREACH OF DUTY

Once it is established that the auditors have breached their duties, the question of remedies naturally arises. The remedy most commonly sought will be damages.

### 4.1 Damages

#### 4.1.1 Loss

The first problem is to establish that the company has suffered a loss. *Galoo* v. *Bright Grahame Murray*[181] was an action against auditors by two companies and their controlling shareholder, who had bought on the faith of the audited accounts, which were alleged to be materially wrong. The company was bought in 1987, and it collapsed in 1992. The loss alleged was that the companies had accepted loans and incurred trading losses. It was held that accepting a loan could not be considered a loss, since the actual acceptance of the loan produced neither an increase nor a decrease in the company's assets, the cash received being exactly matched by the obligation to repay the loan. Other points in the case are considered below.

#### 4.1.1.1 UNLAWFUL DIVIDENDS

A particular difficulty arises where a company has declared unlawful dividends in reliance on improperly prepared accounts which appear to show that there is profit available for distribution. It is not obvious why the payment of a dividend should be regarded as causing a loss to the company. Certainly it appears a strange use of language to describe a lawful dividend in those terms, notwithstanding that money is obviously paid out of the company, and there is no obvious reason why an unlawful

181. [1994] 1 W.L.R. 1360, C.A.

dividend should be different in this context. Despite this, in the two cases where the question has arisen, *Leeds Estate Building and Investment Co* v. *Shepherd*[182] and *Re Thomas Gerrard & Son Ltd*,[183] it was assumed, without argument, that the payment of an unlawful dividend caused a loss to the company. It is submitted that these cases should not be regarded as decisive of the point, since the question was never raised in either case.

#### 4.1.1.2 LIMITATION OF LIABILITY

The Companies Act, s. 310 makes void any term in an agreement between a company and its auditors under which the company agrees to exclude or limit any liability of the auditor for breach of duty in connection with the conduct of the audit. The question of possible limits on auditors' liability has been much discussed. In 1989 the Likierman Report on Professional Liability[184] recommended that the liability of auditors and directors for failures in the accounts should be several and not joint (since it is normally preferable to sue the auditors, who may be expected to have insurance cover) and that auditors should prefer to negotiate as a matter of contract limits to their liabilities for audit work, subject always to the Unfair Contract Terms Act 1977. Neither of these suggestions were adopted in the Companies Act 1989, but the suggestion of several liability has recently been raised again, and the question has been referred to the Law Commission for consideration. An obvious difficulty arising from the proposal is that of deciding in any given case how the responsibility should be apportioned between, for example, the directors on the one hand and the auditors on the other.

### 4.1.2 Causation

Even where it is clear that auditors have been negligent and loss can be established, liability will not arise unless it can also be shown that this advice was the cause of the loss suffered by the plaintiff. This is a general principle in both contract and tort, and its application in the present context is well illustrated in the case of *JEB Fasteners Ltd* v. *Marks Bloom & Co*,[185] where the defendants negligently allowed the inclusion of inflated stock values in a set of statutory accounts, knowing that the company concerned was seeking outside finance. The plaintiffs took over the company, having seen the accounts. On discovering the truth the plaintiffs claimed damages from the defendants, but Woolf J held that the plaintiffs had not in fact relied on the defendants' report because they had effectively decided to acquire the company anyway. Consequently the claim for damages failed. Although it is uncertain whether any duty on the part of the auditors to the plaintiffs would be recognised at the present day,[186] this does not affect the specific point that causation of loss by the defendant's actions must always be established.

More recently, in *Berg Sons & Co* v. *Mervyn Hampton Adams*[187] an action was

---

182. (1887) 36 Ch.D. 787 (Stirling J).
183. [1967] 2 All E.R. 525 (Pennycuick J).
184. HMSO; see also Martyn (1990) 6 P.N. 36.
185. [1981] 3 All E.R. 289 (Woolf J).
186. *Caparo* v. *Dickman* [1990] 1 All E.R. 568 at 579 *per* Lord Bridge.
187. [1993] B.C.L.C. 1045 (Hobhouse J).

brought by an insolvent company against its auditors for failure to qualify the 1982 accounts in relation to the recoverability of certain bills. The company collapsed in 1985. At all material times all shares in the company were under the ultimate beneficial ownership of the sole executive director of the company. Hobhouse J held that the company was entitled only to nominal damages. The executive director had not been misled by the accounts and had not relied on them. Moreover, there was no evidence that the error in relation to the 1982 accounts had contributed to the collapse of the company. This point is emphasised by the decision of the Privy Council in *Deloite Haskins & Sells* v. *National Mutual Life Nominees Ltd.*[188] Plaintiffs were trustees for a licensed deposit-taker in New Zealand. Under local legislation such deposit-takers were required to have a trustee, whose job was to exercise ongoing monitoring of the deposit-taker's activities. The deposit-taker had to deliver to the trustee every half year an auditor's report on the business stating, *inter alia*, whether he had become aware of any breaches of the trust deed (into which various provisions were implied by law) and whether there was any other matter which in his opinion called for investigation by the trustee in the interests of the depositors. The auditor was also under a duty to notify the trustee if at any time he became aware in the course of performing his duties as auditor of anything which might be relevant to the exercise of the powers of the trustee. In early 1986, while preparing the year-end report for 1985, the defendants became concerned about certain aspects of the deposit-taker's financial status. In May 1986 they made a report to the plaintiffs about this, but the company continued to trade until August 1986, when another report relating to an associated company caused the whole group to be put into liquidation. The plaintiffs incurred a liability of $6.75m to depositors, and claimed to be indemnified by the defendants on the ground that the defendants should have reported by March 1986 on the state of the company. The Privy Council held that the duty to report depended upon the actual state of knowledge of the defendants, i.e., they only came under that duty when they had formed the necessary opinion in the course of their duties as auditors. There was no duty for them to be actively on watch for irregularities. For this reason the duty to report had not arisen by March 1986, and in any event the company was insolvent by the end of 1985 at the latest. An earlier report would not have altered that fact; indeed, it would have caused the plaintiffs' liability to depositors to materialise at an earlier stage. The logic of these two cases is difficult to challenge, but its practical effect appears to be that there will be very few cases where mistakes in the accounts will entitle the company to substantial damages.

### 4.1.2.1 TRADING LOSSES

In *Galoo* v. *Bright Grahame Murray*[189] the Court of Appeal held that two companies which had suffered losses through continuing to trade at a time when proper accounts would have shown them to be insolvent could not recover for the trading losses, because these had not been shown to have been caused by the mistakes in the accounts, although the mistakes had provided the background and opportunity for them. On the other hand their parent company, which had invested on the faith of the accounts, could sue for its loss (i.e., the loss of its investment) which was caused by

188. [1993] 2 All E.R. 1015, P.C.
189. See fn. 181 above.

reliance on the accounts.[190] This distinction between acts which cause the loss and acts which merely provide the setting for it is of general importance in this context.

### 4.1.2.2 UNLAWFUL DIVIDENDS[191]

In *Leeds Estate Building and Investment Co* v. *Shepherd*[192] there had been unlawful payments of dividends out of capital. It appeared that the auditors had not checked the accounts properly. The auditors were held liable for these payments because they were a direct consequence of the breach of duty. In *Re Thomas Gerrard & Son Ltd*[193] unlawful dividends were paid because the auditors had for years accepted the word of a fraudulent managing director as to various matters. It was held that the auditors' breach of duty[194] was the direct cause of the loss arising from the unlawful distributions, and this was recoverable from the auditors. Once it is accepted that the payment of the dividends caused a loss to the company,[195] the question of remoteness of damage arises.

### 4.1.3 Remoteness

Because most of the recent reported actions against auditors have failed on the question of causation, there is little authority on the question of remoteness of damage in this specific context. It appears that the general principles of remoteness of damage, laid down for the law of tort in *The Wagon Mound*[196] and for contract in a line of cases from *Hadley* v. *Baxendale* to *Parsons* v. *Uttley Ingham*,[197] will apply to such cases.

### 4.1.4 Burden of proof

In *Re Republic of Bolivia Exploration Syndicate Ltd*[198] it was held that if the audited accounts do not show the true position and loss is occasioned thereby, the onus is on the auditors to show that they have not committed any breach of duty. This appears to suggest that the burden of proof is effectively reversed in these circumstances. It is submitted, however, that the case should not be regarded as establishing so general a proposition. Certainly, errors in the accounts do call for some explanation, but it remains a matter for the court to decide whether there has been any breach of duty. It has already been emphasised that mistakes in the accounts are not of themselves proof of negligence.

In the same case Astbury J said that auditors are prima facie responsible for *ultra vires* payments made on the faith of their balance sheet. The most likely kind of *ultra vires* payment at the present day would be an illegal dividend based on a misconception of the true level of profits. The observations made in the previous paragraph would seem to apply with equal force to this example.

---

190. For the problems arising from a shareholders' attempt to claim reliance on the accounts, see p. 264.
191. See also above under "Loss".
192. (1887) 36 Ch.D. 787 (Stirling J).
193. [1967] 2 All E.R. 525 (Pennycuick J).
194. For further discussion of the breach of duty see p. 272.
195. As to which, see p. 272 above.
196. [1914] 1 Ch. 139 (Astbury J).
197. [1978] Q.B. 791, C.A. Other important cases include *Newman* v. *Victoria Laundry* [1948] 2 All E.R. 806 and *The Heron II* [1969] 1 A.C. 350.
198. [1914] 1 Ch. 139 (Astbury J).

On the other hand Astbury J said in the same case that it is a question of fact to what extent the auditors' failure to spot illegal payments made before the audit is evidence of negligence. If this means that the normal burden of proof on the plaintiff applies to such cases, it is clearly correct. However, the obvious undesirability of having a different burden of proof for the two previous examples serves to emphasise the need to retain the normal burden of proof in all cases.

### 4.1.5 Auditors' negligence and limitation of actions

Even where it is established that the auditors have been negligent and that their negligence has caused loss, the question of limitation of actions may still be relevant. As has been seen above, it is now more or less settled that the only action against auditors is that of the company, which will be an action in contract, and will therefore become time-barred six years after the date on which it accrues. In actions founded on contract time runs from the date of the breach of contract,[199] even of the plaintiff suffers only nominal damage at that point. It appears, however, that in most cases it will be open to the company to sue in tort as an alternative to the contract action.[200] In those rare cases where the action can be brought by someone other than the company the action will obviously have to be in tort. In an action founded on tort time runs from the date when the cause of action accrues,[201] subject to the possibility of relying on the Latent Damage Act 1986. The cause of action accrues when the defendant's breach of duty causes the plaintiff to suffer some loss which is more than merely trivial.[202] In cases of reliance on accounts the loss will almost always be purely economic, and in such cases it is clear from *Forster* v. *Outred & Co*[203] and *Moore* v. *DW Ferrier & Co*[204] that the cause of action accrues as soon as any loss is suffered in reliance on the accounts. Thus, the declaration of the first unlawful dividend based on the accounts would be enough to set time running, even if there are further unlawful dividends later based on the same accounts. At the same time it is clear that each set of negligently audited accounts gives rise to a fresh cause of action. It is also well settled that there will be no cause of action in tort until the plaintiff suffers some loss which is actionable. The difficult questions of causation discussed above lead to the conclusion that by no means all losses can be laid at the door of the auditors. In particular, the kind of ongoing trading loss which would pose difficult limitation questions will not normally be recoverable because of the principle stated in *Galoo* v. *Bright Grahame Murray*, discussed above. It appears that recoverable losses will normally result from a single readily identifiable (and dateable) act of reliance, so that the question of accrual of cause of action will rarely cause much difficulty.

Given that the errors in the auditing of the accounts may not come to light for some time, it is necessary to consider how the Latent Damage Act may help the company. The Act provides an alternative period of limitation of three years from the "starting

199. *Gibbs* v. *Guild* (1882) 8 Q.B.D. 296.
200. *Henderson* v. *Merret Syndicates* [1994] 3 All E.R. 506, H.L., is the latest case on this long-running controversy, and appears to establish for the moment that the law sees no objection to such concurrent rights of action.
201. Limitation Act 1980, s. 2.
202. *Pirelli General Cable Works* v. *Oscar Faber & Partners* [1983] 2 A.C. 1, H.L.
203. [1988] 1 W.L.R. 86, C.A.
204. [1988] 1 All E.R. 418, C.A.

date", i.e., the earliest time when the plaintiff has knowledge (actual or constructive) of all the facts relevant to the cause of action. In most cases of errors in auditing the plaintiff will have no actual knowledge of the errors for some considerable time, but there is a danger that it will be held to have constructive knowledge, since the directors are personally responsible for the accuracy of the accounts and ought to have known the true position anyway. If this argument is accepted as a matter of principle, the result would appear to be that in all cases time will run against the company from the day the auditors express their opinion on the accounts. The same argument does not necessarily apply to any third party who might be able to sue, since there will often be no onus on the third party to know the true position.

### 4.1.6 Revision of defective accounts and reports

The 1989 Act has introduced some new provisions relating to the revision of accounts and reports which are subsequently shown to have been defective in some respect. Prior to this Act there was no provision for amending accounts once they had been audited and approved by the general meeting, even where it subsequently became apparent that the original accounts had been inaccurate. Section 245 empowers the directors of the company to prepare revised accounts or a revised report if they see fit. This may be done by producing an entirely new set of accounts and report or by the less drastic expedient of preparing a supplementary note which can be appended to the original accounts.[205] The detailed rules on this subject are contained in the Companies (Revision of Defective Accounts and Report) Regulations 1990.[206] These require that the revised accounts (or where appropriate, the supplementary note) be prepared as at the date of the original accounts[207] and that they give a true and fair view as at that date.[208] Thus, matters arising between the date of the original accounts and the date when the revision is in fact prepared are to be ignored. The auditors must report on the revision in the same way as they reported on the individual accounts,[209] and must also state whether in their view the original accounts failed to comply with the Act in the respects identified by the directors and relied on by them as the reason for preparing the revision.[210] This is of course a source of potential embarrassment for auditors, who may have reported on the original accounts and expressed the opinion that those accounts did in fact give a true and fair view. When commenting on the revision, they will no doubt be asked to state that the original accounts did not give a true and fair view, the obvious implication of which is that they were mistaken in their first opinion. For this reason it is likely that in most cases different auditors will be asked to report on the revised accounts, though the Regulations[211] do clearly contemplate the possibility that the same auditors will be used.

Under section 245A the Secretary of State is empowered to call upon the directors of a company for an explanation of any matters relating to the accounts or report

205. Companies Act 1985, s. 245(2).
206. S.I. 1990/2570.
207. *Ibid.*, reg. 6.
208. *Ibid.*
209. *Ibid.*, regs 6 and 7.
210. *Ibid.*, reg. 6(3).
211. *Ibid.*, reg. 6.

which raise a question as to whether the accounts have been prepared in accordance with the Act. If he is not satisfied with the explanation given by the directors, he may apply to court for an order under section 245B requiring the directors to prepare revised accounts, and, where appropriate, to have them properly audited. Section 245C allows the Secretary of State to authorise other persons to make application to the court for the same purpose. This power has been exercised in the Companies (Defective Accounts) (Authorised Persons) Order 1991.[212] This order confers the power to make such applications on the Accounting Standards Board, which is a subsidiary organ of the Financial Reporting Council. This power has already been exercised in a small number of cases, all of them relating to public listed companies, and it is inevitable that the cases which attract sufficient controversy and interest to warrant the expense of making an application will relate almost exclusively to such companies, which tend to have a large number of shareholders and whose accounts are subject to considerable critical expert scrutiny in a way which does not happen to private companies.

## 5 OTHER DUTIES OF AUDITORS

### 5.1 Other duties of auditors

Apart from the auditing of the annual accounts, there are a few other situations under the Companies Acts where auditors as such may be called upon to express an opinion on some aspect of the company's affairs. Although auditors cannot be compelled to express such opinions, even where justified in doing so, the fact that, in most cases, the company cannot lawfully undertake a proposed transaction without the benefit of a favourable opinion from the auditors, makes it inappropriate for the auditors to refuse to give proper consideration to the question.

### 5.1.1 Section 271 statement

Where a company wishes to make a distribution of assets (usually but not necessarily in the form of a dividend) the directors will need to consider whether there are sufficient profits available for distribution within the meaning of section 263 of the Companies Act 1985. This question is normally to be decided by reference to the company's last annual accounts.[213] Where the auditors' report on those accounts is not an unqualified report that the accounts have been prepared in accordance with the Companies Act 1985, section 271(4) imposes a further prerequisite to the legality of the distribution. This is that the auditors must have stated in writing whether in their opinion the matter in respect of which their report is qualified is material for the purpose of determining whether the distribution would be unlawful. A copy of their statement on this subject must have been laid before the company in general meeting.

---

212. S.I. 1991/13.
213. Companies Act 1985, s. 271.

This provision gives rise to some practical difficulties. Most qualifications to the annual accounts are capable of affecting some item of the profit and loss account and thus of having some impact on the level of distributable profits. The exact extent of that impact will often be difficult to gauge, with the result that it will be difficult for the auditors to say with confidence that the qualification is not material for distribution purposes. The directors of the company will naturally want them to make such a statement, even though section 271 does not say that the making of a statement in those terms is a prerequisite to the legality of the distribution—the requirement is only that the auditors must have stated *whether* the qualification is material. It is clear that a strict adherence to the letter of the section may create considerable difficulties even for a perfectly legitimate distribution. The solution most commonly adopted to deal with this problem is not to ask the auditors to express an opinion on the effect of their qualification in the abstract, but to wait until the company contemplates a specific distribution and to ask the auditors to confirm that the qualification is not material for the purposes of that distribution; in other words, though the statement will not be phrased in this way, to say that at all events the distribution which is proposed can legitimately go ahead. A statement of this kind can properly be made where the maximum possible effect of the qualification on the level of distributable profit can be calculated and where it can be seen that even allowing for this hypothetical effect there is still enough profit to support the distribution.

There is no authority dealing specifically with possible liabilities incurred by the auditors in connection with the making of a section 271(4) statement. Presumably such liability cannot arise unless the company relies on the statement, since the statement could not otherwise cause loss. Such reliance might take either of two forms—a distribution could be made which would otherwise not have been made, or the company could refrain from making a distribution which it would otherwise have made. In the former case the position would seem to be the same as that which arises where the company relies on unqualified annual accounts as the basis for a distribution which cannot in fact be supported out of profits. In such cases the authorities discussed earlier suggest that the auditors may well be liable for the cost to the company of the unlawful distribution.[214] If the company refrains from making a distribution which could have been made, then the loss will be much harder to quantify. There is no obligation on a company to distribute all its profits, so non-distribution is not in itself a wrong. Moreover, the company will not have lost money by the non-distribution; indeed, it will have preserved its assets. There will no doubt be a loss to shareholders, who are deprived of a dividend which they would otherwise have received, but, as has been seen,[215] it is now settled that the auditors owe no duty to individual shareholders when conducting the audit, and it is suggested that the arguments deployed in *Caparo* v. *Dickman*[216] for rejecting a duty in these circumstances apply with equal force to the making of a section 217 statement, which is certainly intended to help the company in a management decision, i.e., how much to distribute, rather than to help individual shareholders. It therefore seems unlikely

---

214. See the discussion at pp. 274–275.
215. *Caparo* v. *Dickman* [1990] 1 All E.R. 568, H.L.
216. [1990] 1 All E.R. 568, H.L.

that the auditors risk any action beyond a breach of contract claim in which they might be required to repay some or all of the fee which they received for making the statement.

### 5.1.2 Statement in connection with financial assistance

Where a company proposes to give financial assistance for the purpose of its own shares in accordance with Part V, Chapter VI of the Companies Act 1985, section 156 of that Act requires the directors, before the assistance is given, to make a statutory declaration to the effect that in their opinion there will be no ground on which, immediately following the giving of the assistance, the company could be found to be unable to pay its debts and either, if it is intended to commence the winding up of the company within 12 months of that date, that the company will be able to pay its debts in full within 12 months of the commencement of the winding up, or, where there is no intention to commence the winding up within 12 months, that the company will be able to pay its debts as they fall due during the 12 months immediately following the giving of the assistance.[217] The role of the auditors in this process is that the directors' statutory declaration must have annexed to it a report addressed to them by the auditors stating that they have inquired into the affairs of the company and that they are not aware of anything to indicate that the opinion expressed by the directors in their statutory declaration is unreasonable in all the circumstances.[218] The wording of this statement calls for careful consideration. First, the Act gives no further guidance on the nature of the inquiry into the company's affairs which the auditors must conduct. It is submitted that as a matter of principle it is necessary for the auditors to conduct such inquiry as will give them sufficient factual basis to be able to make their statement with reasonable confidence. The purpose of the section is clearly to involve the auditors in checking on the position of the company and on the opinion of the directors. It is a safeguard intended to protect against the making of rash declarations by the directors. This intention cannot be fulfilled unless the auditors take reasonable care in making their investigations. It follows that making a report under section 156(4) without making reasonable inquiry is a breach of the duty which the auditors owe to the company.

In relation to the giving of financial assistance it is easy to see how loss could result from a breach of this duty; if the company's financial position is unreasonably weakened by the giving of assistance which should not have been given, there is obvious loss, and the auditors will be liable if their negligent failure to make proper inquiries is a contributory factor in this loss. It may once again be assumed that there will be no liability to any other party, though it should be noted that in cases of financial assistance the purchaser of the shares will normally be greatly interested in the financial stability of the company and may place some reliance on the auditors' statement. The second point about the subsection concerns the very limited nature of the statement which the auditors are called upon to make. They are not asked to warrant the accuracy of the directors' opinions; they are merely asked to state that they have found nothing to indicate that the opinions are unreasonable. Thus, the

217. Companies Act 1985, s. 156(2).
218. *Ibid.*, s. 156(4).

auditors can in good faith make the statement as long as it appears to them that the opinion is one which the directors could reasonably hold, even though they may think that on the balance of probabilities the opinion is inaccurate. It follows that there will be very few cases where the auditors cannot properly make the necessary statement, so that the risk of liability for negligence in the making of it will in practice be less than might at first sight appear.

An alternative situation of difficulty for the auditors occurs where the directors ask them for a report under section 156 and they refuse to give it, saying that they are not satisfied that the statutory statement is true. If their opinion is a proper one, then there can be no question of any liability to anyone, but it may be alleged that they are negligent in their refusal. In practice the question is often likely to be resolved by the removal of the auditors under section 391(1) of the Companies Act 1985, but even this may not end the matter, since the company may suffer loss if the statement is not made in time to allow a particular deal to be completed. It has been suggested above that auditors are under a duty to make all necessary inquiries to form a proper view on the question, and it would be very odd if they were liable for negligently making the statutory statement but not for negligently refusing to make the same statement. It appears that the company will, as usual, be the only possible plaintiff in these circumstances.

### 5.1.3 Comment on directors' report

Section 235(3) of the Companies Act 1985 requires the auditors to consider whether the information given in the directors' report for the year for which the accounts are prepared is consistent with those accounts. If they think that it is not so consistent they shall state the fact in their report. It is to be noted that there is no positive duty to state that the information is consistent, though it may properly be deduced from the absence of a statement under this subsection that the auditors do consider it consistent, since they would otherwise have been under a duty to make a statement. Auditors should therefore be aware that silence on this point is to be treated as making a positive representation; they should take care to direct their minds to the question of consistency and should not let it go by default. It is also to be noted that section 235(3) imposes no duty on auditors to state in what respects the accounts and the report are inconsistent. Clearly, the auditors' report will be more helpful to the members if it does make this clear.

### 5.1.4 Resignation and removal of auditors

Auditors who resign during their term of office (whether at the annual general meeting or not) or who are removed from office by the company under section 391(1) of the Companies Act 1985 have certain rights and duties.

Auditors who wish to resign are governed by sections 392–394A of the Companies Act 1985. They must deposit a notice of their wish to resign at the company's registered office, and the notice takes effect on the day of deposit or on such later day as may be specified in it.[219] In order to be effective the notice of resignation must be accompanied by the statement required by section 394. This statement must disclose

---

219. *Ibid.*, s. 392(2).

any circumstances connected with the resignation which the auditor considers ought to be brought to the attention of members or creditors. If there are no such circumstances, the notice must state that fact.[220] The notice must be delivered not less than 14 days before the time for next appointing auditors.[221] Failure to deliver the necessary notice at the proper time is an offence.[222]

The auditor may (but is not obliged to) deposit with the notice a signed requisition calling on the directors forthwith to convene an extraordinary general meeting for the purpose of receiving and considering such explanation of the circumstances connected with his resignation as he may wish to place before that meeting.[223] The directors must convene such a meeting within 21 days of receiving the request, and the meeting must be convened for a date no more than 28 days after the date on which the notice is sent out.[224] Failure to comply is an offence punishable by a fine.[225] The auditor may also ask the company to circulate to its members before such a meeting a written statement of reasonable length setting out the circumstances connected with his resignation.[226] Unless the company receives the statement too late for it to do so, it must disclose the existence of the statement in any notice of the meeting given to members of the company and must send a copy of the statement to all members who have received notice of the meeting.[227] If the company does not send out the notice, for whatever reason, the auditor may require that it be read out at the meeting.[228] The only exception to these duties imposed on the company occurs where the court is satisfied on the application of the company or any other aggrieved party that the rights conferred on the auditor under section 392A are being abused to secure needless publicity for defamatory matter. In such a case the court may disapply those rights and may order the auditor to bear the costs of the application.[229]

An auditor may at any time be removed by an ordinary resolution of the company, notwithstanding anything in any agreement between the company and the auditor.[230] This right of the company is without prejudice to any right to compensation (e.g., for breach of contract) which the auditor may have as a result of being removed.[231] An auditor who is so removed retains all the rights conferred on auditors by section 390 of the Companies Act 1985.[232]

Where it is proposed to remove an auditor before the expiry of his term of office or to appoint as auditor someone other than a retiring auditor, special notice must be given to the company,[233] which must immediately send a copy to the auditor proposed to be removed or nor reappointed and, where applicable, to the person proposed to

220. *Ibid.*, s. 392(1).
221. *Ibid.*, s. 394(2).
222. *Ibid.*, s. 394A(1).
223. *Ibid.*, s. 392A(2).
224. *Ibid.*, s. 392A(5).
225. *Ibid.*
226. *Ibid.*, s. 392A(3).
227. *Ibid.*, s. 392A(4).
228. *Ibid.*, s. 392A(6).
229. *Ibid.*, s. 392A(7).
230. *Ibid.*, s. 391(1).
231. *Ibid.*, s. 391(4).
232. For the details of these rights, see p. 251.
233. Companies Act 1985, s. 391A(1).

be appointed as the new auditor.[234] Section 391A goes on to duplicate the provisions of section 392A in relation to the rights of the (potentially) outgoing auditor to have a copy of his representations as to his removal circulated to the members or read out at the meeting,[235] subject to a power for the court to disapply this right and make orders as to costs in the case of defamatory material.[236]

Under the elective regime for small companies introduced by the Companies Act 1989 it is possible to dispense with the annual appointment of auditors, so that auditors continue in office unless and until removed.[237] When this option has been exercised the removal of the auditors is governed by section 393 of the Companies Act 1985. Under this section any member of the company may deposit at the registered office of the company notice in writing proposing that the appointment of the company's auditors be brought to an end.[238] No member may deposit more than one such notice in any financial year of the company,[239] though there is nothing to prevent the deposit of successive notices by different members of the company. The directors of the company must then within 14 days[240] convene an extraordinary general meeting for a date not more than 28 days after the date on which the notice was given and at that extraordinary general meeting must propose a resolution in a form enabling the company to decide whether or not to terminate the appointment of the auditors.[241] It is suggested that a resolution to remove the auditors will usually be the simplest and most appropriate way to do this. If the directors fail to convene the meeting as required by the section, any one or more of the members depositing the notice may proceed to convene the meeting,[242] which must be held within three months of the date of the deposit of the notice. If the extraordinary general meeting decides that the appointment of the auditors should be brought to an end, the effect is that the auditors will not be deemed to be reappointed when next they would have otherwise been so deemed.[243] Further, if the notice was deposited in the period immediately following the distribution of accounts (up to 14 days after the date on which the annual accounts were sent to the members) the deemed reappointment of the auditors for the financial year following that to which those accounts relate ceases to have effect.[244] As with other provisions relating to the removal of auditors section 393 overrides anything to the contrary contained in any agreement between the company and the auditors.[245] More unusually, the auditors are not entitled to compensation or damages as a result of removal under this section,[246] apparently again irrespective of any agreement between them and the company on the subject.

---

234. *Ibid.*, s. 391A(2).
235. *Ibid.*, s. 391A(4) and (5).
236. *Ibid.*, s. 391A(6).
237. *Ibid.*, s. 386, as substituted by the Companies Act 1989.
238. *Ibid.*, s. 393(1).
239. *Ibid.*
240. *Ibid.*, s. 393(4).
241. *Ibid.*, s. 393(2).
242. *Ibid.*, s. 393(4).
243. *Ibid.*, s. 393(3).
244. *Ibid.*
245. *Ibid.*, s. 393(7).
246. *Ibid.*

## 6 NON-STATUTORY FUNCTIONS OF AUDITORS

### 6.1 Valuations

Apart from the statutory cases mentioned above, there are also situations where the auditors are asked to perform other roles. The most common of these occurs where the company's articles, or a share transfer agreement, provides that the value of the company or its shares for the purposes of the share transfer shall be determined by the auditors. It is clear that this is no part of the statutory audit function, with the result that the rules discussed above concerning the duties and role of the auditors are not applicable. Auditors who undertake such a task should therefore be aware that the relative immunity from suit conferred by the *Caparo* v. *Dickman* line of cases will not necessarily help them.

A further point which follows on from this is that auditors are under no duty to perform this kind of valuation role at all. They will not be parties to the articles nor to any share transfer deal in which their help is likely to be sought. Auditors may wish to consider whether it it really appropriate for them to perform this task.

When the auditors do undertake such a valuation, a number of issues may arise.

### 6.1.1  Liability for negligence

It was for a long time thought that auditors (and other experts) acting as valuers were immune from liability for negligence in the exercise of their functions. The argument in favour of this immunity was that by the nature of their task valuers were likely to upset one party, if not both, and that it was important for them to be able to do their work without fear of a negligence action by the aggrieved party. This view was made more tenable by the general view, based on a series of cases,[247] that a valuation could in any event be challenged in legal proceedings on the basis that it was negligently made. However, in *Arenson* v. *Arenson*[248] the House of Lords held that the immunity from suit extends only to arbitrators and not to valuers. The auditors or other valuers are considered to be acting as arbitrators only where there is a pre-formulated dispute which has been remitted to a third party to resolve through the exercise of judicial functions, the parties having agreed to abide by that person's decision. This requirement will rarely be satisfied in the share valuation cases, since there is normally no pre-formulated dispute. In any event it is usual to provide in the document referring the matter to the auditors (normally the articles of association of the company, though this need not be so) that they are to act as experts not as arbitrators, so that the question of their status does not usually arise. In those few cases where it does arise the parties need to take care how they proceed. In *Leigh* v. *English Property Corp*[249] the plaintiff could by agreement under certain circumstances require the defendant to buy out his shares in the company at a fair value, with the auditors to certify a fair value in default of agreement. The plaintiff sued on

247. These cases include *Frank H Wright (Construction) Ltd* v. *Frodoor Ltd* [1967] 1 All E.R. 433 (Roskill J); *Dean* v. *Prince* [1954] Ch. 409 where Denning LJ suggests that the valuation can be impugned for error; and *Burgess* v. *Purchase & Sons Ltd* [1983] Ch. 216, a decision of Nourse J which follows *Dean* v. *Prince*. See also the discussion below of the finality of the valuers' decision.
248. [1977] A.C. 405, H.L.
249. [1976] 2 Lloyd's Rep. 298, C.A.

the agreement, claiming a particular value for the shares, though at that stage the auditors had not stated a value. The question was whether the auditors acted as valuers or as arbitrators. If the latter, the plaintiff was entitled to continue the action, since the defendant had taken a step and was therefore barred from seeking a stay. By contrast, if the auditors acted as valuers, the action was clearly premature and would probably have been incompetent anyway since the valuation would not normally be open to challenge. The defendant applied under R.S.C., Ord. 18, r. 19 to have the action struck out, alleging that the auditors acted as valuers. It was held that the point was arguable, so that the action should not be struck out. The moral of the case is that a defendant who is confronted with an action of this kind would be well advised to seek a stay of the action immediately, i.e., before taking any other step.

### 6.1.2 Finality of certificate

A question which has given rise to much difficulty over the years is the extent, if any, to which a valuation performed in these circumstances may be challenged by either party. On the one hand it may be said that neither party should be prejudiced by a mistake made by the valuers. On the other hand it may be said that the whole point of submitting the question to a third party is to obtain an impartial opinion which is then binding on both buyers and sellers.

A very important case in the development of this line of authority is *Campbell* v. *Edwards*.[250] This concerned a valuation of a lease on an agreed surrender (not by auditors or accountants). The question was whether the valuation was conclusive, and the Court of Appeal held that it was, having been made in good faith. Although this case does not involve auditors, the general principle which it lays down clearly applies to all cases of expert independent valuation, and the judgments in the case show a clear awareness of the issues relating to the finality of the valuation and a definite decision in favour of finality.

The following year the Court of Appeal had the opportunity to deal with very similar issues in the context of a shares valuation by auditors. The case was *Baber* v. *Kenwood Manufacturing Co Ltd*,[251] where the auditors were expressed to act as "experts not arbitrators". One party declined to accept the valuation, alleging that it was made on the wrong basis. He also sought to sue the auditors for negligence in the valuation, but did not allege bad faith. It was held that the parties must be understood to have accepted the risk of honest error by the auditors and the valuation could not be impugned on this ground. The case may be treated as being authority for the proposition that a non-speaking valuation (i.e., one in which no reasons for the valuation are given) cannot be challenged for honest error.

The most recent and most authoritative consideration of this question may be found in *Jones* v. *Sherwood Computing*[252] where a share sale agreement required accountants (not auditors) to be appointed by each side to agree a valuation, with reference to a third firm if the first two could not agree. The third firm were called in and made a valuation, which accepted entirely the conclusions of one of the first two firms, though no reasons for the conclusion were stated in the final valuation. One

250. [1976] 1 All E.R. 785, C.A.
251. [1978] 1 Lloyd's Rep. 175, C.A.
252. [1992] 1 W.L.R. 277, C.A.

party now wished to challenge the valuation for error. The Court of Appeal refused to allow this. In the light of previous cases the conclusion is unsurprising, but the case is interesting for a number of observations by Dillon LJ:

(1) The conclusive nature of the valuation as between the parties is easier to understand and to justify now that the expert's former immunity from negligence liability has been ended. A party who is aggrieved by the valuation must accept it for the purposes for which it was made, but may seek redress by suing the valuer.

(2) There is no material difference between speaking and non-speaking valuations—both are equally conclusive. This may be regarded as extending the principle laid down in *Baber* v. *Kenwood Manufacturing Co Ltd* and brings a desirable element of coherence to this area of the law. The arguments in favour of the finality of the valuation are equally strong whether the valuation gives reasons or not.

(3) The valuation may still be challenged if the expert has not done what he was asked to do, but not if he has done what he was asked to do, but is alleged to have done it negligently. The earlier cases of *Dean* v. *Prince*[253] and *Burgess* v. *Purchase & Sons Ltd*[254] which suggested a general discretion to set aside the valuation were disapproved. As an example of the class of case where the valuation can be challenged, Dillon LJ cited *Jones* v. *Jones*,[255] in which the instructions to the valuer were that he should instruct an appropriate expert to value a particular item of property. Instead he valued this item himself, and it was held that this valuation could be set aside.

### 6.1.3 Effect where valuation disregarded

A point which did not arise in *Jones* v. *Sherwood Computing* was the effect of disregarding a valuation because of an error of principle such as occurred in *Jones* v. *Jones*. On the face of it the result would seem to be that there has been no effective valuation and the parties must start again and obtain a proper valuation. This is obviously likely to be both time-consuming and expensive, and the parties may well want the court, having set aside the original valuation, to substitute its own decision. This occurred in *Smith* v. *Gale*,[256] where on the dissolution of a partnership final accounts were to be taken according to specified principles, and the resultant accounts were to be "binding" on the partners. A dispute arose as to whether the accounts had been properly prepared. The plaintiffs wanted the accountant's certificate, based on his understanding of the relevant agreement, to be set aside. The defendant claimed that the certificate was "binding", so that the other partners could not challenge it. Goulding J held that the certificate could not be binding because it had been based on a misunderstanding of the agreement. It would therefore be set aside. The judge went on to decide that in the circumstances the court had jurisdiction to order the payment of the sums which would have been revealed had the accounts been properly prepared. Although it is not in every case that this can be

---

253. [1954] Ch. 409.
254. [1983] Ch. 216.
255. [1971] 1 W.L.R. 840.
256. [1974] 1 All E.R. 401 (Goulding J).

done, it was possible here because it was clear that one of two bases must be correct, and it was clear what would be the result of the adoption of either basis. In the absence of these facts it would presumably have been necessary to remit the matter to the accountant for the production of a new certificate on the correct basis.[257]

### 6.1.4  Nature of certificate

In *Shorrock Ltd* v. *Meggitt plc*[258] auditors were called upon to certify a net asset value for the company as part of a sale agreement. They issued a certificate which stated a value but also drew attention to unresolved uncertainties about the basis of the valuation. The certificate was challenged. The Court of Appeal held that it was invalid. A certificate must state the position with certainty. If the auditors felt unable to do this, they must either resolve the uncertainty or refuse to issue a certificate at all. On the face of it this principle does not appear to be limited to auditors. On the other hand it may be doubted whether it necessarily applies to every certificate. Presumably attention must be paid to the nature and purpose of the certificate.

### 6.1.5  Standard of care

In *Whiteoak* v. *Walker*[259] a share transfer clause in the articles of a private company provided for valuation of the shares by the auditor. The question was as to the standard of care and skill to be expected of the auditor when performing this task. For the plaintiffs it was argued that the standard was that of an expert valuer, whereas the argument for the defence was that the standard should only be that of a reasonably competent accountant in general practice and acting as auditor. It was held that the latter standard was correct. On construction of the articles it was clear that what the parties had contemplated in these circumstances was a quick solution, to be achieved by the auditor applying his own skills, which would inevitably be limited. The decision must be regarded as turning on the wording of the particular articles. However, it is significant that the task was expressly entrusted to the *auditor* as such. Provisions of this kind are quite common, and it is suggested that the same result would normally be reached.

## 7  OTHER MATTERS

This section deals with a variety of other legal issues which may arise in connection with the rights and duties of auditors.

---

257. See also *Frank H Wright (Constructions) Ltd* v. *Frodoor Ltd* [1967] 1 All E.R. 433 (Roskill J); *Dean* v. *Prince* [1953] 2 All E.R. 636 (Harman J); *Dinham* v. *Bradford* (1869) 5 Ch.App. 519; *Thomas* v. *Hamlyn & Co* [1917] 1 K.B. 527.
258. [1991] B.C.C. 471, C.A.
259. (1988) 4 B.C.C. 122 (Cullen QC).

## 7.1 Litigation

### 7.1.1 Ownership of documents

In *Chantry Martin* v. *Martin*[260] an audit clerk sued his employers for wrongful dismissal, alleging that he had been dismissed for refusing to cover up fraud discovered in the course of an audit. They said he left without notice. He sought discovery of the papers relating to the company where the fraud was said to have taken place. They claimed that these papers belonged to the company not to them. It was held that working accounts and other papers created by them for the purposes of the audit were the auditors' property and therefore subject to discovery. Although this decision appears to be correct on its facts, it must be noted that it is limited to documents brought into existence for the purposes of the audit and not communicated or intended to be communicated to third parties. Any document which did not satisfy this test would, it is submitted, belong to the company not to the auditors.

### 7.1.2 Professional privilege

In *Plummers Ltd* v. *Debenhams plc*[261] accountants were engaged by the defendants to report on the state of the plaintiff's business, as the defendants had the right to do under an earlier sale agreement. The defendants had in mind to serve a demand for the whole of an outstanding debt owed to them by the plaintiffs, but the plaintiffs did not realise this and therefore co-operated with the investigation. In due course the defendants served the demand. In the resulting litigation the plaintiffs wanted sight of the report but the defendants claimed litigation privilege. Millett J upheld the defendants' claim, relying on *Waugh* v. *BRB*[262]—the document had been brought into existence for the purpose of contemplated litigation, and was therefore privileged from discovery.

### 7.1.3 Liens on documents

In *Woodworth* v. *Conroy*[263] the defendant accountants claimed a lien on files and papers relating to the plaintiff's tax affairs. The lien was for unpaid fees. The plaintiff disputed that the fees were due, but the defendants counterclaimed for these. The defendants objected to producing the files and papers for inspection, saying that this would render their lien worthless since the plaintiff would then be entitled to copy them. The Court of Appeal held that the defendants did have a particular lien on the papers, but that despite this inspection was necessary in order to allow the action for unpaid fees to be properly dealt with in accordance with R.S.C., Ord. 23. It appears that the result might have been different if the defendants had simply resisted the claim for the documents and had not at that stage sued for their fees.

---

260. [1953] 2 Q.B. 286, C.A.
261. [1986] B.C.L.C. 447 (Millett J).
262. [1979] 2 All E.R. 1169, H.L.
263. [1976] Q.B. 884, C.A.

### 7.1.4 *Right to conduct the audit*

In *Cuff* v. *London & County Land & Building Co Ltd*[264] the company alleged that negligence by the auditors had enabled the ex-secretary to commit fraud and was suing the auditors, who had refused a request to resign. The company also refused to hand the books over to the auditors for the annual audit (having apparently passed them to another firm) and the auditors sought a mandatory injunction, which Eve J granted. The company appealed. It was held that the injunction should be discharged. The question would be left to the shareholders to decide, though it is not at all clear from the report quite which question was being left to the shareholders. At the present day the position seems fairly straightforward. So long as the auditors remain in office, they are surely entitled and bound to carry out the audit. Section 391(1) of the Companies Act 1985 allows the company to remove its auditors at any time by means of an ordinary resolution, and a company which is no longer happy with its auditors can always use this section to resolve the matter. Unless and until it does so, the auditors remain the auditors and are entitled to the information necessary to carry out the audit, in accordance with section 389A of the Companies Act 1985.[265]

## 7.2 Investigations under the Insolvency Act 1986

Sections 234–237 of the Insolvency Act 1986 make provision for the investigation of the affairs of a company which is in administration, administrative receivership or liquidation. The powers conferred by these sections may in some cases be of concern to auditors.

Section 234 allows the court to order the delivery up to the company of any books, papers or records to which the company appears to be entitled and which are in the possession of some other person. Auditors will of course at various times have such documents in their possession for audit purposes, and it follows that an order could be made against them under this section. Two points should be noted. First, the power is discretionary, so that the court will not necessarily order the delivery up of documents if the audit is in progress at the relevant time or if there is other good reason why the order should not be made. Secondly, the power applies only to items to which the company is entitled. As appears from *Chantry Martin* v. *Martin*,[266] working papers brought into existence by auditors for the purposes of the audit are their property and the company is not entitled to them. An order under section 234 should therefore not include such documents. However, section 234(3) and (4) does give protection to an administrator, administrative receiver or liquidator (collectively referred to as the "office-holder") who seizes documents under the reasonable but mistaken belief that he is entitled to them (whether under an order of the court or otherwise). These subsections provide that the office-holder is not liable to anyone for loss or damage resulting except in so far as it results from his own negligence, and that he has a lien on them for the expenses incurred in seizing them.

---

264. [1912] 1 Ch. 440, C.A. (Eve J).
265. For the details of this section see p. 250.
266. See fn. 255 above.

Section 235 applies in the same circumstances as does section 234 and imposes a duty to co-operate with the office-holder by providing such information as may reasonably be requested and attending on the office-holder when reasonably called upon to do so. The duty is imposed[267] on those who have at any time been officers of the company, but the term "officers" has the same meaning as in section 744 of the Companies Act 1985[268] and it is therefore submitted that it does not include auditors.[269] The duty is also imposed[270] on those who have been in the employment of the company (including employment under a contract for services) within one year before the commencement of the administration, administrative receivership or liquidation and who are in the office-holder's opinion capable of giving information which he requires. It appears that auditors are capable of falling within this definition, since they will be employed under a contract for services. They will be subject to the section if they acted as auditors within the one-year period mentioned and if the office-holder thinks that they can help with his investigations. In the nature of their role the auditors will often have been privy to information about the financial state of the company and may have been consulted about the company's solvency at some point before it failed.

Section 236 applied in the same circumstances as does section 234 and in cases where the company has been wound up on the order of the court. On the application of the office-holder the court may summon to appear before it any officer of the company, any person known or suspected to have in his possession any property of the company or any person whom the court thinks capable of giving information relating to the affairs of the company. For reasons discussed above auditors should not be regarded as falling within the first of these categories. They may be in the second category and will often be in the third category. A number of issues arise about the basis on which the power of the court may be exercised.

### 7.2.1 Purpose of section

In *Re British & Commonwealth Holdings plc*[271] Hoffmann J held that the purpose of section 236 was exclusively to allow the reconstruction of the company's state of knowledge at the relevant time. To the extent that the documents here requested went beyond that, the application would be refused.

### 7.2.2 Privilege against self-incrimination

In *Re Arrows Ltd*[272] the court was concerned with the powers of the Serious Fraud Office to demand production of information arising from the examination of directors under the Insolvency Act 1986 section 236. Obviously, the SFO wanted the information in connection with possible criminal proceedings against the directors concerned, and for the same reasons the directors were anxious to keep the information out of the hands of the SFO. The court therefore had to consider the

267. Insolvency Act 1986, s. 235(3)(a).
268. *Ibid.* s. 251.
269. See the discussion on this point at p. 262.
270. Insolvency Act 1986, s. 235(3)(c).
271. [1992] B.C.L.C. 314 (Hoffmann J).
272. [1993] 3 All E.R. 861, C.A.

powers of the SFO under the Criminal Justice Act 1987 to demand access to the information. It was held that statements made by directors in section 236 applications are admissible in any court proceedings (civil or criminal). The 1987 Act gives the SFO power to require production of these documents without giving any undertakings as to the use to be made of them. It is irrelevant to the exercise of this power whether or not criminal proceedings have been instituted against the director (i.e., there is no relevant privilege against self-incrimination). There is no public interest immunity which could be used to restrain the disclosure of documents in these circumstances to the regulatory authorities. Although this case concerns directors rather than auditors, the position is apparently the same where auditors are made respondents to a section 236 application. In *London & County Securities* v. *Nicholson*[273] the plaintiffs had obtained information from the auditors in connection with a DTI inquiry; it had been supplied under promises of confidentiality, but the plaintiffs now wanted to use it in an action against the auditors. It was held that the evidence was admissible. There is a general principle that the court will always admit relevant evidence. This can be overridden for good reason, but no such reason could be identified in the present case. Although this case pre-dates the Insolvency Act 1986, it appears that the same result would be reached under the present legislation.

### 7.2.3 Oral or written proceedings

In *Re Norton Warburg Holdings Ltd*[274] the liquidators wanted to question the auditors about the circumstances surrounding a corporate failure. The immediate issue was whether the procedure should be oral or written. Auditors wanted written notice of questions so that they could check in the files, but the liquidator wanted to be able to conduct an oral examination so as to pursue further any points which might arise. The court said that this issue needed very careful consideration on the facts of each case. The parties should collaborate so as to refine and reduce the outstanding issues and to define them as closely as possible. Only then should there be an oral examination, and only in relation to issues which could not be dealt with in any other way. This very sensible approach to the question should be regarded as being still good law.

## 7.3 Disciplinary aspects

In addition to their possible legal liabilities, auditors may face disciplinary action from their professional bodies if they are negligent in the conduct of an audit.

### 7.3.1 Disciplinary proceedings while litigation ongoing

In *R* v. *ICAEW, ex parte Brindle*[275] the ICAEW wished to take disciplinary proceedings against the applicant arising out of the BCCI collapse. However, a number of civil actions were pending, some of them in jurisdictions which still had jury trial for such matters. The applicant sought judicial review of the decision to

---

273. [1980] 3 All E.R. 861 (Browne-Wilkinson J).
274. (1983) 1 B.C.C. 127.
275. [1993] B.C.C. 736.

institute the proceedings, claiming that this would be unfairly prejudicial to his interests. It was held that on the facts there was no likelihood of prejudice to the applicant. It was also to be noted that the proceedings arose out of an exceptionally spectacular and serious banking failure. It is hard to see why the last point is relevant. It was no doubt important that the professional conduct aspects of the matter should be properly investigated, but the applicant's argument was only that this process should be delayed, not that it should be abandoned entirely. What is clear from the case is that the disciplinary powers may in an appropriate case be exercised even though litigation arising from the matter has not been settled. The outcome of the case would presumably have been different if the court had been satisfied that the continuance of the disciplinary proceedings did pose a serious risk of unfair prejudice to the defendant. It must be emphasised, however, that *unfair* prejudice is required. To be subjected to professional discipline for misconduct is not unfair prejudice. Brindle would have had to show that the trial of the litigation was likely to be made significantly more difficult or expensive for him by the presence of the disciplinary proceedings. Clearly, there will be few cases where prejudice of this kind can be established.

The seriousness with which disciplinary proceedings in general should be treated is underlined by the outcome of the proceedings relating to the BCCI collapse. Three members of the ICAEW were expelled and ordered to pay substantial costs. The effect of their expulsion is that they will no longer be qualified to act as auditors.

## 7.4 Criminal liabilities

### 7.4.1 Auditor as officer

In *R v. Shacter*[276] the auditor of a company was found to have presented misleading accounts to the bank for the purpose of obtaining further finance. He was convicted of various offences under the Companies Act and the Larceny Act which can only be committed by an "officer" of the company. He appealed against conviction, contending that an auditor as such is not an officer of the company. The Court of Criminal Appeal held that an auditor is an officer. The Companies Act refers to auditors "holding office"[277] and the only office which they can plausibly be thought to hold is an office within the company. Although this decision seems plausible at first sight, it must be doubted whether it is correct at the present day. Section 744 of the Companies Act 1985 is the main definition section for the purposes of the companies legislation, and this states that the term officer "includes a director, manager or secretary". The definition is of course not exhaustive, since it uses the word "includes" rather than the word "means", but it seems unlikely that auditors would not have been mentioned if it had been intended that they should fall within the term. Although all the section 744 definitions are stated to apply only where the context permits, the most likely conclusion is that auditors are not normally officers of the company where that term is used in the companies legislation. On the other hand section 27 of the Companies Act 1989, dealing specifically with eligibility for appointment as auditor, declares that an auditor is not to be regarded as an officer of

276. [1960] 1 All E.R. 61, C.C.A.
277. Now in the Companies Act 1985, s. 235 and the Companies Act 1989, s. 28.

the company for the purposes of that section, a provision which is otiose unless the auditor would otherwise have been so regarded. The answer to this problem is probably that an auditor may be an officer for some purposes without necessarily being one for all purposes. In the particular context of false accounting it is to be observed that the relevant provisions are now to be found in sections 17–20 of the Theft Act 1968 (which was not in force at the date of *R* v. *Shacter*), and that section 744 of the Companies Act 1985 does not apply to the interpretation of these sections. Sections 18 and 19 of the Act deal specifically with the position of company officers. Section 18 imposes liability for false accounting by a company on any "director, manager, secretary or other similar officer" with whose consent or connivance the offence was committed, whilst section 19 applies to any "officer" of a body corporate who publishes or concurs in publishing a false statement about its affairs with the intention of deceiving members or creditors. As to section 18 it may be said that an auditor, even if arguably an "officer" of the company, is not "similar" to a director, manager or secretary, since his functions are entirely different. The wording of section 18 appears to be designed to catch those running the company, whatever title the company chooses to give them, but not to catch auditors. The offence created by section 19, by contrast, is one to which auditors could well be party, and the term "officer" is not qualified in the same way as in section 18. It may well be that auditors are "officers" for the purposes of section 19.

### 7.4.2 Acting while disqualified

Section 28 of the Companies Act 1989 creates an offence of acting as auditor while disqualified,[278] whether the disqualification was in force at the time of the original appointment or whether it arose thereafter, but section 28(5) allows a defence where the person charged did not know and had no reason to believe that he was ineligible for appointment. *Secretary of State for Trade & Industry* v. *Hart*[279] concerned an earlier version of the same provision. The defendant was charged with acting as auditor while knowing that he was disqualified. He knew the relevant facts, i.e., that he was a director of the company concerned, but did not appreciate their legal significance. It was held that the section was ambiguous as to what knowledge was required, so the interpretation most favourable to the defendant would be adopted. He was therefore acquitted. It is submitted that this result could not be reached under the current legislation. The defendant would need to show that he had no reason to be aware of his disqualification, and it seems unlikely that the court would accept this test as being satisfied where the error was one of law. A person who acts as auditor ought to be under an obligation to find out the relevant legal rules before taking on the role, and this alone provides a reason why he should know the position.

## 8 THE FUTURE

Although the discussion in this chapter might seem to lead to the conclusion that auditors in practice run relatively little risk of liability for the conduct of the audit and

---

278. For the qualifications to act as auditor, see p. 245 above.
279. [1982] 1 All E.R. 817, D.C.

other related functions, there can be no doubt that at the time of writing of this chapter the auditing profession faces a major crisis resulting from substantial ongoing claims. Some of these are very large claims arising from major collapses (BCCI, Barings and Maxwell are perhaps the best-known examples) but a steady flow of other smaller claims is also having its impact. Recent proposals to abolish joint liability for auditors seem unlikely to have much impact, since auditors will presumably retain a substantial degree of responsibility in most cases where they would at present be liable. Some modest relief may come from the relaxation of the audit requirements for very small companies, though the claims to be expected in such cases would presumably have been small in any event, and the relief from liability will be balanced by the loss of fee income.

It may well be suggested that the auditing profession cannot go on as it has been doing over the past decade with ever-increasing numbers of claims. It seems unlikely, however, that the arguments in favour of limiting liability, whether by a standard cap on *quantum* or by allowing negotiation in individual cases, will succeed. On this assumption it is necessary to ask how else the liability problem might be addressed. It is suggested that much of the present problem results directly from a mismatch between the expectations of users of accounts about what the audit does and the perceptions of auditors about what their responsibilities are. On the one hand users need to remember that auditing of accounts is not a guarantee of their accuracy,[280] the audit process does not and cannot involve checking every single transaction entered into by the company. It would be useful also if the limits of the notion of the true and fair view[281] could be more generally understood. On the other hand users of the accounts need to be able to rely within reasonable limits on the substantial accuracy of the accounts, and in this context it is suggested that auditors may need to devote rather more resources to the auditing process than they do at present. This is in part a cost issue, since the constant downward pressure on audit fees is a major cause of the cost-cutting practices which have imperilled the quality of the audit process. In the end there are only two choices. Either the audit must be done properly or it must be abandoned—to keep the present arrangement of audits of variable and unreliable quality is to have the worst of all worlds. Abolition is not a possibility at a national level, since the matter is subject to European Law.[282] It follows that the task will have to be done to a higher standard, that companies will have to accept the cost implications of these higher standards, and that auditors will have to accept the liability implications of being properly paid for doing the job. It is greatly to be regretted that at present the debate is still about limiting liability rather than about improving standards.

ANDREW McGEE

---

280. See pp. 262–263 above.
281. See p. 263 above.
282. The Fourth and Seventh Company Law Directives. See p. 264 above.

294

CHAPTER 6

# BARRISTERS

## 1 INTRODUCTION

### 1.1 The function and role of barristers

Barristers like surgeons are members of a referral profession.[1] The Code of Conduct of the Bar of England and Wales, published by the General Council of the Bar, confirms that the ordinary scope of a barrister's practice consists of advocacy, drafting pleadings and other legal documents and advising on questions of law.[2] It states[3]:

"A barrister acts only on the instructions of a professional client, and does not carry out any work by way of the management, administration or general conduct of a lay client's affairs nor the management, administration or general conduct of litigation nor the receipt or handling of client's money."

In most instances "professional client" in this context is a solicitor although the professional Code of Conduct referred to above now permits direct professional access by the members of other accredited professions, principally surveyors, chartered accountants and planning professionals.[4] In such cases, barristers are subject to more stringent obligations to retain copies of briefs and instructions and to observe statutory or other time-limits which pertain to the matter. Direct professional access remains confined principally to advisory work.[5]

Outwith these more unusual circumstances, most barristers rely upon solicitors to supervise and manage the lay client's affairs and receive instructions in connection with an ongoing matter only on a periodic basis. Depending on the sphere of work, those instructions might be notionally addressed to the barrister *qua* advocate or the barrister *qua* specialist adviser. As with professionals working within the building industry the system at best provides the lay client with a professional team in which the members complement and support each other. At worst, the division of responsibility breaks down causing duplication of effort and misunderstanding.

---

1. The analogy has some foundation in the similar treatment of the two professions: see *Rondel* v. *Worsley* [1969] 1 A.C. 191 at 198C–199A.
2. 1990 edition as amended at Annexe H, para. 2.1.
3. *Ibid.*
4. See the Code of Conduct of the Bar of England and Wales (1990 edn, as amended) at paras 305, 901 and Annexe E.
5. Paragraph 3 of Annexe E of the Code of Conduct of the Bar of England and Wales (1990 edn, as amended).

Until recently barristers enjoyed a privileged monopoly in respect of advocacy in the Supreme Court. The Courts and Legal Services Act 1990 swept away much of this privilege and solicitor advocates willing to undergo a rigorous training programme are permitted to appear alongside barristers.[6] An important distinction remains the operation of the so-called "cab-rank rule" whereby a barrister is obliged to accept instructions from a client willing to pay a proper fee unless the instructions fall outside the sphere in which he is accustomed to practise.[7]

## 1.2 A non-contractual framework for liability

Unlike the other professionals considered in this work, barristers do not contract with those clients by whom they are retained and they are precluded from suing for their fees. Bar Council rules forbid the making of such a contract with solicitors for barristers in England and Wales.[8] Nor, as a matter of standard custom, does there exist any direct contract between the barrister and the lay client.[9] The origins of the rule are well established, if obscure.[10] Further, while section 61(1) of the Courts and Legal Services Act 1990 abolished the rule of law which prevented a barrister from entering into a contract for the provision of services, section 61(2) went on to state that the Bar Council would remain free to restrict such contracts by its rules. Thus, unlike solicitors, the liability of barristers has made no contribution to the interesting debate on concurrent liability in tort and contract considered elsewhere in this work.[11]

## 1.3 Liability in tort—a duty of care

The principle that a professional person may owe a duty of care in tort regardless of contract was restated and reaffirmed in the important decision of *Hedley Byrne & Co Ltd* v. *Heller & Partners Ltd*,[12] but derives from the earlier Privy Council case of *Nocton* v. *Lord Ashburton*.[13] Of unique interest for the liability of barristers is whether the underlying rationale for liability in such cases, the voluntary assumption of responsibility, can be reconciled with the "cab-rank rule", or whether a barrister's

6. By s. 31(1) of the Act barristers' rights of audience are confirmed and the Code of Conduct is duly approved. At the date of writing, some 150 solicitors have acquired rights of audience in the higher courts with some 140 or so in the pipeline: see the Annual Report of the General Council of the Bar for 1994. They, however, appear without wigs: *Practice Direction (Court Dress)* [1994] 1 W.L.R. 1056.

7. Code of Conduct of the Bar of England and Wales (1990 edn, as amended) at para. 209.

8. The Code of Conduct of the Bar of England and Wales (1990 edn, as amended) at Annexe D provides for standard terms of work on which barristers offer their services to solicitors. By para. 25, it is provided that a barrister who offers services on those terms has no intention to create legal relations or to enter into any contract or other obligation binding in law. Although barristers and solicitors are now permitted to accept certain instructions on a contingency basis, this principle remains intact.

9. *Ibid.* at recital (3). In *Mostyn* v. *Mostyn* (1870) 5 Ch.App. 457, the court held that a solicitor's promise to pay counsel's fees did not bind the client.

10. Lord Nottingham's note on Coke on Littleton (Co.Inst. (1628)), volume 1, p. 293; Viner's Abridgement (1741–56), volume 6, p. 478; Blackstone's Commentaries (17th edn, 1830), volume 3, p. 28; *Thornhill* v. *Evans* (1742) 2 Atk. 330; *Turner* v. *Phillipps* (1792) Peake 166; *Morris* v. *Hunt* (1819) 1 Chit. 544 and *In re Le Brasseur and Oakley* [1896] 2 Ch. 487. In *Wells* v. *Wells* [1914] P. 157 it was held that unpaid fees due to counsel could not be attached by a garnishee order, even though received by the solicitor from the client, because counsel was unable to sue the solicitor for them. There was no "attachable debt".

11. At p. 45.

12. [1964] A.C. 465.

13. [1914] A.C. 932.

inability to reject work from a client abrogates the voluntary acceptance of responsibility. This was one strand of argument of counsel for the respondent barrister in the key decision in *Rondel* v. *Worsley*,[14] who argued that just as on the facts of *Hedley Byrne* it was open to a party expressly to negative the duty of care which would otherwise arise from the giving of advice, so the commonly observed practice and understanding whereby a barrister enjoyed immunity, as to which see below, was capable of being an implied disclaimer of responsibility. The argument was expressly rejected by Lord Upjohn who was content to state that prima facie a barrister fell within the general principle that a duty of care was owed.[15] Outside the scope of the immunity, this must be correct.

The question then arises whether the duty is owed to the professional client, the lay client or to both. The problem may be more apparent than real as the professional client suffers no loss which is not in truth a loss which he is entitled to pass on to his lay client. Unlike solicitors[16] it is difficult to envisage any circumstances in which a barrister could be held to owe a duty of care to a third party[17] and, in line with this, in *Orchard* v. *South Eastern Electricity Board*[18] the Court of Appeal rejected the proposition that members of the Bar owe any independent duty to their lay client's opponent.

## 1.4 Immunity

Unique amongst the professional persons dealt with in this work, barristers have traditionally enjoyed immunity from suit arising from their negligence in certain circumstances.[19] As an exception from the established fault principle that wrongs occasioned by a person's negligence must be compensated by that person, the immunity must be fully justified. Furthermore, the suggestion by Lord Pearce in *Rondel* v. *Worsley*[20] that the immunity may be justified in part at least by the difficulty of the barrister's task is unlikely to be favourably received by other professionals burdened by heavy workloads and expensive professional indemnity premiums.

14. [1969] A.C. 191 at 210F–211E.
15. [1969] 1 A.C. 191 at 280F–281C. Cf. the views of Lord Pearce at 264A–D.
16. In *Gran Gelato Ltd* v. *Richcliff (Group) Ltd and others* [1992] Ch. 560, Sir Donald Nicholls V-C rejected the contention that in a conveyancing transaction the solicitor acting for the vendor might owe a duty of care to the buyer when answering inquiries before contract, but left open the possibility of there being special features where a solicitor might assume direct responsibility towards a third party. See also *Al-Kandari* v. *JR Brown & Co (a firm)* [1988] Q.B. 665 at 672 and *Allied Finance and Investments Ltd* v. *Haddow & Co* [1983] N.Z.L.R. 22.
17. The facts of *Mathew* v. *Maughold Life Assurance Co Ltd* (1985) 1 P.N. 142 (Leonard J), (1987) 3 P.N. 98, C.A. were somewhat unusual and provide an exception to the principle stated in the text.
18. [1987] 1 Q.B. 565 at 571F–H.
19. It has been observed that the immunity is not itself unique in that police officers are protected from suits arising from their investigation of crime, and certain regulators enjoy a degree of protection from claims arising from the performance by them of statutory functions—J Powell QC, "Barrister's Immunity—Time to Go" in the March/April 1995 edition of *Counsel—the Journal of the Bar of England and Wales* at p. 10. However, as the learned author notes, the underlying policy considerations are wholly different. On the immunity of the police, see *Hill* v. *Chief Constable of West Yorkshire* [1989] A.C. 53 and, recently, *Osman* v. *Ferguson* [1993] 4 All E.R. 344. Furthermore, as observed below at p. 306, the immunity extends to solicitors and to others who lawfully provide legal services in connection with proceedings—Courts and Legal Services Act 1990, s. 62.
20. [1969] 1 A.C. 191 at 274.

## 2 IMMUNITY FROM SUIT

### 2.1 The origins of the immunity

Despite inconclusive *dicta* to the contrary in *Bradish* v. *Gee*,[21] the first suggestion that a barrister was immune from suit for his own negligence appears to have been in *Fell* v. *Brown*[22] where Lord Kenyon observed, *obiter*, that an action against a barrister could not be maintained. He added that "he believed this action was the first, and hoped it would be the last, of the kind".[23] Similarly, in 1845 in *Purves* v. *Landell*[24] *dicta* indicates that Lord Campbell presupposed without giving reasons that a barrister could not be sued for incorrect or inaccurate advice.

By 1860, in the decision in *Swinfen* v. *Lord Chelmsford*,[25] an attempt was being made to justify the perceived immunity by reference both to the absence of any contract between barrister and client and also the wider obligations owed by a barrister to the court and to the public at large. The case, however, was concerned with the apparent authority of a barrister to bind his client rather than an action for negligence *per se* and the observations of Pollock CB on this point[26] are accordingly *obiter*. Whatever the true basis for the early case-law, it was not until 1967 and the judgment of the Court of Appeal in *Rondel* v. *Worsley*[27] that public policy was articulated to be the basis of the immunity.

### 2.2 The modern basis for the immunity

In *Rondel* v. *Worsley*[28] the respondent barrister undertook to act on behalf of the appellant on a dock brief in connection with a criminal charge of causing bodily harm with intent to do so. The appellant was convicted and sent to prison. In 1965, almost six years later, the appellant, acting in person, issued a writ claiming damages for professional negligence. The question whether an action for negligence lay against a barrister was heard as a preliminary issue upon the respondent's application to strike out the statement of claim. Without determining whether there was negligence in fact,[29] the House of Lords reaffirmed the existence of the immunity and the public policy grounds upon which it was to be justified in modern times. Lord Reid said:

"For the reasons which I have given I am of the opinion that it is in the public interest to retain the existing immunity of barristers from action by their clients for professional negligence, at

21. (1754) 1 Amb. 229 *per* Lord Hardwicke: "When a decree is made by consent of counsel there lies not an appeal or rehearing, though the party did not really give his consent; but the remedy is against his counsel".
22. (1791) Peake 131. In the earlier case of *Perring* v. *Rebutter* (1842) 2 M. & R. Rob. 429, a case of alleged negligence against a special pleader, Lord Abinger CB stated without deciding that the special pleader was not distinguishable from a barrister, against whom no action would lie.
23. *Ibid.* at 132.
24. (1845) 12 Cl. & Fin. 91 at 103.
25. (1890) Exch. Rep. 890.
26. *Ibid.* at 920–923.
27. [1967] 1 Q.B. 443.
28. [1969] 1 A.C. 191.
29. By way of an irrelevant but interesting aside, at the time of the assault the appellant claimed to be in the employ of a Mr Rachman, described by Lord Pearce (*ibid.* at 254) as "the well-known slum landlord" and one of the particulars of alleged negligence was the respondent's failure to call Mr Rachman on the question of whether the appellant was accustomed to use a knife.

least so far as it relates to their work in conducting litigation. And that would be sufficient to require the dismissal of the present appeal."

He continued:

"The main reasons on which I have based my opinion relate to the position of counsel while engaged in litigation, when his public duty and his duty to his client may conflict. But there are many kinds of work undertaken by counsel where no such conflict would emerge, and there I see little reason why the liability of counsel should be different from that of members of any other profession who give their professional advice and services to their clients. The members of every profession are bound to act honourably and in accordance with the recognised standards of their profession. But that does not, in my view, give rise to any such conflict of duties as can confront counsel while engaged in litigation."[30]

The order striking out the statement of claim as disclosing no cause of action was upheld. It was thus firmly established that in the light of *Hedley Byrne & Co Ltd* v. *Heller & Partners Ltd*[31] it could no longer be argued that the immunity was justified by the rule that a barrister did not contract with his clients and was unable to sue for his fees.[32] At the same time, the special considerations giving rise to the immunity were linked squarely to the barrister as advocate and four of their Lordships were accordingly satisfied that public policy did not require there to be a blanket immunity.[33]

Although the existence of the immunity was not in issue in the subsequent House of Lords' decision in *Saif Ali* v. *Sydney Mitchell & Co*,[34] the speeches provide an additional support for those seeking to justify the immunity. The plaintiff claimed damages for professional negligence against the defendant firm of solicitors arising from their conduct of an action for damages for personal injury arising out of a road traffic accident. The plaintiff had been a passenger in a van driven by another when it collided with a car driven by a wife and owned by her husband. Proceedings were issued against the husband as owner of the car which were eventually discontinued. By that time, any claim by the plaintiff against the drivers of the respective vehicles was statute-barred. The defendants issued a third party notice claiming indemnity against the barrister who had settled the proceedings and advised throughout the proceedings. A majority of the House of Lords ruled in favour of the plaintiff and against the barrister on whether the allegations fell within the scope of the latter's immunity on the ground that the advice given on joinder and amendment was not sufficiently closely connected with the conduct of the case in court.

## 2.3 Justifications for the immunity[35]

As a bald statement justifying the immunity, "public policy" appears a poor refuge against the charge of protectionism by judges appointed almost exclusively from the

30. *Ibid.* at 231.
31. [1964] A.C. 465.
32. [1969] 1 A.C. 191 at 232 *per* Lord Reid; *ibid.* at 246–247 *per* Lord Morris; *ibid.* at 260–263 *per* Lord Pearce and *ibid.* at 280–281 *per* Lord Upjohn.
33. See the observations of Lord Wilberforce in *Saif Ali* v. *Sydney Mitchell & Co* [1980] A.C. 198 at 212–213 on the *obiter* but none the less persuasive status of the observations made by their Lordships on the extent of the immunity.
34. [1980] A.C. 198. Lord Diplock referred to an "unsatisfactory feature" of the case that their Lordships did not have the benefit of "a more radical submission" that the immunity was no longer to be upheld—*ibid.* at 223F–G.
35. See C Miller, "The advocate's duty to justice, where does it belong?" (1981) 97 L.Q.R. 127.

Bar. Unsurprisingly, it is possible to discern different strands of argument from these two House of Lords' decisions. The arguments can be conveniently paraphrased and considered in turn.

### 2.3.1 The overriding duty owed by barristers to the court

The point here is neatly summarised by Lord Reid in *Rondel* v. *Worsley*[36]:

"Every counsel has a duty to his client fearlessly to raise every issue, advance every argument, and ask every question, however distasteful, which he thinks will help his client's case. But, as an officer of the court concerned in the administration of justice, he has an overriding duty to the court, to the standards of his profession, and to the public, which may and often does lead to a conflict with his client's wishes or with what the client thinks are his personal interests. Counsel must not mislead the court, he must not lend himself to casting aspersions on the other party or witnesses for which there is no sufficient basis in the information in his possession, he must not withhold authorities or documents which may tell against his clients but which the law or the standards of his profession require him to produce. And by so acting he may well incur the displeasure or worse of his client so that if the case is lost, his client would or might seek legal redress if that were open to him."

The thesis may be one which is of particular resonance in a legal system founded upon the adversarial principle, but Lord Diplock in *Saif Ali* was robust in suggesting that reliance upon the duty owed by a barrister to the court may be seen to be "a pretentious way of saying that when a barrister is taking part in litigation he must observe the rules; and this is true of all who practise any profession".[37] There are two aspects to the argument: first, it presupposes that there is a sufficient number of disgruntled clients who will unjustifiably seek to accuse counsel who fulfils his duty to the court as negligent to justify the rule. However, on a practical note, the costs of embarking upon all proceedings and the screen of legal aid entitlement are themselves disincentives to frivolous or weak actions. Moreover, if the barrister negligently misunderstands the rules then arguably there is no ground to shield him with the cloak of immunity because to do so runs counter to the administration of justice. As long as his conduct is measured against the standard of the reasonably competent barrister, there is more than adequate room for the barrister's duty to the court to be accommodated in reaching a finding of fact on the question of breach of duty.

Secondly, it is implied that the immunity is necessary because without it certain barristers might be tempted to compromise their duty to the court with that owed to their client. It has been observed that this argument "sells counsel short".[38] Certainly, it is a curious logic which argues for immunity from suit to protect those barristers who might have difficulty meeting the rigorous standards imposed upon them by the profession.

Properly separated from these strands, the overriding duty of a barrister to the court is little more than a statement that barristers work in conditions where they are often called upon to make and act on judgments speedily and in the highly stressful

36. [1969] 1 A.C. 191 at 227–228. See also *ibid.* at 247–248 *per* Lord Morris; *ibid.* at 272 *per* Lord Pearce; *ibid.* at 282–283 *per* Lord Upjohn and *ibid.* at 293 *per* Lord Pearson.

37. [1980] A.C. 198 at 219H–220F.

38. K Nicholson, "The immunity of barristers from suit in negligence—the Australian experience" (1989) 4 P.N. 124 at 126.

courtroom arena. Against this, as observed by Lord Diplock in *Saif Ali*,[39] the common law allows both of errors of judgment short of negligence and account to be taken of the circumstances in which those judgments are made. Further, it is submitted that there is no objection to the court affording priority to the barrister's duty to the court at the stage of determining breach of duty.

### 2.3.2 Re-litigation

This is arguably the most compelling of the arguments in favour of immunity.[40] A client is unlikely to wish to sue his counsel where a successful result was achieved. Thus, it is argued, it will be a *sine qua non* of an allegation of negligence that but for the fault of the barrister, the client would have enjoyed a favourable (or on quantum, more favourable) result. The point is good for civil and criminal litigation. The argument runs that a subsequent court would be obliged to speculate and determine what would have happened in the earlier proceedings if the case had been competently handled. Outside the process of appeal to a superior court, it is objectionable and contrary to the proper administration of justice for proceedings to be the subject of collateral attack.

First, it must be accepted that this argument is denuded of force where no trial or hearing in fact took place, for example, because the alleged negligence lead to the dismissal or striking out of the action at an interlocutory stage.[41] Secondly, it has been argued convincingly that a finding of negligence does not in itself imply that the decision of the previous court was wrong provided one accepts that the earlier decision was made on the basis of the information then before it.[42] Far from undermining public trust in the administration of justice, it is argued that the second decision goes some way to restoring confidence and the judicial system gains credit for acknowledging its earlier mistake. Thirdly, the re-litigation objection is accepted to have greater force in criminal proceedings especially having regard to the less burdensome burden of proof which would apply in the subsequent civil action. Thus, it is argued that a finding of negligence will inevitably prompt calls for a reconsideration of the underlying conviction and the finality of litigation will be irreparably undermined.[43] Interestingly, there was no attempt in *Saif Ali* v. *Sydney Mitchell & Co* to suggest that the *ratio decidendi* of *Rondel* v. *Worsley* should be interpreted strictly and thereby to restrict the immunity to criminal proceedings.

39. [1980] A.C. 198 at 220D–F.

40. *Rondel* v. *Worsley* [1969] 1 A.C. 191 at 249A–250B *per* Lord Morris; Lord Reid, *ibid.* at 230B–D, thought the argument had weight but was not conclusive; *Saif Ali* v. *Sydney Mitchell & Co* [1980] A.C. 198 at 222D–223D and 235G–236A.

41. *Saif Ali* v. *Sydney Mitchell & Co* [1980] A.C. 198 at 223E; cf. *ibid.* at 235H.

42. K Nicholson, "The immunity of barristers from suit in negligence—the Australian experience" (1989) 4 P.N. 124 at 127–128. The author of that article accepts that the argument presupposes that the appeal process has been exhausted. For a recent examination of the circumstances in which the acts or omissions of counsel may provide ground for appeal in criminal proceedings see RSJ Marshall, "Blame it on the barrister" (1994) S.J. 154.

43. *Rondel* v. *Worsley* [1969] 1 A.C. 191 at 249A–251A and 251G. K Nicholson, above at pp. 127–128 argues that the objections to collateral attack by subsequent proceedings apply most strongly to an allegation of negligence in a criminal action where the appeal process has been exhausted and the client remains convicted. Where the client is successful on appeal he argues that the client has the strongest case for claiming against negligent counsel because the final decision on appeal is confirmed. In such a case, the mitigating effect of the decision on appeal would presumably be relevant to the measure of damages awarded.

Finally, the public interest in finality of litigation is in any event capable of independent protection which does not involve the grant of immunity. In *Somasundaram* v. *M Julius Melchior & Co*,[44] an allegation of negligence was made by a man convicted and sentenced to imprisonment against a firm of solicitors for their conduct of the criminal proceedings.[45] The Court of Appeal held that it was an abuse of process to bring proceedings which would impugn the correctness of a decision of a court of competent jurisdiction, whether civil or criminal, and ordered the action to be struck out.[46] More recently in *Walpole* v. *Partridge & Wilson*[47] the Court of Appeal held that the principle admitted of exceptions where, for example, fresh evidence was relied upon because such a collateral attack would demonstrate no more than that a court might go wrong in law. There was in such a case no risk of the administration of justice being brought into disrepute.[48] There exists then a viable alternative to the immunity in cases where abuse of process is a genuine fear.

### 2.3.3 Prolixity and defensive practices

The first is discernible as a distinct theme in the speeches of Lord Reid and Lord Pearce in *Rondel* v. *Worsley*.[49] The argument runs that stripped of their immunity barristers would be tempted to raise every argument, call every witness, and put every question so as to avoid any criticism from their client. Put another way, barristers would practise defensively, in order to avoid exposure to a claim in negligence. The consequential lengthening of trials and increased costs would be contrary to the interests of justice.

As a justification for the immunity, this argument is open to the objections first, that it sells both counsel *and* judges short.[50] The former are after all subject to their overriding duty to the court as discussed above and, in the words of Lord Reid, "most experienced counsel would agree that the golden rule is—when in doubt stop".[51] It is open to the judges to apply vigorously their power to control proceedings in court to curb excessive loquaciousness of counsel and to penalise counsel in costs for time wasted.[52] Secondly, and more importantly, fears of defensive practice have been fully rehearsed in the context of the common law liability of other professionals, especially medical practitioners. Whilst it is conceded that the rise in professional negligence actions is a matter for genuine concern with wide implications for

---

44. [1988] 1 W.L.R. 1394.

45. The alleged negligence concerned the conduct of the defendant solicitors in "pressurising" the plaintiff to plead guilty. Although it was accepted that this advice was intimately connected with the conduct of the trial so as to be capable of falling within the immunity of an advocate, the solicitors were not in fact engaged as advocates when they gave the advice—*ibid.* at 1403D–1404A.

46. Applying *Hunter* v. *Chief Constable of the West Midlands Police* [1982] A.C. 529, H.L.(E.).

47. [1994] 1 All E.R. 385.

48. The principle was recently affirmed by the Court of Appeal, albeit a different conclusion reached, in *Smith* v. *Linskills (a firm)* (1996) *The Times*, 7 February. See S Fennell, "Solicitors' immunity from suit: *Walpole* v. *Partridge and Wilson*" (1994) 10 P.N. 89.

49. [1969] 1 A.C. 191 at 228F–229B and 272F–273F respectively.

50. K Nicholson, "The immunity of barristers from suit in negligence—the Australian experience" (1989) 4 P.N. 124 at 126–127.

51. *Rondel* v. *Worsley* [1969] 1 A.C. 191 at 228G.

52. See below at p. 311.

resource management, there are no grounds for believing that the Bar has a stronger case for immunity on this ground.

### 2.3.4 Immunity of judges, court officials, witnesses and jurors from suit

This argument is explored most fully by Lord Pearce in *Rondel* v. *Worsley*.[54] If, as is undoubtedly the case, judges and witnesses and others involved in the process of a case in court enjoy immunity from suit,[55] why should a barrister be treated differently? Lord Pearce accepted as a premise that immunity would create hardship for a client who believed the barrister had acted negligently. However, the legal process inevitably creates hardships.[56] Thus, he argues, a man subjected to a baseless claim by a plaintiff endures hardship by incurring expense and injury to his reputation and, further, a defendant suffers hardship if he is slandered in court by a disreputable witness, especially if that evidence is persuasive in leading a judge or jury to find against him.

It may be that this argument goes more to the scope of an advocate's immunity rather than to its existence because the principle that judges, witnesses and counsel are immune from actions arising from statements in court is well established and was not challenged in either of the leading House of Lords' cases on immunity. Outwith the narrow scope of what is said in court, it is doubtful that Lord Pearce's analysis is acceptable as a justification for a general immunity in litigation. There exist sound and largely uncontroversial reasons why judges, witnesses and counsel should speak freely in court unencumbered by the fear of an action for negligence or slander. Where it is possible to protect this public policy objective by a narrowly formulated rule, there is no logical or other basis for defining the scope of immunity in wider terms.

### 2.3.5 The cab-rank principle

Several of their Lordships in *Rondel* v. *Worsley*[57] found additional justification for the immunity from the principle that barristers are obliged to accept work which they are competent to perform. For justice to be both done and seen to be done, it was essential that barristers should act for, and, where necessary, defend those who were disreputable, unreasonable and lacking in apparent merit. Their Lordships feared that in the absence of immunity, barristers would be unwilling to take the risk of acting for such clients.[58]

---

54. [1969] 1 A.C. 190 at 267G–271C. See also Lord Diplock in *Saif Ali* v. *Sydney Mitchell & Co* [1980] A.C. 198 at 222A–D. However, Lord Russell in the same case, at 233C–D, rejected any connection with the immunity afforded to judges, witnesses and jurors.

55. *Scott* v. *Stansfield* (1868) L.R. 3 Ex. 220 (judges); *Marrinan* v. *Vibart* [1963] 1 Q.B. 528; *Hargreaves* v. *Bretherton* [1959] 1 Q.B. 45; *Palmer and Another* v. *Durnford Ford and Another* [1992] 1 Q.B. 483; *Landall* v. *Dennis Faulkner & Alsop and others* [1994] 5 Med.L.R. 268; *X and others (minors)* v. *Bedfordshire County Council* [1995] 3 All E.R. 353 (witnesses); *Munster* v. *Lamb* (1883) 11 Q.B.D. 588 (immunity of advocate for slander).

56. See also the comments of May LJ in *Somasundaram* v. *M Julius Melchior & Co* [1988] 1 W.L.R. 1394 at 1400A–B.

57. [1969] 1 A.C. 191 at 227D–F *per* Lord Reid; 274G–276D *per* Lord Pearce and at 281D–G *per* Lord Upjohn.

58. Cf. *Saif Ali* v. *Sydney Mitchell & Co* [1980] A.C. 198 at 221B–F *per* Lord Diplock and at 236B *per* Lord Keith.

Leaving aside whether the cab-rank principle has any place given the reality of modern practice, there are several objections to its use as a reason for immunity. First, it presupposes that unpleasant or difficult clients are more predisposed to generate litigation. If so, the immunity is a large shield with which to protect the profession against what is surely a small risk. Secondly, it ignores the power which exists by statute and pursuant to the inherent jurisdiction of the court for any action to be struck out if it is regarded as being frivolous and vexatious or otherwise an abuse of the process of the court.[59] Thirdly, the cab-rank principle is considerably diluted by the need for lay clients to retain a solicitor to act on their behalf in instructing counsel.[60]

### 2.3.6 Conclusion

The immunity is not without its critics.[61] However, it must not be thereby inferred that there exists any real momentum for reform whether from within the profession or otherwise.[62] Indeed, critics argue that the adversarial system itself works to preserve the immunity "by shielding it from any developed submission that it should no longer be upheld".[63]

## 2.4 Other jurisdictions

Amongst the major common law countries, there exists a divided approach to the question of immunity. Aside from its importance in determining the scope of the immunity, the judgment of McCarthy P in *Rees* v. *Sinclair*[64] confirmed that the requirements of public policy in New Zealand were broadly similar to those which influenced the House of Lords in *Rondel* v. *Worsley*.[65] Australia, too, has adopted a conservative position in favour of immunity, albeit in a decision of a bare majority of the High Court in *Giannarelli* v. *Wraith*.[66] To this extent, there is no discernible distinction on grounds of principle between so-called "fused" and divided professions.

In Canada, the immunity was however firmly rejected in *Demarco* v. *Ungaro*.[67] It is scarcely surprising that on an important issue of public policy Canada is allied more closely to the approach adopted in the USA where no immunity exists. The stated

59. R.S.C., Ord. 19, r. 18.
60. Cf. *Rondel* v. *Worsley* [1969] 1 A.C. 191 at 275F–276B.
61. M Zander, *Legal Services for the Community* (1978) at pp. 134–136; K Nicholson, "The immunity of barristers from suit in negligence—the Australian experience" (1989) 4 P.N. 124; CJ Veljanovski and CJ Whelan, "Professional negligence and the quality of legal services—an economic perspective" (1983) 46 M.L.R. 700; Hayes and Poll, "Lawyers' Immunity: The wider English and European framework" (1991) 7 P.N. 184; J Powell QC, "Barrister's immunity—time to go" (1995) March/April *Counsel* 10. For a reply to Powell and a rare defence of the immunity, see R Jackson QC, "Disappointed litigants and doubtful actions" (1995) May/June *Counsel* 16.
62. Such an opportunity was afforded by the Courts and Legal Services Act 1990.
63. Hayes and Poll, "Lawyers' Immunity: the wider English and European framework" (1991) 7 P.N. 184 at 186.
64. [1974] 1 N.Z.L.R. 180.
65. Both McCarthy P and Macarthur J considered that the duties owed by a barrister to the court and the relitigation arguments were of greatest force—*ibid.* at 182–184 and 189 respectively.
66. (1988) 62 A.L.J.R. 611; K Nicholson, "The immunity of barristers from suit in negligence—the Australian experience" (1989) 4 P.N. 124; K Nicholson, "Professional negligence in Australia 1984–1994" (1994) 10 P.N. 128 at 129–130.
67. (1979) 95 D.L.R. (3d) 385; see also *Banks* v. *Reid* 81 D.L.R. (3d) 730.

grounds for the decision are in fact more pragmatic in that the court found no empirical evidence of a serious conflict between the duties owed by counsel to the court and to his client.

No immunity exists elsewhere in Europe.[68]

## 2.5 Scope of the immunity

### 2.5.1 The limits of the immunity

In *Rondel* v. *Worsley*[69] the observations of the House of Lords on the scope of the immunity were *obiter* and there are significant differences in the formulations of their Lordships as to the circumstances in which the immunity would apply.[70] While the language used in each case was not uniform, the common thread echoed the earliest cases on immunity in focusing on barristers' work in court. Having regard to the expansive developments in the tort of negligence in the period since *Rondel* v. *Worsley*, it was unsurprising that the House of Lords was presented with an opportunity to define and clarify the extent of the immunity in *Saif Ali* v. *Sydney Mitchell & Co*.[71] The majority sought a more precise formulation for the immunity and derived assistance in this regard from the words of McCarthy P in the New Zealand Court of Appeal in *Rees* v. *Sinclair*[72]:

"I cannot narrow the protection to what is done in court: it must be wider than that and include some pre-trial work. Each piece of before-trial work should, however, be tested against the one rule; that the protection exists only where the particular work is so intimately connected with the conduct of the cause in court that it can fairly be said to be a preliminary decision affecting the way that cause is to be conducted when it comes to a hearing. The protection should not be given any wider application than is absolutely necessary in the interests of the administration of justice, and that is why I would not be prepared to include anything which does not come within the test I have stated."

Although there is a legitimate concern as to the application of this principle at its margins,[73] there is no empirical evidence to suggest any such difficulties in practice.[74]

---

68. *International Encyclopaedia of Comparative Law*, volume XI (Torts), chapter 6 (Professional Liability) at p. 46.

69. [1969] 1 A.C. 191.

70. For Lord Reid the immunity was justified only insofar as it related to barristers' work "in conducting litigation"—[1969] 1 A.C. 191 at 231D although later he added that the same would apply "when drawing pleadings or conducting subsequent stages in a case" (at 231G) and "at a stage when litigation is impending". Lord Morris posed the question whether immunity was justified "so far as concerns what is said or done in the conduct or management of a case in court" (at 247D). Lord Pearce gave the widest formulation in finding no distinction between "litigation and his other non-litigious work as a barrister" (at 265B). Lord Upjohn's position was close to that of Lord Reid in that public policy necessitated the immunity "in matters pertaining to litigation" (at 281D). He went on to find that as "a matter of practicality" the immunity should start with the letter before action (at 285G–286A). Lord Pearson questioned whether the immunity applied to "pure paper work" (at 294B) a distinction which also featured in the judgment of Lord Morris (at 249A).

71. [1980] A.C. 198.

72. [1974] 1 N.Z.L.R. 180 at 187.

73. Compare for example the views of Bridge LJ in the Court of Appeal in *Saif Ali* v. *Sydney Mitchell & Co (a firm)* [1978] Q.B. 95 with those of Lord Wilberforce in the House of Lords [1980] A.C. 198.

74. In *Mathew* v. *Maughold Life Assurance Co Ltd* (1985) 1 P.N. 142, a barrister was held liable at first instance for advice given orally in conference. The finding was reversed by the Court of Appeal ((1987) 3 P.N. 98) on the grounds that the barrister was entitled to rely upon solicitors and an accountant who were also present to ensure that the lay clients understood the advice. It is submitted that advice given orally in conference presents particular evidential difficulties for barristers' liability given that the barrister often relies upon the solicitor to make a full and accurate note of the advice given.

Conduct which has been held to fall within the scope of the immunity includes: failing to introduce allegations of misconduct in an application for maintenance[75]; compromising a claim at court[76]; failure to plead and ask for interest at trial[77]; and advice as to a plea on a criminal charge.[78] On the other hand, in *Saif Ali* v. *Sydney Mitchell & Co*,[79] the majority of the House of Lords was satisfied that the failure to consider the consequences of adding the negligent driver prior to the expiry of the limitation period fell well outside the immunity area.[80]

### 2.5.2 Solicitors as advocates

Four of their Lordships in *Rondel* v. *Worsley* were clear that the same public policy justifications for immunity for barristers applied to solicitors when acting as advocates.[81] Although the House of Lords favoured a more restrictive scope for the immunity overall in *Saif Ali*, a majority of their Lordships nevertheless confirmed that the same immunity attached to the solicitor advocate as to a barrister.[82] As solicitors increasingly make use of their extended rights of audience the scope of the immunity, in this regard at least, may be seen to enlarge.

By section 62 of the Courts and Legal Services Act 1990, "a person (a) who is not a barrister; but (b) who lawfully provides any legal services in relation to any proceedings, shall have the same immunity from liability for negligence in respect of his acts or omissions as he would have if he were a barrister lawfully providing those services".[83]

### 2.5.3 The forum for the operation of the immunity

This question has received little judicial comment. While it is clear that the immunity extends to proceedings, including interlocutory proceedings,[84] in the constituent courts of the Supreme Court and to county courts, it remains to be seen whether the immunity extends to the work of advocates in other tribunals such as employment tribunals, social security tribunals and in arbitrations. It is submitted that to the extent that the public policy justifications for the immunity are accepted, the same

75. *Rees* v. *Sinclair* [1974] 1 N.Z.L.R. 180.
76. *Biggar* v. *McLeod* [1978] 2 N.Z.L.R. 9; *Landall* v. *Dennis Faulkner & Alsop* [1994] 5 Med.L.R. 268 *per* Holland J at 274: "It is difficult to conceive of an activity that is so intimately connected with court proceedings as advising at the court door". Cf. *Donellan* v. *Watson* (1990) 21 N.S.W.L.R. 335, where the negligent making of a compromise when not instructed to do so was held to be outside the scope of a solicitor-advocate's immunity.
77. *Keefe* v. *Marks* (1989) 16 N.S.W.L.R. 713.
78. *Somasundaram* v. *M Julius Melchior & Co* [1988] 1 W.L.R. 1394.
79. [1980] A.C. 198.
80. *Ibid.* at 216B–C *per* Lord Wilberforce; at 224F–G *per* Lord Diplock and at 232F–G *per* Lord Salmon; cf. at 234A–C *per* Lord Russell.
81. [1969] 1 A.C. 191 at 232D–F *per* Lord Reid; at 243F–244A *per* Lord Morris; at 267F *per* Lord Pearce and at 284D–285D. Lord Pearson declined to rule on the question—*ibid.* at 294C–G.
82. [1980] A.C. 198 at 215G–H *per* Lord Wilberforce; at 224A *per* Lord Diplock and at 227H *per* Lord Salmon.
83. In effect, this extends immunity to persons with rights of audience granted pursuant to the Act—see s. 119 and, generally, JR Midgley, "Statutory reforms affecting lawyers' liability in negligence" (1991) 7 P.N. 17. For the position of employees of the Crown Prosecution Service, see *Welsh* v. *Chief Constable of Merseyside* [1993] 1 All E.R. 692.
84. *Saif Ali* v. *Sydney Mitchell & Co* [1980] A.C. 199 at 215F–G.

considerations apply and the immunity should apply. However, as the pressure for forms of alternative dispute resolution through, for example, mediation, gain momentum the line defining barristers' work in connection with proceedings is liable to become increasingly blurred.

## 3 BREACH OF DUTY

Outside the scope of the immunity, it is a mixed question of law and fact to decide whether there has been a breach of the requisite standard of care. It is important to stress that immunity must be kept quite separate from any defences which are otherwise available to the barrister.[85] As with other professional persons what is the requisite standard of care is a complex inquiry requiring a balance to be struck between the utility of the function carried out and the public interest in being free from harm.[86]

Although there is some *obiter* support in the case-law for the application of a stricter standard of care to apply to barristers such that only gross negligence would suffice,[87] the better view is that no such rule applies. The reasonable man test gives way to a reasonable professional test and the barrister, no less than the member of any other profession, is to be judged against the standards of those who profess to have the same skill and expertise.[88] As with the medical profession, increasing specialisation and differences of opinion between practitioners provide for interesting theoretical questions to be posed as to whether a given act or omission falls below this standard, but a dearth of decided authority suggests that, with barristers, the line may be a clear-cut one in practice.[89]

No doubt proper account is required to be given to the context in which advice is given and, in particular, the nature of interaction between solicitor and barrister is such that special account should be taken of the scope of the latter's instructions. It is consistent with the status of the Bar as a referral profession that much of its work involves the exercise of judgment on questions susceptible of more than one answer.[90] A mere error of judgment will not suffice.[91]

Although it is unlikely that a barrister would be held negligent for failing to advise on a point not raised by his instructions, or *a fortiori*, for failing to advise at all when

---

85. In *Saif Ali* v. *Sydney Mitchell & Co* [1980] A.C. 198 at 214–215, Lord Wilberforce was at pains to distinguish between (i) privilege as to statements made in court, (ii) defences, and (iii) immunity, and stressed that only the latter rested on public policy considerations.

86. See chapter 2.

87. Lord Upjohn in *Rondel* v. *Worsley* [1969] 1 A.C. 191 at 287A–B citing *Purves* v. *Landell* [1845] 12 Cl. & Fin. 91 expressed support for the view that *crassa negligentia* or gross negligence by some really elementary blunder was required but this was not a view supported by any other of their Lordships.

88. *Mathew* v. *Maughold Life Assurance Co Ltd* (1987) 3 P.N. 98 at 103.

89. Doubts have been expressed in the context of solicitors' negligence actions as to the utility and appropriateness of expert evidence from other lawyers on the grounds that the judge is well placed to determine whether the practitioner fell below the requisite standard of care—*Midland Bank Trust Co Ltd* v. *Hett Stubbs & Kemp* [1979] Ch. 384. However, it is submitted that in certain specialised areas of law a judge may derive considerable assistance from such evidence and it is to be noted that in *Mathew* v. *Maughold Life Assurance Co Ltd* (1987) 3 P.N. 98 evidence was received from two QCs practising in revenue law. Cf. *Brown* v. *Gould & Swayne* (1996) New Law Digest, 24 January.

90. *Saif Ali* v. *Sydney Mitchell* [1980] A.C. 198 at 214G.

91. *Ibid.* at 215H and 231C–D; *Cook* v. *S* [1966] 1 W.L.R. 635.

instructed only to settle pleadings, the question is likely to be one of degree. It is not difficult to imply into any retainer that if the barrister observes a fundamental error he is under a duty to alert the solicitor to the point and that failure to do so would be negligent. Although a barrister ought generally to be entitled to assume that his solicitor has established all the pertinent facts, it would be unwise to rely upon instructions which are incomplete on their face.

In non-contentious areas of practice, it is reasonable to suppose that a barrister will be liable for negligence in much the same circumstances as a solicitor. This author's view is that barristers who undertake the drafting of wills, trust deeds, leases or commercial agreements must assume responsibility for ensuring that the documents are in line with modern precedent and case-law and that they achieve the desired objective. Outside the scope of his immunity, a barrister can expect to be held liable for negligence in connection with contentious matters if he advises a claim or defence to be pursued where there is no proper basis in law for doing so. Once proceedings are contemplated, counsel must act diligently and carefully within the rules of court and may be held liable for any delays or errors of advice or pleading which lead to a client losing an opportunity to bring or defend a claim. However, in the context of proceedings, many decisions fall to be taken which in hindsight may be "wrong" but which are not negligent. For example, counsel for a plaintiff may recommend that an application for summary judgment should be made on the grounds that the defence of the defendant is "shadowy" and lacking in substance and the costs of proceeding to trial will be large. That the application fails is no guide to whether the advice was negligently given. Similarly, advice on the terms of settlement of an action or on the overall merits will rarely be capable of being found to be so wrong as to be negligent.

## 4 DAMAGES

The general measure of damages in tort is that the plaintiff is entitled to be restored to the position he would have been in but for the negligence.[92] Although there is no decided authority on the point, there is no reason to believe that this principle requires any special application to barristers' negligence save that it must be remembered that in the absence of contractual liability, damage is a necessary ingredient of the cause of action. A more interesting question arises on causation because, as has been seen, in normal circumstances there is a division of responsibility and labour between solicitor and barrister. It has been held that a solicitor who instructs counsel is not thereby entitled to abdicate that responsibility in favour of the barrister,[93] and many cases will concern allegations against both professionals. For example, it is not unreasonable to suppose that both barrister and solicitor should be mindful of the limitation period which applies to the client's action and where that period is allowed to elapse, responsibility may attach to both. Although the point has not arisen for decision in any decided case, in principle

92. See chapter 2.
93. *Locke* v. *Camberwell Health Authority* [1991] 2 Med.L.R. 249. See also *Ridehalgh* v. *Horsefield* [1994] 3 W.L.R. 467 at 483B–C and the analysis in Jackson and Powell, *Professional Negligence* (3rd edn, 1992) at paras 4–65 to 4–69.

barrister and solicitor may be joint tortfeasors in which case responsibility *inter se* would be subject to the Civil Liability (Contribution) Act 1978.

## 5 DISCIPLINARY PROCEDURES

### 5.1 Internal regulation

The Code of Conduct of the Bar of England and Wales regulates the conduct of all barristers within that jurisdiction whenever called to the Bar.[94] Subject to the power of the General Council of the Bar to waive the duties imposed by the Code, the Bar thereby regulates its members and requires them to comply with the standards thereby set. As with other professional bodies, a key factor in achieving compliance lies in the power of the Bar Council to hear and determine complaints against its members and, where necessary, to impose disciplinary measures.

The Professional Conduct Committee of the Bar Council ("the PCC") has a twofold role:

(i) to interpret and make rulings on the meaning of the Code of Conduct; and
(ii) to investigate complaints against barristers.

While its role at (i) above is relevant to this work as a monitor of the standards of care and conduct expected of barristers, the second role is of greater interest in providing an alternative forum for professional liability disputes.

Upon receiving a complaint the PCC must determine whether prima facie professional misconduct has been disclosed.[95] The PCC has three principal options:

(i) In cases which are insufficiently serious to merit further referral, the PCC has power to require a barrister to attend and for an oral or written admonition to be given. There is no power at this stage to require a barrister to repay or forgo fees and, further, the findings of the PCC are not published.[96]

(ii) To prefer charges and to deal with the complaint summarily.[97] This option is appropriate for cases involving no disputes of fact which are not suitable for summary determination and where none of the charges, if proved or admitted, would be likely to lead to a sentence of disbarment. The sentencing powers available include partial or total suspension, imposition of a fine payable to the Bar Council, reprimand and advice as to future conduct as well as the admonishment power referred to above.

(iii) To direct that the complaint should be the subject matter of a charge before a disciplinary tribunal.[98] This is a committee comprising usually a judge, a lay representative and three barristers in independent practice of

94. 1990 edn as amended.
95. Such a complaint may be from an outside body or person or initiated by the Bar Council of its own motion. In addition, although outside the scope of this work, the PCC receives complaints from barristers about their treatment in chambers and has jurisdiction to consider them if heads or members of chambers are in breach of their obligations under the Code of Conduct.
96. The Professional Conduct Committee Rules, r. 3(e)(vi) reproduced as Annexe M to the Code of Conduct of the Bar of England and Wales (1990 edn, as amended).
97. The Professional Conduct Committee Rules, r. 3(e)(vii) and the Summary Procedure Rules reproduced as Annexe P to the Code of Conduct.
98. The Professional Conduct Committee Rules, r. 3(e)(viii).

not less than five years' standing established under the Disciplinary Tribunals Regulations 1993.[99] Such a reference is appropriate in cases which are not suitable for summary determination under the procedure at (ii) above.[100] In this event, the PCC has power to appoint counsel and solicitors for the purpose of formulating charges and representing it before the tribunal. Hearings are held in private unless a contrary direction is given.[101] In addition to its powers of admonishment and reprimand, the tribunal has power to disbar, suspend, order payment of a fine to the Bar Council of up to £5,000 and to order the barrister to repay or forgo fees.[102] Appeal against a decision of the tribunal lies to the Visitors to the Inns of Court.[103]

Not all complaints relate to matters which are properly termed "professional misconduct". Further, it is to be noted that the Bar Council has no power to order a barrister to compensate a claimant. In September 1994 the Standards Review Body, established for this purpose by the Bar Council, proposed the establishment of a new complaints system for the Bar to include a Barristers' Complaints Bureau with powers to investigate complaints of poor work and unsatisfactory service. The new Bureau, it is envisaged, will operate alongside the existing disciplinary procedure and will comprise adjudication panels consisting of lay and barrister members. The adjudication panel will have powers to require a barrister to give a formal apology, to forgo or repay fees and to pay compensation to the claimant, limited to £2,000.[104]

## 5.2 The Legal Services Ombudsman[105]

In addition to having a role in overseeing the Professional Conduct Committee of the Bar Council, the Legal Services Ombudsman has power to recommend that barristers pay compensation to complainants and to publicise any failure to do so.[106] Complaints must however be referred in the first instance to the General Council of the Bar and it is only where a complainant is not satisfied with the way in which the

99. Reproduced as Annexe N to the Code of Conduct.

100. In practice, "serious" in this context is likely to mean conviction of a criminal offence. By way of example, a barrister convicted of theft and making a false statement pursuant to s. 1 of the Forgery and Counterfeiting Act 1981 and sentenced to a period of imprisonment was disbarred in July 1994. The third charge arose from his failure to report the criminal conviction to the Bar Council—see *Counsel, The Journal of the Bar of England and Wales*, May/June 1995 at p. 33.

101. Disciplinary Tribunals Regulations 1993, reg. 11.

102. *Ibid.* at reg. 18(2).

103. Under the Hearings Before the Visitors Rules 1991—se Annexe O of the Code of Conduct of the Bar of England and Wales (1990 edn, as amended). Such an appeal is heard by a single judge of the High Court or the Court of Appeal nominated by the Lord Chief Justice save that where the appeal is in relation to an order for disbarment or is from a tribunal which was itself presided over by a judge of the High Court, the appeal is heard by three judges of the High Court or the Court of Appeal so nominated—*ibid.* at r. 10. See *R* v. *Visitors to the Inns of Court, ex parte Calder and Persaud* [1993] 2 All E.R. 876 for an analysis of the jurisdiction of the Visitors.

104. The Final Report of the Complaints System Working Group was delivered in August 1995 and was due to be considered by the Bar Council in autumn 1995.

105. See R James and M Seneviratne, "The Legal Services Ombudsman—Form versus Function?" (1995) 58 M.L.R. 187.

106. Sections 21–26 of, and Sch. 3 to the Courts and Legal Services Act 1990. The Legal Services Ombudsman is appointed for a three-year period and cannot be a barrister, solicitor, licensed conveyancer or notary.

matter is dealt with by that body that a reference to the Legal Services Ombudsman occurs.[107] Initially, at least, the Legal Services Ombudsman investigates the handling of the complaint by that body, but the underlying complaint may also be investigated.

The remit of the Legal Services Ombudsman is otherwise a wide one which seeks to uphold standards of service beyond the purely disciplinary code of the Bar Council. Of the investigations completed during 1994, 80 complaints related to barristers with a further 32 awaiting final report. Of the completed investigations, only five resulted in an order that the barrister should pay compensation and one involved a recommendation that the General Council of the Bar should reconsider its original decision.[108]

## 6 LIABILITY FOR WASTED COSTS

### 6.1 A statutory framework[109]

By section 51(6) of the Supreme Court Act 1981, as substituted by section 4 of the Courts and Legal Services Act 1990, the court is empowered to disallow or order the legal or other representative concerned to meet the whole of any wasted costs or such part of them as may be determined in accordance with rules of court. By subsection (6) "wasted costs" is defined to mean "any costs incurred by a party (a) as a result of any improper, unreasonable or negligent act or omission on the part of any legal or other representative or any employee of such a representative; or (b) which, in the light of any such act or omission occurring after they were incurred, the court considers it unreasonable to expect that party to pay". Further guidance is given by R.S.C., Ord. 62, r. 11.

Prior to the 1990 Act, some confusion had arisen as to whether section 51 as originally drafted extended to barristers and also over the test which was to be applied in each case.[110] Thus, although as has already been noted,[111] section 62 of the

---

107. The Legal Services Ombudsman cannot investigate an allegation while the complaint is being investigated by the relevant professional body or where either an appeal is pending or the time for such an appeal has not expired: Courts and Legal Services Act 1990, s. 22(5). However, the above does not apply if the allegation relates to the conduct of that professional body in investigating the complaint or where he is satisfied that an investigation is nevertheless justified: *ibid.* s. 22(6).

108. Fourth Annual Report of the Legal Services Ombudsman 1994. The average amount of compensation awarded in 1993 (including cases against solicitors and licensed conveyancers) was £427. The principal complaints related to what was broadly termed "client care" issues, poor communication with lay clients and poor record keeping. In addition, the report notes concern over late "returned briefs" where cases are switched at the last minute to another counsel owing to non-availability of the barrister originally briefed.

109. See S Fennell, "Wasted costs after the Courts and Legal Services Act" (1993) 9 P.N. 25 and P Jones and N Armstrong, "Living in fear of wasted costs" (1994) 13 C.J.Q. 208 and the addendum *ibid.* at p. 225.

110. The history of the jurisdiction is set out in detail in *Ridehalgh* v. *Horsefield* [1994] 3 W.L.R. 462. Prior to 1960 when a new rule (the forerunner of R.S.C., Ord. 62, r. 8(1)) was introduced, the better view is that there was no general jurisdiction to order a legal representative to pay wasted costs and that the matter was one for the inherent jurisdiction of the court. By the 1980s applications against solicitors were becoming more frequent: see *Davy-Chiesman* v. *Davy-Chiesman* [1984] 2 W.L.R. 291; but as recognised in *Orchard* v. *South Eastern Electricity Board* [1987] Q.B. 565 at 572 no claim could be made against counsel. In 1986 the Rules of the Supreme Court were amended. However, doubt arose as to whether the rule introduced a lesser standard of negligence (see *Sinclair-Jones* v. *Kay* [1989] 1 W.L.R. 114 at 121–122 and *Gupta* v. *Comer* [1991] Q.B. 629) or whether gross neglect or serious dereliction of duty was required (see *Holden & Co (A Firm)* v. *Crown Prosecution Service* [1990] 2 W.L.R. 1137).

111. Above, at p. 297, fn. 19.

1990 Act expressly preserved the immunity of advocates in relation to their conduct of court proceedings, the power to order an advocate guilty of "improper, unreasonable or negligent" conduct in that context to pay wasted costs provides an alternative remedy while preserving the formal immunity principle at law.[112] Such costs are in the discretion of the court.[113] It is now accepted that an order for wasted costs may be made against counsel as well as solicitors.[114] At the outset, however, it must be noted that jurisdiction is not generally exercised to order a barrister or other advocate to compensate his own client and there is no obvious overlap with the previous sections in this chapter. Yet, like the issue of immunity, public policy considerations can be seen to shape the jurisdiction as appears from the important decision of the Court of Appeal in *Ridehalgh* v. *Horsefield*.[115] As Sir Thomas Bingham MR put it[116]:

"The argument we have heard discloses a tension between two important public interests. One is that lawyers should not be deterred from pursuing their clients' interests by fear of incurring a personal liability to their clients' opponents; that they should not be penalised by orders to pay costs without a fair opportunity to defend themselves; that wasted costs orders should not become a back-door means of recovering costs not otherwise recoverable against a legally aided or impoverished litigant; and that the remedy should not grow unchecked to become more damaging than the disease. The other public interest, recently and clearly affirmed by Act of Parliament, is that litigants should not be financially prejudiced by the unjustifiable conduct of litigation by their or their opponents' lawyers."

The Court of Appeal went on to propound a three-stage test to be applied when a wasted costs order is contemplated[117]:

(i) Has the legal representative of whom complaint is made acted improperly, unreasonably or negligently?

(ii) If so, did such conduct cause the applicant to incur unnecessary costs?

(iii) If so, is it in all the circumstances just to order the legal representative to compensate the applicant for the whole or any part of the relevant costs?

### 6.2 "Improper, unreasonable or negligent"

Improper conduct was defined in *Ridehalgh* v. *Horsefield*[118] to include a significant breach of professional conduct and to this extent conduct which would be sufficient to justify the disbarment of a barrister under the disciplinary procedures referred to above would also merit an award of wasted costs. However, the Court of Appeal indicated that irrespective of whether the conduct violated the relevant professional code, it could be "improper" according to the consensus of professional and judicial opinion.

Unreasonable conduct was held to be that which is "vexatious, designed to harass

---

112. In *Ridehalgh* v. *Horsefield* [1994] 3 W.L.R. 462 at 481G, the court noted the anomaly which would arise if the wasted costs jurisdiction over barristers was subject to immunity in relation to the conduct of cases in court.

113. Section 51(1) of the Courts and Legal Services Act 1990.

114. *R* v. *Secretary of State for the Home Department, ex parte Abassi* (1992) *The Times*, 6 April, C.A.; *Ridehalgh* v. *Horsefield* [1994] 3 W.L.R. 462.

115. *Ibid.*

116. *Ibid.* at 472C–E.

117. *Ibid.* at 477D–E.

118. [1994] 3 W.L.R. 462.

the other side rather than advance the resolution of the case, and it makes no difference that the conduct is the product of excessive zeal and not improper motive".[119] The acid test was said to be whether the conduct permitted of a reasonable explanation.

The term "negligent" was recognised to be the most controversial. Unsurprisingly, the Court of Appeal rejected the proposition that the conduct must necessarily involve an actionable breach of duty to his own client as to have done so might have significantly reduced the scope of the new provision. Instead, negligence is to be understood in an "untechnical" way to mean failure to act with the competence reasonably to be expected of ordinary members of the profession. However, the court went on somewhat elliptically to discount the notion that anything less than that required in an action for negligence would suffice.[120]

In the case of barristers, the court expressly acknowledged the impact of the cab-rank principle and confirmed that it would not be improper, unreasonable or negligent merely to act for a party who pursued a claim or defence which was plainly doomed to fail.[121] The position is otherwise if he lends his assistance to proceedings which are an abuse of the process of the court.[122] Furthermore, in a clear echo of the justifications for the immunity from civil suit, the Court of Appeal cautioned judges to have regard to the fact that an advocate makes decisions in court quickly and under pressure.[123]

Specifically, the court in *Ridehalgh* v. *Horsefield* confirmed the following further safeguards in applying the wasted costs regime:

(i) Allowance must be made for the inability of lawyers to tell the whole story owing to their obligation to preserve their client's legal professional privilege.[124]

(ii) Demonstration of a causal link between the improper, unreasonable or negligent conduct is essential.[125]

(iii) The threat of proposed applications for wasted costs should not be used as a means of intimidation.[126]

---

119. *Ibid.* at 478C–D. See also *R* v. *Horsham District Council, ex parte Wenman* [1994] 4 All E.R. 681, where it is apparent that Brooke J would have been willing to make an order against counsel in the context of judicial review proceedings but for the fact that most of the errors pre-dated the new wasted costs regime.

120. *Ibid.* at 478H–479A. For a recent example, see *R* v. *Stuart* [1993] Crim.L.R. 767 and *Barrister (Wasted Costs Order) (No 4 of 1992)* (1992) *The Times*, 15 March.

121. The court in *Ridehalgh* recognised the particular vulnerability of practitioners who acted on behalf of legally aided clients to applications for wasted costs. See also *Symphony Group plc* v. *Hodgson* [1994] Q.B. 179 at 194 and *Sampson* v. *John Boddy Timber Ltd* (1995) 145 N.L.J. 851, C.A.

122. The court gave the example of a barrister pursuing a case which he knew to be dishonest or knowingly failing to make full disclosure on an *ex parte* application. A barrister must not raise an allegation of fraud unless he has clear instructions to do so and has before him reasonably credible material which establishes a prima facie case of fraud: para. 606(a) of The Code of Conduct of the Bar of England and Wales (1990 edn, as amended). It is submitted that to do so in the absence of such credible evidence could be regarded as improper and the barrister mulcted in costs.

123. [1994] 3 W.L.R. 462 at 482B–C.

124. *Ibid.* at 482D–H.

125. *Ibid.* at 482H–483A; *Re a Barrister (Wasted Costs Order) (No 1 of 1991)* [1993] Q.B. 293.

126. *Ibid.* at 483D; *Orchard* v. *South Eastern Electricity Board* [1987] Q.B. 565.

(iv) Save in exceptional circumstances, applications for wasted costs should not be sought after trial so as to avoid depriving the opposing party of the legal representative of his choice.[127]

(v) The court should be slow itself to initiate the inquiry as to whether a wasted costs order should be made having regard to the time-consuming, difficult and embarrassing issue on costs which may arise.[128]

(vi) The procedure on such applications should be as simple and summary as fairness permits and hearings should be measured in hours rather than days or weeks.[129]

(vii) Discretion should be exercised actively both at the initial stage of deciding whether a barrister should be ordered to "show cause" and at the final stage of deciding whether an order for payment of wasted costs should be made.[130]


## 7 INSURANCE

It is a prerequisite to a barrister supplying legal services in independent practice that he should be a member of the Bar Mutual Indemnity Fund Limited ("BMIF") a company limited by guarantee, and that he should thereafter pay the appropriate premium so as to be insured against professional negligence.[131] BMIF was formed in 1988 following the failure of one of the major underwriters who had previously provided professional indemnity insurance for the Bar. By establishing its own mutual insurance company, the Bar sought to provide certainty and stability and, most importantly, provided a mechanism whereby it controlled its own insurance.

As at 31 March 1994 the sum retained and available to meet outstanding claims amounted to £7,142,912 and, as with most of the other professions which are the subject of this work, BMIF reported a rising level of claims and a substantial increase in premium rates.[132] Premiums are calculated by reference to levels of income and areas of practice based upon the statistical claims exposure.[133] Save in the case of wasted costs orders where a deductible of £250 per claim applies, members of BMIF are not subject to an excess and claims history is disregarded.

LESLEY ANDERSON

127. *Ibid.* at 483F; *Filmlab Systems International Ltd* v. *Pennington* [1994] 4 All E.R. 673.
128. In *Re Freudiana Holdings* (1995) C.L. 432 Jonathan Parker J ordered that the application for wasted costs should not proceed where the application was made in the context of a minority shareholder's unfair prejudice petition which had lasted 165 days.
129. *Ibid.* at 484B–C.
130. *Ibid.* at 484D–H.
131. The Code of Conduct of the Bar of England and Wales (1990 edn, as amended) at para. 302.
132. See the Chairman's Report comprised in the Directors' Report and Financial Statements for the year ended 31 March 1994. 472 new claims files were opened in that year, which represents a threefold increase on the number six years earlier.
133. An analysis of the claims experience of BMIF since 1988 identified that 20 per cent of all files and 23 per cent of payments related to incorrect analysis or application of legal principles or precedents, a problem which is perceived by BMIF to apply in particular to barristers who practise on the fringe of their own expertise. Three per cent of all files related to vexatious claims. A basic contribution sufficient to provide £2,500,000 cover is compulsory.

# CHAPTER 7

# ESTATE AGENTS

## 1 INTRODUCTION

The first part of this chapter sets out to provide a context for discussion of the specific professional liabilities and regulation of estate agents, by considering the nature and incidents of the legal relationship which such agents have with their clients. After a general introduction, there is an examination of the unusually limited type of agency which is involved, and a brief account of the major principles which govern the remuneration of estate agents. The two main sections of the chapter which follow consider the liabilities to which estate agents may be subject at common law (notably for professional negligence and for breach of fiduciary duty), and the regulatory regime to which they have been subjected since the implementation of the Estate Agents Act 1979. For the sake of completeness, the chapter concludes with a brief note of other statutory provisions which are of particular relevance to this area of professional work.

### 1.1 Estate agency in context

The essence of estate agency may be defined as work carried out in order to secure the introduction of one person who wishes to dispose of an interest in land to another person who wishes to acquire such an interest.[1] It is a notable feature of the property industry in the United Kingdom that any person may lawfully set up in business to carry out such work; there is no professional closed shop in the sense of entry qualifications or restrictions upon practice. True, there is power under section 22 of the Estate Agents Act 1979 to issue statutory instruments imposing "minimum standards of competence" upon anyone carrying on estate agency work, but successive governments have rejected pleas from various quarters (including the major professional bodies representing estate agents) to implement this provision, on the ground that it would unduly hamper competition.[2] The alternative approach which is favoured by the government is that of professional self-regulation through a voluntary Code of Practice, but this has as yet failed to convince even the major estate agency professional organisations, let alone the substantial number of agents who are independent of any professional body.

Although no formal qualification is required to practise estate agency, many

---

1. See the Estate Agents Act 1979, s. 1.
2. See the Department of Trade and Industry's *Review of Estate Agency* (June 1989). The Office of Fair Trading takes a similar line: see the OFT's *Report on Estate Agency* (March 1990).

agents are in fact members of a professional organisation, of which the largest are the Royal Institution of Chartered Surveyors ("RICS"), the Incorporated Society of Valuers and Auctioneers ("ISVA") and the National Association of Estate Agents ("NAEA").[3] Each of these bodies imposes a code of regulations upon its members which covers such matters as client accounts, conflict of interests and so on. However, the expulsion of a member for breach of such regulations means merely expulsion from the organisation concerned, not from the practice of estate agency itself.

A significant feature of the 1980s property boom was the growth of the corporate estate agency sector, as many banks, building societies and insurance companies diversified into this area of activity, often by purchasing and renaming existing firms of agents. Consumer concern about potential conflicts of interest in this sector led to the designation of certain practices as "undesirable" under the Estate Agents Act 1979.[4] A further consequence, a response by the corporate sector itself, was the setting up of an Ombudsman scheme to deal with consumer complaints.[5]

## 1.2 The estate agency relationship

The place of estate agents within the general law of agency is somewhat unusual for a number of reasons. First, there is considerable doubt as to the nature of the legal relationship between estate agent and client. Secondly, the extent to which an estate agent can affect a client's legal relationship with third parties (something which lies at the very heart of agency) is extremely limited. Thirdly, while the rules which govern the remuneration of estate agents are in principle no different from those which apply to other agents, disputes over estate agents' commission have generated a highly specialised body of case-law.

### 1.2.1 A unilateral contract?

Some uncertainty as to the nature of the relationship between estate agent and client stems from *dicta* of the House of Lords in *Luxor (Eastbourne) Ltd* v. *Cooper*.[6] According to these *dicta*, an estate agent's mandate imposes no positive duty on the agent to act,[7] but merely sets out the conditions which, if satisfied, will entitle the agent to recover commission. This suggests that the normal relationship between estate agent and client consists of a "unilateral contract", that is to say, one which does not ripen into a contract in the full sense until the agent "accepts" the client's "offer" by bringing about whatever event is specified.[8]

Such an interpretation, if logically correct, would have some undesirable practical

---

3. In addition to these associations, which commonly act (either jointly or individually) as spokesmen for estate agents generally, there are various smaller bodies, many of which represent specialist sectors of estate agency.

4. See p. 339.

5. The details of this scheme are described in Morris, "The Ombudsman for Corporate Estate Agents" (1994) *Civil Justice Quarterly* 337.

6. [1941] A.C. 108. According to Lord Russell of Killowen (at 124): "The contracts are merely promises binding on the principal to pay a sum of money upon the happening of a specified event, which involves the rendering of some service by the agent". Similar views, though less unequivocally expressed, may be found in the speeches of Viscount Simon LC (at 117) and Lord Romer (at 153).

7. See p. 321.

8. See *Chitty on Contracts* (27th edn, 1994), para. 2–057; *Bowstead on Agency* (15th edn, 1985), pp. 234–235; Murdoch, "The Nature of Estate Agency" (1975) 91 *Law Quarterly Review* 357.

implications, notably in undermining the status of the "confirming letter" which estate agents have traditionally used to communicate their terms of business. The "unilateral contract" view presupposes that the "offer" emanates from the client; hence, any communication from the agent which purports to vary the terms of that offer would take effect as a counter-offer and would thus destroy the original offer.[9] More importantly, unless the relationship is fully contractual from the outset there appears no room for the implication of terms under sections 13–15 of the Supply of Goods and Services Act 1982.

Notwithstanding the high authority of the *dicta* on which the unilateral contract view of estate agency is based, the view itself has not passed without challenge. It has been pointed out[10] that the courts have from time to time imposed liability for breach of contract upon an estate agent in respect of actions carried out before the occurrence of any commission-earning event.[11] It also appears that, quite apart from potential liability for negligence (which might arise independently of any contract) an estate agent can be liable for disobeying an express instruction from the client.[12] Finally, it may be noted that section 18 of the Estate Agents Act 1979, which requires estate agents to notify clients of certain information, clearly assumes that the agency relationship is contractual from the outset.[13]

Even if the view of estate agency as a unilateral contract can survive such attacks, it does not appear applicable where the agent in question is given a sole agency or sole selling rights.[14] There is authority for regarding such cases as involving a bilateral contract, under which the agent impliedly undertakes to use best endeavours to find a purchaser.[15]

## 1.2.2 The limits of authority

In legal terms, the essence of agency lies in the authority of the agent to affect the principal's legal relations with third parties. The most notable feature of estate agency is that the agent is almost entirely bereft of such authority, except in so far as it is expressly conferred by the client. In *Thuman* v. *Best*,[16] Parker J stated:

"Estate agents as such have no general authority to enter into contracts for their employers. Their business is to find offers and submit them to their employers for acceptance."

In recognition of this very restricted authority, estate agency is sometimes referred to as an example of "incomplete agency".[17]

The most striking limitation upon the implied authority of an estate agent lies in

9. Whether or not a confirming letter is treated as a counter-offer, the need to identify the client's acceptance of its terms has caused problems in the past: see *Way & Waller Ltd* v. *Ryde* [1944] 1 All E.R. 9; *John E Trinder & Partners* v. *Haggis* (1951) 158 E.G. 4; cf. *Toulmin* v. *Millar* (1887) 3 T.L.R. 836.

10. CR McConnell, "Engaging an estate agent; is it really a unilateral contract?" (1983) 265 *Estates Gazette* 547.

11. Particular emphasis is placed upon the decision of the Court of Appeal in *Keppel* v. *Wheeler* [1927] 1 K.B. 577.

12. See p. 321.

13. "A contract ... under which the agent *will engage* in estate agency work on behalf of the client" (emphasis added).

14. *Bowstead on Agency* (15th edn, 1985), p. 235.

15. See p. 322.

16. (1907) 97 L.T. 239.

17. *Bowstead on Agency* (15th edn), p. 11.

the fact that, unless specifically authorised,[18] such an agent is unable to create a contract of sale[19] or lease[20] which will bind the client. This is certainly the case where the agent is instructed to find a purchaser or a tenant; where the word "sell" is used the position is less clear.[21] It appears moreover that, even where an estate agent *is* authorised to make a contract, this can be no more than an open contract; to negotiate special conditions would require specific authorisation from the client.[22]

Apart from the inability to bind the client to a contract, it appears that an estate agent as such has no authority to accept a pre-contract deposit as the client's agent,[23] although the Court of Appeal has twice held a landlord liable when an estate agent without any express instruction demanded an illegal premium from a tenant.[24] Nor, it appears, may the agent appoint a sub-agent to act on the client's behalf without express authority.[25]

An estate agent who deals with a third party in excess of whatever authority is expressly or impliedly conferred may incur personal liability to that third party for breach of warranty of authority.[26] The agent's disobedience may also entitle the client to refuse payment of commission, for example where a purchaser is introduced by a sub-agent whose appointment by the main agent was unauthorised.[27]

The one aspect of estate agency work in which the agent has implied authority to affect the client's legal position relates to the task of describing the property to be sold or leased. It appears that a misrepresentation made by an estate agent will be treated as emanating from the vendor, except where a contract term or notice explicitly denies that the agent is authorised to make such a statement,[28] and may thus entitle the purchaser to rescind the sale[29] or claim damages under section 2 of the Misrepresentation Act 1967.[30] Losses incurred by the client in this way may be recovered from the agent as damages for breach of duty.[31]

18. As would be the case, for example, where the agent sells by auction.

19. *Hamer* v. *Sharp* (1874) L.R. 19 Eq. 108; *Chadburn* v. *Moore* (1892) 61 L.J.Ch. 674; *Lewcock* v. *Bromley* (1920) 127 L.T. 116.

20. *Thuman* v. *Best* (1907) 97 L.T. 239.

21. *Dicta* in *Rosenbaum* v. *Belson* [1900] 2 Ch. 267 and *Keen* v. *Mear* [1920] 2 Ch. 574 suggest that "sell" confers the requisite authority; the opposite view appears from *Chadburn* v. *Moore* (1892) 61 L.J.Ch. 674, *Lewcock* v. *Bromley* (1920) 127 L.T. 116 and *Wragg* v. *Lovett* [1948] 2 All E.R. 968.

22. See *Keen* v. *Mear* [1920] 2 Ch. 574; *Wragg* v. *Lovett* [1948] 2 All E.R. 968.

23. *Sorrell* v. *Finch* [1977] A.C. 728, in which the House of Lords overruled a line of Court of Appeal decisions including *Ryan* v. *Pilkington* [1959] 1 All E.R. 689; *Burt* v. *Claude Cousins & Co Ltd* [1971] 2 Q.B. 426; and *Barrington* v. *Lee* [1971] 3 All E.R. 1231. The statutory rules governing deposits paid to estate agents are discussed at p. 332.

24. *Navarro* v. *Moregrand Ltd* [1951] 2 T.L.R. 674; *Saleh* v. *Robinson* [1988] 2 E.G.L.R. 126.

25. *Maloney* v. *Hardy and Moorshead* (1970) 216 E.G. 1582; *McCann & Co* v. *Pow* [1975] 1 All E.R. 129. It may be noted, however, that in neither case was any serious attempt made to establish a trade custom permitting delegation.

26. See, for example, *Godwin* v. *Francis* (1870) L.R. 5 C.P. 295.

27. So held by the Court of Appeal in *McCann & Co* v. *Pow* [1975] 1 All E.R. 129. Unless, however, the unauthorised delegation prejudices the client's position, it is with respect difficult to see why commission should be forfeited, since the client achieves the desired result.

28. Such notices have twice been held effective to absolve the vendor from responsibility: *Overbrooke Estates Ltd* v. *Glencombe Properties Ltd* [1974] 3 All E.R. 511; *Collins* v. *Howell-Jones* [1981] 2 E.G.L.R. 108. In *Overbrooke* it was further held that a term or notice denying the agent's authority is not subject to what is now the Unfair Contract Terms Act 1977; see, however, *South Western General Property Co Ltd* v. *Marton* [1982] 2 E.G.L.R. 19.

29. *Mullens* v. *Miller* (1882) 22 Ch.D. 194.

30. *Gosling* v. *Anderson* (1972) 223 E.G. 1743. The agent, however, has no implied authority to give a warranty having contractual force: *Lawrence* v. *Hull* (1924) 41 T.L.R. 75; *Hill* v. *Harris* [1965] 2 Q.B. 601.

31. *Whiteman* v. *Weston* (1900) *The Times*, 15 March.

## 1.2.3 Estate agents' commission[32]

The essence of an estate agent's commission agreement lies in the fact that the agent receives an agreed fee if, and only if, he or she is successful in bringing about a specified result.[33] In *Howard Houlder & Partners Ltd* v. *Manx Isles Steamship Co Ltd*,[34] McCardie J stated[35]:

"It is a settled rule for the construction of commission notes and the like documents which refer to the remuneration of an agent that a plaintiff cannot recover unless he shows that the conditions of the written bargain have been fulfilled. If he proves fulfilment he recovers. If not, he fails. There appears to be no halfway house, and it matters not that the plaintiff proves expenditure of time, money and skill."

It follows from this "settled rule" that an estate agent[36] who wishes to charge a fee or expenses irrespective of whether or not a transaction is concluded must ensure that this is clearly stated in the agency agreement.[37]

Many of the reported cases on estate agents' commission have turned on the question of what event must take place in order to trigger the agent's entitlement to be paid.[38] While this is of course a matter of interpretation of the individual agency agreement, a study of the authorities reveals a fairly consistent judicial approach. It appears that, in the absence of clear words to the contrary,[39] commission will be earned when either a sale is completed or, following the making of a binding contract of sale,[40] an applicant introduced by the agent remains willing and able to complete but the vendor-client defaults.[41] Commission clauses which have been interpreted in this way include "completion of the sale",[42] "find a purchaser",[43] "on a sale being effected",[44] and those which make reference to payment out of the purchase price.[45]

Although the above represents the prevalent construction of estate agents'

---

32. See *Bowstead on Agency* (15th edn, 1985), art. 58.

33. Where an estate agent is employed to carry out professional *services*, rather than to procure a result, there is a strong judicial presumption that payment will be on the basis of the time and trouble expended: *Upsdell* v. *Stewart* (1793) Peake 255; *Drew* v. *Josolyne* (1888) 4 T.L.R. 717; *Faraday* v. *Tamworth Union* (1917) 86 L.J.Ch. 436. See generally, Murdoch, "Professional Fees—How Much is Reasonable?" [1981] Conv. 424 at 425–428.

34. [1923] 1 K.B. 110.

35. *Ibid.* at 113.

36. Including an auctioneer: *John Meacock & Co* v. *Abrahams* [1956] 3 All E.R. 660.

37. The statutory duty to inform clients of such charges (under s. 18 of the Estate Agents Act 1979) is considered at p. 334.

38. Where the agent's efforts result in a transaction which is different from what was originally envisaged (e.g., a long lease rather than a sale), entitlement to commission depends upon the doctrine of substantial performance: see Murdoch, *Law of Estate Agency and Auctions* (3rd edn, 1994), pp. 147–152.

39. "It is possible that an owner may be willing to bind himself to pay a commission for the mere introduction of one who offers to purchase at the specified or minimum price, but such a construction of the contract would, in my opinion, require clear and unequivocal language" (*Luxor (Eastbourne) Ltd* v. *Cooper* [1941] A.C. 108 at 129 *per* Lord Russell of Killowen).

40. A contract which is voidable for misrepresentation is not "binding" for this purpose: *Peter Long & Partners* v. *Burns* [1956] 1 W.L.R. 413, 1083. Whether the contract must also be capable of specific performance is unclear: see *Murdoch Lownie Ltd* v. *Newman* [1949] 2 All E.R. 783 at 789; *Fowler* v. *Bratt* [1950] 2 K.B. 96 at 105; *McCallum* v. *Hicks* [1950] 2 K.B. 271 at 274. Cf. *Sheggia* v. *Gradwell* [1963] 3 All E.R. 114.

41. In *Blake & Co* v. *Sohn* [1969] 3 All E.R. 123 it was held that a vendor's inability to prove title did not constitute "default" for this purpose.

42. *Luxor (Eastbourne) Ltd* v. *Cooper* [1941] A.C. 108.

43. *Poole* v. *Clarke & Co* [1945] 2 All E.R. 445.

44. *Martin* v. *Perry & Daw* [1931] 2 K.B. 310.

45. *Beningfield* v. *Kynaston* (1887) 3 T.L.R. 279; *Beale* v. *Bond* (1901) 17 T.L.R. 280.

commission agreements, it is perfectly possible for the parties to agree that payment shall be tied to some other event. It is not uncommon, especially in the commercial sector, for commission to be made payable on exchange of contracts, irrespective of whether or not the transaction proceeds to completion or who is to blame if it does not.[46] More controversially, it now appears settled that clauses such as "on the introduction of a person ready, willing and able to purchase" may entitle an estate agent to commission on the mere introduction of a suitable applicant, even though the vendor subsequently withdraws without entering into a contract of sale.[47] In such circumstances, whether or not the applicant fulfils the stated criteria is a question of fact.[48]

In addition to showing that a specified event has occurred, an estate agent claiming commission must normally be able to establish that it is his or her efforts which have brought about that event.[49] The court must be satisfied that the agent's introduction of the parties, or subsequent negotiation,[50] is not only a *causa sine qua non* of whatever transaction is entered into, but is its "effective" or "efficient" cause. This question, which is at root a matter of judicial impression, is responsible for a high proportion of the commission disputes which reach the stage of litigation. Such disputes frequently (though by no means always) arise where more than one agent claims responsibility for the effective introduction of the purchaser, or where there is a long delay between the introduction of a purchaser and the actual sale.[51]

It is possible for a commission agreement to be drafted in such a way as to outflank the "effective cause" requirement.[52] The most obvious example of this is where an estate agent is appointed on "sole agency" terms.[53] Traditionally, an agent deprived of the opportunity to earn commission by a sale in breach of a sole agency agreement has been compensated by an award of damages.[54] The more recent approach,

---

46. The Court of Appeal, albeit somewhat reluctantly, has twice held such a clause effective: *Midgley Estates Ltd* v. *Hand* [1952] 2 Q.B. 432; *Sheggia* v. *Gradwell* [1963] 2 All E.R. 114.

47. *Christie Owen & Davies* v. *Rapacioli* [1974] 2 All E.R. 311; *AA Dickson & Co* v. *O'Leary* [1980] 1 E.G.L.R. 25. It is submitted that the view repeatedly expressed by Lord Denning MR (e.g., in *McCallum* v. *Hicks* [1950] 2 K.B. 271 at 276), that a person cannot be described as "willing to purchase" unless he actually purchases, should now be ignored.

48. "Ability" is largely concerned with finance (see *James* v. *Smith* [1931] 2 K.B. 317n at 322, *per* Atkin LJ). However, a potential purchaser of a leasehold interest cannot be described as "able" where the landlord refuses consent to an assignment: *Dellafiora* v. *Lester*; *Lester* v. *Adrian Barr & Co Ltd* [1962] 3 All E.R. 393. As to the meaning of "prepared to enter into a contract", see *AL Wilkinson Ltd* v. *Brown* [1966] 1 All E.R. 509 at 511, *per* Harman LJ.

49. See *Bowstead on Agency* (15th edn, 1985), art. 59.

50. See *FP Rolfe & Co* v. *George* (1969) 210 EG 455; *Hoddell* v. *Smith* [1976] 2 E.G.L.R. 38.

51. The cases are collected, and the different factual situations described, in Murdoch, *Law of Estate Agency and Auctions* (3rd edn, 1994), pp. 152–159.

52. Auctioneers commonly seek to protect their position by providing in their standard terms of business that commission is payable on any private treaty sale within a specified period "whether or not effected by the auctioneers": see *Bernard Thorpe & Partners* v. *Snook* [1983] 1 E.G.L.R. 37; *Barnard Marcus & Co* v. *Ashraf* [1988] 1 E.G.L.R. 7; cf. *Fairvale Ltd* v. *Sabharwal* [1992] 2 E.G.L.R. 27. For an example of successful evasion outside the auction context, see *Brian Cooper & Co* v. *Fairview Estates (Investments) Ltd* [1987] 1 E.G.L.R. 18.

53. "Sole agency" as such prohibits the client from selling through another agent, but not from selling privately: *Bentall, Horsley & Baldry* v. *Vicary* [1931] 1 K.B. 253. Private sales are prohibited where the agent is given "sole selling rights": *Chamberlain & Willows* v. *Rose* (1924), unreported but summarised at [1931] 1 K.B. 261n.

54. See, for example, *Hampton & Sons Ltd* v. *George* [1939] 3 All E.R. 627.

however, is to provide that the agent in such circumstances is entitled to commission.[55]

Where an estate agent has done whatever is necessary to earn commission, the amount which is payable depends upon the terms of the particular commission agreement. Such agreements commonly make provision for a scale of fees or for a percentage of the price realised; fixed fee agreements are also found. In the absence of an express provision as to the amount of commission, the agent will normally be entitled to a reasonable sum.[56]

## 2 PROFESSIONAL LIABILITY OF ESTATE AGENTS

### 2.1 Duties of performance

Although direct authority is sparse, it appears to be generally accepted that an estate agent is obliged to comply with all lawful instructions from the client, and will be liable for any loss resulting from a failure to do so. In *Papé* v. *Westacott*,[57] for example, an agent was instructed to give a client's tenant written permission to assign his lease, provided that the tenant first paid off all arrears of rent. The agent in fact gave the licence to the tenant in return for a cheque, which was subsequently dishonoured, and the agent was held liable to the client for the money lost. Similarly, in *Hunt* v. *Beasley Drake*,[58] a potential purchaser agreed to pay commission to an estate agent for introducing suitable properties, provided that the agent gave an assurance that the published details of those properties were accurate. It was held that although, in normal circumstances, a purchaser's estate agent would not be expected to check the vendor's sale particulars, the agent in this case had expressly undertaken such an obligation and was liable for failure to carry it out.

The question of whether or not an estate agent owes any *positive* duty of performance to the client is one which goes to the very nature of the relationship between them. As noted earlier,[59] the decision of the House of Lords in *Luxor (Eastbourne) Ltd* v. *Cooper*[60] provides some authority for the view that this relationship is a unilateral contract, and *dicta* in the case in question strongly deny that the estate agent is under any duty to act. Thus[61]: "I doubt whether the agent is bound, generally speaking, to exercise any standard of diligence in looking for a possible purchaser". Again[62]: "No obligation is imposed on the agent to do anything". And, most explicitly[63]: "The respondent was not employed by the

55. An approach given credence by the wording of the Estate Agents (Provision of Information) Regulations 1991: see p. 334.
56. In assessing a reasonable sum in such circumstances, the courts have shown a preference for a figure related to the agent's time and trouble, rather than to the result achieved: see, e.g., *Reiff Diner & Co* v. *Catalytic International Inc* [1978] 1 E.G.L.R. 16; *Sinclair Goldsmith* v. *Minero Peru Comercial* [1978] 2 E.G.L.R. 28.
57. [1894] 1 Q.B. 272. See also *Edmonds* v. *Andrew & Ashwell* [1982] 1 E.G.L.R. 36 (unauthorised handing over of keys to prospective purchasers); *Benham & Reeves* v. *Christensen* [1979] C.L.Y. 31 (unauthorised erection of "Sold By" board).
58. [1995] N.P.C. 35.
59. See p. 316.
60. [1941] A.C. 108.
61. *Luxor (Eastbourne) Ltd* v. *Cooper* [1941] A.C. 108 at 117, *per* Viscount Simon LC.
62. *Ibid.* at 124 *per* Lord Russell of Killowen.
63. *Ibid.* at 153 *per* Lord Romer.

appellants to find a purchaser. He was not employed to do anything at all, and would have committed no breach of his agreement with the appellants had he remained entirely inactive".

Despite the strength of these remarks, it would be unwise to assume that an estate agent can never incur liability for failing to act on a client's behalf. In *Prebble & Co* v. *West*,[64] an estate agent who was sued for negligence argued (on the basis of *Luxor* v. *Cooper*) that, if there was no liability for nonfeasance, there could equally be none for any misfeasance which did not leave the client in a worse position than a failure to act would have done. This proposition was emphatically rejected by two members of the Court of Appeal, who asserted that an estate agent would owe a positive duty to pass on to the client any offers received for a property, at least where the agent was aware of the client's desire for a quick sale.[65]

Whether or not estate agents in general are under any positive duty to act, there is some authority for the view that such a duty is imposed upon one who is appointed as a "sole agent" or given "sole selling rights". In seeking to explain the undoubted enforceability of the agent's *rights* under such an arrangement, the courts have on occasion suggested that there is an implied undertaking by the agent to use "best endeavours" to find a purchaser.[66] While this is a convenient explanation, it may be noted that neither of the decisions most relied upon is fully reported. Moreover, in *Glentree Estates Ltd* v. *Gee*,[67] where a client attempted to list the specific duties comprised in "best endeavours", Ewbank J expressed strong doubts as to whether any of these duties actually existed.

## 2.2 Duty of care and skill

The precise nature of the legal relationship between estate agent and client may remain a matter of controversy, but it is none the less well settled that the agent owes the client a duty of care and skill. This duty covers every aspect of estate agency work, although in practice allegations of professional negligence arise mainly in two particular areas.[68]

First and foremost, an estate agent will be liable where, through negligent advice, valuation or marketing, the client is led into a transaction which does not reflect the true market value of the property.[69] In the common case of an estate agent acting for a vendor, the result of such negligence (for example in overlooking a potential demand for the property in question) will normally be that a sale takes place at an

---

64. (1969) 211 E.G. 831.

65. Failure to pass on offers is now an "undesirable practice" under the Estate Agents Act 1979 (see p. 335), although this does not create any civil remedy for the client.

66. See *E Christopher & Co* v. *Essig* [1948] W.N. 461; *Mendoza & Co* v. *Bell* (1952) 159 E.G. 372.

67. [1981] 2 E.G.L.R. 28.

68. For examples which do not belong in either of these categories, see *Edmonds* v. *Andrew & Ashwell* [1982] 1 E.G.L.R. 36 (duty of agent letting residential property to see that prospective purchasers do not take unauthorised possession) and *Hellings* v. *Parker Breslin Estates* [1995] 2 E.G.L.R. 99 (duty of agent letting residential property to ensure that landlord will be able to recover possession at end of term).

69. Such allegations frequently surface as a counterclaim when the agent seeks commission on a completed transaction. Recent examples, in which negligence was not established, include *Knight Frank & Rutley* v. *Randolph* [1991] 1 E.G.L.R. 46 and *Watson* v. *Lane Fox & Partners Ltd* [1991] 2 E.G.L.R. 21. See also *Letgain Ltd* v. *Super Cement Ltd* [1994] 1 E.G.L.R. 43, where an agent who failed to advertise the client's property escaped liability on the surprising ground that this was in accordance with the client's instructions.

undervalue.[70] However, in the unusual case of *Kenney* v. *Hall, Pain & Foster*,[71] an estate agent who negligently *overvalued* a client's house was held liable for thus encouraging the client into a disastrous course of action which led him to the verge of bankruptcy. Believing that the agent's valuation left a substantial safety margin, the client obtained bridging finance for the purchase of another property, only to find that his own was unsaleable at anything like the suggested price.

An estate agent retained to find a suitable property for a potential purchaser or tenant must take reasonable steps to obtain sufficient information to enable the client to make an informed decision.[72] Agents have accordingly been held liable for negligence in over-estimating the size of office accommodation[73] and in failing to discover an error in the rateable value of office premises quoted by landlords.[74]

The second major area of negligence claims against estate agents concerns the finding of suitable tenants on behalf of a prospective landlord. An agent in this connection should, it appears, take reasonable steps to obtain references,[75] and should be alert for any indication of a lack of solvency.[76] Failure in this respect may render the agent liable for loss of rent, legal costs incurred in recovering possession, and damage caused by the tenant to the premises.[77]

## 2.3 Fiduciary duties

Notwithstanding the limited nature of their ability to bind the client,[78] estate agents are fully subject to the fiduciary duties which the law imposes upon every agent. These duties, although capable of appearing as an itemised list, are in truth all aspects of the general principle that an agent must not allow any personal interest, or the interests of others, to conflict with the obligations which are owed to the client. In the context of estate agency, two aspects are of particular importance: a duty to make full and frank disclosure of all relevant facts concerning an actual or potential conflict of

70. See, for example, *Bell Hotels (1935) Ltd* v. *Motion* (1952) 159 E.G. 496; *Cuckmere Brick Co Ltd* v. *Mutual Finance Ltd* [1971] Ch. 949. For (unsuccessful) complaints about agents' general handling of a transaction, see *Lough Eske Holdings* v. *Knight Frank & Rutley* [1991] E.G.C.S. 18 and *Berkowitz* v. *MW (St John's Wood) Ltd* [1995] 1 E.G.L.R. 29.

71. [1976] 2 E.G.L.R. 29.

72. What is reasonable is a question of fact, and the functions of the client's other professional advisers are important. Thus an estate agent need not carry out a personal check of the planning register to ascertain the permitted use, since it can be assumed that the client's solicitors will do so (*GP & P Ltd* v. *Bulcraig & Davis* [1986] 2 E.G.L.R. 148, affirmed [1988] 1 E.G.L.R. 138). See also *Holt* v. *Payne Skillington* [1995] E.G.C.S. 201.

73. *Carreras Ltd* v. *DE & J Levy* (1970) 215 E.G. 707. The clients recovered only nominal damages, however, since it appeared that, notwithstanding the discrepancy, the agreed rent was no higher than the true market rental value.

74. *Computastaff Ltd* v. *Ingledew Brown Bennison & Garrett* [1983] 2 E.G.L.R. 150. The decision, while unimpeachable on the question of liability, is highly suspect on the measure of damages: the agents were held liable for all the extra rates payable by the clients during the tenancy, despite evidence that the transaction took place at market value.

75. Although not, in the absence of grounds for suspicion, to *check* those references: *Bradshaw* v. *Press* (1982, unreported).

76. *Heys* v. *Tindall* (1861) 30 L.J.Q.B. 362; *Brutton* v. *Alfred Savill, Curtis & Henson* (1971) 218 E.G. 1417; *Faruk* v. *Wyse* [1988] 2 E.G.L.R. 26; cf. *Cunningham* v. *Herbert Fulford & Chorley* (1958) 171 E.G. 285.

77. *Murray* v. *Sturgis* [1981] 2 E.G.L.R. 22.

78. See p. 317.

interest, and a duty to refrain from making any "secret profit" out of the agency relationship.

The derivation of an agent's fiduciary duties lies in the controls placed by equity upon trustees, and the duties are therefore applicable whether or not the agency relationship is contractual. However, where there is a contract between agent and client, the agent's fiduciary duties may be treated as implied terms of that contract, which may affect the remedies available in respect of a breach.

Although the roots of fiduciary duties thus lie in equitable ideas of good faith, it is well established that the duties themselves involve strict liability. An agent may thus be in breach where a conflict of interest arises, even though the agent has acted in good faith and without seeking to profit from the situation.[79]

An agent's fiduciary duties do not arise until the agency relationship is established; there is thus no duty of disclosure at the time when agency terms are being negotiated.[80] Once in place, however, the duties remain in force until a binding contract of sale or lease is executed[81] or until the agency is terminated. Nor can an estate agent avoid the consequences of a conflict of interest by first terminating the agency relationship, unless full disclosure is made to the client.[82]

Of the various ways in which these fiduciary duties apply in practice, the most fundamental is the principle that an agent may neither acquire property from,[83] nor transfer property to,[84] the client, unless the agent's position is made perfectly clear.[85] Nor, in general, may an agent act for both parties to a transaction without the informed consent of both "clients".[86] However, the latter principle has been applied by modern courts with some flexibility, so as not to disentitle an agent to commission where an undisclosed potential conflict of interest is shown not to have damaged the client.[87]

Potential conflicts of interest are not limited to cases in which parties are on

79. *Harrods Ltd* v. *Lemon* [1931] 2 K.B. 157. The agent's state of mind may, however, be relevant in determining the remedies available: see *Keppel* v. *Wheeler* [1927] 1 K.B. 577.

80. *Pilkington* v. *Flack* (1948) 152 E.G. 366. An estate agent's client was there held bound by a commission agreement which the Court of Appeal described as "scandalous", on the ground that she had signed it. The position would no doubt have been different if the estate agent had positively misrepresented the contents of the document: *Jaques* v. *Lloyd D. George & Partners Ltd* [1968] 2 All E.R. 187; *Homebuyers Estates (Fylde) Ltd* v. *Laycock* (unreported), 8 May 1981, C.A.

81. Agreement "subject to contract" does not release the agent: *Keppel* v. *Wheeler* [1927] 1 K.B. 577; *Dunton Properties Ltd* v. *Coles, Knapp & Kennedy Ltd* (1959) 174 E.G. 723.

82. Thus in *Regier* v. *Campbell-Stuart* [1939] 1 Ch. 766, an estate agent instructed to find a house for a client was held liable to account for a secret profit made by buying a suitable property through a nominee, terminating the agency and reselling the property to the client.

83. *McPherson* v. *Watt* (1877) 3 App.Cas. 254.

84. *Gillett* v. *Peppercorne* (1840) 3 Beav. 78; *Salomons* v. *Pender* (1865) 3 H. & C. 639; *Regier* v. *Campbell-Stuart* [1939] 1 Ch. 766; *Headway Construction Co* v. *Downham* [1975] 1 E.G.L.R. 35.

85. It should be noted that an intention on the agent's part to profit is not essential to liability although, where an agent does obtain a "secret profit", this in itself entitles the client to hold the agent to account in an action for money had and received: see p. 325.

86. *Andrews* v. *Ramsay & Co* [1903] 2 K.B. 635; *Fullwood* v. *Hurley* [1928] 1 K.B. 498. Such consent was obtained in *Harrods Ltd* v. *Lemon* [1931] 2 K.B. 157.

87. Examples are *Meadow Schama & Co* v. *C Mitchell & Co Ltd* (1973) 228 E.G. 1511, where estate agents received a fee from the other party's agent after their own work was complete; *Christie Owen & Davies* v. *Brown* (1983, unreported), where sub-agents of the vendor became agents of the purchaser; and *Druce Investments Ltd* v. *Thaker* [1988] 2 E.G.L.R. 229, where agents acting respectively for vendor and purchaser agreed to divide their combined commission equally (an agreement described by the court as "unwise").

opposite sides of a transaction. In *Eric V Stansfield* v. *South East Nursing Home Services Ltd*,[88] for example, it was recognised that an estate agent who is retained by more than one client to look for similar property should disclose the potential conflict, at least once more than one client had shown "a real intent to buy". Indeed, it may be argued that the normal case of estate agency necessarily creates a potential conflict of interests, in that estate agents routinely act simultaneously for a number of vendors, more than one of whose properties may suit a prospective purchaser. This problem was explicitly recognised by the Privy Council in *Kelly* v. *Cooper*,[89] where it was held that an estate agent's duty to one vendor-client cannot compel the disclosure of information which is confidential to another.[90]

The cases cited above are merely examples of the general prohibition against any undisclosed conflict of interests. This prohibition has also been invoked so as to impose liability upon estate agents who failed to inform their client about an intended resale of the property by a potential purchaser[91]; who unduly favoured one potential purchaser on the ground that this purchaser would employ them in future transactions[92]; who falsely claimed to have employed a sub-agent to effect an introduction, in order to charge the client a higher level of commission[93]; and who charged their client for advertising costs at the full rate without revealing that they had in fact received a discount.[94]

Where an agent is guilty of a breach of fiduciary duty, the client may make use of a wide range of legal remedies. Any transaction which is tainted by the breach may be rescinded[95]; damages may be claimed to compensate the client for any loss suffered[96]; and the agent may be compelled to hand over any secret profit which has been obtained.[97] In addition, the agent will in principle forfeit the right to any commission

88. [1986] 1 E.G.L.R. 29.

89. [1993] A.C. 205. See also *Robinson Scammell & Co* v. *Ansell* [1985] 2 E.G.L.R. 41, where an estate agent's attempt (on fearing that an arranged sale was about to collapse) to sell the purchaser another house was held by the Court of Appeal to be a breach of duty to the first client.

90. Ironically, disclosure of this information (that a potential purchaser wished to acquire *both* properties) would have enabled both clients to take advantage of the "marriage value" of the properties and thus to negotiate higher prices.

91. *Keppel* v. *Wheeler* [1927] 1 K.B. 577; *Dunton Properties Ltd* v. *Coles, Knapp & Kennedy Ltd* (1959) 174 E.G. 723; *Price* v. *Metropolitan House Investment and Agency Co Ltd* (1907) 23 T.L.R. 630. In *Heath* v. *Parkinson* (1926) 42 T.L.R. 693 an estate agent was held liable for concealing the existence of potential purchasers who were prepared to pay more than an applicant introduced by the agent, but whose introduction would not entitle the agent to commission.

92. *Smith (Henry) & Son* v. *Muskett* [1978] 1 E.G.L.R. 13.

93. *Ian Scott & Co* v. *Medical Installations Co Ltd* [1981] 1 E.G.L.R. 23.

94. *Hippisley* v. *Knee Bros* [1905] 1 K.B. 1.

95. There appears to be no direct authority on the point in an estate agency context, but see, generally, *Bowstead on Agency* (15th edn), pp. 160, 170, 188.

96. *Keppel* v. *Wheeler* [1927] 1 K.B. 577; *Dunton Properties Ltd* v. *Coles, Knapp & Kennedy Ltd* (1959) 174 E.G. 723. The principles on which such damages fall to be assessed were reconsidered by the House of Lords in *Target Holdings Ltd* v. *Redferns* [1995] 3 All E.R. 785.

97. *Andrews* v. *Ramsay & Co* [1903] 2 K.B. 635; *Price* v. *Metropolitan House Investment and Agency Co Ltd* (1907) 23 T.L.R. 630; *Regier* v. *Campbell-Stuart* [1939] 1 Ch. 766. If the secret profit consists of a "bribe" from a third party (which in this context is not limited to corrupt payments), the client may also recover damages or the amount of the bribe from the third party (see *Mahesan s/o Thambiah* v. *Malaysia Government Officers' Co-operative Housing Society Ltd* [1979] A.C. 374).

earned,[98] although the courts have held that, where the agent's breach does not involve any lack of honesty or good faith, commission remains payable.[99]

## 2.4 Liability to third parties

The circumstances in which a vendor's estate agent may incur personal liability to an actual or prospective purchaser are necessarily limited, since the agent will only exceptionally be a party to the resulting contract of sale.[100] Nevertheless, some potential heads of personal liability may be found. For example, an estate agent who, while lacking the necessary authority from the vendor, purports to make a binding contract of sale on the latter's behalf may be liable to the purchaser for breach of warranty of authority.[101] Furthermore, an agent who receives a pre-contract deposit from a prospective purchaser "as stakeholder" is personally liable to return it on demand.[102]

The situation most likely to result in legal action against an estate agent is where that agent gives inaccurate information about a property to a prospective purchaser. The agent in such circumstances cannot be held liable under the Misrepresentation Act 1967.[103] However, proof of a deliberate lie would surely found an action in deceit, and it seems in principle that liability may also arise in the tort of negligence, although there are only two reported cases in which the United Kingdom courts have been called upon to address this issue.

In *Computastaff Ltd* v. *Ingledew Brown Bennison & Garrett*[104] the plaintiff company, when seeking to rent office accommodation, was shown letting particulars drawn up by the landlords' agents which seriously understated the rateable value of the property. When the amount quoted was queried, the plaintiffs instructed their own estate agents and their solicitors to investigate; this simply resulted in an approach to the landlords' agents which confirmed the erroneous figure. It was held that both the plaintiffs' estate agents and their solicitors were liable in negligence to their clients[105]; however, both defendants were entitled to recover 50 per cent of the damages from the landlords' agents[106] on the ground that the latter could also have been held liable to the plaintiffs for breach of a duty of care in tort.[107]

---

98. *Salomons* v. *Pender* (1865) 3 H. & C. 639; *Andrews* v. *Ramsay & Co* [1903] 2 K.B. 635; *Price* v. *Metropolitan House Investment and Agency Co Ltd* (1907) 23 T.L.R. 630; *Heath* v. *Parkinson* (1926) 42 T.L.R. 693; *Fullwood* v. *Hurley* [1928] 1 K.B. 498; *Smith (Henry) & Son* v. *Muskett* [1978] 1 E.G.L.R. 13. In *Hocker* v. *Waller* (1924) 29 Comm.Cas. 296 it was held that, even with full disclosure, an agent contracting with the client can only recover commission if there is an explicit agreement to this effect.

99. *Keppel* v. *Wheeler* [1927] 1 K.B. 577 [1927] 1 K.B. 577; *Robinson Scammell & Co* v. *Ansell* [1985] 2 E.G.L.R. 41.

100. *Davies* v. *Sweet* [1962] 1 All E.R. 92 is a rare example.

101. *Godwin* v. *Francis* (1870) L.R. 5 C.P. 295.

102. *Rayner* v. *Paskell & Cann* (1948) 152 E.G. 270.

103. It has been held that the Act applies only to a statement made by one contracting party to another: *Resolute Maritime Inc* v. *Nippon Kaiji Kyokai* [1983] 2 All E.R. 1.

104. [1983] 2 E.G.L.R. 150.

105. Liability was apportioned at 60 per cent to the agents and 40 per cent to the solicitors.

106. Under the Civil Liability (Contribution) Act 1978.

107. McNeill J relied on *Hedley Byrne & Co Ltd* v. *Heller & Partners Ltd* [1964] A.C. 465.

In the second case, *McCullagh* v. *Lane Fox & Partners Ltd*,[108] the plaintiff purchased a substantial residential property following a misstatement (originally found in the defendant estate agents' sale particulars, but later confirmed orally by an employee of the agents) as to the size of the plot on which it stood. The Court of Appeal held unanimously that, since the true basis of liability for negligent misstatement was "assumption of responsibility",[109] a clear disclaimer in the defendants' sales particulars operated to exclude any duty of care.[110] The effect of this disclaimer also extended to the oral statement, since it could not realistically have been supposed that the agents were assuming responsibility for something for which in the particulars they had specifically disclaimed responsibility.[111]

It was further held by a majority of the court that, even without the disclaimer, the defendants would not have been liable in the present circumstances. This was because, when the misstatement was made, the defendants did not expect it to be relied upon; they would expect the plaintiff to rely upon his own solicitors' enquiries and (possibly) to commission a survey. Although they subsequently realised that the plaintiff would indeed rely on their statement, since the vendor wished to exchange contracts immediately, they were still unaware that it was untrue.

In contrast to this slender body of authority in English law, claims by purchasers against estate agents have featured much more frequently in other Commonwealth jurisdictions. In applying *Hedley Byrne* to this relationship, courts in Canada, New Zealand and Australia have imposed liability upon negligent agents for misstatements as to a property's size[112]; such physical characteristics as its location,[113] boundaries,[114] sewerage[115] and soundproofing[116]; the size of the existing mortgage on the property[117]; the use to which it could lawfully be put[118]; and the income and expenditure in which that use might be expected to result.[119] However, claims have

---

108. [1995] 1 E.G.C.S. 195.

109. Reverting to *Hedley Byrne & Co Ltd* v. *Heller & Partners Ltd* [1964] A.C. 465 in preference to later authorities such as *Smith* v. *Eric S Bush*; *Harris* v. *Wyre Forest D.C.* [1990] 1 A.C. 831 and *Caparo Industries plc* v. *Dickman* [1990] 2 A.C. 605.

110. The court accepted that this disclaimer was subject to the Unfair Contract Terms Act 1977, but ruled that it would be fair and reasonable to allow the defendants to rely on it.

111. In excluding a duty of care in this case, the Court of Appeal nevertheless specifically rejected the analogy of the vendor's solicitors who, it appears, owes no duty of care in a normal conveyancing transaction: *Cemp Properties (UK) Ltd* v. *Dentsply Research & Development Corporation* [1989] 2 E.G.L.R. 192; *Gran Gelato Ltd* v. *Richcliff (Group) Ltd* [1992] 1 E.G.L.R. 297; cf. *Wilson* v. *Bloomfield* (1979) 123 S.J. 860.

112. *Thompson* v. *Nanaimo Realty Co Ltd* (1973) 44 D.L.R. (3d) 254; *Komarniski* v. *Marien* (1979) 100 D.L.R. (3d) 81.

113. *Grisack* v. *Smith & Lyle Real Estate Ltd* (1985) 59 A.R. 238.

114. *Richardson* v. *Norris Smith Real Estate Ltd* [1977] 1 N.Z.L.R. 152.

115. *Barrett* v. *JR West Ltd* [1970] N.Z.L.R. 789.

116. *Roberts* v. *Montex Development Corporation* (1979) 100 D.L.R. (3d) 660.

117. *Avery* v. *Salie* (1972) 25 D.L.R. (3d) 495.

118. *Hopkins* v. *Butts* (1967) 65 D.L.R. (2d) 711; *Bango* v. *Holt* (1971) 21 D.L.R. (3d) 66; *Alessio* v. *Jovica* (1973) 34 D.L.R. (3d) 107; *Hauck* v. *Dixon* (1975) 64 D.L.R. (3d) 201; *Betker* v. *Williams* (1991) 86 D.L.R. (4th) 395.

119. *Dodds and Dodds* v. *Millman* (1964) 45 D.L.R. (2d) 472; *Olsen* v. *Poirier* (1980) 111 D.L.R. (3d) 512; *Roots* v. *Oentory Pty Ltd* [1983] 2 Qd.R. 745; *Spiewak* v. *251268 Ontario Ltd* (1988) 43 D.L.R. (4th) 554.

failed where the purchaser could not be shown to have relied on information provided by an estate agent,[120] and also where such reliance would not have been reasonable.[121]

A somewhat contentious aspect of this requirement of "reasonable reliance" arises where an estate agent passes on information of a kind which does not fall within any special area of skill or competence of the agent. Commonwealth courts have on occasion ruled that such circumstances will not support a duty of care under *Hedley Byrne*[122]; however, a number of estate agents have been held liable for merely passing on information from a client without subjecting this to any kind of check.[123]

## 3 REGULATION OF ESTATE AGENCY UNDER THE 1979 ACT[124]

Statutory regulation of estate agency in the United Kingdom is a recent development.[125] The first indication by any government that it might favour legislation in this area was revealed in a Green Paper published in 1975.[126] The main suggestion in that document was for a licensing scheme similar to the one in operation under the Consumer Credit Act 1974 and, like that scheme, to be administered by the Director General of Fair Trading. However, consultations stimulated by the Green Paper led to the devising of a different scheme, commonly known as "negative licensing", under which entry to estate agency would be largely unrestricted but subject to a power for the Director General of Fair Trading in certain circumstances to ban an unsuitable individual or firm. This approach, which avoided both the creation of a professional "closed shop" and the need for an expensive administrative bureaucracy, attracted support across the political spectrum and ultimately formed the basis of the Estate Agents Act 1979.

A general point worth making is that successive governments have regarded the 1979 Act, not as a matter of professional regulation, but rather as one of consumer protection; protection, moreover, against dishonesty and sharp practice, rather than against incompetence. In consequence, the Act itself contains relatively little in the way of detailed controls upon the conduct of estate agency business, save in relation to the handling of deposits, the notification of charges and the disclosure of personal interest. However, the legislators were careful to include in the Act a power to deal

---

120. *Reichl and Weisz* v. *Rutherford-McRae Ltd* (1965) 51 D.L.R. (2d) 332; *Hatlelid* v. *Sawyer and McClocklin Real Estate* [1977] 5 W.W.R. 481; *Norris* v. *Sibberas* [1990] V.R. 161.

121. *John Bosworth Ltd* v. *Professional Syndicated Developments Ltd* (1979) 97 D.L.R. (3d) 112; *Semkuley* v. *Clay* (1982) 140 D.L.R. (3d) 489.

122. See *Jones* v. *Still* [1965] N.Z.L.R. 1071, *Alessio* v. *Jovica* (1973) 34 D.L.R. (3d) 107 and (especially) *Presser* v. *Caldwell Estates Pty Ltd* [1971] 2 N.S.W.L.R. 471.

123. See *Barrett* v. *JR West Ltd* [1970] N.Z.L.R. 789; *Bango* v. *Holt* (1971) 21 D.L.R. (3d) 66; *Roots* v. *Oentory Pty Ltd* [1983] 2 Qd.R. 745.

124. Murdoch, *Estate Agents and Property Misdescriptions Acts* (3rd edn, 1993); Card, *Estate Agents Act 1979* (1979); Douglas & Lee, *Estate Agents Act 1979* (Current Law Statutes Annotated, 1979).

125. Of the 14 Private Members' Bills introduced between 1888 and 1965 which sought to set up a registration scheme for estate agents, none succeeded in attracting government support.

126. *The Regulation of Estate Agency: a Consultative Document*, published by the Department of Prices and Consumer Protection.

with abuses which might come to light in the future by designating them as "undesirable practices" and thus subjecting them to the statutory regime. Following the publication of reports by the Director General of Fair Trading[127] and the Department of Trade and Industry,[128] this power has been used to impose rules of a much more detailed kind to govern the way in which estate agency work is carried on.

As mentioned above, the scheme of regulation introduced by the Estate Agents Act 1979 does not in general place restrictions upon persons wishing to set up in practice as estate agents.[129] However, section 22 of the Act provides power to prescribe, by way of statutory instrument, minimum standards of competence[130] for anyone seeking to practise on his own account. This provision, which appears somewhat inconsistent with the general philosophy which underlies the 1979 Act (that of avoiding a closed shop), currently commands support from all the main professional bodies representing estate agents; notwithstanding increasing pressure from that quarter, however, successive governments have continued to insist that there is no justification for implementing section 22.

## 3.1 Scope of the Estate Agents Act 1979

It is worth emphasising that the 1979 Act does not seek to control all the activities which are commonly associated with estate agents, but merely the central "broking" function of estate agency, that of bringing about transactions involving the transfer of certain interests in land. This restricted area of operation is defined by the first two sections of the Act. Section 1 provides a general definition of "estate agency work" and excludes a number of matters which might at first sight appear to fall within it. Section 2 describes the interests in land whose transfer attracts the statutory controls.

### 3.1.1 Estate agency work

Section 1(1) provides:

"This Act applies, subject to subsections (2) to (4) below to things done by any person in the course of a business[131] (including a business in which he is employed) pursuant to instructions[132] received from another person (in this section referred to as 'the client') who wishes to dispose of or acquire an interest in land—
　　(a)　for the purpose of, or with a view to, effecting the introduction[133] to the client of a third person who wishes to acquire or, as the case may be, dispose of such an interest; and

---

127. *Review of the Estate Agents Act 1979*, Office of Fair Trading, December 1988.

128. *Review of Estate Agency*, Department of Trade and Industry, June 1989.

129. The main exception to this general principle is that an undischarged bankrupt may not carry on estate agency work other than as an employee, on pain of criminal sanctions: s. 23.

130. The wording of s. 22(2) suggests that "competence" for this purpose is to be shown either by the holding of designated qualifications or by having acquired a prescribed degree of practical experience.

131. The Act does not provide a definition of "business". There is, moreover, no requirement that the business in question should be a estate agency business.

132. The Act provides no definition of "instructions", and certainly does not impose any requirement as to the form which they take. Nevertheless, until "instructions" are received, nothing done will satisfy the definition of "estate agency work". Consequently, an estate agent "touting" for instructions (even where this involves giving misleading information to a potential client) is not subject to the Act.

133. It is submitted that the word "introduction", although clearly used with private treaty sales in mind, will nonetheless include transactions brought about by auction or tender.

(b) after such an introduction has been effected in the course of that business, for the purpose of securing the disposal or, as the case may be, the acquisition of that interest;

and in this Act the expression 'estate agency work' refers to things done as mentioned above to which this Act applies."

The specific reference to both acquisitions and disposals of interests in land makes it clear that the Act applies to estate agents acting for prospective purchasers and tenants, as well as to those representing vendors or landlords.[134] However, anything which is done after the parties have been introduced is only "estate agency work" if it is carried out by the agent responsible for that introduction. Consequently, where (as frequently occurs in relation to commercial property) an estate agent is brought in to negotiate the detailed terms of a transaction which has already been agreed in principle, that agent's work is not governed by the 1979 Act.

As mentioned above, various activities commonly carried on by estate agents are specifically excluded from the operation of the Act. Of these, credit brokerage[135] and insurance brokerage[136] are excluded because they are subject to other statutory controls.[137] Also excluded, though for less obvious reasons, are surveys and valuations,[138] at least where these are not carried out as an integral part of estate agency work,[139] and things done in connection with applications and other matters arising under planning legislation.[140]

A number of other matters are excluded from the application of the Act, apparently in the belief that, without such exclusion, the general definition of estate agency work might catch persons who are not estate agents at all. While this may well be so, it should be noted that the wording of each exclusion is apt to remove the statutory controls from certain activities or relationships, irrespective of whether or not an estate agent is involved. The matters in question are things done by the following persons: someone whose *only* "estate agency work" consists of the publication of advertisements or the dissemination of information[141]; a practising solicitor or an employee of a solicitor[142]; a receiver appointed under a mortgage[143]; a person acting in the course of employment on behalf of his own employer[144]; and a person acting on behalf of his own employee (provided that this is done by reason of the employment).[145]

---

134. However, some of the specific duties imposed by subordinate legislation made under the Act are so worded as to apply only to agents acting for vendors or landlords.

135. Excluded by s. 1(2)(b). The effect is that mortgage-broking in respect of residential premises is not governed by the Estate Agents Act.

136. Excluded by s. 1(2)(c).

137. Under the Consumer Credit Act 1974, s. 145(2) and the Insurance Brokers (Registration) Act 1977, ss. 2 and 4, respectively.

138. Section 1(2)(d).

139. As they would be in the case of an estate agent offering a "free" valuation to potential vendors.

140. Section 1(2)(e).

141. Section 1(4). Newspapers are thus excluded; so are those "property shops" and house-finding agencies which offer nothing more than a list of available properties.

142. Section 1(2)(a). This means that, even where a practising solicitor is carrying on a full-scale estate agency business (as is common in Scotland), this will not be subject to the 1979 Act.

143. Section 1(3)(b). No equivalent exception was thought necessary for liquidators, trustees in bankruptcy, executors and the like, since it was believed that such persons, who sell property by virtue of their office and not "pursuant to instructions", are in any case beyond the scope of the Act.

144. Section 1(3)(a).

145. Section 1(3)(c).

Of the exclusions noted above, it is the last two which are the most controversial. Although it would clearly be undesirable to subject employers and employees in non-estate agency businesses to all the statutory controls merely because they render assistance to each other in house purchase, it seems that the legislature may have thrown the baby of consumer protection out with the bath water. While section 1(1) makes clear that every employee of an estate agent must in principle comply with the Act, the effect of section 1(3)(a) is that this will not apply where the estate agent himself is the "client". Similarly, an estate agent who assists his own employee (as a "perk" of employment) in buying or selling a house will be outside the Act.

The scope of the 1979 Act is open to considerable doubt in one relatively common area of estate agency practice, namely, the use of sub-agents. As a matter of general law, such sub-agents, even if appointed with the authority of the client, nonetheless operate as agents to the main agent and have no direct contractual relationship with the client. However, the definition of estate agency work contained in section 1 of the Act treats the agent's client as the "person who wishes to dispose of or acquire an interest in land". Hence, unless the main agent can be regarded as fulfilling this definition (albeit as an agent for someone else), it seems that the sub-agent does not carry out estate agency work and is not covered by the Act.[146]

### 3.1.2 Interests in land

As originally conceived, the Estate Agents Act was to apply only to property which was wholly or substantially residential. However, this restriction was removed during the parliamentary passage of the Bill and, in consequence, transactions involving all types of real property are subject to the statutory controls.

Section 2 sets out the particular interests in land whose acquisition or disposal is subject to the 1979 Act. First and foremost is the transfer of "a legal estate in fee simple absolute in possession". This form of words describes the most common form of estate agency work and, in so doing, effectively excludes a subsale by someone who has agreed to purchase the freehold.[147]

The second type of transaction dealt with by section 2 is the transfer or creation of "a lease which, by reason of the level of the rent, the length of the term or both, has a capital value which may be lawfully realised on the open market". "Lease" in this context includes both equitable and legal interests,[148] but not any interest created by way of mortgage.[149] The major uncertainty inherent in the statutory wording, however, lies in its reference to the "capital value" of the lease. This qualification was originally introduced simply to exclude Rent Act lettings, on which it was generally unlawful to charge a premium.[150] However, it is strongly arguable that all leases at full

---

146. To treat the sub-agent as acting pursuant to instructions from the "real" client, which are received via the main agent, provides only a partial solution. Some of the statutory obligations are thereby brought into play, but not s. 18 (the obligation to inform the client about charges), since this specifically requires a contract between agent and client.

147. What the sub-purchaser receives in such a case is an equitable right to call for a conveyance of the property.

148. The rights and obligations which arise under an agreement to grant a lease are specifically included by s. 2(2).

149. Section 2(3)(a).

150. It was believed that such transactions were already subject to sufficient statutory controls.

rental value (whether of residential or commercial property) are excluded, since such leases by definition have no capital value.

A further difficulty in the wording of section 2 concerns its geographical limits. Many estate agents in the United Kingdom market property which is situated overseas, and it would seem desirable that they should be subject to the same statutory regulations as apply to domestic property. However, the fact that section 2 makes specific provision for Scotland[151] and that its general language is that of English land law suggests that the Act does not extend to property outside the UK.[152]

## 3.2 The statutory requirements

The statutory regulation of estate agents has from the outset been regarded by government as a matter of general consumer protection. In contrast to those duties which arise under the general law of agency, therefore, the specific obligations created by the 1979 Act and its supporting orders and regulations are as much for the benefit of third parties who deal with an estate agent as for the agent's client.

It is perhaps worthy of note that the 1979 Act itself contains very little by way of detailed controls upon the manner in which estate agency work is carried on. It was only in 1991, with the designation of a number of "undesirable practices", that the legislators attempted to address various specific criticisms which had been raised by consumer organisations and others.

### 3.2.1 Clients' money

The consumer protection philosophy of the Estate Agents Act 1979 finds its clearest expression in those provisions which deal with clients' money. The Act and its supporting regulations seek to ensure that estate agents deal properly with such money and that, in the event of an agent's default, the public is protected as far as possible against any resulting loss. It should be noted however that the definition of "clients' money" for this purpose is a narrow one; section 12 limits it to deposits (both contractual and pre-contractual) which are paid to an estate agent in respect of the acquisition of an interest in land in the United Kingdom or in respect of a connected contract.[153] Such a deposit is "clients' money", irrespective of the capacity (e.g., as agent or stakeholder) in which the money is received.[154]

In an attempt to protect deposit money from being lost in the event of an estate agent's insolvency, section 13 provides that such money is held by the agent on trust for the person who is entitled to it or, where the money is received "as stakeholder", for the person who will ultimately become entitled to it on the occurrence of the event against which it is held.[155] In effect, this means that a pre-contract deposit will

151. The interests covered are defined in s. 2(1)(c).

152. This is the view of the regulatory authorities: see the Office of Fair Trading's "Estate Agency Guide" (July 1991), p. 3.

153. A "connected contract" is one which is conditional upon such an acquisition, such as a contract to acquire the existing curtains and carpets: s. 12(4).

154. The Members' Accounts Rules of most professional bodies define clients' money in a much broader sense. Estate agents who are members of such bodies must effectively comply with two separate codes, since the 1979 Act requires rigid separation of deposits from all other monies.

155. However, specific provisions under ss. 14 and 15 replace the normal duties of a trustee in respect of investment, keeping of accounts and accounting for interest: s. 13(3).

be held on trust for the prospective purchaser, except where the agent has been expressly authorised to receive the money as agent for the vendor.[156] A contract deposit, on the other hand, will be held for the vendor where it has been received "as agent"[157]; if it is received "as stakeholder", the identity of the beneficiary will not be known until either the sale is completed or it falls through.[158]

A number of provisions under the Estate Agents Act either restrict or remove the ability of an estate agent to seek or receive clients' money. Of these provisions, the most wide-ranging is section 21(4), which prohibits an agent from seeking or receiving either a contract or pre-contract deposit in respect of land in which the agent has a personal interest.[159] Oddly, however, this provision does not appear to cover the most extreme example, namely, the sale of a property owned exclusively by the estate agent. In such circumstances the agent does not act "pursuant to instructions" as required by section 1, so that the 1979 Act does not apply. The only other provision currently in force which places controls on deposits is section 20 (which bans pre-contract deposits where estate agency work is carried out in Scotland).[160]

The detailed handling of clients' money is governed generally by section 14(1), which requires it to be paid without delay into a client account,[161] and in more depth by the Estate Agents (Accounts) Regulations 1981.[162] These Regulations make detailed provision as to the circumstances in which money may lawfully be paid into or out of a client account; the form in which accounts and records must be kept; and the obligation to have the client account audited annually by a qualified person.[163]

The question of interest which is or which could be earned upon clients' money is dealt with by section 15 of the Act and by regulation 7 of the Estate Agents (Accounts) Regulations 1981.[164] These provisions[165] impose a basic obligation on the agent to account for interest to the person "who is for the time being entitled" to the clients' money in question.[166] They also explain how the interest is to be computed, depending on the type of account (if any) in which the money is held. The obligation to account does not arise unless the clients' money exceeds £500 and the interest payable to a particular person is at least £10; moreover, the obligation may be modified or excluded altogether by an "arrangement in writing" made between the estate agent and a person who would be entitled to interest.

156. *Sorrell* v. *Finch* [1977] A.C. 728. In such circumstances it will be held on trust for the vendor.
157. *Ellis* v. *Goulton* [1893] 1 Q.B. 350.
158. It has been suggested that, in the absence of contrary evidence, an estate agent receives a contract deposit "as agent" for the vendor: *Ojelay* v. *Neosale Ltd* [1987] 2 E.G.L.R. 167. This, however, seems open to doubt, given that an auctioneer is presumed to be a stakeholder: *Furtado* v. *Lumley* (1890) 6 T.L.R. 168.
159. For the definition of personal interest, see p. 336.
160. Two further provisions which have not been brought into force are s. 16 (estate agents not to accept clients' money unless bonded, on pain of criminal penalties) and s. 19 (power to make Regulations prescribing the maximum size of pre-contract deposits in England, Wales and Northern Ireland).
161. Defined as an account with an "authorised institution" which is in the name of a person engaged in estate agency work and which includes the word "client" in its title: s. 14(2).
162. Breach of either s. 14 or the Regulations is a criminal offence: s. 14(8).
163. The auditor's report must be made available on demand to a duly authorised officer of an enforcement authority: reg. 8(9).
164. These rules are practically exhaustive, in that s. 15(3) provides that there is no other liability to account for interest on money held in a general client account.
165. Which, unlike the other rules governing clients' money, carry no criminal sanction.
166. There is no duty to account in respect of any period during which the money is held as stakeholder pending an event. As to who is otherwise entitled, see p. 332.

### 3.2.2 Written notification of terms of business

The statutory provisions which govern the relationship between estate agent and client are primarily designed to ensure transparency of dealing. It is accordingly provided[167] that, before entering into any contract to provide estate agency services, an estate agent must give the prospective client certain information concerning the terms of business. The prescribed information, which is to be set out in writing,[168] must be given "when communication commences between the estate agent and the client or as soon as is reasonably practicable thereafter provided it is a time before the client is committed to any liability towards the estate agent".[169] It is further provided that, if the parties subsequently agree to vary the terms of their agreement, the estate agent must give written notice of the new terms.[170]

The most important information which must be given to the client under these provisions relates to the estate agent's proposed charges. The agent must explain at what point remuneration will become payable,[171] and set out either the precise amount of that commission or the method by which it will be assessed. The agent must also give details of any potential charges which do not constitute "remuneration",[172] stating either the exact amount of each charge or the method of assessment together with an estimate.[173]

For the most part, section 18 and the 1991 Regulations simply specify the information which is to be given to clients, leaving it to the estate agent to decide on how that information is to be expressed. In relation to three frequently used estate agency terms, however, a more prescriptive approach is adopted. The Regulations contain definitions of "sole agency", "sole selling rights" and "ready, willing and able purchaser"[174] and require an estate agent who wishes to employ any of these terms to use the statutory definitions when explaining them to the client.[175] Where an estate agent employs a term having "a similar purport or effect" to one of those specified, the agent must use a suitably amended version of the statutory definitions. It is further provided[176] that, if the circumstances render a statutory explanation misleading, the agent must use a suitably amended version so as to ensure accuracy.

In its original form, section 18 applied only to an estate agent's proposed fees and other charges. Since 1991, however, an estate agent is also required to inform the client about certain services which the agent offers or intends to offer to a prospective purchaser.[177] These are defined as "any services to a prospective purchaser for

---

167. Section 18.
168. Estate Agents (Provision of Information) Regulations 1991, reg. 4.
169. *Ibid.*, reg. 3(1).
170. Section 18(3) and reg. 3(2).
171. For the various events on which an estate agent may become entitled to commission, see p. 319.
172. This obviously includes those expenses which are separately charged. It has also been held to include an estate agent's "secret profit" (a discount for advertising which the agent did not pass on to the client): *Solicitors Estate Agency (Glasgow) Ltd* v. *MacIver* 1993 S.L.T. 23.
173. The view of the Office of Fair Trading is that the agent must provide, so far as practicable, an itemised list of such charges; a global total of expenses is not sufficient.
174. It may be noted that the statutory definitions are not entirely consistent with the interpretations which the courts had previously placed upon these terms: see Murdoch, *Law of Estate Agency and Auctions* (3rd edn, 1994), pp. 204–206.
175. Reg. 6 seeks to ensure that the statutory definitions are not hidden away in small print.
176. Reg. 5.
177. A "purchaser" for this purpose includes a tenant: reg. 1.

consideration, which are such as would ordinarily be made available to a prospective purchaser in connection with his acquisition of an interest in land or his use or enjoyment of it".[178] The duty to inform the client[179] applies to services personally provided by the estate agent, those provided by a "connected person"[180] and those out of whose provision the estate agent or a connected person will derive a financial benefit.

In addition to providing a trigger for the enforcement powers of the Director General of Fair Trading, failure by an estate agent to comply with the requirements of section 18 may result in a financial penalty. It is provided by section 18(5) that, unless the prescribed information has been given at the correct time and in the correct manner, the contract is unenforceable, either by legal action or by the exercise of a lien over the client's money, without a court order. Furthermore, where such an order is sought, the court may, having regard to the prejudice caused to the client by non-compliance and the degree of culpability of the agent, either dismiss the claim altogether or reduce the amount of commission payable.[181]

### 3.2.3 Other information to clients

The statutory theme of transparency of dealing between estate agents and their clients finds further expression in the Estate Agents (Undesirable Practices) (No 2) Order 1991. This identifies three events during the course of an agency relationship, on whose occurrence the agent is required to give certain information to the client. In each case, failure by the agent to give the prescribed information to the client "promptly and in writing" is designated an "undesirable practice" and is thus a trigger for the enforcement powers of the Director General of Fair Trading.[182]

The first of these events concerns the provision of services to prospective purchasers. As noted above,[183] an estate agent who intends to offer such services must inform the client at the outset. The Undesirable Practices Order provides that, irrespective of whether or not this has been done, the agent must notify the client if a prospective purchaser, who has been introduced to the client and who has made an offer for the property,[184] actually makes an application for services, unless that application is immediately refused.[185]

The second obligation imposed on an estate agent under this heading is to forward to the client accurate details of any offer which the agent receives from a prospective

---

178. The Regulations give as examples the provision of financial and insurance services, and also the marketing of the prospective purchaser's existing property.

179. The time and manner of compliance are the same as for fees and charges.

180. The meaning of "connected person" is discussed at p. 336.

181. Estate Agents Act 1979, s. 18(6). In *Solicitors Estate Agency (Glasgow)* v. *MacIver*, 1993 S.L.T. 23, an agent's commission was reduced by one half on this ground. See also *Fiesta Girl of London Ltd* v. *Network Agencies* [1992] 2 E.G.L.R. 28; *Connell Estate Agents* v. *Begej* [1993] 2 E.G.L.R. 35.

182. Estate Agents Act 1979, s. 3(1)(d). It is submitted that the mechanism of designating undesirable practices rather than creating obligations will operate to exclude any civil claim for damages based on breach of statutory duty.

183. See p. 334.

184. Including a conditional offer: Sch. 2, para. 2.

185. "Services" for this purpose mean the same as under the earlier provision. The rules as to "connected persons" and "financial benefit" are also applicable.

purchaser. This obligation specifically includes conditional offers; however, it is capable of being limited where the client has indicated in writing that certain types of offer, or certain details, need not be forwarded.

The third duty of disclosure concerns potential conflicts of interest between estate agent and client. It arises in two situations: where the agent "has, or is seeking to acquire, a beneficial interest in the land or in the proceeds of sale of any interest in the land", and where the agent "knows that any connected person[186] has, or is seeking to acquire" such an interest. In each of these situations, the estate agent must inform the client promptly and in writing of the interest in question.[187]

### 3.2.4 Disclosure of personal interest

Section 21 of the Estate Agents Act 1979 imposes certain duties of disclosure upon agents who have, or are deemed to have, a personal interest in land which is being marketed. It may be immediately pointed out that these statutory obligations differ in at least three respects from the equitable duty to disclose conflicts of interest which was considered earlier.[188] First, while the equitable duty is owed only to the client,[189] section 21 requires disclosure to persons with whom the agent "enters into negotiations". This *may* include the client, for example where an estate agent is seeking to purchase the client's property[190]; however, in most situations it will be the other party to the transaction to whom disclosure must be made. Secondly, the statutory definition of "personal interest" is limited to cases in which the agent[191] has a beneficial interest in land. Thirdly, the only sanction for a breach of section 21 is that it may be used as a trigger for the enforcement powers of the Director General of Fair Trading; there is no other criminal or civil remedy.[192]

The obligations created by this provision apply where an estate agent has, or expects to acquire, a "personal interest in land". According to section 21(5), this will occur in two situations: first, where the agent "has a beneficial interest in the land or in the proceeds of sale of any interest in it"[193] and secondly, where the agent "knows or might reasonably be expected to know that any of the following persons has such a beneficial interest, namely (i) his employer or principal, or (ii) any employee or agent of his, or (iii) any associate of his or of any person mentioned in subparagraphs (i) and (ii) above".[194]

The breadth of this provision, which is considerable, derives from the statutory definition of "associate". According to section 32, this includes a spouse[195] and any

186. The meaning of "connected person" is discussed below.

187. This provision covers a wide range of permutations. It applies both where the agent already has an interest in property and where he wishes to acquire one. It also applies to agents acting on behalf of purchasers and tenants as well as to those marketing property on behalf of vendors and landlords.

188. See p. 324.

189. So that an auctioneer (and presumably an estate agent) can sell property without disclosing to the purchaser that it belongs to him: *Flint* v. *Woodin* (1852) 9 Hare 618.

190. Such a situation would not normally fall within the Act at all, since the estate agent would not be acting "pursuant to instructions" as required by s. 1. However, s. 21(3) applies the duty of disclosure to cases where the agent is "negotiating on his own behalf".

191. Or a person connected with the agent.

192. Estate Agents Act 1979, s. 21(6).

193. It need not be the estate agent's interest which is being marketed.

194. An identical list of persons linked to the estate agent is used in relation to the provision of "tie-in services" (see p. 334); those on it are there given the generic title of "connected persons".

195. Including a former spouse and a reputed spouse.

one of a wide circle of relatives.[196] It also covers "business associates"[197] and their spouses and relatives. Finally, complex provisions govern the possibility that two partnerships, two companies or two unincorporated associations may be "associates" where certain natural persons are common to both organisations.[198]

Where an estate agent has a personal interest in land as defined above, section 21(1) provides that the agent "shall not enter into negotiations with any person with respect to the acquisition or disposal by that person of any interest in that land until the estate agent has disclosed to that person the nature and extent of his personal interest in it".[199] The Act itself does not specify how or when disclosure is to be made, but it has since been made clear that this is to be done "promptly and in writing".[200]

Section 21(2) extends the duty of disclosure to situations in which an estate agent has no initial personal interest in the relevant land but where, as the result of a proposed disposal "or of such a proposed disposal and other transactions", the agent would acquire such an interest. This clearly applies where an agent is seeking personally to purchase the client's property; however, it does not appear to include purchases by an "associate" of the agent, unless the agent can be said in such a case to "enter into negotiations" with the client.[201] The provision will also cover the case where an estate agent appears to a vendor to be purchasing property on behalf of an independent client, whereas in reality the agent intends to acquire the property personally or for a connected person.[202] In such circumstances the agent must reveal the true position to the vendor.[203]

### 3.2.5 Dealing with purchasers

Although in most cases an estate agent is primarily responsible to the vendor, there are a number of respects in which the legislation seeks to ensure that prospective purchasers are fairly dealt with. Apart from the agent's obligation to disclose personal interest which was noted above, two particular causes for concern are identified as "undesirable practices"[204] and thus as potential triggers for the enforcement powers of the Director General of Fair Trading.[205]

First, as part of the general controls on the provision by estate agents of "tie-in"

196. "Brother, sister, uncle, aunt, nephew, niece, lineal ancestor or linear [sic] descendant". Illegitimate relationships and those of the half-blood are also included.
197. According to s. 31, this effectively means the directors and controllers of a company; the partners of a partnership and the officers of an unincorporated association. In each case the natural person is a "business associate" of the organisation. In addition, a partner is the business associate of each of the other partners.
198. However, it is not possible for one type of organisation, such as a limited company, to be the "associate" of another type, such as a partnership, by virtue of common members.
199. Thus, for example, an estate agent instructed by a tenant to market the leasehold interest must disclose to prospective purchasers (though not to the tenant) that a relative of one of the agent's employees is the freehold owner of the property.
200. Estate Agents (Undesirable Practices) (No. 2) Order 1991, Sch. 1, para. 1.
201. It further seems that an estate agent who intends (directly or indirectly) to bid for the client's property is under no obligation to disclose this fact to the prospective purchasers with whom he is thus competing.
202. Whether this includes the common situation of a known agent bidding at auction is unclear, since such conduct may well not constitute "entering into negotiations".
203. Although there is no specific requirement to do so "promptly and in writing".
204. Estate Agents (Undesirable Practices) (No. 2) Order 1991.
205. Estate Agents Act 1979, s. 3(1)(d).

services to purchasers,[206] the 1991 Order identifies as an undesirable practice "discrimination against a prospective purchaser by an estate agent on the grounds that that purchaser will not be, or is unlikely to be, accepting services". "Discrimination" for this purpose is not further defined; "services", however, bears the same meaning as previously discussed.[207]

Secondly, in order to prevent estate agents playing off one prospective purchaser against another (for example by suggesting that the other has made a higher offer), the 1991 Order makes it an undesirable practice for an estate agent to make any misrepresentation "(a) as to the existence of, or details relating to, any offer[208] for the interest in the land; or (b) as to the existence or status of any prospective purchaser of an interest in the land". This applies to all false or misleading statements, whether made in writing or orally; however, an agent is only in breach where the offending statement is made "knowingly or recklessly".[209]

### 3.3 Enforcement of the Act

While the Director General of Fair Trading is generally responsible for supervising the working of the Estate Agents Act 1979,[210] the specific duty of enforcing the Act is imposed upon both the Director and local weights and measures authorities.[211] However, while the latter may well be the first to hear of complaints about estate agents in their locality, their powers to deal personally with those complaints is restricted to those matters which constitute criminal offences under the Act.[212] Only the Director may take action in relation to the statutory requirements discussed above[213]; the function of trading standards officers in respect of these will simply be to pass on relevant information to the Director.

"Enforcement" of the Act consists generally of deciding, after due investigation, whether the conduct of a particular estate agent (or estate agency firm) justifies the issue of an order prohibiting that agent from carrying on estate agency work.[214] Where such an order is issued,it may prohibit an individual or firm from engaging in estate agency work altogether[215]; alternatively, the order may be limited to estate

---

206. As noted earlier (p. 334), an estate agent must inform the client about the provision or intended provision of such services.

207. See p. 334.

208. Including a conditional offer.

209. The right of an auctioneer to bid on behalf of the vendor is specifically preserved, provided that the auctioneer complies with the provisions of the Sale of Land by Auction Act 1967, s. 6. See Murdoch, *Law of Estate Agency and Auctions* (3rd edn, 1994), pp. 363–369.

210. Estate Agents Act 1979, s. 25(1). This includes reporting to the Secretary of State on estate agency in general and the Act in particular, and also making public relevant information and advice.

211. *Ibid.*, s. 26(1).

212. These are in effect the provisions relating to clients' money and those which require persons to co-operate with the enforcement authorities. In investigating these matters, the enforcement authorities have wide powers of entry, search and seizure: s. 11.

213. I.e. ss. 15 and 18–21 of the Act, and the 1991 Regulations and Orders.

214. Practising estate agency work in contravention of such an order is a criminal offence: s. 3(8).

215. Estate Agents Act 1979, s. 3(2)(a).

agency work of a particular description[216] or to a particular part of the United Kingdom.[217] However, there is no power to prescribe that an order shall be of limited duration.[218]

In certain circumstances, where the grounds for issuing a prohibition order against an estate agent exist, the Director General of Fair Trading is given the alternative of an order warning the agent that future transgressions will lead to a prohibition order.[219] The procedure involved in such a case is identical to that required for a prohibition order.[220] If, after such an order has been made, the agent is guilty of a further breach,[221] the Director may proceed automatically to issue a prohibition order.

Before deciding to issue a prohibition order against an estate agent, the Director must be satisfied that the person or firm concerned "is unfit to carry on estate agency work generally or of a particular description".[222] It is important to note that, in coming to this conclusion, the Director is not restricted to considering that person's conduct of estate agency work. Of equal relevance is whether the agent, in the course of *any* business activity, has engaged in "any practice which involves breaches of a duty owed by virtue of any enactment, contract or rule of law".[223]

Apart from a general finding of unfitness, the issue of an order requires the occurrence of one or more of certain events, which are specified by section 3(1) as "triggers" for the Director's powers. These events are of four types: a conviction of the agent for certain criminal offences[224]; a ruling by an appropriate tribunal that the agent has been guilty of racial or sex discrimination in the course of estate agency work (other than as an employer)[225]; breach by the agent of any of the specific duties imposed by sections 15 and 18 to 21 of the 1979 Act[226]; and the commission by the agent of an "undesirable practice".[227]

As to the criminal offences involved, these again are divided into groups: those involving fraud, dishonesty or violence (whether or not in the course of estate agency

---

216. *Ibid.*, s. 3(2)(b). This could apply, for example, to the holding of clients' money.

217. *Ibid.*, s. 3(5).

218. There is a procedure whereby an estate agent against whom an order has been made may apply to have it revoked: *ibid.*, s. 6 and Sch. 2, para 2.

219. The availability of this option depends upon the grounds on which a prohibition order would be based. There is no power to issue a warning order where the relevant grounds consist of a criminal conviction (s. 3(1)(a)) or a finding of racial or sex discrimination (s. 3(1)(b)).

220. See below.

221. If the warning order is based on a breach of ss. 15 and 18–21 of the 1979 Act, a further breach of *any* of those sections may trigger a ban. If the order is based on an "undesirable practice", however, it must be the *same* practice which recurs.

222. In relation to a warning order, the Director must be satisfied that such unfitness *would* be found in the event of a further transgression.

223. Estate Agents Act 1979, s. 3(2). Section 9 gives the Director extensive powers (backed by criminal sanctions) to demand relevant information from any person. The confidentiality of information so collected is protected by s. 10.

224. Other than those which are treated as "spent" by the Rehabilitation of Offenders Act 1974.

225. The particular rulings (under the Race Relations Act 1976 and the Sex Discrimination Act 1975) which constitute "discrimination" for this purpose are listed in Sch. 1. On the expiry of five years these rulings cease to operate as triggers under the Estate Agents Act.

226. See pp. 332–338.

227. Under the Estate Agents (Undesirable Practices) Order 1991.

work)[228]; most of the offences created by the Estate Agents Act itself; and any offences specified by statutory instrument.[229]

The procedure to be followed by the Director General of Fair Trading in issuing a prohibition or warning order is laid down in Schedule 2 to the Estate Agents Act. The person or firm against whom an order is in contemplation must be duly notified and given the opportunity to make written representations or to demand an oral hearing. If the decision is then taken to issue an order, the person or persons affected must again be notified and informed of their statutory right to appeal against the order.[230]

Any prohibition or warning order made under the Estate Agents Act 1979, and any decision of the Director on an application for revocation or variation of such an order, is recorded in a register which is open for public inspection.[231] It is the duty of the Director to ensure that this register is kept up to date and that any change of circumstances[232] is noted.

## 4 OTHER STATUTORY CONTROLS

### 4.1 Property Misdescriptions Act 1991[233]

A recurring theme in various official reviews of estate agency has been the need to offer consumers some protection against the misleading advertising of properties being sold.[234] For some time it was the government's expressed intention to extend the Trade Descriptions Act 1968 so as to include false or misleading statements about land and buildings and, until such time as this might be done, to designate the making of such statements as an "undesirable practice" under the Estate Agents Act 1979.[235] However, the introduction in 1990 of a Private Members' Bill entitled the Estate Agents (Property Misdescriptions) Bill provided a convenient alternative solution which attracted government support. This Bill, having been widened to include statements made in the course of a property development business, was duly enacted as the Property Misdescriptions Act 1991.

228. In *Antonelli* v. *Secretary of State for Trade and Industry* [1995] N.P.C. 68 it was held that a 1973 conviction for arson in the USA could be used as a trigger, notwithstanding that this took place outside the jurisdiction of the English courts, that it was prior to the coming into operation of the Estate Agents Act or that the "violence" was directed at property rather than persons.

229. Some 50 offences have so far been specified: see the Estate Agents (Specified Offences) (No. 2) Order 1991 and the Estate Agents (Specified Offences) (No. 2) (Amendment) Order 1993.

230. Appeals are governed by s. 7 of the Act. An appeal lies primarily to the Secretary of State (in practice to a tribunal of three persons appointed from a panel). The procedures followed on such an appeal are laid down by the Estate Agents (Appeals) Regulations 1981. A further appeal (on a point of law) lies to the High Court: s.7(4). Quite separately from this, a person in respect of whom a prohibition or warning order has been made may apply to the Director General of Fair Trading seeking its revocation or variation: s. 6.

231. Section 8.

232. E.g., the expiry of a relevant period under the Rehabilitation of Offenders Act 1974.

233. Murdoch, *Estate Agents and Property Misdescriptions Acts* (3rd edn, 1993); Bragg, "Regulation of Estate Agents: A series of Half-hearted Measures?" (1992) 55 M.L.R. 368.

234. See, for example, *Review of the Estate Agents Act 1979*, Office of Fair Trading, December 1988; *Review of Estate Agency*, Department of Trade and Industry, June 1989.

235. See p. 339. For the extent to which the Trade Descriptions Act could apply to such statements, see Stephenson, "Estate Agents and Trade Descriptions" [1980] Conv. 249.

### 4.1.1 The offence of property misdescription

The effect of the 1991 Act[236] is to create a criminal offence of strict liability.[237] Section 1(1) provides:

"Where a false[238] or misleading statement about a prescribed matter is made in the course of an estate agency business or a property development business, otherwise than in providing conveyancing services, the person by whom the business is carried on shall be guilty of an offence under this section."

The centrepiece of this provision, that of a "statement", is widely defined; according to section 1(5)(c), it includes both written and spoken words, pictures and "any other method of signifying meaning".[239] However, the requirement that a statement be made means that liability cannot arise out of a pure omission. The Act therefore does not create a positive duty to disclose known defects in a property, although partial silence may of course have the effect that something which is literally true becomes misleading.[240]

The Property Misdescriptions Act applies only to a statement about a "prescribed matter", which means any matter relating to land which is specified by statutory instrument.[241] At the time of writing, only one such instrument has been issued,[242] but the 33 items which this contains provide virtually comprehensive coverage of both the physical and the legal aspects of property being sold.

In order to attract liability under this provision, a statement must be made in the course of either an estate agency or a property development business.[243] The former of these is defined in such a way that, with one important exception, it coincides with the definition of "estate agency work" contained in section 1 of the Estate Agents Act 1979.[244] The exception is that, while a practising solicitor who is also an estate agent is not subject to the 1979 Act,[245] such a person falls within the 1991 Act.[246]

The wording of section 1(1) is such that liability falls primarily, not upon the person who *makes* a false or misleading statement, but upon the person carrying on the business in the course of which the statement is made.[247] In addition, section 1(2) provides that, where the making of an offending statement is due to the act or default

---

236. Which came into force on 4 April 1993.
237. A contravention of the Act does not in itself give rise to any civil liability: s. 1(4).
238. "False" means false to a material degree: s. 1(5)(a).
239. E.g., a model or a show house.
240. A statement is misleading if (though not false) what a reasonable person may be expected to infer from it, or from any omission from it, is false: s. 1(5)(b).
241. Section 1(5)(d).
242. The Property Misdescriptions (Specified Matters) Order 1992, S.I. 1992/2834.
243. Defined by s. 1(5)(f) as a business concerned wholly or substantially with the development of land: the Act applies only to a statement which is made with a view to selling a building constructed or renovated in the course of that business.
244. See p. 329.
245. See p. 330.
246. But only while acting as an estate agent; hence the specific exclusion of things done "in providing conveyancing services".
247. Section 4 deals with the attribution of liability to individuals in cases where the business is carried on by a company.

of an employee,[248] he or she may be prosecuted whether or not proceedings are taken against the employer.

### 4.1.2 The defence of due diligence

Although the offence of property misdescription is in principle one of strict liability, section 2(1) provides that it shall be a defence for a person prosecuted "to show that he took all reasonable steps and exercised all due diligence to avoid committing the offence". On the assumption that the courts approach this in a similar fashion to the defence contained in section 24 of the Trade Descriptions Act 1968,[249] it is likely that "reasonable steps" and "due diligence" will be treated as cumulative requirements; that a defendant will be required to show that he has done something positive to avoid the commission of an offence; and that this will normally involve the setting up and periodic monitoring of a system designed to ensure compliance.

Section 2 gives more detailed treatment to one particular application of "due diligence", namely, a claim by a defendant to have relied upon information from another person.[250] A defendant who seeks to rely on the statutory defence in such circumstances must show that reliance on the information was reasonable in all the circumstances. Furthermore, regard will be had in this context to what steps (if any) were taken to check the information; what steps (if any) might reasonably have been taken to check it; and whether there was any reason to disbelieve the information.

In *Enfield L.B.C.* v. *Castles Estate Agents Ltd*,[251] the defendant was held justified in relying, without making any further enquiries, upon the vendor's assurance that a bungalow erected in the garden of a house had the benefit of planning permission, since there was nothing to lead an estate agent to suspect that this might not be the case.

### 4.1.3 Enforcement of the Act

Responsibility for enforcing the Property Misdescriptions Act 1991 is conferred by the Schedule to the Act upon the trading standards departments of local authorities. The relevant provisions, which include powers of entry, search and seizure and which make the obstruction of officers a criminal offence, are in general similar to those found in the Estate Agents Act 1979. A limitation on these powers which may prove important in practice is that an enforcement officer has no right to enter premises used only as a dwelling, even where an alleged offence concerns a misdescription of that dwelling.

## 4.2 Accommodation Agencies Act 1953

While the normal basis on which estate agency work is carried on in the United Kingdom is that the agent acts on behalf of the vendor or landlord, there is in general

---

248. This wording again may catch, not only an employee who actually makes a false statement, but also one who fails to prevent a statement from being made (e.g., by failing to check sales particulars before publication).
249. On which see Parry & Rowell, *Butterworths Trading and Consumer Law*, para. 250 *et seq.*
250. A defendant in such circumstances must assist the prosecution authorities in identifying the person on whom he claims to have relied: s. 2(3) and (4).
251. [1996] E.G.C.S. 30.

nothing to prevent a prospective purchaser or tenant from appointing an estate agent to look for suitable property. However, this is subject in one respect to a statutory restriction, albeit one which is honoured as much in the breach as in the observance.[252] The statute in question is the Accommodation Agencies Act 1953, section 1 of which makes it a criminal offence for any person to demand or accept payment for registering or undertaking to register the requirements of anyone seeking the tenancy of a house, or for supplying or undertaking to supply addresses or other particulars of houses to let.[253]

The 1953 Act does not prohibit an estate agent from charging a fee for finding residential accommodation for a tenant, providing that no payment is due unless and until such accommodation is found and accepted.[254] However, to demand payment in advance (even on the basis that it is a deposit which will be refunded if no suitable accommodation is found) is an offence under the Act.[255] Nor can the agent escape liability by pointing to other "services" rendered, such as arranging for the client to view the property or negotiating with the landlord, if the substantial consideration for the fee paid is in truth the mere supply of the address to the client.[256]

In addition to the potential criminal sanctions involved, a breach of the Accommodation Agencies Act means that the agency agreement itself is an illegal contract. In consequence, the client is entitled to refuse payment of the agent's fees and to recover any money which has been paid.[257]

## 4.3 Miscellaneous

Of the other statutory measures which impinge on the work of estate agents, two seem of particular relevance. The first concerns the way in which estate agents' boards are dealt with under the rules of planning law which control advertisements. According to section 222 of the Town and Country Planning Act 1990, planning permission is deemed to have been granted for the display of any advertisement for the sale or letting of the land or premises on which the advertisement is displayed,[258] provided that it complies with Regulations made under section 220.[259] These Regulations place strict limitations upon such matters as the size of a board or the lettering on it, and the degree to which it may project from a building. They also make it clear that only one advertisement per property is permitted; if more than one board is displayed, the "deemed consent" applies to whichever is first erected.[260]

252. "The provisions of the 1953 Act are not nearly as well known as they ought to be": *Crouch & Lees* v. *Haridas* [1971] 3 All E.R. 172 at 176 *per* Edmund Davies LJ.

253. The Act was drafted as a short-term answer to a specific problem, namely, the exploitation of persons seeking accommodation to let. Originally due to expire at the end of 1957, it was thereafter renewed on an annual basis and was eventually made permanent by the Expiring Laws Continuance Act 1969, s. 1.

254. *Saunders* v. *Soper* [1975] A.C. 239.

255. *McInnes* v. *Clarke* [1955] 1 All E.R. 346.

256. *Lawrence* v. *Sinclair-Taylor* (1973) 228 E.G. 1922.

257. *Crouch & Lees* v. *Haridas* [1971] 3 All E.R. 172.

258. This in itself would not include an advertisement to the effect that the land has been sold or let, but an agent is specifically permitted to add such a statement to an existing board, provided that it is removed within 14 days of the completion of the sale or lease.

259. Town and Country Planning (Control of Advertisements) Regulations 1992, S.I. 1992/666, reg. 6, Sch. 3, Part I.

260. For the problems caused by two boards under an earlier set of regulations, see *Porter* v. *Honey* [1988] 3 All E.R. 1045.

The second statutory provision of which many estate agents have fallen foul in the past is section 22 of the Solicitors Act 1974,[261] which makes it a criminal offence for an unqualified person to draw or prepare certain instruments relating to the transfer of land, unless he proves that this was not done for any fee, gain or reward. The instruments in question include a deed of conveyance or lease[262] and any contract for the sale or other disposition of land, but not a contract for such a lease as may validly be made without using a deed.[263]

JOHN MURDOCH

261. And its predecessors from the Stamp Duty Act 1804.
262. An estate agent may not avoid liability by drawing the instrument but not affixing a seal: *Harte* v. *Williams* [1934] 1 K.B. 201; *Kushner* v. *Law Society* [1952] 1 K.B. 264.
263. I.e., short leases as defined by the Law of Property Act 1925, s. 54(2).

CHAPTER 8

# INSURANCE INTERMEDIARIES

## 1 CLASSIFICATION OF INSURANCE INTERMEDIARIES

Until the middle of the 1970s those involved on the selling and advising on insurance were thought of as being either insurance agents or insurance brokers. In the minds of the general public the former worked for insurance companies and the latter were independent. But things began to change in the mid-1970s. The Insurance Brokers (Registration) Act 1977 was passed creating the status of registered insurance broker. The immediate side-effect of that development was that non-registered independents could no longer call themselves brokers but they were free to use any other title they chose. Insurance agents did not comprise a generic group. They might be full-time or part-time employees of a particular insurer or they might be "independent" in the sense that they held agency agreements with one or several companies.

Now we have, in addition to the 1977 Act, the Financial Services Act 1986.

The origins of the Act are to be found in the Review of Investor Protection—the Gower Report.[1] It was concerned with investor protection and, therefore, did not cover what we can call general insurance business, such as accident, motor, marine, house buildings and contents, travel, etc. What the Act is concerned with is "investment business" and that includes, in particular, long-term insurance contracts and pension contracts.

If an intermediary intends to give advice on choosing an investment product or a particular company, then he is said to be carrying on investment business. If that is so then the Act requires him to have some form of authorisation. Without it he will be committing a criminal offence. Authorisation can be obtained from three sources. An individual application can be made directly to the Securities and Investment Board ("SIB") which is the supreme agency designated under the Act.[2] Alternatively, authorisation can come from membership of a Self-Regulatory Organisation ("SRO") or from a Recognised Professional Body ("RPB"). Both SROs and RPBs must first be recognised by the SIB.

Whichever method an intermediary uses he will then be subject to very detailed rules of business behaviour.

Just as the Insurance Brokers (Registration) Act 1977 created a new classification of insurance intermediary so, too, the Financial Services Act 1986 introduces new

---

1. Review of Investor Protection: Report, Part 1 (Cmnd. 9125).
2. A route which independent intermediaries would not chose to take.

terminology. It also subjects the intermediary to extensive administrative supervision and controls on the way he does business. The problem facing an intermediary is whether his business in the future will be classified as investment business or whether he will prefer to limit it to general/commercial insurance business.

If he decides to include investment advice as part of his portfolio then authorisation is necessary. But he can decide not to seek independent authorisation. He can avoid the cost and administrative problems by choosing to become a company representative. (A firm or company deciding to follow this path is called an appointed representative.) This, however, will often require a change of business practice because a representative can only give advice or sell the products of one company or group. He will be required to give up agencies he has with other companies. In relation to investment business it is now incorrect to talk of "tied agents".

Another change is the creation of a category of intermediaries known as "introducers". This covers people who, when asked for investment advice, choose to refer the applicant to a third party who will then take over full responsibility for the applicant. Those who choose to become introducers might be those who were acting as part-time insurance agents alongside their main occupations, such as solicitors or accountants.

Where investment business provided an important source of income through commissions, such people may decide, however, to opt to become representatives of one company or fully fledged authorised independent intermediaries. If this person is involved in a professional calling it might serve the best interests of his professional reputation to act only as an introducer and have links with reputable firms of authorised insurance intermediaries and thereby present his client with an unbiased opinion.

Broking business at Lloyd's of London deserves a separate mention. This unique insurance market place has rules built up by customary usage spanning 300 years. In recent years, however, many of the practices have been scrutinised by the courts. In addition to the courts' statements those working in the Lloyd's market have been subjected to a flurry of Lloyd's byelaws, often following on from detailed internal working papers, affecting every aspect of their working life. Major financial losses at Lloyd's have also led to numerous legal actions in the 1990s which tell us much more about the legal relationships between the various parties operating in the Lloyd's market place.

The discussion which follows is concerned with insurance intermediaries, for want of a better description, whose work involves various aspects of insurance advice, and might include both investment business commercial and general business or one to the exclusion of the others.


## 2 AGENCY LAW AND THE INTERMEDIARY

It is not intended here to attempt to deal fully with the complexities of the general law of agency. It is necessary, however, to deal briefly with certain aspects which more directly affect the present topic and which will be taken up more specifically below.

Commercial life is impossible without reference to agency. Insurance is sold by means of agents, claims are settled by means of agents. An explanation of how the principal-agent relationship is created is called for together with a brief explanation of the legal relationships between the principal, the agent and third parties.

## 2.1 Creation of agency

There are four main methods of establishing a principal-agent relationship: by an agreement between the two parties; by ratification; by estoppel; by operation of law. Only the first three really concern insurance intermediaries.

The normal situation is that the insurer will either have a contract of employment with his employees or an agency agreement with independent agents and brokers. The contents of that agreement and the construction given to it by the courts, in case of conflict between the parties, will be the main determining factors on which will hang the rights and duties of the parties.

It is possible for someone to act on behalf of another person without sufficient authority and for that person to ratify what has been done in his name or on his behalf. This may be done both where the agent has some authority from the principal but exceeds it, and also where he had no authority at all to act as an agent for that person.

Thus an intermediary may hold an agency from an insurer which is limited in certain ways, such as the types of insurance that he may market or the limits within which he may operate. If he deals in classes of insurance beyond his mandate, the insurer can, if he so wishes, ratify what the intermediary has done. If he holds no agency agreement with that insurer, but the customer presses for cover with that particular company, any resulting arrangement can be ratified if the company so wishes. When this is done the ratification clothes the agent with authority from the time he so acted on behalf of the principal.

But it is necessary that the agent was purporting to act on behalf of another person and not on his own behalf. In *Watson* v. *Swann*[3] a broker was asked to insure goods on certain terms. Unable to arrange those terms, the broker insured the goods on a policy that he already had with the insurers. When a loss occurred the owner of the goods was not allowed to ratify what the broker had done because the broker had insured them on his own behalf, and there was no evidence to show that he was insuring on behalf of a particular principal or one of a class of persons which would include that particular person.

The Privy Council decision in *Siu Yin Kwan* v. *Eastern Insurance Co Ltd*[4] throws interesting light on the question of the rights of undisclosed principals. A shipping company appointed A as their worldwide agents and this included obtaining their various insurance requirements. A particular ship was insured by A and this included the compulsory employers liability cover for its employees. However, A did not declare the name of the shipowner and A signed the proposal form in their own name. The insurers were unsuccessful in their attempts to avoid their liability. An undisclosed principal could sue and be sued on a contract made by its agent when acting within the scope of his authority if there was nothing in the contract that prevented this. It is perhaps crucial to the decision that the trial judge found that the insurers had no real interest in knowing the real identity of the shipowner. As long as

---

3. (1862) 11 C.B.N.S. 756.
4. [1994] 1 Lloyd's Rep. 616, [1994] 1 All E.R. 213.

the questions on the proposal form relating to past insurance history were correctly stated there was no material breach of good faith. In some classes of insurance the identity of the insured is crucial to the underwriter. In such a situation it may well be that the present decision would be inapplicable.

*Watson* v. *Swann* (above), *Grover & Grover Ltd* v. *Mathews* (below) and *Williams* v. *North China Insurance Co* (below) were referred to in *National Oilwell (UK) Ltd* v. *Davy Offshore Ltd*,[5] where the judge held *obiter*, that he would not have followed the decisions in *Grover & Grover* or *Williams*. *National Oilwell (UK) Ltd* is a long complicated case involving several insurance principles. For present purposes it can be narrowed down to the question of whether a sub-contractor could be regarded as an assured under a policy taken out by the main contractor. The answer to that question was that he could be classed as an assured even though the wording of the policy could be such that his rights were not necessarily co-extensive with those of the main assured. In order to be an assured they needed to show either that they were undisclosed or unnamed principals of the main assured or that they were entitled and did ratify the policy. It would be necessary to show that at the time that the policy was taken out the main assured intended to effect insurance on their behalf.[6]

Ratification may be express or implied. Implied ratification arises where the conduct of the principal shows that he adopts or recognises the transaction.

There are two particular problems relating to insurance contracts and ratification. If ratification has the effect of sanctioning the agent's work from the date the work was carried out, what if there has been a loss under the policy prior to the act of ratification? Originally the answer appeared to depend on whether it was a marine or non-marine policy.

In *Williams* v. *North China Ins Co*[7] a broker effected a freight policy without authority on behalf of his principal. After the loss occurred, and to the knowledge of the principal, he successfully ratified the policy enforcing it against the underwriters. Section 86 of the Marine Insurance Act 1906, an Act which codified existing law, states that:

"Where a contract of marine insurance is in good faith effected by one person on behalf of another, the person on whose behalf it is effected may ratify the contract even after he is aware of a loss."

This approach would appear to be sensible as reflecting commercial requirements within the field of insurance, but in *Grover & Grover Ltd* v. *Mathews*[8] it was said that the rule should not be extended beyond the area of marine insurance on the ground that it was "an anomalous rule which it was not, for business reasons, desirable to extend". *Grover* has not been followed in other common law jurisdictions and, ironically, the reason often given is that it is sound business practice to allow such ratification, thus reflecting what often happens in reality. But *National Oilwell (UK) Ltd* (above), after referring to Canadian, American and Australian decisions, considered the English rule to be outdated and that it was undesirable to have different rules for marine and non-marine insurance.

---

5. [1993] 2 Lloyd's Rep. 582.
6. See *Petrofina (UK) Ltd* v. *Magnaload* [1983] 2 Lloyd's Rep. 91; *Mark Rowlands* v. *Berni Inns Ltd* [1985] 3 All E.R. 473.
7. (1876) 1 C.P.D. 757.
8. [1910] 3 K.B. 401.

The second problem area is where the original act of the intermediary relates to an "illegal" insurance contract. There are major problems with the definition of "illegality" in English contract law. If the subject-matter of the insurance is illegal in the sense that courts would not or could not enforce the contract, then ratification cannot untie the illegality. For instance, where there is a lack of insurable interest under the Life Assurance Act 1774, ratification of such a contract will not legalise the original transaction.[9]

But recent cases referring to unauthorised insurers raise problems. Under the insurance companies legislation it is necessary to obtain government authorisation before carrying out insurance business in the UK.

In *Bedford Ins Co* v. *Instituto de Resseguros do Brasil*[10] the plaintiffs were Hong Kong insurers who instructed London brokers to obtain reinsurance within certain financial limits. Neither party was authorised in accordance with UK legislation. The brokers reinsured with the defendant company beyond the limits of their authority. The plaintiffs purported to ratify the contracts while the defendants argued that the ratification was invalid. The plaintiffs failed on the grounds that the contracts were illegal and void and, therefore, ratification would not legitimate them.

It must be noted, however, that this interpretation given to the effect of illegal contracts by unauthorised insurers was not followed in *Stewart* v. *Oriental Fire and Marine Ins Co Ltd*[11] but here ratification was not in question.

Agency by estoppel arises where one person represents to another person, either by words or conduct, that a particular individual is his agent in such a way that it would be inequitable for the person making such representations to deny the agency. It arises in situations where there is no formal agency agreement and also where the authorised agent has been permitted to go beyond his original remit.

It might be argued that by arming an intermediary with proposal forms and explanatory literature an insurer should be stopped from denying most things that are said by the salesman while attempting to convince the customer to enter into the contract. This view is rarely adopted by the courts and, therefore, the buyer of the policy will often find himself without an effective remedy in situations where he has been misled by inaccurate statements and predictions. One reason is that the proposal wording may state specifically that the intermediary has limited powers. A more worrying reason is that such words of caution only appear in the policy documentation, but by the time this reaches the customer the harm has been done.

Thus, in *Comerford* v. *Britannic Ass Co*[12] a superintendent of one of the defendant company's branch offices discussed a policy that the plaintiff wished to take out on her husband. An indorsement to the policy stated that it would pay out certain sums in each of the first five years of cover up to a final total of £150. The superintendent, however, told the plaintiff that the full £150 would be payable at any time within the first five years if death resulted from an accident. The assured drowned after two years and the company was held liable to pay only £75 on the grounds that the advice

9. In *Tenant* v. *Elliot* (1797) 1 Bos. & Pul. 3 it was held that the premium could be recovered from the broker as money had and received. The "insured" would not, however, be able to reclaim from the insurer.
10. [1985] Q.B. 966, [1984] 1 Lloyd's Rep. 210.
11. [1985] Q.B. 988, [1984] 2 Lloyd's Rep. 109—now overruled in *Phoenix General Insurance Co of Greece SA* v. *ADAS* [1987] 2 All E.R. 152, C.A. discussed in greater detail below.
12. (1908) 24 T.L.R. 593.

given could not contradict the wording of the policy and that it was not normal for a local superintendent to have authority to validate such promises as he had made.

Hard though it may be on contracting parties, there can be no doubt that English law does allow later documentation to include the core of the contractual agreement as long as reference is made to its existence in the earlier negotiations. American law has gone a long way in protecting the insured in such situations of misleading statements by intermediaries by what has been termed the doctrine of detrimental reliance.

It is difficult to see how English law can change without legislative action.[13] Insurance is contained almost exclusively in standard form contracts, certainly with regard to consumer policies, and the courts show a reluctance to interfere in the insurance area.[14]

In an important non-insurance case involving agency, the House of Lords has recently attempted to give clear guidelines on the ostensible and apparent authority of an agent. In *Armagas Ltd* v. *Mundogas SA (The Ocean Frost)*,[15] Lord Keith said:

"Ostensible authority comes about where the principal by words or conduct has represented that the agent has the requisite actual authority, and the party dealing with the agent has entered into a contract with him in reliance on that representation. The principal in these circumstances is estopped from denying that actual authority existed. In the commonly encountered case, the ostensible agent is general in character, arising when the principal has placed the agent in a position which in the outside world is generally regarded as carrying authority to enter into transactions of the kind in question. Ostensible general authority may also arise where the agent has had a course of dealings with a particular contractor and the principal has acquiesced in this course of dealings and honoured transactions arising out of it. Ostensible general authority can, however, never arise where the contractor knows the agent's authority is limited so as to exclude entering into transactions of the type in question, and so cannot have relied on any contrary representation by the principal."

In his judgment Lord Keith referred to a Canadian insurance case[16] where an agent when dealing with the plaintiff's application for motor insurance explained that he would need authorisation from head office because of the plaintiff's earlier record. The plaintiff later asked if this had been given and the agent wrongly said that it had and issued the plaintiff with a temporary cover note. An accident occurred before the defendant insurers had made a decision. A divided court held the insurers liable on the grounds that the agent had been clothed by the company with the trappings of authority, particularly the ability to issue cover notes. Lord Keith agreed, with some reservations, that the decision was correct because of the wide powers given to the agent. The agent's formal agreement with the insurers stated that he had "authority to sign and deliver such policies and renewal certificates of the company as are supplied to the agent and subject to the company's underwriting instructions, to bind the company and to issue 'cover notes' and/or 'policies' as are designated for use".

While it will always depend on the particular facts of each case, it can be argued here that, generally, an agent will bind his principal if he has acted within what appears to be the ostensible authority of such an agent in that branch of insurance. Even where the customer knows that a particular problem needs to be referred to

13. This has been done in Australia (Insurance Contracts Act 1984). But how will the Unfair Terms in Consumer Contracts Regulations 1994 affect the position?
14. See *Roberts* v. *Plaisted* [1989] 2 Lloyd's Rep. 341 (below).
15. [1986] 2 Lloyd's Rep. 109, H.L.
16. *Berryere* v. *Firemans Fund Ins Co* (1965) 51 D.L.R. (2nd) 603.

higher authority he can rely on the answer given by the agent on the assumption that this is the answer the agent has himself received.[17]

Another useful illustration of the court's interpretation of ostensible authority is afforded by the New Zealand case of *Blackley* v. *National Mutual Life Association of Australasia Ltd*.[18] The insured had a life policy that was loaded because he had earlier had a cancerous mole removed from his face. He asked the defendant's agent to arrange a second policy. The agent in turn asked the insured to have a medical examination. This revealed a second mole and the insured was advised to have it removed and have it subjected to pathological examination. This led to a serious operation of which the agent was aware. The agent continued to process the insurance application. The insured's doctor informed the defendant's branch office of the illness and the company repudiated the policy on the grounds of non-disclosure. The insured died and his widow argued that sufficient information had been given to the agent and this knowledge was the company's knowledge.

The court accepted this argument on the grounds that the agent had ostensible authority to grant the cover and the company were therefore estopped from denying knowledge. The court adopted a practical business-like approach to the problem. They asked how disclosure could be made to an artificial entity such as an insurance company, and answered it by saying that such communication could only be through one of its agents. The only problem was to discover if this particular agent had been entrusted with authority to receive such disclosures. The judge said that he did not find it necessary to inquire whether the terms of his actual appointment expressly or impliedly gave him, as between himself and the company, such authority. What was of more importance was to look at the facts of the case and to determine whether or not the agent was clothed with ostensible authority by the company to receive disclosures. By holding out the agent as a person competent to arrange life cover, the company was estopped from denying receipt of the knowledge of the illness.

If, of course, the customer knew that the agent had limited powers then the rule would not apply. Neither must the *Blackley* decision be interpreted broadly to mean that all information obtained by any category of intermediary in any circumstances will automatically be imputed to the principal. In any effort to do justice to a plaintiff in a given situation, the courts would always be concerned not to create absurd results. Thus knowledge obtained by a mere introducer of business which was not relayed to the company would not bind the company.

An additional problem for the customer is where the proposal/policy wording sets out different powers and duties for the agent and thus the information is contractually relayed to the insured. Where the intermediary is an independent adviser, the insured may be able to sue him for negligent advice or for breach of his contract to effect insurance. Because of professional indemnity insurance the chances are that the insured will recover his losses if successful in his allegation. The real problem is where the intermediary is really classed as an employee of the insurer. Although it would be possible to sue him directly there will be less chance of any legal success translating itself into monetary compensation.

17. *Armagas* was considered in another non-insurance decision which contains statements of general principle which would much benefit a modern interpretation of insurance agency rules: *First Energy (UK) Ltd* v. *Hungarian International Bank Ltd* [1993] 2 Lloyd's Rep. 194.
    18. [1972] N.Z.L.R. 1038.

Where the agency relationship is clear-cut, there will almost always be a prohibition on delegating the authority to others. This is an obvious business necessity. If the insurer has trained his employee or has carefully vetted the independent intermediary, it would be to no avail if the work could then be passed down to others not known to the insurer.

In *O'Keefe* v. *London and Edinburgh Ins Co Ltd*,[19] an agent appointed by the defendant insurers decided to appoint another person as his local agent without first obtaining the insurer's approval. He sent the plaintiff's fire proposal to the authorised agent who issued a policy. The answers failed to disclose an earlier fire claim. The "sub-agent" knew of that claim and the plaintiff argued that his knowledge should be imputed to the insurer. The court rejected the argument on the grounds that the sub-agent was not the insurer's agent and even if he had been their agent his earlier knowledge of the plaintiff's loss could not be imputed to the insurer. The court explained the basic principles of commercial agency. A principal can only be liable for the acts of others as agents if they are acting within the scope of the authority given to them by the principal. If the principal is to be bound by the act of a sub-agent then two matters must be established. First, the agent must have either express or implied authority from the principal to delegate his authority and appoint the sub-agent and, secondly, the agent must have express or implied authority from his principal to constitute the relationship of principal and agent between the principal and the sub-agent and it must have been the intention, as between agent and sub-agent, that such a relationship was to be formed.

Thus it is not possible for the sub-agent to bind an insurer if he did not act on behalf of that insurer but only on behalf of the originally authorised agent. That was important in this case because the particular insurer's business practice was to allow their agents to appoint sub-agents. This met the first requirement above, but evidence did not support the second requirement.

## 2.2 Duties owed by agent to his principal

The contract of employment or the agency agreement will provide the basis of the relationship and therefore the rights and duties between the principal and his agent. Some documentation may be detailed, leaving little room for uncertainty. But with the modern tendency in many commercial areas to simplify matters in an attempt to set out clearly the relationship, ambiguities and uncertainties often creep in, thus thwarting the original desired aim for simplicity.

Some duties may be so obvious an outcome of the appointment that they do not appear at all in the contract and if one party attempts to deny their existence it will be left for the other party to ask the court to imply their existence. More problematic are those situations where the intermediary is truly independent and his principal is the customer. In such a situation there would often not be a contract between them setting out any obligations. It is more likely at the present time that, in the event of a dispute, an action would be brought in the tort of negligence rather than in contract.[20]

The basic duties owed by the intermediary to his principal include obeying any specific instructions given to him and carrying out those instructions with reasonable

19. (1928) N.I. 85.
20. But see *Henderson*'s case discussed in chapter 2.

skill and judgment. He must deal honestly with his principal and account for any money received by him for his principal. It will be a matter of fact in each case whether or not the intermediary has reached the required standard.

The crucial factor will be the precise requirements placed by the principal on him. As long ago as 1833 in *Chapman* v. *Walton*,[21] the court stated that the test of reasonable and proper care, skill and judgment was to ask whether other persons exercising the same profession or calling would or would not have come to the same conclusion as did the individual in question. It may be that the relationship between the parties points to the intermediary doing the best he can in the circumstances rather than guaranteeing to achieve a specific result. But there is little doubt that the burden of professional competence on the independent intermediary is an increasingly heavy one following the House of Lords' decision in *Hedley Byrne* v. *Heller & Partners*.[22]

When handling his principal's money the intermediary must obey any specific instructions or act in accordance with any customs or usages that apply.

So, in *Hine Bros* v. *Steamship Insurance Syndicate Ltd*[23] the plaintiff instructed a broker to settle his claim against the defendant insurers for cash in accordance with recognised custom. Contrary to both requirements the broker accepted a bill of exchange at three months' payment. It was eventually paid to the broker but he failed to pay the plaintiff and was later declared bankrupt. The plaintiff sued the insurers for non-payment and succeeded. The court found that it was contrary to recognised custom for insurers to pay in this way and even though the bill was met it did not amount to cash payment.

While little sympathy can be extended to the brokers in this case, perhaps some can be shown for them in *Vehicle and General Ins Co Ltd* v. *Elmbridge Insurances*.[24] The insurers entered into an agency agreement with the brokers which stated that:

"all monies received on behalf of the company in your capacity as an agent of the company are at all times the property of, and received for, and on account for and in trust, to pay the same to the company and can in no way form part of your personal estate or have any connection with any business you may transact apart from that done on behalf of the company".

The insurers went into liquidation and the broker was holding £216 as premiums received for Vehicle and General policies. The broker used that money to obtain fresh cover for those clients. The insurer's liquidator claimed the £216. The court found for the liquidator on the basis of the above agency condition.

This case exposed the thorny problem of a broker acting for two principals. It is an unhappy state of affairs and has been criticised by the courts on many occasions. Here the broker was clearly intent on caring for the interests of his private clients.

The Vehicle and General liquidation also created fiduciary problems for the broker in *Wilson* v. *Avec Audio-Visual Equipment Ltd*.[25] The brokers arranged cover for the defendants with Vehicle and General a few months prior to liquidation. The

---

21. (1833) 10 Bing. 57.
22. [1964] A.C. 465; [1963] 1 Lloyd's Rep. 485. This decision, however, must be read in the light of the House of Lords decision in *Caparo Industries plc* v. *Dickman* [1990] 1 All E.R. 568, discussed in chapter 2.
23. (1895) 72 L.T. 79.
24. [1973] 1 Lloyd's Rep. 325.
25. [1974] 1 Lloyd's Rep. 81, C.A.

brokers asked for the premiums in order to pay them over to the liquidator. The defendants offered to pay a pro rata sum reflecting the months when they had effective cover. The broker paid the full amount on the direction of the liquidator and then claimed the full amount from the defendants.

The Court of Appeal held against the broker on the grounds that he had assumed a personal liability when he need not have done so because the communication from the defendants to the broker had revoked his authority to pay. The court explained that it would require clear and precise evidence of a very special relationship before an agent could be rendered personally liable in respect of a contract entered into on behalf of his principal. Here he was an ordinary agent who had laboured under a mistaken belief as to his legal position in the transaction. As Lord Scarman said:

"insurance business is a complicated affair and different rights and liabilities are assumed by brokers in different spheres of that business. In particular there is no certainty that the rights and liabilities of a broker dealing with a company are the same or are co-extensive with the rights and liabilities of a broker dealing with a Lloyd's underwriter".

Here, Lord Scarman is alluding to the custom at Lloyd's whereby Lloyd's brokers are personally responsible for the premiums.[26]

Where an intermediary is acting for one principal and receives payment for him he should pay that sum over to him without delay. Even if he honestly believes that others have an interest in the money it is not for him to ignore his basic duty to his principal. This was the situation in *Roberts* v. *Ogilby*[27] where the court held that it was his duty to pay over the money to his principal. To rule otherwise would be commercially chaotic because it would place an unfair burden on intermediaries to investigate each and every claim from outsiders who objected to the payment to his principal.

Problems relating to secret commissions or bribes received by intermediaries are by no means new even if in recent years they have generated much heated controversy. Clearly, an intermediary must not breach the fiduciary obligations he owes to his principal by taking an illicit payment or other reward from the other party. A declaration by the intermediary to his principal of the level of commission that he is to receive is obviously the safest course to take. But the courts have adopted a sensible business-like approach wherever possible and not every payment is automatically classified as a secret commission.

It is useful to compare *Great Western Ins Co* v. *Cunliffe*[28] with *Green & Son (Ltd)* v. *Tunghan & Co*[29] In the first case the plaintiffs were American insurers who employed London agents to settle claims in England and also to arrange their reinsurance business. For settlements the plaintiffs paid a fixed percentage but no mention was made of payment for arranging the reinsurance. The agents received what was customary at that time on the London market, namely five per cent plus a further 12 per cent at the end of the year of any profit that occurred on the account between agent and underwriter. The agent declared the five per cent in his accounts with the plaintiffs. After several years the plaintiffs discovered the additional commission.

26. See below.
27. (1821) 9 Price 269.
28. (1874) 9 Ch.App. 525.
29. (1913) 30 T.L.R. 64.

They did not object for a further two years but finally sued to recover all the earlier additional commission together with interest.

The Court of Appeal rejected their claim. It was pointed out that the plaintiffs paid nothing for the work done by the agents on the reinsurance contracts and it was for the agents to arrange for their own profit margins. It was well known in the London market that 12 per cent was paid in accordance with the above formula. Thus if the principal knows that the agent must be receiving some commission, and that must be obvious if the principal is not paying any remuneration himself, then it is for him to make inquiries of his agent about the level of, or method of, commission he is receiving.

In *Green's* case the brokers received five per cent commission plus a 10 per cent discount and a further 25 per cent on two particularly large pieces of business. The broker however disclosed the five per cent to the principal but not the two larger commissions. The court considered this to be an act of dishonesty and the principal was entitled to receive all commissions received.

It is possible to receive rewards from both contracting parties without breaching the rules of secret commissions. The crucial factor will again be whether or not the complainant knew or should have known that this was the situation. Thus in *Norreys* v. *Hodgson*[30] the defendant broker was asked by the plaintiff to arrange a loan. This was done by means of a life policy. The plaintiff agreed to pay the broker one per cent commission based on the value of the loan. The insurance company also paid the broker £210 commission. When the plaintiff discovered this he demanded the commission from the broker. The Court of Appeal rejected the claim on the basis that the plaintiff knowing that the loan was to be secured by means of an insurance policy must have realised that commission would be payable to the broker. The payment could not be classified as a secret commission.

Presents or gifts received by the agent may not necessarily be regarded as bribes or secret commissions. They may reflect assistance given by the agent to the third party. But the dividing line may be difficult to draw, and the greater the value of the gift in comparison with the help given the more dangerous is the agent's position. Again the best policy to adopt is to inform the principal as to what is happening.

It should also be borne in mind that criminal offences may be committed by both the giver and receiver of any bribe. The Prevention of Corruption Act 1906, section 1(1), states:

"If any agent corruptly accepts or obtains or agrees to accept or attempts to obtain from any person, for himself or for any other person, any gift or consideration as an inducement or reward for doing or forbearing to do, or for having done or forborne to do any act in relation to his principal's affairs or business, or for showing or forbearing to show favour or disfavour to any person in relation to his principal's affairs or business he shall be guilty of a misdemeanour."

The punishment can be imprisonment and/or a fine.

## 2.3 Agent's rights against his principal

An agent has the right to expect a payment, normally in the form of commission, for the work he has done. The principal should not put obstacles in his way preventing

---

30. (1897) 13 T.L.R. 421.

him from earning his remuneration. The method of calculating the remuneration will normally be set out in the agreement between the parties but custom or usage in a particular branch of insurance may also have its part to play, as illustrated in the *Great Western* case, above.

The decision in *Sun Alliance Pensions Life and Investment Services Ltd* v. *RJL and Anthony Webster*[31] provides a rare example in an insurance setting of an attempt to imply a term into the agency agreement. The defendant company had agreed to be an appointed representative of the plaintiff company. Considerable sums of money were advanced to the defendant at the beginning of the agency agreement. When the defendant experienced serious financial difficulties the plaintiff company sued for sums advanced. One of several defences raised argued that the plaintiffs had not expeditiously processed proposal forms forwarded to them by the defendant, thus preventing them from earning commission. The defendants argued that a term should be implied into the agency agreement whereby the plaintiffs should not reject proposals without any reasonable grounds. The argument was rejected by the court who found for the plaintiffs. The judge explained that implying a term into a contract can only be done to give business efficacy to that agreement. But the consequences of so doing in the present relationship would have unfortunate and unacceptable results. The agency agreement spelt out clearly that commission would only become payable when the plaintiffs had carried out their underwriting assessment and then issued a policy. To imply a term would, in the court's opinion, fetter the underwriting judgment. Thus if a proposal was rejected by the plaintiffs which the defendants thought should have been accepted then an implied term would possibly interfere with the plaintiffs' commercial judgment. If an implied term puts into a contract something which both parties would have agreed to if their minds had been directed to the problem at the time the contract was negotiated, there was clearly no way in which the plaintiffs would have agreed to such a fetter on their decision-making. The only remedy available to the defendants who felt that they were being unfairly treated would be for them to terminate the agency agreement. Even if that agency agreement was felt to be wanting in its wording by the defendant, it could not be cured by implying a term of the type for which they presently contended.

Problems can arise in the case of commissions for renewals. Normal practice is for the intermediary to receive commission at each renewal. But this is obviously a reflection of the work done by the intermediary.

In *McNeil* v. *Law Union and Rock Ins Co*,[32] the plaintiff broker was instrumental in setting up and renewing annually an employer's liability policy. After several years problems arose concerning the collection of premiums and the broker asked the insurers to send one of their inspectors to see the insured. This was done but only on the basis that the arrangement then became an "own case" agency. By this method the commission was paid to the inspector who in turn was contractually obliged to return it to the insurers. No commission was paid to the broker who then sued the insurers. The court said that if the broker could be described as actively participating in the renewal, which on the facts he could, then he was entitled to his commission. This must be the correct approach. Any other technique could lead effectively to

---

31. [1991] 1 Lloyd's Rep. 410.
32. (1925) 23 Ll.L.Rep. 314.

eliminating the intermediary once he had completed the initial burdensome task of setting up the policy in the first year.

Thus, in *Gold* v. *Life Ass Co Pennsylvania*,[33] it was held that an agent was entitled to the commission on the first year's premium even though his agency had been terminated prior to the payment of that premium.

Agency agreements usually spell out the renewal commission relationship, but even where this is not the case an agent would be entitled to claim a *quantum meruit* for a payment to reflect the amount of work he had done.

When an intermediary has arranged cover for his principal and has paid premiums or incurred expenses on his behalf, he has a lien over the policy documents until he is paid. In marine insurance this lien is set out in section 53(1) of the Marine Insurance Act 1906.

An explanation of the working of a lien in insurance law was given by the Lord Chancellor in *Fisher* v. *Smith*.[34] He said the broker:

"is the person who effected the policies he either paid the premium or became liable for the premiums and his was the labour and the care through which the insurances were effected. According to the well-known rules of law he would be entitled, by common law, for his labour and care and his money expended, to a lien in the nature of holding possession of the policies, and he would be entitled to that lien against every person—against the owner of the goods for whose benefit the policies were effected and against any intermediary who might have intervened between the owner of the goods and himself".

It must be remembered, however, that it is possible for the parties contractually to supersede the effectiveness of the general lien. For instance, where a life policy was deposited with a bank as a security for an overdraft, but specifically stating that it should only apply up to a stated amount, the bank's general lien could not extend beyond that amount.

## 2.4 Termination of authority[35]

An agency agreement would normally set out the circumstances in which the agency comes to an end. Possible examples would include failing to meet the minimum standards of competence as required by the insurer, legislation or applicable codes of practice; failing to service and develop and realise the full potential of the agency from the point of view of the insurer; deliberately overcharging a policyholder; failure to keep proper accounts or mishandling the insurer's money; and backdating or otherwise falsifying cover notes.

An insurer will reserve the right to terminate the relationship often without giving reasons but on giving reasonable notice to the intermediary. The meaning of what is "reasonable" may be a cause of concern.

In certain circumstances the agreement may list occasions when automatic termination would apply. These would normally include death, bankruptcy of the intermediary or his partners, compounding with creditors or being convicted of a

33. [1971] 2 Lloyd's Rep. 164.
34. (1878) 4 App.Cas. 1.
35. The decision in *Yasuda Fire and Marine Insurance* v. *Orion Marine Insurance Underwriting Agency Ltd* [1995] 1 Lloyd's Rep. 525 concerned rights and duties following the termination of an underwriting agency agreement. Although not a case involving insurance intermediaries in the sense used in this chapter, it is a decision of some importance in illustrating the enduring obligations of agents generally.

criminal offence which the insurer deems sufficiently serious to affect the commercial relationship.

Commission will normally cease at the same time as termination takes effect. The intermediary thus loses his right to renewal commissions. The payment of commission is usually tied to the receipt of the first premium and, therefore, if termination took effect prior to that receipt the agreement would effectively cancel the right to payment of that commission. But it would clearly be unfair where a lot of preparatory work had been undertaken by the intermediary and, in the unlikely event of the insurer refusing to pay, even though he has later issued a policy to the insured and taken the premium, a claim on *quantum meruit* could be made.

Although termination of agency effectively carried out will sever the relationship between principal and agent, third parties may still obtain rights against the principal. Where the third party has been led to believe that an agent has authority to effect an insurance but the relationship has been terminated unknown to him, the principal will be bound to the contract. This is an example of "apparent authority".

The burden is on the principal to notify third parties. So, in *Willis, Faber & Co Ltd* v. *Joyce*[36] the defendant underwriter employed an agent to underwrite policies with a proviso that such authority was to terminate at the end of 1909. No notice was given to any other persons nor to Lloyd's concerning this time limitation. The plaintiff sued on policies effected by the agent after the 1909 deadline. The court held that the defendant was estopped from denying the agent's authority to act.

## 2.5 Torts committed by the agent

Apart from the principal's legal liability for his agent, it is possible to hold the agent personally liable. This is unusual but not impossible in contract for the simple reason that the agent is not normally a party to the contract. He arranges the contract on behalf of his principal and drops out.

In tort, however, the agent usually owes a duty of care towards both principal and third party and, in situations that amount to negligent misrepresentations, the typical area bearing in mind the work of insurance agents, an action under *Hedley Byrne* v. *Heller & Partners*[37] may arise. This is dealt with in more detail below.

Liability in other branches of tort law are possible although relatively infrequent. In *McEntire* v. *Potter & Co*[38] defendant brokers arranged cover for a client's ship. The ship was lost and a claim made. Before payment was received by the broker, and unknown to him, the client was adjudicated bankrupt and the plaintiff became the assignee of the estate. The brokers paid the proceeds over to the client and were successfully sued by the plaintiff for that sum. The broker is then left in the unenviable position of seeking an indemnity from his client.

A more unusual extension of tortious liability is seen in the Australian decision in *Colonial Mutual Life Ass Soc* v. *Producers and Citizens Co-operative Ass Co.*[39] The defendant insurers employed someone to act as a canvasser and general agent. A condition of the employment was that the "agent will not in any circumstances

36. (1911) 104 L.T. 576.
37. [1964] A.C. 465.
38. (1889) 22 Q.B.D. 438.
39. (1931) 46 C.L.R. 41.

whatsoever use language or write anything respecting any person or institution which may have the effect of reflecting upon the character, integrity or conduct of such person or institution, or which may tend to bring the same into disrepute or discredit".[40] The agent when selling on behalf of his new employers slandered the plaintiff insurers for whom he had previously worked. A divided court held the defendant insurers liable on the grounds that the wrong committed arose from the mistaken or erroneous manner in which he exercised the actual authority given to him. The case is clearly on the borderline of vicarious liability. The minority judgments rested on the fact that they felt that his terms of engagement and method of working placed him more in the category of an independent agent rather than an employee-agent. If this view had represented the majority opinion the insurers would not have been liable but the agent would have been personally liable.

As it is, there is nothing to prevent the employer in such a case from seeking an indemnity from the agent for breach of contract of employment. It has been stressed above that whether or not the agent held his own professional indemnity cover would be a major determining factor in deciding whether to institute proceedings against the agent. It is possible to buy a "defamation extension" to most professional indemnity policies.

## 2.6 Crimes committed by an agent

As noted earlier, the contract of employment or agency agreement will normally come to an end if the agent is found guilty of a crime. The seriousness of the offence will usually be the determining factor. But what crimes can be particularly associated with an agent by virtue of the position be holds? The obvious answer is offences of dishonesty. Agents often hold large sums of money, either belonging to the client or insurer.

The intricacies of the Theft Act 1968 present agents with problems which may surprise them. Section 1(1) states that "a person is guilty of theft if he dishonestly appropriates property belonging to another with the intention of permanently depriving the other of it". Section 5(3) states that "where a person receives property from or on account of another and is under an obligation to the other to retain and deal with that property or the proceeds in a particular way, the property or proceeds shall be regarded (as against him) as belonging to the other". The combination of these two sections places a heavy burden on the agent to take the utmost precautions in relation to any money that he is handling.

The wording of his contract with the insurer is of great importance. In *R* v. *Robertson*[41] an insurance agent was charged with the theft of premiums held by him and for which he did not account in full to his principals, the insurance company. In his direction to the jury the judge explained that their task was to decide whether Robertson was merely an agent of the company and under no obligation to keep separate accounts or whether his contract did require him to keep the insurer's money separately from other money. If separation was called for then he would be guilty of theft if he used the money for other purposes. On the evidence, the jury acquitted.

40. See the Codes of Practice below and in Appendix 1.
41. [1977] Crim.L.R. 629.

In reality, the contract between the insurer and the agent will invariably contain detailed provisions for the handling of money and the setting up and use of a bank account. The rights of withdrawal from that account[42] will normally be very restricted and a second bank account is usually opened for the payment of commission. Robertson's case was special to its facts and *R* v. *Brewster*[43] is probably a truer reflection of the agent's position. Here the accused was the agent of several insurance companies. A clause common to all of his agency agreements stated that premiums received by him, as agent, were for his principals and such payments would vest and remain in these companies. Over a considerable period of time Brewster had used the premiums as working capital to support his own business. The business had not prospered and he was charged with the theft of £6,100. He was found guilty. The prosecution called witnesses from the insurance companies concerned who conceded that it was accepted and understood in the insurance world that agents were not expected to hand over to their principals the actual (i.e., specific) monies or proceeds of cheques received from those taking out or renewing policies. They admitted that it was well known to them that agents as a matter of common practice did use such monies received by way of premiums for the purposes of their businesses and that they were expected to account to the insurers for equivalent amounts.

Brewster unsuccessfully argued that section 5(3) did not operate to invest the insurers with the title to the actual money. The court accepted that at first glance it was a plausible argument, but ultimately a fallacious one. This was so because the contract of agency was the legal foundation of the parties' relationship. That relationship could be altered or modified by the course of dealings between the parties. That was a matter of evidence in each particular case. But here it was more a question of an indulgence accorded by the insurers to the agent rather than behaviour which changed the contractual relationship. But no indulgence could be implied to justify the dishonest conversion of the premiums.

This decision must come as a shock to many agents. As the insurers admitted, it was common practice for agents to use the insurers' monies in the daily running of their businesses. But what this decision illustrates is that by condoning this practice the insurers could be exposing the agent to an allegation of theft. Only where he could prove that the original contract rights of the insurer had in some way been surrendered, would he be on safer ground. It does seem unfortunate for criminal charges to be brought to penalise situations which themselves have grown out of common practice between the parties. The more acceptable answer is that the agent should remain the debtor of the insurer.

## 3 THE INSURANCE EMPLOYEE, "TIED" INTERMEDIARIES OR COMPANY REPRESENTATIVES

In this part we are not concerned with registered brokers, insurance consultants or other truly independent intermediaries. The Financial Services Act 1986 has brought about changes in terminology and will require changes in business practice. These were referred to above. It is necessary to emphasise here that if the insurance

---

42. See in particular the P.I.A. Rules.
43. [1979] Crim.L.R. 798.

business transacted is not classified as "investment business" under that Act then the idea of "tied" agents survives. By "tied" agent we refer to those who have agency agreements with one or more insurers. This category will include those working on a part-time basis, although some of them, if caught by the Financial Services Act, may choose to become introducers.

Also included in this part is the employee-agent of the insurance company. He is now referred to as a company representative under the 1986 Act and that phrase will also include a previously independent agent who decides to forgo that independence and transact investment business with one insurer only.

The legal position of these agents will clearly depend on their contract of employment or their agency agreement. It is usual however to incorporate into those contracts the relevant "codes" that have been established in recent years aimed at providing the public with a sounder basis for their insurance dealings with the industry.

### 3.1 The codes[44]

Strictly speaking, it is perhaps incorrect to call an employee of an insurance company an intermediary. He certainly does not stand between insurer and assured in the same way as a broker. He clearly is the representative of the company. However, the Life Association's code of selling practice for non-registered intermediaries defines "intermediaries" as "all those persons, including employees of a life office, selling life assurance". The Association of British Insurers' general business code of practice[45] does not attempt any definition, although it specifically excludes registered insurance brokers. Both codes add a further classification complication by differentiating between intermediaries and introducers; the latter's function is merely to introduce a prospective policyholder to a company and then take no further part in the selling transaction. The wording of the Financial Services Act 1986 also leads to the concept of introducer.

Both codes provide useful guidelines as to the responsibilities expected of the agent. It must be stressed, however, that neither code has the force of law[46] and the policing of them is left in the hands of the particular company concerned.[47] Thus an individual insurer's sense of professionalism and what image it wishes to create in the minds of the public will be the main control mechanism. Where the Financial Services Act applies detailed rules have been drafted by the Securities and Investment Board, the SROs and RPBs.

Although the responsibility for enforcing compliance with the codes resides primarily with those insurance companies who are members of the ABI, the Association has published reports on the Code relating to General Insurance. The chairman of the Monitoring Committee stated in the 1991 report that the Committee was encourged by the way the code was operating and that it was pleased by the responsible and practical approach taken both by the ABI and its member companies. The areas of complaint under the code relate to ensuring that the policy

44. See Appendix 1 to this chapter.
45. *Ibid.*
46. See *Harvest Trucking Co Ltd* v. *PB Davies* [1991] 2 Lloyd's Rep. 638 (below).
47. Subject also to the views of the Insurance Ombudsman Bureau.

meets the needs and resources of the policyholder; explaining the essential provisions of the policy; drawing attention to the restrictions and exclusions in policies; not imposing any charges in addition to the premium; not withholding any documentation and passing on claims expeditiously to insurers.

With regard to the need for professional indemnity insurance to be held by intermediaries who are subject to the code the Register now has approximately 7500 entries.

The Department of Trade and Industry considers that the code is working well although both the DTI and the Committee call for greater awareness of the code and that additional advertising should be used to achieve this goal.

In January 1993 the Monitoring Committee published its first full report on the working of the General Business Code of Practice. The purpose of the Committee was to monitor the effectiveness of the first three years of the code in its revised form (the original code had been issued in 1981). The Report explains that the code covers two types of non-broker intermediary; the independent intermediary and the company agent who can represent up to six companies, although special dispensation can be given. The independent intermediary acts for his client, the insured, and is responsible to him for the advice and service given.[48] In the case of the company agent the insurers must accept responsibility for his conduct. Membership of the ABI, however, brings with it the need to see that the code is adhered to and the ABI gives guidelines to its members relating to the appointment and the supervision of such intermediaries. Non-ABI insurers are encouraged to implement the code. There is, however, no way by which this can be legally enforced. Neither does the code apply to Lloyd's, but underwriters have agreed to abide by its wording.

A major concern, in addition to enforcing the code in a general way, is what, if anything, can be done about an intermediary who is found to be failing in his duties as set out in the code. The code is silent on this point. Responsibility falls on the shoulders of the insurers to see that as much compliance as possible is maintained.

An attempt to achieve this can be carried out by careful selection of intermediaries and continual monitoring of their performance. The sanction exercisable by insurers is cancellation of the agency agreement and general warning. Where a company agent is concerned then information concerning cancellation of the agreement should be given to the other insurers for whom that person acted. However, it was felt, after legal advice had been taken, that in the case of independent intermediaries, wide publication should not be given unless some form of exemption from legal liability could be granted to the informant, similar to that which is given to self-regulatory bodies under the Financial Services Act. An additional problem was seen to be that there is no appeal body to whom the "named" intermediary could turn.

Having received submission from various interested groups, the Committee's final recommendations included reference to various areas of insurance about which action should be taken; the suggestion that all insurers should participate in a recognised adjudicator scheme for the settlement of disputes; that the annual review procedure of the Committee should continue and that the code should remain on a non-statutory basis.

48. See below.

The Insurance Ombudsman referred in some detail to the code in his 1993 Annual Report. It has to be remembered that the IOB jurisdiction concerns only insurance companies (and Lloyd's) and then only those companies who have chosen to join the Bureau. It has no direct control over other intermediaries. However, as seen above insurers, by virtue of their membership (also voluntary) of the ABI, must abide by the Code of Selling. In so doing their failure to see that the code is followed by those who sell their products may, by a somewhat circuitous route, be grounds for a complaint to the IOB by an insured.

Part I of both codes deals with the intermediary who is involved in selling and servicing the product. Part II deals with the intermediary who acts only as an introducer. The elementary requirement is that the intermediary should act with the utmost good faith and integrity.

Examples are given of how the sales procedure should evolve. Where possible, appointments to call should be made. Where unsolicited calls are made they should be at an hour likely to be suitable to the prospective policyholder. The intermediary should identify himself and explain that he wishes to discuss insurance matters. He must attempt to make clear to the customer his legal status. Thus he should explain that he is an employee of a particular insurance company or an agent of one or of a number of companies for whose conduct that company or those companies accept responsibility, or that he is an independent intermediary who acts on behalf of the customer, in which case the company with whom the contract is made does not accept responsibility for his acts.

He should ensure, as far as possible, that the policy suggested is suitable to the needs and resources of the client. To that end he should advise only on matters about which he is knowledgeable and he should seek or recommend specialist advice where appropriate.

All information given by the client should be treated in the strictest confidence. The codes state that the agent should not make inaccurate or unfair criticisms of any insurer; should not make comparisons with other types of policies unless he brings out the differing characteristics of each policy; finally, he should not say that the client's name has been given to him by another person unless he is prepared to divulge that name if requested and has permission to divulge it.

The guideline that the agent must give competent advice is expanded upon in Part B of both codes. The Association of British Insurers' general business code states that the insurance company must be identified and the agent must then explain all the essential provisions of the cover provided in that particular policy, drawing attention to the restrictions and exclusions applicable. The overall aim being fully to inform the prospective policyholder about the cover that he is buying. The agent is warned that in attempting to meet what are at times exacting standards and difficulties of interpretation he should seek specialist advice from the company whenever necessary. No additional charge may be made other than the premium unless the agent discloses the amount together with an explanation of the purpose of such charge. If he is an independent intermediary he must disclose his commission if requested to do so by the customer.

The Life Association[49] spells out in more detail the agent's responsibilities when

---

49. See also the SIB Rules.

explaining life assurance contracts. The code covers industrial and ordinary long-term insurance, including all types or annuities, pension contracts and permanent health insurance. In particular the agent should explain the meaning and effect of long-term policies and the problems posed by early discontinuance and surrender values. Of the greatest importance is the explanation of how future benefits are calculated and that variations in both directions are possibilities. It is this area of advice that presents a legal minefield for agents.

Part C of both codes concentrates on the completion of the proposal form. The agent is warned to avoid influencing the prospective policyholder in this matter and to make it clear to him that the answers or statements are those of the client. The agent is also to ensure that the consequences of non-disclosure and inaccuracies are explained. Again, this is an area fraught with difficulties for the agent and dangers for the client as the cases below will demonstrate.

Part D of the codes refers to the handling of money by the agent. It states that where the agent has authority under the terms of his appointment to collect monies then he must keep proper account of all financial transactions involving transmission of money; acknowledge receipt of all money received and distinguish premiums from any other charges; and remit such monies in strict conformity with his agency appointment.

Part E of the general business code requires the agent to make available to the policyholder all documentation relating to the insurance contract. Part F applies the relevant parts of the code to existing policyholders as well as to prospective clients.

Part G of the general code deals with the role of an intermediary when a claim is made. Where the policyholder advises him of a potential claim, the intermediary must inform the company, within three working days. He must also give prompt advice as to the company's claims requirements.

The requirements of the code must be incorporated into all letters of appointment of non-broker intermediaries.

Part II of the both codes refers to the duties to be observed by introducers. Such a person must only give advice on matters within his area of competency and seek advice from the company whenever necessary. At the earliest opportunity he must transmit inquiries to the company and a qualified representative must explain the policy to prospective policyholders. The agent must not solicit insurance business outside the terms of his agency agreement and he must not attempt to influence the answers given on the proposal form.

Both codes appear to place a great burden of professional competence on the shoulders of agents. As policies become more sophisticated and numerous that burden increases in complexity. Under the Financial Services Act 1986 the problem is particularly acute for those giving advice within the terms of the Act.

The effect of the general code was referred to in *Harvest Trucking Co Ltd* v. *Davis*.[50] The plaintiff was a haulage contractor who had arranged his various business insurance needs through the agency of the defendant insurance intermediary. One of the plaintiff's lorries was stolen and the insurers successfully avoided liability on the grounds that one of the policy conditions was not met, namely that the lorry was unattended at the time of the loss. In earlier years of the policy, both plaintiff and

---

50. [1991] 2 Lloyd's Rep. 638.

defendant had successfully negotiated that such a requirement should be omitted from the policy on the grounds that it was impracticable for the plaintiff to conform with it. However, when the plaintiff expanded his business and purchased two larger lorries capable of carrying a more expensive load, the conditions had been reintroduced.

The plaintiff argued that the defendant intermediary had either failed to renegotiate successfully on his behalf or had failed to inform him of the condition. On the evidence before the court the plaintiff succeeded.

The judge explained the effect that the Insurance Brokers (Registration) Act 1977[51] had had on the classification of intermediaries. By virtue of that Act, they were now to be seen either as registered brokers or intermediaries (although at various parts in his judgment he interchanged the two words). Irrespective of which classification applied, the ordinary function of the intermediary was to exercise reasonable skill and care in obtaining his client's insurance needs. This did not mean that the law requires an "extraordinary degree of skill but only such a reasonable and ordinary degree as a person of average capacity and ordinary ability in his situation and profession might fairly be expected to exert". This might require him to construe or interpret the policy for the client, but the court did not regard this as a universal rule. Everything would depend on the particular circumstances of the case, which would include the type of working arrangement the intermediary and his client had. Here, the limitation clause was of special significance because it had been successfully removed in earlier insurances with the same insurer.

The defendant admitted that he had received the ABI code. The judge referred in particular to the section stating that the intermediary should "ensure as far as possible that the policy proposed is suitable to the needs and resources of the prospective policyholder". He also referred to the section stating that an explanation should be given relating to all the essential provisions of the cover and that the intermediary should draw attention to any restrictions or exclusions that applied to the policy.

Having itemised parts of the code which would appear to be specifically relevant to the facts before him, the judge then added that the code was not binding on him, because it was merely a voluntary code of practice, and that his decision could only be arrived at on the basis of legal principle. However, the court did admit that the code was helpful in two ways. First, because it described the context in which an intermediary had to operate. Secondly, it was helpful to refer to the code to ensure that the standard of care which the court intends to apply is not considered to be unrealistic by the insurance industry. The court was wary of adopting a too high or perfectionist standard of behaviour.

Fortunately the code reflects what the cases have illustrated over many years to be the duty owed by an insurance intermediary. This judgment is important as it reflects a judicial approach enforcing the principle that brokers and non-registered independent intermediaries should be judged by the same standards.

51. See below.

### 3.2 The agency agreement

The wording of agency agreements varies. The majority are quite short and follow a pattern. Some make specific reference to the various codes of practice. Thus an example taken from one company states:

"It is a condition of your appointment as agent that:—

(1) If you are an insurance broker by virtue of being registered or listed under sections 2 or 4 of the Insurance Brokers (Registration) Act 1977, you shall conform with the Code of Conduct contained in the Insurance Brokers Registration Council (Code of Conduct) Approval Order 1994 as may be varied from time to time.

(2) If you are not an insurance broker as defined above, you shall conform with any Code of Practice issued by the Life Offices Association as may be varied from time to time. The terms contained in any Codes of Conduct or Practice shall be regarded as forming part of this appointment.

(3) If it should come to the notice of the Company that it has assumed a risk through you whilst the above Codes were not conformed with, then you shall indemnify the Company at its option against any sums expended by the Company arising from such assumed risk."

Where this direct application of the codes is not the method used to spell out the relationship of agent to insurer, the normal pattern of powers and duties tends to cover a basic set of requirements. In particular, an agent is not empowered to give cover for any risk unless expressly authorised to do so by the company nor is the agent empowered to bind the company by any statement, written or oral, unless authorised by the company to do so. This is basically a limitation of his authority as agent and has led to numerous problems as is shown by the cases below. The company can give an agent wider than normal powers but certainly, in the class of business with which the vast majority of agents are concerned, it is only rarely done.

Companies seem to have been able to carve out for themselves a considerable degree of protection by limiting agents in this way and, although criticised by both the courts and the Law Reform Committee (1957),[52] little has been done to improve the position of the insured.

The remaining core of obligations in the agency agreement is concerned with certain administrative and financial arrangements. Thus the agent must forward proposal forms as soon as possible to the company and promptly advise the company of any claims made. Depending on the particular agency agreement, agents may be empowered to settle claims in the general business area up to certain financial limits. Many agreements, however, will not give such power of settlement to the agent.

Financial arrangements will depend on whether the agent has a cash or credit agency. If a cash agency, then the agent may not retain monies on behalf of the company and premiums received from clients must be transmitted immediately upon receipt. The agent is forbidden to issue evidence of payment on behalf of the company. Normally, documents are retained by the insurer until payment has been received by them. If it is a credit agency, then all monies received by the agent are to be regarded as the property of the company and the agreement will state that it is held on trust on behalf of the company. Such monies are normally to be kept in properly designated bank accounts in such a way that they can be readily identified as those of the company; agents are usually warned that any credit extended by them to a

52. Cmnd. 62.

customer is at their own risk and they will have no right of indemnification against the company. The agreement will spell out the method of calculating commission and of forwarding monies to the company.

The various grounds for terminating the agency will be set out. These usually include bankruptcy, compounding with creditors and death of the agent. The company invariably reserves the right to terminate the agency without explanation, whereupon the right to commission and allowances will cease apart from those earned prior to such notification.

To hold an agency appointment from a particular insurer does not necessarily put beyond question the precise classification of an individual. Companies are desirous of obtaining good business under any legitimate circumstances and this can occasionally lead to complex employment situations.

In *Massey* v. *Crown Life Insurance Co*,[53] the appellant was employed by the insurers as a branch manager from 1971 until 1973 under contract. The contract treated him as an employee and he was paid a salary and PAYE and pension scheme deductions were made. In 1973 his accountant advised him that for various tax reasons he should seek to be self-employed. The insurers agreed to this change and his tax position was altered with the agreement of the Inland Revenue. In 1975 the insurers dismissed him and he claimed unfair dismissal. Such claims are only possible if the person dismissed can be classified as an employee working under a contract of service. The Court of Appeal held that Massey was not an employee and his claim failed. The answer comes from looking at all the surrounding circumstances. He was paid on commission, he could work for other brokers and the 1973 agreement sought, successfully, to classify him as an independent contractor. As Lord Denning MR said, "Having made his bed as being self-employed, he must lie on it".

It is important to remember, however, that merely describing a person in a particular way will not be decisive to the outcome of the question: is he an employee or an independent agent? The court will look closely at all aspects of the agreement. This is how the Privy Council approached an appeal from Australia in *Australian Mutual Provident Society* v. *Allan*.[54]

The plaintiff had worked for eight years for the insurance company. He claimed compensation under the Long Service Leave Act 1967 on termination of employment. The question was whether or not he was to be classified as an "employee". The legislation provided for the possibility of a person being an employee even if paid on commission. The contract itself provided that the relationship was that of principal and agent and not master and servant.

The Privy Council, overturning the Australian courts, held that the plaintiff was not an employee. The description used in the employment contract was not the only factor to be taken into account. All aspects of the working relationship had to be weighed together. Those which influenced the decision were the fact that the plaintiff could form a partnership, or he could even incorporate himself. He was allowed to appoint sub-agents and this power of sub-delegation is a crucial indication of a person's independence. Additional indicators were the fact that he did not need to tell the insurers where he was; when he was working, he worked from his own house;

---

53. [1978] I.C.R. 590.
54. (1978) 44 S.A.I.R. 354.

he could employ others and he had a high incidence of expenses which he was allowed to set against tax.

In *Excess Life Ass Co Ltd* v. *Fireman's Ins Co of Newark New Jersey*,[55] the plaintiff insurers had taken out with the American defendant insurers a policy to cover dishonest and fraudulent behaviour of "employees". The question arose as to whether independent salesmen could be regarded as "employees". The type of work undertaken was mainly concerned with selling life policies. After analysing the working relationship between the plaintiff and the sales force, who were clearly employed by a distinct company, the court decided that they were employees of the plaintiff insurers and, therefore, covered by the terms of the defendant's policy.

The court said that even if the intermediaries could be regarded in some respects as agents of the policyholders that would not preclude the possibility of them also being, in the same transaction, agents of Excess. "In my view there is nothing in English law and practice which is inconsistent with the Group being Excess's agents, even if they described themselves as 'brokers' " (Webster J). The problem that arises in such a situation is that, in acting for both sides, the intermediary is in grave danger of being in breach of his duty to one or other party, or both parties, should a conflict of interest arise between them.

These three cases help to illustrate how the courts view the relationship between insurer and agent. The great majority of cases that reach the courts, however, are concerned with the relationship of insurer with insured. Those problems often concern the role played by the agent or employee in the formation of the contract or the settlement of claims. The next section looks in some detail at the problems that have arisen.

### 3.3 Cases involving the insured

The following cases involve both the employee/agent of particular insurers and the "tied" agent of one or more insurers. It is convenient to group the decisions under four main agency functions: (i) failure to follow the customer's instructions to insurers; (ii) advising the customer as to his particular insurance requirements; (iii) completing the proposal form; and (iv) wrongful behaviour with regard to procedural matters.

### 3.3.1 *Failure to follow the customer's instructions to insurers*

We saw earlier that an agent owes a number of duties to his principal. These include a duty to carry out the transaction; a duty to obey instructions; and a duty to act with reasonable skill and to exercise reasonable judgement. The first problem that arises is that an agent may owe these duties to both insurer and customer, depending on the particular task he is performing. Thus it is possible that a tied agent may have a contract with the customer to oversee his insurance requirements.

In *United Marketing Co* v. *Hasham Kara*,[56] a shopkeeper, finding himself

55. [1982] 2 Lloyd's Rep. 599.
56. [1963] 1 Lloyd's Rep. 331, [1963] 1 W.L.R. 523, P.C.

uninsured following a fire, argued that the fault lay with the agent. The argument was that for a number of years the agent had arranged his insurance requirements with a particular company. Premiums were paid to the agent by the unsatisfactory method of off-setting the money against purchases by the agent from the plaintiff's shop. The agent's defence was that there was no agreement that he should continue, without specific instructions, to renew the insurance. Faced with a conflict of evidence the court accepted the plaintiff's argument. They were persuaded by the agent's behaviour after the fire when he appeared to consider that there were no problems with regard to the policy and attempted to pay into the company's account a sum equivalent to the premium.

Clearly, the outcome of any litigation will depend on how the court interprets the understanding between the parties on the evidence available. Even where an agent acts gratuitously in agreeing to arrange insurance he still owes a duty of care to the other party.

The point is illustrated in the old case of *Wilkinson* v. *Coverdale*.[57] The vendor of property agreed with the purchaser to have his policy assigned to the purchaser. He charged the purchaser with the costs of the premium but failed correctly to assign the policy and the purchaser failed in his claim against the company. In an action against the vendor the purchaser failed to prove negligence, but the court was of the opinion that if a person is so negligent in effecting an insurance then the fact that he was acting without payment would provide no defence.

On the other hand even an agent's failure to follow his principal's instructions precisely and thus cause loss to either party to the contract may not mean the agent is liable. In *Holland* v. *Russell*,[58] the agent of a foreign shipowner failed to inform the plaintiff's insurer of existing damage to the ship. The insurers later paid out on a loss. The agent handed the money to the shipowner. When the insurers subsequently discovered the error they sought to recover the sum from the agents. They failed, the court holding that the original mistake was neither fraudulent nor negligent but an honest mistake and, as the insurers knew throughout the transaction that the agent was acting as agent of the shipowner, they could not look to the agent for reimbursement.

### 3.3.2 Advising the customer as to his particular insurance requirements

Here we have an area fraught with difficulties and dangers, although, as the cases illustrate, it is often the customer who suffers. In these cases the agent is usually the agent of the insurer. The problem stems from the fact that many agents who have contact with the customer have much more limited powers of negotiation than the public think they have. When the agent exceeds the authority given to him by his principal he no longer binds the principal to the contract.

It would be possible, at least since the House of Lords' decision in *Hedley Byrne* v. *Heller*,[59] to sue the agent in negligence. But if the agent does not carry professional indemnity insurance it may prove to be an illusory legal remedy.[60]

---

57. (1793) 1 E.S.P. 74.
58. (1863) 4 B. & S. 14.
59. [1964] A.C. 465.
60. The ABI Codes of Selling and the IBRC Code require the intermediary to carry professional indemnity insurance.

The main hope of the customer is that the agent is clothed with sufficient authority to bind his principal. That is a matter of construction of his agency agreement. But, as we have seen above, the normal terms of the agreement limit his powers.

It may be of importance to ask whether or not the agent's advice was innocently or fraudulently given. After some initial conflict between decisions it now seems that, if the misleading advice is innocently given, the company will not be ordered to return premiums.

The decision of the Supreme Court of Canada in *Fletcher* v. *Manitoba Public Insurance Co*[61] is of considerable interest in this area. The insured applied for motor insurance from the defendants. The clerk did not explain to him the problems and significance of a situation where the other party to an accident might be underinsured. Company literature was available at that time but this was not brought to the plaintiff's attention. On renewal the documentation referred, in small print, to the problem. The plaintiff did not read this documentation and did not purchase the extended cover. He was injured by an underinsured driver. He successfully sued the defendant insurer for breach of their duty to advise him correctly as to his insurance needs.[62] For the present discussion the relevant question posed by the Supreme Court was: did a (Government-owned) insurer selling compulsory insurance directly to a client have a duty to advise that person of the existence, nature and extent of underinsured motor cover and if such a duty did exist had the insurer fulfilled its duty?

In answer to the first question it was clear the decision in *Hedley Byrne* v. *Heller* has been applied to insurer-insured situations.[63] Thus the principle in *Hedley Byrne* would be applicable in the present case if the insured relied on the information given by their insurer; that reliance was reasonable and the insurers knew or ought to have known that the insured would rely on the information. Applying those ingredients to the situation in question the court held that the insured did rely on the advice given by the insurer and that such reliance was entirely reasonable because a few prospective insureds would have sufficient familiarity with insurance requirements and they "expect employees serving them to tell them about the risks against which they must insure and against which they may insure and what it will cost them to do so". Finally, it was clear to the insurer that such insureds would reasonably rely on the information given.

It might be argued that a different emphasis should be placed on private agents and brokers compared with public insurance personnel (an unknown distinction, of course, in the UK). As the court stressed, however, private insurance agents and brokers are regarded by the insurance industry as more than mere salespeople. Thus it is also entirely appropriate to hold such people to a stringent duty to provide both information and advice to customers. They are licensed professionals (again, in the UK, this phrase would not at present be used to describe all insurance intermediaries) who specialise in helping with risk assessment and in tailoring insurance policies to fit the particular needs of such clients. Subtle differences in the forms of

---

61. 74 D.L.R. (4th) 636.
62. Admittedly the factual situation in this case could not arise in the UK in that there is unlimited liability for personal injuries arising from road accidents.
63. *Cherry* v. *Allied Insurance Brokers* [1978] 1 Lloyd's Rep. 274; *General Accident Fire and Life Ass Corp* v. *Tanter (The Zephyr)* [1984] 1 Lloyd's Rep. 58.

coverage available are frequently difficult for the average person to understand. Agents and brokers are trained (in the UK?)[64] to understand these differences and to provide individualised insurance advice. It is both reasonable and appropriate to impose upon them a duty to provide counsel and advice.

This Canadian decision provides an extensive and comprehensive approach to the duty owed by intermediaries. It is to be hoped that it will also be used as a benchmark for the various bodies and organisations presently occupied with drawing up standards of competence, in the UK, in their task of deciding what the correct levels of responsibilities should be for insurance intermediaries.

In a case of innocent misrepresentation the remedy of rescission is not always that useful to the plaintiff because the right to rescind is too easily lost. But, in *Mutual Reserve Life Ins Co* v. *Foster*,[65] the House of Lords showed sympathy with the predicament in which the insured found himself. The insurer's agent had misrepresented a highly complex life policy to the plaintiff, above all failing to explain that premiums increased as age increased. On discovering the true situation the plaintiff tried to argue that the policy should continue along the lines that he had been led to believe applied. This delay in seeking rescission of the contract would normally prove fatal, but the House accepted his reasons for trying to keep alive the policy and, therefore, granted rescission and return of premiums.

If the agent's advice is fraudulent, presumably to gain a commission, the insurer will be bound at least to refund premiums, although not bound to honour the policy itself. In *Hughes* v. *Liverpool Victoria Legal Friendly Soc*,[66] the agent fraudulently advised the plaintiff that she had an insurable interest in certain lives. The plaintiff later discovered that this was not so and the court held that she was entitled to recover the premiums from the insurer. The Court of Appeal advised insurers how they should conduct their business. Swinfen Eady LJ said that if insurance agents were carefully instructed not to procure or accept proposals where there is no insurable interest there would be far fewer claims for return of premiums. Phillimore J added that it was not for insurers to argue that their collectors or superintendents were acting beyond the scope of their authority and thus their actions were not binding on them and yet at the same time claim that they could retain the premiums obtained by such methods.

So, in *Kettlewell* v. *Refuge Ass Soc Ltd*,[67] a policyholder who intended to give up her policies was persuaded by the company agent that if she continued with them she would be eligible for a free policy. The court found that this was a fraudulent statement and she was entitled to a refund on the premiums paid to the company.

It is unusual in life policies to spell out the requirements of insurable interest. In policies which do set out certain benefits the insurer will not normally be bound by alterations made to those conditions by the agent during his negotiations with the customer.

In *Horncastle* v. *Equitable Life Ass Soc of United States*,[68] an agent told a customer that while the benefits under a policy were stated to be worth £5,000 they would in

---

64. But see the Chartered Insurance Institute examinations and the 1995 PIA requirements.
65. (1904) 20 T.L.R. 715, H.L.
66. [1916–1917] All E.R. Rep. 918.
67. (1909) 53 Sol.J. 339, H.L.
68. (1906) 22 T.L.R. 735, C.A.

fact be worth £7,390 after 15 years. The policy stated that no changes in the wording were possible unless authorised in writing by certain specified officers of the company. The agent was not one of those officers. On maturity the policy was worth £6,106 and the plaintiff sued the company. The Court of Appeal rejected the claim, holding that the policy was intended to be the complete and final statement of the transaction. Even if the agent had authority to make such statements the court was of the opinion that they would have been inconsistent with the wording of the policy and, therefore, would have been of no assistance to the policyholders.

When the policy does not narrow the insurer's obligations by specific conditions there can be no doubt that the agent and therefore his principal do owe a duty to give careful and considered advice. What meets this requirement will vary with the complexity of the policy on offer. To prove negligence requires evidence that the agent acted in a way in which other competent agents would not have acted.

In *Rust* v. *Abbey Life Assurance Co Ltd*,[69] the plaintiff wished to invest £90,000. She inquired about the defendant's property bonds and spoke to their agent on a number of occasions. She explained that easy withdrawal facilities were important to her and these were explained to her by the agent but she saw no printed details until she received the policy documentation. However, the agent spoke to the plaintiff's accountant and explained the arrangements and he approved the plan. Six months after the money was invested, the plaintiff sought to withdraw a large amount. The insurers were not prepared to return this sum and the plaintiff was not prepared to accept the surrender value offered. The plaintiff therefore sued the insurers arguing that she had made it plain throughout the negotiations that she intended it to be a short-term investment, that she had been misled by the agent and that he had exercised undue influence over her.

On the evidence the court rejected her claim, finding no negligence on the part of the agent. But the judge added that an agent in such a transaction was under a duty of care to give adequate explanations of the nature of such bonds and of the liquidity facilities. The duty involved a separate and more positive and extensive duty than not to make misrepresentations. The duties imposed by the Financial Services Act 1986 will now be more onerous on advisers on such business investments.

Silence could itself amount to negligence in response to specific questions. The Canadian case of *Myers* v. *Thompson and London Life Insurance Co*,[70] affords a useful example of the scope of the duty of care in negligence and also illustrates the limits of the relationship between principal and agent. A solicitor asked the first defendant, who was an agent of the second defendant, to convert an existing life policy held by one of the solicitor's clients in such a way as to avoid certain tax duties. The agent visited the client to arrange matters. He failed however to inform his principals of the exact requirements, and the result was that the intended alterations to the policy were not made.

The court held that even though the agent was acting gratuitously, he had breached his duty of care to the insured. He had been a general insurance agent for 30 years and was, therefore, a person upon whom others could rely to exercise due care. The insurers, however, were not vicariously liable for their agent's negligence on the

69. [1978] 2 Lloyd's Rep. 386.
70. 63 D.L.R. (2nd) 476.

grounds that his contract of employment was limited to "solicit applications and receive premiums for the Company upon the terms, within the limits and under the instructions contained in the Agents' Manual". In a situation such as this the existence of professional indemnity cover would be crucial to both parties.

Another area of difficulty, and yet one which must commonly face both tied agents and independent intermediaries, is where the customer asks for help in understanding the policy wording. We have seen in *Horncastle* v. *Equitable Life*[71] that the insured is often prevented from successfully alleging that he has been misled by the agent by the simple argument that the policy states clearly that it can not be altered without senior management approval. But what of the situation where help is requested in determining the meaning of words in phrases in the policy?

In *Re Hooley Hill Rubber and Chemical Co Ltd and Royal Insurance Co Ltd*,[72] manufacturers of explosives discussed with the insurer's agent the extent of the policy and particularly the meaning of exclusion clauses in the policy. The manufacturers alleged that they had been misled by the agent's answers, and therefore the insurers were estopped from denying that the policy had the meaning given to it by the agent.

The judge rejected this defence. He did so even though he was of the opinion that an intelligent businessman would have been misled by the statements made by the agent. The difficulty confronting the judge was the rule that while misleading statements of fact may allow one party a remedy a misstatement of law will not. He had the further difficulty of deciding whether the statements were ones of fact or law. He considered that the matter was finely balanced,[73] but what tipped the decision against the insured was that the agent made specific references to one of the conditions in the policy and in so doing he was giving his view as to the interpretation of the legal document. In consumer contracts the ABI Statements of Insurance Practice place a clear burden on the intermediary to explain the policy wording. The Statements are discussed below.

## 3.4 Completing the proposal form

If the last section exposes the customer to difficulties in his relationship with the insurers, then the present topic illustrates an even more lamentable situation. The agent may well be individually liable, but again this may be of little comfort to the customer in the absence of indemnity insurance held by the agent.

There is a considerable conflict of judicial opinion in the cases that follow. The basic fact situation is one that must occur on a regular basis. The customer is faced with a proposal form for completion. Although there has been an attempt in recent times to simplify such forms,[74] many customers still find them a trying experience. The agent, eager to help or perhaps eager to speed up the exercise, often offers to complete the form for the customer. Wrong answers are entered and, when a claim is later made, the insurers plead misrepresentation or non-disclosure by the customer.

71. See above.
72. [1920] 1 K.B. 257.
73. The law report states that the present legal point was not raised on appeal, the parties having come to an agreement. Perhaps the words of the judge had convinced the parties that a comprise was the best course of action.
74. Attempts at simplicity can in fact lead to ambiguity.

There are various permutations possible. It may be that correct answers were given by the customer to the agent but he, innocently, negligently or fraudulently, entered an incorrect answer. The position of the agent may be that of either limited powers or he may be vested with authority to complete proposals. The proposal form may contain a proviso that, if an agent assists in completing the form, he is to be treated as acting as agent of the customer and not the agent of the insurer for this purpose.

The starting-point in analysing the cases is *Bawden* v. *London, Edinburgh and Glasgow Ass Co.*[75] In completing a proposal for accidental injury cover, the plaintiff stated that he had no physical infirmity and that there were no circumstances that rendered him peculiarly liable to accidents. In fact the plaintiff was blind in one eye. The agent knew this but did not relay the information to the insurers. The court was given no explanation as to the terms of the agency agreement. The court found for the plaintiff. Lord Esher MR explained the situation clearly. He said that the agent was the agent of the company. His function was to negotiate terms with a view to completing a contract. He was not merely an agent to take a piece of paper to the company. Knowledge that he possessed was deemed to be the knowledge of the company. This commonsense description of an insurance agent must surely commend itself as a reflection of what the general public believe to be the situation.[76]

Unfortunately for insureds *Bawden* was soon distinguished in later judgments. In *Biggar* v. *Rock Life Ass Co,*[77] the customer gave the correct answers to the agent who incorrectly transcribed them. The customer did not check over the completed form. He failed in his action against the insurer. The decision in this, and later cases, is based on the argument that one is bound by one's signature and failing to read over a document before signing it is a fault that should rest squarely on that person's shoulders.

As a general statement of legal principle, such an argument is unassailable. But does it reflect the reality of insurance sales using proposal forms? Surely the agent knows that reliance is being placed on him and, having carelessly or negligently filled in answers which had been correctly given, it does not seem to reflect the public's reasonable expectations when the courts reject claims. The judge did show some sympathy with the plaintiff when he said that the most that the plaintiff could ask for was that the contract be declared void on the grounds of fraud, if proved, or mistake. But even if this could be done, only the return of premiums would be possible and not a claim to the insurance money.

In *M'Millan* v. *Accident Ins Co Ltd,*[78] the proposal form specifically stated that the company should not be liable for any knowledge acquired by their agent unless such information was communicated to the company, and acknowledged by them to the customer, in writing. An inspector failed to complete the proposal form accurately. The customer admitted that he had not read over the proposal because he had relied on the agent to do his job properly. Again, the customer failed. The reason being that it is the proposer's form and, therefore, his responsibility to see that the answers are accurate. If he allows a person to complete the form then that person acts as his agent for that task and not as agent of the insurers. The court found the reasoning in

---

75. [1892] 2 Q.B. 534, C.A.
76. See *Roberts* v. *Plaisted* [1989] 2 Lloyd's Rep. 341, C.A.
77. [1902] 1 K.B. 516.
78. 1907 S.C. 484.

*Bawden's* case unacceptable, adding that it would be most unjust to hold that a policy was valid on the grounds that an agent of the insurer knew a fact which was contrary to a statement in the form signed by the proposer.

These cases clearly reduce the role of agent to that of errand boy. There is an implied rejection of any professional competence. Although these cases arose long before any attempt was made in this country to provide a modicum of consumer protection, some judges did attempt to provide a basis of protection.

In *Thornton-Smith* v. *Motor Union Ins Co*,[79] the plaintiff, when seeking motor cover, told the agent that he had been refused a renewal of his policy by another company. When he later completed the proposal form he was asked whether he had been refused insurance on any previous occasion. He did not complete this question once the agent assured him that he would "make it all right". When the company attempted to reject a later claim, the court held that the insurers were bound, as a full disclosure had been made to the agent and there was no suggestion of collusion between the proposer and the agent.

Similarly, in *Ayrey* v. *British Legal and United Provident Ass Co*,[80] in an application for a life policy the proposer correctly stated that he was a trawlerman. But he also told the agent that he was a member of the Royal Naval Reserve. The agent referred the matter to the district manager and the policy was issued without alteration. Despite the fact that the policy stated that the agent was to be regarded as the insured's agent when receiving information, the court found that the policy was valid. It was considered to be a reasonable expectation that, when information is given to a person with the status of district manager, this is equivalent to informing head office. The acceptance of premiums by the district manager with full knowledge of the facts amounted to a waiver by the company of any objection by them that there had been a concealment of a material fact.

Here the court is using two methods to place responsibility on the company for their agent's neglect. The first is to look closely at the status of the agent and determine whether or not he is sufficiently senior so that knowledge on his part can be regarded as knowledge of the company. The other technique used is that of waiver or estoppel. This arises where the insurers, in full knowledge of the facts, act in such a way as to show that they are not intent on raising any objections and thereby convince the insured that he is fully covered.

*Keeling* v. *Pearl Ass Co Ltd*[81] provides another illustration of these techniques. The agent discussed with a wife life assurance on the life of her husband. True answers were given to health questions, but the agent filled in incorrect answers. There was also an inconsistency between the "date of birth" and the "age next birthday" questions. The company attempted to avoid liability on the death of the husband.

The court rejected the defence. It was found that the agent had authority from the company to negotiate and complete proposal forms and was therefore the agent of the insurer for this purpose. The discrepancy between the date of birth and age answers was something which the company should have detected. It was a staring inaccuracy and if companies insist that the answers are crucial to their judgement of

---

79. (1913) 30 T.L.R. 139.
80. [1918] 1 K.B. 136.
81. [1923] All E.R. Rep. 307.

the risk, they cannot avoid the consequences of their own negligence in not recognising the mistake.

Any glimmer of hope from these two cases that an agent may be regarded as agent of the insurer when completing proposal forms and that this was to be the way forward, was, however, crushed by the Court of Appeal in *Newsholme* v. *Road Transport and General Ins.*[82]

The agent discussed insurance of the plaintiff's motor-bus. The customer gave the agent correct answers which the agent incorrectly entered on the proposal form. The court found for the insurer. The agent had authority to obtain completed proposal forms, and to receive premiums. But he had no authority to complete the forms and no authority to issue cover notes. In completing the form he was, according to Scrutton LJ, the amanuensis of the customer.

The conflict between the earlier cases was explained as a desire in some situations to hold an insurer liable for anything that an agent does in procuring business and a desire in other cases to uphold the contention that a person who signs a promise that his written statements are true and are to be regarded as the basis of his contract cannot claim to vary his contract by omitting that promise and disclaiming misstatements. The court distinguished *Bawden's* case[83] by arguing that it did not apply where the agent completed the proposal at the request of the customer. If that is the situation, then according to Scrutton LJ, the agent must be the agent of the customer for that specific purpose.

Insurance companies are quick to learn from any adverse judicial decisions and to adapt their approach accordingly. While *Newsholme* clearly favoured them, it still left open the problem that, in certain circumstances, as in *Keeling*, an agent might have authority to complete answers and thus remain the agent of the insurer. The modern technique therefore used by many insurers is to state on the proposal form that, when an agent helps to complete a proposal, he is to be regarded as the agent of the customer. The form must be signed by the customer and thus he assents to this role of the agent.[84]

This is what happened in *Facer* v. *Vehicle and General Ins Co Ltd.*[85] The plaintiff wanted to insure his car. He did not have a great ability in completing forms. The sub-agent of the insurer's agent completed the form and no mention was made of the fact that the plaintiff had lost one eye. The plaintiff argued that this fact was well known to the sub-agent as he had known him for 18 months prior to his application for insurance and, consequently, the knowledge of the agent should be imputed to the insurers.

The court was faced with the *Bawden/Newsholme* conflict. Marshall J found that *Bawden* had not been followed in English cases and had been criticised in Scotland, Ireland and in the USA. *Newsholme*, on the other hand, had been accepted as correctly stating the law. In addition, the signed agreement stating that the agent was to be regarded as the customer's agent put the matter beyond doubt and the plaintiff's claim failed.

While the courts seemed to accept the correctness of *Newsholme*, the decision is

---

82. [1929] 2 K.B. 356.
83. [1892] 2 Q.B. 534, C.A.
84. This role is favoured by the ABI Code of Practice, para. (C).
85. [1965] 1 Lloyd's Rep. 113.

clearly so contrary to what the general public would expect the legal position to be[86] that it was inevitable that, in the days of mounting demands for consumer protection, a change should be advocated. This was first seen as far back as 1957 in a Law Reform Committee Report. The recommendation was that "any person who solicits or negotiates a contract of insurance shall be deemed for the purpose of the formation of the contract, to be the agent of the insurers, and that the knowledge of such person shall be deemed to be the knowledge of the insurers". In 1976 a Committee of Inquiry into the Insurance Industry in Ireland proposed similar changes to Irish law.

In 1980 the Law Reform Commission of Australia in their Report[87] on Insurance Agents and Brokers said in relation to agents:

"The additional cost to the industry and, ultimately, to the public of imposing on insurers civil responsibility for the acts of their agents would be very small. All members of the insuring public who deal through agents would obtain additional security against the risk of heavy personal loss resulting from their errors. Contractual clauses seeking to limit the responsibility of insurers for the misrepresentations or other conduct of their agents should be rendered ineffective. The responsibility of an insurer should extend to all matters connected with a proposal or policy in respect of which the insured can show that he actually relied on the agent."

This has manifested itself in the Australian Insurance (Agents and Brokers) Act 1984. Section 11 states that an insurer is responsible for the conduct of his agent or employee where the customer could reasonably be expected to rely and did rely in good faith on any matter relating to the insurance. This liability applies even where the agent has acted outside the scope of his authority. The insurer cannot avoid this obligation in any way. Where the customer has been misled in these circumstances, the insurer must make good any losses. Section 13 goes on to penalise any misrepresentations made by agents and employees of insurers and also of insurance intermediaries. The type of conduct covered is where misleading statements are made about premiums and other amounts payable in respect to an intended contract, and also situations where the agent or employee misleads the customer as to his duty to disclose or as to the content of his duty of disclosure. However, the liability only covers situations where the agent or employee's conduct has been wilful with an intent to deceive.

New Zealand legislated to change the situation in their Insurance Law Reform Act 1977 along lines similar to the English Law Reform Committee's recommendations. Canadian Provinces have also enacted changes that shift the burden onto the shoulders of the insurers. It is surely impossible to criticise such proposals and reforms. But in England nothing has been done legislatively to implement the suggested changes of 1957.

The only inroad into the *Newsholme* rule has been made by the Court of Appeal in *Stone* v. *Reliance Mutual Ins Co*.[88] The appellant insured his flat against fire and theft with the respondent insurers, the premiums paid weekly to collectors. A year later a fire occurred and the appellant was indemnified. The policy later lapsed and an inspector visited the appellant with a view to reviving the policy. He convinced the

---

86. See *Roberts* v. *Plaisted* (above).
87. Report No. 16.
88. [1972] 1 Lloyd's Rep. 469, C.A.

appellant's wife to renew. The inspector was empowered to complete proposal forms and amazingly he did not record the earlier claim or that the original policy had lapsed. When a later theft occurred the appellant declared on his claims form both the fire and the lapse of policy. An assessor was sent and a figure agreed.

Premiums were collected for a further three months before the respondent insurers rejected the claim on the grounds of non-disclosure. To avoid the negligence of their own inspector they argued that the proposal form contained a declaration stating that "I further declare insofar as any part of this proposal is not written by me the person who has written same has done so by my instructions and as my agent for that purpose". In other words, it was a *Facer* defence. Oddly enough, *Facer*[89] was not referred to in the judgment.

The Court of Appeal rejected the defence and found for the appellant. Lord Denning MR found that the mistake was that of the inspector. He had not asked any questions about earlier claims nor had he checked the company's records. The appellant's wife was also at fault in not reading the proposal before signing. But this was excused by Lord Denning on the grounds that she was poorly educated and she assumed that the agent would have known about the earlier claim. The real crux of his judgment, and the method used to distinguish *Newsholme*, was to say that the agent, by his conduct, impliedly represented that he had filled in the form correctly and, therefore, he needed no further information from her. The wife relied on these representations and signed without reading over the answers entered by the agent. In *Newsholme* the agent had no authority to enter the answers on the form.

Lord Denning approved the *Bawden*[90] decision, so long in the abyss, commenting that it would be most unjust if a company was allowed to repudiate its liability on such facts. To use his words:

"It was their own agent who made the mistake. It was he who ought to have known better. It was he who put the printed form before the wife for signature. It was he who thereby represented to her that the form was correctly filled in and that she could safely sign it. She signed it trusting to him."

The dialogue between the insurer's counsel and the court that followed the decision is illustrative of the vexations that have crept into this important area of the law. In asking for leave to appeal to the House of Lords, a request which was rejected by the Court of Appeal, counsel pointed out that the decision would seriously upset the law as it was previously understood to be. He explained that it was the practice in this type of cover for agents to complete forms and therefore "countless thousands of policies" will be affected. Megaw LJ had little sympathy with the point. He thought it to be most unfair to poorly educated consumers that they should be caught by the clause purporting to shift the agent's mistakes from the insurer's shoulders onto those of the customer.

The problem now remains as to the present state of the law with regard to answers filled in erroneously by agents. In *Stone* the agent had such authority to complete the answers, and that is often not the case. Will the case be extended to this wider area? In *Stone* the company had records showing the earlier claim, and although waiver was

---

89. See fn. 85 above.
90. [1892] 2 Q.B. 534, C.A.

not pleaded by the customer, the fact must have been in the mind of the court.[91] Strangely, there appears to be no recent English case following up on this problem.

In Australia the High Court has shown a dislike of the *Newsholme* decision and in Canada a similar preference for the *Stone* approach has been seen in *Blanchette* v. *CIS Ltd*,[92] a decision of the Supreme Court of Canada. Here the insured had completed insurance cover with the defendant insurer but later informed its agent that he wanted to change it to include other property. He signed a blank proposal having instructed the agent about the changes. The agent filled in the wrong answers. The majority of the court found for the insured, but they were not prepared to say that *Newsholme* was wrongly decided. They sought to distinguish between a situation where the answers are filled in before the proposer is asked to sign and a situation where, as here, the form was signed and then sent away to be completed by someone who had authority to complete the answers, and who could be expected to display professional competence.

The High Court of Australia took a commercially realistic and pro-consumer stance to the present problem in *Deaves* v. *CML Fire and General Insurance Co Ltd*.[93] Stephen J explained that while the insurer's representative who has called on the insured at his request might lack authority to complete the proposal form he did however receive as part of his function as the insurer's agent, information relevant to the risk. In the particular circumstances the insurer was to be treated as itself possessing that knowledge. On the broader issue and referring to other defence points taken by the insurer, Murphy J said the insurers had taken every possible point to avoid paying a modest sum of money even though the claimant had acted reasonably and honestly. He was of the opinion that the situation was such that every householder and small businessman would need to be guided at every step of even a modest insurance transaction by an expert insurance consultant or counsel.

These conflicting decisions clearly demonstrate the urgent need for legislative reform. In an age of consumer protection it is surprising that nothing has been achieved. The Law Reform Committee recommendations of 1957 gather dust. But in New Zealand and Australia the necessary changes were introduced in 1977 and 1984. Section 10 of the New Zealand Insurance Law Reform Act 1977 states:

"(1) A representative of an insurer who acts for the insurer during the negotiation of any contract of insurance, and so acts within the scope of his actual or apparent authority, shall be deemed, as between the insured and the insurer and at all times during the negotiations until the contract comes into being to be the agent of the insurer.

(2) An insurer shall be deemed to have notice of all matters material to a contract of insurance known to a representative of the insurer concerned in the negotiation of the contract before the proposal of the insured is accepted by the insurer."

When the Australian Law Reform Commission reported in 1980 they commented on the above section, "despite fears expressed at the time of the enactment inquiries by the Commission have not revealed any problems in its application". Australia was thus able to implement the changes referred to above.

---

91. See, however, *Malhi* v. *Abbey Life Ass Co Ltd* (1994) *The Times*, 2 June. In an age of computerised record-keeping the minority judgment surely is more convincing?
92. 36 D.L.R. (3rd) 561.
93. (1979) 53 A.L.J.R. 382.

The Insurance Ombudsman in this country has made reference to the difficulties of the present legal position:

"Whether a remark uttered in the heat of the sales pitch can be binding on the insurer is sometimes an exceedingly nice question, in the philosophical sense. It turns on the extent, to which, if at all, the agent—which can in certain circumstances include a so-called independent—'holds himself out', by express words or conduct, as speaking, on behalf of the company or underwriter." (1988 Report.)

With the Court of Appeal criticism in *Roberts* v. *Plaisted*[94] in mind, he said:

"I am now prepared, in appropriate cases, to hold insurers responsible for the defaults of intermediaries. Speculation as to exactly what will prove an appropriate case appears fruitless." (1989 Report.)

However in his 1992 Report he commented:

"A complaint against an insurer on these grounds (wrong advice) will not ... be upheld as valid if the warning or advice was given (or not) by an independent intermediary or other person for whom the insurer has no responsibility."

### 3.5 Wrongful behaviour with regard to procedural matters

An agent may fail in a number of ways to service the insurance contract. Whether or not such failure will adversely affect the customer will depend on the powers and duties the agent possesses. Thus the problem remains that of defining the scope of a particular agent's relationship with the insurer.

In *Acey* v. *Fernie*[95] the agent had limited powers with regard to the collection of premiums. He was permitted to receive payments within 15 days of the due date but was to give immediate notice if such payment was not made. The company practice was to debit the agent's account. The customer failed to pay on a renewal and the agent failed to inform the company. The court held that there had been no renewal. The fact that the company had debited the agent's account was only a penalty exacted by the company against the agent and was not a sign of company renewal.

Similarly, where the company instructs its agent that payment must be made by a certain method or prohibits payment by certain methods then an ordinary agent cannot vary these instructions. In *London and Lancashire Life Ass Co* v. *Fleming*,[96] the agent accepted payment of a premium by a promissory note specifically against instructions. It was held that this did not signify that the policy was then in force.

It is often the close relationship between agent and customer that leads to difficulties. The agent may well wish to help the customer overcome personal problems with regard to payments, but, by so doing, the agent, perhaps unwittingly, creates a false sense of security in the mind of the customer. In *British Industry Life Ass Co* v. *Ward*,[97] the agent was permitted to accept premiums up to four weeks in

94. [1989] 2 Lloyd's Rep. 341, discussed below.
95. (1840) 7 M. & W. 151.
96. [1897] A.C. 499, P.C.
97. (1856) 17 C.B. 644.

arrears. He accepted payments 11 weeks late. The contract contained a forfeiture clause. It was held that the policy lapsed and the agent had no authority to waive a forfeiture clause. Instructions by the company to the agent also required him to return lapsed policies after four weeks of non-payment.

It may be possible to argue that the agent has sufficient authority to alter certain conditions in the policy and, by so doing, bind the company.

In *Wing* v. *Harvey*,[98] it was a condition in a life policy that it should become void if the insured left Europe. He went to live in Canada but the agent continued to accept premiums and told the assignee of the policy that the policy was still valid. The company was held bound by the policy on the grounds that notice to the agent amounted to constructive notice to them.

The court in *Newsholme*'s case accepted the correctness of this decision on the grounds that the directors of the company had sufficient notice of the change of country and continued to accept the premiums.

*Wing* was followed in *Holdsworth* v. *Lancashire and Yorkshire Ins Co*.[99] The insured took out employer's liability cover using the company agent. It was explained to the agent that the proposer was a joiner and builder but the agent chose only to enter the description of joiner. The proposer did not read the form before signing. At this stage it is clear from the general trend of the above cases that the company would not be liable for the proposer's failure to read over the answers. But when he received the policy the proposer noticed the mistake. He objected to the description used. The chief clerk of the branch office added the word "builder" and the proposer then paid the premiums. No notification of the change was communicated to head office. In the event of a later claim, the court held that the policy was good and knowledge by the agents was to be imputed to the company. Bray J said that he was quite unable to avoid the decision in *Wing* v. *Harvey*.

It would be unusual, however, for an ordinary local agent to be vested with sufficient authority to grant a policy. His normal powers would be limited to passing proposals to a higher authority for a decision to be made. So, in *Linford* v. *Provincial Horse and Cattle Ins Co*,[100] the plaintiff sought a livestock policy and paid a premium to the company's local agent who failed to transmit it to head office. The company was not liable on the policy, the court finding that the particular relationship did not extend to the agent "a power to grant or contract to grant policies of assurance".

Such limited authority is probably the normal situation with agents, as opposed to brokers or fully independent intermediaries. It is possible, however, to find occasional cases where the agent has wider than normal authority.

In *Murfitt* v. *Royal Ins Co*,[101] the court found, on the evidence of the documents disclosed at the trial, that the agent did have authority to give an oral assurance of temporary cover until a final decision was made by the company. The agent had offered to hold the plaintiff covered on condition that he did not approach other companies. A fire occurred a week later, and the company refused the proposal on the grounds that they were not interested in that type of business. The company, however, was unaware of the fire at the time they made their decision.

98. (1854) 5 De G.M. & G. 265.
99. (1907) 23 T.L.R. 521.
100. (1864) 34 Beav. 291.
101. (1922) 38 T.L.R. 334.

The court decided in favour of the plaintiff and McCardie J's approach is of special interest. He said that while the agent was not a salaried official of the company, he was a full as opposed to a casual or intermittent agent. The casual agent pays over premiums as soon as he receives them, while the full agent runs an account with the company and usually pays over premiums on a quarterly basis and retains or receives his commission. There was no evidence that the agent had authority to make contracts. But was there a holding out by the company that the agent had such authority? There was none. But was there an implied authority? If the company gives the agent forms for making insurances the agent will then have sufficient authority to make agreements within the terms of the documentation. In particular, fire insurance necessitates the business requirement of verbal cover[102] and, as the branch manager had on previous occasions allowed the agent to give verbal cover, pending a final decision by the company, the plaintiff was insured at the time the fire occurred. The working agreement as to verbal temporary cover between the branch manager and the agent is probably crucial to the court's finding for the plaintiff.

Where an agent is only a part-time or a casual agent of an employer it is normal for the company to limit his authority considerably.

In *Wilkinson* v. *General Accident Fire and Life Assurance Corp Ltd*,[103] a garage owner was an occasional agent for the defendant company. The agency agreement allowed him to issue short-term cover notes. Motor certificates and policies were prepared and issued at the company office. The plaintiff insured his car through the company agent. He later sold the car with the agent's knowledge. The agent sent him a renewal notice which was paid even though the plaintiff no longer owned a car. When an accident occurred while the plaintiff was driving another person's car, he claimed that the agent had assured him that he was covered against third party risks if driving with the owner's consent.

The court dismissed the plaintiff's claim finding that no such representation had been made. Even if the assurance had been given by the agent, it would not have bound the company because the agent had only limited authority and the suggestion made would have been outside such a limitation. The knowledge of the agent about the sale of the car would not be imputed to the company because the knowledge came to him as a garage owner involved in the sale transaction and not in his capacity as insurance agent.

When making a claim the insured should follow whatever instructions appear in his policy. But it is understandable that he will often rely heavily on an agent for assistance, particularly where that agent helped in arranging the original policy or a renewal. Unless there are stipulations to the contrary, the client can assume that the agent does have sufficient authority to deal with the claim.

Even where the agent has ceased to be employed by the insurer, notice to him has been held sufficient notice to the company. In the case of *Marsden* v. *City and County Assurance Co*,[104] the plaintiff insured his plate glass through the insurers' local agent. The insurers later transferred their business to another agency. The plaintiff was not aware of this and he presented his claim to the former agent who processed it for him.

102. I.e., in terms of speed.
103. [1967] 2 Lloyd's Rep. 182.
104. (1865) L.R. 1 C.P. 232.

This was considered to be sufficient notice even though the policy wording called for notice to be made "to the manager, or to some known agent of the company".

But, equally, decisions have gone the other way. If that is the situation then the agent would be exposed to individual liability.

In *Brook* v. *Trafalgar Ins Co Ltd*[105] a motor-vehicle policy provided that notice of any accident or loss should be given in writing to the company's head office within seven days of the loss. The car was destroyed by fire and notice was given by the insured to the company's provincial agent the following day. The agent gave him a claims form which was completed just over two weeks later and sent to the agent who forwarded it to the company. The Court of Appeal held that the claim was out of time and that the agent had no authority to waive the express conditions relating to notice.

This is a correct interpretation of the policy condition which leads to harsh results. It would, hopefully, be modified today by the insurers following the spirit of the Statement of Insurance Practice. Although the Statement makes no specific mention of the role of the agent in making claims it does say that the policyholder should not be asked to do more than report a claim as soon as reasonably possible. It must be remembered by insurers that the general public assimilates the agent with the company and, therefore, the company practice should reflect this belief.

### 3.6 Legislation

So far, legislative intervention on behalf of the assured during the difficult time of contract completion has been infrequent. The Industrial Assurance Act 1923, as amended, provides some assistance, but only for those contracts covered by the Act.[106]

The contracts covered by the 1923 Act are "assurances upon human life, premiums in respect of which are received by means of collectors", the premiums being collected at intervals of less than two months. In 1853 a House of Commons select committee saw the functions of such insurance as a method of extending some financial protection to the "humbler classes". Certainly the policies have remained unsophisticated in their aims and their cover.

Protection for the customer comes in two ways. A collector (agent) must be someone who is regularly employed, whether full-time or part-time, by the collecting society or company. In this way the employing company will retain direct control over its agents. The more important protection concerns the completion of proposal forms. If the form is filled in wholly or partly by a collector, the society or company cannot question the validity of any misstatement in it.

There are three exceptions. There will be no liability if the misstatement is due to the fraud of the proposer. If the misstatement refers to the age of the proposer, then the policy provisions will be adjusted to make the policy reflect the true age of the person concerned. If the misstatement concerns the health of the assured, then the validity of the policy can be questioned if this is done within two years from the date of issue.

---

105. (1946) 79 Ll.L.Rep. 365, C.A.
106. See, e.g., the Financial Services Act 1986, s. 139.

There seems little reason why the protection afforded here could not be extended to all types of consumer transactions and thereby avoid the confusion presently created by the *Newsholme/Stone* decisions.

Section 73 of the Insurance Companies Act 1982 was repealed and replaced by provisions in the Financial Services Act 1986. These concern misleading statements. It is made a criminal offence for a person to make a statement, promise or forecast which he knows to be misleading, false or deceptive or to conceal dishonestly any material fact or to make, recklessly, dishonestly or otherwise, a statement, promise or forecast which is misleading, false or deceptive for the purpose of inducing another person to enter into or refrain from entering into an investment agreement or contract of insurance. The penalties possible under these provisions are imprisonment for up to seven years or a fine or both.

It is also an offence under section 74 of the Insurance Companies Act 1982 for a "connected person" to invite another person to enter into an insurance contract without first giving certain information to that person about his connection with the particular insurer. Section 129 of and Schedule 10 to, the Financial Services Act 1986 deal with the potential overlap between the 1982 Act and the 1986 Act.

The definition of "connected person" and details of the information that must be given are set out in the Insurance Companies Regulations 1981.

A "connected person" covers a wide range of people from senior management of insurance companies down to certain categories of agents. We are concerned here only with this last group. It excludes agents employed under a contract of employment with that insurer and, therefore, the great majority of agents would not be regarded as "connected persons". But it includes tied agents who work only on a commission basis because such a relationship is not regarded as a contract of employment. A list of such "connected persons" must be included in companies' annual returns to the Department of Trade.

The information that the person must give to the customer depends on the mode of the invitation to do business. If it is made in writing, then the information describing the connection must be made at the same time. If the invitation is made orally, then an oral explanation must be made at that time, together with a written statement containing the same information. These requirements can be met simply by making the invitation to do business on stationery which prominently displays the name of the intermediary and the insurance company, and a clear statement of the relationship between the two. Lloyd's brokers merely need to show that the policy will be underwritten at Lloyd's.

These requirements apply only where the customer is ordinarily resident in the UK. If the insurance company is not authorised to do business in the UK their intermediary must indicate this to the customer.[107]

Of particular importance is the fact that customers of such companies are not protected by the Policyholders' Protection Act 1975.[107a] This Act provides financial compensation to an insured who holds a policy with an insurance company which goes into liquidation. It would have been a considerable advance in protection if this point was also spelt out at this stage of the proceedings. The present requirements

---

107. The problems of unauthorised insurers has recently been considered in a number of decisions and is referred to above.

107a. See *Scher* v. *Policyholders Protection Board* [1993] 3 All E.R. 384, H.L.

demand some information while omitting to ask that it is presented in a more meaningful way.

Certain classes of insurance business are exempt from the "connected person" disclosures. The regulations do not apply to renewals or amendments to policies taken out before 11 October 1976 nor to policies renewed or amended after that date, if there has been no significant change of circumstance in facts previously given.

Certain classes of insurance are also exempt on the basis that the insured are (presumably) not in need of the protection. This is so where the premium exceeds £1,000 p.a., or where the business relates to motor and fire and other damage to property and the first premium exceeds £5,000 p.a. Reinsurance, marine and transport and aviation are completely exempt, together with any business effected with a registered friendly society.

Where the insurance contract meets the definition of investment business in the Financial Services Act 1986, the rules made by the Securities and Investments Board ("SIB"), the Self-Regulatory Organisations ("SROs") and Recognised Professional Bodies ("RPBs") are drafted to provide a wealth of protection to the customers.

## 4 THE INDEPENDENT ADVISER

Reference has been made above to the difficulty of classification and nomenclature of those involved in the marketing of insurance. So far we have dealt with those who are clearly tied to a particular identifiable insurer, or who are termed company representatives under the Financial Services Act 1986.

We now deal with other problems. While the Insurance Brokers (Registration) Act 1977[108] provided a major reform in this area, it also had the side-effect of creating an additional group of intermediaries who were not eligible for registration as brokers or who chose not to register even if eligible. No single group name exists to describe such people. "Insurance consultants" seems to be a much used description together with "insurance adviser".

We are here concerned with the legal position of anyone who can truly be described as "independent" of a particular insurer in the sense that he has no employment contract with an insurer. It clearly includes brokers and insurance consultants. Lloyd's brokers, because of the working practices at Lloyd's are dealt with separately below.

There is one reported case that deals with the liability of a non-broker independent intermediary.[109] Such a person will be treated in accordance with the same standards as brokers have been in the recent past. This assumption is adopted on the grounds that it would be unfair, unjust and unworkable if the courts created a middle ground of liability for non-broker intermediaries.

It is proposed for the sake of brevity when referring to future development to use the words "insurance adviser" to describe both brokers registered under the 1977 Act and those professionals who are independent advisers but who have not registered as brokers. The word "broker" will be used when dealing with cases prior to registration on the grounds that this was the description used by the court.

108. See below.
109. *Harvest Trucking Co Ltd* v. *PB Davies* [1991] 2 Lloyd's Rep. 638.

It is commonly said that the insurance adviser is the agent of the insured. That being so, then there would normally be a contractual relationship between the two parties. But the cases below show that, in certain aspects of a tripartite insurance transaction, the insurance adviser may also act as agent of the insurer and is thus contractually bound also to that insurer.

However, it is the possible tortious relationship between the insurance adviser and others that is the more potentially dangerous for the adviser because this liability is made difficult to define and, potentially, more wide-ranging in effect.

The fact that the insurance adviser may have both a contractual and a tortious relationship with the plaintiff does not mean that the plaintiff must make a choice between such options. Concurrent liability is possible and many of the cases which follow illustrate this fact. Failure in one, because of some technical reason, and success in the other is possible. Damages cannot, of course, be won twice over although they might be assessed differently. The extent of the contractual duty owed will depend on the wording of the contract itself, together with any enforceable limitations of liability expressed in it; if the contract is purely or partly oral, the problem of determining the extent of the contractual duty is even greater, because the parties' intentions may be unclear. The question of concurrent liability had greatly vexed the courts throughout the 1980s and early 1990s. The idea that a professional person, whose relationship with his client was considered to be founded in contract could, as it seemed, be exposed to greater liability in negligence, was considered unacceptable by some judges.[110] After a number of contradictory views in the High Court and in the Court of Appeal finally we have the House of Lords' decision in *Henderson* v. *Merrett Syndicates, Arbuttnott* v. *Feltrim Underwriting Agencies*,[111] on the matter endorsing the possibility of concurrent liability.

Liability in negligence for negligent advice leading to economic loss was not considered as covered by the general principle of *Donoghue* v. *Stevenson*.[112]

While purely economic loss often arises from advice given in a contractual relationship, it is possible to envisage fact situations arising outside of that type of relationship and, therefore, the question was whether the tort of negligence could take on board such claims.

The answer came with the House of Lords in *Hedley Byrne* v. *Heller & Partners*.[113] It was decided that where there existed between an adviser and the recipient of the advice a special relationship, then a duty of care could arise whereby the adviser should exercise reasonable care in the circumstances in the giving of that advice. Courts throughout the Commonwealth seized upon this breakthrough with enthusiasm. The position of the professional adviser in particular became more onerous.

Although the facts of *Hedley Byrne* were concerned with a bank as adviser, the words of Lord Pearce are particularly apposite for insurance intermediaries. He said:

"if persons holding themselves out in a calling or situation or profession take on a task within that calling or situation or profession, they have a duty of skill and care".

The impact of the decision in *Hedley Byrne* merits close attention particularly from

110. See, in particular, Lord Scarman's views in *Tai Hing Cotton Mill Ltd* v. *Liu Chong Hing Bank Ltd* [1986] A.C. 80.
111. [1994] 3 All E.R. 506, H.L. (see chapter 2).
112. [1932] A.C. 562.
113. [1964] A.C. 465.

the point of view of how it has been received in other cases and how it has been reworked by the House of Lords in their decision in *Caparo Industries plc* v. *Dickman*[114] and to assess the effect in relation to the liability of independent intermediaries for negligent advice.

When looking at later cases it must first be asked what effect the Unfair Contract Terms Act 1977[114a] may have on the decision in *Hedley Byrne*. This Act bans the use of exclusion clauses where they attempt to avoid liability for death or personal injury arising from an act of negligence.

In relation to exclusion clauses which attempt to avoid financial liability arising from breach of contract or a tortious act, the rule is that the exclusion will only be valid if it can meet the test of "reasonableness" as defined in the Act. Reasonableness is tested by asking if it was fair and reasonable wording to be included in the contract or in any non-contractual notice having regard to the circumstances which were or ought reasonably to have been known or in the contemplation of the parties.

Let us first look at how the decision in *Hedley Byrne* was received in later cases and then look briefly at the effect that *Caparo* may have in this area.

In *O'Leary* v. *Lamb*,[115] an Australian decision, the defendant was the manager of a finance company who advised the plaintiff investors. The advice turned out to be negligent and as the defendant stood to gain financially from the recommended investment by virtue of his brokerage interest in the recommended company, he was liable to the plaintiffs.

In a Canadian case, *Creyke* v. *Royal Trust Corp of Canada*,[116] a defendant estate agent knowing that the plaintiff had only very limited ability to pay monthly repayments on a mortgage was held liable in negligence in giving advice that led to a serious financial burden for the plaintiff.

Again, in *Elliot* v. *Ron Dawson and Assoc*,[117] an insurance agent wrongly advised the plaintiff that her house contents policy would cover loss of baggage and, therefore, she need not take out extra travel insurance. The plaintiff's failure to read her existing policy did not prevent her successfully suing the agent in negligence.

In *Farish* v. *National Trust Co*,[118] the plaintiff contributed to a retirement savings plan. The defendant trust company failed to advise him on a tax-free annuity scheme so that he was finally exposed to a tax loss. The court held the defendant liable not only for breach of a fiduciary relationship but also for breach of a duty owed by a professional to a layman in such an area as this.

Similarly, in *Manuge* v. *Prudential Ass Co*,[119] the defendants were liable for misleading the plaintiffs as to the value of an insurance pension plan that they were recommending. In another Canadian case,[120] the seller of a lorry required the conditional buyer to insure the lorry with an indorsement in favour of the seller. The seller checked with the defendant's insurance agent who wrongly stated that the

114. [1990] 1 All E.R. 568 (see chapter 2).
114a. In relation to consumer contracts see also the Unfair Terms in Consumer Contracts Regulations 1994.
115. (1973) 7 S.A.S.R. 159.
116. (1980) 17 R.P.R. 298.
117. 139 D.L.R. (3rd) 323.
118. 54 D.L.R. (3rd) 426.
119. 81 D.L.R. (3rd) 360.
120. *General Motors Accept Corp of Canada* v. *Fulton Insurance Agencies Ltd*, 24 N.S.R. (2nd) 114.

indorsement had been arranged. The defendant was held liable to reimburse the seller's losses when the lorry was destroyed.

One important obstacle for the plaintiff to overcome, however, is to prove to the court's satisfaction that he did in fact rely on the defendant's statement. In the case of a member of the public looking for insurance advice it would not usually present a difficulty. But where the plaintiff was more commercially sophisticated his dependency on the advice given might be less obvious.[121]

While no one doubts that it was *Hedley Byrne* that provided the great push forward in this area of professional liability, it is of interest to note that 20 years earlier Hallett J was accurately prophesying what was to come in *Sarginson Bros* v. *Moulton*.[122]

There, brokers had been asked by the plaintiffs to obtain insurance for their stock of timber. The brokers advised wrongly that because of wartime regulations cover was unobtainable. While the court did not consider that a broker was required to know all the technicalities of the law, more was required of them before giving the answer that they did. The judge said that:

"if people occupying a professional position take it upon themselves to give advice upon a matter directly connected with their own profession then they are responsible for seeing that they are equipped with a reasonable degree of skill and a reasonable stock of information so as to render it reasonably safe for them to give that particular piece of advice".

The above cases illustrate how *Hedley Byrne* has been adopted in various common law jurisdictions to establish the liability of insurance advisers. It is important to consider whether the more limited approach to liability for negligent statements expressed by the House of Lords in the case of *Caparo Industries* will alter the legal position of intermediaries. The judgment will be seen as a potential check on the expansive interpretation of *Hedley Byrne* during the intervening years since that decision was given. The new approach is to warn against expansion of liability on a general front and to suggest that cases should be looked at in the subject areas or groupings of fact situations and decisions made accordingly. Thus the implication is that various classes of advisers exist and each should be treated separately from one another before making a decision on liability.

While the *Caparo* decision must lead to a limiting of liability under the *Hedley Byrne* principle it is unlikely to be of great importance to insurance intermediaries. The relationship of adviser and customer is so close, the parties readily identifiable and the reliance so reasonable, that the adviser must be under a duty not to advise negligently.

The decisions in *Hedley Byrne* and in *Caparo* were referred to in *Pryke* v. *Gibbs Hartley Cooper Ltd*.[123] Atlas Underwriters Ltd had held a binding authority for some 20 years prior to 1985 whereby they wrote insurance business in the USA on behalf of Lloyd's underwriters and Excess Insurance Co. At all material times the defendant Lloyd's brokers, Gibbs Hartley Cooper Ltd, acted in relation to that business.

In 1983 Atlas issued a policy which was outside the scope of their mandate with Lloyd's underwriters and was not the kind of policy that Excess would normally write. These financial guarantee policies were in fact a forbidden form of policy at Lloyd's. The defendant brokers were unaware at that stage that Atlas were issuing

---

121. See *JEB Fasteners Ltd* v. *Marks Bloom & Co* [1983] 1 All E.R. 583, C.A.
122. (1943) 73 Ll.L.Rep. 104.
123. [1991] 1 Lloyd's Rep. 602.

such a policy. Some months later all parties became aware of what had happened. Atlas were then asked to cancel the policy *ab initio*. The defendant brokers investigated the situation and were told by Atlas that the form of policy had been changed to one of physical damage and that while it had been impossible to cancel *ab initio* it had in fact been cancelled from the later date of the underwriters' instructions. Atlas also stated that there was no real risk of claims under the original policy. The underwriters were also informed of the new situation.

The underwriters took no further action and did not inform the following market. Atlas did not cancel the policy and in 1985 the primary insured went bankrupt and very large claims were in the pipeline. The underwriters denied liability on the grounds of Atlas' lack of authority and on the grounds of misrepresentation and fraudulent procurement. The action in the USA was ultimately settled in 1987. The underwriters then commenced the present action against the brokers either for indemnification in full or for a contribution to the underwriters' losses. The grounds for the action were three: (i) the defendants were aware before the date the underwriters became aware of the situation created by Atlas and were thus in breach of their duty in failing to disclose, at that earlier date, the true situation; (ii) that the defendants should have been aware that Atlas had breached their promise to cancel the policy and were thus in breach of their duty to the underwriters to inform them of this; (iii) and if they had informed the underwriters they in turn would have been in a position to avoid all liabilities or at least substantially to reduce them.

Waller J found for the Lloyd's underwriters on the grounds that they would have reacted immediately to avoid or reduce their liability. Waller J found for the defendants in the Excess action on the grounds that such a policy was not forbidden, that Excess realised that there was an exposure and thus they had not relied on the defendants in taking action which they would not otherwise have done.

In approaching the potential liability of the brokers to the underwriters it is particularly important to note Waller J's finding of fact that, although all business was originally contemplated as flowing through the defendants from about 1974 onwards, the underwriters had such trust in Atlas that they no longer required this to be done and it was indeed not required during the year in which the troublesome policy was negotiated and issued by Atlas. Thus having relieved the defendant brokers of at least some responsibilities during those years, the question arose as to how liability was to be imputed to them. The basic argument of the plaintiffs was that the defendants came into possession of vital information at a time when they could have alerted the plaintiffs sufficiently for them to have taken evasive action. That boiled down to a long drawn-out question of evidence.

The judge analysed the plaintiff's case as a "broad case in contract and a broad case in tort and ... a narrower case in tort".

The broad case in contract: this argument was that there was a contract between the parties to administer the binding authority for brokerage of five per cent to include reasonable skill and care and to communicate all matters which the plaintiffs would reasonably require to know, and similarly on renewals. There was agreement by all that, as a broker acts for the insured, then the defendants were acting for Atlas throughout. But because of the more unusual way the business was placed the plaintiffs argued that there was a concurrent implied contractual duty owed by the defendants to the plaintiffs. This argument was itself dependent on an alleged custom at Lloyd's. This found no favour with Waller J. Even though the payment of brokerage comes from the insurer this did not mean that the broker was undertaking to perform any obligation in favour of the underwriter. The obligations carried out were done so under his contractual obligations to the cover holder (Atlas). The court was prepared to allow, however, that in certain cases it might be possible to find a concurrent contractual liability between insurer and insured, but not on the facts of the present case. It could not be so found by basing the argument on Lloyd's custom because the custom was uncertain and unreasonable.

The broad case in tort: having found no broad case in contract Waller J was equally certain that no broad case in tort existed. No detailed explanation of why this was so was given. Perhaps this was partly dictated by his findings on the third head of claim—the narrow claim in tort.

The narrow case in tort: although admitting the idea of voluntary assumption of responsibility had been questioned by the House of Lords as recently as *Smith* v. *Bush*[124] and *Caparo Industries plc* v. *Dickman*,[125] Waller J was prepared to consider that it was a useful phrase where an agent voluntarily undertakes some personal responsibility to a particular party, in which case he should exercise reasonable care in so doing particularly when he appreciates reliance will be placed upon him. This is especially so when the agent's principal should supply such information accurately. However, there was no basic duty on the defendants to carry out an investigation into Atlas' dealings on behalf of the plaintiffs. But the defendants chose to carry out such investigations. In so doing they created a duty of care towards the plaintiffs whereby the twin requirements of foreseeability and proximity were met. Thus whereas *Empress Assurance*[126] and *Glasgow Corporation*[127] had additionally said that no duty of care could be owed by a broker to underwriters, those views based on *Le Lievre* v. *Gould*[128] could no longer stand after *Hedley Byrne & Co Ltd* v. *Heller & Partners*.[129]

Lloyd's underwriters succeeded in their claim on the grounds that reliance on the broker's skill and judgement was proved, whereas Excess failed on this point because the type of insurance being underwritten while not particularly favoured by them was not forbidden as it was at Lloyd's. Once Excess knew of the original placing, appreciated the risk but continued with the policy, the underwriter was clearly making an underwriting judgement that such risk was minimal. Thus they were not placing reliance on the defendants in the same way that Lloyd's had done.

We need now to examine further the extent of the duty of care in negligence in the area of independent insurance advisers. The answer depends on what the courts consider to be reasonable in the circumstances of the case.

The broker's closest relationship is usually the one he has with his assured, and we will consider the extent of his duty in this area first. We will then look at the relationship between insurance adviser and insurer and, finally, whether or not a duty is owed beyond this close circle of connected parties.

124. [1989] 2 All E.R. 514, H.L.
125. [1990] 1 All E.R. 568, H.L.
126. (1906) 11 Com.Cas. 107.
127. (1911) 16 Com.Cas. 109.
128. [1893] 1 Q.B. 491.
129. [1963] 1 Lloyd's Rep. 485.

## 4.1 The insurance adviser and his client

Normally the insurance adviser's relationship with his client is in both contract and tort. But it rarely happens that a formal contract is made between the adviser and the lay client and, therefore, it might be easier for the client to argue that the adviser was in breach of a duty of care owed towards him in tort.

The cases that follow show how the courts have perceived the standard that they consider necessary for insurance advisers. But it should be remembered that the Code of Conduct Regulations of 1978 and, later, 1994 under the Insurance Brokers (Registration) Act 1977 also give guidance to which the courts will presumably pay some heed in future cases. There would appear to be no good reason why the courts should not expect similar standards from non-broker insurance advisers.[130]

Codes of Conduct for members of the Association of British Insurers[131] and Life Associations[132] have been referred to above.

It is worth recalling some of the main points of the Insurance Brokers Registration Council's Code of Conduct. The code explains that the courts will, where necessary, adjudicate on allegations of negligence but the Council recognises that gross negligence or repeated cases of negligence may amount to unprofessional conduct. It should be stressed, however, in order that the broker is not misled by the Council's words, that gross negligence is not a phrase used by the courts when discussing cases of negligence in civil cases, nor would there need to be repeated acts of negligence for a broker to be liable in tort.

The general principles of professional conduct are stated to be that brokers shall at all times conduct their business with the utmost good faith and integrity; that they shall do everything to satisfy the insurance requirements of their clients and thus place these requirements above all other considerations; and that brokers must avoid all misleading or extravagant advertising. These are general principles and, therefore, to add strength to them, a list of 33 specific examples is added by way of illustration. Only some of these can be regarded as specifically referable to allegations of negligence. One example given in the code concerns the matter of "material facts". It is a basic requirement of insurance contract law[133] that the insured disclose all facts which would be considered by a prudent insurer as material to the judgement of the risk. The close relationship that might exist between client and broker, perhaps built up over many years, may lead the broker to possess information about his client that conflicts with the information now being given by the client about the risk to be insured.

In such a situation the code states that the broker should request his client to make a true, fair and complete disclosure. If this is not forthcoming then the broker should consider whether or not to continue to act.

One example that might help to assist a client in any action he wishes to bring in negligence or for breach of a fiduciary relationship is that the broker should provide objective and independent advice and that he should, on a request from the client, explain the difference in cover and cost between the principal types of insurance available. To achieve this end, the broker must ensure that he uses a sufficient

---

130. See *Harvest Trucking Co Ltd* v. *PB Davis* [1991] 2 Lloyd's Rep. 638.
131. See Appendix 1.
132. *Ibid.*
133. *Carter* v. *Boehm* (1766) 3 Burr. 1905.

number of insurers to satisfy clients' needs. This may well require a technical know-how on the part of the broker as to the client's business environment.

In *Beattie* v. *Furness-Houlder Insurance (Northern) Ltd*,[134] a solicitor arranged insurance cover for an hotel through defendant brokers, asking for cover to extend to "all business risks". The broker acknowledged the instructions and arranged temporary cover. Before a permanent policy was completed the hotel was destroyed by fire. There was no cover for loss of profits. The brokers were sued for both breach of contract and negligence in the sum of £7,500.

The court held that while there was no breach of contract, there was negligence. But the plaintiff had not proven to the court's satisfaction that the loss was £7,500. However, they awarded £100 for the loss of opportunity to make a claim against the insurers. The court was of the opinion that the insurers might have made an *ex gratia* payment even if there was no strong evidence of loss of profits, merely to avoid the nuisance element of dealing with and investigating the claim of a disgruntled client. The broker's negligence had deprived the client of this opportunity.

Even where it is clear that the intermediary has been negligent in the conduct of his customer's requirements, it is not always easy to predict the measure of damages that will be awarded. In *Ramwade Ltd* v. *WJ Empson & Co*,[135] the plaintiffs instructed the brokers to obtain comprehensive cover for one of their skip lorries. The brokers negligently obtained only third-party cover. The lorry was written off in an accident. At that time the plaintiffs could not afford to purchase a replacement lorry immediately and in order to carry out the work they had to hire lorries. The plaintiffs claimed the cost of the lorry together with the hire charges that they had incurred. The Court of Appeal disallowed the claim for the hire charges and these were not the foreseeable result of the broker's breach of duty.

It is important to note that the intended comprehensive policy would not have included any hire charge provisions so the broker's negligence had not deprived the plaintiffs of anything other than the cost of the lorry. Any late payment of compensation by the brokers would entitle the plaintiff to interest on that sum up to the date of judgment, but that figure was not to be arrived at by equating it to the cost of hiring other lorries. It could be argued that *Ramwade* would not be followed in the future.[136]

The case of *Newbury International Ltd* v. *Reliance National Insurance Co (UK) Ltd*[137] provides an unusual insurance setting. The policies involved were "prize indemnity" policies dependent upon the outcome of a sporting event. The brokers involved were held to be guilty of non-disclosure in not describing the past successful record and general reputation of a Formula Ford driver. The insured argued that the failure to succeed under the policies was due to their broker's negligence. However, it was clear that the insureds' contractual undertaking was to pay over sums only if they received those sums from the insurer. If the insurer was able to avoid liability on the grounds of misrepresentation and lack of insurable interest[138] the only loss caused to

134. 1976 S.L.T., 5 November.
135. [1987] R.T.R. 72.
136. This part of the decision rested on the decision in *Leisbosch Dredger* v. *SS Edison* [1933] A.C. 448. That decision has been criticised in a number of recent cases. An insurance scenario is provided in *Mattocks* v. *Mann* [1993] R.T.R. 13.
137. [1994] 2 Lloyd's Rep. 83.
138. An essential requirement for a valid policy.

them by the broker was nominal and the brokers were accordingly liable for nominal damages.

A further illustration is the Canadian case of *Fine's Flowers Ltd* v. *General Accident Ass Co.*[139] The plaintiff ran a flower and plant business in Ontario. He asked his insurance agent (Canada used the word "agent" to cover both broker and non-broker) to see that he was fully insured. The agent failed to obtain cover for losses caused by the shutdown of the heating system in the greenhouses. The shutdown was due to a technical failure in one of the water pumps which tripped circuitry resulting in a loss of electricity supply to other pumps.

The court held the agent liable on the grounds that the plaintiff had relied on the agent to see that he was adequately insured. Even if the type of cover required for that particular loss was unobtainable, it being largely a "wear and tear" failure, it was still on the shoulders of the agent to advise the plaintiff that such cover was not possible so that the plaintiff knew the situation he was in more precisely. The agent should have realised the financial dangers to which the plaintiff was potentially exposed by the lack of insurance on the machinery.

This case probably states the liability in its broadest terms. The court recognised the fact, based on the English marine insurance case of *James Vale & Co* v. *Van Oppen & Co,*[140] that certain businesses or trades would only intend certain aspects of their business to be insured even when asking to be insured "against all risks". Failure in such situations to obtain the fullest available cover would not necessarily be negligent.

While a broker would be unable to deny that he owed a duty of care to his client, he might argue that his alleged failure to obtain the right type of cover did not amount to a breach of that duty. Breach is always a difficult matter for the court to assess. It constitutes falling below the standard that can be expected of someone professing to exercise that trade or profession.

There do not appear to be any reported cases involving insurance intermediaries on this point. Two helpful cases from very different factual settings can be offered as a guide. In one case[141] the plaintiff had agreed to sit with the defendant learner driver during his practice session. The defendant crashed the car and injured the plaintiff. The question that arose was what standard of care can be expected from a learner driver? The answer was that it is the standard of the competent and experienced driver and not the lower standard of the average learner driver.

The second case[142] involves medical standards of competence. A young and therefore inexperienced doctor mistakenly inserted a catheter into a newly born child's vein rather than an artery. The doctor asked a registrar to check what he had done and the registrar failed to detect the error and in fact replicated the error himself at a later stage. The defence in relation to the young doctor's negligence was that he should be judged by a less exacting standard than more experienced medical staff.

The Court of Appeal rejected this argument. The standard demanded by the law was that of the ordinary skilled person exercising and professing to have that special

---

139. 81 D.L.R. (3rd) 139. See also *Fletcher* v. *Manitoba Public Ins Co*, 74 D.L.R. (4th) 636.
140. (1921) 37 T.L.R. 367, 6 Ll.L.Rep. 167.
141. *Nettleship* v. *Weston* [1971] 2 Q.B. 691.
142. *Wisher* v. *Essex AHA* [1986] 3 All E.R. 801.

skill. That standard was to be assessed not according to his rank or status but according to the act he had elected to perform. In this case the young doctor had acted correctly in seeking the advice of his registrar immediately following the insertion and it was the registrar who was at fault.

Where does this leave the insurance adviser? From the viewpoint of consumer protection it would be wrong to treat the High Street adviser more leniently than a major firm of brokers. The public expects expertise, and commission rates payable by insurers to advisers do not officially vary between those who are experienced and those who are not. Policies increase in number and in their complexity but the adviser must aspire to a standard that the competent insurance adviser elsewhere maintains.

The medical case illustrates that where inexperienced advisers are given responsibility for a client's needs it may be necessary for a more experienced colleague to satisfy himself that an acceptable level of ability has been displayed. Nor would it be a defence for the adviser to argue that the client should have detected the adviser's error.

In *Dickson & Co* v. *Devitt*,[143] the plaintiff instructed brokers to insure goods against war risks on named ships. The broker's clerk made a mistake and failed to name more than one ship. The completed documents were sent to the plaintiff and he failed to detect the error. The court held the broker liable when a loss occurred. It was said that a client was entitled to rely on his broker to carry out his instructions, particularly where the client might quite easily overlook a difference which ought to be perfectly plain to a person who had a special knowledge of insurance matters. There was no obligation on the client to examine the broker's work in this area.[144]

In *Seavision Investments SA* v. *Evennett and Puckle*[145] brokers were asked to obtain marine cover. The request was made by a company registered in Switzerland which was a wholly owned subsidiary of a Swiss company the shares of which were owned by a French national. With that background information in mind the broker wrongly decided that the risk qualified for certain facilities available in the London market. Insurance was obtained on the basis that the assured was German. In fact the ship was owned by a Panamanian registered company and flew the Liberian flag. The ship was hit by an Exocet missile near Kharg Island. The lead underwriter and others, apart from the first defendant, indemnified the plaintiff. The first defendant argued that he was entitled to repudiate his share because the assured was wrongly described. If that argument was successful the brokers as second defendants accepted that they were liable to the plaintiff. The court held that there was a breach of warranty in that the ship was not in German ownership. The brokers were, therefore, liable. The fact that other underwriters had paid their share did not prevent the first defendant from availing himself of a legal defence which was open to him.

This is further illustrated by the decision in *General Accident Fire and Life Ass* v. *JH Minet*.[146] The plaintiff insurers instructed their brokers to obtain reinsurance on their behalf. In relation to part of that placing the brokers had misrepresented or concealed certain aspects of one of the policies they were seeking to reinsure. The

---

143. (1916) 86 L.J.K.B. 315.
144. For questions of contributory negligence see: *Youell* v. *Bland Welch* [1990] 2 Lloyd's Rep. 431.
145. [1990] 2 Lloyd's Rep. 418.
146. 74 Ll.L.Rep. 1.

immediate effect was that the reinsurer was not liable to the plaintiffs. The plaintiffs therefore sued the brokers.

The question of crucial importance was what instructions and information had the brokers been given by the plaintiffs? It often happens in complicated commercial disputes that the memories of witnesses are hazy and, if the evidence is unsupported by any documentary evidence from the time in question, the court is left to decide between conflicting evidence. In the present case, the court accepted the evidence of the plaintiffs that sufficient information had been given to the brokers. The brokers then defended their position by arguing that the plaintiffs had approved the reinsurance wording and therefore had ratified the broker's mistake. This argument also failed on the basis that the plaintiff was under no duty to check the reinsurance arrangements that the broker had made.

This approach is quite supportable where the plaintiff is a person unskilled in the ways of insurance. But, in the *Minet* case, the plaintiff was himself an insurer, although, according to the court, one who appeared to know little about the complexities of the particular policy in question.

A different approach to the problem can be seen in *Youell* v. *Bland Welch & Co.*[147] Lloyd's brokers had been instructed to obtain reinsurance for the plaintiff insurers. The reinsurance proved to be an inadequate security and the plaintiffs failed in the action on that policy. In a second action they sued their brokers and the brokers who had been appointed to assist the first brokers on the grounds that if they had been told of the limitations in the reinsurance they would not have taken such a large initial risk and that, in any case, they had been told that the reinsurance reflected the original risk. The brokers defended, arguing that all the relevant information was to be found in the correspondence and it was to be expected of an insurer that he would read the reinsurance conditions. Alternatively, if they were liable, the brokers argued that the plaintiffs were at least contributorily negligent.

The court decided that both brokers were in breach of the duty of care to the plaintiffs in not explaining the importance of the more limited cover found in the reinsurance policy, a clause inserted by the brokers without instructions from their clients. They were also in breach of their duty in not advising as to how the consequences of the reinsurance wording could be avoided. The brokers' defence that the plaintiffs were under a duty to check the wording of the policy was rejected on the grounds that it was not justified that a client who was the cause of the brokers' commission should be saddled with the very responsibility that was the brokers' in the first place. Phillips J explained the duty owed[148]:

"When a Lloyd's broker accepts instructions from a client he implicitly undertakes to exercise reasonable skill and care in relation to his client's interests in accordance with the practice at Lloyd's. The general duty will normally require the broker to perform a number of different activities on behalf of the client, but the performance of those activities constitute no more than the discharge of the duty to exercise reasonable skill and care. Failure to perform one of the activities will normally constitute a breach of that duty of care, not a breach of an absolute obligation. The breaches of duty for which I have held the brokers liable all represent breaches of the general duty owed by the broker to exercise reasonable skill and care, not breaches of absolute obligations."

147. [1990] 2 Lloyd's Rep. 431.
148. For instance a doctor's duty is not an absolute duty to cure his patient but to exercise reasonable skill and care in treating the patient.

Having rejected the brokers' defence on liability the court did however decide that the plaintiff was contributorily negligent under the Law Reform (Contributory Negligence) Act 1945. This argument had worked in the earlier case of *Vesta* v. *Butcher*[149] where Hobhouse J had set out his three-point classification of how concurrent liability[150] in contract and tort was to be meshed with the 1945 Act. It is suggested that Phillips J's allotment of responsibility of 80 per cent negligence on the part of the brokers and 20 per cent on the part of the plaintiff-insurer is a more realistic reflection of responsibilities than the ratio in *Vesta* v. *Butcher*.[151] The insurers were contributorily negligent because, in the words of Phillips J, they were:

"Lloyd's agent. The personnel involved were marine insurers of great experience. An insurer who was exercising reasonable skill and care in relation to the business he was conducting would have noticed the [problematical] clause and would have queried its presence and effect with the brokers".

Both the *Fine Flowers* case and *Youell* were referred to in *O'Brien* v. *Hughes-Gibb & Co and BBA (Ireland) Ltd*.[152] The plaintiffs ran a successful stud in Ireland. They purchased three shares in the highly prized racehorse, Shergar, at £280,000 per share. The plaintiffs wishing to insure their financial interest in the horse instructed the second defendant, BBA, who were a blood stock agency, to obtain insurance at Lloyd's. As BBA were not Lloyd's brokers they approached the first defendants, Hughes-Gibb & Co who could place such business. BBA held a binding authority from the first defendants who they had used on many previous occasions. The cover provided under this authority included loss by proven theft. However, this method of placing was not used in the case of Shergar and Hughes-Gibb placed the insurance on the open market and that policy did not include cover against theft. Shergar was stolen and never recovered. The plaintiffs alleged that both defendants had been negligent in not obtaining theft cover. The plaintiffs' action failed. At first sight this may seem surprising. After all cover against theft was included in the original binder. It seems, however, that prior to the theft of Shergar such a loss was not regarded as a significant risk.[153] Those who gave evidence, owners, brokers and underwriters, all agreed. It is not uncommon for insurers to put into a policy a "freebie" or a "goody", particularly when there is little chance of that event occurring.

Rattee J referred to the scope of the duty of an insurance intermediary used by Phillips J in *Youell*, namely that the intermediary should ascertain his client's needs, use reasonable skill and care to procure the cover his client has asked for, either expressly or by implication and if he cannot obtain suitable cover then to report back to his client and seek alternative instructions. While not an exclusive list of duties the judge did not consider that Hughes-Gibb was in breach of any of the above requirements. The plaintiffs had sought insurance against the death of Shergar and this was what the policy had provided. They had not sought, expressly or impliedly, cover against theft. It could not be accepted that the plaintiffs assumed that theft cover was included because it had been included in the earlier binding authority on

149. [1986] 2 Lloyd's Rep. 179.
150. The question of concurrent liability is considered in more detail in chapter 2.
151. [1986] 2 Lloyd's Rep. 179.
152. [1995] L.R.L.R. 90.
153. For similar reasons, see *Bates* v. *Barrow Ltd* [1995] 1 Lloyd's Rep. 680, and below.

the grounds that it had not been shown that the plaintiffs were ever aware of the scope of the binder.

Plaintiffs' counsel relied on *Fine Flowers* arguing that case assumed a wider role of responsibility for an intermediary beyond that set out in *Youell*. Rattee J, however, was able to distinguish *Fine Flowers* on the grounds that in the Canadian decision the intermediary had been instructed to obtain "full cover". In the present case narrower and more specific instructions were found to have been given and these had been fulfilled. BBA's duty of care was found to be the same as Hughes-Gibb. This was so despite the finding that at that time an extension of the policy to cover theft was obtainable at no extra cost to the insured.

Another illustration given in the Code of Conduct regulations is that the broker shall use his skill objectively in selecting an insurer suitable to the best interests of his client. This could be widely interpreted, especially where the client's interests are themselves wide-ranging. Certainly it would be a requirement of the broker that he should not recommend any insurer over whom hangs any solvency or trading doubts.

In *Osman* v. *Moss*,[154] the plaintiff was Turkish with a limited command of English. He asked the defendant broker to arrange motor cover, and the broker recommended a company that was known in the industry to be in serious financial difficulties. A 60-day cover note was issued and the premium paid. After the note expired, the broker received notification from the insurers that the policy was effective. Five days later the winding-up proceedings were started. The broker wrote to the plaintiff informing him that he was insured "and would suggest you insure with another company". The plaintiff failed to understand the meaning of this contradictory letter and when an accident occurred he found himself uninsured. The Court of Appeal held the broker liable in negligence for failure to warn the plaintiff of the insurer's shaky financial position.

Three recent conflicting decisions should cause some concern for insurance advisers. They concern the choice of an insurer.

In order to carry on insurance business in the UK it is necessary for the insurer to be authorised under the relevant legislation. In *Bedford Insurance Co Ltd* v. *Instituto de Resseguros do Brasil*[155] and *Stewart* v. *Oriental Fire and Marine Insurance Co Ltd*[156] contracts were made with unauthorised insurers and the question arose concerning the validity and enforceability of such contracts.

In the *Bedford* case, the plaintiff Hong Kong insurance company instructed London brokers to act as their agents in writing and reinsuring marine contracts in the UK. Neither was authorised to carry on such business in this country. The defendants were reinsurers. When claims were made on the reinsurers they refused to meet them arguing that the original contracts were illegal because of the lack of authorisation. This defence succeeded. The brokers were not being sued for negligence but clearly they had behaved in a "negligent" fashion.

In *Stewart*, the plaintiff was a representative member of a Lloyd's syndicate who had reinsured its primary risk with a foreign, unauthorised company. The court held that the intention of the legislation was not to invalidate such contracts, whereby the

---

154. [1970] 1 Lloyd's Rep. 313, C.A.
155. [1985] Q.B. 966, [1984] 1 Lloyd's Rep. 210.
156. [1985] Q.B. 988, [1984] 2 Lloyd's Rep. 109.

innocent insured (the Lloyd's underwriter) would lose. The purpose of the legislation was to protect innocent insureds.

It is important to stress that here the court decided that the plaintiffs were unaware of the defendant's lack of authorisation, whereas in the *Bedford* case the London brokers and the Hong Kong insurers were in collusion and had misled both the UK and Hong Kong authorities.

There was no suggestion in *Stewart* of negligence, and the case was brought with the active participation of the defendant insurers in order to test the soundness of the *Bedford* decision, which had caused consternation in the insurance market. Such conflicting views clearly left the insurance market in a state of confusion. Fortunately a third case was appealed to the Court of Appeal.

In *Phoenix General Insurance Co of Greece* v. *ADAS*,[157] the plaintiff insurance company was authorised to carry on marine, aviation and transport business. But the Insurance Companies (Classes of General Business) Regulations 1977 changed the categories and groupings of insurance business with the result that aviation contingency insurance no longer formed part of MAT but fell within a category described as "miscellaneous financial loss". The plaintiffs had reinsured part of this business with the defendant Romanian reinsurers. The defendants alleged that the plaintiffs were not authorised to conduct that class of business and, therefore, the reinsurance contracts were not enforceable.

The Court of Appeal, after a detailed analysis, decided that the plaintiffs were authorised and, therefore, the defendants were liable. But the court also dealt in detail with the problems that arose from the two earlier conflicting decisions as to the effect on the parties in a situation where there was an absence of authorisation.

In *Stewart* the court had stressed the public policy issue that if authorisation was meant as a safeguard for those doing business with insurers then it would be wrong to hinder their actions against such insurers on the basis that the contracts they made were illegal. As counsel for the plaintiffs stressed, good public policy and common sense demanded that such contracts should not be invalidated. To do so would mean that the original assureds might not receive their monies if the plaintiff insurer was unable to claim from the reinsurer. The Court of Appeal was sympathetic to this argument but unfortunately felt unable to accept it.

The court accepted the views expressed in *Bedford* that the language of the legislation clearly showed that contracts made by unauthorised insurers are prohibited in the sense that they are illegal and void and, therefore, unenforceable by either party, irrespective of the innocence of either party. In arriving reluctantly at this construction of the legislation, Kerr LJ recognised that it might well result in an unfortunate state of affairs for the insurance market. His only consolation was to be found in the fact that counsel for both sides had never heard of a case where an insurer had used his own illegality as a defence to a claim for payment. Only the future will tell whether this faith in the insurance market will hold good.

While these cases were not concerned specifically with the role of the broker it must remain a distinct possibility that, if a broker placed business with an unauthorised insurer, he would be liable in negligence to his client. He should have the business expertise to know who is authorised to carry on the business he is trying

---

157. [1986] 2 Lloyd's Rep. 582, [1987] 2 All E.R. 152, C.A.

to place. In addition, the Code of Conduct makes specific reference to unauthorised insurers. Paragraph 13 states that both in recommending or in accepting a client's wish to be insured with a company which is not authorised in the UK great care must be taken by the broker that the client appreciates the possible risks involved. The suggestion is made that the warnings should be put in writing.

The Financial Services Act 1986[158] has also added to the debate. It must be remembered that it is only concerned with controlling contracts that fall within the Act's definition of "investment business". But if a transaction meets that requirement then section 3 states that no person shall carry on such business unless authorised to do so under the provisions of the Act.

Section 5 then takes up the matter by stating that where an unauthorised agreement is made it shall be unenforceable against the other party and that party shall be entitled to recover any money or other property paid or transferred by him under the agreement together with compensation for any loss suffered as a result of having parted with it. But the court does have a discretion to enforce an unauthorised agreement or permit money or property transferred to be retained in a number of circumstances. Thus, where the person entering into the transaction reasonably believed that his behaviour did not constitute a contravention of section 3 or where an authorised person, having acted in a prohibited fashion, did not know that he was in contravention of the Act, it is just and equitable for the agreement to be enforced or the money or property to be retained. Where the innocent party elects not to perform the agreement he must repay or return any money or property he has received under that agreement.

Section 132 is concerned with insurance contracts made in contravention of section 2 of the Insurance Companies Act 1982 (restrictions on carrying on business unless authorised) and it is not concerned with those agreements covered by section 5 of the Financial Services Act.

It is section 132 that attempts to settle the problems posed by the judgments in the above three cases. It says that where the contract is entered into by an unauthorised insurer it shall be unenforceable against the other party and that party shall be entitled to recover any money or property paid or transferred under the contract together with compensation for any loss suffered. The court has a similar discretion to that under section 5 to save the transaction where the unauthorised person reasonably believed he was authorised and it is just and equitable for the contract to be enforced.

Both section 5 and section 132 state that their contravention shall not make the contract of insurance illegal or invalid to any greater extent than provided for in the section wording. Section 132 further adds that the validity of reinsurance contracts based on the unauthorised contract is not in question.

Problems relating to the interpretation of illegality under the Insurance Companies Acts and the interrelation with section 132 of the Financial Services Act and the obligations of the insurance adviser in such a situation were considered in *Bates* v. *Barrow Ltd & Others*.[159]

The plaintiffs were Lloyd's Names who had taken out stop-loss cover. The

---

158. See below.
159. [1995] 1 Lloyd's Rep. 680. See also *Deutsche Ruckversicherung AG* v. *Walbrook Insurance Co Ltd* [1996] 1 All E.R. 791, C.A.

placement with several insurers was made by the first defendant brokers. Cover obtained was with a reputable Finnish reinsurer who, however, was not authorised to carry on such business in the UK. The two main questions for the court were, first, whether section 132 of the Financial Services Act 1986 would save the contracts in the sense that they would be enforceable by the plaintiffs and, secondly, whether the brokers were negligent in placing the business. The answer to the first question was that section 132 was intended to reverse the problems caused by the *Bedford* and *Phoenix* decisions. The section allows enforcement of "illegal" contracts by the insured but not against the insured save for the limited circumstances set out in section 132(3). It was further held that the section has retrospective effect.

The answer to the second question concerning the liability of the brokers in placing the business with unauthorised insurers was broken down into two parts. First, was the broker under a duty to use reasonable care to ensure that policies did not infringe UK legislation? The answer was that a reputable intermediary owed such a duty even though at the time there might have been some doubt in the insurance market as to the precise implications of the interrelationship between the Insurance Companies legislation and section 132 of the Financial Services Act 1986. If there was any doubt in the mind of the brokers as to the appropriateness of their scheme they should have taken legal advice.[160]

The second part of the question, however, was whether the breach of duty had led to foreseeable losses to Names, assuming that the interpretation of section 132 proved to be incorrect. Here the court found for the brokers. This was so because the court found that brokers operating in the 1980s would not have considered it to be a serious possibility that a reputable insurer, which the Finnish insurer was acknowledged to be, would have taken the illegality point.[161]

In the words of Gatehouse J:

"Considering the real world and ethos of the insurance market at that period, and discounting the wisdom of hindsight, it seems to me that Barrow would not have contemplated such an eventuality as a real danger."

Perhaps the most important example in the Insurance Brokers Registration Council Code of Conduct that affects the discussion of negligence is that concerned with the completion of documents. It states:

"In the completion of the proposal form, claim form, or any other material document, insurance brokers shall make it clear that all the answers or statements are the client's own responsibility. The client should always be asked to check the details and told the inclusion of incorrect information may result in a claim being repudiated."

This approach sounds very similar to the warning given to applicants for insurance by companies acting through their agents. It could be argued that such an applicant when he chooses to approach a broker rather than a company agent does so partly because he wants more detailed professional assistance.

The guidance given to the broker in this example is to avoid completing the form himself and to throw that burden on to the client's shoulders. While it may be good advice in helping to avoid accusations of negligence, just how practical is it? An independent adviser may feel that he should assist in the completion of forms

160. See *Sarginson Bros* v. *Moulton* (1943) 73 Ll.L.Rep. 104.
161. For similar reasoning, see *O'Brien* v. *Hughes-Gibb & Co* [1995] L.R.L.R. 90.

because he knows this is one reason why many clients choose to approach him in the first place. Sometimes the adviser may choose to do so merely to speed up the transaction. Presumably the example was drafted with the many cases in mind where the adviser has been held liable for negligently completing insurance forms. Assuming that many advisers will still choose to maintain their existing work methods, it is important that they realise that by so doing they risk the accusation of negligence being levelled at them by their client.

It is submitted that the code's example on this point is not in the best interests of the profession's image. If the advice is that the broker throws back on the client the responsibility of accuracy in completing the documentation then the broker absolves himself from liability in that part of the transaction that is potentially the most traumatic for the average client. The suggestion here is not that the broker should be liable for misrepresentations made by the client to the broker but that the broker should be liable to the client for any negligence that derives from the broker's own failure to maintain professional standards.

A good illustration is provided by the Irish Supreme Court decision in *Chariot Inns Ltd* v. *Assicurazioni Generali SpA and Coyle Hamilton Hamilton Phillips Ltd*.[162] The plaintiff had stored part of his furniture at another party's premises. A fire destroyed the premises and the insurers of those premises paid out a sum which included the value of the plaintiff's property. This sum was paid over to the plaintiff. At a later date the plaintiff instructed brokers to obtain fire cover for his own premises. The broker knew of the earlier fire. The proposal form asked questions relating to claims experience during the last five years. The broker when completing the form himself failed to declare the earlier fire apparently on the grounds that he did not consider that it was material to the present application. The Supreme Court found the insurers not liable on the grounds of non-disclosure and misrepresentation, but held the broker liable for breach of contract and in negligence to their client. The view of expert witnesses was that even if the particular broker did not consider that the earlier fire was material to the risk it would be normal practice to have disclosed it. The court also rejected the broker's argument that if they were negligent then the plaintiffs were equally culpable since it should have been obvious to them that the earlier fire should have been disclosed. The court was of the opinion that the plaintiffs having employed brokers as their professional advisers were entitled to rely on any advice given to them in relation to the completion of the proposal form. "The reasonable man who goes to the trouble of obtaining professional advice normally acts in accordance with it."

According to one decision of the Court of Appeal, even that standard may not be as high as the client would have hoped. In *O'Connor* v. *BDB Kirby & Co*,[163] the plaintiff approached the defendant broker to arrange motor insurance. The broker completed the proposal based on questions and answers between him and the client. It was stated on the form that the car was garaged, whereas it later transpired that it was parked on the street. The insurers avoided liability and the client sued the brokers and failed.

The court considered that the duty owed by the broker was to take reasonable care

---

162. [1981] I.R. 199.
163. [1971] 2 All E.R. 1415

in the circumstances. The client had given the correct answer to the broker and then had been asked to read the completed form before signing, but he failed to detect the broker's mistake. The court's view was that the duty of care did not extend as far as guaranteeing that every answer was correctly recorded.

Care should be taken in assessing the value of this decision. If the broker's mistake was due to an act that could be classed as less than negligent, then the decision is sound. It may well be that the court was influenced by the hint of a conspiracy between broker and client at the time of the claim against the insurer, and felt that in the circumstances the loss should remain on the car owner.

If the general attitude towards negligent advice displayed by the courts in various professional cases is anything to go by, then insurance advisers who negligently and thus incorrectly enter client's accurate answers to questions will be liable for any losses suffered, and thus the decision in *O'Connor* should be limited in its interpretation.

The law reports abound with cases where clients have failed in their allegations of negligence against their insurance advisers. This is so because no reasonable man would brand the adviser as negligent on the facts in question.

For instance, in *King* v. *Chambers*,[164] the client wanted an "all risks" policy on jewellery and furs. The insurers made it a condition that the objects be kept in one of several safe places when not being worn. The client asked her brokers to renegotiate this condition in relation to certain items. They were unable to change the insurers' mind. When a loss occurred the insurers were not liable and neither were the brokers because they had informed their client of their inability to obtain the terms that she requested.[165]

Again in *Avondale Blouse Co Ltd* v. *Williamson & Town*,[166] having arranged various insurance covers for his client the intermediary was told that part of the business should be relocated. He arranged with the insurers that cover would extend to the new premises. The insurers were not prepared to extend the burglary cover until they had surveyed the new premises. This was explained to the client. A theft occurred before the survey took place and the client sued the brokers for negligence. The action failed on the grounds that the broker had explained the situation and that temporary cover would also have been almost impossible to find.

The insurance adviser's duty is to do his best in the circumstances and display professional skill. It is not incumbent on him to meet the exact requirements of the client if they are unobtainable. In *Sarginson Bros* v. *Moulton*,[167] the brokers were negligent because they wrongly informed their client that the required cover was unobtainable whereas in *King* they had relayed the information that the insurers were not prepared to alter their condition, and this could hardly be regarded as professional negligence.

*United Mills Agencies Ltd* v. *Harvey, Bray & Co*[168] looks at the intermediaries' duties from a different angle. Here the question was how pro-active an intermediary should be in advising his client on his insurance needs. The plaintiff required

164. [1963] 2 Lloyd's Rep. 130.
165. This can usefully be compared with *Harvest Trucking* v. *PB Davis* [1991] 2 Lloyd's Rep. 638.
166. (1948) 81 Ll.L.Rep. 492.
167. (1943) 73 Ll.L.Rep. 104.
168. [1951] 2 Lloyd's Rep. 631.

insurance for goods destined for export. The policy arranged by his intermediary covered the goods from "warehouse to warehouse". This description did not include the time while the goods were at the packers' place of business. A fire at these premises destroyed the plaintiff's goods. The plaintiff's argument really came down to the complaint "you failed to advise us properly, as to our real insurance requirements". The judge rejected the argument in strong terms. His view was that an intermediary should be able to expect that a businessman conducts his business in a prudent fashion and that he has sufficient insurance to cover those parts of his business which are not subject to the specific instructions given at a particular time. In the light of movements from the late 1970s onwards whereby there has been an effort to "professionalise" the insurance intermediaries' role by means of various codes of conduct, the decision in *United Mills* looks somewhat outmoded. In advising the client on insurance of his goods for export it is not appropriate or necessary, for instance, to review the client's vehicle insurance. But where policies draw lines at points which would not automatically be clear even to an alert businessman, then perhaps more should be expected of an insurance adviser.

It must be stressed that references to the Insurance Brokers Registration Council's Code of Conduct are merely by way of example of what might be considered as negligent by the courts. It is now necessary to look at past situations on a more general basis as reflections of what the courts have considered to be negligent behaviour. The main areas are where the insurance adviser fails to carry out the client's instructions or fails to instruct the client as to his true needs. It should act as a general warning to the adviser that often the cause of complaint stems from poor office practices.

In *London Borough of Bromley* v. *Ellis*[169] the first defendant found himself uninsured in a motor collision case brought by the plaintiff. He joined the brokers as third party. The defendant had purchased the car from the original owner and the agreement between them was that the insurance on the car should be transferred to the defendant. The brokers who had handled that original insurance were contacted and were asked to arrange the transfer. The defendant completed a proposal form and was issued with a 30-day cover. The brokers failed to send off this proposal form. Two more renewals were issued by the brokers. Finally, the proposal was sent off and was questioned by the insurers. The brokers did not respond and the insurers told them not to issue any more cover notes. The brokers failed to inform the defendant.

The court held that the brokers were liable in negligence. Quite why the brokers advised that a transfer of insurance was the most suitable way to effect cover for the plaintiff is not spelt out in the judgment. It certainly seems poor professional advice to suggest that it was the best way to proceed. Apart from that it was clearly negligent of the brokers not to inform their client that the cover had lapsed.

In *Cherry* v. *Allied Insurance Brokers*,[170] the defendant brokers had handled the plaintiff company's business for over 50 years. The plaintiffs were unhappy at the size of the premium in the light of a low claims record. They instructed the brokers to terminate all policies and informed them that they intended putting their business in the hands of other brokers. New policies were arranged by the new brokers when the

---

169. [1971] 1 Lloyd's Rep. 97.
170. [1978] 1 Lloyd's Rep. 274.

defendant brokers reported that the present insurers would not agree to cancel mid-term. The plaintiff being double-insured cancelled the new policies but did not inform the defendants. At a later date the original insurers agreed to cancel, but the defendants did not relay this fact to the plaintiffs who were now uninsured. A major loss occurred and the plaintiffs claimed in negligence from the defendant brokers who were held liable.

It is interesting to note that neither party told the other of the changed circumstances, but clearly the court's view was that the brokers were professional advisers and it was their negligence that was the sole cause of the loss. The measure of damages was the amount covered by the original, cancelled policy.

However, it is not immediately easy to reconcile *Cherry* with *Argy Trading Development Co Ltd* v. *Lapid Developments Ltd*,[171] which, while not a case involving a professional insurance adviser as defendant, does raise the issue of what reliance can be placed on statements or actions that imply to another that the relevant insurance exists. The defendants leased property to the plaintiffs and the tenants agreed by a term of the lease to insure the property for fire risks. In fact the defendants arranged the insurance on all the property in the block and passed on the premiums to the plaintiffs. The policy was later renewed and the plaintiffs were informed that, in future, the insurance arrangements would be handled by the defendants' brokers and they were to be invoiced accordingly. This decision was later changed, but the plaintiffs were not informed and, in consequence, the insurance lapsed so that when a fire occurred they discovered that they were uninsured. They sued the defendants arguing that although the defendants had gratuitously arranged the original insurance, they owed the plaintiffs a duty of care to continue the insurance or to inform them that it was to be cancelled.

The action failed. There was no contractual duty to continue the insurance because there was no consideration to support such a contract. The action under *Hedley Byrne* also failed and it is this point that is perhaps surprising. The court argued that, although the relationship between the parties was such as to create a special relationship as required by *Hedley Byrne*, the extent of such a duty was not to give negligent information. The original information had been correct, namely, that the defendants would arrange the insurance cover, but the court considered that the duty did not go so far as advising that there was then to be a change of plan on the expiration of the insurance.

The difference between *Cherry* and *Argy* might be that the court is prepared to place a greater burden on an insurance adviser to maintain his duty of care to a former client than it is to place such a duty on someone who does not profess any professional expertise in insurance matters.

A matter closely related to the termination of the cover as illustrated in the last two cases is the question of renewals and the insurance adviser's duty towards his client. This is not an easy area wherein precise rules can be stated. The relationship between insurer and insurance adviser, set out in contractual terms, will be a deciding factor. This may indicate whether or not days of grace apply and the method of account between the two is also an important indicator whether late renewals will be valid.

This relationship is crucial to the adviser/client relationship and will help dictate

---

171. [1977] 1 Lloyd's Rep. 67.

the extent of the duty owed by the insurance adviser to his client. The first question to ask is what is the extent of the adviser's duty at renewal time? Assuming that the insurance contract is for a set period of time, usually for one year, there is no legal obligation on the insurers to advise the insured that the policy is due for renewal. The situation would be different if the policy expressly stated that the insurers would give such notice. But does the adviser have a greater duty to warn the client about renewal dates? *Cherry's* case would imply that such a duty exists. Section 58 of the Australian Insurance Contracts Act 1984 is of interest in that it requires an insurer to give at least 14 days' notice that a policy is to expire. If he fails to do so and the insured has not arranged insurance elsewhere, the original policy is automatically renewed on the same terms. It could be implied from the Statement of General Insurance Practice[172] that insurers must send renewal notices to the insured. The Statement does not however have legal force.

Further guidance can be taken from the Court of Appeal decision in *Fraser* v. *B Furman (Productions) Ltd*.[173] The plaintiffs instructed their brokers to arrange employer's liability insurance and it was common ground between the parties that the Eagle Star Insurance Co would be the insurers. The brokers failed to arrange cover. The plaintiffs were ordered to pay damages to an injured employee and, on seeking an indemnity, discovered that they were uninsured. They commenced proceedings against their broker for breach of contract. The brokers argued that an exclusion clause in the Eagle Star policy would have allowed the insurers to avoid liability and, therefore, the broker's omission had not caused any loss to the plaintiffs.

The court rejected their argument on the grounds that it was "highly improbable that as a matter of business a company of high reputation, wishing to obtain business, would conceivably take the wholly unmeritorious point in a claim of this kind". The court awarded the plaintiffs damages representing the total sum that had been awarded against them in the employee's claim.

Here the failure was to obtain the initial cover required by the client, but it would not stretch the principle too far to add that the insurance adviser should continue to see that his client's insurance requirements were up to date. Inevitably, there is a limit to such a duty. If the adviser sends his client renewal questions and these are unanswered by the client, then there would seem to be no answer to the adviser's claim that he had done all that was reasonable in the circumstances.

In the Canadian case of *Morash* v. *Lockhart & Ritchie Ltd*,[174] the intermediaries had looked after the plaintiff's insurance affairs for more than 20 years. This included carrying out renewals without always waiting for instructions. On one occasion the renewal of a fire policy was not effected and 18 months later a fire loss occurred. The court held the intermediary liable on the grounds that the past self-imposed conduct of renewing the policies had created a duty towards the plaintiff. The damages were recuced by 25 per cent to reflect the plaintiff's failure over an 18-month period to realise that he was uninsured.

A further illustration of renewal problems can be seen in *Mint Security* v. *Blair*.[175] It is also concerned with the problem of possible sub-agency when more than one

---

172. Para. 3.
173. [1967] 2 Lloyd's Rep. 1.
174. (1978) 95 D.L.R. (3rd) 647.
175. [1982] 1 Lloyd's Rep. 188.

broker is used. The third defendant brokers were instructed by the clients to obtain cash in transit cover. They in turn asked the second defendant broker to approach the market and a slip was initialled by the first defendant insurers. The policy contained a limitation of £50,000 on any one vehicle. The policy was renewed. During the second year of the policy, the plaintiffs decided to expand their business and again all the above parties were approached, as before, with a view to increasing cover. The insurers were only prepared to take part of the enlarged risk, but the third defendant broker failed to inform the client of the limitation. The addition to the new slip was dated to incorporate the original policy specifications in relation to the original vehicles. Again the clients were not informed of this. A loss of £85,000 occurred. The plaintiffs were unsuccessful in their claim against the insurers because of breach of policy warranties.

In the alternative the plaintiff sued both sets of brokers. The second defendants were held to be in breach of their duty of care in that no copy of the slip had been passed on. The third defendants were not liable because there was no breach of duty on their part. The damages were limited to £20,000 as set out on the policy. But why were the third defendants not liable for the negligence of the second defendants? This was answered by Staughton J in the following way:

"There might have been an interesting question as to whether the second defendants were true sub-agents, owing a duty to the third defendants only; or whether they were agents of the plaintiffs appointed as such by the third defendants on the plaintiff's behalf. However, the second defendants accept that in the circumstances of the case and in particular in view of the fact that they issued a brochure jointly with the third defendant they owed a duty of care directly to the plaintiffs, both in contract and tort. Nobody else has argued otherwise. I am the last to complain that an interesting academic issue does not need to be decided. If the second defendants had been true sub-agents, the third defendants would have been vicariously liable for the second defendant's negligence."

Another interesting point raised in this case was that the plaintiffs had rejected the insurer's offer to settle the original action at £20,000 and commenced the unsuccessful action against them. In the light of these facts the second defendants argued that the plaintiffs were guilty of failing to mitigate their losses. This defence, however, was also rejected by the judge. He explained that the plaintiffs had not acted unreasonably because they knew little if anything about the circumstances which surrounded the placing of the insurance business. Thus it was understandable that they should test the validity of the policy itself. It would have been different if the insurers had admitted liability on the policy.

Finally, it should be said that section 13 of the Supply of Goods and Services Act 1982 states that:

"In a contract for the supply of a service where the supplier is acting in the course of a business, there is an implied term that the supplier will carry out the service with reasonable care and skill."

This would clearly apply to an intermediary who has a contract with his client. Such implied term can be negated or varied under section 16 but it would have to meet the "reasonableness" provisions of the Unfair Contracts Terms Act 1977.[176]

Office practice is of vital importance. The broker will need to know when any one of his many clients' policies is about to terminate and he will need to convince the

---

176. See also the Unfair Terms in Consumer Contracts Regulations 1994.

court that a renewal notice was sent out if the client's argument is that none was received. The ever-increasing office technology available to the market should make life easier than before for the adviser to keep abreast of his clients' needs.

The approach used in *Fraser* v. *Furman* whereby the court made an assessment of what insurers might have done in a given situation was adopted in *Dunbar* v. *A & B Painters Ltd & Others*.[177]

The plaintiff was an employee of the first defendant. The employer had for a number of years obtained his employer's liability policy from the Eagle Star Group. When his premium doubled the employer instructed his brokers, the third defendants, to insure elsewhere. His insurance was placed with the Economic Insurance Co. In completing the proposal form, serious misstatements were made. It was stated that no insurer had ever asked for an increased premium and two earlier claims for £10,000 and £20,000 were shown as claims for £5,000 and £250. The exact circumstances whereby these answers were given are not clearly set out in the judgments, but in the trial court the deputy judge held the brokers at fault on the grounds that although they were endeavouring to negotiate cover at the cheapest rates for their clients they unfortunately allowed their standards to fall below that which was acceptable. But the brokers then raised a defence similar to that in *Fraser's* case. The policy with Economic contained an exclusion clause which stated that no indemnity would be paid if the employee was injured while working at a height in excess of 40 feet. The plaintiff received serious injuries, compensated by an award of £125,000, when he fell from a height a little in excess of 40 feet. The brokers therefore argued that even if they had correctly completed the proposal form the employer would not have obtained his indemnity from Economic.

The trial court rejected this argument on the basis that no respectable insurance company would have taken the height defence in these circumstances. The Court of Appeal, while agreeing with the trial judge's decision on the facts, stated that the correct approach would be for the judge to assess the chances that the insurers might attempt to utilise their exclusion clause to negotiate a settlement. In which case the brokers should be made liable for whatever assessment the judge estimated as a likely outcome of such negotiations. Here the brokers were liable for the full compensation awarded to the plaintiff employee.

The placing of the heavier burden on the shoulders of the broker rather than equally or more so on the client is further illustrated by the Court of Appeal decision in *Warren* v. *Henry Sutton & Co*.[178]

The plaintiff planned a driving holiday in France and wanted a friend included as an additional driver. This was arranged for an additional premium of £2 and presumably the brokers received the relevant commission. The additional driver was represented as having a clean driving record, which was not the case. The insurers were able to avoid their liability for the property damage that followed on the grounds of the misrepresentation. The plaintiff sued his brokers arguing that they were responsible for the misrepresentation in that they had failed to ask the relevant questions concerning the claims history of the additional driver. The brokers defended by arguing that it was not they who had made the misrepresentation but the plaintiff and it was for him to have divulged his friend's bad driving record.

177. [1986] 2 Lloyd's Rep. 38.
178. [1976] 2 Lloyd's Rep. 276, C.A.

The Court of Appeal by a majority decided the brokers were liable. The representation was made by the brokers over the telephone to the insurers without first checking with the plaintiff. The brokers had volunteered the statement "no accidents, convictions or disabilities". Because of the dilatoriness of the brokers the plaintiff had also contacted the insurers but no questions had been asked of him concerning his friend and no information volunteered. The question then remained as to whether the plaintiff should have told the brokers what he knew of his friend's previous record or whether the brokers should have asked.

The majority of the court felt that the brokers' misrepresentation was due to their failure to ask the client the relevant questions. Lord Denning MR in a strong dissent argued that it was the duty of the client not to mislead the broker and that by failing to inform the broker he was the author of his own misfortune. The financial implications of this decision presumably go beyond the cost of the repair damages. The accident involved a personal injury claim. The insurers were bound to pay that by virtue of their membership of the Motor Insurers' Bureau. But, having paid out, they would look to the car owner for an indemnity who in turn would add this to his claim against the brokers.

The true extent to which the client places himself in the hands of his adviser, and relies on him for professional advice, extends to conversations prior to actually filling in the proposal. This clearly is a potentially dangerous period for the adviser.

In *McNealy* v. *Pennine Insurance Co and West Lancashire Insurance Brokers Ltd*,[179] the plaintiff approached brokers to arrange comprehensive motor insurance. The Pennine were offering motorists special low rates. The plaintiff was a property repairer and qualified for their insurance. He was also a part-time musician and this made him unacceptable to the insurers. The brokers knew of the insurers' rejection list of certain occupations but they failed to ask the plaintiff whether he had any part-time occupation. When an accident occurred the insurers were able to repudiate liability for non-disclosure. The brokers, however, were held liable. Knowing of the insurers' condition concerning certain part-time occupations, it was not sufficient for them merely to accept the plaintiff's main trade. They should have gone one step further and questioned him as to any part-time work. The brokers had completed the proposal and the plaintiff had signed it. No questions as to part-time work appeared on the form and the plaintiff's answer "property repairer" to the occupation question was correct on the face of it. There was nothing that should have put him on the alert. The prohibited occupations only appeared in the insurer's instructions to brokers.

Lord Denning MR also gave judgment in this case. But, unlike *Warren's* case, he had no criticisms of the plaintiff. Full responsibility fell on the brokers. The brokers should have gone through the list of unacceptable occupations with the client. In failing to do so they did not do all that was reasonable to see that their client was properly insured.

A decision which illustrates a number of problems arising from the adviser-client relationship referred to above, can be seen in *Sharp and Another* v. *Sphere Drake Insurance plc*.[180] The decision covers a number of insurance questions including wrongful signing of the proposal form.

---

179. [1978] 2 Lloyd's Rep. 18.
180. [1992] 2 Lloyd's Rep. 501.

In part it was alleged that there had been a non-disclosure in that the proposal form had never been signed by the applicant for insurance but by an employee of the D3, the brokers. The court found for the insurers but against the brokers.

As to the question of the bogus signature, how did it come to be that S had not signed the proposal form and that it had been signed by an employee of the broker, who incidentally had the same name as S, although the judgment does not labour the point? The boat was moored in Majorca and the brokers knew that S wanted to sail to Puerto Banus within a few days. Renewal of the policy was an urgent matter and communication by post was slow and difficult. There would seem little doubt from the evidence that the broker's intention was to speed things up with the client's interests at heart. However, understandably, the underwriters argued that the broker was in gross breach of his duty of good faith owed as the insured's agent to the insurers. Expert witnesses were called by both sides to give their opinions as to the signing. Most agreed that only the true proposer's signature would be satisfactory although one underwriter witness said that he might have held covered while time was taken to obtain that true signature. The judge explained that there appeared to be no earlier authority covering this exact situation and therefore approached the matter with a general review of Lord Mansfield's leading judgment on good faith in *Carter* v. *Boehm*.[181] From the authorities he was of the opinion that "given the width of the general principle of utmost good faith there can be no justification for confining material circumstances to those which are directly relevant to the assessment of the risk". Provided that it is established that such circumstances would influence the mind of the prudent insurer in deciding whether to take the risk, they ought to have been disclosed and if they were not the insurer can avoid the policy. In the light of these findings the first plaintiff's claim against the insurers failed.

The first plaintiff also alleged that if there had been a failure to disclose the presence of the crew aboard during the lay-up period then that failure was due to his broker's failure to exercise his professional duty to his client. A similar argument was directed to the broker's failure in relation to the signing of the proposal form. The judge made reference to the words of Phillips J in *Youell* v. *Bland Welch & Co.*[182] The problem facing the court was to decide on the level of professional care required in the circumstances of the particular case. The difficulty of differing levels of expertise within a particular profession was referred to by Megarry J in *Duchess of Argyll* v. *Beuselinck*[183] when discussing alleged solicitors negligence. Deputy Judge Colman explained that:

"it is appropriate to require that a non-specialist marine broker should bear no greater skill than that which would be expected from a reasonably skilled non-specialist broker. This is not the same thing as saying that the standard is that of a marine broker substantially inexperienced in the insurance of large yachts. It is rather the standard of a broker who has such general knowledge of the yacht insurance market and the cover available in it as to be able to advise his client on all matters on which a lay client would in the ordinary course of events predictably need advice, in particular in the course of the selection of cover and the completion of the proposal".

In order to answer the question whether or not the broker had fallen below the

181. (1766) 3 Burr. 1905.
182. [1990] 2 Lloyd's Rep. 431 at 445.
183. [1972] 2 Lloyd's Rep. 172 at 183.

required standard it was important to evaluate what information he had at hand and how he came to have it. The plaintiff and the broker spoke over the telephone. The broker did not read over all of the questions. They spoke in general terms about living abroad and on that information the broker considered that a negative answer should be given to the question relating to the "house boat" clause. The plaintiff, however, alleged that the broker had failed properly to construe that clause, and failed to give to it the importance it deserved. The judge explained: "There is no doubt that a broker is not necessarily in breach of his duty of professional skill and care merely because he has given to a document relevant to the placing of the risk a meaning which on its proper construction such a document does not bear". He was of the opinion that the essential point was to ask whether or not other persons exercising the same profession would or would not have reached the same conclusion. The real problem was whether the "house boat" question should be read as referring only to the plaintiff and family living on board or whether it should be read as referring to crew. In the face of conflicting expert evidence, the court accepted the view that it was the presence of anyone living on board, apart perhaps than occasional occupancy, that was required by the question and therefore the broker was negligent in not asking for more details about the crew.

As to the signing of the plaintiff's name this was held to be a "radical departure" from the standard practice of insurance broking.

Was the plaintiff to be held contributorily negligent? When he finally saw the completed proposal, should he have realised that the "house boat" clause had not been accurately answered? The court rejected this line of argument on the grounds that the way the original question had been posed over the telephone whereby the plaintiff had been asked if he and his wife would live on board, meant that he had no reason to assume that specific mention of the crew was required. As a layman the plaintiff was "clearly entitled to rely on [the broker's] skill and judgement as a professional broker in identifying what kind of information was required. It was no part of his duty to second guess his own professional adviser".

No reference was made at this point in the judgment to *Youell* v. *Bland Welch & Co* or *Vesta* v. *Butcher*[184] where contributory negligence against the client was successfully raised by the defendant brokers. In both cases, however, the plaintiffs were professional insurers in their own right and hopefully the present case marks the boundary between lay client responsibility and that of professional clients in the vetting of the insurance documentation.

The difficulties of watching over the affairs of clients who are at a distance and particularly where communication is difficult led the brokers in the present case to take an unfortunate and expensive shortcut. It would seem, at least from one expert witness, that one way out would be to explain the situation fully to the underwriters and ask for them to hold covered while the completed proposal form finds its way from one party to the other. On the facts of the present case, however, even that solution would not avail the broker if he falls below the standard of professional competence in the way he construes the questions on the proposal form and fails to instruct or advise his client as to their true meaning.

The decision in *Verderame and Others* v. *Commercial Union and Another*[185] also

184. [1990] 2 Lloyd's Rep. 431 and [1986] 2 Lloyd's Rep. 179 respectively.
185. (Unreported) 24 March 1992, C.A.

raises questions of alleged brokers' negligence. The first two plaintiffs were sole shareholders and directors of the third plaintiff company and they appealed against a striking-out of part of their claim. The Commercial Union did not appear, the second defendants were the brokers. The plaintiffs ran a garage trading as V & A Garage. The policy issued by Commercial Union was under, *inter alia*, a policy against loss or damage by theft and loss of profits resulting from interruption or interference with the business carried on by the policyholder. Losses occurred within the wording of the policy. Part-payment was made by Commercial Union to the first plaintiff who received it for and on behalf of the company and paid over that sum to the company. However, the plaintiffs alleged that due to the failure to receive compensation in full the company, V & A Garage, went out of business.

The individual directors continued the case in their own names. This however, *per* Balcombe LJ, raised "a number of insuperable objections". The most important of which was the fact that the directors were seeking to go behind the corporate status of the company. The plaintiff directors were in reality arguing that if the brokers had failed to obtain adequate cover for the company then they were in breach of a duty to the directors individually. If such an argument was allowed then as Balcombe LJ said, "the principles of the leading case of *Salomon* v. *Salomon & Co*[186] would become a dead letter". This would then "permit directors and shareholders to circumvent the rules governing the winding up of companies and would expose brokers, and others dealing with a company to the risk of having to make double restitution".

In even more forceful language Nourse LJ, in a short judgment, stated that the proposition that a broker when acting for a small private company or quasi-partnership might owe a duty of care to the individual director, even though the broker was dealing directly with them, was:

"not only novel but startling ... it would have wide-ranging consequences, not only in relation to insurance brokers, but also to others who provide services to small private companies, solicitors, accountants, estate agents and so forth. Not only would it pierce the corporate veil on a vast scale it would lead to quite unjustifiable procedural impracticabilities and right or potential rights of double recovery".

Apart from the great dangers of piercing the corporate veil Balcombe LJ had earlier in his judgment relied heavily on the House of Lords' judgment in *Caparo Industries plc* v. *Dickman*[187] in illustrating the appellate court's more restrictive approach to actions in negligence leading to economic loss.

It has been stressed that the tort of negligence has been willing to take on board new situations where one person's negligence causes loss to another. This seems particularly prevalent where the defendant is a professional person. It is not easy, however, to estimate just how far the courts are willing to go, particularly in the light of the new, more limited approach seen in *Caparo Industries*.

In *Hedley Byrne* and several cases dependent upon it, the courts have stressed that only where the professional is acting within the scope of his professional duties will they impose a duty to be careful. It is the "gravity of the inquiry" that must be looked at and in Lord Denning's words "representations made during a casual conversation

186. [1897] A.C. 22.
187. [1990] 2 A.C. 605.

411

in the street; or in a railway carriage; or impromptu opinion given offhand; or 'off the cuff' on the telephone" would not create liability. This is what the Americans call "kerb stone" advice.

One can visualise cases, however, where the parties involved will see the conversation from different perspectives. The plaintiff will argue that he thought he was entitled to act on the advice given. The defendant will argue that the plaintiff was wrong to do so in the conditions prevailing at that time. Professionals would be wise to preface their remarks to other parties with suitable caution. By so doing, they will then be able to argue that it should have been clear to the reasonable man that no duty of care was being accepted by the speaker at that point.

Even where the courts find that a duty exists, the plaintiff may still fail to prove that the advice was negligent. The fact that advice turns out to be incorrect is not necessarily the same as saying that it is negligent.[188]

The decision in *Macmillan* v. *Knott Becker Scott & Others*[189] illustrates a novel point concerning the liability of a broker. It is a requirement that all registered brokers, and therefore Lloyd's brokers, should carry professional liability insurance that can then meet the award of any damages made against them. The plaintiffs in this case were clients of a Lloyd's broker against whom they alleged negligence. The broker, however, was then in liquidation and it was assumed that action could commence against his professional indemnity insurers once liability had been assessed. It was discovered, however, that the brokers who had placed the original brokers' E and O (errors and omissions) policy had themselves acted negligently in placing that insurance with the effect that there was no valid professional indemnity insurance. The preliminary point in issue therefore was whether the plaintiffs could sue the broker's brokers. The court went to some lengths in explaining the mandatory requirements of professional indemnity insurance that brokers must have under section 12 of the Insurance Brokers (Registration) Act 1977.[190]

It was readily conceded by the court that the protection of the public was its paramount concern and that for Lloyd's brokers such requirement had predated the 1977 Act by more than a hundred years.[191] Despite such a concession, the plaintiffs failed in their argument. The problem was that the claim was one for economic loss based in negligence. The law in this area has been in considerable turmoil for many years. Present House of Lords' thinking is such that pure economic claims are, subject to narrow exceptions, unsustainable.[192] Thus, while it might be said that the defendant broker could foresee that by the negligent failure to obtain professional indemnity cover loss would be caused to the present plaintiffs, such foreseeability alone was insufficient to expose them to liability to such plaintiffs. The plaintiffs were unable to bring themselves within the ambit of the decision in *Hedley Byrne* because there had been no statement or failure to speak by the defendants.

Also, there was no "duty to speak" in these circumstances.[193] The duty of the

---

188. See *Briggs* v. *Gunner* (1978) 129 N.L.J. 116.
189. [1990] 1 Lloyd's Rep. 98.
190. See below.
191. Lloyd's Act 1871, s. 24.
192. See *Murphy* v. *Brentwood DC* [1990] 2 All E.R. 908; *Caparo Industries plc* v. *Dickman* [1990] 1 All E.R. 568.
193. See the Court of Appeal judgment as set out in *The Good Luck* [1991] 3 All E.R. 1, H.L. and *La Banque Financiere de la Cite SA* v. *Westgate Insurance Co Ltd* [1988] 2 Lloyd's Rep. 513.

defendants was a contractual duty only to their clients, the first brokers. Although the court could see some merit in allowing an uninsured client to proceed against the negligent E and O broker, in the final analysis it was decided that the liquidator of the insolvent broker should exercise his rights against the second broker. While this would presumably result in some compensation going to the plaintiffs it does not guarantee total compensation. The amount of compensation would depend on the assets held by, and claims made to, the liquidator.

## 4.2 The insurance adviser and the insurer

In the above section the question was whether or not the adviser was liable to the client when the insurers were able to avoid their liability to the "assured". In this section we are concerned with situations where the insurer is liable but is entitled to turn on the adviser and seek indemnification on the ground of the adviser's negligence or breach of agency.

The cases show that this is possible and they thus illustrate that the adviser owes a duty of care to both parties whom he is attempting to put into a contractual relationship. But the situation is not without its complications as to whose agent the adviser is at a particular time during the transaction. The problem is particularly acute when cover notes are being issued by an adviser or when he is dealing with changes to existing cover. It is more likely than not that he is acting as agent of the insurers for part of this time. If this is the case and any negligence occurs on the part of the adviser, then the insurers will be liable to the assured, but in all probability the insurer can seek reimbursement from the adviser for any breach of their relationship.

In *Stockton* v. *Mason & Others*,[194] the first defendant's father had his Ford Anglia insured with the second defendant, Vehicle and General, through the agency of the third defendants. The owner's wife telephoned the brokers to explain that her husband had sold the Anglia and had replaced it with an MG Midget. She asked for the insurance to be transferred. A clerk in the broker's office told her that everything would be all right and that they would see to it. The owner took this to mean that the same terms and conditions applied as previously. A week later the brokers informed the owner that driving must be restricted to the owner only. A few hours before that information reached the owner, his son negligently caused an accident while driving the car and damages of £46,000 were awarded to the plaintiff. Who was to pay?

The difficulty of analysing the legal position of the broker in this transaction is reflected in the fact that the county court judge's view was overruled by the Court of Appeal. What was the role of the broker at the moment he gave information over the telephone to Mrs Mason? The judge considered that he was not yet acting as an agent of the insurers. The broker owed a personal duty of care to the client and was in breach of that. The Court of Appeal saw it differently. The relationship between insurer and broker in non-marine insurance is such that the broker can have implied authority to enter into interim insurance and to issue cover notes.

The vast majority of the motoring public believe that a telephone call to a broker will result in immediate temporary cover, sufficient to drive a newly acquired car

194. [1978] 2 Lloyd's Rep. 430, C.A.

immediately. The industry practice reflects those assumptions and, therefore, the broker's conversation with Mrs Mason had the effect of granting temporary cover and therefore they were agents of the insurers. The plaintiff's case against the insurers succeeded and the court's earlier judgment against the brokers was reversed.

It is clear that in the client-broker relationship much will depend on what was said and understood. That is a matter of evidence for the court to deal with having seen and heard the witnesses. In *Stockton*'s case the decision hinges on the court's interpretation of a telephone conversation that can only have lasted a minute or two.

In the broker-insurer relationship there is more chance that conversations will have been written down or recorded in some way. This may present the court with clearer evidence on which to base their decision. But even here inadequate office administration can lead to unhappy results for one of the parties.[195]

In both *Stockton* and *Hadenfayre* the disputed statements were made in what one might call "office hours and office environment". But the broker would not deny that his working environment goes beyond those parameters. So, too, do his legal responsibilities to both insurer and client.

This is well illustrated in *Woolcott* v. *Excess Insurance and Others*[196] (see also *Woolcott* v. *Sun Alliance*).[197] The plaintiff had a number of criminal convictions, including one of 12 years' imprisonment for armed robbery. He set up a business and several insurance policies were effected for the business through the third party defendant brokers. The business was put into a creditors' voluntary liquidation. But before this occurrence the plaintiff asked the brokers to arrange a household comprehensive policy. This was placed with the first party defendant insurers in accordance with the authority given to the brokers by the insurers. When a subsequent loss occurred due to fire the insurers repudiated liability on the grounds of non-disclosure of the plaintiff's criminal record.

The plaintiff argued that the brokers were aware of his previous record and consequently as agents of the insurers in effecting the policy the brokers' knowledge was imputed to the insurers. If that argument was sound then the insurers argued that the brokers were liable to indemnify them for failing to relay this crucial information. This the brokers were obliged to do by virtue of the "binding authority" issued by the insurers to the brokers whereby it was an implied term of that authority that such matters as previous criminal convictions must be brought to the attention of the insurers. What then was the extent of the brokers' knowledge and by what means were they in possession of it? The plaintiff first argued that when the brokers visited his company, prior to its liquidation, it was common knowledge among the company's employees that the plaintiff had a criminal record. This knowledge came into the possession of the broker. Secondly, it was argued that on a social occasion this knowledge had also been passed on to the broker when dancing with a lady later to become the plaintiff's wife. The resolving of these crucial issues led to a judgment by the High Court, an appeal to the Court of Appeal and an order by them for a retrial.

This sequence of events, while not unheard of, is certainly unusual, and expensive

---

195. See *Hadenfayre Ltd* v. *British National Insurance Society* [1984] 2 Lloyd's Rep. 393 and *Icaron plc* v. *Peek Puckle (International) Ltd* [1992] 2 Lloyd's Rep. 600.
196. [1979] 1 Lloyd's Rep. 23, C.A., [1978] 1 Lloyd's Rep. 633.
197. [1978] 1 Lloyd's Rep. 629.

in a civil matter. No intricate question of law was involved only the evaluation of the witnesses' evidence. In the retrial the judge admitted as much when he confessed that "the decision ultimately depends on my human and therefore fallible judgement as to which of two witnesses I believe" (referring to the testimony of the broker and Mrs Woolcott). The judge preferred the evidence of Mrs Woolcott that on a social occasion she had confirmed the broker's suspicions of the plaintiff's previous criminal record. This knowledge was therefore imputed to the insurers by the finding by the court that the brokers were acting as agent of the insurers under their binder with them. This being the case, then the brokers were in breach of their contract of agency with the insurer. Why they did not pass on this important information to the insurers was, as the judge said, "one of the mysteries and tragedies of this case". The outcome then was that the plaintiff succeeded in his claim against the insurers while the insurers were successful in their claim for an indemnity from the brokers.

There is no doubt however that the "classical" relationship between potential policyholder, independent adviser and insurer is that the adviser is the agent of the policyholder. This reflects the fact that the customer approaches the adviser with a request that the adviser arrange a policy on his behalf. But the policyholder is well aware that he does not pay directly for this service, at least not in normal consumer insurance. Every party to the transaction knows that commission is paid by the insurer to the adviser. It is therefore not surprising that the policyholder thinks that the information he has given to the adviser should automatically be implied to the insurer. The above case illustrates that this can be the situation in certain circumstances, especially where the adviser has the right to issue cover notes, or acts under a binder.

The Court of Appeal decision in *Roberts* v. *Plaisted*,[198] however, contains strong criticism of the so called "classical" position. Although the court found that the insured was not in breach of the duty of disclosure, and therefore the insurers were liable for fire damage to a hotel complex, one of the plaintiff's arguments in the alternative was that the broker had sufficient knowledge of the risk for this to be imputed to the insurers. Purchas LJ dealt with the argument in the following way:

"Full and frank disclosure to the Lloyd's broker concerned in presenting on behalf of the proposed assured the proposal to the insurers as against an insurer who complains of non-disclosure and repudiates on that ground avails the proposed insured in no sense at all. To the person unacquainted with the insurance industry it may seem a remarkable state of the law that someone who describes himself as a Lloyd's broker who is remunerated by the insurance industry and who presents proposals and suggested policies on their behalf should not be the safe recipient of full disclosure; but that is undoubtedly the position in law as it stands at the moment. Perhaps it is a matter which might attract the attention at an appropriate moment of the Law Commission."

## 4.3 The insurance adviser and third parties

Perhaps another significant impact of the *Hedley Byrne* decision for brokers is the potential liability that it may place on them when dealing with third parties. At the same time it must be admitted that there are few cases that so far illustrate this point.

198. [1989] 2 Lloyd's Rep. 341.

We have seen above that the relationship that binds the broker to his client and to the insurer may be contractual as well as tortious. Here we are concerned with situations where no contractual relationship can be shown between the parties.

The problem that faces the court was illustrated in the words of Cardozo CJ in the *Ultramares* case.[199] The House of Lords' answer to that problem in *Hedley Byrne* was to demand a special relationship between the parties in order to narrow the field of potential litigants. In the Court of Appeal decision on the non-insurance case of *Dutton* v. *Bognor Regis Urban District Council*,[200] Lord Denning MR said that: "Nowadays since *Hedley Byrne* it is clear that a professional man who gives guidance to others owes a duty of care not only to the client who employs him but also to another who he knows is relying on his skill to save him from harm".[201]

If we translate this to the insurance environment we can pose the situation where a broker or insurer negligently issues a life policy whereby the beneficiary of that policy, not being the assured, loses the expected benefit because of an error in the policy. Would not that beneficiary have a legitimate right of complaint?

The extent of the broker's duty of care to third parties has been considered by the Court of Appeal in *Punjab National Bank* v. *De Boinville*.[202]

The decision concerned the extent of the duties owed by insurance brokers in contract and in negligence. The plaintiffs were bankers for a customer who exported $17m of gas-oil to the Sudan. The sales were on C and F terms and payment was to be by confirmed irrevocable letters of credit opened by the Bank of Sudan with the plaintiff bank. The letter of credit expressly requested the plaintiff bank to add its confirmation. However, because of the uncertainties of the funding arrangements, two insurance policies were taken out covering the first shipments of gas-oil and two policies in respect of the second shipment. The policies were obtained via brokers X and Y, the first and second defendants, who changed their employers several times during the transactions. Originally they worked for A & Co, the third defendants; for three months they worked for B & Co, the fifth defendants; after which they returned to working for A & Co for a short period before moving to C & Co, the fourth defendants. All three firms were Lloyd's brokers.

Four slips were obtained. The first two slips were exclusively A & Co slips and the third and the fourth slips were ultimately C & Co slips. In the first two policies the assured was described as the Punjab National Bank A/C Esal (Commodities) Ltd, i.e., the exporters, using the bank's address. The third and fourth policies described the assured as Esal (Commodities) Ltd using their trading address.

The Sudan Bank failed to remit funds and the plaintiff bank claimed under all four policies. The underwriters did not resist payment under the first two policies but they resisted payment under the remaining two policies on the grounds of misrepresentation and non-disclosure.

The plaintiff bank sued the brokers, arguing that the brokers were in breach of their duty to the bank or Esal. They further argued that the assignment by Esal to

199. (1931) 174 N.E. 441.

200. [1972] 1 Q.B. 373, overruled by *Murphy* v. *Brentwood DC* [1990] 2 All E.R. 908, but the general gist of the quotation still applies. It remains to be seen whether the decision will be allowed to stand alongside *Murphy*. See chapter 2.

201. See the House of Lords' decision in *White* v. *Jones* [1995] 1 All E.R. 691 and chapter 2.

202. [1992] 1 Lloyd's Rep. 7.

them was sufficient to transfer to the bank the right to sue the brokers for any breach of the brokers' duty to Esal. The brokers denied that the plaintiff bank was the assured under the policies.

Hobhouse J held that the plaintiff bank was the assured under policies one and two and Esal was the assured under policies three and four. The assignment had not transferred any cause of action to the plaintiff bank. There was a contractual relationship between the plaintiff bank and A & Co in respect of the first two policies, and between the plaintiff bank and A & Co and C & Co with regard to the other two policies. Duties of care were owed to the plaintiff bank by A & Co, C & Co and the two individual brokers. The claim against B & Co was struck out, together with claims against other defendants who were companies with whom the two individual brokers had interests. All the defendants who had been held liable appealed.

The Court of Appeal rejected all of the appeals. Staughton LJ was of the opinion that the words "a/c Esal" did not detract from the fact that the bank was the assured under the first two policies. In addition there was a contractual relationship between the bank and A & Co and this was to be gleaned by looking at the instructions given by the bank to A & Co and the way A & Co responded to those instructions. There was no evidence that A & Co positively declined to accept the bank's instructions or to repudiate the inference that the bank was regarded as their client.

With regard to the third and fourth policies the judge considered that the correspondence between the bank and the individual brokers illustrated a continued broking contract. The fact that the brokers had changed employers from A & Co to C & Co did not relieve A & Co of responsibility because the bank had not been informed by A & Co of the changed circumstances. A contract was later formed between the bank and C & Co when C & Co sent a cover-note and the bank responded by sending the premium to them.

Perhaps the most interesting legal aspects of the judgment centre on the alleged duty of care owed to the bank. This was important for two reasons. C & Co formed a contractual relationship on a specific day, but did they owe a duty of care prior to that date when the individual broker went to work for them? Secondly, the brokers themselves did not have a contract with the bank and therefore did they owe a duty of care? As Staughton LJ explained, the court was faced yet again with claims for pure economic loss. C & Co argued that the question to be answered was whether the relationship between the parties fitted into a recognised category of liability and, if not, was it justifiable to enlarge the category to include the defendants? Quoting Lord Bridge in *Caparo Industries plc*, where he said that:

"In advising the client who employs him the professional man owes a duty to exercise that standard of skill and care appropriate to his professional status and will be liable both in contract and tort for all losses which his client may suffer by reason of any breach of that duty ...",

Staughton LJ was of the opinion that the principle applied equally to insurance brokers.

The question remained, however, as to whether the bank was to be seen as a client of C & Co in the period prior to the formation of their contractual relationship. The answer to that question was that the bank was not a client at the time of the placing of the third and fourth policies because the bank was not knowingly giving instructions to C & Co. Was it justifiable, however, for the court to allow an incremental growth or expansion of liability on the facts of the present case? The court considered that it was justifiable because at all times throughout the negotiations the individual brokers knew the importance to the bank of all four policies. The moment the brokers went to work for C & Co their knowledge should be attributed to C & Co. The important legal development in the judgment in Staughton LJ's words is:

"It seems to me a justifiable increment to hold that an insurance broker owes a duty of care to the specific person who he knows is to become an assignee of the policy, at all events if (as in this case) that person actively participates in giving instructions for the insurance to the broker's knowledge."

Having found that C & Co owed a duty of care, the remaining question was the liability of the individual brokers. Staughton LJ explained that the answer depended on the job the employee was employed to do and that not every employee of a company providing professional services owed a personal duty of care. The court had no doubt, however, that when one looked at the close relationship of the individual brokers and the bank, the brokers were clearly liable.

### 4.4 The independent adviser and limitation periods[203]

If the independent adviser can be shown to owe a duty of care to another person, we have seen above that he may be able to argue that that person is in some way contributorily negligent and the court will then reduce the damages accordingly.

It may be that the adviser has a complete defence in arguing that the case has been brought too late and the complainant is barred by the statutory limitation period. Such periods within which the writ must be issued vary from one legal topic to another and sometimes within the legal topic itself. This arises in both contract and the tort of negligence. Recent legislation, the Latent Damage Act 1986, has eased the problem somewhat but in fact another area has complicated it still further. Thus while it has made life easier for plaintiffs, who can sue the adviser in negligence, by introducing a limitation period of three years from the date of knowledge of the act of negligence, the Act has been held not to affect the previous law relating to actions framed in contract; whereby the period runs from the date of breach even though the plaintiff may not be aware of the breach.

Two cases involving brokers can be used to illustrate the point. In *Iron Trades Mutual Insurance Co* v. *JK Buckenham Ltd*,[204] the defendant brokers sought to have the plaintiffs' claim struck out as time-barred. The plaintiffs were insurers and underwriting agents who had engaged the defendants at various dates to obtain quota share reinsurance. This reinsurance was placed with a Portuguese insurer. That insurer failed to pay out on claims and alleged non-disclosure, misrepresentation and breach of warranty. The plaintiffs therefore argued that such mistakes made in placing the reinsurance business were made by the brokers. The plaintiffs sued the brokers in both contract and tort. It was common ground between the parties that the

203. See chapter 2.
204. [1989] 2 Lloyd's Rep. 85.

accrual of action in contract dated from the last date an amendment had been made to the reinsurance contract and that was more than six years before the writ was issued and was thus time-barred under section 5 of the Limitation Act 1980. The question then arose as to whether the plaintiffs could continue their action in negligence. The timing of the present action was such that the plaintiffs were forced to argue two limitation points. They agreed that they did not suffer damage in tort until the reinsurer chose to avoid their obligations in 1984, and the limitation period ran from that date. This would mean that the plaintiffs were not time-barred on any of the claims. Alternatively, if the argument failed, the plaintiffs relied on the Latent Damage Act 1986 in relation to the last year in which the brokers had acted on their behalf. The defendants in turn argued that the time-barred action in contract could not be side-stepped by framing the action in negligence.

The court framed three questions to answer:

(a) When did the plaintiffs suffer damage such to give rise to their cause of action in tort?

(b) Does the Latent Damage Act 1986 apply to actions for breach of contract where the breach of contract is simply a breach of an implied duty of care?

(c) Did the plaintiffs have sufficient knowledge to trigger the three-year limitation period under the 1986 Act before the time at which they issued their writ?

The defendants argued in relation to the first question that numerous authorities clearly indicated that damage was suffered at the moment the contract, which results in financial loss, is entered into, even though the innocent party may not discover this until some years later. The defendants took care to illustrate how the decisions in these financial loss cases were, and had been, distinguished from the building cases as exemplified in the House of Lords' decision in *Pirelli General Cable Works Ltd* v. *Oscar Faber & Partners*.[205] The court was persuaded by the defendants' argument and held that, subject to the Latent Damage Act 1986 application below, the answer to the first point was that damages accrued when the voidable reinsurance policies were concluded, not when discovered by the plaintiff.

The second question to be answered was fundamental to questions where concurrent liability is pleaded.

The Latent Damage Act 1986 introduced a new three-year period of limitation to date from the earliest time when the plaintiff had both the knowledge required for bringing an action for damages and a right to bring such an action. Does the Act cover actions brought in both contract and tort or in one as opposed to the other? The court carefully analysed the wording of the relevant sections of the 1986 Act, and came to the conclusion that as the wording of the Limitation Act 1980 expressly preserves the distinction between actions in tort and in contract, it was clear that section 14A was not intended to apply to actions framed in contract. Thus if "negligence" in section 14A refers only to the tort of negligence, then the plaintiffs action in contract failed.

The third question was whether the plaintiffs had sufficient knowledge to set in motion the new limitation period of three years prior to 1984. Although the answer was always a question of fact, the court set out the question along the following lines:

---

205. [1983] A.C. 1.

"When was the earliest date upon which the plaintiffs had knowledge of such facts about the damage as would lead a reasonable person who had suffered such damage to consider it sufficiently serious to justify his instituting proceedings for damages against a defendant who did not dispute liability and was able to satisfy a judgment?"

The answer to that question, however, was not a matter that the court could deal with at this particular stage of the case.

*Iron Trade Mutual* was followed by Evans J in *Islander Trucking Ltd* v. *Hogg Robinson Gardner Mountain (Marine) Ltd.*[206]

The plaintiffs, in 1980, instructed the defendant brokers to obtain "goods in transit" cover for them. In 1985 the insurers avoided liability on the grounds of non-disclosure and misrepresentation and in 1986 the plaintiffs sued the first two brokers for breach of contract and/or negligence in failing to obtain adequate insurance cover. These brokers argued that they were acting as sub-agents of other brokers, who were then joined as third defendants in 1989.

The sole issue in the case was whether the action against the third defendant brokers should be dismissed as being out of time by virtue of the Limitation Act 1980. The crucial dates, therefore, for triggering the six-year limitation period under the 1980 Act were either in 1980, being the policy date, or 1985, when the plaintiffs became liable to claimants under the policies which, in turn, were rejected by the insurers.

It was accepted that an action in contract would date from when the contract of insurance was completed in 1980, and such claim was statute-barred. However, it was also accepted that the plaintiffs would have a cause of action in the tort of negligence. The crucial question for dating the commencement of the limitation period in the negligence claim was when was damage suffered? This was either 1980 or 1985. The court opted for 1980 as being the determining date and the plaintiffs failed in their action against the third defendants. Evans J regarded it as a satisfactory conclusion that the same date should be used as the starting date for limitation periods in actions based in contract and tort. In future, the Latent Damage Act 1986 will, however, come to the aid of plaintiffs who are innocently ignorant of their rights and who have a case in negligence.

## 4.5 Insurance intermediaries and the European Community[207]

In 1976 the European Community introduced the Insurance Intermediaries Directive, to take effect from June 1978. One of the great strengths of the UK insurance market is the expertise and international orientation of its salesforce, in particular insurance brokers and, more particularly, Lloyd's brokers. It is therefore of the greatest importance to them that the European Community markets should be open to their skills. This Directive helps to achieve those goals by introducing measures to allow freedom of establishment and freedom to provide services by such persons.

Article 4 calls for the mutual recognition of academic qualifications or work experience. In fact the UK's Insurance Brokers (Registration) Act 1977 requires more stringent requirements for registration of a UK broker than those called for by the Directive. Proof of compliance with the conditions required for recognition as an

---

206. [1990] 1 All E.R. 826.
207. See *Insurance Intermediaries in the EEC* (Lloyd's of London Press Ltd, 1992) and chapter 1.

insurance broker, agent or sub-agent shall be a certificate issued by the competent authority or body in the Member State of origin. Each State must inform the others as to which bodies have the power of granting such certificates of competency. The Directive is transitional in nature in that it will remain applicable only until there is a co-ordination of national rules concerning the taking up and pursuit of these activities.

In December 1991 the European Commission published its Recommendation on Insurance Intermediaries.[208] A Recommendation does not have binding force on Member States but it clearly has the psychological effect of directing their minds towards what the Commission would like to see happen in a particular case. The Recommendation is of special importance in that the European Single Market for insurance is now complete with the adoption of the Third Non-Life Directive in June 1992 and the Third Life Directive in November 1992.[209] These Directives should create a fully competitive market in insurance and therefore methods of distribution of insurance within the Community is of crucial importance.

Insurance intermediaries are defined in Article 2, paragraph 1(a) to (c) of Council Directive 77/92/EEC, the Insurance Intermediaries Directive.[210] Article 2 of the present Recommendation states that all such insurance intermediaries are subject to the Recommendation other than those who offer cover against loss or damage to goods supplied by that person and where the principal professional activity of that person is other than providing advice on and selling insurance. The example given in the Department of Trade and Industry Consultative Document is where an optician sells cover for loss of contact lenses. The argument is that such selling requires no detailed insurance ability on the part of the seller. However, a car salesman selling motor insurance would not be exempt from meeting the Recommendation's requirements on the grounds that this type of insurance cover is more complex in its nature.

Article 2.3 requires the management of an undertaking exercising the activity of an insurance intermediary to have an adequate number of persons who have commercial and professional knowledge and ability. There is, however, no definition of what is envisaged by the phrase "adequate number". The Article calls upon such undertakings to provide relevant basic training for those employees involved in advising on insurance products. Article 4 elaborates on this requirement. Intermediaries must possess general, commercial and professional knowledge and ability although this may vary depending on the type of intermediary involved. Crucially the standard of such ability shall be determined by the Member States. However, these standards can also be determined and administered by professional organisations recognised by Member States. Thus the role of the Insurance Brokers Registration Council would presumably be retained in relation to registered brokers. An insurance agent working for a specific insurance company who has assumed responsibility for that person can, subject to the supervision of the Member State, undertake this obligation in relation to that agent.

The intermediary must have professional indemnity insurance or the undertaking

---

208. 92/48/EEC
209. See *EC Insurance Directives* (LLP Limited, looseleaf).
210. *Ibid.*

accepting responsibility for that person must provide such cover. No explanation is given as to the required level of such professional indemnity cover.

The intermediary must be of good repute and must not be a declared bankrupt.

Article 5 requires that all intermediaries who fulfil the requirements of professional competence set out in the previous Article must be registered in their Member State. Such registration is a prerequisite to pursuing the activity of an insurance intermediary. It is the responsibility of each Member State to appoint a competent body to administer such registration. Such competent bodies can include professional bodies and insurance undertakings where relevant. Registers of intermediaries shall be available to the Member States' administrative bodies. Intermediaries must inform the public that they are so registered. If one central register exists, it must distinguish between independent and dependent intermediaries.

Adequate sanctions must exist in Member States which can be applied to those who act as insurance intermediaries without proper registration.

Article 3 refers to independent intermediaries. It requires them to divulge to prospective policyholders any direct or economic connections they have with an insurance undertaking or any shareholding in or by such undertakings. It is also required that such intermediaries declare to the competent authority the spread of their business with different insurance undertakings over the previous year.

The great majority of the requirements set out in the Commission's Recommendation are already in place in the UK. However, the source of such requirements are something of a mish-mash. Some are statutory in nature while some are on a voluntary basis. If the UK intends to implement the Recommendation it will require the political willpower to reorganise the present system and to put it on a more coherent basis.

## 5 THE LLOYD'S BROKER AND THE LAW

Broking insurance business at Lloyd's requires separate treatment to reflect the unique rules that apply (although many of the cases referred to above also concern Lloyd's brokers). "Rules" may in fact be a misleading word as much of what goes on is governed by usage and custom stretching back over several centuries. In recent years, however, there has been a flood of Lloyd's byelaws and regulations following various working party reports and recommendations.[211]

Lloyd's brokers are subject to the supervision of both the Insurance Brokers (Registration) Act 1977 and the Lloyd's Act 1982, and the byelaws made under the Act. These supervisory powers are discussed below.

### 5.1 Formation of the insurance contract

Just as we have seen how the formation of the insurance contract involves three parties—the insurance company, an insurance intermediary or a tied/company

---

211. See *Lloyd's Acts, Byelaws and Regulations* (LLP Limited, looseleaf) and *Ellis: Regulation of Insurance* (Kluwer, looseleaf).

representative and the client—so too at Lloyd's three parties are involved: the underwriters, the Lloyd's broker and the client.

The law regulating the various rights and duties of the parties to a "Lloyd's contract" is, however, sometimes rather obscure, uncertain and at times different from that applying to contracts between insurance companies and clients. This is largely due to the customs and usage of the Lloyd's market. In recent years, however, the courts have been asked to review the uncertainties relating to formation of the contract and the interrelationship of the parties.[212]

Although it may be of little consolation to the insured, it is possible for a Lloyd's broker to be guilty of misconduct under various byelaws. While it may expose such persons to disciplinary proceedings under the byelaws it will not necessarily mean that the party who has suffered a detriment will be successful in any civil action against the wrongdoer.

The basic definitions of misconduct are set down in the Misconduct Penalties and Sanctions Byelaw No 9 of 1993. Thus the byelaw states that a Lloyd's broker, among others, will be guilty of misconduct if he conducts himself in a manner which is detrimental to the interests of a Lloyd's policyholder or conducts any insurance business in a discreditable manner or with lack of good faith or conducts himself in any way which is dishonourable, disgraceful or improper. Most of these descriptions would also apply to the conduct of the Lloyd's broker employee. Furthermore, the Misconduct (Reporting) Byelaw No 11 of 1989 places a person under a duty to report promptly to the deputy chairman and chief executive of the Society any situation where he knows of any actual or proposed misconduct or believes or has reason to believe that any misconduct is likely to occur or is likely to have occurred unless it is of a minor nature.

Where the above byelaws apply, a person against whom disciplinary proceedings have been successful may be subject to exclusion or suspension from the Society, or in the case of a Lloyd's broker revocation or suspension of permission to broke insurance business at Lloyd's. Such a person may also be suspended permanently or temporarily, fined, or censured and reprimanded.

## 5.2 Custom and usage

The earliest references to Lloyd's Coffee House date from around 1688 and it is understandable that early transactions were governed by the usages and customs existing between merchants trading together in London where the subject-matter invariably referred to marine risks often involving foreign parts.

What it clear is that the usages may apply between underwriter and broker but do not necessarily affect the rights of the insured. This is partly because a Lloyd's broker is treated as a principal by the underwriter and not merely as an agent of the client. More importantly, usage cannot bind a person who is not coversant with such usage or custom. Both points are illustrated in the old case of *Scott* v. *Irving*.[213]

---

212. See *La Banque Financiere de la Cite SA* v. *Skandia (UK) Insurance Co and Westgate Insurance Co* [1990] 2 Lloyd's Rep. 377, [1990] 2 All E.R. 947, H.L. The Commercial Court and Court of Appeal judgments are also illustrative of the problems found at Lloyd's. See [1987] 1 Lloyd's Rep. 69 and [1988] 2 Lloyd's Rep. 513.
213. (1830) 1 B. & Ad. 605.

The assured in Glasgow employed the broker to recover his insurance monies from the London underwriter. Payment was made by the underwriter setting off as against the broker premium payments owed by the broker and then paying the balance in cash. The broker became bankrupt and the unpaid assured claimed from the underwriter who in turn argued that such a method of account with the broker was part of the custom.

The court rejected this defence on the grounds that an assured cannot be bound by a custom without first proving that he knew of it. He could not, however, recover the cash balance because he had authorised the broker to receive that money as his agent.

If it could be shown that the assured did know and did accept this method of setting off payments then he would be bound, but that remains a question of evidence in each particular case. Merely including a reference in the policy that payments will be recoverable according to Lloyd's custom would not be sufficient to bind the assured if he could show that he did not know what those customs were. The setting off of accounts between broker and underwriter reflects the normal course of business at the present time and no problems usually arise because the likelihood of bankruptcy of either party is rare, although not unknown.

Custom precludes the underwriter looking to the assured for his premium. As was said in *Universo Ins Co of Milan* v. *Merchant Maritime Ins Co*[214]:

"the underwriter to whom in most instances the assureds are unknown, looks to the broker for payment, and he to the assured. The latter pays the premium to the broker only, and he is a middleman between the assured and the underwriter. But he is not solely agent; he is a principal to receive the money from the assured and to pay it to the underwriter".

In addition to the above, Lloyd's Insurance Intermediaries Byelaw 1990 deals with business placed at Lloyd's by non-Lloyd's intermediaries. Such business can only be done within the limits set out in the byelaw and one requirement is that the Lloyd's broker agrees with the managing agent of the syndicate in question to indemnify the members of the syndicate against non-payment of the premium. The Lloyd's broker would then need to pursue his claim against the other intermediary.

The decision in *Merrett* v. *Capitol Indemnity Corporation*[215] dealt with the single question: when an insured had been paid directly for his loss, or part of it, by his brokers, can that insured nevertheless also make a claim on the insurer? The plaintiffs were reinsured under policies issued by the defendant company. Under an arbitration the plaintiffs were awarded a certain sum and the arbitrators found that the plaintiffs' brokers had part of that award and therefore they went on to award the unpaid amount against the defendants. The plaintiffs appealed, arguing that the full amount of the sum claimed should be paid by the defendants irrespective of the sum paid by the brokers.

Steyn J held for the plaintiffs. He found that the brokers were under no legal liability to pay any part of the award but had done so to save themselves work later and to maintain the goodwill of their clients, the plaintiffs. Apparently such payments are not uncommon in the Lloyd's market and they are seen as a loan for a period of time until the insurance monies are paid over. Despite this practice the

214. [1897] 2 Q.B. 93.
215. [1991] 1 Lloyd's Rep. 169.

arbitrators came to the conclusion, reversed by Steyn J, that this was not what had happened in the instant case, and that what had taken place was an out-and-out payment by the brokers to the plaintiffs.

The court stressed that the judgment would not mean that the plaintiffs would be overcompensated. Counsel for the plaintiffs was at pains to stress that they would in turn account to the brokers for the original payment made once the defendants were held liable for the full amount.

## 5.3 Necessity of using a Lloyd's broker

It is commonly stated that business can only be placed at Lloyd's through a Lloyd's broker because only such a person has access to the underwriting room.

If a client in Manchester who normally uses a local broker wants to place some of his business at Lloyd's, or his local broker advises that this is the most appropriate place for a particular risk, then the local broker must contact a Lloyd's broker for this purpose. The commission will be shared between them on an agreed basis. Each would owe the other a duty of care in the work undertaken.

With the growth of the Lloyd's market into areas other than marine, aviation and other large commercial risks, the market practice has had to adapt to provide an efficient service. Apart from the method of using two or more brokers, new methods known as umbrella agreements have recently been considered in some detail by the court in *Johns* v. *Kelly*.[216]

An umbrella arrangement is "an arrangement between a Lloyd's broker and a non-Lloyd's broker whereby business is transacted at Lloyd's by the directors, partners, or employees of the non-Lloyd's broker acting as if they were directors, partners etc. of the Lloyd's broker itself, using the Lloyd's broker's slips". Such arrangements are known more colloquially as piggybacks or flags of convenience.

The number of umbrella arrangements seen to exist at the time *Johns* v. *Kelly* was before the courts was one of the reasons why the Council introduced the Umbrella Arrangements Byelaw No 6 of 1988.[217] Such an arrangement must be distinguished from a sub-agency agreement which allows direct dealing at Lloyd's.[218] An umbrella arrangement is appropriate in situations where a non-Lloyd's broker intends to apply for registration as a Lloyd's broker at a later date, but during the interim period wishes to be involved in placing business there.

Complicated problems similarly arise, apart from umbrella agreements, when the Lloyd's broker deals with other intermediaries as part of a chain of people placing business.

In *The Okeanis*,[219] the plaintiffs wanted to insure their ship and approached their London agents who in turn contacted the defendant Lloyd's brokers who regularly placed their marine business. The Lloyd' brokers were instructed to place part of the risk with Italian underwriters. To achieve this the Lloyd's brokers approached an Italian intermediary to place part of the risk. On renewal, the Italian insurers

---

216. [1986] 1 Lloyd's Rep. 468.
217. This byelaw was amended by the Umbrella Arrangements (Amendment) Byelaw No.7 of 1990.
218. See Lloyd's Brokers Byelaw No. 5 of 1988 as amended, and Insurance Intermediaries Byelaw No. 8 of 1990, as amended.
219. [1986] 1 Lloyd's Rep. 195.

required a higher rate of premium and the business was, therefore, transferred to a different Italian insurer.

The ship was damaged. The London underwriters agreed the level of compensation and the defendant Lloyd's brokers set about claiming a share from the Italian insurers through the Italian intermediary. The response from the Italian intermediaries was that a direct request should be made to the insurers on the grounds that the intermediaries did not regard themselves as agents of the Italian insurers. The Lloyd's brokers were then informed by the insurers that they had credited the Italian intermediaries with the sum required. The plaintiffs sued the Lloyd's brokers claiming that they had received the money for the plaintiffs' use.

The question therefore in issue was the status of the Italian intermediaries. Were they sub-brokers and thus agents of the defendant brokers; were they agents of the Italian insurers or were they acting for both brokers and insurers at different stages of the transaction?

The Commercial Court held that the Lloyd's brokers were not liable to the plaintiffs for any sums received by the Italian intermediaries. The business relationship pointed to the Italian intermediaries being agents of the Italian insurers and not agents of the Lloyd's brokers. The signing of the slips and the payment of premiums directly to the insurers were consistent with that view and were further reinforced by the important fact that there was no evidence that suggested that the Italian intermediaries had any authority from either the Lloyd's brokers or the plaintiffs to receive cash or to settle accounts by mutual set-off so as to discharge the Italian insurers.

The defendants had done nothing to deprive the plaintiffs of their right to recover directly from the Italian insurers. All that the defendants were liable for was to repay to the plaintiffs any premiums still held by them for the Italian insurers. If the Italian intermediaries had been regarded as sub-agents of the Lloyd's brokers then the brokers would have been liable for any money received by the sub-agents for the principal.

Clearly, the biggest problem in an involved chain such as this is to classify the relationships. The court accepted the argument that under Italian law it was a relatively new idea that agents acted for assureds. The Lloyd's brokers relied on this argument by stating that throughout the proceedings they always assumed that the Italian intermediaries were acting on behalf of the Italian insurers.

## 5.4 The slip[220]

The formation of the insurance contract at Lloyd's is unique and therefore so too is the broker's role. A number of recent cases has helped to clarify previously unclear areas. The broker is the agent of the client and must divulge all relevant facts to the underwriter when seeking cover. Thus, despite his description of "Lloyd's broker", it does not mean that information that he possesses will be implied to the underwriter.[221]

---

220. For a detailed analysis, see Bennett, "The role of the slip in marine insurance law" [1994] L.M.C.L.Q. 94.
221. See *Roberts* v. *Plaisted* [1989] 2 Lloyd's Rep. 341 where the Court of Appeal was critical of this situation.

The procedure for obtaining cover is that the broker prepares a "slip" which is a document setting out the main aspects of the risk requiring cover. The information entered on the slip obviously varies from one class of business to another and, even then, the language is heavily abbreviated.

The broker should have a professional view of the various areas of specialisation offered by certain syndicates and will then approach an underwriter offering the class of business required. The first signature to the slip will usually become the lead underwriter and his initialling will help to convince others who are approached by the broker to follow his lead.

Each underwriter will accept a percentage of the total cover. It is possible that a subsequent subscriber will take a larger percentage than the lead underwriter.

It is also possible for later underwriters to add amendments to the wording of the original cover and then problems arise as to the position of the earlier subscribers. The amendments would be shown to them in the expectation that they will accept the modifications. If this is not done, it may be necessary for the broker to prepare more than one contract on differing terms.

It is also possible for the slip to be oversubscribed in which case it will be necessary for the broker to arrange a proportional scaling down.

Where the slip is undersubscribed, then the policy will go ahead for only a proportion of the originally desired cover and the insured is deemed to be his own insurer for the balance.

The slip or slips are then sent to the Lloyd's Policy Signing Office where language which is almost unintelligible from the client's point of view is put into a formal policy which should be intelligible.

Throughout the operation the broker is clearly required to act with the highest professional competence and integrity in order to acquaint the various underwriters with all details of the risk he is attempting to place. Failure to meet the high standards required will expose him to an accusation of negligence by the underwriters. Failure to meet the legitimate expectations of the client will similarly place him in a potentially dangerous legal situation.

It is instructive to look in some detail at the cases involving Lloyd's brokers and more generally at the formation of a contract at Lloyd's because of some of the unusual features described above.

In *Rozanes* v. *Bowen*,[222] Scrutton LJ went out of his way to explain the placing of business at Lloyd's on the grounds that the plaintiff was a foreign national who would probably be unfamiliar with the system. The plaintiff had declared previous claims for burglary losses to an agent in Paris who failed to inform the Lloyd's broker. When the contract was avoided following a later claim, the plaintiff sued the underwriter and failed.

It was explained that while there might be problems with the legal position of an intermediary working with a non-Lloyd's insurer in receiving information from the client no such doubt existed within the Lloyd's market. The broker does not know when he starts to approach the underwriters which, if any, will agree to subscribe to the slip. It is not possible, therefore, to argue that the agent in Paris is the agent of

---

222. (1928) 32 Ll.L.Rep. 98, C.A.

Lloyd's, for in the beginning he does not know who at Lloyd's will ultimately subscribe to the slip.

In *American Airlines Inc* v. *Hope*,[223] Lord Diplock's judgment provides an excellent review of the Lloyd's broker's position in the market. He said:

"Contracts of insurance are placed at Lloyd's by a broker acting exclusively as agent for the assured. It is he who prepares the slip in which he undertakes in the customary 'shorthand' to obtain the cover that the assured requires. He takes the slip in the first instance to an underwriter whom he has selected to deal with as leading underwriter, i.e., one who has a reputation in the market as an expert in the kind of cover required and whose lead is likely to be followed by other insurers in the market. If it is the first contract of insurance covering that risk in which a particular underwriter has acted as leading underwriter it is treated as an original insurance. The broker and the leading underwriter go through the slip together. They agree on any amendments to the broker's draft and fix the premium. When agreement has been reached, the leading underwriter initials the slip for his proportion of the cover and the broker then takes the initialled slip round the market to other insurers who initial it for such proportions of the cover as each is willing to accept. For practical purposes all the negotiations about the terms of the insurance and the rate of premium are carried out between the broker and the leading underwriter alone. Where, as is often the case, the slip gives the assured options to cover additional aircraft or additional risks during the period of cover, it does so on terms to be agreed with the leading underwriter."

Lord Diplock also dealt with renewals of an original cover. He explained that where there are no substantial alterations the expiring slip is shown to the lead underwriter and the only matter for negotiation is usually the renewal premium. In such cases it is normal practice for the broker to indicate that no substantial changes are required by adding the words "as expiring" to the renewal slip.

It is the broker's obvious duty to inform that underwriter of any changes, just as it is his duty to inform him fully of all relevant details when negotiating the original cover. Brokers keep copies of all slips and policies issued to their clients whereas it is not customary for the leading underwriter to do so.

The *Fennia Patria* case[224] helps to clear up earlier doubts relating both to the contractual position of the parties to a partially subscribed slip or where later underwriters made amendments to the wording of the slip.

*Jaglom* v. *Excess Insurance Co Ltd*[225] had suggested that where the slip was not fully subscribed there was no concluded contract between the various underwriters and the assured. The *Fennia Patria* case, however, has stated that each signature to the slip concludes a binding contract between the parties for the percentage of the risk shown, assuming of course that the underwriter has not attached any conditions to his acceptance. There must be an unqualified acceptance.

If the underwriter does amend the broker's details on the slip, this becomes a counter-offer and the broker will be put in a position, as agent of the intending assured, to accept or reject the alteration. Before reaching his decision he should refer back to his principal (the "assured") for instructions or explain the situation to him.

Would the assured be in a position to withdraw from the contract prior to the slip

223. [1974] 2 Lloyd's Rep. 301, H.L.
224. [1983] 2 Lloyd's Rep. 287.
225. [1972] 2 Q.B. 250, [1971] 2 Lloyd's Rep. 171.

being fully subscribed? The Court of Appeal recognised that underwriters often permit the assured to do this but added that such a practice did not have the force of law and was not therefore a binding custom.

## 5.5 Dual agency

We have discussed earlier the situation where an independent adviser appears to act for both parties to the insurance contract.[226] The common situation is where the intermediary has a "binder" from an insurer to write cover on behalf of that insurer within certain specified limits without the need to go back to the insurer for approval. At the other end of the transaction some intermediaries have the power to settle claims, again within certain limits.

The decision in *Forsikringsaktieselskapet Vesta* v. *Butcher*[227] provides an illustration of the dual role of a broker in a more complex fact situation. The plaintiffs were Norwegian insurers who had insured their customer's fish farm against loss of fish. They sought 90 per cent reinsurance cover on the London insurance market using Lloyd's brokers. The first interesting aspect of the case is that the particular policy that provided this type of reinsurance cover was a policy which had been pioneered not by the underwriters but by the brokers themselves. They had decided that there was a worldwide demand for this specialist type of cover and they had proceeded to establish a subsidiary company to develop it. Having done so they were then in a position to sell the idea to the underwriters. In the words of Sir Roger Ormrod in the Court of Appeal:

"the brokers were certainly not acting in the conventional role of Lloyd's brokers, i.e., exclusively as agents for their clients [Vesta] seeking an insurance cover. On the contrary, they, through their subsidiary Aquacultural Insurance Services Ltd [the third defendant] were the prime movers. They designed the form of words to be used in contracts for the insurance of fish farms. They negotiated with underwriters and obtained their approval to this form of words and arranged that the business would be done in the form of reinsurance at a time when they had no actual clients and no 'original' insurance to be reinsured. One could not help wondering, whether brokers acting exclusively for Vesta would have allowed the disastrous situation in which they may be to arise in the first place."

The disastrous situation referred to is concerned with complications of insurance/reinsurance/conflict of laws/construction matters beyond the scope of the present discussion. One point, however, does concern us in particular. The reinsurance contract required that there was to be a 24-hour watch on the fish farm. The insured realised that they could not provide such security and they instructed their Norwegian insurers, Vesta, to inform the brokers of the problem. The brokers did not reply to Vesta's request and the reinsurance contract remained unaltered. Following a major storm loss, Vesta paid out on their policy and sought to enforce the reinsurance contract. They succeeded but only after a long battle through the courts.

---

226. See the discussion of *Stockton* v. *Mason* [1978] 2 Lloyd's Rep. 430, C.A. (below).

227. All three courts found for the plaintiff. The discussion at each level concentrated on various legal rules. It is worth noting each court's reference: High Court [1986] 2 Lloyd's Rep. 179, [1986] 2 All E.R. 488; Court of Appeal [1988] 1 Lloyd's Rep. 19, [1988] 2 All E.R. 43; and the House of Lords, which did not have to deal with the role of the broker, [1989] 1 Lloyd's Rep. 331, [1989] 1 All E.R. 402.

They proceeded also initially, however, against the brokers to cover the event of their possible failure to enforce their claim against the reinsurers.

The courts had no doubt that despite their dual role in the transaction the brokers did owe a duty of care to Vesta. This duty was both in contract and in tort; Hobhouse J, having held the reinsurers liable, awarded £1 nominal damages against the brokers. However, he went on to consider what would have been the liability of the brokers to Vesta if Vesta had failed in their original action against the reinsurers. This required him to examine the complex question of the applicability of the Law Reform (Contributory Negligence) Act 1945 to the facts of the case.

One might wonder why the question was relevant in the first place. The brokers argued that when Vesta failed to receive any reply to their request that the 24-hour watch condition be removed the onus was back on them to follow up with more inquiries. There is no real discussion in the judgments of why a client should shoulder the burden of seeing that the other party performs his professional and contractual duties. Such a burden was, however, assumed to exist by Hobhouse J. Thus it was then possible for the brokers to allege that Vesta was guilty of contributory negligence if the 1945 Act could be held to apply to the situation.[228]

The judge held that it did apply and somewhat surprisingly he then proceeded to apportion the blame 75 per cent against Vesta and 25 per cent against the brokers.

A more realistic apportionment was awarded by Phillips J in *Youell and Others* v. *Bland Welch & Co* (the *Superhulls Cover* case).[229]

Insurers in the London market had failed on a reinsurance claim and now brought an action against the firms of brokers who had obtained the reinsurance alleging negligence by them. Although the facts relating to the reinsurance are complex, the basis for the allegation of negligence was that the reinsurance cover did not run for the same length of time as the original insurance.

The plaintiff insurers argued that if they had been informed that the reinsurance did not cover their basic exposure they would not have accepted the reinsurance and they would not have accepted so large an exposure on the original insurance. The brokers raised numerous defences, mainly built around the proposition that the plaintiffs must have been aware of the wording of the reinsurance. Their final defence was that if they were liable then the plaintiffs were contributorily negligent.

Two groups of brokers had been involved in the arranging of the reinsurance cover but they later merged and, as Phillips J said, the merger had at least removed the potential division of responsibility between the two groups.

The court found for the plaintiffs under a number of headings. First, the brokers were in breach of their duty in failing to obtain for the plaintiffs adequate reinsurance cover. Secondly, the brokers had been responsible for drafting the contractual wording of the policy. They had failed to exercise reasonable skill and care when undertaking that task. Thirdly, having obtained inadequate cover, the brokers failed to warn the plaintiffs of the inadequate performance of their initial obligation. They should also have attempted to obtain an extension of the reinsurance so that it matched the requirements of the initial insurance cover.

---

228. This matter is dealt with in chapter 2.
229. Sir Roger Ormrod in the Court of Appeal: "His ratio 75:25 surprised me somewhat." The other judges made no comment on the apportionment despite the fact that Vesta had questioned the division as being wholly unreasonable.

One of the lines of defence was that the plaintiffs, particularly as they were themselves insurers, should have checked the wording of the reinsurance and would then have detected the mistake. In failing to do so the defendants alleged that there was a break in the chain of causation. This argument had been rejected in *Dickson* v. *Devitt*[230] and in *General Accident Fire and Life Assurance Corp Ltd* v. *Minet*[231] and was no more successful in the present case. Phillips J held that there was no justification for imposing a duty on the client to check that what he had instructed his broker to do had been efficiently accomplished.

However, the defendants' argument based on contributory negligence was successful. In reaching that conclusion the judge dealt in some detail with the court's judgment in *Vesta* v. *Butcher*.[232] The relationship of the parties in the present case was similar to that in *Vesta* v. *Butcher* and fell within category (3) in that case.

In arriving at a finding of 20 per cent contributory negligence on the part of the plaintiffs, Phillips J explained:

"There is no question in this case of the insurers' negligence breaking the chain of causation. Whether considered from the viewpoint of blameworthiness or causative potency, the majority of the liability for the insurers' loss must fall on the brokers. They were wholly responsible for the insurers' initial over-exposure. They were primarily responsible for the failure on the part of themselves and the insurers to wake up to the implications of the 48-month clause. They were primarily responsible for the consequent failure to put in place a mechanism that would have led to the obtaining of extensions of cover when the 48-month periods elapsed. They were primarily responsible for the failure to obtain those extensions. In all those respects they were in breach of a contractual duty to exercise skill and care. The insurers were guilty of a failure to exercise reasonable care in carrying out what they accepted were customary checks on the manner in which the brokers had performed their duty."

In both *Vesta* and *Youell* the plaintiffs were themselves insurers whose contributory negligence reflected their position in the insurance market. It is to be hoped that there would be no finding, except perhaps in the most glaring of situations, that a non-specialist insured would be guilty of contributory negligence. There should be no "customary checks" on seeing that a professional person had done what the consumer expects of him.

## 6 REINSURANCE AND THE BROKER[233]

Reinsurance is the method whereby the original insurer(s) of a risk "lay off" part or even all of that risk with other insurers. This is a sophisticated branch of insurance practice. The burden on the broker (it is not only Lloyd's brokers or Lloyd's that deal with reinsurance) is a heavy one. Not only will he be dealing in large sums, but his role is complicated in that he deals as agent of both the ceding insurer and the reinsurer at various stages of the transaction and thus problems of conflict of interest may arise. Some of the cases that follow are not necessarily concerned with Lloyd's brokers[234] but with the role of brokers generally in reinsurance.

---

230. (1916) 86 L.J.K.B. 315.
231. 74 Ll.L.Rep. 179.
232. [1986] 2 Lloyd's Rep. 179.
233. See *Reinsurance Practice and the Law* (LLP Limited, looseleaf), chapter 2.
234. See *Vesta* v. *Butcher* and *Youell* v. *Bland Welch*, discussed above.

Reference should first be made to marine reinsurance because the duty here appears not to reflect the duty owed in non-marine cases. In *Empress Assurance Corp Ltd* v. *Bowring*,[235] a broker effected reinsurance for the ceding company with the plaintiff. The premiums were to be the same as those received by the ceding company although, unknown to the plaintiff, the broker's commission was first deducted. When this was later discovered the plaintiff sued the broker arguing that he was in breach of a duty to the plaintiff in not advising the plaintiff as to the true premium figure.

The court found that in marine insurance no such duty existed. All that was required of the broker was a duty to act honestly. The suggestion was also made that neither would there be liability for negligence, although such suggestion might not be good today, particularly where dual agency would appear to be more common. The early cases, however, bear out the suggestion of limited liability.

In a case involving burglary insurance in 1925 Scrutton LJ stated that it was elementary marine insurance law that earlier refusals by an insurer need not be disclosed to a later underwriter whereas in all other branches of insurance such information is regarded as material to be risk.

Scrutton LJ followed Bowring in *Glasgow Ass* v. *Symondson & Co*[236] and used a more graphic example of the unique position of the broker in marine insurance. He said that even when the broker is paid commission by the underwriter and prepares the documentation it would generally be erroneous to assume that he has become the underwriter's agent and owed him any duty other than to be honest in his dealings with him.

In *Mackenzie* v. *Whitworth*,[237] it was further held that the broker is under no duty to disclose that the marine risk which he is seeking to reinsure is in fact a reinsurance. The defendant reinsurer argued that it was the invariable practice in such matters to declare the true position. The court was quick to point out that until 1864 reinsurance contracts were prohibited by statute and therefore there could hardly be an invariable practice built up in so short a time. Despite the passage of time, it is assumed that it remains unnecessary to make such a declaration because the court further found that such an omission does not vary the nature of the risk itself and is, therefore, not material.

It would seem, therefore, that marine insurance practice may hold a special place and not be affected by the sweeping demands of the rule in *Hedley Byrne* v. *Heller*, whereby professional people owe a duty of care in negligence based on foreseeability and proximity of relationship. But the position is further complicated by a statement by Hobhouse J in *The Zephyr*[238] where he said that both *Symondson* and *Bowring* were decisions that were no longer authoritative after *Hedley Byrne* and he reinforced this view by pointing out that a broker's errors and omissions policy wording supported his view that the market felt that it was subject to the rule in *Hedley Byrne*. This matter was not commented upon when *The Zephyr* was heard in the Court of Appeal (the case is dealt with in some detail below).

The view of Hobhouse J was referred to by Waller J in *Pryke* v. *Gibbs Hartley*

235. (1905) 11 Com.Cas. 107.
236. (1911) 104 L.T. 254.
237. (1875) 1 Ex.D. 36.
238. [1984] 1 Lloyd's Rep. 58.

*Cooper Ltd*[239] when the judge agreed that after the decision in *Hedley Byrne*, the earlier cases depending as they did on *Le Lievre* v. *Gould*[240] could no longer be regarded as good law on this point.

Although *CTI* v. *Oceanus Mutual Underwriting Ass (Bermuda) Ltd*[241] is not a reinsurance case, mention should be made of it here because it reflects the complications faced by the Lloyd's broker when negotiating marine insurance with successive but different insurers. In essence the plaintiffs ran a container leasing business and wanted to insure against damage to their containers. Their claims experience with American insurers was so bad that their American brokers contacted Lloyd's brokers with a view to placing the business on the London market. This was done and the basis of the quotations partly relied on the American experiences. Lloyd's underwriters' experience was subsequently such that new insurers were required by the Lloyd's brokers and the business was placed with Oceanus. Both the American and Lloyd's underwriters' experience was used as the basis of negotiation. In both sets of negotiations there was a failure by the brokers to disclose fully all the relevant earlier information.

There was no allegation of fraud or dishonesty but merely an argument that the broker had failed to meet the obligations of section 19 of the Marine Insurance Act 1906. This requires that an agent must disclose to an insurer every material circumstance which is known to him and that an agent is deemed to know every circumstance which in the ordinary course of business ought to be known by or to have been communicated to him, and every material circumstance which the assured is bound to disclose, unless it comes to his knowledge too late to communicate it to the agent.

The undeclared facts were clearly material. One line of defence was that the individual placing broker did not personally have the relevant information at the time. But his head office did. Clearly this can provide no sound defence. The Court of Appeal said that if the broker's firm chose to organise its business in such a way that material information did not reach a particular broker acting on its behalf this would provide no excuse. Obviously this applies to any firm of intermediaries. It is essential that the head office, highly computerised as it may be for receiving information, must provide the facilities for transmitting that information to its personnel in the field.

Of particular importance in this case is the way the Court of Appeal dealt with the marine rule that earlier refusals of cover are not relevant and need not be disclosed to later underwriters. This rule was to be distinguished from the situation where the broker or assured gave some information relating to the earlier insurance history. Once some information was given it might well amount to a misrepresentation if a true and complete explanation of earlier dealings were not divulged. Thus to offer no information, unless asked, is safer than giving only limited information. The court relied on *Sibbald* v. *Hill*[242] where a policy was vitiated when the assured incorrectly stated that early cover had been offered at a certain premium on a certain risk.

In non-marine reinsurance, however, the broker's role may carry with it greater

---

239. [1991] 1 Lloyd's Rep. 602 at 618. The decision is dealt with in more detail below.
240. [1893] 1 Q.B. 491.
241. [1984] 1 Lloyd's Rep. 476, C.A. See, however, the House of Lords' decision in *Pan Atlantic Ins Co* v. *Pine Top Ins Co* [1994] 3 All E.R. 581.
242. (1814) 2 Dow. 263.

obligations to the reinsurer. In *Equitable Life Ass Soc* v. *General Accident Ass Corp*,[243] the plaintiff company had insured a life for £2,000. The insured had correctly described himself as a driver of motor cars and admitted taking part in motor races (in 1900!). The plaintiff asked the brokers to reinsure the whole sum. The broker arranged this with the defendant company who paid his commission. In this transaction the original insured's occupation was given as "gentleman". He was killed during a race.

The Scottish court held that the defendants were not liable because of the misrepresentation. Even though the broker was in full possession of the true facts and was acting at least in part for the defendants, his knowledge should not be imputed to the defendants. The imputation of knowledge is a difficult area particularly in situations where the broker is acting in this dual role of agent for both sides.

The dividing line of when there is or is not liability is shown in two cases involving the same ceding company.

In *Blackburn Low & Co* v. *Vigors*,[244] the plaintiffs instructed brokers to arrange insurance on an overdue ship. Before doing so the brokers received information that the ship had been lost but they did not tell the plaintiffs. Reinsurance went ahead using the brokers' London agents. At a later date the plaintiffs effected a second reinsurance "lost or not lost". Such cover is enforceable even if the ship has been lost prior to insuring but not if the insured knows of the loss and the insurer does not. The second contract was arranged through different brokers. Crucially then the problem was whether or not the broker's knowledge was to be imputed to the plaintiffs.

The *Vigors* case is concerned with the second reinsurance and *Blackburn Low & Co* v. *Haslam*[245] concerns the first policy. The court held that, in *Vigors*, the plaintiffs were not saddled with the first broker's knowledge when they were acting through a second firm of brokers. In *Haslam*, however, the policy of reinsurance was void because the broker was acting for the plaintiffs and his knowledge must be imputed to his principals.

What was attempted by the defendant in *Vigors* was to argue that the plaintiffs had constructive notice of the ship's loss on the basis that the broker, who no longer represented them, knew of it. As one member of the court said, it had frequently been held by judges that the doctrine of constructive notice ought not to be extended and to do so here would be a dangerous extension of the doctrine.

*Vigors* was referred to in *Simner* v. *New India Assurance Co Ltd*.[246] The plaintiff claimed under a stop loss reinsurance policy effected with the defendant company who themselves sued on a counterclaim to include the plaintiff's brokers as third parties. The defence argument was that they had been induced to enter into the contract by material misrepresentations made to them by the plaintiff's brokers. The court found for the plaintiffs.

Reference was made to the "good faith" requirements set out in sections 17–19 of the Marine Insurance Act 1906 (which apply equally to non-marine policies). In particular section 19, entitled "Disclosure by agent effecting insurance", reads:

243. (1904) 12 S.L.T. 348.
244. (1877) 17 Q.B.D. 553, C.A.
245. (1888) 21 Q.B.D. 144.
246. (1994) *The Times*, 21 July.

"Subject to the provisions of the preceding section as to circumstances which need not be disclosed, where an insurance is effected for the assured by an agent, the agent must disclose to the insurer—

(a) every material circumstance which is known to himself and an agent to insure is deemed to know every circumstance which in the ordinary course of business ought to be known by, or to have been communicated to him; and

(b) every material circumstance which the assured is bound to disclose, unless it comes to his knowledge too late to communicate it to the agent."

However, the court stressed that neither the 1906 Act nor any authority suggests that in order to make a fair representation it is necessary for the assured to make inquiries or investigations as to facts outside his knowledge. In the present case the assured had no relevant information to pass on. Of crucial importance was the fact that the defendant made no inquiries of the assured which might have required the assured to make such investigations in order to answer fairly any such questions. The defendant's behaviour was considered by the brokers to be "foolish", in that they were prepared to underwrite without seeking further and better particulars.

The court set out the assured's position in such a situation: he is under no duty of care not to cause financial loss to the insurer; he is under no duty to advise the insurer whether or not to write the risk. The insurer is presumed to know his own business and to be capable of forming his own judgement.

But where the broker is clearly representing his principal, his knowledge is the knowledge of the principal. This is further illustrated in *Eagle Star Ins Co* v. *Spratt*,[247] a case which also shows the functions of the Lloyd's Policy Signing Office ("LPSO"), and the brokers' involvement. The LPSO's function is to put the slip's wording into an intelligible policy format. The broker's duty is to check that this policy accords with the slip.

In *Spratt* the plaintiffs reinsured using two Lloyd's brokers. Several underwriters raised objections about the policies and a steering committee was established to iron out the problems. New agreements were reached and the brokers took these terms to underwriters for initialling. One underwriter objected that there had been an unauthorised initialling on behalf of his syndicate and that the LPSO had exceeded their authority in stamping the policy. The broker, it was alleged, knew of these flaws and his knowledge must be imputed to his principals.

The Court of Appeal agreed, holding the defendant underwriter not liable on his share of the cover. The brokers had presumptive knowledge of the situation and this must be imputed to their principals, the ceding company. The court were also of the opinion that, as Eagle Star knew from their own correspondence with the underwriter that a true agreement on all matters had not been reached, any policy issued by LPSO exceeded their authority.

Problems created by the changing role of the broker in complex insurance and reinsurance placings together with an analysis of sections 18 and 19 of the Marine Insurance Act 1906[248] were the subject-matter of complex litigation in *Société Anonyme d'Intermediaries Luxembourgeois* v. *Farex Gie and Others*.[249]

SAIL were captive brokers in the AIG group of companies. SAIL wanted to

247. [1971] 2 Lloyd's Rep. 116, C.A.
248. These sections also apply to non-marine insurance.
249. [1995] L.R.L.R. 116, C.A. See also fn. 159.

arrange a facility for reinsurance of risks underwritten by AIG. This would allow SAIL to broke an increased amount of business for AIG. To achieve this SAIL instructed brokers Heath Fielding ("HF") to arrange the reinsurance facility. HF approached St Paul Fire & Marine. While declining the reinsurance offer St Paul expressed an interest in retrocession insurance (i.e., reinsurance of reinsurance) if a suitable reinsurer could be found. A "mock slip" was signed by St Paul. HF then approached Farex who explained that they would consider a line slip if suitable retrocession was obtained by HF. Eventually, Farex signed the line slip for the reinsurance of SAIL adding the words "subject to reinsurance and security". HF purported to confirm retrocession arrangements with St Paul.

To recap it can be seen that SAIL have instructed HF; HF then approached St Paul; HF then approached Farex. HF issued a cover note to SAIL confirming reinsurance placed with Farex having erased the proviso about "confirmation". Eventually, St Paul claimed that it was not bound by any retrocession arrangements with Farex on the grounds that an underwriter of St Paul who had accepted the retrocession from HF had no authority to do so and this fact was known to HF.

Farex in turn claimed that they were not liable under the reinsurance agreements because no suitable retrocession existed. One part of their defence was that in law SAIL was deemed or presumed to have had HF's knowledge that the St Paul underwriter had no authority to commit St Paul to the retrocession with Farex.

If Farex had been misled by HF as to the validity of the retrocession was SAIL responsible for HF's misrepresentation? Hoffmann LJ held that HF acted as agents for Farex and not for SAIL when it concluded or purported to conclude the retrocession agreement. In addition, the status of the retrocession between Farex and St Paul was not a material circumstance, within sections 17, 18 and 19 of the Marine Insurance Act 1906, which needed to be disclosed in arranging the reinsurance between SAIL and Farex. Thus it was not necessary for the court to decide whether HF's knowledge of the invalidity of the retrocession would be imputed to SAIL under section 18 or disclosable by HF under section 19. HF's knowledge could not be imputed to SAIL for the purposes of section 18.[250]

Saville LJ summed up the point in issue here by saying[251]:

"It simply does not follow that everything which the agent ... does in order to carry out his instructions is to be treated as done on behalf and with the authority of his principal; and the fact that the principal knows what the agent is going to do makes no difference. Were the law otherwise, then it would mean, for example, that a broker who (to the knowledge of the intending assured) had to take on additional staff in order to carry out the principal's instructions would be employing them on behalf of the principal, to whom they could look for their wages etc. This self-evidently can not be so ... a broker carrying out instructions on behalf of an intending assured may have to undertake obligations to others in order to perform his mandate. In the present case it is to my mind clear that in obtaining (or purportedly obtaining) retrocession from St Paul and in informing (or misinforming) Farex that this had been done, Heath Fielding were acting as brokers to Farex and carrying out (or purporting to carry out) instructions that they had received, not from SAIL, but from Farex. There is simply nothing to suggest that SAIL gave any authority to Heath Fielding to act on behalf of SAIL in making or

250. The court preferred the reasoning of *Blackburn Low & Co* v. *Vigors* (1887) 12 App.Cas. 531 at 542 to that expressed in *Deutsche Ruckversicherung AG* v. *Walbrook Insurance Co Ltd* [1995] 1 Lloyd's Rep. 153; see also [1996] 1 All E.R. 791, C.A.

251. In the final analysis the court answered several points addressed to it which are not specifically in point here.

reporting the making of retrocession for Farex. The knowledge of SAIL that this would be done does not amount to authority from SAIL to do it on their behalf."

Case illustrations used throughout this chapter do not always show intermediaries as parties to the legal action even though the outcome of that action often hinges on their behaviour during the transaction. This does not mean that they will escape liability. When the principal finds himself uninsured and that resulted from the intermediary's clear-cut negligence then there is little to be gained by incurring further legal expenses by protracted litigation. A settlement will be hammered out. Apart from a saving on legal fees it does neither party much good to be seen locked in legal battle.

However, even these two commonsense reasons will be to no avail when the intermediary refuses to accept that he is legally responsible. The quality of his defence may well vary as the following two reinsurance cases show.

In *Everett* v. *Hogg, Robinson and Gardner Mountain (Ins) Ltd*,[252] the plaintiff underwriter instructed Lloyd's brokers to effect reinsurance of one of the plaintiff's policies. A crucial question asked of the brokers was whether the insured stored plastics at his factory. An assurance that no plastics were stored was given. This was untrue and the reinsurers successfully repudiated liability. When sued for negligence, the brokers raised two defences.

First, they said that they had been given the wrong information by the plaintiff. Clearly, this was a matter of evidence for the court, but the case illustrates that keeping proper records may be crucial to success or failure. This is particularly so when communication is face to face or over the telephone.[253] Here the court found that an alleged telephone call had not been made. The court was influenced by an admittance by the broker that, on that particular Friday afternoon, he was under a lot of pressure. Such a statement may provide some sympathy; but it does not provide a legal defence.

The second line of defence and the way the court dealt with it is of special interest. The brokers argued that even if they were negligent the reinsurers would have additionally been able to repudiate because the plaintiffs had themselves given incorrect information with regard to their previous claims experience. The court rejected this argument. It pointed out that the relationship between cedant and reinsurer was good and, therefore, in the judge's opinion, the reinsurer would not have taken this point in order to repudiate the policy but would have come to a compromise on the figure claimed. This the judge put at two-thirds of the sum claimed. Thus the brokers were liable for that sum.

This is an unusual approach, but a similar view was taken by the Court of Appeal in *Fraser* v. *Furman*[254] and *Dunbar* v. *A & B Painters*.[255] The court in these three cases had no evidence on which to base their assessments. The judgments must be reconciled, if possible, with the earlier decision in *Thomas Cheshire & Co* v. *Vaughan Bros & Co*[256] (which is not a reinsurance case).

The plaintiffs as warehouse owners instructed brokers to obtain a policy ("policy

252. [1973] 2 Lloyd's Rep. 217.
253. See *Hadenfayre* v. *British National Insurance Society* [1984] 2 Lloyd's Rep. 393.
254. [1967] 2 Lloyd's Rep. 1.
255. [1986] 2 Lloyd's Rep. 38, discussed above.
256. [1920] 3 K.B. 240.

proof of interest") on goods arriving from South America. Such shipments at that time were controlled by the British Government and were liable to deviation at any time at the Government's dictate. The brokers failed to inform the insurers of this fact and when a deviation took place and the plaintiffs claimed for their loss of expected profits the insurers successfully defended the claim on the grounds of non-disclosure. The plaintiffs then sued their brokers and lost.

The probable distinction between this finding and the previous three cases, where brokers were liable on contracts successfully avoided by insurers, is that here such a policy was null and void for want of insurable interest, a fatal drawback for a valid insurance contract. Therefore, to hold the brokers liable would in some way legitimate a contract which Parliament had declared invalid and to that extent be against public policy.[257]

An important decision illustrating the complexities facing the Lloyd's broker when arranging reinsurance is seen in the judgments given in *The Zephyr*.[258]

The case shows how the Lloyd's broker may serve more than one principal and the complications that may arise when the broker offers to obtain a "signing down" on the slip. The plaintiffs insured the *Zephyr* and paid out on its constructive total loss. They then sought to recover against four defendant underwriters who had accepted reinsurance lines and the four defendants claimed against the brokers, the fifth defendant.

The factual background leading to the disagreements deserves mention because it further illustrates the working practices at Lloyd's which have not previously been subject to close examination by the courts. When an insurer is asked to quote on a risk it will be important to him to know if and at what rate he will be able to obtain reinsurance. It is therefore not unusual for brokers to seek quotes on the reinsurance before the original insurance is concluded.

This was done here. This led to the reinsurers' first defence, namely, that the brokers were arranging reinsurance of a non-existent policy and therefore they had no principals. This matter was dealt with shortly in the Commercial Court and not pursued in the Court of Appeal. Hobhouse J said that English law recognised that, where two parties intend to create a legal relationship of a commercial character, it would be wrong to frustrate their intentions on the grounds of some analytical difficulties.

The second line of argument is more important to our discussion. The first four defendant reinsurers alleged negligence and breach of contract by the brokers in arranging the reinsurance. The basis for this argument was the allegation that the broker had given clear signing down indications to the reinsurers which were not met, thus exposing them to a much greater share of the loss than anticipated.

Signing down occurs when the slip is oversubscribed. If the broker continues to seek subscriptions in excess of the 100 per cent he needs, then the practice is that each line is scaled down. Thus if 200 per cent is obtained each subscriber will have his line halved.

The broker here had a reputation at Lloyd's of heavily oversubscribing his slips and then signing down. On the original cover he had obtained 282 per cent

257. Marine Insurance Act 1906, s. 4(2)(b).
258. [1984] 1 Lloyd's Rep. 58.

subscription and thus the written line was signed down to about 35 per cent. But on the reinsurance slip, due to pressure of work, only a slight oversubscription was obtained so that it signed down to 88 per cent, whereas the reinsurers alleged that they had been given an indication that it would sign down to 33 per cent.

Hobhouse J agreed with this argument and held the brokers liable to all four reinsurers. On appeal by the brokers that they had given no such indication to the second and third reinsurers, the Court of Appeal allowed the appeal. No appeal was made by the brokers with regard to their liability to the other two reinsurers. The contract issue for the brokers revolved around their obligations when presenting the slip.

Mustill LJ in the Court of Appeal considered that there were three main issues for consideration. First, does a signing indication by a broker to an underwriter involve the broker in any legally enforceable obligation? Secondly, if the answer is that it does, is that obligation to be characterised as contractual, tortious or both? Thirdly, and very important in this case, can a signing indication given to one underwriter create obligations towards other underwriters who subsequently initial the slip? The relationship, Mustill LJ decided, was contractual in this case.

This was so because the broker made a promise implicit in the signing, in return for the reinsurer's subscription of the slip, whereby the broker would earn his remuneration. This would meet the essential requirements of a collateral contract which ran alongside the primary contracts between insurer and reinsurer. Hobhouse J, however, had rejected this type of analysis in the Commercial Court.

Could there exist a relationship in tort, particularly within the compass of *Hedley Byrne* v. *Heller*? Hobhouse J thought that there could on the basis that there had been a gradual expansion in the cases of a generalised duty of care sufficient to cover the present relationship and dealings between broker and underwriter.

Mustill LJ agreed there had been a general growth of liability but he felt that it did not go so far as to cover the facts of this case. The general expansion of the duty of care required a person to avoid doing something or to avoid doing something badly. In the present case the broker was giving a bare promise "in circumstances where the parties stood in no relationship other than one where one party is speaking to the other about a transaction being effected between that other and a third party" (the original insurer).

In order to consider whether or not a duty could be owed to the second and third defendants, the Court of Appeal accepted that in certain circumstances it might be possible to recognise a tortious obligation even in the absence of contract. Would that obligation then extend to those to whom no signing down indication had been given?

Mustill LJ decided that no such obligation would be owed. To find otherwise would lead to the possibility of a broker's liability arising from another underwriter overhearing the conversation between the broker and the first underwriter or even where the first underwriter repeated the statements made to him to the second underwriter. Existing legal rules would not admit such a liability.

The question then arose as to whether there was anything in the London insurance market that created its own special rules. This could be argued in three ways. First, that the lead underwriter was somehow to be regarded as an agent for later underwriters. This was totally rejected by the court.

Secondly, can a misrepresentation to the lead underwriter entitling him to avoid the contract give similar rights to those who follow him on the slip? There was the suggestion that such a right did exist. Mustill LJ was not, however, convinced and, if it did, he did not consider it still to be good law.

The third possibility was that Lloyd's had created its own special duties and obligations between the parties whereby the subscribers were mutually dependent on one another. This was also rejected. The court was not prepared to recognise a practice amounting to a legally enforceable rule that a promise to one underwriter was by inference to be regarded as being made to other underwriters who follow on the slip.

The moral of the story is that each underwriter must ask those questions of the broker which he regards as crucial for his decision as to whether to accept the risk and as to what conditions to impose and what premium to charge.

## 7 FRONTING[259]

Brief mention should be made here of the use of "fronting", a device used in the insurance market which involves the active participation of brokers. The matter was considered in *Sedgwick Tomenson Inc* v. *PT Reasuransi Union Indonesia.*[260]

The first plaintiffs were insurance brokers in Canada who held open covers issued by the second defendants in the name of the first defendants. The second group of plaintiffs were fishing vessel owners who were insured under the open cover. Claims for losses were made by the insured against the insurers. Alternatively, if they were not liable on the grounds that the cover was outside the scope of the second defendant's authority, then they made a claim against those defendants for breach of warranty of authority. Evans J explained the use of "fronting":

"The meaning of 'fronting' is clear. When one insurer is willing to take a risk but either is unable to do so, not being licensed to do business in the territory in question, or is not acceptable to the assured, for part or all of the risk, either for commercial (security) reasons or perhaps on political grounds, then another insurer may 'front' for him, by underwriting the insurance in full and then reinsuring part or all of the risk with him. There may be standing arrangements to this effect when a number of insurers belong to a group or pool and for whatever reason the insurance is accepted by one or more insurers but the risk is shared by them with others under built-in reinsurance agreements.

The usual form of remuneration for the fronting insurer is an 'overriding commission' of say, one per cent. No one doubts that the named insurer is liable in full to the assured, in accordance with the contract and regardless of the reinsurance arrangements though in the normal course he would recover an indemnity, depending on the terms agreed, with the reinsurer."

In the present case the first defendants had limited the authority that they had given to the second defendants to a certain financial ceiling. The authority also contained a fronting clause. The second defendants argued that they were therefore permitted to exceed the financial limit if fronting arrangements were made. The problem arose that the reinsurers of the fronting arrangement failed and therefore the first defendants were liable unless the fronting arrangement was beyond the

---

259. "Fronting" at Lloyd's is usually referred to as an "umbrella agreement".
260. [1990] 2 Lloyd's Rep. 334; see also *Wace* v. *Pan Atlantic Group Inc* [1981] 2 Lloyd's Rep. 339, *SunCorp Insurance and Finance* v. *Milano Assicurazioni SPA* [1993] 2 Lloyd's Rep. 225.

scope of the second defendant's authority. On construction of the arrangement between the two defendants, the court held that the first defendants were not liable beyond the financial limits they had contracted the second defendants to observe.

A more unusual problem arising from a fronting arrangement is to be seen in *Harris & Dixon (Insurance Brokers) Ltd* v. *Graham & Co.*[261] The plaintiffs were Lloyd's brokers who had entered into an umbrella agreement with the defendant non-Lloyd's brokers. The arrangement was to last for five years but provided for automatic termination should the Committee or Council of Lloyd's express their disapproval of it. Unlike the *Johns* v. *Kelly* case,[262] this arrangement provided for extension to the plaintiffs' E & O policy so as to include the defendants.

Towards the end of the five-year period, the Committee of Lloyd's expressed disapproval of the arrangement and gave instructions that it should be terminated. The plaintiffs then claimed various balances owed to them by the defendants. One claim related to business placed by the defendants at the request of the plaintiff for a P & I club now in liquidation. The effect of this placing with a Lloyd's underwriter and, by virtue of the umbrella agreement, the fronting and section 53 of the Marine Insurance Act 1906 was that the plaintiff and not the defendant was debited with the premiums due. In turn the plaintiffs debited the defendants' account with them. The P & I club had failed to pay their premiums.

The question therefore arose as to who should be responsible for the loss of the premium. The Court of Appeal found for the plaintiffs holding that the defendants could not set off that sum against the plaintiffs. An analysis of the agreement between the two parties pointed to the liability of the defendants even though the agreement was to share the commission equally and that the plaintiff had introduced the new (insolvent) client to the defendants. It would be possible to reverse the liability in such a situation by a carefully worded contract, but in an umbrella arrangement it is assumed that the Lloyd's broker has the superior negotiating position.

## 8 SETTLEMENTS AND CLAIMS

Another area of potential conflict of the broker's interest and duty to his client, the assured, is in the handling of claims.

Lloyd's practice in this matter has been seriously criticised by the courts. The practice has been for the underwriter to discharge his liability to the assured by altering the running account that he has with the broker. Thus the underwriter credits the account of the broker thus debiting that amount from what the broker owes the underwriter by way of premiums. Such practice dates back a long way but for more than 160 years it has been criticised by the courts.

In *Scott* v. *Irving*,[263] the court held that the general rule was that while the broker was the debtor of the underwriter with regard to the premium the underwriter was the debtor of the assured for the loss. In *Matveieff* v. *Crossfield*,[264] it was held that an

261. (Unreported) December 1989.
262. [1986] 1 Lloyd's Rep. 468—see above at p. 425.
263. (1830) 1 B. & Ad. 605.
264. (1903) 51 W.R. 365.

assured could not be bound by such practice unless it could be shown that it was "known and notorious" to the parties.

It would appear from the cases that the courts are slow to fix the assured with such knowledge. Perhaps evidence of a long course of dealings including a number of claims payments in the Lloyd's market might convince the court that in a particular case the assured was bound by a settlement between broker and underwriter.

Conflict of interest arises at Lloyd's when there is a dispute as to liability on the policy. In such a situation it is customary for the broker to handle the claim, apparently for both protagonists.

In *Anglo-African Merchants Ltd* v. *Bayley*,[265] a claim was made under a theft policy and the underwriters argued non-disclosure by the assured. During the investigation of the claim the assured's brokers had made their files available to the underwriters and their solicitors but when asked by the assured's solicitors for the same facility, this was refused.

Megaw J considered that such behaviour was not justified and that such a sorry state of affairs should not be allowed to arise again. He reinforced the general rule that a broker is the agent of the assured when placing business. The underwriters agreed but argued that when it came to claims the broker also could and did usually act for the underwriter. Megaw J reasoned that this view was only acceptable in the very precise circumstances where the broker, before he accepts instructions to place the insurance, discloses to his client that he wishes to be free to act in this dual role. Even then it must be shown that the assured fully appreciates the implications of such a collaboration between the two parties. Without evidence of such express and fully informed consent it would amount to a breach of duty on the part of the broker.

Without such requirements, potential dangers and undesirable consequences might well follow. In the words of Megaw J: "Such a relationship with the insurer inevitably invites suspicion that the broker is hunting with the hounds whilst running with the hare". The way to avoid these problems is for the underwriter to appoint his own assessors or investigators. Even if it could be shown to be a generally accepted method of dealing with claims, the court considered that such a custom could not be upheld by the courts in this country because it is in direct violation of one of the basic rules of the law of agency that an agent may not serve two masters when in actual or potential opposition to one another.

The matter was again dealt with in *North and South Trust Co* v. *Berkeley*[266] and the strictures of Megaw J were approved. The plaintiffs insured goods in transit from Buenos Aires to Paraguay. A local agent arranged the cover using a Lloyd's broker. The underwriters rejected a claim and, when pressed by the plaintiffs, they instructed the brokers to arrange for assessors to investigate the claim.

In accordance with Lloyd's practice, the report went direct to the underwriters while the brokers kept a copy for their files. The claim was again rejected. In the action on the policy the underwriters claimed that the assessors' report was privileged and need not be disclosed to the plaintiffs. The plaintiffs therefore asked their brokers for their copy of the report and the underwriters sought an injunction preventing such disclosure.

---

265. [1970] 1 Q.B. 311, [1969] 1 Lloyd's Rep. 268.
266. [1970] 2 Lloyd's Rep. 467, [1971] 1 W.L.R. 471.

The court strongly criticised the practice adopted by Lloyd's of using brokers in this way but at the same time held that the brokers need not divulge the contents of the report. This was because the report was not acquired in the service of the plaintiffs or in discharge of any duty to them.

Despite the lack of success by the plaintiff, the importance of the decision is the attack on the broker's role in the claim settlement process. Donaldson J explained that there was ample evidence that the practice was widespread not only at Lloyd's but in the insurance industry generally. It was only in 1969 in *Bayley's* case that the practice was challenged. Donaldson J expressed surprise that the Committee of Lloyd's had not immediately reacted to the criticisms either by requiring an alteration to the practice or by means of a friendly test action to seek the views of the Court of Appeal. The judge expressed the hope that now that he was adding his support to the views of Megaw J the changes would be forthcoming.

The Fisher Report (1980) pointed out that by that date still no reforms were forthcoming. Finally, however, the matter has been addressed in the Lloyd's Code of Practice for Lloyd's Brokers.

*Taylor* v. *Walker*[267] is not concerned with brokers but is worthy of mention as reflecting the agency problem in claims settlement. The plaintiff was injured in a road accident. A claims settlement firm offered to negotiate damages on behalf of the plaintiff explaining that their fee was 10 per cent of the damages. They in turn instructed an assessor to carry out the negotiations. The claim was settled but the plaintiff was not told that the assessor had received £42 from the insurers as his fee and that the fee was dependent on the figure suggested being accepted by the plaintiff.

When this was later discovered the plaintiff was successful in having the agreement set aside and received damages three times greater than the original figure. The insurers argued that they normally expected to pay a fee to whoever negotiated with them on behalf of claimants and that it rarely happened that the claimant was informed. The court stated that such a practice was an entirely wrong mode of operation.

The decision in *Merrett* v. *Capitol Indemnity Corporation*,[268] where it was held that payments by the broker to the insured did not relieve the insurer from his liability to the insured, has been referred to above.

There is no doubt, however, that there is a burden on a broker to see his client's insurance affairs through to settlement. This obligation can be based either on custom or by reading an obligation to do so into the contractual relationship between the parties. Thus brokers regularly accept this to be their role without expecting an additional fee. It might be possible, particularly in the case of a very complex claim, for the intermediary to negotiate an additional fee. If this had been the original understanding between the parties then the problem would not be too great. If, however, it could be shown that it was customary for this facility to be offered to the client then the greater additional burden might have to be carried without expectation to additional fees.

Paragraph 12 of the Lloyd's Code of Practice for Lloyd's Brokers under the

---

267. [1958] 1 Lloyd's Rep. 490.
268. [1991] 1 Lloyd's Rep. 169.

heading of "Servicing" sets out such an obligation to provide any relevant service requested by the client. As Mance QC (now Mance J) has pointed out[269] hitherto brokers have kept somewhat flimsy placing files on their clients' business. In cases of long-tail business, e.g., asbestosis claims, serious problems may arise. He provides the vivid story of one major firm of brokers who are reputed to have 26 miles of records in respect of long-term business.

In *Grace* v. *Leslie & Godwin Financial Services Ltd*[270] the plaintiffs had placed retrocession business using the defendants' brokers. Some of the business dated back to the 1950s and concerned claims in the 1980s relating to various losses. In attempting to make those claims the brokers found that they had no records of who the retrocessionaires were at those earlier dates. The plaintiffs therefore commenced proceedings in both contract and tort against the brokers seeking to claim in damages the sums that they argued they had lost on those policies.

The majority of expert witnesses, mainly brokers, explained that the normal procedure would be for the broker to check with the principal the acceptability of the intended retrocessionaire before formalising any such business. To that extent the principal would have been given and would have approved those names. However, the greater duty would lay with the broker to retain such information because it would be normal practice for the brokers to process any claims on behalf of their clients. There was also no evidence of any policies having been given to the plaintiffs for their retention. This, according to Lloyd's practice, was not unusual because the cover note indicated that the claims would be paid as and when they occurred and thus the wording would have been the same as the plaintiffs' original liability policies.

What duty in contract does a broker owe in these circumstances? First, the evidence in the market indicated that it was the normal practice for Lloyd's brokers to collect claims when called upon to do so. Thus the commission paid is acknowledged to cover not only the placing of the insurance but also the following up of the claim. Clarke J was prepared to imply into the contract all reasonable care and skill in collecting such claims. To this end the broker must be in a position to carry out in an efficient manner this obligation and that would clearly involve knowing against whom a claim could be made. How long such information should be retained was a matter to be decided in the light of the facts of each case. Once a time comes when it can be shown that no reasonable broker would consider that a claim could be made under the policy then his duty to retain the information would come to an end. Although the slip, as opposed to the policy, is the property of the broker once it is acknowledged that no policy came into existence then the duty on the broker was that he should not destroy the slip without seeking the instructions of his principal. The defendants, however, argued that the long-tail business associated with asbestosis claims was not known in the market until the early 1980s and thus it was not realised that events dating back to the 1950s might be the subjects of claims. Evidence indicated that the documents in question had not been thrown away but had been lost. The majority view of the expert witnesses was that by the 1970s and certainly by the 1980s the dangers of long-tail claims were more generally appreciated in the market and thus earlier documentation should be kept. The judge

269. "Insurance brokers negligence" (*British Insurance Association Journal*, May 1993, No. 82).
270. (Unreported) 16 May 1995.

accepted this view and the brokers were liable for breach of their duty to their principal to be in a position to make claims on the early policies.[271]

The defendants' argument that the plaintiffs had been contributorily negligently was also rejected. At the time in question it was not normal practice for the principal to keep a record of who were the retrocessionaires because it was always assumed that the placing broker would do so in keeping with the normal practice of processing claims.

The assessment of damages raised a problem which the court appeared to deal with quite shortly. The burden of proof for breach of contract lay with the plaintiffs. As it was not known who were the retrocessionaires it was not known if they were all in existence at the time the claims would have been made. The defendants showed that of the companies with whom they normally placed only 43 per cent were still meeting claims. The judge therefore chose this figure as the one by which to assess damages.

What of the situation where the broker has reason to suspect that the insured is making a fraudulent claim? His first duty is to his client and he might argue that it would be a breach of confidentiality to divulge any information to another party, even when that other party is an underwriter. However, paragraph 9.2 of the Lloyd's Code of Practice for Lloyd's Brokers states:

"If a Lloyd's broker has reason to believe that the notification of the facts of a claim by a client is not true, fair and complete, he should request him to make the necessary true, fair and complete disclosure. In the absence of such agreement, the broker should consider whether he should decline to continue acting for the client and what obligations he has to insurers or any regulatory authority."

There is no reason to believe that this advice should not equally apply to non-Lloyd's broker intermediaries. The major problem in any given case will be in making the decision as to whether there is sufficient evidence of bad faith on the part of the client.

Unfortunately, there are instances where the intermediary becomes embroiled in the fraudulent claim. This is illustrated by *Black King Shipping* v. *Massie (The Litsion Pride)*,[272] a marine insurance case where both the insured and the brokers were found to have made fraudulent claims for the loss of the ship. The basic element of the fraud was to try to argue that a letter notifying entry into a war zone had been sent before the loss of the ship had occurred. In the judge's view quite apart from fraudulent misrepresentations made by the broker to the underwriter the broker was also "guilty of the most culpable concealment of the relevant facts and documents known to him ..."

In this case both insured and broker were found to have been involved in the fraudulent presentation of the claim. But if only the broker had been guilty what effect would that have had on the insured's claim? That was also answered in the case. Hirst J said:

"In my judgement it is plain that in the present case the presentation of the claim to the underwriters was the very matter delegated by the owners to the brokers at the relevant stage. Consequently, on the authority of the *Blackburn Low* case, I hold that the brokers really did represent the owners at that stage, and that therefore any fraud by the brokers during the course of carrying out that responsibility is attributable to the owners."

271. In the light of this finding the court did not deal with the claim in tort.
272. [1985] 1 Lloyd's Rep. 437.

# 9 SUPERVISION OF INSURANCE INTERMEDIARIES

No area affecting the working conditions of the insurance intermediary has changed so dramatically in recent years as that concerned with his supervision. The aim has been to improve his standing in the commercial sector and by so doing to provide the consumer and the insurer with higher quality service. The changes have come from different directions and have been made by different organisations. Some changes have been necessitated by legislation while others reflect attempts by interested bodies to enhance the industry's reputation in the eyes of the public by means of self-regulation.

## 9.1 Insurance Brokers (Registration) Act 1977

Before the introduction of this Act,[273] anyone could call himself an "insurance broker". To the general public this probably implied that the person was a truly independent adviser on all insurance matters who would be capable of displaying considerable skill in advising the client on his insurance needs and which company was the most suitable for him. Obviously this must have been true of many such brokers, but equally there must have been many who were masquerading behind the title of insurance broker. It was a desire from brokers themselves as much as from the Government that some form of official status be given to this important section of the insurance industry.

The Act breaks down into the main headings of registration and training; regulation of conduct; disciplinary matters, and penalties. The important supervisory role is placed in the hands of the Insurance Brokers Registration Council established by section 1 of the Act. The Council was then given the responsibility of drawing up a code of conduct,[274] establishing, maintaining and publishing a register of insurance brokers and bodies corporate, and setting up a disciplinary machinery.

The qualifications for registration as an insurance broker are a combination of both educational attainment and practical experience.

Section 10 gives power to the Council to draw up a code of conduct, transgression of which may constitute unprofessional conduct. The code was published in 1978 and rewritten in 1994 and a number of its provisions have been dealt with above.

One of the longest sections of the Act is concerned with the requirements for carrying on business. This refers mainly to accounting and working capital provisions and has led to a detailed statutory instrument setting out the precise requirements.[275]

Of particular importance is the requirement that practising insurance brokers and enrolled bodies corporate shall ensure that the number of insurance companies with whom they place business, and the amount of insurance business which each places with each insurance company, is such as to prevent their business from becoming

---

273. See Hodgin, *Insurance Intermediaries: Law and Regulation* (LLP Limited, looseleaf) at paras 6.701 and 6.702.

274. The code of conduct is set out in Appendix 2.

275. Hodgin, *op. cit.*, at para. 6.707.

unduly dependent on any particular insurance company. In order to show compliance with this requirement, the broker must show with how many companies he has placed business (if over 10 he merely has to state "over 10"); he must also state the largest percentage of the brokerage derived from a single insurance company, but if that is under 15 per cent he need only state "under 15 per cent"; if he has placed business with four or less insurers or he has placed 35 per cent or more with any one company then he must state why it is considered that the business is not unduly dependent on any one company.

Obviously these are important requirements to support the truly independent status of a broker. The requirements not merely ask how many company proposal forms he may have in his filing cabinet, but go deeper and require information as to how many he actually uses.

A sign of professionalism is the requirement for a professional indemnity insurance scheme to provide compensation to an aggrieved party when the broker strays from the path of professional competence. This is mandatory under the Act, which also provides for the establishment of a fund administered by the Council to compensate clients who are unable to obtain compensation from the individual broker, for instance, where he has failed to meet his obligation to obtain professional indemnity insurance or where the policy is unenforceable by him for some reason.

Although the Council does have, at its absolute discretion, the power to make grants to applicants who are outside the approved list, the general thrust of the Act is in the direction of consumer protection and, therefore, it is extremely unlikely that insurance companies alleging non-payment of premiums would be likely candidates for compensation from the fund. It does, however, include those who sought and were given advice even though no contract of insurance followed.

This is important because it recognises the point that the broker's duty of care starts the moment the first contact is made with the intending insured. His liability is not restricted merely to those who take out a policy. Inevitably this must mean that the duty exists even in situations where no commission is paid to the broker.

Having established certain standards and imposed certain conditions for brokers and enrolled firms, the Act then allows for disciplinary proceedings to be brought. An Investigating Committee has been established to carry out preliminary investigation of allegations that a name should be erased from the register on the grounds that he has been convicted of a criminal offence sufficient to render him unfit to remain on the register or where there is an allegation by a member of the public of unprofessional conduct.

If preliminary investigations point to a possible case for erasure from the list or register then the matter is dealt with by the Disciplinary Committee. In particular failure to observe the requirements for carrying on business, i.e., financial obligations or failure to meet the professional indemnity rules, can lead to an allegation of being unfit to remain on the list or register.

The sanctions or penalties enforceable under the Act fall into two groups. The Council can erase the name from the register or list and that person cannot call himself an insurance broker. This does not mean that he is debarred from the insurance arena. One of the difficulties created by the Act is that while it controls and supervises insurance brokers there is no control of other titles that individuals or firms choose to use. There are also criminal sanctions. Any person or firm who wilfully uses the title insurance broker or implies that he is registered or enrolled when he is not, is liable on conviction to a fine. Successful prosecutions have been brought under this heading.

The Council has been active in carrying out its functions under other sections of the Act. As a reflection on how well they have exercised their powers only two cases have been appealed to the courts, and both decisions found that the Council had acted correctly.[276]

The Financial Services Act 1986 calls for certain alterations to the wording and workings of the Insurance Brokers (Registration) Act 1977. The Financial Services Act will only apply to those brokers who need authorisation to conduct investment business as defined in the Act. Where the Insurance Brokers (Registration) Act calls for proof as to character and suitability of the applicant as prerequisites of registration, the Council must accept as proof the fact that the broker has received authorisation under the Financial Services Act, or that he is a member of a partnership or unincorporated association which has been so authorised.

The rules relating to code of conduct requirements for carrying on business set down under the Insurance Brokers (Registration) Act must now take account of the fact that the Financial Services Act has similar provisions for such authorised persons. Thus, to prevent overlapping with the Insurance Brokers (Registration) Act's indemnity requirements, the Financial Services Act substitutes for "The Council shall" make rules relating to indemnity and grants the words "The Council may" make such rules.

Section 15 of the 1977 Act now has added to it new subsections (2A) and (2B) by virtue of section 138 of the 1986 Act. The section is concerned with the erasure of names from the register or list. The new provisions allow the Council to take notice of the fact that a person has been found in breach of the 1986 Act sufficient to merit erasure under the 1977 Act, thus avoiding the necessity for a second investigation into the matter by the Council. The Council is required to share its information with any supervisory body established under the Financial Services Act.

## 9.2 Lloyd's broker

The market place at Lloyd's has been under intense scrutiny for a number of years. The changes so far made have not pleased everyone and the changes still to come will probably equally find a mixed reception.

The main changes revolve around a system of self-regulation but without the impartiality of the Securities and Investment Board as is found in the Financial Services Act 1986. The Neill Report 1987 (Regulatory Arrangements at Lloyd's) stated that it had detected a number of shortcomings in particular areas of regulation. This led them to the opinion that Lloyd's arrangements fell below the standards that will be acceptable elsewhere in the financial sector.

Numerous specific changes affecting Lloyd's brokers have now been implemented by the means of Lloyd's byelaws.[277]

276. *Pickles* v. *I.B.R.C.* [1984] 1 W.L.R. 748; *James* v. *I.B.R.C.* (1984) *The Times*, 16 February.
277. See *Lloyd's Acts, Byelaws and Regulations*, and Hodgin, *Insurance Intermediaries: Law and Regulation*, both looseleaf (LLP Limited).

The Lloyd's Act 1982 directs the Council to establish a Disciplinary Committee and an Appeals Tribunal to whom Lloyd's brokers are answerable. The Committee has powers to investigate a wide range of behaviour that might amount to acting against the interests of policyholders, the Corporation of Lloyd's, members of Lloyd's, other Lloyd's brokers, underwriting agents or others doing business at Lloyd's. Where guilt is proven that person may be suspended from doing business at Lloyd's, permanently or temporarily; he may be fined, reprimanded or a notice of censure may be posted in the Room.

Lloyd's Brokers Byelaw paragraph 20 gave powers to the Council to introduce a code of practice for Lloyd's brokers and the code came into force on 1 November 1988. There is a strong inter-relationship between the Lloyd's code and that issued by the Insurance Brokers' Registration Council because a prerequisite for registration as a Lloyd's broker is that the applicant must be registered under the Insurance Brokers (Registration) Act 1977. Thus throughout the Lloyd's code certain examples issued in the IBRC code are reproduced to illustrate the fundamental principles that were the basis of the earlier code. The three basic principles are:

(i) insurance brokers must at all times conduct their business with utmost good faith and integrity;

(ii) they must do everything possible to satisfy the insurance requirements of their clients, and must place the interests of those clients before all other considerations, but subject to those requirements and interests, must have proper regard for others;

(iii) statements made by or on behalf of insurance brokers when advertising must not be misleading or extravagant.

The introduction to the Lloyd's code stresses that due regard will be paid to these three underlying principles when considering whether a person is a fit and proper person for registration.

The code is subdivided under a number of major headings. The first is concerned with the relationship with the client. It is the duty of the Lloyd's broker to take steps to see that the client understands the Lloyd's broker's role when placing business at Lloyd's. He must know his client's needs and attempt to understand his client's awareness of risk and insurance provisions. The broker should aim to put things in writing for his client, including those recommendations that have been declined by the client. The broker should not act in such a way that he is in conflict with his duties to another client.

A second topic relates to remuneration. The broker should disclose his remuneration to the client if requested to do so. Where a broker intends to charge his client for work to be undertaken, he should declare the amount before the work commences. If the recognised practice in a particular area of insurance is that the broker deducts commission from any claim that is payable to the client, the broker should declare this and the percentage that might be deducted before he commences any work for that client. Similarly, any departure from the normal return of premiums practice should be notified at the time instructions are given by the client.

With regard to the ever-present problem of confidentiality, the code accepts that a broker is likely to build up a considerable file of information relating to his client. In such a situation, the broker must take great care with its use and not act in a way that is adverse to his client's interests. The broker should not divulge information in relation to his client's affairs unless permitted to do so by that client or unless it is available in the market generally. However there are specific cases, for instance under the Information and Confidentiality Byelaw No 4 of 1983, as amended, when the broker must give relevant information to the appropriate committee of Lloyd's even though it may affect his client.

The code stresses that a Lloyd's broker must act as an independent adviser. Thus he should not allow any connection he has with anyone offering cover to prejudice the performance of his duty as an adviser. Where the broker intends to advise the client to place his insurance requirements with an insurer not authorised in the EU he should, bearing in mind his client's experience of insurance, advise him in writing of certain drawbacks. These would include the fact that the management and solvency of that insurer is not supervised by an appropriate EU authority; that he would not be covered by the financial support of the Policyholders Protection Act 1975; and that the client might have difficulty in suing or executing judgment against that particular insurer. The client's written acknowledgement of these points should be obtained. If the client decides to ignore the broker's advice, the broker should similarly seek written proof of this.

The Lloyd's broker should explain the doctrine of the duty of good faith law and seek to give a fair representation of his client's position. The broker should not normally complete proposal forms but where he does so complete it he should declare this to the insurer. He should see that slips and other placing information is clear and unambiguous. He should employ staff who are sufficiently competent to deal with reasonable questions about the risk in question. He should be quick to relay to the client any request from the insurer for further particulars.[278]

The client should be informed, as soon as the contract of insurance is made, of the name of the insurer. Any changes in the contract should be notified at the earliest opportunity. Cover notes, other than temporary motor cover, should be signed by senior personnel, and it is good practice for the person signing to be someone other than the person who placed the contract so that a check can be made of the details. The broker should provide his client as soon as possible with written confirmation and details of any insurance that has been placed, although this requirement is subject to any lien that the broker may have. If he exercises such a lien he should inform the client accordingly.

The client should be informed early in the business arrangement of his obligation to pay the premiums. Such payments must be kept in an Insurance Broking Account and the broker is entitled to retain any interest thereon. He must observe dates of payment to the insurer and he must account to his client promptly for any monies received. He must exercise good judgement as to when he pays over money received if it derives from several sources.

Where a Lloyd's broker has binding authority to place business, this poses a potential conflict of interest. He must be certain that in using his binding authority with a particular insurer he is acting in his client's best interests. If he accepts business in this way he must disclose this to his client and, where the client so requests, he must inform him of the financial advantage he has gained. A broker accepting a binding

---

278. See *Vesta* v. *Butcher* (above).

authority should remind the insurer in question that his fundamental obligation is to his client rather than to that insurer.

In the matter of claims the client should be advised that prompt claims notification is essential and that all material facts must be disclosed. If the broker is of the opinion that the client has failed in this duty he should request further information and, failing that, he should consider whether he can continue to act for that client. He should further consider what obligations he may owe to the insurer and any supervisory authority if such a situation arises.

The specific problems referred to in *Anglo-African Merchants* case[279] and *North and South Trust* case[280] are dealt with in the code. Paragraph 9.6 states that:

"a Lloyd's broker should not, without the fully informed consent of both parties, act for both the client and insurers during the claims settling process if by doing so he would be undertaking duties to one principal which are inconsistent with those owed to the other. In any event, a Lloyd's broker who receives or holds on behalf of the insurers concerned an adjuster's report or similar document relating to an insurance claim made by his client should only do so on the basis that the information in the report may be imparted to the client".

Similarly, where the broker has authority to settle a claim, he has a potential conflict of interest. He should refer back to the insurers for instructions where he feels he cannot reconcile his client's best interests with his obligations to the insurer. There might also be a conflict of interest where the broker is acting for two or more clients in relation to the same claim. In such circumstances the code calls upon the broker to take appropriate steps to represent each client's position fairly. No guidance is given as to how this might be accomplished.

The broker should remind his client of renewal dates and that the duty of good faith and disclosure applies as much to renewals as it does when taking out the original cover.

Where a client wishes to change brokers, it is the duty of the prior broker to provide the new broker with all relevant documentation concerning the client's insurance position.

An efficient complaints procedure should be established by the Lloyd's broker whereby senior management handle complaints, and complainants should also be advised that they can write to the Council of Lloyd's. A notice displaying this fact, together with a notice advising parties that the Insurance Brokers Registration Council handles complaints against brokers, must be displayed in the public part of the broker's office.

The broker must ensure that his staff are adequately trained and are aware of the standards expected of them in the code of practice. He should also ensure that the broking business is under the control of day-to-day supervision of a registered broker. He should not attempt to handle business in which he is not competent.

Mention should be made here of two further innovations aimed at dealing with complaints and providing general supervision at Lloyd's. The Members' Ombudsman Byelaw No 13 of 1987 established an Ombudsman to receive written complaints from any member of the Society in relation to any action taken by or on

279. [1969] 1 Lloyd's Rep. 268 (above).
280. [1970] 2 Lloyd's Rep. 467 (above).

behalf of the Society. Thus the byelaw is concerned with allegations of maladministration by the Society and its employees and it has no concern with policyholder complaints. The task of the Ombudsman is to facilitate the satisfaction, settlement or withdrawal of any complaint. This can involve the recommendation of an *ex gratia* payment. The Ombudsman reports his recommendation to the Council and to the complainant. There are certain limitations on his powers of investigation. Thus he would not normally deal with matters which are more than two years old unless he is convinced that there is good reason to do so and he may not investigate where the matter is subject to judicial proceedings, to arbitration or is subject to certain internal Lloyd's investigations.

The Insurance Ombudsman Bureau Byelaw No 1 of 1989 paved the way to Lloyd's joining the Insurance Ombudsman Bureau that had been established by individual insurance companies in 1981. By 1989 the great majority of personal lines insurers were members, and the addition of Lloyd's Council helped to cement the undoubted success of the Bureau as a provider of a free dispute resolution service for individual policyholders.

The terms of reference of the Bureau do not give it powers over the behaviour of insurance intermediaries. As we have seen earlier, an insurer will not normally be legally responsible for the negligence or incompetence of an independent intermediary, whether or not a registered broker, but, in the 1989 annual report of the Bureau, the Insurance Ombudsman explained that he had decided to hold insurers liable for acts of independent intermediaries when he considered that the facts warranted it. Presumably, if he maintains his position, he may hold underwriters responsible for certain acts of Lloyd's brokers. One major difference between the power of the Insurance Ombudsman under his terms of reference and the wording of the present byelaw is that the byelaw gives the Society the power to require a Lloyd's broker to provide information to the Ombudsman.

Lloyd's brokers together with other registered brokers are, of course, subject to the disciplinary procedures of the Insurance Brokers Registration Council.

## 10 FINANCIAL SERVICES ACT 1986[281]

References have been made to the Act at a number of places in this chapter. It is worthwhile repeating here the application of the Act in relation to the scope of this chapter. It is concerned with regulating, with the safety of the consumer in mind, investment business. This covers a wide range of dealings including: shares in UK or foreign companies; debentures including loan stock; futures contracts if made for investment and not commercial purposes; and especially from our point of view, long-term insurance contracts and unit trusts or other collective investment schemes.

Long-term insurance is defined in the Insurance Companies Act 1982 and covers: life and annuity contracts; contracts in excess of one year to pay out on marriage or the birth of a child; linked long-term policies; permanent health insurance; tontines;

---

281. For an overview of the Act in relation to the role of insurance intermediaries, see Hodgin, *op. cit.*, chapter 7.

capital redemption contracts and pension fund management contracts. It must be stressed, therefore, that the 1986 Act is not concerned with general insurance business such as fire, motor, house buildings or contents, accident, property damage or the other examples set out in the 1982 Act under "General Business".

The type of activity that is subject to the 1986 Act includes advising on investments, and it is this activity that is most applicable to the insurance intermediary.

## 10.1 Authorisation

Control over those involved in marketing investment business is achieved by the necessity to seek authorisation. This can be done in three ways. The applicant can apply directly to the Securities and Investment Board ("SIB") which has the overall responsibility, as the designated agency, for the implementation of the Act, subject to the Secretary of State. An alternative method, favoured by the SIB, is for intending applicants to apply to one of the self-regulating organisations ("SRO") for membership and such membership will carry with it the necessary authorisation. A third method is to hold a certificate issued by a recognised professional body ("RPB"). Such a body must regulate the practice of a profession and must not wholly or mainly carry on investment business.

Insurance companies and friendly societies are dealt with separately. To carry on business in the UK it is necessary for an insurance company to be authorised under the 1982 Act and this authorisation automatically gives it authorisation under the Financial Services Act in respect of investment business. Authorisation under the Friendly Societies Act 1992 has the same effect. Lloyd's is exempt from the requirements of authorisation under the Financial Services Act despite strong criticism and much lobbying during the passage of the Bill in 1986.

It should be remembered that only a very small percentage of Lloyd's business would come within the definition of investment business. If the general insurance business of other insurance companies is outside the Financial Services Act then so too would be the great part of Lloyd's interests.

Under the Financial Services Act, an intermediary who is involved with the marketing of investment business will fall into one of three categories with varying responsibilities and liabilities. If he is a truly independent intermediary he will need to be authorised, and the most obvious route will be by means of his membership of one of the SROs.

Alternatively, he may be an appointed representative. This refers to anyone who is employed by an authorised person under a contract for services to carry on investment business. This must be contrasted with a person who is employed under a contract of service, i.e., an employee of that particular company.

The company intermediary is really a tied agent and his principal must accept responsibility for his behaviour when advising or attempting to procure people to enter into investment agreements with his principal. His contractual relationship may recognise that he can utilise the facilities of other authorised persons. The fact that the principal is responsible for the behaviour of the representative means that he is treated as though he was an employee of the principal. The representative must make it clear to the client that he is not able to give truly independent advice but that he represents the interests of one particular company or companies. The fact that the company representative need not be authorised on an individual basis means that he is within the description of "exempted person" in the Financial Services Act.

The third possibility is that the representative is an employee of one insurance company. If this is so then he does not need to be authorised; he is not in the exempt category but is not regarded as a person carrying on investment business. His employer is the person who must be authorised and bear responsibility for his employees' actions.

Once authorisation has been granted then the person authorised will be subject to very detailed rules of doing business. The SIB drafted their original rules which the SROs and RPBs were expected to adopt and adapt to cover the type of membership falling under their jurisdiction.

## 10.2  Statements of principles

The Statements of Principles issued by the SIB came into force in April 1990. The principles apply to all authorised persons whether directly authorised by the SIB or members of SROs or RPBs. They are intended to be a universal declaration of expected standards and they set a high moral tone in commercial dealing. However, they are not meant to be exhaustive of the standards expected and, crucially, compliance with them does not absolve a person to whom they are directed from a failure to observe any other requirements of competent practice in any given area. The introduction to the Statements of Principles stresses that the failure to observe them will not give rise to an action in damages but could lead to disciplinary actions or intervention by the regulatory body concerned. Where the principles refer to customers, the reference includes potential customers.

The principles are here set in their entirety.

### 10.2.1  Introduction

1. These principles are intended to form a universal statement of the standards expected. They apply directly to the conduct of investment business and financial standing of all authorised persons ("firms"), including members of recognised self-regulating organisations and firms certified by recognised professional bodies.

2. The principles are not exhaustive of the standards expected. Conformity with the principles does not absolve a failure to observe other requirements, while the observance of other requirements does not necessarily amount to conformity with the principles.

3. The principles do not give rise to actions for damages, but will be available for purposes of discipline and intervention.

4. Where the principles refer to customers, they should be taken to refer also to clients and to potential customers, and where they refer to a firm's regulator, they mean SIB, or a self-regulating organisation or professional body which regulates the firm.

5. Although the principles may be taken as expressing existing standards, they come into force formally, with additional sanctions resulting, on 30 April 1990.

THE PRINCIPLES

*Integrity*

1. A firm should observe high standards of integrity and fair dealing.

*Skill Care and Diligence*

2. A firm should act with due skill, care and diligence.

*Market Practice*

3. A firm should observe high standards of market conduct. It should also, to the extent endorsed for the purpose of this principle, comply with any code or standard as in force from time to time and as it applies to the firm either according to its terms or by rulings made under it.

*Information about Customers*

4. A firm should seek from customers it advises or for whom it exercises discretion any information about their circumstances and investment objectives which might reasonably be expected to be relevant in enabling it to fulfil its responsibilities to them.

*Information for Customers*

5. A firm should take reasonable steps to give a customer it advises, in a comprehensible and timely way, any information needed to enable him to make a balanced and informed decision. A firm should similarly be ready to provide a customer with a full and fair account of the fulfilment of its responsibilities to him.

*Conflicts of Interest*

6. A firm should either avoid any conflict of interest arising or, where conflicts arise, should ensure fair treatment to all its customers by disclosure, internal rules of confidentiality, declining to act, or otherwise. A firm should not unfairly place its interests above those of its customers and, where a properly informed customer would reasonably expect that the firm would place his interests above its own, the firm should live up to that expectation.

*Customer Assets*

7. Where a firm has control of or is otherwise responsible for assets belonging to a customer which it is required to safeguard, it should arrange proper protection for them, by way of segregation and identification of those assets or otherwise, in accordance with the responsibility it has accepted.

*Financial Resources*

8. A firm should ensure that it maintains adequate financial resources to meet its investment business commitments and to withstand the risks to which its business is subject.

*Internal Organisation*

9. A firm should organise and control its internal affairs in a responsible manner, keeping proper records, and where the firm employs staff or is responsible for the conduct of investment business by others, should have adequate arrangements to

ensure that they are suitable, adequately trained and properly supervised and that it has well-defined compliance procedures.

*Relations with Regulators*

10. A firm should deal with its regulator in an open and co-operative manner and keep the regulator promptly informed of anything concerning the firm which might reasonably be expected to be disclosed to it.

### 10.3 Insurance Brokers Registration Council (RPB)

The Insurance Brokers Registration Council became a Recognised Professional Body by virtue of the Financial Services Act. It issued its rules in June 1988.

It must be stressed that not all registered brokers or enrolled bodies corporate under the Insurance Brokers (Registration) Act 1977 are subject to the RPB rules. They concern only those who are carrying on investment business as defined by the Financial Services Act. The definition of such business is complex, and the IBRC's guidance notes advise members to seek legal advice as to whether their activities are caught by the Financial Services Act. Many insurance brokers who are heavily involved in investment business joined FIMBRA, and now the PIA.

The Council's certification as a RPB allows it to certify brokers whose business includes: (i) buying, selling or subscribing for life policies or unit trusts as agents; (ii) making, or offering or agreeing to make, arrangements with a view to clients taking out or surrendering life policies or buying or selling unit trusts, or arrangements with third parties with a view to the third parties buying or selling any investments; and (iii) giving advice to clients in relation to life policies and unit trusts.

Where a broker wishes to go beyond the type of business listed above he should look to PIA or to the SIB for his authorisation, although direct authorisation by the SIB is extremely rare.

An equally important limitation on the Council's power to give authorisation as a RPB is the so-called "49 per cent rule". Where the broker's income, together with any appointed representative's income, from investment business exceeds 49 per cent of the broker's total income from all sources, the Council will not normally issue a certificate. If the figure is exceeded in occasional years the Council may exercise its discretion but, if the figure is regularly exceeded, PIA is the appropriate body to issue authorisation.

A further important consideration for the broker considering certification by the IBRC relates to his handling of client money. If he seeks such certification he must not hold client money unless that money is payable to the firm for its own account. Any money received should otherwise be returned immediately with an explanation that the client should pay it directly to the intended recipient. If money is intended to go to a client, for instance the payment of insurance monies, then the broker must pay it directly to the client and not put it through his own account. The only exception to this last point is where a cheque is endorsed to the client, or as he may direct, and is not passed by the broker through a bank account. Where the broker receives cheques on behalf of clients, pays such cheques into his own bank account and then writes separate cheques for his clients, certification by the Council is inappropriate. It is similarly inappropriate if premiums are retained in the broker's account and a cheque is periodically written on that account and sent to the life office.

Assuming, however, that the IBRC as a RPB is the appropriate source of certification, a survey of its rules is necessary. They broadly break down into four main headings: (i) certification procedures; (ii) conduct of investment business; (iii) client relations; and (iv) records.

### 10.3.1 Certification

A certificate may be issued to carry on investment business of the kind above. A firm may not become an appointed representative for the obvious reason that it would cease to give independent advice. It is possible however for a firm to appoint representatives under section 44 of the Financial Services Act (which deals with appointed representatives) who are either individuals, or companies which have only one or two directors or employees and which do not carry on investment business except as the firm's appointed representative.

Those eligible for certification are sole practitioners carrying on the business of insurance broking at the time of issue of the certificate; a partnership in which at least one of the partners is a practising insurance broker and each of the partners permitted to bind the partnership is either a practising insurance broker, or subject to the rules of another RPB in carrying on a profession which he is entitled to practise, or an enrolled body corporate.

The Council has the power to suspend, withdraw or impose conditions on a certificate in a number of circumstances. These include any circumstances that indicate that the firm is not a fit and proper person to carry on investment business, or where it has breached any rules or terms under the Insurance Brokers (Registration) Act 1977, or where it has returned false, inaccurate or misleading information to the Council. The discretionary powers may also be exercised where any partner's name has been erased from the register or where any director's name has been erased from the enrolled body corporate's list. Similarly where a Lloyd's broker loses that status or there is a contravention of the Insolvency Act 1986, the Council may exercise powers under this paragraph of the rules.

Where the Council suspends a certificate, this may be for a specified period or until specified conditions are met.

Where the Council refuses to grant a certificate, or refuses to review the withdrawal or suspension of a certificate or acts in any way which prevents an applicant from conducting investment business, such applicant will have 28 days from notification to make an appeal to the Certification Appeal Committee which has the power to vary, increase, decrease or revoke any decision of the Council.

RAY HODGIN

# CODES OF CONDUCT

# ASSOCIATION OF BRITISH INSURERS' GENERAL INSURANCE BUSINESS CODE OF PRACTICE FOR ALL INTERMEDIARIES (INCLUDING EMPLOYEES OF INSURANCE COMPANIES) OTHER THAN REGISTERED INSURANCE BROKERS

Introduced January 1989 (replacing earlier versions)

This code applies to general business as defined in the Insurance Companies Act 1982, but does not apply to reinsurance business. As a condition of membership of the Association of British Insurers, members undertake to enforce this code and to use their best endeavours to ensure that all those involved in selling their policies observe its provisions.

It shall be an overriding obligation of an intermediary at all times to conduct business with the utmost good faith and integrity.

In the case of complaints from policyholders (either direct or indirect, e.g., through a trading standards officer or citizens advice bureau) the insurance company concerned shall require an intermediary to co-operate so that the facts can be established. An intermediary shall inform the policyholder complaining that he can take his problem direct to the insurance company concerned.

## PART I

This part applies to the selling and servicing of general business insurance policies, but not where the intermediary is acting solely as an introducer.

### A. General sales principles

1. The intermediary shall:
   - (i) where appropriate make a prior appointment to call. Unsolicited or unarranged calls shall be made at an hour likely to be suitable to the prospective policyholder;
   - (ii) when he makes contact with the prospective policyholder, identify himself and explain as soon as possible that the arrangements he wishes to discuss could include insurance. He shall make it known that he is:

(a) an employee of an insurance company, for whose conduct the company accepts responsibility;

(b) an agent of one or a number of companies (as the case may be) for whose conduct the company/companies accept responsibility; or

(c) an independent intermediary seeking to act on behalf of the prospective policyholder, for whose conduct the company/companies do not accept responsibility;

(iii) ensure as far as possible that the policy proposed is suitable to the needs and resources of the prospective policyholder;

(iv) give advice only on those insurance matters in which he is knowledgeable and seek or recommend other specialist advice when necessary; and

(v) treat all information supplied by the prospective policyholder as completely confidential to himself and to the company or companies to which the business is being offered.

2. The intermediary shall not:

(i) inform the prospective policyholder that his name has been given by another person unless he is prepared to disclose that person's name if requested to do so by the prospective policyholder and has that person's consent to make that disclosure;

(ii) make inaccurate or unfair criticisms of any insurer; or

(iii) make comparisons with other types of policies unless he makes clear the differing characteristics of each policy.

## B. Explanation of the contract

The intermediary shall:

(i) identify the insurance company;

(ii) explain all the essential provisions of the cover afforded by the policy, or policies, which he is recommending so as to ensure as far as possible that the prospective policyholder understands what he is buying;

(iii) draw attention to any restrictions and exclusions applying to the policy;

(iv) if necessary, obtain from the insurance company specialist advice in relation to items (ii) and (iii) above;

(v) not impose any charge in addition to the premium required by the insurance company without disclosing the amount and purpose of such charge; and

(vi) if he is an independent intermediary, disclose his commission on request.

## C. Disclosure of underwriting Information

The intermediary shall, in obtaining the completion of the proposal form or any other material:

(i) avoid influencing the prospective policyholder and make it clear that all the answers or statements are the latter's own responsibility;

(ii) ensure that the consequences of non-disclosure and inaccuracies are pointed out to the prospective policyholder by drawing his attention to the relevant statement in the proposal form and by explaining them himself to the prospective policyholder.

### D. Accounts and financial aspects

The intermediary shall, if authorised to collect monies in accordance with the terms of his agency appointment:

    (i) keep a proper account of all financial transactions with a prospective policyholder which involve the transmission of money in respect of insurance;

    (ii) acknowledge receipt (which, unless the intermediary has been otherwise authorised by the insurance company, shall be on his own behalf) of all money received in connection with an insurance policy and shall distinguish the premium from any other payment included in the money; and

    (iii) remit any such monies so collected in strict conformity with his agency appointment.

### E. Documentation

The intermediary shall not withhold from the policyholder any written evidence or documentation relating to the contract of insurance.

### F. Existing policyholders

The intermediary shall abide by the principles set out in this code to the extent that they are relevant to his dealings with existing policyholders.

### G. Claims

If the policyholder advises the intermediary of an incident which might give rise to a claim, the intermediary shall inform the company without delay, and in any event within three working days, and thereafter give prompt advice to the policyholder of the company's requirements concerning the claim, including the provision as soon as possible of information required to establish the nature and extent of the loss. Information received from the policyholder shall be passed to the company without delay.

### H. Professional indemnity cover for independent intermediaries

The intermediary shall obtain, and maintain in force, professional indemnity insurance in accordance with the requirements of the Association of British Insurers as set out in the Annex, which may be updated from time to time.

### I. Letters of appointment

This code of practice shall be incorporated verbatim or by reference in all letters of appointment of non-registered intermediaries and no policy of the company shall be sold by such intermediaries except within the terms of such a letter of appointment.

ABI GENERAL INSURANCE BUSINESS CODE

ANNEX

## Code of Practice for the Selling of General Insurance

### Professional Indemnity Cover Required for Non-Registered Independent Intermediaries

As from 1 January 1989 (new agents) and by 1 July 1989 (existing agents) all non-registered independent intermediaries must take out and maintain in force professional indemnity cover in accordance with the requirements set out below.

The insurance may be taken out with any authorised UK or EEC insurer who has agreed to:

(a) issue cover in accordance with the requirements set out below,

(b) provide the intermediary with an annual certificate as evidence that the cover meets the ABI requirements, this certificate to contain the name and address including postcode of the intermediary, the policy number, the period of the policy, the limit of indemnity, the self-insured excess and the name of the insurer;

(c) send a duplicate certificate to ABI at the time the certificate is issued to the intermediary;

(d) inform ABI, by means of monthly lists, of any cases of non-renewal, cancellation of the cover mid-term or of the cover becoming inadequate.

The requirements are as follows:

### A. Limits of indemnity

The policy shall at inception and at each renewal date, which shall not be more than 12 months from inception or the last renewal date, provide a **minimum limit** of indemnity of either:

(a) a sum equal to three times the annual general business commission of the business for the last accounting period ending prior to inception or renewal of the policy, or a sum of £250,000, whichever sum is the greater. In no case shall the minimum limit of indemnity be required to exceed £5m, and a minimum sum of £250,000 shall apply at all times to each and every claim or series of claims arising out of the same occurrence; or

(b) a sum equal to three times the annual general business commission of the business for the last accounting period ending prior to inception or renewal of the policy, or a sum of £500,000 whichever sum shall be the greater. In no case shall the minimum limit of indemnity be required to exceed £5m.

### B. Maximum self-insured excess

The maximum self-insured excess permitted in normal circumstances shall be one per cent of the minimum limit of indemnity required by paragraph A(a) or A(b) above as the case may be. Subject to the agreement of the professional indemnity insurer, the self-insured excess may be increased to a maximum of two per cent of such minimum limit of indemnity.

461

*C. Scope of policy cover*

The policy shall indemnify the insured:
  (a) against losses arising from claims made against the insured:
      (i) for breach of duty in connection with the business by reason of any negligent act, error or omission; and
      (ii) in respect of libel or slander or in Scotland defamation, committed in the conduct of the business by the insured, any employee or former employee of the insured, and where the business is or was carried on in partnership any partner or former partner of the insured; and
      (iii) by reason of any dishonest or fraudulent act or omission committed or made in the conduct of the business by any employee (other than a director of a body corporate) or former employee (other than a director of a body corporate) of the insured; and
  (b) against claims arising in connection with the business in respect of:
      (i) any loss of money or other property whatsoever belonging to the insured or for which the insured is legally liable to consequence of any dishonest or fraudulent act or omission of any employee (other than a director of a body corporate) or former employee (other than a director of a body corporate) of the insured; and
      (ii) legal liability incurred by reason of loss of documents and costs and expenses incurred in replacing or restoring such documents.

*D.   General business only*

The above requirements relate only to the intermediary's general insurance business.

# INSURANCE BROKERS REGISTRATION COUNCIL (CODE OF CONDUCT) APPROVAL ORDER 1994 (S.I. 1994/2569) (REVOKING THE 1979 CODE OF CONDUCT)

SCHEDULE
Regulation 2

## CODE OF CONDUCT DRAWN UP BY THE INSURANCE BROKERS REGISTRATION COUNCIL PURSUANT TO SECTION 10 OF THE INSURANCE BROKERS (REGISTRATION) ACT 1977

Words and expressions used in this Code of Conduct shall have the meaning ascribed to them by the Insurance Brokers (Registration) Act 1977 ("the Act") except that:

"insurance broker" means practising insurance broker, registered insurance broker or enrolled body corporate;

"insurance broking business" and references to businesses carried on by an insurance broker shall mean all aspects of the business conducted by a practising insurance broker or enrolled body corporate and includes, for example, investment business as defined by the Financial Services Act 1986, Schedule 1;

"insurer" means a person or body of persons carrying on insurance business;

"advertisement" shall have the meaning ascribed to it by section 207(2) of the Financial Services Act 1986 and "advertising" shall be construed accordingly;

"appointed representative" shall have the meaning ascribed to it by section 44 of the Financial Services Act 1986;

"relevant investment business" shall have the meaning ascribed to it by the Insurance Brokers Registration Council (Conduct of Investment Business) Rules 1988.

1. The Act provides for the registration of insurance brokers and for the regulation of their professional standards. The objective of the Code of Conduct is to establish a recognised standard of professional conduct to which all insurance brokers should, in the interests of the public and in the performance of their duties, conform and in doing so they should bear in mind this objective and the underlying spirit of this Code.

The Code is not exhaustive or all embracing and while it shall serve as a guide to insurance brokers and other persons concerned with their conduct nevertheless the mention or the lack of mention in it of a particular act or omission shall not be taken as conclusive of any question of professional conduct.

Apart from this Code insurance brokers authorised by the Council to advise or effect transactions on relevant investment business are also required to comply with any rules made by the Council for the conduct of investment business under the Financial Services Act 1986.

Claims against insurance brokers for compensation arising from acts or omissions amounting to negligence are matters for determination by the courts. Nevertheless, acts of gross negligence or repeated acts of negligence may amount to unprofessional conduct and notwithstanding that the matter may be the subject of legal proceedings, the Council may still investigate the conduct of the insurance broker.

2. In the opinion of the Council, the fundamental principles governing the professional conduct of insurance brokers are shown below in paragraphs A to H. Any act or omission done or made by insurance brokers in breach of these fundamental principles may, in the opinion of the Council, constitute unprofessional conduct.

A. Insurance brokers shall at all times conduct business with utmost good faith and integrity.

B. Insurance brokers shall do everything possible to satisfy the requirements of clients and shall, subject to Principle C, place the interests of clients before all other considerations. Subject to these requirements and interests, insurance brokers shall have proper regard for *others*.

C. Insurance brokers shall not directly or indirectly do anything in the course of practising as insurance brokers which compromises or impairs, or is likely to compromise or impair, the good repute of insurance brokers or the insurance broking profession.

D. Statements made by or on behalf of insurance brokers when advertising shall not be misleading or extravagant.

E. Insurance brokers shall conduct their relationship with the Council, their professional body, with propriety.

F. Insurance brokers shall organise and control the internal affairs of their insurance broking business in a responsible manner, and where staff are employed ensure that they are competent, suitable, and under adequate day-to-day supervision by a registered insurance broker.

G. Insurance brokers should be familiar with, and in carrying on business should be mindful of guidance as to proper professional conduct contained in any Practice Notes issued or endorsed by the Council.

H. Insurance brokers who are authorised by the Council to conduct relevant investment business shall comply with any statements of principle issued under section 47A of the Financial Services Act 1986.

The following are some specific examples of the application of these principles:

(1) In the conduct of business and in the choice of an insurer or investment, insurance brokers shall provide advice objectively and independently in the best interests of the client.

(2) Insurance brokers shall not act in any way which is contrary to law or a principle of professional conduct.

(3) If insurance brokers have reason to believe that the disclosure of material facts by the client or the notification of the facts of a claim by a client is not true, fair and complete, they should request the client to make the necessary true, fair and complete disclosure. In the absence of such disclosure, insurance brokers should consider whether they should decline to continue acting for the client.

(4) If insurance brokers are placed in the position where their interests or the interests of a third party to whom the insurance broker owes a duty conflict with the interests of the client, they should withdraw from the matter unless after full disclosure all relevant parties agree in writing that they should continue.

(5) Insurance brokers shall only use or permit the use of the description "insurance broker" in connection with a business provided that business is carried on in accordance with the requirements of the Rules made by the Council under sections 11 and 12 of the Act.

(6) Insurance brokers shall ensure that their employees are made aware of and adhere to this Code.

(7) Insurance brokers shall, upon request, disclose to any client who is an individual and who is, or is contemplating becoming, the holder of a policy of insurance the amount of commission paid by the insurer under any relevant policy of insurance. In respect of investment business as defined by the Financial Services Act 1986, insurance brokers shall observe the disclosure requirements under the Rules made pursuant to that Act by their regulatory body for that purpose.

(8) Before effecting a contract for insurance or investment, insurance brokers shall disclose and identify in writing any amount, or if the amount is not known the basis on which it will be calculated, they propose to charge to the client and which will be in addition to the insurance contract or investment for any service or work relating to that contract of insurance or investment or their placement.

(9) Insurance brokers shall disclose to a client in writing any payment which they receive or will receive in addition to commission as a result of effecting a contract of insurance or investment or as a result of securing on behalf of that client any service additional to the arrangement of a contract of insurance or investment.

(10) Insurance brokers may not become an appointed representative of any authorised person, including an insurer, under section 44 of the Financial Services Act 1986 if by doing so and carrying on business as such they would be unable to comply with any of the provisions of the Code.

(11) Insurance brokers shall explain to the client the differences in, and the relative costs of, the principal types of insurance, relevant investment business, or if appropriate, any other investments, which in the opinion of the insurance broker, would suit the client's needs. In doing so, insurance brokers may take into consideration the knowledge held by the client when deciding to what extent it is in the client's interest to have the terms and conditions of the policy or investment explained to him.

(12) In order to satisfy the requirements of their clients, insurance brokers shall take care not to limit unduly the number of insurers they are able to use.

(13) If insurance brokers recommend to a client, or are requested by such a client, to place his insurances with an insurer who is not authorised or permitted to carry on or provide insurance of the relevant class in the UK, great care must be taken to ensure that at the time of the recommendation or the request, the client appreciates the possible risks involved and such should be put in writing to the client if the insurance broker reasonably believes it would be appropriate having regard to the client's experience of insurance. In such a case either definitive instructions should be obtained from the client in writing, or confirmation of such instruction should be given to the client in writing.

(14) Insurance brokers shall not withhold from the client any written evidence or documentation relating to the contract of insurance or investment without adequate and justifiable reasons being disclosed in writing and without delay to the client. If an insurance broker withholds documents from the client by way of lien he shall provide advice to the client in writing of this at the time that the documents are withheld.

(15) When inviting renewal of insurance policies for individuals, insurance brokers shall forward to the client promptly the original of all available insurers' renewal invitations which are accepted as being accurate and complete.

(16) If a premium for a policy is being paid by instalments, insurance brokers shall ensure that evidence of cover and the basis of payments is given to the client at the commencement of the risk, or on any renewal.

(17) Insurance brokers shall inform a client of the name of all insurers with whom a contract of insurance is placed. This information, or any changes thereafter, shall be advised to the client at the earliest opportunity.

(18) Insurance brokers shall have a proper regard for the wishes of a policyholder or client who seeks to terminate their appointment as insurance brokers.

(19) Any information acquired by insurance brokers from their client shall not be used or disclosed except in the normal course of negotiating, maintaining, or renewing a contract of insurance, or in handling a claim for that client unless the consent of the client has been obtained or the information is required by a court of competent jurisdiction.

(20) In the completion of the proposal form, claim form, or any other material document, insurance brokers shall make it clear that all answers or statements are the client's own responsibility. The client should always be asked to check the details and told that the inclusion of incorrect information may result, inter alia, in a claim being repudiated. On request, a client shall be supplied with a copy of the proposal form or other relevant document at the time of completion.

(21) When giving a quotation for a policy of insurance, insurance brokers shall

take due care to ensure its accuracy and their ability to place at the quoted price: if any premium is reduced by a commission rebate that amount should be disclosed.

(22) When a claim arises on an insurance policy effected by an insurance broker he shall on request give reasonable assistance to the client in pursuing that claim.

(23) Advertisements made by or on behalf of insurance brokers shall comply with the applicable parts of the British Code of Advertising Practice published by the Advertising Standards Authority and for this purpose the British Code of Advertising Practice shall be deemed to form part of this Code of Conduct.

(24) Advertisements made by or on behalf of insurance brokers shall distinguish between contractual benefits, that is those that the contract of insurance is bound to provide, and non-contractual benefits, that is the amount of benefit which it might provide. Where such advertisements include a forecast of non-contractual benefits, insurance brokers shall restrict the forecast to that provided by the insurer concerned.

(25) Advertisements made by or on behalf of insurance brokers shall not be restricted to the policies of one insurer except where the reasons for such restriction are fully explained in the advertisement, the insurer named therein, and the prior approval of that insurer obtained.

(26) When advertising their services directly or indirectly either in person (e.g., by canvassing) or in writing insurance brokers shall disclose their identity, occupation and purpose before seeking information or before giving advice.

(27) Registered insurance brokers who commence to carry on business either as a sole proprietor or in partnership with others shall submit forthwith the appropriate documentation of their change in status as required by the Rules made pursuant to section 8 of the Act to the Council in order that the Registrar may amend their entry to that of practising insurance brokers.

(28) Insurance brokers who wish to relinquish membership of the profession must submit to the Registrar a statutory declaration as required by the Rules made pursuant to section 8 of the Act and any other necessary documentation required by the Council in order that their names may be removed from the Register/List in good order.

(29) Insurance brokers shall ensure that they reply promptly or procure a prompt reply to all correspondence.

(30) Registered insurance brokers who are directors of an enrolled body corporate shall ensure that the company complies with all the requirements under the Act and its subordinate legislation, including the Rules, and, if applicable the Financial Services Act 1986 and similarly its subordinate legislation.

(31) Insurance brokers shall display in any office where they are carrying on business and to which the public have access a notice to the effect that a copy of the Code of Conduct is available upon request and that if a member of the public

wishes to make a complaint or requires the assistance of the Council in resolving a dispute, he may write to the Insurance Brokers Registration Council at its offices at 15 St Helen's Place, London EC3A 6DS.

(32) Where the interests of clients would be significantly affected by the death or incapacity of an insurance broker arrangements must be made to protect the interests of clients in that event.

(33) If acting as an agent for another insurance broker or insurance intermediary, insurance brokers shall disclose this in writing to their clients.

# CHAPTER 9

# MEDICAL PRACTICE AND PROFESSIONAL LIABILITY

## 1 INSTITUTIONAL STRUCTURES, PERSONNEL AND FORMS OF LIABILITY

### 1.1 Introduction

A knowledge of the breadth and complexity of the medical professions and the organisational structure of the modern health delivery service is vital in terms of considering the numerous issues that will be discussed in this chapter. Matters of mainly tortious but also contractual and criminal liability will be seen to be affected by the changing face of the health service. Of importance in this chapter will be a recognition that while traditional legal notions will continue to be a necessary area of knowledge for those concerned with matters of medical professional liability, the complex nature of medical practice, and the wide variety of factual situations that can arise have slowly led these traditional legal notions through a metamorphosis. Nowhere will this be seen more clearly than the medical negligence action. Of importance also is a further recognition of the potential number of professionals who can become defendants in this arena of professional practice. Any list of specialisms in medicine would be considerable, but a sample list indicates the variety of practical situations that can arise to task the litigator.[1]

One should further note that there are a number of very specific pieces of legislation controlling a variety of aspects of many of these professions.[2] Most of these statutes are, however, designed to facilitate the development of lists of those deemed to be competent to practice. Of more significance in the present context is that these statutes do create regulatory functions that include a disciplinary role.[3]

### 1.2 The registered medical practitioner

In the broadest sense liability of whatever form will only attach to a medical person who is designated a "registered medical practitioner" or persons who falsely declare

---

1. Doctors, surgeons, nurses, physiotherapists, pharmacists, health visitors, midwives, anaesthetists, dentists, paramedics, alternative therapists. It should also be noted that surgeons, for example, can be divided up into a considerable range of specialities.
2. Three examples should suffice at this stage; the Pharmacy Act 1954, the Nurses, Midwives and Health Visitors Act 1979, and the Dentists Act 1984.
3. See section 8 of this chapter on general legal aspects of the disciplinary structures in existence.

themselves to be so qualified. Criminal liability will attach to an individual practising medicine without being so recognised.

Section 49 of the Medical Act 1983 provides that:

"... any person who wilfully and falsely pretends to be or takes or uses the name or title of physician, doctor of medicine, licentiate in medicine or surgery, bachelor of medicine, surgeon, general practitioner or apothecary, or any name, title, addition or description implying that he is registered under any provision of this Act, or that he is recognised by law as a physician or surgeon or licentiate in medicine and surgery or a practitioner in medicine or an apothecary, shall be liable on summary conviction to a fine."

This section should be read in conjunction with section 3, which might be termed the "registration" section.[4]

Kennedy and Grubb make the useful introductory point that "being a fully registered medical practitioner confers on a doctor as a matter of public policy the privilege of doing certain things to other people which would otherwise be prima facie unlawful".[5] *R* v. *General Medical Council, ex parte Virik*[6] provides both an example of the difficulties where traditional pathways of medical education are not undertaken and the process of registration with the involvement of the General Medical Council ("GMC"). A doctor applied to quash a decision of the GMC to refuse to allow full registration as a medical practitioner. Initially the doctor was granted limited registration as someone who had acceptable foreign qualifications.[7] He required a full registration to practise. He could, the GMC decided, so register if he became a member of the Royal College of Surgeons. The GMC was also aware that the doctor had never held the post of registrar in this country. A domestically trained doctor was not required to meet these conditions. The application for *certiorari* was upheld (but with a recognition that enforcement through declaratory relief would be impossible) because the review board of the GMC was mistaken in interpreting its guidelines as creating a higher standard for certain overseas qualified doctors. The lack of experience expressed by the review board in its decision was not unacceptable for the purposes of registration.

## 1.3 Institutional structure

The complexities of the structure of the modern National Health Service are sufficient to tax the most diligent researcher, but a basic knowledge of this structure is important, and relates primarily back to the issue of who to sue, and whether to do so as a matter of an allegation of direct or vicarious liability.

Newdick has effectively analysed the changing structure of the National Health Service.[8] In terms of professional liability within the medical professions, such

---

4. "Subject to the provisions of this Act any person who—
    (a) holds one or more primary United Kingdom qualifications and has passed a qualifying examination and satisfied the requirements of this Part of this Act as to experience; or
    (b) being a national of any member State of the Communities, holds one or more primary European qualifications;
is entitled to be registered under this section as a fully registered medical practitioner."
5. I Kennedy and A Grubb, *Medical Law; Text with Materials* (2nd edn, 1994, Butterworths), p. 38.
6. (1995) *The Times*, 17 February (Q.B.D., Carnwath J).
7. In accordance with the Medical Act 1983, s. 22.
8. See C Newdick, *Who Should We Treat?* (1995, OUP, Oxford).

reforms have had a noticeable impact. The essence of this impact lies in the number, variety and complexity of managerial/operational tasks that need to be performed, with the "knock-on" effect that has on the complexity of any litigation which results from the inadequacy in the performance of any one of those myriad roles. Issues of primary and vicarious liability then rear their heads—in essence the vital decision on where those representing the plaintiff in a medical negligence action should direct their fire.[9]

Further support for the need to consider the essential features of the modern health care system come from Newdick's description of a recent survey[10]:

"Concern has been expressed about the standard of care in some accident and emergency units. In a survey of the treatment of skeletal trauma following serious accidents, the British Orthopaedic Association studied 800 patients selected at random. Medical assessors were asked to decide how many patients suffered morbidity following treatment and whether it would have been preventable using proper methods of management. Their results were as follows.

50 per cent of patients had no morbidity at all, often as a result of good treatment. 30 per cent were judged to have morbidity which was inevitable regardless of facilities, treatment etc. However, in some 20 per cent of patients the assessors judged that the morbidity could have been less with ideal treatment and in 12 per cent this was of significant proportions affecting the quality of their life, work, independence etc.

The assessors were asked to judge how treatment could have been improved ... Of the 98 patients (12 per cent) with severe preventable morbidity, our assessors felt that 55 patients had been treated by people with inadequate training and special interest to achieve a good result."

With surveys such as these it is essential to be aware of the law as it affects the medical profession. It seems likely that the amount of personal injury litigation in this context will increase, as will the demand of the medical professionals involved in retaining those with an understanding of the available law as well as an understanding of the operational underpinnings of the modern health service.

The general governing legislation at present is the National Health Service Act 1977 in combination with the National Health Service and Community Care Act 1990. These pieces of legislation give the Secretary of State a number of powers and duties in relation to the organisational structuring and priorities of the National Health Service.[11]

The main alterations effected by the 1990 Act were the establishment of NHS Trust hospitals and GP fund-holding.[12] This has tended to "devolve decision-making power down the chain of authority towards GPs and hospitals so that many of the supervisory and administrative functions of RHAs to set objectives and monitor performance have declined".[13] Criticism of Trusts, fund-holding and the creation of

---

9. "Apart from their patients, doctors have to consider a variety of other matters. Clinical decisions may be subject to medical audit; business plans may have to be agreed; financial budgets and targets may have to be agreed. This means that clinical discretion may now involve considerations which differ from those in the past." (Newdick, *op. cit.*, at p. 3.)

10. C Newdick, *op. cit.*, at pp. 79–80.

11. The establishment of Regional Health Authorities (National Health Service Act 1977, s. 8(1A)(a)); the establishment of District Health Authorities (1977 Act, s. 8(1A)(a), as amended by the National Health Service and Community Care Act 1990, ss. 1(1), 66(2) and Sch. 10); the establishment of Family Health Service Authorities (1977 Act, s. 19, as amended by the National Health Service and Community Care Act 1990, ss. 2(1) and 3(a)).

12. See the 1990 Act, ss. 14–17.

13. C Newdick, *op. cit.*, at p. 41.

the internal market is relevant for our purposes in that there has been an increased trend to litigate on the basis of clinical decisions which appear on the surface to have been made on a determination of need in an era of scant resources. Such attempts to litigate here are worthy of consideration, even having acknowledged that none has been successful in terms of substantive law, due to the fact that such judicial reluctance to allow the plaintiff to succeed has been tempered with sympathetic comments on the plight of patients. One can tentatively state that the courts may not have closed the door on such actions.

The actions in question have been either against the relevant health authority or even the Secretary of State and will be considered after an introductory analysis of the medical professional's relationship with that person's employer and patient.[14]

The legal relationship is between a doctor and the newly formed Family Health Service Authority ("FHSA"). The duty incumbent upon the FHSA is to "arrange as respects their locality with medical practitioners to provide medical services for all persons in the locality who wish to take advantage of the arrangement".[15] The arrangement is by way of the production of the "medical list" of those general practitioners who carry out services.

The legal relationship between the medical practitioner and the FHSA is complex. It is uncertain what branches of law regulate this area. In the words of Kennedy and Grubb[16]:

"There are a number of options. First, the relationship is one of contract, which, in this situation, would undoubtedly be a contract for services since the GP could never be viewed as an employee of an FHSA. Secondly, the relationship is one which is *sui generis* defined by statute and lying in the realm of public law. Thirdly, their relationship may be a hybrid, being a creature in part of private law (though not contract) and in part public law."

This fell to be directly considered by the courts in the case of *Roy* v. *Chelsea and Kensington FPC*.[17] Dr Roy was accused of not devoting enough time to his general practice under the NHS. As a result his practice allowance was reduced by 20 per cent. Dr Roy contended that his relationship with the Family Practitioner Committee (the forerunner to the FHSA) was contractual, and further, that he had fulfilled his obligation under that contract by providing a locum during his absences. He thus contended that the reduction amounted to a breach of contract by the FPC. The FPC applied to have the action struck out as an abuse of the process of the court.

At first instance his Honour Judge White held that Dr Roy could not proceed. Both the action and the relationship had contractual "echoes", but such echoes were deceptive. The rights and duties were dependent on statute. The duties of the FPC existed in the realm of public law. Dr Roy's action would thus be for judicial review.

On appeal it was argued that the relationship was governed by Schedule I, Part II to the 1974 Regulations. The form used under these Regulations constitutes an offer to perform general medical services upon terms. If the FPC accept the application, the communication of that acceptance (whether by letter, or by the inclusion of the doctor's name on the medical list) amounts to a contract. The consideration relates to the promise to perform these general medical services in return for payment in

14. See "Primary Duty of the Secretary of State" at p. 475.
15. National Health Service Act 1977, s. 29, as amended.
16. Kennedy and Grubb, *op. cit.*, note 5, at p. 39.
17. [1990] 1 Med.L.R. 328, C.A., [1992] 1 A.C. 624, H.L.

accordance with the Statement of Fees and Allowances. According to Balcombe LJ, "If the relationship were not contractual it is difficult to see what else it could be".[18]

It was left to the House of Lords to resolve this difficulty. Lord Lowry set out the unanimous view:

"... under the statutory arrangements the doctor on the one side and each of the FPC and medical committee on the other have rights and obligations conferred by statute rather than by contract. It is not necessary and we think it wrong to seek to import a contract into a scheme of things which is governed by the very detailed statutory arrangements made by neither the FPC or the medical committee."

Notwithstanding such a comment however, Lord Lowry went on to state:

"The actual or possible absence of a contract is not decisive against Dr Roy. He has in my opinion a bundle of rights which should be regarded as his individual private law rights against the Committee, arising from the statute and regulations and including the very important private law right to be paid for the work that he has done."

A general practitioner may be removed from the medical list where there is a breach of the terms of service under Schedule 2 to the Medical Regulations. Where a GP is found to be in breach of the terms of service, with such a breach making continued inclusion "prejudicial to the efficiency of the service", the FHSA may refer the case to a tribunal set up under section 46 of, and Schedule 9 to, the National Health Service Act 1977.[19]

## 1.4 Hospital doctors

Obviously the legal responsibility of the hospital doctor is to the Health Authority or the NHS Trust. The development of the NHS Trust can have implications for hospital doctors. Section 6 of the National Health Service and Community Care Act 1990 allows the newly created Trust to take over the disciplinary procedures of the hospital. What the section also does is allow the Trust to negotiate its own terms and conditions, with the obvious opportunity for variation.

The contract is one of service. Such a contractual relationship is part of national negotiation.[20] Of importance at this stage is the interesting observation of Bell[21]:

"The common law draws an important distinction between treatment under the NHS and private treatment. The House of Lords has held [*Pfizer v. Ministry of Health* [1965] A.C. 512] that where services are provided pursuant to a statutory obligation there is no contractual relationship, for the element of compulsion is inconsistent with the consensual basis of contract. The fact that the patient makes some payment is irrelevant. Thus the NHS patient can only sue in tort."

Tort then lies at the heart of professional liability in medicine.

18. Nourse and Neill LJJ agreed. It is perhaps unfortunate that the court was not referred to the case of *Wadi v. Cornwall and Isles of Scilly FPC* [1985] 1 C.R. 492. The E.A.T. here found that the relationship was not contractual.

19. National Health Service (Service Committees and Tribunal) Regulations 1992, S.I. 1992/664, reg. 24.

20. "The Red Book" or "Terms and Conditions of Service of Hospital Medical and Dental Staff (England and Wales)".

21. "The Doctor and the Supply of Goods and Services Act 1982" (1984) 4 L.S. 175.

## 2 DUTIES

### 2.1 Introduction

It is vitally important to establish when a duty of care comes into existence for the purposes of contract, but more particularly here, for the purposes of an action in tort. It is the fundamental aspect of the legal relationship between medical professional and patient. Kennedy and Grubb set the general scene[22]:

"While the coincidence of a 'request' by an individual and a resulting 'undertaking' by a doctor adequately captures the normal case, in fact there are situations in which the legal relationship will come into existence without there having been a request on the part of the individual. The doctor, however, must always have given an undertaking of some sort or other before the law will recognise the legal relationship and his duty which flows from it. Examples of these latter situations are where a parent seeks medical care on behalf of a young child or where an emergency arises and the individual is unconscious."

A doctor may withdraw an undertaking to a patient but cannot abandon the patient. Paragraphs 9–11 of the terms of service state the manner of withdrawal needed:

"9.(1) A doctor may have any person removed from his list and shall notify the FHSA in writing that he wishes to have a person removed from his list, subject to subparagraph (2), the removal shall take effect—
    (a)  on the date on which the person is accepted by or assigned to another doctor; or
    (b)  on the eighth day after the FHSA receives the notice, whichever is the sooner ...

10. Where the doctor informs the FHSA in writing that he wishes to terminate his responsibility for a temporary resident, his responsibility for that person shall cease in accordance with paragraph 9, as if the temporary resident were a person on his list.

11.(1) A doctor with whom an arrangement has been made for the provision of any or all of the maternity medical services mentioned in regulation 31(1)(a) may agree with the woman concerned to terminate the arrangement, and in default of agreement the doctor may apply to the FHSA for permission to terminate the arrangement.
(2) On an application under paragraph (1), the FHSA, after considering any representations made by either party and after consulting the Local Medical Committee, may terminate the arrangement.
(3) Where a doctor ceases to provide any or all of the maternity medical services mentioned in regulation 31(1)(a), he shall inform any woman for whom he has arranged to provide such services that he is ceasing to provide them and that she may make a fresh arrangement to receive those services from another doctor."

It should be noted that the doctor's undertaking continues until it is reasonable for another doctor to give a separate undertaking. Liability may occur where this does not take place.

### 2.2 The establishment of the duty of care

The literature on medical negligence and liability in general in relation to the medical profession centres discussion of the duty of care with the term "undertaking".[23] One of the classic early expositions of medical negligence by Lord Nathan focused the

---

22. *Op. cit.*, at p. 64.
23. The concept of undertaking was succinctly put by Lord Hewart CJ in *R* v. *Bateman* [1925] 94 L.J.K.B. 791, C.C.A.

discussion of duty on the assumption of responsibility for the particular patient. Whatever particular phraseology may be utilised, the matter at hand turns upon whether the judicial mind is expansive or constrictive in its notion of when a duty arises. There is a line along which legal duty may travel. The line begins with the individual patient requiring a form of medical treatment, and ends with completed treatment. There are a number of potentially legally significant events along this journey to which may be attached the formation of a legal responsibility—a duty of care.

It may be perceived as overly restrictive, but with the benefit of certainty, that the duty of care only arises when some form of official admissions procedure has been complied with. At the other end of the scale it may be decreed that the hospital itself may have made an implicit automatic undertaking to treat anyone who enters the surgery or hospital, notwithstanding the fact that an admissions procedure has not been complied with. Broadly speaking, the available case-law does not clearly indicate the time at which the vital issue of the duty of care arises.

## 2.3 Primary duty of the Secretary of State

In specific terms the 1977 Act imposes upon the Secretary of State a[24]:

"duty to continue the promotion in England and Wales of a comprehensive health service designed to secure improvement (a) in the physical and mental health of the people of those countries, and (b) in the prevention, diagnosis and treatment of illness, and for that purpose to provide or secure the effective provision of services in accordance with this Act."

Section 3 sets out the statutory duties of the Secretary of State in some detail[25]:

"It is the Secretary of State's duty to provide to such an extent as he considers necessary to meet all reasonable requirements—
   (a) hospital accommodation;
   (b) other accommodation for the purpose of any service provided under this Act;
   (c) medical, dental, nursing and ambulance services;
   (d) such other facilities for the care of expectant mothers and nursing mothers and young children as he considers are appropriate as part of the health service;
   (e) such facilities for the prevention of illness, the care of persons suffering from illness and the after-care of persons who have suffered from illness as he considers are appropriate as part of the health service;
   (f) such other services as are required for the diagnosis and treatment of illness."

The specific enforceability of such duties have taxed the courts on a few occasions; to date without success. A consideration of the prospects of success if such an action were contemplated begins with the first case to consider the scope of section 3(1), that of *Hincks*.[26]

The applicants in this case were orthopaedic patients who had been waiting for treatment for a period beyond that which was medically advisable for their illness due to a shortage of facilities, this shortage being due to financial constraints. The action sought was against the Secretary of State, the Regional Health Authority and the Area Health Authority for breach of the section 1 duty to provide a comprehensive service, and section 3 for the failure to provide the facilities to eventuate this. The

---

24. Section 1.
25. Section 3(1).
26. *R* v. *Secretary of State for Social Services, ex parte Hincks* (1992) B.M.L.R. 93.

Secretary of State accepted the need for an increase in such orthopaedic services, but in terms of priority, the project could not be expected to start within the next 10 years (the case was decided in 1980).

The basis of the action was stated as being, "If the Secretary of State needs money to do it, then he must see that Parliament gives it to him. Alternatively, if Parliament does not give it to him, then a provision should be put in the statute to excuse him from his duty."[27]

The patients failed in their action. Wien J, while sympathising with the anguish of the patients stated that, "I have come to the conclusion that it is impossible to pinpoint anywhere a breach of duty on the part of the Secretary of State ... It all turns on the matter of financial resources. If the money is not there then the services cannot be met in one particular place". The matter was thus one for Parliament to address. The clear point made was that the phrase in terms of duty was "to such an extent as he considers necessary". Such a phrase leant itself to the exercise of discretion in the Secretary's obligations. On appeal this decision was upheld, but with the key notion being the use of the concept of "reasonable" in the legislation. Nevertheless the comment was made that the possibility existed in the future of the Secretary of State making a decision within that discretion that was so unreasonable that no Minister would have made it; the invocation of the principle of "unreasonableness".

Much the same result was achieved in the later case of *Walker*.[28] The factual background was that a baby had been born prematurely and required a heart operation. On a number of occasions the child's operation was cancelled. The affidavit set out the reasons:

"Apparently the problem is a shortage of specially trained nurses for the intensive unit that my baby would have to go in after the operation. There are six beds in this unit but currently four trained nurses. There has to be a trained nurse for each bed in use. The four beds are occupied by other babies and, in the period that my baby has been at the hospital, whenever a bed has come free, which has been rare, Mr Giovanni and Mr Sethi have told me that, unfortunately, more urgent cases than my baby's have had to be admitted to the free beds."

According to McPherson J:

"I find it impossible to say that there is any decision made by the health authority or by the surgeons who act on their behalf, any illegality nor any procedural defect, nor any such unreasonableness. The fact that the decision is unfortunate, disturbing and in human terms distressing, simply cannot lead to a conclusion that the court should interfere in a case of this kind."

Once more the confirmation was that if there were issues to be raised then they would be properly raised in the political arena and not the court of law.

While rejecting another attempt to resurrect the action in the Court of Appeal, Sir John Donaldson MR did raise the issue of *Wednesbury*[29]:

"The court could only intervene where it was satisfied that there was a *prima facie* case, not only of failing to allocate resources in the way that others would think that resources should be allocated, but of a failure to allocate resources to an extent which was *Wednesbury* unreasonable."[30]

27. *Ibid.* at 95 *per* Lord Denning MR.
28. *R* v. *Central Birmingham Health Authority, ex parte Walker* (1987) 3 B.M.L.R. 32 (reported before, but decided much later than, *Hincks*).
29. *Associated Provincial Picture House Ltd* v. *Wednesbury Corporation* [1948] 1 K.B. 223.
30. *Walker* (1987) 3 B.M.L.R. 32 at 35.

This option for a failure to provide what may be termed essential medical services through the realms of public law, does remain an availability, but with little real prospects for success. Given that this possibility nevertheless exists in the judicial mind, the exact parameters of this possibility in public law as it applies to clinical decision making needs to be addressed.

The judicial review alternative was considered applicable[31]:

"... to a decision which is so outrageous in its defiance of logic or of accepted moral standards that no sensible person who had applied his mind to the question to be decided could have arrived at it. Whether a decision falls within this category is a question that judges by their training and experience would be well equipped to answer, or else there would be something badly wrong with our system."

In *R* v. *Central Birmingham Health Authority, ex parte Collier*[32] a four-year-old child was suffering from a hole in the heart. The consultant involved in the clinical management of the child described him as "desperately needing surgery". The child was placed on top of the waiting list in September 1987. By the end of January 1988, the operation had been cancelled a number of times. Unless the operation was performed, with an intensive care bed being made available, then the likelihood was that the child would die. The Court of Appeal stance was that:

"... even assuming that [the evidence] does establish that there is an immediate danger to health, it seems to me that the legal principles to be applied do not differ from *Walker*. This court is in no position to judge the allocation of resources by this particular health authority ... there is no suggestion here that the hospital authority have behaved in a way which is deserving of condemnation or criticism. What is suggested is that somehow more resources should be made available to enable the hospital authorities to ensure that the treatment is immediately given."

A number of useful matters come out of litigation concerning the modern management of health care and the existence of legal duties of hospitals. The future may see whether *Wednesbury* is utilised more vigorously in clinical decision-making combined with the reasonableness of the allocation of particular resources. Newdick[33] points out evidence of a more aggressive judicial stance on the issue of whether clinical decision-making should be dominated by resource allocation decisions from Lord Donaldson MR in the recent case of *Re J*.[34] "Health authorities are supported by medical and administrative staff. In the context of medical decisions, it would be perverse for it to act otherwise than in accordance with the advice of its medical staff when the advice was unanimous."

To all of the above considerations one must now add the well-publicised case of child B.[35] The case concerned a 10-year-old girl with leukaemia. The child had been in the medical care of the relevant authority since 1990. The prognosis in 1995 was very poor. The girl was expected to die within months without treatment. The health authority had refused this remedial treatment. The argument was based on a rough

31. *Council of Civil Service Unions* v. *Minister for the Civil Service* [1985] A.C. 374 at 410 *per* Lord Diplock.

32. Lexis transcript, 6 January 1988. See also Newdick, *op. cit.*, at pp. 124–125.

33. *Op. cit.*, at p. 129.

34. [1992] 4 All E.R. 614 at 619.

35. *R* v. *Cambridge District Health Authority, ex parte B* [1995] 2 All E.R. 129. See Newdick, *op. cit.*, at p. 131. See also M. Davies, "Resource Allocation in Medicine and Professional Liability—the Final Nail?" (1996) 12 P.N. 15.

cost-benefit analysis. The cost of the treatment of £75,000 was stated to be too high with marginal benefit clinically to be expected. At first instance Laws J invited the health authority to reconsider its evidence for its refusal in the following terms[36]:

"...merely to point to the fact that resources are finite tells us nothing about the wisdom, or ... the legality of the decision to withhold funding in a particular case ... Where a question is whether the life of a 10-year-old child might be saved, by however slim a chance, the responsible authority must do more than toll the bell of tight resources. They must explain the priorities that have led them to decline to fund the treatment."

Not unexpectedly the finding of the judge of first instance was overruled in the Court of Appeal on the same day. It appears that the court accepted that there were sufficient clinical reasons not to treat.[37]

The action in negligence against the Secretary of State has also been attempted in the significant litigation surrounding the Factor VIII vaccine.[38]

It will be remembered that 962 haemophiliacs had developed AIDS or would do so after being treated with Factor VIII concentrate from the USA. The negligence was alleged to have been the failure of the Secretary of State to ensure that the country was self-sufficient in blood supplies. This failure caused the plaintiffs to be infected with the contaminated supplies from the USA. The plaintiffs applied to the court requiring an order for the production of documents which the Government had argued attracted public interest immunity because they related to the formulation of Government policy debating the possible merits in maintaining self-sufficiency in blood products.

The plaintiffs' appealed on the basis that Rougier J, at first instance, should not have excluded certain documents from the order that was made. That order had distinguished between "performance" and "breach" related negligence.

The crux of the issue was described by Ralph Gibson LJ as to whether "the rejection of the claim for breach of statutory duty must of itself negative any coterminous claim in negligence ..."

The court went on to hold that[39]:

"the plaintiffs have at least made out an arguable case. It is obvious that it would be rare for a case of negligence to be proved having regard to the nature and duties under the 1977 Act, and to the fact that, in the law of negligence, it is difficult to prove a negligent breach of duty when the party charged is required to exercise discretion and to form judgements upon the allocation of public resources. That, however, is not sufficient, in my judgement, to make it clear for the purposes of these proceedings, that there can in law be no claim in negligence. Nor, on the allegations of fact, can it be said that the plaintiffs have not alleged a case which could be upheld if in law the claim is viable".

Therefore, while there may be evidential difficulties and matters of departmental and Ministerial operational discretion fatal to a claim in negligence in such potentially wide-ranging actions, the possibility of success as a matter of law, exists.

36. Newdick, *op. cit.*, at pp. 131–132.
37. Note that at the time of writing the child is receiving treatment as a result of an anonymous donation. The father is considering an action in negligence against the health authority.
38. *Re HIV Haemophiliac Litigation* (1990) N.L.J.R. 1349, C.A.
39. Gibson LJ, in reaching this decision, sought to rely on the pragmatism inherent in *Rowling* v. *Takaro Properties Ltd* [1988] A.C. 473; and *Murphy* v. *Brentwood DC* [1991] 1 A.C. 398, H.L.

## 2.4 Duty of care and hospitals

The obvious issue to consider here is the primary liability of the hospital authority in negligence. Potential duties were identified by Picard[40] in relation to Canada, but would appear generally applicable for English Law:

> "(a) to select competent and qualified employees;
> (b) to instruct and supervise them;
> (c) to provide proper facilities and equipment;
> (d) to establish systems necessary to the safe operation of the hospital".

In English law, the notion of primary liability of hospitals has not received a great deal of judicial encouragement. Nevertheless Browne-Wilkinson V-C gave the matter some thought in the significant case of *Wilsher* v. *Essex Area Health Authority*[41]:

"... I agree with the comments of Mustill LJ as to the confusion which has been caused in this case both by the pleading and by the argument below which blurred the distinction between the vicarious liability of the health authority for the negligence of its doctors and the direct liability of the health authority for negligently failing to provide skilled treatment of the kind that it was offering to the public. In my judgement, a health authority which so conducts its hospitals that it fails to provide doctors of sufficient skill and experience to give the treatment offered at the hospital may be directly liable in negligence to the patient. Although we are told in argument that no case has ever been decided on this ground and that it is not the practice to formulate claims in this way, I can see no reason why, in principle, the health authority should not be so liable if its organisation is at fault."

It is also worth considering the more positive tone on primary liability in *Bull* v. *Devon AHA*.[42] In this case Mrs Bull sued the health authority both on her own behalf and that of her disabled son. Mrs Bull's claim was that her son's asphyxia-caused disability was due to her son's delivery being delayed by the absence of an attendant doctor. This, it was claimed, was due to the hospital maintaining services on two sites. This was found to have led to a breakdown in the established system of summoning doctors.

According to Slade LJ:

"The duty of a hospital is to provide a woman admitted in labour with a reasonable standard of skilled obstetric and paediatric care, in order to ensure as far as reasonably practicable the safe delivery of the baby or babies and the health of the mother and offspring thereafter."

He continued:

"It is possible to imagine hypothetical contingencies which would have accounted for a failure, without any avoidable fault in the hospital's system or any negligence in its working, to secure to Mrs Bull attendance by any obstetrician to deliver the ... [plaintiff's son] ... In my judgement, however, all the most likely explanations for this failure point strongly either:
> (1) to inefficiency in the system for summoning the assistance of the registrar or consultant, in operation at the hospital in 1970, or
> (2) to negligence by some individual or individuals in the working of that system."

---

40. (1981) 26 McGill LJ 997.
41. [1986] 3 All E.R. 801, C.A.; [1987] Q.B. 730. For the facts and a further analysis of this important case, see p. 498 in this chapter.
42. [1993] 4 Med.L.R. 117, C.A.

## 2.5 Vicarious liability

Having noted the existence of the possibility of a direct duty on the hospital, Ellen Picard[43] feels that traditional rules of vicarious liability "do not fit the hospital and its professional staff. But most courts try to stretch the old garments to fit the new flesh". The reason behind this is that the central concept underlying vicarious liability is that of "control". As Picard continues:

"An employer of a professional such as a doctor may know nothing about the practice of medicine. He is not only not in a position to control the doctor, but if he attempts to do so will find that the employee has exercised his own form of control over the situation and quit."

This difficulty of a "control" analysis has been recognised by case-law. In both *Evans* v. *Liverpool Corporation*[44] and *Hillyer* v. *St Bartholomew's Hospital*[45] it was held that the absence of control in relation to clinical (as opposed to administrative) duties meant that the employer would not be vicariously liable for such activities.

The fiction of dividing aspects of the doctor's work, controlling the one at law but not the other, was recognised finally in *Gold* v. *Essex County Council.*[46] In *Cassidy* v. *Minister of Health*[47] Denning LJ found that the "hire and fire" power of an employer was indicative of a broader notion of control. This change of approach was also explained as a recognition that the private or charity-sponsored hospitals were less prevalent compared with the state-supported system, therefore there was less need for the protectionism inherent in the old control test.

*Roe* v. *Minister of Health*[48] expanded vicarious liability to cover part-time assistants at a hospital. This general law would also apply to the private sector.

As Kennedy and Grubb correctly indicate[49]:

"Outside the NHS, the steady growth of the private sector will inevitably mean that the courts will be faced with issues of respondent superior."

The key is to determine in the medical context the general issue of organisation and control. Denning LJ phrased it in the following terms[50]:

"One feature which seems to run through the instances is that, under a contract of service, a man is employed as part of the business and his work is done as an integral part of the business; whereas, under a contract for services, his work, although done for the business is not integrated into it, but is only accessory to it."

The case of *Razell* v. *Snowball* clarified the emerging question of the position of the consultant[51]:

"... whatever may have been the position of a consultant in former times nowadays since the National Health Service Act 1946, the term 'consultant' does not denote a particular relationship between a doctor and a hospital. It is simply a title denoting his place in the hierarchy of the hospital staff. He is a senior member of the staff, and is just as much a member

43. E Picard, "Liability of Hospitals in Common Law Canada" (1981) 26 McGill LJ 997 at pp. 1016–1017.
44. [1906] 1 K.B. 160.
45. [1909] 2 K.B. 820.
46. [1942] 2 K.B. 293.
47. [1951] 1 All E.R. 574.
48. [1954] 2 Q.B. 66.
49. *Op. cit.*, p. 433.
50. *Stevenson Jordan and Harrison Ltd* v. *MacDonald and Evans* [1952] 1 T.L.R. 101 at 111.
51. [1954] 3 All E.R. 429, [1954] 1 W.L.R. 1382.

of the staff as the house surgeon is. Whether he is called specialist or consultant makes no difference."

## 2.6 Duties in private medicine

The ambit of duty in private medicine is generally determined by contractual form. It is apparent that the emergency situation will be the same whether one is considering a scenario involving private medicine or treatment in the public sector.

The contractual matters are determined by simple ideas of what constitutes an offer, and what an acceptance: "Is it the patient who offers to pay if the doctor agrees to treat, or the patient who accepts the doctor's offer by agreeing to pay?"[52]

Usually express contractual terms are contained in the consent form.[53]

The main area of contention in the contractual realm is the breadth of implied terms in undertaking medical treatment. The usual contractual difficulties of implied terms in contract are exacerbated by the relative inexactitude of medical procedures. The *locus classicus* in relation to this matter can be found in *Thake* v. *Maurice*.[54]

The plaintiffs did not wish to have any more children. The defendant was advised of this fact. The first plaintiff decided to have a vasectomy and duly signed a consent form to this effect. Two years after this operation the second plaintiff became pregnant. By the time this was discovered it was too late for an abortion and the second plaintiff gave birth. The action was brought on a number of contractual grounds. First, the contract was to sterilise, and this was breached when the second plaintiff fell pregnant; in the alternative, that the plaintiffs had been induced to enter into the contract by a false warranty or innocent misrepresentation. The defendant was held at first instance to be in breach of contract. The defendant appealed to the Court of Appeal.

It was admitted that the defendant never used the word "guarantee". The plaintiffs' contention was that the actions of the consultant would have led a reasonable person to the conclusion that the effect of the operation would be permanent sterility.

Counsel for the plaintiffs placed great reliance on the fact that the consultant frequently described the operation as "irreversible". The defendant had in fact agreed at trial that the effect of such terminology would have been understood by the plaintiffs as "irreversible by God or man".

In response to such assertions, Neil LJ remained unpersuaded:

"It is the common experience of mankind that the results of medical treatment are to an extent unpredictable and that any treatment may be affected by the special characteristics of the particular patient. It has been well said that 'the dynamics of the human body of each individual are themselves individual'."

Neil LJ concluded that the reasonable person, in the absence of an express guarantee, would not have expected 100 per cent success.

An increase in the number of claims during the late 1980s for failed sterilisations led to private medicine adopting the cautious consent form wording of the

---

52. Kennedy and Grubb, *op. cit.*, at p. 69.
53. A specimen form is the Department of Health's "A Guide to Consent for Examination or Treatment" (H.C. (90) 22).
54. [1986] 1 All E.R. 497.

Department of Health, any reading of which would appear to close the door on such actions in future[55]:

"I understand
that the aim of the operation is to stop me having any children and it might not be possible to reverse the effects of the operation.
that sterilisation/vasectomy can sometimes fail, and that there is a very small chance that I may become fertile again after some time.
For vasectomy I understand
that I will have to use some other contraceptive method until two tests in a row show that I am not producing sperm, if I do not want to father any children
that I may remain fertile or become fertile again after some time."

Notwithstanding this development in private practice there will be continuing debate on the ambit of implied contractual terms in relation to elective/cosmetic surgery. One example, from Canada, indicates the possibility of founding an action in contract. In *LaFleur* v. *Cornelis*[56] the defendant was a cosmetic surgeon who operated on the plaintiff to reduce the size of her nose. The allegation was of breach of contract, due to his failure to inform her of a 10 per cent risk of scarring. Both contractual and negligence claims succeeded.

Barry J indicated the difference between a cosmetic and an "ordinary" doctor:

"He is selling a special service and he is more akin to a businessman. Therefore, this is not the ordinary malpractice case. Normally a doctor contracts to use the best skill he possesses and he is expected to exercise at least the methods ordinarily employed by similarly trained professionals. If he does not do so, he may be guilty of negligence in carrying out his contract, as I have found in the present case.

In the instant case, that was not the kind of contract which the defendant entered into with the plaintiff. The latter told the defendant what she wanted, namely a smaller nose. The defendant drew a sketch on his note to show the changes he would make if the plaintiff paid him a fee of $600. There was no misunderstanding whatever. Both parties were *ad idem* as to what each was to do. The plaintiff paid the fee and the defendant failed to carry out his part of the contract. Negligence is not a factor in a straight breach of contract action. There is no law preventing a doctor from contracting to do that which he is paid to do. I appreciate that usually there is no implied warranty of success, in the absence of special circumstances. In this case, the defendant stated to the plaintiff—'no problem. You will be very happy'. He made an express agreement, which he was not required to, without explaining the risk.

I find that the parties made a contract, and the defendant breached it, leaving the plaintiff with a scarred nose with a minimal deformity."

## 2.7 Duties and emergencies

There has long been an acceptance that the English law is uncomfortable with a recognition of the "Good Samaritan", whereas some jurisdictions make acting in such a laudable manner a legally enforceable obligation. More recently there has been apparent less animosity toward acting in an emergency without the consent of the patient. In *Re F*[57] Lord Goff justified emergency treatment without consent thus:

"Such action is sometimes said to be justified as arising from an emergency; in Prosser and Keaton, *Hornbook on Torts*[58] ... the action is said to be privileged by the emergency."

55. "A Guide to Consent for Examination or Treatment" ((1991) NHS Management Executive; Appendix A(2)).
56. (1979) 28 N.B.R. (2d) 569 (New Brunswick). See the further discussion of this case in M. Jones, *Medical Negligence* (1991).
57. [1990] 2 A.C. 1, [1989] 2 All E.R. 545, H.L.
58. (5th edn, 1984), p. 117.

However, as stated in relation to private practice, the key issue is when an obligation arises. It may turn on the concept of "undertaking" or even be defined as when the individual becomes known as a "patient". The key case on this area remains that of *Barnett* v. *Chelsea and Kensington Hospital Management Committee.*[59] The facts come from the judgment of Nield J:

"At about 5 am on 1 January 1966, three night watchmen drank some tea. Soon afterwards all three men started vomiting. At about 8 am the men walked to the casualty department of the defendant's hospital, which was open. One of them, the deceased, when he was in the room in the hospital, lay on some armless chairs. He appeared ill. Another of the men told the nurse that they had been vomiting after drinking tea. The nurse telephoned the casualty officer, a doctor, to tell him of the men's complaint. The casualty officer, who was himself unwell, did not see them, but said that they should go home and call in their own doctors. The men went away, and the deceased died some hours later from what was found to be arsenical poisoning."

The defendants argued that the existence of an open casualty ward was not a general invitation to treat anyone who entered.

Nield J cited with general approval Denning LJ in *Cassidy* v. *Ministry of Health*[60] with reference to hospital authorities that "Once they undertake the task they come under a duty to use care in the doing of it, and that is so whether they do it for reward or not". A little confusion can be found in the judgment of Nield J. During the course of his consideration he pointed out that casualty departments could be abused from time to time; therefore there was not necessarily a duty to see all who presented themselves. An unfortunately vague analysis of the situation, given that the opportunity existed for a more considered theory on when the legal duty comes into existence rather than a vague comment as to when it does not.

Some further illumination of judicial attitude may be available from the earlier *Barnes* v. *Crabtree.*[61] The plaintiff here claimed that on Christmas day she felt unwell and called at the defendant's surgery for treatment, as she believed she was registered with this particular doctor. He informed her that there was no surgery, and in any case, she was no longer on his list. She reacted by lying down on the doorstep until the doctor called the police to remove her. The defendant disputed this evidence and stated that she was still on his list. In addition he informed Barnes that she was fine and if she wasn't satisfied she could go to another doctor. He then closed the door. The jury intervened, so the judge directed them on the relevant points of law:

"In a case of real acute emergency a doctor under the National Health Service scheme was under an obligation to treat any patient who was acutely ill; for example, if there was a motor accident and someone was lying seriously injured. The obligation of a doctor under the health scheme to a patient on his list was to render all necessary and proper treatment to his patient. To ascertain what treatment was necessary and proper he had to exercise reasonable skill in diagnosis. But in a case of chronic illness when he had been seeing the patient frequently that did not mean that he was required to make a full clinical examination every time the patient asked for it."

The jury were unanimously of the opinion that there was no case for the doctor to answer.

59. [1969] 1 All E.R. 1068.
60. [1951] 1 All E.R. 574.
61. [1955] 2 B.M.J. 1215.

One should not, however, overlook a limited exception to the sometimes seen antipathy towards a "Good Samaritan" law; namely paragraph 4 of the GP's Terms of Service:

"4. (1)(h) ... persons to whom he may be requested to give treatment which is immediately required owing to an accident or other emergency at any place in his practice area, provided that—

  (i) he is not, at the time of the request, relieved of liability to give treatment under paragraph 5 (i.e., elderly or infirm), and

  (ii) he is not, at the time of the request, relieved, under paragraph 19(2), of his obligation to give treatment personally (i.e., by reason of having employed a deputy), and

  (iii) he is available to provide such treatment,

and any persons by whom he is requested, and agrees, to give treatment which is immediately required owing to an accident or other emergency at any place in the locality of any FHSA in whose medical list he is included, provided there is no doctor who, at the time of the request, is under an obligation otherwise than under this head to give treatment to that person, or there is such a doctor but, after being requested to attend, he is unable to attend and give treatment immediately required ..."

## 2.8 Specific aspects of duty of care

### 2.8.1 Duty of care and the unborn child

The important focus case on this aspect of duty is that of *Burton* v. *Islington Health Authority*.[62] Here the medical staff of a hospital run by the defendants carried out an operation on the plaintiff's mother when she was pregnant. The plaintiff, at birth, was found to be suffering from numerous disabilities. The female newborn brought an action which alleged that the gynaecological operation was the cause of her injuries while *in utero*. Further, that such an operation should not have been carried out on a pregnant woman, and that the medical staff had been negligent in failing to ascertain whether the woman was pregnant at the time of the operation. The refutation of this allegation from the health authority was based on the fact that there was no reasonable cause of action, as the injuries caused to the plaintiff were *in utero*, and therefore caused before the plaintiff had a legal status. Without such a legal status, it was alleged, no duty to care could be owed at law.

Potts J held in this case that there was no reason why the court could not, as a preliminary point, find that the child could claim in negligence. This was despite the fact that at the time of the injury she was a foetus. Later cases have questioned whether *B* v. *Islington* turns "on a legal fiction".

The grounds for the decision of Potts J are reasonably simple. The defendants had sought to rely on the persuasive case of *Watt* v. *Rama*.[63] Particular weight was put on part of the judgment that:

"... the defendant owed no duty of care to the infant plaintiff she being at the time of the collision *en ventre sa mere*, not an existing person and merely part of her mother. When an act or omission involving fault which might otherwise be regarded as founding an action occurs, there must, in order for such an act or omission to be regarded as negligent, be then and there in existence some legal person to sue or be sued. There must then and there be in existence a legal person having a legal right and another legal person having at the time a corresponding legal duty. Since the infant plaintiff was at the time of the accident *en ventre sa mere* she was not

62. [1991] 1 All E.R. 825.
63. (1972) V.R. 353.

then a person or human being *in esse* and in fact had no legal separate existence apart from her mother. Accordingly, she was not a legal person to whom a legal duty could be owed."

Potts J considered this *dictum* in the light of the passing of the Congenital Disabilities (Civil Liability) Act 1976, which at the time of *B* v. *Islington* was the only vague type of authority to contemplate such actions. The Act was passed to "make provision as to civil liability in the case of children born disabled in consequence of some person's fault".

Section 1 reads as follows:

"(1) If a child is born disabled as the result of such an occurrence before its birth as is mentioned in subsection (2) below, and a person (other than the child's own mother) is under this section answerable to this child in respect of the occurrence, the child's disabilities are to be regarded as damage resulting from the wrongful act of that person and actionable accordingly at the suit of the child.

(2) An occurrence to which this section applies is one which—

    (a) affected either parent of the child in his or her ability to have a normal, healthy child; or

    (b) affected the mother during her pregnancy, or affected her or her child in the course of its birth, so that the child is born with disabilities which would otherwise not have been present.

(3) ... a person ... is answerable to the child if he was liable in tort to the parent or would, if sued in due time, have been so; and it is no answer that there could not have been such liability because the parent suffered no actionable injury, if there was a breach of legal duty which, accompanied by injury, would have given rise to the liability ..."

The 1976 Act, however, did not apply in the present case because the Act only applied to children born after the passing of the Act. B was born before this date. Therefore Potts J was forced to fall back on general medical negligence precedent and the status approach to the duty of care and the unborn child.

The well-known case of *Paton* v. *Trustees of BPAS*[64] was unequivocal. Baker P stated that "The foetus cannot, in English law, in my view, have any right of its own at least until it is born and has a separate existence from the mother".

This was followed a number of times[65] thus appearing to preclude the actions of the newborn for pre-natal injuries outside the ambit of the 1976 Act. Indeed as Potts J was forced to admit, "I proceed on the basis that in England and Wales the foetus has no right of action, no right at all until birth".

However, having considered the recent developments in the duty of care in negligence generally, Potts J went on to argue that the hospital staff, when considering the D & C operation on the plaintiff's mother, should have reasonably foreseen that any embryo which might have been carried by the mother at the time would have been damaged by this gynaecological procedure, and any living child resulting from this embryo would be liable to be born injured.

The crux of the judgment comes in the following statement:

"In my view, the actual damage suffered by the plaintiff, i.e., being born suffering from physical abnormalities, was 'potential damage which was foreseeable' and was the result of the breach of a 'possible duty'. The fact that the plaintiff was undefined in law and without status when the train of events which resulted in that damage was set in motion is neither here nor there ... In my view there is no requirement in this branch of English law for the plaintiff and defendant to possess correlative rights and duties at the time of the wrongful act."

64. [1979] Q.B. 276.
65. *C* v. *S* [1987] 1 All E.R. 1230 at 1235; *Re F (in utero)* [1988] 2 All E.R. 193 at 196.

This case and the similar case of *De Martell* v. *Merton and Sutton HA*[66] went to the Court of Appeal. Dillon LJ give the unanimous view of the court. While recognising the force of the argument of Baker P in *Paton* v. *BPAS*, contrasted it with the fact that "There are contexts ... in which the courts have adopted as part of English law the maxim of the civil law that an unborn child shall be deemed to be born when its interests require it."

Weight was given to the principle that emerged from *Montreal Tramways* v. *Leveille*[67] that a child could be cloaked with the rights of action in the civil law upon birth as if those causes of action, which in actual fact were caused *in utero*, were caused when it had legally recognised rights; i.e., the child was born. The essential fact to be revealed from these decisions is that the child only needs to be born to maintain an action in negligence for pre-natal injury. The action crystallises upon birth.

### 2.9 Common law duty of confidence

#### 2.9.1 The duty of confidentiality

The general law still corresponds essentially to the ethical duty imposed by the Hippocratic oath; namely that:

"Whatsoever things I see or hear concerning the life of men in my attendance on the sick or even apart therefrom, which ought not to be noised abroad, I will keep silence thereon, counting such things to be sacred secrets."

The general duty to maintain a confidence at common law and the relevant features of that duty were laid down in the seminal case of the *Attorney-General* v. *Guardian Newspapers Ltd (No 2)*.[68] This decision established the notion of a public interest in maintaining a legally enforceable duty of confidence. Lord Goff set out the preconditions for the establishment of a common law duty[69]:

"... a duty of confidence arises when confidential information comes to the knowledge of a person (the confidant) in circumstances where he has notice, or is held to have agreed, that the information is confidential, with the effect that it would be just in all the circumstances that he should be precluded from disclosing the information to others. I have used the word 'notice' advisedly, in order to avoid the question of the extent to which actual knowledge is necessary, though I of course understand knowledge to include circumstances where the confidant has deliberately closed his eyes to the obvious. The existence of this broad general principle reflects the fact that there is such a public interest in the maintenance of confidences, that the law will provide remedies for their protection. I realise that in the vast majority of cases, in particular those concerned with trade secrets, the duty of confidence will arise from a transaction or relationship between the parties, often a contract, in which event the duty may arise by reason of either an express or an implied term of that contract. It is in such cases as these that the expression 'confider' and 'confidant' are perhaps most aptly employed. But it is well settled that a duty of confidence may arise in equity independently of such cases."

Although there have been relatively few cases concerning the legal aspects of the confidential nature of the doctor/patient relationship, in *Hunter* v. *Mann*[70] the basis

---

66. [1992] 3 All E.R. 833.
67. [1933] 4 D.L.R. 337.
68. [1990] 1 A.C. 109, [1988] 3 All E.R. 545.
69. [1988] 3 All E.R. 545 at 658.
70. [1974] Q.B. 767; [1974] 2 All E.R. 414 at 417.

was stated as being that "... the doctor is under a duty not to [voluntarily] disclose, without the consent of the patient, information which he, the doctor, has gained in his professional capacity".

In terms of disciplinary procedures in the medical profession, there is a strict adherence to the notion of confidentiality.[71]

Common law adherence to the duty has been augmented by statute, which indicate the breadth of the obligation in medical practice.[72]

### 2.9.2 Changing the nature of the obligation

A significant case in the context of medical confidentiality worthy of focal analysis is that of *Egdell*.[73]

W was detained as a patient in a secure hospital unit for reasons of public safety, having killed five people and wounded two others. As was his right, he applied for review by a mental health review tribunal for discharge or transfer with a view to discharge. The Secretary of State opposed the application, whereas W's responsible medical officer felt his condition (schizophrenia) could be controlled by drugs, and therefore supported W's application. W's solicitors instructed E to review W and produce a report to support this application.

E's report opposed transfer and the report was sent to W's solicitors with a view to its consideration by the tribunal. W withdrew his application. E considered that the report would not be included on W's records. He therefore sent a copy to the medical director of the hospital. A copy also turned up at the Home Office. W thus brought actions in equity and contract alleging a breach of the duty of confidence.

At trial Scott J argued that the crux of the matter[74]:

"... is not whether Dr Egdell was under a duty of confidence; he plainly was. The question is as to the breadth of that duty. Did the duty extend so far as to bar disclosure to the medical director of the hospital? Did it bar disclosure to the Home Office?"

Scott J went on to confirm Lord Goff in the *Spycatcher* case that there was a balancing act to be performed between "... weighing the public interest in maintaining confidence against a countervailing public interest favouring disclosure".[75]

Scott J focused on the disciplinary rules for doctors, with the GMC's jurisdiction being found in the Medical Act 1983. Paragraphs (b) and (g) of Rules 80–82 on Professional Confidences set up the tenor of judicial attitude to the duty of confidence:

"(b) Confidential information may be shared with other registered medical practitioners who participate in or assume responsibility for the clinical management of the patient. To the extent that the doctor deems it necessary for the performance of their particular duties, confidential information may also be shared with other persons (nurses and other health care

71. See "Professional Conduct and Discipline: Fitness to Practice" ("The Blue Book") para. 76.
72. National Health Service (Venereal Disease) Regulations 1974, S.I. 1974/29; Abortion Regulations 1991, S.I. 1991/499; Human Fertilisation and Embryology Act 1990, s. 33.
73. *W* v. *Egdell* [1990] 1 All E.R. 835, C.A.
74. [1989] 1 All E.R. 1089 at 1101.
75. [1988] 3 All E.R. 545 at 658–659.

professionals) who are assisting and collaborating with the doctor in his professional relationship with the patient. It is the doctor's responsibility to ensure that such individuals appreciate that the information is being imparted in strict professional confidence ...

(g) Rarely, disclosure may be justified on the ground that it is in the public interest which in certain circumstances such as, for example, investigation by the police of a grave or very serious crime, might override the doctor's duty to maintain his patient's confidence..."

In this case the Court of Appeal decided that in the balance of public interests the particular interest of the protection of the physical safety of the public outweighed the interest in maintaining patient confidence.

Bingham LJ clearly sets out the parameters of disclosure in the public interest.

(1) Disclosure should be limited to those to whom the information is vital.

(2) The risk, if disclosure did not take place, must be "real", i.e., substantiated.

(3) It may be that such substantiated threat must be of physical, as opposed to any other sort of, harm.

### 2.9.3 Consent to disclosure

An obvious point, but still worthy of recognition, is the fact that consent in broad terms needs to be free and rational. In other words the consent to disclose details needs to be made by a person deemed rational at law to make that decision. The GMC "Blue Book" (1993) at paragraph 77 sets out the medical obligation:

"Where a patient, or a person properly authorised to act on the patient's behalf, consents to disclosure, information to which the consent refers may be disclosed in accordance with that consent."

It is clear from the tone of this paragraph that unless a consent is one which encompasses all records with regard to that particular patient, a consent should be treated as specific in ambit. Notwithstanding the fact, with the complexity of modern clinical management of the patient there is a development in the concept of implied consent. A typical example being the number of trainee doctors, nurses, consultants, anaesthetists and others who may need to be cognisant of the clinical factors that go to make up the patient's condition, prognosis and thus medical needs.

Paragraph 79 of the "Blue Book" confirms this view:

"Most doctors in hospital and general practice are working in health care teams, some of whose members may need access to information, given or obtained in confidence about individuals, in order to perform their duties. It is for doctors who head such teams to judge when it is appropriate for information to be disclosed for that purpose. They must leave those whom they authorise to receive such information in no doubt that it is given to them in professional confidence. The doctor also has the responsibility to ensure that arrangements exist to inform patients of the circumstances in which information about them is likely to be shared and to give patients the opportunity to state any objection to this."

### 2.9.4 Statutory modification of the duty

There are a number of statutory modifications to this duty,[76] but given the nature of liability under discussion here it is proposed to focus on the modifications possible

76. For example, the Abortion Regulations 1991, S.I. 1991/499; see s. 5 Public Health (Control of Disease) Act 1984; see ss. 10 and 11 and the supplements contained in the Public Health (Infectious Diseases) Regulations 1988, S.I. 1988/1546; National Health Service (Venereal Diseases) Regulations 1974, S.I. 1974/29; Police and Criminal Evidence Act 1984, ss. 9, 11 and 12.

where HIV infection is in issue, as well as providing a further opportunity to consider the strict way the courts view the maintenance of the confidential quality of information. A pertinent example is the important case of *X* v. *Y*,[77] a case which gained some notoriety.

In essence the names of two doctors who were being treated in hospital for AIDS were disclosed by a national newspaper. Despite the plaintiff obtaining an order restraining publication an article was written under the headline "Scandal of Docs with AIDS". The plaintiffs sought:

(1) an injunction restraining the defendant from publishing the identity of the two doctors;

(2) disclosure by the defendants of their sources.

The obvious issue was whether the newspaper could publish the information on the grounds of public interest.

Rose J began his consideration by stating that:

"Under the National Health Service (Venereal Diseases) Regulations 1974 the plaintiffs and their servants have a statutory duty to take all necessary steps to secure that any information capable of identifying patients examined or treated for AIDS shall not be disclosed except to a medical practitioner, or a person under his direction, in connection with and for the purpose of treatment, or prevention of the spread, of the disease. Confidentiality is of paramount importance to such patients, including doctors."

Rose J went on to acknowledge the notion of the freedom of the press and that there was a form of public interest in knowing the information sought to be published. Despite this Rose J argued that[78]:

"The public in general and patients in particular are entitled to expect hospital records to be confidential and it is not for any individual to take it upon himself or herself to breach that confidence whether induced to do so by a journalist or otherwise."

Rose J concluded that there was insufficient evidence for enforced disclosure of the source of the information; there was sufficient public interest in the maintenance of such a confidence to allow a permanent injunction.

### 2.9.5 *Remedies for a breach of confidence*

As seen above the injunction is the most pertinent remedy available. It is only necessary to note here that, as is well established, there can be an award of damages, not necessarily nominal, for breach of confidence, even though there has been no harm suffered. The symbolic importance of the maintenance of confidences, particularly in this area, allows for such awards.

### 2.10 Duty to keep up with professional developments

The dynamic of advances in medicine and medical technological developments and techniques necessitates the medical professional being concerned with current theories and literature generally. The question which flows from this is the extent to which the doctor has to keep abreast of such matters. While the level of knowledge

77. [1988] 2 All E.R. 648.
78. *Ibid.* at p. 665.

needed at law will also be a matter of the relevant professional standard, there has to be a threshold duty level. This matter was considered in the case of *Crawford* v. *Board of Governors of Charing Cross Hospital.*[79]

The plaintiff was admitted to hospital for removal of his bladder. This involved a blood transfusion. The method was to extend the arm at an angle away from the body for this purpose. After the operation the plaintiff found that the arm was paralysed. The essence of the allegation was that some seven months earlier an article had appeared in *The Lancet*, which appeared to cast doubt on this method of transfusion. On appeal Denning LJ held that while the defendant doctor did not read the article, a medical man would not be expected to read every piece of literature generally available. In essence the case turned on Denning LJ's well-known sympathy for the medical profession:

"It would, I think, be putting too high a burden on a medical man to say that he has to read every article appearing in the current medical press: and it would be quite wrong to suggest that a medical man is negligent merely because he does not at once put into operation the suggestions which some contributor or other might make in a medical journal. The time may come in a particular case when a new recommendation may be so well proved that it should be adopted. But that was not this case ... It is a misfortune for the hospital and the doctors concerned that they should have been put to the burden of defending this action when they have served the patient so well."

As Mason and McCall Smith confirm, this is not to say that a medical man can ignore a series of signposts in current literature which strongly suggest a different form of medical intervention. One also needs to be aware of the following comment that[80]:

"The practice of medicine has ... become increasingly based on principles of scientific elucidation and report and the pressure on doctors to keep abreast of current developments is now considerable. It is no longer possible for a doctor to coast along on the basis of long experience; as in many professions and callings, such an attitude has been firmly discredited."

### 2.11 Protecting the patient from self-harm and causing harm to others

There has developed over the years a strong line of cases establishing the duty on doctors, nurses and other health care professionals to prevent a disturbed patient from harm through the impact of the medical condition. One should be aware, however, that the cases have not all gone the same way. This is itself indicative of a tension over what precautions to take in circumstances where often the threat may appear to be illusory or the assessment of the condition difficult to accurately measure in terms of a prediction over future conduct by the patient.

In the case of *Thorn* v. *Northern Group Hospital Management Committee*[81] a husband told a nurse at the hospital where his wife was being kept, that his wife was threatening suicide. There was a suspicion that the wife was a depressive, and therefore was moved to a convalescent ward. The next day she was due to be moved as there was difficulty finding any medical origin for her condition. While the nurse and ward sister left the wing temporarily the wife walked out of the hospital, went home and committed suicide. The husband brought an action in negligence based on

---

79. (1953) *The Times*, 8 December.
80. Mason and McCall Smith, *Law and Medical Ethics* (Butterworths, London, 4th edn, 1995), p. 202.
81. (1964) 108 Sol.J. 484.

the perceived lack of supervision of the deceased woman. The defendants' denial of liability was based on evidence adduced that threats of suicide were communicated to medical staff so that more strict supervision would take place. There was no evidence that the threats by the wife had actually been communicated to medical staff.

In finding for the defendants, Edmund Davies J argued that:

"As later events showed, the patient was set upon making her escape for the purpose of self-destruction, and it was highly conceivable that she kept a wary eye on the nurses and seized her opportunity immediately their backs were turned and they had absented themselves temporarily. That did not connote negligence on the part of the nurses."

In addition Edmund Davies J argued that it would be unrealistic to expect a member of the hospital staff to keep a constant vigil.

In the next case of *Selfe* v. *Ilford and District Hospital Management Committee*[82] the plaintiff had been admitted to hospital as the result of a drug overdose. The patient was known to have suicidal tendencies, but the three nurses monitoring the patient all left to attend to other duties, each failing to tell the other of the intended absence. The plaintiff climbed through the ground floor window of his room, walked up some steps to the roof and threw himself off. His injuries reduced him to a paraplegic state. As the report in the *British Medical Journal* indicates:

"Mr Selfe had been placed on a ground floor ward with a window at the back of his bed. There were 27 other patients in the ward, four of whom, being suicide risks, were grouped together at one end. The degree of care owed by the hospital was proportionate to both the degree of risk and the magnitude of the harm that might be occasioned, and his Lordship felt that reasonable care in these circumstances demanded continuous observation by duty nurses on the ward. 'To look after four suicide risks with adequate care,' he said, 'would require three nurses as an absolute minimum in a ward containing 27 patients'."

A different result was reached in *Hyde* v. *Tameside Area Health Authority*.[83] The plaintiff here tried to kill himself. In the middle of the night, while on ward, he smashed a window, moved on to a parapet and then threw himself to the ground. As a result of this fall he suffered severe injuries. The evidence showed that the plaintiff was convinced that he had incurable cancer. The centre of the allegation once more was lack of supervision by the nursing staff. Lord Denning MR argued that it was a matter of deciding between whether the patient was merely depressed by pain or the patient was determined to end his life. The decision was based essentially on the standard of care to be expected of the nursing staff. On the basis of the evidence before the court of the attendance of nurses at the ward, the finding was that there was no negligence, and the nurses had discharged the duty incumbent upon them. It is further interesting to note that Lord Denning MR made it perfectly clear that he found it distasteful to award damages in cases of suicide. In a forthright manner he stated, "I would disallow them altogether—at the outset—rather than burden the community with them".[84]

In *Holgate* v. *Lancashire Mental Hospitals Board*[85] a duty of care in the

---

82. [1979] 4 B.M.J. 754, (1970) 114 S.J. 935.

83. (1981) C.L.Y. 1854, 2 P.N. 26, C.A.

84. Further examples are *Swiecicki* v. *Camden and Islington A.H.A.* (unreported, 1983); see also *Newnham* v. *Rochester Hospital Board* (1936) in Nelson-Jones and Burton, *Medical Negligence Case Law* (Fourmat Publishing, 1990), p. 279, where a child was left unsupervised and fell out of an open window, and the hospital found negligent. But as to Lord Denning's attitude to suicide, see *Kirkham* v. *CC of Greater Manchester* [1990] 3 All E.R. 246, C.A.

85. [1937] 4 All E.R. 19.

circumstance where a dangerous prisoner was negligently released on licence and assaulted the plaintiff was found to be focused around the notion of control. The case was seen to be analogous to the relationship between a prisoner and prison officer. The case also makes it clear that the issue of duty of care in these circumstances would rarely centre around the concept of the proximity of the relationship between the plaintiff and defendant, a matter which would invariably be obvious in its presence.

## 2.12  Duty to write prescriptions clearly

Sometimes a focus of ironic humour when in receipt of a poorly written prescription, the duty to write one legibly is a significant one, with the potential for serious consequences of illegibility. In *Prendergast* v. *Sam and Dee Ltd*[86] the court held that the doctor owes a duty to a patient to write a prescription clearly. The specific aspect of this duty was found to be that the prescription must be sufficiently legible to allow for mistakes by those who may be processing the prescription. In similar vein, it was held that the pharmacist would be found to be in breach of duty where the prescription was of sufficient clarity to put that person on warning that they may be prescribing the wrong drug. In this case the doctor was found to be 25 per cent liable, while the pharmacist was found the remaining 75 per cent vicariously to blame. The plaintiff here suffered permanent brain damage when a diabetic drug was dispensed instead of a drug to ease the effects of asthma and a chest infection. The pharmacist, it was held, should have noticed that there was something wrong by the dosage placed after the Amoxil (or Daonil as the pharmacist appears to have read it).

In *Dwyer*[87] the doctor prescribed pain-killing drugs after the plaintiff had complained of severe headaches. While a useful drug, it could have severe side-effects if the maximum dosage were exceeded. The plaintiff on taking a course of the tablets became increasingly ill. A partner of the defendant doctor called upon request at the plaintiff's home, but failed to spot the drug being taken. The plaintiff, as a result of poisoning by the drug, became permanently crippled. In this case the judge found that the doctor was 45 per cent to blame for a poorly written prescription and the pharmacist 40 per cent for failing to spot the error, with the partner doctor 15 per cent for attending without Mrs Dwyer's medical notes.

## 2.13  Duty to inform the patient of adverse results

The following two cases would appear to directly contradict each other, and indeed they do appear to be difficult to reconcile. It should be remembered that the allegation of negligence lies not in the treatment itself, which, it has to be accepted is not always a complete success, even with the use of the utmost skill. The negligence is alleged to have arisen through a failure to tell the patient what has gone wrong.

In *Gerber* v. *Pines*[88] the plaintiff was left with part of a broken needle in her body, which appeared to have been due to a muscle spasm at the time of the injection. Du Parq J argued, according to the report, "That a patient in whose body a doctor found

---

86. (1988) *The Times*, 24 March; see also *Dwyer* v. *Roderick* (N.L.J., 25 February 1982).
87. See fn. 86 above.
88. (1935) 79 Sol.J. 13.

that he had left some foreign substance was entitled to be told at once. That was a general rule, but there were exceptions. In this case he held that there was a breach of duty and negligence on the doctor's part in not at once informing the patient or her husband on the day of the accident". Damages in the sum of five guineas were awarded.

In *Daniels* v. *Heskin*[89] a different result was reached. The plaintiff having just given birth at home, required some stitches. While the attending doctor was inserting those stitches the needle broke. The doctor could not find the broken part so completed the stitching, leaving the broken portion in the woman's body. The doctor, as in the previous case, decided not to tell the patient or her husband. Meanwhile the midwife was informed to look for any unusual symptoms, but if the needle was not found to have the patient x-rayed in six weeks' time. This duly happened and an operation was performed to remove the portion of the needle. On appeal by the plaintiffs it was held that there was first no evidence that the breaking of the needle was caused by negligence. Secondly, it was decided that the defendant in deferring the operation to remove the needle part was acting reasonably. Thirdly, it was decided that the broken part did not cause damage and the non-disclosure of its existence did not amount to negligence. According to Kingsmill Moore J:

"I cannot admit any abstract duty to tell patients what is the matter with them or, in particular, to say that a needle has been left in their tissues. All depends on the circumstances—the character of the patient, her health, her social position, her intelligence, the nature of the tissue in which the needle is embedded, the possibility of subsequent infection, the arrangements made for future observation and care and innumerable other considerations."

This case appears to run counter to a number of recent cases on the issue of consent, which together make it clear that there is a general duty to keep the patient informed. Contrary to what the learned judge stated, this is precisely the type of case where a general duty to fully inform the patient of the adverse consequences of treatment could be simply enunciated.

This enunciation, while far from complete, has been attempted in the next two, rather more recent cases.

In *Lee* v. *South West Thames HR*[90] Lord Donaldson felt that "... a doctor is under a duty to answer his patient's questions as to the treatment proposed". This he found applied to the adverse results of treatment. In *Naylor* v. *Preston AHA*[91] the same judge declared:

"... that in professional negligence cases, and in particular in medical negligence cases, there is a duty of candour resting on the professional man. This is recognised by the legal profession in their ethical rules requiring their members to refer the client to other advisers, if it appears that the client has a valid claim for negligence. This also appears to be recognised by the Medical Defence Union, whose view is that 'the patient is entitled to a prompt, sympathetic and above all truthful account of what has occurred' (*Journal of the MDU* (1986) vol. 2, no. 2, p. 2.)"

More forcefully his Lordship continued:

"I was disturbed to be told during the argument of the present appeals that the view was held in some quarters that whilst the duty of candid disclosure, to which we were referred, might give rise to a contractually implied term and so benefit private fee-paying patients, it did not

89. (1954) I.R. 73.
90. [1985] 2 All E.R. 385, C.A.
91. [1987] 2 All E.R. 353, [1987] 1 W.L.R. 958, C.A.

translate into a legal or equitable right for the benefit of National Health Service patients. This I would entirely repudiate. In my judgement ... it is but one aspect of the general duty of care, arising out of the patient/medical practitioner or hospital authority relationship and gives rise to rights both in contract and tort."

## 3 STANDARD OF CARE IN MEDICINE

### 3.1 Introduction

While Margaret Brazier may be generally correct in her assessment that "a patient claiming against his doctor ... usually has little difficulty in establishing that the defendant owes him a duty of care"[92] the same cannot, by any stretch of the imagination, be said about establishing that the medical practitioner has breached that duty of care by acting in such a manner as to have fallen below the standard of medical care prescribed by law. There is a wealth of both case-law and critical legal literature on this aspect of professional negligence in medicine. It would not be inaccurate to say that as a result of a review of the general law, it will become apparent that along with the difficulties of causation, breach of duty is the main stumbling block for the plaintiff and the main protector of the defendant doctor. A comprehensive analysis of the case-law will prove also to be indicative of the wide variety of factual situations that can be faced in medical professional negligence actions.

### 3.2 General principles

In considering the standard of care generally in negligence actions the case usually considered an effective introduction is that of *Nettleship* v. *Weston*.[93] For the purposes of the present discussion the seminal case is that of *Bolam* v. *Friern Hospital Management Committee*.[94]

The plaintiff in this case was suffering from mental illness. It was decided that he should undergo electro-convulsive therapy. During the course of the therapy no relaxant drugs were used, and apart from manual control of the lower jaw, the plaintiff was unrestrained. There were two bodies of opinion at that time, one which supported the use of some sort of control, whether by drugs or manually, and another which found such an approach generally dangerous. Again, there was also a difference of professional opinion over whether to issue a warning to the patient of the risk of fracture or wait for the patient to ask to be specifically warned about such risks. In the course of this particular treatment, the patient sustained dislocation of both hip joints and fractures of the pelvis. During his finding that the doctors in the case had not breached their duty of care, McNair J made a number of statements that have been repeated with approval on numerous occasions, and broadly can be seen as general propositions of law on the standard of care in professional practice. Having confirmed the existence of the man on the Clapham omnibus, McNair J considered why he could not be used where professional liability was in issue:

92. "Medicine, Patients and the Law" (2nd edn, 1992), pp. 117–118.
93. [1971] 3 All E.R. 591, C.A., [1971] 2 Q.B. 691.
94. [1957] 2 All E.R. 118, [1957] 1 W.L.R. 582 (McNair J).

"... where you get a situation which involves the use of some special skill or competence, then the test of whether there has been negligence or not is not the test of the man on the Clapham omnibus, because he has not got this special skill. The test is the standard of the ordinary skilled man exercising and professing to exercise that special skill. A man need not possess the highest skill at the risk of being found negligent. It is well-established law that it is sufficient if he exercises the ordinary skill of an ordinary man exercising that particular art."

Further on McNair established that[95]:

"A doctor is not guilty of negligence if he has acted in accordance with a practice accepted as proper by a responsible body of medical opinion of medical men skilled in that particular art."

One of the most significant cases in medical negligence, particularly in terms of the standard of care and the issue of causation, that of *Whitehouse* v. *Jordan,*[96] confirmed the views of McNair J, and thus elevated the decision to the status of an established proposition of law. Another significant case has also confirmed that the "Bolam test" applies to the areas of diagnosis, advice and treatment.[97]

### 3.3 Compliance with a professional practice

Kennedy and Grubb rightly note the significance of this issue in terms of the role of the judiciary and the role of the medical profession in professional liability litigation[98]:

"... who sets the legal standard of care to which doctors must comply? Is it, as you would expect, the law; or is it the medical profession? If it be the latter, this would mean that the medical profession would not only be offering evidence of good practice (a factual matter) but also determining what doctors ought to do (a legal matter)."

It will soon become apparent that it is the latter.

In *Marshall* v. *Lindsey County Council*[99] Maugham LJ held that the action of a doctor, which accorded with the general practice of the profession at the time, could not be judged to be negligent. While acting in a manner perceived to be correct by the profession appears at first glance to accord with logic, it does not necessarily remain so when one considers the possibility that the practice of the whole profession could be deemed incorrect. In *Clarke* v. *Adams,*[100] for example, it was successfully argued that the warning given to a patient having heat treatment to inform the doctor if it got too warm was inadequate, despite the fact that the warning was given in standard form used by the profession.

Similarly, in *Hucks* v. *Cole*[101] Sachs LJ found that a failure to treat a patient with penicillin in the particular circumstances was negligent notwithstanding medical evidence which suggested it was professional practice to do what this doctor did.

It may be that these latter two cases are the exception rather than the rule in that they are extremely difficult to reconcile with the rule contained in *Bolam*.

95. [1957] 2 All E.R. 118 at 121.
96. [1981] 1 All E.R. 267, [1981] 1 W.L.R. 246.
97. *Sidaway* v. *Bethlem Royal Hospital Governors* [1985] 1 All E.R. 643.
98. *Op. cit.*, at p. 449.
99. [1935] 1 K.B. 516, C.A.; approved in *Whiteford* v. *Hunter* [1950] W.N. 553.
100. (1950) 94 S.J. 599.
101. (1968) 118 N.L.J. 469.

### 3.4 Differences of professional practice

As already seen in the facts of *Bolam*, and apparent throughout the development of medicine, there are often a number of views on the best clinical management and procedures to benefit a particular patient. Once more McNair J established the ground rules, using the Scottish case of *Hunter* v. *Hanley*[102] which lead directly on from his previous pronouncement:

"In the realm of diagnosis and treatment there is ample scope for genuine difference of opinion, and one man clearly is not negligent merely because his conclusion differs from that of other professional men, nor because he has displayed less skill or knowledge than others would have shown. The true test for establishing negligence in diagnosis or treatment on the part of a doctor is whether he has been proved to be guilty of such failure as no doctor of ordinary skill would be guilty of it acting with ordinary care."

Overall the case-law indicates that the courts will not intervene and judge between different medical practices. In *Chapman* v. *Rix*[103] Romer LJ forcefully stated that:

"... I am aware of no case in which a medical man has been guilty of negligence when eminent members of his own profession have expressed on oath their approval of what he had done."

*Sidaway*[104] has proved an important case in terms of ethical and legal aspects of consent. What the case has also done is to debate the merits of the *Bolam* test, at least in the context of the amount of information a doctor is required to give in order to gain consent to treatment which has a risk of harm.

Lord Bridge began his analysis with emphasising that the doctor was not only there to provide treatment, but was also there to diagnose and advise. He then went on to confirm that the *Bolam* test applied to the giving of information and advice. There was, however, one phrase which appeared to cast some doubt on the application of *Bolam simpliciter*, namely that there would be no breach of duty if the doctor acted in accordance with a responsible body of professional opinion. Lord Bridge put matters thus:

"... whether non-disclosure in a particular case should be condemned as a breach of the doctor's duty of care is an issue to be decided *primarily* [my emphasis] on the basis of expert medical evidence, applying the *Bolam* test. But I do not see that this approach involves the necessity to hand over to the medical profession the entire question of the scope. Of course if there is a conflict of evidence as to whether a responsible body of medical opinion approves of non-disclosure in a particular case, the judge will have to resolve that conflict. But even in a case where, as here, no expert witness in the relevant medical field condemns the non-disclosure as being in conflict with accepted and responsible medical practice, I am of the opinion that the judge might in circumstances come to the conclusion that disclosure of a particular risk was so obviously necessary to an informed choice on the part of the patient that no prudent medical man would fail to make it."

It can be seen clearly from this statement that where the allegation of professional negligence involves the failure to impart sufficient information for the patient to make an informed choice, then the judiciary will be willing, on occasion, to intervene, and thereafter possibly criticise a professional practice. It should be recognised that this may well be due to the fact that the judicial mind is rather more comfortable with this less technical issue. That this may well be a new formulation of *Bolam*, in relation

102. (1955) S.L.T. 213 at 217.
103. (1958) *The Times*, 10 November.
104. [1984] 1 All E.R. 1018, [1985] 1 All E.R. 643, [1985] 1 A.C. 871.

to consent issues at least, is confirmed by the comment of Lord Donaldson that "The duty is fulfilled if the doctor acts in accordance with a practice *rightly* accepted as proper by a body of skilled and experienced medical men". [My emphasis.]

## 3.5 Departure from established practice/innovative treatment

In *Hunter* v. *Hanley*[105] the action concerned a patient who had been injured when a hypodermic needle broke while she was receiving a injection. In the course of his ordering of a retrial, Lord President Clyde indicated the court's view of deviation from normal professional practice. He prefaced his remarks by stating "such a deviation [from professional practice] is not necessarily negligence".

He went on to establish a test to establish liability in circumstance of such a deviation. First, the plaintiff needs to show that there is in existence a common professional practice. Secondly, it needs to be shown that the defendant has not adopted such a practice. Thirdly, it needs to be shown that the doctor has acted in such a manner as no person of ordinary skill would have done if acting with ordinary care.

In *Clark* v. *MacLennan*[106] the legal effect of deviation from professional practice was considered. The plaintiff was admitted to hospital expecting a child. Soon after the child was born, the mother was found to be suffering from the temporary and fairly common ailment of stress incontinence. In the plaintiff's case this was acute. The conventional treatment failed to alleviate the condition, therefore the defendant gynaecologist decided to perform an anterior colporrhaphy operation. Current practice demanded that the operation should not be performed until a minimum of three months after the birth to reduce the risk of haemorrhage. Such haemorrhage occurred causing the operation to break down, and finally resulting in the incontinence becoming a permanent disability. In giving judgment for the plaintiff, Peter Pain J discussed the plaintiff's submissions which were:

"... that, if the plaintiff could show (1) that there was a general practice not to perform an anterior colporrhaphy until least three months after birth, (2) that one of the reasons for this practice was to protect the patient from the risk of haemorrhage and a breakdown of the repair, (3) that an operation was performed within four weeks, and (4) that haemorrhage occurred and the repair broke down, then the burden of showing that he was not in breach of duty shifted to the defendants."

Peter Pain J responded positively by concluding that:

"... a general duty of care arises and there is a failure to take a precaution, and that very damage occurs against which the precaution is designed to be a protection, then the burden lies on the defendant to show that he was not in breach of duty as well as to show that the damage did not result from his breach of duty."

While there has been criticism of the idea that this is a reversal of the burden of proof in favour of the plaintiff,[107] it is safe to say that the plaintiff, if it can be shown that there was failure and specific damage, has proved the case in the absence of a response from the defendant.

---

105. (1955) S.C. 200, Court of Session (Inner House).
106. [1983] 1 All E.R. 416, Q.B.D.
107. See *Wilsher* v. *Essex Area Health Authority* [1986] 3 All E.R. 801 at 815 *per* Mustill LJ.

### 3.6 Special units and standards of care

The case of *Wilsher* is a useful one, in that it indicates the complexity of modern treatment, the numerous professionals involved in unit treatment and the difficulties of setting a standard of care in such a professional setting. The case also developed notoriety in the context of causation, which was the exclusive consideration of the House of Lords and will be considered later.

Martin Wilsher was born prematurely, and was found to be suffering from a number of illnesses, the most prominent being oxygen deficiency. Due to his poor prognosis, it was decided to place him in a special baby care unit. The medical team involved in the unit consisted of two consultants, a senior registrar, several junior doctors and trained nurses. The plaintiff, while in the unit, was monitored by a junior and inexperienced doctor. The doctor mistakenly placed a catheter into the plaintiff's vein rather than an artery. The insertion was checked by the senior registrar, who failed to spot the error. It was even the case that some hours later the registrar did exactly the same as the junior doctor had done. The catheter monitor therefore failed to register accurately the amount of oxygen in the blood with the result that the plaintiff was given excess oxygen. The plaintiff was later found to be almost blind, the result of a condition known as retrolental fibroplasia (RLF), one of the possible causes of the condition being an excess of oxygen. It was contended that this condition arose out of a want of care for the plaintiff. The central question for the Court of Appeal to consider was what was the standard of care required of the members of the unit.

Mustill LJ began his consideration of the law surrounding the breach of duty issue by recognising the difficulties inherent in complex medical treatment "... the duty of care is not a warranty of a perfect result".[108]

A number of fundamental issues were considered in setting the legal standard required by the unit:

(1) *The "unit" standard and primary liability*

The argument here would be that the defendants owed a direct duty to the plaintiff to ensure that the special baby care unit functioned to a legally recognised reasonable standard. The focus would move away from individual standards of the doctors and nurses involved and move on to the unit as a whole. It might have been argued that "... if the junior doctors did not have sufficient skill or experience to provide the special care demanded by such a premature baby, the defendant authority were at fault in appointing them to the posts which they held".[109] This, it needs to be understood, was never claimed by the plaintiff, merely posited by Mustill LJ as a possible line of attack.

(2) *The "team" standard*

This issue was live in the appeal and amounted to counsel's assertion that "... each of the persons who formed the staff of the unit held themselves out as capable of undertaking the specialised procedures which the unit set out to perform."

Mustill LJ responded negatively to this assertion because it would mean a junior nurse being judged by the same legal yardstick as the highly skilled consultant.

---

108. *Ibid.* at 810.
109. *Ibid.* at 811.

### (3) *Individualised standard*

This proposition calls for a consideration of the actual expertise of the individual alleged to have been negligent. Simply put, the junior doctor, who may be in a special baby care unit, will be expected to act according to his actual factual level of ability. This it was recognised by the Court of Appeal, would mean that the plaintiff's chances of success at law would depend on "recruitment and rostering". As Mustill LJ again put it[110]:

"... this notion of a duty tailored to the actor rather than the act which he elects to perform, has no place in the law of tort ... Public hospital medicine has always been organised so that young doctors and nurses learn on the job ... The long-term interests of patients as a whole are best served by maintaining the present system, even if this may diminish the legal rights of the individual patient, for, after all, medicine is about curing, not litigation."

### (4) *The "post" standard*

This was the proposition which found favour with the court. The standard to be expected of a junior doctor would be the standard of a junior doctor working in a specialist environment and offering a specialist service. It is something of a hybrid in that there is an element of individuation as regards the inexperienced doctor, but this is tempered by the recognition that there is nevertheless a complex procedure undertaken which requires a minimum standard of competence.

### 3.7 The error of clinical judgement

The classic case on this "doubtful concept" and another example of the complexities of modern medical negligence litigation is that of *Whitehouse* v. *Jordan*.[111] This case concerned a defendant who was a senior registrar concerned with the plaintiff, a child due to be delivered at the end of a high risk pregnancy. The mother had been in labour for some 22 hours, when the defendant doctor carried out a test to see whether forceps could be used to assist the delivery. This decision itself came from the head of department, a consultant professor of obstetrics. The defendant pulled five or six times with the forceps, and then, worried for the health of the mother, delivered the child by means of Caesarean section. The allegation was that the defendant had pulled too hard and too long with the forceps, which itself caused the baby to get stuck in the birth canal, with the unwedging causing the child to suffer from asphyxia and thence cerebral palsy.

Lord Denning found that "It was at worst an error of clinical judgement" and held that errors of judgement and negligence were not the same concept. Lord Donaldson dissented from this view strongly in arguing that the concept of the error was a false antithesis. An error of clinical judgement may or may not be negligent, this would depend on the nature of the error. Lord Edmund Davies confirmed this view in the House of Lords decision in *Whitehouse* when he stated[112]:

"... it is high time that the unacceptability [of the Denning concept of error of clinical judgement] be finally exposed. To say that a surgeon committed an error of clinical judgement is wholly ambiguous, for, while some such errors may be completely consistent with the due exercise of professional skill, other acts or omissions in the course of exercising 'clinical

110. *Ibid.* at 813.
111. [1980] 1 All E.R. 650, C.A.
112. [1981] 1 All E.R. 267 at 276.

499

judgement' may be so glaringly below proper standards as to make a finding of negligence inevitable."

His Lordship then went on to confirm the relevance of the *Bolam* test of the standard of care required.

On a broader front the decision to dismiss the plaintiff's appeal, and the form in which it was done was regarded as being based on a readily discernible policy. As Gerald Robertson explained[113]:

"When the desire to implement a particular policy, such as discouraging medical negligence claims, reaches such an extent as to conflict with the dispassionate consideration of the individual case on its own merits, then there is cause for genuine concern."

Robertson concludes in strident fashion that the case[114]:

"... represents all that is wrong with the present system of compensating victims of medical accidents. It emphasises the delay inherent in the system ... It emphasises the expense of the system ... Above all it illustrates how much of a lottery personal injury litigation is and how heavily the odds are stacked against the plaintiff if an allegation of medical negligence is involved."

### 3.8 Standards in diagnosis

The general law on the standard of care in medical practice is applicable here.[115] Once more, however, it is worth noting that a misdiagnosis may or may not be adjudged to be negligent; it depends on whether the reasonable medical practitioner exercising reasonable skill, could have come to the same (if incorrect) decision on the clinical nature of the patient's condition.

Failures that have attracted liability have involved misdiagnosis due to inadequately considering the patient's medical history. In *Chin Keow* v. *Government of Malaysia*[116] the failure was to inquire into a possibility that the patient was allergic to penicillin. Mason and McCall Smith once more utilise *Barnett* to indicate the hazards of diagnosis over the telephone.[117] Attendance, perusal of medical history and adequate consideration of a patient's comments all would appear to be required as a benchmark standard of care expected at law.

Two cases illustrate the possibility of successfully claiming against a doctor who has failed or attempted inadequately to diagnose. In *Tuffil* v. *East Surrey Area Health Authority*[118] the doctor failed to diagnose the condition of amoebic dysentery, despite the fact that the patient had spent many years in a tropical climate. Similarly, in *Langley* v. *Campbell*[119] a patient returning from Africa went to his doctor, who failed to diagnose malaria. Interestingly, the evidence indicated that members of the plaintiff's family had actually canvassed the possibility of malaria with the doctor.

As was the case with the junior doctor in *Wilsher* when doubtful about a diagnosis a doctor should consult a specialist and obtain a second opinion in order to discharge the duty that now exists.

---

113. Gerald Robertson, "Medical Negligence Retried" (1981) 44 M.L.R. 457 at p. 459.
114. *Ibid.* at p. 461.
115. See *Crivon* v. *Barnet Group Hospital Management Committee* (1958) *The Times*, 18 November.
116. [1967] 1 W.L.R. 813, P.C.
117. *Op. cit.*, at p. 203.
118. (1978) *The Times*, 15 March.
119. (1975) *The Times*, 6 November.

Recently matters of misdiagnosis were considered by the Outer House in the case of *Morrison* v. *Forsyth*[120] where a wife brought an action after her husband had died from what had been thought to have been a minor condition. He had attended at a casualty department and was diagnosed as suffering from a viral infection. He was told to go home and contact his doctor if things got any worse. His condition soon worsened to the extent that he requested a neighbour to telephone his doctor. This doctor made a telephone diagnosis and made arrangements for a prescription. Only a few hours after this, the condition had seriously deteriorated and an ambulance was called. The patient was found to be dead on arrival at the hospital.

The wife's allegation was that the doctor had been cursory in his telephone questions and subsequent diagnosis; her husband's condition demanded a house call. The wife's claim failed. It was accepted that in certain circumstances there could be a duty to seek further clarification through questioning the patient, the doctor was found to have acted in a reasonably competent manner. In the particular circumstances enough information had been elicited to make an informed diagnosis. On the facts of the case, moreover, it was shown that the condition was rare and unlikely to be one encountered in general practice.[121]

### 3.9 Obstetric standards

In *Robertson (an infant)* v. *Nottingham HA*[122] it was held that no reasonably competent registrar in the defendant's position would have done as this doctor had. The plaintiff child alleged negligence against the defendant health authority. The mother, in the seventh month of pregnancy, noticed a decrease in foetal movement. She was taken to hospital for foetal heartbeat monitoring. Early traces indicated a decrease of heartbeat. Later traces indicated the possibility of abnormalities. It was admitted that overall the quality of the traces was poor. After a number of tests it was decided by the registrar to perform a Caesarean section. This took place after the mother had been in hospital for four days. The plaintiff was born suffering severe disabilities and illness. The allegation was that the Caesarean took place after unnecessary delay, and a reasonably competent doctor would have performed it after a few tests as opposed to the number taken here.

It was held that there was a one and a half to two-hour delay which was the registrar's fault. The case, however, failed on the issue of causation.[123]

### 3.10 Standard of care and anaesthetics

A good general starting-point here is the case of *Roe* v. *Minister of Health*.[124] As well as concerning anaesthetic practice, it also establishes when the standard of care issue is judged.

Two patients were operated on for minor ailments, the anaesthetic was injected by

120. (1995) 23 B.M.L.R. 11.
121. On failure to detect breast cancer, see *Judge* v. *Huntingdon HA* [1995] 6 Med.L.R. 223; on failure to spot symptoms of pneumonia, see *Bova* v. *Spring* [1995] 4 Med.L.R. 120.
122. (1995) 22 B.M.L.R. 49, Q.B.D.
123. On the failure to detect the correct lie of twins, see *Bowers* v. *Harrow HA* [1995] 6 Med.L.R. 16. On a Caesarean section causing cerebral palsy, see *Parry* v. *NW Surrey HA* [1994] 5 Med.L.R. 259.
124. [1954] 2 Q.B. 66.

lumbar puncture. The nupercaine itself was stored in glass ampoules stored in phenol. After the operation both patients suffered from spastic paraplegia. This was found to have been caused by the percolation of phenol into the ampoules by means of microscopic cracks, undetectable by visual inspection.

On the plaintiff's appeal it was held significantly that[125]:

"applying the test of what was the standard of medical knowledge in 1947 in respect of the detection of the presence of the phenol in the ampoules, at the time of the operation neither the anaesthetist nor any member of the hospital staff had been guilty of negligence"

A book on lumbar puncture and spinal anaesthetics published in 1951 had drawn attention to the risk of molecular flaws in the glass, but in 1947 the risk had yet to be discovered.

In a not unusual case a doctor failed to find the vein of the arm of a patient described as "extremely fat". The arm was damaged during the course of the doctor's attempts. The doctor was found not to be negligent in that a reasonably competent doctor would find such an activity difficult to perform in similar factual circumstances.[126]

A case on both the standard of care and the issue of the proof of negligence, which makes a number of interesting points is that of *Saunders* v. *Leeds Western Health Authority*.[127] During a four-year-old girl's operation, her heart stopped beating for over 30 minutes and she suffered brain damage. Mann J found for the plaintiff, indicating that a heart does not stop without negligence. It was also held that the hospital had not provided a satisfactory alternative explanation.

Charles Lewis helpfully points out the increase in the number of reported cases which have been concerned with allegations that the patient was aware of the operation supposedly performed under general anaesthetic. While claims appear numerous, success does not. Nevertheless in *Ackers* v. *Wigan Health Authority*[128] the plaintiff received £21,000 for nervous shock arising from consciousness during the course of an operation. Similarly in *Phelan* v. *East Cumbria Health Authority*[129]:

"A patient who had been aware of intense pain and fright during an operation for a serious leg injury that involved deep cutting and drilling into the bone was awarded £15,000 of which £5,000 was for the actual experience on the operating table and, it appears, the rest for the after-effects."[130]

---

125. *Ibid.* at 66.
126. *Williams* v. *North Liverpool Hospital Management Committee* (1959) *The Times*, 17 January.
127. (1985) 82 L.S. Gazette 1491.
128. [1991] 2 Med.L.R. 232.
129. [1991] 2 Med.L.R. 418.
130. Lewis, *op. cit.*, p. 384. Of the many cases to have failed note *Ludlow* v. *Swindon Health Authority* [1989] 1 Med.L.R. 104, which appears typical. The judge was not convinced that the patient had been awake during, rather than at the end of, the operation. See also *Muzlo* v. *NW Herts Health Authority* [1995] 6 Med.L.R. 184; *Jacobs* v. *Great Yarmouth and Waveney Health Authority* [1995] 6 Med.L.R. 192; *Hepworth* v. *Kerr* [1995] 6 Med.L.R. 139; *Glass* v. *Cambridge Health Authority* [1995] 6 Med.L.R. 91.

## 4 CAUSATION[131]

### 4.1 Introduction

The general law concerning factual and legal causation in relation to negligence generally having already been explained, it is here necessary to consider the application of that general law to the area of medical practice. The breach-harm link obviously needs to be established at law. In medical negligence litigation it is a major hurdle, and at times for the plaintiff can appear to be an insurmountable one. At the centre of the discussion is the case of *Wilsher* in the House of Lords[132] which was exclusively concerned with complex and significant issues of causation. A simple, but valuable starting-point, however, is the case of *Barnett*[133] considered earlier in this chapter.

### 4.2 General principles in medical causation

It will be remembered that this case involved the arsenic poisoning of the plaintiff's husband. The defendants argued that notwithstanding that they were under a duty of care to the deceased and had breached it by the doctor failing to consider the patient personally, the deceased as a matter of fact would have died even in the absence of this negligent behaviour. The facts relevant to a determination of this issue were that the deceased entered the hospital casualty department at 8.05–8.10 am. If the doctor had attended at that time, the deceased, nevertheless, would not have been in a ward before 11 am, the drip would not have been utilised until 12 noon and the potassium loss, indicative of this type of poisoning, would not have been discovered until 12.30 pm. An expert, Dr Goulding, stated significantly:

"The only way to deal with this [poisoning] is to use the specific BAL. I see no reasonable prospect of the deceased being given BAL before the time at which he died . . ."

Nield J completed his judgment by saying[134]:

"I find that the plaintiff has failed to establish, on the grounds of probability, that the defendants' negligence caused the death of the deceased."

Kennedy and Grubb regard *Barnett* as an example of one of the difficulties of factual causation which may be peculiar to litigation involving medical practice[135]:

". . . Whether in the particular case the harm *did* arise from the doctor's or other's conduct."

The case of *Kay* v. *Ayrshire and Avon Hospital Board*[136] illustrates the other difficulty

---

131. The case of *McGhee* laid the general ground rules that persist in causative matters in negligence litigation where it was put in the following manner ([1973] 1 W.L.R. 1 at 5): "It has often been said that the legal concept of causation is not based on logic or philosophy. It is based on the practical way in which the ordinary man's mind works in the everyday affairs of life. From a broad and practical viewpoint I can see no substantial difference between saying that what a defendant did materially increased the risk of injury to the plaintiff and saying what the defendant did made a material contribution to his injury".
132. [1988] 1 All E.R. 871, [1988] A.C. 1074, H.L.
133. *Barnett* v. *Chelsea and Kensington Hospital Management Committee* [1969] 1 All E.R. 1068.
134. *Ibid.* at p. 1074.
135. *Op. cit.*, note 5, at p. 468.
136. [1987] 2 All E.R. 417, H.L.

involved here "... the need to show that the doctor's or other's conduct *could* cause the plaintiff harm as a medical fact".[137]

A child was admitted to the hospital with pneumococcal meningitis. It was admitted that during the course of the treatment the patient was given an overdose of penicillin. Remedial treatment for this overdose was given after recovery from the original illness, but the child was found to be deaf. The respondents brought forward evidence to indicate that there was no recorded case in which a penicillin overdose had caused this type of damage. On the other hand, their evidence stated, deafness had often been known to result from meningitis. In the House of Lords the appellant argued that[138]:

"the overdose had created an increased risk of neurological damage, that since deafness was a type of neurological damage and the causes of it were unclear the increased risk of neurological damage was sufficient to establish that the overdose had made a material contribution to the neurological damage which had in fact resulted, namely deafness".

The House of Lords held, however, that where there were competing claims of cause, the tortious cause would not receive favourable treatment, and the court would not find in favour of it unless it was first proved that the tortious cause was capable of causing or aggravating damage. In this case the House accepted that penicillin had never caused the deafness complained of.[139]

A case which has been considered *in extenso* by a number of authors on the matter of factual causation, and indeed, heavily criticised by some is that of *Wilsher*.[140] It will be recalled that a child suffered RLF, leading to blindness, alleged by the plaintiff to have been caused by a negligent excess of oxygen. It was suggested in the course of the expert evidence that there were five other common conditions that could affect a premature baby's sight. All five had occurred in the case of the plaintiff. On the issue of causation the health authority appealed to the House of Lords from the decision of the Court of Appeal that, notwithstanding that the existence and extent of the contribution made by the hospital's breach of duty could not be ascertained, the hospital were to be taken to have caused the injury.

In the House of Lords it was decided that the breach and injury could not create a presumption of causation. The burden remained on the plaintiff to establish a causative link. The House did, however, concede that the inferential link was capable of being drawn from evidence in a case. Here, the plaintiff had failed to discharge the burden of proof of causation. The case was thus ordered for retrial on the basis of the health authority's successful appeal.

It is useful to note the concluding comment of Lord Bridge[141]:

"Many feel that such a result [a retrial] serves to highlight the shortcomings of a system in which the victim of some grievous misfortune will receive substantial compensation or none at all according to the unpredictable hazards of the forensic process."

137. Kennedy and Grubb, *op. cit.*, note 5, at p. 468.
138. [1987] 2 All E.R. 417 at 417.
139. The case of *McGhee* v. *NCB* [1972] 3 All E.R. 1008, [1973] 1 W.L.R. 1, H.L.; allowing the court to draw an inference of negligence where there were competing causes, could not be used here. The allegedly tortious agent was capable of causing the injury complained of. Obviously the evidence in *Kay* indicated that the agent could not.
140. [1988] 1 All E.R. 871, H.L.
141. *Ibid.* at 883.

A case of even more factual causative complexity concerning the pertussis vaccine is that of *Loveday* v. *Renton*.[142] Nevertheless the judiciary has found itself unable to move away from the rule established in *Wilsher*.[143]

The variety of possible causes of adverse results of treatment will continue to lead to the same result.[144]

### 4.2.1  Loss of chance of a better medical result

Walter Scott introduces the causative issue in question[145]:

"Advances in modern medicine increasingly provide patients with opportunities of cure which would hitherto have been impossible. If a patient can show that the doctor's negligence caused him to lose that opportunity, the question arises of how to quantify the damage in a way that is just for both parties."

The choice for the courts would be to resolve such cases either through a proportionate or absolute assessment of liability and damages. It is the latter approach that has been adopted by the courts. In *Kenyon* v. *Bell*[146] a girl suffered an eye injury. The allegation was that subsequent negligent treatment lost the girl the chance to have her sight saved. The medical evidence was important because it showed the chances of saving the sight in the injured eye were less than 50 per cent, even with effective medical treatment. The rule adopted was that if the chance of saving the eyesight with non-negligent treatment was more than 50 per cent then the plaintiff could have full damages on the basis of achieving the threshold of the balance of probabilities. This, as already stated, was not achieved, therefore no damages were awarded.

The House of Lords have now considered the matter in *Hotson* v. *East Berkshire Area Health Authority*.[147] A boy injured his hip in a fall. He was taken to hospital and examined, but negligently, in that there was no x-ray taken, therefore a fracture remained undiagnosed. The fracture was of a type which could develop into avascular necrosis. His GP sent him back to the hospital five days later and the correct diagnosis was finally made and treatment given. Medical evidence at trial indicated, however, that even if the correct diagnosis had been made initially, there was still a 75 per cent chance that the necrosis would develop.

The House of Lords, having reviewed the development of case-law in this area, came to the conclusion that the plaintiff had failed to show, on the balance of probabilities, that the negligence caused the avascular necrosis.

142. [1990] 1 Med.L.R. 117.

143. Lord Bridge concluded in *Wilsher* (at p. 883) that: "Whether we like it or not, the law requires proof of fault causing damage as the basis of liability in tort."

144. Some encouragement may be derived from the award of £2.75m to a plaintiff who suffered brain damage after receiving pertussis vaccine: *Best* v. *Wellcome Foundation* (unreported) 3 June 1992, Irish Supreme Court. See also C Dyer, "Man Awarded Damages after Pertussis Vaccination" (1993) 306 B.M.J. 1365.

145. Scott, "Causation in Medico-Legal Practice: A Doctor's Approach to the 'Lost Opportunity' Cases" (1992) 55 M.L.R. 68.

146. (1953) S.C. 125 (Outer House).

147. [1987] 2 All E.R. 908.

### 4.2.2 Supervening cause

The general law as applied to the medical negligence action is identified by the case of *Hogan* v. *Bentnick West Hartley Collieries Ltd.*[148] A workman, who had injured his thumb had it unnecessarily amputated. It was found that the ill-advised operation eclipsed the original negligence of his employers in causing the injury to the thumb.[149]

### 4.2.3 Proving medical negligence

The main features from a consideration of the development of medical negligence case-law are suspicions that in this area of professional liability there has been and continues to be a tendency for the medical profession to "close ranks" combined with judicial antipathy towards finding the medical profession negligent. The latter is particularly apparent from the reluctance to utilise *res ipsa loquitur*.

Charles Lewis has been fairly strident in his criticism of the "closing ranks" syndrome[150]:

"The usual reason given for this [difficulty in finding a doctor negligent] is that you cannot find an expert who is willing to accuse a colleague ... It no doubt contributes to plaintiffs' difficulties, particularly where the speciality concerned is a narrow one, for its practitioners will almost certainly all know each other, so that the reluctance to accuse of negligence is all the more pronounced."

The suspicion which has sometimes appeared substantiated is that whereas in negligence litigation generally the burden of proof is on the balance of probabilities, in medical negligence actions[151]:

"A charge of negligence against a professional man was serious. It stood on a different footing to a charge of negligence against the driver of a motor car. The consequences were far more serious. It affected his professional status and reputation. The burden of proof was correspondingly greater. As the charge was so grave, so should the proof be clear."

Such statements have been offset somewhat by *Ashcroft* v. *Mersey Regional Health Authority*[152] where it was clearly stated that no special rules on the burden of proof should apply in medical negligence actions.

*Res ipsa loquitur* is potentially extremely valuable in actions involving surgical intervention. Usually when the allegedly negligent action takes place, the plaintiff is unaware of how matters are proceeding due to anaesthesia. The evidential gaps apparent in many negligence actions against doctors could be bridged by the utilisation of *res ipsa loquitur*.

The classic case expounding the rule in the medical context is that of *Cassidy* v. *Ministry of Health.*[153] The plaintiff went into hospital for an operation on his left hand. While undergoing treatment he was under the care of a number of medical professionals, including the operating surgeon, an assistant medical officer, a house surgeon and members of the nursing staff. When the treatment was completed it was found that the left hand was completely useless.

---

148. [1949] 1 All E.R. 588.
149. See also *Emeh* v. *Kensington and Chelsea and Westminster Area Health Authority* [1985] Q.B. 1012, under "Wrongful Conception" at pp. 509–510.
150. *Op. cit.*, at p. 261.
151. *Hucks* v. *Cole* (1968) *The Times*, 9 May.
152. [1983] 2 All E.R. 245.
153. [1951] 1 All E.R. 574, [1951] 2 K.B. 343.

It was held here that the doctrine of *res ipsa loquitur* applied. The onus lay on the defendant hospital authority to prove that there had been no negligence. This onus had not been discharged. As Denning LJ illustrated in his well-known passage[154]:

"If the plaintiff had to prove that some particular doctor or nurse was negligent, he would not be able to do it. But he was not put to that impossible task; he says, 'I went into the hospital to be cured of two stiff fingers. I have come out with four stiff fingers and my hand is useless. That should not have happened if due care had been used. Explain it, if you can'."

In *Saunders* v. *Leeds Western Health Authority and Robinson*[155] a four-year-old girl had an operation for a congenitally dislocated hip. During the course of the operation her heart stopped, and attempts to start it again were only successful after 35–40 minutes. The child suffered brain damage, quadriplegia and blindness. The plaintiff sought to rely on *res ipsa loquitur*. The defendant replied that there was evidence of "a paradoxical air embolism travelling from the site of the operation to block a coronary artery".[156]

Mann J found that:

"The plaintiff's reliance on *res ipsa loquitur* makes it unnecessary for her to suggest a specific cause for the cardiac arrest. It is plain from evidence called on her behalf that the heart of a fit child does not arrest under anaesthesia if proper care is taken in the anaesthetic and surgery processes."

The PMILL commentary regards this case as a positive outcome for the development of anaesthetic practices. This view is based on an expert commentary that[157]:

"The acceptance by the judge of *res ipsa loquitur* makes the presentation of any anaesthetic case for the plaintiff that much simpler. Although the doctrine has been applied before in similar cases, a more definitive reasoning in an anaesthetic case has not been given ... "

One should, however, be aware of the general reluctance to apply the doctrine. Mason and McCall Smith use the case of *Fletcher* v. *Bench*[158] to reassert this reluctance:

"[If one were to accept that negligence was inevitably proved if something went wrong and it was unexplained] few dentists, doctors and surgeons, however competent, conscientious and careful they might be, would avoid the totally unjustified and unfair stigma of professional negligence probably several times in the course of their careers."

In the "swab" case of *Mahon* v. *Osborne*[159] it was found that where a swab or other instrument is left in the body of a patient, then the clinician involved should be required to produce an explanation.[160]

---

154. See also *Roe* v. *Ministry of Health* [1954] 2 Q.B. 66. The same point was made by Denning LJ. Here, however, the Ministry was asked to provide a non-negligent explanation, and did so.

155. (1985) 82 L.S.Gaz. 1491.

156. (1986) PMILL (January), p. 82.

157. For other examples of the successful application of the doctrine in medical negligence actions, see *Cavan* v. *Wilcox* [1973] 44 D.L.R. (3d) 42; *Holmes* v. *Board of Hospital Trustees of the City of London* [1977] 81 D.L.R. (3d) 67.

158. (1973) unreported, C.A.; cited in 4 B.M.J. 117. Mason and McCall Smith, *Law and Ethics in Medicine op. cit.* at p. 209.

159. [1939] 2 K.B. 14.

160. See also the cases of *Cavan* v. *Wilcox* [1973] 44 D.L.R. (3d) 42; *Clarke* v. *Worboys* (1952) *The Times*, 18 March; *Garner* v. *Morrell* (1953) *The Times*, 31 October; contra *Fish* v. *Kapur* [1948] 2 All E.R. 176.

It should be remembered that there are inherent risks in numerous clinical procedures. If the injury suffered is recognised by means of expert evidence as a manifestation of such an inherent risk, then the doctrine will not apply. *Ludlow* v. *Swindon Health Authority*[161] confirms the difficulty of proof which remains.

As a final example, where a defendant actually agreed that *res ipsa loquitur* should apply where brain damage occurred during a normal operation through hypoxia, then attempted to respond by arguing that this was due to a non-negligent cause, namely silent regurgitation of gastric content. This was unsuccessful and the plaintiff won the action.[162]

## 5 PROFESSIONAL LIABILITY FOR WRONGFUL CONCEPTION AND BIRTH

### 5.1 Introduction

The increasing number of medical negligence actions claiming in respect of the performance of sterilisation operations warrants separate consideration of this variant of the "typical" medical negligence action. A number of legal issues can arise out of such operations. In essence, the cases will contain one or more of the following allegations:

(1) The operation, through negligence on the part of the operating "team", has proved unsuccessful, and the plaintiff has become pregnant.

(2) The plaintiff (individual or couple) was not told of the risk of a natural reversal of the process of sterilisation, failed to take other contraceptive measures during the period when reversal was a risk, and has become pregnant.

(3) The sterilisation was stated as making the plaintiff sterile. Through natural reversal the plaintiff has become pregnant. The action is for a breach of a contractual guarantee of sterility.

(4) The mother of a handicapped child was not informed, due to negligent oversight, that the child while *in utero*, might be disabled. The mother was therefore not afforded the opportunity of choosing to have a therapeutic abortion. The mother claims damages for the birth and upbringing of the child.

(5) The mother of a healthy child born as a result of an unsuccessful abortion or sterilisation operation chose, when informed of her pregnancy, not to have an abortion. The mother now claims damages for the birth and upbringing of this healthy child.

### 5.2 The contractual action

The type of claim is exemplified clearly by the cases of *Eyre* v. *Measday*[163] and *Thake* v. *Maurice*.[164] In *Eyre* the plaintiff and her husband did not want to have any more

161. [1989] 1 Med.L.R. 104.
162. [1991] 2 Med.L.R. 301.
163. [1986] 1 All E.R. 488, C.A.
164. [1986] 1 All E.R. 497, C.A., [1986] Q.B. 644.

children. The plaintiff consulted the defendant, who was a gynaecologist, requesting a sterilisation operation. The defendant explained the procedure, laying particular stress on the irreversible nature of the operation. The defendant failed to inform the couple that there was a small risk that the procedure could naturally reverse itself. A year later the plaintiff became pregnant. The plaintiff alleged that the couple should receive damages in contract as the representation of permanent sterility was a breach of a term or an express or implied collateral warranty.

The Court of Appeal found against the plaintiff. In the course of his judgment, Slade LJ found that the inference of a warranty of sterility could not be drawn here. In the absence of an express guarantee of sterility the only matter which could be implied would be that the operation would be carried out with care and skill, as was the case.

The contractual issue occurred again in the case of *Thake* which concerned a vasectomy operation. This operation took place in 1975. The operation failed in circumstances where the plaintiff was again not told of the possibility of natural reversal. As well as the "simple" breach of contract allegation as in *Eyre*, the alternative allegation was that the plaintiff couple were induced to enter into the contract by means of a false warranty or innocent misrepresentation. Counsel for the plaintiffs had sought on a number of occasions to emphasise that the doctor had used the word "irreversible". The attitude of Nield LJ became clear when he stated that, as has been emphasised on numerous occasions in this chapter, the practice of medicine is still to a degree surrounded by elements of uncertainty.

He continued:

"I do not consider that a reasonable person would have expected a responsible medical man to be intending to give a guarantee . . . The reasonable man would have expected the defendant to exercise all the proper skill and care of a surgeon in that speciality; he would not in my view have expected the defendant to give a guarantee of 100 per cent success."

## 5.3 Negligence

As with actions in negligence generally, a plaintiff here will have to show that had he or she been given adequate information, contraceptive methods would have been used to avoid the risk of conception. An interesting issue of legal causation appeared in *Emeh* v. *Kensington and Chelsea and Westminster Area Health Authority*.[165]

The plaintiff underwent an operation to terminate a pregnancy in combination with a sterilisation operation. Two doctors performed the operation in a negligent manner and the plaintiff became pregnant. This pregnancy was discovered at 20 weeks' gestation. The plaintiff did not wish to undergo another termination. She eventually gave birth to a child suffering from congenital abnormality.

The plaintiff's claim was for the loss of future earnings, maintenance of this child, pain, suffering and loss of amenity and additional care for the handicapped child. At the trial stage it was held that the plaintiff's refusal to have an abortion was so

---

165. [1984] 3 All E.R. 1044, C.A., [1985] Q.B. 1012.

unreasonable as to be a *novus actus interveniens* which broke the chain of causation. Damages would therefore be limited to the time when it was discovered that the plaintiff was pregnant.

In allowing the plaintiff's appeal, Slade LJ argued that the defendants had no right to expect the plaintiff to undergo an operation to abort at over 20 weeks' gestation. The negligent operation had "faced her with the very dilemma which she had sought to avoid by having herself sterilised". He continued that only in the rarest of circumstances could the court find such a refusal to undergo such an operation unreasonable and so break the chain of causation.[166]

### 5.4 The issue of damages

The main matter which has taxed the courts in relation to such actions is the assessment of damages. A number of important issues of public policy have been canvassed in numerous cases, but for the purpose of brevity one need only concentrate[167] on the recent decision of Brooke J in *Allen* v. *Bloomsbury Health Authority*.[168] The case considers both the development of the common law in this area as well as listing the current legal principles applicable.

(1) From *Emeh*[169] the basic principle was expounded that where a child is born as the result of a foreseeable breach of duty on the part of the doctor, "the law entitles the mother to recover damages for the foreseeable loss and damage she suffers in consequence of the doctor's negligence".

(2) The damage recoverable in such an action is for discomfort and pain that goes with the continuation of the pregnancy and the delivery of the child. This needs, however, to be offset against the benefit of avoiding the discomfort of an abortion.[170]

(3) The plaintiff is further entitled to damages described as "associated with her own physical injury", namely:

> (i) financial loss having to feed, clothe, house and educate the child until it becomes an adult;
> (ii) financial loss through her own loss of earnings or her own expenses which flow from having the unwanted child.

(4) While the mother may suffer from a general lowering in lifestyle by the birth of the unwanted child, where a healthy child is born, such tiredness and so forth will generally be offset by the pleasure of seeing a healthy child born and grow to maturity.

(5) Where the plaintiff gives birth to a handicapped child, the law recognises that damages should be awarded for the additional burdens. Such burdens are not to be financially offset as in (4) because there is no countervailing benefit derived.

(6) Where negligence against a doctor is proved, and the existing children of the plaintiff have been, or are being, educated in the private sector, it may be that the

---

166. Unsurprisingly, Slade LJ did not (one suspects could not) give an example where a refusal would be so unreasonable.

167. As Kennedy and Grubb have usefully done (*op. cit.*, pp. 991–992).

168. [1993] 1 All E.R. 651, [1992] 13 B.M.L.R. 47.

169. *Op. cit.*, note 165.

170. See *Garner* v. *Montfield* (1989) 5 B.M.L.R. 1; *Emeh* v. *Kensington and Chelsea and Westminster Area Health Authority* [1985] Q.B. 1012 at 1028 *per* Purchas LJ; *Thake* v. *Maurice* [1986] 1 All E.R. 497 at 508 *per* Kerr LJ.

health authority has to pay such costs for this additional child. Brooke J argued that if this were thought to be an inappropriate policy, then it would be a matter for Parliament to alter it.

The main matter of continuing controversy is the payment of damages for the upkeep of a healthy child to maturity. In *Udale* v. *Bloomsbury Area Health Authority*[171] the policy against the award of damages in such circumstances was submitted by defendant counsel as being that it would be "... intolerable ... if a child ever learned that a court had publicly declared him so unwanted that medical men were paying for his upbringing because their negligence brought him into the world". The court found that while the plaintiff could claim for pain, suffering, inconvenience and anxiety, public policy demanded that there could be no damages for the upkeep of a healthy child.

A different (and many regard more acceptable) conclusion was reached in *Thake* v. *Maurice* and now represents the law. Damages will be paid for the upkeep of a healthy child (subject to the offset acknowledged in *Allen* v. *Bloomsbury*). This is based on the policy expounded by Peter Pain J that " ... every child has a belly to be filled and a body to be clothed. The law relating to damages is concerned with reparation in money terms and this is what is needed for the maintenance of a baby".

## 6 CONSENT OF THE PATIENT TO MEDICAL TREATMENT

### 6.1 Introduction

This is a significant area for the medical lawyer, given that the legal issues surrounding consent cover aspects of contractual, tortious and even criminal liability. It is useful to understand that there is a strong legal recognition of the ethical importance of the notion of bodily integrity. The law has attempted to develop in line with the classic view of Cardozo J that[172]:

"Every human being of adult years and sound mind has a right to determine what shall be done with his own body; and a surgeon who performs an operation without the patient's consent commits an assault."

One should note the last word in this statement. "Assault" is a recognition that issues of criminal liability for unauthorised touching can arise, but more significantly for present purposes is the possibility of an action for battery in the civil law. As with issues of medical negligence generally, and confidentiality specifically, the relationship between doctor and patient is at the heart of the duties, scope and potential liabilities where consent to medical treatment is being considered. Allegations against the medical profession here can take a number of potential forms. These include:

(1) The patient was either merely not consulted or was not considered competent to make a decision, and was therefore treated without consent. The allegation will be of a crime or tort of battery.[173]

---

171. [1983] 2 All E.R. 522, [1983] 1 W.L.R. 1098, Q.B.D.
172. *Schloendorf* v. *Society of New York Hospital* (1914) 211 N.Y. 125.
173. The criminal liability aspects of medical practice will be considered in the next section.

(2) The patient was only told in the broadest of terms what was involved in the operation, therefore the consent was invalid. Again an action in battery.

(3) As an alternative, the patient was not told enough about the risks inherent in an operation to make an informed consent to the treatment undertaken. The risk became a reality and the patient makes an allegation in negligence for the resultant injury.

As a starting-point it is useful to be reminded of the comments of Kennedy and Grubb[174]:

"In reality, consent or lack of it is only an issue of the civil law of torts. Although theoretically, a doctor who ordinarily acts without obtaining a patient's consent may not only be exposed to liability in tort, but also runs the risk of facing a criminal prosecution for the crime of battery, there is little or no chance that this will happen in the ordinary course of ordinary practice of medicine in good faith."

## 6.2 The action in the tort of battery[175]

One can do better than begin with Professor Fleming's definition of the tort[176]:

"Of the various forms of trespass to the person the common is the tort known as battery, which is committed by intentionally bringing about a harmful or offensive contact with the person of another. The action, therefore, serves the dual purpose of affording protection of the individual not only against bodily harm but also against any interference with his person which is offensive to a reasonable sense of honour and dignity. The insult in being touched without consent has been traditionally regarded as sufficient, even though the interference is only trivial and not attended with actual physical harm."

As mentioned earlier this is both a recognition of the legal scope of the tort of battery, and an emphasis of its symbolic importance.

The paucity of case-law in this area does appear to indicate strongly that an action in the tort of battery would be relatively rare. The advantages of framing an allegation as one of battery are obvious. There is no need to establish loss as a result of being touched by a doctor without consent. There is no difficulty of the high hurdle of factual causation of injury that exists in negligence. All direct damages are recoverable in damages, not merely those that are reasonably foreseeable. There have been instances of battery actions succeeding,[177] but the following case clearly shows the predominant judicial attitude.[178]

Mrs Chatterton was treated by the defendant for chronic pain around an abdominal operation scar. This was by way of injection. The first was unsuccessful, as was the second, which had the further effect of rendering her right leg numb. The plaintiff claimed that consent was vitiated by the failure to inform her of the risk of

---

174. *Op. cit.*, at p. 90.

175. This potential form of action is important because the Crown Indemnity Scheme only applies to actions in negligence. The health authority arguably would not cover damages awarded for a battery action against one of its doctors.

176. *The Law of Torts* (8th edn, 1992), p. 24.

177. *Hamilton* v. *Birmingham Regional Health Board* [1969] 2 B.M.J. 456; *Michael* v. *Molesworth* [1950] 2 B.M.J. 171; *Cull* v. *Royal Surrey County Hospital* [1932] 1 B.M.J. 1195. Charles Lewis (*op. cit.*, at p. 274) usefully points out an unreported case of a Mrs Potts who recovered £3,000 damages for assault when she was injected with Depo-Provera without her consent, during the course of a termination.

178. *Chatterton* v. *Gerson* [1981] 1 All E.R. 257, [1981] Q.B. 432, Q.B.D.

512

numbness. Her claim in battery (as well as negligence) failed. Bristow J described the applicable law in the following terms[179]:

"In my judgement once the patient is informed in broad terms of the nature of the procedure which is intended, and gives her consent, that consent is real, and the cause of the action on which to base a claim for failure to go into risks and implications is negligence, not trespass. Of course, if information is withheld in bad faith, the consent will be vitiated by fraud."

In an emergency situation, even though there is no direct authority on the matter, it appears that the lack of consent will be justified on the basis that the situation itself amounts to a form of immunity from a prima facie unlawful act. In the case of *Wilson* v. *Pringle*[180] the Court of Appeal found that:

"The patient cannot consent, and there may be no next-of-kin available. Hitherto it has been customary to say in such cases that consent is to be implied for what would otherwise be a battery on the unconscious body. It is better simply to say that the surgeon's action is acceptable in the ordinary conduct of everyday life and not a battery."

## 6.3 The action in negligence

The case of *Sidaway*[181] confronts a considerable number of issues in consent; so much so that it deserves central consideration here.[182]

The plaintiff had suffered a number of recurrent pains in the neck, right shoulder and arms. To relieve such problems an operation was performed by the senior neuro-surgeon of the defendant hospital. This operation, even if carried out with the necessary skill, carried an inherent risk, of some one to two per cent, of damage to the spinal column and the nerve roots. The risk of spinal column damage was less than the possibility of damage to the nerve roots. The more remote possibility became real and the plaintiff was severely disabled.

The plaintiff claimed significant damages on the basis that the defendant employee failed to disclose the risks involved in the operation that had been advised. At first instance Skinner J found that the defendant had failed to indicate that the operation was one which was not a necessity, but a matter of choice. Although the defendant, in addition, did inform the patient that there was the possibility of disturbing the nerve root, there was nevertheless a failure to tell the patient of the possibility of damage to the spinal cord. Further, at the time there was a responsible body of medical opinion that would have so informed the patient. Utilising the *Bolam*[183] formulation of the standard of care, the plaintiff had acted in accordance with a responsible body of opinion, notwithstanding that there was a contrary expert view as to disclosure of such a risk. The Court of Appeal affirmed this view, but the matter went to the House of Lords.

One of the many questions of concern to the House was whether a different criterion applied in the realm of disclosure of risk rather than performance of the

179. The more recent case of *Hills* v. *Potter* [1983] 3 All E.R. 716 was more strident in its view that the judge found himself ". . . deploring reliance on these torts in medical cases of this kind. The proper cause of action, if any, is negligence".
180. [1987] Q.B. 237.
181. [1984] 1 All E.R. 1018, C.A.; [1985] 1 All E.R. 643, [1985] A.C. 871, H.L.
182. As well as significance in relation to the legal issues surrounding consent, it is another example of the modern process of the medical negligence litigation action.
183. [1957] 2 All E.R. 118, [1957] 1 W.L.R. 582.

operation. Lord Bridge recognised that there were two legal postures which could be taken in the context of the disclosure of risk. First, "It could be argued that, if the patient's consent is to be fully informed, the doctor must warn him of all risks in the treatment offered, unless he has some sound clinical reason not to do so". His Lordship disapproved of such an approach, contending that "there is no need to warn of the risks inherent in all surgery under general anaesthesia".

His Lordship recognised that there was another extreme which could be taken:

"Once the doctor has decided what treatment is, on balance of advantages and disadvantages, in the patient's best interests, he should not alarm the patient by warning of any risk involved, however grave and substantial, unless specifically asked by the patient."

This view has found some acceptance in Commonwealth authority,[184] but the House of Lords found such an analysis to be "impractical". The reasons given were that it was not a recognition of the reality of the doctor-patient relationship. The factors influencing the disclosure or non-disclosure of particular pieces of information regarding the proposed medical procedure is a matter of clinical judgement in the particular circumstances of the particular case:

"The doctor cannot set out to educate the patient to his own standard of all the relevant factors involved ... If it is to be left to the individual judges to decide for themselves what a 'responsible person in the patient's position' would consider a risk of sufficient significance that he should be told about it the outcome of litigation in this field would be quite unpredictable."

His Lordship went on to consider that the *Bolam* test was "primarily" the test of how to judge the level of information to be disclosed.

As a matter of evidence his Lordship found that "... the non-disclosure complained of accorded with a practice accepted as proper by a responsible body of neuro-surgical opinion afforded the respondents a complete defence to the appellant's claim".

The House in this matter was not *ad idem* on the application of the *Bolam* principle, however, and the possibility (albeit slight) remains that such principle has less force where the allegation is of non-disclosure of information as opposed to another allegation of negligence on the part of the medical practitioner. It should be remembered that Lord Bridge analysed *Bolam* in the sense that this test of liability was "primarily" the one to be utilised. It thus appears from this that the *Bolam* test *simpliciter* does not offer the sanctity the medical profession may have hoped for in the area of pre-operative advice.

Compare the above case with that of *Gold* v. *Haringey Health Authority*.[185] The plaintiff became pregnant, having agreed with her husband not to have any more children. The consultant obstetrician, employed by the defendant health authority, suggested a sterilisation, without mentioning the possibility of the husband having a vasectomy or indeed of the risk that there was a chance of the sterilisation operation failing. It is useful here to note that the percentage chance of the sterilisation failing was higher than that of the vasectomy. The plaintiff, having had a sterilisation operation, became pregnant. The obvious action was that there had been inadequate information given as to the possibility of the operation being subject to natural

184. See *Canterbury* v. *Spence* (1972) 464 F. 2d 772, D.C.
185. [1987] 2 All E.R. 888, [1988] Q.B. 481, C.A.

reversal. The trial judge found that the information had been given in a non-therapeutic context and that there was a negligent misrepresentation that the operation would be "irreversible". On appeal by the defendants *Bolam* was considered in this context. While allowing the appeal it was held by Lloyd LJ that:

"... a distinction between advice given in a therapeutic context and advice given in a non-therapeutic context would be a departure from the principle on which the *Bolam* test is itself grounded. The principle does not depend on the context in which any act is performed or an advice given. It depends on the man possessing skill or competence in a field beyond that possessed by the man on the Clapham omnibus. If the giving of contraceptive advice required no special skill, then I could see no argument that the *Bolam* test should not apply. But that was not, and could not have been, suggested."

It is apparent, therefore, that there may be a variant opinion that can be placed on the strict applicability of the *Bolam* test *simpliciter* in the realms of advice.

Usefully, Kennedy and Grubb[186] compare the decision in *Gold* with *The Department of Health Guide to Consent for Examination or Treatment*.[187] As a matter of potential evidence it is worthy of reproduction:

"Patients are entitled to receive sufficient information in a way that they can understand about the proposed treatments, the possible alternatives and any substantial risks, so that they can make a balanced judgement. Patients must be allowed to decide whether they will agree to the treatment, and they may refuse treatment at any time.

Enough information must normally be given to ensure that they understand the nature, consequences and any substantial risks of the treatment proposed so that they are able to take a decision based on that information. The patient's ability to appreciate the significance of the operation should be assessed.

A doctor will have to exercise his or her professional skill and judgement in deciding what risks the patient should be warned of and the terms in which the warning should be given. However, a doctor has a duty to warn patients of substantial or unusual risks inherent in any proposed treatment.

Care should be taken to respect the patient's wishes.

Where treatment carries a substantial risk the patient must be advised of this by the doctor so that consent may be well informed, and the doctor's advice must be formally recorded.

Oral consent may be sufficient for the vast majority of contacts with patients by doctors and nurses and other health professionals. Written consent should be obtained for any procedure or treatment carrying any substantial risk or substantial side-effect.

It should be noted that the purpose of obtaining a signature on the consent form is not an end in itself. The most important element of consent procedure is the duty to ensure that patients understand the nature and purpose of the proposed treatment.

Where a patient has not been given appropriate information then consent may not always have been given despite the signature on the form."

### 6.4 The remaining questions

Given that there still does not appear to be unanimity on the level of information to be disclosed, there can only at present be a view as to the specific elements contained in the judgment of their Lordships in *Sidaway*. For example, Kennedy and Grubb pertinently question the ambit of the phrase "substantial risk of grave adverse consequences".[188] Yet this term may appear little more than a general questioning of the pertinence of applying *Bolam* in its basic form. Lord Bridge appeared to be

---

186. *Op. cit.*, at p. 187.
187. H.C. 90 (22).
188. Kennedy and Grubb, *op. cit.*, at p. 188.

swayed by the fact that there were certain risks that ought to be disclosed in order that the patient could make an informed choice as to treatment. It might further be suggested that this is another attempt to refine the test for the standard of disclosure to suit the myriad of possible factual circumstances that may confront the courts. Lord Templeman, on the other hand sought to distinguish between "general" and "special" risks. The plaintiff would be expected to be aware of the general risks associated with surgery/anaesthesia, whereas the latter would be risks peculiar to a particular form of medical intervention, and therefore would be deserving of specific disclosure by the doctor in discussing the operative procedure with the patient. One should once more not place too much significance on such judicial remarks. The likelihood is that these pronouncements will not be seen as variants of the *Bolam* test, but will be interpreted subsequently as merely different forms of stating the traditional test.

The difficulty is still by what standard to measure the amount of information a patient requires. Lord Scarman opted for what Kennedy and Grubb describe as the "prudent patient" test as opposed to the "particular patient" test.[189] It has already been noted that his Lordship decided on the former analysis; namely what a reasonable patient, in the circumstances of the plaintiff, would need to know to make a valid consent. Lord Bridge's emphasis, and that of the House as a whole, remained with the medical profession.

More recently in the case of *Moyes* v. *Lothian Health Board*[190] there was a reassertion of the relevance of *Bolam* (albeit at first instance). The patient had not been told of certain risks inherent in an angiography. The court found that in 1981, at the time of the incident, responsible medical opinion had it that such risks were not disclosed.

In *Heath* v. *West Berkshire Health Authority*[191] the same decision was reached. The failed allegation was that there should have been warning of risk of damage to the lingual nerve during a wisdom tooth extraction. A "prudent patient" test was applied.

### 6.5 Duty to answer questions

An early case, indicative of judicial attitude at the time was that of *Hatcher* v. *Black*.[192] Mrs Hatcher was a BBC broadcaster who required an operation on her thyroid. She was reassured that there was no risk to her voice. During the course of the operation her nerve was damaged, with the devastating result that she was unable to speak properly and thus broadcast again. In giving judgment for the defendant Denning LJ appeared to be condoning the therapeutic lie. He accepted the argument of the doctor that while he knew of the slight risk, he decided that this would unduly worry the plaintiff.[193]

Such an attitude would be unlikely to be condoned today. As Lord Bridge announced in *Sidaway*, "When questioned specifically by a patient apparently of

189.  *Ibid.* at pp. 190–201.
190.  [1990] 1 Med.L.R. 463.
191.  [1992] 3 Med.L.R. 57.
192.  (1954) *The Times*, 2 July.
193.  It now appears fascinating that Denning LJ could declare during the course of his judgment that "this is not a court of morals, but a court of law"!

sound mind about risks involved in a particular treatment proposed, the doctor's duty must, in my opinion, be to answer both truthfully and as fully as the questioner requires".

Even in the realms of the therapeutic lie, it appears that the doctor may still in certain circumstances be justified at law for not disclosing information, even when specifically asked. In *Lee* v. *South West Thames Regional Health Authority*[194] Sir John Donaldson MR found that the duty of disclosure "... is subject to the exercise of clinical judgement as to the terms in which the information is given and the extent to which, in the patient's interests, information should be withheld".

Much the same was said by the Court of Appeal in *Blyth* v. *Bloomsbury Health Authority*.[195] This case has gained some notoriety in that it was decided soon after *Sidaway*, and also appeared to reveal a determined shift back to the attitudes apparent in the decision of *Hatcher* v. *Black*.

The plaintiff, Mrs Blyth, became pregnant. She attended a consultant for ante-natal advice. It was found that she had no rubella immunity, but it was too late in the pregnancy to administer a vaccination. It was decided therefore, that both her and the baby would be vaccinated post-natally. Mrs Blyth, after the birth of the baby, received two injections. The first was a vaccination against rubella. The second was an injection of Depo-Provera, which was to provide contraceptive cover for three months because the rubella vaccination could harm any foetus conceived within these three months.

The plaintiff's complaints were as follows.

(1) She was given insufficient information on the possible side-effects of Depo-Provera when in the hospital.
(2) If she had been informed more fully about the possible side-effects then she would not have agreed to the injection of the Depo-Provera.
(3) The injection caused her to suffer from a number of side-effects.

In finding against the plaintiff Kerr LJ stated:

"The question of what a plaintiff should be told in answer to a general inquiry cannot be divorced from the *Bolam* test, any more than when no such inquiry is made. In both cases the answer must depend upon the circumstances, the nature of the inquiry, the nature of the information which is available, its reliability, relevance, the condition of the patient and so forth."

The evidence in this case however indicated that those involved were not accurately answering direct questions, and perhaps even more seriously were not aware of research material available in their consultant's file on the case.

## 6.6 Consent and causation

The distinct difficulty for the courts here has been to decide between a subjective and objective approach to the question of whether, on the balance of probabilities, the patient would have undergone the operation knowing of the risk or risks which were not disclosed, but came to fruition. The case of *Chatterton* v. *Gerson*[196] took a

194. [1985] 2 All E.R. 385, C.A., [1985] 1 W.L.R. 845.
195. [1993] Med.L.R. 151, C.A., (1985) C.L.Y. 2321.
196. [1981] Q.B. 432.

517

subjective line where Bristow J stated, "When the claim is based on negligence the plaintiff must prove not only the breach of duty to inform but had the duty been broken she would not have chosen to have the operation".

The current approach is a mixture of the subjective and the objective. An effective English authority is that of *Smith* v. *Barking, Havering and Brentwood Health Authority*.[197]

The plaintiff underwent an operation to relieve severe symptoms caused by a cyst on the spinal column. Some nine years later the symptoms began to recur, and the same doctor decided to perform another cyst drainage operation. It was accepted in evidence that the operation was extremely difficult, and the doctor was extremely reluctant to undertake it. The operation was unsuccessful, and Mrs Smith was left tetraplegic. The allegation she made was that if she had been warned of the risks that were inherent in the operation, she would have decided against having it. The court was invited to consider which test to apply. Against the subjective test was the fact that it would be open to the abuse of hindsight. Mrs Smith's reflections, it was contended by the court, would be coloured by her present condition. The other option would be to use a reasonable patient test. The problem with this test is that it cannot take any idiosyncratic features of the individual patient into account, which may have affected their choice when compared to the patient "on the Clapham omnibus". The court, in deciding on a middle course, developed a test which judged the causation issue by the standard of the reasonable patient but imbued with characteristics of the particular patient in question which might have affected their decision. Despite this the tenor of the argument in finding against Mrs Smith was that the plaintiff's evidence would be treated with caution when combined with the reasonable patient's hypothetical posture.

## 6.7 Disclosure post-treatment

The case of *Lee*[198] indicates that *Sidaway* levels of disclosure apply where the patient actually asks what treatment they have had. The question is really whether the doctor is under a legal duty to inform the patient of any mistakes that might have been made during the course of the operation. Gerald Robertson addresses the real problem as being "... where the doctor's failure to tell the patient what has happened does not cause any additional physical injury, but merely keeps the patient ignorant of a possible cause of action against the doctor".[199]

The case of *Naylor*[200] appears to confirm Robertson's view that such a duty does exist. Sir John Donaldson MR argued that, it will be remembered, a duty of disclosure has been recognised by professional rules, and therefore this should be translated into information about what has happened. The possibility thus arises, subject to the usual legal difficulties already encountered in this chapter, of actions in contract and tort.

197. (Unreported) 29 July 1989, Q.B.D.
198. See fn. 194 above.
199. G Robertson, "Fraudulent Concealment and the Duty to Disclose Medical Mistakes" (1987) 25 Alberta L.R. 215.
200. *Naylor* v. *Preston Area Health Authority* [1987] 2 All E.R. 353, [1987] 1 W.L.R. 958, C.A.

## 6.8 Refusing consent to treatment

A large volume of case-law has developed where patients have refused consent to medical treatment, often life-saving treatment. The question here is whether there is legal authority for the doctor to treat in the face of a refusal, so protecting the doctor from a form of professional liability, or indeed whether a doctor treating against the patient's wishes is to be exposed to civil, or even criminal liability. Not all of the case-law can be considered here, that would require a book of its own. It is sufficient for present purposes to give some factual examples of the situations likely to arise, the possible arguments that can be raised and the trend of judicial authority in this contentious and highly emotive area.

The recent case of *Re R*[201] is important in two respects. First, it is a consideration of the concept of the "mature minor", therefore a consideration of the approach taken in *Gillick*.[202] Secondly, the case turned on the legal authority to override a refusal of treatment. The case involved a 15-year-old girl, whose increasingly disturbed behaviour required sedative treatment. At times, however, the girl appeared coherent and rational, and at those times refused to take her medication. The wardship was attempted on the basis that then the anti-psychotic drugs could be given with or without consent. The Court of Appeal was swift to note the extent of the power given to a ward. It was clear that the best interests of the patient were predominant, and certainly would override any refusal. The court found that the capacity approach of *Gillick* would not be appropriate, because, as Mason and McCall confirm, "*Gillick* was concerned with the developing maturity of a normal child; the test elaborated in that case could not be applied to a child whose mental state fluctuated from day to day".[203] Lord Donaldson MR went on to establish the idea of the key to the therapeutic door. There are two keyholders the child and the parents (or ward). Consent of either of these parties would enable treatment to be lawfully given.

In *Re W*[204] the significance of the decision in *Re R* for the medical professional in terms of liability as an issue becomes clear. Lord Donaldson MR again makes the point.

"On reflection I regret my use ... of the keyholder analogy ... because keys can lock as well as unlock. I now prefer the analogy of the legal 'flak jacket' which protects from claims by the litigious whether he acquires it from his patient who may be a minor over the age of 16, or a 'Gillick' competent child under that age or from another person having parental responsibilities which include a right to consent to treatment of the minor. Anyone who gives him a 'flak jacket' (i.e., consent) may take it back, but the doctor only needs one and so long as he continues to have one he has the legal right to proceed."

Adults have been known to refuse life-saving treatment on occasion. The usual reason being a religious objection to the treatment. What is the doctor to do in the face of such a refusal? The issue arose for consideration in the case of *Re T*.[205]

201. *Re R (a minor) (wardship: medical treatment)* [1992] Fam. 11, [1992] B.M.L.R. 147, C.A.
202. *Gillick* v. *West Norfolk and Wisbech Area Health Authority* [1985] 3 All E.R. 402. The case decided that a child was to be judged capable of consenting if he or she had the general capacity to understand the nature and implication of a particular medical action, as opposed to having a particular status.
203. *Op. cit.*, at p. 226.
204. *Re W (a minor) (medical treatment)* [1992] 4 All E.R. 627.
205. *Re T (adult: refusal of treatment)* [1992] 4 All E.R. 649, C.A.

An adult woman, declaring herself to be a Jehovah's Witness, refused to allow a life-saving blood transfusion to take place. The Court of Appeal found the refusal invalid on the facts because of strong evidence of the undue influence of the mother. Although not required to do so the court considered what would have been the position if the woman had been a Jehovah's Witness and no influence had been apparent. Lord Donaldson MR quite clearly stated that her choice "... is not limited to decisions which others might regard as sensible. It exists notwithstanding that the reasons for making the choice are rational, irrational, unknown or even non-existent ..."

It needs to be emphasised that the doctor who treats a patient in the face of a refusal by a patient (an adult or *Gillick* competent child) may be liable under the criminal law, or for damages in the tort of battery. There appears little doubt that this tort will apply whatever definition one applies to battery. The act is a directly hostile one, because, not only is there a lack of consent, here there is active refusal. What may turn out in the future to become the judicial counterpoint to this view, and enable the doctor to treat, will be a questioning not of the belief-system itself, but subtly using the existence of that belief-system as an indicator of irrationality to the extent that the patient is not competent to make rational decisions generally. This is at present, merely hypothesis, and treatment in such circumstances should not be undertaken without some judicial authority.[206]

A variant on the issue of refusing treatment can be seen in the case of *Re S*.[207] The application made was for a declaration to authorise a surgeon and other staff to carry out an emergency operation on S. S was a 30-year-old woman who had been admitted in labour. The only way to deliver the child, and also save the life of the mother, was to perform a Caesarean section. Mrs S had refused the operation, describing herself (and her husband) as "born again Christian". The case before the court was an emergency, with the doctor giving evidence saying that they were concerned with minutes rather than hours. Sir Stephen Brown P made the order sought. There was a recognition that no English authority existed to justify the decision, but one might tentatively perceive it to be that the interests of the unborn child were considered preferable to those of the mother.

## 6.9 Mental incompetence and consent to treatment

It is not the place to discuss statutory arrangements to treat the mentally disordered for their condition.[208] This statutory arrangement does not, however, apply to treatment which is not for the mental disorder itself, but for some other physical ailment. The most useful area of medical practice of relevance here is where there is a proposal to sterilise a mentally incompetent individual, or abort the foetus of a mentally incompetent person. The case of *Re F*[209] considers the issues of relevance.

A woman, aged 36, suffered from a serious mental disability. Her verbal capacity was that of a two-year-old, and her general mental capacity was of a four- to five-year-old child. While a voluntary in-patient at a mental hospital she formed a

206. See also AN Wear and D Brahams, "To Treat or Not To Treat: The Legal, Ethical and Therapeutic Implications of Patient Refusal" (1991) 17 J.Med. Ethics 131.

207. *Re S (adult: refusal of medical treatment)* [1992] 4 All E.R. 671, (1992) B.M.L.R. 69.

208. Governed by the Mental Health Act 1983.

209. *Re F (mental patient: sterilisation)* [1990] 2 A.C. 1; *sub nom. F* v. *West Berkshire Health Authority* [1989] 2 All E.R. 545.

sexual relationship with a male patient. Psychiatric evidence was to the effect that it would be a disaster if she were to become pregnant. Existing contraceptive measures were unreliable as far as this patient was concerned, or in combination with the drugs being taken for the mental condition, could prove dangerous. The medical staff felt that it would be best if she were sterilised. The mother sought a declaration that the absence of consent would not make the sterilisation unlawful. It was conceded that the court had no power to give consent on behalf of F (*parens patriae* jurisdiction not applying to adults). The trial judge, Scott-Baker J, was prepared to see all treatments for physical conditions given to mental patients in good faith and in their best interests to be an exception to battery. This was repeated in effect in the Court of Appeal where Lord Donaldson felt that such treatment "fell within generally accepted standards". The House of Lords were concerned with the procedural as well as legal elements involved. It was confirmed that the *parens patriae* jurisdiction no longer had any effect in this country. They thus proceeded by way of declaration. It was reiterated that a doctor acting in the best interests of the patient would not be acting unlawfully. "Best interests" meant carried out in order to save a life, secure improvement or prevent deterioration in physical and/or mental health.

Now matters are governed by a *Practice Note*,[210] which makes a number of useful points to guide both the doctor, the health workers and those charged with advising on the legality of a proposed sterilisation:

(1) The sterilisation of a minor or mentally incompetent adult will, in virtually all cases, require prior sanction by a High Court judge.
(2) It would be preferable in the case of a minor that the court invoke its inherent jurisdiction when an application is made.
(3) An application in the case of an adult should be done by way of originating summons issued out of the Family Division of the High Court.
(4) Prior to a substantive hearing there will be a summons for directions.
(5) The purpose of the proceedings is to establish whether or not the proposed sterilisation is in the best interests of the patient. The judge needs to be satisfied that those proposing sterilisation are seeking it in good faith and that their paramount concern is for the patient's best interests rather than their own, or the public's convenience. In straightforward cases, the matter can be disposed of at the summons for directions without hearing oral evidence.
(6) Although not exhaustive, the following should be established at the hearing;
   (a) The patient is incapable of making a decision about sterilisation.
   (b) The patient is unlikely to develop sufficiently to make an informed judgement in the foreseeable future; but it should be borne in mind that because a person is legally incompetent for some purposes, it does not mean that they are incompetent for the purposes of a sterilisation decision.[211] It should also be borne in mind, where the sterilisation of the young is being considered, that the potential for development may be impossible to predict.

210. [1993] 3 All E.R. 222.
211. This was specifically included to stop a patient detained under the Mental Health Act 1983 having that fact used as an indication of "blanket" incompetence.

(c) There is a likelihood that the condition sought to avoid will occur.

(d) There is a likelihood that the patient will suffer substantial trauma or psychological damage greater than that resulting from the sterilisation itself.

(e) The person is incapable of looking after a child.

(f) No other form of treatment short of sterilisation will avoid the risk of pregnancy.

## 7 MEDICAL PRACTICE AND CRIMINAL PROFESSIONAL LIABILITY

### 7.1 Introduction

It goes without saying that those involved in medical practice are not above the general criminal law. It is the case that there have been a number of developments in the criminal law which directly affect the activities of doctors. Of even more relevance for the purposes of this work there are a number of statutes and aspects of the common criminal law which govern the activities of medical practitioners. Criminal liability attracts obvious sanctions of the utmost seriousness to these professionals, but in addition attracts professional disciplinary liability and sanctions which can include dismissal from the profession. It thus becomes vital to consider in some detail these aspects of the criminal law.

### 7.2 Consent and criminal assault

As well as potential actions for the tort of battery and the action in negligence, the doctor acting without a legally recognised consent can be left open to liability in the criminal law. It is worth noting that the general issues raised in relation to the tort of battery apply. The key to the criminal aspect is the intention behind the touching and whether it can be regarded as "hostile".[212] There have been criminal prosecutions where there have been false representations as to the purpose behind the "touching".[213]

### 7.3 Homicide and medical practice

This issue is particularly important in two main respects. Recent prosecutions in the criminal courts have proved successful against medical practitioners, therefore the practices involved as well as the legal rules that have been considered are of more than passing significance:

(1) Manslaughter by gross negligence.

---

212. Although the current trend is to consider whether the conduct was acceptable in the ordinary course of everyday events; namely the ordinary practice of medicine in good faith.

213. See, for example, *R* v. *Williams* [1923] 2 K.B. 340, where sexual intercourse was falsely represented as a form of clinical examination.

(2) Murder/"mercy killing".

(3) Neonaticide.

## 7.4 Manslaughter by gross negligence

There has long been a recognition that the practice of medicine is far from certain and mistakes do occur. The negligence action recognises negligent behaviour in circumstances of medical practice, but what may not be so apparent is that the law relating to manslaughter recognises a form of negligence, that of "gross negligence". As far back as 1874, an attendant at a mental hospital who released boiling water into a bath was convicted for gross negligence manslaughter.[214] In the more well-known case of *Bateman*[215] the test was whether the negligence was over and above that required for civil liability for negligence. It has to show a "disregard for the safety of others" that warrants the sanction of the criminal law.

Most recently in the case of *Adomako*[216] the House of Lords has re-established the existence of the concept of gross negligence manslaughter. An anaesthetist failed to notice, during the course of an operation, that the patient was in obvious distress. There was some evidence which appeared to suggest that he may even have been out of theatre. It is interesting to note that while some have welcomed this particular conviction and the resurrection of gross negligence manslaughter, Mason and McCall Smith argue that if the anaesthetist had not been out of theatre but had nevertheless not noticed the distress "it might be more difficult to argue for his conviction of manslaughter, although undoubtedly, professional sanctions would be needed."[217]

The test to be applied now is:

(a) whether there was a duty of care in existence;

(b) whether there was a breach of this duty of care towards the victim;

(c) whether the breach of duty caused the death of the victim;

(d) whether the breach of duty amounted to gross negligence.

The duty issue will be interpreted along the lines of the pronouncement in *Bateman* by Lord Hewart CJ:

"If a person holds himself out as possessing special skill and knowledge, and he is consulted, as possessing such skill and knowledge, by or on behalf of a patient, he owes a duty to the patient to use due caution in undertaking the treatment. If he accepts the responsibility and undertakes the treatment and the patient submits to his discretion and treatment accordingly, he owes a duty to the patient to use diligence, care, knowledge, skill and caution in administering the treatment. No contractual relation is necessary, nor is it necessary that the service be rendered for reward."

Importantly, during the course of his judgment in *Adomako* Lord Mackay LC succinctly sets out the test of gross negligence. It was found to depend[218]:

"... on the seriousness of the breach of duty committed by the defendant in all the circumstances in which he was placed when it occurred and whether, having regard to the risk

214. *R* v. *Finney* (1874) 12 Cox.C.C. 625.
215. *R* v. *Bateman* (1925) 94 L.J.K.B. 791.
216. *R* v. *Adomako* [1995] 1 A.C. 171.
217. *Op. cit.*, at p. 216.
218. [1995] 1 A.C. 171 at 323.

of death involved, the conduct of the defendant was so bad in all the circumstances as to amount in the jury's judgement to a criminal act or omission."

## 7.5 Murder and mercy killing

While the media continues to debate the ethical boundaries of the concept of euthanasia, the criminal law still has to consider the medical practitioner who administers some lethal drug to the terminally ill, comatose, or pain-ridden patient. There has, once more, been a considerable amount of literature written on the euthanasia debate. For the purposes of an analysis of professional criminal liability in this area one is able to focus attention on a small number of nevertheless significant cases for medical practice.

A Dr Cox[219] was charged and convicted of attempted murder of his patient Lillian Boyes. Boyes was suffering from a severe form of arthritis, which was becoming less amenable to control through pain-killing medication. Dr Cox injected Boyes with a lethal dose of potassium chloride and she died within minutes. A nurse discovered Cox's notes and informed the hospital authorities, who in turn contacted the police. He was tried for attempted murder because the body had been cremated before a post-mortem could take place and there was thus no evidence that the injection had been the actual cause of death.

The defence attempted to argue that the potassium chloride was given only to relieve the suffering, but the evidence proved that this drug could have no analgesic effect. Ognall J, sentencing Cox to a year of imprisonment, suspended, said that the doctor had allowed his professional duty to be overridden by his compassion for his patient. He concluded, "What you did was not only criminal, it was a total betrayal of your unequivocal duty as a physician".[220]

It was accepted during the course of the judgment, however, that there could be circumstances where[221]:

"If a doctor believes that a certain course is beneficial to the patient, either therapeutically or analgesically, then even though he recognises that that course carries with it a risk to life, he is fully entitled none the less, to pursue it. If in those circumstances the patient dies, nobody could possibly suggest that in that situation the doctor was guilty of murder or attempted murder."

Dr Cox was reprimanded by the General Medical Council, but was not struck off.

The general law applicable to such situations is also contained in the judgment of Devlin J in his summing-up to the jury in the trial of Dr Bodkin Adams[222] for murder by the injection into the deceased of a massive dose of opiates:

"If the acts done intended to kill and did, in fact, kill, it did not matter if a life were cut short by weeks or months, it was just as much murder as if it were cut short by years."

One must accept this as a correct proposition of law. Notwithstanding this, however, the judge went on to direct that:

219. (1992) 12 B.M.L.R. 38.
220. *R* v. *Cox* (1992) 12 B.M.L.R. 38.
221. *Ibid.* at 39.
222. *R* v. *Adams* (1957) C.L.R. 365, C.C.C.

"If the first purpose of medicine, the restoration of health, can no longer be achieved, there is still much for the doctor to do, and he is entitled to do all that is proper and necessary to relieve pain and suffering, even if the measures he takes may incidentally shorten life."

The notion effectively introduced here is one of double effect. While the opiates did have an analgesic effect, Devlin J in essence legally discounted the significance of the fact that they also shortened life.

## 7.6 Neonaticide

The main decisions of the courts in this area are further indicators that the judiciary will allow a degree of latitude in allowing a doctor to undertake a particular course of clinical management which, in circumstances outside the profession, would be highly likely to attract the attention of the criminal courts.

The case of Leonard Arthur proves instructive as a starting-point.

A child was born with what was described in evidence as "uncomplicated Down's Syndrome". The parent, on being informed of this fact, rejected the child. Dr Arthur thereafter wrote in the medical notes, "Parents do not wish it to survive. Nursing care only". Some 69 hours later the child was dead. Dr Arthur was eventually acquitted of the reduced charge of attempted murder. This, it has been widely claimed, is an anomalous decision, because it reveals a stark protectionist policy towards the medical profession, whereas the summing-up revealed a blatant side-stepping of the legal issues. The *actus reus* and *mens rea* for murder were apparent, as was the possibility of a manslaughter conviction. Even more apparent was the distinct possibility of a breach of the Children and Young Persons Act 1933. The true nature of the decision comes from the summing-up to the jury by Farquharson J where he stated, "I imagine that you will think long and hard before concluding that doctors, of the eminence we have heard, have evolved standards that amount to committing a crime."[223]

A clarification (and reduction in the impact of the anomalous decision in *Arthur*) can be found in *Re J*.[224]

Here the child was severely brain damaged, suffered frequent violent fits and phases where breathing stopped and ventilation was required. The matter brought to the court was whether, if the breathing stopped again, it would be lawful not to undertake ventilation, with the inevitable consequence of death. The court emphasised that while one should presume in favour of life generally, consideration had to be given to matters of pain, dignity and the continuance of intrusive treatment. While it would be difficult and not without its detractors, the court also felt that it should look at the issue from the perspective of the neonate; initiating a form of "substituted" judgment in relation to the child. While allowing the application not to ventilate the court continued to emphasise that[225]:

"The court can never sanction steps to terminate life. That would be unlawful. There is no question of approving, even in the case of the most horrendous disability, a course aimed at

---

223. *R* v. *Arthur* (1981) *The Times*, 6 November, (1981) 12 B.M.L.R. 1 at 22.
224. *Re J (a minor) (wardship: medical treatment)* [1990] 3 All E.R. 930, (1990) 6 B.M.L.R. 25.
225. [1990] 3 All E.R. 930 at 943.

terminating life or accelerating death. The court is concerned only with the circumstances in which steps should not be taken to prolong life."

## 7.7 Liability for terminating life support

In order to avoid professional liability for such an action, which appears to have become, unfortunately, a more frequent aspect of the work of the medical practitioner, it is necessary to consider and follow the guidance of the House of Lords in the case of *Bland*.[226]

It will be recalled that Anthony Bland was a spectator at the ill-fated football match at Hillsborough. He was one of the victims of the disaster. He suffered a severe crushed chest injury which gave rise to hypoxic brain damage. He deteriorated into a persistent vegetative state. The issue was whether the artificial feeding and antibiotic drugs could be lawfully withdrawn from the patient with the knowledge that death would ensue. The allegation of the Official Solicitor for the purposes of the appeal to the House of Lords was that it was "... an act intended to lead to the death of Anthony Bland. In the result, the withdrawal of the feeding regime would amount to unlawful killing and would in fact be the crime of murder".

Their Lordships spent a great deal of the time considering the ethical aspects of the case. The legal considerations are contained in the judgment of Butler-Sloss LJ. As confirmed earlier the right of a patient to accept or reject treatment can be rational or irrational. This could also be done in the consideration of future circumstances, by advance directive. Again, as mentioned in relation to consent, here it is necessary to be aware that any treatment undertaken without the consent of the patient is a battery, the well-known exception being the emergency concerning the unconscious patient. The legal difficulty was that Bland had not expressed any views on what should be done if such a situation were to arise. The case-law had already confirmed that the family did not have the power to consent on this adult's behalf. The case-law did, however, provide the court with the power to make a declaration that a particular clinical activity would not be unlawful.

Where a patient is unable, for whatever reason, to give instructions, then there is a legal duty on the medical professional to act in the best interests of the patient. This general duty is set in accordance with the activities of a responsible and competent body of medical opinion as expressed in *Bolam*.

With regard to the patient in a persistent vegetative state, it was felt that *Bolam* itself was not adequate when such a grave decision was being made, as opposed to a decision merely concerned with the usefulness of future treatment. The principle of the best interests of the patient in the present case encompasses wider consider-ations, including some degree of monitoring of the medical decision. In duty of care terms there was a great deal of support of the decision of Lord Donaldson in *Re J*. In reality it had to be part of the doctor's duty to undertake a balancing exercise when considering the best interests of the patient.

As already stated, the Official Solicitor sought to argue that a doctor owes a duty to treat or provide artificial nutrition. A failure to do so would be a criminal breach of duty. Here it was found that in the circumstances encountered in *Bland* there would be no duty to continue treatment as it was not in the best interests of the patient,

---

226. *Airedale NHS Trust* v. *Bland* [1993] 1 All E.R. 821.

therefore there was no *mens rea* in relation to the alleged unlawful act or omission. It was held simply that the issue of *mens rea* did not arise here. The case of *Cox* was different in that there was a lethal dose designed to cause death. It was an external and intrusive act which was not in accordance with the duty of a doctor.

In conclusion it was stated that the termination of the hydration and feeding should not be a matter for the medical profession alone and should be put before the High Court for determination.

Lord Goff, speaking for the House of Lords pertinently pointed out that:

"A murder prosecution is a poor way to design an ethical and moral code for doctors who are faced with decisions concerning the use of costly and extraordinary life-support measures."

Lord Browne-Wilkinson discussed in more detail the criminal issues involved. In general an omission to prevent death is not an *actus reus* and cannot give rise to a conviction for murder. But, where the accused is under a duty to the deceased to do an act which he omits to do, such an omission can constitute the *actus reus* of homicide. In response to the Official Solicitor's arguments it was decided that:

"The removal of the tube itself does not cause the death since by itself it did not sustain life. Therefore, even if, contrary to my view, the removal of the tube is to be classified as a positive act, it would not constitute the *actus reus* of murder, since such positive act would not be the cause of death."

What of the position of the doctor where the patient is conscious, rational yet still refuses life-sustaining treatment? The general considerations surrounding consent apply. It is a battery to treat a patient without their consent, so the doctor would appear to be legally protected if there is no medical intervention as the patient requests. The justification for this view can clearly be seen in the case of *Blaue*,[227] where it was recognised that a Jehovah's Witness can refuse life-saving treatment.

## 7.8 Termination of pregnancy

The issue here concerns the professional liability of those involved in a procedure as well as the pre-conditions for the performance of a termination. It has already been seen that there may be negligence in the performance of the abortion. While one would be correct in stating that current legislation sets up what may be described as a liberal abortion regime, there is still the possibility of a criminal conviction if one strays outside the ambit of the law. The abortion legislation is also relevant where a member of the medical "team" has a conscientious objection to involvement in the abortion process.

## 7.9 The current abortion legislation

The 1967 Abortion Act has been amended by section 37 of the Human Fertilisation and Embryology Act 1990. The Act provides that no offence will be committed under the law relating to abortion[228] where pregnancy is terminated by a registered medical

---

227. *R* v. *Blaue* [1975] 1 W.L.R. 1411.
228. This being defined by s. 6 (the interpretation section) as ss. 58 and 59 of the Offences Against the Person Act 1861.

practitioner in circumstances where two such persons have formed the opinion in good faith that one of the following conditions is in existence:

(1) that the pregnancy has not exceeded 24 weeks, and that the continuance would involve risk, greater than if the pregnancy were terminated, of injury to the physical or mental health of the pregnant woman or any existing children of her family[229];

(2) that the termination is deemed to be necessary to prevent grave permanent injury to the physical or mental health of the pregnant woman[230];

(3) that continuance of the pregnancy would involve risk to the life of the woman, greater than if the pregnancy were terminated[231];

(4) that there is a substantial risk that the child if born would suffer from such severe physical or mental abnormalities as to be seriously handicapped.[232]

Whereas two medical practitioners would normally be required to form an opinion in relation to the above, this will not apply where one medical practitioner forms an opinion in good faith that termination is necessary to save the life or prevent grave permanent injury to the pregnant woman. This is a legislative recognition of the possibility of an emergency.

The courts have only been called on to consider the issue of good faith in abortion procedure in *Smith*,[233] and this was in the very specific area of certification of the abortion. Nevertheless, the case is of interest as one of the rare convictions under modern abortion legislation.

Dr Smith, in performing an abortion on a patient, was accused of breaching the (unamended) Abortion Act 1967. The claim was that he had not properly examined the patient to ascertain the necessity of an abortion and had not acted in good faith in asking his anaesthetist for the required second opinion when the patient was in theatre. Evidence was that the young woman was healthy, and practitioners called to give evidence commented that normally careful inquiries would be made. Dr Smith was charged with the unlawful procuring of an abortion, contrary to section 58 of the Offences Against the Person Act 1861. Those representing Dr Smith argued amongst other things that he had formed what was termed an "honest" opinion of the need for an abortion. Nevertheless he was convicted.

The 1967 Act (as amended) makes provision for those involved in the abortion process to object on moral grounds to their participation in the procedure. Section 4 of the Act provides that "No person shall be under a duty, whether by contract or by statutory or other legal requirement, to participate in any treatment authorised by this Act to which he has a conscientious objection". The section goes on to state that, in legal proceedings, the person claiming to object has the burden of showing that it is a conscientious objection.

The section also clarifies the fact that it does not affect the duty of practitioners to participate in treatment which would be necessary to save life or prevent grave permanent injury to the physical or mental health of the pregnant woman. A refusal

---

229. Section 1(1)(a).
230. Section 1(1)(b).
231. Section 1(1)(c).
232. Section 1(1)(d).
233. *R v. Smith (John)* [1974] 1 All E.R. 376.

therefore would lead to possible dismissal from employment, and if the refusal has a detrimental physical impact on the woman, then a criminal prosecution would seem likely. The practical result of a refusal by a doctor in a non-emergency situation is that the doctor would be under a duty to advise, even if this was merely to refer the patient to another practitioner willing to carry out the procedure.

The only issue to come before the court in relation to this section is in relation to the ambit of the phrase "participate in any treatment". It fell to be considered in the case of *Janaway* v. *Salford Health Authority*.[234] Given the complexity of the structure of the modern hospital or clinic, involvement in the abortion process can take a number of forms, from the person on the reception desk to the nurse and medical practitioner more intimately involved in the clinical process of termination. Mrs Janaway was employed as a secretary/receptionist at a health centre. She was asked by a doctor to type a letter referring a patient to a consultant for advice on a possible abortion. Mrs Janaway was a practising Roman Catholic, and had a moral objection to the performance of abortion. She therefore refused to type the letter. Her refusal to give a reassurance that there would be no similar incident in the future lead to her dismissal on the grounds of misconduct. There was an attempt to rely on the existence of section 4. The House decided quite correctly that the term "participate" meant participation in the medical process of abortion itself and thus her termination of employment was lawful.

A lawful abortion may only be carried out by a registered medical practitioner. Modern abortion techniques do not necessitate the continuous presence of the doctor with the patient. The legality of the involvement of nurses in the contemporary process of abortion was considered extensively by the House of Lords.[235]

Aside from the initial surgical intervention of the doctor in the termination by Prostaglandin,[236] the practitioner has little involvement in the rest of the process compared to nursing staff. Nursing staff, through the Royal College of Nurses, started this action because they were anxious about the danger of acting contrary to the 1967 Act, in that they were unsure whether they came within the term "medical practitioner". If they did not, then their liability would be nullified in addition to the obvious criminal liability under the Offences Against the Person Act 1861.

Lord Diplock argued that the Act was designed both to state the broad grounds for a lawful abortion, and of particular relevance here, to ensure that such abortions were carried out with the necessary skill and in hygienic conditions. He then went on to recognise modern abortion practice as a team effort. The interpretation to be placed on the Act should therefore take that practicality into account. The registered medical practitioner retains general control and responsibility. If medical practice commonly demands that a particular act be performed by the medical practitioner then that must be done. Similarly, where it is common ground that doctors routinely instruct others to perform particular acts as part of the abortion process, then that too should be done. In essence, the practitioner or that person's substitute should be available throughout the abortion process. If these guidelines are followed then the "pregnancy is terminated by a registered medical practitioner" and lawful provided the other requirements of the law are satisfied.

234. [1988] 3 All E.R. 1079, H.L.
235. *Royal College of Nursing UK* v. *DHSS* [1981] 1 All E.R. 545, H.L.
236. A drug which stimulates the muscles to contract and premature labour to begin.

### 7.10 Surrogate arrangements and criminal liability

Such arrangements and the potential for criminal professional liability are governed by the Surrogacy Arrangements Act 1985. The Act has distinctly limited aims. It is directed towards the criminalisation of commercial surrogacy arrangements. The Act criminalises those who commercially arrange surrogacy. Private/altruistic surrogacy arrangements are not regulated. The doctor who participates by giving advice as part of employment would, however, be guilty under the Act.

### 7.11 Transplantation and the criminal law

With regard to the transplantation from live donors, two issues of potential significance to the medical professional arise: first, the validity of an individual consenting to donate non-regenerative tissue; secondly, commercial transactions necessitating the participation of the medical practitioner.

The particular difficulty with consent in the context of live donor transplantation is that the consent of the donor is to perform an operation which is of no therapeutic value to the donor. There is a well-established rule of the common law, which has been confirmed recently by the House of Lords,[237] that there cannot be consent to being injured where such injury is contrary to the public interest. Nevertheless, Mason and McCall Smith argue "... consent to a surgical operation which is, in itself, non-therapeutic will be valid so long as the consequent infliction of injury can be shown to be in the public interest".[238]

Aspects of live donor transplantation are regulated by the Human Organ Transplants Act 1989. This makes it an offence to undertake a live donor transplant, where the persons are genetically unrelated.[239] Specifically the Act prohibits the exchange of money other than legitimate expenses where a live transplant is under consideration.[240] The interpretation of the legislation by the medical profession is revealed by the guidance provided by the General Medical Council[241]:

"In no circumstances may doctors participate in or encourage in any way the trade in human organs from live donors. They must not advertise for donors nor make financial or medical arrangements for people who wish to sell or buy organs ... Doctors must also satisfy themselves that consent to a donation has been given without undue influence of any kind, including the offer of financial or material benefit."

## 8 MEDICAL PRACTICE AND PROFESSIONAL DISCIPLINE

### 8.1 Introduction

As mentioned earlier, the doctor found liable in negligence, or for some other form of liability in relation to his professional activities, may well attract additional sanctions from one of the bodies which regulate the medical professions. In addition *Ham et al.* point out the importance for the purposes of discussion that[242]:

237. *R* v. *Brown* [1993] 2 W.L.R. 556, [1993] 1 A.C. 212.
238. *Op. cit.*, at p. 294.
239. Unless agreement is made with the Unrelated Live Transplant Regulatory Authority (s. 2).
240. Section 1(1).
241. GMC, "Guidance for Doctors on Transplantation of Organs from Live Donors" (1992).
242. C Ham, R Dingwall, P Fenn and D Harris, "Medical Negligence; Compensation and Accountability" (1988), pp. 16–17. Quoted in Kennedy and Grubb, *op. cit.*, at p. 566.

"accountability lies at the heart of the criticism voiced against tort law by organisations representing patients and their relatives. The argument advanced by these organisations is that doctors are accountable to patients only in a weak sense and that changes are needed to ensure that adequate explanations are given when things go wrong and that appropriate action is taken against the doctors concerned."

One should be aware at this stage however, as far as the patient is concerned, that these complaint and disciplinary procedures are generally regarded as unsatisfactory, and there is a strong move for some fundamental reforms of said procedures. Christopher Newdick lays out the difficulties[243]:

"An aggrieved patient wishing to pursue a complaint against a doctor faces a procedural maze of considerable complexity; first, in the varied institutional structure of the NHS, covering general practice and community health as well as hospitals; second, in the distinction which has to be made between clinical and non-clinical complaints."

## 8.2 The General Medical Council

This body has wide disciplinary powers that can have the most profound effect on the career of the registered medical practitioner. The statutory powers are set out in section 36 of the Medical Act 1983:

"(1) Where a fully registered medical person—
  (a) is found by the Professional Conduct Committee to have been convicted in the British Islands of a criminal offence, whether while so registered or not; or
  (b) is judged by the Professional Conduct Committee to have been guilty of serious professional misconduct, whether while so registered or not;
the committee may, if they think fit, direct—
    (i) that his name shall be erased from the register;
    (ii) that his registration in the register shall be suspended (that is to say, shall not have effect) during such period not exceeding twelve months as may be specified in the direction; or
    (iii) that his registration shall be conditional on his compliance, during such period not exceeding three years as may be specified in the direction, with such requirements so specified as the Committee thinks fit to impose for the protection of members of the public or in his interests."

The phrase "serious professional misconduct" can describe a multitude of sins. Given the consequence that may flow from the doctor being so described, it is vital to have some idea of what will amount to this level of behaviour. According to the somewhat dated case of *Allinson* v. *General Council of Medical Education and Registration*[244]:

"If it be shown that a medical man, in the pursuit of his profession, has done something with regard to it which would be reasonably regarded as disgraceful or dishonourable, by his professional brethren of good repute and competence, then it is open to the General Medical Council to say that he has been guilty of infamous conduct in a professional respect."[245]

A modern interpretation of the term can be found in the case of *Doughty* v. *General Dental Council*.[246] A dentist was charged with various forms of misconduct,

---

243. C Newdick, *op. cit.*, at p. 241, quoting the Review of the Parliamentary Commissioner and Health Service Commissioner Schemes (Reading Centre for Ombudsman Studies, Evidence to the Select Committee on the Parliamentary Commissioner for Administration 1993), para. 14.

244. [1894] 1 Q.B. 750, C.A. See also *McCandless* v. *GMC* [1996] 1 W.L.R. 167.

245. *Ibid.* at 760.

246. [1987] 3 All E.R. 843, P.C., [1988] A.C. 164.

including failing to retain radiographs of patients for a reasonable period and failing to deliver them to the Dental Estimates Board when specifically asked to do so. With regard to six patients is was alleged that there had been a failure to exercise reasonable care and skill. This also applied to four other patients accepted for treatment later.

At first instance, so to speak, the Professional Conduct Committee directed that the dentist's name be erased from the register. Counsel for the appellant at the Privy Council argued that it had to be shown that the appellant held an opinion with regard to the latter groups of patients, that could not be honestly held by him or any dentist. The allegation then was that the misconduct had to be dishonest.[247] In response their Lordships simply stated their view of the phrase "serious professional misconduct". Lord Mackay considered there to be two parts to the test:

> "1. Did the doctor's conduct fall short, by act or omission, of the standard expected among doctors? If yes, then:
> 2. Was this 'falling short' serious?"[248]

How does this square with negligent behaviour on the part of the medical practitioner? Traditionally, the GMC has not considered the issue of medical negligence to be within its overall jurisdiction. Paragraph 38 of the "Blue Book" indicates the true extent of the potential jurisdiction:

"The council is concerned with errors of diagnosis or treatment, and with the kind of matters which give rise to action in the civil courts for negligence, only when the doctor's conduct in the case has involved such a disregard of professional responsibility to patients or such a neglect of professional duties as to raise a question of serious professional misconduct."

It is apparent then that the GMC will consider negligence issues, but only ones which can in addition be considered to amount to serious misconduct. A tentative example of what may come within the jurisdiction can be seen in the case of *McEniff* v. *General Dental Council*.[249] The dentist here was alleged to have allowed unqualified members of his staff to insert fillings after he had drilled the teeth. The appeal was on the basis that there had been unsound legal advice to the General Dental Committee. The decision in this case approved the distinction between merely negligent conduct and conduct which reasonable members of the profession itself (i.e., the members of the General Dental Council) would consider to be infamous or disgraceful conduct.

Part II of the "Blue Book" lists some examples of what it considers may amount to "serious professional misconduct":

(1) neglect or disregard of personal responsibilities to patients for their care and treatment;
(2) abuse of professional privileges or skills;
(3) personal behaviour which is derogatory to the reputation of the medical profession;
(4) self-promotion, advertising and canvassing.

247. See *Felix* v. *General Medical Council* [1960] 2 All E.R. 391 in support of this view.
248. Kennedy and Grubb, *op. cit.*, at p. 577.
249. [1980] 1 All E.R. 461, [1980] 1 W.L.R. 328, P.C.

## 8.3 Complaints within the NHS

Aside from the GMC, general practitioners are also subject to procedures set up under regulations.[250] These regulations stipulate the types of conduct that can lead to a complaint and the procedure to be followed. It should be noted that the complaint must relate to an alleged breach of the GP's Terms of Service.[251]

The FHSA, on receiving the complaint has a number of options. The first option is to solve the problem and satisfy the complainant by informal means. If this fails then there is a formal system to deal with complaints. The FHSA has service committees for the different areas of clinical specialisms. The medical service committee is relevant here, and is required to note that the complaint should be made within 13 weeks of the complained of incident. There will then be consideration by the chairman of the service committee whether the information before him discloses evidence of clinician failure. Where a formal hearing takes place, a complainant may ask for someone to assist, but that person cannot speak at the hearing itself. There is no legal aid available. The FHSA receives the result of the hearing and then can do the following. It can limit the number of patients the doctor himself is allowed to treat, or it can recommend to the Department of Health that the doctor receive an official warning to comply with the terms of service or withhold payment. What it cannot do, however, is award compensation to the complainant.

Kennedy and Grubb point out[252] that the 1992 Regulations do not apply to hospital doctors. The nature of the system is dependent upon whether the complaint relates to clinical or non-clinical matters. In any event, the Complaints Procedure Act 1985 makes it the duty of the Secretary of State to give directions regarding arrangements to deal with complaints by current or past patients, and to publicise such arrangements.[253]

## 8.4 Non-clinical complaints

The Department of Health circular, "Health Service Management Hospital Complaints Procedure"[254] makes it a requirement that there be a "designated officer to receive and act on complaints". In general terms the complaint should be made within three months of the incident (although this period may be extended where there is good cause). The circular itself really only provides the broadest of brushstrokes on procedure. Of interest is the relevance of non-clinical complaints in private medicine. According to the "Patient's Charter"[255]:

"… [DHAs or GP fund-holders] must stipulate in their contracts that any complaints about services by or on behalf of patients will be dealt with in accordance with procedures similar to those prescribed in directions made in reference to the Hospital Complaints Procedure Act 1985."[256]

---

250. National Health Service (Service Committees and Tribunal) Regulations 1992, S.I. 1992/664.
251. As governed by the National Health Service (General Medical Services) Regulations 1992, S.I. 1992/635.
252. *Op. cit.*, at p. 591.
253. Complaints Procedure Act 1985, s. 1(1).
254. H.C. (88) 37.
255. (Department of Health, 1991).
256. "Implementing the Patient's Charter" (HSG (92) 4, NHSME 1992) annex 3, quoted in C Newdick, *Who Should We Treat?* (OUP, 1995) at p. 243.

Newdick[257] considers that this system must be voluntary, as "the contract will be between the hospital and the health authority or GP fund-holder. The patient will not be a party to it so will have no action for breach of contract. One suspects that the NHS purchasers will have limited time and energy to pursue the complaints on the patients' behalf."

## 8.5 Clinical complaints

The current system was introduced in 1981.[258] It has been criticised by Newdick[259] on the ground that "the current complaints system in the NHS seems designed for the convenience of providers of the service rather than of complainants". Nevertheless, the complaints system is composed of three stages:

(1) The consultant involved deals with the issue directly, in person or in writing. This is intended to take place "within a matter of days".

(2) If the complainant is still not satisfied the complaint goes to the DHA, to an administrator or again to the consultant. In any event the matter has to go before the Regional Medical Officer.

(3) The next stage is one of independent review. It still has to be the case that court action would be unlikely. The Regional Medical Officer will get a second opinion on the clinical management of the case. Two independent consultants, still in active practice, will provide such an opinion. They must be specialists in the particular field in question.

It is the case that at the end of such an inquiry, the complainant has no automatic right to see the findings of such an independent review. There is further no compulsion on the medical staff in question to co-operate with any stage of the review of the case. Margaret Brazier recognises that "... it is a strange situation where an employer cannot require his employee to explain conduct that has resulted in injury to the clients of the business".[260]

If this last comment were not enough to raise suspicions about the fairness of the system, there is no obligation to engage the system where there is a possibility of medical negligence litigation. This activity (or lack of it) has been approved in *R* v. *Canterbury and Thanet District Health Authority and South East Thames Regional Health Authority, ex parte F & W.*[261] The court approved of the fact that the procedure was designed to get a second opinion on the matter in question and to provide for the possibility of change in medical practice. If litigation were to be spotted on the horizon, then it would be unreasonable to expect the complained-of consultant to assist in a voluntary exercise. The litigation itself would be far more likely to be a searching inquiry.

257. *Ibid.*
258. "Memorandum of an Agreement for Dealing with Complaints Relating to the Exercise of Clinical Judgment by Hospital Medical and Dental Staff" (HC (81) 5).
259. *Op. cit.*, at p. 244 quoting the Select Committee on the Parliamentary Commissioner for Administration. The Powers, Work and Jurisdiction of the Ombudsman (HC 33–1, Session 1993–94, para. 101).
260. *Medicine, Patients and the Law* (Penguin, 1992), p. 207.
261. [1994] 5 Med.L.R. 132.

### 8.6 The Ombudsman

In the medical sphere the relevant Parliamentary Commissioner has a fairly typical role. Once more, however, potential power has been undermined by the fact that complaints regarding the exercise of clinical judgement are outside the scope of power. Once more Newdick has provided useful evidence that there may be a slight side-stepping around this limitation[262]:

"... a failure to diagnose a fracture following inadequate X-rays has been criticised, as has the failure to diagnose the psychosis of a patient who was subsequently left alone and committed suicide. Similarly, he condemned a failure to obtain the consent of a 23-year-old woman who had been admitted for an abortion but who, after discussion with her parents, was sterilised without her knowledge. She only discovered the fact some years later after she had married and wanted a baby."

MICHAEL DAVIES

---

262. *Op. cit.*, at p. 248.

# CHAPTER 10

# SOLICITORS

## 1 STRUCTURE OF THE PROFESSION

Although this chapter deals with the solicitors' profession, it is important to realise at the outset that the acts or omissions which may found liability will by no means all be attributable to solicitors. The structure of a typical solicitors' firm is likely to include:

(a) partners;

(b) assistant solicitors;

(c) consultants;

(d) trainee solicitors (formerly known as articled clerks);

(e) legal executives;

(f) "paralegals"—that is, those who are employed to work on clients' files but have no formal qualification;

(g) general or outdoor clerks, part of whose work will involve potentially negligent tasks relating to clients' files;

(h) personal assistants, secretaries and word-processing staff whose oral and/or written work may affect the progress of the client's transaction;

(i) accounts staff (at various levels of qualification and expertise) whose handling of clients' money may potentially be negligent;

(j) purely administrative staff whose tasks involve only the running of the office as a business with no encounter with clients or their files or transactions.

In considering the liability of a firm, one is in fact considering the liability of the partners who are the proprietors of the business.

Partners are divided into two types: equity partners and salaried partners. Salaried partners are, as the name suggests, paid a salary each year (which may be fixed or variable) and are not entitled to share the profits or obliged to share the losses of the partnership. Since they are held out to the outside world as partners, they are responsible for the partners' debts but are commonly given an indemnity by the proprietor partners against the liabilities of the partnership.

Those proprietors are the equity partners of the firm. They own the capital of the firm and share the profits or losses of the firm in the proportions specified in a partnership agreement.

The device of appointing salaried partners is of relatively recent origin and the current fashion for it is certainly new. The purpose of it is presumably to give the appearance of a firm with broad-based capital resources. In the days when the number of partners determined the premium for indemnity insurance[1] this apparent breadth of capital resources presumably counter-balanced the consequent increase in the premium. Salaried partners are not proprietors of the business. From their point of view the apparent prestige of partnership must be balanced against the risk of the equity partners failing to give an effective indemnity against the debts of the firm.

Aspects of vicarious liability and the indemnity from employed to employer in case of the employee's negligence are considered on page 570 below.

The term "legal executive" is widely and incorrectly used as an alternative to paralegal. There is, however, an Institute of Legal Executives which admits individuals to Membership or Fellowship after a rigorous training process.

In the non-contentious field there is a Council of Licensed Conveyancers set up by the Courts and Legal Services Act 1990 which again admits individuals into membership after training criteria are met.[2]

It is important in considering liability for negligence to keep in mind the structure and sanctions of the regulatory process applying to the professions in question.[3]

Again, the contents of this chapter in relation to duty, breach and damage are intended to apply (unless the contrary is expressly noted) to the acts and omissions of any of the participants referred to above.

## 2 THE BASIS OF THE RELATIONSHIP BETWEEN CLIENT AND SOLICITOR—THE RETAINER

### 2.1 The law

The retainer of a solicitor by a client is effectively the contract for employment of the solicitor and is the source of the solicitor's duties in relation to the client. The retainer may be in writing, oral or inferred from the conduct between the parties. The solicitor is authorised by the acceptance of the retainer to act for the client and to bind the client in relation to third parties in respect of dealings within the limits of the solicitor's authority.

The retainer cannot impose an open-ended obligation on the solicitor to consider the interests of the client generally. This is clear from the case of *Midland Bank Trust Co Ltd* v. *Hett Stubbs and Kemp*[4] where Oliver J said "The extent of his duties depends upon the terms and limits of the retainer and any duty of care to be applied must be related to what he is instructed to do".

The other leading and seminal case of *Groom* v. Crocker[5] makes the same point:

"The retainer when given puts into operation the normal terms of the contractual relationship, including in particular the duty of the solicitor to protect the client's interest and carry out his instructions in the matter to which the retainer relates by all proper means ... the solicitor shall

1. See pp. 598–601 below.
2. These are dealt with in outline on pp. 601–603 below.
3. This will be dealt with in relation to all those mentioned above in pp. 601–603 below.
4. [1978] 3 All E.R. 571.
5. [1939] 1 K.B. 194, C.A.

consult with his client on all questions of doubt which do not fall within the express or implied discretion left to him and shall keep the client informed to such extent as may be reasonably necessary according to the same criteria."

## 2.2 Solicitors Practice Rule 15

Whatever the common law has to say about the constitution of a retainer, client care now effectively determines the manner in which the retainer is recorded. Practice Rule 15, introduced in May 1991, provides as follows:

**"Rule 15 (Client care)**
(1) Every principal in private practice shall operate a complaints handling procedure which shall, *inter alia*, ensure that clients are informed whom to approach in the event of any problem with the service provided.
(2) Every solicitor in private practice shall, unless it is inappropriate in the circumstances:
  (a) ensure that clients know the name and status of the person responsible for the day-to-day conduct of the matter and the principal responsible for its overall supervision;
  (b) ensure that clients know whom to approach in the event of any problem with the service provided; and
  (c) ensure that clients are at all relevant times given any appropriate information as to the issues raised and the progress of the matter."

The Law Society publication *Civil Litigation—A guide to good practice* (April 1990) also sets out model standards in relation to the conduct of civil litigation.

It is likely to be important in any case for a solicitor to be able to show that any act or step carried out was within the terms of the retainer. If it was not, the client may escape liability to a third party leaving that liability upon the solicitor alone and the unauthorised act, if it has adverse consequences for the client, may provide compelling evidence of breach of duty.

## 2.3 Legal Aid Board franchising arrangements

A further impetus to the recording in writing of the terms of a retainer is given by the onerous documentary requirements of solicitors who are awarded franchises by the Legal Aid Board. The franchise permits a firm of solicitors in one or more areas (e.g., personal injury, family law, employment, housing law) to take advantage of streamlined procedures for authorisations under the Legal Advice (Green Form) Scheme, the grant or amendment of legal aid certificates and in relation to payment.

## 3 NATURE OF THE DUTY

The duty of a solicitor to a client arises both in equity and at common law. For the purposes of this chapter, the latter is the more important although equitable considerations influenced some members of the House of Lords in *White* v. *Jones*.[6]

The equitable duty obliges a solicitor to act with strict fairness and openness towards the client.

The equitable duty is a fiduciary duty, but one which constitutes a solicitor for all

---

6. [1995] 1 All E.R. 691, referred to in detail on pp. 547–552 below.

purposes a trustee of his client: *Oswald Hickson Collier & Co* v. *Carter-Ruck*,[7] *Finers* v. *Miro*.[8]

In that case Lord Denning MR said[9]:

"... as the relationship between a solicitor and client is a fiduciary relationship, it would be contrary to public policy that he should be precluded from acting for a client when that client wanted him to act for him, especially in pending litigation. The client ought reasonably to be entitled to the services of such solicitor as he wishes. That solicitor no doubt has a great deal of confidential information available to him. It would be contrary to public policy if the solicitor were to be prevented from acting for him by a clause of this kind."

The fiduciary duty is not one which constitutes a solicitor for all purposes a trustee of his client: *Finers* v. *Miro*.[10] In that case the Court of Appeal held that the privilege of the client is lost by the criminal or fraudulent intent of the client, whether or not the solicitor was aware of that intent, following *Gamlen Chemical Co (UK) Ltd* v. *Rochem Ltd*.[11]

The duty was further defined by the Privy Council in *Mouat* v. *Clark Boyce*[12] on an appeal from New Zealand thus:

"A fiduciary duty concerns disclosure of material facts in a situation where the fiduciary either has a personal interest in the matter to which the facts are material or acts for another party who has such an interest. It cannot be prayed in aid to enlarge the scope of contractual duties."

This case is also referred to in relation to conflict of interest on pages 585–588.

At common law the duty of a solicitor is to act with skill and care and to put at the disposal of the client his relevant knowledge and, if he is unwilling to reveal his knowledge to his client, he should not act for him: *Spector* v. *Ageda*.[13]

A question which has exercised the courts is whether the nature of the duty is simply as set out above or whether there are specific duties to take particular steps as part of the retainer. Although this is of theoretical interest, it may be of great practical importance where the answer to the question will determine whether or not the action for professional negligence is statute-barred.

The point arose in the *Midland Bank Trust Co Ltd* case.[14] The defendant solicitors had failed to register an option granted to the son of the owner of the farm. The option was granted in 1961 and defeated (since it was in fact unregistered) in 1967 when the owner sold the farm to his wife for a nominal sum.

The solicitors claimed that any action against them for the son's loss (more accurately the loss belonged to his estate since he had by then died) was statute-barred since proceedings against them were not issued within six years of a reasonable time to register the option after its grant.

The trial judge, Oliver J, said that the contract between the solicitor and client gave rise to a complex of rights and duties of which the exercise of reasonable care and skill was only one. He continued:

7. [1984] 2 All E.R. 15, C.A.
8. [1991] 1 All E.R. 182.
9. [1984] 2 All E.R. 15 at 18.
10. [1991] 1 All E.R. 182.
11. [1980] 1 All E.R. 1049, C.A.
12. [1993] 3 W.L.R. 1021 at 1029.
13. [1973] Ch. 30 at 48F.
14. [1978] 3 All E.R. 571.

"If one were to seek to write out in longhand the obligations which Mr Stubbs senior assumed when he was engaged to act in the matter of the grant of the option, they were (1) to draw and have completed a proper and enforceable option agreement which would bind the parties; (2) to take such steps as were necessary and practicable to ensure that it was binding on the land into whosoever hands it might come before any third party acquired a legal estate; (3) to carry out his work with the skill and care which a normally competent practitioner would bring to it."

The second obligation was a continuing one until the sale of the farm in 1967 ended the opportunity to register the option.

This case marks the high point of judicial analysis of the relationship between solicitor and client as a series of relatively detailed obligations.

The analysis of the duty as a number of details as carried out by Oliver J may well have been influenced by the essentially self-contained obligation upon the solicitors, that is to register an option. The analysis of two specific steps and a general requirement for skill and care is almost impossible to replicate in a complex piece of litigation where literally hundreds of steps, whether procedural, tactical or strategic might require in some cases to be taken and in all cases to be considered. Apart from the requirement to issue proceedings within the limitation period and to obey the directions of the court, it is hard to see how it would be practicable or desirable to analyse the duties imposed by the retainer in detail rather than regard each step taken (or indeed not taken) as evidence of compliance or failure on the part of the solicitors to exercise reasonable skill and care.

The more modern cases which will be reviewed below appear to favour this latter approach.

A somewhat amplified version of the general duties is to be found in the Canadian case of *Tiffin Hldg Ltd* v. *Millican*[15]:

"The obligations of a lawyer are, I think, the following:
  (1)  to be skilful and careful;
  (2)  to advise his client on all matters relevant to his retainer, so far as may be reasonably necessary;
  (3)  to protect the interest of his client;
  (4)  to carry out his instructions by all proper means;
  (5)  to consult with his client on all questions of doubt which do not fall within the express or implied discretion left to him;
  (6)  to keep his client informed to such an extent that may be reasonably necessary, according to the same criteria."

## 4 SOURCE OF THE DUTY

The very existence of the retainer upon which duties are based and under which rights accrue make it certain that there is a liability of solicitor to client in contract.

What of a duty of care in tort? It is clear from older cases such as *Davies* v. *Hood*[16] that there was assumed to be a duty in tort owed to the client as well. The case of *Groom* v. *Crocker*,[17] however, purported to establish that the duty owed by a solicitor to a client was in contract only and arose only out of the retainer. This case remained

15.  49 D.L.R. (2d) 216.
16.  (1903) 88 L.T. 19 (K.B.D.) 20.
17.  [1939] 1 K.B. 194.

as an established precedent although subject to occasional doubts judicially expressed for example by Lord Denning in *Esso Petroleum Co Ltd* v. *Mardon*.[18]

The law was returned to the original position in the *Midland Bank Trust Co Ltd* case where Oliver J decided that *Groom* v. *Crocker* was no longer good law, principally since it was largely inconsistent with the decision in *Hedley Byrne* v. *Heller & Partners Ltd*[19] and that the plaintiff had a good cause of action in negligence as well as for breach of contract.

This case was followed shortly afterwards in *Ross* v. *Caunters*[20] and was approved by the Court of Appeal in *Forster* v. *Outred & Co.*[21]

The rather unusual situation has now developed wherein concurrent liability is generally conceded by the defendant despite less than whole-hearted enthusiasm from the bench (e.g., *Bell* v. *Peter Browne & Co*[22]), a suggestion that the time was right for the subject to be reviewed (in *Lee* v. *Thomson*[23]) and adverse analysis from some academic commentators.[24]

The position has been largely clarified by the recent House of Lords' decision arising out of the Lloyd's litigation in *Henderson and others* v. *Merrett Syndicates Ltd and others*.[25] This decision is dealt with in detail in chapter 2.

The importance for solicitors, particularly in the present context, is that the case makes clear that, where there is assumption of responsibility by a solicitor and a concomitant reliance by the client or the person for whom the benefit was rendered on the solicitor, a tortious duty of care arises whether or not there is a contractual relationship between the parties. Lord Goff pointed out that, given the availability of concurrent remedies in contract and tort against the medical profession, the same remedies should be available against other professions whatever form the damage may take. He agreed with the analysis in *Central Trust Co* v. *Rafuse*,[26] following Oliver J in *Midland Trust Co Ltd*[27]:

"A concurrent or alternative liability in tort will not be admitted if its effect would be to permit the plaintiff to circumvent or escape a contractual exclusion or limitation of liability for the act or omission that would constitute the tort. Subject to this qualification, where concurrent liability in tort and contract exists the plaintiff has the right to assert the cause of action that appears to be the most advantageous to him in respect of any particular legal consequence."

He noted that the trend in all common law jurisdictions is towards concurrent remedies. He dealt with Mr Kaye's article[28] by regarding the historical argument against concurrent liability as of no direct relevance in the light of subsequent

18. [1976] Q.B. 801 at 819.
19. [1964] A.C. 465.
20. [1980] Ch. 297 at 308.
21. [1982] 1 W.L.R. 86.
22. [1990] 2 Q.B. 495.
23. [1989] 2 E.G.L.R. 151. "So far as I know *Groom* v. *Crocker* has never been overruled. It may be that the time is now ripe for *Groom* v. *Crocker* and *Midland Bank* to be looked at together in the light of subsequent cases ... " *per* Lloyd LJ at 153G–H.
24. The last is most comprehensively argued in J M Kaye, "The Liability of Solicitors in Tort" (1984) 100 L.Q.R. 680.
25. [1994] 3 All E.R. 506, H.L., and further considered by the Court of Appeal in two cases in December 1995: *Holt* v. *D.E. Groot Collis and Another* (unreported) and *McCullogh* v. *Lane Fox & Partners* (1995) *The Times*, 22 December.
26. (1986) 31 D.L.R. (4th) 481 at 522.
27. *Ibid.* at 530.
28. Referred to at fn. 21 above.

developments of principle. Lord Goff also refuted Mr Kaye's assertion that the principle in *Hedley Byrne* of assumption of responsibility is restricted to cases where there is no contract. Liability in tort is therefore available unless the relevant parties have explicitly contracted their dealings out of it.

Lord Browne-Wilkinson said[29]:

"The existence of an underlying contract (e.g., as between solicitor and client) does not automatically exclude the general duty of care which the law imposes on those who voluntarily assume to act for others. But the nature and terms of the contractual relationship between the parties will be determinative of the scope of the responsibility assumed and can, in some cases, exclude any assumption of legal responsibility to the plaintiff for whom the defendant has assumed to act. If the common law is not to become again manacled by 'clanking chains' (this time represented by causes, rather than forms, of action), it is in my judgment important not to exclude concepts of concurrent liability which the courts of equity have over the years handled without difficulty. I can see no good reason for holding that the existence of a contractual right is in all circumstances inconsistent with the co-existence of another tortious right, provided that it is understood that the agreement of the parties evidenced by the contract can modify and shape the tortious duties which, in the absence of contract, would be applicable."

The significance of concurrent liability in contract and tort is mainly relevant to: (1) establishment of the correct date of limitation in respect to any claim, and (2) to the proper measure of damages recoverable.

The limitation date, for example, in a claim based on contract, is at the latest six years after termination of the retainer. In tort, however, it will be six years after all elements of duty, breach and damage are present. The recent case of *Hopkins* v. *McKenzie*[30] neatly illustrates the difference.

The normal measure of damages for breach of contract is the estimated loss directly resulting in the ordinary course of events from the breach. Recovery of damage in negligence is governed by the criterion of remoteness and in addition recovery of damages for pure economic loss is not possible save under the theories of assumption of responsibility and/or reliance to which we will return later.

## 5 EXTENT OF THE DUTY

### 5.1 To the client

As discussed above there is a straightforward duty on the part of the solicitor to the client in contract and in negligence. A solicitor also has the duty to observe the standards of conduct appropriate to and required of a member of the profession and to conform to disciplinary regulations made in respect of it.[31]

A solicitor is under an obligation not to disclose any confidential information obtained in the process of acting as solicitor to the client. The role of agent, in addition to the other duties peculiar to the profession, imposes upon the solicitor the duty of utmost good faith to the client.

A solicitor may not receive any fee, profit, commission or other benefit without the agreement of the client. This and the matters referred to in the last paragraph can be seen as reflecting the fiduciary quality of the relationship.

29. [1994] 3 All E.R. 506 at 544.
30. [1995] 6 Med.L.R. 26, dealt with at pp. 557 and 558.
31. Regulation and the consequences of breach are discussed on pp. 588–591 below.

A solicitor in accepting a retainer in relation to a particular matter makes a representation that he or she has adequate skill and knowledge properly to undertake it.

### 5.2 To third parties

It is clear that a solicitor can have no contractual liability to a non-client third party since there is of course no retainer to form a contract and the only possible cause of action will consequently be that in negligence. This is an extremely fruitful area for claims against solicitors which now has the benefit of two clarifying decisions of the House of Lords in *White* v. *Jones*[32] and *Target Holdings Ltd* v. *Redferns*.[33]

To proceed by exclusion, the simplest case is the question whether a duty of care is owed to the opponent of the solicitor's client in a transaction or in litigation. The general rule appears to be that the solicitor does not owe such a duty of care. Sir John Donaldson MR in *Orchard* v. *South Eastern Electricity Board*[34] seriously doubted the existence of such a duty of care but pointed out the duty of the solicitor to conduct the litigation with propriety. Breach of such duty could enable the court to order compensation by the solicitor to the injured party.

In the more recent case of *Gran Gelato Ltd* v. *Richcliff Ltd*[35] a vendor's solicitors who had answered an inquiry before contract incorrectly were found not to be liable to the purchaser and the Vice-Chancellor held that there is in general no such duty of care in normal conveyancing transactions. The purchaser might well, of course, be liable to the seller for misrepresentation and if so, the seller might have rights against his own solicitors.

Scott J in *Business Computers International Ltd* v. *Registrar of Companies*[36] concluded that "the safeguards against impropriety are to be found in the rules and procedure that control litigation and not in tort" and dismissed the action on that ground. The existence of this rule was accepted in *Al-Kandari* v. *JR Brown & Co.*[37] Here the solicitors incurred liability by accepting responsibility of holding a passport. The court concluded that this was outside the normal run of solicitors' business and that the solicitors had accepted that responsibility towards both their own client and her opponent. Lord Donaldson MR said[38]:

"A solicitor acting for a party who is engaged in 'hostile' litigation owes a duty to his client and to the court, but he does not normally owe any duty to his client's opponent (see *Business Computers International Ltd* v. *Registrar of Companies* [1987] 3 All E.R. 465, [1987] 3 W.L.R. 1134). This is not to say that, if the solicitor is guilty of professional misconduct and someone other than this client is damnified thereby, that person is without a remedy, for the court exercises a supervisory jurisdiction over solicitors as officers of the court and, in an appropriate case, will order the solicitor to pay compensation (see *Myers* v. *Elman* [1939] 4 All E.R. 484, [1940] A.C. 282). That said, it should be emphasised that in the present case there is no allegation and no suspicion of any misconduct on the part of the defendant solicitors.

I would go rather further and say that, in the context of 'hostile' litigation, public policy will

32. [1995] 1 All E.R. 691.
33. [1995] 3 All E.R. 737.
34. [1987] 1 Q.B. 565.
35. [1992] Ch. 560.
36. [1988] Ch. 229.
37. [1988] 1 All E.R. 833.
38. *Ibid.* at 835–836.

usually require that a solicitor be protected from a claim in negligence by his client's opponent, since such claims could be used as a basis for endless relitigation of disputes (see *Rondel* v. *Worsley* [1967] 3 All E.R. 993, [1969] 1 A.C. 191).

This case is, however, different, because the passport was not only that of Mr Al-Kandari, the defendants' client. It was also the passport of the two children who were in the custody, care and control of the plaintiff. In voluntarily agreeing to hold the passport to the order of the court, the solicitors had stepped outside their role as solicitors for their client and accepted responsibilities towards both their client and the plaintiff and the children. One such responsibility was quite clearly a duty not to hand the passport to Mr Al-Kandari on his request and, of course, there was no breach of this duty. The issue is whether there was a wider responsibility.

For my part I regard the plaintiff as falling squarely (if she will forgive the term) within Lord Atkin's concept of the defendant solicitors' 'neighbours' (see *Donoghue* v. *Stevenson* [1932] A.C. 562, [1932] All E.R. Rep. 1 at 11), and accordingly, in the absence of contra-indications, of which there are none, the law required the solicitors to take reasonable care to avoid acts or omissions which they could reasonably foresee would be likely to injure the plaintiff. Thus I am in complete agreement with the judge that the defendants owed the plaintiff a duty in tort. Quite what was the relevant scope of that duty is, I think, more conveniently considered under the head of breach."[39]

In the field of criminal law a prosecuting solicitor (in this case employed by the Crown Prosecution Service) was considered in *Welch* v. *Chief Constable of Merseyside*[40] to owe a duty to a defendant.

A more general and difficult question is whether non-clients have rights against solicitors for damages caused by negligent misstatement. The House of Lords had in *Hedley Byrne & Co Ltd* v. *Heller & Partners Ltd*[41] established liability in certain circumstances for financial loss caused or materially contributed to by the defendant's negligent misstatement. A generation later the principles properly to be deduced from that case were set out in the speech of Lord Oliver in *Caparo Industries plc* v. *Dickman*.[42] The four conditions to found liability are:

(1) the advice is required for a purpose, whether particularly specified or generally, which is made known, either actually or inferentially, to the adviser at the time when the advice is given;

(2) the adviser knows either actually or inferentially, that his advice will be communicated to the advisee, either specifically or as a member of an ascertainable class, in order that it should be used by the advisee for that purpose;

(3) it is known, actually or inferentially, that the advice so communicated is likely to be acted upon by the advisee for that purpose without independent inquiry; and

(4) it is so acted upon by the advisee to his detriment.

Lord Oliver went on to say that these conditions simply represented the basis of the decision in *Hedley Byrne* and not a final or exhaustive definition of preconditions for the existence of a liability in respect of negligent statements. Subsequent cases adhere strictly to these conditions.

39. This point is dealt with further in relation to conflict of interest on pp. 585–588 below.
40. [1993] 1 All E.R. 692.
41. [1964] A.C. 465.
42. [1990] 2 A.C. 605.

The need for reliance in such cases is surely to limit the numbers and classes of potential plaintiffs.

No such limit (and therefore no such reliance) is required in the case of those who have lost their intended benefit under a will owing to the negligence of the solicitors instructed to produce that will. Such intended beneficiaries are clearly identifiable and limited in number.

The starting-point here is the proposition that a solicitor is not liable to a non-client. Doubts about this proposition began to grow and reached a head in the leading case of *Ross* v. *Caunters*.[43] Here the solicitors had failed to warn a beneficiary that the will should not be witnessed by her husband so that (when it was) the legacy to the plaintiff failed. The only live issue was the existence of a duty to the non-client, negligence having been admitted.

Sir Robert Megarry V-C concluded that:

"a solicitor who is instructed by his client to carry out a transaction that will confer a benefit on an identified third party owes a duty of care towards that third party in carrying out that transaction, in that the third party is a person within his direct contemplation and someone who is likely to be so closely and directly affected by his acts or omissions that he can reasonably foresee that the third party is likely to be injured by those acts or omissions."

Thus, the decision was intended to be rooted in the "neighbour" principle of Lord Atkin in *Donoghue* v. *Stevenson*.[44]

The decision in *Ross* v. *Caunters* has provoked an academic debate. It was not followed in Scotland in *Weir* v. *JM Hodge & Son*[45] but has been generally applied in Commonwealth cases. It was accepted without argument in *Clarke* v. *Bruce Lance & Co.*[46]

The way *Ross* has been treated in the English courts has been apparently bound up in the debate over the decision in *Anns* v. *Merton Borough Council.*[47]

The decision in *Ross* may be interpreted either (as set out above) as an application of the *Donoghue* principle to financial loss or as an extension of the *Hedley Byrne* principle. That latter seems now to be untenable since there was no reliance by the beneficiary on the solicitor which, on the analysis by Lord Oliver in *Caparo* referred to above, is an essential precondition for liability.

Founding the case on the *Donoghue* principle necessitates a view being taken on the identification of the ambit of the "neighbour" principle in relation to economic loss. At the time of *Ross* the guiding principle was to be found in *Anns*: if there is sufficient proximity between the parties liability will be assumed unless there are policy reasons which should negative it. This principle had been very widely criticised and the House of Lords formally departed from it in *Murphy* v. *Brentwood District Council.*[48]

In *Murphy* the House of Lords inclined to the alternative view expressed in an Australian case, *Shire of Sutherland* v. *Heyman*,[49] where Brennan J uttered the words which have become the bedrock of the *Anns*—reformers:

43. [1980] 1 Ch. 297.
44. [1932] A.C. 562.
45. 1990 S.L.T. 266.
46. [1988] 1 W.L.R. 881.
47. [1978] A.C. 728.
48. [1991] 1 A.C. 398.
49. (1985) 157 C.L.R. 424.

"It is preferable, in my view, that the law should develop novel categories of negligence incrementally and by analogy with established categories, rather than by massive extension of a *prima facie* duty of care restrained only by indefinable 'considerations which ought to negative, or to reduce or limit the scope of the duty or the class of person to whom it is owed'."

Thus the *Donoghue* principle now provides less support for the existence of a third party liability towards a non-client than it would have, had *Anns* remained intact.

Is negligence towards a disappointed beneficiary an established category of negligence within this principle? Since the Court of Appeal appeared to use it as a benchmark in a case relating to insurance brokers: *Punjab National Bank* v. *De Boinville*[50] and it was relied upon at first instance in *Pryke* v. *Gibbs Hartley Cooper Ltd*[51] and *Kecskemeti* v. *Rubens Rabin & Co*,[52] it probably is. The precise standing of the decision in *Ross* is of lesser importance since the decision of the House of Lords on 16 February 1994 in *White* v. *Jones*.[53]

In that case the testator asked solicitors to amend his will after a dispute within the family had been resolved. Unfortunately, however, the legal executive entrusted with this task negligently delayed carrying it out for so long that the testator died with the original will unamended. The plaintiffs were the testator's two daughters who would have been the beneficiaries under the new will.

In 1990 Turner J dismissed the claim. The judgment is unreported so that the basis for the dismissal is not clear. The Court of Appeal upheld the plaintiffs' appeal.

The House of Lords upheld the decision of the Court of Appeal and found the solicitors negligent by a majority of 3–2.

The first opinion against finding liability came, unsurprisingly, from Lord Keith who argued that imposing liability would in effect give the plaintiffs the benefit of a contractual arrangement into which they had not entered or of a reliance which they had not in fact made. In relation to the *Anns* question, he considered that for the purpose of *Murphy* v. *Brentwood* the category of negligence argued for by the plaintiff was so far removed from the original duty set out in *Hedley Byrne* and in *Henderson* v. *Merrett Syndicates Ltd*[54] that it could not be described as an incremental or analogous development. He said[55]:

"I am unable to reconcile the allowance of the plaintiffs' claim with principle, or to accept that to do so would represent an appropriate advance on the incremental basis from decided cases.

The contractual duty which Mr Jones owed to the testator was to secure that his testamentary intention was put into effective legal form promptly. The plaintiffs' case is that precisely the same duty was owed to them by Mr Jones in tort. To admit the plaintiffs' claim in the present case would in substance, in my opinion, be to give them the benefit of a contract to which they were not parties."

The three Law Lords who comprised the majority were Lords Goff, Browne-Wilkinson and Nolan.

Lord Goff, whilst reflecting that the demands of practical justice required that the plaintiffs should not go without a remedy, regarded the simple *Donoghue*-inspired principle of *Ross* as inappropriate and decided that there was a *lacuna* which needed

50. [1992] 1 Lloyd's Rep. 7 and see chapter 8.
51. [1991] 1 Lloyd's Rep. 602 and see chapter 8.
52. (1992) *The Times*, 31 December.
53. [1995] 2 W.L.R. 187.
54. [1984] 3 All E.R. 506.
55. [1995] 2 W.L.R. at 190–191.

to be filled. His preferred method of filling it was to extend the reliance principle of *Hedley Byrne* so that the assumption of duty by solicitor to client and the reliance by client on solicitor both be extended to the intended beneficiary who would foreseeably be deprived of the intended benefit by the negligence of the solicitor. The undoubted liability of solicitor to client (or his estate) would be valueless since neither would have suffered an actionable loss. This would frustrate proper social purposes since legacies were an important means of transfer of resources and solicitors were relied on generally for this purpose. There would be no injustice for the negligent solicitor to be sued successfully.

The answer was to extend to the intended beneficiary a remedy under the *Hedley Byrne* principle by deciding that the assumption of responsibility of a solicitor towards his client should be held in law to extend to the beneficiary foreseeably deprived by the solicitor's negligence.

Favourable consequences of his approach are that:

(a) there is no circumvention of principle in relation to economic loss;

(b) liability can be excluded by the terms of the agreement between solicitor and client subject to the Unfair Contract Terms Act 1977 and the Unfair Terms in Consumer Contracts Regulations 1994;

(c) the *Hedley Byrne* principle covers omissions as well as commissions;

(d) damages for loss of an expected benefit would be irrecoverable in tort under the *Hedley Byrne* principle but recoverable in contractual negligence— there is no relevant distinction. Expectation loss may well occur when a professional person such as a solicitor has assumed responsibility for the affairs of another.

His opinion contained the following passages[56]:

"It has been recognised on all hands that *Ross* v. *Caunters* [1980] Ch. 297 raises difficulties of a conceptual nature, and that as a result it is not altogether easy to accommodate the decision within the ordinary principles of our law of obligations.

It is right however that I should immediately summarise these conceptual difficulties. They are as follows.

First, the general rule is well established that a solicitor acting on behalf of a client owes a duty of care only to his client. The relationship between a solicitor and his client is nearly always contractual, and the scope of the solicitor's duties will be set by the terms of his retainer; but a duty of care owed by a solicitor to his client will arise concurrently in contract and in tort.

But, when a solicitor is performing his duties to his client, he will generally owe no duty of care to third parties.

A plaintiff is entitled to damages if, and only if, he can establish a breach of contract by the defendant. First, the plaintiff's claim is one for purely financial loss; and as a general rule, apart from cases of assumption of responsibility arising under the principle in *Hedley Byrne & Co Ltd* v. *Heller & Partners Ltd* [1964] A.C. 465 no action will lie in respect of such loss in the tort of negligence. Furthermore, in particular, no claim will lie in tort for damages in respect of a mere loss of an expectation, as opposed to damages in respect of damage to an existing right or interest of the plaintiff.

A third, and distinct, objection is that, if liability in tort was recognised in cases such as *Ross* v. *Caunters* [1980] Ch 297, it would be impossible to place any sensible bounds to cases in which such recovery was allowed. In particular, the same liability should logically be imposed in cases where an *inter vivos* transaction was ineffective and the defect was not discovered until the donor was no longer able to repair it. Furthermore, liability could not logically be restricted to

56. *Ibid.* at 195–196 and 206–207.

cases where a specific named beneficiary was disappointed, but would inevitably have to be extended to cases in which wide, even indeterminate, classes of persons could be said to have been adversely affected.

Furthermore, for the reasons I have previously given, the *Hedley Byrne* principle cannot, in the absence of special circumstances, give rise on ordinary principles to an assumption of responsibility by the testator's solicitor towards an intended beneficiary. Even so it seems to me that it is open to your Lordships' House, as in the *Lenesta Sludge* case [1994] 1 AC 85, to fashion a remedy to fill a *lacuna* in the law and so prevent the injustice which would otherwise occur on the facts of cases such as the present. In the *Lenesta Sludge* case, as I have said, the House made available a remedy as a matter of law to solve the problem of transferred loss in the case before them. The present case is, if anything, *a fortiori*, since the nature of the transaction was such that, if the solicitors were negligent and their negligence did not come to light until after the death of the testator, there would be no remedy for the ensuing loss unless the intended beneficiary could claim. In my opinion, therefore, your Lordships' House should in cases such as these extend to the intended beneficiary a remedy under the *Hedley Byrne* principle by holding that the assumption of responsibility by the solicitor towards his client should be held in law to extend to the intended beneficiary who (as the solicitor can reasonably foresee) may, as a result of the solicitor's negligence, be deprived of his intended legacy in circumstances in which neither the testator nor his estate will have a remedy against the solicitor. Such liability will not of course arise in cases in which the defect in the will comes to light before the death of the testator, and the testator either leaves the will as it is or otherwise continues to exclude the previously intended beneficiary from the relevant benefit. I only wish to add that, with the benefit of experience during the 15 years in which *Ross* v. *Caunters* has regularly applied, we can say with some confidence that a direct remedy by the intended beneficiary against the solicitor appears to create no problems in practice."

Lord Browne-Wilkinson, on the other hand, concluded that the duty of care which the solicitor owed to the plaintiffs derived from an incremental extension to the *Hedley Byrne* principle of assumption of responsibility. It is interesting that both of their Lordships looked at *Hedley Byrne* more in the light of assumption of responsibility than of reliance by the non-client plaintiff.

He argued following *Nocton* v. *Lord Ashburton*[57] that:

(a) A special relationship between the parties can give rise to an assumption of duty where such a duty would not otherwise exist.

(b) Fiduciary duty is one such duty but not the only duty.

(c) By assuming to act in B's affairs A has a fiduciary duty to B. The extent of that duty varies but the duty of care arises in every case.

(d) A special relationship giving rise to the assumption of responsibility does not therefore depend on mutual dealings or contracts between A and B. B need not depend on the actions of A: what matters is that A knows not that B is consciously relying upon him but that B's economic well-being depends on A being careful in relation to B's affairs.

(e) *Nocton* was treated as the starting-point in *Hedley Byrne*. In that case the House of Lords was adding to fiduciary duties, not substituting for them.

(f) Because *Hedley Byrne* was a case of misstatement, it was inevitable that there was reliance and therefore foreseeability.

(g) In relation to negligent action or inaction the special relationship did not depend upon reliance but on foreseeability. If in fact damage can be foreseen and is caused, that is enough.

---

57. [1914] A.C. 932.

(h) *Hedley Byrne* shows that by assuming to act a duty is created.

(i) The assumption of responsibility for a task creates a special relationship and a duty to carry out the task carefully. The assumption is of responsibility for the task, not of legal liability.

(j) There is a duty of care where the special relationship is fiduciary or where the defendant voluntarily supplies skilled advice or services knowing that the plaintiff will rely upon them. The defendant, by involving himself assumes responsibility to carry the matter through. The relationship arises even where the defendant acts in the plaintiffs affairs presumed to a contract with a third party. In this respect the court is entitled to identify a new special relationship by close analogy with existing categories.

He said[58]:

"The law of England does not impose any general duty of care to avoid negligent misstatements or to avoid causing pure economic loss even if economic damage to the plaintiff was foreseeable. However, such a duty of care will arise if there is a special relationship between the parties. Although the categories of cases in which such special relationship can be held to exist are not closed, as yet only two categories have been identified, *viz* (1) where there is a fiduciary relationship and (2) where the defendant has voluntarily answered a question or tenders skilled advice or services in circumstances where he knows or ought to know that an identified plaintiff will rely on his answers or advice. In both these categories the special relationship is created by the defendant voluntarily assuming to act in the matter by involving himself in the plaintiff's affairs or by choosing to speak. If he does so assume to act or speak he is said to have assumed responsibility for carrying through the matter he has entered upon. In the words of Lord Reid in *Hedley Byrne* ([1964] A.C. 465 at 486) he has 'accepted a relationship ... which requires him to exercise such care as the circumstances require', although the extent of the duty will vary from category to category, *some* duty of care arises from the special relationship. Such relationship can arise even though the defendant has acted in the plaintiff's affairs pursuant to a contract with a third party.

I turn then to apply those considerations to the case of a solicitor retained by a testator to draw a will in favour of an intended beneficiary. As a matter of contract, a solicitor owes a duty to the testator to use proper skill in the preparation and execution of the will and to act with due speed. But as the speech of Lord Goff demonstrates that contractual obligation is of little utility. Breach by the solicitor of such contractual duty gives rise to no damage suffered by the testator or his estate: under our existing law of contract, the intended beneficiary, who has suffered the damage, has no cause of action on the contract.

Has the intended beneficiary a cause of action based on breach of a duty of care owed by the solicitor to the beneficiary? The answer to that question is dependent upon whether there is a special relationship between the solicitor and the intended beneficiary to which the law attaches a duty of care. In my judgement the case does not fall within either of the two categories of special relationships so far recognised. There is no fiduciary duty owed by the solicitor to the intended beneficiary. Although the solicitor has assumed to act in a matter closely touching the economic well-being of the intended beneficiary, the intended beneficiary will often be ignorant of that fact and cannot therefore have relied upon the solicitor.

However, it is clear that the law in this area has not ossified. Both Viscount Haldane LC (in the passage I have quoted from *Nocton* v. *Lord Ashburton* [1914] A.C. 932 at 948) and Lord Devlin (in the *Hedley Byrne* case [1964] A.C. 465 at 530–531) envisage that there might be other sets of circumstances in which it would be appropriate to find a special relationship giving rise to a duty of care. In *Caparo Industries plc* v. *Dickman* [1990] 2 A.C. 605 at 618 Lord Bridge of Harwich recognised that the law will develop novel categories of negligence 'incrementally

---

58. *Ibid.* at 212–214.

and by analogy with established categories'. In my judgement, this is a case where such development should take place since there is a close analogy with existing categories of special relationship giving rise to a duty of care to prevent economic loss.

The solicitor who accepts instructions to draw a will knows that the future economic welfare of the intended beneficiary is dependent upon his careful execution of the task. It is true that the intended beneficiary (being ignorant of the instructions) may not rely on the particular solicitor's actions. But, as I have sought to demonstrate, in the case of a duty of care flowing from a fiduciary relationship liability is not dependent upon actual reliance by the plaintiff on the defendant's actions but on the fact that, as the fiduciary is well aware, the plaintiff's economic well-being is dependent upon the proper discharge by the fiduciary of his duty. Second, the solicitor by accepting the instructions has entered upon, and therefore assumed responsibility for, the task of procuring the execution of a skilfully drawn will knowing that the beneficiary is wholly dependent upon his carefully carrying out his function. That assumption of responsibility for the task is a feature of both the categories of special relationship so far identified in the authorities. It is not to the point that the solicitor only entered on the task pursuant to a contract with the third party (i.e., the testator). There are therefore present many of the features which in the other categories of special relationship have been treated as sufficient to create a special relationship to which the law attaches a duty of care. In my judgement the analogy is close.

Moreover there are more general factors which indicate that it is fair just and reasonable to impose liability on the solicitor. Save in the case of those rash testators who make their own wills, the proper transmission of property from one generation to the next is dependent upon the due discharge by solicitors of their duties. Although in any particular case it may not be possible to demonstrate that the intended beneficiary relied upon the solicitor, society as a whole does rely on solicitors to carry out their will-making functions carefully. To my mind it would be unacceptable if, because of some technical rules of law, the wishes and expectations of testators and beneficiaries generally could be defeated by the negligent actions of solicitors without there being any redress. It is only just that the intended beneficiary should be able to recover the benefits which he would otherwise have received".

The third Law Lord in the majority, Lord Nolan, simply found that the criteria laid down in *Caparo* and *Murphy* (see above) had been satisfied in relation to a pragmatic case-by-case approach to negligence. Both contractual and tortious liability depend on the assumption of liability—in the case of contract it is defined by the terms of the contract and in tort assumed by the undertaking of a potentially harmful activity. The existence of a contract does not exclude liability in tort. Here the assumption was in relation to the activities of the family solicitor. The fact that the complaint was an omission rather than an action was irrelevant after a duty of care was assumed. *Ross* v. *Caunters* had stood for 15 years and should not be overruled.

Lord Mustill dissenting pointed out that *Ross* was decided in the light of *Anns* two years before. *Hedley Byrne* had four themes:

(a) a non-contractual mutuality between plaintiff and defendant;
(b) a defendant could have a special relationship giving rise to a duty to the plaintiff;
(c) it was foreseeable that reliance would be placed on the defendant;
(d) the defendant voluntarily undertook reliability.

Thus the only basis for accretion of liability—*Hedley Byrne* and *Henderson*—was not apt to found liability in these circumstances. The only alternative was to invent a special duty. This would be wrong, however, since it would be applicable to any case where B pays A to do something where it was foreseeable that C would obtain a benefit, if A carried out the task properly.

The two Law Lords (Lords Goff and Browne-Wilkinson) who based themselves on the assumption of responsibility had to go on to accept that any such liability to non-clients would be subject to any restrictions or limits placed by the actual retainer between the solicitor and client so that the tortious duty to a non-client will precisely shadow that owed to the client. Thus, for example, if the testator fails in his lifetime to act to remedy a known defect or agrees to a long delay in the carrying out of his instructions, the liability to the non-client will be negatived by the client's default or acquiescence.

The case seems to reinforce the view that there is no duty of care to the opponent of the client or to those with a contrary interest to that of the client and that there is no liability to intended beneficiaries of lifetime gifts or other transactions. The decision appears to be limited (at least by Lords Goff and Browne-Wilkinson) to the preparation of wills. It is, of course, open to question whether the analytical passages of the speeches will be relied upon by others in future for the purpose of an incremental increase to the categories of negligence known to the law.

In relation to lifetime gifts it was decided in *Hemmens* v. *Wilson Browne (A firm)*[59] that solicitors who had drafted an unenforceable document in relation to the intended beneficiary of a settlement owed no duty to that intended beneficiary since the settlor was still alive and could rectify the mistake, if he so desired—in fact he did not. If, however, the document had been irrevocable and the benefit was conferred on the wrong person, the intended beneficiary who was thus deprived might have the benefit of a duty on the part of the solicitors.

## 6 STANDARD OF THE DUTY

We have already seen that the duty of a solicitor is to act with reasonable skill and care. A trial judge, when required to find that an error of omission or commission amounts to a failure so to act is unlikely to have a precedent entirely in point. Assistance may, however, be derived from the growing body of claims information collected by the Solicitors Indemnity Fund and others with an interest in indemnity insurance. Such evidence is clearly suggestive rather than determinative of the law.

What is clear is that the standard required is not that of perfection: the mere fact of an error does not constitute negligence. Solicitors who advised their clients to complete a purchase after a survey carried out after a binding contract had been entered into on the ground that failure to complete would expose them to severely adverse financial consequences were held not to have been negligent in their advice although the contract could in fact have been rescinded by reason of the vendor's fraudulent misrepresentation: *Neighbour* v. *Barker*.[60]

Oliver J in *Midland Bank Trust Co Ltd* set out the test of reasonable skill and care as "what the reasonably competent practitioner would do having regard to the standards normally adopted in his profession". Some flesh was put upon these bones in the case of *Tiffin Hldgs Ltd* referred to above[60a]: the general duty included providing advice on all matters relevant to the ambit of the retainer, protecting the

59. [1994] 2 W.L.R. 323.
60. (1992) 40 E.G. 140.
60a. On p. 541.

client's interest, consulting the client on matters of doubt and keeping the client reasonably informed.

The solicitor is properly judged by the standards of the time of the act or omission complained of without the advantage of hindsight on the part of the court.

A solicitor is not expected to know all the law but should be able to gain access to sufficient resources to answer the questions which arise in the areas in which he or she chooses to practise.

Some old cases establish that the solicitor is not expected to have perfect judgement: this is probably no more than saying that the expectation is of reasonable skill and care. As compliance with general practice of the profession in relation to a particular matter is likely (but not certain) to rebut negligence, so failure to comply is likely to found a successful action for negligence.

There is one case which appears to go against the proposition. It is a Privy Council case from Hong Kong, *Edward Wong Finance Co Ltd* v. *Johnson, Stokes & Master*.[61] The solicitors had completed the purchase of a factory using the plaintiff's mortgage money. Standard practice in Hong Kong was for the purchaser's solicitor to hand over the purchase money in return for an undertaking to provide the title deeds within a specified number of days. The vendor's solicitor defaulted on his undertaking and the plaintiff's charge over the property was valueless.

The Privy Council found that, although the method of completion was standard practice, the risk inherent in it was foreseeable and avoidable and The Law Society of Hong Kong in fact foresaw it in an earlier report on conveyancing and procedures. The solicitors did, however, in all respects comply with general practice but were still found liable. This case is clearly a radical departure from the general understanding but does not seem to have influenced English practice over the last 10 years.

More complicated is the case where a solicitor accused of negligence has adopted one of a choice of practices current in the profession. By analogy with the medical negligence case of *Bolam* v. *Friern Hospital Management Committee*,[62] a solicitor who has acted in accordance with a practice accepted as proper by a responsible body of those skilled in that particular art will not be found negligent. To paraphrase *Bolam*: "... Putting it the other way round, a [doctor] is not negligent, if he is acting in accordance with such a practice, merely because there is a body of opinion which takes a contrary view".

It is the custom for each party to call expert evidence in relation to the proper professional and practical approach to the matter in question. The object of this is to allow the court to test whether the actions contended for by the respective parties do in fact represent or are in fact supported by a practice accepted as proper by a responsible body of opinion within the profession. It does, however, remain for the judge to decide as a matter of law whether the result of the weighing of both factual and expert evidence by the parties does or does not amount to negligence.

There has been a tendency in recent years in the solicitors' profession, in common with that in many other professions, to attempt to standardise the provision of service. How much bearing this will have on the law of negligence of solicitors remains to be seen: much of the standardisation relates to organisational procedures

61. [1984] A.C. 296.
62. [1957] 1 W.L.R. 582.

as opposed to uniform method of carrying out particular legal tasks. Even so, a clear breach of, for example, the National Conveyancing Protocol may well be accepted as evidence of failure to comply with a proper standard although in *Johnson* v. *Bingley*,[63] BA Hytner QC decided that breach of The Law Society's Guide to Professional Conduct did not necessarily prove negligence. The Guide set out a code of proper and accepted practice but its provisions were not mandatory. Presumably the same would apply to breaches of the Civil Litigation Guide to Good Practice. We have already seen above that Practice Rule 15 may well help to define the nature and extent of the retainer.

The obligation to act with reasonable care and skill, whilst on one level objective, does certainly involve tailoring the level of skill and care to the identity of the solicitor in question. Thus, a solicitor claiming particular expertise (and, no doubt, remuneration appropriate to it) is judged by a higher standard in relation to that area of practice than would be a general practitioner.

There is authority for this in the case of *Duchess of Argyle* v. *Beuselinck*[64] where Megarry J said:

"the essence of the contract of retainer, it may be said, is that the client is retaining the particular solicitor or firm in question, and he is therefore entitled to expect from that solicitor or firm a standard of care and skill commensurate with the skill and experience which that solicitor or firm has. The uniform standard of care postulated for the world at large in tort hardly seems appropriate when the duty is not one imposed by the law of tort but arises from a contractual obligation existing between the client and the particular solicitor or firm in question".

This appears perfectly acceptable in principle and proper in practice by reference to the particular contractual duty imposed by the retainer rather than the more general duty owed in negligence.

Conversely, the standard to be expected of a non-qualified person engaged on legal work (as opposed to purely administrative work) is that reasonably expected of a person of that description. The corollary of this is, of course, that the retainer must specify the rank or grade of person who in fact performs the legal services specified by the retainer and that the rank or grade (and the individual within it) must be appropriate to the task in question.

The legal profession is generally categorised by description rather than distinction, although a move towards a greater hierarchy has been made by the introduction by The Law Society of specialist panels. The test for negligence in respect of work undertaken by a person claiming expertise or specialism is presumably that of the reasonably competent specialist practitioner in the field of law in question.

## 7 TYPES OF BREACH OF DUTY

We have seen above that there are different theories of liability in respect of which the law now appears relatively settled.

The retainer may well impose express terms breach of which will found a purely contractual liability.

63. (1995) *The Times*, 28 February.
64. [1972] 2 Lloyd's Rep. 172.

The objective requirement to exercise reasonable skill and competence will create a liability (which is entirely extra-contractual) to the client. Any liability (within the limits discussed above) to a non-client is also clearly extra-contractual. Breach of a term implied into the contract of retainer in the usual way will create liabilities in both contract and negligence.

For the sake of completeness, there remains the possibility of breach of the relationship of trust between solicitor and client (which is more likely to involve a breach of professional ethics than negligence) and breach of the solicitor's duty to the court. Either of these may confer upon the client the right to compensation by the solicitor.

Before examining by category the various types of activity and conduct on the part of solicitors which may give rise to a liability to the client or a third party it will be useful to inject a practical note by reproducing an analysis of the types of matter or error giving rise to claims against the Solicitors Indemnity Fund over the last three years. This is done as much for its prophylactic as its pedagogic effect.

## 7.1 Negligence in litigation

A solicitor engaged in litigation is expected to show reasonable competence and familiarity with the procedures of the court: *Heywood* v. *Wellers*.[65] In *Langley* v. *North West Water Authority*[66] the plaintiff's solicitor failed to comply with a local practice direction in relation to documents to be served with the particulars of claim and was ordered to pay the wasted costs.

A solicitor should obtain evidence of actual authority to commence proceedings. Without that authority the action is not properly constituted, can be stayed at any time and the solicitor will be personally liable for the costs incurred: *Danish Mercantile Co Ltd* v. *Beaumont*.[67] It is open to the client to ratify proceedings once commenced: *Bolton* v. *Lambert*.[68] In the recent case of *Presentaciones Musicales SA* v. *Secunda*[69] such ratification was permitted outside the limitation date.

In relation to corporate clients a solicitor must clearly be sure to obtain instructions from a person or persons actually authorised to give them.

It is likely to be negligent to issue proceedings without checking the basic facts upon which the proceedings are founded (*Losner* v. *Michael Cohen & Co*)[70] and the identity of the correct parties.

A solicitor will be liable for errors in (as opposed to refusing slavishly to follow the client's wishes relating to) pleadings drafted by the solicitor.

A solicitor must consider and advise the client of all remedies open on the facts. For example, solicitors were found negligent who failed to advise their client to issue an application to remove their estranged husband from the matrimonial home notwithstanding that his presence there was apparently causing serious harm to the children of the family: *Dickinson* v. *Jones Alexander & Co*.[71]

65. [1976] Q.B. 446, C.A.
66. [1991] 1 W.L.R. 697, C.A.
67. [1951] 1 All E.R. 925.
68. (1889) 41 Ch.D. 295.
69. [1994] 2 All E.R. 737.
70. (1975) 119 S.J. 340, C.A.
71. (1990) 6 P.N. 205.

## DISTRIBUTION OF CLAIMS BY TYPE OF WORK
### 1 SEPTEMBER 1987 to 31 AUGUST 1994

| CATEGORY | % OF CLAIMS | | % OF SETTLEMENT AMOUNT | | % OF OUTSTANDING RESERVES | | % OF CLAIMS PAYMENTS AND RESERVES | |
|---|---|---|---|---|---|---|---|---|
| | AS AT 31/8/94 | AS AT 31/8/93 | AS AT 31/8/94 | AS AT 31/8/93 | AS AT 31/8/94 | AS AT 31/8/93 | AS AT 31/8/94 | AS AT 31/8/93 |
| NOT CLASSIFIED | 3.02 | 4.58 | 0.77 | 3.72 | 1.34 | 2.30 | 1.20 | 2.69 |
| COMMERCIAL | 5.98 | 5.96 | 12.81 | 11.49 | 18.68 | 19.00 | 16.95 | 17.07 |
| LANDLORD AND TENANT | 7.73 | 7.86 | 7.42 | 7.63 | 7.24 | 7.64 | 7.31 | 7.63 |
| TOWN AND COUNTRY PLANNING | 0.42 | 0.38 | 0.55 | 0.35 | 0.50 | 0.48 | 0.52 | 0.46 |
| CONVEYANCING | 46.26 | 45.43 | 51.53 | 49.19 | 45.45 | 43.89 | 46.81 | 44.96 |
| INHERITANCE TAX AND TAXATION | 1.37 | 1.35 | 1.34 | 1.24 | 1.48 | 1.30 | 1.45 | 1.31 |
| TRUST AND PROBATE | 4.96 | 4.84 | 3.99 | 4.40 | 4.64 | 4.50 | 4.48 | 4.52 |
| MATRIMONIAL | 3.91 | 3.82 | 1.45 | 1.43 | 1.52 | 1.40 | 1.59 | 1.50 |
| PERSONAL INJURY | 11.27 | 10.97 | 10.49 | 10.17 | 6.72 | 6.68 | 7.77 | 7.51 |
| OTHER LITIGATION | 10.86 | 10.90 | 6.42 | 6.57 | 8.41 | 9.25 | 7.98 | 8.65 |
| EMPLOYMENT | 0.49 | 0.41 | 0.11 | 0.09 | 0.33 | 0.23 | 0.26 | 0.19 |
| CRIME | 0.14 | 0.11 | 0.03 | 0.00 | 0.08 | 0.18 | 0.07 | 0.13 |
| DEBT COLLECTION | 0.36 | 0.27 | 0.12 | 0.09 | 0.16 | 0.13 | 0.15 | 0.12 |
| OTHER CATEGORIES | 3.23 | 3.12 | 3.16 | 3.63 | 3.45 | 3.01 | 3.44 | 3.25 |
| TOTAL | 100.00 | 100.00 | 100.00 | 100.00 | 100.00 | 100.00 | 100.00 | 100.00 |

Source: Solicitors Indemnity Fund Seventh Annual Report 1994.

Whilst a solicitor's agreement to commence litigation cannot be a guarantee of their success, the solicitor may be liable if, on the material before him at the time, it should be clear to a reasonably competent solicitor practising in that field that the proceedings are hopeless. The Legal Aid Board is entitled to similar advice in legally aided matters: *Davey-Chiesman* v. *Davey-Chiesman*.[72] May LJ said[73]:

"In my judgement this failure by the solicitor to question counsel's advice let alone to report the situation on his own to the Legal Aid Committee, as in any event I think that he should have done, was a substantial failure on his part to fulfil his duty to the court to promote in his particular sphere the cause of proper administration of justice."

A solicitor should take all reasonable steps to trace potential witnesses with a view to deciding whether they should be called to give evidence: *Holden & Co* v. *Crown Prosecution Service*.[74] Lord Lane CJ described failure to notify a defendant to a criminal charge that his case was in the warned list as a "serious dereliction of a solicitor's duty".

A solicitor must exercise reasonable competence in the selection of an expert prospective witness and will be liable for selection of a prospective expert whose experience or expertise is inadequate to the role that solicitor asks him to perform.

After the dismissal of a claim for want of prosecution or for breach of a peremptory order of the court, "it follows, almost inevitably, that the solicitors for the plaintiff were at fault and are liable for negligence" (*per* Lord Denning MR in *Reggentim* v. *Beecholme Bakeries Ltd*).[75] Liability can be avoided if the dismissal is for delay caused or consented to by the client: *Allen* v. *Sir Alfred McAlpine & Sons Ltd*.[76] In a personal injury case where a solicitor has failed to issue proceedings within three years the exercise by the court of its discretion under section 33 of the Limitation Act 1980 to extend the primary limitation period is affected by the respective prejudice to the parties in extending or not extending time. The availability of a claim against a solicitor for negligent delay is clearly relevant to the prejudice to the plaintiff although even a case against a solicitor described by Lord Diplock in *Thompson* v. *Brown Construction (Ebbw Vale) Ltd*[77] as "cast iron" does not automatically result in the discretion being exercised in the defendant's favour.

In the case of *Hopkins* v. *Mackenzie*[78] the plaintiff issued medical negligence proceedings in February 1982 in respect of treatment in February 1979. The action was struck out for want of prosecution on 27 January 1986. The plaintiff instructed new solicitors who issued proceedings against the first solicitors on 27 January 1992. The first solicitors alleged that the plaintiff's claim was time-barred because six years before the issue of the writ against the first solicitors, the medical negligence claim was all but certain to be struck out for want of prosecution and thus its value reduced to all but zero. The plaintiff had therefore sustained damage by reason of the solicitors' breach of their duty of care more than six years before the issue of a writ against them. This argument succeeded before the deputy judge and the plaintiff appealed.

72. [1984] Fam. 48, C.A.
73. *Ibid.* at 66B.
74. [1990] 2 Q.B. 261.
75. [1968] 2 Q.B. 276.
76. [1968] 2 Q.B. 229.
77. [1981] 2 All E.R. 296 at 301.
78. [1995] 6 Med.L.R. 26.

The question for the Court of Appeal was when the cause of action arose. It rejected the defendant's submission that loss or damage should be treated as having occurred when it could be shown to be probable or inevitable that it would occur. It further rejected the submission that, as the negligent conduct of the solicitors continued, so the value of the claim decreased and a loss was thereby continuously incurred on the ground that the plaintiff was not suing for the continuing diminution of the value of his claim but for the loss of it on it being struck out.

The court distinguished *Melton* v. *Walter & Stanger*,[79] *Baker* v. *Ollard & Bentley*,[80] *Moore (DW) & Co* v. *Ferrier*[81] and *Bell* v. *Peter Browne & Co*[82] as all showing that actual (and not future, even if inevitable) loss or damage is necessary to complete the cause of action. The actual loss here was the loss of the ability to advance the claim and this did not occur until it was struck out.

Solicitors cannot hide behind the delays of counsel, but must chase them regularly and, if necessary, pass the papers to another counsel: *Mansouri* v. *Bloomsbury Health Authority*.[83]

The modern approach of the court involving itself more in the achievement of procedural deadlines and timetables is such that escaping dismissal for want of prosecution or breach of order will not prevent the solicitor being penalised by not recovering his costs and probably by being ordered to pay the costs of his opponent in respect of the delays complained of.

This approach was confirmed in the well-known dictum of Lord Griffiths in *Ketteman* v. *Hansel Properties Ltd*[84]:

"We can no longer afford to show the same indulgence towards the negligent conduct of litigation as was perhaps possible in the more leisured age. There will be cases in which justice will be better served by allowing the consequences of negligence of the lawyers to fall upon their own heads rather than by allowing an amendment to a very late stage of a proceedings."

It is reasonable to suppose that even these strictures will be as nothing compared to the penalties to be visited upon those who fail to comply with the new express regime foreshadowed in the interim report of Lord Woolf in June 1995 into access to civil justice.

There is a dearth of authority in relation to liability for negligent settlement of proceedings. The case of *Waugh* v. *HB Clifford & Sons Ltd*[85] is authority for the proposition that the solicitor has ostensible authority to compromise litigation on the client's behalf so as to bind the client provided that the settlement does not comprise an agreement outside the subject-matter of the action. Notwithstanding this, a solicitor would be rash who did not seek specific approval from the client to the proposed terms of settlement.

Solicitors who failed to advise clients who were unsuccessful on a rent review arbitration (and who made it clear that they were unhappy about it) regarding an appeal were negligent: *Corfield* v. *DS Bosher & Co*.[86]

79. (1981) 125 Sol.J. 861.
80. (1982) 126 Sol.J. 593.
81. [1988] 1 W.L.R. 267.
82. [1990] 2 Q.B. 495.
83. (1987) *The Times*, 20 July.
84. [1987] A.C. 189.
85. [1982] Ch. 374, C.A.
86. [1992] 1 E.G.L.R. 163.

The last 10 years have seen the increasingly common use of structured settlements for large personal injury and medical negligence claims. These guarantee the plaintiff an annuity for life designed to cover inflation. Given the danger of failure of investments into which lump sum damages are placed and ample evidence that the return on such investments is unlikely fully to compensate the plaintiff for life in real terms, failure on the part of a plaintiff's solicitor at least to consider the relative attractions of lump sum versus structured settlement and advise the plaintiff may very well be found to be negligent, notwithstanding the fact that, despite the recommendations of the Law Commission, there is still no statutory basis on which such arrangements can be made.

In *Griffiths* v. *Dowson & Co*[87] solicitors negligently advised a wife that she could apply for a financial settlement after a decree absolute of divorce had been made. The wife instructed her solicitor not to allow the decree to be made absolute until the financial circumstances had been investigated since she was unhappy with the amount on offer. The husband offered maintenance if the wife did not oppose the decree absolute and was told by the wife's solicitor that he had no instructions to oppose the decree absolute. A consent order was made. The court held that the first step for any competent solicitor would have been to file an application under section 10 of the Matrimonial Causes Act 1973 and to hold up the ground of decree absolute until investigation of the husband's position had been completed. The solicitors should have discovered the terms of the husband's pension scheme to see whether an application could have been made under section 24(1)(c) of the Act. As his pension fund could not be commuted the wife would have received a lump sum to compensate her for the loss of pension rights with which she could have bought an annuity.

## 7.2 Non-contentious work

### 7.2.1 Probate matters

The law in relation to this topic has been discussed (mainly in the context of claims by disappointed beneficiaries) at some length above. Whilst claims by testators may be less important (because a testator is under a duty to mitigate any damage discovered in his or her lifetime and because the estate is unlikely to have suffered any loss in respect of errors discovered thereafter), the solicitor is under a duty: (a) properly to explain and obtain the consent of the client to the terms of the will; (b) properly to explain the effect of the provisions; (c) to act promptly in the context of the client's known medical condition; (d) properly to explain the rules for execution of the will and the consequences of failure so properly to execute it.

The theoretical difficulty in showing actionable damage referred to above is borne out by the fact that the category in the SIF statistics for trust and probate claims represents only 4.96 per cent of total claims and 3.99 per cent of the settlement amounts as at 31 August 1994.

---

87. [1993] 2 F.L.R. 315.

### 7.2.2 Conveyancing

Claims in respect of allegedly negligent conveyancing form by far the largest category of claims to the SIF. As at 31 August 1994 they comprised 46.26 per cent of all claims and 51.35 per cent of the settlement amount. Given that almost the whole of England and Wales is now subject to compulsory registration of title, this provides a somewhat lamentable picture. The size of the problem cannot be explained away by dishonesty since claims relating to dishonest partners (claims against dishonest sole practitioners or where all partners have been dishonest being paid out of the Compensation Fund) have amounted to 7.9 per cent of all claims payments during the seven years from 1 September 1987 during which the SIF has operated.

There are a number of areas in which errors in conveyancing can amount to negligence.

### 7.2.3 Failure to keep to time-limits

Many conveyancing transactions are intended to be simultaneous sales and purchases. Given that a contract for either is not binding until exchange with the other party, exchanging contracts on a sale but not the purchase or vice versa can very easily lead to the client being committed to his vendor but having no commitment from his purchaser or vice versa. Exchange of one contract without exchanging the other would, unless specifically authorised by the client after receiving a proper warning, surely amount to negligence.

The practicality of a simultaneous exchange of contracts is that it can only be done by telephone in circumstances where the client's purchaser has authorised the release of his purchase contract to the solicitor who can then exchange on the client's own purchase with the client's vendor's solicitor safe in the knowledge that the solicitor is still in a position forthwith to complete the exchange of the sale contract. The practice of exchanging contracts by telephone was specifically approved by the Court of Appeal in *Domb* v. *Isoz*.[88]

In order to take advantage of the priority period given by a clear Land Registry search against a title, it is of course necessary to present to the Registry the application for registration of the transaction in question within the priority period. Failure so to do resulting in postponement of the interest to the client or his or her mortgagee would certainly be classified as negligence.

Solicitors who reported to a building society that the title of the security was good but failed to notice that the land certificate did not contain the whole of the charged property contained in the valuer's report were found negligent: *Mercantile Building Sociey* v. *JW Mitchell Dodds & Co*.[89]

Another fruitful source of claims is the failure by solicitors to keep to the strict time-limits under the Landlord and Tenant Act 1954, Part II for notices in relation to claims for a new business tenancy of premises and for applications to the county court for a new business tenancy of the premises. Since the SIF report specifically disclaims precision in the categorisation of subject-matter of claims, pointing out that similar

88. [1980] Ch. 548.
89. [1993] N.P.C. 99, C.A.

claims might have been variously classified as "landlord and tenant", "conveyancing" or even "other litigation", the position may be even worse than just set out above.

### 7.2.4 Searches and inquiries

A solicitor must make all relevant searches and inquiries, consider the replies to them and fully and fairly advise the client of the nature of those replies and any risks which they import into the transaction.

In *Allan* v. *Clark* Mellor J said[90]:

"It is clear negligence if an attorney suffers himself to be misled by the apparent respectability of the vendor, and thereby neglects his obvious duty of making reasonable inquiries into his title."

More recently, solicitors failed when acting for their client on the purchase of empty land to make a commons search in the Register even though the consensus was that the chance of it showing any registered rights of common was slim: *G & K Ladenbau (UK) Ltd* v. *Crawley and De Reya*.[91] Mocatta J said[92]:

"This decision does not mean that a solicitor is in peril of an action for negligence unless he searches the register in every case ... There is clearly room for some discretion for example in relation to densely built up land ... "

Solicitors who had failed exactly to establish the extent of land comprised in a sale so that their clients had subsequently to purchase a "ransom strip" were found liable: *McManus Developments Ltd* v. *Barbridge Properties Ltd*.[93]

Solicitors who accepted the wrong form of purported release of a notice under the Matrimonial Homes Act 1967 which proved in the event ineffective to remove the notice of the rights in question from the title were found liable: *Holmes* v. *Kennard & Son*.[94]

The solicitor acting for a vendor of property who answers any inquiries raised by the purchaser's solicitor must take reasonable care to ensure that the replies are accurate since, if they are not, they may well give rise to liability on the vendor (which the vendor will of course wish to pass on to the solicitor) for misrepresentation or under the Property Misdescriptions Act 1991. The solicitor will not be liable for reasonably relying on information given by way of an instruction from the client.

Solicitors in *Simmons* v. *Pennington*[95] were perhaps lucky to escape an action for negligence when they replied to a requisition regarding breaches of a restrictive covenant in a form which the court held to be standard for the profession but which was in fact inaccurate: "There appear to have been breaches of covenant as to user but no notice of breach has been served". The purchaser was entitled to rescind the purchase contract by reason of this incorrect reply and the vendor sued the solicitors who had given the incorrect reply. Little is known about the information in the vendor's solicitor's possession regarding the covenant and how clear it should have been to the solicitor that the standard reply was in fact wrong. The standard reply had

90. (1863) 7 L.T. 781.
91. [1978] 1 W.L.R. 266.
92. *Ibid.* at 289.
93. [1992] E.G.C.S. 50.
94. (1984) 128 S.J. 854, C.A.
95. [1955] 1 W.L.R. 183.

been in use for many years and the consequence of resession was not reasonably foreseeable when the reply was given. Mere compliance with a standard has never been sufficient to avoid liability since the test for the court to apply is whether the solicitor has acted with reasonable skill and care. It would be very odd indeed if mere slavish adoption of a generally used form of words was sufficient to discharge this burden.

In *Faragher* v. *Gerber*[96] solicitors acting on the purchase of a flat failed to make inquiries which would have revealed plans for a major new highway in front of the property. This was held to be negligent and damages for the diminution in the capital value of the property were awarded. No deduction was made for the plaintiff's right to claim under the Land Compensation Act 1973 because of its speculative nature. The plaintiff also received £6,000 plus interest for damages to the quality of her life.

As mentioned above, The Law Society has introduced a National Protocol for domestic conveyancing dating back to March 1990. The accompanying Law Society Council Statement describes the Protocol as preferred practice.

The Society has also in its Guide to Professional Conduct promulgated standard forms for exchange of contracts by telephone and postal completions. Whilst failure to comply with the terms of these, if agreed between the parties, would almost certainly constitute negligence, a failure to incorporate them into the arrangements would surely of itself not.

### 7.2.5 Security

A solicitor who acts for purchaser and lender on the security of purchase property owes a separate duty to each client. A solicitor is obliged to disclose to the lender any information relevant to the status of the borrower or of the security: *Scholes* v. *Brook*[97]; *Anglia Hastings and Thanet Building Society* v. *House & Son*.[98]

In *Glantz* v. *Polikiff & Co (a firm)*[99] a solicitor acted on the purchase of a flat and its immediate resale at double the price. He paid over deposit money supplied by the plaintiff moneylender to the order of the purchaser after exchange of contracts. The contract fell through when the bank refused to lend the capital to the new purchaser on suspicion of fraud and the deposit was forfeited. The solicitor was unaware of the fraud but was sued for money lost by the moneylender. The court held that he was liable in equity. Once he had received the plaintiff's money he became a trustee of it which put him under a duty to act prudently. Had he acted prudently, he would not have paid over the money without looking into doubtful circumstances existing at that date. The judge decided that the solicitor was not liable in negligence as the moneylender had not established a sufficient duty of care.

In *Boston & Co* v. *Roberts*,[100] solicitors failed to obtain a secured guarantee and instead accepted a bare guarantee with neither protection nor security for costs from a guarantor who clearly presented a risk of defaulting on his liability for costs. They

96. [1994] E.G.C.S. 122.
97. (1981) 63 L.T. 837.
98. (1981) 260 E.G. 1128.
99. [1993] N.P.C. 145.
100. (1995) *The Times*, 17 March, C.A.

were held to fall well below the professional standards expected of competent litigators.

In *Target Holdings Ltd* v. *Redferns Ltd*[101] there has been a recent clear statement from the House of Lords regarding the duty of solicitors acting for a lender as trustee of the loan monies.

Redferns acted as solicitors both for Crowngate Developments Ltd and for Target Holdings Ltd. The latter was to lend approximately £1.5m to finance the purchase of two properties on secured loans. The properties had been overvalued at £2m. Crowngate had arranged to purchase the same properties through intermediate companies (under the same control as Crowngate) for £700,000 and £750,000. Neither Crowngate nor their solicitors informed Target of this.

Redferns paid the mortgage monies before completion to the two intermediate companies. Part of this was handed over to the owners of the property to complete the purchase. Redferns notified Target that the purchase and Target's charge over the properties had been completed prior to actual completion. The intermediate companies retained the balance of the loan monies. Three years later Target was obliged to sell the properties to enforce its charge but realised only £500,000 for them and sued Redferns for negligence and breach of trust.

An application for summary judgment was made under R.S.C., Ord. 14. Redferns admitted breach of trust and that they had received the loan money from Targets as its agent pending authority from Target to release the money to Crowngate. Redferns admitted transferring the money prior to authority and actual completion to the intermediate companies but denied that Target had suffered any loss (having eventually obtained the charges to which it was entitled to secure the loan monies) as a result of that breach of trust.

At first instance Redferns were given leave to defend conditional on payment of £1m to Target in respect of the claim for breach of trust and were given unconditional leave to defend the action in respect of negligence.

Redferns appealed to the Court of Appeal on the ground that Target had suffered no loss resulting from the breach of trust and therefore Redferns should have been given unconditional leave to defend the breach of trust claim. Target entered a cross-appeal for final judgment on the breach of trust claim.

By a majority the Court of Appeal dismissed Redferns' appeal and allowed Target's cross-appeal. Redferns were ordered to pay Target's claim after credit had been given for Target's actual recovery from the sale of the properties.

The majority of the Court of Appeal (Peter Gibson and Hirst LJJ) held that liability for breach of trust was not subject to the principles of causation, foreseeability and remoteness to be found in the law of negligence: all that was required was a causal connection between breach of trust and loss. Where, however, the breach of trust was the wrongful payout of trust money, "the but-for" test, whether the loss would have happened in the absence of a breach of trust, did not fall to be considered. Here there was a clear immediate loss causally connected to the breach of trust. Peter Gibson LJ said, "if this appears harsh treatment of a defaulting trustee, it has to be acknowledged that equity has always treated a defaulting trustee severely".

---

101. [1995] 3 All E.R. 737, H.L.

In his minority judgment Ralph Gibson LJ agreed that the liability of a trustee for breach of trust to restore the trust fund could not be limited by the contractual and tortious doctrines relating to causation of damage, but held that there had to be a causal connection between the breach of trust and the loss claimed. The "but-for" test of causation had to be applied. He was of the opinion that Redferns had raised a triable issue: would Target have suffered the same loss whether or not the breach of trust had taken place?

The judgment of the House of Lords comprised one speech by Lord Browne-Wilkinson. He said it was necessary for Target to prove that the transaction would not have gone ahead at all, but for the breach of trust by Redferns. Since the appeal arose out of an Ord. 14 application, it was necessary to assume, pending a trial of the action, that the transaction would in fact have gone ahead.

Lord Browne-Wilkinson differed from the Court of Appeal which had decided that Redferns would be liable, even if the breach of trust had not caused the loss, on the ground that, if the reasoning of the Court of Appeal was correct, solicitors who had made an entirely innocent and honest mistake (in his example such as a mistake caused by an unforeseeable failure in their computer system) would be liable for the entire loss incurred by the client without any fault on their part.

He decided that the principles governing causation and quantification of loss were the same in equity as at common law: the wrongful act of the defendant must have caused the damage complained of and the plaintiff should then be put in the same position which would have obtained, if he had not sustained the wrong.

The holding of client's money by a solicitor amounted to a bare trust in favour of the client. A solicitor would be liable to restore to the client account any money wrongly paid out in breach of trust before the appropriate conveyancing transaction had been completed. Once that transaction had in fact been completed the client was only entitled to recover from the solicitor the loss suffered "which, using hindsight and common sense, can be seen to have been caused by the breach".

The Court of Appeal had taken strongly into account an unreported decision in *Alliance & Leicester Building Society* v. *Edgestop Ltd*,[102] referred to in *Target Holdings Ltd* v. *Redferns*[103] where the client was awarded damages against the solicitors for breach of trust. Lord Browne-Wilkinson distinguished that case where there had been a finding of fact that, if the building society had known the true facts, it would not have made the loan. In *Target Holdings Ltd*, owing to the nature of the application under R.S.C., Ord. 14, Redferns were entitled to an assumption pending trial of the action that the loan would have gone ahead in any event. In effect, the House of Lords remitted the case for trial of the question whether or not the transaction would have gone ahead, but for Redferns' breach of trust. Any compensation found to be payable should be assessed at the date of judgment rather than at the date of wrongful payment. Thus, Redferns' appeal was successful and the matter will in due course come on for trial, if not settled. In the meantime a potentially vast exposure to claims for damages for innocent and guilty lapses alike has been averted to the collective relief of the solicitors' profession and its insurers.

Lord Browne-Wilkinson summarised the case as follows:

---

102. (Unreported) 18 January 1991.
103. [1995] 3 All E.R. 737, H.L.

"For these reasons I reach the conclusion that, on the facts which must currently be assumed, Target has not demonstrated that it is entitled to any compensation for breach of trust. Assuming that monies would have been forthcoming from some other source to complete the purchase from Mirage if the monies had not been wrongly provided by Redferns in breach of trust, Target obtained exactly what it would have obtained had no breach occurred, i.e., a valid security for the sum advanced. Therefore, on the assumption made, Target has suffered no compensatable loss. Redferns are entitled to leave to defend the breach of trust claim."

### 7.2.6 Giving or failing to give advice

A solicitor who gives incorrect advice on a point which is not obscure and which is governed by clear law will be liable in negligence: *Romsey* v. *Owen, White and Catlin.*[104]

The position is more controversial where the law is not clear. The Scottish case, *Bell* v. *Strathairn & Blair*,[105] suggests that a reasonable opinion on such a difficult point is likely to exonerate the solicitor from negligence, the more particularly if the difficulty of the point is drawn to client's attention.

The practice of solicitors being used as general advisers by their clients on non-legal matters is much less common than of old. The position here seems to be that a solicitor who does undertake the provision of such advice will be liable for obvious error but not for a mere error of judgement: *Bryant* v. *Goodrich*.[106] The more the advice given is of a legal (rather than general) nature and is based on legal (rather than practical or general) considerations, the more likely it will be (if wrong) to found a successful negligence claim.

Another variant of the problem is the solicitor giving incomplete advice. In the well-known case of *Crossnan* v. *Ward Bracewell & Co*[107] a solicitor had given correct advice about penalties for a traffic offence and the cost of representation but had failed to tell the client that the costs of representation would be covered by the plaintiff's motor insurers. This was held to be negligent. The wrong in this category may be simply giving incomplete advice or it may be failing to give particular advice which a solicitor of reasonable skill and competence should have given in the particular circumstances to the particular client.

If, as seems probable (as discussed above), the nature of the duty of solicitor to client is a general duty, implicit in the general duty is the obligation to take all necessary steps on the client's behalf. If so, failure to give advice as to the action to be taken may well be an almost identical breach of the retainer (or the common law duty) as failure to take the step itself.

A solicitor must communicate to the client important points (not every single piece of information) which come to the attention of the solicitor and are relevant to the subject of the retainer. Case-law concentrates on conveyancing examples: the planning position on the property to be purchased, a right of way over it and a defective title are all matters which it would be negligent not to bring to the attention of the client.

104. (1978) 245 E.G. 225, C.A.
105. (1954) 104 L.J. 618.
106. (1966) 110 S.J. 108.
107. (1989) 5 P.N. 103.

The duty to inform the client is now, in common with the modern trend, formulated or standardised in a Law Society Professional Standard dating back to 1985:

"The solicitor should keep his client informed both of the progress of his matter and of the reason for any serious delay which occurs. This may often be assisted by sending to the client copies of letters. Requests for information [from the client] should be answered promptly."

This standard reflects the *dictum* in *Groom* v. *Crocker*[108]:

"It is an incident of that duty that the solicitor shall consult with his client in all questions of doubt which do not fall within the express or implied discretion left him, and shall keep the client informed to such an extent as may be reasonably necessary according to the same criteria."

This affects to some extent the basic quality of the retainer: the process is dynamic and the client cannot properly instruct the solicitor without appreciation of the relevant and important aspects of the matter being dealt with.

Perhaps remarkably, solicitors escaped liability for negligence to an injured workman whom they advised in relation to statutory remedies but not a common law claim for damages against the employer: *Griffiths* v. *Evans*.[109] The decision was on the basis that the solicitors had been asked specifically to advise on compensation under the Workers Compensation Acts 1925 to 1943. Denning LJ dissented on this point on the ground that the solicitor possessed special knowledge denied to the client.

In *Goody* v. *Baring*[110] solicitors acting on the purchase of a partly tenanted property made standard inquiries into the passing rents but failed to check that these were not in excess of registered rents. They were and the client had to repay the excess rent. The solicitors were liable for failing to make the necessary inquiries and to communicate them to the client. The court held that the mere making of standard inquiries might well be insufficient and[111]:

"it is still the duty of a purchaser's solicitor to make the appropriate requisitions and inquiries after the contract is signed, even if the preliminary inquiries have been so complete that it is only necessary to ask whether the answers received are still complete and accurate".

In another well-known case, the Court of Appeal (whilst allowing the solicitors' appeal on another ground) expressed the opinion that it would not be negligent in all cases for a solicitor to fail to advise a couple whose wills they made that the wills would be revoked by their subsequent marriage to each other. Each case would depend on its own facts. In this case there were no express instructions regarding an impending marriage from the clients although the plaintiffs' son teased the couple about it whilst sitting in on their giving the instructions for the wills: *Hall* v. *Meyrick*.[112]

In relation to the giving of advice different standards will apply to different types of client. An example of the "specialist or expert client" is *Carradine Properties Ltd* v. *DJ Freeman & Co*.[113] In this case a substantial property company with experienced

---

108. [1938] 2 All E.R. 394.
109. [1953] 1 W.L.R. 1424.
110. [1956] 2 All E.R. 11.
111. *Ibid.* at 16I.
112. [1957] 2 Q.B. 455.
113. (1989) 5 Cons.L.J. 267, (1985) 1 P.N. 41.

directors instructed solicitors to make claims against both builders and the estate agents who had advised the selection of those builders. The property company did not tell the solicitors that it was insured against the damage in respect of which the claim was to be made. The solicitors were not asked to consider the insurance position and did not ask questions or offer advice about insurance. The finding for the solicitors at first instance was upheld in the Court of Appeal with weight being given to the experience of the managing director of the plaintiff company.

Donaldson LJ underlined the variable standard required:

"an inexperienced client will need and will be entitled to expect the solicitor to take a much broader view of the scope of his retainer and of his duties than will be the case with an experienced client".

Conversely, a solicitor has a clear duty to bring to the attention of the client (even if it is outside the strict terms of the retainer) risks which are obvious to him with his special expertise but which will not be apparent to a lay client: *Boyce* v. *Rendells*.[114]

In *Welton Sinclair* v. *Hyland*[115] a landlord informed the solicitors who had acted for the tenant on the assignment of a lease of the premises in question that he had served a notice on the tenant to bring the lease to an end. The court decided that the solicitors owed a duty to the tenant to advise him about the strict time-limits in relation to an application to the court for a new lease, although the tenant had placed no reliance on the solicitors in relation to that matter, as opposed to the original assignment.

Another important aspect of the duty in relation to advice is the duty to explain and interpret legal documentation to the lay client. Here again the matter has become the object of a professional standard: "The solicitor should explain to the client the effect of any important and relevant document".[116]

This goes further than the leading case on the subject, *Sykes* v. *Midland Bank Executor & Trustee Co Ltd*,[117] where the judge held that the duty of a solicitor was "... to call his client's attention to clauses in an unusual form which may affect the interests of his client as he knows them".

This case was followed in *County Personnel (Employment Agency) Ltd* v. *Alan R Pulver & Co*.[118] That case involved an unusual rent review clause. The solicitors acting for the underlessee attempted unsuccessfully to persuade the court that the problem in the case was not the legal consequences of the lease but the financial implications of the rent review structures.

Conversely, in *Reeves* v. *Thrings & Long*,[119] solicitors who advised a commercial purchaser of the legal nature of an unsatisfactory means of access to a hotel were held not to be liable for failure to explain the commercial consequences of those shortcomings. His retainer was limited to the purchase of the hotel and did not include advice regarding its development. He had advised the client of the terms of

114. (1983) 268 E.G. 268.
115. (1992) E.G. 112.
116. Law Society Guide to Professional Conduct.
117. [1971] 1 Q.B. 113, C.A.
118. [1987] 1 W.L.R. 916.
119. 12 February 1992, Queen's Bench Division, MacPherson of Cluny J, reported in *Professional Negligence*, vol. 9, No. 2, 1993.

the licence for access. Since the client was an experienced businessman it was not necessary to explain the provisions of the licence further. The judge found that the plaintiff would have proceeded with the purchase in any event. Even if the solicitor were liable, recovery would have been limited to the cost of acquiring the access rights which the plaintiff had assumed he was purchasing and not amounted to recovery of his investment[120]:

"I cannot believe that the defendants, whose negligence was purely in relation to the means of access, should pay more than the proper and reasonable costs of achieving permanent access."

In *Forbouys* v. *Gadhavi*[121] a person who conducted the business of buying and selling leasehold reversions agreed to buy a lease knowing that there was a rent review clause but not knowing about its timing. He agreed to sell it to a sub-purchaser but after exchange contracts agreed to release that sub-purchaser who had discovered that the rent review would produce a rent of £14,000 (as opposed to the present rent of £6,250) per annum which it could not afford. The dealer sued his solicitor for negligence as he had had to pay £60,000 to his vendor for non-completion of the purchase. The court decided that the solicitor was not guilty of negligence as his duty did not extend to preventing his client who was a businessman with considerable experience who knew the significance of rent reviews from taking the commercial risk of proceeding without the knowledge of the figure under the rent review.

The duty to explain important and relevant documents does not oblige a solicitor to give a fully detailed explanation of every document, particularly where the document in question is widely used and contains standard conditions, for example the National Conditions of Sale: *Walker* v. *Boyle*.[122] Dillon J said[123]:

"It is of course the duty of a solicitor to advise his client about any abnormal or unusual term in a contract, but I think it is perfectly normal and proper for a solicitor to use standard conditions of sale ... I do not think he is called on to go through the small print of those somewhat lengthy conditions with a tooth comb every time he is advising a purchaser or to draw the purchaser's attention to every problem which on a careful reading of the conditions might in some circumstance or other conceivably apply. I cannot believe that purchasers of home property throughout the land would be overjoyed at having such lengthy explanations of the National Conditions of Sale ritually foisted on them."

The preponderance of authority is in favour of the proposition that advice on a future time-limit, once firmly given, need not be repeated: *West London Observer* v. *Parsons*,[124] followed in *Yager* v. *Fishman & Co.*[125] The decision was to the contrary in *RP Howard Ltd* v. *Woodman Matthews*.[126] In that case the solicitors gave a warning about time-limits under the Landlord and Tenant Act 1954, Part II at the outset but failed to repeat it after they had conducted negotiations on behalf of their client before the time-limit for application to the court for a new tenancy had passed.

120. *Ibid.* at p. 103.
121. [1993] N.P.C. 122.
122. [1982] 1 All E.R. 634.
123. *Ibid.* at 645a.
124. (1955) 166 E.G. 749.
125. [1944] 1 All E.R. 552.
126. [1983] BCLC 117.

## 8 THE LIABILITY SHARED

The solicitor's liability may be shared either with the client or with another solicitor or other professional involved in the same matter giving rise to the liability.

It is most unusual to have contributory negligence by the client since in the normal transaction the client relies upon the professional skill and competence of the solicitor.

The only reported English case involving solicitor and client is *McLellan* v. *Fletcher*.[127] In that case the solicitor was told by his client that the client had arranged an endowment insurance policy and had arranged to pay the premium. The solicitor was found negligent in failing to confirm with the insurers of, or the lenders to, the client that the insurers were on risk. The client was, however, found 75 per cent contributorily negligent for incorrectly believing that he had paid the first premium and so informing the solicitor.

In *Clark Boyce* v. *Mouat*[128] the Privy Council reversed the decision of the New Zealand Court of Appeal that, in acting for their client and her son, the defendant solicitors were subject to a major conflict of interest and so liable but that their client who had been advised but failed to take independent advice should bear 50 per cent responsibility.[129]

It is more common for considerations of sharing of liability between professionals to arise.

This may be either between different firms of solicitors involved in the same matter (usually sequentially) or between the solicitor and other professionals involved in the matter.

It is not uncommon for a client to change solicitors either because dissatisfied with the first or for reasons such as geographical convenience, increased specialised expertise, lower charging rates etc.

Thus the first solicitor may be wholly blameless. If the conduct of one solicitor alone has caused a loss (e.g., a missed limitation date), that solicitor alone will be liable.

Equally, each solicitor may be liable either for discrete acts of negligence or may share liability for similar acts of negligence.

As an example of the first type, in a simple debt recovery action, negligent delay by the first solicitor may cause the client to retain a second solicitor. The client could look to the first solicitor for any interest on the monies claimed which was disallowed against the defendant because of the plaintiff's first solicitor's delay. If the second solicitor missed a limitation date or allowed the claim to be dismissed for want of prosecution or sued a defendant who was not liable, the second solicitor would be liable for the damages flowing from that negligence.

As an example of the second type, the first solicitor may miss the primary and secondary limitation dates in a personal injuries action. The client may move on to a second solicitor who takes the view that an application to the court to exercise its discretion under section 33 of the Limitation Act 1980 should be made to mitigate the

---

127. (1987) 3 P.N. 202.
128. [1993] 3 W.L.R. 1021; see p. 586 below.
129. This is discussed in relation to the principles governing conflict of interest in pp. 585–588 below.

loss. The second solicitor may then negligently delay or even fail to make the application. If the court on the trial of the negligence action takes the view that a timely application under section 33 would have failed, the negligence of the second solicitor will have caused no damage (save for any costs paid fruitlessly by the client to the second solicitor and subject to the question of damages for distress discussed below).

If, on the other hand, the court decides that a timely section 33 application would have succeeded, the second solicitor will be the cause of all the loss except damages for interest foregone by reason of the delay from the date on which the client would have received any damages to that on which the judge finds he would have been entitled in the main action, but for the negligence of the first solicitor and any costs thrown away.

As a rule of thumb, a successor solicitor who has to take on a case which may have become urgent owing to lapse of time is likely to have a greater ability to commit actionable negligence than the first solicitor since, by definition, the second solicitor has undertaken to exercise reasonable skill and care in relation to the circumstances (including urgency) obtaining at the time of his retainer. These are really questions of causation where the usual "but-for" test is applied.

Although all solicitors are insured (at least to a certain level of cover under the same indemnity policy), it is necessary to apportion the damages between the solicitors concerned for reasons of claims experience, deductibles and total cover per firm.[130]

Even if all the negligence complained of takes place within one firm of solicitors, different individuals may be at fault. As seen above the partners are liable as principals and insure their liability. Under the normal principles of vicarious liability, the partners will be liable for the negligent acts and omissions of their staff provided those acts and omissions occur within the normal scope of their employment. Indeed, the cover provided by the Solicitors Indemnity Fund, as will be seen, goes further than common law principles of vicarious liability. Whilst, therefore, any client is likely in anything but the most extraordinary case to have a good claim (assuming negligence) against the partners backed by unavoidable indemnity insurance of the Compensation Fund (as appropriate), questions have recently been raised as to the liability of employed staff to indemnify the partners against the consequences of negligent acts or omissions on the part of those staff members. There is as yet no law on this. The motive of the partners is presumably to salvage deductibles and/or to improve their claims record and the legal basis presumably an express or implied covenant by the staff member in his or her contract of employment to act with reasonable skill and care.

Solicitors frequently act (particularly in commercial or property matters) in concert with other professionals such as accountants, surveyors and architects.

In this case the rule of thumb is that a mistake common to both or all professionals will result in the sharing of liability (on the face of it on an equal basis). If only one professional commits an act of negligence, only that one will be liable. If more than one professional commits different acts of negligence, the court will have to decide what damages are required to compensate the client for each individual act of

---

130. As discussed on pp. 598–601 below.

negligence. Where the aggregation of the damages which would separately be recoverable exceeds the total of the client's loss the court will have to make an apportionment on an equitable basis of the amount of the loss between the negligent professionals. Again, the "but-for" test for causation will be applied.

An example of the apportionment process is *Anglia Hastings and Thanet Building Society* v. *House & Son*,[131] where solicitors and valuers who had acted for the plaintiff building society in relation to the mortgage of two properties were both found to be negligent in relation to insufficient security for the loan.

The valuers had reported to the building society a valuation which was dramatically wrong. The solicitors had not been directly concerned in the valuation, but had failed to protect the interests of the building society over an extended period of time. The court apportioned liability 70 per cent to the solicitors and 30 per cent to the valuer. It is perhaps surprising that the solicitors came off that badly since presumably, if the valuers had produced a reasonably accurate valuation, the loan never would have been made and the solicitors' failure to protect the building society would not have been an effective cause of loss.

The Law Commission is considering the feasibility of reviewing the law on joint and several liability. This is likely to be welcome to insured professionals where the extent of their obligation to pay may well in practice often exceed their proportion of liability.[131a]

## 9 THE LIABILITY REBUTTED

It is of course for the plaintiff to prove all the necessary facts and elements required to found an action for negligence. The solicitor has, in addition, a number of specific defences to such a claim.

### 9.1 Immunity from suit

A solicitor advocate is entitled to the same immunity against a claim for negligence as that afforded to a barrister. This principle is now enshrined in section 62(1) of the Courts and Legal Services Act 1990 which provides:

"a person—
    (a) who is not a barrister; but
    (b) who lawfully provides any legal services in relation to any proceedings,
shall have the same immunity from liability for negligence in respect of his acts or omissions as he would have if he were a barrister lawfully providing those services".

This immunity covers both the actual advocacy in court and any pre-trial work such as advice on a plea to a criminal charge.

The test applied in *Saif Ali* v. *Sidney Mitchell & Co*[132] (a case which concerned the

---

131. (1981) 260 E.G. 1128.
131a. But the initial recommendation in the recently published Consultation Paper is to leave the law unchanged.
132. [1980] A.C. 198.

liability of a barrister but which is equally applicable to solicitors) was that any such pre-trial work must be "so intimately connected with the conduct of the cause in court that it can fairly be said to be a preliminary decision affecting the way that cause is to be conducted when it comes to a hearing".

The immunity is against liability for breach of contract or in negligence and is confirmed by the exclusion order disapplying the obligation to act with reasonable care and skill imposed by section 13 of the Supply of Goods and Services Act 1982 to the services of an advocate in court or before any tribunal, inquiry or arbitrator and in carrying out preliminary work directly affecting the conduct of the hearing: Supply of Services (Exclusion of Implied Terms) Order 1982.[133]

### 9.2 Abuse of process

It appears that, if a solicitor negligently allows his client to lose a civil case or be convicted in a criminal case, the client cannot subsequently sue the solicitor. In *Somasundaram* v. *Julius Melchior & Co*[134] the Court of Appeal found that the claim for negligence was an abuse of process involving an attack on the final decision of another court.

In that case the allegation was that the solicitors had "over-persuaded" the plaintiff to plead guilty to a charge of assault. He had in fact already completed his sentence and was in effect attempting to vindicate his reputation and claim compensation. Thus the plaintiff's purpose may well have been to relitigate a closed issue.

This doctrine has recently been reviewed in the leading case of *Walpole* v. *Partridge & Wilson*[135] where solicitors failed to advise a convicted defendant to lodge an appeal, despite having advice from counsel that there were good grounds for such an appeal. The solicitors invited the court to strike the claim out as an abuse of process. The Court of Appeal refused and recognised four exceptions to the general rule:

(a) where the prior decision of the court which the plaintiff wished to challenge had been obtained by fraud, collusion or perjury;

(b) where there is such fresh evidence that the character of the case is entirely changed;

(c) where the complaint is that the solicitors had failed to prosecute an appeal;

(d) where the previous court had not in fact made a decision on the merits of the case.

The court decided that the action was not a collateral attack on the criminal conviction and therefore not an abuse of process. A claim that a solicitor's negligence deprived the plaintiff of his right to appeal against a conviction in a criminal case does not constitute an attempt to reopen the initial issue which, because of the negligence, had never been fully litigated. The motive of the plaintiff in bringing the action for negligence is a factor to be taken into account but not decisive in determining it.

133. S.I. 1982/1771.
134. [1988] 1 W.L.R. 1394.
135. [1993] 3 W.L.R. 1093, and see also *Smith* v. *Linskills* (1996) *The Times*, 7 February, C.A.

## 9.3 Reliance on counsel's advice

One hundred and fifty years of authority suggest it will be a good defence to action for negligence, if a solicitor relies upon and follows the advice of counsel properly instructed. It does not matter if counsel's advice is wrong.

A modern example of this is *Francis* v. *Francis and Dickerson*[136] where Sachs J said, " ... as a general rule a solicitor acting on the advice of properly instructed counsel can hardly be said to be acting unreasonably—save perhaps in some very exceptional circumstances".

This defence will not prevail where the solicitor has instructed counsel who is clearly not competent to give the advice required, or where a counsel who has been instructed on a point which the solicitor should have dealt with without counsel or on a claim for breach of the retainer agreement where the action advised by counsel is contrary to the client's instructions to the solicitor.

The long history of this doctrine largely reflects a more hierarchical distinction between solicitors and barristers than exists today. Solicitors' firms set their sights far more than previously on dealing with complicated matters including advocacy without resource to counsel. Many who would previously have gone to the Bar now choose the solicitors' profession whether because of the perceived financial rewards, for greater security, for better support systems or other reasons.

The consequence of this is that the reflexive reaching for and reliance upon counsel is far less prevalent amongst solicitors than before.

The gradual shift in the "balance of power" between the professions led the Court of Appeal in *Davey-Chiesman* v. *Davey-Chiesman*[137] to modify the general rule where solicitors continued the prosecution of a financial application in matrimonial proceedings which were clearly doomed to failure simply (it appears) because they were following counsel's advice. May LJ said:

"However, [the general rule] does not operate so as to give a solicitor an immunity in every such case. A solicitor is highly trained and rightly expected to be experienced in his particular legal field. He is under a duty at all times to exercise that degree of care, to both client and the court, that can be expected of a reasonably prudent solicitor. He is not entitled to rely blindly and with no mind of his own on counsel's views."

In *Locke* v. *Camberwell HA*[138] the plaintiff's solicitor in a medical negligence case relied on a short positive advice by counsel described by the court as "cavalier" and written without counsel having the plaintiff's medical records in front of him. He then instructed leading counsel and had a consultation with leading and junior counsel and the plaintiff again without the medical records. When counsel saw the medical records they wrote a joint advice saying that the plaintiff's legal aid should be withdrawn. The plaintiff's solicitor was liable for: (1) failing to inspect the medical records; (2) failing to instruct counsel properly (in particular by not supplying the medical records with the instructions); and (3) for relying upon counsel's advice in those circumstances.

The immunity of a barrister under the principle in *Saif Ali* is limited to advocacy

136. [1956] P. 87.
137. [1984] Fam. 48.
138. [1990] 1 Med.L.R. 253, [1991] 2 Med.L.R. 249.

and pre-trial advice. It is now not unknown for solicitors faced with a negligence action or an application for a wasted costs order (see below) to bring third party proceedings against counsel.

### 9.4 Following instructions of the client

Since the duty of a solicitor under the terms of the retainer is to act in accordance with the client's instructions, if the solicitor gives advice according to the standard referred to above, he or she will not be liable if the client chooses to insist upon the instructions being carried out, ignoring the advice on the risks inherent in that course of action: *Okafor* v. *Malcolm Slowe & Co.*[139]

If, however, the solicitor's advice to the client is not sufficient by the standards referred to above, the defence of following instructions will not be available to the solicitor: *Morris* v. *Duke-Cohan & Co.*[140]

The solicitors in *FG Reynolds (Whitchurch) Ltd* v. *Joseph*,[141] enterprisingly but unsuccessfully sought to rebut liability for providing an inferior service on the ground that the client was tardy in settling invoices for fees.

## 10 PRINCIPLES OF RECOVERY

The principles governing recovery of damages for a solicitor's negligence or breach of contract are no different from those generally applicable: the breach of contract or duty must have caused loss of a type recognised by the law and that loss must have been foreseeable (or not too remote).

In relation to causation, the test is to ask whether the loss would have occurred, but for the breach of duty or contract in question.

For example, if an action for damages against a third party is struck out owing to the solicitor's breach but that action would on the balance of probabilities have failed at trial, the causation test is not satisfied and the disappointed client cannot recover from the solicitor the damages which he or she was claiming from the third party. The client may, of course, have the right to recover any additional expenses incurred as a result of the breach.

Similarly, if negligent advice by a solicitor does not affect the action taken by the client, there is no causation of damage. In *Sykes* v. *Midland Bank Executor & Trustee Co Ltd*[142] solicitors negligently advised a client in respect of a proposed underlease. The Court of Appeal decided as a matter of fact that the client would have entered into the underlease, even if it had been given proper non-negligent advice and thus only nominal damages were recoverable.

Clients sued their solicitor in *Nash* v. *Phillips*[143] for damages after their solicitor's negligence had resulted in their inability to buy the house which they wanted. The house which they ended up buying was less convenient than the one they were unable to buy and they claimed damages for the loss of convenience. The claim was rejected

139. (1968) 207 E.G. 345.
140. (1975) 119 S.J. 826.
141. (1992) *The Times*, 6 November.
142. [1971] 1 Q.B. 113.
143. (1974) 232 E.G. 1219.

on the ground that the cause of the inconvenience was not the negligence but the purchase of the house in question.

The negligence must be the proximate cause of the loss: in a business tenancy case solicitors negligently failed to protect the clients' right to renew a lease. On termination of the contractual lease the landlords were entitled to dilapidations under the tenant's repairing covenant. The clients' claim against their solicitors for the cost of the dilapidations failed on the ground that the cause of the payment was not the negligence but the obligation to pay for any want of repair at the end of the lease: *Clark and Another* v. *Kirby-Smith*.[144]

In *Law* v. *Cunningham & Co (a firm)*[145] the client claimed damages against her solicitors in relation to the sale of a property. The solicitors raised issues of causation and *novus actus interveniens*. The judge decided in favour of the plaintiff on the ground that, although the solicitor did not guarantee a particular result, hazards should have been pointed out to the client and the duty was all the greater when the client was inexperienced. The solicitor had to make sure that the client understood the nature of the matter. Whilst the client was entitled to manage her own affairs, she should not be allowed to do so on inadequate advice from the solicitor and in this case the solicitor had failed to identify the risk to the client of the agreement entered into. The client had been left to negotiate on her own and it was not adequate for the solicitors simply to say that they were carrying out their client's instructions.

The chain of causation between the negligence and loss may be broken by subsequent or intervening events. In order for the chain to be broken it is probably necessary that the intermediate event constitutes negligence on the part of someone besides the solicitor: *Cook* v. *Swinfen*.[146] This largely reflects the discussion of shared liability in section 8 above.

The mirror image of the requirement that the causal link between negligence and damage must be preserved is that the damage complained of must be foreseeable at the time of breach (whether of contract or of the duty of care).

Since the solicitor will be in possession of the instructions and thus presumably the intentions of the client, it will generally be the case that there should be little difficulty in fixing the solicitor with foresight of the losses which may occur, if a breach is committed.

A leading recent case is *Hayes* v. *James and Charles Dodd*.[147] The defendants negligently failed to advise their client that there was no right of way over the only access to the property. It took their clients at least five extra years to sell the property and they claimed ancillary expenses of holding on to it such as legal costs, interest on their loan, rates on the property and even redundancy payments. Because the solicitors knew that the plaintiffs had purchased the property for business purposes it was held that these losses were not too remote and the plaintiffs therefore secured judgment for them. In this case damages for anguish and vexation arising out of a breach of contract were not recoverable unless the object of the contract was to provide peace of mind and freedom from distress. This was not appropriate in the case of a purely commercial contract.

144. [1964] 1 Ch. 506.
145. [1993] E.G.C.S. 126.
146. [1966] 1 W.L.R. 635.
147. [1990] 2 All E.R. 815.

Damages for the psychological consequences of the solicitors' breach were awarded in *Malyon* v. *Lawrence, Messer & Co*.[148] The defendants had allowed a claim in respect of a car accident in Germany to become time-barred. The plaintiff was to the defendants' knowledge suffering a severe anxiety state which the plaintiff's neurologist expected to clear up once the claim was settled. Brabin J said[149]:

"What is said is, that unless that situation exists initially, solicitors cannot be made liable for any exacerbation or injury caused to the plaintiff through their subsequent conduct. I disagree with that submission. A solicitor's obligation is a continuing one while his retainer is still in operation, and I do not accept that his obligations are always dictated by, and confined to, the situation existing at the moment he first sees his client. In many cases where the solicitor is giving his continuing care to the case other circumstances supervene, which might require that a solicitor take certain action. He contracts to use his skill and care and gives an implied undertaking to act as a reasonably careful solicitor. The defendants in this case admit, that for several years they were in breach of that undertaking in many respects. From the earliest time it must have been obvious to Mr Herbert that the plaintiff was suffering from a nervous condition. It must have been obvious that, as a natural and probable consequence of negligence in not prosecuting the action, the plaintiff's condition would not improve. Not only was it not unlikely to be the result, it was—I would have thought—an obvious result that would follow. I consider that a solicitor acting with reasonable skill and care would know, in the circumstances of this case, that it was necessary to proceed with reasonable expedition to bring the plaintiff's case to finality when, in fact, the solicitor is fully aware that that is required in the plaintiff's best interest. One has not to look at this with hindsight obtained from later medical reports, which I do not find it necessary to deal with in detail. But hindsight does not arise where the anxiety state was still continuing, where it was directly due to the accident, where it was affected by the long, drawn-out litigation, where it was said, as in 1960 that the anxiety state, which is directly due to the accident, will persist until the case is settled. This was confirmed in a later report where the doctor pointed out that the plaintiff was a stable individual beforehand, that his symptoms will persist until the case is settled, adding: 'I am sure they will clear up completely', in other words according to authoritative medical opinion, this is one of those cases where the courts will provide a therapy which medicine has been unable to do. In my view it must have been, as I have said, obvious to the defendants that the plaintiff's condition was worsening, certainly not improving, by reason of the inordinate delays admittedly due to the defendants' negligence, and I think that the plaintiff is entitled to damages in that respect. He has had nearly six years since the curtain would have come down if a trial had taken place in Germany. If the trial had taken place at the proper time the plaintiff by now would have had this neurosis behind him, he would have been completedly cured on the medical evidence, but instead of that, he has been kept in the condition that I have seen and in the condition spoken to by his friends, who knowing him years ago at the time of the accident saw a marked change in him initially brought about, as I find, by this accident."

(See also *McLeish* v. *Amoo Gottfried & Co*.)[150]

The plaintiff was entitled to be put financially as far as possible in the position which would have obtained but for the negligence complained of.

In *Dickinson* v. *Jones Alexander & Co*[151] the solicitors advised a wife to leave the matrimonial home although she had grounds for an ouster injunction. The trainee solicitor (supported by partner) advised her that the only asset available for distribution was the matrimonial home, ignoring the share holdings in the family business and inheritance prospects. No steps were taken to obtain full disclosure of the husband's position and a consent order was made on a clean-break basis. The

148. [1968] 2 Lloyd's Rep. 539.
149. *Ibid.* at 551.
150. (Unreported) 23 July 1993, discussed on p. 580 below.
151. [1993] 2 F.L.R. 521.

wife was advised to buy a small house and obtain a mortgage against which she could claim tax relief although she in fact had no income at the time against which to offset any tax liability. The solicitors admitted negligence but argued that there should be a discount for litigation risk and accelerated payment, that her damages should reflect her net loss because it would not attract liability to tax, that credit should be given for state benefits paid to the wife as in personal injury cases and the damages for mental stress claimed by the wife were too remote to be recoverable.

The court decided that the damages would be assessed on what the husband would have been ordered to pay on the application of the Matrimonial Causes Act 1973, section 25. The most likely award would be one-third of the husband's income. The wife should receive the full amount without any discount in case the Inland Revenue should argue that the income portion represented taxable income in her hands. The state benefits would be clawed back from her by the state, so there should be no discount:

"The damages claimed for mental distress, anxiety and vexation were a direct and foreseeable consequence of the solicitors' negligence, who had been aware of her mental state when she instructed them and will be assessed at £5,000."

Damages are assessed as at the date of the breach unless assessment as at another date may not more fairly and accurately compensate the plaintiff: *County Personnel Ltd* v. *Alan R Pulver & Co.*[152]

Non-financial loss is compensated as general damages to the extent recoverable in the normal way and using any "tariffs" applicable at the date as at which damages are to be assessed. Again in the normal way the plaintiff must give credit against the claimed loss for any benefit which is attributable to the breach. The benefit must (as with the loss) not be too remote.

An example of the approach of the court to deduction of benefits is *Teasdale* v. *Williams & Co.*[153] A solicitor negligently achieved for his client a seven-year lease at an initial rental of £19,000 per annum for the first two years and £26,500 per annum for the next five years. The client had intended to acquire a lease for five years at a fixed rent of £20,000 per annum.

The plaintiff was awarded damages comprising three years' extra rent (years three to five) in a total sum of £19,500 less the benefit to him in years one and two of £2,000. There was no award for the apparent gain in years six and seven attributable to the rent review coming at the year end of seven rather than at the end of year five. This was because that gain would be offset by the rent review at the end of year seven being expected to produce a higher rent than it would have produced at the end of year five.

In the right of way case, *Hayes* v. *Dodd*,[154] the property in question increased in value during the years of delay in achieving a sale. The gain in value was not deducted from the damages claimed as a benefit except to the extent credit was in effect given by disallowing the claim for mortgage interest charges for the period in question. Thus the plaintiff was entitled to the capital appreciation less the cost of servicing the loan which made that appreciation possible.

152. [1987] 1 W.L.R. 916.
153. (1984) 269 E.G. 1040.
154. [1990] 2 All E.R. 815.

The courts have tended to deal with lack of certainty in relation to the plaintiff's future conduct, absent the breach complained of, by discounting the otherwise recoverable damages by a percentage designed to reflect the chance that the plaintiff would not in fact have behaved in such a way that the causal connection between breach and loss was made out: *Nash* v. *Phillips*[155] where a discount of 10 per cent was applied to reflect the fact that, although owing to the breach they had lost the chance of purchasing a particular property, they might not have gone ahead with the purchase in any event.

In a case three years earlier already referred to (*Sykes* v. *Midland Bank Executor & Trustee Co Ltd*) the Court of Appeal chose to approach the matter on a simple balance of probabilities test and found the chain of causation broken.

Interestingly, the view promulgated by the Court of Appeal in *Wilsher* v. *Essex Area Health Authority*[156] interpreting the House of Lords decision in *McGhee* v. *National Coal Board*[157] as establishing that the burden of proof that the outcome would have been the same in any event passed to the defendant once the plaintiff had proved breach of duty, was firmly overruled by the House of Lords[158] and has a parallel in solicitors' negligence cases: *Heywood* v. *Wellers*.[159]

The client is under a duty in the normal way to mitigate all losses caused by the negligence. The courts have, however, taken a robust view in relation to the steps which the plaintiffs should reasonably have taken, as opposed to the steps urged upon them by defendants in their attempt to minimise or avoid any damages being payable. The basis for this is presumably that the plaintiff is *ex hypothesi* only innocently in the position having to make choices between different possible steps of mitigation owing to the culpability of the defendant.

For example, in *Transportation Agency Ltd* v. *Jenkins*[160] the plaintiffs had, owing to their solicitors' negligent advice, purchased a lease of restaurant premises which contained a covenant against cooking! The defendants argued unsuccessfully that the plaintiff should have taken all possible steps to mitigate their loss by coming to an accommodation with the landlord.

A plaintiff is not generally under a duty to begin fresh litigation in order to mitigate a loss. The difficulty and expense and prospects of success of such new proceedings are relevant factors to be taken into account. It is sometimes the practice of negligent defendants or their insurers to seek to take proceedings in the plaintiff's name to protect the position on damages and it is likely that the plaintiff's refusal to lend his name to the action (if satisfactorily indemnified against the risks and costs of litigation) would be an unreasonable failure to mitigate.

---

155. (1974) 232 E.G. 1219, and see also *Allied Maples Group Ltd* v. *Simmons & Simmons* [1995] 4 All E.R. 907, C.A., followed in *Stovold* v. *Barlows*, 12 October 1995, C.A., adopting the same approach where the plaintiff's loss arose from the hypothetical act of a third party: e.g. if the defendant solicitor had not been negligent, would the plaintiff's purchaser have completed the purchase at the intended price?
156. [1987] 2 W.L.R. 425.
157. [1970] 1 W.L.R. 1, H.L.
158. [1990] A.C. 1074.
159. [1976] Q.B. 446.
160. (1972) 223 E.G. 1101.

# 11 TYPES OF DAMAGES RECOVERABLE

## 11.1 Plaintiff unable to have prior claim adjudicated

This may occur either by failure to issue proceedings before the limitation date or by allowing the action to be struck out for want of prosecution or breach of peremptory order.

The court trying the negligence action must be convinced on the balance of probabilities that the plaintiff had a cause of action which would have resulted in a successful or trial settlement (a nuisance value is not enough): *Kitchen* v. *Royal Airforce Association*.[161] If the case is either certain to succeed or certain to fail the task of the court is easy. Almost all cases, however, fall somewhere in between. The approach of the Court of Appeal in *Kitchen* was that:

"... assuming that the plaintiff has established negligence, what the court has to do in such a case ... is to determine what the plaintiff has lost by that negligence. The question is: has the plaintiff lost some right of value, some chose in action of reality and substance? In such a case it may be that its value is not easy to determine, but it is the duty of the court to determine that value as best it can."

Thus the court must take a robust view of the value of the forgone claim: in practice multiplying the likely damages by the likely prospects of success may provide a useful guide. This reflects the fact that any civil claim which is not bound to fail has a financial value. This is true (as a matter of practice, if not logic) even of a claim whose prospects of success do not exceed 50 per cent.

The time for the assessment is the date upon which the court finds the original action would have been tried or settled with interest running on the value of the claim from that date at judgment rate.

In evaluating the prospects of success, the court must also consider which items of damages claimed would in fact have satisfied the causation test and therefore been recoverable.

In *Yardley* v. *Coombs*[162] the trial judge decided that in relation to proving liability the plaintiff had a fair chance of success and that his chance of establishing causation or aggravation of a pre-existing condition was not hopeless. He awarded one-third of the full value of the claim, assuming that the aggravation was proved.

In *MacNamara* v. *Martin Mears & Co*[163] it was recognised that no litigation is certain to succeed and therefore that a discount (however small) for the risks of litigation may be appropriate.

Other practical considerations relate to the ability of the original defendant to satisfy the judgment against him and to the influence of exposure to costs (both own costs which are irrecoverable and opponent's costs, if the plaintiff fails) on the settlement process. There appear, however, to be no authorities on these points. Perhaps the correct approach would be for the defendants in the negligence action to advance these arguments in relation to *quantum* and seek to persuade the trial judge in the negligence action that they are factors properly to be taken into account in the particular case.

---

161. [1958] 1 W.L.R. 563.
162. (1963) 107 S.J. 575.
163. (1983) 127 S.J. 69.

There is a precedent in *Cutler* v. *MN*[164] where the irrecoverable costs of pursuing a claim for an industrial tribunal for unfair dismissal were deducted from the likely award of compensation for that dismissal.

If a solicitor negligently fails to file a defence, similar considerations apply and the court in the negligence action must evaluate the chance of the defence succeeding and the value to the defendant of such success.

## 11.2 The effect on the plaintiff

If as a result of the negligence of the solicitor the client sustains a compensatable loss (e.g., of earnings or of the type of psychological injury which sounds in damages), those damages will be recoverable over and above the value of the lost original claim.

The successful plaintiff is entitled to an indemnity against future liabilities to third parties arising out of his solicitor's negligence. This may be by way of a declaration of liability for an indemnity as in *Transportation Agency Ltd* v. *Jenkins*[165] or by deferring final assessment of damages in the negligence action until the rights of third parties against the client have been quantified.

## 11.3 Liability under the criminal law

A client who is convicted of an offence as a result of a solicitor's negligence can, in addition to any other damages, recover the penalties imposed by the criminal court. In addition, in *McLeish* v. *Amoo Gottfried & Co*[166] it was decided that breach of an implied term in the retainer agreement to ensure the peace of mind of the client entitled the defendant in criminal proceedings to damages for distress arising out of the damage to his reputation caused by the negligence of his solicitor leading to his criminal conviction. Negligence was admitted. The solicitors had failed to interview potential witnesses, proof them and ensure that they attended trial. Counsel was not briefed until the morning of the trial. He was inexperienced and made a series of errors in the conduct of the case. Damages for loss of reputation could not be recovered as a separate head of damage but, insofar as any loss of any reputation was an integral part of the client's mental distress, it was a matter that could properly be taken into account. Quantification of damages is clearly difficult since there is no possibility of settling criminal proceedings so that in theory damages should be on an all or nothing basis.

Scott Baker J said[167]:

"Mr Goodman for the plaintiff contends that, subject to the normal rules of remoteness and mitigation, damages for distress may form part of an award in cases of professional negligence, irrespective of whether the plaintiff chooses to frame his case in contract or tort. Whilst mental distress is not in itself sufficient damage to ground an action in tort, Mr Doggett for the defendants accepts that the plaintiff is entitled to damages in contract under this head and refers me to the judgment of Bingham LJ in *Watts* v. *Morrow* [1991] 4 All ER 937 at 959, where he says:

'A contract-breaker is not in general liable for any distress, frustration, anxiety,

164. (Unreported) 1979.
165. (1972) 223 E.G. 1101.
166. 26 July 1993, Q.B.D. (Scott Baker J), reported in *Professional Negligence* (1994), vol. 10, No. 3.
167. *Ibid.* at pp. 103–104.

displeasure, vexation, tension or aggravation which his breach of contract may cause to the innocent party. This rule is not, I think, founded on the assumption that such reactions are not foreseeable, which they surely are or may be, but on considerations of policy.

But the rule is not absolute. Where the very object of a contract is to provide pleasure, relaxation, peace of mind or freedom from molestation, damages will be awarded if the fruit of the contract is not provided or if the contrary result is procured instead. If the law did not cater for this exceptional category of case it would be defective. A contract to survey the condition of a house for a prospective purchaser does not, however, fall within this exceptional category.

In cases not falling within this exceptional category, damages are in my view recoverable for physical inconvenience and discomfort caused by the breach and mental suffering directly related to that inconvenience and discomfort. If those effects are foreseeably suffered during a period when defects are prepared I am prepared to accept that they sound in damages even though the cost of the repairs is not recoverable as such. But I also agree that awards should be restrained, and that the awards in this case far exceeded a reasonable award for the injury shown to have been suffered.'

The very essence of the contract to act for the plaintiff in preparation for and at his trial was to ensure his peace of mind by taking all appropriate steps to secure his acquittal, if possible, and if not, to make the best possible case for him. I have no doubt it was foreseeable that he would suffer mental distress if the defendants conducted the preparations and trial negligently.

Whilst I am satisfied that damages for loss of reputation cannot be recovered in this case as a separate head of damage, it seems to me that where a plaintiff is wrongly convicted as a consequence of his solicitor's negligence it is very difficult to draw a clear line between mental distress on the one hand and loss of reputation on the other. Insofar as any loss of reputation is an integral part of the plaintiff's mental distress, I think that it is a matter that can properly be taken into account. If the vicar's wife is, through her solicitor's negligence, wrongfully convicted of shoplifting and her mental anguish is increased by what she believes the parishioners think of her, I cannot see why that does not enhance her damages. Mental distress that sounds in damages comes in different forms in different categories of case and it is necessary to look at the nature of the particular distress for which the plaintiff is to be compensated.

There are no remotely similar cases in the reports. I have to do my best to put into terms of money something that cannot truly be quantified in financial terms. I regard awards in libel cases as irrelevant. I have been referred to the case of *Dickinson* v. *Jones Alexander & Co*, a decision of Douglas Brown J reported in *Professional Negligence* for December 1990, at p. 205. In that case he made an award on 16 October 1989 of £5,000 for mental distress suffered by a woman whose solicitors in matrimonial proceedings failed to obtain proper financial relief. They knew she was suffering from ill-health as a consequence of matrimonial pressures and the sum included the figure of £1,000 for failing to remove the husband from the matrimonial home.

In my judgment, the appropriate figure for general damages in the present case is £6,000 with the agreed special damage of £250. The total award, therefore, is £6,250, and there will be judgment accordingly."

## 11.4 Reduction of value of property

If the value of a property acquired by a client is diminished by a solicitor's negligence, the measure of damages will be the difference between the price paid by the client and the actual value of the property, both calculated as on the date of purchase. This method of valuation is familiar to the courts from negligence actions against surveyors. It was, however, said by Bingham LJ in *County Personnel (Employment Agency) Ltd* v. *Alan R Pulver & Co*[168]:

168. [1987] 1 W.L.R. 916.

"That is not, however, an invariable approach, at least in claims against solicitors, and should not be mechanistically applied in circumstances where it may appear inappropriate."

In some cases plaintiffs have been compensated for loss of use of the property where the intended use has been made known to the solicitor before the purchase: *King* v. *Hawkins & Co.*[169]

The difference between price paid and market value is not always the determinant. In *ComputaStaff Ltd* v. *Ingledew Brown Bennison & Garrett*[170] the solicitors mis-informed the client of the rateable value of office premises. The solicitors sought to avoid liability on the basis that the premises which the client had in fact acquired represented good value for the rates payable. This was unsuccessful on the basis that, if it had known of the error, the client would not have proceeded to take the lease as it could have acquired other premises at the rateable value for which it wished to be liable.

If the negligent error by the solicitors affects the client's business, that loss (as well as the difference in value) will sound in damages: *Simple Simon Catering Ltd* v. *Binstock Miller & Co.*[171]

In the case of *Murray* v. *Lloyd*[172] the client was unable to obtain a statutory tenancy of a property on the expiry of a lease since her solicitor had negligently advised her to take the tenancy in the name of a company. There was evidence that the value of a statutory tenancy was one-quarter of the vacant possession value of the property and she was compensated on that basis. The principle that the object of an award of damages was to put the injured party in the same position as he would have been if he had not suffered the wrong meant that the proper measure of damages was the cost of putting her in that position by paying to acquire what she had lost.

## 11.5 Failure to acquire a property

The measure of damages here is *prima facie* the difference between the true value of the property and the price which the purchaser would have paid for it but for the negligence of the solicitor. Clearly, a purchaser who is prevented by a solicitor's negligence from acquiring a property at an excessive price will recover only nominal damages.

In a "ransom" situation, where a purchaser is unable owing to a solicitor's negligence to complete a purchase of property but is able to purchase it later, he or she can recover the difference between the total cost of purchasing it at the later date and the total cost for which it could have been purchased on the first occasion: *Simpson* v. *Grove Tompkins & Co.*[173]

If the loss of property cannot be precisely valued the court simply has to do its best to award a fair figure: *Bryant* v. *Goodrich.*[174]

---

169. (1982) *The Times*, 28 January.
170. (1983) 268 E.G. 906.
171. [1958] 1 W.L.R. 563.
172. [1989] 1 W.L.R. 1060.
173. (1982) *The Times*, 17 May.
174. (1966) 110 S.J. 108.

## 11.6 Business tenancies

The Solicitors Indemnity Fund confirms that missing deadlines imposed by the Landlord and Tenant Act 1954, Part II is a very common source of claims for negligence.

A client who fails entirely owing to a solicitor's negligence to obtain a new tenancy is entitled to the value of the tenancy foregone. If a client has to take a tenancy on less advantageous terms because of the solicitor's negligence the measure of damages will be the difference between the value of the tenancy which he or she could have obtained (but for the negligence) and that of the tenancy actually obtained. Valuation of tenancies will be a matter for expert valuation evidence.

## 11.7 Solicitors' costs

The client is entitled to recover any costs paid to a solicitor if the services provided in return for those costs have no value (or perhaps a disproportionately small value).

In addition, other expenditure simply wasted by the client as result of the solicitor's negligence is recoverable in addition to legal costs as is the cost, if ascertainable, of putting right the mistake.

## 11.8 Wasted Costs Orders

There has always been provision for solicitors to bear (or pay to the client or opponent) costs incurred as a consequence of the solicitors' misconduct.

Until the introduction of R.S.C., Ord. 62, r. 11 in 1986 the provision (the former Ord. 62, r. 8) reflected the inherent jurisdiction of the court which was thought to be limited to make orders of this type only in cases of serious misconduct going beyond mere negligence.

Order 62, r. 11 introduced the test that "costs have been incurred unreasonably or improperly in any proceedings or have been wasted by failure to conduct proceedings with reasonable competence and expedition".

There were conflicting decisions of the Court of Appeal on the question whether the words of the rule should be given their normal simple English meaning or whether they were intended to enshrine the previous law.

The question became academic on 1 October 1991 when section 4 of the Courts and Legal Services Act 1990 introduced new provisions as follows:

"(6) In any proceedings mentioned in the sub-section (1), the court may disallow or (as the case may be) order the legal or other representative concerned to meet, the whole of any wasted costs or such part of them as may be determined in accordance with rules of court.

(7) In subsection (6) 'wasted costs' means any costs incurred by a party—

    (a) as a result of any improper, unreasonable or negligent act or omission on the part of any legal or other representative or any employee of such a representative; or

    (b) which, in the light of any such act or omission occurring after they were incurred, the court considers it is unreasonable to expect that party to pay."

These changes are incorporated in a new R.S.C., Ord. 62, r. 11 and in relation to the criminal courts.

The new jurisdiction has provoked a welter of applications and threatened applications for wasted costs orders.

Guidance was finally given by the Court of Appeal in *Ridehalgh* v. *Horsefield*.[175]

In that case the Court of Appeal allowed appeals from solicitor and counsel who had either been ordered to pay or to show cause why they should not pay the costs of their opponents.

The case established that a solicitor or barrister may be ordered to bear another party's costs in two circumstances:

    (1) where proceedings are launched, defended or carried on without the authority of the client;

    (2) where costs flow from any improper unreasonable or negligent act or omission on the part of that solicitor or barrister.

The first ground is surely an extension of the principle of breach of the implied warranty of authority. It is the second ground where the decision is of interest on the interpretation of the 1990 Act.

The court attempted to explain the use in the statute of three adjectives (improper, unreasonable and negligent). No acute differentiation between them was either useful or necessary or intended by Parliament.

"Improper" included conduct which would:

"ordinarily justify disbarment, striking off, suspension from practice or other serious professional penalty as well as any significant breach of a substantial duty imposed by a relevant code of professional conduct and also conduct which would be regarded as improper according to the consensus of professional (including judicial) opinion ... whether or not it violates the letter of a professional code."

"Unreasonable", on the other hand, meant "vexatious, designed to harass the other side rather than advance the resolution of the case" but did not necessarily entail an inevitably unsuccessful result or a result which could have been avoided by a more cautious approach. Was there a reasonable explanation for the actual conduct of the practitioner?

"Negligent" had the ordinary meaning discussed at length in this chapter: that is failure to achieve the competence reasonably to be expected of ordinary members of the profession. Whilst it is clear that "improper" has its own meaning, common lawyers will probably find difficulty in envisaging negligent conduct which is not also unreasonable.

That part of the definition of "improper" which uses the consensus of professional (including judicial) opinion as its yardstick may be thought to be similar to the *Bolam* test in relation to medical negligence referred to above. Is the "consensus" of all solicitors (or barristers), those practising as advocates, those practising in the same field or of all right-thinking professionals generally? The argument in favour of simplicity suggests that it is the consensus of solicitors generally (since they are governed by the same rules and regulations), but this is little more than speculation.

The Court of Appeal went on to point out the particular position of those acting for legally aided clients, that the doctrine of immunity of an advocate did not apply (although the particular pressures on an advocate would be taken into account), that it was essential to demonstrate a causal link between the conduct complained of and the actual waste of costs and that in the normal way the party aggrieved rather than

---

175. [1994] 3 All E.R. 848, C.A.

the court should make the application which should be left until after the end of the trial. The procedure for disposing of the application should be short and fair and not give rise to full-blown derivative litigation.

In a recent case following *Ridehalgh (C v. C (Wasted Costs Order))*[176] Ewbank J described the relevant solicitors advice as "fanciful and unreasonable" and as the "precursor" (note—rather than (as in *Ridehalgh*) the cause) of the waste of costs.

In two other cases, *Re A Minor (Wasted Costs Application)*[177] and *Turner* v. *Plasplagus Ltd*[178] the judges hearing the applications concluded that the behaviour of the solicitor had not amounted to negligence.

In the first case the action complained of was the making of an application to discharge a care order which stood very little chance of success. In the second there was failure to advise further searches in relation to a patent application. The searches in question were unusual, very expensive and their accuracy was by no means guaranteed.

The court laid particular emphasis on the necessity of demonstrating a causal link between the conduct complained of and the costs wasted.

Threats of applications for wasted cost orders have been a relatively common weapon used by litigators. The case of *Orchard* v. *South Eastern Electricity Board*[179] (under the previous regime) condemns the practice. The Court of Appeal in *Ridehalgh* was prepared to countenance such a threat by advisers who genuinely believed that the necessary criteria for the award of wasted costs had been complied with.

## 11.9 Conflict of interest

We have already seen in section 5.2 that there is no general duty of care by a solicitor to the opponent of his client.

The position, however, frequently arises where a solicitor acts for more than one party, e.g., a borrower and a lender. Where the interests of those two clients are not entirely in harmony, fulfilment of the duty to one is bound to lead to a breach of the duty to act in the best interests of the other.

This was first briefly considered by the Court of Appeal in *Wills* v. *Wood*[180] where one client of a solicitor had made a loan to another. The court decided that this may not be objectionable, if the terms of the loan and all other matters were entirely agreed before the solicitors were instructed but, where one client sought advice on the terms of the loan or other matters (which would of necessity involve a potential conflict, if not breach) "the solicitors were exposing themselves to the risk of criticism".

176. [1994] 2 F.L.R. 34.
177. [1994] 2 F.L.R. 842.
178. (Unreported) 5 May 1995, Patents County Court. In *Tolstoy Miloslavasky* v. *Aldington* (1995) *The Times*, 27 December, the Court of Appeal decided that acting pro bono should not of itself expose a solicitor to a wasted costs order although one would be made in this case since the solicitor should have realised that his client's case was hopeless and no reasonable solicitor would have instituted proceedings. In *Re A Solicitor (Wasted Costs Order)* [1996] 1 F.L.R. 40, a solicitor who issued a witness summons against a local authority on behalf of a defendant on a charge of alleged sexual abuse was ordered to pay the costs of the authority.
179. [1987] 2 Q.B. 565.
180. (1984) *The Times*, 24 March.

Solicitors were held negligent when sued by a building society in *Anglia, Hastings & Thanet* v. *House & Son*[181] for failure to inform the building society that they had reason to doubt the good faith of their borrower client.

The Privy Council considered the question in *Clark Boyce* v. *Mouat*.[182] The plaintiff had agreed to charge her home to provide for her son's business. The son approached entirely new solicitors who warned the mother that she might lose her home if her son failed to make the repayments, and recommended that she should take independent advice before proceeding. She told the solicitors that she realised the consequences of default by her son and that she did not want any further advice. Inevitably, the son went bankrupt leaving his mother with a large debt.

The Privy Council rejected the allegation that the defendants were under a contractual duty to the plaintiff to ensure that she did actually receive independent advice or to refuse to act for both her and her son, if she would not take it. It also dismissed allegations of breach of fiduciary duty in relation to some minor matters of fact.

There is no general rule of law to the effect that a solicitor should never act for both parties in a transaction where their interests may conflict. The Board stated that it is acceptable for solicitors to act for parties whose interests conflict provided they all give their informed consent and the solicitor can in fact properly carry out his instructions from all his clients irrespective of the conflict. Informed consent was defined as:

"consent given in the knowledge that there is a conflict between the parties and that as a result the solicitor may be disabled from disclosing to each party the full knowledge which he possesses as to the transaction or may be disabled from giving advice to one party which conflicts with the interests of the other."

In determining whether a solicitor has obtained informed consent it is essential to determine precisely what services are required of him by the parties. In this case the defendant was instructed simply to explain the legal implications of the mortgage and to perfect it: he had no role in providing advice to the plaintiff. If the duty of disclosure to the lender applied (as it did in the *Anglia* case) the defendant here could not have fulfilled it. The Privy Council observed that the overriding legal rule was that a solicitor must be able to act fairly and adequately for all his clients and, if he cannot, must decline to act[183]:

"When a client in full command of his faculties and apparently aware of what he is doing seeks the assistance of a solicitor in the carrying out of a particular transaction, that solicitor is under no duty whether before or after accepting instructions to go beyond those instructions by proffering unsought advice on the wisdom of the transaction. To hold otherwise could impose intolerable burdens on solicitors."

In *Perry* v. *Edwin Co (a firm)*,[184] the court decided that a solicitor engaged to act on behalf of joint clients, one of whom was not contractually bound to pay the solicitor,

---

181.  (1981) 260 E.G. 1128.
182.  [1993] 4 All E.R. 268.
183.  *Ibid.* at 275b *per* Lord Jauncey.
184.  (1994) *The Independent*, 1 April, and see *Halifax Mortgage Services Ltd* v. *Stepsky and Another*, 24 November 1995, C.A.

was in serious breach of duty when he withheld information from that client and acted on instruction from one to the detriment of the first.

The matter has recently come before the Court of Appeal in *Mortgage Express Ltd v. Bowerman & Partners.*[185] The court decided that in circumstances where a solicitor acts for both borrower and lender in a domestic conveyancing transaction, although the implied duty of the solicitor extends beyond reporting on matters of title to the lender, it extends only to disclosing information which might have a material bearing on the potential security given to the lender or its decision whether or not to advance the loan. If the information concerned is confidential to the borrower, the solicitor must either obtain the consent of the borrower to disclose it to the lender, or decline to act for the lender or for both parties.

At first instance the trial judge held that the duty of a solicitor is to protect the respective interests of his clients when carrying out their instructions, reporting all relevant information to the lender and any information which puts him on inquiry as to the accuracy of the valuation obtained by the lender.

The Court of Appeal upheld the result on narrower grounds as set out above. Information containing the sale price and the existence of a sub-sale could not be said to be confidential to the borrower and was of equal importance to both borrower and lender. It was not the duty of the solicitor to comment on the valuation report, but the solicitor should disclose information which might cause the lender to doubt the accuracy of the valuation, if it came into his possession.

The problems raised by this doctrine in practice are likely to increase as instructions from lenders to solicitors become more detailed and exacting.

The other area where conflict of interest is of relevance relates to the question whether a firm of solicitors who has acted for a former client could thereafter act for another client against the former client.

This was considered in *Re a Firm of Solicitors*[186] where the Court of Appeal decided that there was no such general rule, but the firm of solicitors would not be permitted to act for an existing client against a former client if a reasonable man with knowledge of the facts would reasonably anticipate that there was a danger that information gained while acting for the former client would be used against him or there was some degree of likelihood of mischief. Parker LJ said[187]:

"In my judgment any reasonable man with knowledge of the facts, in the present case, including the proposals for a 'Chinese Wall' would consider that some confidential information might permeate the wall and would indeed regard it as astonishing that the plaintiff should be faced with solicitors on the other side to whom, over a considerable period, they had forwarded much confidential information concerning matters being investigated in the main action."

The court followed the provisions of The Law Society's Guide to the Professional Conduct of Solicitors (1990) which provided in paragraph 11.02:

"If a solicitor or a firm of solicitors has acquired relevant knowledge concerning a former client during the course of acting for him, he or it must not accept instructions to act against him."

---

185. (1995) *The Times*, 1 August.
186. [1992] 1 All E.R. 353.
187. *Ibid.* at 359f.

The court decided by a majority that it was only in exceptional cases that a Chinese Wall would be a satisfactory barrier against the risk of conflict.

The question came before the Court of Appeal again in *Re a Firm of Solicitors*.[188] In that case a partner in the intellectual property department of firm A acted for certain plaintiffs. A partner in that department left firm A and joined firm B. Two and a half years later the defendants in the same action approached firm B to act for them. The partner had not, whilst a partner in firm A, acted for the plaintiffs or been involved in their matters. The plaintiffs applied to the Chancery Division to stop firm B acting for the defendants. Firm B contended that the burden of proof was on the plaintiffs on the balance of probabilities to show that the partner possessed relevant confidential information and in particular that communication of that information to him had taken place. The plaintiffs' contention was that they only had to show that there was a real risk that such confidential information had been communicated.

The decision of the court was that the contract of retainer created a close fiduciary relationship between the client and solicitors and each partner in the firm and therefore the burden was on any person who was a partner in a firm which was retained while he occupied that position and which in the course of such retainer became possessed of confidential information to establish that there was no risk of his misusing confidential information before he could thereafter act against that client. The solicitor had to show that there was no reasonable prospect of any conflict between his duty to his previous client and his personal interest in obtaining the new retainer and his duty to the new client and accordingly not merely that he was not in possession of any relevant confidential information, that there was no real risk that he had such information. On the facts there was no real risk that the solicitor would be in possession of any confidential relevant or recallable information and therefore firm B was permitted to act for the defendant.

The judge reflected that the law needed to balance the interest of a client to the fullest confidence in his solicitor (including non-disclosure of information) against freedom of choice of solicitor for others. The basis of intervention by the court is not a possible perception of impropriety: it is the protection of confidential information which is entitled to special protection given the special importance for the relationship of confidence between solicitor and client. Only information which is confidential and relevant is entitled to protection and it is for the plaintiff to show that this is the case.

## 11.10  Regulation of the profession

The consolidating Solicitors Act 1974 is the principal measure governing the profession.

In order to be qualified to act as a solicitor, a person must:

(1)  have been admitted as such (section 88(1));
(2)  have his or her name on the Roll of Solicitors at the time in question (section 88(2));
(3)  have in force a practising certificate issued by the Law Society.

---

188. [1995] 3 All E.R. 482. See also in relation to information belonging to an opponent innocently but wrongly coming into a solicitor's hands: *Ablitt* v. *Mills of Reeve*, Blackburne J (unreported) 24 October 1995.

Under the Courts and Legal Services Act 1990, section 89(9) The Law Society must also keep a register of foreign lawyers who are entitled to enter into partnerships (known as multi-national partnerships) whose members consist of one or more foreign lawyers registered under section 89 or incorporated practices formed under the Administration of Justice Act 1985, section 9 of, and Schedule 18, paragraph 54(3) to, the Courts and Legal Services Act 1990.

A foreign lawyer who wishes to be registered for this purpose must apply to the Society for registration in accordance with specified requirements. The powers of the Society to make rules and to regulate the solicitors' profession extends to the regulation of foreign lawyers, including its power of intervention, maintenance of a compensation fund, requirement of accountants' reports and the jurisdiction of the Solicitors Disciplinary Tribunal.[189]

The Law Society, in addition to its regulatory role, is also a members organisation incorporated under Royal Charter in 1845. Any person whose name is on the Roll of Solicitors (whether or not holding a practising certificate) may be elected by the Council of The Law Society into membership. Membership is voluntary.

The President, Vice President and Deputy Vice President of the Society are elected annually by the membership. 1995 saw the first contested election in living memory: the practice before had been for the Council to propose for election unopposed a Deputy Vice President who would in succeeding years become the Vice President and then the President. The effects of the election of the current President and Vice President on a "populist" platform have yet to be seen.

Under the Solicitors Act the Society is required to keep up to date the Roll of Solicitors and the Practising Certificate Register.

Under sections 32–34 of the Act the Council of The Law Society must, with the concurrence of the Master of the Rolls, make rules in relation to solicitors keeping accounts with banks or building societies for clients' money and for the keeping of accounts of the money received or held or paid by them for or on account of their clients; a similar obligation in relation to money comprised in controlled trusts and in relation to monies to be kept on deposit for the benefit of clients or the payment to clients of an appropriate sum by way of interest forgone, if such monies are not placed on deposit for the benefit of the client.

The Council must also make rules in relation to the provision to the Society on an annual basis of accountants' reports showing an examination of the solicitor's accounts material and satisfaction (or lack of it) of compliance with the Solicitors' Accounts rules.

The obligation in relation to indemnity insurance is considered in pp. 598–601.

The Council has an additional power to make any rules approved by the Master of the Rolls in relation to the professional practice, conduct and discipline of solicitors and in relation to the education and training of those seeking admission or to practise as solicitors.

The Law Society must under section 36(1) of the Act maintain and administer a Compensation Fund out of which the Council may make grants to relieve loss or hardship suffered in consequence of dishonesty on the part of a solicitor or the employee of a solicitor in connection with that solicitor's practice or purported

---

189. See pp. 593–594 below.

practice (section 36(2)(a)) or in consequence of a failure on the part of a solicitor to account for money which has come into his hands in connection with his practice or purported practice (section 36(2)(b)).[189a]

A payment may also be made to a solicitor who has suffered or is likely to suffer loss or hardship by reason of his liability to any of his or his firm's clients in consequence of some act or default of any of his partners or employees in circumstances where but for the liability of that solicitor a grant might have been made out of the Compensation Fund to some other person (section 36(2)(c)). Such latter grant may be made by way of loan including terms and conditions as to repayment, interest and security (section 36(3)).

Under section 36(4) in relation to any outright grant or to a loan whose repayment has been waived or in respect of which the borrower has defaulted, The Law Society is subrogated to the rights of the person to whom the grant was made and is entitled, having given a sufficient indemnity, to require that person to sue on behalf of the Society to recover the monies laid out by the Society from the Fund.

The case of *R* v. *The Law Society, ex parte Reigate Projects Ltd*[190] established that the Society is entitled to adopt a policy to exclude compensation for consequential loss under section 36(2)(a).

An application for compensation from the Fund must be made within six months of the applicant becoming aware of the loss or potential loss.

The Compensation Fund is now administered by the Solicitors Complaints Bureau which in 1994 received 2,298 applications, a rise of 28.4 per cent on 1993. The Bureau's 1994 report shows that the value of applications was £4,969,000 in 1993 (it seems that the figure for 1994 is not yet available) which is somewhat lower than the 1992 record.

Under section 35 of the Act the Society has powers to intervene in a solicitor's practice in specified circumstances including suspected dishonesty, breach of Accounts Rules, bankruptcy, being struck off the Roll or suspended from practice or undue and unexplained delay in dealing with a client matter.

These powers are now also exercised on behalf of the Society by the Solicitors Complaints Bureau which in 1994 intervened in 192 solicitors' practices, a considerable increase from the total of 85 in 1993 and (although there is some doubt whether the figures are truly comparable) the figure of 49 in 1988.

Under the Training Regulations 1990 a person before qualifying as a solicitor must have taken either a qualifying law degree or the Common Professional Examination and the Legal Practice Course.

Under the Training Regulations articles of clerkship have been replaced by training contracts of two years' duration. A professional skills course must be passed during the course of the training contract in order to ensure admission as a solicitor.

Requirements for continuing professional education have been introduced, and are being gradually extended to those admitted in less recent years and will be universal requirements as from 1 November 1998.

---

189a. The practice of the Law Society to exercise its discretion to make payments only in cases where the defaulting solicitor has not himself received any benefit is being tested in Judicial Review proceedings brought by Mortgage Express Ltd and Alliance & Leicester Building Society: *Law Society Gazette*, vol. 93/04, 31 January 1996, p. 1.
190. [1992] 3 All E.R. 232, D.C.

Sections 19 and 20 of the Courts and Legal Services Act 1990 and Schedules 1 and 2 established the Lord Chancellor's Advisory Committee on Legal Education and Conduct. The Committee has a chair and 16 members of whom nine must be neither judges, barristers, solicitors nor law teachers!

The general duty of the Committee is to assist in the maintenance and development of standards for the education, training and conduct of those offering legal services, to review continuing education, training and the academic and practical training necessary to ensure effective exercise of rights of audience and rights to conduct litigation.

Subject to passing the necessary examinations, satisfactory completion of the training contract and prior enrolment with The Law Society a person is entitled to be admitted a solicitor on application with the prescribed fee, but The Law Society is able to object and the Master of the Rolls will hear any objection.

Any change of name by any solicitor requires amendment of the roll. No barrister can be admitted solicitor without first being disbarred. A solicitor is not qualified to act as such unless in possession of a practising certificate issued by The Law Society. A person without a practising certificate cannot recover any costs in respect of any action or matter in which he or she has acted.

Under section 10 of the Act the Society must issue a practising certificate within 21 days of receipt of an application provided it is satisfied that the solicitor's name is on the Roll, he is not suspended from practice, he has delivered a duly completed application in the prescribed form, he is complying with such training regulations as may apply to him, he is complying with or is exempt from compliance with any indemnity rules and he has paid to the Society his annual contribution to the Compensation Fund and any special levy in addition thereto.

Section 12(1) of the Act specifies 12 circumstances in which the Society has a discretion whether to grant the practising certificate. These are principally concerned with first applications, return to practice after a gap, disciplinary or financial defaults, illness, imprisonment or insolvency.

In these cases six weeks' notice of the application is required and the Society may issue a certificate subject to conditions and there is a right for the applicant to appeal.

Where a certificate is refused, there is an appeal to the Master of the Rolls who has complete freedom of action in respect of the appeal.

## 11.11 Solicitors Complaints Bureau

In 1986 The Law Society established an independent Solicitors Complaints Bureau to delegate to it its powers under the Solicitors Act. This was partly a response to severe and prolonged criticism arising from its failure to take disciplinary proceedings against one of its own Council members in respect of spectacular over-charging so that the complainant was forced to issue a motion in the Chancery Division of the High Court to obtain redress.

We have seen that the Bureau has responsibility for interventions into solicitors' practices and for the administration of the Compensation Fund. It is also charged with the investigation of regulatory breaches and complaints of inadequate professional service and of misconduct, forensic inspection of solicitors' accounts, the imposition and removal of restrictions on practising certificates and prosecution in the independent Solicitors Disciplinary Tribunal. Membership of the committees of the Bureau appears to be equally divided between lay members and solicitors, some of whom are members of The Law Society Council. Complaints regarding inadequate professional service are always dealt with by a committee whose majority is of lay members.

The 1994 report of the Bureau shows that approximately 20,000 complaints were received. Apparently more than 50 per cent of complaints of inadequate professional service resulted from non-compliance with The Law Society's professional standards and/or lack of information about costs. Three-quarters of complaints are dealt with through mediation.

The Bureau received approximately 6,300 new matters in 1994 relating to its functions other than complaints about professional service.

Sanctions which can be imposed by the Bureau for inadequate professional services include:

(a) a determination of the costs to which the solicitor is entitled, coupled with a requirement to refund the whole or part of any amount already paid by the client or a requirement to remit the whole or part of those costs or a requirement to waive, in whole or in part, the right to recover those costs;

(b) a direction to the solicitor to secure the rectification at the expense of the solicitor or his firm of any specified error, omission or other deficiency arising in connection with the matter;

(c) a direction to pay specified compensation to the client;

(d) a direction to take such an action in the interest of the client at the solicitor's expense as it may specify.

There is power in connection with the investigation of any complaint of professional misconduct or in relation to the quality of professional services provided to require the solicitor to produce files relevant to the complaint for inspection.

In its annual report for 1994 the Bureau considers that 75 per cent of complaints received fall into the category of "shoddy work" rather than misconduct and specifically cites delay, poor communication, failure to explain and unresponsiveness to clients' needs. Forty-three per cent of complaints were referred back to firms for resolution under Practice Rule 15. Thirteen per cent were sent back to the Bureau unsolved by this means. The Bureau sees as its goal effective dispute resolution through conciliation and mediation rather than apportionment of blame.

From 1 August 1995 a new procedure has been introduced. Every complaint received by the Bureau will be sent back to the firm concerned. The firm will be given six weeks to resolve the dispute. The firm will be encouraged and supported in using its own Complaints Procedure under Practice Rule 15. Failure on the part of the solicitor to comply with the Rule will be formally investigated. A reasonable response by the firm to the complainant which fails to resolve the complaint will be very likely to lead the Bureau to decide to take no further action. The President of the Law Society for 1995/96 has announced his wish to abolish the Bureau and revert to the position where unresolved complaints are adjudicated upon by the Law Society itself. It was announced in March 1996 that the Bureau is to be replaced in September by an Office for the Supervision of Solicitors. This will comprise a client relations committee with a lay majority and a lay chairman, and a professional regulation committee. The Office will be independent and its director will be accountable to the Secretary General of the Law Society.

## 11.12 Solicitors Disciplinary Tribunal

The proceedings of this Tribunal are governed by the Solicitors (Disciplinary Proceedings) Rules 1994.[191]

The Tribunal is composed of both lay and solicitor members all of whom are appointed by the Master of the Rolls.

Grounds for disciplinary proceedings are divided into statutory and non-statutory grounds. The statutory grounds are:

(1) material false statement in an application for practising certificate;
(2) false statement in relation to change of place or business;
(3) failure to comply with the Solicitors Practice Rules 1990 or the Solicitors Accounts Rules;
(4) failure to comply with rules relating to accountants' reports;
(5) employment or remuneration of a solicitor who is struck off or suspended from practising;
(6) knowingly contravening an order in respect of, or conditions relating to, the employment of a solicitor's clerk;
(7) failure to comply with regulations relating to training contracts or a defect in admission or enrolment procedure;
(8) being guilty of corrupt practice in connection with a parliamentary or local election.

These are mainly technical grounds and in respect of them The Law Society brings the complaint.

A complaint may be made on non-statutory grounds by any person. The conventional complaint is that the solicitor has been guilty of conduct unbecoming a solicitor.

Conviction of a serious criminal offence is generally accepted as unbecoming conduct. The offence need not be one of dishonesty: it may be one of violence or a sexual offence. It need not be committed by the solicitor in connection with his practice, if it brings discredit on the profession generally.

Unbefitting conduct in relation to the court or to legal aid or to The Law Society itself may suffice.

Two further categories of unbecoming conduct are unbefitting conduct in relation to practice (for example, a solicitor practising without a practising certificate or whilst suspended or breach of conditions attached to a practising certificate, or failing properly to organise his office) and in relation to clients (for example continuing to act where a conflict of interest had been established, misleading the client, taking advantage of the client's ignorance, abusing a power of attorney or making arrangements adverse to the interest of the client). There may also be unbefitting

---

191. S.I. 1994/288.

conduct in relation to persons other than clients (for example, other solicitors, counsel, a bank etc).

An application is made to the Tribunal by The Law Society or other complainant supported by affidavit evidence. A quorum is three, provided one lay member is present and solicitor members outnumber lay members. Decisions are published and filed with The Law Society. The hearings are held in public but a party may apply on notice for a hearing in private.

If the Tribunal finds the complaint proved it may order:

(1) the solicitor to be struck off;
(2) the solicitor to be suspended from practice for a set period;
(3) payment of a penalty of up to £5,000 to the Treasury;
(4) restoration to the Roll of a solicitor previously struck off,

and in any case may make provision for the costs of the application.

The Tribunal may refer the application at any stage to The Law Society or to the Adjudication and Appeals Committee of the Solicitors Complaints Bureau. Presumably this will be rare in practice since it is, of course, the Complaints Bureau which prosecutes most of the applications through the Disciplinary Tribunal and the Bureau will presumably have come to a conclusion as to the proper means by which the complaint should be dealt with.

There is an appeal from the Tribunal to the Divisional Court of the Queen's Bench Division by way of rehearing. No appeal lies from the determination of the High Court without leave of that Court or of the Court of Appeal.

An appeal against the decision on an application by a former solicitor to be restored to the Roll or for the revocation of an order restricting the employment of a solicitor's clerk lies to the Master of the Rolls only.

If the High Court orders a solicitor to be struck off the Roll, there is an appeal without leave to the Court of Appeal.

In 1994 the Bureau resolved to commence disciplinary proceedings in 334 cases, an increase of 84 from the total for 1993. During 1994 the Tribunal reached decisions in 211 matters referred by the Bureau which resulted in 129 solicitors being struck off or indefinitely suspended.

## 11.13  Legal Services Ombudsman

The Lord Chancellor may under section 21 of the Courts and Legal Services Act 1990 appoint a Legal Services Ombudsman for a renewable term of not more than three years. The functions of the office are to investigate any allegation properly made relating to the manner in which a complaint made to a professional body concerning an authorised advocate, authorised litigator (these two categories including solicitors), licensed conveyancer, registered foreign lawyer, recognised body or notary public has been dealt with by his or her professional body (section 22(1)).

The investigation cannot take place while the complaint is being investigated by the professional body concerned or an appeal therefrom is pending (section 22(5)). The Ombudsman cannot investigate any issue which is being or has been determined by a court, the Solicitors Disciplinary Tribunal or any tribunal specified by the Lord Chancellor by Order (section 22(7)).

On completing an investigation, the Ombudsman may under section 23 send a written report of his conclusions to the complainant, the person about whom the complaint was made, any other person affected by recommendation and the professional body concerned.

The recommendation may be:

(a) that the relevant professional body reconsider the complaint;
(b) that it or any other relevant disciplinary body should consider exercising its powers in relation to the person complained about;
(c) that that person pay compensation of a specified amount to the complainant for loss, inconvenience or distress suffered as a result of the matter of complaint;
(d) that the relevant professional body pay compensation on the same basis arising out of the way in which that body handled the complaint;
(e) that the professional body which is the object of the recommendation should make a separate payment to compensate the complainant for the cost of making the allegation.

If the person fails to comply with the recommendation, he must publicise the failure and the reasons for it. The Ombudsman may alternatively publicise the failure to comply with the recommendation and recover the expenses so incurred. Publication of any report and publicity relating to failure to comply are absolutely privileged for defamation purposes.

The Ombudsman may make recommendations to any professional body about the arrangements which it has in force for the investigation of complaints concerning those over whom it has control. The professional body concerned must have regard to those recommendations. The Ombudsman may refer to the Lord Chancellor's Advisory Committee on Education and Conduct any matters which come to his notice which appear to be relevant to the functions of that committee (section 24).

## 11.14 Publicity

The Solicitors Practice Rules 1990 have substantially relaxed the rules relating to publicity of and by solicitors. The general principle is now that a solicitor must not do anything in the course of practising which compromises or impairs:

(a) his own independence or integrity;
(b) a person's freedom to instruct the solicitor of his choice;
(c) his duty to act in the best interest of his client;
(d) the good repute of himself or of his profession;
(e) his proper standard of work;
(f) his duty to the court (Rule 1).

Subject to these standards and the Solicitors Publicity Code 1990 a solicitor may publicise his practice at his discretion (Rule 2).

The remainder of these Practice Rules deal with the preservation by a solicitor of proper independence in the context of his relationship with other professionals and the introduction of work and potential conflict of interests.

The Solicitors Publicity Code 1990 permits advertising which is not in bad taste,

595

inaccurate or misleading, which complies with the general law and codes of advertising practice. A claim to specialisation must be justified, but publicity may not refer to a solicitor's success rate or make a direct comparison in relation to the charges or quality of service of any other identifiable solicitor.

The Code does not authorise any breach of any other practice rule or other professional obligation or requirement. A solicitor cannot delegate responsibility for publicity and must withdraw it forthwith on becoming aware of any impropriety in it.

The adequacy of this Code has been called into question by the practice of sensational advertisements suggesting free and easy recovery of damages in product liability or employers' liability cases. The position is apparently under review by The Law Society, but there are no present plans to change the Code. A Code relating to introduction and referral by solicitors was also introduced in 1990, non-compliance with or evasion or disregard of which may lead to a breach of the Solicitors Practice Rules and to unbecoming conduct.

## 11.15 Practice Management Standards

The Law Society intends in 1996 to introduce a voluntary system of certification of practice management standards (PMS).

These are devised specially for solicitors and are claimed to combine the systematic approach of ISO 9000 (the former BS5750) with what the Society describes as the "the people focus of Investors in People".

If a practice decides to seek PMS certification, it may seek it by itself from the Society or with ISO 9000 or with Investors in People.

The Society will issue these certificates but will use the existing ISO 9000 and Investors in People certification bodies to carry out the assessments.

The assessment will be preceded by a self-assessment checklist and a voluntary pre-certification audit.

The assessment itself will be carried out by means of:

(1) any available appropriate credit in particular areas, for example from approval by Investors in People, ISO 9000 or franchising;

(2) a certificate from the accountants of the practice that the practice complies with the financial information and time recording standards;

(3) a document check to see that appropriate procedures have been devised.

This will be combined with interviews with relevant personnel in the practice to check that procedures have been understood and implemented.

The first certificates will be issued in a block at the end of 1996.

## 11.16 Rights of audience

The Courts and Legal Services Act 1990, Part II sets out to develop advocacy, litigation, conveyancing and probate services by new and better means and to give a wider choice to clients whilst maintaining the proper and efficient administration of justice.

For the old rules is substituted the principle that the grant of a right of audience should be determined by reference only to whether the person concerned has been granted a right of audience for the proceedings by an authorised body. The advocate must be qualified in relation to educational and training requirements appropriate to the court and be a member of a professional or other body with an effective mechanism for enforcing proper rules of conduct. Refusal by that person to offer services on the ground that the nature of the case is objectionable to him or to any section of the public or that the conduct, appearance or beliefs of the prospective clients are unacceptable to him or to any section of the public or on any ground relating to the source of any financial support which may properly be given to the prospective client for the proceedings in question is precluded. The rules of conduct of that body must be appropriate in the interests of the proper and efficient administration of justice.

The Law Society has applied to the Lord Chancellor and been granted designation as an authorised body for the purposes of the Court and Legal Services Act 1990.

Accordingly, solicitors have rights of audience before a court where that right of audience has been granted by The Law Society.

The Society has established a qualification for solicitors as advocates in the higher criminal and civil courts. Those solicitors who have not obtained these qualifications are not allowed to practise in open court in the High Court except before the Official Referees, but in applications rather than trials or in emergency or informal and unopposed proceedings.[192]

The Lord Chancellor has in mid-1995 acknowledged that applications for appointment as Queen's Counsel from a solicitor will be entertained, although it is thought that it will be some years before any have had a chance to obtain the appropriate experience pursuant to their advocacy qualifications. Recently published figures show that a lower proportion of candidates achieve qualification in civil matters with each examination.

### 11.17 Solicitors as officers of the Supreme Court

In addition to professional regulations, solicitors are subject to the disciplinary jurisdiction of the Supreme Court of which they are officers. This jurisdiction is exercisable against a solicitor for his or her own acts and those of his or her employees. Action may be taken on the court's own motion pursuant to section 66(1) of, and Schedule 20 to, the Courts and Legal Services Act 1990 which prohibit a solicitor from acting as agent for any unqualified person (apart from those in multi-disciplinary and multi-national practices or in incorporated associations).

If any solicitor deliberately interferes with the administration of justice, he or she is guilty of a criminal contempt of court. A number of old cases give as examples defying a judge in open court, using improper language to the judge or the opponent or destruction of documents.

There is also a civil liability for contempt of court where a solicitor fails to perform an undertaking given as an officer of the court or fails without reasonable excuse to inform the client of an order against him, for example for discovery of documents.

An undertaking given by a solicitor acting professionally for a client may be enforced on application for committal in the county court or by motion in the

---

192. *Practice Direction* [1986] 2 All E.R. 226, which also permits a solicitor to read out a statement in open court to conclude an action for defamation.

Chancery Division of the High Court. An undertaking properly given by the solicitor binds the solicitor even after the death of the client, the client's instruction not to perform it or after notice that the client has changed his solicitor.

The case of *Udall* v. *Capri Lighting Ltd*[193] established that where the conduct of the solicitor was inexcusable, the court might make a compensatory order of a disciplinary nature. The seriousness of the court's reliance upon its officers was shown in *Rooks Rider* v. *Steel*,[194] where even the fraudulent intention of a client in entering into a transaction did not vitiate the undertaking in question or release the defendant solicitors who gave it from their obligations. Knox J said:

"In human terms one can well see that they may have regarded it as adding insult to injury to be required to pay the costs of the solicitors acting for a company engaged in fraud which, although unsuccessful, has cost their client dear, even though not as dear due to the plaintiffs' skill as it might have done."

Even so, the undertaking was enforceable since (1) the undertaking was given by them to the other solicitors direct and not to their client, (2) the dishonest client was not a party—the only parties were the two solicitors, and (3) the plaintiff firm was innocent of any complicity in their client's dishonesty and, being untainted with any dishonesty, were not vulnerable to any defence by the undertaking firm of illegality.

Undertakings which are enforceable may be given either in connection with litigation or non-contentious matters. They are equally enforceable when clearly given. A solicitor has a right of indemnity in respect of any loss sustained in the performance of an undertaking given with the authority and upon the instructions of the client. Experience shows this may be cold comfort.

Undertakings by licensed conveyancers are not treated in the same way.

## 11.18 Indemnity insurance

The modern regime for solicitors indemnity insurance began with the Solicitors Indemnity Rules 1987 made under section 37 of the Solicitors Act 1974 and section 9 of the Administration of Justice Act 1985 by the Council of The Law Society with the concurrence of the Master of the Rolls.

These Rules which have been renewed each year with amendments, form the bedrock of the current indemnity insurance arrangements.

The Society is authorised to establish and maintain a fund for the purpose of providing indemnity against loss in respect of annual indemnity periods beginning on 1 September in each year (beginning in 1987). The Rules apply to a practice carried on by solicitors, a multi-national partnership, a recognised body and a recognised body in partnership with one or more solicitors and/or one or more recognised bodies.

The fund is managed by Solicitors Indemnity Fund Limited ("SIF Ltd").

The indemnity covers present and former solicitors and registered foreign lawyers practising in partnership with solicitors, their employees, recognised bodies and

193. [1987] 3 All E.R. 262, C.A.
194. [1993] 4 All E.R. 716.

former recognised bodies and their officers and employees. The indemnity is against loss arising from claims in respect of civil liability incurred in the private practice of the above.

On receipt of the initial contribution due, the practice and each of its members becomes entitled to an indemnity from the Fund against all loss including costs arising at any time directly from any claim first made or intimated against the practice or any of its members during the indemnity period in question in respect of any description of civil liability whatsoever incurred by the practice or a member of such practice or (in the case of a principal) as a principal in any previous practice.

An indemnity is also provided against loss arising directly from any claim in respect of civil liability made or intimated against the practice or any of its members during or after the indemnity period in question arising out of circumstances notified to SIF Ltd during the indemnity period as circumstances which might give rise to such a claim. There is further indemnity against the costs of defending, settling or compromising any such claim.

There is no indemnity in respect of any loss arising out of a claim for death, personal injury or loss of, or damage to, property except property not owned or occupied by the practice but held by it in the course of its business (presumably for its clients or third parties), for a breach of partnership agreement, claims in respects of employment matters, trading debts in respect of any undertakings given for the benefit of any principal or close relation of any principal in the practice, in respect of any dishonest or fraudulent act or omission (but any innocent member of the practice is entitled to be indemnified against the acts or omissions of other guilty members of the practice), in respect of any liability incurred in connection with an overseas practice or arising out of any circumstances which had been notified prior to 1 September 1987 or in respect of any act or omission of a principal acting on behalf of a practice or any member thereof of which he or she was a principal.

The indemnity is provided either by payment in or towards satisfaction of the claim and/or the claimant's costs and expenses either to the claimant or to the person claimed against (in which case it may include the costs and expenses incurred in respect of the defence or settlement or compromise of the claim).

The indemnity shall lie and be made exclusively out of and against the Fund and SIF Ltd has no obligation to provide indemnity save to the extent that it can be provided out of the Fund. No claim shall lie against the Society or the Council.

The indemnity limit is £1,000,000 each and every claim (including claimants' costs).

All claims arising from the same act or omission (whether or not made or intimated or arising out of circumstances notified during the same indemnity period and whether or not involving the same or any number of different practices and/or members of such practices) shall be regarded as one claim.

This last matter is of concern to those acting for numerous plaintiffs in a group action (e.g., against a pharmaceutical manufacturer). SIF Ltd has apparently recently told one such firm that it regards the group action as one claim for the purpose of these Rules so that the indemnity limited will be £1,000,000, notwithstanding the fact that there are potentially hundreds of plaintiffs. No doubt the point will be argued forcefully on behalf of the profession.

Indemnity is conditional on written notification as soon as practicable of any claim made or intimated during the indemnity period or of receipt by a practice or principal of notice of any intention to make any such claim. The practice or any of its members may also give notice in writing to SIF Ltd of any circumstances of which it or he shall become aware which may give rise to any such claim during or after the indemnity period in question. This is voluntary and not mandatory. A subsequent claim arising out of the facts notified is treated as a claim made on the date of notification. A practice and its members shall not admit liability for or settle any claim without the prior consent of SIF Ltd which may not be unreasonably held.

SIF Ltd is entitled at any time to take over conduct of a claim and may thereafter conduct it as it thinks fit in its absolute discretion save that a practice shall not be required by SIF Ltd to contest any legal proceedings unless a Queen's Counsel has advised that the proceedings should be contested.

There is the usual duty to inform, consult with and co-operate with SIF Ltd, whether or not the claim is taken over by the Fund.

The Fund explicitly waives any rights of subrogation against any member of the practice, save where those rights arise in connection with a dishonest or criminal act by that member or where the member has received a net benefit to which he is not entitled.

If the practice or member makes a claim knowing it to be false or fraudulent (whether or not in relation to the amount claimed), the claim to indemnity is forfeited.

If contribution is unpaid, the indemnity is provided but the practice must thereafter on request reimburse SIF Ltd any increase in the total payable out of the Fund, including costs and expenses as a result of such failure together with interest.

If non-compliance by the practice or member results in some potential prejudice to the handling or settlement of any claim, the practice or member must reimburse SIF Ltd any extra expense occasioned by such prejudice.

The Fund can, require "innocent principals" in a practice to take all reasonable steps at the Fund's expense to reobtain reimbursement from any member of the practice concerned in dishonesty or fraud.

The Fund may appoint a panel of solicitors to act on its behalf and on behalf of the practice or any member thereof. It must act on the sole direction of the Fund and disclose to the Fund as required any statement or information becoming known to it in the course of so acting.

Indemnity is subject to a deduction in respect of each claim paid as a self-insured excess. The deduction is one per cent of the gross fees notified to SIF Ltd on the annual return, subject to a minimum standard deduction of £3,000 and a maximum deduction of £150,000, irrespective of the number of principals in the firm. The deduction is additionally subject to an aggregate limitation on the amount a practice can be asked to pay (it is currently three times the standard deduction) in respect of claims notified in an indemnity year. It is possible to delete the deduction on payment of an additional annual contribution. The deduction is disregarded when a payment is made in respect of any claim against an insolvent or bankrupt person for whom indemnity is provided.

The deduction is calculated by reference to the regime in force when the claim was first made or intimated or, at the option of SIF Ltd, at the time when the practice or its members first became aware of the circumstances giving rise to the potential claim.

There are detailed provisions governing the setting up of new practices, the acquisition of an existing practice by another existing practice and the transfer of a principal from one practice to another taking a proportion of the clientele (and thus gross fees) of the old firm.

The provision of information of gross fees earned by the practice has for a number of years been the basis for calculation of the premium, the proportion of gross fees payable declining from 6.20 per cent of fees up to £70,000 to 0.36 per cent of fees over £150 million for the year 1995/6.

The 1995 Rules introduce material for the provision of a database over the next three years to provide for risk banding in relation to different types of fee-earning work. It is anticipated that factors will be applied loading or diminishing the premium rate applicable to high- or low-risk activities. The latter are anticipated to include criminal law, debt collection, children work, mental health tribunal work, immigration work, welfare work and the administration of oaths.

As a result of an increase in gross fees, a reduction in management costs and a projected increase in investment income a five per cent reduction in the contribution requirement for 1995–96 appears possible. The data collected by SIF Ltd shows that in the eight years to 31 August 1994 practices with one, two and three principals contributed 29.1 per cent of the contribution, but accounted for 48.2 per cent of the total claims by amount. In the result, since the average gross fee income of a three-principal firm was £430,000, the proportion of gross fees payable by way of initial contribution up to £500,000 are left unchanged, the 5 per cent saving being spread over all the gross fee bands above this figure.

It is intended to introduce a composite package of penalties including claims loading based on loss ratios up to 200 per cent, penalty deductions and low claims discounts perhaps up to 20 per cent in the year 1996–97.

It is clear that the Fund, given the imperfections in relation to failure to relate size of firm, types of work and claims record to contribution payable, provides protection which a firm (or its non-dishonest or non-fraudulent principals) is unable to lose, however it conducts its affairs. It has unsurprisingly given rise to very little litigation and no reported cases.

There have been recent but unsuccessful attempts to exclude "cut-price conveyancing solicitors" from the protection of the Fund on the ground that such work apparently gives rise to a disproportionate number of claims.

### 11.19 Incorporated practices

The intention of the Government to increase the range of bodies providing legal services, particularly in relation to conveyancing services by banks, building societies, insurance companies and others under the Courts and Legal Services Act 1990, sections 34–52 has led to the Solicitors Incorporated Practice Order 1991.[195]

This in turn placed upon The Law Society the obligation to regulate the management and control by solicitors (or multi-national partnerships) of bodies corporate carrying on businesses consisting of the provision of professional services such as provided by solicitors or multi-national partnerships, prescribing criteria for recognition of such bodies as suitable bodies for the provision of such legal services,

---

195. S.I. 1991/2684.

prescribing conditions to be satisfied for continued recognition and regulating the affairs of the bodies themselves.

These broadly relate to accounts rules (including the provision for interest on clients' money), accountants' reports, a compensation fund, control of employment of persons convicted of offences of dishonesty, inadequate professional services, examination of files and complaints to the Solicitors Disciplinary Tribunal and power to inspect files and intervention by The Law Society.

These are broadly similar to the regulations affecting solicitors and will not be rehearsed in detail.

The current regulations are the Solicitors Incorporated Practice Rules 1988, and the Solicitors Indemnity (Incorporated Practice) Rules 1991, as amended by the Solicitors Indemnity (Incorporated Practice) Amendment Rules 1992.

## 11.20 Regulation of licensed conveyancers

The Administration of Justice Act 1985, Part II provides for the regulation of the provision of conveyancing services by those holding licences in force under that Act.

The Act establishes the Council for Licensed Conveyancers whose general duty is to ensure that standards of competence and professional conduct among persons who practise as licensed conveyancers are sufficient to secure adequate protection for consumers and that the conveyancing services provided by such persons are provided both economically and efficiently.[196]

The Council must make rules for the education and training of those seeking to practise as licensed conveyancers, including provision for examinations and practical training and experience.

An application for a licence to practise as a licensed conveyancer must be made to the Council of Licensed Conveyancers in the manner prescribed by the Council.

The Council must, if satisfied that the training rules have been complied with, ensure that adequate professional indemnity has been arranged and that the applicant is a fit and proper person, issue a licence, either unconditional or conditional. If not so satisfied, the application must be refused. The criteria for issue of a conditional licence follow closely those for solicitors relating to conditional practising certificates.

Conditions may be imposed upon a licence, once granted. The licence is immediately suspended at any period during which the licensed conveyancer is adjudicated bankrupt or the holder becomes a patient within the meaning of the Mental Health Act 1983.

The Council must keep a register of all licences granted.

In pursuance of the Government policy of increasing the provision of legal services, the Council has the powers necessary to enable it to become:

(a) an authorised body for the purposes of granting rights of audience and rights to conduct litigation;

(b) an approved body for the purposes of granting exemption from the provisions relating to the preparation of probate papers. Separate licences for these purposes are granted.

196. Section 12(1).

The Council must make rules regulating the professional practice, conduct and discipline of licensed conveyancers and for a professional indemnity insurance scheme.

There are further provisions for regulating the establishment and keeping of accounts, for the payment of interest on clients' money and for the establishment of an Investigating Committee and a Discipline and Appeals Committee to investigate and adjudicate upon alleged disciplinary offences.

There is power in the Council to intervene in a licensed conveyancer's practice:

(a) on suspicion of dishonesty;
(b) following the death of a sole practitioner;
(c) for failure to comply with accounts rules;
(d) for insolvency;
(e) for committal to prison;
(f) for incapacity by illness or accident of a sole practitioner;
(g) for the mental disorder of a licensed conveyancer; or
(h) if the licence has been revoked or suspended, by an order of the Discipline and Appeals Committee, or has expired without a further licence being issued.

There are ancillary powers in relation to money and documents and redirection of mail and for examination of files.

The Council has full powers of disciplinary control over recognised bodies[197] and may also revoke recognition, if satisfied that the recognition has been granted as a result of any fraud or error.

## 11.21 Authorised Conveyancing Practitioners Board

This is a body corporate consisting of a chairman and at least four and not more than eight other members appointed by the Lord Chancellor. Appointees should be considered in the light of the desirability of experience or knowledge in:

(a) the provision of conveyancing services;
(b) financial arrangements associated with the conveyancing;
(c) consumer affairs; *or*
(d) commercial affairs.

The Lord Chancellor should attempt a proper balance between practitioners and consumers of the relevant services. Detailed provisions are set out in Schedule 5 to the Courts and Legal Services Act 1990. The Board has a general duty:

(a) to seek to develop competition in the provision of conveyancing services and
(b) to supervise the activities of authorised practitioners in connection with the provisions by them of such services. The functions are conferred by the Courts and Legal Services Act 1990.[198]

The Board must consider any matter referred to it by the Lord Chancellor

---

197. Under the Administration of Justice Act 1985, s. 32.
198. Sections 36–39, 43 and Sch. 7.

connected with the provision of conveyancing services by authorised practitioners or the organisation or practice of authorised practitioners and report to the Lord Chancellor. The Lord Chancellor may give directions to the Board if he has reasonable grounds for believing that it has failed in any way to carry out its duties.

There are detailed provisions, none of which are yet in force, relating to the authorisation of practitioners, the competence and conduct of authorised practitioners, the refusal or approval or imposition of conditions, the revocation and suspension of authorisation, the establishment of the Conveyancing Appeals Tribunal and appeals therefrom, the conveyancing Ombudsman scheme, a compensation scheme, investigative powers, intervention powers, tying-in arrangements in connection with loans, offences, enforcement and advice from the Director General of Fair Trading on rules and regulations.

MARK MILDRED

# CHAPTER 11

# SURVEYORS AND VALUERS

## 1 INTRODUCTION

This chapter deals with the professional responsibilities of those whose work involves the inspection and appraisal of land and buildings, in order to report to a client on their condition and/or value. It is not concerned with those other persons, albeit sometimes referred to as "surveyors" or "valuers", whose expertise relates to other kinds of property such as ships,[1] shares or chattels.[2]

There are no statutory controls upon surveying or valuation, in the sense of minimum entry qualifications or membership of any particular professional body.[3] However, the great majority of those who carry out such work are members of either the Royal Institution of Chartered Surveyors ("RICS") or the Incorporated Society of Valuers and Auctioneers ("ISVA"). Membership of these bodies, which permits use of the respective appellations "chartered surveyor" and "incorporated valuer", requires both academic qualifications[4] and a period of practical experience, the latter culminating in a formal assessment of professional competence.

Both the RICS and the ISVA (and certain smaller professional bodies to which surveyors and valuers belong) impose a code of regulations upon their members which covers such matters as client accounts, conflict of interests and so on. However, the expulsion of a member for breach of such regulations means merely that that person is excluded from the organisation concerned; there is nothing to prevent him or her from continuing to practise as a surveyor or valuer.[5]

## 2 RELATIONSHIP WITH THE CLIENT

### 2.1 Liability in contract

The contract under which a client engages the services of a surveyor or valuer is not required by the law to be made in any particular form—it may be written or oral, or

---

1. It is notable that in *Marc Rich & Co AG* v. *Bishop Rock Marine Co Ltd* [1995] 3 All E.R. 307, where the House of Lords considered whether a marine surveyor could be liable for negligence to a non-client, the wealth of previous cases dealing with this point in the context of building surveys was not even mentioned.
2. Notably fine art and antiques.
3. However, valuations for certain purposes must be carried out by a person who holds a designated professional qualification: see the R.I.C.S. *Appraisal and Valuation Manual*, Practice Statement 5.
4. Traditionally the passing of examinations set by the professional body, although the trend in recent years has been towards the obtaining of exemption through approved degree or diploma courses.
5. Though not as a "chartered" surveyor or an "incorporated" valuer.

even inferred from conduct. However, it is clearly good practice to ensure either that the contract itself is made in writing or, if made orally, that written evidence (such as a confirming letter) is available to establish its terms.[6]

The extent of a surveyor or valuer's liability to the client is primarily determined by the contract between them, which will identify the services which are to be provided.[7] However, such contracts do not usually define expressly the *standard* of care and skill which is to be shown in the performance of these services, unless, perhaps, in an attempt to exclude or restrict liability.[8] Where this is not done, a term will be implied to the effect that the services will be carried out with reasonable care and skill.[9] As Judge Hordern QC said in *Kerridge* v. *James Abbott & Partners*[10]:

"[The defendant] was obliged to survey the property to the standard of a reasonably competent surveyor exercising due skill, care and diligence and possessing the necessary knowledge and experience."

In the common situation where a client enters into a contract with a firm of surveyors rather than with an individual practitioner, it is the firm which will owe a duty of reasonable care and skill. That duty will be "non-delegable", at least in the sense that any negligence by an employee will in itself render the firm guilty of a breach of contract. It is submitted moreover that the firm will normally be deemed to have assumed responsibility for any non-employee (such as a consultant) to whom it entrusts the particular work.[11]

## 2.2 Liability in tort

The question whether a client may choose to frame a professional negligence action in tort rather than in contract, in order to obtain the benefit of a longer limitation period, appears finally to have been settled by the House of Lords in *Henderson* v. *Merrett Syndicates Ltd*.[12] There seems no reason to doubt that their lordships' ruling in favour of concurrent liability will apply to actions involving surveyors and valuers. Nonetheless, pending a specific decision to that effect, it may be noted that earlier *dicta* in such cases in support of concurrent liability[13] have far outweighed those against it.[14] However, in the few reported cases where the ability to claim in tort has been crucial to the success of a client's action, the possibility that such a claim might

6. Written confirmation of instructions is a professional requirement: see the R.I.C.S. *Appraisal and Valuation Manual*, Practice Statement 2.

7. The role of instructions in determining whether or not there is negligence is considered at p. 627.

8. For the rules governing disclaimers, see p. 666.

9. Supply of Goods and Services Act 1982, s. 13. There will also be an implied obligation to carry out the services within a reasonable time: *ibid.*, s. 14(1).

10. [1992] 2 E.G.L.R. 162.

11. There appears to be no direct authority on this point in the surveying or valuation context. See, however, *Luxmoore-May* v. *Messenger May Baverstock* [1990] 1 All E.R. 1067, where the Court of Appeal held that a firm of auctioneers would be liable for the negligence of an independent consultant.

12. [1994] 3 All E.R. 506.

13. E.g., *Leigh* v. *Unsworth* (1972) 230 E.G. 501; *McIntyre* v. *Herring Son & Daw* [1988] 1 E.G.L.R. 231; *Howard* v. *Horne & Sons* [1990] 1 E.G.L.R. 272; *Smith* v. *Eric S Bush*; *Harris* v. *Wyre Forest D.C.* [1990] 1 A.C. 831 at 870; *Pfeiffer* v. *E & E Installations* [1991] 1 E.G.L.R. 162; *CIL Securities Ltd* v. *Briant Champion Long* [1993] 2 E.G.L.R. 164; *Nyckeln Finance Co Ltd* v. *Stumpbrook Continuation Ltd* [1994] 2 E.G.L.R. 143 at 146.

14. See *Heatley* v. *William H Brown Ltd* [1992] 1 E.G.L.R. 289; *Nykredit Mortgage Bank plc* v. *Edward Erdman Group Ltd* [1996] 02 E.G. 110, Mayor's and City of London Court.

not be available does not appear to have been explicitly considered.[15] Moreover, in most of the cases where the client has adopted the common practice of pleading both breach of contract and tort, the court has simply held the surveyor or valuer liable without identifying the basis of that liability.[16]

## 2.3 Remuneration

The right of a surveyor or valuer to be paid for professional services depends in principle upon the contract with the client.[17] If that contract makes express provision as to the amount of remuneration and the circumstances in which it is to be paid, the parties will with one qualification be bound by their agreement. The qualification is that, where professional services are concerned with litigation, an agreement to pay a fee dependent on success is champertous, unlawful and therefore unenforceable.[18]

Where the contract with the client is silent on the question of remuneration, an obligation to pay a reasonable fee will normally be implied.[19] In assessing what is reasonable, a court will endeavour to ascertain and give effect to the intentions of the parties.[20] In so doing, the courts have almost invariably related fees to the time and trouble expended and have resisted strongly any suggestion that remuneration for professional services should be based on the value of property to which those services relate.[21] In particular, attempts by surveyors to claim that "reasonable remuneration" for expert witness work or other litigation services work should be based on a professional scale of charges have repeatedly been rejected.[22]

Where professional services are negligently carried out and are consequently worthless, the client is under no obligation to pay for those services, and may indeed recover any payments already made on the basis that there has been a total failure of consideration.[23] Thus in *Whitty* v. *Lord Dillon*,[24] where the plaintiff's valuation of the

15. See *Anglia Hastings & Thanet Building Society* v. *House & Son* [1981] 2 E.G.L.R. 17; *Secretary of State for the Environment* v. *Essex, Goodman & Suggitt* [1985] 2 E.G.L.R. 168; *Westlake* v. *Bracknell D.C.* [1987] 1 E.G.L.R. 161; *Kitney* v. *Jones Lang Wootton* [1988] 1 E.G.L.R. 145; *Horbury* v. *Craig Hall & Rutley* [1991] E.G.C.S. 81; *Whitley (FG) & Sons Co Ltd* v. *Thomas Bickerton* [1993] 1 E.G.L.R. 139.

16. See, for example, *Fisher* v. *Knowles* [1982] 1 E.G.L.R. 154; *London & South of England Building Society* v. *Stone* [1983] 3 All E.R. 105; *Wilson* v. *Baxter Payne and Lepper* [1985] 1 E.G.L.R. 141; *Lucas* v. *Ogden* [1988] 2 E.G.L.R. 176; *Hacker* v. *Thomas Deal & Co* [1991] 2 E.G.L.R. 161; *United Bank of Kuwait* v. *Prudential Property Services Ltd* [1994] 2 E.G.L.R. 143.

17. In the unlikely event that there is no contract (even one implied from the conduct of the parties), the doctrine of restitution would presumably provide the basis for a claim for the value of the services.

18. This principle is restricted to proceedings in a court of law. It is lawful to agree a contingency fee for negotiating with the district valuer a reduction in the rateable value of a clients' property, (*Pickering* v. *Sogex Services (UK) Ltd* [1982] 1 E.G.L.R. 42) or for obtaining planning permission (*Picton Jones & Co* v. *Arcadia Developments Ltd* [1989] 1 E.G.L.R. 43).

19. Supply of Goods and Services Act 1982, s. 15(1).

20. In *Francis* v. *Harris* [1989] 1 E.G.L.R. 45, where the evidence of the parties' intentions was hopelessly unclear, the Court of Appeal was compelled to order a new trial.

21. Except where it is possible to prove a binding custom justifying such an assessment (*Wilkie* v. *Scottish Aviation Ltd* 1956 S.C. 198 at 205 *per* Lord Clyde; *Buckland and Garrard* v. *Pawson & Co* (1890) 6 T.L.R. 421). There may be a further exception in cases where the professional services bring about a valuable result for the client (see *Graham & Baldwin* v. *Taylor, Son & Davis* (1965) 109 S.J. 793).

22. *Upsdell* v. *Stewart* (1793) Peake 255; *Debenham* v. *King's College, Cambridge* (1884) 1 T.L.R. 170; *Drew* v. *Josolyne* (1888) 4 T.L.R. 717; *Faraday* v. *Tamworth Union* (1917) 86 L.J.Ch. 436. See, generally, Murdoch, "Professional Fees—How Much is Reasonable?" [1981] Conv. 424 at 425–428.

23. *Heywood* v. *Wellers* [1976] Q.B. 446.

24. (1860) 2 F. & F. 67.

timber on a certain estate was inaccurate by some 40 to 50 per cent because he erroneously included saplings in his calculations, it was held that the client was not liable to pay the agreed fee, since the work was of no value to him. However, where professional services, albeit negligently carried out, remain of some value to the client, the latter is not relieved of the obligation to pay fees.[25] It appears that the doctrine of abatement, which applies to sales of goods[26] and to contracts for work and materials[27] does not operate in this context.[28]

In the surveying context, the principles outlined above have occasionally served to defeat a negligent surveyor's claim for payment[29] or to entitle a client to recover fees already paid.[30] However, the issue has seldom been contested; in most cases where a negligent surveyor has claimed or counterclaimed for fees, the entitlement has either been expressly conceded by the client[31] or has been accepted by the court without apparent argument.[32]

## 3 LIABILITY TO THIRD PARTIES

Until 1963, English law insisted that liability for financial loss caused by negligent advice could arise only where relationship between the parties was either contractual[33] or fiduciary.[34] Without such a relationship, it mattered not that the adviser actually knew that an identified plaintiff intended to rely on a report,[35] nor that the adviser's fee for professional services would ultimately (albeit indirectly) be paid by the plaintiff, as in the common case of a house buyer paying for a mortgage valuation.[36] Moreover, it was held that the principle laid down in *Donoghue* v. *Stevenson*[37] applied only to cases of physical injury, and could not be extended to cover the financial losses suffered by one who entered into some transaction in reliance on a negligently prepared report.[38]

Given the refusal of the courts to recognise a duty of care in tort, it is hardly surprising that many of the cases reported at that time turned on attempts by persons other than the primary client to establish a contractual relationship with a surveyor or

25. *Moneypenny* v. *Hartland* (1826) 1 C. & P. 352.
26. Sale of Goods Act 1979, s. 53.
27. *Mondel* v. *Steel* (1841) 8 M. & W. 858.
28. *Hutchinson* v. *Harris* (1978) 10 B.L.R. 19.
29. *Hill* v. *Debenham Tewson and Chinnocks* (1958) 171 E.G. 835; *Sincock* v. *Bangs (Reading)* (1952) 160 E.G. 134; *Buckland* v. *Watts* (1968) 208 E.G. 969.
30. *Chong* v. *Scott Collins & Co* (1954) 164 E.G. 662.
31. See, for example, *Last* v. *Post* (1952) 159 E.G. 240; *Bell Hotels (1935) Ltd* v. *Motion* (1952) 159 E.G. 496; *Corisand Investments Ltd* v. *Druce & Co* [1978] 2 E.G.L.R. 86; *Bigg* v. *Howard Son & Gooch* [1990] 1 E.G.L.R. 173.
32. As in *Conn* v. *Munday* (1955) 166 E.G. 465.
33. 75 years earlier, in *Cann* v. *Willson* (1888) 39 Ch.D. 39, Chitty J held a valuer who had been instructed by a prospective borrower liable to the lender for negligence. However, this path-breaking decision was soon overruled by the Court of Appeal (*Le Lievre* v. *Gould* [1893] 1 Q.B. 491), and was only vindicated by the House of Lords in *Hedley Byrne & Co Ltd* v. *Heller & Partners Ltd* [1964] A.C. 465.
34. *Nocton* v. *Lord Ashburton* [1914] A.C. 932.
35. *Scholes* v. *Brook* (1891) 63 L.T. 837 (where the plaintiff in fact succeeded in establishing the existence of a contract); *Love* v. *Mack* (1905) 92 L.T. 345.
36. *Odder* v. *Westbourne Park Building Society* (1955) 165 E.G. 261; *Davis* v. *Sprott & Sons* (1960) 177 E.G. 9.
37. [1932] A.C. 562.
38. *Old Gate Estates Ltd* v. *Toplis* [1939] 3 All E.R. 209.

valuer.[39] Such cases are now much less common; the availability of a claim in tort has rendered the presence or absence of a contract largely unimportant.[40] Indeed, some recent judgments leave unresolved the question of which of two parties is to be regarded as the client of a surveyor in the contractual sense.[41]

## 3.1 The basis of liability

The seminal decision of the House of Lords in *Hedley Byrne & Co Ltd* v. *Heller & Partners Ltd*[42] established that, provided certain conditions were satisfied, liability in tort could arise in respect of financial loss resulting from negligent advice. In coming to this conclusion, their lordships were unanimously of the opinion that a duty of care in respect of words must be more narrowly defined than that in respect of deeds, in view of the risk that a defendant might otherwise be exposed to liability "in an indeterminate amount for an indefinite time to an indeterminate class". It was accordingly ruled that a duty of care would not automatically arise merely because a defendant could foresee that the plaintiff might rely on what was said; it would arise only where there was a "special relationship" between the parties.

In seeking to identify the defining characteristics of such a relationship, the House of Lords gave support to the notion of a "voluntary assumption of responsibility" by the defendant. However, it has since been made clear that this should not be interpreted literally; it can "only have real meaning if it is understood as referring to the circumstances in which the law will deem the maker of the statement to have assumed responsibility to the person who acts on the advice".[43] As to what those circumstances might be, it appears that a duty of care will be imposed "if it is foreseeable that if the advice is negligent the recipient is likely to suffer damage, that there is a sufficiently proximate relationship between the parties and that it is just and reasonable to impose the liability".[44]

That "proximity" in this context requires something more than mere "foreseeability" appears from the decision of the Court of Appeal in *Shankie-Williams* v. *Heavey*.[45] That case arose when the defendant, who traded as a "dry rot surveying specialist", was instructed to inspect a ground floor flat in a house which had recently been converted into three flats. The defendant's instructions came from the developer responsible for the conversion, but he knew that the developer wanted a

---

39. Cases in which house buyers were successful in establishing a contract with the mortgagee's surveyor include *Gurd* v. *A Cobden Soar & Son* (1951) 157 E.G. 415 and *Wooldridge* v. *Stanley Hicks & Son* (1953) 162 E.G. 513. For the converse situation (a contract between a mortgagee and a valuer paid by the mortgagor), see *Scholes* v. *Brook* (1891) 63 L.T. 837; affirmed (1892) 64 L.T. 674.

40. Unusually, in *Banque Bruxelles Lambert SA* v. *Eagle Star Insurance Co Ltd* [1995] 2 All E.R. 769 a lending bank attempted (unsuccessfully) to establish a contract with valuers who were instructed and paid by the borrower.

41. See, for example, *Beaumont* v. *Humberts* [1990] 2 E.G.L.R. 166; *Peach* v. *Iain G Chalmers & Co* [1992] 2 E.G.L.R. 135.

42. [1964] A.C. 465.

43. *Smith* v. *Eric S Bush; Harris* v. *Wyre Forest D.C.* [1990] 1 A.C. 831 at 862, *per* Lord Griffiths.

44. *Ibid.* at 865. See also *Caparo Industries plc* v. *Dickman* [1990] 2 A.C. 605; *James McNaughton Papers Group Ltd* v. *Hicks Anderson & Co* [1991] 1 All E.R. 134 at 143 *per* Neill LJ (both cases involving auditors preparing company accounts).

45. [1986] 2 E.G.L.R. 139. See also *Bourne* v. *McEvoy Timber Preservation* [1976] 1 E.G.L.R. 100.

report which could be shown to a prospective purchaser. In these circumstances it was held that the defendant owed a duty of care to the purchasers of the ground floor flat which he had inspected, although those purchasers' claim failed because they were not shown to have relied on the report. However, no duty of care was owed to the purchaser of the first floor flat, who claimed to have assumed that, if there was no evidence of dry rot on the ground floor, the rest of the house would likewise be free from infestation.

In most of the cases where a surveyor or valuer has been held liable in the absence of a contract, the defendant has had actual knowledge both of the identity of the person concerned and of the fact that that person was likely to rely on the surveyor or valuation report. Without such knowledge, establishing a duty of care will be more difficult, as emphasised by Lord Griffiths in *Smith* v. *Eric S Bush; Harris* v. *Wyre Forest DC*[46]:

> "I would certainly wish to stress that, in cases where the advice has not been given for the specific purpose of the recipient acting upon it, it should only be in cases where the adviser knows that there is a high degree of probability that some other identifiable person will act upon the advice that a duty of care should be imposed. It would impose an intolerable burden upon those who give advice in a professional or commercial context if they were to owe a duty not only to those to whom they give the advice but to any other person who might choose to act upon it."

Notwithstanding such *dicta*, a duty of care has on occasion been held to exist where a surveyor or valuer merely *ought* to have realised that a third party might rely on a report.[47] Thus, for example, where the prospective purchaser of a flat arranged for a valuation to be carried out and submitted to a building society, a Scottish court had little hesitation in holding that the valuer's duty of care extended to an individual (of whom he knew nothing) who entered the scene as a joint purchaser.[48]

In cases where the defendant has neither actual nor inferential knowledge of the plaintiff's likely reliance, no duty of care will be owed. This was acknowledged in *Beaumont* v. *Humberts*,[49] although the Court of Appeal disagreed as to whether the defendant should have realised that the plaintiff would rely upon his report. The point also proved decisive in *Le Lievre* v. *Gould*,[50] where the defendant surveyor was employed by a builder to issue a series of certificates as to the progress of certain building works. Without the defendant's knowledge (either actual or constructive), the builder passed on these certificates to the plaintiff, a mortgagee of the land in question, who thereupon advanced instalments of the mortgage loan. In these circumstances it was held by the Court of Appeal that no duty of care was owed by the defendant to the plaintiff.[51]

---

46. [1990] 1 A.C. 831 at 865.
47. In setting out the criteria for a duty of care in respect of advice, Lord Oliver referred repeatedly to what the adviser knows "actually or inferentially": *Caparo Industries plc* v. *Dickman* [1990] 2 A.C. 605 at 638. See also *UCB* v. *Dundas & Wilson* 1989 S.L.T. 243, where it was held sufficient for the plaintiff to allege that valuers "knew or ought to have known" of the likelihood of reliance by a particular person.
48. *Smith* v. *Carter*, 1994 S.C.L.R. 539.
49. [1990] 2 E.G.L.R. 166.
50. [1893] 1 Q.B. 491.
51. The Court of Appeal's general ruling, that there could be no liability in the absence of a contract, is clearly no longer law. However, a majority of the House of Lords in *Hedley Byrne & Co Ltd* v. *Heller & Partners Ltd* took the view that the actual decision in *Le Lievre* v. *Gould* was correct on its facts.

## 3.2 Claims by house buyers

The purchase of residential property is commonly financed, wholly or partly, by a loan from an institutional mortgagee such as a bank, building society or local authority which is secured on the property. Before making such a loan, the mortgagee will almost invariably require a valuation of the property to be made, either by an employee of the mortgagee or by an independent valuer. It is currently common practice for the valuer's report to be shown by the mortgagee to the prospective purchaser, although this was not formerly the case. In either event, the controversial question which has arisen is to what extent the purchaser of the property, having relied on the valuer's report or on the mere fact that the valuation has been carried out and the loan made, may recover damages from the valuer or the mortgagee in the event of a negligent over-valuation.[52]

### 3.2.1 Liability of valuer

The seminal case of *Yianni* v. *Edwin Evans & Sons*[53] arose out of the purchase in 1975 by the plaintiffs of a modest house, built at the turn of the century, for £15,000. The plaintiffs applied to a building society for a mortgage loan of £12,000 and the building society duly commissioned a valuation of the property from the defendant firm of valuers and surveyors (charging the plaintiffs a valuation fee in the process). The defendants reported to the building society that the house was worth £15,000 and was suitable for maximum lending (i.e., 80 per cent of the valuation). The plaintiffs did not see this report, which they were informed was confidential to the building society; however, they assumed that it must have been satisfactory, since they received the required loan of £12,000. Within a year of purchase the plaintiffs discovered serious structural damage due to subsidence, which the defendant's "grossly incompetent and negligent survey" had failed to detect, and which meant that the house was in truth worth little more than its site value.

When sued by the plaintiffs, the defendant valuers admitted negligence in their inspection and subsequent report to the building society. However, the defendants denied that they owed any duty of care to the plaintiffs, on the basis of clear statements in the building society's literature (which the plaintiffs had received) to the effect that no responsibility was accepted for the condition of the property; that the offer of mortgage did not imply any warranty that the purchase price was reasonable[54]; that the plaintiffs should not assume that the property was free from undisclosed defects; and that the plaintiffs were recommended to obtain their own survey before agreeing to purchase.

Park J, relying on expert evidence to the effect that some 90 per cent of purchasers at the lower end of the market ordinarily ignored such warnings, concluded that the defendants must have known that the plaintiffs would rely on their valuation and held that this was sufficient to subject them to a duty of care. In so deciding, the judge

---

52. Prior to the decision in *Hedley Byrne* v. *Heller*, any such claim was dependent upon the purchaser's ability to establish a contractual or fiduciary relationship: see p. 608.

53. [1982] Q.B. 438.

54. This was intended to exclude a deemed warranty which would otherwise have arisen under the (since repealed) Building Societies Act 1962, s. 30.

was at pains to reject claims by counsel for the defendants that this would impose an unacceptably onerous burden upon professionals[55]:

"[Counsel] also submitted that if the defendants were held liable to the plaintiffs no professional man would be able to limit his liability to a third party, even if he could do so to his own client. He would be at the mercy of a client who might pass on his report to a third party and, as defects in the property he had surveyed might not manifest themselves for many years, he would be unlikely to remain under a liability for those defects he ought to have detected for a very long period, and at the end of that period, for an unlimited amount by way of damages. In my view, the only person to whom the surveyor is liable is the party named in the building society's 'Instructions to Valuer' addressed to him. That party, as well as the building society, has to be regarded as his client. That does not seem to me to be unreasonable, since, to his knowledge, his fee for the valuation is paid by that party to the building society which hands it over to him. On this submission, it can also be said that the surveyor's report is concerned with the valuation of a dwelling-house, the condition of which is important only in so far as it affects its value at that time. It is common knowledge that in the ordinary way, the market value of a dwelling-house is not static. Consequently, a valuation made at one time for the purpose of assessing its suitability as security for a loan would be of limited use."

The decision in *Yianni*, though subjected to some criticism on the ground of its "inherent judicial weakness",[56] achieved a high level of acceptance by the courts in subsequent cases.[57] However, the issue was not finally settled until 1989, when two conflicting decisions of the Court of Appeal, in *Smith* v. *Eric S Bush* and *Harris* v. *Wyre Forest DC*, were taken together to the House of Lords.[58] The decision of their Lordships in those cases confirmed that a mortgage valuer will in most circumstances owe a duty of care to a house purchaser.[59]

*Smith* v. *Bush* concerned the purchase in 1980 by the plaintiff of a small house for £18,000, of which the plaintiff sought to raise £3,500 by way of a mortgage loan from a building society. As in *Yianni*, the society commissioned a mortgage valuation from an independent firm of surveyors and charged the plaintiff an inspection fee, having first made clear (by a declaration in the application form which the plaintiff had signed) that neither the building society nor the valuer would accept any responsibility for the contents of the valuer's report. With this caveat, the valuer's report (which valued the house at £16,500 and stated that no essential repairs were needed) was actually passed on to the plaintiff, who relied on it in agreeing to purchase the property. Some 18 months later it was discovered that the valuer had failed to notice

---

55. [1982] Q.B. 438 at 456.

56. See *Harris* v. *Wyre Forest D.C.* [1988] Q.B. 835 at 851 *per* Kerr LJ.

57. *Ward* v. *McMaster* [1985] I.R. 29; *Curran* v. *Northern Ireland Co-Ownership Housing Association Ltd* (1986) 8 N.I.J.B. 1; *Westlake* v. *Bracknell D.C.* [1987] 1 E.G.L.R. 161 (in all of which cases the decision was expressly followed); *Hadden* v. *City of Glasgow D.C.* 1986 S.L.T. 557; *Martin* v. *Bell-Ingram* 1986 S.L.T. 575; *Duncan* v. *Gumleys* [1987] 2 E.G.L.R. 263; *Nash* v. *Evens & Matta* [1988] 1 E.G.L.R. 130; *Smith* v. *Eric S Bush* [1987] 3 All E.R. 179, C.A.; *Davies* v. *Idris Parry* [1988] 1 E.G.L.R. 147; *Green* v. *Ipswich B.C.* [1988] 1 E.G.L.R. 239.

58. [1990] 1 A.C. 831. The conflict between the cases related to the effectiveness of disclaimers in documentation produced by the mortgagee and the question of whether this was subject to the Unfair Contract Terms Act 1977: see p. 669.

59. Given the range of facts in the two appeals, it appears that the existence of a duty of care will not be affected by the status of the mortgagee (e.g., a bank, building society, or local authority); the size of the mortgage loan in relation to the purchase price; whether the valuation is carried out by an independent valuer or by an employee of the mortgagee; or whether or not the valuer's report is disclosed to the purchaser.

and report that the chimneys of the house had been left without support following the removal of chimney breasts.

*Harris* v. *Wyre Forest* concerned the purchase in 1978 by the plaintiffs of a small house for £9,000, prior to which the plaintiffs applied to the defendant local authority for a loan on mortgage. The application form which the plaintiffs signed made it clear that, while the defendants would obtain a valuation of the property, this would remain confidential to them; moreover, the defendants disclaimed any responsibility for the value or condition of the property. The house was duly inspected by a member of the defendants' staff who valued it at £9,450 and recommended it as suitable security for a loan of 90 per cent, subject to a condition that the purchasers should undertake to carry out certain repairs. The plaintiffs, on being offered a loan of £8,505 subject to this condition, assumed that the property must have been valued at not less than £8,505 and that no serious defects had been found; they thereupon agreed to purchase. Some three years later, when the plaintiffs attempted to sell the house, they discovered that it was subject to settlement, required extensive and expensive underpinning work and was effectively unsaleable.

The House of Lords, expressly approving the decision in *Yianni*, held unanimously that a duty of care was owed to the purchasers in each of these cases. In so deciding, the three judges who delivered speeches clearly regarded two factors as critical: the mortgage valuer's knowledge that the purchaser was likely to rely (directly or indirectly) on the valuation, and the fact that the valuer's fee would ultimately be paid by the purchaser. As Lord Templeman stated[60]:

"In general, I am of the opinion that in the absence of a disclaimer of liability the valuer who values a house for the purpose of a mortgage, knowing that the mortgagee will rely and the mortgagor will probably rely on the valuation, knowing that the purchaser mortgagor has in effect paid for the valuation, is under a duty to exercise reasonable skill and care and that duty is owed to both parties to the mortgage for which the valuation is made."

Lord Griffiths, having referred to the threefold test of foreseeability, proximity and just and reasonableness,[61] continued[62]:

"In the case of a surveyor valuing a small house for a building society or local authority, the application of these three criteria leads to the conclusion that he owes a duty of care to the purchaser. If the valuation is negligent and is relied on damage in the form of economic loss to the purchaser is obviously foreseeable. The necessary proximity arises from the surveyor's knowledge that the overwhelming probability is that the purchaser will rely on his valuation, the evidence was that surveyors knew that approximately 90 per cent of purchasers did so, and the fact that the surveyor only obtains the work because the purchaser is willing to pay his fee. It is just and reasonable that the duty should be imposed for the advice is given in a professional as opposed to a social context and liability for breach of the duty will be limited both as to its extent and amount. The extent of the liability is limited to the purchaser of the house: I would not extend it to subsequent purchasers.[63] The amount of the liability cannot be very great because it relates to a modest house."

Lord Jauncey, while agreeing in the decision, adopted a more cautious approach, for example expressing doubts as to whether the position of a mortgagee's staff valuer should really be equated with that of an independent professional. More

---

60. [1990] 1 A.C. 831 at 848.
61. See p. 609.
62. [1990] 1 A.C. 831 at 865.
63. On this point see also Lord Jauncey: [1990] 1 A.C. 831 at 872.

importantly, Lord Jauncey drew attention to the type of property with which both appeals were concerned[64]:

"I would not therefore conclude that the mere fact that a mortgagee's valuer knows that his valuation will be shown to an intending mortgagor of itself imposes on him a duty of care to the mortgagor. Knowledge, actual or implied, of a mortgagor's likely reliance on the valuation must be brought home to him. Such knowledge may be fairly readily implied in relation to a potential mortgagor seeking to enter the lower end of the housing market but *non constat* that such ready implication would arise in the case of a purchase of an expensive property whether residential or commercial."

In the light of *Smith* v. *Bush* there can be no doubt that, at least where "modest" residential properties are concerned, a mortgage valuer will owe a duty of care to the purchaser.[65] Indeed, in virtually all subsequent cases the existence of this duty has been either expressly conceded by the defendant or assumed by the court.[66] Furthermore, although the House of Lords recognised the possibility that a valuation of industrial or commercial property, or even of a very expensive house, might justify a different conclusion,[67] this line of argument appears to have been pursued in only one subsequent case, where it failed.[68]

In *Saddington* v. *Colleys Professional Services*[69] an unsuccessful attempt was made to extend the *Smith* v. *Bush* principle to a case where the plaintiffs, a married couple, remortgaged their house in order to raise capital for the husband's business. When the business failed, the wife sued the mortgage valuers on the basis that, due to their negligent over-valuation of the property, she had incurred a liability to repay the mortgage loan. The Court of Appeal held that the valuers were not liable: it was impossible to regard either the plaintiff's acceptance of the loan, or her giving of security for the loan, as a "loss", and the defendants could not be said to have caused the loss of the money through failure of the business.

It is worth noting that the duty of care which a mortgage valuer owes to a house purchaser is quite independent of the duty which is owed to the mortgagee, and there is no reason in principle why a negligent valuer should not be made to pay damages to both parties. In view of this risk, a valuer sued by a house purchaser may wish to ensure that the lender is informed of the progress of the litigation.[70]

---

64. [1990] 1 A.C. 831 at 872.

65. This is apparently limited to the particular purchaser whose mortgage application led to the valuation which is challenged: [1990] 1 A.C. 831 at 865 *per* Lord Griffiths; at 872 *per* Lord Jauncey. See also *Yianni* v. *Edwin Evans & Sons* [1982] Q.B. 438 at 456.

66. See *Gibbs* v. *Arnold Son & Hockley* [1989] 2 E.G.L.R. 154; *Bere* v. *Slades* [1989] 2 E.G.L.R. 160; *Whalley* v. *Roberts & Roberts* [1990] 1 E.G.L.R. 164; *Lloyd* v. *Butler* [1990] 2 E.G.L.R. 155; *Henley* v. *Cloke & Sons* [1991] 2 E.G.L.R. 141; *Peach* v. *Iain G Chalmers & Co* [1992] 2 E.G.L.R. 135.

67. See *Smith* v. *Eric S Bush*; *Harris* v. *Wyre Forest D.C.* [1990] 1 A.C. 831 at 859–860 *per* Lord Griffiths; at 872 *per* Lord Jauncey.

68. In *Qureshi* v. *Liassides* (unreported) 22 April 1994, Official Referees' Business, a negligence action was based on a valuation for mortgage purposes of a small greengrocer's shop. Mr Recorder Anthony Thornton QC regarded the case as indistinguishable from *Smith* v. *Bush*.

69. [1995] E.G.C.S. 109.

70. If this is done, the lender may be able in turn to ensure that any damages received by the borrower are used in repayment of the mortgage loan, thus reducing the likelihood of an action by the lender against the valuer.

### 3.2.2 Liability of mortgagee

The possibility that a lender who commissions a mortgage valuation might be held responsible for any negligence on the part of the valuer has been considered by the courts on a number of occasions. Their response, at least in principle, has been generally hostile, for reasons explained by Lord Jauncey in *Smith* v. *Eric S Bush*; *Harris* v. *Wyre Forest DC*[71]:

"The fact that A is prepared to lend money to B on the security of property owned by or to be acquired by him cannot *per se* impose upon A any duty of care to B. Much more is required. Were it otherwise a loan by A to B on the security of property, real or personal, would *ipso facto* amount to a warranty by A that the property was worth at least the sum lent."

Nor, it appears, does the buyer's claim gain strength by being based on an alleged breach of contract by the mortgagee.[72] As pointed out by Gibson LJ in the Northern Ireland Court of Appeal[73]: "Generally, a mortgage contract in itself imports no obligation on the part of a mortgagee to use care in protecting the interests of a mortgagor."

While such comments might suggest that a mortgagee can never be liable for a negligent valuation, the actual decisions tell a very different story, at least where the valuation concerned is carried out by an employee of the mortgagee. The courts in such cases have tended to focus their attention on the tort which is committed by the individual valuer and then to hold the mortgagee vicariously liable *qua* employer for it; in this way the weakness of the house buyer's claim against the mortgagee *qua* mortgagee is simply ignored.[74] In the light of this approach, the liability of mortgagees for in-house valuations has been generally accepted.[75]

Where a mortgage valuation is commissioned from an independent valuer, there can be no question of imposing vicarious liability as such on the mortgagee for any negligence.[76] The mortgagee may nevertheless be held responsible to the house buyer for any negligence on its part in appointing or instructing the valuer

---

71. [1990] 1 A.C. 831 at 872 (endorsed by Lord Templeman at 847 and Lord Griffiths at 865). See also the views of Kerr LJ when *Harris* v. *Wyre Forest D.C.* was before the Court of Appeal: [1988] Q.B. 835 at 851.

72. It is in any event not clear whether the provision of a mortgage valuation is to be regarded as part of the contract between mortgagor and mortgagee. Such an interpretation is supported by the decision in *Melrose* v. *Davidson & Robertson* 1993 S.L.T. 611 and by *dicta* of Lord Templeman and Lord Griffiths in *Smith* v. *Eric S Bush; Harris* v. *Wyre Forest D.C.* [1990] 1 A.C. 831 at 847 and 865 respectively. However, a contrary decision was reached in *Hadden* v. *City of Glasgow D.C.* 1986 S.L.T. 557, and serious doubts were expressed by Parker LJ in *Beresforde* v. *Chesterfield B.C.* [1989] 2 E.G.L.R. 149. In most of the cases where the potential liability of the mortgagee has been considered, the courts appear simply to have assumed that any claim lies in tort: see, for example, *Stevenson* v. *Nationwide Building Society* [1984] 2 E.G.L.R. 165; *Ward* v. *McMaster* [1985] I.R. 29; *Westlake* v. *Bracknell D.C.* [1987] 1 E.G.L.R. 161; *Beaton* v. *Nationwide Building Society* [1991] 2 E.G.L.R. 145.

73. *Curran* v. *Northern Ireland Co-ownership Housing Association Ltd* (1986) 8 N.I.J.B. 1.

74. Some of the judgments are less than clear on this issue, wavering between the duty of the valuer and the duty of the mortgagee: see, for example, *Smith* v. *Eric S Bush; Harris* v. *Wyre Forest D.C.* [1990] 1 A.C. 831 at 847 *per* Lord Templeman; at 865–866 *per* Lord Griffiths.

75. Both before the decision in *Smith* v. *Bush* (*Stevenson* v. *Nationwide Building Society* [1984] 2 E.G.L.R. 165; *Hadden* v. *City of Glasgow D.C.* 1986 S.L.T. 557; *Westlake* v. *Bracknell D.C.* [1987] 1 E.G.L.R. 161) and after it (*Beaton* v. *Nationwide Building Society* [1991] 2 E.G.L.R. 145).

76. "The mortgagee will not be held liable for the negligence of the independent valuer who acts as an independent contractor": *Smith* v. *Eric S Bush; Harris* v. *Wyre Forest D.C.* [1990] 1 A.C. 831 at 865 *per* Lord Griffiths. See also *Halifax Building Society* v. *Edell* [1992] Ch. 436 at 454 *per* Morritt J.

concerned.[77] Furthermore, there is some authority for the view that a mortgagee which "adopts" the report of an independent valuer (for example by sending a copy of it to the purchaser on the mortgagee's own notepaper) may thereby render itself liable for any negligence on the part of the valuer.[78]

### 3.3 Claims by mortgage lenders

Where mortgage loans are made on the security of commercial property, it is common for the prospective borrower to commission and pay for a valuation of the property which is then shown to one or more prospective lenders. In a number of cases decided around the turn of the century it was held that, in the absence of a contract between the valuer and the mortgagee,[79] there could be no liability if the mortgagee relied on the valuation which proved to have been negligently carried out.[80]

Since *Hedley Byrne & Co Ltd* v. *Heller & Partners Ltd*,[81] it appears to have been assumed on all sides that the relationship between valuer and mortgagee will support a duty of care in tort, provided only that the valuer is aware of the purpose for which the valuation is required and that it has not been provided to the client under an explicit condition that it is not to be shown to or relied on by any other party.[82] In most of the reported cases, the valuer has known the actual identity of the proposed mortgagee; it is common practice among institutional lenders to require any report originally commissioned by the mortgagor to be readdressed to the mortgagee. However, even without such specific knowledge, the existence of a duty of care has seldom been put in issue. Thus, a duty of care has been conceded by valuers in respect of valuations which they addressed to "the lending principals" and sent either to solicitors[83] or to mortgage brokers.[84]

The assumption that a duty of care exists in this situation[85] is so strong that, even in

77. "The mortgagee in such a case, knowing that the mortgagor will rely on the valuation, owes a duty to the mortgagor to take reasonable care to employ a reasonably competent valuer": *Smith* v. *Eric S Bush*; *Harris* v. *Wyre Forest D.C.* [1990] 1 A.C. 831 at 865 *per* Lord Griffiths. See also *Ward* v. *McMaster* [1985] I.R. 29.

78. In *Beresforde* v. *Chesterfield B.C.* [1989] 2 E.G.L.R. 149, the Court of Appeal refused to strike out a claim of this kind as disclosing no reasonable cause of action, while drawing attention to the "formidable difficulties" which lay between the plaintiffs and ultimate success. See also *Tipton & Coseley Building Society* v. *Collins* [1994] E.G.C.S. 120.

79. Such a contract was found to exist in *Scholes* v. *Brook* (1891) 63 L.T. 837; affirmed (1892) 64 L.T. 674.

80. *Le Lievre* v. *Gould* [1893] 1 Q.B. 491 (overruling *Cann* v. *Willson* (1888) 39 Ch.D. 39); *Love* v. *Mack* (1905) 92 L.T. 345.

81. [1964] A.C. 465.

82. As it was in *Commercial Financial Services Ltd* v. *McBeth & Co* (unreported) 15 January 1988, Court of Session.

83. *Corisand Investments Ltd* v. *Druce & Co* [1978] 2 E.G.L.R. 86.

84. *Swingcastle Ltd* v. *Alastair Gibson* [1991] 1 E.G.L.R. 157. In *Assured Advances Ltd* v. *Ashbee & Co* [1994] E.G.C.S. 169, valuers instructed by mortgage brokers argued that they owed no duty of care to an unknown lender, specialising in high-risk loans, to whom the valuation was shown. It was held that, since the valuers knew that the valuation would be used to make a decision on mortgage lending, they would owe a duty of care to any lender, even if the valuation "passed from hand to hand until a lender could be found".

85. Which frequently leads defendants to concede the existence of the duty: see *Singer & Friedlander Ltd* v. *John D Wood & Co* [1977] 2 E.G.L.R. 84; *HIT Finance Ltd* v. *Lewis & Tucker Ltd* [1993] 2 E.G.L.R. 231; *Craneheath Securities Ltd* v. *York Montague Ltd* [1994] 1 E.G.L.R. 159.

those cases where the evidence might support a contractual relationship,[86] the courts have tended to ignore this in favour of the duty in tort.[87] The assumption has moreover received support from the highest level, in the speech of Lord Templeman in *Smith* v. *Eric S Bush; Harris* v. *Wyre Forest DC*[88]:

"A valuer who values property as security for a mortgage is liable either in contract or in tort to the mortgagee for any failure on the part of the valuer to exercise reasonable skill and care in the valuation. The valuer is liable in contract if he receives instructions from and is paid by the mortgagee. The valuer is liable in tort if he receives instructions from and is paid by the mortgagor but knows that the valuation is for the purpose of a mortgage and will be relied on by the mortgagee."

In *Banque Bruxelles Lambert SA* v. *Eagle Star Insurance Co Ltd*[89] the plaintiffs made a number of very large loans to companies on the security of commercial properties which the latter had recently acquired. In each case the plaintiffs placed reliance on a valuation of the property concerned by a firm of valuers who were instructed and paid by the borrowing companies. In addition, the plaintiffs required insurance cover against the risk of default by the borrowers; the relevant mortgage indemnity guarantee policies were issued by Eagle Star Insurance Co Ltd, which also relied on the valuations before agreeing to underwrite the risk. It was held that, in carrying out the relevant valuations, the valuers owed a duty of care, not only to the mortgagees (which they conceded), but also to Eagle Star (which they had strenuously denied).

### 3.4 Independent experts and arbitrators

A contract may provide that, in the event of a dispute arising, the parties will submit that dispute for determination by an independent third party with appropriate expert knowledge and, further, that they will treat the third party's decision as binding. Depending on the terms of the contract, the third party may be an arbitrator or merely an "independent expert",[90] and may be appointed by the parties themselves or by some other person.[91] As far as surveyors and valuers are concerned, such procedures are adopted most frequently in rent reviews, although a surveyor might also be appointed to determine the surrender value of a lease[92] or the market value of property which the parties have agreed in principle to buy and sell.[93] It appears that

---

86. See, for example, *Mount Banking Corporation Ltd* v. *Brian Cooper & Co* [1992] 2 E.G.L.R. 142; *European Partners in Capital (EPIC) Holdings BV* v. *Goddard & Smith* [1992] 2 E.G.L.R. 155; *Nykredit Mortgage Bank plc* v. *Edward Erdman Group Ltd* [1996] 02 E.G. 110, Mayor's and City of London Court; *United Bank of Kuwait* v. *Prudential Property Services Ltd* [1994] 2 E.G.L.R. 100.

87. See *PK Finans International (UK) Ltd* v. *Andrew Downs & Co Ltd* [1992] 1 E.G.L.R. 172; *Allied Trust Bank Ltd* v. *Edward Symmons & Partners* [1994] 1 E.G.L.R. 165.

88. [1990] 1 A.C. 831 at 844.

89. [1995] 2 All E.R. 769.

90. Many leases provide expressly that an independent surveyor appointed under a rent review provision shall act "as an expert and not as an arbitrator". Though highly persuasive, such a provision is not conclusive, since "You cannot make a valuer an arbitrator by calling him so, or vice versa": *Taylor* v. *Yielding* (1912) 56 S.J. 253 *per* Greer LJ. In the absence of an express provision, the status of the surveyor may depend upon interpretation of the lease as a whole: see, for example, *Langham House Developments Ltd* v. *Brompton Securities Ltd* [1980] 2 E.G.L.R. 117; *North Eastern Co-operative Society Ltd* v. *Newcastle upon Tyne CC* [1987] 1 E.G.L.R. 142; *Safeway Food Stores Ltd* v. *Banderway Ltd* [1983] 2 E.G.L.R. 116.

91. Commonly the President of an appropriate professional body such as the R.I.C.S. or the I.S.V.A.

92. As in *Campbell* v. *Edwards* [1976] 1 All E.R. 785.

93. As in *Arenson* v. *Casson, Beckman, Rutley & Co* [1977] A.C. 405.

an appointment of this kind creates a trilateral contract[94] and, subject to what is said below, the third party will owe a duty of care in both contract and tort to each of the other parties.[95]

A decision of an arbitrator is subject to a limited right of appeal on a point of law.[96] By contrast, a determination by an independent expert is virtually unimpeachable,[97] except where the expert's appointment is itself invalid (e.g., because it is out of time).[98] As Knox J explained in *Nikko Hotels (UK) Ltd* v. *MEPC plc*[99]:

"If parties agree to refer to the final and conclusive judgment of an expert an issue which either consists of a question of construction or necessarily involves the solution of a question of construction, the expert's decision will be final and conclusive and, therefore, not open to review or treatment by the courts as a nullity on the ground that the expert's decision on construction was erroneous in law, unless it can be shown that the expert has not performed the task assigned to him. If he has answered the right question in the wrong way, his decision will be binding. If he has answered the wrong question, his decision will be a nullity."

The extent to which an independent decision-maker may incur liability to the parties for negligence is not entirely clear, although two propositions appear reasonably well settled. First, someone who is formally appointed as an arbitrator is immune from negligence claims arising out of his decision.[100] Secondly, a "mere" independent expert has no such immunity and thus owes a duty of care to both parties.[101]

The area of uncertainty concerns the possibility that a person who is not an arbitrator in the formal sense may nevertheless be immune from claims in negligence if he is required to act in a "judicial" role and not merely to carry out a valuation.[102] The existence of such immunity has twice been recognised by the House of Lords,[103] although defining the circumstances in which it will arise has proved difficult. The

---

94. *K/S Norjarl A/S* v. *Hyundai Heavy Industries Co Ltd* [1992] Q.B. 863 at 885 *per* Sir Nicolas Browne-Wilkinson, V-C. This analysis is not universally accepted: see Mustill & Boyd, *Commercial Arbitration* (2nd edn, 1989), pp. 220–223.

95. In the unlikely event that the expert is in a contractual relationship (carrying responsibility for fees) with only one of the parties, a duty of care in tort would presumably be owed to the other party.

96. Arbitration Act 1979, s. 1.

97. *Campbell* v. *Edwards* [1976] 1 All E.R. 785; *Baber* v. *Kenwood Manufacturing Co* [1978] 1 Lloyd's Rep. 175. This is so even where a reasoned decision contains patent errors of law: *Jones* v. *Sherwood Computer Services plc* [1992] 2 All E.R. 170, overruling *Burgess* v. *Purchase & Sons (Farms) Ltd* [1983] 2 All E.R. 4.

98. See *Darlington B.C.* v. *Waring & Gillow (Holdings) Ltd* [1988] 2 E.G.L.R. 159.

99. [1991] 2 E.G.L.R. 103 at 108; followed in *Pontsarn Investments Ltd* v. *Kansallis-Osake-Pankki* [1992] 1 E.G.L.R. 148.

100. *Arenson* v. *Casson, Beckman, Rutley & Co* [1977] A.C. 405. The implied duty of care and skill in contracts for services (Supply of Goods and Services Act 1982, s. 13) is specifically excluded in relation to "services rendered by an arbitrator" (Supply of Services (Exclusion of Implied Terms) Order 1985, S.I. 1985/1).

101. "An expert owes the parties a duty to carry out the valuation with reasonable professional skill. If he does not, he will be liable in damages to the party who, in consequence, has to pay more or receive less than he would have done": *Zubaida* v. *Hargreaves* [1995] 1 E.G.L.R. 127 *per* Hoffmann LJ. The existence of a duty of care was also accepted in *Campbell* v. *Edwards* [1976] 1 All E.R. 785; *Belvedere Motors Ltd* v. *King* [1981] 2 E.G.L.R. 131; and *Wallshire Ltd* v. *Aarons* [1989] 1 E.G.L.R. 147. However, in no reported case has a plaintiff yet succeeded in establishing negligence against a surveyor acting as an independent expert.

102. The term "quasi-arbitrator" is often used in this context, but has been criticised: see *Arenson* v. *Casson, Beckman, Rutley & Co* [1977] A.C. 405 at 424 *per* Lord Simon.

103. *Sutcliffe* v. *Thackrah* [1974] A.C. 727; *Arenson* v. *Casson, Beckman, Rutley & Co* [1977] A.C. 405.

most complete attempt was made by Lord Wheatley in *Arenson* v. *Casson, Beckman, Rutley & Co*[104]:

"The indicia are as follows: (a) there is a dispute or difference between the parties which has been formulated in some way or another; (b) the dispute or difference has been remitted by the parties to the person to resolve in such a manner that he is called on to exercise a judicial function; (c) where appropriate, the parties must have been provided with an opportunity to present evidence and/or submissions in support of their respective claims in the dispute; and (d) the parties have agreed to accept his decision."

In *Palacath Ltd* v. *Flanagan*,[105] an independent surveyor appointed to carry out a rent review claimed immunity as a "quasi-arbitrator" when sued by the landlords, who alleged that he had negligently fixed the rent at too low a level. Having studied the terms of the lease,[106] Mars-Jones J confessed that he had at one time thought that the case contained all the criteria identified by Lord Wheatley. However, further reflection led the judge to a change of mind[107]:

"I am satisfied that the provisions of [the rent review clause] were not intended to set up a judicial or quasi-judicial machinery for the resolution of this dispute or difference about the amount of the revised rent. Its object was to enable the defendant to inform himself of the matters which the parties concerned were relevant to the issue. He was not obliged to make any finding or findings accepting or rejecting the opposing contentions. Nor indeed, as I see it, was he obliged to accept as valid and binding on him matters on which the parties were agreed. He was not appointed to adjudicate on the cases put forward on behalf of the landlord and the tenant. He was appointed to give his own independent judgment as an expert, after reading the representations and valuations of the parties (if any) and giving them such weight as he thought proper (if any). That being so, there can be no basis for conferring immunity on the defendant in respect of a claim for damages for negligence in and about giving that independent expert view."

## 3.5 Other cases

Apart from the types of cases described above, which are the ones most often encountered, the question whether the relationship between the surveyor or valuer and a particular third party is sufficiently proximate to found a duty of care has been raised in a number of other situations. First, as a general point, the courts have for the most part been willing to utilise a tortious duty of care to outflank technical arguments as to whether a company, or the individual who controls it, is the client of a negligent surveyor or valuer.[108] In *Miro Properties Ltd* v. *J Trevor & Sons*[109] this enabled a claim in respect of a negligent survey which was commissioned by the promoters of a company to be brought by the company, despite the fact that it had not been incorporated at the time when the survey was carried out.

Turning to more specific situations, the first is where a survey of property to be sold is commissioned by the vendor, with the intention of making the surveyor's report

104. [1977] A.C. 405 at 428.
105. [1985] 2 All E.R. 161.
106. Which included a provision that, in determining the rent (upon certain stated assumptions), the surveyor: "(1) will act as an expert and not as an arbitrator; (2) will consider any statement of reasons or valuation or report submitted to him as aforesaid but will not be in any way limited or fettered thereby; (3) will be entitled to rely on his own judgment and opinion".
107. [1985] 2 All E.R. 161 at 166.
108. See *Freeman* v. *Marshall & Co* (1966) 200 E.G. 777; *Kendall Wilson Securities* v. *Barraclough* [1986] 1 N.Z.L.R. 576; cf. *Old Gate Estates Ltd* v. *Toplis* [1939] 3 All E.R. 209.
109. [1989] 1 E.G.L.R. 151.

available to prospective purchasers.[110] Although direct authority is lacking, the courts have recognised a duty of care in a somewhat similar situation, where a specialist in the detection and treatment of rot and damp issued a report or guarantee to someone whom he knew to be preparing a property for sale.[111] However, the argument that a surveyor in such circumstances would be placed in an impossible position, given the conflict of interest between vendor and purchaser, gains some support from the courts' refusal in conveyancing cases to hold a vendor's solicitor liable to the purchase for negligent misstatements.[112]

A second possible area of liability concerns a surveyor or valuer who, in advising a lender on the sale of a repossessed property, negligently causes the property to be sold at below its true value. It is established that, in such circumstances, the mortgagee will be held responsible for any loss suffered to the mortgagor, and judges in a number of cases have suggested that the mortgagor might also take action directly against the professional adviser concerned.[113] However, it was recently held in *Huish* v. *Ellis*[114] that this is not so, and that the adviser's duty of care in this context is owed to the mortgagee alone.[115]

A third situation, which does not appear to have featured in any reported case, concerns the possibility of a claim by a vendor who loses a sale, or is forced to sell at a reduced price, following an adverse survey or mortgage valuation. While a *deliberate* untruth contained in such a report could undoubtedly support a claim in the tort of malicious falsehood,[116] it is submitted that the relationship between the vendor and a surveyor instructed by either the purchaser or a mortgage lender is not sufficiently proximate to give rise to a duty of care.

## 4 THE STANDARD OF CARE AND SKILL

A negligence claim arising out of a survey almost invariably relates to a physical defect in the property concerned.[117] The essence of the complaint may be that the surveyor through negligence has failed to observe the defect altogether; or has

110. This practice, found mainly in the context of sales by auction, was at one time put forward in a Law Commission consultation paper (*Caveat Emptor in Sales of Land*—1988) as part of a general reform of *caveat emptor*. However, it was not included in the Law Commission's final recommendations (*Let the buyer be well informed*—1989).

111. *Shankie-Williams* v. *Heavey* [1986] 2 E.G.L.R. 139; *Bourne* v. *McEvoy Timber Preservation* [1976] 1 E.G.L.R. 100.

112. See *Cemp Properties (UK) Ltd* v. *Dentsply Research & Development Corporation* [1989] 2 E.G.L.R. 192; *Gran Gelato Ltd* v. *Richcliff (Group) Ltd* [1992] 1 E.G.L.R. 297. On the other hand, a vendor's *estate agent* has been held directly liable to a purchaser: *Computastaff Ltd* v. *Ingledew Brown Bennison & Garrett* [1983] 2 E.G.L.R. 150; cf. *McCullagh* v. *Lane Fox & Partners Ltd* [1995] E.G.C.S. 195.

113. See *Cuckmere Brick Co Ltd* v. *Mutual Finance Ltd* [1971] Ch. 949; *Johnson* v. *Ribbins* [1975] 2 E.G.L. 78; *Commercial & General Acceptance Ltd* v. *Nixon* (1981) 152 C.L.R. 491; *Garland* v. *Ralph Pay and Ransom* [1984] 2 E.G.L.R. 147.

114. [1995] N.P.C. 3.

115. The judge held that given the conflict of interest involved, and the fact that the mortgagor could claim against the mortgagee, the creation of an additional duty of care would not be just or reasonable.

116. See *Mayer* v. *Pluck* (1971) 223 E.G. 219.

117. However, the courts in assessing damages are concerned, not with the cost of rectifying such defects, but with their effect on the value of the property: see p. 644.

observed it but failed to recognise or understand its significance; and/or has failed to report adequately on the defect and its significance. A negligence claim arising out of a valuation may likewise be based on a failure by the valuer to observe or recognise a physical defect in the property. However, it may also relate to other factors such as a lack of awareness of the property market (either generally or locally), failure to understand and apply the correct methods of valuation, inadequate selection of comparables, the making of inappropriate assumptions or errors in calculation.

It should be emphasised that all these issues are essentially questions of fact and dependent upon all the circumstances of a particular case. A judicial decision that a surveyor or valuer is or is not in breach of duty does not therefore constitute a binding precedent, but is at best a guide as to how a future court might view a broadly similar factual situation.

In reaching a decision as to whether or not a surveyor or valuer is in breach of the duty of care and skill, a court will pay close attention to the evidence of expert witnesses called by the parties[118] or (less commonly) by the court.[119] Such a witness is commonly called to assist the court on two issues: whether the defendant's error was one which a reasonably competent practitioner would not have made,[120] and whether procedures or techniques adopted by the defendant reflected those of the profession in general.[121] In giving evidence on these issues, the expert should possess qualifications and experience which are at least equal to those of the defendant, and which are of direct relevance. In *Whalley* v. *Roberts & Roberts*,[122] which concerned a mortgage valuation, Auld J said[123]:

"In my view, it is only the evidence of the surveyors that may be of value on this issue. [The civil engineer and architect], however competent they may be in their respective professions, cannot speak with authority on what is to be expected of the ordinarily competent surveyor."

It follows that, while a surveyor in general practice with relevant local experience may be a suitable expert witness in a case involving a negligent valuation, a chartered building surveyor should be instructed in a case arising out of a structural or building survey.

Since the question of breach is essentially one of fact, a plaintiff will very rarely be entitled in a disputed case to summary judgment under RSC Order 14. This is

118. Valuable guidance on the role of the expert witness was given by Cresswell J in *National Justice Compania Naviera SA* v. *Prudential Insurance Co Ltd, The "Ikarian Reefer"* [1993] 2 Lloyd's Rep. 68, [1993] 2 E.G.L.R. 182n.

119. The principles on which a court will decide whether or not to appoint its own expert were considered by the Court of Appeal in *Abbey National Mortgages plc* v. *Key Surveyors Nationwide Ltd* [1996] E.G.C.S. 23.

120. "A valuer will only be liable if other qualified valuers, who cannot be expected to be harsh on their fellow professionals, consider that taking into consideration the nature of the work for which the valuer is paid and the object of that work, nevertheless he has been guilty of an error which an average valuer, in the same circumstances, would not have made": *Smith* v. *Eric S Bush; Harris* v. *Wyre Forest D.C.* [1990] 1 A.C. 831 at 851 *per* Lord Templeman.

121. In *Strover* v. *Harrington* [1988] Ch. 390 a purchaser's surveyor, relying on what he was told by the vendor, reported that the property was served by main drainage (when in truth the drains led to a cesspool). The plaintiffs led no evidence as to what would be normal professional practice in this situation, a failure which was held to be fatal to their claim.

122. [1990] 1 E.G.L.R. 164.

123. *Ibid.* at 169, applying what was said by Slade LJ in *Investors in Industry Ltd* v. *South Bedfordshire D.C.* [1986] 1 All E.R. 787 at 808–809.

especially so where allegations of professional negligence involve a conflict of opinion between professionally qualified persons. In *European Partners In Capital (EPIC) Holdings BV v. Goddard & Smith*,[124] which concerned an allegedly negligent valuation of commercial property for mortgage purposes, Scott LJ said[125]:

"In my judgement, issues of professional opinion, which must be chosen between if liability in negligence is to be established, will not as a general rule be issues suitable to be resolved on a summary judgment application ... If it has been made clear ... that the defendants propose to stand by and contend for the competence of, let alone the correctness of, their expression of professional opinion, it would be a very unusual case in which it would be right to deny them the opportunity of so doing at trial."

## 4.1 General principles

### 4.1.1 The basic standard

The yardstick by which a defendant falls to be judged in a professional negligence action is that described by McNair J in *Bolam* v. *Friern Hospital Management Committee*[126]:

"Where you get a situation which involves the use of some special skill or competence, then the test whether there has been negligence or not is ... the standard of the ordinary skilled man exercising and professing to have that special skill. A man need not possess the highest expert skill. It is well established law that it is sufficient if he exercises the ordinary skill of an ordinary competent man exercising that particular art."[127]

The emphasis which is thus placed upon "ordinary" skill raises the issue of what standard is to be expected of a person or firm claiming to possess specialist skills or additional expertise within a particular profession. The question of whether a higher standard is demanded in such circumstances has not directly arisen in any case concerning a surveyor or valuer. Surprisingly, perhaps, the balance of authority in cases relating to other professions appears to favour the application of the "ordinary" standard.[128]

Whatever the true position of those who possess additional qualifications or expertise, it is clear that inexperience or lack of qualifications will provide no defence against a charge of professional negligence. In *Freeman* v. *Marshall & Co*,[129] where a surveyor was sued for failing to report on rising damp, the defendant said that he was unqualified; had undergone no organised course of training nor passed any professional examination in surveying; had become a member of the Valuers Institution through election, not examination; and had only a working knowledge of structures from the point of view of buying and selling. It was held that, since the

---

124. [1992] 2 E.G.L.R. 155.
125. *Ibid.* at 157.
126. [1957] 2 All E.R. 118 at 121.
127. See also the remarks of Lord Diplock in *Saif Ali* v. *Sidney Mitchell & Co* [1980] A.C. 198 at 220: "No matter what profession it may be, the common law does not impose on those who practise it any liability for damage resulting from what in the result turn out to be errors of judgment, unless the error was such as no reasonably well-informed and competent member of that profession could have made".
128. See *Duchess of Argyll* v. *Beuselinck* [1972] 2 Lloyd's Rep. 172 (solicitors); *Andrew Master Homes Ltd* v. *Cruikshank and Fairweather* [1980] R.P.C. 16 (patent agents); *Wimpey Construction (UK) Ltd* v. *Poole* [1984] 2 Lloyd's Rep. 499 (engineers).
129. (1966) 200 E.G. 777.

defendant had held himself out as a surveyor, he must be deemed to have the skills of a surveyor and would be judged upon those skills.[130]

In *Baxter* v. *F W Gapp & Co Ltd*,[131] the defendant valuer was instructed to carry out a valuation of a bungalow for mortgage purposes. The defendant was experienced in the general sense but had no particular knowledge of values in the locality.[132] A local practitioner would almost certainly have been aware that close to the bungalow there was a similar house for sale and also a smaller house which had been for sale for over a year. It was held[133] that, if the valuer did not know enough about the property market or property values at the place where the bungalow was situated, he should have taken steps to inform himself of such matters. As Goddard LJ pointed out:[134]

"It would be no defence, for instance, to say: I made this valuation, but the reason why my valuation has proved incorrect, if it has proved incorrect, is that I was not a person, as you know, who practised in that locality."

The standard demanded of a surveyor or valuer, that of the "ordinary skilled man", applies whether or not a fee is charged for the professional services which are called in question.[135] Nor is this standard lessened if the valuation is carried out in difficult circumstances, as where the market is showing signs of collapsing into a depression.[136] There is moreover no reason why, just because a mortgage loan is taking place at the risky end of the market, the lender should not be entitled to receive advice from an expert valuer arrived at after the exercise of proper care and skill.[137]

In deciding whether a defendant has complied with the required standard, "the court must have regard to the circumstances and knowledge current at the time of the survey. The court must be careful to guard against hindsight and determine the surveyor's skill and competence on the knowledge and information available to him at the time of the survey".[138] While this approach may operate to the defendant's benefit, in preventing the court from being "wise after the event",[139] it also means that a defendant may be adjudged negligent for failing to keep up to date with what is common knowledge in the profession.[140] Surveyors have been held liable on this basis for failing to appreciate the problems associated with ventilation in flat roofs[141] and with precast reinforced concrete houses of the "Dorran" type.[142]

One aspect of the need to keep up to date relates to the legal knowledge which a

---

130. See also *Kenney* v. *Hall, Pain & Foster* [1976] 2 E.G.L.R. 29, where the defendant estate agents were held liable for a free valuation given by one of their sales negotiators who had no formal qualifications and whose experience of estate agency was limited to six months in New Zealand and three months with the defendants.

131. [1938] 4 All E.R. 456.

132. Lack of relevant local knowledge constitutes breach of a professional requirement: R.I.C.S. *Appraisal and Valuation Manual*, Practice Statement 5.

133. By Goddard LJ, whose decision was affirmed by the Court of Appeal: [1939] 2 K.B. 271.

134. [1938] 4 All E.R. 457 at 459.

135. *Kenney* v. *Hall, Pain & Foster* [1976] 2 E.G.L.R. 29 at 33 *per* Goff J.

136. *Private Bank & Trust Co Ltd* v. *S (UK) Ltd* [1993] 1 E.G.L.R. 144 at 146 *per* Judge Rice. See also *Singer & Friedlander Ltd* v. *John D Wood & Co* [1977] 2 E.G.L.R. 84 at 85–86 *per* Watkins J.

137. *Britannic Securities & Investments Ltd* v. *Hirani Watson* [1995] E.G.C.S. 46.

138. *Private Bank & Trust Co Ltd* v. *S (UK) Ltd* [1993] 1 E.G.L.R. 144 at 146 *per* Judge Rice.

139. See *Hill* v. *Debenham, Tewson and Chinnocks* (1958) 171 E.G. 835 *per* Judge Carter QC.

140. The need for valuers to be aware of market movements is discussed at p. 635.

141. *Hooberman* v. *Salter Rex* [1985] 1 E.G.L.R. 144.

142. *Peach* v. *Iain G Chalmers & Co* [1992] 2 E.G.L.R. 135.

surveyor or valuer is expected to possess. That some knowledge of the law is required was specifically recognised as long ago as 1855, in an action for negligence which arose out a valuation of dilapidations in a rectory.[143] The valuer concerned based his valuation upon an erroneous view of the law, in allowing only for rendering the premises habitable (as in the case of normal tenants) and not for putting them into good and substantial repair. The trial judge told the jury that the defendants were under no duty to supply any skill in, or knowledge of, the law, whereupon the jury found them not liable. On appeal to the Court of Common Pleas, a new trial was ordered, and Jervis CJ said[144]:

"The defendants could not be expected to supply minute and accurate knowledge of the law; but we think that, under the circumstances, they might properly be required to know the general rules applicable to the valuation of ecclesiastical property, and the broad distinction which exists between the cases of an incoming and an outgoing tenant, and an incoming and outgoing incumbent."

Liability for failing to keep abreast of developments in the law arose specifically in *Weedon* v. *Hindwood, Clarke & Esplin*,[145] where the defendants were retained to act for a client in compulsory purchase negotiations. Shortly before these negotiations began, a well-publicised decision of the Court of Appeal[146] altered the law as to the date on which property should be valued for this purpose, and this new rule was confirmed by the House of Lords before the defendants agreed a figure on behalf of their client.[147] Despite this change, which would have been very favourable to their client, the defendants allowed themselves to be persuaded by the district valuer to agree upon a figure which was clearly based on the old law, and were held liable in negligence for the resulting loss.

### 4.1.2 Practice Statements and Guidance Notes

In considering whether or not a surveyor or valuer has achieved the standard of a reasonably competent practitioner, a court may find assistance in Guidance Notes or other documents published by the relevant professional bodies. The status of such publications was considered in *PK Finans International (UK) Ltd* v. *Andrew Downs & Co Ltd*,[148] where it was suggested by Sir Michael Ogden QC that:

"These Guidance Notes are not to be regarded as a statute. I suspect they are as much for the protection of surveyors as anything else, in that they set out various recommendations which, if followed, it is hoped will protect the surveyor from the unpleasantness of being sued. In any event, mere failure to comply with the Guidance Notes does not necessarily constitute negligence."

Although evidence that a surveyor or valuer did or did not comply with Guidance Notes is thus not conclusive in an action for professional negligence, it is likely to

143. *Jenkins* v. *Betham* (1855) 15 C.B. 168.
144. *Ibid.* at 189.
145. [1975] 1 E.G.L.R. 82. See also *Corisand Investments Ltd* v. *Druce & Co* [1978] 2 E.G.L.R. 86, where the defendants' valuation of an hotel was held negligent because they failed to take account of the provisions of the Fire Precautions Act 1971 relating to the need for obtaining a fire certificate.
146. *West Midland Baptist Trust Association (Incorporated)* v. *Birmingham Corporation* [1968] 2 Q.B. 188.
147. [1970] A.C. 874.
148. [1992] 1 E.G.L.R. 172 at 174.

prove highly persuasive, not least because a court will be readily convinced that such notes represent general and approved practice within the profession. In recent years, such evidence has been important in determining such matters as how a building survey should be carried out,[149] what inquiries a valuer should make and what information the valuer should communicate to the client,[150] and (most significantly) on what basis a valuation should be made.[151]

In the field of valuations,[152] the most important professional guidance is to be found in the RICS *Appraisal and Valuation Manual*, published in September 1995 and applicable to valuations carried out from 1 January 1996. This major undertaking results from the amalgamation and substantial revision of two previous RICS publications,[153] which accordingly cease to have effect from the latter date.

The RICS *Appraisal and Valuation Manual* is in two sections. The first contains Practice Statements, compliance with which is mandatory for members of the Royal Institution of Chartered Surveyors,[154] the Incorporated Society of Valuers and Auctioneers and the Institute of Revenues Rating and Valuation (subject to the right of a member to justify departure).[155] Apart from exposing a member to possible disciplinary action, it is the view of the RICS that "failure to comply with Practice Statements is likely to be adjudged negligent". The second section contains Guidance Notes, which apply to all valuations[156] and which seek to provide further material and information on good valuation practice. Compliance with these Guidance Notes is not a professional requirement, and the RICS takes the view that a member will not automatically be adjudged negligent in not following practices recommended therein. However, it is also emphasised that such recommended practices should not be departed from without good reason, and that a court in a negligence action is likely to require an explanation from a valuer who has done so.

Of the 22 Practice Statements contained in the RICS *Appraisal and Valuation Manual*, the first seven are of general application; the remainder provide additional mandatory requirements in respect of valuations for particular purposes. The aim throughout is to ensure that valuers establish and understand the requirements of their clients; that they are equipped to meet those needs; and that they provide in an unambiguous and comprehensible form the advice and information which is

149. At first instance in *Watts* v. *Morrow* [1991] 1 E.G.L.R. 150, Judge Bowsher QC was highly critical of a surveyor who (contrary to the R.I.C.S. Guidance Note *Structural Surveys of Residential Property*) dictated his report while on site, rather than making notes and drafting the report later. In *Hacker* v. *Thomas Deal & Co* [1991] 2 E.G.L.R. 161, a surveyor who failed to use a torch and mirror to look behind a kitchen cupboard was held not to have been negligent, since the relevant R.I.C.S. Guidance Note stated specifically that a decision on whether or not to carry a mirror was a matter of individual preference.

150. *PK Finans International (UK) Ltd* v. *Andrew Downs & Co Ltd* [1992] 1 E.G.L.R. 172.

151. See *Predeth* v. *Castle Phillips Finance Co Ltd* [1986] 2 E.G.L.R. 144 (definitions of "open market value" and "forced sale value"; *Craneheath Securities Ltd* v. *York Montague Ltd* [1994] 1 E.G.L.R. 159 (mortgage valuer entitled to base valuation of restaurant on "open market value"; *Allied Trust Bank Ltd* v. *Edward Symmons & Partners* [1994] 1 E.G.L.R. 165 (valuer entitled to include "hope value" on mortgage valuation of country house ripe for development).

152. Including the R.I.C.S./I.S.V.A. Home Buyers' Survey and Valuation Scheme, but not building or structural surveys.

153. *Statements of Asset Valuation Practice* (the "Red Book", 3rd edn, August 1990) and *Manual of Valuation Guidance Notes* (the "White Book", 3rd edn April 1992).

154. R.I.C.S. Byelaw 19(7) and Conduct Regulation 17.1.

155. In which case there must be a clear declaration in writing giving details of and reasons for the departure.

156. Including those specifically excluded from Section One by Practice Statement 1.3.

required. The *Manual* is not principally concerned with valuation theory or methods, but with the mechanics of practice, including the assembly, interpretation and reporting of information relevant to the task of valuation.[157]

The matters which are dealt with in the generally applicable Practice Statements are as follows:

*PS1 Application of the Practice Statements*  This is widely drawn ("the provision by valuers of appraisals, valuations, revaluations, valuation reviews and calculations of worth in respect of property in all countries for all purposes"). However, a number of matters are specifically excluded.[158] Moreover, a member may depart from a Practice Statement where appropriate, provided that the reasons for this departure are contained in a clear written statement in the report.

*PS2 Conditions of engagement*  The basic principle is that the client's requirements are to be established, clarified and properly recorded. In addition, the Practice Statement sets out a list of items to be covered as a minimum in written conditions of engagement.[159]

*PS3*  The different purposes for which valuations may be required and the base on which each is to be carried out.

*PS4*  Detailed definitions of each of the valuation bases and the related assumptions which are involved.

*PS5*  Qualifications of the valuer (including competence and knowledge of the relevant market) and the special qualifications and disqualifications applicable to certain types of valuation. This Practice Statement also covers the question of potential conflicts of interest.

*PS6 Inspections and material considerations*  This makes clear that, in the absence of clear contrary agreement, a valuer must always carry out an inspection of the property in question. The Practice Statement also contains a minimum list of relevant matters to be taken into account (while recognising that certain types of valuation may involve additional matters), and deals with the extent of the valuer's obligation to verify information used in a valuation.

*PS7 Reports*  The primary aim is that every report should convey a clear understanding of the opinions being expressed, the basis of valuation used and the assumptions and information on which it is based. To this end the Practice Statement provides a list of items which, as a minimum, every report should contain.[160]

157. R.I.C.S. *Appraisal and Valuation Manual*, Introduction.

158. Among the exclusions are valuations in anticipation of evidence in legal and quasi-legal proceedings; valuations carried out by arbitrators or independent experts; valuations for the purposes of taxation or assessment of compensation; and valuations in the course of estate agency work.

159. The R.I.C.S. *Appraisal and Valuation Manual* elsewhere provides Model Conditions of Engagement for the following: Valuation of Residential Property (Practice Statements, Appendix 2); Valuation of Residential Properties for Mortgage Purposes (Practice Statement 9, Annex B); Valuation of Commercial and Industrial Property (Practice Statements, Appendix 4); Valuation and Appraisal of Commercial Land and Buildings for Secured Lending Purposes (Practice Statements, Appendix 8); R.I.C.S./I.S.V.A. Home Buyers' Survey and Valuation Scheme (Practice Statements, Appendix 12).

160. In addition, Practice Statements Appendices 9–11 contain Model Report Forms for Mortgage Valuations, Reinspections and Valuations for Further Advances, all in relation to residential property.

## 4.2 The client's instructions

The question whether or not a surveyor or valuer has been guilty of negligence is one which cannot be answered in the abstract, but only in relation to the professional task which the defendant is instructed to carry out. Thus, for example, the extent and depth of the inspection to which a property is subjected is very different according to whether the client requires a mortgage valuation, a Home Buyers' Survey and Valuation or a full structural or building survey.[161]

Members of the RICS and ISVA are required by their professional bodies to confirm all instructions in writing,[162] something which would in any event be a prudent and sensible practice to adopt. In a number of cases involving valuations, proof of the unusual nature of the client's instructions has provided a defence to a charge of negligence.[163] In *Predeth* v. *Castle Phillips Finance Co Ltd*[164] a finance company which had repossessed a house on the mortgagor's default asked a valuer for a "crash sale valuation" of the property.[165] The valuer provided a figure of £5,750 and the finance company then sold the property for £6,000, only to be held liable to the mortgagor for failing to take reasonable care to obtain the best available price.[166] The finance company then claimed, in third party proceedings, that the valuer was negligent in failing to advise on the property's true market value, but this was rejected by the Court of Appeal on the ground that the task carried out by the valuer was precisely what the client had requested.[167]

In *Sutcliffe* v. *Sayer*[168] the defendant, an estate agent with no surveying qualifications but with considerable experience of the local housing market, was instructed and paid by prospective purchasers to comment on whether the asking price of a particular retirement bungalow was right. The defendant confirmed that the price was right but failed to identify that the property was built on a substratum of peat. On finding that the bungalow was effectively impossible to resell, the purchasers sued the defendant for negligence, but their claim was rejected by the Court of Appeal on the ground that the purchasers had received exactly what they had paid for.

A common feature of the decisions noted above is that the court in each case held that the valuer owed no duty to the client to go beyond limited instructions and warn the client of potential problems. This is in marked contrast with the case of *McIntyre* v. *Herring Son & Daw*,[169] where the defendant rating valuers were instructed to act for a private client in seeking a reduction in the rateable value of the

---

161. See p. 628.
162. R.I.C.S. *Appraisal and Valuation Manual*, Practice Statement 2.
163. See, however, *South Australian Asset Management Corporation* v. *York Montague Ltd* [1995] 2 E.G.L.R. 219, where the defendants argued unsuccessfully that what the clients had requested was not an open market valuation of a development site, but rather an appraisal of the development project in the hands of a joint venture.
164. [1986] 2 E.G.L.R. 144.
165. The term "crash sale valuation" is not in general use within the valuation profession, but was taken to mean a forced sale valuation.
166. This was held by the court to be £8,500.
167. See also the odd case of *Tenenbaum* v. *Garrod* [1988] 2 E.G.L.R. 178, where a client requested a "tactically jaundiced" view of a property for use in negotiations with the vendor. When the client's low offer was rejected by the vendor, the client sued the valuer for negligence, but without success.
168. [1987] 1 E.G.L.R. 155.
169. [1988] 1 E.G.L.R. 231.

client's leasehold house. The defendants, having negotiated what the expert witnesses agreed was a satisfactory reduction, advised their client that the expense involved in seeking through legal proceedings to secure a further reduction could not be justified, given the slim chance of success. The defendants were held to have been negligent in failing to alert the client to the fact that a comparatively slight further reduction would bring the property within the financial limits of the Leasehold Reform Act 1967 and thus give the client a valuable right of enfranchisement, notwithstanding the fact that the client's instructions made no mention of enfranchisement.[170]

## 4.3 Surveys

In the vast majority of cases in which a surveyor is accused of negligence, the gist of the complaint is that the defendant failed to draw the attention of the client (or the third party, where a claim arises in tort) to some physical defect in the property concerned. This failure may have come about because the surveyor did not inspect (or did not inspect with thoroughness) the relevant part of the property. Alternatively, it may be that the surveyor (through inadvertence or negligence) misunderstood the significance of what was discovered in the course of the inspection. In either case, the crucial question for a court is simply whether a reasonably competent surveyor would have discovered, understood and reported on that defect.[171]

### 4.3.1 Types of inspection

In order to answer this question, a court must first ascertain what type of inspection the surveyor was instructed to carry out. Such inspections vary considerably, in both extent and depth, between a full structural or building survey and a mortgage valuation. Somewhere between these two extremes lies the Home Buyers' Survey and Valuation, or HBSV[172]; this consists of a more limited inspection than a full survey, although the surveyor is expected to show the same level of expertise as would be required for a full inspection.[173]

There are at present no standard conditions of engagement covering full surveys, and the particular terms used by the surveyor must therefore be examined in order to

---

170. It is submitted that, if this decision can be justified, it is on the ground that the defendants held themselves out as experts in the rating field and that the plaintiff was a layman. For an example of a court's reluctance to impose a duty on a valuer to warn a commercially experienced client, see *PK Finans International (UK) Ltd* v. *Andrew Downs & Co Ltd* [1992] 1 E.G.L.R. 172.

171. The method of preparing a survey report came under scrutiny at first instance in *Watts* v. *Morrow* [1991] 1 E.G.L.R. 150 at 153–154, where Judge Bowsher was highly critical of a surveyor who dictated his report into a dictating machine while on site. In the judge's view, this led to the report being "lengthy and diffuse and to its conclusions being inadequate ... strong on immediate detail but excessively, and I regretfully have to say, negligently weak on reflective thought".

172. Replacing the former House Buyers' and Flat Buyers' Reports.

173. *Cross* v. *David Martin & Mortimer* [1989] 1 E.G.L.R. 154 at 155 *per* Phillips J.

ascertain any limits on what is to be inspected[174] or how this is to be done.[175] The Standard Conditions of Engagement for the HBSV inspection make clear that the surveyor is not expected to lift carpets or look into unexposed or inaccessible areas and further, that services will only be visually inspected where they are accessible and will not be tested.[176]

The extent of inspection which a surveyor is required to carry out has received the closest judicial attention in the context of mortgage valuations.[177] In *Roberts* v. *J Hampson & Co*,[178] Kennedy J stated[179]:

"What is the extent of the service that a surveyor must provide in performing a building society valuation? The service is, in fact, described in the Halifax's brochure. It is a valuation and not a survey but any valuation is necessarily governed by condition. The inspection is, of necessity, a limited one. Both the expert surveyors who gave evidence before me agreed that with a house of this size they would allow about half an hour for their inspection on site. That time does not admit of moving furniture, nor of lifting carpets, especially where they are nailed down. In my judgement, it must be accepted that where a surveyor undertakes a scheme 1 valuation it is understood that he is making a limited appraisal only. It is, however, an appraisal by a skilled professional man. It is inherent in any standard fee work that some cases will colloquially be 'winners' and others 'losers', from the professional man's point of view. The fact that in an individual case he may need to spend two or three times as long as he would have expected, or as the fee structure would have contemplated, is something that he must accept. His duty to take reasonable care in providing a valuation remains the root of his obligation. In an extreme case . . . a surveyor might refuse to value on the agreed fee basis, though any surveyor too often refused to take the rough with the smooth would not improve his reputation. If, in a particular case, the proper valuation of a £19,000 house needs two hours' work that is what the surveyor must devote to it."

The limited nature of a mortgage valuation was further acknowledged in *Lloyd* v. *Butler*[180] by Henry J, who described it as "an inspection which on average should not take longer than 20 to 30 minutes. It is effectively a walking inspection by someone with a knowledgeable eye, experienced in practice, who knows where to look . . . to detect either trouble or the potential form of trouble".

Given such limitations, in *Nash* v. *Evens & Matta*[181] a mortgage valuer was held not to have been negligent in failing to discover wall tie failure. In *Whalley* v. *Roberts &*

---

174. In the absence of contrary agreement, the surveyor is expected to examine all visible parts of the building. It is, however, common to provide that unexposed parts will not be inspected, or that services such as electricity, gas, water and drainage will not be tested. Even without express provision, it is highly doubtful whether a surveyor would be expected to uncover or open up unexposed areas: see *Kerridge* v. *James Abbott & Partners* [1992] 2 E.G.L.R. 162 (no duty to remove stonework of parapet wall in order to check concealed part of roof).

175. Cases in which the courts have considered whether a surveyor was required to use a particular method of inspection include *Fryer* v. *Bunney* [1982] 2 E.G.L.R. 130 (damp meter); *Eley* v. *King & Chasemore* [1989] 1 E.G.L.R. 181 (long ladder to gain access to roof); *Hacker* v. *Thomas Deal & Co* [1991] 2 E.G.L.R. 161 (torch and mirror to check for damp behind kitchen units).

176. In *Howard* v. *Horne & Sons* [1990] 1 E.G.L.R. 272, however, a surveyor who stated in a HBSV report that "electrical wiring is in PVC cable" was held negligent for implying that the wiring was modern and gave no cause for concern, whereas in truth much of the wiring was old, exposed and dangerous.

177. This has been described as "work at the lower end of the surveyor's field of professional expertise": *Smith* v. *Eric S Bush*; *Harris* v. *Wyre Forest D.C.* [1990] 1 A.C. 831 at 858 *per* Lord Griffiths.

178. [1989] 2 All E.R. 504.

179. *Ibid.* at 510; this was described as "of general application" by Lord Templeman in *Smith* v. *Eric S Bush*; *Harris* v. *Wyre Forest D.C.* [1990] 1 A.C. 831 at 850.

180. [1990] 2 E.G.L.R. 155 at 160.

181. [1988] 1 E.G.L.R. 130.

*Roberts*[182] it was said that a mortgage valuer would not normally be expected to carry and use a spirit level. However, it appears that even an inspection of this kind requires the surveyor to carry out a "head and shoulders" examination of any accessible roof space.[183]

As noted earlier, a Practice Statement binding upon members of the RICS and ISVA requires instructions to be agreed or confirmed in writing.[184] In a number of earlier cases, where such written confirmation was absent or inadequate, disputes have arisen as to the nature of the inspection to be carried out.[185] In *Stewart* v. *H A Brechin & Co*,[186] for example, surveyors were instructed orally to carry out a valuation of a property and to report upon its general condition. In considering these instructions, Lord Cameron said[187]:

"I am of opinion that all the defenders were under contract to do was to make such valuation of the property and to carry out such visual inspection as was reasonably practicable in the circumstances, reporting anything of significance to their client if such should be found."[188]

Similarly, in *Fisher* v. *Knowles*[189] it was held that what the defendant had undertaken to do (and had done negligently) was more than a bare valuation but less than a full survey.[190]

Drawing the limitations of a proposed inspection to the client's attention is not necessarily sufficient to absolve the surveyor from what might otherwise have amounted to negligence. In *Heatley* v. *William H Brown Ltd*,[191] for example, the defendant surveyors' written conditions of engagement emphasised the inevitable limitations of a report where parts of a property are unexposed or inaccessible, and their subsequent report pointed out that they had been unable to gain access to roof voids. The defendants were nevertheless held negligent for describing the property as "in a reasonable condition for its age" and not advising the clients to delay their purchase until access to the roof could be obtained.[192] In *Strover* v. *Harrington*,[193] on the other hand, where a surveyor was held not liable for failing to discover that the property had no mains drainage, the Court of Appeal was clearly influenced by the fact that the client had declined the surveyor's invitation to commission (at an additional cost) specialist tests on all services including the drains.

---

182. [1990] 1 E.G.L.R. 164.
183. See *Gibbs* v. *Arnold Son & Hockley* [1989] 2 E.G.L.R. 154; *Ezekiel* v. *McDade* [1994] 1 E.G.L.R. 255.
184. R.I.C.S. *Appraisal and Valuation Manual*, Practice Statement 2.
185. See *Sincock* v. *Bangs (Reading)* (1952) 160 E.G. 134; *Sinclair* v. *Bowden Son and Partners* (1962) 183 E.G. 95.
186. 1959 S.C. 306.
187. *Ibid.* at 308.
188. The defendants were held to have failed in their duty by not inspecting the roof space of an old house and thus failing to discover extensive woodworm.
189. [1982] 1 E.G.L.R. 154.
190. For unsuccessful attempts by defendants to argue that the client's instructions required less than a full survey, see *Moss* v. *Heckingbottom* (1958) 172 E.G. 207 and *Buckland* v. *Watts* (1968) 208 E.G. 969.
191. [1992] 1 E.G.L.R. 289.
192. See also *Syrett* v. *Carr & Neave* [1990] 2 E.G.L.R. 161, where a surveyor who failed to discover a very bad infestation of death-watch beetle, movement in some of the walls and severe damp was held negligent, notwithstanding a clause in the report stating that "my survey is restricted to items of major expenditure which would affect your intention to purchase or the price offered".
193. [1988] Ch. 390.

### 4.3.2   The trail of suspicion

It is generally accepted that all forms of survey consist in principle of a visual inspection of what is visible in a property, and that there is no inherent obligation upon a surveyor to uncover or open up other parts for examination.[194] However, where what is visible is enough to alert a reasonably competent surveyor to the possibility of concealed defects, the exercise of reasonable care and skill may require the taking of further steps.[195] In *Roberts* v. *J Hampson & Co*,[196] Kennedy J stated[197]:

"As it seems to me, the position that the law adopts is simple. If the surveyor misses a defect because its signs are hidden, that is a risk that his client must accept. But if there is specific ground for suspicion and the trail of suspicion leads behind furniture or under carpets, the surveyor must take reasonable steps to follow the trail until he has all the information which it is reasonable for him to have before making his valuation."[198]

Although the principle which is embodied in the phrase "follow the trail" has been endorsed and applied in a number of subsequent cases involving both mortgage valuations[199] and full surveys,[200] there remains a degree of uncertainty as to its precise legal significance. It would appear from a passage in the judgment of Kennedy J which was quoted earlier[201] that his lordship regarded it in an almost literal sense in that, once alerted to the possibility of trouble, a surveyor would be expected to spend whatever time was necessary at the property in carrying out further investigations. In most of the other cases, however, the "trail of suspicion" has had a more subtle effect. It means that it is no answer for a surveyor who fails to detect dry rot, for example, to say simply that dry rot was not visible, if what *was* visible would have provoked a reasonably competent surveyor into suspecting dry rot and putting in motion the more detailed examination which would have confirmed its existence.[202]

It is submitted that the true significance of the injunction to "follow the trail" lies not so much in what a surveyor does on site as in how the surveyor reports to the client. Provided that the client is alerted in unequivocal terms to the presence of symptoms of potential trouble, and is left in no doubt of the need for further

194. In addition to the cases cited above, support for this proposition may be found in *Ker* v. *John H Allan & Son* 1949 S.L.T. 20; *Bishop* v. *Watson, Watson and Scoles* (1973) 224 E.G. 1881; *Bere* v. *Slades* [1989] 2 E.G.L.R. 160.

195. Surveyors have occasionally been held negligent for failing to discover defects which had been deliberately camouflaged, on the ground that evidence of very extensive redecoration or refurbishment may in itself give reason for suspicion: *Morgan* v. *Perry* (1973) 229 E.G. 1737; *Hingorani* v. *Blower* [1976] 1 E.G.L.R. 104; cf. *Whalley* v. *Roberts & Roberts* [1990] 1 E.G.L.R. 164.

196. [1989] 2 All E.R. 504.

197. *Ibid.* at 510.

198. This approach was accepted as correct by the Court of Appeal in *Sneesby* v. *Goldings* [1995] 2 E.G.L.R. 102, where a mortgage valuer noticed that a chimney breast in the kitchen of a converted property had been removed. Had the valuer then looked up the cooker hood or opened a cupboard, he would have seen clear signs that the chimney had been left with inadequate support. It was held that, even if a valuer on such an inspection would not normally be expected to look up a cooker hood or open kitchen cupboards, the need to ensure that the chimney had been given adequate alternative support required such steps to be taken. It was not enough for the valuer merely to have checked the room above for signs of distress.

199. See, for example, *Hipkins* v. *Jack Cotton Partnership* [1989] 2 E.G.L.R. 157; *Bere* v. *Slades* [1989] 2 E.G.L.R. 160; *Lloyd* v. *Butler* [1990] 1 E.G.L.R. 155; *Sneesby* v. *Goldings* [1995] 2 E.G.L.R. 102.

200. See, for example, *Hacker* v. *Thomas Deal & Co* [1991] 2 E.G.L.R. 161.

201. See p. 629.

202. See *Grove* v. *Jackman and Masters* (1950) 155 E.G. 182; *Wooldridge* v. *Stanley Hicks & Son* (1953) 162 E.G. 513; *Hill* v. *Debenham, Tewson and Chinnocks* (1958) 171 E.G. 835.

investigations before any transaction (such as a purchase or a mortgage loan) is entered into, the surveyor will have fulfilled his duty of care.[203]

Support for this view of the surveyor's duty, at least in the context of a mortgage valuation, may be found in the judgment of Henry J in *Lloyd* v. *Butler*[204]:

"He does not necessarily have to follow up every trail to discover whether there is trouble or the extent of any such trouble. But where such an inspection can reasonably show a potential trouble or the risk of potential trouble, it seems to me it is necessary . . . to alert the purchaser to that risk, because the purchaser will be relying on that valuation form."

It appears moreover that a similar principle applies in the context of a full survey. In *Eley* v. *King & Chasemore*[205] the defendants' report to a prospective purchaser of a house which stood on a clay subsoil drew attention to the inherent risk of subsidence, noted particularly the proximity of a tall fir tree and advised the client to seek insurance protection against subsoil movement. When, a year after purchase, the property suffered structural movement and required underpinning, the client claimed that the defendants were negligent in not advising him against purchase on account of this risk. The Court of Appeal, however, agreed with the conclusion of the trial judge that, far from being negligent, the defendant had given the client the best possible advice on how to deal with the risk of subsidence.

### 4.3.3 Major problem areas

As stated earlier, the crucial issue in a case involving an allegedly negligent survey is whether a reasonably competent surveyor would have discovered, understood and reported on the particular defect which the defendant has overlooked. Given the essentially factual nature of this question, there is little to be gained from a detailed examination of the cases in which it has arisen. Nevertheless, it may be worthwhile drawing attention to those areas in which the majority of claims against surveyors have arisen.

Statistics prepared by the insurers to the RICS professional indemnity insurance scheme indicate that approximately one-third of all claims arising out of surveys relate to some form of timber defect.[206] Furthermore, it is in relation to this type of claim that the "follow the trail" principle is most often relevant: the gist of the complaint is that the individual surveyor (perhaps through inexperience) failed to recognise clear symptoms of dry rot, or wrongly believed that evidence of woodworm or beetle related to an infestation which was no longer active.[207]

---

203. Warning the client in this way is even more likely to be held sufficient in a case where further investigation of the building presents difficulties, for example because it is furnished and occupied: see *Ker* v. *John H Allan & Son* 1949 S.L.T. 20; *Thorne* v. *Harris & Co* (1953) 163 E.G. 324.

204. [1990] 1 E.G.L.R. 155 at 160.

205. [1989] 1 E.G.L.R. 181.

206. Such defects include wet and dry rot, penetrating or rising damp and infestation by woodworm, deathwatch beetle etc.

207. Cases involving a substantial consideration of timber defects include *Ker* v. *John H Allan & Sons* 1949 S.L.T. 20 (dry rot); *Tew* v. *WM Whitburn and Sons* [1952] C.P.L. 111 (wet rot); *Wooldridge* v. *Stanley Hicks & Son* [1953] C.P.L. 700 (dry rot); *Thorne* v. *Harris and Co* (1953) 163 E.G. 324 (wet and dry rot); *Tremayne* v. *T Mortimer Burrows and Partners* (1954) 165 E.G. 232 (dry rot); *Conn* v. *Munday* (1955) 166 E.G. 465 (woodworm in cellar); *Hill* v. *Debenham, Tewson & Chinnocks* (1958) 171 E.G. 835 (extensive timber defects—damp, wet and dry rot, beetle, woodworm); *Stewart* v. *HA Brechin & Co* 1959 S.C. 306 (woodworm infestation); *Hood* v. *Shaw* (1960) 176 E.G. 1291 (various defects); *Sinclair* v. *Bowden Son*

The second most common type of claim against surveyors is one which concerns defects in the roof of a property. Such defects may relate simply to the condition of the roof[208]; more common, however, are allegations of errors in design or construction.[209] In most cases the basic complaint against the surveyor is either failure to inspect the roof properly or insufficient knowledge of construction technology.[210]

The third main category of claims against surveyors, amounting to some 10 per cent of the total,[211] consists of those involving structural damage due to subsidence or other ground movement. As with timber defects, this is an area in which a surveyor is called upon to exercise professional skill and judgement in interpreting symptoms such as cracks and distinguishing the signs of past settlement from those which foretell future movement and damage.[212] In a number of cases, the question of the surveyor's liability has turned, at least in part, upon awareness of the potential effect of nearby trees upon a building's stability.[213]

Apart from these three problem areas, a significant number of claims arise out of a simple failure to observe defects in the way in which a building has been

---

*and Partners* (1962) 183 E.G. 95 (wet rot and weevil); *Freeman v. Marshall & Co* (1966) 200 E.G. 777 (rising damp, wet and dry rot in basement); *Hardy v. Wamsley-Lewis* (1967) 203 E.G. 1039 (dry rot); *Fisher v. Knowles* [1982] 1 E.G.L.R. 154 (rot in window frames, defects in ceiling joists and door joinery); *Roberts v. J Hampson* [1989] 2 All E.R. 504 (dry rot); *Gibbs v. Arnold Son & Hockley* [1989] 2 E.G.L.R. 154 (various timber defects in old house); *Lloyd v. Butler* [1990] 2 E.G.L.R. 155 (woodworm); *Watts & Watts v. Morrow* [1991] 1 E.G.L.R. 150 (ORB) (defects in floor timbers and windows); *Hacker v. Thomas Deal & Co* [1991] 2 E.G.L.R. 161 (dry rot under kitchen floor); *Heatley v. William H Brown Ltd* [1992] 1 E.G.L.R. 289 (wide-ranging defects); *Kerridge v. James Abbott & Partners* [1992] 2 E.G.L.R. 162 (dry rot); *Oswald v. Countrywide Surveyors Ltd* [1994] E.G.C.S. 150 (death-watch beetle).

208. In *Allen v. Ellis & Co* [1990] 1 E.G.L.R. 170, for example, the defendant surveyor was held negligent for failing to appreciate that the asbestos sheet roof of a garage was "brittle or fragile, likely to split or crack, scantily supported, much repaired and right at the end of its useful life".

209. See, for example, *Cross v. David Martin & Mortimer* [1989] 1 E.G.L.R. 154.

210. In addition to the cases cited above, roof defects have also been considered in *Last v. Post* (1952) 159 E.G. 240 (disintegration of tiling); *Leigh v. Unsworth* (1972) 230 E.G. 501 (various defects); *Perry v. Sidney Phillips & Son (A Firm)* [1982] 1 All E.R. 1005 (leaking roof); *Hooberman v. Salter Rex (A Firm)* [1985] 1 E.G.L.R. 144 (defective roof construction leading to dry rot); *Eley v. King & Chasemore (A Firm)* [1989] 1 E.G.L.R. 181 (various defects); *Lloyd v. Butler* [1990] 2 E.G.L.R. 155 (various defects); *Watts & Watts v. Morrow* [1991] 1 E.G.L.R. 150 (defects in roof and chimneys); *Heatley v. William H Brown Ltd* [1992] 1 E.G.L.R. 289 (various defects).

211. This overall figure conceals wide fluctuations from year to year, depending upon weather conditions.

212. Where cracking is progressive, a court may have to decide how clear the symptoms were at the time when the defendant inspected the property. The difficulty of this task will be greatly increased if there is a long time between the survey and the trial: see *Leigh v. Unsworth* (1972) 230 E.G. 501 (seven years).

213. Cases in this category include *Parsons v. Way and Waller* [1952] C.P.L. 417 (serious distortion and cracking); *Franses v. Barnett* (1956) 168 E.G. 425 (front wall cracked and defective); *Lawrence v. Hampton & Sons* (1964) 190 E.G. 107 (cracking requiring underpinning); *Daisley v. B S Hall & Co* (1972) 225 E.G. 1553 (risk of subsidence from poplar trees and soil type); *Morgan v. Perry* (1973) 229 E.G. 1737 (serious subsidence and settlement); *Hingorani v. Blower* [1976] 1 E.G.L.R. 104 (cracking in brickwork camouflaged); *Nash v. Evens & Matta* [1988] 1 E.G.L.R. 130 (cracking in walls); *Davies v. Idris Parry* [1988] 1 E.G.L.R. 147 (evidence of settlement and structural damage); *Cross v. David Martin & Mortimer* [1989] 1 E.G.L.R. 154 ("hump" in floor); *Eley v. King & Chasemore (A Firm)* [1989] 1 E.G.L.R. 181 (subsidence); *Hipkins v. Jack Cotton Partnership* [1989] 2 E.G.L.R. 157 (evidence of settlement); *Whalley v. Roberts & Roberts* [1990] 1 E.G.L.R. 164 (evidence of settlement camouflaged); *Henley v. Cloke & Sons* [1991] 2 E.G.L.R. 141 (distortion and cracking in front bay); *Beaton v. Nationwide Building Society* [1991] 2 E.G.L.R. 145 (risk of subsidence); *Matto v. Rodney Broome Associates* [1994] 2 E.G.L.R. 163 (risk of future subsidence).

constructed.[214] Moreover, recent cases have highlighted the duty of a surveyor, even when carrying out a mortgage valuation, to be alert to the possibility that what appears to be an ordinary building may conceal an unconventional method of construction.[215] Finally, it may be noted that, although defects in services (gas, electricity, water and drainage) account for a relatively large number of claims against surveyors which are notified to insurers, many of these claims fail at the outset on proof that the survey in question did not include any obligation to test the services.[216]

### 4.4 Valuations

#### 4.4.1 The nature of a valuation

In *Singer & Friedlander Ltd* v. *John D Wood & Co*[217] Watkins J said[218]:

"Whatever conclusion is reached, it must be without consideration for the purpose for which it is required. By this I mean that a valuation must reflect the honest opinion of the valuer of the true market value of the land at the relevant time, no matter why or by whom it is required, be it by merchant bank, developer or prospective builder. So the expression, for example, 'for loan purposes' used in a letter setting out a valuation should be descriptive only of the reason why the valuation is required and not as an indication that were the valuation required for some other purpose a different value would be provided by the valuer to he who seeks the valuation."

It is submitted that, if this passage is intended to suggest that a property can only have a single "value" at any given time, then it cannot be supported. Documents such as the RICS Appraisal and Valuation Manual[219] make it quite clear that valuations which are carried out for different purposes may require the valuer to make different assumptions.[220]

214. See, for example, *Hood* v. *Shaw* (1960) 176 E.G. 1291 (defective brickwork); *Bishop* v. *Watson, Watson and Scales* (1972) 224 E.G. 1881 (damp caused by defective construction); *Leigh* v. *Unsworth* (1972) 230 E.G. 501 (defective construction of foundations and ceilings); *Lees* v. *English and Partners* [1977] 1 E.G.L.R. 65 (bad "tie" between old and new brickwork); *Bolton* v. *Puley* [1983] 2 E.G.L.R. 138 (defective boundary wall); *Marder* v. *Sautelle & Hicks* [1988] 2 E.G.L.R. 187 (bungalow's external walls built of blocks of cement and aggregate); *Gibbs* v. *Arnold Son & Hockley* [1989] 2 E.G.L.R. 154 (structural defects in old property); *Bere* v. *Slades* [1989] 2 E.G.L.R. 160 (defective wall construction); *Smith* v. *Eric S Bush* [1990] 1 A.C. 831 (chimney breasts removed and flues left unsupported).
215. *Peach* v. *Iain G Chalmers & Co* [1992] 2 E.G.L.R. 135 (mortgage valuer liable for describing a "Dorran" type bungalow, consisting of thin concrete panels bolted together, as "concrete block built, harled". See also *Spencer-Ward* v. *Humberts* [1995] 1 E.G.L.R. 123 (mortgage valuer failed to mention that bungalow was of a "Woolaway" construction).
216. Cases on defective services include *Gurd* v. *A Cobden Soar & Son* (1941) 157 E.G. 415 (defective drains); *Leigh* v. *Unsworth* (1972) 230 E.G. 501 (defective drainage system); *Fryer* v. *Bunney* [1982] 2 E.G.L.R. 130 (water leaks from central heating tank and pipes); *Howard* v. *Horne & Sons (A Firm)* [1990] 1 E.G.L.R. 272 (electrical wiring); *Lloyd* v. *Butler* [1990] 2 E.G.L.R. 155 (wiring and heating problems). For the type of examination required where central heating system *was* to be tested, see *Pfeiffer* v. *E & E Installations* [1991] 1 E.G.L.R. 162.
217. [1977] 2 E.G.L.R. 84.
218. *Ibid.* at 85.
219. See p. 625.
220. However, there appears no justification for the view expressed in *Corisand Investments Ltd* v. *Druce & Co* [1978] 2 E.G.L.R. 86, namely, that a valuation for mortgage purposes requires the open market value to be discounted by an arbitrary 20 per cent so as to exclude the "speculative content" which might not be realisable in the event of a forced sale.

It is perhaps inevitable that claims against valuers tend to increase in the aftermath of a collapse in the property market and, moreover, that some clients will attempt to blame a valuer for not having foreseen that collapse. However, it is important to recognise the limits of the valuer's duty in this respect. As was stated by Sir Thomas Bingham MR in *Banque Bruxelles Lambert SA* v. *Eagle Star Insurance Co Ltd*[221]:

"In the absence of special instructions it is no part of V's [the valuer's] duty to advise L [the lender] on future movements in property prices, whether nationally or locally. The belief among buyers and sellers that prices are likely to move upwards or downwards may have an effect on current prices, and to that extent such belief may be reflected by V in his valuation. But his concern is with current value only. He is not asked to predict what will happen in future. His valuation is not sought to protect L against a future decline in property prices."[222]

Clearly, then, a valuation is a "snapshot" of a property at a given time,[223] and it is only where an impending market fall is sufficiently obvious and imminent to affect current values that a valuer can be adjudged negligent for failing to take it into account. The courts, moreover, have shown no great readiness to hold valuers liable on this basis. In *Private Bank & Trust Co Ltd* v. *S (UK) Ltd*,[224] for example, where the defendants were sued in respect of an office development valuation carried out in June 1990, the court accepted that "in June 1990, though the market was going through a difficult period, on the information then available nobody could predict the decline that was to follow in the second half of the year".[225]

### 4.4.2 The margin of error

The courts have repeatedly emphasised that, while a valuer must carry out his task with reasonable care and skill, the valuation process is one which includes a strong subjective element.[226] It follows that not every error of judgement will amount to negligence, a point made by Goddard LJ in *Baxter* v. *FW Gapp & Co Ltd*[227]:

"Valuation is very much a matter of opinion. We are all liable to make mistakes, and a valuer is certainly not to be found guilty of negligence merely because his valuation turns out to be wrong. He may have taken too optimistic or too pessimistic a view of a particular property. One has to bear in mind that, in matters of valuation, matters of opinion must come very largely into account."

Similar sentiments were expressed by Watkins LJ in *Singer & Friedlander Ltd* v. *John D Wood & Co*[228]:

221. [1995] 2 All E.R. 769 at 840.
222. See also *Nykredit Mortgage Bank plc* v. *Edward Erdman Group Ltd* [1996] 02 E.G. 110.
223. See *Credit Agricole Personal Finance plc* v. *Murray* [1995] E.G.C.S. 32, where it was pointed out that a prudent valuer will nevertheless alert the client to clear adverse market trends.
224. [1993] 1 E.G.L.R. 144. See also *Corisand Investments Ltd* v. *Druce & Co* [1978] 2 E.G.L.R. 86. Cf. *Scotlife Homeloans (No 2) Ltd* v. *Kenneth James & Co* [1995] E.G.C.S. 70, where a valuer was held to have taken insufficient account of the fact that the residential property market "had come off the boil and was falling".
225. *Ibid.* at 148. The view of an expert witness was that the crucial factor was Iraq's invasion of Kuwait in August 1990, when the London office development market dried up overnight.
226. "Valuation is not a science; it is an art, and the instinctive 'feel' for the market of an experienced valuer is not something which can be ignored": *Craneheath Securities Ltd* v. *York Montague Ltd* [1996] 07 E.G. 141 *per* Balcombe LJ.
227. [1938] 4 All E.R. 457 at 459.
228. [1977] 2 E.G.L.R. 84 at 85. See also *Corisand Investments Ltd* v. *Druce & Co* [1978] 2 E.G.L.R. 86 at 92 *per* Gibson J.

"The valuation of land by trained, competent and careful professional men is a task which rarely, if ever, admits of precise conclusion. Often beyond certain well-founded facts so many imponderables confront the valuer that he is obliged to proceed on the basis of assumptions. Therefore, he cannot be faulted for achieving a result which does not admit of some degree of error. Thus, two able and experienced men, each confronted with the same task, might come to different conclusions without anyone being justified in saying that either of them has lacked competence and reasonable care, still less integrity, in doing his work."

One consequence of such judicial attitudes is that, as acknowledged by Hoffmann LJ in *Zubaida* v. *Hargreaves*[229]:

"In an action for negligence against an expert, it is not enough to show that another expert would have given a different answer. Valuation is not an exact science; it involves questions of judgement on which experts may differ without forfeiting their claim to professional competence."[230]

Recognition that, for any given property on a given date, there is a range of values which might be given by competent valuers using reasonable care and skill has led to the suggestion that a valuation which falls within the permitted range, or "bracket", cannot found liability in negligence. This idea appears to have originated in *Singer & Friedlander Ltd* v. *John D Wood & Co*,[231] where Watkins J stated[232]:

"Valuation is an art, not a science. Pinpoint accuracy in the result is not, therefore, to be expected by he who requests the valuation. There is, as I have said, the permissible margin of error, the 'bracket' as I have called it. What can properly be expected from a competent valuer using reasonable skill and care is that his valuation falls within this bracket."

The precise status of the "bracket" in legal terms is not entirely clear. According to Watkins J,[233] a valuation which falls outside the permitted range "brings into question the competence of the valuer and the sort of care he gave to the task of valuation".[234] On the other hand, while various *dicta* assert that a valuation within the bracket may nevertheless be adjudged negligent (for example where the valuer has overlooked physical defects in the property),[235] it is difficult to see how a plaintiff in such circumstances can establish that any loss has resulted from that negligence.[236]

The expert evidence which was led in *Singer & Friedlander* v. *John D Wood & Co* suggested that the permissible margin of error would normally be 10 per cent either

---

229. [1995] 1 E.G.L.R. 127 at 128.

230. Similarly, "different competent valuers will produce different opinions": *Banque Bruxelles Lambert SA* v. *Eagle Star Insurance Co Ltd* [1995] 2 All E.R. 769 at 789 *per* Phillips J. For an extreme statement of this view see *Campbell* v. *Edwards* [1976] 1 All E.R. 785 at 789 *per* Geoffrey Lane LJ: "Where the only basis of criticism is that another valuer has subsequently produced a valuation a third of the original one it does not afford, in my view, any ground for saying that Chestertons' valuation must have been or may have been wrong".

231. [1977] 2 E.G.L.R. 84.

232. *Ibid.* at 86.

233. *Ibid.* at 85.

234. It is not however suggested that this justifies a formal invocation of the doctrine of *res ipsa loquitur*.

235. "There is no proposition of law that in valuation cases a valuer is not negligent if his valuation falls within such a bracket": *McIntyre* v. *Herring Son & Daw* [1988] 1 E.G.L.R. 231 at 233 *per* Mr EA Machin QC, sitting as a deputy judge. See also *Henley* v. *Cloke & Sons* [1991] 2 E.G.L.R. 141 at 144–145 *per* Judge Thayne Forbes QC.

236. *Mount Banking Corporation Ltd* v. *Brian Cooper & Co* [1992] 2 E.G.L.R. 142; *Craneheath Securities Ltd* v. *York Montague Ltd* [1996] 07 E.G. 141. See also *Matto* v. *Rodney Broom Associates* [1994] 2 E.G.L.R. 163 at 168 *per* Ralph Gibson LJ: "If a surveyor fails to appreciate the extent of past damage, or to carry out the investigations which proper care and skill required, he will, in the absence of very special circumstances, commit no breach of duty in giving advice which is right and consistent with his having exercised proper care and skill. A professional man is entitled to be lucky".

side of the "correct" figure,[237] but that this could be extended to 15 per cent in exceptional circumstances.[238] The courts have subsequently shown themselves receptive to pleas for a bracket of 15 per cent where a valuation is especially difficult, either because the property in question is unusual and there are few comparables[239] or because the property market is in a period of rapid movement.[240]

### 4.4.3 Methods of valuation

The view which has traditionally been taken by the courts is that there is no single "correct" method of valuation. As Kekewich J stated in *Love* v. *Mack*[241]:

"The law does not say that in any breach of intelligent operation, intelligent skill, there is necessarily one defined path which must be strictly followed, and that if one departs by an inch from that defined path one were necessarily at fault ... There is no absolute rule as regards the proper method of ascertaining the value in this case, and [the defendant] adopted methods which, if they are not perfect, if they are not the best, if they might have been improved upon, still are methods which a man of position, endeavouring to do his duty, might fairly adopt without its being said he was wanting in reasonable care and skill."

Such judicial reluctance to prescribe working methods for valuers is also strongly reflected in *Corisand Investments Ltd* v. *Druce & Co*,[242] where Gibson J acknowledged that a valuer might legitimately base conclusions simply upon comparables, without any further calculation, or even upon his experienced instinct and awareness of the market, in which case any comparables would be indirect and unavailable for scrutiny.[243]

In most modern cases involving valuers, the courts have adopted a more prescriptive approach towards valuation methodology.[244] A classic description of what constitutes a proper valuation was given by Watkins J in *Singer & Friedlander Ltd* v. *John D Wood & Co*[245]:

"It consists of four fairly distinct stages of activity, namely, firstly, the sometimes tedious and laborious but vital approach work; secondly analysing the information thereby gained, and so be enabled by the exercise of experience and judgement to accept facts and make assumptions; thirdly, applying the detailed discount method with comparables or some other justified by the

237. "That in itself seems, in my uninstructed opinion, a high standard to impose": *Beaumont* v. *Humberts* [1990] 2 E.G.L.R. 166 at 168 *per* Staughton LJ.

238. In *Banque Bruxelles Lambert SA* v. *Eagle Star Insurance Co Ltd* [1995] 2 All E.R. 769 at 789, Phillips J noted the expert witnesses' agreement that, when valuations are based on comparables, one competent valuation may differ from another by as much as 20 per cent.

239. As in *Credit Agricole Personal Finance plc* v. *Murray* [1995] E.G.C.S. 32; *Scotlife Homeloans (No 2) Ltd* v. *Kenneth James & Co* [1995] E.G.C.S. 70; *BNP Mortgages Ltd* v. *Barton Cook & Sams* (unreported) 18 February 1994, Official Referees' Business, where the court also took the view that the "bracket" on a standard house on an estate might be as low as five per cent.

240. As in *Private Bank & Trust Co Ltd* v. *S (UK) Ltd* [1993] 1 E.G.L.R. 144; *Nykredit Mortgage Bank plc* v. *Edward Erdman Group Ltd* [1996] 02 E.G. 110.

241. (1905) 92 L.T. 345 at 349.

242. [1978] 2 E.G.L.R. 86 at 89–90.

243. Cf. *Baxter* v. *FW Gapp & Co Ltd* [1938] 4 All E.R. 457, where Goddard LJ, at 462, regarded it as "not very helpful" for a valuer simply to say: "The only thing I did was to go and look at the place". See also *Johnson* v. *Ribbins* [1975] 2 E.G.L.R. 78 for strong judicial criticism of an expert witness who merely stated a figure without supporting evidence.

244. This may reflect increased reliance upon evidence given by expert witnesses.

245. [1977] 2 E.G.L.R. 84 at 88.

circumstances as an alternative, or as a check, to the findings, and thereby produce the valuation; and fourthly, informing the client of it."

In the *Singer & Friedlander* case itself, the defendants' negligence consisted in the main of failure in the first stage, that of gathering all relevant information about the property to be valued. The property there was a development site in Gloucestershire, and the judgment of Watkins J contains a detailed list of the inquiries which a competent valuer would have made in order to prepare for such a valuation.[246] A similar exercise, in relation to residential property, was undertaken by Mr B Walsh QC, sitting as a deputy judge in *Axa Equity & Law Home Loans Ltd* v. *Hirani Watson*.[247] According to recent cases, the price at which the property has recently changed hands is potentially the most cogent evidence of its market value, so that (in the absence of specific instructions to disregard it), a valuer who gives an open market valuation without considering the implications of a recent sale is negligent.[248]

Although it appears that a valuer is expected to gather the relevant information personally,[249] it does not follow that he cannot rely on what he is told by other persons. It would seem in principle that the valuer should treat information from those who have a personal interest with a degree of healthy scepticism, although the reported cases do not suggest that negligence in this respect will be readily inferred.[250]

As mentioned earlier, the courts in recent years have displayed a much greater willingness to examine in detail the method of valuation adopted by a particular defendant and to scrutinise, with the assistance of expert witnesses called by the parties, the assumptions, comparables and yields which have been selected.[251] In consequence, a body of case-law is developing to provide some guidance as to the appropriate methodology for various types of valuation, including development sites,[252] hotels and restaurants,[253] shops,[254] insurance,[255] rating,[256] freehold investment properties[257] and rent reviews.[258]

246. *Ibid.* at 86. See also *Mount Banking Corporation Ltd* v. *Brian Cooper & Co* [1992] 2 E.G.L.R. 142 at 145.

247. [1994] E.G.C.S. 90.

248. *Banque Bruxelles Lambert SA* v. *Eagle Star Insurance Co Ltd* [1995] 2 All E.R. 769 at 789–791 *per* Phillips J. See also *Nyckeln Finance* v. *Stumpbrook Continuation Ltd* [1994] 2 E.G.L.R. 143; *BNP Mortgages Ltd* v. *Goadsby & Harding Ltd* [1994] 2 E.G.L.R. 169.

249. In *Old Gate Estates Ltd* v. *Toplis* [1939] 3 All E.R. 209 it was conceded by the defendants that "it would be negligent for a valuer to value a property without himself collecting the material upon which the valuation is made, such as the income and the outgoings".

250. For cases where negligence by a valuer or surveyor was alleged but not established, see *Love* v. *Mack* (1905) 92 L.T. 345 (mortgagor exaggerated income from business); *Strover* v. *Harrington* [1988] 1 E.G.L.R. 173 (vendor claimed falsely that house enjoyed mains drainage); and *PK Finans International (UK) Ltd* v. *Andrew Downs & Co Ltd* [1992] 1 E.G.L.R. 172 (developer misrepresented planning position).

251. This process appears likely to increase following the publication of the R.I.C.S. *Appraisal and Valuation Manual*, which contains Practice Statements and Guidance Notes relating to different types of valuation.

252. *Singer & Friedlander Ltd* v. *John D Wood & Co* [1977] 2 E.G.L.R. 84. For analysis and scrutiny of the "residual valuation" method, see *Mount Banking Corporation Ltd* v. *Brian Cooper & Co* [1992] 2 E.G.L.R. 142; *Nykredit Mortgage Bank plc* v. *Edward Erdman Group Ltd* [1996] 02 E.G. 110.

253. *Corisand Investments Ltd* v. *Druce & Co* [1978] 2 E.G.L.R. 86; *Craneheath Securities Ltd* v. *York Montague Ltd* [1994] 1 E.G.L.R. 159; affirmed [1996] 07 E.G. 141.

254. *Qureshi* v. *Liassides* (unreported) 22 April 1994, Official Referees' Business.

255. *Beaumont* v. *Humberts* [1990] 2 E.G.L.R. 166.

256. *McIntyre* v. *Herring Son & Daw* [1988] 1 E.G.L.R. 231.

257. *Macey* v. *Debenham Tewson & Chinnocks* [1993] 1 E.G.L.R. 149.

258. *Zubaida* v. *Hargreaves* [1995] 1 E.G.L.R. 127.

# 5 DAMAGES

Where a surveyor or valuer is sued in contract, proof of breach will in itself entitle the client to an award of nominal damages, whether or not any loss has resulted. By contrast, an action in tort (whether brought by the client or by a third party) can only succeed on proof of loss or damage. In either case, however, a plaintiff who seeks substantial damages will have to satisfy the court that reliance on the defendant's negligent advice has caused some injury, loss or damage and, furthermore, that this is not too remote a consequence of the negligence in question. This section examines the general principles governing the award of damages, before considering the application of those principles to particular types of claim against surveyors and valuers.

## 5.1 General principles

### 5.1.1 Causation and remoteness

"The court, before making any award in a plaintiff's favour, must be satisfied, albeit upon the narrowest balance of probabilities, that the breach of duty caused or contributed to the loss."[259] If the court concludes that the loss in respect of which damages are claimed results solely from some other extraneous factor, or *novus actus interveniens*, the defendant cannot be held responsible for it.[260] One particular aspect of this principle is the doctrine of mitigation, which precludes a claim for any part of the loss suffered which the plaintiff could have avoided by taking reasonable steps.[261]

In approaching the issue of causation, the courts frequently ask whether the plaintiff would have suffered the loss in question "but for" the negligence of the defendant. If that loss would have been suffered in any event, then the defendant's negligence has not "caused" it. Thus in *Thomas Miller & Co* v. *Richard Saunders & Partners*,[262] where surveyors acting for a tenant on a rent review negligently failed to place certain evidence before the arbitrator, they were held not liable for the tenant's losses, since the court was convinced that the arbitrator's decision would have been the same if the relevant evidence had been presented to him.

Where causation is in issue in a case involving a surveyor or valuer, the dispute usually turns on the question of whether or not the plaintiff relied on the defendant's negligent advice. In the absence of such reliance, the defendant cannot be held liable

---

259. *Thomas Miller & Co* v. *Richard Saunders & Partners* [1989] 1 E.G.L.R. 267 at 272 *per* Rougier J. It is for the plaintiff to plead and prove the causal link: thus, it is for a mortgage lender to prove that a proper valuation would have resulted in no loan at all, rather than for the valuer to prove that there would still have been a smaller loan: *Mount Banking Corporation Ltd* v. *Brian Cooper & Co* [1992] 2 E.G.L.R. 142. (As to the importance of this distinction, see p. 654.)

260. In *PK Finans International (UK) Ltd* v. *Andrew Downs & Co Ltd* [1992] 1 E.G.L.R. 172, a lending bank claimed that valuers had negligently failed to warn of the need to verify the planning assumptions on which their valuation was based. It was held that the defendants' failure did not constitute negligence. Had it done so, the judge would have treated the plaintiff's own failure to show the valuation to their solicitors, not as a *novus actus interveniens*, but as contributory negligence, and would have held the plaintiffs responsible for 80 per cent of their own losses.

261. For the operation of this doctrine in cases of house buyers and mortgage lenders, see pp. 653 and 661 respectively.

262. [1989] 1 E.G.L.R. 267.

for the plaintiff's loss.[263] However, it is not necessary for the plaintiff to have relied exclusively upon the defendant's advice, provided that it affected his judgement to a material degree.[264] Indeed, it is common to find that a negligent valuation is only one of the factors which led the plaintiff to enter into a transaction. As pointed out by Wright J in a commercial lending case[265]:

"One of the elements of the scheme of protection that a lender sets up when negotiating an advance of this kind, in order to protect himself against loss should the borrower default, is an assurance as to the value of his security. It would only be in a most exceptional set of circumstances that the negligent valuer would not be at least in part responsible for the consequential loss suffered by the lender upon the failure of the borrower to honour his obligations."[266]

In *Kenney* v. *Hall, Pain & Foster*[267] the plaintiff was assured by the defendants that his current house was worth at least £100,000. He therefore put the house on the market at that price and, leaving what he believed to be an adequate safety margin, committed himself to the purchase and renovation of another property. By the time that he took this step, the plaintiff had clearly come to realise that the defendant's valuation of his house was too high; moreover, his belief was supported by warnings given to the plaintiff by a local estate agent and by his bank manager. Nevertheless, Goff J held that the plaintiff had continued to rely, at least in part, on the defendants' valuation[268]:

"Certainly ... he had come to suspect that [the defendants'] valuation was rather high; he was also exercising his own judgement, in the light of all the factors known to him, but one of those factors remained [the defendants'] advice, and I am satisfied that the plaintiff was still relying substantially on that advice, in the sense that, even allowing for the fact that he suspected [the defendants'] figure to have been rather high, still the valuation made him feel that he could safely commit himself to spending £65,000 on Wickham Lodge and cover his commitments by achieving a quick sale of Culverlands House by a dramatic reduction of 25 per cent in the asking price. He felt that, in the light of the advice that he had received from [the defendants], even allowing that his valuation might have been rather high, this was a risk that he could safely take."[269]

It seems clear that, where a person enters into a loss-making transaction after having received negligent professional advice, the inference that the advice was

---

263. If it is unreasonable for the plaintiff to rely on the defendant's advice, the defence of contributory negligence may apply: see p. 673.

264. "As long as a misrepresentation plays a real and substantial part, though not by itself a decisive part, in inducing a plaintiff to act, it is a cause of his loss and he relies on it, no matter how strong or how many are the other matters which play their part in inducing him to act": *JEB Fasteners Ltd* v. *Marks Bloom & Co* [1983] 1 All E.R. 583 at 589 *per* Stephenson LJ.

265. *HIT Finance Ltd* v. *Lewis & Tucker Ltd* [1993] 2 E.G.L.R. 231, at 234. See also *Nyckeln Finance Co Ltd* v. *Stumpbrook Continuation Ltd* [1994] 2 E.G.L.R. 143 at 147–148 *per* Judge Fawcus.

266. In *Banque Bruxelles Lambert SA* v. *Eagle Star Insurance Co Ltd* [1995] 2 All E.R. 769, the plaintiff lenders were held to have relied on a negligent valuation of the property to be mortgaged, even though they would not have agreed to lend without first obtaining a mortgage indemnity guarantee policy from an insurance company. In *Charterhouse Bank Ltd* v. *Rose* [1995] N.P.C. 108, where the plaintiffs requested and were given an endorsement by one qualified valuer of an earlier (negligent) valuation given by another, it was held that the plaintiffs had relied on both valuations in deciding to lend.

267. [1976] 2 E.G.L.R. 29.

268. *Ibid.* at 35.

269. It was nevertheless held that, to the extent that the costs incurred by the plaintiff in renovating the new property exceeded what was reasonable, these could not be regarded as having been caused by the defendants' negligence.

relied upon will not easily be displaced.[270] However, claims against surveyors or valuers have occasionally failed for lack of evidence of reliance. In *Rona* v. *Pearce*,[271] for example, the purchaser of a bungalow failed in an action for negligence against the defendant who surveyed the property for him, since Hilbery J "could not believe ... that the report was a factor which influenced [the plaintiff] in buying the bungalow". So too, in *Shankie-Williams* v. *Heavey*,[272] where the vendor of newly converted flats obtained a report from a "dry rot surveying specialist" which negligently gave the property a clean bill of health, the specialist was held not liable to the purchasers of one of those flats, since the Court of Appeal could find no evidence to show that the purchasers had been shown the report before deciding to purchase.[273]

Even where causation is established, a plaintiff's claim will still fail if the loss suffered is too remote a consequence of the defendant's breach of duty. However, the fact that remoteness of damage is based upon foreseeability[274] means that it is not usually a live issue in cases involving surveyors or valuers, since the kinds of loss in respect of which claims are normally made are precisely what would be expected to result. Indeed, even where the point is specifically raised, it seldom enables a defendant to escape liability; thus in *Allen* v. *Ellis & Co*,[275] for example, it was held that the defendant surveyors should have foreseen the possibility that a house purchaser might rely on their report as justifying his decision to stand on the asbestos roof of his garage.[276] Exceptionally, however, in *Morgan* v. *Perry*[277] it was held on the facts that an unprecedented rise in house prices in the early 1970s was not something which could have been foreseen by a surveyor in 1968.[278]

270. In *Allen* v. *Ellis & Co* [1990] 1 E.G.L.R. 170, for example, where a house purchaser stood on his garage roof with disastrous results, Garland J found sufficient "reliance" on a surveyor's report, despite the plaintiff's admission that he did not have that report in mind at the time. See also *Oswald* v. *Countrywide Surveyors Ltd* [1994] E.G.C.S. 140: p. 648.

271. (1953) 162 E.G. 380.

272. [1986] 2 E.G.L.R. 139.

273. In *Banque Bruxelles Lambert SA* v. *Eagle Star Insurance Co Ltd* [1995] 2 All E.R. 769, a claim in respect of one mortgaged property failed because Phillips J was satisfied that the plaintiffs were in fact highly sceptical about the defendants' valuation and that their decision to go ahead with the loan transaction was based entirely on commercial considerations which had nothing to do with it.

274. In contract, loss is too remote if it is not at the time of the contract reasonably foreseeable as liable to result from the breach: *Victoria Laundry (Windsor) Ltd* v. *Newman Industries Ltd* [1949] 2 K.B. 528. In tort, loss is too remote if it is not at the time of breach reasonably foreseeable as a consequence of that breach: *Overseas Tankship (UK) Ltd* v. *Morts Dock and Engineering Co Ltd, The Wagon Mound* [1961] A.C. 388.

275. [1990] 1 E.G.L.R. 170.

276. In *Drinnan* v. *CW Ingram & Sons* 1967 S.L.T. 205, however, the judge, while refusing to strike out a house buyer's claim against a surveyor, expressed the "gravest doubts" as to whether it could reasonably be foreseen that she would suffer hypertension, leading to the loss of her job, as a consequence of a negligent survey report.

277. (1973) 229 E.G. 1737.

278. Whether a court today would take a similar view must be doubted. As Sir Thomas Bingham MR pointed out in *Banque Bruxelles Lambert SA* v. *Eagle Star Insurance Co Ltd* [1995] 2 All E.R. 769 at 841: "It has not been argued that [the lender's] claim for any part of his loss, including that part attributable to the fall in the property market, is too remote. The reason is obvious. [The lender] and [the valuer] know, as everyone knows, that in any market prices may move upwards or downwards. That is the essence of a market. No one in recent times has expected property prices to remain stable over a prolonged period".

### 5.1.2  Collateral benefits

A question which has arisen in a number of cases concerning surveyors and valuers is whether the plaintiff's entitlement to damages is affected by a benefit (usually money) received from some third party. The approach commonly adopted by the courts is to ask whether the benefit in question is to be regarded as *res inter alios acta* ("something between other people"), in which case it will be ignored in assessing damages.[279] This principle was considered by Phillips J in *Banque Bruxelles Lambert SA* v. *Eagle Star Insurance Co Ltd*[280]:

"Whatever circumstances *res inter alios acta* embraces, they have, I believe, one thing in common. They are circumstances in which a third party, or an extraneous event, intervenes to provide a plaintiff with some form of indemnity, in whole or in part, for the loss which the defendant has caused. The law ignores the intervention so that the plaintiff remains entitled to recover from the defendant the full amount of the loss or damage initially suffered."

One important application of *res inter alios acta* is the well-established general principle that, in assessing the damages to be awarded to a plaintiff, no deduction is to be made in respect of any benefits which that plaintiff has received by virtue of an insurance policy. This principle, which is well established in tort generally, is most commonly encountered in relation to the building insurance policy taken out by house owners; however, it is equally relevant where a mortgage lender sues a negligent valuer in respect of losses which are in fact covered by a mortgage indemnity guarantee policy.[281]

Apart from insurance, it appears that any statutory grants received by the plaintiff will also be ignored, at least where the award of such grants is a matter for the discretion of the public authority concerned. In *Treml* v. *Ernest W Gibson and Partners*[282] the plaintiff, having purchased a house in reliance on the defendants' negligent survey report, subsequently received a grant from the local authority towards the cost of repairing the serious defects which the defendants had failed to detect. The defendants' claim that the amount of this grant should be deducted from the plaintiff's damages was rejected by Popplewell J:

"I am clearly of the view that the sum does not fall to be deducted. First, because it is irrelevant to a claim where the difference in value is the measure of damage and, secondly, because, to use legal shorthand, it is a collateral benefit which does not have to be taken into account."

In *Marder* v. *Sautelle and Hicks*[283] the plaintiffs, having purchased a house in reliance on the defendants' survey report, subsequently discovered that (unnoticed by the defendants) it was of inferior construction and was unlikely to remain inhabitable for very long. The plaintiffs recovered damages from the defendants which reflected the difference between what they had paid for the property (£33,000) and what it was actually worth (£13,500, that being its site value less the cost of demolition). In effect, therefore, the court had declared the property to be worthless. When the defendants learned that the plaintiffs had sold the property for £70,000, they sought to appeal out of time, but their arguments failed to convince the Court of

---

279.  This formulation, although convenient, conceals a decision based on the judge's view as to whether the benefit in question *ought* to be taken into account.
280.  [1995] 2 All E.R. 769 at 802.
281.  *Banque Bruxelles Lambert SA* v. *Eagle Star Insurance Co Ltd* [1995] 2 All E.R. 769.
282.  [1984] 2 E.G.L.R. 162.
283.  [1988] 2 E.G.L.R. 187.

Appeal. As Staughton LJ pointed out, there were various possible explanations for the price obtained by the plaintiffs, such as the hope of increased development value due to a change in the local planning climate, or merely a rise in property values generally. Moreover, if the truth was that the new purchasers had simply paid too much, "that would be a collateral matter for which the defendants could claim no credit".[284]

The limits of the doctrine of *res inter alios acta* were explored in *Banque Bruxelles Lambert SA* v. *Eagle Star Insurance Co Ltd*[285] where the plaintiff bank, having agreed to make very substantial mortgage loans on the security of commercial properties valued by the defendants, then syndicated those loans to a group of other banks. When the plaintiffs brought an action for negligence against the defendants, a question which arose was whether the plaintiffs' damages should reflect the total loss on any given loan, or whether the share of that loss which was borne by the other banks should be deducted. In holding that the latter view was correct, Phillips J stated[286]:

"The principle of *res inter alios acta* requires the court to disregard an indemnity received by the plaintiff from a third party in respect of the loss caused by the defendant. It does not require or permit the court to assess damages on the basis of a fiction; to treat losses sustained by third parties as if they had been sustained by the plaintiff. The intervention of the syndicate banks did not indemnify BBL (the plaintiffs) in respect of consequences of entering into the loan transactions. It resulted in the syndicate banks suffering those consequences in place of BBL. The loss claimed by BBL is not loss suffered by BBL prior to syndication, but loss suffered by all the syndicate banks after syndication. The principle of *res inter alios acta* does not permit BBL to recover damages in respect of the losses sustained by the syndicate banks."[287]

### 5.1.3 *Interest*

Where a court awards damages for negligence against a surveyor or valuer, it has a discretion to order that the basic sum shall bear simple interest for a period ending with the date of judgment.[288] This discretion will normally be exercised in the plaintiff's favour, unless there is some compelling reason why this should not be so.[289] The court's discretion applies to both the rate of interest and the period (the maximum being from the accrual of the cause of action until the date of judgment); it is usual for interest to run from the date on which the plaintiff suffers the loss for which the damages are awarded.

As to the rate of interest, it would seem in principle that, where the interest is

284. *Ibid.* at 189.
285. [1995] 2 All E.R. 769.
286. *Ibid.* at 802.
287. In *BM Samuels Finance Group plc* v. *Countrywide Surveyors Ltd* (unreported) 15 June 1994, Official Referees' Business, mortgage loans arranged by the plaintiffs were syndicated in full among a number of client companies. It was held that, in instructing the defendant mortgage valuers, the plaintiffs had acted purely as agents for the other companies; it was accordingly to those companies *and not to the plaintiffs* that the valuers' duty of care was owed.
288. Supreme Court Act 1981, s. 35A(1).
289. In *Morgan* v. *Perry* (1973) 229 E.G. 1737, house purchasers were awarded damages against a negligent surveyor equivalent to the full price which they had paid for the property. The basis of the award thus was that the house was worth nothing, but the plaintiffs were still living in it at the date of trial. The judge refused to award interest on the principal sum, in recognition that the plaintiffs had in truth received some value from their "worthless" investment.

intended to compensate the plaintiff for being deprived of a capital sum until judgment, a reasonable commercial borrowing rate should be selected.[290] This view has been taken in cases involving both house purchasers[291] and commercial lenders.[292] However, the courts in some recent cases[293] have instead applied the rate laid down under the Judgments Act 1838 for interest on judgment debts, which seems unduly harsh upon defendants.[294]

In *Watts* v. *Morrow*,[295] where the trial judge had applied the Judgments Act rate of interest, Bingham LJ questioned the use of this rate in professional negligence actions[296]:

"Since the award of interest on damages is intended to compensate a plaintiff for being kept out of money lawfully due to him, there is much to be said for applying a rate of interest which reflects the cost or value of money over the relevant period rather than a flat rate fixed under the Judgments Act which has remained fixed over a number of years despite fluctuations in interest rates during that time."

Notwithstanding these views, however, Bingham LJ agreed with Ralph Gibson LJ and Sir Stephen Brown P that the choice of rate was an exercise of the trial judge's discretion which could not be challenged.[297]

## 5.2 Purchasers

### 5.2.1 Basic measure of damages

Two different methods of assessing damages have been suggested as appropriate in cases where a person has purchased property in reliance on a surveyor's or valuer's negligent report.[298] The first,[299] which has been advocated mainly in cases involving full building surveys, is based on the argument that the purchaser relies on the surveyor's report, not only as a guide to the property's value, but also for reassurance that there are no hidden defects which will require expensive repair work. Hence, it is

290. The rate of interest on damages for "inconvenience" (see p. 650) will almost invariably be two per cent, by analogy with general damages in personal injury cases.

291. *Treml* v. *Ernest W Gibson and Partners* [1984] 2 E.G.L.R. 162; *Wilson* v. *Baxter Payne and Lepper* [1985] 1 E.G.L.R. 141.

292. *Corisand Investments Ltd* v. *Druce & Co* [1978] 2 E.G.L.R. 86; *Swingcastle Ltd* v. *Alastair Gibson* [1991] 1 E.G.L.R. 157; *HIT Finance Ltd* v. *Lewis & Tucker Ltd* [1993] 2 E.G.L.R. 231. In *Nykredit Mortgage Bank plc* v. *Edward Erdman Group Ltd* [1996] 02 E.G. 110, Mayor's and City of London Court, the plaintiffs themselves suggested that such a rate would be fair.

293. E.g., *Bigg* v. *Howard Son & Gooch* [1990] 1 E.G.L.R. 173; *Heatley* v. *William H Brown Ltd* [1992] 1 E.G.L.R. 289.

294. The Judgments Act rate is set at a deliberately high level in order to coerce defendants into paying what is due.

295. [1991] 4 All E.R. 937.

296. *Ibid.* at 960.

297. Applying the earlier decision of the Court of Appeal in *Pinnock* v. *Wilkins & Sons* (1990) *The Times*, 29 January.

298. In addition to this basic measure, which is likely to constitute the bulk of the damages awarded, a person who completes a purchase may recover for certain incidental expenses incurred (see p. 649) and for inconvenience or discomfort (see p. 650). Where, by contrast, a prospective purchaser discovers the truth in time to avoid completing the purchase, a claim for damages will be limited to any wasted expenditure incurred (see p. 650).

299. Usually referred to as "cost of repair".

claimed, a purchaser who would not have purchased at all without such reassurance should be entitled, on discovering defects which a competent survey would have revealed, to be compensated for the full cost of repairing the relevant defects, even where this exceeds the difference between the property's values in its assumed and its actual condition.

The second proposed method of assessment[300] is based on the view that the purchaser's true complaint is of having paid too much for the property. Seen in this light, the purchaser's basic loss consists of the difference between the price which has been paid in reliance on the survey or valuation and the true value of the property at the date of purchase.[301]

Until some 40 years ago, the weight of judicial authority in cases of negligent surveys favoured "cost of repair" as the appropriate measure of damages. However, the law has undergone a fundamental change following three decisions of the Court of Appeal, the first of which was *Philips* v. *Ward*.[302] The plaintiff in that case purchased a house for £25,000 on the basis of a survey carried out by the defendant, which negligently failed to discover the ravages of death-watch beetle and woodworm. The evidence before the court indicated that, although the necessary repair work would have cost £7,000 at the time of purchase, the property was actually worth £21,000 at that date. The Court of Appeal upheld the decision of the trial judge to award the plaintiff £4,000 and not £7,000 as damages for the negligent survey, for reasons clearly stated by Denning LJ[303]:

"I take it to be clear law that the proper measure of damages is the amount of money which will put the plaintiff into as good a position as if the surveying contract had been properly fulfilled ... Now if the defendant had carried out his contract, he would have reported the bad state of the timbers. On receiving that report, the plaintiff either would have refused to have anything to do with the house, in which case he would have suffered no damage, or he would have bought it for a sum which represented its fair value in its bad condition, in which case he would pay so much less on that account. The proper measure of damages is therefore the difference between the value in its assumed condition and the value in the bad condition which should have been reported to the client ... In this action, if the plaintiff were to recover from the surveyor £7,000, it would mean that the plaintiff would get for £18,000 (£25,000 paid less £7,000 received) a house and land which were worth £21,000. That cannot be right. The proper amount for him to recover is £4,000."

A similar view was taken by Morris LJ[304]:

"The plaintiff must not be placed in a better position by the award of damages than he would have been in had the defendant given a proper report. If the plaintiff had received £7,000 damages in 1952 on the basis of what it would then cost him to do the repair work, and if the plaintiff instead of doing the work had sold the property for £21,000, which was its value, he would have profited to the extent of £3,000."

*Philips* v. *Ward* was followed in *Perry* v. *Sidney Phillips & Son*,[305] where the plaintiff paid £27,000 for a house which was stated by the defendant surveyors, in the course of their report, to be worth £28,500. The defendants had negligently

300. Usually referred to as "difference in value".
301. The sum awarded on this basis will bear interest between the date of purchase and the date of judgment: see p. 643.
302. [1956] 1 All E.R. 874.
303. *Ibid.* at 875–876.
304. *Ibid.* at 878.
305. [1982] 3 All E.R. 705.

overlooked a number of serious structural defects in the property, and the trial judge[306] awarded damages against them based on the cost of repairing those defects, assessed at the date of judgment. When the defendant appealed against this award the plaintiff, who had meanwhile sold the property for £43,000, accepted that an assessment based on the cost of repair could no longer be justified. However, the plaintiff claimed instead that the appropriate measure of damages was the difference *at the date of judgment* between the value of the property in its assumed condition and in its actual condition. This argument was unanimously rejected by the Court of Appeal, which regarded *Philips* v. *Ward* as authority for awarding the difference between the price paid for the property and its true value *at the date of purchase*. As Oliver LJ pointed out: "The position ... is simply this, that the plaintiff has been misled by a negligent survey report into paying more for the property than that property was actually worth".

Notwithstanding these clear rulings by the Court of Appeal, the argument that "cost of repair" more fairly reflects the loss caused to a purchaser by a negligent surveyor surfaced again in *Watts* v. *Morrow*.[307] That case concerned a survey by the defendant of a substantial farmhouse, which the plaintiffs purchased for £177,500, intending to make it their second home. It was discovered that the defendant had negligently overlooked a number of defects, to repair which would cost some £34,000; however, the evidence established that, even in its defective state, the property was still worth £162,500. On being satisfied that, had they known the truth, the plaintiffs would not have purchased the farmhouse at all, the trial judge[308] held that they were entitled to recover the full cost of repair. In so deciding, the judge relied on *dicta* of Bingham LJ[309] to the effect that "difference in value" is not the invariable measure of damages against a negligent surveyor and should not be mechanistically applied; he accordingly held that, since the plaintiffs' decision to retain the property and to repair it was a reasonable one, they were entitled to recover all their ensuing costs.

On appeal, this departure from the principles laid down in *Philips* v. *Ward* and *Perry* v. *Sidney Phillips & Son* was roundly condemned, and the judge's award of damages replaced by one which would reflect merely the excessive amount which the plaintiffs had been led to pay for the property. Once again, the need to avoid over-compensating the plaintiff was stressed, this time by Bingham LJ[310]:

"The plaintiffs paid £177,500, the value of the house as it was represented to be. The value of the house in its actual condition was £162,500, a difference of £15,000. The actual cost of repairs was (in rounded-up figures) £34,000. If the plaintiff were to end up with the house and an award of £34,000 damages he would have obtained the house for £143,500. But even if the defendant had properly performed his contract this bargain was never on offer. The effect of the award is to put the plaintiffs not in the same position as if the defendant had properly performed but in a much better one."

In delivering the leading judgment in *Watts* v. *Morrow*, Ralph Gibson LJ exposed

---

306. [1982] 1 All E.R. 1005.
307. [1991] 4 All E.R. 937.
308. [1991] 1 E.G.L.R. 150.
309. *County Personnel (Employment Agency) Ltd* v. *Alan R Pulver* [1987] 1 All E.R. 289 at 297.
310. [1991] 4 All E.R. 937 at 959.

what he regarded as the underlying fallacy in the argument for "cost of repair" damages, namely, that it does not accurately reflect what a surveyor undertakes to do for the client. As his lordship pointed out[311]: "The task of the court is to award to the plaintiffs that sum of money which will, so far as possible, put the plaintiffs into as good a position as if the contract for the survey had been properly fulfilled". Given that task, it is obviously critical to identify what is included in "the contract for the survey", and this is where the "cost of repair" argument goes astray[312]:

"From his [i.e., the plaintiff's] point of view, it would indeed be better if the surveyor could be treated as having warranted that no repairs, beyond those described as indicated in the survey report, would be required within some period of time. No such warranty, however, was given in this case, or said to have been given, and, in the absence of such a warranty, there is no basis for awarding the cost of repairs."

In the light of these three cases it now appears, subject to an appeal to the House of Lords, that the basis on which damages fall to be assessed is undeniably "difference in value". However, the cost of repairing defects which a surveyor or valuer has negligently overlooked retains some relevance in litigation when it comes to assessing the value of the property in its defective condition. As was pointed out by Purchas LJ in *Steward* v. *Rapley*[313]:

"There is no objection to a person who wishes to present a professional assessment of a market value from arriving at that market value by taking a value based on a good state of condition in the house and then deducting from it, either fully or appropriately discounted, the cost of putting it into an acceptable marketable condition."[314]

As to precisely what is meant by "difference in value" in the present context, the formulations used by the courts reveal a certain ambiguity. A number of judgments have regarded the relevant difference as that between the value of the property as stated or implied in the surveyor's report and its value in its actual condition at the date of purchase.[315] Others, however, concentrate on "the difference between the price actually paid for the property on the basis that the advice was good, and the price at which it would be bought as it was in fact".[316]

311. *Ibid.* at 950.
312. *Ibid.* at 954.
313. [1989] 1 E.G.L.R. 159 at 161.
314. Although the principle thus stated seems unobjectionable, its application in *Steward* v. *Rapley* is open to argument. The case concerned the purchase by the plaintiff of an old house for £58,500 after the defendant surveyor had found no signs of dry rot. When dry rot was subsequently discovered, the plaintiff's expert took the view that the defendant should have recognised it and should have valued the property at £50,000 (presumably on the basis of what remedial work would then have been thought necessary). However, the Court of Appeal held that the best available evidence of the extent to which the dry rot diminished the property's "value" was the full cost of eradicating it (£26,800), even though it was not until remedial work was started that the full extent of the dry rot was discovered. With all due respect, it is difficult to see how the value of a property in the market can be affected by the cost of repairs which, at the date of valuation, are not understood to be required.
315. See, for example, *Philips* v. *Ward* [1956] 1 All E.R. 874 at 876 *per* Denning LJ; at 878, *per* Morris LJ. In actions brought by lenders, the courts have rejected the argument that the lower figure should be, not the true value of the property, but the highest value which could have been attributed to it without negligence: see *United Bank of Kuwait* v. *Prudential Property Services Ltd* [1994] 2 E.G.L.R. 100; *Scotlife Homeloans (No 2) Ltd* v. *Kenneth James & Co* [1995] E.G.C.S. 70.
316. *Simple Simon Catering Ltd* v. *Binstock Miller & Co* [1973] 228 E.G. 527 at 529 *per* Lord Denning MR. To similar effect is *Watts* v. *Morrow* [1991] 2 E.G.L.R. 152 at 155, *per* Ralph Gibson LJ: "The diminution in value rule is more accurately to be expressed as the difference between the price paid and the value in its true description". See also *Ford* v. *White & Co* [1964] 2 All E.R. 755 at 758 *per* Pennycuick J.

In most of the reported cases, the potential difference between these two formulations has been obscured by the fact that the price paid and the defendant's valuation have been identical. Where this is not so, because the purchaser has managed to acquire the property for less than its stated value, it is submitted that damages should reflect the price actually paid; if they do not, the purchaser will receive compensation for a "loss" which has not in fact been suffered.[317]

In the converse situation, where a purchaser agrees to pay more for the property than the value placed on it by the surveyor or valuer, it is submitted that damages should in principle reflect the lower figure (the valuation rather than the price), since it is difficult to see how the purchaser can claim to have relied on the surveyor's report in deciding to pay more than the value given therein.[318] However, this approach has not been consistently followed by the courts. In *Oswald* v. *Countrywide Surveyors Ltd*,[319] for example, where the plaintiffs purchased a house for £225,000 after the defendant surveyors had valued it at £215,000, the judge decided that damages for "diminution in value" should be based upon the purchase price rather than the valuation. The judge was satisfied that "the excess of £10,000 which the price paid represents over [the defendants'] valuation cannot reasonably be said not to be attributable to [the defendants'] default. In short, I am satisfied that by reason of the report [the plaintiffs] were caused to pay £225,000 for Bell Farm".[320]

The "difference in value" principle has a number of further implications. First, where the valuation evidence before a court establishes that, defects notwithstanding, the property in question has been purchased for no more than its market value, the purchaser will have suffered no loss; hence, an action for breach of contract should result in an award of nominal damages and an action in tort should fail altogether (because the tort of negligence is not complete unless and until damage is suffered). Such an argument was accepted in *Upstone* v. *GDW Carnegie & Co*,[321] with the result that the defendant surveyors, although negligent, were liable only for nominal damages.[322]

A second implication is seen in cases where a property is subject to a progressive defect such as dry rot. If a surveyor negligently fails to discover such a defect, with the result that it becomes far more expensive to remedy, there appears to be no way in which the surveyor can be held liable for the purchaser's increased loss.[323] Thus in *Hooberman* v. *Salter Rex*,[324] where the cost of remedying dry rot had increased

317. The effect will also be to treat the surveyor's report as a warranty as to the value of the property.

318. In *Hardy* v. *Wamsley-Lewis* (1967) 203 E.G. 1039, where the plaintiff paid £4,600 for a house which the defendant surveyor had valued at £4,300 (and which was in reality worth only £3,500), it was held that the appropriate measure of damages was £800 (i.e., £4,300 less £3,500). See also *Morgan* v. *Perry* (1973) 229 E.G. 1737; *Hingorani* v. *Blower* [1976] 1 E.G.L.R. 104.

319. [1994] E.G.C.S. 150.

320. See also *Shaw* v. *Halifax (SW) Ltd* [1994] 2 E.G.L.R. 95, where a mortgage valuer negligently valued a house at £37,000 when it was worth only £32,000. The plaintiff purchased the property two months later for £42,000, by which time it was actually worth £37,000. Damages of £5,000 were awarded.

321. 1978 S.L.T. 4.

322. Cf. the decision of the Official Referee in *Howard* v. *Horne & Sons* [1990] 1 E.G.L.R. 272, where a purchaser who bought a house at what the expert witnesses agreed was its true market value was nevertheless awarded £1,500 for "loss of the opportunity to negotiate a reduction in price". With respect, this is difficult to understand since, if a reduction in price could indeed have been negotiated on the basis of an accurate surveyor's report, it was surely the price thus reduced which represented the market value of the property.

323. *Morgan* v. *Perry* (1973) 229 E.G. 1737.

324. [1985] 1 E.G.L.R. 144.

fourfold by the time the purchaser discovered it, the judge held that this additional cost was undoubtedly caused by the negligence of the defendant surveyor, but that the purchaser was restricted to recovering the "difference in value" at the date of purchase, with interest on that sum.

Thirdly, "difference in value" can occasionally operate to increase the damages awarded to a purchaser. In *Daisley* v. *BS Hall & Co*,[325] for example, the plaintiff paid £1,750 more than the true market value of a property, in reliance on a survey carried out by the defendants which failed to report on damage caused by soil shrinkage. By the time the case came to trial it was clear that the risk of further damage to the property had receded, and that the problem could be permanently solved by works costing no more than £250. It was nevertheless held by Bristow J that "what is sauce for the goose is sauce for the gander", and that the plaintiff was entitled to damages of £1,750.

### 5.2.2 *Incidental losses and expenses*

A person who purchases property in reliance on a negligent survey or valuation is entitled, in addition to the basic measure of damages described above, to any costs incurred in extricating himself from the transaction. Thus, a plaintiff who chooses to leave the property[326] or who is forced to leave it (for example because it is repossessed by a mortgagee[327]) will be entitled to recover the legal costs and other expenses incurred in moving into and out of the property.[328]

Where a purchaser chooses to remain in the property and to rectify the defects which were negligently overlooked by the surveyor or valuer, the question of incidental expenses is rather less clear. As noted earlier, the cost of repair itself is certainly not recoverable; moreover, the Court of Appeal in *Watts* v. *Morrow*[329] specifically rejected an argument that at least part of the cost of repair might be recovered as a substitute for the cost of resale. Despite this, there is considerable authority[330] for an award of damages to cover certain incidental expenses incurred by the purchaser in taking reasonable action to deal with defects.[331] However, the courts have stressed the need to exclude any items which ought properly to be regarded as part of the cost of repair, since this is not recoverable,[332] and any which are already reflected in the diminution in value of the property.[333]

---

325. (1972) 225 E.G. 1553.

326. See *Philips* v. *Ward* [1956] 1 All E.R. 874 at 879 *per* Romer LJ; *Watts* v. *Morrow* [1991] 2 E.G.L.R. 152 at 157 *per* Ralph Gibson LJ; at 160 *per* Bingham LJ; *Heatley* v. *William H Brown Ltd* [1992] 1 E.G.L.R. 289.

327. See *Ezekiel* v. *McDade* [1994] 1 E.G.L.R. 255.

328. In *Hardy* v. *Wamsley-Lewis* (1967) 203 E.G. 1039 the plaintiff was awarded his solicitors' costs on resale but not on purchase, but this seems incorrect.

329. [1991] 4 All E.R. 937.

330. Albeit only at first instance: in *Watts* v. *Morrow* [1991] 4 All E.R. 937 at 956, Ralph Gibson LJ in the Court of Appeal noted the point but declined to express an opinion upon it.

331. For judicial recognition that such an award may not be entirely logical, see *Cross* v. *David Martin & Mortimer* [1989] 1 E.G.L.R. 154 at 159 *per* Phillips J.

332. *Shaw* v. *Halifax (SW) Ltd* [1994] 2 E.G.L.R. 95.

333. "If such an award [i.e., for the cost of accommodation during the period of repairs] is ever appropriate it is not so when the likely need for and probable cost of vacating the premises during repair, as foreseeable by a purchaser buying at the relevant date with knowledge of the defects, has been taken into account in assessing what price he would have been prepared to pay": *Bigg* v. *Howard Son & Gooch* [1990] 1 E.G.L.R. 173 at 175 *per* Judge Hicks QC.

The items for which damages have been awarded on this basis include costs incurred[334] and "management time" wasted[335] in investigating the defects and in carrying out temporary works of an emergency nature in order to render the property safe.[336] During the period of repairs, plaintiffs have been held entitled to recover the cost of alternative accommodation for themselves[337] or for their children[338]; the expense of removing and storing furniture[339] (including the damage suffered by carpets through shrinkage)[340]; and the cost of removing and reinstalling a burglar alarm.[341] Awards have also been made for loss of rent[342] and a general award for loss of use of the plaintiffs' home.[343] Finally, where a surveyor negligently failed to warn purchasers to postpone works of decoration until a problem of damp had been rectified, the plaintiffs recovered their wasted expenditure on plastering and decorations.[344]

Where a purchaser discovers the negligence of a surveyor or valuer in time to avoid completing the proposed purchase, damages should in principle extend to all the wasted expenditure incurred in reliance on the report. This will include any deposit which has been forfeited to the vendor,[345] and the purchaser's conveyancing costs.[346] It is submitted that the surveyor or valuer may also be held liable for any expense incurred by the purchaser in investigating the defects which have been overlooked before taking the decision to withdraw from the purchase.

### 5.2.3 Damages for inconvenience

Plaintiffs in negligence actions against surveyors and valuers frequently include a claim for compensation for what judges have variously referred to as "distress, worry,

---

334. *Morgan* v. *Perry* (1973) 229 E.G. 1737.

335. *Broadoak Properties Ltd* v. *Young & White* [1989] 1 E.G.L.R. 263.

336. *Treml* v. *Ernest W Gibson and Partners* [1984] 2 E.G.L.R. 162; *Broadoak Properties Ltd* v. *Young & White* [1989] 1 E.G.L.R. 263; *Heatley* v. *William H Brown Ltd* [1992] 1 E.G.L.R. 289. In *Martin* v. *Bell-Ingram* 1986 S.L.T. 575, the plaintiffs recovered the cost of certain unsuccessful attempts at repair which were undertaken at the defendants' suggestion.

337. *Hood* v. *Shaw* (1960) 176 E.G. 1291; *Collard* v. *Saunders* (1972) 221 E.G. 797; *Treml* v. *Ernest W Gibson and Partners* [1984] 2 E.G.L.R. 162; *Cross* v. *David Martin & Mortimer* [1989] 1 E.G.L.R. 154; cf. *Gibbs* v. *Arnold Son & Hockley* [1989] 2 E.G.L.R. 154.

338. *Hunter* v. *J & E Shepherd* 1992 S.L.T. 1096. However, accommodation for a 19-year-old son was held too remote: *Cross* v. *David Martin & Mortimer* [1989] 1 E.G.L.R. 154.

339. *Hill* v. *Debenham Tewson and Chinnocks* (1958) 171 E.G. 835; *Treml* v. *Ernest W Gibson and Partners* [1984] 2 E.G.L. 162; *Cross* v. *David Martin & Mortimer* [1989] 1 E.G.L.R. 154.

340. *Fryer* v. *Bunney* [1982] 2 E.G.L.R. 130.

341. *Syrett* v. *Carr & Neave* [1990] 2 E.G.L.R. 161.

342. *Tremayne* v. *T Mortimer Burrows and Partners* (1954) 165 E.G. 232; *Freeman* v. *Marshall & Co* (1966) 200 E.G. 777.

343. *Gibbs* v. *Arnold Son & Hockley* [1989] 2 E.G.L.R. 154.

344. *Hill* v. *Debenham Tewson and Chinnocks* (1958) 171 E.G. 835.

345. *Parsons* v. *Way and Waller Ltd* (1952) 159 E.G. 524; *Buckland* v. *Watts* (1968) 208 E.G. 969. Although direct authority is lacking, it would presumably extend to any damages for breach of contract for which the purchaser is liable to the vendor.

346. Solicitors' fees were recovered in *Buckland* v. *Watts* (1968) 208 E.G. 969. Fees paid to a building society for inspecting the property (following which it refused to lend) were denied in *Parsons* v. *Way and Waller Ltd* (1952) 159 E.G. 524, but this seems incorrect.

inconvenience and trouble"[347]; "vexation and discomfort"[348]; "disturbance and disruption"[349]; "heartache and upheaval"[350]; and "bother".[351] It was held by the Court of Appeal in *Perry* v. *Sidney Phillips & Son*[352] that such claims are in principle acceptable. This ruling has been applied in numerous subsequent cases arising out of both structural surveys[353] and a *House Buyers' Report and Valuation*.[354] Moreover, it has been held on several occasions that a negligent mortgage valuer may also be liable for such damages,[355] although courts have seldom explicitly considered whether the fact that the action is based in tort rather than in contract could or should make any difference to the legal position.[356]

As a general rule,[357] damages for breach of contract cannot include compensation for purely mental distress. However, there are certain exceptions to this general rule, notably where the contract in question has as a specific object the provision of pleasure (as in the "defective package holiday" cases[358]) or the removal of displeasure (as where a solicitor should have obtained an injunction to protect a client from being molested).[359] A crucial question is whether contracts for surveys or valuations fall into one of these exceptional categories, or whether the "inconvenience" for which a surveyor or valuer may be held liable bears a more limited meaning.

In *Perry* v. *Sidney Phillips & Son*[360] Lord Denning MR appeared to support the former view, by citing the "exceptional" cases mentioned above and emphasising that a purchaser who discovered that a house was in a deplorable condition would naturally be "most upset", especially if he could not afford to repair it. A similar line is taken by a small number of subsequent cases in which the plaintiff's "distress" appears unrelated to any physical inconvenience suffered.[361]

347. *Perry* v. *Sidney Phillips & Son* [1982] 3 All E.R. 705 at 709 *per* Lord Denning MR.
348. *Ibid.* at 710 *per* Oliver LJ.
349. *Roberts* v. *J Hampson & Co* [1988] 2 E.G.L.R. 181 at 187 *per* Ian Kennedy J.
350. *Westlake* v. *Bracknell D.C.* [1987] 1 E.G.L.R. 161 at 163 *per* Mr PJ Cox QC.
351. *Fryer* v. *Bunney* [1982] 2 E.G.L.R. 130 at 135 *per* Judge Newey QC.
352. [1982] 3 All E.R. 705. Earlier examples of such awards include *Moss* v. *Heckingbottom* (1958) 172 E.G. 207 (£250 for physical inconvenience) and *Sinclair* v. *Bowden Son and Partners* (1962) 183 E.G. 95 (£100 for "inconvenience and discomfort for a family man").
353. By the Court of Appeal in *Watts* v. *Morrow* [1991] 4 All E.R. 937, and at first instance in *Fryer* v. *Bunney* [1982] 2 E.G.L.R. 130; *Treml* v. *Ernest W Gibson and Partners* [1984] 2 E.G.L.R. 162; *Wilson* v. *Baxter Payne and Lepper* [1985] 1 E.G.L.R. 141; *Hooberman* v. *Salter Rex* [1985] 1 E.G.L.R. 144; *Broadoak Properties Ltd* v. *Young & White* [1989] 1 E.G.L.R. 263; *Hipkins* v. *Jack Cotton Partnership* [1989] 2 E.G.L.R. 157; *Syrett* v. *Carr & Neave* [1990] 2 E.G.L.R. 161; *Hacker* v. *Thomas Deal & Co* [1991] 2 E.G.L.R. 161 and *Heatley* v. *William H Brown Ltd* [1992] 1 E.G.L.R. 289.
354. *Cross* v. *David Martin & Mortimer* [1989] 1 E.G.L.R. 154.
355. By the Court of Appeal in *Ezekiel* v. *McDade* [1994] E.G.C.S. 194, and at first instance in *Martin* v. *Bell-Ingram* 1986 S.L.T. 575; *Westlake* v. *Bracknell D.C.* [1987] 1 E.G.L.R. 161; *Roberts* v. *J Hampson & Co* [1988] 2 E.G.L.R. 181; *Whalley* v. *Roberts & Roberts* [1990] 1 E.G.L.R. 164; *Henley* v. *Cloke & Sons* [1991] 2 E.G.L.R. 141; *Shaw* v. *Halifax (SW) Ltd* [1994] 2 E.G.L.R. 95.
356. In *Shaw* v. *Halifax (SW) Ltd* [1994] 2 E.G.L.R. 95 it was held that the nature of the action was irrelevant.
357. Based on *Addis* v. *Gramophone Co* [1909] A.C. 488.
358. See *Jarvis* v. *Swan Tours Ltd* [1973] 1 Q.B. 233.
359. See *Heywood* v. *Wellers* [1976] Q.B. 446.
360. [1982] 3 All E.R. 705 at 709.
361. See *Bolton* v. *Puley* [1983] 2 E.G.L.R. 138; *Whalley* v. *Roberts & Roberts* [1990] 1 E.G.L.R. 164; *Hacker* v. *Thomas Deal & Co* [1991] 2 E.G.L.R. 161. In *Ezekiel* v. *McDade* [1994] E.G.C.S. 194, the undoubted inconvenience and distress suffered by the plaintiffs appeared to result from the loss of their home through repossession, rather than from any physical discomfort inherent in its defective condition.

The weight of authority, however, favours a narrower definition of "inconvenience". In *Perry* v. *Sidney Phillips & Son* itself, Oliver LJ referred to the plaintiff's "vexation, that is the discomfort and so on suffered by the plaintiff as a result of having to live for a lengthy period in a defective house".[362] Kerr LJ was even more specific[363]:

"So far as the question of damages for vexation and inconvenience is concerned, it should be noted that the deputy judge awarded these not for the tension or frustration of a person who is involved in a legal dispute in which the other party refuses to meet its liabilities ... He awarded these damages because of the physical consequences of the breach, which were all foreseeable at the time."

These views were unequivocally endorsed by the Court of Appeal in *Watts* v. *Morrow*.[364] Ralph Gibson LJ, having denied that contracts for surveys fall into the "exceptional" categories described above, concluded that "in the case of the ordinary surveyor's contract, damages are recoverable only for distress caused by physical consequences of the breach of contract".[365] A similar view was adopted by Bingham LJ, whose judgment contains a clear summary of the present legal position[366]:

"A contract-breaker is not in general liable for any distress, frustration, anxiety, displeasure, vexation, tension or aggravation which his breach of contract may cause to the innocent party. This rule is not, I think, founded on the assumption that such reactions are not foreseeable, which they surely are or may be, but on considerations of policy. But the rule is not absolute. Where the very object of a contract is to provide pleasure, relaxation, peace of mind or freedom from molestation, damages will be awarded if the fruit of the contract is not provided or if the contrary result is procured instead. A contract to survey the condition of a house for a prospective purchaser does not, however, fall within this exceptional category. In cases not falling within this exceptional category, damages are, in my view, recoverable for physical inconvenience and discomfort caused by the breach and mental suffering directly related to that inconvenience and discomfort. If those effects are foreseeably suffered during the period when defects are repaired I am prepared to accept that they sound in damages even though the cost of the repairs is not recoverable as such."

Awards of damages under this heading are subject to a number of limitations. First, the emphasis on personal physical discomfort means that such damages will not be awarded to a plaintiff whose interest in the property is purely commercial.[367] Secondly, in order to avoid double counting, no damages for inconvenience will be awarded in a case where this factor has already been taken into account in assessing the reduced value of the house.[368] Thirdly, where a plaintiff ought reasonably to have remedied defects, and thus removed the source of inconvenience, at an earlier

362. [1982] 3 All E.R. 705 at 710.
363. *Ibid.* at 712.
364. [1991] 4 All E.R. 937.
365. *Ibid.* at 956–957.
366. *Ibid.* at 959–960.
367. Direct authority on the point is lacking, although the courts have taken this line in actions against solicitors (*Hayes* v. *Dodd* [1990] 2 All E.R. 815), architects (*Hutchinson* v. *Harris* (1978) 10 B.L.R. 19) and builders (*Michael* v. *Ensoncraft Ltd* [1990] E.G.C.S. 156).
368. *Bigg* v. *Howard Son & Gooch* [1990] 1 E.G.L.R. 173. Note, however, the view expressed by Oliver LJ in *Perry* v. *Sidney Phillips & Son* [1982] 3 All E.R. 705 at 710: "I do not think that that is a realistic view at all, and I should be extremely surprised to find any valuer who is prepared to say that that is a factor which he took into account in making his valuation".

date, damages for inconvenience may fall to be reduced under the doctrine of mitigation.[369]

Apart from these specific limitations, the courts have stated repeatedly that awards of damages for inconvenience should be modest in amount.[370] In deciding what sum is appropriate, the major factors are the severity of the inconvenience and its duration or likely duration.[371] Consideration of these factors led in *Goodwin* v. *Phillips*[372] to an award of £12,500 to a diabetic husband and wheelchair-bound wife for the extreme physical inconvenience suffered by them for two-and-a-half years in a seriously defective house, followed by four more years in unsuitable alternative accommodation (a mobile home). The size of that award is, however, unusual; the great majority of plaintiffs have received no more than £1,000 under this heading.[373]

### 5.3 Vendors

Where a valuer advising a potential vendor negligently undervalues the property concerned, the natural consequence is that the property will be sold for less than it is worth. In such circumstances it appears, by analogy with the case of a purchaser,[374] that the basic measure of damages should be the difference between the sale price and the true market value of the property at the time when it is sold.[375] However, in one of the few cases in which this question has arisen, a different (and, it is submitted, erroneous) measure was used. This was in *Bell Hotels (1935) Ltd* v. *Motion*,[376] where the defendant valuer told the plaintiffs that their hotel and its contents were worth approximately £20,000 and that it would not attract brewery companies as potential purchasers. Relying on this advice, the plaintiffs sold the property for £21,730 to a private purchaser, who resold it within a week to a brewery company for £25,000. Having held that the defendant's advice was negligent, Byrne J awarded the plaintiffs

369. *Cross* v. *David Martin & Mortimer* [1989] 1 E.G.L.R. 154, where the plaintiffs had left unremedied for four years a hole in the hall floor caused by subsidence. However, a plaintiff who cannot afford to carry out the necessary repairs may not be regarded as unreasonable, especially where the defendant has persisted in denying liability and thus left the plaintiff without any assurance that the expense will ultimately be recovered: see *Perry* v. *Sidney Phillips & Son* [1982] 3 All E.R. 705 at 711 *per* Oliver LJ; at 712 *per* Kerr LJ.

370. There is, however, no arbitrary ceiling or conventional amount. For useful summaries of awards, see Franklin, "Damages for Heartache" (1988) 4 Const.L.J. 264 and "More Heartache" (1992) 8 Const.L.J. 318.

371. *Watts* v. *Morrow* [1991] 4 All E.R. 937 at 958 *per* Ralph Gibson LJ. In *Collard* v. *Saunders* (1972) 221 E.G. 797 an award was increased on medical evidence that the inconvenience and discomfort suffered was affecting the plaintiff's health. See, however, *Drinnan* v. *C W Ingram & Sons* 1967 S.L.T. 205, where the judge expressed the "gravest doubts" as to whether a negligent surveyor ought reasonably to have foreseen hypertension leading to loss of the plaintiff's employment: see p. 641.

372. (Unreported) 17 June 1994, Official Referees' Business.

373. Awards of £8,000 and £6,000 to plaintiff married couples have been reduced by the Court of Appeal to £1,500 and £4,000: *Watts* v. *Morrow* [1991] 4 All E.R. 937 and *Ezekiel* v. *McDade* [1994] E.G.C.S. 194 respectively. Other awards of more than £1,000 were made in *Oswald* v. *Countrywide Surveyors Ltd* [1994] E.G.C.S. 150 (£2,000 each to husband and wife) and *Heatley* v. *William H Brown Ltd* [1992] 1 E.G.L.R. 289 (£1,500 to husband, £3,000 to wife).

374. See p. 644.

375. This was accepted as the correct measure in *Shacklock* v. *Chas Osenton, Lockwood & Co* (1964) 192 E.G. 819 where, however, the allegation of negligence failed on the facts. It was also applied in *Weedon* v. *Hindwood, Clarke & Esplin* [1975] 1 E.G.L.R. 82, where valuers conducting compulsory purchase negotiations on behalf of a landowner negligently advised their client to accept too low a figure from the local authority.

376. (1952) 159 E.G. 496.

£5,000 damages, though without stating explicitly how this figure was arrived at. If (as seems likely) it represents the difference between the sale price and the defendant's valuation, it is submitted that the decision is incorrect; the plaintiff's loss was in fact £3,270, that being the difference between what they actually received and what they should have received on the sale.

Very unusually, a vendor in *Kenney* v. *Hall, Pain & Foster*[377] complained of a negligent *over-valuation* of his property. Relying on the defendants' assurances as to the price which could be obtained for his house, and leaving what appeared to be a sensible safety margin, the plaintiff obtained a bridging loan in order to purchase and renovate two other properties. When the plaintiff's house, which had been greatly overvalued, proved virtually impossible to sell, the plaintiff's venture overstretched him to the verge of bankruptcy. The difficult task of assessing damages in this situation was eased when the parties agreed that, had the plaintiff been properly advised, he would have sold his house and purchased a replacement at much lower prices, thus losing only some £10,000 as a result of a fall in the property market. The plaintiff's damages were accordingly assessed so as to cover all the losses resulting from his disastrous course of action, less the £10,000 which he would have lost in any event.

## 5.4 Mortgage lenders

### 5.4.1 Basic measure of damages

In defining the basic loss suffered by a mortgage lender who relies on a negligent over-valuation of the mortgaged property, the courts in recent years have identified a crucial distinction between cases where, given an accurate valuation, there would still have been a mortgage advance, albeit at a lower level, and those where no loan transaction at all would have resulted. These two categories are commonly described as "successful-transaction" and "no-transaction" cases.[378] The category into which a particular case falls may be determined, not only by the lender's criteria for making loans on mortgage, but also by evidence of whether the borrower would have been prepared to accept a smaller loan.[379] It appears that a lender who seeks damages on a "no-transaction" basis bears the onus of proving that the case falls into that category.[380]

The basic measure of damages in a "successful-transaction" case consists of the difference between what has been lent and lost in reliance on the negligent valuation and the hypothetical loss which the lender would still have suffered if given an

---

377. [1976] 2 E.G.L.R. 29.

378. *Banque Bruxelles Lambert SA* v. *Eagle Star Insurance Co Ltd* [1995] 2 All E.R. 769 at 840 *per* Sir Thomas Bingham MR, adopting the terminology used by Staughton LJ in *Hayes* v. *Dodd* [1990] 2 All E.R. 815 at 818–819.

379. See, for example, *Banque Bruxelles Lambert SA* v. *Eagle Star Insurance Co Ltd* [1995] 2 All E.R. 769; *Nyckeln Finance Co Ltd* v. *Stumpbrook Continuation Ltd* [1994] 2 E.G.L.R. 143; *HIT Finance Ltd* v. *Lewis & Tucker Ltd* [1993] 2 E.G.L.R. 231.

380. *Mount Banking Corporation Ltd* v. *Brian Cooper & Co* [1992] 2 E.G.L.R. 142 at 144 *per* Mr RM Stewart QC.

accurate valuation of the property.[381] If the latter situation would not have resulted in any loss at all (because the smaller loan would have remained fully secured), then the valuer is liable for the full amount of the loan less whatever the lender is able to recover from the borrower or from repossession and resale of the property. However, if the property would not have provided sufficient security even for the smaller loan, the basic measure of damages becomes simply the difference between the loan which has been made and that which would have been made.[382]

In a "no-transaction" case there is no "hypothetical loss" to be offset since, by definition, there would have been no mortgage loan at all if the true value of the property had been known. It might therefore seem inevitable that the lender's damages will include everything which has been lent and lost in reliance on the negligent valuation.[383] While this principle has been generally accepted as correct, there is one exceptional issue which has provoked considerable judicial disagreement, namely, whether the damages awarded should exclude any losses which are attributable to a fall in the property market in general, subsequent to the making of the loan.

The valuer's argument in support of such an exclusion is that, while a negligent valuation may have resulted in a loan being less than fully secured, it is not the legal cause of that part of the lender's over-exposure which results from a fall in market values.[384] The lender, on the other hand, reasons that since, but for the valuer's negligence, there would have been no mortgage loan at all, the valuer must accept liability for all the losses which flow from the making of that loan. These losses consist simply of the amount of the loan less whatever is recovered by the lender, and there is no justification for making any further deduction.

Until recently, the weight of authority in "no-transaction" cases has undoubtedly been in favour of permitting the lender to recover the full amount lent,[385] with no deduction other than in respect of amounts recovered (for example on realisation of the security).[386] Nevertheless, the question of market losses was not specifically addressed in any case prior to December 1993, when two conflicting High Court decisions were published within a period of 10 days.[387] In *United Bank of Kuwait* v.

---

381. The argument that the hypothetical "smaller loan" should be based on the highest non-negligent valuation which could have been given has been rejected: see *United Bank of Kuwait* v. *Prudential Property Services Ltd* [1994] 2 E.G.L.R. 100; *Scotlife Homeloans (No 2) Ltd* v. *Kenneth James & Co* [1995] E.G.C.S. 70.

382. This measure was agreed as correct by the parties in *Singer & Friedlander Ltd* v. *John D Wood & Co* [1977] 2 E.G.L.R. 84. It was subsequently applied by the courts in *Corisand Investments Ltd* v. *Druce & Co* [1978] 2 E.G.L.R. 86 and *Allied Trust Bank Ltd* v. *Edward Symmons & Partners* [1994] 1 E.G.L.R. 165. As noted by Sir Thomas Bingham MR, the effect of this is "to treat the difference between what was advanced and what would have been advanced on a proper valuation as the upper limit of what the lender can recover in damages": *Banque Bruxelles Lambert SA* v. *Eagle Star Insurance Co Ltd* [1995] 2 All E.R. 769 at 854.

383. The lender's loss "may be expressed as the difference between what the lender advanced and what the lender would have advanced if properly advised (which is always nil)": *Banque Bruxelles Lambert SA* v. *Eagle Star Insurance Co Ltd* [1995] 2 All E.R. 769 at 854 *per* Sir Thomas Bingham MR.

384. A related argument is that, since lenders do not rely on valuers to offer any sort of protection against market movements, such movements cannot legitimately be regarded as within the risk to which a particular lender has been exposed by the valuer's negligence.

385. *Baxter* v. *F W Gapp & Co Ltd* [1939] 2 All E.R. 752; *London & South of England Building Society* v. *Stone* [1983] 3 All E.R. 105; *Swingcastle Ltd* v. *Alastair Gibson* [1991] 2 A.C. 223.

386. See p. 659.

387. There is nothing in either judgment to suggest that the judge was aware of the other litigation.

*Prudential Property Services Ltd*[388] Gage J held that there was no justification for excluding such losses from a lender's damages[389]; in *Banque Bruxelles Lambert SA* v. *Eagle Star Insurance Co Ltd*[390] Phillips J came to the opposite conclusion. His Lordship, having held that the previous cases were not binding upon him,[391] considered that it would be unfair to hold the valuer responsible for something unrelated to his negligent advice[392]:

"Whether the cause of the loss of an advance is clearly foreseen or not reasonably foreseeable I do not see how the negligent adviser can fairly be said to have caused that loss unless his advice has been relied upon as providing protection against the risk of that loss."[393]

In a number of subsequent cases, judges at first instance applied *BBL* in preference to *United Bank of Kuwait*.[394] However, early in 1995 appeals in six cases were heard together by the Court of Appeal, which reversed the trend. The decisions in *United Bank of Kuwait* and one earlier case[395] were accordingly upheld; those in *BBL* and three other cases[396] were overturned.

In delivering the judgment of the Court of Appeal, Sir Thomas Bingham MR stressed that it is no part of a mortgage valuer's duty to advise the lender on likely future movements in property prices.[397] However, having set out the general principles on which damages are assessed in a "no-transaction" case, the learned Master of the Rolls pointed out that the exclusion of market losses from an award could not be justified on grounds of remoteness[398] and that no attempt had been made to justify it on grounds of policy. It followed that the only possible basis for exempting the valuer from liability for market losses would be that those losses had not been

388. [1994] 2 E.G.L.R. 143.
389. Gage J regarded himself as bound by the decision of the Court of Appeal in *Baxter* v. *F W Gapp & Co Ltd* [1939] 2 All E.R. 752.
390. [1995] 2 All E.R. 769.
391. On the somewhat unconvincing ground that, while this was a "no-transaction" case in the strict sense, it fell into that category only because the *borrowers* would not have contemplated a smaller loan.
392. [1995] 2 All E.R. 769 at 809.
393. The question of how particular risks *ought* to be allocated between the parties had also been addressed by the judge at 806–807: "Where a party is contemplating a commercial venture that involves a number of risks and obtains professional advice in respect of one head of risk before embarking on the adventure, I do not see why negligent advice in respect of that head of risk should, in effect, make the adviser the underwriter of the entire adventure. More particularly, where the negligent advice relates to the existence or amount of some security against risk in the adventure, I do not see why the adviser should be liable for all the consequences of the adventure, whether or not the security in question would have protected against them."
394. *Axa Equity & Law Home Loans Ltd* v. *Goldsack & Freeman* [1994] 1 E.G.L.R. 175; *Axa Equity & Law Home Loans Ltd* v. *Hirani Watson* [1994] E.G.C.S. 90; *BNP Mortgages Ltd* v. *Goadsby & Harding Ltd* [1994] 2 E.G.L.R. 169; *BNP Mortgages Ltd* v. *Key Surveyors Nationwide Ltd* (unreported) 19 July 1994, Official Referees' Business. See also *Mortgage Express Ltd* v. *Bowerman & Partners* [1994] 2 E.G.L.R. 156 (a solicitors' negligence case).
395. *Nykredit Mortgage Bank plc* v. *Edward Erdman Group Ltd* [1996] 02 E.G. 110, Mayor's and City of London Court.
396. *BNP Mortgages Ltd* v. *Goadsby & Harding Ltd* [1994] 2 E.G.L.R. 169; *BNP Mortgages Ltd* v. *Key Surveyors Nationwide Ltd* (unreported) 19 July 1994, Official Referees' Business; *Mortgage Express Ltd* v. *Bowerman & Partners* [1994] 2 E.G.L.R. 156.
397. "The belief among buyers and sellers that prices are likely to move upwards or downwards may have an effect on current prices, and to that extent such belief may be reflected by V in his valuation. But his concern is with current value only. He is not asked to predict what will happen in future. His valuation is not sought to protect L against a future decline in property prices. In no sense is he a guarantor of L's investment decision": [1995] 2 All E.R. 769 at 840.
398. See p. 641.

caused by the valuer's negligence and, after an examination of both English and Commonwealth authority, that possibility was emphatically rejected[399]:

"If ... a fall in the property market between the date of the transaction and the date of realisation contributes to the lender's overall loss sustained as a result of entering into the transaction, it would seem to us, on a straightforward application of the restitutionary principle, that the lender should be entitled to recover that element of his loss against the negligent party ... Since the valuer's negligence caused the lender to enter into the transaction, which he would not otherwise have done, and because he cannot escape from the transaction at will, we regard that negligence as the effective cause of the loss which the lender suffered as a result. The market fall cannot realistically be seen as a new intervening cause ... In the result, we do not think that a fall in the market can be said to have broken the link between the valuer's negligence and the damage which the lender has suffered."[400]

### 5.4.2 Incidental losses and expenses

In addition to the basic loss of capital described above, a lender may suffer consequential losses, notably those incurred in taking proceedings against the defaulting borrower to repossess and sell the mortgaged property. In a "successful-transaction" case[401] it should not normally be possible for the lender to recover damages in respect of such losses, since they would (presumably) have been incurred in any event.[402] In "no-transaction" cases,[403] by contrast, damages for such losses have been routinely awarded[404]; indeed, while defendants may dispute an individual item,[405] the lender's basic entitlement does not appear to have been challenged in any reported case.[406]

### 5.4.3 Interest

A lender who succeeds in a negligence action against a valuer is entitled to recover compensation, not only for the capital sum lost, but also for having been deprived of interest on that sum. It has been suggested[407] that such compensation is in fact

---

399. [1995] 2 All E.R. 769 at 855. The Court of Appeal held itself bound by *Baxter* v. *FW Gapp & Co Ltd* [1939] 2 All E.R. 752, which it regarded as having been upheld (save on the specific question of interest) by the House of Lords in *Swingcastle Ltd* v. *Alastair Gibson* [1991] 2 A.C. 223.

400. For an argument (in relation to an earlier case) that the approach adopted by the Court of Appeal erroneously equates factual causation with legal responsibility, see Dugdale, "Causation and the professional's responsibility" (1991) 7 P.N. 78. For a suggestion that, notwithstanding its denials, the Court of Appeal in *BBL* effectively made the negligent valuer a "guarantor of the lender's investment decision", see Murdoch, "Damages and *BBL*: a better way?" [1995] 10 E.G. 115.

401. I.e., one where, if an accurate valuation of the property had been given, a smaller loan would have been made.

402. "The plaintiffs would have been taking proceedings with equal lack of utility in respect of the smaller loan they would have made if they had received a valuation which was not in breach of the defendants' duty": *Corisand Investments Ltd* v. *Druce & Co* [1978] 2 E.G.L.R. 86 at 101 *per* Gibson J.

403. I.e., one where, if an accurate valuation of the property had been given, no loan at all would have been made.

404. See, for example, *Baxter* v. *FW Gapp & Co Ltd* [1938] 4 All E.R. 457; affirmed [1939] 2 All E.R. 752; *Swingcastle Ltd* v. *Alastair Gibson* [1991] 2 A.C. 223.

405. E.g., *HIT Finance Ltd* v. *Lewis & Tucker Ltd* [1993] 2 E.G.L.R. 231 (overpayment to estate agents handling the resale).

406. It may nevertheless be argued that to award damages under this head raises a similar problem to that of the falling market (see p. 656). The cause of these losses is that the borrower has defaulted; yet it can hardly be suggested that a lender looks to the valuer for an assurance that this will not happen.

407. *Banque Bruxelles Lambert SA* v. *Eagle Star Insurance Co Ltd* [1995] 2 All E.R. 769 at 817 *per* Phillips J.

comprised of two separate elements: damages reflecting unearned interest on the entire capital sum between the date of the loan and the date on which the security was realised, and interest on the capital lost in accordance with the court's statutory discretion between the date on which the security was realised and the date of judgment.[408] Whether or not this analysis is correct, it is normal practice to award simple rather than compound interest.

The appropriate measure of damages for lost interest was considered by the House of Lords in *Swingcastle Ltd* v. *Alastair Gibson*.[409] The plaintiff finance company there lent £10,000 to high risk borrowers on the security of a house, following a valuation of £18,000 by the defendant which was subsequently held to be negligent. The rate of interest payable under the mortgage contract was more than 36 per cent, rising to some 45 per cent on any default in repayment. When the borrowers fell into arrears, the plaintiffs repossessed the property and sold it for £12,000. They then sued the defendant to recover everything which they had lost, including accrued interest at the default rate. This claim succeeded in the county court; the Court of Appeal,[410] despite an acknowledgment by Neill LJ that "to award damages on this basis is in effect to treat the valuer as the guarantor of the contract of loan", held unanimously that it was bound by *Baxter* v. *FW Gapp & Co Ltd*[411] to uphold the award.

On further appeal by the valuer, the House of Lords unanimously overturned the decision of the Court of Appeal and overruled *Baxter* v. *Gapp* on the point in issue. The only speech was delivered by Lord Lowry, who pointed out[412]:

"The approach [adopted in *Baxter* v. *Gapp*], if carefully scrutinised, seems contrary to principle: the aggrieved party was entitled to be placed in the same position as if the wrong had not occurred, and not to receive from the wrongdoer compensation for lost interest at the rate which the borrower had contracted to observe ... What the lenders lost, in addition to their other damages, was the use of the £10,000 while it was perforce locked up in the loan ... My Lords, it is clear that the lenders ought to have presented their claim on the basis that, if the valuer had advised properly, they would not have lent the money. Where they went wrong was to claim not only correctly that they had to spend all the money which they did but incorrectly that the valuer by his negligence deprived them of the interest which they would have received from the borrowers if the borrowers had paid up. The security for the loan was the property, but the lenders did not have a further security consisting of a guarantee by the valuer that the borrowers would pay everything, or indeed anything, that was due from them to the lenders at the date, whenever it occurred, on which the loan transaction terminated. The fallacy of the lenders' case is that they have been trying to obtain from the valuer compensation for the borrowers' failure and not the proper damages for the valuer's negligence."

Having thus analysed the true nature of what the lenders had lost, the House of Lords awarded damages based on a calculation of interest at 12 per cent.[413]

The principle laid down in *Swingcastle* was applied in *HIT Finance Ltd* v. *Lewis & Tucker Ltd*.[414] The plaintiff there was a wholly owned subsidiary of two public companies, which were the only source of funds for its mortgage lending operations. In an action against a negligent valuer the plaintiff claimed that, since it was obliged

---

408. Supreme Court Act 1981, s. 35A(1).
409. [1991] 2 A.C. 223.
410. [1990] 3 All E.R. 463.
411. [1938] 4 All E.R. 457; affirmed [1939] 2 All E.R. 752.
412. [1991] 2 A.C. 223 at 238.
413. See below.
414. [1993] 2 E.G.L.R. 231.

to account to its parents for all interest received from the borrower, its loss in a "no-transaction" case consisted of everything which the borrower should have paid. This argument was rejected by Wright J who concluded that the underlying reality was that the plaintiff was a mere puppet and that the parent companies had in truth suffered the relevant loss. And, since there was no evidence to show precisely how the parent companies raised the money to fund the plaintiff's activities, they were entitled merely to a rate of interest designed to compensate them for being kept out of their money.[415]

In considering what rate of interest should be adopted, the courts have recognised three main possibilities. The first (which is by far the least likely) arises where a lender can show, in a "no-transaction" case, that the money could have been lent to a different borrower who would not have defaulted and who would have paid a high contractual rate of interest. As was pointed out by the Court of Appeal in *Swingcastle Ltd* v. *Alastair Gibson*[416]:

"The lender could be awarded a sum equivalent to the amount he would have earned on another loan if he had the money available for this purpose. In my view, however, such an award should not be made in the absence of evidence that the money lent would have been used for another transaction. This evidence would have to be directed to proving an unsatisfied demand for loans and I anticipate that such evidence might seldom be forthcoming."

A lender who produces no evidence as to how the loan in question was funded runs the risk that the court will adopt a rate of interest close to the Special Account rate. In *Swingcastle Ltd* v. *Alastair Gibson*[417] this produced a rate of 12 per cent; in the earlier "successful-transaction" case of *Corisand Investments Ltd* v. *Druce & Co*[418] it resulted in an award of 9 per cent.[419] However, the adoption of such a rate is by no means inevitable; in *HIT Finance Ltd* v. *Lewis & Tucker Ltd*,[420] for example, Wright J applied a rate of one per cent above base rate, on the basis that commercial organisations can be presumed to fund their activities on a normal commercial basis.

In most cases, the lender will be able to provide evidence as to how the money to finance the loan was raised. In such circumstances, it appears that the court will adopt either the lender's actual borrowing rate[421] or a normal commercial borrowing rate.[422]

### 5.4.4 Offsets against damages

In seeking to assess a lender's net loss, certain sums received by the lender may fall to be deducted from the total figure which is arrived at using the principles described above. In a "no-transaction" case,[423] the most important of these sums will be the

415. Wright J calculated damages on the basis of interest at one per cent over base rate: see below.
416. [1990] 3 All E.R. 463 at 469 *per* Neill LJ.
417. [1991] 2 A.C. 223; see also *BNP Mortgages Ltd* v. *Chadwick Bird* (unreported) July 1994, Official Referees' Business.
418. [1978] 2 E.G.L.R. 86.
419. This was based on the Short Term Investment Account, the predecessor of the Special Account.
420. [1993] 2 E.G.L.R. 231.
421. See, for example, *Nykredit Mortgage Bank plc* v. *Edward Erdman Group Ltd* [1996] 02 E.G. 110, Mayor's and City of London Court.
422. In *Banque Bruxelles Lambert SA* v. *Eagle Star Insurance Co Ltd* [1995] 2 All E.R. 769, the plaintiffs were awarded one per cent above base rate as ("fair compensation for being deprived of the use of money"), despite the defendants' claim that the Special Account rate should be used.
423. See p. 654.

amount recovered by the lender on sale of the repossessed property. It would seem logical also to deduct the amount of any repayments of capital and/or interest made by the borrower prior to default, although the Court of Appeal has been divided on this issue.[424] In addition to these receipts, the lender must give credit for any income, such as rent, which the mortgaged property produces from its repossession by the mortgagee until its resale.[425]

In a "successful-transaction" case,[426] by contrast, it would seem logical to ignore both the amount recovered on resale and any repayments made by the borrower in calculating the lender's loss, at least where it is reasonable to assume that these sums would equally have been received by the lender in the event of a smaller loan. However, in *Corisand Investments Ltd* v. *Druce & Co*,[427] where the borrowers had made interest payments of some £9,000 under the mortgage prior to default, Gibson J held that the correct approach was to calculate the difference between the loan actually made (£60,000) and the smaller loan which would have been made (£16,300) and to deduct the £9,000 from the figure so arrived at.[428]

Apart from making deductions in respect of sums actually received by the lender, a question which has provoked a range of judicial views concerns the extent, if any, to which account should be taken of sums which the lender *might* recover, most importantly by taking action against the borrower to enforce the personal covenant to repay the loan.

This question first arose in *Eagle Star Insurance Co Ltd* v. *Gale and Power*,[429] where the plaintiffs lent £3,015 on the security of a house valued by the defendants at £3,350, on terms that the mortgagor would after four years repay £1,500 of the loan out of his retirement gratuity. The house, which had been negligently over-valued, was in truth worth only £1,600; however, provided that the mortgagor duly made the promised repayment, the outstanding loan would then be fully secured on the property. In assessing damages against the valuers, Devlin J held that, while the mortgagor's covenant could not be ignored as *res inter alios acta*, this was not a case in which nominal damages would be appropriate.[430] Devlin J accordingly awarded the plaintiffs damages of £100 as an indemnity against such contingencies as the house collapsing or the borrower proving unable to fulfil his covenant.

In *London & South of England Building Society* v. *Stone*[431] the plaintiff building society lent £11,800 on the security of a house, in reliance on a valuation carried out

424. In *London & South of England Building Society* v. *Stone* [1983] 3 All E.R. 105, this view was taken by Stephenson LJ (at 119, applying *Baxter* v. *F W Gapp & Co Ltd* [1938] 4 All E.R. 457; affirmed [1939] 2 All E.R. 752, and Sir Denys Buckley (at 118). The *dictum* of O'Connor LJ (at 116) that the lender's loss "has not been diminished by the small repayment of capital" seems, with respect, impossible to justify.

425. In *Banque Bruxelles Lambert SA* v. *Eagle Star Insurance Co Ltd* [1995] 2 All E.R. 769, the plaintiffs simply totalled the income received and set this against the total of the damages claimed. The valuers argued that credit should be given on a running account basis, so that early receipts would operate so as to reduce the capital outstanding. However, the plaintiffs' approach was held to be appropriate and fair, given that they were claiming interest on a simple and not a compound basis.

426. See p. 654.

427. [1978] 2 E.G.L.R. 86.

428. This award, with respect, seems incorrect. It was, however, explained in *Assured Advances Ltd* v. *Ashbee & Co* [1994] E.G.C.S. 169 as resting on the impossibility of knowing for certain what would have happened if a smaller loan had been made.

429. (1955) 166 E.G. 37.

430. As the defendants had argued.

431. [1983] 3 All E.R. 105.

by the defendant. This valuation was subsequently found to have been negligent, in that the defendant had failed to discover that the house, which was built on the site of a filled quarry on a hillside, was in danger of collapsing as the quarry fill slid downwards. The plaintiffs paid for the necessary repairs at a cost of £29,000 (which was considerably more than the total value of the house). They then announced that they would take no action against the house owners on their personal covenant to repay the loan.[432]

In assessing the damages to which the building society was entitled, Russell J at first instance[433] held that the basic measure was the amount of the mortgage loan, but that a deduction should be made in recognition of the alternative means by which the plaintiffs might have protected their position. The judge thought that although, in terms of honour and commercial good sense, it was reasonable for the plaintiffs not to have pursued the purchasers for the full amount of their debt, it was not reasonable to have let them off completely. Russell J therefore deducted £3,000.

The Court of Appeal, by a majority, reversed this ruling and held that no deduction should be made.[434] However, the judges who reached this decision did so for different reasons. O'Connor LJ simply stated that money owing from the mortgagor did nothing to diminish the plaintiff's loss.[435] Stephenson LJ, by contrast, regarded the question as essentially one of mitigation of damage[436]:

"[Valuing the chance of repayment] can be justified only if it was reasonable for the respective plaintiffs to enforce the borrowers' covenant to pay; for what the borrowers might pay could only be taken into account in mitigation of the plaintiffs' damage if the plaintiffs ought to have mitigated that loss and damage by enforcing the borrowers' covenants ... It seems to me the wrongdoer must show that the wronged party's reasoned choice to waive his contractual rights against the third party is unreasonable in the ordinary course of events in the particular field of commercial business and in all the circumstances, it may be some special, of the particular case."

On the facts before him, Stephenson LJ held that the plaintiffs' refusal to enforce the borrowers' covenant was not "an act of unreasonable benevolence or forgiveness", that there was accordingly no failure to mitigate their loss and that no deduction should be made from the damages awarded.

## 5.5 Other cases

The wide range of claims to which a negligent surveyor or valuer may be subject does not permit the application of a universal test for the assessment of damages.

432. The building society's decision appears to have been taken partly out of a sense of moral responsibility for the conduct of its chosen valuer and partly as a public relations exercise.

433. [1981] 1 E.G.L.R. 139.

434. [1983] 3 All E.R. 105. Sir Denys Buckley, dissenting, agreed with the trial judge's deduction on the basis that the contingency of repayment or non-repayment by the purchasers had to be taken into account in evaluating what the plaintiffs had lost: *ibid.* at 118.

435. *Ibid.* at 116.

436. *Ibid.* at 121. A similar view was taken by Judge Byrt QC in *Nykredit Mortgage Bank plc* v. *Edward Erdman Group Ltd* [1996] 02 E.G. 110, Mayor's and City of London Court. Once again, however, the lender's decision not to pursue the borrower was held to be reasonable, since the latter was "engulfed in debt with no significant assets" and was thus not worth suing. In *Nyckeln Finance Co Ltd* v. *Stumpbrook Continuation Ltd* [1994] 2 E.G.L.R. 143, it was held that a lender's delay in repossessing and selling the security following the mortgagor's default, against the background of a rapidly falling commercial property market, was an unreasonable failure to mitigate.

However, a court will normally attempt to place the claimant, so far as money can achieve this, in the position he would have occupied if the professional work had been properly carried out. In *Beaumont* v. *Humberts*,[437] for example, where it was alleged that a surveyor had negligently advised a client to insure a property against fire damage for too low a figure, damages would have reflected the difference between what the client received when claiming on the insurance policy and what would have been received had the property been insured for its true value.[438] Similarly in *Whitley (FG) & Sons Co Ltd* v. *Thomas Bickerton*,[439] where surveyors negligently failed to pursue appeals on behalf of their clients against a refusal of planning permission, the resulting damage was perceived as the depreciation in value of the clients' site at the moment when it became too late to rectify the situation.

In the majority of situations, the approach described above means that the court will in effect compare the capital value of what the plaintiff has with what he ought to have had. This was applied in the context of rent review work in *Rajdev* v. *Becketts*,[440] where the defendant surveyor's negligent failure to make proper representations on behalf of a tenant resulted in the determination by an independent expert of a surprisingly high rent. It was held that the tenant's damages should reflect the difference in value of a lease at this rent and a lease at the rent which ought to have been fixed if the defendants had performed their work properly. Similarly, in *Knight* v. *Lawrence*,[441] where a mortgagee's receiver negligently failed to trigger certain rent reviews, it was held that the landlords were entitled to the extra value which their properties would have realised if the rent reviews had been carried out.[442]

The "capitalisation" approach, though common, is not invariably adopted, and "should not be mechanically applied in circumstances where it may appear inappropriate".[443] Thus, for example, other rent review cases involving negligent surveyors and solicitors have resulted in damages based on the amount of rent lost to a landlord over the rental period,[444] the loss to a landlord of the *chance* of obtaining a higher rent,[445] and the cost to a tenant company of extracting itself from the disadvantageous underlease into which it had entered on its solicitors' advice.[446]

# 6 DEFENCES

Even where the various elements of liability discussed above are present, a surveyor or valuer may yet be able to rely on certain defences so as to avoid or reduce that

---

437. [1990] 2 E.G.L.R. 166.
438. In fact the defendants were held not to have been negligent.
439. [1993] 1 E.G.L.R. 139.
440. [1989] 2 E.G.L.R. 144.
441. [1991] 1 E.G.L.R. 143.
442. In fact the judge went one stage further by investigating how the plaintiffs' ultimate financial position would have differed if the properties had in fact been sold at that higher price.
443. *County Personnel (Employment Agency) Ltd* v. *Alan R Pulver* [1987] 1 All E.R. 289 at 297 *per* Bingham LJ.
444. *CIL Securities Ltd* v. *Briant Champion Long* [1993] 2 E.G.L.R. 164.
445. *Corfield* v. *D S Bosher & Co* [1992] 1 E.G.L.R. 163.
446. *County Personnel (Employment Agency) Ltd* v. *Alan R Pulver* [1987] 1 All E.R. 289.

liability. A plaintiff's delay in bringing legal proceedings may mean that the action becomes statute-barred; contract terms or other disclaimers may exclude or restrict liability; and a plaintiff's failure to take sufficient care of his own interests may lead to a finding of contributory negligence. Finally, though this is not a defence as such, a negligent surveyor or valuer may be able to recoup some of the damages payable from another negligent adviser, such as a solicitor, in an action for contribution.[447]

## 6.1 Limitation of actions

The general principles under which an action may become statute-barred by lapse of time were discussed in chapter 2. What follows is a brief examination of the way in which those principles operate in cases involving surveys and valuations. Such cases almost invariably arise out of negligence, and the resulting legal action is therefore framed in contract or tort. However, other types of liability may occasionally be relevant, notably an action for fraud[448] or a claim for contribution by one professional adviser against another.[449]

### 6.1.1 Claims in contract and tort

It is trite law that, where a surveyor or valuer is sued for breach of contract, the accrual of the plaintiff's cause of action (and therefore the start of the limitation period under section 5 of the Limitation Act 1980) occurs at the moment of breach. The first such moment is likely to be when the defendant carries out an inadequate inspection of a property or makes an error in a calculation of value. However, in most cases a negligent valuer or surveyor will also commit a second breach of contract when a misleading report (based on the negligent inspection or calculation) is submitted to the client. There seems no reason to doubt that the client may base an action on this second breach, in order to obtain a contractual limitation period of six years from the date of the report.

Where an action is brought in the tort of negligence,[450] the accrual of the plaintiff's cause of action (and therefore the start of the limitation period under section 2 of the Limitation Act 1980) occurs at the moment when the plaintiff suffers relevant loss or damage.[451] In *Secretary of State for the Environment* v. *Essex, Goodman & Suggitt*,[452] which concerned a survey of commercial property carried out on behalf of prospective tenants, it was held that the plaintiffs suffered loss as soon as they entered into a legally binding contract to acquire the property.[453] A similar principle

447. Civil Liability (Contribution) Act 1978, s. 1(1). See *Anglia Hastings & Thanet Building Society* v. *House & Son* [1981] 2 E.G.L.R. 17 (decided on the Law Reform (Married Women and Tortfeasors) Act 1935); *UCB* v. *Dundas & Wilson* 1989 S.L.T. 243.

448. See, for example, *Alliance & Leicester Building Society* v. *Edgestop Ltd (No 3)* [1994] 2 E.G.L.R. 229. In such a case, the period of limitation does not begin to run against a plaintiff until he discovers or could with reasonable diligence have discovered the fraud: Limitation Act 1980, s. 32(1)(a).

449. Such claims are subject to a special limitation period of two years from when the right to contribute arises: Limitation Act 1980, s. 10.

450. The ability of a *client* to frame an action in tort for limitation purposes is discussed at p. 606.

451. Subject to the question of "latent damage": see p. 664.

452. [1985] 2 E.G.L.R. 168.

453. This accords with the principle on which damages are assessed, namely, the difference between the true value of a property and the price which is paid for it on the basis of a negligent surveyor's report: see p. 644.

has been assumed to apply to a survey for a purchaser[454] and to a mortgage valuation commissioned by a building society but relied on by the purchaser[455]; it would appear equally apt where a vendor complains that a negligent over-valuation has resulted in a sale at an undervalue.

The "date of transaction" approach used in these cases, though often appropriate, is not necessarily so. It was held by the Court of Appeal in *First National Commercial Bank plc* v. *Humberts*[456] that, where a mortgagee would not have entered into a mortgage transaction at all but for a negligent over-valuation of the subject property, the mortgagee's "loss" for limitation purposes is suffered when the subject property does not afford security for the amount outstanding.[457] It is therefore only where the initial loan exceeds the true value of the property that the limitation period runs from the date of the mortgage; in other circumstances it will be necessary to trace the fluctuations in both the size of the debt and the value of the mortgaged property.

In cases where the work of a surveyor or valuer does not lead to a "transaction" as such, the identification of sufficient loss or damage to start the limitation period in tort will be a question of fact to be deduced from all the evidence. In *Whitley (FG) & Sons Co Ltd* v. *Thomas Bickerton*,[458] for example, where the plaintiffs alleged that the defendant surveyors had negligently failed to prevent their conditional planning permission for mineral extraction from lapsing, it was held that the plaintiffs' loss was suffered, not when the planning permission actually expired, but at the earliest time at which the obviously deteriorating planning prospects for the site would have an adverse effect upon its value.[459]

## 6.1.2 *Latent damage*

Section 14A of the Limitation Act 1980[460] makes special provision for any action for damages for negligence[461] (other than one involving personal injuries) where there is a gap between the date on which the plaintiff's cause of action accrues and the date on which the plaintiff[462] first has both the right to bring an action and also actual or constructive knowledge of certain material facts about the damage suffered and the potential defendant. The general effect of this provision is that the plaintiff's writ will be in time if issued either within six years of when the cause of action accrues[463] or within three years of the date on which the plaintiff has the relevant "knowledge".

There can be no doubt that these provisions are potentially applicable to cases

454. *Horbury* v. *Craig Hall & Rutley* [1991] C.I.L.L. 692.
455. *Felton* v. *Gaskill Osbourne & Co* [1993] 2 E.G.L.R. 176; *Campbell* v. *Meacocks* [1995] E.G.C.S. 143.
456. [1995] 1 E.G.L.R. 142.
457. Although not specifically stated, this must presumably be taken to include the cost of realising the security.
458. [1993] 1 E.G.L.R. 139.
459. See also *Kitney* v. *Jones Lang Wootton* [1988] 1 E.G.L.R. 145, where the plaintiff tenant lost the right to renew a lease through breach of a repairing covenant, despite having appointed defendant surveyors to identify and supervise all necessary works of repair. The tenant's loss was held to arise when the lease ended, rather than 10 years later when a court ruled (in an action between landlord and tenant) that the right to renew had indeed been lost.
460. Inserted by the Latent Damage Act 1986, s. 1.
461. This means an action in tort: *Iron Trades Mutual Insurance Co Ltd* v. *J K Buckenham Ltd* [1990] 1 All E.R. 808; *Société Commerciale de Reassurance* v. *ERAS (International) Ltd, Re ERAS EIL appeals* [1992] 2 All E.R. 82n.
462. Or any person in whom the cause of action was previously vested: s. 14A(5).
463. As to the accrual of the cause of action, see p. 663.

involving building surveys[464] and mortgage valuations.[465] This has for the most part simply been assumed, although the counter-argument, that section 14A was intended to apply only to negligent design or construction, has been specifically rejected by the courts on two occasions.[466]

As to what amounts to "knowledge" for the purpose of section 14A, each case turns on its own facts.[467] However, some general guidance may be gleaned from the great emphasis given by the Court of Appeal in *Spencer-Ward* v. *Humberts*[468] to remarks of Lord Donaldson MR in the personal injury case of *Halford* v. *Brookes*[469]:

"In this context 'knowledge' clearly does not mean 'know for certain and beyond possibility of contradiction'. It does, however, mean 'know with sufficient confidence to justify embarking on the preliminaries to the issue of a writ, such as submitting a claim to the proposed defendant, taking legal and other advice and collecting evidence'. Suspicion, particularly if it is vague and unsupported, will indeed not be enough, but reasonable belief will normally suffice."

A point of great practical importance in this context is whether, when a surveyor or valuer has overlooked more than one defect in a property, a plaintiff is fixed with "knowledge" as soon as the first error is discovered. In *Horbury* v. *Craig Hall & Rutley*[470] it was held that this was indeed the position, on the basis that a plaintiff's claim against a negligent surveyor is "one single cause of action, not a bundle of causes of action relating to different defects in the house and different elements of inconvenience as they arise". In consequence, the plaintiff's awareness that her surveyor had overlooked a fairly minor defect[471] operated to bar her claim in respect of devastating dry rot which was not discovered until several years later. In *Felton* v. *Gaskill Osbourne & Co*,[472] by contrast, it was held that what the statute requires is knowledge of "the damage in respect of which damages are claimed", so that the plaintiff may always sue in respect of something which has come to light only within the last three years, irrespective of his knowledge of other items of damage.[473]

464. *Horbury* v. *Craig Hall & Rutley* [1991] E.G.C.S. 81.

465. *Felton* v. *Gaskill Osbourne & Co* [1993] 2 E.G.L.R. 176; *Spencer-Ward* v. *Humberts* [1995] 1 E.G.L.R. 123; *Higgins* v. *Hatch & Fielding* [1996] 10 E.G. 162; *Campbell* v. *Meacocks* [1995] E.G.C.S. 143; *Heathcote* v. *David Marks & Co* [1996] 03 E.G. 128.

466. In *Horbury* v. *Craig Hall & Rutley* [1991] E.G.C.S. 81 and (at first instance) in *Campbell* v. *Meacocks* [1993] C.I.L.L. 886.

467. In most of the cases so far reported, the plaintiff's knowledge (of defects which the defendant has failed to observe or report) has been held sufficient to trigger the three-year period. In *Horbury* v. *Craig Hall & Rutley* [1991] E.G.C.S. 81 this included awareness that chimney breasts had been removed (a defect rectified at a cost of £132). In *Heathcote* v. *David Marks & Co* [1996] 03 E.G. 128, the plaintiffs' argument that they did not know the identity of the mortgage valuer was rejected, since a simple inquiry would have revealed this. The exceptional case is *Campbell* v. *Meacocks* [1995] E.G.C.S. 143, where receipt by the plaintiffs of a letter from loss adjusters about subsidence damage to an adjoining house was held insufficient to fix the plaintiffs with knowledge that their own mortgage valuer had been negligent.

468. [1995] 1 E.G.L.R. 123.

469. [1991] 3 All E.R. 559 at 573.

470. [1991] E.G.C.S. 81.

471. Chimney breasts had been removed leaving the flues without support (a defect which the plaintiff put right at a cost of £132).

472. [1993] 2 E.G.L.R. 176.

473. It is respectfully submitted that, while the "single cause of action" view adopted in *Horbury* is correct in principle, both these decisions are based on an erroneous approach to the problem. Since the "damage" caused by a negligent survey or valuation is defined as the excessive amount paid for the property (see p. 645), what matters is when the plaintiff first has "knowledge" that he or she has been led to pay more for the property than its true market value by a misleading report (i.e., one which overlooks a defect of sufficient importance to affect market value).

### 6.1.3 Personal injuries

Personal injury cases,[474] whether framed in contract or tort, are given special treatment under the Limitation Act 1980. First, section 11 prescribes a time-limit of three years from either the accrual of the cause of action or (if later) the plaintiff's "knowledge" of certain relevant facts. Secondly, section 33 gives a court a general discretion to disapply even this extended period where it would be equitable to do so.

These special rules are applicable to any action where the damages claimed "consist of or include" damages for personal injuries. As a result, where a negligent survey causes a person both personal injury and economic loss, an action to recover under both heads may be brought at a time when a claim for economic loss alone would be statute-barred.[475]

### 6.1.4 Deliberate concealment

Section 32(1)(b) of the Limitation Act 1980 provides that, where any fact relevant to the plaintiff's right of action has been deliberately concealed from him by the defendant, the limitation period appropriate to the claim shall not begin to run until the plaintiff has discovered the concealment or could with reasonable diligence have discovered it.[476] This provision was applied in the surveying context in *Westlake* v. *Bracknell DC*,[477] where the plaintiff house purchasers obtained a local authority mortgage from the defendants, following an inspection of the property by one of the defendants' staff surveyors. Having purchased the house in 1975, the plaintiffs became concerned by signs of structural movement, but were assured by the same surveyor that all movement had ceased. On discovering several years later that the concrete floor slab was seriously defective, the plaintiffs in 1983 issued a writ against the defendants, who pleaded that the action was statute-barred. It was held, however, that the statements made by the surveyor on his return visit amounted to "deliberate concealment",[478] so that the limitation period did not begin to run until the plaintiffs learned the truth about the defects.

## 6.2 Exemption clauses and disclaimers

### 6.2.1 General principles

The basic principles of law which govern attempts by professional persons to exclude or restrict their liability for negligence were considered in chapter 2. At this point we

474. Though unusual, it is not unheard of for such actions to be brought against surveyors: see, for example, *Allen* v. *Ellis & Co* [1990] 1 E.G.L.R. 170.

475. It appears from the Scottish case in *Drinnan* v. *C W Ingram & Sons* 1967 S.L.T. 205 that a plaintiff has a separate cause of action for each type of loss, injury or damage suffered in a single incident. Hence, in the (admittedly unusual) situation where time has run out on a plaintiff's action for personal injury but not on a claim for economic loss, the latter may still be pursued.

476. In *Sheldon* v. *R H M Outhwaite (Underwriting Agencies) Ltd* [1995] 2 All E.R. 558, it was held by a bare majority of the House of Lords (reversing a majority decision of the Court of Appeal) that this provision is not restricted to cases where the defendant's breach of duty is concealed from the outset. It can also apply (so as to give the plaintiff a new six year period) where the concealment occurs at a later date, even when the original period is about to expire.

477. [1987] 1 E.G.L.R. 161.

478. Defined by the judge as including "conduct involving recklessness or turning a blind eye or unconscionable conduct".

are concerned with the question of how those principles apply in the case of valuers and surveyors. This is a somewhat complex issue, partly because the general term "disclaimer" is used loosely to describe a range of contract terms and non-contractual notices which in fact impact upon a person's potential liability in a variety of ways.

The first, and simplest, type of disclaimer is a contract term which purports to exclude or to restrict in some way[479] the potential liability of one party to the other for a breach of that contract.[480] Such terms are seldom if ever used by surveyors or valuers, and have not featured in any reported case. However, there seems no reason in principle why they should not be effective, provided of course that they comply with the common law rules which govern exemption clauses[481] and subject to the provisions of the Unfair Contract Terms Act 1977.

The second (and far more common) type of disclaimer is one which seeks to ensure that a professional person does not incur liability in the tort of negligence to any third party. For example, reports from surveyors and valuers to their clients frequently contain a provision to the effect that they are for the use only of the client (and sometimes also the client's other professional advisers), and that no responsibility is undertaken towards any other person. Similarly, standard form correspondence between mortgagees and house buyers often attempts to ensure that, even if the latter is shown a copy of the mortgage valuation report, the valuer concerned cannot be held liable for its content.

Once again it appears that, subject to the Unfair Contract Terms Act,[482] such non-contractual notices may be effective to exclude a duty of care which would otherwise have arisen.[483] In *Hadden* v. *City of Glasgow DC*,[484] for example, where a local authority mortgagee brought a clear disclaimer to the attention of a house buyer at the time when the latter applied for a mortgage, this was held to prevent any implication of a duty of care owed by the mortgage valuer.[485] This was followed in *Commercial Financial Services Ltd* v. *McBeth & Co*,[486] where a valuers' report to developer clients stated: "This valuation is for the use only of the parties to whom it is addressed and no responsibility is accepted to any third party for the whole or any part of its contents". The valuation was shown to and relied on by a mortgagee, who subsequently brought an action for negligence, but it was held that the defendants had successfully disclaimed any responsibility which they might otherwise have incurred.

The types of disclaimer described above are intended to operate as a direct denial of responsibility. An alternative, more subtle, approach seeks to remove an essential element of liability (usually reliance by the plaintiff) by qualifying what is contained

---

479. E.g., by placing a financial ceiling limit on any claim, or imposing a time-limit within which it must be brought.

480. In so far as such a term is effective, it will probably apply with equal force to any concurrent liability which may exist in tort.

481. See *Chitty on Contracts* (27th edn, 1994), para. 14–005 *et seq*.

482. See p. 668.

483. See *Hedley Byrne & Co Ltd* v. *Heller & Partners Ltd* [1964] A.C. 465 at 492 (*per* Lord Reid); at 504 (*per* Lord Morris); at 511 (*per* Lord Hodson); at 533 (*per* Lord Devlin); and at 540 (*per* Lord Pearce).

484. 1986 S.L.T. 557.

485. In *Martin* v. *Bell-Ingram* 1986 S.L.T. 575, by contrast, terms in building society literature which purported to exclude a valuer's liability were not shown to the plaintiff house buyer until after contracts had been exchanged. The terms were held to be of no effect.

486. (Unreported) 15 January 1988, Court of Session.

in a report to a client. A valuation report, for example, may state that the valuer has not personally checked certain underlying facts, such as planning consents or questions of title. Likewise, a survey report may state that it has not been possible to obtain access to, or to inspect thoroughly, certain parts of the property. Such qualifications may, by restricting the matters in respect of which anyone may justifiably claim to rely on the report, limit the scope of any future negligence action arising out of it. However, to be effective, clear wording is required: thus surveyors who failed to make a proper inspection of parts of a property where dry rot might be inspected were not protected by a statement in their report that "in view of the prevalence of dry rot in London it is impossible to guarantee every property is free".[487]

### 6.2.2 Unfair Contract Terms Act 1977

#### 6.2.2.1 SCOPE OF THE ACT

The exclusion or restriction of a person's liability for negligence, by means of either a contract term or a non-contractual notice, is subject to the provisions of the Unfair Contract Terms Act 1977.[488] The effect, broadly, is that any attempt to exclude or restrict liability for causing death or personal injury will be void; furthermore, any term or notice which purports to affect other types of loss or damage will be subject to a statutory test of reasonableness.[489]

As noted earlier, surveyors and valuers do not in practice seek to exclude or restrict liability to their clients; if they did so, there can be no doubt that any relevant provision in the terms of engagement would be caught by the 1977 Act. There is, however, one situation in which disclaimers are routinely used, namely, that of an inspection and valuation carried out on behalf of a prospective mortgage lender. It has been common practice for at least 20 years for the standard documentation issued to borrowers by banks, building societies, local authorities and other lenders to disclaim responsibility on the part of both the lender and the mortgage valuer and to advise borrowers to obtain their own survey of the property before agreeing to purchase. The wording of such disclaimers varies from one lender to another, but typical are the clauses which appeared in *Smith* v. *Eric S Bush; Harris* v. *Wyre Forest DC*.[490] In *Smith* v. *Bush*, which arose out of a mortgage valuation carried out on behalf of a building society by an independent chartered surveyor, the house buyer had signed a building society application form stating:

"I understand that the society is not the agent of the surveyor or firm of surveyors and that I am making no agreement with the surveyor or firm of surveyors. I understand that neither the society nor the surveyor or the firm of surveyors will warrant, represent or give any assurance to me that the statements, conclusions and opinions expressed or implied in the report and mortgage valuation will be accurate or valid and the surveyor's report will be supplied without any acceptance of responsibility on their part to me."

487. *Lowy* v. *Woodroffe, Buchanan and Coulter* (1950) 156 E.G. 375.
488. See generally *Chitty on Contracts* (27th edn, 1994), para. 14–045 *et seq*. Prior to the Law Reform (Miscellaneous Provisions) (Scotland) Act 1990, s. 68, the Unfair Contract Terms Act 1977 did not apply in Scotland to non-contractual disclaimers. For the significance of this, see *Robbie* v. *Graham & Sibbald* [1989] 2 E.G.L.R. 148; *Melrose* v. *Davidson & Robertson*, 1993 S.L.T. 611.
489. The onus of proving the reasonableness of a contract term, or the reasonableness of reliance on a non-contractual notice, is on the person who seeks to rely on that term or notice: s. 11(5).
490. [1990] 1 A.C. 831. Other aspects of this important case are discussed at pp. 609 *et seq*.

In *Harris* v. *Wyre Forest DC*, which concerned a local authority mortgage and a valuation carried out by a staff valuer, the plaintiff purchasers had signed an application form containing the following clause:

"I/We understand ... that the valuation is confidential and is intended solely for the benefit of Wyre Forest District Council in determining what advance, if any, may be made on the security and that no responsibility whatsoever is implied or accepted by the council for the value or condition of the property by reason of such inspection and report."

Whether such disclaimers are subject to the Unfair Contract Terms Act was, until 1990, a matter of dispute. The Court of Appeal in *Smith* v. *Eric S Bush*[491] held that they were[492]; in *Harris* v. *Wyre Forest DC*,[493] however, a differently constituted Court of Appeal held that the Act applied only to terms and notices which sought to exclude *liability* and not to those which sought to exclude a *duty of care*. This was in spite of the provision in section 13(1) of the Act that, to the extent that section 2 prevents the exclusion or restriction of any liability, it also prevents "excluding or restricting liability by reference to terms and notices which exclude or restrict the relevant obligation or duty".

The conflict was finally settled by the House of Lords when appeals in the two cases were heard together.[494] Noting that the interpretation given to the Act in *Harris* would emasculate its effect, their Lordships held that the wording of section 13(1) was "entirely appropriate to cover a disclaimer which prevents a duty coming into existence".

## 6.2.2.2 THE REASONABLENESS TEST

The decision of the House of Lords in *Smith* v. *Eric S Bush; Harris* v. *Wyre Forest DC*[495] means, not only that the disclaimers commonly found in the mortgage valuation context are subject to the Unfair Contract Terms Act 1977, but also that, in normal circumstances, such disclaimers will fail the statutory test of reasonableness and will thus provide no defence to the house buyer's claim. In reaching the latter conclusion, Lord Templeman first summarised the defendants' arguments in favour of the disclaimers[496]:

"(1) The exclusion clause is clear and understandable and reiterated and is forcefully drawn to the attention of the purchaser.

(2) The purchaser's solicitors should reinforce the warning and should urge the purchaser to appreciate that he cannot rely on a mortgage valuation and should obtain and pay for his own survey.

(3) If valuers cannot disclaim liability they will be faced by more claims from purchasers some of which will be unmeritorious but difficult and expensive to resist.

(4) A valuer will become more cautious, take more time and produce more gloomy reports which will make house transactions more difficult.

(5) If a duty of care cannot be disclaimed the cost of negligence insurance for valuers and therefore the cost of valuation fees to the public will be increased.

---

491. [1988] Q.B. 743.

492. This decision was followed in *Davies* v. *Parry* [1988] 1 E.G.L.R. 147. Disclaimers were also struck down as unreasonable in *Green* v. *Ipswich B.C.* [1988] 1 E.G.L.R. 239 and *Roberts* v. *J Hampson & Co* [1988] 2 E.G.L.R. 181 where, however, the applicability of the Act was not disputed.

493. [1988] Q.B. 835.

494. *Smith* v. *Eric S Bush; Harris* v. *Wyre Forest D.C.* [1990] 1 A.C. 831.

495. [1990] 1 A.C. 831.

496. *Ibid.* at 851–852.

[Counsel for the valuers] also submitted that there was no contract between a valuer and a purchaser and that, so far as the purchaser was concerned, the valuation was 'gratuitous', and the valuer should not be forced to accept a liability he was unwilling to undertake."

These arguments were then decisively rejected:

"All these submissions are, in my view, inconsistent with the ambit and thrust of the 1977 Act. The valuer is a professional man who offers his services for reward. He is paid for those services. The valuer knows that 90 per cent of purchasers in fact rely on a mortgage valuation and do not commission their own survey. There is great pressure on a purchaser to rely on the mortgage valuation. Many purchasers cannot afford a second valuation. If a purchaser obtains a second valuation the sale may go off and then both valuation fees will be wasted. Moreover, he knows that mortgagees ... are trustworthy and that they appoint careful and competent valuers and he trusts the professional man so appointed. Finally, the valuer knows full well that failure on his part to exercise reasonable skill and care may be disastrous to the purchaser. If, in reliance on a valuation, the purchaser contracts to buy for £50,000 a house valued and mortgaged for £40,000 but in fact worth nothing and needing thousands more to be spent on it, the purchaser stands to lose his home and to remain in debt to the building society for up to £40,000 ... The public are exhorted to purchase their homes and cannot find houses to rent. A typical London suburban house, constructed in the 1930s for less than £1,000 is now bought for more than £150,000 with money largely borrowed at high rates of interest and repayable over a period of a quarter of a century. In these circumstances it is not fair and reasonable for building societies and valuers to agree together to impose on purchasers the risk of loss arising as a result of incompetence."

Lord Griffiths, whose remarks on this issue were endorsed by Lord Jauncey,[497] rejected as impossible any attempt to draw up an exhaustive list of the factors to be taken into account when deciding on the "reasonableness" of a disclaimer. None the less, his lordship suggested[498] that certain factors will always be relevant. These include:

(1) whether the parties are of equal bargaining power;
(2) in cases of advice, whether it would have been reasonably practicable to obtain the advice from an alternative source, taking into account considerations of costs and time. His Lordship noted that a house buyer commissioning his own inspection and report would in effect have to pay twice for the same advice and that this would place a considerable financial strain on young buyers at the bottom of the market;
(3) the difficulty of the task being undertaken for which liability is being excluded. In this context his Lordship regarded a mortgage valuation as "work at the lower end of the surveyor's field of professional expertise";
(4) the practical consequences of the decision on reasonableness (in particular the availability of insurance and its effect in spreading the risk of negligence over a wider area and thus lessening its impact).

Additionally, in the present context, Lord Griffiths regarded it as very important that:

"The surveyor is only appointed in the first place because the purchaser wishes to buy the house and the purchaser in fact provides or contributes to the surveyor's fees. No one has

497. *Ibid.* at 873–874.
498. *Ibid.* at 858–859.

argued that, if the purchaser had employed and paid the surveyor himself, it would have been reasonable for the surveyor to exclude liability for negligence, and the present situation is not far removed from that of a direct contract between the surveyor and the purchaser."

Although their Lordships were thus very firm in their opinion that reliance upon the disclaimers under consideration would not be reasonable, they were at pains to point out that this would not necessarily always be the case. Lord Griffiths, with whose remarks Lord Templeman expressly agreed, suggested an important limitation upon the scope of the decision[499]:

"It must, however, be remembered that this is a decision in respect of a dwelling-house of modest value in which it is widely recognised by surveyors that purchasers are in fact relying on their care and skill. It will obviously be of general application in broadly similar circumstances. But I expressly reserve my position in respect of valuations of quite different types of property for mortgage purposes, such as industrial property, large blocks of flats or very expensive houses. In such cases it may well be that the general expectation of the behaviour of the purchaser is quite different. With very large sums of money at stake prudence would seem to demand that the purchaser obtain his own structural survey to guide him in his purchase and, in such circumstances with very much larger sums of money at stake, it may be reasonable for the surveyors valuing on behalf of those who are providing the finance either to exclude or limit their liability to the purchaser."

The suggestion that the extent of a professional's exposure to liability might justify a different approach to exemption clauses surfaced elsewhere in Lord Griffiths' speech, where it was not restricted to cases of mortgage valuations:

"I would not, however, wish it to be thought that I would consider it unreasonable for professional men in all circumstances to seek to exclude or limit their liability for negligence. Sometimes breathtaking sums of money may turn on professional advice against which it would be impossible for the adviser to obtain adequate insurance cover and which would ruin him if he were to be held personally liable. In these circumstances it may indeed be reasonable to give the advice on a basis of no liability or possibly of liability limited to the extent of the adviser's insurance cover."

The House of Lords' ruling on disclaimers in mortgage valuation cases is so clear that this issue has been conspicuously absent from subsequently reported cases.[500] Moreover, in *Beaton* v. *Nationwide Building Society*,[501] the one reported case in which reliance was placed on a disclaimer, the defence failed. It was held that neither the fact that the house buyers had been advised by their solicitors to have a full survey, nor that they had been told by the estate agents of previous underpinning work, was a sufficient ground on which to distinguish *Smith* v. *Bush*. In addition, the judge rejected the defendants' argument that a notice, given to a house buyer so as to exclude the warranty as to the reasonableness of the purchase price which would otherwise be implied,[502] was also effective to exclude a duty of care at common law.

One earlier reported case in which liability was successfully disclaimed[503] was *Stevenson* v. *Nationwide Building Society*.[504] The wording of the disclaimer in that

---

499. *Ibid.* at 859–860.

500. In *Henley* v. *Cloke & Sons* [1991] 2 E.G.L.R. 141, which concerned a substantial detached house purchased in 1984 for £74,000, the defendant valuers conceded that a standard disclaimer in building society literature provided them with no defence.

501. [1991] 2 E.G.L.R. 145.

502. Under the Building Societies Act 1962, s. 30 (repealed by the Building Societies Act 1986).

503. By a building society sued in respect of a negligent in-house mortgage valuation.

504. [1984] 2 E.G.L.R. 165.

case, which was cited in argument in *Smith* v. *Bush* but was not referred to in their Lordships' speeches, was for the most part almost identical to that in *Harris* v. *Wyre Forest DC*; it further emphasised that the inspection by the building society's valuer was not a structural survey and stated that such a survey could be provided by the society, albeit at an additional cost to the purchaser. Having considered the provisions of the Unfair Contract Terms Act, the trial judge held that it was reasonable for the building society to rely on the disclaimer and thus to exclude its liability.

It is submitted that two crucial features of the *Stevenson* case enable it to be reconciled with *Smith* v. *Bush*. The first is that the plaintiff was himself an estate agent who was familiar with such disclaimers and with the range of surveys and valuations which were available. The second, and perhaps the more significant, is that what was purchased was not "a dwelling-house of modest value", but a relatively expensive (£52,000) property consisting of two shops, a maisonette and a flat.

## 6.3 Contributory negligence

The possibility of apportioning responsibility between a plaintiff and a defendant who are both guilty of unreasonable conduct arises in English law by virtue of section 1 of the Law Reform (Contributory Negligence) Act 1945. This provides:

"Where any person suffers damage as the result partly of his own fault and partly of the fault of any other person or persons, a claim in respect of that damage shall not be defeated by reason of the fault of the person suffering the damage, but the damage recoverable in respect thereof shall be reduced to such extent as the court thinks just and equitable having regard to the claimant's share in the responsibility for the damage."

Until comparatively recently, this statutory provision was seldom encountered in professional negligence cases.[505] However, the defence of contributory negligence is now routinely pleaded by valuers, especially in the context of claims by commercial mortgage lenders. It appears settled that the 1945 Act is in principle applicable to a negligence action against a valuer or surveyor,[506] irrespective of whether the plaintiff's claim is pleaded in contract or tort.[507] However, the Act cannot provide a defence to an action in deceit, even to a defendant (such as an employer held vicariously liable for an employee's fraud) who is personally innocent of moral blame.[508]

Allegations of contributory negligence in valuation cases tend to take one of two lines: either that it was unreasonable for the plaintiff to believe or to rely upon the defendant's report, or that, while reliance on the report was reasonable, the

505. Perhaps because it seems inherently implausible to suggest that a client ought to "second guess" professional advice which he or she has received.

506. *United Bank of Kuwait plc* v. *Prudential Property Services Ltd* [1995] E.G.C.S. 190. Cf. *Davies* v. *Idris Parry* [1988] 1 E.G.L.R. 147. In rejecting a mortgage valuer's claim that a house buyer was contributorily negligent for not commissioning an independent survey, McNeill J said: "Either the defendant was to blame or the plaintiffs were wholly responsible. There is, in my view, no middle way such as a division of fault would imply."

507. So held in *Forsikringsaktieselskapet Vesta* v. *Butcher* [1986] 2 All E.R. 488 by Hobhouse J, whose analysis of the statute was upheld by the Court of Appeal ([1988] 2 All E.R. 43). However, the Act does not apply to an action for breach of a contractual provision which does not depend on negligence by the defendant: *Barclays Bank plc* v. *Fairclough Building Ltd* [1994] 3 W.L.R. 1057.

508. *Alliance & Leicester Building Society* v. *Edgestop Ltd* [1994] 2 All E.R. 38.

plaintiff's decision to enter into a transaction (such as a mortgage loan) was imprudent for other independent reasons.[509] While recognising that these are not separate categories of case in any legal sense, it is convenient for the purpose of discussion to deal separately with them.[510]

### 6.3.1 Unreasonable reliance

There are formidable difficulties in the way of a valuer or any other professional adviser who seeks to argue that a reasonable client would have disregarded his advice. Thus: "No court will lightly hold a plaintiff at fault for relying on advice given by a professional adviser who owes a duty of care to the plaintiff".[511] Again: "It lies ill in the mouth of a professional valuer, who is giving a valuation for mortgage lending purposes, to say that it was unreasonable for the party to whom such valuation was given to rely on it."[512]

In spite of such cautionary judicial statements, valuers have succeeded on at least two occasions[513] in convincing a court that a mortgage lender's uncritical acceptance of a negligent valuation (in circumstances where there were good reasons for treating it with circumspection) amounted to contributory negligence.[514] In each of these cases, the defendants' negligence consisted in placing a value on certain commercial property greatly in excess of the price at which the borrowers had just acquired that property, without offering any justification or explanation for the difference. However, on proof that the plaintiff lenders were equally aware of the discrepancy between valuation and price, it was held that they had fallen below the standard of reasonably prudent bankers in going ahead with the mortgage transactions without first seeking a convincing explanation.[515]

509. "There is clearly a distinction between a finding that a person reasonably relies on a valuation, and a consideration of whether that person is then at fault in lending a particular sum of money in the light of that valuation": *Nyckeln Finance Co Ltd* v. *Stumpbrook Continuation Ltd* [1994] 2 E.G.L.R. 143 at 148 *per* Judge Fawcus QC.

510. A somewhat bizarre case, which does not fit conveniently into either category, is *Craneheath Securities Ltd* v. *York Montague Ltd* [1994] 1 E.G.L.R. 159. The plaintiff finance company there alleged that the defendants, in valuing a restaurant as a going concern, had negligently overestimated the profits. It emerged at trial that the defendants had not been shown the most recent accounts of the business; the plaintiffs had obtained those accounts but had inexplicably chosen not to show them to the defendants. Jacob J made it clear that, if he had held the defendants guilty of negligence, a finding of contributory negligence would have been extremely likely.

511. *Banque Bruxelles Lambert SA* v. *Eagle Star Insurance Co Ltd* [1995] 2 All E.R. 769 at 824 *per* Phillips J.

512. *Nyckeln Finance Co Ltd* v. *Stumpbrook Continuation Ltd* [1994] 2 E.G.L.R. 143 at 148 *per* Judge Fawcus QC.

513. *Banque Bruxelles Lambert SA* v. *Eagle Star Insurance Co Ltd* [1995] 2 All E.R. 769; *Nyckeln Finance Co Ltd* v. *Stumpbrook Continuation Ltd* [1994] 2 E.G.L.R. 143.

514. In addition to the two cases cited, one of the reasons given for reducing damages by 25 per cent in *South Australian Asset Management Corporation* v. *York Montague Ltd* [1995] 2 E.G.L.R. 219 was that the mortgage lenders "had not subjected the valuers' report to a properly detailed scrutiny". Reference may also be made to *PK Finans International (UK) Ltd* v. *Andrew Downs & Co Ltd* [1992] 1 E.G.L.R. 172, where valuers did not emphasise to the plaintiffs, a financial institution considering a £1m mortgage of a development site, that it was necessary to check certain planning assumptions on which their valuation was based. The valuers' failure was held not to amount to negligence, since they were entitled to rely on the commercial experience and awareness of the lenders; however, had it been held negligent, the judge would have held the lenders 80 per cent responsible for failing to send the valuation report to their solicitors.

515. In *Banque Bruxelles*, the lenders suffered a reduction in their damages of 30 per cent. In *Nyckeln*, where there had been at least a token attempt to investigate the discrepancy, the reduction was 20 per cent.

Notwithstanding the decisions cited in the previous paragraph, it appears highly unlikely that a court would penalise a lay person (such as a house purchaser) for placing unqualified reliance upon professional advice from a surveyor or valuer. The point arose in *Yianni* v. *Edwin Evans & Sons*,[516] where a mortgage valuer argued that the plaintiff house buyers were guilty of contributory negligence "because they failed to have an independent survey; made no inquiries with the object of discovering what had been done to the house before they decided to buy it; also failed to read the literature provided by the building society, and generally took no steps to discover the true condition of the house". In refusing to treat the plaintiffs' failures as negligent, Park J pointed out that they had simply relied on the defendant to make a competent valuation of the house.[517]

In *Allen* v. *Ellis & Co*[518] the plaintiff, before deciding whether or not to purchase a house, commissioned a survey of the property from the defendants. The defendants' report stated, among other things, that the detached garage was in good condition; it did not reveal (as was in fact the case) that the corrugated asbestos roof of the garage was brittle and in need of replacement. When the plaintiff, having purchased the house, stepped on to the garage roof to investigate a leak and fell through, it was held by Garland J that his injuries could be attributed to the defendants' negligence and, moreover, that his decision to climb onto the roof did not amount to contributory negligence.[519]

### 6.3.2 *Other carelessness by lenders*

As noted above, it is quite possible for a valuer or surveyor to argue that, while it was perfectly reasonable for the plaintiff to trust his report, the plaintiff's subsequent decision to enter into a particular transaction was negligent for other reasons. The cases so far reported in which such an argument has been put forward have all concerned mortgage loans made by commercial lending institutions. Moreover, while various aspects of the lenders' conduct have been tested against the standard of the reasonably prudent banker, by far the most common accusation has been that the lender has failed sufficiently to investigate the financial stability of the proposed borrower.

The obligations of a lender in this respect were subjected to careful judicial analysis in *HIT Finance Ltd* v. *Lewis & Tucker Ltd*.[520] Wright J there observed that, while a lender would obviously prefer only to deal with a reliable and compliant borrower, it is precisely because not all borrowers fall into that category that the lender requires the loan to be adequately secured. In the particular case, a loan of £1.54m had been made on the security of property which was valued by the defendants at £2.2m, but

---

516. [1982] Q.B. 438. See also *Davies* v. *Idris Parry* [1988] 1 E.G.L.R. 147; *Whalley* v. *Roberts & Roberts* [1990] 1 E.G.L.R. 164.

517. His Lordship did however suggest that, had the building society's documentation included a warning that it would be dangerous to rely on the valuer's report, the position might have been different.

518. [1990] 1 E.G.L.R. 170.

519. "The plaintiff is a layman. He knows nothing, or virtually nothing, about building or property ... I find it impossible to hold him contributorily negligent. If he were unaware of the risk—and I accept his evidence that he was unaware of the risk—then it cannot be said that he was negligent in failing to comprehend it."

520. [1993] 2 E.G.L.R. 231.

which was subsequently found to have been worth only £1.35m. As the judge pointed out[521]:

"The 'cushion' apparently provided by the property on the basis of the defendants' valuation was accordingly £660,000. In such circumstances, even if the borrowers turned out to be complete men of straw, the lenders were entitled to regard themselves as being more than adequately covered not merely in respect of the capital sum lent, but also any likely loss of interest, and indeed all the costs and expenses likely to be incurrred in foreclosing upon and realising the security. In such circumstances, although the hypothetical lender might not unreasonably feel irritated at being put to the trouble of having to realise his security rather than enjoying the fruits of his investment in a peaceful manner and in accordance with the terms of his contract, it is very difficult to see how such a lender could properly be characterised as 'imprudent'."

This emphasis on the value of the property as the lender's primary security was subject only to the qualification that "a prudent lender must not shut his eyes to any obvious lack of integrity or substance in his borrower". And since the evidence did not suggest any substantial reason for suspicion as to the borrower's honesty, it followed that the lenders were not guilty of contributory negligence.[522]

The obvious reluctance of Wright J to impose too heavy a burden upon a lender has also been apparent in a number of similar cases, where expert evidence of banking practice has convinced the courts that lenders have not acted unreasonably.[523] However, a different view was taken in *Credit Agricole Personal Finance plc* v. *Murray*,[524] where a borrower whose business affairs were uncertain and whose income fluctuated wildly was none the less granted a mortgage loan on a self-certification basis. The mortgage valuers were in fact held not to have been negligent; however, it was made clear that, had negligence been established, the lenders would have lost 15 per cent of their damages for contributory negligence.

An important question which arises in this context is whether, where the lender's solicitors are aware that a borrower shows unsatisfactory characteristics, their knowledge may be attributed to the lender so as to establish contributory negligence. It has twice been accepted in principle that such attribution is possible,[525] although on each occasion the argument failed on the facts.[526] By contrast, in *BFG Bank AG* v. *Brown & Mumford Ltd*[527] it was held (correctly, it is submitted) that a lender's

521. *Ibid.* at 235.

522. In reaching this conclusion, Wright J distinguished the somewhat similar New Zealand case of *Kendall Wilson Securities* v. *Barraclough* [1986] 1 N.Z.L.R. 576 on the ground that the lender there, a solicitors' nominee company, was acting as a trustee of clients' money and was accordingly subject to extra obligations of prudence and caution.

523. See *United Bank of Kuwait* v. *Prudential Property Services Ltd* [1995] E.G.C.S. 190; *Nykredit Mortgage Bank plc* v. *Edward Erdman Group Ltd* [1996] 02 E.G. 110, Mayor's and City of London Court; *Britannic Securities & Investments Ltd* v. *Hirani Watson* [1995] E.G.C.S. 46.

524. [1995] E.G.C.S. 32.

525. *HIT Finance Ltd* v. *Lewis & Tucker Ltd* [1993] 2 E.G.L.R. 231; *Axa Equity & Law Home Loans Ltd* v. *Goldsack & Freeman* [1994] 1 E.G.L.R. 175.

526. Neither judge was satisfied that the solicitors' duty extended to passing on the information concerned.

527. [1995] E.G.C.S. 21.

contributory negligence should be judged on the basis of actual and not imputed knowledge, since it would be hopelessly unrealistic to test the reasonableness of a party's conduct by reference to knowledge which that party does not actually possess.[528]

JOHN MURDOCH

---

528. Such considerations did not, however, preclude a ruling that, since the presence of mortgage indemnity guarantee insurance was to be ignored (as *res inter alios acta*) in computing the lenders' damages, it must also be ignored in deciding whether or not they were guilty of contributory negligence. In consequence, the question to be asked was whether a reasonably prudent merchant bank would have made the loans in question without the insurance cover which the plaintiffs in fact had: *Banque Bruxelles Lambert SA* v. *Eagle Star Insurance Co Ltd* [1995] 2 All E.R. 769 at 819–820 *per* Phillips J.

# CHAPTER 12

# INSURANCE OF PROFESSIONAL
# INDEMNITY RISKS

In modern times the insurance market has sought to meet the needs of professional practitioners by indemnifying them under professional indemnity insurance covers in respect of their professional liabilities.

The last 30 years have witnessed a phenomenal growth in the sale and purchase of this type of insurance and this has been mirrored by a similar growth in the size and frequency of claims against professional practitioners. There are many reasons behind the claims development during this period, notably the rise of consumerism and a change of public attitude which now subscribes to the view that if a commercial venture fails or expectations are not realised then through the medium of litigation someone must pay. It is an unfortunate feature of modern society that due to the operation of joint and several liability, the party who has to pay is usually the professional adviser. Professional firms tend to stay in existence longer than commercial organisations and also, by means of insurance, professional firms tend to have "the deepest pockets".

As demand has increased, the cost of professional indemnity insurance premiums has tended to rise, with the result that for many professional firms their largest overhead, after salaries, is their professional indemnity premium.

Furthermore, in recent years many professional bodies have included some form of compulsory insurance as part of their regulation of the profession so that the choice of whether to have insurance or not is no longer available for most professionals today. Thus for many professional practitioners the availability of a certificate to practise is linked to their ability to produce evidence of insurance in the required form.

Before attempting any detailed consideration of how the professional indemnity insurance market meets the needs and requirements of professional practitioners, it is first necessary to understand some of the basic characteristics of professional indemnity insurance in the UK. Every professional indemnity policy that is issued in this country will be written on a "claims made" basis and it is necessary to understand the significant consequences for professional firms which flow from underwriters' use of this particular method of underwriting risks. This basis of underwriting is particularly significant for professional practitioners because of the long-tail nature of professional liability.

Before investigating the detail of professional indemnity policies it is necessary to have some understanding of the way in which underwriters express limits of indemnity and self-borne contributions from the insured in the event of a claim (an "excess") and in particular to have some idea of the importance attached to claims notification and how professional indemnity policies distinguish between "claims" and "circumstances".

It will then be possible to consider in detail how professional indemnity policies are designed to meet the needs of practitioners and to explore the extent of cover on a clause-by-clause basis.

Finally, no review of professional indemnity insurance would be complete without attempting to set the concept of professional indemnity underwriting in the context of the mid-90s. It will be necessary, therefore, to take some account of the pressures which are mounting both in the UK and abroad to ease the burden on professional firms by way of legal reform and incorporation of those still operating as unlimited partnerships. This mid-90s characteristic has been brought about by the realisation on the part of Government and lobby groups that without reform we can expect a crop of unacceptable and spectacular bankruptices, together with a flight by senior staff from those areas of professional activity involving high risk. There is also a growing appreciation that high-calibre staff may decline to proceed to partnership status because of the unacceptable prospect of unlimited liability. One should also bear in mind when considering these characteristics the volatile nature of insurance cycles in the professional indemnity market.

Inevitably in any short general review of professional indemnity insurance some sacrifices have to be made and thus there will be no consideration of the basic principles of insurance nor of insurance contracts nor of the way in which underwriters assess or handle risks and apply risk-management programmes. Similarly, no consideration is given to the techniques of placing larger risks by way of layering; use of captive insurance companies; and reinsurance.

It is for underwriters to choose the basis on which they will underwrite a policy. Many third party liability policies (other than professional indemnity policies) are written on an "occurrence" basis. A policy written on an "occurrence" basis means that the insurance in force at the time a negligent act occurred is the policy which will respond to any claim made in respect of that act. Thus, for example, when a writ is received if this is the first notification of the claim, then the claim will be related back to the policy in force when the negligent act was committed.

There are obvious disadvantages of underwriting business on this basis, particularly when one considers that a writ may be issued some years after the occurrence and by then with the passage of time the limits of indemnity, terms and condition of the original policy may appear to be inadequate. It is also conceivable that the insurer is no longer in business. From an underwriting point of view this basis of providing cover with its obvious time gap makes reserving for unknown future losses very difficult, and particularly in inflationary times, very unattractive. When one considers that since the late 1960s professional indemnity claims have increased in both number and size, coupled with the fact that many practitioners find their actions or omissions tested at the cutting edge of judicial decision, then it will be appreciated that this particular method of underwriting liability risks has serious disadvantages.

As an alternative, professional indemnity insurance can be written on what is termed a "claims made" basis.

This means that it is the policy in force when a claim is actually made that provides the cover. It follows, therefore, that there must be a policy in force at the time when the claim is made for indemnity under the insurance policy to be triggered. If a professional indemnity policy has been allowed to lapse, has not been renewed, or has been cancelled before the claim is made, then there is in fact no insurance which will respond to that claim. Similarly, it follows that if a professional indemnity policy on a "claims made" basis in in force at the time when the claim is made, then it is that policy which will provide the cover regardless of any insurance which might have been in place at the time of the alleged error or omission.

The effect of making a valid claim on a "claims made" policy is that such notification attaches to that policy and it is that policy which will pay the claim regardless of the actual date of settlement or when the legal action takes place.

Perhaps "claims made" *cover* is best explained by way of a simple example. Assuming for the sake of the example that the cover is written on a 12-month basis which corresponds with the calendar year, if a professional practitioner is negligent in say 1993, but the client only becomes aware of his loss and the negligence in 1995 and thereupon seeks redress (either by way of letter of claim or writ) *in 1995*, it is the 1995 cover which will respond to that claim.

Underwriters under the 1995 policy will remain potentially exposed to that claim until it is settled or until a legal action is fought to judgment, however far in the future that may be. The underwriters who will pay the claim if settlement is achieved or judgment given are the underwriters in 1995 and not underwriters involved in the insurances before or after that year.

In view of the nature of "claims made" cover a problem arises when a professional practitioner discovers that a mistake, error or omission has occurred but as yet is not in receipt of any claim or notification that a claim will be made. Under a "claims made" policy special provision has to be included in the wording in order to deal with this situation. Thus the insured will be required to give notice to underwriters of any "circumstance" of which the insured becomes aware during the period of the insurance which may give rise to a loss or claim against the insured. For example an accountant while reviewing one of his client's files realises for the first time that he has made a mistake, or may have omitted to advise his client of the consequences of a certain course of action. The insurer will expect the insured to report the matter as though it were an actual claim. It will be for the insurers to decide how to handle the matter. The golden rule is that "if in doubt, report it".

The policy wording will also provide that notification of a "circumstance" will be deemed to be a claim for the purposes of that policy. Thus the "circumstance" will fall to be dealt with under the policy in force when it was notified regardless of when the claim is ultimately made. Clearly, many notifications of circumstances will not result in a subsequent claim just as many actual claims may be made but are not necessarily pursued.

The choice by underwriters of a "claims made" basis of underwriting professional indemnity insurance produces a number of significant consequences for insured practitioners. These may be summarised as follows:

*The insured practitioner must renew cover.* The choice of a "claims made" basis of underwriting professional indemnity insurance means that if a policy lapses, is not renewed, or is cancelled, for any reason then there will be no policy cover to which a future claim or the discovery of a "circumstance" can be attached.

*Provision will need to be made within the current policy document for former partners, predecessors in business, and the past liability of the practice.* In this connection it is relevant to consider the implications of joint and several liability in the context of partnership.

*It is the limit and terms of the policy in force when a claim or circumstance is first notified to underwriters which will apply when that claim is subsequently settled or judgment is given in a legal action.* At the time of settlement, therefore, it is the limit and terms of the policy in force at the time that the claim was first made which apply and which will need to be adequate in order to deal with the claim when it is settled. Subsequent increases or alteration in terms in later policies are irrelevant when the claim comes to be settled. A current policy limit has to be adequate in order to deal with liability for actions or omissions in the past but in respect of which the legal decision or settlement regarding those actions or omissions may not be given or achieved until some date far into the future.

*An insured needs to comply very strictly with the claims notification requirements of his policy both in relation to actual claims and also "circumstances"* as subsequent insurers will exclude claims arising from matters of which the insured is already aware. Thus claim notification assumes a particular importance in relation to "claims made" policies.

Professional indemnity insurance may be classified as a specialist form of liability insurance. By definition it concerns liability which flows from the exercise by or on behalf of any person having a professional qualification of the professional skill associated with such qualification.

Liability may be judged, therefore, according to the standard of care which is expected of a qualified professional practitioner in the exercise of his calling or profession.

It follows that the appropriate standard of care will be much higher than that expected of the layman and that evidence of the standard of care may be sought in the testimony of expert witnesses having similar qualifications.

In this context qualification means a qualification granted after examination by an appropriate professional body incorporated by statute or by royal charter, for example, qualification as a solicitor or as an accountant.

A qualified professional practitioner may belong to a single discipline practice such as a firm of solicitors, chartered accountants, certified accountants etc. or may belong to a multi-discipline practice, for example property developers, engineering consultants, auctioneers, valuers, surveyors and estate agents or a corporate entity which employs a variety of qualified professionals and hires out their various skills and services.

Regardless of whether one is dealing with a single discipline practice, a multi-discipline practice, or professional consultants, the appropriate form of cover will be based on legal liability to pay damages in respect of claims resulting from any negligent act, error or omission in the exercise of the professional skills associated with the appropriate professional qualifications.

In the early professional indemnity policies, underwriters sought to define the extent of cover in relation to the actual profession of the insured, for example against liability at law arising from negligence or the negligent performance of professional duties as a solicitor or accountant, etc.

As the demand for protection grew, policies were widened to cover any negligent act, error or omission in connection with the exercise of the insured's professional duties.

In the mid-1970s a trend was started towards granting cover in respect of any civil liability of whatsoever nature (including claimants' costs) incurred in connection with the conduct of any professional business carried on by or on behalf of the insured.

Use of a civil liability basis of indemnification has now become widespread or indeed mandatory for many of the more traditional professions.

Thus, underwriters have moved from a position of defining the scope of the cover and activities in a precise or narrow form, to granting cover on as broad and wide a basis as possible, even to the extent of covering the conduct of any professional business carried on by or on behalf of the insured.

At this point it is worth noting that even in the widest form underwriters may impose some restriction or limitation. For example, cover may be subject to the proviso "provided that the fees if any are included in the fees declaration". Thus cover is conditional on the fees for the work involved being included in the declaration of fees in the proposal form which is usually required annually (or in the equivalent renewal proposal form or renewal declaration which will include a declaration of fees). It is traditional for underwriters to base the premium upon the level of fees and other factors.

The reference to fees "if any" relates to the fact that many professional practitioners undertake honorary work for charity or sports associations for which either no fee is paid or the fee is waived. Nevertheless, in these instances the absence of any fee does not necessarily guarantee the absence of legal action if it is felt that the work has been carried out negligently or in an unprofessional manner and that loss has been caused as a result.

Underwriters will express the extent of their exposure in the form of a "limit of indemnity" (i.e., the financial extent of cover available under the policy) and the extent of the insured's own involvement in the risk in the form of a self-borne, self-insured "excess" (i.e., the level of cover borne by the insured) which is usually expressed as a financial sum each claim.

In the event of the payment of a claim under the policy this self-insured "excess" will be separate from any settlement or payment met by underwriters.

The "limit of indemnity" sets out the limit of the insured's exposure in the event of a claim. The amount of this limit may represent the maximum amount that the underwriters will grant cover for in respect of that particular risk, or the amount which the insured has requested and is willing to pay for. A further factor today involves the amount of indemnity which is required for the purposes of compulsory insurance laid down by the appropriate professional body. For example, the Institutes of Chartered Accountants in England and Wales, of Scotland, and in Ireland require a minimum limit of £50,000 for a sole practitioner or £100,000 for a partnership and/or a limit of 2.5 per cent gross fees, up to a maximum of £1m in the aggregate.

The factors which influence the choice of limit may be summarised as:

(a) what the insured can afford;
(b) what the insured feels exposed to by way of financial amount;
(c) what is advised by a specialist broker or insurance adviser;
(d) other factors such as, the degree of specialisation and the average fee per client (which will show whether there are a large number of small potentially low-risk clients or a small number of larger higher-risk clients);
(e) the nature of the work undertaken by the practice and whether this is generally regarded as high risk or not;
(f) the maximum limit which insurers will underwrite for a particular risk.

In any consideration of limits, however, the amount of such limit is only one segment of the limit of indemnity, the other being the qualification of that financial limit as either aggregate or aggregate with a single (or more) reinstatements or an each-and-every-claim basis. An each-and-every-claim basis means that the total limit of indemnity is available to meet claims as they arise during the policy period. It follows that theoretically one could have an unlimited number of such claims until the end of the policy period.

An aggregate limit may be variously described as: "in the aggregate"; "in the annual aggregate"; "in the aggregate for the period of insurance" or "any one claim and in all" (i.e., an aggregate description). Alternatively, cover which is written on an each-and-every-claim basis may be expressed as "each and every claim" or "any one claim" during the policy period.

The past 20 years has seen the rise of the "self-borne" or "self-insured" excess which is now virtually universal for all professional indemnity policies. Prior to this the prevailing view was that if an insured decided to buy insurance then his premium should cover any sum which had to be paid without contribution. Conversely, an excess was imposed when there were special features relating to the risk or when an adverse claims' experience justified underwriters involving the insured in this way. Older senior partners tended to take the view that if one purchased "a dog" then one should not be expected to "bark" oneself.

The rise in the number and value of claims has enabled underwriters to prevail in their view that the insured should contribute towards any claim under the policy as this gives the insured an interest in avoiding claims and also reduces administrative costs. From an underwriter's point of view, the cost of opening a claim file and investigating a claim is very similar whether the claim is small or large. Clearly, as a claim progresses then this progression may well involve greater investigation or the need for legal assistance, but in the initial stages the basic costs of administering all claims are the same.

In view of this it is clearly in the underwriter's interest to attempt to avoid small claims which will be costly to administer. Thus the majority of policies will have a minimum excess of, say, £500 or £1,000 and for many professions the minimum may be as much as £5,000–£10,000 or more. Underwriters may also use the self-insured excess as a means of granting premium saving or discount if the insured is prepared to take a higher excess than the underwriters have stipulated for that particular risk in return for a discount.

In a similar way to a limit of indemnity, the excess may be expressed as any one claim and in all (aggregate) or each and every claim.

The difference between an aggregate excess and an each-and-every-claim excess is of course significant. For example, if the excess were, say, £5,000 in the aggregate then that sum is the maximum which the insured may be required to pay regardless of the number of claims within the policy period. Thus this would be true of the excess whether the insured had one large claim to which the insured had to contribute £5,000 in full or whether he suffered a series of claims. The total amount of £5,000 would not be exceeded however many claims are made.

By contrast, if the excess were £5,000 each-and-every-claim then regardless of the amounts involved assuming that these were greater than £5,000 the insured would have to contribute £5,000 on each claim which arose during that policy period.

It is possible to "cap" the excess, for example, a £5,000 each-and-every-claim excess could be "capped" at, say, £45,000, so that the maximum which the insured would have to contribute in any policy period would be £45,000 regardless of the number of claims. Thus if the insured had 10 claims the last claim would be excess-free.

This form of capping is usually expressed as, for example, "£5,000 each and every claim but limited to £45,000 in the annual aggregate". Underwriters might impose a further excess once the annual aggregate is reached of a smaller sum so that although the excess is capped there is some small contribution on each claim thereafter, for example, "£5,000 each and every claim but limited to £45,000 in the annual aggregate subject thereafter to £750 each and every claim".

As the frequency and amount of settlement of professional indemnity claims has increased rapidly so has the importance of securing an adequate indemnity limit. In this connection professional practitioners tend to take a very limited view of their potential exposure. Claim settlements are related to the amount of damages which may be awarded by the court. What many professional practitioners fail to realise is that the courts rely upon the law of evidence and expert witnesses in coming to a decision. Thus the amount of damages awarded in court often surprises practitioners and many would regard the outcome as akin to a lottery.

To any amount awarded by the courts one must add third-party costs and interest. As a result the final total to be paid by the unsuccessful defendant will often exceed by several times what the professional practitioner may have regarded as "a reasonable amount" when considering his potential liability exposure.

Most professional advisers and professional bodies rely upon some form of multiplier such as two-and-a-half times fees or three times fees as a guide to a minimum limit of indemnity. In dealing with any form of specialisation, however, the accepted multiplier would need to be very much higher, for example five or 10 times fees, and if the practitioner is involved in high-risk work then it should be related to the current or estimated level of damages being awarded by the courts for claims in respect of that type of work.

Failure adequately to insure can cripple a professional firm and lead to either bankruptcy of the partners or the sale of the practice. Sometimes, as in the case of the largest practitioners, an inadequate sum insured may arise because of their inability to obtain insurance anywhere in the world beyond a certain figure despite substantial self-borne excesses. The amount by which the sum insured falls short of the amount of final settlement is termed "under-insurance".

Most policies provide for payment of legal costs in proportion to the amount which

683

the sum insured bears to the final settlement. In other words, the legal costs which underwriters will pay will be reduced in proportion in the event of under-insurance.

The clauses relating to claims notification are important in any form of insurance policy but have a special significance as already mentioned in a "claims made" policy.

In the field of professional indemnity insurance the earlier policies required the insured as "a condition precedent to their right to be indemnified" to give underwriters *immediate notice* in writing of any claim or circumstance likely to give rise to a claim. Most practitioners would find this requirement impossible to fulfil in reality and thus potentially as a result of this wording most insured would face being in breach of policy conditions in relation to claims. In more recent professional indemnity policies this harsh requirement has been modified so that currently in at least a substantial number of policies the insured is required to notify claims and circumstances "as soon as practical". Some policies go even further and provide protection to policy-holders in the event of "innocent non-disclosure" of claims or circumstances. In these policies it is usual for the policy to allow underwriters to deduct any amount by which they have been prejudiced due to late notice, but the onus is placed on the insurer rather than the insured to establish that they have been prejudiced.

The protection which some policies afford in respect of non-disclosure or misrepresentation of facts goes beyond claims or "circumstances" and may extend to alleged untrue statements in a proposal form provided the insured can establish to the underwriters' reasonable satisfaction that such alleged non-disclosure or untrue statement was free of fraudulent conduct or intent to deceive. This is a valuable protection in the event of an innocent non-disclosure in a proposal form.

In connection with failure to inform underwriters of any circumstance of which the insured was aware then underwriters usually restrict the indemnity to the same indemnity as would have been available under the previous insurance which would have been the appropriate insurance had the circumstance been properly notified. In those situations in which the insured should have notified the circumstance and this notification would have been prior to any increase in the limit of indemnity or other variation, then the indemnity available will be limited to the previous indemnity or the terms prior to the variation. In that sense it could be said that some insurers operate a "proportionality" approach. In other words the policy exists as a safeguard on which underwriters will respond if they choose to. Thus in the event of a relatively small claim which might reflect a lax attitude to compliance with the policy terms, or unacceptable "housekeeping" standards on the part of the insured, the underwriter may decide to pay the claim but to decline to renew the policy. If there is a matter of principle then the underwriter may decide to adopt a strict policy interpretation or to use the full force of the law relating to utmost good faith.

However, it should be noted that there is considerable variety in the wording of such clauses and indeed in many policies clauses offering protection for innocent non-disclosure are conspicuous by their absence.

One of the most difficult situations which faces underwriters in connection with the interpretation of a policy arises where there are a number of different claimants or where a loss has been sustained by one or more persons comprising the assured.

Most policies will attempt to clarify complex, multi-party claims. For example a professional indemnity policy may define the insured as the partners of a firm, the former partners, the employees and specified consultants. A claimant may issue writs against each individual partner, former partner, employee, consultant etc. In that event the policy wording provides that these various writs are to be considered as one claim. Similarly although each writ may disclose different causes of action, if they arise out of one occurrence (or out of a series of occurrences having the same original cause or source) they are to be deemed to be one claim, or loss.

A similar interpretation applies if the writs emanate from different claimants.

In any professional indemnity insurance the precise nature and extent of the exclusions and conditions contained within the policy will depend upon the individual preference and choice of each controlling underwriter.

The most likely exclusions will include those dealing with the jurisdictional or territorial limits, for example, excluding actions brought overseas or actions brought in the courts of the USA and also what may be termed "boundary" exclusions which define the limits of professional indemnity cover in relation to covers such as public liability, employers' liability or third-party insurance. Thus in professional indemnity policies one would expect to find exclusions relating to death or bodily injury which are more properly the subject of public liability covers as are claims relating to physical loss of or damage to property.

In addition, one would expect to find exclusions relating to indemnity under any other policy so that the insured would not be indemnified in respect of any claim or loss of which the insured was entitled to indemnity under any other insurance. The exclusion might go on to modify this by covering any claim or loss in respect of any excess beyond the amount which would have been payable under such insurance if the current policy had not been effected.

In addition, in accordance with the agreement made with the Home Office many years ago all policies exclude claims or loss directly or indirectly caused by nuclear activity or from war and invasions and similar hostilities. These clauses appear in all liability policies as the risks involved are considered to be uninsurable.

Under the conditions section of the policy, underwriters would make it clear that the insured should not admit liability for or settle any claim or incur any costs or expenses without their written consent. Underwriters consider that if they are going to pay claims then they should have total control of them and that their freedom to decide how to deal with a claim should not be inhibited by any prior admissions or attempts to settle on the part of the insured.

There is usually also an exclusion relating to any claim which the insured knows to be false or fraudulent which will carry the sanction that the policy will become void if such a claim is preferred by the insured and all claims under the policy shall be forfeited.

It is also in this area of the policy that one is likely to find any arbitration procedure set out in detail.

Generally under the headings "Exclusions" and "Conditions" underwriters group the standard exclusions and conditions found in the majority of policies or those which are peculiar to that underwriter and which he will include in all the policies issued under his name. More specific exclusions and conditions and any warranties will probably be included elsewhere in the policy in relation either to the operative clause of the policy or in related clauses setting out extensions of cover under the policy terms. In relation to policy interpretation, therefore, the sections headed

"Exclusions" and "Conditions" should not be regarded as in any way definitive of exclusions and conditions under that particular policy.

Throughout the 1980s and 1990s there has been a steady rise in the number and value of claims against professional practitioners, together with an increasing trend towards closer regulation of all the professions by their appropriate professional body. Currently it is accepted that a prerequisite for obtaining a certificate of compliance in order to be able to practise is the production of evidence of insurance in the appropriate form and in the specified manner and amount.

As most professional practices are built on stability and continuity, professional firms tend to have a longevity beyond the short lifespan of most commercial enterprises. From a practitioner's viewpoint, therefore, the unfortunate consequence is that due to the operation and principle of joint and several liability it is the professional adviser who pays 100 per cent of the damages, while the other participants in the enterprise are likely either to have gone out of business, or, in the case of directors, to have no adequate insurance.

Even a casual reading of the press will highlight many instances of spectacular awards in the courts leading in some cases to possible bankruptcy of partners, so that it is not surprising that there is a growing groundswell of support for law reform, particularly in the area of joint and several liability.

Many practitioners consider that until the law is reformed and a form of proportionate liability is introduced, the scales of justice weigh unfairly against them. Similarly, various methods of self-help, such as agreeing with clients to limit liability in advance (usually a multiplier based on the fee for the particular job) or persuading clients to purchase specific separate insurance in a high-risk area, such as audit, are already finding passionate supporters.

For similar reasons there is currently a noticeable trend within professional structures towards a greater specialisation, merger or purchase by the more successful firms as a means of expansion and in order to achieve greater protection by means of size. By contrast, sole practitioners and the smaller partnerships are seeking to unburden themselves of the weight of past liability and unlimited liability exposures by selling the practice to the larger firms.

In those professions in which unlimited partnerships are still common, such as accountancy and firms of solicitors, there is now a growing acceptance that following the proposed changes in taxation by 1997 the larger firms, and those in high-risk areas of business, will incorporate thereby avoiding the possibility of individual partners becoming bankrupt and facilitating the distribution of a deceased partner's estate by executors and administrators.

ROY PARR

# INDEX